CH. #	CHAPTER TITLE	FOCUS COMPANY	MANAGERIAL FOCUS	CONTRAST COMPANIES	KEY RATIOS
8	Reporting and Interpreting Cost of Goods Sold and Inventory	DELL INC. Dell Inc. (Direct-sale computer vendor)	Manufacturing management	Gateway IBM	**Inventory Turnover**
9	Reporting and Interpreting Property, Plant, and Equipment; Natural Resources; and Intangibles	WESTJET WestJet Airlines Ltd. (Major Canadian airline)	Planning productive capacity	Southwest Airlines Jet Blue Airways	**Fixed Asset Turnover**
10	Reporting and Interpreting Current Liabilities	PETRO-CANADA. Petro-Canada (Oil and gas company)	Capital structure	Suncor Energy Imperial Oil	**Current Ratio** **Accounts Payable Turnover**
11	Reporting and Interpreting Bonds	PETRO-CANADA. Petro-Canada (Oil and gas company)	Long-term debt financing	Suncor Energy Imperial Oil	**Financial Leverage** **Times Interest Earned**
12	Reporting and Interpreting Owners' Equity	Sun Life Financial Sun Life Financial (Protection and wealth accumulation company)	Corporate ownership	Great-West Lifeco Fairfax Financial	**Earnings per Share** **Dividend Yield**
13	Analyzing Financial Statements	THE HOME DEPOT The Home Depot Inc. (Home improvement retailer)	Financial statement analysis	Canadian Tire RONA	**Ratio Summary**

P9-DDV-668

Third CANADIAN Edition

Financial Accounting

Robert Libby
Cornell University

Patricia A. Libby
Ithaca College

Daniel G. Short
Miami University

George Kanaan
Concordia University

Maureen Gowing
University of Windsor

Toronto Montréal Boston Burr Ridge, IL Dubuque, IA Madison, WI New York
San Francisco St. Louis Bangkok Bogotá Caracas Kuala Lumpur Lisbon London
Madrid Mexico City Milan New Delhi Santiago Seoul Singapore Sydney Taipei

The McGraw-Hill Companies

McGraw-Hill
Ryerson

Financial Accounting
Third Canadian Edition

Copyright © 2008, 2006, 2003, by McGraw-Hill Ryerson Limited, a Subsidiary of The McGraw-Hill Companies. All rights reserved. Copyright © 2007, 2004, 2001, 1998, 1996, by The McGraw-Hill Companies, Inc. All rights reserved. No part of this publication may be reproduced or transmitted in any form or by any means, or stored in a data base or retrieval system, without the prior written permission of McGraw-Hill Ryerson Limited, or in the case of photocopying or other reprographic copying, a license from The Canadian Copyright Licensing Agency (Access Copyright). For an Access Copyright licence, visit www.accesscopyright.ca or call toll free to 1-800-893-5777

ISBN-13: 978-0-07-098096-9
ISBN-10: 0-07-098096-9

2 3 4 5 6 7 8 9 10   DOW   0 9

Printed and bound in the United States of America.

Care has been taken to trace ownership of copyright material contained in this text; however, the publisher will welcome any information that enables them to rectify any reference or credit for subsequent editions.

Editorial Director: Joanna Cotton
Senior Sponsoring Editor: Rhondda McNabb
Developmental Editors: Sarah Fulton and Suzanne Simpson Millar
Marketing Manager: Joy Armitage Taylor
Senior Editorial Associate: Christine Lomas
Copy Editor: Erin Moore
Senior Production Coordinator: Paula Brown
Cover and Interior Design: Michelle Losier/Fine Lines
Cover Image Credits: Grapes: © Goodshoot/Punchstock;
Coffee Cup: © Randy Allbritton/Getty Images; Plane: © Flat Earth Images;
Basketball: © Stockbyte/Getty Images
Page Layout: S R Nova Pvt Ltd., Bangalore, India.
Printer: R. R. Donnelley/Willard

Library and Archives Canada Cataloguing in Publication

Financial accounting / Robert Libby ... [et al.]. — 3rd Canadian ed.

Includes index.
ISBN 978-0-07-098096-9

1. Accounting—Textbooks.   2. Corporations—Accounting—Textbooks.
3. Financial statements—Textbooks.   4. Cash management—Textbooks.
5. Inventories—Accounting—Textbooks.   I. Libby, Robert

HF5635.F43 2008   657   C2007-907441-3

Robert Libby

Robert Libby is the David A. Thomas Professor of Management at the Johnson Graduate School of Management at Cornell University, where he teaches the introductory financial accounting course. He has previously taught at the University of Illinois, Pennsylvania State University, University of Texas at Austin, University of Chicago, and University of Michigan. He received his B.S. from Pennsylvania State University and his M.A.S. and Ph.D. from the University of Illinois; he is also a CPA. Bob is a widely published author specializing in behavioural accounting.

Patricia A. Libby

Patricia Libby is Chair of the Department of Accounting and Associate Professor of Accounting at Ithaca College, where she teaches the undergraduate financial accounting course. She has previously taught graduate and undergraduate financial accounting at Eastern Michigan University and the University of Texas. Before entering academe, she was an auditor with Price Waterhouse (now Pricewaterhouse-Coopers) and a financial administrator at the University of Chicago. She received her B.S. from Pennsylvania State University, her M.B.A. from DePaul University, and her Ph.D. from the University of Michigan; she is also a CPA. Pat conducts research on using cases in the introductory course and other parts of the accounting curriculum.

Daniel G. Short

Daniel Short is Professor of Accounting and Dean of the M.J. Neeley School of Business at Texas Christian University in Fort Worth, Texas. Formerly, he was Dean at the Richard T. Farmer School of Business at Miami University (Ohio) and the College of Business at Kansas State University. Prior to that, he was Associate Dean at the University of Texas at Austin, where he taught the undergraduate and graduate financial accounting courses. He has also taught at the University of Michigan and the University of Chicago. Dan received his undergraduate degree from Boston University and his M.B.A. and Ph.D. from the University of Michigan. He has won numerous awards for his outstanding teaching abilities and has published articles.

George Kanaan

George Kanaan is Associate Professor of Accountancy and Associate Dean at the John Molson School of Business at Concordia University, where he teaches the introductory financial accounting course. George previously taught undergraduate and graduate courses at other universities in Canada, China, and Lebanon. He received his B.A. from the Lebanese University, his M.A. from Southern Illinois University at Carbondale, and his Ph.D. from the University of Wisconsin–Madison. He has conducted research on disclosures related to pension accounting, deferred income taxes, and the effects of changing prices. George's research has been published in *The Journal of Accounting, Auditing and Finance,* and *Managerial Finance.*

Maureen Gowing

Maureen Gowing is Assistant Professor of Accounting at the Odette School of Business at the University of Windsor. She has taught accounting research methods at the Ph.D. level, as well as financial and managerial accounting and accounting theory at both the M.B.A. and undergraduate levels. She has co-authored and published articles on ethics in accounting in the *Journal of Business Ethics,* and the *International Journal of Business Research.* Maureen has also conducted research on the effectiveness of technological and pedagogical strategies in teaching different content in accounting courses. She is also the Canadian author of a managerial accounting text. She worked for several years as an analyst in the oil and securities industries and at the Vancouver Stock Exchange doing forensic accounting. Maureen obtained her B.A. from Carleton University, her M.B.A. from the University of Toronto, and her Ph.D. from Queen's University.

Contents in Brief

Contents

CHAPTER **TWO**

Investing and Financing Decisions and the Balance Sheet   44

CHAPTER **THREE**

Operating Decisions and the Income Statement   100

CHAPTER **FIVE**

Reporting and Interpreting Cash Flows   231

FOCUS COMPANY: ANDREW PELLER LIMITED—
MANAGING PRODUCTION AND CASH FLOWS IN A
SEASONAL BUSINESS   231

CHAPTER **SIX**

Communicating and Interpreting Accounting Information   288

CHAPTER SEVEN

Reporting and Interpreting Sales Revenues, Receivables, and Cash 343

CHAPTER **EIGHT**

Reporting and Interpreting Cost of Goods Sold and Inventory   403

CHAPTER **NINE**

Reporting and Interpreting Property, Plant, and Equipment; Natural Resources; and Intangibles 461

CHAPTER **TEN**

Reporting and Interpreting Current Liabilities   526

CHAPTER **ELEVEN**

Reporting and Interpreting Long-term Liabilities   568

CHAPTER **TWELVE**

Reporting and Interpreting Owners' Equity 626

CHAPTER **THIRTEEN**

Analyzing Financial Statements   673

FOCUS COMPANY: HOME DEPOT: FINANCIAL
ANALYSIS: BRINGING IT ALL TOGETHER   673

*F*inally, a textbook on which both students and instructors can agree. The authors of *Financial Accounting,* third Canadian edition, continue to make financial accounting more relevant and interesting to students. How? By helping the instructor and student become partners in learning, using a remarkable learning approach that keeps students engaged and involved in the material from the first day of class.

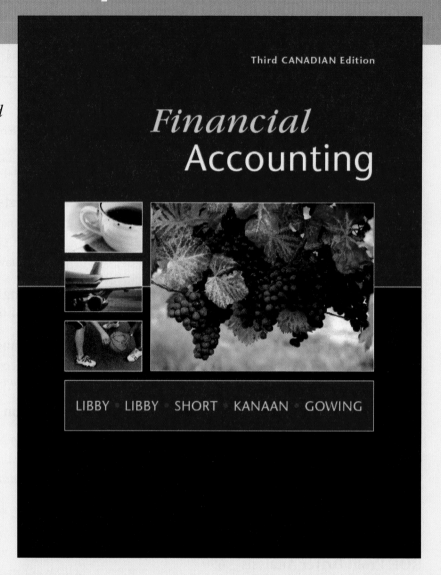

Financial Accounting's distinctive focus-company method motivates students by involving them in the business decisions of a real company, demonstrating how financial accounting makes a difference in the success of a firm. That, combined with pedagogical features and technology tools that serve a variety of learning styles, makes Libby/Libby/Short/Kanaan/ Gowing the textbook that both students and instructors agree is the best of its kind on the market today.

# of students and instructors alike.

Financial Accounting*'s success is based on three key attributes:*

RELEVANCE. The authors' use of real-world focus companies is the best tool for demonstrating the relevance of financial accounting topics. Ethics continues to be a crucial topic within accounting, and *Financial Accounting* integrates coverage of ethical issues throughout the book. Furthering its real-world applicability, the end-of-chapter cases tie into the annual reports of Van Houtte Inc. and the Forzani Group Limited. This gives students valuable practice in reading and interpreting real financial data. Finally, Real-World Excerpts expand important chapter topics with insight into how real firms use financial accounting to their competitive advantage.

CLARITY. Do students complain that their textbook is hard to read? They don't if they're reading *Financial Accounting*. It is the proven choice for presenting financial accounting in a clear, relevant approach that keeps students engaged throughout the course. To continue to meet the changing needs of financial accounting instructors and students, the organization of the material has been refined to ensure maximum readability for students and flexibility for instructors.

TECHNOLOGY AIDS. Today's students have diverse learning styles and numerous time commitments, and they want technology supplements that help them study more efficiently and effectively. Lyryx Assessment, and *i*Study—an interactive online study guide—both provide your students with powerful tools tied directly to *Financial Accounting,* third Canadian edition. These tools will help them maximize their study time and make their learning experience more enjoyable.

Proven Learning Solutions

Financial Accounting offers a host of pedagogical tools that complement the way you like to teach and the ways your students like to learn. Some offer information and tips that help you in presenting a complex subject; others highlight issues relevant to what your students read online and in the papers, or see on TV. Either way, *Financial Accounting*'s pedagogical support will make a real difference in your course and in your students' learning.

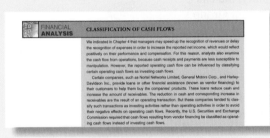

FINANCIAL ANALYSIS

The **Financial Analysis** sections tie important chapter concepts covered in each chapter to real-world decision-making examples. They also highlight alternative viewpoints and add to the critical thinking skills and decision-making focus of the text.

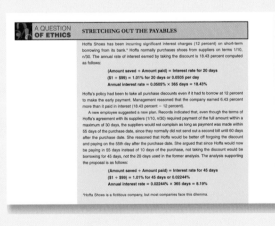

INTERNATIONAL PERSPECTIVE

As our Canadian instructors are acutely aware, the Canadian Generally Accepted Accounting Principles will converge with the International Financial Reporting Standards by the year 2011. Because of the rapid increase in global competition, the **International Perspective** sections make students aware of the differences in accounting methods used around the world. International issues are included in the end-of-chapter material as well.

A QUESTION OF ETHICS

The more students are exposed to ethical situations, the more likely they will consider the effects their choices will have on others. **A Question of Ethics** boxes appear throughout the text, conveying to students the importance of acting responsibly in business practice. Recent events in the accounting profession have made ethics awareness more crucial than ever.

SELF-STUDY QUIZZES

This learning feature engages the student, provides interactivity, and promotes efficient learning. Research shows that students learn best when they are actively engaged in the learning process. These **Self-Study Quizzes** ask students to pause at strategic points throughout each chapter to ensure they understand key points before moving ahead.

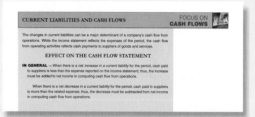

FOCUS ON CASH FLOWS

Each of chapters 2 through 12 includes **Focus on Cash Flows**, a discussion and analysis of changes in the cash flow of the focus company and an exploration of the decisions that caused those changes. The early and consistent coverage of cash flows encourages students to think more critically about the decisions they will face as managers and the impact those decisions will have on the company's cash flow.

KEY RATIO ANALYSIS

Students will be better prepared to use financial information if they understand how to evaluate elements of financial performance while learning how to measure and report them. For this reason, we include relevant key ratios in the **Key Ratio Analysis** sections. Each Key Ratio Analysis box presents a ratio analysis for the focus company in the chapter as well as for comparative companies. Cautions are also provided to help students understand the limitations of certain ratios.

REAL WORLD EXCERPT

These insightful excerpts appear throughout the text and include annual report information from the focus companies as well as numerous other companies, news articles from various publications, analysts' reports, and press releases.

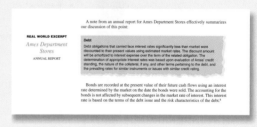

Proven Learning Solutions

ORGANIZATION OF THE CHAPTER

A unique feature of Libby *Financial Accounting*, this framework provides a powerful visual schematic of each chapter's content, easily enabling students to identify the topics covered.

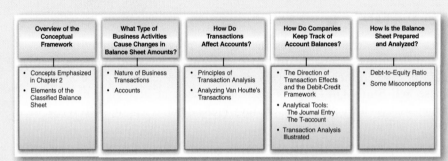

Overview of the Conceptual Framework	What Type of Business Activities Cause Changes in Balance Sheet Amounts?	How Do Transactions Affect Accounts?	How Do Companies Keep Track of Account Balances?	How Is the Balance Sheet Prepared and Analyzed?
• Concepts Emphasized in Chapter 2 • Elements of the Classified Balance Sheet	• Nature of Business Transactions • Accounts	• Principles of Transaction Analysis • Analyzing Van Houtte's Transactions	• The Direction of Transaction Effects and the Debit-Credit Framework • Analytical Tools: The Journal Entry The T-account • Transaction Analysis Illustrated	• Debt-to-Equity Ratio • Some Misconceptions

ALL JOURNAL ENTRIES TIED TO THE ACCOUNTING EQUATION

Journal entries in early chapters marked with (A), (L), (SE), (R), (E), or X, (if a contra account) and + and − signs assist students in transaction analysis. In addition, following each journal entry is a summary of the effects of each transaction on the fundamental accounting equation.

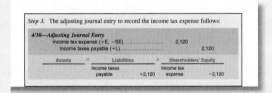

Step 3. The adjusting journal entry to record the income tax expense follows:

4/30—Adjusting Journal Entry
Income tax expense (+E, −SE)............... 2,120
Income taxes payable (+L)................. 2,120

Assets	=	Liabilities	+	Shareholders' Equity
		Income taxes payable +2,120		Income tax expense −2,120

LEARNING OBJECTIVES CROSS-REFERENCED

Outlined at the beginning of each chapter, Learning Objectives are cross-referenced to the end-of-chapter material.

ICONS

Easily identifiable margin icons indicate what types of skills are being addressed in the end-of-chapter material.

 • International Perspectives: An assignment that includes an international element.

 • Ethics: An ethical dilemma that the student must consider.

 • Cash Flows: An exercise that requires the student to complete a cash flow analysis.

 • Ratio Analysis: An assignment that includes ratio analysis.

 • Written Communication: An assignment that requires the student to do written work, developing their communication skills.

 • Excel templates: Exercises which can be solved using an Excel template.

 • Analysis icon: Identifies problems and cases that require analysis, developing the skills students require to use financial information to guide their business decisions.

Flexible End-of-Chapter Content and Organization

Each chapter is followed by an extensive selection of end-of-chapter assignments that examine single concepts or integrate multiple concepts presented in the chapter. To maintain the real-world flavour of the chapter material, they are often based on real Canadian, U.S., and international companies, and require analysis, conceptual thought, calculation, and written communication. Assignments suitable for written individual or group projects and oral presentations are included in strategic locations.

Chapter Take-Aways   Bulleted, end-of-chapter summaries that correspond with the learning objectives outlined at the beginning of the chapter.

Key Ratios   Summary of the key ratios presented in the chapter.

Finding Financial Information   Highlights the chapter's key concepts in an easy to review graphic. The graphic includes Balance Sheet, Income Statement, Cash Flow Statement, and Note Information.

Key Terms   Key terms introduced in each chapter are referenced to the chapter text.

Questions   Allow students and faculty to ensure that chapter concepts have been grasped.

Exercises   Assignments that cover multiple learning objectives from each chapter.

Problems   Detailed assignments that integrate various topics discussed in the chapter. They are cross-referenced in blue to the Alternate Problems.

Alternate Problems   Similar in level and content to the end-of-chapter problems. They are cross-referenced in blue to the Problems.

Cases and Projects   This section includes Finding and Interpreting Financial Information, Financial Reporting and Analysis Cases, Critical Thinking Cases, and a Financial Reporting and Analysis Team Project.

Annual Reports   The annual reports of two dynamic Canadian companies, Van Houtte Inc. and The Forzani Group Ltd., are referenced in the text's problem material. The annual report for Van Houtte is included as an appendix to the text, while The Forzani Group's annual report is posted online for student study.

There are several ways to identify end-of-chapter materials to use when achieving the learning objectives. We have

- included applicable Learning Objective numbers in the margin;
- arranged assignments by increasing level of difficulty in learning objective order;
- included a number of assignments that focus on understanding the effects of transactions, rather than producing journal entries;
- included user-oriented analytical materials;
- incorporated the text themes: international, ethics, cash flows, ratio analysis, real world, written communication, team project, broadening research skills, comparing companies within and across industries and over time, finding financial information, and interpreting the financial press.

What's New in the Third Canadian Edition?

Based on market feedback, the primary goals of the third Canadian edition are

- to simplify explanations of complex topics;
- to make the end-of-chapter material match instructor and student needs better;
- to accurately reflect the exciting changes taking place in the accounting environment; and
- to provide instructors with more flexibility in key topical coverage.

As a result, the authors have made the detailed revisions noted in the following sections.

Chapter One
- Changed the focus company to Vincor International, Canada's largest wine producer.
- Improved the presentation of material in the chapter by introducing a few graphical illustrations both in the body of the page and on the page margins that help students in understanding key concepts in business and accounting.
- Added a new self-study quiz related to the statement of retained earnings.
- Revised the discussion related to the price earnings ratio and clarified the relevance of this ratio to the chapter's content.
- Added an exhibit that summarizes the content of the four financial statements.
- Revised the content of the International Perspectives box to highlight the growing importance of the international accounting standards in financial reporting worldwide.
- Updated the information related to new regulations on management responsibility over internal controls and financial reporting.
- Updated and revised a substantial number of exercises, problems and cases.
- Upgraded Team Project to follow the concept of a continuous project from prior and subsequent chapters.

Chapter Two
- Updated the coverage related to the focus company, Van Houtte, Inc.
- Revised the Question of Ethics box which focuses on environmental liabilities.

- Added a new exhibit showing a list of typical account titles.
- Rewrote sections of the chapter for added clarity.
- Substantially revised the end of chapter exercises, problems, and cases, and added new problems and cases.
- Upgraded Team Project to follow the concept of a continuous project from prior and subsequent chapters.

Chapter Three
- Updated the coverage related to the focus company, Van Houtte, Inc.
- Reorganized the learning objectives.
- Reorganized the presentation of material in the chapter material.
- Added the preparation of an income statement.
- Moved the Key Ratio Analysis to the end of the chapter.
- Added an International Perspectives box.
- Created a new chapter supplement that discusses discontinued operations and extraordinary items.
- Added a new section called Nonrecurring Items.
- Included an expanded discussion in the Focus on Cash Flows box.
- Added a self-study quiz related to ratio analysis to strengthen the user perspective.
- Substantially revised the end of chapter exercises, problems, and cases, and added new problems and cases in response to reviewer feedback.
- Upgraded Team Project to follow the concept of a continuous project from prior and subsequent chapters.

Chapter Four
- Updated the coverage related to the focus company, Van Houtte, Inc.
- Revised the learning objectives.
- Revised the chapter opening to focus on the need for adjustments at the end of the period.
- Realigned the discussion on adjustments by Revenues (deferred and accrued) and Expenses (deferred and accrued) versus Deferrals (revenues and expenses) and Accruals (revenues and expenses) in the 2nd edition.
- Improved on the presentation of material by reorganizing parts of the chapter.
- Added the Return on Equity Key Ratio Analysis toward the end of the chapter.
- Added two self-study quizzes.
- Revised the closing process by adding the Income Summary account.
- Expanded on the requirements of the Demonstration Case to show how the omission of adjustments affects elements of financial statements.
- Substantially revised the end of chapter exercises, problems, and cases, and added new exercises, problems and cases in response to reviewers' comments.
- Upgraded Team Project to follow the concept of a continuous project from prior and subsequent chapters.

Chapter Five
- Changed the focus company to Andrew Peller Limited (formerly Andrés Wines).
- Improved on the presentation of the material by inserting procedural steps that are common to both the direct and indirect methods.

- Revised the method of computation of cash receipts and payments (within the direct method) that will enhance students' understanding of these computations.
- Added a new self-study quiz.
- Moved discussion of direct method to a chapter supplement.
- Added a chapter supplement that discusses how gains and losses are reported on the cash flow statement.
- Substantially revised the end of chapter exercises, problems, and cases, including a new case based on the cash flow statement of an Italian company (Geox) that uses International Financial Reporting Standards.
- Upgraded Team Project to follow the concept of a continuous project from prior and subsequent chapters.

Chapter Six
- Changed the focus company to Forzani Group Ltd., Canada's largest retailer of sporting goods.
- Revised the learning objectives.
- Improved on the presentation of material by reorganizing parts of the chapter and updating information related to corporate governance.
- Deleted the Key Ratio Analysis related to the Return on Equity based on reviewers' comments, and relocated this ratio to Chapter 4.
- Revised the content of the International Perspective box to highlight the growing importance of the international accounting standards in financial reporting worldwide.
- Revised the content of A Question of Ethics to highlight the growing importance of sustainability reporting by companies.
- Changed the company used in the Demonstration case from Sleeman Breweries to Canadian Tire.
- Significantly revised the end-of-chapter material, resulting in a smaller, but more focused set of questions, exercises, problems, and cases that relate primarily to the topics covered in the chapter.

- Upgraded Team Project to follow the concept of a continuous project from prior and subsequent chapters.

Chapter Seven
- Updated the information related to the focus company, Gildan Activewear Inc.
- Rewrote certain sections of the chapter to improve on readability of the text.
- Added a new self-study quiz.
- Updated the requirements related to internal control over financial reporting and added a real world excerpt from Gildan's annual report.
- Substantially revised the end-of-chapter exercises, problems, and cases based on reviewers' feedback, and added new exercises and problems.
- Upgraded Team Project to follow the concept of a continuous project from prior and subsequent chapters.

Chapter Eight
- Updated the information related to the focus company, Dell, Inc.
- Reorganized the chapter and related Supplement A based on CICA Handbook Section 3031, which is consistent with International Financial Reporting Standard 2 on "Inventories."
  - Removed discussion of LIFO from the body of the chapter to Supplement B.
  - Incorporated discussion of the perpetual FIFO and weighted average costing methods that were previously covered in Supplement A.
  - Expanded on the discussion of lower of cost and market by focusing on the net realizable value as the only concept of market value permitted in Section 3031.
- Replaced the algebraic relationship between cost of goods sold and inventory with a relationship based on statement format, similar to the changes made in Chapter 5 for relationships between accrual and cash basis items.
- Converted the section on estimation of inventory to a Financial Analysis box.

- Added summary tables showing detailed computation of the cost of goods sold under different inventory control systems and different costing methods to complement the graphical presentations in the exhibits.
- Substantially revised the end-of-chapter exercises, problems, and cases based on reviewers' feedback, and added new exercises and cases.
- Upgraded Team Project to follow the concept of a continuous project from prior and subsequent chapters.

Chapter Nine
- Updated the information related to the focus company, WestJet Airlines.
- Rewrote certain sections of the chapter to improve on readability of the text, and updated the information related to the various exhibits and real world excerpts.
- Revised the coverage of revenue and capital expenditures to highlight the differences between ordinary repairs and maintenance versus extraordinary repairs and betterments.
- Expanded on the discussion of asset impairment.
- Moved discussion of changes in amortization estimates from chapter supplement into body of text.
- Substantially revised the end-of-chapter exercises, problems, and cases based on reviewers' feedback, and added, new exercises and alternate problems.
- Upgraded Team Project to follow the concept of a continuous project from prior and subsequent chapters.

Chapter Ten
- Updated the information related to the focus company, Petro-Canada.
- Rewrote certain sections of the chapter to improve on readability of the text, and updated the information related to the various exhibits and real world excerpts.

- Moved the discussions related to Lease Liabilities and Present Value Concepts and Chapter Supplement B to Chapter 11 as per reviewers' suggestions.
- Added a new A Question of Ethics box.
- Substantially revised the end-of-chapter exercises, problems, and cases based on reviewers' feedback, and added new exercises, problems, alternate problems, and cases.
- Upgraded Team Project to follow the concept of a continuous project from prior and subsequent chapters.

Chapter Eleven
- Changed the focus company to Petro-Canada to provide a continuation of the discussion of liabilities introduced in Chapter 10.
- Expanded the content of the chapter to include lease liabilities, asset retirement obligations, and employee retirement obligations.
- Reorganized the discussion of discount or premium amortization for a better comparison between the straight-line and effective-interest amortization methods.
- Added a chapter supplement that focuses on present value concepts.
- Revised the end-of-chapter exercises, problems, and cases based on reviewers' feedback, adding a substantial number of new exercises, problems, alternate problems, and cases.
- Upgraded Team Project to follow the concept of a continuous project from prior and subsequent chapters.

Chapter Twelve
- Changed the focus company to Sun Life Financial Inc.
- Revised the Learning Objectives.
- Reorganized the chapter's content to discuss common shares first before focusing on preferred shares.
- Added a Key Ratio Analysis on earnings per share and deleted the Key Ratio Analysis related to the dividend payout ratio.
- Added a brief section on accounting and reporting for income trusts.
- Substantially revised the end-of-chapter exercises, problems, and cases based on reviewers' feedback, adding nine new exercises, problems, and cases.
- Upgraded Team Project to follow the concept of a continuous project from prior and subsequent chapters.

Chapter Thirteen
- Updated the information related to the focus company, Home Depot.
- Rewrote certain sections of the chapter to improve on readability of the text, and updated the information related to the various exhibits and real world excerpts.
- Substantially revised the end-of-chapter exercises, problems, and cases based on reviewers' feedback, and added new assignment material.
- Upgraded Team Project to follow the concept of a continuous project from prior and subsequent chapters.

Chapter-Specific Online Supplements Supplemental topics specific to chapter content are also included on the OLC, for instructors who wish to cover this material.

- *The Formal Recordkeeping System:* This appendix, supplemental for Chapters 2 to 4, describes and illustrates the use of the General Journal and General Ledger during the accounting period, the construction of the worksheet at year-end, and the use of reversing entries at the beginning of the next accounting period.

- *Comparison of the Direct and Indirect Methods of Preparing the Cash Flow from Operating Activities Section of the Cash Flow Statement:* For use in Chapter 5, this simplified example—both a mini-chapter and an illustrative Excel spreadsheet, illustrates the difference between the computation of cash flow from operating activities using two methods: the direct method and the indirect method.

- *Canadian Capital Markets:* To supplement Chapter 6, this document helps define capital markets and the role of capital markets in Canada.

- *Comprehensive Income:* This supplement to Chapter 6 provides an overview of the Statement of Comprehensive Income and presents illustrative real-world excerpts from recent annual reports.

- *Accounting for Goodwill and Other Intangible Assets:* For use with Chapter 9, this supplement explains how businesses account for goodwill and other intangible assets as well as impairment in the value of goodwill.

- *Financial Instruments:* After reading this supplement to Chapter 10, students will understand the important differences among financial instruments.

- *Future Value Concepts:* For use with Chapter 11, this supplement explains the concept of future value cash flows and related computations.

- *Expanding the ROE Profit Driver Analysis: The Scott Formula:* To supplement Chapter 13. This expanded analysis of the ROE model provides additional insights into the operating, investing, and financing activities of a business.

- *Reporting and Interpreting Investments in Other Corporations:* This supplement is a complete chapter that describes the classification, recording, and disclosure of corporate investments in other corporations.

Teaching and Learning with Technology

Financial Accounting's technology learning solutions complement the textbook every step of the way, giving students the extra help they need while providing instructors with tools for teaching a stimulating and rewarding class.

LYRYX ASSESSMENT FOR FINANCIAL ACCOUNTING

A COMPLETE ONLINE ASSESSMENT SYSTEM

Lyryx Assessment for Financial Accounting, is an online learning and assessment tool that has captured the attention of post-secondary institutions across the country while improving student success in financial accounting.

The assessment takes the form of a homework assignment called a **Lab, which corresponds to the chapters in the Libby text**.

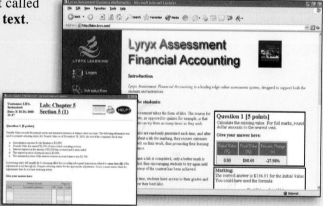

Key variables within the Labs are **algorithmically generated and automatically graded**, so students get instant scores and feedback—no need to wait until the next class to find out how well they did!

New Labs are randomly generated each time, providing the student with unlimited opportunities to try a type of question. After they submit a Lab for marking, students receive **extensive feedback** on their work, thus promoting their learning experience. Student motivation is high with these Labs because they can be **tied to assessment** and because they can try as many times as they want prior to the due date, with only their best grade being recorded.

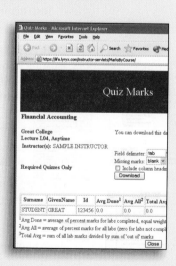

After registering their course with us, instructors can create Labs of their choice by selecting problems from our test bank, and setting a deadline for each one. Instructors have access to all the students' marks and can view their best Labs. Instructors can also download the class grades at any time to analyze individual and class performance.

If students do their financial accounting practice and homework, they *will* improve their performance in the course. Recent research regarding the use of Lyryx has shown that when Labs are tied to assessment, even if worth only a small percentage of the total grade for the course, students will do their homework—and more than once. *The result is improved student success in introductory financial accounting!*

Please contact your *i*Learning Sales Specialist for additional information on *Lyryx Assessment for Financial Accounting*.

Supplements

FOR THE STUDENT

iSTUDY

Available 24/7: providing instant feedback when you want, how you want, and where you want. This online *i*Study space was developed to help you master the concepts and achieve better grades. With all the learning tools you've come to expect, Libby's *i*Study includes tips on what you really need to know, an audio glossary, matching exercises, and self-study quizzes. *i*Study simply offers the best, most convenient way to interact, learn, and succeed.

*i*Study can be purchased through the online Student Success Centre or by purchasing a PIN code card through the campus bookstore. Instructors: Please contact your *i*Learning Sales Specialist for more information on how to make *i*Study part of your students' success.

ONLINE LEARNING CENTRE

Available at **www.mcgrawhill.ca/olc/libby**, the Online Learning Centre provides a range of resources, including numerous chapter-specific supplements (as outlined on page xxiv), Excel templates tied to selected end-of-chapter material, and self-study quizzes to help you succeed in your studies.

FOR THE INSTRUCTOR

INSTRUCTOR'S CD-ROM

This Instructor's CD-ROM includes:

- **PowerPoint® Presentations.** These slides for use in your classroom are completely customized for the third Canadian edition of *Financial Accounting*.
- **Solutions Manual.** Provides solutions for end-of-chapter questions, mini-exercises, exercises, problems, and cases.
- **Instructor's Manual.** Includes a chapter outline, detailed lecture notes, suggested activities and a reading list for each chapter.
- **Computerized Test Bank.** Includes over 1700 True/False, Multiple Choice, and Essay questions. Algorithmic questions also available.
- **Instructor's Excel® Template Solutions.** These Excel template solutions accompany the templates available to students in the Online Learning Centre.

ONLINE LEARNING CENTRE

www.mcgrawhill.ca/olc/libby

Select Instructor Resources are available for download on the Instructor's Centre of the Online Learning Centre. These include the PowerPoint® Presentations, Solutions Manual, Instructor's Manual, and Excel® Template Solutions.

CONTENT FOR COURSE MANAGEMENT SYSTEMS

Content cartridges are available for course management systems. Please contact your local McGraw-Hill Ryerson *i*Learning Sales Specialist for details.

PRIMIS CUSTOM PUBLISHING CASE OPTIONS

Through McGraw-Hill Ryerson's custom publishing division, **Primis**, instructors are able to select cases to accompany Financial Accounting in a number of ways. Create your own case set, or browse the selection of cases that correspond to the chapter material. Contact your McGraw-Hill Ryerson *i*Learning Sales Specialist for more information.

Acknowledgements

Writing and adapting a successful textbook requires a team effort and we have enjoyed working with excellent team-mates. Throughout the process of writing this textbook, many people stepped forward with tremendous efforts that allowed us to accomplish our stated goals. First and fore-most, we are deeply indebted to Robert Libby, Patricia Libby and Daniel Short, the authors of the U.S. book for developing the pedagogical approach used in this text. Their approach helped us tremendously in shaping this third Canadian edition. We would like to recognize the sincere and devoted efforts of the many people who added their input to the process of developing this book. We received invaluable advice and suggestions during the manuscript development and revision process. For this assistance, we thank the following colleagues:

THIRD EDITION REVIEWERS

Francois Brouard	Carleton University
H. Donald Brown	Brock University
Anthony Chan	Ryerson University
Liang-Hsuan Chen	University of Toronto at Scarborough
Ann Clarke-Okah	Carleton University
John Currie	Humber College
Sandra Daga	University of Toronto at Scarborough
Robert Ducharme	University of Waterloo
Allan W. Foerster	Wilfrid Laurier University
George Gekas	Ryerson University
Colin Haime	Malaspina University College
Sandy Hilton	University of Alberta
Susan Hogan	Capilano College
Gordon Holyer	Malaspina University College
Ian R. Hutchinson	Acadia University
Deborah Jarvie	University of Lethbridge
Winston Marcellin	George Brown College
Jeanbih Pai	University of Manitoba
William Richardson	McMaster University
Sandra M. Robinson	Concordia University
Catherine Seguin	University of Toronto at Mississauga
Joan Wallwork	Kwantlen University College
Shu-Lin Wong	Memorial University

PREVIOUS EDITION REVIEWERS

Teresa Anderson	University of Ottawa
Rick Bates	University of Guelph
Hilary Becker	Carleton University
Sandra Daga	University of Toronto
Greg Dunning	University of Windsor
Gerry Dupont	Carleton University
Dave Eliason	Southern Alberta Institute of Technology
Larry Goldsman	McGill University
Elizabeth Grasby	University of Western Ontario
Melissa Harty	University of Western Ontario
Ian Hutchinson	Acadia University
Heather Johnston	Brandon University
Hilary Johnston	Brandon University
Stuart Jones	University of Calgary
Duane Kennedy	University of Waterloo
Michael Konopaski	Trent University
Valorie Leonard	Laurentian University
Jingyu Li	Brock University
Marie Madill-Payne	George Brown College
Vanessa Magness	Ryerson University
David McConomy	Queen's University
Muriel McKenna	Seneca College
Cameron Morrill	University of Manitoba
Joe Pidutti	Durham College
Jo-Anne Ryan	Nipissing University
Mervat Saleh	Concordia University
Catherine Seguin	University of Toronto
Bob Sproule	University of Waterloo
Carol Tristani	Seneca College
Mike Welker	Queen's University
Elisa Zuliani	University of Toronto
Cecile Ashman	Algonquin College
Rick Bates	University of Guelph
David Carter	University of Waterloo
Don Drury	McGill University
Gary Dupont	Carleton University
Gary Entwistle	University of Saskatchewan
Leo Gallant	St. Francis Xavier University
Marilyn Glynn	Ryerson University
Mahlon Harvey	University of Winnipeg
Darrell Herauf	Carleton University

David Hiscock	University of Waterloo
Stuart Jones	University of Calgary
Valorie Leonard	Laurentian University
Carol McKeen	Queen's University
Cameron Morrill	University of Manitoba
Fred Phillips	University of Saskatchewan
Lloyd Seguin	Wilfrid Laurier University
Mohamed Shehata	McMaster University
Chris Wright	Lakehead University

We also received invaluable input and support through the years from present and former colleagues and students.

We are also indebted to the following individuals who helped adapt, critique, and shape the ancillary package for the Canadian market: Allan Foerster, Wilfrid Laurier University; Melissa Jean, University of Western Ontario; Deborah Mortimer, University of Manitoba; Robert Ducharme, University of Waterloo; and Ian Feltmate, Acadia University.

The extraordinary efforts of a talented group of individuals at McGraw-Hill Ryerson made all of this come together. We especially thank Rhondda McNabb for her guidance throughout this project; Suzanne Simpson Millar for initiating the developmental work for this edition; Sarah Fulton who followed through the whole process tirelessly until the final printing; Kelly Dickson who managed the final production of this book, and all the marketing and sales people who helped bring this book to both instructors and students. We also thank all those who worked behind the scenes to ensure the successful completion of this book. Special thanks to Erin Moore who edited our work.

We thank Van Houtte Inc. and The Forzani Group Ltd. for permitting us to use their annual reports to provide students with real-world examples of financial statements and accompanying notes. We are also grateful to all the focus companies that allowed us to use excerpts from their financial statements and notes to illustrate the main ideas in each chapter.

Special thanks go to our families for their support, patience and understanding while we worked on completing this third edition of the book. We dedicate the book to them.

George Kanaan
Maureen Gowing

To Our Student Readers

This book is aimed at two groups of readers:

1. *Future managers*, who will need to interpret and use financial statement information in business decisions.

2. *Future accountants,* who will prepare financial statements for those managers.

Future managers need a firm basis for using financial statement information in their careers in marketing, finance, banking, manufacturing, human resources, sales, information systems, or other areas of management. Future accountants need a solid foundation for further professional study.

Both managers and accountants must understand how to *use financial statements in making real business decisions* to perform their duties successfully. The best way to learn this is to study accounting in real business contexts. This is the key idea behind our *focus company approach*, which we introduce in the first chapter. Each chapter's material is integrated with a focus company, its decisions, and its financial statements. The focus companies are drawn from 10 different industries, providing you with a broad range of experience with realistic business and financial accounting practices. In each chapter, *you will actually work with these real companies' statements* and those of additional contrast companies.

When you complete this course, you will be able to read and understand financial statements of real companies. We help you achieve this goal by:

1. Selecting learning objectives and content based on the way that seasoned managers use financial statements in modern businesses. *We emphasize the topics that count.*

2. Recognizing that students using this book have no previous exposure to accounting and financial statements

and often little exposure to the business world. We take you through the financial statements three times at increasing levels of detail (in Chapter 1, Chapters 2 through 5, and Chapters 6 through 13). This is the secret to our *"building block approach."*

3. Helping you *"learn how to learn"* by teaching efficient and effective approaches for learning the material. Keep these learning hints in mind throughout.

4. Providing regular feedback in *Self-Study Quizzes*, which occur throughout each chapter. *Complete the quizzes before you move on.* Then check your answers against the solutions provided at the end of the chapter. If you are still unclear about any of the answers, refer back to the chapter material before moving on.

5. Highlighting the *Key Terms* in bold print and repeating their definitions in the margins. You should pay special attention to the definitions of these terms and review them at the end of the chapter. A handy index is provided at the end of the book.

6. Introducing the *Key Financial Ratios* used to assess different elements of financial performance at the same time you are learning how to measure and report those elements. These will show you what kinds of accounting information managers use and how they interpret it.

7. At the end of each chapter, test what you have learned by working through the Demonstration Cases. *Working problems is one of the keys to learning accounting.*

Good luck in your financial accounting course.

George Kanaan
Maureen Gowing

Financial Statements and Business Decisions

1

After studying this chapter, you should be able to:

FOCUS COMPANY:

Vincor International Inc.

VALUING AN ACQUISITION USING FINANCIAL STATEMENT INFORMATION

I n June 2006, Constellation Brands Inc., the world's biggest wine maker, purchased Vincor International Inc.—Canada's largest wine producer—for $1.58 billion. Vincor has wineries in British Columbia, Ontario, Quebec, New Brunswick, California, Washington State, Western Australia, and New Zealand, and is one of the largest wine importers, marketers, and distributors in the United Kingdom. Vincor markets wines produced from grapes grown in the Niagara Peninsula of Ontario, the Okanagan Valley of British Columbia, and vineyards around the world. The company makes and sells several brands, including Inniskillin ice wine, a specialty wine made from grapes picked frozen on the vine. In addition to its premium wines, Vincor also sells cider and wine coolers. The company's estate wineries are supported by an international distribution network and dedicated sales and marketing forces.

The price Constellation Brands paid was decided by considering the value of the economic resources owned by Vincor International, its debts to others, its ability to sell goods for more than the cost to produce them, and its ability to generate the cash necessary to pay its current bills. Much of this assessment was based on financial information that Vincor provided to Constellation in the form of financial statements.

THE OBJECTIVES OF *FINANCIAL ACCOUNTING*

Determining the price that Constellation Brands was willing to pay for Vincor International is typical of the economic decisions that are made based on financial statements. Businesses use financial statements as the primary means to communicate financial information to parties outside the organization. The purpose of this text is to help you develop the ability to read and interpret financial statements of business organizations and understand the system that produces those statements. This book is aimed at two groups of readers: *future managers*, who will need to interpret and use financial statement information in business decisions, and *future accountants*, who will prepare financial statements for those managers. The book provides future managers with a firm basis for using financial statement information in their careers in marketing, finance, banking, manufacturing, human resources, sales, information systems, and other areas of management. It also provides future accountants with a solid foundation for further professional study.

Both managers and accountants must understand *financial statements* (what the statements tell you and what they do not tell you about a business enterprise), *business operations*, and *the use of financial statements in decision making* to perform their duties successfully. As a consequence, we integrate actual business practice in our discussions, starting with Chapter 1. We examine the fundamentals of financial accounting in a variety of business contexts relevant to your future careers. Each chapter's material is integrated around a *focus company* (in this chapter, Vincor International). The focus companies are drawn from nine different industries, providing you with a broad range of experience with realistic business and financial accounting practices. When appropriate, the focus company's operations and financial statements are then compared to those of the *contrast companies*. When you complete this book, you will be able to read and understand financial statements of real companies.

The way that seasoned managers use financial statements in modern businesses has guided our selection of learning objectives and content. At the same time, our teaching approach recognizes that students using this book have no previous exposure to accounting and financial statements and often little exposure to the business world. The book also is aimed at helping you learn how to learn by teaching efficient and effective approaches for learning the material.

UNDERSTANDING THE BUSINESS

THE PLAYERS

The success story of Vincor began in 1874 with the establishment of The Niagara Falls Wine Company. The company was founded by Thomas G. Bright and Francis A. Shirriff who invested a major portion of their savings, becoming the sole owners of the company. As is common in new businesses, the founders also functioned as managers of the business (they were *owner-managers*).

Bright's leadership in wine research and development in Canada helped bring Canadian wines to their position of respect around the world. As a result of their success, the founders soon discovered that they needed additional money to develop their business. So they borrowed money from a local bank and other lenders, or *creditors*, and used the funds to expand the business. Subsequent acquisition of other companies and consolidations in the wine industry led to the creation of Vincor International in 1993. Today, Vincor has established itself as a major participant in the North American super-premium wine market. By acquiring other companies, Vincor has fuelled growth in its sales from $114 million in 1995 to $654 million in 2005. The company's success attracted the attention of its competitors. On September 27, 2005, Constellation Brands, Inc. announced its intention to buy Vincor and subsequently acquired the company in June 2006.

Investors—such as Constellation Brands, which bought an entire company, or individuals who buy small percentages of large corporations—make their purchases hoping to gain in two ways. They hope to receive a portion of what the company earns in the form of cash payments called *dividends*, and they hope to eventually sell their share of the company at a higher price than they paid.

Creditors lend money to a company for a specific length of time. They gain by charging interest on the money they lend. When Vincor exchanges money with its lenders and owners, these are called *financing activities*. When Vincor buys or sells property such as vineyards used in producing grapes and extracting wine, these are called *investing activities*.

THE BUSINESS OPERATIONS

To understand any company's financial statements, you must first understand its operations. As noted, Vincor produces and markets wine, cider, and wine coolers for personal consumption. Vincor's wines are manufactured from grapes through a natural fermentation process. To produce the wine and bottle it for sale, Vincor needs raw materials such as apples, bulk wine, grape juice concentrate, and yeast for fermentation of the crushed grapes, kegs to store the wine during the fermentation process, and packaging materials such as glass bottles, caps, corks, labels, and cardboard cartons. Vincor purchases these ingredients and accessories from other companies, referred to as *suppliers*.

Vincor distributes its wines through its own distribution network in Canada, the United States, Australia, and the United Kingdom. It sells its products to wine retailers, or *customers*, either directly or through wholesale distributors.

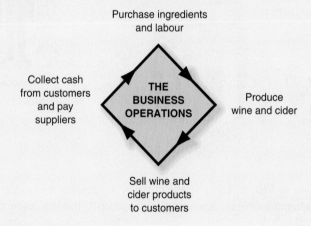

THE ACCOUNTING SYSTEM

Like all businesses, Vincor has an **accounting** system that collects and processes financial information about an organization and reports that information to decision makers. Vincor's managers (often called *internal decision makers*) and parties outside the firm such as the managers at Constellation Brands and the bank's loan officer (often called *external decision makers*) use reports produced by this system. Exhibit 1.1 outlines the two parts of the accounting system. Internal managers typically require continuous detailed information because they must plan and manage the day-to-day operations of the organization. Developing accounting information for internal decision makers is called *managerial* or *management accounting* and is the subject of a separate accounting course. The focus of this text is accounting for external decision makers, called *financial accounting*, and the four basic financial statements and related disclosures that are the output of that system.

We begin this process with a brief but comprehensive overview of the four basic financial statements and the people and organizations involved in their preparation and use. This overview provides you with a context in which you can learn the more detailed material that is presented in the following chapters. In particular, we focus on how two primary users of the statements, investors (owners) and creditors (lenders), relied on each of Vincor's four basic financial statements in their decisions to invest

ACCOUNTING is a system that collects and processes (analyzes, measures, and records) financial information about an organization and reports that information to decision makers.

■ LEARNING OBJECTIVE 1

Recognize the information conveyed in each of the four basic financial statements and how it is used by different decision makers (investors, creditors, and managers).

EXHIBIT **1.1**

**The Accounting
System and Decision
Makers**

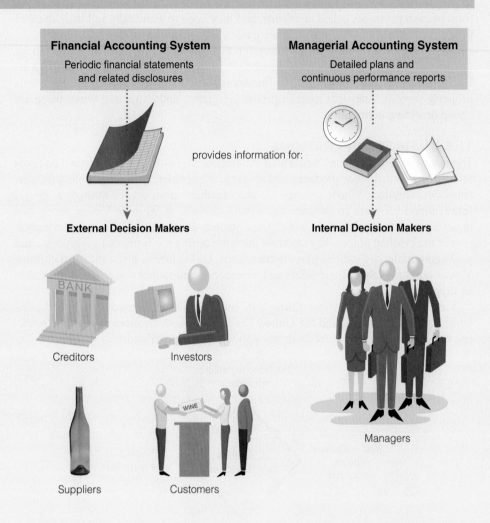

in or lend money to Vincor. Later in the chapter, we discuss a broader range of uses of financial statement data in marketing, management, human resources, and other business contexts.

To understand the way that Constellation Brands used Vincor's financial statements in its decision, we must first understand what specific information is presented in the four basic financial statements for a company such as Vincor.

We present many new business and financial statement terms in this chapter. **Instead of trying to memorize the definitions of every term used in this chapter, focus your attention on learning the general structure and content of the statements.** Specifically, you should focus on these questions:

1. What categories of items (often called *elements*) are reported on each of the four statements? (What type of information does a statement convey, and where can you find it?)

2. How are the elements within a statement related? These *relationships* are usually described by an equation that tells you how the elements fit together.

3. Why is each element important to managers', owners', or creditors' decisions? (How important is the information to decision makers?)

The *Self-Study Quizzes* that occur throughout the chapter will test your ability to answer these questions. Remember that since this chapter is an overview, each concept discussed in this chapter will be discussed again in Chapters 2 through 5.

ORGANIZATION OF THE CHAPTER

The Basic Financial Statements	Using Financial Statements to Determine Vincor's Value	Responsibilities for the Accounting Communication Process
• The Balance Sheet • The Income Statement • The Statement of Retained Earnings • The Cash Flow Statement • Relationships among the Four Statements • Notes to Financial Statements	• Determining Vincor's Purchase Price	• Generally Accepted Accounting Principles (GAAP) • Management Responsibility and the Demand for Auditing • Ethics, Reputation, and Legal Liability

THE FOUR BASIC FINANCIAL STATEMENTS: AN OVERVIEW

The four basic financial statements include the *balance sheet*, the *income statement*, the *statement of retained earnings*, and the *cash flow statement*.[1] These are the basic statements normally prepared by profit-oriented corporations for use primarily by investors, creditors, and other external decisions makers. They summarize the financial activities of the business. They can be prepared at any point in time and can apply to any time span (such as one year, one quarter, or one month). Like most companies, Vincor prepares financial statements for investors and creditors at the end of each quarter (known as *quarterly reports*) and at the end of the year (known as *annual reports*).

The organization for which financial data are to be collected, called an **accounting entity**, must be precisely defined on all the financial statements. The accounting entity itself, not the business owners, is viewed as owning the resources it uses and as owing its debts.

> An **ACCOUNTING ENTITY** is the organization for which financial data are to be collected.

THE BALANCE SHEET

The purpose of the **balance sheet** is to report the financial position (amount of assets, liabilities, and shareholders' equity) of an accounting entity at a particular point in time. We can learn a lot about what the balance sheet reports just by reading the statement from the top. The balance sheet of Vincor presented by its former owners to Constellation Brands is shown in Exhibit 1.2.

Structure   The *heading* of the balance sheet identifies four significant items related to the statement:

1. *name of the entity*—Vincor International Inc.
2. *title of the statement*—Balance Sheet
3. *specific date of the statement*—At March 31, 2005
4. *unit of measure*—(in thousands of dollars)

The heading of the statement indicates the time dimension of the report. The balance sheet is like a financial snapshot indicating the entity's financial position *at a specific point in time*—in this case, March 31, 2005—which is stated clearly on the balance sheet. Financial reports are normally denominated in the currency of the country in which they

> A **BALANCE SHEET (STATEMENT OF FINANCIAL POSITION)** reports the financial position (assets, liabilities, and shareholders' equity) of an accounting entity at a point in time.

BALANCE SHEET

Assets = Liabilities + Shareholders' Equity

---

[1] The income statement and the statement of retained earnings are sometimes combined into the statement of earnings and retained earnings.

EXHIBIT **1.2**

Balance Sheet

VINCOR INTERNATIONAL INC.		
Balance Sheet		
At March 31, 2005		
(in thousands of dollars)		
Assets		
Cash		$ 40,968
Accounts receivable		115,014
Inventories		257,076
Prepaid expenses		10,370
Plant and equipment		219,738
Intangible assets		528,689
Total assets		$1,171,855
Liabilities		
Bank indebtedness	$ 22,362	
Accounts payable	126,052	
Income taxes payable	9,930	
Long-term debt	311,980	
Future income taxes	40,800	
Total liabilities		$ 511,124
Shareholders' Equity		
Share capital	$438,875	
Retained earnings	221,856	
Total shareholders' equity		660,731
Total liabilities and shareholders' equity		$1,171,855

The notes are an integral part of these financial statements.
This balance sheet is an adaptation of Vincor's actual balance sheet.

amount of cash in the company's bank accounts
amounts owed by customers from prior sales
bottled wine, bulk wine, and packaging materials
rent and insurance paid in advance
factories and production equipment
economic resources that lack physical substance

amounts owed to banks within one year
amounts owed to suppliers for prior purchases
amount of taxes owed to the government
amounts owed on written debt contracts after one year
liabilities that resulted from differences between accounting and tax rules

amounts invested in the business by shareholders
past earnings not distributed to shareholders

are located, in this case Canadian dollars. Similarly, U.S. companies report in U.S. dollars and Mexican companies in Mexican pesos. Medium-sized companies often report in thousands of dollars; that is, they round the last three digits to the nearest thousand. The cash amount of $40,968 on Vincor's balance sheet actually means $40,968,000.

Vincor's balance sheet first lists the company's assets. Assets are economic resources legally controlled by the entity. Assets are followed by liabilities and shareholders' equity. They are the sources of financing or claims against the company's economic resources. Financing provided by creditors creates a liability. Financing provided by owners creates owners' equity. Because Vincor is a corporation, its owners' equity is designated shareholders' equity. Since each asset must have a source of financing, a company's assets must, by definition, equal the sum of its liabilities and shareholders' equity.[2] The **basic accounting equation**, often called the **balance sheet equation**, is written as

BASIC ACCOUNTING EQUATION (BALANCE SHEET EQUATION):
Assets = Liabilities + Shareholders' Equity.

Assets	=	Liabilities + Shareholders' Equity
Economic resources (e.g., cash, inventory)		Sources of financing for the economic resources Liabilities: from creditors Shareholders' Equity: from shareholders

[2]A corporation is a business that is incorporated under the federal or provincial laws. The owners are called **shareholders** or **stockholders**. Ownership is represented by shares of capital that usually can be bought and sold freely. The corporation operates as a separate legal entity, separate and apart from its owners. The shareholders enjoy limited liability; they are liable for the debts of the corporation only to the extent of their investments. Chapter Supplement A discusses forms of ownership in more detail.

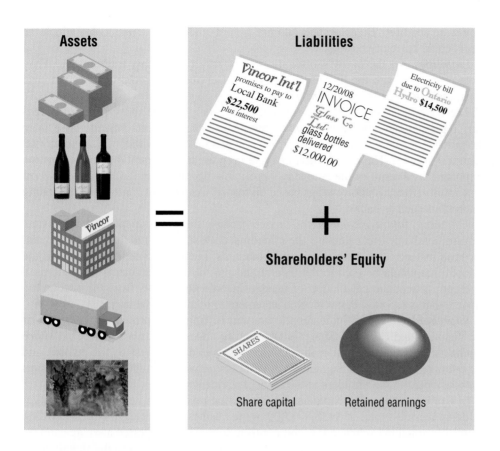

The basic accounting equation shows what we mean when we refer to a company's *financial position*: the economic resources that the company owns and the sources of financing for those resources.

Elements   *Assets* are economic resources controlled by the entity as a result of past transactions and from which future economic benefits can be obtained. Vincor lists six items under the category assets. The exact items listed as assets on a company's balance sheet depend on the nature of its operations. The six items listed by Vincor are the economic resources needed to produce and sell wine and cider to its customers. Each of these economic resources is expected to provide future benefits to the company. To prepare for the fermentation process, Vincor first needed *cash* to purchase *land* on which to develop vineyards, build manufacturing facilities, and install production machinery (*plant and equipment*). Vincor needs to have insurance to protect its resources against potential losses; advance payment of any insurance premiums gave rise to *prepaid expenses* **that reflect future economic benefits (i.e., insurance protection)**. Vincor then began making its wine and cider products, which led to the balance assigned to *inventories*. When Vincor sells its wine and cider to retailers and wholesalers, it sells them on credit and receives promises to pay called *accounts receivable*, which are collected in cash later. Vincor also owns patents, trademarks, and franchises. These are called *intangible* assets because they do not have physical existence.

Every asset on the balance sheet is initially measured at the total cost incurred to acquire it. For example, the balance sheet for Vincor reports Plant and equipment at $219,738; this is the amount paid (in thousands) for these assets when they were acquired. Balance sheets do not generally show the amounts for which the assets could currently be sold.

Liabilities are the entity's obligations that result from past transactions. They arise primarily from the purchase of goods or services on credit and through cash borrowings to finance the business.

There are five types of liabilities listed on Vincor's balance sheet. *Bank indebtedness* represents an amount borrowed from banks. The *accounts payable* arise from the purchase of goods and services from suppliers on credit without a formal written contract (or note). The *income taxes payable* represent an amount due to the taxation authorities as a result of the company's profitable operations in 2005. The *long-term debt* results from cash borrowings based on formal written debt contracts with lending institutions such as banks.

The term "*future income taxes*" arises because the governments that collect tax require companies to calculate their income tax using the federal and provincial tax laws instead of specific accounting standards. Future income taxes represent the amount that would be paid to the federal and provincial governments if they ceased to require a separate calculation of taxable income that differs from the accounting income that is reported in the income statement to other external users.

Shareholders' equity indicates the amount of financing provided by owners of the business and earnings. Shareholders' equity arises from two sources: (1) *share capital*, or the investment of cash and other assets in the business by the owners, and (2) *retained earnings*, or the amount of earnings reinvested in the business (and thus not distributed to shareholders in the form of dividends).

In Exhibit 1.2, the Shareholders' Equity section reports two items. Vincor's shareholders invested a total of $438,875,000 in the business and received over 33 million shares of capital in exchange for their contributions. This is reported as share capital.[3] Vincor's total earnings (or losses incurred) less all dividends paid to the shareholders since formation of the corporation equalled $221,856,000 and is reported as retained earnings. Total shareholders' equity is the sum of the proceeds received on issuing shares to owners plus the retained earnings.

FINANCIAL ANALYSIS   **INTERPRETING ASSETS, LIABILITIES, AND SHAREHOLDERS' EQUITY ON THE BALANCE SHEET**

Assessment of Vincor's assets was important to its creditors, and to its prospective investor, Constellation Brands, because assets provide a basis for judging whether the company has sufficient resources available to operate the business. Assets are also important because they could be sold for cash in the event that Vincor went out of business.

Constellation Brands was interested in Vincor's debts because of its concern whether the company had sufficient sources of cash to pay its debts. Vincor's debts were also relevant to its bankers' decisions to lend money to the company because existing creditors share the bankers' claims against Vincor's assets. If a business does not pay its creditors, they may force the sale of assets sufficient to meet their claims. The sale of assets often fails to cover all of a company's debts, and some creditors may take a loss.

Vincor's shareholders' equity or net worth is important to creditors because their claims legally come before those of owners. If Vincor goes out of business and its assets are sold, the proceeds of that sale must be used to pay back creditors before the shareholders receive any money. Thus, creditors consider shareholders' equity a protective cushion.

---

[3]It should be noted that the amounts in share capital on Vincor's balance sheet did not change when Vincor's shareholders sold their shares to Constellation Brands since the transaction did not involve an additional contribution of cash or other assets to Vincor. This transaction, which took place between Vincor's original owners and Constellation, occurred outside of the accounting entity, Vincor, and thus was not recorded by its accounting system.

A Note on Format   A few additional formatting conventions are worth noting here. Assets are listed on the balance sheet by ease of conversion into cash. Liabilities are listed by their maturity (due date). Most financial statements include the monetary unit sign (in Canada, the $) beside the first dollar amount in a group of items (e.g., the cash amount in the assets). Also, it is common to place a single underline below the last item in a group before a total or subtotal (e.g., intangible assets). A dollar sign is also placed beside group totals (e.g., total assets) and a double underline below. The same conventions are followed in all four basic financial statements.

SELF-STUDY **QUIZ 1-1**

1. Vincor's *assets* are listed in one section and *liabilities* and *shareholders' equity* in another. Notice that the two sections balance in conformity with the basic accounting equation. In the following chapters, you will learn that the accounting equation is the basic building block for the entire accounting process. Your task here is to verify that the shareholders' equity of $660,731,000 is correct, using the numbers for assets and liabilities presented in Exhibit 1.2 and the basic accounting equation in the form

Assets − Liabilities = Shareholders' Equity

2. Learning which items belong in each of the balance sheet categories is an important first step in understanding their meaning. Mark each balance sheet item in the following list as an asset (A), liability (L), or shareholders' equity (SE), without referring to Exhibit 1.2.

_____ Accounts payable		_____ Inventories	
_____ Accounts receivable		_____ Prepaid expenses	
_____ Cash		_____ Long-term debt	
_____ Share capital		_____ Retained earnings	
_____ Plant and equipment			

After you complete your answers, check them with the solutions on page 27. If you are unclear about any of the answers, you should refer back to the chapter material preceding the quiz before moving on.

THE INCOME STATEMENT

Structure   The **income statement (statement of income, statement of earnings, or statement of operations)** reports the accountant's primary measure of performance of a business: revenues generated less expenses incurred during the accounting period. While the term profit is commonly used in our language for this measure of performance, accountants prefer to use the technical terms *net income* or *net earnings*. Vincor's net income measures its success in selling wine and cider for more than it cost to generate those sales.

A quick reading of Vincor's income statement (Exhibit 1.3) provides an indication about its purpose and content. The heading of the income statement again identifies the name of the entity, the title of the statement, and the unit of measure used in the statement. Unlike the balance sheet, which reports financial information as of a certain date, the income statement reports information for a *specified period of time* (for the year ended March 31, 2005). The time period covered by the financial statements (one year in this case) is called an **accounting period**.

Notice that Vincor's income statement has three major captions: revenues, expenses, and net income. The income statement equation that describes this relationship is

Revenues − Expenses = Net Income

The **INCOME STATEMENT (STATEMENT OF INCOME, STATEMENT OF EARNINGS, STATEMENT OF OPERATIONS)** reports the revenues less the expenses of the accounting period.

The **ACCOUNTING PERIOD** is the time period covered by the financial statements.

EXHIBIT **1.3**

Income Statement

name of the entity
title of the statement
accounting period
unit of measure

revenue earned from sale of wine and cider products

cost to produce the wine and cider sold
expenses related to sales distribution and
administration not related to production
cost of using borrowed funds

income taxes on the period's pretax income

VINCOR INTERNATIONAL INC.
Income Statement
For the Year Ended March 31, 2005
(in thousands of dollars)

Revenues		
Sales revenue	$653,915	
Total revenues		$653,915
Expenses		
Cost of goods sold	365,005	
Selling and administrative expense	198,905	
Interest expense	24,650	
Total expenses		588,560
Income before income taxes		65,355
Income tax expense		16,666
Net income		48,689

The notes are an integral part of these financial statements.
This income statement is an adaptation of Vincor's actual income statement for 2005.

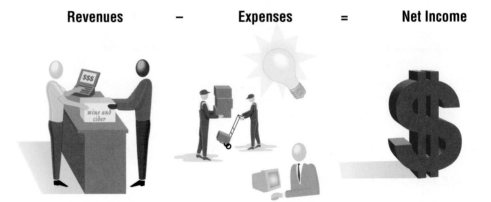

Revenues   –   Expenses   =   Net Income

Elements   Companies earn *revenues* from the sale of goods or services to customers (in Vincor's case, from the sale of wine and cider). Revenues are normally reported on the income statement when the goods or services are sold to customers **whether or not they have been paid for**. Retail stores such as Wal-Mart or McDonald's often receive cash at the time of sale. However, when Vincor sells its wine and cider to supermarkets and convenience stores, it receives a promise of future payment called an account receivable, which is collected in cash at a later date. In either case, the business recognizes total sales (cash and credit) made during a specific accounting period as revenue for that period. Various terms are used in financial statements to describe different sources of revenue (e.g., provision of services, sale of goods, rental of property). Vincor lists only one source, *sales revenue,* for wine and cider delivered to customers.

Expenses represent the dollar amount of resources the entity used up, or consumed, to earn revenues during the period. Vincor lists four items as expenses on the income statement. The **cost of goods sold** is the total cost to Vincor to produce the wine and cider delivered to customers during the year. These include the costs of ingredients used in production, wages paid to the factory workers, and even a portion of the cost of vineyards, storage tanks, and equipment used to produce the goods that were sold (called *amortization*). **Selling expenses** include a variety of expenses such as the salaries of sales staff and expenses related to distribution of wine and cider and the development of new markets. *Administrative expenses* also include many items such as the salaries of management personnel, plus other general costs of operating the company not directly related to production.

Vincor also reported *interest expense,* which reflects the cost of using borrowed funds. Finally, as a corporation, Vincor must pay income tax to the government. Vincor's *income tax expense* is approximately 25 percent of its pretax income.

Expenses may require the immediate payment of cash, a payment of cash at a future date, or the use of some other resource such as an inventory item that may have been paid for in a previous period. For accounting purposes, the expense reported in one accounting period may actually be paid for in another accounting period. Nevertheless, the company recognizes all expenses (cash and credit) incurred during a specific accounting period regardless of the timing of the cash payment. For example, let us assume that Vincor owes $50,000 in sales commissions to salespeople who sold wine and cider to retailers in March 2005, but did not pay the $50,000 until April 2005. In this case, the sales commissions would be recognized as expenses for the accounting period ending on March 31, 2005, because during March 2005 the salespeople exerted the efforts that resulted in commissions for their success at selling wine and cider.

Net income or net earnings (often called *profit* or *the bottom line*) is the excess of total revenues over total expenses. If total expenses exceed total revenues, a net loss is reported. (Net losses are normally noted by parentheses around the income figure.) When revenues and expenses are equal for the period, the business has operated at breakeven.

We noted earlier that revenues are not necessarily the same as collections from customers and expenses are not necessarily the same as payments to suppliers. As a result, net income normally **does not equal** the net cash generated by operations. This latter amount is reported on the cash flow statement discussed later in the chapter.

ANALYZING THE INCOME STATEMENT: BEYOND THE BOTTOM LINE

FINANCIAL **ANALYSIS**

Investors such as Constellation Brands and creditors closely monitor a firm's net income because it indicates the firm's ability to sell goods and services for more than they cost to produce and deliver. Investors buy the company's shares when they believe that future earnings will improve and lead to a higher share price. Lenders also rely on future earnings to provide the resources to repay loans. The details of the statement also are important. For example, Vincor had to sell $654 million worth of wine and cider to earn about $49 million. If a competitor were to lower prices just 10 percent, forcing Vincor to do the same, or if Vincor had to triple market development to catch up to a competitor, its net income could easily turn into a net loss. These factors and others help investors and creditors estimate the company's future earnings.

SELF-STUDY **QUIZ 1-2**

1. Learning which items belong in each of the income statement categories is an important first step in understanding their meaning. Mark each income statement item in the following list as a revenue (R) or an expense (E) without referring to Exhibit 1.3.

   _____ Cost of goods sold   _____ Selling and administrative

   _____ Sales

2. During the period 2005, Vincor delivered wine and cider to customers for which the customers paid or promised to pay in the future amounts totalling $653,915,000. During the same period, it collected $603,811,000 in cash from its customers. Without referring to Exhibit 1.3, indicate which of the two amounts will be shown on Vincor's income statement as *sales revenue* for 2005. Explain.

3. During the period 2005, Vincor *produced* wine and cider with a total cost of production of $401,759,000. During the same period, it *delivered* to customers wine and cider that had cost a total of $365,005,000 to produce. Without referring to Exhibit 1.3, indicate which of the two amounts will be shown on Vincor's income statement as *cost of goods sold* for 2005. Explain.

After you complete your answers, check them with the solutions on page 27.

THE STATEMENT OF RETAINED EARNINGS

The **STATEMENT OF RETAINED EARNINGS** reports the way that net income and the distribution of dividends affected the financial position of the company during the accounting period.

Structure   Vincor prepares a separate **statement of retained earnings**, shown in Exhibit 1.4. The heading identifies the name of the entity, the title of the statement, and the unit of measure used. Like the income statement, the statement of retained earnings covers a specific period of time (the accounting period), which in this case is one year. The statement of retained earnings reports the way that net income and the distribution of dividends affected the company's financial position during the accounting period. Net income earned during the year increases the balance of retained earnings. The declaration of dividends to the shareholders decreases retained earnings.[4] The retained earnings equation that describes these relationships is

Beginning Retained Earnings + Net Income − Dividends = Ending Retained Earnings

Elements   The statement begins with Vincor's retained earnings at April 1, 2004 (the beginning of the accounting period). The net income reported on the income statement for the current period is added and dividends declared during the year are subtracted from this amount. During 2005, Vincor earned $48,689,000, as shown in Exhibit 1.3. Also during 2005, Vincor declared and paid a total of $20,000,000 in dividends to its shareholders.[5] The net result is that retained earnings at March 31, 2005 (the end of the accounting period) increased by $28,689,000 (=$48,689,000−$20,000,000), or the portion of net income reinvested in the business.

The ending retained earnings amount of $221,856,000 is the same as that reported in Exhibit 1.2 on Vincor's balance sheet. Thus, the statement of retained earnings shows the relationship between the income statement and the balance sheet.

EXHIBIT 1.4

Statement of Retained Earnings

	VINCOR INTERNATIONAL INC.
name of the entity	**Statement of Retained Earnings**
title of the statement	**For the Year Ended March 31, 2005**
accounting period	**(in thousands of dollars)**
unit of measure	
last period ending retained earnings	Retained earnings, April 1, 2004 .... $193,167
net income reported on the income statement	Net income for 2005 48,689
dividends declared during the period	Dividends for 2005 .... (20,000)
ending retained earnings on the balance sheet	Retained earnings, March 31, 2005 .... $221,856

The notes are an integral part of these financial statements.
This statement is an adaptation of Vincor actual statement of retained earnings for 2005.

---

[4]Net losses are subtracted. The complete process of declaring and paying dividends is discussed in a later chapter.

[5]Vincor did not declare dividends since its formation, preferring to reinvest earnings in the business in order to sustain its growth. Nevertheless, we assume that dividends were declared in 2005 for illustrative purposes.

INTERPRETING RETAINED EARNINGS

FINANCIAL ANALYSIS

Reinvestment of earnings, or retained earnings, is an important source of financing for Vincor, representing about one-fifth of its financing. Creditors closely monitor a firm's statement of retained earnings because the firm's policy on dividend payments to its shareholders affects its ability to repay its debts. Every dollar Vincor pays to shareholders as a dividend is not available for use in paying back its debt to creditors. Investors examine retained earnings to determine whether the company is reinvesting a sufficient portion of earnings to support future growth.

SELF-STUDY QUIZ 1-3

Vincor's statement of retained earnings reports the way that the net income and the distribution of dividends affected the financial position of the company during the accounting period. In a prior period Vincor's financial statements reported the following amounts (in thousands): beginning retained earnings $126,900, total assets $885,700, dividends $16,800, cost of goods sold expense $235,200, net income $46,300. Without referring to Exhibit 1.4, compute ending retained earnings.

After you complete your answer, check it with the solution on page 27.

THE CASH FLOW STATEMENT

Structure　Vincor's cash flow statement is presented in Exhibit 1.5. The cash flow statement divides Vincor's cash inflows (receipts) and outflows (payments) into three primary categories of cash flows in a typical business: cash flows from operating,

EXHIBIT 1.5

Cash Flow Statement

VINCOR INTERNATIONAL INC.			
Cash Flow Statement			*name of the entity*
For the Year Ended March 31, 2005			*title of the statement*
(in thousands of dollars)			*accounting period*
			unit of measure
Cash flows from operating activities			*directly related to earning income*
Cash collected from customers	$ 603,811		
Cash paid to suppliers and employees	(545,306)		
Cash paid for interest	(16,894)		
Cash paid for taxes	(11,751)		
Net cash flow from operating activities		$29,860	
Cash flows from investing activities			*purchase/sale of productive assets*
Cash received for sale of short-term investment	$ 166,086		
Cash paid to purchase plant and equipment	(33,939)		
Cash paid to purchase long-term investment	(159,904)		
Net cash flow from investing activities		(27,757)	
Cash flows from financing activities			*from investors and creditors*
Repayment of long-term debt	$(267,604)		
Increase in bank indebtedness	324,396		
Cash received from issuance of share capital	2,073		
Cash paid for dividends	(20,000)		
Net cash flow from financing activities		38,865	
Net decrease in cash during the year		40,968	*change in cash during the period*
Cash at beginning of year		-0-	*last period's ending cash balance*
Cash at end of year		$40,968	*ending cash on the balance sheet*

investing, and financing activities. The heading identifies the name of the entity, the title of the statement, and the unit of measure used. Like the income statement, the cash flow statement covers a specified period of time (the accounting period), which in this case is one year.

As discussed earlier in this chapter, reported revenues do not always equal cash collected from customers because some sales may be on credit. Also, expenses reported on the income statement may not be equal to the cash paid out during the period because expenses may be incurred in one period and paid for in another. As a result, net income (revenues minus expenses) does *not* usually equal the amount of cash received minus the amount paid during the period. Because the income statement does not provide any information concerning cash flows, accountants prepare the **cash flow statement** to report inflows and outflows of cash.

The cash flow statement equation describes the causes of the change in cash reported on the balance sheet from the end of the last period to the end of the current period:

$$+/-\ \textbf{Cash Flows from Operating Activities}$$
$$+/-\ \textbf{Cash Flows from Investing Activities}$$
$$+/-\ \textbf{Cash Flows from Financing Activities}$$

$$\textbf{Change in Cash}$$

Note that each of the three cash flow sources can be positive or negative.

Elements *Cash flows from operating activities* are cash flows that are directly related to earning income. For example, when retailers pay Vincor for the wine and cider it has delivered to them, Vincor lists the amounts collected as cash collected from customers. When Vincor pays salaries to its salespeople or pays bills received from suppliers of packaging materials, it includes the amounts in cash paid to suppliers and employees.[6]

Cash flows from investing activities include cash flows related to the acquisition or sale of the company's productive assets. This year, Vincor had two cash outflows for investing activities: the purchase of additional plant and equipment to meet the growing demand for its wine and cider and the purchase of long-term investments. It also received cash for selling short-term investments. *Cash flows from financing activities* are directly related to the financing of the company itself. They involve both receipts and payments of cash to investors and creditors.

The **CASH FLOW STATEMENT** reports cash inflows and outflows that are related to operating, investing, and financing activities during the accounting period.

Cash Flow
Statement

+/− CFO
+/− CFI
+/− CFF
—————
Change in Cash

FINANCIAL ANALYSIS   **INTERPRETING THE CASH FLOW STATEMENT**

Many analysts believe that the cash flow statement is particularly useful for predicting future cash flows that may be available for payment of debt to creditors and dividends to investors. Bankers often consider the Operating Activities section to be most important because it indicates the company's ability to generate cash from sales to meet its current cash needs. Any amount left can be used to repay the bank debt or expand the company.

Shareholders will invest in a company if they believe that it will eventually generate more cash from operations than it uses so that cash will become available to pay dividends and to expand. The Investing Activities section shows that Vincor has made heavy investments in new manufacturing capacity, a good sign if demand continues to increase. The Financing Activities section indicates that Vincor was able to pay dividends to shareholders and repay part of its notes payable because it generated cash from operating activities.

---

[6]Alternative ways to present cash flows from operating activities are discussed in Chapter 5.

This year, Vincor paid $267,604,000 on long-term debt, and $20,000,000 in dividends to the company's shareholders. It also received $2,073,000 from shareholders and $324,396,000 through borrowing from banks.

SELF-STUDY **QUIZ 1-4**

1. During the period 2005, Vincor delivered wine and cider to customers that paid or promised to pay in the future amounts totalling $653,915,000. During the same period, it collected $603,811,000 in cash from its customers. Without referring to Exhibit 1.5, indicate which of the two numbers will be shown on Vincor's cash flow statement for 2005.

2. Learning which items belong in each cash flow statement category is an important first step in understanding their meaning. Mark each item in the following list as a cash flow from operating activities (O), investing activities (I), or financing activities (F), without referring to Exhibit 1.5. Also place parentheses around the letter only if it is a cash *outflow*.

_____ Cash paid for dividends

_____ Cash paid for interest

_____ Cash received from bank indebtedness

_____ Cash paid for taxes

_____ Cash paid to purchase plant and equipment

_____ Cash paid to suppliers and employees

_____ Cash collected from customers

After you complete your answers, check them with the solutions on page 27.

RELATIONSHIPS AMONG THE FOUR STATEMENTS

Our discussion of the four basic financial statements focused on the different elements reported in the statements, how the elements are related through the equation for each statement, and how the elements are important to the decisions of investors, creditors, and other external users. We have also discovered how the statements, all of which are outputs from the same system, are related to one another. In particular, we learned that:

1. Net income from the income statement results in an increase in ending retained earnings on the statement of retained earnings.

2. Ending retained earnings from the statement of retained earnings is one of the two components of shareholders' equity on the balance sheet.

3. The change in cash on the cash flow statement added to the cash balance at the beginning of the year equals the balance of cash at the end of the year, which appears on the balance sheet.

Thus, as external users, we can think of the income statement as explaining, through the statement of retained earnings, how the operations of the company improved its financial position during the year. The cash flow statement explains how the operating, investing, and financing activities of the company affected the cash balance on the balance sheet during the year. These relationships are illustrated in Exhibit 1.6 for Vincor's financial statements.

NOTES TO FINANCIAL STATEMENTS

At the bottom of each of Vincor's four basic financial statements is this statement: *"The notes are an integral part of these financial statements."* This is the accounting equivalent of the warning on a package of cigarettes. It warns users that failure to read the **notes** (or footnotes) to these financial statements will result in an incomplete picture of the company's financial health. Notes provide supplemental information about the financial condition of a company, without which the financial statements cannot be fully understood.

NOTES (footnotes) provide supplemental information about the financial condition of a company, without which the financial statements cannot be fully understood.

EXHIBIT **1.6**

**Relationships among
Vincor's Statements**

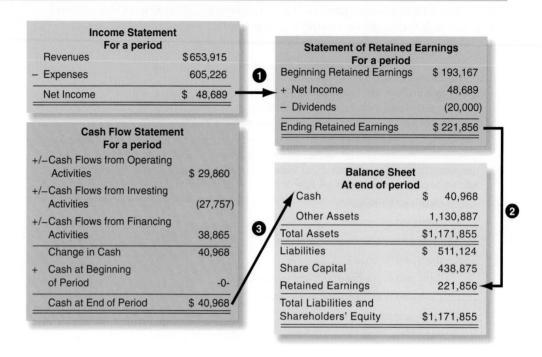

Income Statement For a period	
Revenues	$653,915
– Expenses	605,226
Net Income	$ 48,689

Statement of Retained Earnings For a period	
Beginning Retained Earnings	$ 193,167
+ Net Income	48,689
– Dividends	(20,000)
Ending Retained Earnings	$ 221,856

Cash Flow Statement For a period	
+/–Cash Flows from Operating Activities	$ 29,860
+/–Cash Flows from Investing Activities	(27,757)
+/–Cash Flows from Financing Activities	38,865
Change in Cash	40,968
+ Cash at Beginning of Period	-0-
Cash at End of Period	$ 40,968

Balance Sheet At end of period	
Cash	$ 40,968
Other Assets	1,130,887
Total Assets	$1,171,855
Liabilities	$ 511,124
Share Capital	438,875
Retained Earnings	221,856
Total Liabilities and Shareholders' Equity	$1,171,855

FINANCIAL ANALYSIS

MANAGEMENT USES OF FINANCIAL STATEMENTS

In our discussion of financial analysis thus far, we have focused on the perspectives of investors and creditors. In addition, managers within the firm often make direct use of financial statements. For example, Vincor's **marketing managers** and **credit managers** use customers' financial statements to decide whether to extend credit to them for their purchases of bottled wine and cider. Vincor's **purchasing managers** analyze financial statements of suppliers to judge whether the suppliers have the resources to meet Vincor's demand for ingredients and to invest in the development of new ingredients. Both Vincor's **human resource managers** and the **employees' union** use the company's financial statements as a basis for contract negotiations over pay rates. The net income figure even serves as a basis for computing **employee bonuses**.

When Vincor's managers examine the financial statements of the company's customers and suppliers, they rely on these statements as the best source of financial information available to external users because they do not have access to internal financial information produced by their customers and suppliers. However, when they make internal decisions regarding Vincor's operations, they rely on more detailed financial information obtained through the company's managerial accounting system.

There are three basic types of notes. The first type provides descriptions of the accounting rules applied in the company's statements. The second presents additional detail about a line on the financial statements. For example, Vincor's inventory note indicates the costs of packaging materials and supplies, bulk wine and cider that is in the process of being fermented, and bottled wine and cider that is ready for sale to customers. The third type of note presents additional financial disclosures about items not listed on the statements themselves. For example, Vincor leases some of its production facilities; terms of the lease are disclosed in a note. We will discuss many note disclosures throughout the book because understanding their content is critical to understanding the company.[7]

SUMMARY OF THE FOUR BASIC FINANCIAL STATEMENTS

We learned a lot about the content of the four basic statements. Exhibit 1.7 summarizes this information. Take a few minutes to review the information in the exhibit before you move on to the next section of the chapter.

EXHIBIT **1.7**

Summary of Four Basic Financial Statements

Financial Statement	Purpose	Structure	Examples of Content
Balance Sheet (Statement of Financial Position)	Reports the financial position (economic resources and sources of financing) of an accounting entity *at a point in time.*	BALANCE SHEET Assets = Liabilities + Shareholders' Equity	Cash, accounts receivable, plant and equipment, notes payable, share capital
Income Statement (Statement of Income, Statement of Earnings, Statement of Operations)	Reports the accountant's primary measure of financial performance *during the accounting period.*	Income Statement Revenues − Expenses Net Income	Sales revenue, cost of goods sold, selling expense, interest expense
Statement of Retained Earnings	Reports the way that net income and the distribution of dividends affected the financial position of the company *during the accounting period.*	Statement of Retained Earnings Beginning RE + Net Income − Dividends Ending RE	Net income is taken from the income statement; Dividends are distributions to shareholders
Cash Flow Statement (Statement of Cash Flows)	Reports inflows (receipts) and outflows (payments) of cash *during the accounting period* in the categories operating, investing, and financing.	Cash Flow Statement +/− CFO +/− CFI +/− CFF Change in Cash	Cash collected from customers, cash paid to suppliers, cash paid to purchase equipment, cash borrowed from banks

---

[7]The four basic financial statements and related notes are part of more elaborate documents called *annual reports* that are produced by public companies. Annual reports are normally split into two sections. The first section is a non-financial section that usually includes a letter to shareholders from the chairperson of the company's board of directors and the chief executive officer; descriptions of the company's management philosophy, products, its successes (and occasionally its failures); exciting prospects and challenges for the future; as well as beautiful photographs of products, facilities, and personnel.

The second section includes the core of the report. The principal components of this financial section include summarized financial data for five or 10 years, management's discussion and analysis of the company's financial condition and results of operations, the four financial statements and related notes, the auditor's report, recent stock price information, a summary of quarterly financial data, and a list of directors and officers of the company.

USING FINANCIAL STATEMENTS TO DETERMINE VINCOR'S VALUE

DETERMINING VINCOR'S PURCHASE PRICE

Even at this early stage of your study of accounting, we can illustrate part of the process Constellation Brands went through to determine the price it was willing to pay for Vincor. The price Constellation paid was decided by considering a variety of factors, including the value of Vincor's assets, its debts to others, its ability to sell goods for more than their production cost, and its ability to generate the cash necessary to pay its current bills. These factors are the subject matter of the balance sheet, income statement, and cash flow statement.

In general, investors use prior year's financial performance to make projections about future performance. They will be willing to pay for a firm that reported high net income in the past if they believe it will produce higher income in the future.

One method for estimating the value of a company is with a *price/earnings ratio* (or *P/E ratio* or *P/E multiple*). The P/E ratio measures the multiple of current year's earnings that investors are willing to pay for the company's shares. A high P/E ratio means that investors have confidence in the company's ability to produce higher profits in future years.

Competitors' P/E ratios often serve as a starting point in analyzing the price that should be paid for a company or its shares. Other companies in the same industry with similar performance and past growth were selling for 21 times their current year's earnings. Accordingly, the price Constellation paid could be determined using the following computation:

$$\text{Price / Earnings Ratio} = \frac{\text{Market Price}}{\text{Net Income}}$$

$$\text{Market (Purchase) Price} = \text{P / E Ratio} \times \text{Net Income}$$

$$= 21 \times \text{Net Income}$$

$$= 21 \times \$48,689,000$$

$$= \$1,022,469,000$$

The price that Constellation paid to acquire Vincor—$1.58 billion—is much higher than the price suggested by the above formula. In some cases, companies are willing to pay a higher amount in order to acquire special assets that are valuable to the acquiring company. In this case, the acquisition of Vincor increased Constellation's global presence and strengthened the company's position as the largest wine company in the world. Constellation paid 39 times last year's earnings because they believe that this acquisition will improve the company's earnings in future years.

A difficult part of this analysis is deciding what price/earnings multiplier is appropriate for this situation. Constellation carefully considered this issue, and its analysis involved more than this simple formula. However, the P/E ratio provides an estimation of the market value of Vincor's net assets.[8]

RESPONSIBILITIES FOR THE ACCOUNTING COMMUNICATION PROCESS

■ LEARNING OBJECTIVE 2

Identify the role of generally accepted accounting principles (GAAP) in determining the content of financial statements.

Effective communication means that the recipient understands what the sender intends to convey. For the decision makers at Constellation to use the information in Vincor's financial statements effectively, they had to understand what information each statement conveys.

---

[8]The role of net income in determining the value of a company will be discussed in more detail in your corporate finance course and more advanced courses in financial statement analysis. See, for example, K.R. Palepu, P.M. Healy, and V.B. Bernard, *Business Analysis and Valuation*. Cincinnati, OH: South-Western, 2004, Chapter 11.

They also needed to know that the amounts reported in the statements fairly represent what is claimed. Financial statements that do not represent what they claim to are meaningless and cannot be used effectively to make decisions. For example, if the balance sheet lists $2,000,000 for a factory that does not exist, that part of the statement does not convey useful information.

Decision makers also needed to understand the *measurement rules* applied in computing the numbers on the statements. A swim coach would never try to evaluate a swimmer's time in the "100 freestyle" without first asking if the time was for a race in metres or in yards. Likewise, a decision maker should never attempt to use accounting information without first understanding the measurement rules that were used to develop the information. These measurement rules are based on **generally accepted accounting principles**, or **GAAP**. These encompass broad principles, specific rules, practices, and conventions of general application that are used by organizations to record transactions and report financial statement information to interested users.

GENERALLY ACCEPTED ACCOUNTING PRINCIPLES (GAAP)

How Are Generally Accepted Accounting Principles Determined? The accounting system that we use today has a long history. Its foundations are normally traced back to the works of an Italian monk and mathematician, Fr. Luca Pacioli. In 1494, he described an approach developed by Italian merchants to account for their activities as owner-managers of business ventures. Many others wrote works on accounting after Pacioli, but prior to 1933, each company's management largely determined its financial reporting practices. Thus, little uniformity in practice existed among companies.

Following the dramatic stock market decline of 1929, the Securities Act of 1933 and The Securities Exchange Act of 1934 were passed into law by the U.S. Congress. These acts created the **Securities and Exchange Commission (SEC)** and gave it broad powers to determine the measurement rules for financial statements that companies must provide to shareholders. In Canada, provincial securities legislation created securities commissions, most notably the **Ontario Securities Commission (OSC)**, to regulate the flow of financial information provided by publicly traded companies whose shares trade on Canadian stock exchanges, such as the Toronto Stock Exchange. Similar to the SEC, the OSC plays an influential role in promotion, surveillance, and enforcement of sound accounting practices by publicly traded companies, especially after the collapse of big corporations, such as Enron and WorldCom, due to fraudulent managerial behaviour.

Since their establishment, these securities commissions have worked with organizations of professional accountants to establish groups that are given the primary responsibilities to work out the detailed rules that become generally accepted accounting principles. The current Canadian group that has this responsibility is the **Accounting Standards Board (AcSB)** of the Canadian Institute of Chartered Accountants. The AcSB is responsible for establishing standards of accounting and reporting by Canadian companies and not-for-profit organizations. These standards or recommendations, which are published in the *CICA Handbook*, have expanded over time because of the increasing diversity and complexity of current business practices.

Most managers do not need to learn all of the details included in these standards. Our approach is to focus on those details that have the greatest impact on the numbers presented in financial statements and are appropriate for an introductory course.

Why Is GAAP Important to Managers and External Users? Generally accepted accounting principles (GAAP) are of great interest to the companies that must prepare the statements and to the readers of these statements. GAAP provide guidance

GENERALLY ACCEPTED ACCOUNTING PRINCIPLES (GAAP) are guidelines for the measurement rules used to develop the information in financial statements.

The **SECURITIES AND EXCHANGE COMMISSION (SEC)** is the U.S. government agency that determines the financial statements that public companies must provide to shareholders and the measurement rules that they must use in producing those statements.

The **ONTARIO SECURITIES COMMISSION (OSC)** is the most influential Canadian regulator of the flow of financial information provided by publicly traded companies in Canada.

The **ACCOUNTING STANDARDS BOARD (AcSB)** is the private-sector body given the primary responsibility to work out the detailed rules that become accepted accounting standards.

to companies in selecting the accounting methods that best reflect the results of their operations and financial situation. At the same time, generally accepted accounting methods help prevent managers from deliberately manipulating income figures that serve their interests by using accounting practices that are not in conformity with GAAP. Widely divergent accounting practices reduce the comparability of financial information produced by different companies; hence, GAAP limits the number of acceptable alternative accounting methods in order to enhance the comparability of financial information across companies and over time. Furthermore, understanding GAAP enables external users to assess the quality of the information presented in the financial statements and related notes.

Companies and their managers and owners are most directly affected by the information presented in the financial statements. Companies incur the cost of preparing the statements and bear the major economic consequences of their publication. These economic consequences include, among others:

1. effects on the selling price of a company's shares.
2. effects on the amount of bonuses received by management and employees.
3. loss of competitive advantage over other companies.

INTERNATIONAL PERSPECTIVE

THE INTERNATIONAL ACCOUNTING STANDARDS BOARD AND GLOBAL CONVERGENCE OF ACCOUNTING STANDARDS

REAL WORLD EXCERPT

Canadian Institute of Chartered Accountants

WEB SITE

Financial accounting standards and disclosure requirements are set by national regulatory agencies and standard-setting bodies. However, since 2002, the International Accounting Standards Board (IASB) has progressed quickly to fulfill its responsibility to produce International Financial Reporting Standards (IFRS).

In January 2006, the Accounting Standards Board publicized its strategic plan that will guide the Board in carrying out its standard-setting mandate for the period 2006–2011[9]:

> For public companies, the AcSB's objective is to move to a single set of globally accepted high-quality standards. The AcSB has concluded that this objective is best accomplished by converging Canadian GAAP with International Financial Reporting Standards (IFRSs) over a transitional period. Australia and the European Union have already adopted IFRS and other countries have convergence programs underway. The AcSB will develop and publish a detailed implementation plan for achieving convergence later this year.... The AcSB expects that the transition period will take approximately five years, but the precise timing will depend on many factors, and will be continuously monitored throughout the process. At the end of that period, Canadian GAAP will cease to exist as a separate, distinct basis of financial reporting for public companies.

In addition to Australia and the European Union, New Zealand has adopted the international standards in 2007, and the Financial Accounting Standards Board (FASB) in the United States has formally stated its intent to harmonize U.S. standards with the IFRSs. Japan and Canada currently accept IFRS financial statements if they are reconciled to the domestic accounting standards,

Canadian public companies will continue to prepare their financial statements in accordance with Canadian accounting standards until the transition to the international standards takes place.

[9]*Accounting Standards in Canada: New Directions—Strategic Plan*, Canadian Institute of Chartered Accountants, 2006, page 1.

Recall that the amount that Constellation was willing to pay to purchase Vincor was determined in part by net income computed in accordance with GAAP. This presents the possibility that changes in accounting standards can affect the price buyers are willing to pay for companies. Employees who receive part of their pay based on reaching stated targets for net income are directly concerned with any changes in how net income is computed. Managers and owners often are concerned that publishing more information in financial statements will give away trade secrets to other companies that compete with them. As a consequence of these and other concerns, changes in accounting standards are actively debated, political lobbying often takes place, and the accounting standards that are eventually issued are often a compromise among the wishes of interested parties.

MANAGEMENT RESPONSIBILITY AND THE DEMAND FOR AUDITING

Who is responsible for the accuracy of the numbers in Vincor's financial statements? Primary responsibility for the information in the financial statements lies with management, as represented by the highest officer of the company and its highest financial officer. Companies take three important steps to assure investors that the company's records are accurate: (1) they develop and maintain a system of internal controls over both the records and the assets of the company, (2) they hire outside independent auditors to attest to the fairness of the statement presentations, and (3) they form a committee of the board of directors to oversee the integrity of these two safeguards. These responsibilities are often reiterated in a formal **report to management** or **management certification** in the annual report. These three safeguards and a management certification are required for companies with publicly traded shares. Managers of companies that prepare fraudulent financial statements are subject to criminal and civil penalties.

■ LEARNING OBJECTIVE 3

Identify the roles of managers and auditors in the accounting communication process.

Three steps to ensure the accuracy of records:

System of Controls   External Auditors   Board of Directors

The **REPORT TO MANAGEMENT (MANAGEMENT CERTIFICATION)** indicates management's primary responsibility for financial statement information and the steps to ensure the accuracy of the company's records.

The role of the independent auditor is described in more detail in the **audit report**, or **report of independent auditors** (Exhibit 1.8). The audit report describes the auditor's opinion of the fairness of the financial statements and the evidence gathered to support that opinion. It is important to note that the main difference between the report of management and the report of the independent auditors concerns the responsibility for the financial information included in the company's annual report. As the report of the independent auditors indicates, the auditor's responsibility is to express an opinion on the Vincor financial statements that have been prepared by its accounting personnel and reviewed by the *audit committee* of the *board of directors* that assumes responsibility for these financial statements.

The **AUDIT REPORT (REPORT OF INDEPENDENT AUDITORS)** describes the auditors' opinion of the fairness of the financial statement presentations and the evidence gathered to support that opinion.

In Canada, an accountant may be designated as a *Chartered Accountant* (CA), a *Certified General Accountant* (CGA), or a *Certified Management Accountant* (CMA). These accounting designations are granted by the respective professional accounting organizations on completion of specific educational programs and experience requirements.[10] Professional accountants can offer various accounting services to the public, but only CAs and CGAs (in most Canadian provinces[11]) are permitted to issue audit reports of publicly traded companies because they have certain responsibilities that extend to the general public as well as to the specific business that pays for their services.

An **audit** involves the examination of the financial reports (prepared by the management of the entity) to ensure that they represent what they claim and conform with GAAP. In performing an audit, the independent auditor examines the underlying transactions and the accounting methods used to account for these transactions. Because of the enormous number of transactions involving a major enterprise such as Wal-Mart that total billions of dollars each year, the auditor does not examine each transaction. Rather, professional approaches are used to ascertain beyond reasonable doubt that transactions were measured and reported properly.[12]

An **AUDIT** is an examination of the financial reports to ensure that they represent what they claim and conform with generally accepted accounting principles.

EXHIBIT **1.8**

Auditors' Report

REAL WORLD EXCERPT

Vincor International Inc.

ANNUAL REPORT

Auditors' Report to Shareholders

We have audited the consolidated balance sheets of Vincor International Inc. as at March 31, 2005 and 2004 and the consolidated statements of operations, retained earnings and cash flows for the years then ended. These financial statements are the responsibility of the Company's management. Our responsibility is to express an opinion on these financial statements based on our audits.

We conducted our audits in accordance with Canadian generally accepted auditing standards. Those standards require that we plan and perform an audit to obtain reasonable assurance whether the financial statements are free of material misstatement. An audit includes examining, on a test basis, evidence supporting the amounts and disclosures in the financial statements. An audit also includes assessing the accounting principles used and significant estimates made by management, as well as evaluating the overall financial statement presentation.

In our opinion, these consolidated financial statements present fairly, in all material respects, the financial position of the Company as at March 31, 2005 and 2004 and the results of its operations and its cash flows for the years then ended in accordance with Canadian generally accepted accounting principles.

KPMG, LLP
Chartered Accountants
Toronto, Canada
May 13, 2005

---

[10]Refer to the following Web sites for details of the educational and experience requirements for the respective designations:

  Chartered Accountant: **www.cica.ca**

  Certified General Accountant: **www.cga-canada.org**

  Certified Management Accountant: **www.cma-canada.org**

[11]At the date of publication of this book, CGAs had limited audit rights in Québec. However recent legislative changes suggest that CGAs and CMAs have the right to practice public accounting if they meet stringent competency criteria. In British Columbia, CMAs are permitted to do assurance audits upon successful application to the Audit Certification Board.

[12]The Auditing and Assurance Standards Board of the Canadian Institute of Chartered Accountants sets standards for auditing of public companies, commonly referred to as Generally Accepted Auditing Standards (GAAS). Similar to Canadian GAAP, the Canadian auditing standards are also expected to converge to the International Standards on Auditing in the near future.

Many unintentional and intentional opportunities exist for managers to prepare misleading financial reports. An audit performed by an independent auditor is the best protection available to the public. When that protection fails, however, the independent auditor is sometimes found liable for losses incurred by those who rely on the statements. In this regard, the Canadian Public Accountability Board was created in 2003 to provide public oversight for auditors of public companies.

ETHICS, REPUTATION, AND LEGAL LIABILITY

If financial statements are to be of any value to decision makers, users must have confidence in the fairness of the information. These users will have greater confidence in the information if they know that the people who were associated with auditing the financial statements were required to meet professional standards of ethics and competence.

> ■ **LEARNING OBJECTIVE 4**
>
> Appreciate the importance of ethics, reputation, and legal liability in accounting.

The three Canadian professional accounting organizations require all of their members to adhere to professional codes of ethics. These broad principles are supported by specific rules that govern the performance of audits by members of these organizations. These organizations stress how important it is for each member to behave in ways that enhance the reputation of the profession by voluntarily complying with ethical codes. For example, the Canadian Institute of Chartered Accountants places ethical behaviour and professionalism as the most important of the pervasive competencies possessed by its members.[13] The Certified General Accountants Association of Canada notes in its *Code of Ethical Principles and Rules of Conduct* that an accountant's actions will have an influence not only on the welfare of society but also on that of the profession.[14] The Society of Management Accountants of Canada has also issued a few publications related to ethical conduct, such as *Codes of Ethics, Practice and Conduct* and *Implementing Ethics Strategies within Organizations*.[15] Failure to comply with professional rules of conduct can result in serious penalties for professional accountants, including rescinding the professional designation of an offending member. The potential economic effects of damage to reputation and malpractice liability, however, provide even stronger incentives to abide by professional standards. Thus, the profession recognizes that its members' reputations for ethical conduct and competence are their most important assets.

Financial statements fraud is a fairly rare event, due in part to the diligent efforts of practising professional accountants. In fact, many such frauds are first identified by the firm's accounting staff or its external auditors who advise regulatory authorities of possible wrongdoing. In doing so, these "whistle blowers" place the interest of the public at large ahead of their own interests and act accordingly. However, in case of malpractice, independent auditors may be held liable for losses suffered by those who relied on the audited financial statements.

It is important to note that the vast majority of managers and owners do act in an honest and responsible manner. However, when the top officers in an organization collude to deceive other parties, they may temporarily succeed. In many cases, even the most diligent audit may not immediately uncover the results of fraud involving collusion of the top officers of a corporation, such as occurred in a number of well-publicized cases like YBM and Livent in Canada, Enron and WorldCom in the United States, and Parmalat in Italy. However, those who were involved in fraudulent behaviour were eventually identified and were sanctioned for their behaviour by the appropriate legal authorities.

Misrepresentations by managers highlight the crucial importance of the public accounting profession in ensuring the integrity of the financial reporting system. The

---

[13]*The CA Competency Map.* The Canadian Institute of Chartered Accountants, Toronto: Canada, 2004, pp. 17–21, accessible through the CICA's Web site: **www.cica.ca**.

[14]*Code of Ethical Principles and Rules of Conduct.* Certified General Accountants Association of Canada, Vancouver: Canada, 2004, accessible through the CGA's Web site: **www.cga-online.org**.

[15]These publications are accessible through the Society's Web site: **www.cma-canada.org**.

recent failures in public disclosure of financial information that does not conform to existing accounting standards cost billions of dollars to the shareholders, creditors, and employees of these companies. In addition, these fraudulent cases raised many questions about the integrity of managers and auditors. More importantly, these spectacular financial reporting failures led to significant reforms of the accounting profession and the imposition of new government regulations both in Canada and the United States that make it more difficult and costly for company managers to engage in fraudulent activities.

These reforms include the requirement that chief executive officers and chief financial officers of publicly traded companies are required to (1) personally certify the fair presentation of annual reports, (2) have an audit committee that is independent of management and includes members who are financially literate. Moreover, the Canadian Securities Administrators (CSA), which coordinates and harmonizes regulation of the Canadian capital markets among the 13 securities regulators of Canada's provinces and territories, requires all publicly traded companies in Canada to report on the effectiveness of their internal controls over financial reporting, as of December 31, 2007. In this regard, Canada differs significantly from the United States where public companies have been required since 2002 to have an audit of internal control over financial reporting, under the Sarbanes-Oxley Act, or SOX for short. The cost of compliance with SOX's requirement has been higher than anticipated. This led the U.S. legislators to exempt from this requirement any public company with a market capitalization[16] not exceeding US$500 million, including Canadian companies that are listed on U.S. stock exchanges. In Canada, the CSA does not require an external audit of internal control over financial reporting, which saves substantial audit fees for approximately 3,400 Canadian public companies.

DEMONSTRATION **CASE**

At the end of most chapters, one or more demonstration cases are presented. These cases provide an overview of the primary issues discussed in the chapter. Each demonstration case is followed by a recommended solution. You should read the case carefully and then prepare your own solution before you study the recommended solution. **This self-evaluation is highly recommended.**

The introductory case presented here reviews the elements reported on the income statement and the balance sheet and how the elements within the statements are related.

ABC Service Corporation was organized by Able, Baker, and Casella on January 1, 2008. On that date, the investors exchanged $36,000 cash for all of the shares of the company. On the same day, the corporation borrowed $10,000 from a local bank and signed a three-year note, payable on December 31, 2010. Interest of 10 percent is payable each December 31. On January 1, 2008, the corporation purchased supplies for $20,000 cash. Operations started immediately.

At the end of 2008, the corporation had completed the following additional business transactions (summarized):

(a) Performed services and billed customers for $100,000, of which $94,000 was collected by year-end.
(b) Used up $5,000 of supplies while rendering services.
(c) Paid $54,000 for other service expenses.

[16]Market capitalization is calculated by multiplying the number of issued and outstanding shares of a corporation by its share price.

(*d*) Paid $1,000 in annual interest expense on the note payable.
(*e*) Paid $8,000 of income taxes to the Canada Revenue Agency.

Required:

Complete the following two financial statements for 2008 by entering the correct amounts. The suggested solution follows the blank statements.

ABC SERVICE CORPORATION
Income Statement
_____ (date)
(in dollars)

			Computation
Revenues			
Service revenue		$_____	_____
Expenses			
Service expenses	$_____		_____
Interest expense	_____		_____
Total pretax expenses		_____	
Income before income tax		$_____	_____
Income tax expense		_____	_____
Net Income		$_____	

ABC SERVICE CORPORATION
Balance Sheet
_____ (date)
(in dollars)

			Computation
Assets			
Cash		$_____	_____
Accounts receivable		_____	_____
Supplies		_____	_____
Total assets		$_____	
Liabilities			
Note payable (10%)	$_____		_____
Total liabilities		$_____	
Shareholders' Equity			
Share capital	$_____		_____
Retained earnings	_____		_____
Total shareholders' equity		_____	
Total liabilities and shareholders' equity		$_____	

We strongly recommend that you prepare your own answers to these requirements and then check your answers with the suggested solution.

SUGGESTED SOLUTION

ABC SERVICE CORPORATION
Income Statement
For the Year Ended December 31, 2008
(in dollars)

			Computation
Revenues			
Service revenue		$100,000	Total billed to customers
Expenses			
Service expenses	$59,000		$5,000 + $54,000
Interest expense	1,000*		
Total pretax expenses		60,000	
Income before income tax		$ 40,000	
Income tax expense		8,000	
Net Income		$ 32,000	

*This amount equals 10 percent of the amount borrowed ($10,000 × 10%).

Note that the *income before income tax* is the difference between revenues and pretax expenses, and that income tax expense is deducted from income before income tax to arrive at *net income*.

ABC SERVICE CORPORATION
Balance Sheet
At December 31, 2008
(in dollars)

			Computation
Assets			
Cash		$57,000	$36,000 + $10,000 − $20,000 + $94,000 − $54,000 − $1,000 − $8,000
Accounts receivable		6,000	$100,000 − $94,000
Supplies		15,000	$20,000 − $5,000
Total assets		$78,000	
Liabilities			
Note payable (10%)	$10,000		Proceeds of bank loan
Total liabilities		$10,000	
Shareholders' Equity			
Share capital	$36,000		Investment by owners
Retained earnings	32,000*		From income statement
Total shareholders' equity		68,000	
Total liabilities and shareholders' equity		$78,000	

*Given that ABC Service Corporation started on January 1, 2008, and there were no dividends declared in 2008, the ending balance of retained earnings equals the net income for 2008. Hence, there is no need to prepare the statement of retained earnings for 2008.

SOLUTIONS TO **SELF-STUDY QUIZZES**

Self-Study Quiz 1-1

1. Assets ($1,171,855,000) − Liabilities ($511,124,000) = Shareholders' Equity ($660,731,000).
2. L, A, A, SE, A, A, A, L, SE (reading down the columns).

Self-Study Quiz 1-2

1. E, R, E (reading down the columns).
2. Sales revenue in the amount of $653,915,000 is recognized because sales revenue is normally reported on the income statement when the goods or services have been delivered to customers who have either paid or promised to pay for them in the future.
3. Cost of goods sold is $365,005,000 because expenses are the dollar amount of resources used up to earn revenues during the period. Only the wine and the cider that have been delivered to customers are used up. The wine and cider still on hand are part of the asset inventory.

Self-Study Quiz 1-3

Beginning retained earnings ($126,900,000) + net income ($46,300,000) − dividends ($16,800,000) = Ending retained earnings ($156,400,000).

Self-Study Quiz 1-4

1. $603,811,000 is recognized on the cash flow statement because this number represents the actual cash collected from customers related to current and prior years' sales.
2. (F), (O), F, (O), (I), (O), O.

Chapter Supplement A

Types of Business Entities

This textbook emphasizes *accounting for profit-making business entities*. The three main types of business entities are sole proprietorship, partnership, and corporation. A *sole proprietorship* is an unincorporated business owned by one person; it usually is small in size and is common in the service, retailing, and farming industries. Often the owner is the manager. Legally, the business and the owner are not separate entities. However, accounting views the business as a separate entity that must be accounted for separately from its owner.

A *partnership* is an unincorporated business owned by two or more persons known as *partners*. Some partnerships are large in size (e.g., international public accounting firms and law firms). The agreements between the owners are specified in a partnership contract that deals with matters such as division of income among partners and distribution of resources of the business on termination of its operations. A partnership is not legally separate from its owners. Legally, each partner in a general partnership is responsible for the debts of the business (each general partner has *unlimited liability*). The partnership, however, is a separate business entity to be accounted for separately from its several owners.

A *corporation* is a business incorporated federally under the Canada Business Corporations Act or provincially under similar provincial Acts. The owners are called shareholders or stockholders. Ownership is represented by shares of capital that usually can be bought and sold freely. When an approved application for incorporation is filed by the organizers, a charter is issued by either the federal or the provincial government. This charter gives the corporation the right to operate as a legal entity, separate from its owners. The shareholders enjoy *limited liability*. Shareholders are liable for the corporation's debts only to the extent of their investments. The corporate charter specifies the types and amounts of share capital that can be issued. Most provinces require a minimum of two shareholders and a minimum amount of resources to be contributed at the time of organization. The shareholders elect a governing board of directors, which in turn employs managers and exercises general supervision of the corporation. Accounting also views the corporation as a separate business entity that must be accounted for separately from its owners.

In recent years, many Canadian corporations have converted to income trusts. In its basic form, an income trust issues units of securities to the public in exchange for funds that are used to purchase the equity and debt of an operating business. The cash generated from the investment in the debt and equity securities issued by the operating business flows to the income trust, and most of the cash is then distributed to unitholders. By distributing most of the cash received to unitholders, income trusts avoid paying income taxes, which has been the main reason for corporations that converted into income trusts. We discuss income trusts in more detail in Chapter 12.

The rush to convert established corporations to income trusts waned in 2007, after the Canadian federal government promulgated a new law that effectively imposed income taxes on income trusts, thus depriving them from the main advantage of establishing an income trust.

In terms of economic importance, the corporation is the dominant form of business organization in Canada. This dominance is caused by the many advantages of the corporate form: (1) limited liability for the shareholders, (2) continuity of life, (3) ease in transferring ownership (shares), and (4) opportunities to raise large amounts of money by selling shares to a large number of people. The primary disadvantages of a corporation are (1) the loss of control by shareholders, (2) complex reporting procedures for a variety of government agencies, and (3) income may be subject to double taxation (it is taxed when it is earned and again when it is distributed to shareholders as dividends). In this textbook, we emphasize the corporate form of business. Nevertheless, the accounting concepts and procedures that we discuss also apply to other types of businesses. The main differences among these three types of entities appear in the equity section of the balance sheet.

Specific aspects of the three types of business entities are compared in Exhibit 1.9.

EXHIBIT **1.9**

Comparison of Three Types of Business Entities

	Proprietorship	Partnership	Corporation
Number of owners	One owner	Two or more owners	Many owners
Legal status of entity	Not separate from that of its owner	Not separate from that of its owner(s)	Separate legal entity
Responsibility of owners for debts of business entity	Unlimited legal liability	Unlimited legal liability	Owners' liability is limited to their investment
Accounting status	Each entity is separate from its owner(s) for accounting purposes		

Chapter Supplement B

Employment in the Accounting Profession Today

Since 1900, accounting has attained the stature of professions such as law, medicine, engineering, and architecture. As with all recognized professions, accounting is subject to professional competence requirements, is dedicated to service to the public, requires a high level of academic study, and rests on a common body of knowledge. As indicated earlier, three Canadian accounting designations are available to an accountant: CA, CGA, and CMA. These designations are granted only on completion of requirements specified by the respective professional organizations. Although specific requirements vary among the three professional organizations, they include a university degree with a specified number of accounting courses, good character, a minimum of two years of relevant professional experience, and successful completion of a professional examination. Similar accounting designations exist in other countries, most notably the *Certified Public Accountant* (CPA) in the United States.

Accountants usually are engaged in professional practice or are employed by businesses, government entities, and not-for-profit organizations. The accounting profession is continuously changing. While many accountants still provide traditional accounting and tax services to businesses, individual clients, and government organizations, other areas of practice have become increasingly common in the accounting profession today. Demand for value-added accounting services (e.g., financial analysis, evaluation and implementation of new information technology and business processes, management advisory and consulting services, forensic accounting, and environmental accounting) is reshaping the nature of educational programs that prepare students to become professional accountants.[17]

PRACTICE OF PUBLIC ACCOUNTING

Although an individual may practise public accounting, usually two or more individuals organize an accounting firm in the form of a partnership (in many cases, a limited liability partnership, or LLP). Accounting firms vary in size from a one-person office, to regional firms, to the Big Four firms (Deloitte & Touche, Ernst & Young, KPMG Peat Marwick, and PricewaterhouseCoopers), which have hundreds of offices located worldwide. Accounting firms usually render three types of services: assurance services, management consulting services, and tax services.

Assurance Services Audit or assurance services are independent professional services that improve the quality of information, or its context, for decision makers. The most important assurance service performed by professional accountants in public practice is financial statement auditing. The purpose of an audit is to lend credibility to the financial reports, that is, to ensure that they fairly represent what they claim. An audit involves an examination of the financial reports (prepared by the management of the entity) to ensure that they conform with GAAP. Other areas of assurance services include integrity and security of electronic commerce and reliability of information systems.

Management Consulting Services Many independent accounting firms offer management consulting services. These services usually are accounting-based and encompass such activities as the design and installation of accounting, data processing, and profit-planning and control (budget) systems; financial advice; forecasting; inventory controls; cost-effectiveness studies; and operational analysis. This facet of public accounting practice has grown rapidly. The perceived influence of offering such services on auditor independence has recently caused large accounting firms to dissociate their consulting practice from their audit function.

Tax Services Accountants in public practice usually provide income tax services to their clients. These services include both tax planning as a part of the decision-making process and the determination of the income tax liability (reported on the annual income tax return). Because of the increasing complexity of provincial and federal tax laws, a high level of competence is required, which accountants specializing in taxation can provide. The accountant's involvement in tax planning often is quite significant. Most major business decisions have significant tax impacts; in fact, tax-planning considerations often govern certain business decisions.

EMPLOYMENT BY ORGANIZATIONS

Many accountants, including CAs, CGAs, and CMAs, are employed by profit-making and not-for-profit organizations. An organization, depending on its size and complexity, may employ from a few to hundreds of accountants. In a business enterprise, the chief financial officer (usually a vice-president or controller) is a member of the

---

[17]Refer to the following Web site for more details about the types of services and skills that should be provided by accountants in the future: **www.nextgenaccountant.com/research_hili/research_sum.html**.

management team. This responsibility usually entails a wide range of management, financial, and accounting duties.

In a business entity, accountants typically are engaged in a wide variety of activities, such as general management, general accounting, cost accounting, profit planning and control (budgeting), internal auditing, and computerized data processing. A primary function of the accountants in organizations is to provide data that are useful for internal managerial decision making and for controlling operations. The functions of external reporting, tax planning, control of assets, and a host of related responsibilities normally are also performed by accountants in industry.

EMPLOYMENT IN THE PUBLIC AND NOT-FOR-PROFIT SECTORS

The vast and complex operations of governmental units, from the local to the international level, create a need for accountants. The same holds true for other not-for-profit organizations such as charitable organizations, hospitals, and universities. Accountants employed in the public and not-for-profit sectors perform functions similar to those performed by their counterparts in private organizations.

A survey of positions occupied by accounting professionals and related salaries is available at **www.accountemps.com**.

CHAPTER **TAKE-AWAYS**

1. **Recognize the information conveyed in each of the four basic financial statements and how it is used by different decision makers (investors, creditors, and managers). p. 3**

   The *balance sheet* is a statement of financial position that reports dollar amounts for the assets, liabilities, and shareholders' equity at a specific point in time.

   The *income statement* is a statement of operations that reports revenues, expenses, and net income for a stated period of time.

   The *statement of retained earnings* explains changes to the retained earnings balance that occurred during the reporting period.

   The *cash flow statement* reports inflows and outflows of cash for a specific period of time.

   The statements are used by investors and creditors to evaluate different aspects of the firm's financial position and performance.

2. **Identify the role of generally accepted accounting principles (GAAP) in determining the content of financial statements. p. 18**
   GAAP are the broad principles, specific rules, and practices used to develop the information in financial statements. Knowledge of GAAP is necessary for accurate interpretation of the numbers in financial statements.

3. **Identify the roles of managers and auditors in the accounting communication process. p. 21**
   Management has primary responsibility for the accuracy of a company's financial information. Auditors are responsible for expressing an opinion on the fairness of the financial statement presentations based on their examination of the reports and records of the company.

4. **Appreciate the importance of ethics, reputation, and legal liability in accounting. p. 23**
   Users will have confidence in the accuracy of financial statement numbers only if the people associated with their preparation and audit have reputations for ethical behaviour and competence. Management and auditors can also be held legally liable for fraudulent financial statements and malpractice.

In this chapter, we studied the basic financial statements that communicate financial information to external users. Chapters 2, 3, 4, and 5 will provide a more detailed look at financial statements and examine how to translate data about business transactions into these statements. Learning the relationship between business transactions and financial statements is the key to using financial statements in planning and decision making. Chapter 2 begins our discussion of how the accounting function collects data about business transactions and processes the data to provide periodic financial statements, with emphasis on the balance sheet. To accomplish this purpose, Chapter 2 discusses key accounting concepts, the accounting model, transaction analysis, and analytical tools. We examine typical business activities of an actual service-oriented company to demonstrate the concepts in Chapters 2, 3, 4, and 5.

<table>
<tr><td>

BALANCE SHEET
Assets = Liabilities + Shareholders' Equity

</td><td>

INCOME STATEMENT
 Revenues
 − Expenses
 Net Income

</td></tr>
<tr><td>

STATEMENT OF RETAINED EARNINGS
 Retained Earnings, beginning of the period
 + Net Income
 − Dividends
 Retained Earnings, end of the period

</td><td>

CASH FLOW STATEMENT
 +/− Cash Flows from Operating Activities
 +/− Cash Flows from Investing Activities
 +/− Cash Flows from Financing Activities
  Change in Cash

</td></tr>
</table>

FINDING
FINANCIAL INFORMATION

KEY **TERMS**

Accounting p. 3

Accounting Entity p. 5

Accounting Period p. 9

Accounting Standards Board (AcSB) p. 19

Audit p. 22

Audit Report (Report of Independent Auditors) p. 21

Balance Sheet (Statement of Financial Position) p. 5

Basic Accounting Equation (Balance Sheet Equation) p. 6

Cash Flow Statement p. 14

Generally Accepted Accounting Principles (GAAP) p. 19

Income Statement (Statement of Income, Statement of Earnings, Statement of Operations) p. 9

Notes (Footnotes) p. 15

Ontario Securities Commission (OSC) p. 19

Report to Management (Management Certification) p. 21

Securities and Exchange Commission (SEC) p. 19

Statement of Retained Earnings p. 12

QUESTIONS

1. Define *accounting*.
2. Briefly distinguish financial accounting from managerial accounting.
3. The accounting process generates financial reports for both internal and external users. Identify some of the groups of users.
4. Briefly distinguish investors from creditors.
5. What is an accounting entity? Why is a business treated as a separate entity for accounting purposes?
6. Complete the following:

Name of Statement/Report	Alternative Title
a. Income statement	*a.* _____
b. Balance sheet	*b.* _____
c. Audit report	*c.* _____

7. What information should be included in the heading of each of the four primary financial statements?
8. What are the purposes of (a) the income statement, (b) the balance sheet, (c) the cash flow statement, and (d) the statement of retained earnings?
9. Explain why the income statement and the cash flow statement are dated "For the Year Ended December 31, 2008," whereas the balance sheet is dated "At December 31, 2008."
10. Briefly explain the importance of assets and liabilities to the decisions of investors and creditors.
11. Briefly define the following: *net income* and *net loss*.

12. Explain the accounting equation for the income statement. Define the three major items reported on the income statement.
13. Explain the accounting equation for the balance sheet. Define the three major components reported on the balance sheet.
14. Explain the accounting equation for the cash flow statement. Explain the three major components reported on the statement.
15. Explain the accounting equation for the statement of retained earnings. Explain the four major items reported on the statement of retained earnings.
16. Financial statements discussed in this chapter are aimed at *external* users. Briefly explain how a company's *internal* managers in different functional areas (e.g., marketing, purchasing, human resources) might use financial statement information.
17. Briefly describe how generally accepted accounting principles are determined in Canada.
18. Briefly explain the responsibility of company management, the board of directors, and the independent auditors in the internal control and financial reporting process.
19. (Supplement A) Briefly differentiate among a sole proprietorship, a partnership, and a corporation.
20. (Supplement B) List and briefly explain the three primary services that accountants in public practice provide.

EXERCISES

■ **LO1**

Honda Motor Co.

E1–1 Preparing a Balance Sheet

Established less than 50 years ago, Honda Motor Co., Ltd., of Japan is a leading international manufacturer of automobiles and the largest manufacturer of motorcycles in the world. As a Japanese company, it follows Japanese GAAP and reports its financial statements in millions of yen (the sign for yen is ¥). A recent balance sheet contained the following items (in millions). Prepare a balance sheet as at March 31, 2006, solving for the missing amount.

Accounts payable and other current liabilities	¥ 3,989,409
Cash and cash equivalents	747,327
Inventories	1,036,304
Investments	695,085
Long-term debt	1,879,000
Net property, plant, and equipment	1,815,267
Other assets	453,006
Other liabilities	577,522
Retained earnings	3,831,343
Share capital	294,407
Total assets	10,571,681
Total liabilities and shareholders' equity	?
Trade accounts, notes, and other receivables	5,824,692

■ **LO1**

E1–2 Completing a Balance Sheet and Inferring Net Income

Terry Lloyd and Joan Lopez organized Read More Store as a corporation; each contributed $50,000 cash to start the business and received 4,000 shares of capital. The store completed its first year of operations on December 31, 2008. On that date, the following financial items were determined: cash on hand and in the bank, $48,900; amounts due from customers from sales of books, $25,000; unused portion of store and office equipment, $49,000; amounts owed to publishers for books purchased, $7,000; one-year note for $3,000, signed on January 15, 2008 and payable to a local bank. No dividends were declared or paid to the shareholders during the year.

Required:

1. Complete the following balance sheet as at December 31, 2008.
2. What was the amount of net income for the year?

Assets		**Liabilities**	
Cash	$ _____	Accounts payable	$ _____
Accounts receivable	_____	Note payable	_____
Store and office equipment	_____	Interest payable	120
		Total liabilities	$ _____

	Shareholders' Equity	
	Share capital	$ _____
	Retained earnings	12,780
	Total shareholders' equity	_____
Total assets $ _____	Total liabilities and shareholders' equity	$ _____

E1–3 Analyzing Revenues and Expenses and Preparing an Income Statement   ■ LO1

Assume that you are the owner of The University Shop, which specializes in items that interest students. At the end of September 2009, you find (for September only) the following:

a. Sales, per the cash register tapes, of $119,000, plus one sale on credit (a special situation) of $1,000.

b. With the help of a friend (who majored in accounting), you determined that all of the goods sold during September had cost $40,000 to purchase.

c. During the month, according to the chequebook, you paid $38,000 for salaries, rent, supplies, advertising, and other expenses; however, you have not yet paid the $600 monthly utilities for September.

Required:
On the basis of the data given, what was the amount of income for September (disregard income taxes)? Show computations. (*Hint:* A convenient form to use has the following major side captions: Revenue from Sales, Expenses, and the difference—Net Income.)

E1–4 Preparing an Income Statement and Inferring Missing Values   ■ LO1

Wal-Mart Stores, Inc., is the largest retail chain in the United States, operating more than 2,000 stores. A recent annual income statement contained the following items (in millions). Solve for the missing amounts and prepare a condensed income statement for the year ended March 29, 2006. (*Hint:* First order the items as they would appear on the income statement and then solve for the missing values.)

Wal-Mart

Cost of sales	240,391
Interest costs	1,172
Net income	?
Net sales	315,654
Operating, selling, and general and administrative expenses	56,733
Provision for income taxes*	5,803
Total costs and expenses excluding income taxes	?
Income before income tax	?

E1–5 Analyzing Revenues and Expenses and Completing an Income Statement   ■ LO1

Home Realty, Incorporated, has been operating for three years and is owned by three investors. J. Doe owns 60 percent of the 9,000 shares that are outstanding, and is the managing executive in charge. On December 31, 2008, the following financial items for the entire year were determined: commissions earned and collected in cash, $150,000; rental service fees earned and collected, $15,000; expenses paid included salaries, $62,000;

---

*In Canada and the United States, "provision for income taxes" is a common synonym for "income tax expense."

commissions, $35,000; payroll taxes, $2,500; rent, $2,200; utilities, $1,600; promotion and advertising, $8,000; income taxes, $18,500; and miscellaneous expenses, $500. At December 31, there were $16,000 of commissions earned but not collected yet, and the rent for December ($200) was not paid. Complete the following income statement:

_____
_____
_____

Revenues		
Commissions	$ _____	
Rental service fees	_____	
Total revenues		$ _____
Expenses		
Salaries	$ _____	
Commission	_____	
Payroll tax	_____	
Rent	_____	
Utilities	_____	
Promotion and advertising	_____	
Miscellaneous	_____	
Total expenses (excluding income taxes)		_____
Income before income taxes		$ _____
Income tax expense		_____
Net income		$ _____

■ LO1

E1–6 Inferring Values Using the Income Statement and Balance Sheet Equations

Review the chapter explanations of the income statement and the balance sheet equations. Apply these equations in each independent case to compute the two missing amounts for each case. Assume that it is the end of 2007, the first full year of operations for the company.

(*Hint:* Organize the listed items as they are presented in the balance sheet and income statement equations and then compute the missing amounts.)

Independent Cases	Total Revenues	Total Expenses	Net Income (Loss)	Total Assets	Total Liabilities	Shareholders' Equity
A	$100,000	$82,000	$	$150,000	$70,000	$
B		80,000	12,000	112,000		60,000
C	80,000	86,000		104,000	26,000	
D	50,000		13,000		22,000	77,000
E		81,000	(6,000)		73,000	28,000

■ LO1

E1–7 Preparing an Income Statement and Balance Sheet

Ducharme Corporation was organized by five individuals on January 1, 2008. At the end of January 2008, the following monthly financial data are available:

Total revenues	$150,000
Total expenses (excluding income taxes)	100,000
Income tax expense (all unpaid as at January 31)	15,000
Cash balance, January 31, 2008	20,000
Receivables from customers (all considered collectable)	25,000
Merchandise inventory (by inventory count at cost)	32,000
Payables to suppliers for merchandise purchased from them (will be paid during February 2008)	11,000
Share capital (2,600 shares)	26,000
Dividends declared in January 2008	10,000

Required:
Complete the following three statements:

DUCHARME CORPORATION
Summary Income Statement

Total revenues	$ _____
Less: Total expenses (excluding income tax)	_____
Income before income tax	_____
Less: Income tax expense	_____
Net income	_____

DUCHARME CORPORATION
Statement of Retained Earnings

Retained earnings, January 1, 2008	$ _____
Net income for January	_____
Dividends declared during January	_____
Retained earnings, January 31, 2008	$ _____

DUCHARME CORPORATION
Balance Sheet

Assets

Cash	$ _____
Receivables from customers	_____
Merchandise inventory	_____
Total assets	$ _____

Liabilities

Payables to suppliers	$ _____
Income taxes payable	_____
Total liabilities	_____

Shareholders' equity

Share capital	$ _____
Retained earnings	_____
Total shareholders' equity	_____
Total liabilities and shareholders' equity	$ _____

E1–8 Preparing a Statement of Retained Earnings   ▪ LO1

Sultan Inc. was organized on January 1, 2008. It reported the following for its first two years of operations:

Net income for 2008	$ 36,000
Net income for 2009	45,000
Dividends for 2008	15,000
Dividends for 2009	20,000
Total assets at end of 2008	125,000
Total assets at end of 2009	242,000

Required:
Prepare a statement of retained earnings for Sultan Inc. for 2009. Show computations.

E1–9 Analyzing and Interpreting an Income Statement and Price/Earnings Ratio   ▪ LO1

Pest Away Corporation was organized by three individuals on January 1, 2007, to provide insect extermination services. At the end of 2007, the following income statement was prepared:

ANALYSIS

PEST AWAY CORPORATION
Income Statement
For the Year Ended December 31, 2007

Revenues		
Service revenue (cash)	$192,000	
Service revenue (credit)	24,000	
Total revenues		$216,000
Expenses		
Salaries	$ 76,000	
Rent	21,000	
Utilities	12,000	
Advertising	14,000	
Supplies	25,000	
Interest	8,000	
Total expenses		156,000
Income before income tax		$ 60,000
Income tax expense		21,000
Net income		$ 39,000

Required:

1. What was the average amount of monthly revenue?
2. What was the amount of monthly rent?
3. Explain why supplies are reported as an expense.
4. Explain why interest is reported as an expense.
5. What was the average income tax rate for Pest Away Corporation?
6. Can you determine how much cash the company had on December 31, 2007? Explain.
7. If the company had a market value of $468,000, what is its price/earnings ratio?

■ LO1

Dell Computer

E1–10 Focus on Cash Flows: Matching Cash Flow Statement Items to Categories

Dell Computer is a leading designer and manufacturer of personal computers. The following items were taken from its recent cash flow statement. Note that different companies use slightly different titles for the same item. Without referring to Exhibit 1.5, mark each item in the list as a cash flow from operating activities (O), investing activities (I), or financing activities (F). Place parentheses around the letter only if it is a cash outflow.

_____ (1) Cash paid to suppliers and employees

_____ (2) Cash received from customers

_____ (3) Income taxes paid

_____ (4) Interest and dividends received

_____ (5) Interest paid

_____ (6) Proceeds from sale of investment in Conner Peripherals, Inc.

_____ (7) Purchases of property, plant, and equipment

_____ (8) Repayment of borrowings

■ LO1

E1–11 Preparing a Cash Flow Statement

NITSU Manufacturing Corporation is preparing the annual financial statements for the shareholders. A cash flow statement must be prepared. The following data on cash flows were developed for the entire year ended December 31, 2008: cash inflow from operating revenues, $270,000; cash expended for operating expenses, $180,000; sale of unissued NITSU shares for cash, $30,000; cash dividends declared and paid to shareholders during the year, $22,000; and payments on long-term notes payable, $80,000. During the year, a tract of land was sold for $15,000 cash (which was the same price that NITSU had paid for the land in 2007), and $38,000 cash was expended for two new machines. The machines were used in the factory. The beginning-of-the-year cash balance was $63,000.

Required:
Prepare a cash flow statement for 2008. Follow the format illustrated in the chapter.

E1–12 **Comparing Income and Cash Flows from Operations (A Challenging Exercise)**

 LO1

Paul's Painters, a service organization, prepared the following special report for the month of January 2007:

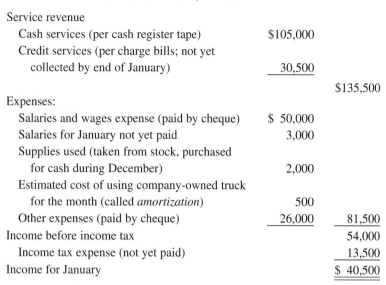

Service Revenue, Expenses, and Income

Service revenue		
Cash services (per cash register tape)	$105,000	
Credit services (per charge bills; not yet collected by end of January)	30,500	
		$135,500
Expenses:		
Salaries and wages expense (paid by cheque)	$ 50,000	
Salaries for January not yet paid	3,000	
Supplies used (taken from stock, purchased for cash during December)	2,000	
Estimated cost of using company-owned truck for the month (called *amortization*)	500	
Other expenses (paid by cheque)	26,000	81,500
Income before income tax		54,000
Income tax expense (not yet paid)		13,500
Income for January		$ 40,500

Required:

1. The owner (who knows little about the financial part of the business) asked you to compute the amount by which cash had increased in January 2007 from the operations of the company. You decided to prepare a detailed report for the owner with the following major captions: Cash Inflows (collections), Cash Outflows (payments), and the difference—Net Increase (or Decrease) in Cash.

2. Reconcile the difference—net increase (or decrease) in cash—you computed in requirement 1 with the income for January 2007 by filling in the following chart.

Reconciliation with income:	
Income	$40,500
Non cash services	(?)
Non cash expenses (? + ? + ? + ?)	?
Net increase (decrease) in cash	$29,000

PROBLEMS

P1–1 **Preparing an Income Statement and a Balance Sheet** (AP1–1)

 LO1

Assume that you are the president of Nuclear Company. At December 31, 2007, the end of the first year of operations, the following financial data for the company are available:

Cash	$ 25,000
Receivables from customers (all considered collectable)	12,000
Inventory of merchandise (based on physical count and priced at cost)	90,000
Equipment owned, at cost less used portion	45,000
Accounts payable owed to suppliers	47,370
Salary payable for 2007 (on December 31, 2007, this was owed to an employee who was away because of an emergency and will return around January 10, 2008, at which time the payment will be made)	2,000
Total sales revenue	140,000
Expenses, including the cost of the merchandise sold (excluding income taxes)	89,100
Income taxes expense (at 30% of pretax income); all paid during 2007	?
Share capital, 7,000 shares outstanding	87,000
No dividends were declared or paid during 2007.	

Required (show computations):

1. Prepare a summarized income statement for the year ended December 31, 2007.
2. Prepare a balance sheet at December 31, 2007.

■ **LO1**

ANALYSIS

P1–2 Analyzing a Student's Business and Preparing an Income Statement and a Balance Sheet (AP1–2)

While pursuing her undergraduate studies, Brigitte Lebeau needed to earn sufficient money for the coming academic year. Unable to obtain a job with a reasonable salary, she decided to try the lawn care business for three months during the summer. After a survey of the market potential, Brigitte bought a used pick-up truck on June 1 for $1,500. On each door she painted "Brigitte's Lawn Service, Phone 471-4487." She also spent $900 for mowers, trimmers, and tools. To acquire these items, she borrowed $2,500 cash by signing a note payable, promising to pay the $2,500 plus interest of $75 at the end of the three months (ending August 31).

At the end of the summer, Brigitte realized that she had done a lot of work, and her bank account looked good. This fact prompted her to become concerned about how much profit the business had earned.

A review of the cheque stubs showed the following: bank deposits of collections from customers totalled $12,600. The following cheques had been written: gas, oil, and lubrication, $920; truck repairs, $210; mower repair, $75; miscellaneous supplies used, $80; helpers, $4,500; payroll taxes, $175; payment for assistance in preparing payroll tax forms, $25; insurance, $125; telephone, $110; and $2,575 to pay off the note including interest (on August 31). A notebook kept in the truck, plus some unpaid bills, reflected that customers still owed her $800 for lawn services rendered and that she owed $200 for gas and oil (credit card charges). She estimated that the cost for use of the truck and the other equipment (called *amortization*) for three months amounted to $500.

Required:

1. Prepare a quarterly income statement for Brigitte's Lawn Service for the months of June, July, and August 2007. Use the following main captions: Revenues from Services, Expenses, and Net Income. Because this is a sole proprietorship, the company will not be subject to income tax.
2. Prepare a balance sheet for Brigitte's Lawn Service as at August 31, 2007. Brigitte's business is a proprietorship with one equity item: Brigitte Lebeau, capital.
3. Do you see a need for one or more additional financial reports for this company for 2007 and thereafter? Explain.

■ **LO1**

ANALYSIS

P1–3 Comparing Income with Cash Flow (A Challenging Problem)

New Delivery Company was organized on January 1, 2008. At the end of the first quarter (three months) of operations, the owner prepared a summary of its operations as shown in the first row of the following tabulation:

Summary of Transactions	Computation of Income	Computation of Cash
a. Services performed for customers, $66,000, of which one-sixth remained uncollected at the end of the quarter.	$66,000	$55,000
b. Cash borrowed from the local bank, $30,000 (one-year note).		
c. Small service truck purchased for use in the business: cost, $9,000; paid 30% down, balance on credit.		
d. Expenses, $36,000, of which one-sixth remained unpaid at the end of the quarter.		
e. Service supplies purchased for use in the business, $3,000, of which one-fourth remained unpaid (on credit) at the end of the quarter. Also, one-fifth of these supplies were unused (still on hand) at the end of the quarter.		
f. Wages earned by employees, $21,000, of which one-half remained unpaid at the end of the quarter.		
Based only on the above transactions, compute the following for the quarter:		
Income (or loss)	═══	
Cash inflow (or outflow)		═══

Required:

1. For each of the six transactions given in this tabulation, enter what you consider to be the correct amounts. Enter a zero when appropriate. The first transaction is illustrated.
2. For each transaction, explain the basis for your responses.

P1–4 Evaluating Data to Support a Loan Application (A Challenging Problem)

■ **LO1**

On January 1, 2008, three individuals organized West Company as a corporation. Each individual invested $10,000 cash in the business. On December 31, 2008, they prepared a list of resources owned (assets) and a list of the debts (liabilities) to support the company's request for a loan of $70,000 submitted to a local bank. None of the three investors had studied accounting. The two lists prepared were as follows:

Company resources

Cash	$ 12,000
Service supplies inventory (on hand)	17,000
Service trucks (four practically new)	68,000
Personal residences of organizers (three houses)	190,000
Service equipment used in the business (practically new)	30,000
Bills due from customers (for services already completed)	15,000
Total	$322,000

Company obligations

Unpaid wages to employees	$ 19,000
Unpaid taxes	8,000
Owed to suppliers	10,000
Owed on service trucks and equipment (to a finance company)	50,000
Loan from organizer	15,000
Total	$102,000

Required:

Prepare a short memo indicating:

1. Which of these items do not belong on the balance sheet (bear in mind that the company is considered to be separate from the owners)?

2. What additional questions would you raise about measurement of items on the lists? Explain the basis for each question.

3. If you were advising the local bank on its loan decision, which amounts on the lists would create special concerns? Explain the basis for each concern and include any recommendations that you have.

4. In view of your responses to (1) and (2), calculate the amount of shareholders' equity as at December 31, 2008. Show your computations.

ALTERNATE PROBLEMS

AP1–1 Preparing an Income Statement and a Balance Sheet (P1–1)

■ **LO1**

Assume that you are the president of McClaren Corporation. At June 30, 2009, the end of the first year of operations, the following financial data for the company are available:

Cash	$13,150
Receivables from customers (all considered collectable)	9,500
Inventory of merchandise (based on physical count and priced at cost)	57,000
Equipment owned, at cost less used portion	36,000
Accounts payable owed to suppliers	31,500
Salary payable for 2009 (on June 30, 2009, this was owed to an employee who was away because of an emergency and will return around July 7, 2009, at which time the payment will be made)	1,500
Total sales revenue	90,000
Expenses, including the cost of the merchandise sold (excluding income taxes)	60,500
Income taxes expense (at 30% of pretax income); all paid during 2009	?
Share capital, 5,000 shares outstanding	?
No dividends were declared or paid during 2009.	

Required (show computations):

1. Prepare a summarized income statement for the year ended June 30, 2009.

2. Prepare a balance sheet at June 30, 2009.

■ **LO1**

ANALYSIS

AP1–2 Analyzing a Student's Business and Preparing an Income Statement and a Balance Sheet (P1–2)

Upon graduation from high school, John Abel immediately accepted a job as an electrician's assistant for a large local electrical repair company. After three years of hard work, John received an electrician's licence and decided to start his own business. He had saved $12,000, which he invested in the business. His lawyer had advised him to start as a corporation. First, he transferred this amount from his savings account to a business bank account for Abel Electric Repair Company, Incorporated, and was issued shares. He then purchased a used panel truck for $9,000 cash and second-hand tools for $1,500; rented space in a small building; inserted an ad in the local paper; and opened the doors on October 1, 2007. Immediately, John was very busy; after one month, he employed an assistant.

Although John knew practically nothing about the financial side of the business, he realized that a number of reports were required and that costs and collections had to be controlled carefully. At December 31, 2007, prompted in part by concern about his income tax situation, John recognized the need for financial statements. His wife Jane developed some financial statements for the business. On December 31, 2007, with the help of a friend, she gathered the following data for the three months just ended. Bank account deposits of collections for electric repair services totalled $32,000. The following cheques had been written: electrician's assistant, $8,500; payroll taxes, $175; supplies purchased and used on jobs, $9,500; oil, gas, and maintenance on truck, $1,200; insurance, $700; rent, $500; utilities and telephone, $825; and miscellaneous expenses (including advertising), $600. Also, uncollected bills to customers for electric repair services amounted to $3,000. The $200 rent for December had not been paid. The average income tax rate is 30 percent. John estimated the cost of using the truck and tools (*amortization*) during the three months to be $1,200.

Required:

1. Prepare a quarterly income statement for Abel Electric Repair Company, Incorporated, for the three months of October through December 2007. Use the following main captions: Revenue from Services, Expenses, Income before Income Taxes, and Net Income.

2. Prepare a balance sheet for Abel Electric Repair Company, Incorporated as at December 31, 2007.

3. Do you think that John may have a need for one or more additional financial reports for 2007 and thereafter? Explain.

CASES AND PROJECTS

FINDING AND INTERPRETING FINANCIAL INFORMATION

■ **LO1, 3**

Van Houtte Inc.

ANALYSIS

CP1–1 Finding Financial Information

Refer to the financial statements of Van Houtte Inc. in Appendix B at the end of this book.

Required:

Look at the income statement, balance sheet, and cash flow statement closely and attempt to infer the types of information they report. Then answer the following questions based on the report.

1. What types of products does the company sell?

2. Did the chief executive officer (CEO) believe that the company had a good year?

3. On what day of the year does its fiscal year end?

4. For how many years does it present complete
   a. balance sheets?   *b.* income statements?   *c.* cash flow statements?

5. Are its financial statements audited by independent accountants? How do you know?

6. Did its total assets increase or decrease over the last year?

7. What was the ending balance of inventories?

8. Write out its basic accounting (balance sheet) equation in dollars at year-end.

■ **LO1, 3**

The Forzani Group Ltd.

ANALYSIS

CP1–2 Finding Financial Information

Refer to the financial statements of The Forzani Group Ltd. on the Online Learning Centre Web site at **www.mcgrawhill.ca/olc/libby/student/resources**.

Required:

1. What is the amount of net income for the current fiscal year?
2. What amount of revenue was earned in the current fiscal year?
3. How much inventory does the company have at the end of the current fiscal year?
4. By what amount did cash and cash equivalents* change during the year?
5. Who is the auditor for the company?

CP1–3   Comparing Companies

Refer to the financial statements and the accompanying notes of Van Houtte Inc. given in Appendix B and of The Forzani Group Ltd. on the Online Learning Centre Web site at **www.mcgrawhill.ca/olc/libby/student/resources.**

Required:

1. Both companies report "basic" earnings per share on their income statements and the market price per share of their stock either in their annual reports or on their Web sites. Using current year's earnings per share and the highest stock price per share reported for the most recent year, compute the price/earnings ratio. Which company provided the highest price/earnings ratio for the current year? (*Note:* For Van Houtte, use a market price of $24.70 per share.)

   (*Note:* Some companies will label an annual report for a period that ends within the first few months of the year as being a report for that year. For example, the annual accounting period for the Forzani Group ends in late January 2007 and that of Van Houtte ends in early April 2007, but both companies label their annual reports as Annual Report 2007, even though the reports cover only a few months in 2007. These reports essentially cover the companies' activities in 2006.)

2. Which company do investors believe will have the higher growth in earnings in the future?

■ **LO1**

Van Houtte
vs.
The Forzani Group

ANALYSIS

FINANCIAL REPORTING AND ANALYSIS CASES

CP1–4   Using Financial Reports: Identifying and Correcting Deficiencies in an Income Statement and a Balance Sheet

Performance Corporation was organized on January 1, 2007. At the end of 2007, the company had not yet employed an accountant; however, an employee who was "good with numbers" prepared the following statements at that date:

■ **LO1**

ANALYSIS

PERFORMANCE CORPORATION
December 31, 2007

Income from sales of merchandise	$175,000
Total amount paid for goods sold during 2007	(90,000)
Selling costs	(25,000)
Amortization (on service vehicles used)	(10,000)
Income from services rendered	52,000
Salaries and wages paid	(62,000)

PERFORMANCE CORPORATION
December 31, 2007

Resources		
Cash		$ 32,000
Merchandise inventory (held for resale)		42,000
Service vehicles		50,000
Retained earnings (profit earned in 2007)		30,000
Grand total		$154,000
Debts		
Payable to suppliers		$ 22,000
Note owed to bank		25,000
Due from customers		13,000
Total		$ 60,000
Supplies on hand (to be used in rendering services)	$ 15,000	
Accumulated amortization** (on service vehicles)	10,000	
Share capital, 6,500 shares	65,000	
Total		90,000
Grand total		$150,000

Cash equivalents are short-term investments readily convertible into cash and whose value is unlikely to change.

**Accumulated amortization* represents the cost related to the used portion of the asset and should be subtracted from the asset balance.

Required:

1. List all of the deficiencies that you can identify in these statements. Give a brief explanation of each one.

2. Prepare a proper income statement for Performance Corporation for 2007 (correct net income is $30,000) and a proper balance sheet at December 31, 2007 (correct total assets are $142,000).

■ **LO1**   **CP1–5 Using Financial Reports: Applying the Balance Sheet Equation to Liquidate a Company**

ANALYSIS   On June 1, 2009, Bland Corporation prepared a balance sheet just prior to going out of business. The balance sheet totals showed the following:

Assets (no cash)	$90,000
Liabilities	50,000
Shareholders' equity	40,000

Shortly thereafter, all of the assets were sold for cash.

Required:

1. How would the balance sheet appear immediately after the sale of the assets for cash for each of the following cases? Use the format given here.

		Balances Immediately after Sale				
	Cash Received for the Assets	Assets	–	Liabilities	=	Shareholders' Equity
Case A	$ 90,000	$_____		$_____		$_____
Case B	80,000	$_____		$_____		$_____
Case C	100,000	$_____		$_____		$_____
Case D	35,000	$_____		$_____		$_____

2. How should the cash be distributed in each separate case? (*Hint*: Creditors must be paid in full before owners receive any payment.) Use the format given here:

	To Creditors	To Shareholders	Total
Case A	$_____	$_____	$_____
Case B	$_____	$_____	$_____
Case C	$_____	$_____	$_____
Case D	$_____	$_____	$_____

CRITICAL THINKING CASES

■ **LO1, 3**   **CP1–6 Making Decisions as a Manager: Reporting the Assets and Liabilities of a Business**

Elizabeth Watkins owns and operates Liz's Boutique (a sole proprietorship). An employee prepares a financial report for the business at each year-end. This report lists all of the resources (assets) owned by Watkins, including such personal items as the home she owns and occupies. It also lists all of the debts of the business, but not her personal debts.

ANALYSIS   *Required:*

1. From an accounting point of view, do you disagree with what is being included in and excluded from the report of business assets and liabilities? Explain.

2. Upon questioning, Watkins responded, "Don't worry about it; we use it only to support a loan from the bank." How would you respond to this comment?

■ **LO3**   **CP1–7 Making Decisions as an Owner: Deciding about a Proposed Audit**

You are one of three partners who own and operate Mary's Maid Service. The company has been operating for seven years. One of the other partners has always prepared the company's annual financial statements. Recently you proposed that the statements be audited each year because it would benefit the partners and preclude possible disagreements about the division of profits. The partner who prepares the statements proposed that his Uncle Ray, who has a lot of

ANALYSIS   financial experience, can do the job and at little cost. Your other partner remained silent.

Required:

1. What position would you take on the proposal? Justify your response.

2. What would you strongly recommend? Give the basis for your recommendation.

CP1–8 Evaluating an Ethical Dilemma: Ethics and Auditor Responsibilities

A key factor that an auditor provides is independence. The *codes of professional conduct* typically state that a member in public practice should be independent in fact and appearance when providing auditing and other attestation service.

ANALYSIS

■ LO3, 4

Required:

Do you consider the following circumstances to suggest a lack of independence? Justify your position. (Use your imagination. Specific answers are not provided in the chapter.)

1. Karl Ottman is a partner with a large audit firm and is assigned to the CGI audit. Karl owns 10 shares of CGI.

2. Jane Winkler has invested in a mutual fund company that owns 500,000 shares of Sears Canada Inc. She is the auditor of Sears.

3. Bob Franklin is a clerk/typist who works on the audit of the Bank of Montreal. He has just inherited 50,000 shares of the Bank of Montreal. (Bob enjoys his work and plans to continue despite his new wealth.)

4. Nancy Chen worked on weekends as the controller for a small business that a friend started. Nancy quit the job in midyear and now has no association with the company. She works full-time for a large accounting firm and has been assigned to do the audit of her friend's business.

5. Sylvie Karam borrowed $100,000 for a home mortgage from First City National Bank. The mortgage was granted on normal credit terms. Sylvie is the partner in charge of the First City audit.

FINANCIAL REPORTING AND ANALYSIS TEAM PROJECT

CP1–9 Team Project: Examining an Annual Report

As a team, select an industry to analyze. *Reuters* provides lists of industries and their make-up at **http://today.reuters.com/business/industryprofiles.aspx**. Each group member should acquire the annual report for one publicly traded company in the industry, with each member selecting a different company. (Library files, the SEDAR service at **www.sedar.com**, or the company's Web site are good sources. The Annual Report Gallery at **www.reportgallery.com** provides links to the Web sites of well-known companies.)

ANALYSIS

■ LO1, 3

Required:

On an individual basis, each group member should write a short report answering the following questions about the selected company. Discuss any patterns that you observe as a team. Then, as a team, write a short report comparing and contrasting your companies, using the six attributes listed below.

1. What types of products or services does it sell?

2. On what day of the year does its fiscal year end?

3. For how many years does it present complete
   a. balance sheets?
   b. income statements?
   c. cash flow statements?

4. Are its financial statements audited by independent auditors? If so, by whom?

5. Did its total assets increase or decrease over the last year?

6. Did its net income increase or decrease over the last year?

Investing and Financing Decisions and the Balance Sheet

2

After studying this chapter, you should be able to:

FOCUS COMPANY:

Van Houtte, Inc.

EXPANSION STRATEGY WITH

A SOCIAL CONSCIENCE

Van Houtte (www.vanhoutte.com), founded in 1919, provides more than 100 different flavours of gourmet coffee and Bigelow teas by the cup to Chevron stations, Couche-Tard outlets, hotels, hospitals, and offices from Halifax to Nanaimo in Canada and from Los Angeles, California, to Golfstown, New Hampshire, in the United States. Its current network includes more than 4,426 points of sale in Canada and approximately 720 in the United States. Van Houtte purchases raw coffee beans, roasts them, and then sells them online and in grocery stores across Canada. You can also enjoy a cup of espresso in one of its 60 café–bistros in Quebec.

Van Houtte has grown rapidly as a coffee service company, providing all equipment and supplies to offices where people can brew the coffee of their choice freshly by the cup. The company has executed its growth strategy by acquiring or investing in other companies. Since 1993, Van Houtte has invested over $300 million to grow through acquiring other companies, and by purchasing coffee brewers, roasters, and distribution and retail facilities. The company's balance sheets at March 31, 2007 compared to April 1, 1995 (in thousands of dollars) highlight its growth:

	Assets	=	Liabilities	+	Shareholders' Equity
March 31, 2007	$370,120		$123,925		$246,195
April 1, 1995	133,675		50,716		82,959
Change	$236,445		$ 73,209		$263,236

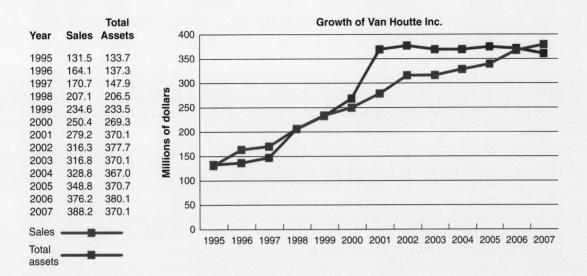

Year	Sales	Total Assets
1995	131.5	133.7
1996	164.1	137.3
1997	170.7	147.9
1998	207.1	206.5
1999	234.6	233.5
2000	250.4	269.3
2001	279.2	370.1
2002	316.3	377.7
2003	316.8	370.1
2004	328.8	367.0
2005	348.8	370.7
2006	376.2	380.1
2007	388.2	370.1

The company's annual growth in sales and total assets since 1995 is highlighted in the graph.

UNDERSTANDING THE BUSINESS

Coffee is a global industry. Coffee consumed by North Americans is produced in and exported from some of the world's poorest countries. Kraft Foods, Nestlé, Sara Lee, and Procter & Gamble capture most of the $65-billion retail coffee market in North America. For the relatively small $3-billion retail market in coffee services, whether they sell by the cup in a convenience store or by the bag online, Tim Hortons, Starbucks, and Van Houtte compete ferociously. Van Houtte distinguishes itself by its unique, single-cup coffee dispensing systems used in offices, gas stations, hotels, and university and college campuses. The most recent dispensing system, Espresso Café™, brews and dispenses cappuccinos and other specialty coffees in less than a minute. The company relies on a strategy of quality for both its products and its services, keeping its business simple and focused on coffee. The company's financial performance, reported in its audited financial statements, helps users to understand how well the company has implemented its strategy in the past and to evaluate future growth potential.

Financial statements for Canadian companies contain estimates of financial value that are developed in accordance with generally accepted accounting principles (GAAP). Financial statements are intended to communicate the economic facts, measured in dollars and cents, in a standardized, formal way. Therefore, by applying accounting principles consistently, accountants formally communicate comparable, reliable estimates that faithfully represent important economic facts about companies like Van Houtte and its competitors. As explained in Chapter 1, financial statements include four components: the balance sheet, the income statement, the statement of retained earnings, and the cash flow statement. In this chapter we focus on the balance sheet, and we examine how this financial statement communicates the results or consequences of Van Houtte's strategy by answering the following questions:

- What type of business activities cause changes in balance sheet amounts from one period to the next?
- How do specific activities affect each of the balance sheet amounts?
- How do companies keep track of these balance sheet amounts?

Once we have answered these questions, we will be able to use the information on the balance sheet to perform two key analytical tasks:

1. Analyze and predict the effects of Van Houtte's business decisions on its financial statements.
2. Identify and compare the financial results of activities that managers of competing companies engaged in during a past period. These latter inferences are a key task in *financial statement analysis*.

In this chapter, we focus on typical asset acquisition activities (often called *investing activities*) in which Van Houtte engages, along with the related *financing activities* such as borrowing funds from creditors and receiving funds from investors to acquire the assets. We examine only those activities that affect balance sheet amounts. In Chapters 3 and 4 we discuss operating activities affecting both income statement and balance sheet amounts. Although these activities are all related, we separate them initially to aid your understanding.

ORGANIZATION OF THE CHAPTER

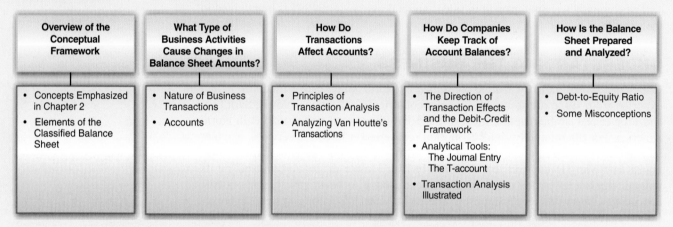

To begin let us return to the basic concepts introduced in Chapter 1.

OVERVIEW OF THE CONCEPTUAL FRAMEWORK

■ **LEARNING OBJECTIVE 1**

Understand the objective of financial reporting and the related key accounting assumptions and principles.

The key accounting terms and concepts we defined in Chapter 1 are part of a theoretical framework developed over many years. The framework prescribes the nature, function, and limitations of both financial accounting and financial statements. The essential elements of this framework are embodied in section 1000 of the *CICA Handbook*, which is a comprehensive set of accounting standards developed in Canada.[1] This conceptual framework is presented in Exhibit 2.1 as an overview with key concepts discussed in the next four chapters. An understanding of the accounting concepts will be helpful as you study because learning and remembering *how* the accounting process works is much easier if you know *why* it works a certain way. A clear understanding of these concepts will also help you in future chapters as we examine more complex business activities.

CONCEPTS EMPHASIZED IN CHAPTER 2

The **PRIMARY OBJECTIVE OF EXTERNAL FINANCIAL REPORTING** is to provide useful economic information about a business to help external parties make sound financial decisions.

Objective of Financial Reporting   The top of the pyramid in Exhibit 2.1 indicates the **primary objective of external financial reporting**, which guides the remaining

_____
[1]Section 1000 will be amended in the near future as Canada harmonizes by the year 2011 its accounting standards with those of the International Accounting Standards Board.

EXHIBIT **2.1**

Financial Accounting and Reporting Conceptual Framework

Primary Objective of External Financial Reporting [Ch. 2]
To provide useful economic information to external users for decision making (for assessing future cash flows).

Elements
Asset, Liability, Shareholders' Equity [Ch. 2]
Revenue, Expenses, Gains, Losses [Ch. 3]

Qualitative Characteristics [Ch. 6]
Understandability
Relevance
Reliability
Comparability

Assumptions
Separate Entity [Ch. 2]
Unit of Measure [Ch. 2]
Continuity (Going-Concern) [Ch. 2]
Periodicity [Ch. 3]

Principles
Historical Cost [Ch. 2]
Revenue Recognition [Ch. 3]
Matching [Ch. 3]
Full Disclosure [Ch. 5]

Constraints
Materiality [Ch. 4]
Cost/Benefit [Ch. 6]
Conservatism [Ch. 6]

EXHIBIT **2.1**

Financial Accounting and Reporting Conceptual Framework

sections of the conceptual framework. The primary objective of financial reporting is to provide useful economic information about a business to help external parties, primarily investors and creditors, make sound financial decisions. The users of accounting information are identified as *decision makers*. These decision makers include average investors, creditors, and experts who provide financial advice. They are all expected to have a reasonable understanding of accounting concepts and procedures (this may be one of the reasons why you are studying accounting). Of course, as we discussed in Chapter 1, many other groups, such as suppliers and customers, also use external financial statements. To achieve this objective, financial reports must enable decision makers not only to assess the amounts, timing, and uncertainty of future cash inflows and outflows but also to understand the financial value of both the assets owned and claims against those assets (liabilities and equity).

The pyramid in Exhibit 2.1 shows how each layer builds upon the lower layer. All the elements of the financial statements (left side of the middle layer) are estimated and reported in accordance with the assumptions, principles, and constraints in the layer below. The objective, however, cannot be achieved simply by reporting any financial value for each element because the amounts must also conform to specific qualities if they are to be useful to decision makers. These qualities, or qualitative characteristics, appear on the right side of the middle layer.

Users are most interested in information to assist them in projecting the future cash inflows and outflows of a business. For example, creditors and potential creditors need to assess an entity's ability to pay interest over time and repay the initial amount borrowed, called the ***principal***. Investors and potential investors want to assess the entity's ability to pay dividends in the future. They also want to evaluate how successful the company might be in the future so that as the share price rises, investors can then sell their shares for more than they paid.

Underlying Assumptions of Accounting   The assumptions of accounting are primarily based on the business environment in which accounting operates. These assumptions reflect the broad scope of decisions external users undertake based on accounting information, and set limits to assure understandability, relevance, reliability, and comparability of reported information. Three of the four basic assumptions that underlie accounting measurement and reporting were discussed briefly in Chapter 1. The fourth assumption, periodicity, will be discussed in Chapter 3. Under the **separate-entity assumption**, each business must be accounted for as an individual organization, separate and apart from its owners, all other persons, and other entities. Separation of the owners' resources (and obligations) from those of the business entity is necessary for a proper evaluation of the entity's results of operations and its

The **SEPARATE-ENTITY ASSUMPTION** states that business transactions are separate from the transactions of the owners.

The **UNIT-OF-MEASURE ASSUMPTION** states that accounting information should be measured and reported in the national monetary unit.

financial position. For example, a building purchased by one of the owners of a real estate development and management company should not be mixed with buildings owned by the company. Under the **unit-of-measure assumption**, each business entity accounts for and reports its financial results primarily in terms of the national monetary unit (dollars in Canada, yen in Japan, pesos in Mexico, etc.), even if the entity has business operations in many countries.

The use of a specific unit of measure allows for meaningful aggregation of financial amounts. Furthermore, accountants assume that the unit of measure has a stable value over time, even though we recognize that the price we pay to purchase a specific item, such as a candy bar, tends to increase over time. Van Houtte's balance sheet includes many assets measured in Canadian dollars from the 1970s, 1980s, and 1990s. The stable monetary unit assumption allows accountants to combine different dollar amounts, even though the purchasing power of the dollar has changed over time.

The **CONTINUITY (GOING-CONCERN) ASSUMPTION** states that businesses are assumed to continue to operate into the foreseeable future.

For accounting purposes, a business normally is assumed to continue operating long enough to carry out its objectives and to meet contractual commitments. This **continuity assumption** is sometimes called the *going-concern assumption* because we expect a business to continue to operate into the foreseeable future. Violation of this assumption means that assets and liabilities should be valued and reported on the balance sheet as if the company were to be liquidated (that is, discontinued, with all assets sold and all debts paid). In all future chapters, unless indicated otherwise, we assume that businesses meet the continuity assumption.

The **COST PRINCIPLE** requires assets to be recorded at the historical cash-equivalent cost, which on the date of the transaction is cash paid plus the current dollar value of all non-cash considerations also given in the exchange.

Basic Accounting Principle The historical **cost principle** states that the cash-equivalent cost needed to acquire an asset (the historical cost) should be used for initial recognition (recording) of all financial statement elements. Under the cost principle, cost is measured on the date of the transaction as the cash paid plus the current dollar value of all non-cash considerations (any assets, privileges, or rights) also given in the exchange. For example, if you trade your computer plus cash for a new car, the cost of the new car is equal to the cash paid plus the market value of the computer. Thus, in most cases, cost is relatively easy to determine and can be verified. A disadvantage of this approach is that, subsequent to the date of acquisition, the continued reporting of historical cost on the balance sheet does not reflect any change in market value, usually because market value is a less verifiable and objective measure than historical cost.

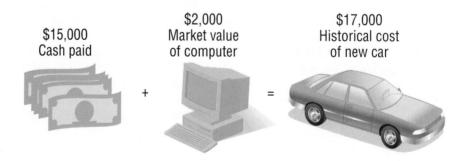

Van Houtte Inc. owns land that cost $1,571,000 when it was acquired several years ago. Although the market price or economic value of the land has risen over time, its recorded value remains unchanged at $1,571,000, because this amount is an objective measure based on an actual exchange that occurred in the past. It would be desirable to show on the balance sheet the land's current market value; that is, the price at which it could either be sold or replaced instead of its outdated historical cost. However, the land's current value may not be reliable if different real estate appraisers produce different values for the same piece of land. For this reason, accountants continue to rely on historical cost measures for reporting purposes because they are factual though they may not be useful for specific decision-making purposes.

Assets, liabilities, and shareholders' equity are the key elements of a corporation's balance sheet, as we learned in Chapter 1. Let us examine the definitions in more detail.

ELEMENTS OF THE CLASSIFIED BALANCE SHEET

When we classify, we group similar things together and arrange them in a specific order. There are three major groups or classifications on a *classified balance sheet*: assets, liabilities, and shareholders' equity. Each of these three large groups is divided into subgroups.

Let us explore Van Houtte's simplified balance sheet, presented in Exhibit 2.2. First, notice the title of the statement, Consolidated Balance Sheet. *Consolidated* means that the classified elements of Van Houtte's balance sheet are combined with those of other companies under its control (e.g., VKI Technologies).[2] For convenience, the amounts for the various balance sheet elements are shown in *thousands of dollars*. Two amounts are shown for each element: one at March 31, 2007, and the other at April 1, 2006, one year earlier. This system allows investors to compare at a glance the value of each classified element from year to year, and

> ■ **LEARNING OBJECTIVE 2**
>
> Define the elements of a classified balance sheet.

EXHIBIT **2.2**

Van Houtte's Balance Sheet

VAN HOUTTE INC.
Consolidated Balance Sheet
(in thousands of dollars)

Assets	March 31, 2007	April 1, 2006
Current assets		
Cash	$ 4,900	$ 5,800
Accounts receivable	56,800	43,000
Inventories	29,500	30,000
Prepaid expenses	3,300	3,600
Other current assets	1,600	1,800
Total current assets	96,100	84,200
Investments	2,600	20,100
Fixed assets, net	116,600	118,500
Goodwill	136,700	135,700
Other long-term assets	18,100	21,600
Total assets	**$370,100**	**$380,100**
Liabilities and shareholders' equity		
Current liabilities		
Accounts payable	$ 39,000	$ 34,400
Accrued liabilities	20,200	2,700
Current portion of long-term debt	1,400	1,500
Total current liabilities	60,600	38,600
Long-term notes payable	51,100	93,600
Other long-term liabilities	12,200	11,300
Total liabilities	123,900	143,500
Shareholders' equity		
Share capital	131,800	129,000
Retained earnings	114,400	107,600
Total shareholders' equity	246,200	236,600
Total liabilities and shareholders' equity	**$370,100**	**$380,100**

Note: These balance sheets are adaptations of Van Houtte's actual balance sheets at those dates. Some of the actual balance sheet elements were combined for illustrative purposes.

---

[2]The rules for consolidation of financial statements are covered in advanced accounting courses.

then analyze these changes to understand if the company's financial position has improved or deteriorated over time.

Van Houtte's balance sheet is shown in *column* or *report* format, with assets listed first, followed by liabilities, and then shareholders' equity. Other companies may choose an account format with the assets listed on the left hand side and liabilities and shareholders' equity listed on the right. Both formats are standard ways of communicating the same information. We now explain the various elements that appear on Van Houtte's balance sheet.

Exhibit 2.2 presents Van Houtte's balance sheet, with amounts rounded to the nearest hundred thousand dollars. Notice that Van Houtte's fiscal year ends on the last Saturday in March, or the first Saturday in April, which was April 1 in 2006 and March 31 in 2007. The choice of year-ends will be discussed in Chapter 4.

ASSETS are economic resources controlled by an entity as a result of past transactions or events and from which future economic benefits may be obtained.

Assets are economic resources controlled by an entity as a result of past transactions or events and from which future economic benefits may be obtained. In other words, these are the resources that the entity has and can use to operate in the future. When reporting conservative information to users, managers use judgment (and past experience) to determine the most likely future benefit. For example, a company may have a list of customers who owe $10,000. However, past experience suggests that only $9,800 will be collected. The more probable or conservative figure is reported to users for projecting future cash flows.

Typically, the assets of a company include:

1. Current assets (short term)
   a. Cash and cash equivalents
   b. Short-term investments
   c. Accounts receivable
   d. Inventory
   e. Prepaid expenses (i.e., expenses paid in advance of use)
   f. Other current assets

2. Non-current assets (long term)
   a. Long-term investments
   b. Property, plant, and equipment (at cost less accumulated amortization)
   c. Intangible assets
   d. Other (miscellaneous) assets

CURRENT ASSETS are assets that will be used or turned into cash, normally within one year. Inventory is always considered to be a current asset, regardless of the time needed to produce and sell it.

Assets are divided into two subgroups, current and non-current assets. **Current assets**, also known as *short-term assets*, are those economic resources that Van Houtte will typically transform into cash or use within the next year or the operating business cycle of the company, whichever is longer. Assets are listed on the balance sheet *in order of liquidity*, which means how soon they can be transformed into cash. Under current assets, *Cash and cash equivalents* (highly liquid investments) appear first because they are the most liquid assets. It should be emphasized that each of the items reported on the balance sheet, such as cash and cash equivalents, is a combination of a number of similar items. For Van Houtte, there were no cash equivalents at April 1, 2006. Furthermore, Van Houtte did not report any *short-term investments*, such as shares of other companies purchased as investments of excess cash.

Any *receivable* represents an amount of money owed to Van Houtte. *Accounts receivable* represent amounts owed by customers who purchased products and services on credit. These amounts are normally collected within one year of the balance sheet date.

Inventory refers to goods that (1) are held for sale to customers in the normal course of business, or (2) are used to produce goods or services for sale. Inventory is always considered to be a current asset, no matter how long it takes to produce and sell.

Van Houtte's inventory would include green and roasted coffee beans not yet sold to distributors, coffee brewing equipment purchased but not yet sold to customers wanting its coffee services, as well as bags of ground coffees and teas. *Prepaid expenses* (e.g., insurance premiums and rent paid in advance of use of a building) reflect available benefits (e.g., monthly insurance protection, office space) that the company will use within one year. *Other assets*, when reported, will include a number of assets with smaller balances that are combined.

ANALYSIS OF CHANGES IN INVENTORY AND ACCOUNTS RECEIVABLE

FINANCIAL
ANALYSIS

Investors analyze the financial statements of a company to decide whether or not to purchase its shares or to lend it money. One important decision factor is how easily a company can access cash to pay both its debts to creditors and its dividends to shareholders. In a normal business cycle, Van Houtte would produce roasted coffee beans for sale to distributors such as Safeway and Provigo. But there is a gap between the time the beans are roasted and the date they are sold. During this time the beans are called *inventory*. The less time the beans remain unsold in inventory, the faster this inventory is transformed into cash from sales. Let us assume for simplicity that Van Houtte's inventory represents these unsold coffee beans, and examine the company's ability to access cash.

Notice the cash balance has decreased from $5.8 million at April 1, 2006 to $4.9 million at March 31, 2007. An investor would also observe that the accounts receivable increased from $43 million at April 1, 2006 to $56.8 million at March 31, 2007, indicating that the company collected less cash from customers who bought merchandise on credit. Investors would examine the cash flow statement to gain clearer insight on how events in the past year resulted in the change in cash (see Chapter 5). For the moment, this brief analysis would reassure an investor that the first two elements reported on the balance sheet are relevant to answering an important question about how easily Van Houtte can access cash to pay its debts to creditors and dividends to shareholders.

Following the Current assets section, Van Houtte reports a number of **non-current assets**. These assets are considered to be long term because they will be used or turned into cash over a period longer than the next year. *Investments* are long-term assets such as shares issued by other companies that will not be used to produce goods and services. *Property, plant, and equipment* includes all land, buildings, machinery, and equipment such as tools, furniture, and other fixtures that will be used to produce Van Houtte's goods and services. These are also called *fixed assets* or *capital assets*—they have a physical form you can touch, and therefore each asset is *tangible*.

Intangible assets have no physical substance but have a long life. They usually are not acquired for resale but are directly related to the operations of the business. Intangible assets include such items as franchises, patents, trademarks, copyrights, and goodwill. Their values arise from the *legal rights* and *privileges* of ownership, and can be identified only as a result of a purchase that transfers ownership. For example, if Van Houtte develops and patents a process for brewing coffee, the value of this intangible asset will not appear on its balance sheet because no transaction with an external party has occurred that lets the accountant identify and verify the asset's value in the marketplace. Van Houtte does report goodwill, a special type of intangible asset related to its purchases of other companies over the years. Intangible assets, including goodwill, are discussed in more detail in Chapter 9.

Other assets, when reported, will include a number of assets that are combined together because of their relatively small values.

NON-CURRENT ASSETS
are considered to be long term because they will be used or turned into cash over a period longer than the next year.

LIABILITIES are probable debts or obligations of the entity that result from past transactions, which will be paid with assets or services.

Liabilities are a corporation's debts and obligations arising from past transactions. They represent future outflows of assets (mainly cash) or services to the *creditors* that provided the corporation with the resources needed to conduct its business. When the corporation borrows money, creditors receive not only full payment of the amount owed to them, but also interest on the borrowed amount.

Typically, the liabilities of a company include:

1. Current liabilities (short term)
   a. Bank indebtedness
   b. Accounts payable
   c. Accrued liabilities
   d. Current portion of long-term debt
   e. Other current liabilities

2. Non-current liabilities (long term)
   a. Notes and mortgages payable
   b. Lease obligations
   c. Bonds payable
   d. Other long-term liabilities

CURRENT LIABILITIES are obligations that will be paid in cash (or other current assets) or satisfied by providing service within the coming year.

Like assets, liabilities are divided into two subgroups, current and non-current. They are listed by *order of time to maturity*, which means how soon an obligation must be paid. **Current liabilities**, known as short-term liabilities, must be paid within the next year or the operating business cycle of the company, whichever is longer. Normally the cash from converting current assets is used to pay current liabilities. The first current liability represents short-term loans from banks. Bank loans are common when the company does not have a sufficient amount of cash to pay its creditors. The second current liability is *Accounts payable*, which represents the total amount owed to suppliers of the raw materials used in making coffee. The third liability, *Accrued liabilities*, is the total amount owed to suppliers for various types of services such as payroll, rent, and other obligations. Current liabilities also include borrowings from banks and other financial institutions that must be repaid within a year. When an entity has long-term debt, the portion that becomes payable within the next year is called the *current portion of long-term debt*. *Other current liabilities*, when reported, will include a number of liabilities with relatively small amounts that are combined.

 **FINANCIAL ANALYSIS**   **ANALYSIS OF CHANGE IN ACCOUNTS PAYABLE**

Using both current assets and current liabilities for Van Houtte, we can improve our analysis of how accessible cash will be to repay debts to creditors and dividends to shareholders.

The company's current liabilities shows that Van Houtte owes $22 million more in current liabilities at March 31, 2007 than it did at April 1, 2006. As investors, we would tentatively conclude that the company has increased its reliance on suppliers to finance its current assets. However, investors must learn far more about the business cycle for coffee services, the outlook for the coffee industry, and Van Houtte's main competitors before coming to a firm conclusion.

At the beginning of this chapter we stated that investors are most interested in relevant information that helps them predict future cash inflows and outflows. From this very preliminary analysis, investors can predict that because Van Houtte has increased its current liabilities by $22 million, a larger amount of cash is needed next year to repay the outstanding debt to creditors than in the current year.

Long-term liabilities are a company's debts having maturities that extend beyond one year from the balance sheet date. They include long-term bank loans, bonds, mortgages, pension liabilities, and lease obligations, among others. At March 31, 2007 Van Houtte's balance sheet showed various types of long-term liabilities, which will be covered in future chapters.

LONG-TERM LIABILITIES are a company's debts that have maturities that extend beyond one year from the balance sheet date.

ENVIRONMENTAL LIABILITIES—THE GREENING OF GAAP

A QUESTION OF ETHICS

For many years, companies faced growing pressure to estimate and disclose environmental liabilities such as the cleanup of hazardous waste. Generally accepted accounting principles (GAAP) require companies to report their best estimate of probable liabilities, including environmental liabilities in notes to the financial statements. For example, Suncor Energy Inc., which mines oil from the tar sands of Northern Alberta, reported environmental liabilities that exceed $800 million in its 2006 financial statements, representing approximately 8 percent of its total liabilities at December 31, 2006. It is estimated, however, that a significant percentage of companies underreport or fail to report such liabilities, often due to the way disclosure rules are applied.

A key economic concern for many Canadian companies is how to manage their resources in an economically sustainable way. Suncor Energy, for example, does so in an extremely sensitive ecological environment. Each year, the company publishes an audited report of financial and non-financial performance indicators that measure its progress towards meeting its sustainable development targets.

Suncor operates in other resource sectors including renewable energy (such as wind turbines), development of natural gas, refining, and marketing. The performance measures of Suncor's operating activities are presented for the company as a whole and then for each area of activity to give the decision maker as much reliable and relevant information as possible. Suncor's comprehensive report on environmental sustainability presents measures of environmental responsibility to augment the financial estimates of environmental liability on its financial statements. Measures of environmental sustainability include levels of air pollution, greenhouse gas emissions, energy consumption, water and waste management, as well as measures of how its activities affect the environment. For example, the company has reduced its greenhouse gas emissions to half the level five years ago, despite an increase in its size of operations.

Suncor's 2007 Report on Sustainability indicates that its management takes its environmental responsibility seriously. The report illustrates how audited, non-financial information is relevant to external decision makers. The fact that the report is audited shows how versatile an accountant must be to provide decision-useful information to external users.

Source: 2007 Report on Sustainability, Stepping Forward Through Innovation and Technology, Suncor Energy Inc. (**www.suncor.com/publications**).

Shareholders' equity (owners' equity or stockholders' equity) is the financing provided to the corporation by both its owners and the operations of the business. One key difference between owners and creditors is that creditors are entitled to settlement of their legal claims on the corporation's assets before the owners receive a penny, even if this consumes all the corporation's assets. Consequently, owners have a residual claim on the corporation's assets.

Owners **invest** (purchase shares) in a company because they expect to receive two types of cash flow: dividends, which are a distribution of the corporation's earnings (a return on shareholders' investment), and gains from selling their shares for more than they paid (known as *capital gains*).

SHAREHOLDERS' EQUITY (OWNERS' EQUITY OR STOCKHOLDERS' EQUITY) is the financing provided by the owners and the operations of the business.

Typically the shareholders' equity of a corporation includes:

1. Share capital (or capital stock)
2. Retained earnings (accumulated earnings that have not been declared as dividends)

SHARE CAPITAL results from owners providing cash (and sometimes other assets) to the business.

Share capital reflects the proceeds received when the corporation issued the shares. Occasionally, shareholders will contribute resources for which they do not receive shares; such contributions are called *contributed surplus*. The sum of share capital and contributed surplus represents the *contributed capital* of the corporation. The 2006 edition of *Financial Reporting in Canada* reports that approximately 73 percent of the 200 companies surveyed had disclosed contributed surplus in their 2005 financial statements.[3] Van Houtte's share capital of $131.8 million has resulted from selling shares to investors at different points in the company's history.

RETAINED EARNINGS refers to the cumulative earnings of a company that are not distributed to the owners and are reinvested in the business.

Most companies that operate profitably retain part of their earnings for reinvestment in their business. The other part is distributed as dividends to shareholders. The annual earnings that are not distributed to shareholders are called **retained earnings**. Van Houtte's retained earnings equal $114.4 million at March 31, 2007 and represent the net amount of earnings that have not been distributed to shareholders since the company was incorporated in 1980. Van Houtte's growth over time has been financed by a substantial reinvestment of retained earnings that represents about 46 percent ($114.4 million/$246.2 million) of its shareholders' equity.

Now that we have reviewed several of the basic accounting concepts and terms, we need to understand the economic activities of a business that result in changes in amounts reported in financial statements and the process used in generating the financial statements.

WHAT TYPE OF BUSINESS ACTIVITIES CAUSE CHANGES IN BALANCE SHEET AMOUNTS?

NATURE OF BUSINESS TRANSACTIONS

■ LEARNING OBJECTIVE 3

Identify what constitutes a business transaction and recognize common balance sheet account titles used in business.

Accounting focuses on specific events that have an economic impact on the entity. Those events that are recorded as a part of the accounting process are called **transactions**. The first step in translating the results of business events to financial statement amounts is determining which events to recognize as transactions. Only transactions are reflected in the statements. As the definitions of assets and liabilities indicate, only economic resources and debts *resulting from past transactions* are recorded on the balance sheet. Transactions include two types of events:

A **TRANSACTION** is (1) an exchange between a business and one or more external parties to a business or (2) a measurable internal event such as adjustments for the use of assets in operations.

1. *External events:* These are *exchanges* of assets and liabilities between the business and one or more other parties. Examples include the purchase of a machine, the sale of merchandise, the borrowing of cash, and the investment in the business by the owners. Transactions that affect balance sheet elements are discussed in this chapter, and those that affect income statement elements will be covered in Chapter 3.

2. *Internal events:* These include certain events that are not exchanges between the business and other parties but nevertheless have a direct and measurable effect on the accounting entity. Examples include losses due to fire or other natural disasters and the use of property, plant, and equipment. Accounting for internal events will be discussed in Chapter 4.

Throughout this textbook, the word *transaction* will be used in the broad sense to include both types of events.

At the same time, some important events that have an economic impact on the company are not reflected in Van Houtte's statements. In most cases, signing a

---

[3]N. Chlala, A. Lavigne, L. Martel, and C. Byrd, *Financial Reporting in Canada* 2006. Toronto: CICA, 2006, p. 356.

contract, which does not involve an exchange of cash, goods, services, or property is not considered to be a transaction because it involves only the exchange of promises, not of assets. For example, if Van Houtte hires a new regional manager and signs an employment contract, no transaction occurs from an accounting perspective because no exchange of assets or liabilities has occurred. Each party to the contract has made promises (the manager agrees to work; Van Houtte agrees to pay in exchange for the manager's work). For each day the new manager works, however, the exchange of services by the employee results in a transaction that Van Houtte must record (as an obligation to pay the manager's salary). Because of their importance, long-term employment contracts, leases, and other commitments may need to be disclosed in notes to the financial statements.

How does the accounting staff at Van Houtte record external and internal events that cause changes in the company's balance sheet amounts? The recording of transactions has evolved over time. Advances in computer hardware and software technology have paved the way for efficient recording of transactions and instantaneous preparation of financial statements. However, the basic system of recording transactions has withstood the test of time, and has been in use for more than 500 years. The basic tenets of manual and computerized recording systems are discussed in this chapter and elaborated on further in Chapters 3 and 4.

ACCOUNTS

An **account** is a standardized record that organizations use to accumulate the financial effects of transactions on each financial statement item. The cumulative result of all transactions that affect a specific account, or its ending balance, is then reported on the appropriate financial statement. Each account has a title and a numeric code to facilitate the recording of similar transactions that affect a specific account. Each company establishes a list of accounts, commonly known as the *chart of accounts,* to facilitate the recoding of transactions. The chart of accounts is organized by financial statement element, with asset accounts listed first (by order of liquidity), followed by liabilities (by order of time to maturity), shareholders' equity, revenue, and expense accounts in that order. In formal recordkeeping systems, including computerized accounting systems, use of appropriate account numbers is essential if the financial effects of similar transactions are to be grouped correctly. Exhibit 2.3 lists account titles that are quite common and are used by most companies. This list is helpful when you are completing assignments and are unsure of an account title.

An **ACCOUNT** is a standardized format that organizations use to accumulate the dollar effects of transactions on each financial statement item.

EXHIBIT **2.3**

Typical Account Titles

Assets	Liabilities	Shareholders' Equity	Revenues	Expenses
Cash	Accounts Payable	Share Capital	Sales Revenue	Cost of Goods Sold
Short-Term Investments	Accrued Expenses	Contributed Surplus	Fee Revenue	Wages Expense
Accounts Receivable	Payable	Retained Earnings	Interest Revenue	Rent Expense
Notes Receivable	Notes Payable		Rent Revenue	Interest Expense
Inventory (to be sold)	Taxes Payable			Amortization Expense
Supplies	Unearned Revenue			Advertising Expense
Prepaid Expenses	Bonds Payable			Insurance Expense
Long-Term Investments				Repair Expense
Equipment				Income Tax Expense
Buildings				
Land				
Intangibles				

You have probably already noticed some regularities in how accounts are named:

1. Accounts with "receivable" in the title are always assets, representing amounts owed to the corporation by customers and others.
2. Accounts with "payable" in the title are always liabilities, representing amounts owed by the corporation to be paid to others in the future.
3. The account Prepaid Expenses is an asset since it represents amounts paid to others for future benefits, such as future insurance coverage or rental of property.
4. Accounts with "unearned" in the title are always liabilities, representing amounts paid in the past by others expecting future goods or services from the company.

Every company has a different chart of accounts, depending on the nature of its business activities. For example, a small lawn care service may have an asset account called Lawn Mowing Equipment, but it is unlikely that the Royal Bank of Canada would need such an account. These differences will become more apparent as we examine the balance sheets of various companies. Because each company has a different chart of accounts, you should *not* try to memorize a typical chart of accounts. **When you prepare homework problems, either you will be given the account names the company uses or you should select appropriate descriptive names.** Once a name is selected for an account, the exact name must be used in all transactions that affect the account.

The accounts you see in the financial statements are actually summations (or aggregations) of a number of more detailed accounts in a company's accounting system. For example, Van Houtte keeps separate inventory accounts for paper supplies, food, and beverages but combines them as Inventories on the balance sheet. Since our aim is to understand financial statements, we focus on aggregated accounts as presented in the statements.

INTERNATIONAL PERSPECTIVE

HARMONIZATION—A PROFESSION'S GLOBAL STRATEGY TO STANDARDIZE ACCOUNT TITLES AND DEFINITIONS

Chapter 1 states that differences in the political, cultural, and economic environment of other countries have produced significant variations in accounting and reporting rules. Recently, however, Canada, the U.S., and Europe have agreed to harmonize their domestic standards to those of the International Accounting Standards Board (IASB). The Canadian Accounting Standards Board, responsible for authorizing accounting standards in Canada, has published its strategic plan indicating the achievement of full harmonization of accounting standards by 2011.

Currently, however, you will find that while the definitions for accounts are very similar, foreign companies often use account titles that differ from those used by Canadian companies. Some also use additional accounts for financial statement items not normally reported under Canadian accounting rules. For example, an Australian company, The News Corporation Limited, headed by K. Rupert Murdoch, follows A-GAAP (Australian generally accepted accounting principles). The principal activities of The News Corporation Limited include printing and publishing books, newspapers, and magazines, television broadcasting, and film production and distribution. Similar Canadian corporations include CanWest Global Communications Corp. and Quebecor Inc. The titles of accounts in a recent balance sheet are similar to those used by Canadian companies, except for liabilities and shareholders' equity:

Australian Accounts	Canadian Equivalents
Liabilities	
Borrowings	Similar to Notes and Bonds Payable
Creditors	Relates to what is owed to suppliers and others, similar to Accounts Payable
Provision	A summary of payables for income tax, dividends, payroll, and other liabilities
Shareholders' Equity	
Retained Profits	Similar to Retained Earnings

SELF-STUDY **QUIZ 2-1**

Wendy's International

The following is a list of accounts from a recent balance sheet for Wendy's International, Inc. Indicate on the line provided whether each of the following is an asset (A), liability (L), or shareholders' equity account (SE).

___ Salaries and Wages Payable   ___ Long-Term Capital Lease Obligations

___ Buildings   ___ Restaurant Equipment

___ Notes Receivable   ___ Retained Earnings

___ Accounts and Drafts Payable   ___ Short-Term Investments

After you complete the schedules, check them with the answers on page 76.

HOW DO TRANSACTIONS AFFECT ACCOUNTS?

Managers make business decisions that often result in transactions affecting financial statements. Typical decisions are to expand the number of stores, advertise a new product, change employee benefit packages, and invest excess cash. Keeping a historical record (like a diary of important events) allows managers to evaluate the effects of past decisions and plan future business activities. In planning, managers are interested in how the implementation of their plans (their decisions) will be reflected on the financial statements. For example, the decision to purchase additional inventory for cash in anticipation of a major sales initiative increases the inventory and decreases cash. If the demand for the inventory does not occur, a lower cash balance reduces the company's flexibility and ability to pay other obligations. Business decisions often involve an element of risk that should be assessed. Therefore, it is necessary for business managers to understand how transactions impact the accounts on the financial statements. The process for determining the effects of transactions is called *transaction analysis* and is discussed next.

■ **LEARNING OBJECTIVE 4**

Apply transaction analysis to simple business transactions in terms of the accounting model: Assets = Liabilities + Shareholders' Equity.

PRINCIPLES OF TRANSACTION ANALYSIS

Transaction analysis is the process of studying a transaction to determine its economic effect on the entity in terms of the accounting equation (A = L + SE, also known as the *accounting model*). We will outline the process in this section of the chapter and create a visual tool representing the process (the transaction analysis model). The basic accounting equation and two fundamental concepts are the foundation for the transaction analysis model. The two concepts underlying the transaction analysis process are that:

TRANSACTION ANALYSIS is the process of studying a transaction to determine its economic effect on the business in terms of the accounting equation.

1. Every transaction affects at least two accounts (duality of effects); it is critical to identify correctly the accounts affected and the direction of the effect (increase or decrease).

2. The accounting equation must remain in balance after each transaction.

Success in performing transaction analysis depends on a clear understanding of how the transaction analysis model is constructed, based on these concepts. **Study this material well. You should not move on to a new concept until you understand and can apply all prior concepts.**

Duality of Effects   The first concept is that every transaction has *at least two effects* on the basic accounting equation. This is known as the *duality of effects*, which is the foundation of the *double-entry system* of recordkeeping. Most transactions with external parties involve an *exchange* of assets, liabilities, and/or equity between the entity and the external party. For example, suppose that Van Houtte purchased some paper napkins for cash. In this exchange, Van Houtte would receive supplies (an increase in an asset) and in return would give up cash (a decrease in an asset).

Transaction	Van Houtte Received	Van Houtte Gave
Purchased paper napkins for cash	Supplies (increased)	Cash (decreased)

In analyzing this transaction, we determined that the accounts affected were Supplies and Cash. As we discussed in Chapter 1, however, most supplies are purchased on credit (that is, money is owed to suppliers). In that case, Van Houtte would engage in *two* transactions: (1) the purchase of an asset on credit and (2) the eventual payment. In the first transaction, Van Houtte would receive supplies (an increase in an asset) and would give in return a promise to pay later, called ***accounts payable*** (an increase in a liability). In the second transaction, Van Houtte would eliminate or receive back its promise to pay (a decrease in the accounts payable liability) and would give up cash (a decrease in an asset).

Transaction	Van Houtte Received	Van Houtte Gave
(1) Purchased paper napkins for credit	Supplies (increased)	Accounts Payable (increased) [a promise to pay]

Transaction	Van Houtte Received	Van Houtte Gave
(2) Paid on its accounts payable	Accounts Payable (decreased) [a promise was eliminated]	Cash (decreased)

As noted earlier, not all important business activities result in a transaction that affects the financial statements. Most important, signing a contract involving the exchange of promises to perform a future business transaction does not result in a transaction that is recorded at the date of signing the contract. For example, consider the case in which Van Houtte and Xerox sign an agreement, with Xerox promising to provide repair service on Van Houtte's copy machines at a price of $50 for each visit during the next year and Van Houtte promising to pay for the service when Xerox provides it. No transaction has taken place yet because Van Houtte and Xerox have exchanged only promises.[4] When Xerox provides service, however, a transaction occurs since service is exchanged for a promise to pay.

---

[4]Contracts of this nature that are likely to result in significant future liabilities must be noted in the financial statements as commitments.

Similarly, if Van Houtte sent an order to its paper supplier for more napkins and the supplier accepted the order, which will be filled the following week, no transaction has taken place for accounting purposes. Only two promises have been exchanged. From the supplier's perspective, the same holds true. No transaction has taken place, so the supplier's financial statements are not affected. As soon as the napkins are shipped to Van Houtte, however, the supplier gives up inventory in exchange for a promise from Van Houtte to pay for the napkins, and Van Houtte exchanges its promise to pay for the napkins that it received as ordered. *One promise* has been exchanged for *goods*, so a transaction has taken place, and the financial statements of both Van Houtte and the supplier will be affected.

Balancing The Accounting Equation   The accounting equation must remain in balance after each transaction. Total assets must equal total liabilities and shareholders' equity. If the correct accounts have been identified and the appropriate direction of the effect on each account has been determined, then the equation should remain in balance. Therefore, in performing the transaction analysis process, you should complete the following steps in this order:

1. *Accounts and effects*
   a. **Identify the accounts affected (by their titles) and classify them by type of account**, making sure that at least two accounts change. Ask yourself what is given and what is received. Classifications are an asset (A), liability (L), or shareholders' equity (SE).
   b. **Determine the direction of the effect** (an increase [+] or decrease [−] on each account).
2. *Balancing*
   c. **Determine that the accounting equation (A = L + SE) remains in balance.**

ANALYZING VAN HOUTTE'S TRANSACTIONS

Let us consider typical transactions and events of Van Houtte, and most other businesses, to illustrate the use of this process. As we stated earlier, only transactions affecting balance sheet accounts are presented in this chapter. Assume that Van Houtte has the following transactions during April 2007 (the month following the balance sheet in Exhibit 2.2). The month will end on April 30. Accounts titles are based on that balance sheet and are summarized in Exhibit 2.4. As stated earlier, each account has a unique numeric code, but we omitted these codes for simplicity.

All of the amounts used in this illustration are in thousands of dollars.

(a) Van Houtte issues shares to new investors in exchange for $1,300 in cash.

1. Identify and classify accounts and effects.	*Cash (A) is received + $1,300. Share certificates are given, Share Capital (SE) + $1,300.*
2. Is the accounting equation in balance?	*Yes. There is a $1,300 increase on the left side and a $1,300 increase on the right side of the equation.*

Assets	=	Liabilities	+	Shareholders' Equity
Cash				**Share Capital**
(a) +1,300	=			+1,300

EXHIBIT **2.4**

Van Houtte's Chart of Accounts

Chart of Accounts (to be used in our Van Houtte example)	**To account for**
Assets (A)	
Cash	— Cash on hand
Accounts Receivable	— Amounts owed by customers, franchisees, and affiliates
Inventories	— Food, beverage, and paper products supplies on hand
Prepaid Expenses	— Benefits or rights to be received in the future (e.g., insurance coverage, rent)
Other Current Assets	— Summary of a number of accounts with smaller balances (current in nature)
Investments	— Amounts invested in securities of other entities
Fixed Assets	— The cost of land, buildings, and equipment to be used in operations in the future
Notes Receivable	— Funds lent to others (e.g., affiliates, employees)
Other Long-Term Assets	— Summary of a number of accounts with smaller balances (long-term in nature)
Liabilities (L)	
Accounts Payable	— Amount owed to suppliers (e.g., for coffee beans, for utility usage)
Accrued Liabilities	— Amount to be paid to others (e.g., wages to employees, interest on debt)
Other Current Liabilities	— Summary of a number of accounts with smaller balances (current in nature)
Long-Term Notes Payable	— Amounts borrowed from banks
Other Long-Term Liabilities	— Summary of a number of accounts with smaller balances (long-term in nature)
Shareholders' Equity (SE)	
Share Capital	— Amount paid by investors in exchange for the company's shares
Retained Earnings	— Accumulated net income not distributed to shareholders as dividends

(b) **The company borrows $1,000 from its local bank, signing a promissory note to be paid in two years.**

1. Identify and classify accounts and effects.	Cash (A) is received + $1,000. A written promise to pay is given to the bank, Notes Payable (L) + $1,000.
2. Is the accounting equation in balance?	Yes. There is a $1,000 increase on the left side and a $1,000 increase on the right side of the equation.

Assets	=	Liabilities	+	Shareholders' Equity
Cash		**Long-Term Notes Payable**		**Share Capital**
(a) +1,300	=			+1,300
(b) +1,000	=	+1,000		

Transactions *(a)* and *(b)* are *financing* transactions. Companies that need cash for *investing* purposes (to buy or build additional facilities as part of their plans for growth) often seek funds by selling shares to investors, as in transaction (a) or borrowing from creditors, usually banks, as in transaction *(b)*.

(c) **For expansion, Van Houtte opened two new company-owned café–bistros. The company purchased $2,200 of new coffee brewers, counters, refrigerators, and other equipment (fixed assets), paying $1,500 in cash and signing a note for $700, payable to the equipment manufacturer in two years.**

1. Identify and classify accounts and effects.	Property and Equipment (A) is received + $2,200. Cash (A) − $1,500 is given and a written promise to pay is also given to the manufacturer, Notes Payable (L) + $700.
2. Is the accounting equation in balance?	Yes, there is a $700 increase on the left side of the equation and a $700 increase on the right side.

Notice that more than two accounts were affected by this transaction.

Assets		=	Liabilities	+	Shareholders' Equity
Cash	Fixed Assets		Long-Term Notes Payable		Share Capital
(a) +1,300		=			+1,300
(b) +1,000		=	+1,000		
(c) −1,500	+2,200	=	+700		

The analysis of transactions (d) through (f) follows. The effects are listed in the chart at the end of Self-Study Quiz 2-2. For transactions (g) and (h), space is left in the chart for your answers to the quiz that follows transaction (f).

(d) Van Houtte lends $450 to new franchisees who sign notes agreeing to repay the loans in 18 months. The franchisees open 25 new restaurants.

1. Identify and classify accounts and effects.	Cash (A) is given − $450. Written promises from the franchisees are received, Notes Receivable (A) + $450.
2. Is the accounting equation in balance?	Yes. The equation remains the same because assets increase and decrease by the same amount.

(e) Van Houtte purchases $3,000 of shares issued by other companies as a long-term investment.

1. Identify and classify accounts and effects.	Cash (A) is given − $3,000. Share certificates from the other companies are received, Investments (A) + $3000.
2. Is the accounting equation in balance?	Yes. The equation remains the same because assets increase and decrease by the same amount.

(f) Van Houtte's board of directors has not declared dividends for shareholders. However, for illustration purposes, we will assume that the first dividend for $200 is declared and paid.

1. Identify and classify accounts and effects.	Cash (A) is given − $200. In this transaction, earnings retained in the business are distributed to investors, Retained Earnings (SE) − $200.
2. Is the accounting equation in balance?	Yes. There is a $200 decrease on the left side of the equation and a $200 decrease on the right side.

SELF-STUDY **QUIZ 2-2**

The most effective way to develop your transaction analysis skills is to practice with many transactions. The key is repeating the steps until they become a natural part of your thought process. Therefore, beginning with the analysis in transactions (a) through (f), complete the transaction analysis steps and following chart for transactions (g) and (h).

(g) Van Houtte collects $300 cash on notes receivable from a number of franchisees. (Hint: Think about what is received and what is given back.)

1. Identify and classify accounts and effects.
2. Is the accounting equation in balance?

(h) Van Houtte paid $400 on the promissory note owed to the local bank.

1. Identify and classify accounts and effects.

2. Is the accounting equation in balance?

Complete the following chart.

		Assets			=	Liabilities	+	Shareholders' Equity	
	Cash	Notes Receivable	Investments	Property and Equipment	=	Long-Term Notes Payable		Share Capital	Retained Earnings
(a)	+1,300				=			+1,300	
(b)	+1,000				=	+1,000			
(c)	−1,500			+2,200	=	+700			
(d)	−450	+450			=				
(e)	−3,000		+3,000		=				
(f)	−200				=				−200
(g)	☐	☐			=				
(h)	☐				=	☐			

After you complete the chart, check it with the solution on page 76.

(i)   Van Houtte's board of directors approved the opening of four café–bistros at a meeting in April 2007 and the granting of $200 of loans to new franchisees that plan to open new café–bistros in May 2007.

Unlike transactions (*a*) through (*h*), which reflect exchanges between Van Houtte and external parties, these two decisions of the board of directors are not transactions because no exchanges have taken place yet. The company's board of directors made commitments that will likely translate into actions in May 2007. Specific balance sheet accounts will be affected only when the actual exchanges occur in May 2007. However, such commitments will normally be disclosed in a financial statement note.

HOW DO COMPANIES KEEP TRACK OF ACCOUNT BALANCES?

■ **LEARNING OBJECTIVE 5**

Determine the impact of business transactions on the balance sheet using two basic tools: journal entries and T-accounts.

Because companies have significantly more transactions every day than those illustrated, recording transaction effects and keeping track of account balances in the manner used in the preceding illustration is impractical for most organizations. We will now expand the transaction analysis model and develop two very important tools that aid in reflecting the results of transaction analysis and performing other financial analysis tasks: journal entries and T-accounts.

These tools are more efficient mechanisms for reflecting the effects of transactions and for determining account balances for financial statement preparation. These efficiencies are important from the standpoint of accounting systems design. **As future business managers, you should develop your understanding and use of these tools in financial analysis. For those studying accounting, this knowledge is the foundation for understanding the accounting system and future coursework.**

THE DIRECTION OF TRANSACTION EFFECTS AND THE DEBIT-CREDIT FRAMEWORK

As we saw earlier, transactions change assets, liabilities, and shareholders' equity. To reflect these effects efficiently, we need to structure the transaction analysis model in a manner that shows the *direction* of the effects. One very useful tool for summarizing the transaction effects and determining the balances for individual accounts is a **T-account**, as shown in Exhibit 2.5. Notice that:

- Each T-account has two sides: a left side, known as the debit side, and a right side, known as the credit side.
- The increase symbol + is located on the left side of the T for accounts that appear on the left side of the accounting equation, and on the right side of the T for accounts that are on the right side of the equation.
- The symbol **dr** or **debit** is always written on the left side of each account, and **cr** or **credit** is always written on the right side. Additions or increases to each type of account are indicated in bold print.

From this transaction analysis model, we can observe the following:

- Asset accounts normally have debit balances (their positive, or increase, side).
- Liabilities and shareholders' equity accounts normally have credit balances (their positive, or increase, side).

As you are learning to perform transaction analysis, you should refer to this model often until you can construct it on your own without assistance.

Many students have trouble with accounting because they forget that the only meaning for **debit** is the left side of an account and the only meaning for **credit** is the right side of an account. Perhaps someone once told you that you were a credit to your school or your family. As a result, you may think that credits are good and debits are bad. Such is not the case. Just remember that **debit means left** and **credit means right**.

If you have identified the correct accounts and effects through transaction analysis, the accounting equation will remain in balance. Moreover, **the total dollar value of all debits equals the total dollar value of all credits** in a transaction. For an extra measure of assurance, add this equality check (Debits = Credits) to the transaction analysis process.

ANALYTICAL TOOL: THE JOURNAL ENTRY

In a bookkeeping system, transactions are initially recorded in chronological order in a *journal* (see our Web site at **www.mcgrawhill.ca/olc/libby/student/resources** for a detailed illustration of formal recordkeeping procedures). The purpose of the journal entry is to record the financial effect of any transaction that affects the financial statements. For a large company such as Van Houtte, the accounting journal is simply the first step in keeping track of the financial effects of thousands of transactions undertaken each year. A bookkeeping system includes more than an accounting journal but the accuracy of this journal is the foundation of all reliable bookkeeping systems. After analyzing the business documents that describe a transaction, the bookkeeper prepares the formal entry in the journal. Using debits and credits, the bookkeeper writes a journal entry for each transaction. The **journal entry** is an accounting tool that summarizes a transaction and its effects on various accounts, using the

The **T-ACCOUNT** is a tool for summarizing transaction effects for each account, determining balances, and drawing inferences about a company's activities.

DEBIT means the left side of an account.

CREDIT means the right side of an account.

A **JOURNAL ENTRY** provides a summary of a transaction and its effects on various accounts, using the double-entry bookkeeping system.

EXHIBIT **2.5**

Transaction Analysis Model

Assets		=	Liabilities		+	Shareholders' Equity			
+	−		−	+					
dr	cr		dr	**cr**					
						Share Capital		**Retained Earnings**	
						−	+	−	+
						dr	**cr**	dr	**cr**
								Dividends	Net Income

double-entry bookkeeping system explained previously. The journal entry for transaction (c) in the Van Houtte illustration is written as follows:

Date or reference	Accounts and explanation	Debit	Credit
April 1, 2007	Fixed assets (+A)................	2,200	
	Cash (−A).....................		1,500
	Long-term notes payable (+L)		700
	Purchased fixed assets paying part in cash and signing a note for the rest.		

Notice the following:

- It is useful to include a date or some form of reference for each transaction.
- The debits are written first (on top); the credits are written below the debits and are indented to the right (both the words and the amounts). The order of the debited accounts or credited accounts does not matter, as long as the debits are on top and the credits are on the bottom and indented.
- Total debits ($2,200) equal total credits ($1,500 + $700).
- Any journal entry that affects more than two accounts is called a *compound entry*. Three accounts are affected by this transaction. Although this is the only transaction in the preceding illustration that affects more than two accounts, many transactions in subsequent chapters will require compound journal entries.

The recording of external transactions in the journal is based on legal documents that highlight the contractual commitments between Van Houtte and other parties. For example, Van Houtte signed a contract with a manufacturer to purchase equipment for $2,200. It issued a cheque for $1,500 to transfer cash to the manufacturer and promised to pay $700 in two years. Consequently, the effects of this transaction are recorded in the journal and reflected in Van Houtte's financial statements. The equipment manufacturer retains legal control of the equipment until it is fully paid after two years. For accounting purposes, however, Van Houtte has control of and will use this resource to generate revenue over the next two years. While the recording of external transactions in the journal requires legal documents, some legal contracts, such as the signing of a contract to hire a new employee, are not reflected in the financial statements.

While you are learning to perform transaction analysis, use the symbols A, L, and SE next to each account title, as is done in the preceding journal entry, including all homework problems. Specifically identifying accounts as assets (A), liabilities (L), or shareholders' equity (SE) clarifies the transaction analysis and makes journal entries easier to write. Throughout subsequent chapters, we include the direction of the effect with the symbol to help you understand the effects of each transaction on the financial statements. For example, if Cash is to be increased, we will write Cash (+A).

We have found that many students try to memorize journal entries without understanding or using the transaction analysis model. The task becomes increasingly difficult as more detailed transactions are presented in subsequent chapters. In the long run, **memorizing, understanding, and using the transaction analysis model** presented here will save you time and prevent confusion.

ANALYTICAL TOOL: THE T-ACCOUNT

By themselves, journal entries do not provide the balances in accounts. After the journal entries have been recorded, the bookkeeper posts (transfers) the dollar amounts to each account affected by the transaction to determine the new account balances. In most computerized accounting systems, this happens automatically upon recording the journal entry.

As a group, the accounts are called a *ledger*. In a manual accounting system used by some small organizations, the ledger is often a three-ring binder with a separate page for each account. In a computerized system, accounts are part of a database and stored on a disk. See Exhibit 2.6 for an illustration of a journal page and the related Cash ledger page. Note that the cash effects from the journal entries have been posted to the Cash ledger page. The three digits under the Posted Ref. column in the General Journal are examples of account codes used in the chart of accounts.

Exhibit 2.7 shows the T-accounts for the Cash and Long-Term Notes Payable accounts for Van Houtte, based on transactions (*a*) through (*h*). Notice that increases in cash (an asset) are on the left and decreases are on the right side of the T-account. For Long-Term Notes Payable, however, increases are on the right and decreases are on the left since notes payable is a liability. Some small businesses still use hand-written or manually maintained accounts in this T-account format. Computerized systems retain the concept but not the format of the T-account.

In Exhibit 2.7, notice that the ending balance is indicated on the "+" side with a double underline. To find the account balances, we can express the T-accounts as equations:

	Cash	Long-Term Notes Payable
Beginning balance	$4,900	$51,100
+ "+" side	+2,600	+1,700
− "−" side	−5,550	−400
Ending balance	$1,950	$52,400

EXHIBIT **2.6**

Illustration of a Journal Page and a Ledger Account in Columnar Format

GENERAL JOURNAL — Page 1

Date	Account Titles and Explanations	Posted Ref.	Debit	Credit
4/1/2005	Cash	101	9,000	
	Share capital	301		9,000
	Issued 1,500 shares to investors (names).			
4/3/2005	Equipment	110	600	
	Cash	101		200
	Notes payable	201		400
	Purchased hand tools (supplier and invoice data			
	indicated), paying part in cash (cheque number			
	indicated) and part on account.			

GENERAL LEDGER

Account Title: Cash — Account Number: 101

Date	Explanation	Posted Ref.	Debit	Credit	Balance
4/1/2005	Investments by owners	1	9,000		9,000
4/3/2005	Hand tools purchased	1		200	8,800
4/4/2005	Land purchased	1		5,000	3,800
4/5/2005	Fuel purchased	1		90	3,710
4/6/2005	Revenue in advance	2	1,600		5,310
4/8/2005	Insurance purchased	2		300	5,010
4/10/2005	Collection from customers	2	3,500		8,510
4/14/2005	Wages paid	3		3,900	4,610
4/18/2005	Note and interest paid	3		740	3,870
4/21/2005	Suppliers paid	3		100	3,770
4/29/2005	Collection from city	4	1,262		5,032

EXHIBIT **2.7**

T-Accounts Illustrated

+ Cash (A) −		− Long-Term Notes Payable (L) +	
Beginning balance 4,900			Beginning balance 51,100
(a) 1,300	(c) 1,500	−400 { (h) 400	(b) 1,000
+2,600 { (b) 1,000	(d) 450		(c) 700 } +1,700
(g) 300	(e) 3,000 } −5,550		
	(f) 200		
	(h) 400		
Ending balance 1,950			Ending balance 52,400

A word on terminology: The words **debit** and **credit** are used as verbs, nouns, and adjectives. For example, we can say that Van Houtte's Cash account was debited (verb) when shares were issued to investors, meaning that the amount was entered on the left side of the T-account. Or we can say that a credit (noun) was entered on the right side of an T-account. Notes Payable may be described as a credit account (adjective). These terms will be used instead of *left* and *right* throughout the rest of the textbook. The next section illustrates the steps to follow in analyzing the effects of transactions, recording the effects in journal entries, and determining account balances using T-accounts.

TRANSACTION ANALYSIS ILLUSTRATED

In this section, we will use the monthly transactions of Van Houtte that were presented earlier to demonstrate transaction analysis and the use of journal entries and T-accounts. We analyze each transaction, checking that the accounting equation remains in balance and that debits equal credits. The amounts from Van Houtte's balance sheet at April 1, 2007, have been inserted as the beginning balances in the T-accounts, located together at the end of the illustration. After reviewing or preparing each journal entry, trace the effects to the appropriate T-accounts using the transaction letters *(a)* to *(h)* as a reference. The first transaction has been highlighted for you.

   Study this illustration carefully (including the explanations of transaction analysis). Careful study of the illustration is *essential* to the understanding of (1) the accounting model, (2) transaction analysis, (3) the dual effects of each transaction, and (4) the dual-balancing system. **The most effective way to learn these critical concepts that affect material throughout the rest of the textbook is to practise, practise, practise**.

(a) **Van Houtte issues shares to new investors in exchange for $1,300 in cash.**

| Cash (+A)............................... | 1,300 | |
| Share capital (+SE).................... | | 1,300 |

Assets	=	Liabilities	+	Shareholders' Equity
Cash +1,300				Share capital +1,300

These effects have been posted to the appropriate T-accounts at the end of the illustration. To post the amounts, transfer or copy the debit or credit amount on each line to the appropriate T-account indicated in order to accumulate balances for each account. For example, the $1,300 debit is listed in the debit (increase) column of the Cash T-account.

(b) **The company borrows $1,000 from its local bank, signing a promissory note to be paid in two years.**

| Cash (+A)............................... | 1,000 | |
| Long-term notes payable (+L)............. | | 1,000 |

Assets	=	Liabilities	+	Shareholders' Equity
Cash +1,000		Long-term notes payable +1,000		

(c) **For expansion, Van Houtte opened two new company-owned café–bistros. The company purchased $2,200 of new coffee brewers, counters, refrigerators, and other equipment (fixed assets), paying $1,500 in cash and signing a note for $700, payable to the equipment manufacturer in two years.**

Fixed assets (+A)............................	2,200	
Cash (−A)		1,500
Long-term notes payable (+L).............		700

Assets		=	Liabilities		+	Shareholders' Equity
Fixed assets	+2,200		Long-term	+700		
Cash	−1,500		notes payable			

(d) **Van Houtte lends $450 to franchisees who sign notes agreeing to repay the loans in 18 months.**

| Notes receivable (+A)..................... | 450 | |
| Cash (−A)............................ | | 450 |

Assets		=	Liabilities	+	Shareholders' Equity
Cash	−450				
Notes receivable	+450				

(e) **Van Houtte purchases $3,000 of shares issued by other companies as a long-term investment.**

| Investments (+A) .... | 3,000 | |
| Cash (−A)............................ | | 3,000 |

Assets		=	Liabilities	+	Shareholders' Equity
Cash	−3000				
Investments	+3000				

(f) **Van Houtte's board of directors has not declared dividends for shareholders. However, for illustration purposes, we will assume that the first dividend for $200 is declared and paid.**

| Retained earnings (−SE)................... | 200 | |
| Cash (−A)............................ | | 200 |

Assets		=	Liabilities	+	Shareholders' Equity	
Cash	−200				Retained earnings	−200

SELF-STUDY **QUIZ 2-3**

For transactions (g) and (h), fill in the missing information, including postings to the T-accounts.

(g) **Van Houtte collects $300 cash on notes receivable from a number of franchisees.**

Write the journal entry		[Post to the T-accounts.]

Assets		=	Liabilities	+	Shareholders' Equity
Cash	+300				
Investments	−300				

(h) **Van Houtte paid $400 on the promissory note owed to the local bank.**

Long-term notes payable (−L)...........	400	[Post to the
Cash (−A)........................		400 T-accounts.]

Assets	=	Liabilities	+	Shareholders' Equity

The following are the T-accounts that changed during the period because of these transactions. The beginning balances are the amounts from Van Houtte's balance sheet at March 31, 2007. The balances of all other accounts remained the same.

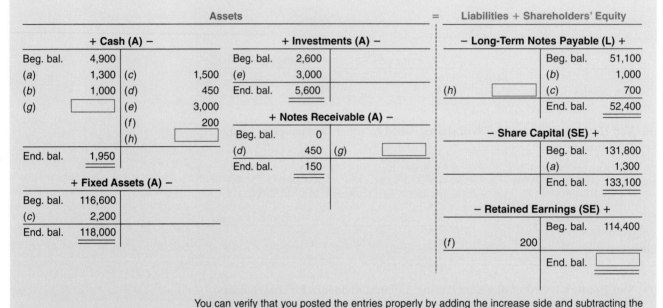

You can verify that you posted the entries properly by adding the increase side and subtracting the decrease side and then comparing your answer to the ending balance for each T-account. You can check your answers with the solutions on page 76.

FINANCIAL ANALYSIS

INFERRING BUSINESS ACTIVITIES FROM T-ACCOUNTS

T-accounts are useful primarily for instructional and analytical purposes. In many cases, we will use T-accounts to determine what transactions a company engaged in during a period. For example, the primary transactions affecting Accounts Payable for a period are purchases of assets on account and cash payments to suppliers. If we know the beginning and ending balances of Accounts Payable and all of the amounts that were purchased on credit during a period, we can determine the amount of cash paid. A T-account will include the following:

− Accounts Payable (L) +

	Beg. bal.	600
Cash payments to suppliers ?	Purchases on account	1,500
	End. bal.	300

Solution:

Beginning Balance	+	Purchases On Account	−	Cash Payments To Suppliers	=	Ending Balance
$600	+	$1,500	−	p	=	$300
		$2,100	−	p	=	$300
				p	=	$1,800

HOW IS THE BALANCE SHEET PREPARED AND ANALYZED?

It is possible to prepare a classified balance sheet at any point in time from the balances in the accounts. The balance sheet in Exhibit 2.8 was prepared using the new balances shown in the T-accounts in the preceding Van Houtte illustration (shaded lines in the exhibit) plus the original balances in the accounts that did not change. It compares the account balances at April 30, 2007, with those at March 31, 2007. Notice that when multiple periods are presented, the most recent balance sheet amounts are usually listed on the left.

At the beginning of the chapter, we presented the changes in Van Houtte's total assets from 1995 to 2007. We questioned what made the accounts change and what the process was for reflecting the changes. Now we can see that the assets have changed again in one month, along with liabilities and shareholders' equity due to the transactions illustrated in this chapter:

> ■ **LEARNING OBJECTIVE 6**
> Prepare a classified balance sheet and analyze it using the debt-to-equity ratio.

	Assets	=	Liabilities	+	Shareholders' Equity
April 30, 2007	$372,500		$125,200		$247,300
March 31, 2007	370,100		123,900		246,200
Change	+$ 2,400		+$ 1,300		+$ 1,100

EXHIBIT **2.8**

Van Houtte's Balance Sheet

VAN HOUTTE INC.
Consolidated Balance Sheet
(in thousands of dollars)

Assets	April 30, 2007	March 31, 2007
Current assets		
Cash	$ 1,950	$ 4,900
Accounts receivable	56,800	56,800
Inventories	29,500	29,500
Prepaid expenses	3,300	3,300
Other current assets	1,600	1,600
Total current assets	93,150	96,100
Note receivable	150	—
Investments	5,600	2,600
Fixed assets, net	118,800	116,600
Goodwill	136,700	136,700
Other long-term assets	18,100	18,100
Total assets	**$372,500**	**$370,100**
Liabilities and shareholders' equity		
Current liabilities		
Accounts payable	$ 39,000	$ 39,000
Accrued liabilities	20,200	20,200
Current portion of long-term debt	1,400	1,400
Total current liabilities	60,600	60,600
Long-term notes payable	52,400	51,100
Other long-term liabilities	12,200	12,200
Total liabilities	125,200	123,900
Shareholders' equity		
Share capital	133,100	131,800
Retained earnings	114,200	114,400
Total shareholders' equity	247,300	246,200
Total liabilities and shareholders' equity	**$372,500**	**$370,100**

KEY RATIO ANALYSIS

THE DEBT-TO-EQUITY RATIO

Users of financial information compute a number of ratios in analyzing a company's past performance and financial condition as input in predicting its future potential. For example, using the elements and classification in the balance sheet, creditors can assess a company's ability to pay off its debt, or see what the company's trend is in taking on more debt. The change in ratios over time and how they compare to the ratios of the company's competitors provide valuable information for users' decisions.

We introduce here the first of many ratios that will be presented throughout the rest of this textbook, with a final summary of ratio analysis in Chapter 13. In Chapters 2, 3 and 4, we present four ratios that provide information about management's effectiveness at managing debt and equity financing (debt-to-equity ratio), controlling revenues and costs (net profit margin), and utilizing assets (total asset turnover ratio and return on assets), all for the purpose of enhancing returns to shareholders. The remaining chapters discuss other ratios that provide valuable information to assess a company's strategies, strengths and areas of concern.

As we discussed earlier in the chapter, companies raise large amounts of money to acquire additional assets by issuing shares to investors and borrowing funds from creditors. These additional assets are used to generate more income. However, since debt must be repaid, taking on increasing amounts of debt carries increased risk. The debt-to-equity ratio provides one measure for analysts to examine the company's financial strategy.

ANALYTICAL QUESTION → As an investor who must decide whether or not to buy shares, it is important to know how much of the company's assets is financed by creditors and how much is financed by the owners. The *debt-to-equity ratio* is used to assess the debt capacity of a business. It is computed as follows:

$$\text{Debt-to-Equity Ratio} = \frac{\text{Total Liabilities}}{\text{Total Shareholder's Equity}}$$

The 2007 ratio for Van Houtte is:

$$\$\,123,900 \div \$\,246,200 = 0.50$$

RATIO AND COMPARISONS

SELECTED FOCUS COMPANY DEBT-TO-EQUITY RATIOS

WestJet Airlines Ltd. 2.30

Dell Inc. 4.60

The Forzani Group Ltd. 1.30

Comparisons over Time			Comparisons with Competitors*	
Van Houtte Inc.			Starbucks	Tim Hortons
2005	2006	2007	2006**	2006
0.60	0.61	0.50	0.99	0.71

INTERPRETATIONS

In General → The debt-to-equity ratio indicates how much debt has been used to finance the company's acquisition of assets relative to equity financing that is supplied by shareholders. A high ratio normally suggests that a company relies heavily on funds provided by creditors. Managers use the ratio to decide if they should finance any additional acquisitions using debt. Creditors use this ratio to assess the risk that a company may not be able to meet its financial obligations during a business downturn. Investors use this ratio to assess the level of financial risk associated with the expected cash flows from their investment (dividends and appreciation in the share value).

*Investors cannot always compare closest competitors. Some companies are privately owned and their financial information is not publicly available. Other close competitors are owned by larger corporations. For example, Second Cup, is owned by a Canadian company, Cara Foods Ltd., which has recently become a private company. Kraft, Nestlé, and Sara Lee compete to sell ground coffee in grocery stores where Van Houtte also sells its coffee; however, these U.S. companies all sell much more than simply coffee.
**The ratios for Starbucks and Tim Hortons are shown for 2006 instead of 2007 because the three companies have different fiscal year ends.

Focus Company Analysis → Van Houtte's debt-to-equity ratio decreased from 0.60 in 2005 to 0.50 in 2007. This indicates that Van Houtte's assets at March 31, 2007 are financed with $0.50 in debt for every $1 of equity. Van Houtte's balance sheet shows that in 2007, the company increased its equity by $10.4 million while its total liabilities also decreased by $19.6 million. These financing decisions helped reduce the ratio to 0.50 at March 31, 2007 compared to previous years. An investor would also read other reports, such as the company's *Annual Information Form,* and carefully review the "Management Discussion and Analysis" section in Van Houtte's annual report to discover why these changes have occurred.

Investors look not only at ratios over time for Van Houtte, but also at the debt-to-equity ratio of competitors for comparison purposes. Both Starbucks and Tim Hortons have higher debt-to-equity ratios than Van Houtte, suggesting that they have higher financial risk. As a result, they may not be in as good a financial position as Van Houtte to generate the cash necessary to meet their financial obligations in case of a business downturn.

A Few Cautions → The debt-to-equity ratio tells only part of the story with respect to risks associated with debt. The ratio is a good indication of debt capacity, but it does not help the investor understand whether the company's operations can support the amount of debt that it has. Remember that debt carries with it the obligation to make cash payments for interest and principal. As a result, most investors would evaluate the debt-to-equity ratio within the context of the amount of cash the company is able to generate from operating activities. While the current ratio indicates whether the accessibility of cash has improved or not, investors can complete a more detailed analysis of relevant information on the cash flow statement, which we introduce later in this chapter.

As you can see, using the relevant financial information from financial statements to calculate a single ratio is only the first step toward understanding whether a company is healthy enough to merit your investment dollar. The real challenges are discovering why the ratios have changed over time, comparing to competitors' ratios, developing a keen understanding of the industry and businesses, and using all this knowledge to predict the future for a company.

SELF-STUDY **QUIZ 2-4**

Wendy's International

Wendy's International, Inc., had the following balances on a recent balance sheet (in thousands):

Liabilities—$1,381,729; Shareholders' equity—$2,058,589

Compute Wendy's debt-to-equity ratio:

What does this tell you about Wendy's financing strategy?

After you complete your answers, check them with the solutions on page 77.

FOCUS ON CASH FLOWS   INVESTING AND FINANCING ACTIVITIES

■ LEARNING OBJECTIVE 7

Identify investing and financing transactions and how they are reported on the cash flow statement.

Recall from Chapter 1 that companies report cash inflows and outflows over a period in their cash flow statement. This statement divides all transactions that affect cash into three categories: operating, investing, and financing activities. Investing and financing activities are covered in this chapter whereas operating activities are covered in Chapter 3.

The eight transactions we have analyzed for Van Houtte included issuing shares, borrowing from a bank, purchasing fixed assets, lending to franchisees, purchasing shares in other companies, declaring and paying dividends, collecting cash payment on a note receivable, and paying down a bank loan (see Exhibit 2.9). All these transactions affected cash. Four of the eight transactions relate to investment activities and the other four relate to financing activities.

The first set includes one transaction that increased cash inflow and three transactions that decreased cash. The collection on notes receivable increased cash by $300. On the other hand, the payment of $1,500 in cash for the purchase of fixed assets; the long-term loan to franchisees for $450; and the investment in shares of other companies for $3,000 resulted in a total cash outflow of $4,950. The net change to cash from investment activities is an outflow of *$4,650*.

The second set of transactions relates to financing activities and includes two transactions that increased cash and two transactions that decreased cash outflow. The issuance of shares for $1,300 and the borrowing of $1,000 from the bank increased cash by $2,300. In contrast, the payment of dividends of $200 and the partial repayment on a bank loan of $400 decreased cash by $600 during the same period. The net change to cash from financing activities is an inflow of *$1,700*. In summary, the change in the cash balance from $4,900 at March 31, 2007 to $1,950 at April 30, 2007 can be explained as follows:

Cash from (used for) investment activities	$(4,650)
Cash from (used for) financing activities	1,700
Net change in cash flow	(2,950)
Cash at beginning of month	4,900
Cash at end of month	$ 1,950

The cash flow statement provides information that not only shows the sources and uses of cash but also helps both investors and creditors predict future cash flows for Van Houtte and make appropriate financial decisions. The pattern of cash flows shown in Exhibit 2.9 (net cash outflows for investing activities and net cash flows from financing activities) is typical of Van Houtte's past several annual cash flow statements. Companies seeking to expand usually report cash outflows for investing activities.

SELF-STUDY **QUIZ 2-5**

Lance, Inc.

Lance, Inc., manufactures and sells snack products. Indicate whether the following transactions from a recent annual cash flow statement were investing (I) or financing (F) activities and show the direction of the effect on cash (+ means increases cash; − means decreases cash):

Transactions	Type of Activity (I or F)	Effect on Cash Flows (+ or −)
1. Paid dividends.	_____	_____
2. Sold property.	_____	_____
3. Sold marketable securities (investments).	_____	_____
4. Purchased vending machines.	_____	_____
5. Repurchased its own shares.	_____	_____

After you complete your work, check it with the solution on page 77.

EXHIBIT **2.9**

Van Houtte's Cash Flow Statement

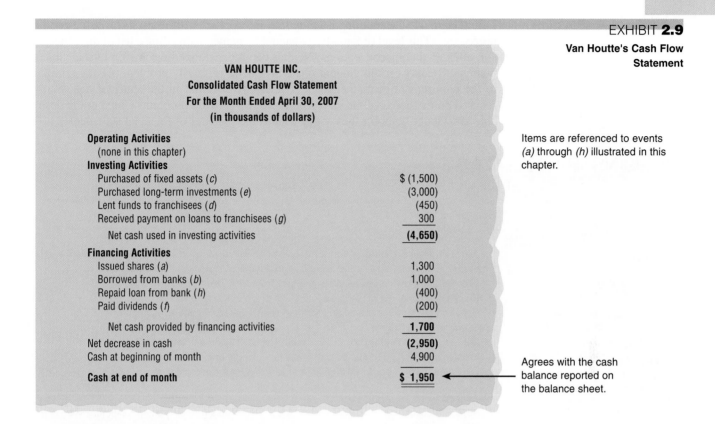

VAN HOUTTE INC.
Consolidated Cash Flow Statement
For the Month Ended April 30, 2007
(in thousands of dollars)

Operating Activities	
(none in this chapter)	
Investing Activities	
Purchased of fixed assets (*c*)	$ (1,500)
Purchased long-term investments (*e*)	(3,000)
Lent funds to franchisees (*d*)	(450)
Received payment on loans to franchisees (*g*)	300
Net cash used in investing activities	**(4,650)**
Financing Activities	
Issued shares (*a*)	1,300
Borrowed from banks (*b*)	1,000
Repaid loan from bank (*h*)	(400)
Paid dividends (*f*)	(200)
Net cash provided by financing activities	**1,700**
Net decrease in cash	**(2,950)**
Cash at beginning of month	4,900
Cash at end of month	**$ 1,950**

Items are referenced to events *(a)* through *(h)* illustrated in this chapter.

Agrees with the cash balance reported on the balance sheet.

SOME MISCONCEPTIONS

Some people confuse bookkeeping with accounting. In effect, they confuse a part of accounting with the whole. Bookkeeping involves the routine, clerical part of accounting and requires only minimal knowledge of accounting. A bookkeeper may record the repetitive and uncomplicated transactions in most businesses and may maintain the simple records of a small business. In contrast, the accountant is a highly trained professional, competent in the design of information systems, analysis of complex transactions, interpretation of financial data, financial reporting, auditing, taxation, and management consulting.

Another prevalent misconception is that all transactions are subject to precise and objective measurement and that the accounting results reported in the financial statements are exactly what happened during that period. In reality, accounting numbers are influenced by estimates, as subsequent chapters will illustrate. Some people believe that financial statements report the entity's market value (including its assets), but they do not. To understand and interpret financial statements, the user must be aware of their limitations as well as their usefulness. One should understand what the financial statements do and do not try to accomplish.

Finally, financial statements are often thought to be inflexible because of their quantitative nature. As you study accounting, you will learn that it requires considerable *professional judgment* on the part of the accountant to capture the economic essence of complex transactions. Accountants develop professional judgment after years of experience in analyzing business transactions and in applying generally accepted accounting principles in preparing and auditing financial reports. Accounting is stimulating intellectually; it is not a cut-and-dried subject. It calls on your intelligence, analytical ability, creativity, and judgment. Accounting is a communication process involving an audience (users) with a wide diversity of knowledge, interest, and capabilities; therefore, it will call on your ability as a communicator. The language of accounting uses concisely written phrases and symbols to convey information about the resource flows measured for specific organizations.

To understand financial statements, you must have a certain level of knowledge of the concepts and the measurement procedures used in the accounting process. You should learn what accounting is really like and appreciate the reasons for using certain procedures. This level of knowledge cannot be gained by reading a list of the concepts and a list of the misconceptions. Neither can a generalized discussion of the subject matter suffice. A certain amount of involvement, primarily problem solving (similar to the requirement in mathematics courses), is essential in the study of accounting focused on the needs of the user. Therefore, we provide problems aimed at the desirable knowledge level for the user as well as the preparer of financial statements.

DEMONSTRATION **CASE**

On April 1, 2007, three ambitious college students started Terrific Lawn Maintenance Corporation. Completed transactions (summarized) through April 30, 2007, for Terrific Lawn Maintenance Corporation follow:

a. Issued 1,500 shares in exchange for $9,000 cash. Each investor received 500 shares.
b. Acquired rakes and other hand tools (equipment) with a list price of $690 for $600; paid the hardware store $200 cash and signed a note for the balance with the hardware store.
c. Ordered three lawn mowers and two edgers from XYZ Lawn Supply, Inc., for $4,000.
d. Purchased four acres of land as a future site of a storage garage. Paid cash, $5,000.
e. Received the mowers and edgers that had been ordered, signing a note to pay XYZ Lawn Supply in full in 30 days.
f. Sold one acre of land to the city for a park. The city signed a note to pay Terrific Lawn Maintenance Corp. $1,250, the cost of the land, by the end of the month.
g. One of the owners borrowed $3,000 from a local bank for personal use.

Required:

1. Set up T-accounts for Cash, Short-Term Notes Receivable (from the city), Equipment (for hand tools and mowing equipment), Land, Short-Term Notes Payable (to equipment supply companies), and Share Capital. Beginning balances are $0; indicate these beginning balances in the T-accounts. Analyze each transaction using the process outlined in the chapter. Prepare journal entries in chronological order. Enter the effects of the transactions in the appropriate T-accounts. Identify each amount with its letter in the preceding list.
2. Use the amounts in the T-accounts developed in requirement 1 to prepare a classified balance sheet for Terrific Lawn Maintenance Corporation at April 30, 2007. Show the account balances for all assets, liabilities, and shareholders' equity. Use the following transaction analysis model:

Assets	=	Liabilities	+	Shareholders' Equity				
+	−	−	+					
dr	cr	dr	**cr**					
				Share Capital			**Retained Earnings**	
				−	+	−	+	
				dr	**cr**	dr	**cr**	
						Dividends	Net Income	

3. Prepare the investing and financing sections of the cash flow statement.

We strongly recommend that you prepare your own answers to these requirements and then check your answers with the solution provided below.

SUGGESTED SOLUTION

1. **Transaction analysis, journal entries, and T-accounts:**

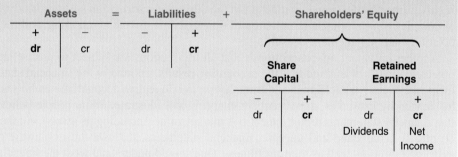

	(a)	Cash (+A)	9,000	
		Share capital (+SE).................		9,000

Assets		=	Liabilities	+	Shareholders' Equity	
Cash	+9,000				Share capital	+9,000

(b)   Equipment (+A).   600
           Cash (−A).   200
           Notes payable (+L).   400

Assets		=	Liabilities		+	Shareholders' Equity
Equipment	+600		Short-term notes			
Cash	−200		payable	+400		

The **historical cost principle** states that assets should be recorded at the amount paid on the date of the transaction. This is $600, not the list price of $690.

(c) **This is not a transaction; no exchange has taken place. No accounts are affected.**

(d)   Land (+A)   5,000
           Cash (−A).   5,000

Assets		=	Liabilities	+	Shareholders' Equity
Land	+5,000				
Cash	−5,000				

(e)   Equipment (+A).   4,000
           Short-term notes payable (+L).   4,000

Assets		=	Liabilities		+	Shareholders' Equity
Equipment	+4,000		Short-term notes			
			payable	+4,000		

(f)   Short-term notes receivable (+A)   1,250
           Land (−A).   1,250

Assets		=	Liabilities	+	Shareholders' Equity
Notes receivable	+1,250				
Land	−1,250				

(g) **This is not a transaction that involves the company. The separate-entity assumption states that transactions of the owners are separate from transactions of the business.**

Assets					=	Liabilities + Shareholders' Equity		

+ Cash (A) −				+ Short-Term Notes Receivable (A) −			− Short-Term Notes Payable (L) +	
Beg. bal.	0			Beg. bal.	0		Beg. bal.	0
(a)	9,000	(b)	200	(f)	1,250		(b)	400
		(d)	5,000	End. bal.	1,250		(e)	4,000
							End. bal.	4,400
End. bal.	3,800							

− Share Capital (SE) +	
Beg. bal.	0
(a)	9,000
End. bal.	9,000

+ Equipment (A) −			+ Land (A) −		
Beg. bal.	0		Beg. bal.	0	
(b)	600		(d)	5,000	(f)	1,250
(e)	4,000		End. bal.	3,750	
End. bal.	4,600				

2. Balance sheet:

TERRIFIC LAWN MAINTENANCE CORPORATION
Balance Sheet
At April 30, 2007

Assets		Liabilities	
Current Assets		*Current Liability*	
Cash	$ 3,800	Short-term notes payable	$ 4,400
Short-term notes receivable	1,250		
Total current assets	5,050	**Shareholders' Equity**	
Equipment	4,600	Share capital	9,000
Land	3,750	Total liabilities and shareholders' equity	$13,400
Total assets	$13,400		

Notice that balance sheets presented earlier in the text listed assets on the top and liabilities and shareholders' equity on the bottom. It is also acceptable practice to prepare a balance sheet with assets on the left side and liabilities and shareholders' equity on the right side, as in the preceding example.

3. Investing and financing effects of the cash flow statement:

TERRIFIC LAWN MAINTENANCE CORPORATION
Cash Flow Statement
For the Month Ended April 30, 2007

Operating Activities	
(none in this case)	
Investing Activities	
Purchased land *(d)*	$(5,000)
Purchased equipment *(b)*	(200)
Net cash used in investing activities	**(5,200)**
Financing Activities	
Issued shares *(a)*	9,000
Net cash provided by financing activities	**9,000**
Change in cash	**3,800**
Beginning cash balance	0
Ending cash balance	**$3,800**

SOLUTIONS TO **SELF-STUDY QUIZZES**

Self-Study Quiz 2-1

Column 1: L; A; A; L. Column 2: L; A; SE; A.

Self-Study Quiz 2-2

(*g*) Cash (A) is received +$300. The franchisees' written promises to pay are "given back" (paid off), Notes Receivable (A) −$300. The equation remains the same because assets increase and decrease by the same amount.

(*h*) Cash (A) is given −$400. Van Houtte's written promise to the bank is "given back" (paid off), Long-Term Notes Payable −$400. There is a $400 decrease on the left side of the equation and a $400 decrease on the right side.

If your answers did not agree with ours, we recommend that you go back to each transaction to make sure that you have completed each of the steps for each transaction.

Self-Study Quiz 2-3

(*g*) Journal entry:

Cash (+A)	300	
Notes receivable (−A).................		300

(*h*) Effects on the Accounting Equation:

Assets		=	Liabilities		+	Shareholders' Equity
Cash	−400		Long-term notes payable	−400		

Self-Study Quiz 2-4

$1,381,729 \div \$2,058,589 = 0.67$.

Wendy's is following a financing strategy that is similar to Van Houtte's. This means that for every dollar of shareholders' equity, creditors supplied $0.67 to acquire assets.

Self-Study Quiz 2-5

1. F −   2. I +   3. I +   4. I −   5. F −

CHAPTER **TAKE-AWAYS**

1. **Understand the objective of financial reporting and the related key accounting assumptions and principles. p. 46**
   - The primary objective of external financial reporting is to provide useful economic information about a business to help external parties, primarily investors and creditors, make sound financial decisions.
   - Key accounting assumptions and principles:
     - *a.* Separate-entity assumption—transactions of the business are accounted for separately from transactions of the owner.
     - *b.* Unit-of-measure assumption—financial information is reported in the national monetary unit.
     - *c.* Continuity (going-concern) assumption—a business is expected to continue to operate into the foreseeable future.
     - *d.* Historical cost principle—financial statement elements should be recorded at their cash-equivalent cost on the date of the transaction.

2. **Define the elements of a classified balance sheet. p. 49**
   - Elements of the balance sheet:
     - *a.* Assets—probable future economic benefits owned by the entity as a result of past transactions.
     - *b.* Liabilities—probable debts or obligations of the entity as a result of past transactions, which will be paid with assets or services.
     - *c.* Shareholders' equity—the financing provided by the owners and the operations of the business.

3. **Identify what constitutes a business transaction and recognize common balance sheet account titles used in business. p. 54**
   A transaction includes:
   - An exchange between a business and one or more external parties to a business.
   or
   - A measurable internal event such as adjustments for the use of assets in operations.
   An account is a standardized format that organizations use to accumulate the dollar effects of transactions of each financial statement item. Typical balance sheet account titles include the following:
   - Assets: Cash, Accounts Receivable, Inventory, Prepaid Expenses, and Property and Equipment.
   - Liabilities: Accounts Payable, Notes Payable, Accrued Liabilities, and Taxes Payable.
   - Shareholders' Equity: Share Capital and Retained Earnings.

4. **Apply transaction analysis to simple business transactions in terms of the accounting model: Assets = Liabilities + Shareholders' Equity. p. 57**
   To determine the economic effect of a transaction on the entity in terms of its accounting equation, each transaction is analyzed as to the accounts (at least two) that are affected. In an exchange, the company receives something and gives something. If the accounts, direction of the effects, and amounts are correctly analyzed, the accounting equation must stay in balance. The transaction analysis model is

Assets		=	Liabilities		+	Shareholders' Equity			
+	−		−	+					
dr	cr		dr	**cr**					
						Share Capital		**Retained Earnings**	
						−	+	−	+
						dr	**cr**	dr	**cr**
								Dividends	Net Income

5. **Determine the impact of business transactions on the balance sheet using two basic tools: journal entries and T-accounts. p. 62**
   - Journal entries express the effects of a transaction on accounts using the debit-credit framework. The accounts and amounts to be debited are listed first. Then the accounts and amounts to be credited are listed below the debits and indented, resulting in debits on the left and credits on the right. A brief description of the transaction is then included for future reference.

(date)	Account	xxx	
	Account.		xxx

   - T-accounts summarize transaction effects for each account. These tools can be used to determine balances and draw inferences about a company's activities.

+	Assets	−		−	Liabilities and Shareholders' Equity	+
Beginning balance						Beginning balance
Increases		Decreases		Decreases		Increases
Ending balance						Ending balance

6. **Prepare a classified balance sheet and analyze it using the debt-to-equity ratio. p. 69**
   Classified balance sheets are structured with

   - Assets categorized as "current assets" (those to be used or turned into cash within the year, with inventory always considered to be a current asset) and non-current assets such as long-term investments, property and equipment, and intangible assets.

   - Liabilities categorized as "current liabilities" (those that will be paid within the next year or the operating cycle, whichever is longer) and long-term liabilities.

   - Shareholders' equity accounts are listed as Share Capital first followed by Retained Earnings. The debt-to-equity ratio (Total Liabilities ÷ Shareholders' Equity) measures the relationship between total liabilities and the shareholders' capital that finance the assets. The higher the ratio, the more debt is used to finance assets. As the ratio (and thus debt) increases, risk increases.

7. **Identify investing and financing transactions and how they are reported on the cash flow statement. p. 72**
   A cash flow statement reports the sources and uses of cash for the period by the type of activity that generated the cash flow: operating, investing, and financing. Investing activities are purchasing and selling long-term assets, making loans, and receiving payment from loans to others. Financing activities are borrowing and repaying loans to banks, issuing and repurchasing shares, and paying dividends.

In this chapter, we discussed the fundamental accounting model and transaction analysis. Journal entries and T-accounts were used to record the results of transaction analysis for investing and financing decisions that affect balance sheet accounts. In Chapter 3, we continue our detailed look at financial statements, in particular the income statement. The purpose of Chapter 3 is to build on your knowledge by discussing concepts for the measurement of revenues and expenses and by illustrating transaction analysis for operating decisions.

KEY **RATIO**

The **debt-to-equity ratio** measures the relationship between total liabilities and the shareholders' capital that finance the assets. The higher the ratio, the more debt is assumed by the company to finance assets. It is computed as follows (p. 70):

$$\text{Debt-to-Equity Ratio} = \frac{\text{Total Liabilities}}{\text{Shareholder's Equity}}$$

FINDING FINANCIAL INFORMATION

BALANCE SHEET

Current Assets
  Cash
  Accounts and
    notes receivable
  Inventory
  Prepaid expenses
Non-Current Assets
  Long-term
    investments
  Fixed assets
  Intangibles

Current Liabilities
  Bank
    indebtedness
  Accounts payable
  Notes payable
  Accrued liabilities
    payable
Non-Current Liabilities
  Long-term debt
Shareholders' Equity
  Share capital
  Retained earnings

INCOME STATEMENT
To be presented in Chapter 3

CASH FLOW STATEMENT

Under Investing Activities
  + Sales of non-current assets for cash
  − Purchases of non-current assets for cash
  − Loans to others
  + Receipt of cash on loans to others
Under Financing Activities
  + Borrowing from banks
  − Repayment of loans from banks
  + Issuance of shares
  − Repurchasing shares
  − Payment of dividends

NOTES
To be discussed in future chapters

KEY TERMS

Account p. 55

Assets p. 50

Continuity (Going-Concern) Assumption p. 48

Cost Principle p. 48

Credit p. 63

Current Assets p. 50

Current Liabilities p. 52

Debit p. 63

Journal Entry p. 63

Liabilities p. 52

Long-Term Liabilities p. 53

Non-current Assets p. 51

Primary Objective of External Financial Reporting p. 46

Retained Earnings p. 54

Separate-Entity Assumption p. 47

Share Capital p. 54

Shareholders' Equity (Owners' Equity or Stockholders' Equity) p. 53

T-account p. 63

Transaction p. 54

Transaction Analysis p. 57

Unit-of-Measure Assumption p. 48

QUESTIONS

1. What is the primary objective of financial reporting for external users?
2. Define the following:
   a. Asset.
   b. Current asset.
   c. Liability.
   d. Current liability.
   e. Share capital.
   f. Retained earnings.
3. Explain what the following assumptions and principle mean in accounting:
   a. Separate-entity assumption.
   b. Unit-of-measure assumption.
   c. Continuity assumption.
   d. Cost principle.
4. Why is it important to have accounting assumptions?
5. How is the debt-to-equity ratio computed and how is it interpreted?
6. For accounting purposes, what is an account? Explain why accounts are used in an accounting system?
7. What are the limitations of using the historical cost principle as a basis for valuation of assets subsequent to acquisition?

8. What is the fundamental accounting model?
9. Define a business transaction in the broad sense and give examples of the two different kinds of transactions.
10. Explain what *debit* and *credit* mean.
11. Briefly explain what is meant by *transaction analysis*. What are the two steps in transaction analysis?
12. What two equalities in accounting must be maintained in transaction analysis?
13. What is a *journal entry*?
14 What is a *T-account?* What is its purpose?
15. What transactions are classified as investing activities in a cash flow statement? What transactions are classified as financing activities?
16. What is the difference between a bookkeeper and an accountant?

EXERCISES

■ **LO3**

E2–1 Identifying Events as Accounting Transactions

Which of the following events results in an exchange transaction for O'Brien Company (Y for yes and N for no)?

_____ (1) O'Brien purchased a machine and signed a note payable in six months.
_____ (2) Six investors in O'Brien Company sold their shares to another investor.
_____ (3) The company lent $150,000 to a member of the board of directors.
_____ (4) O'Brien Company ordered supplies from Office Max to be delivered next week.
_____ (5) The founding owner, Meaghan O'Brien, purchased additional shares in another company.
_____ (6) The company borrowed $1,000,000 from a local bank.

■ **LO3**

E2–2 Identifying Account Titles

The following are independent situations.

a. A company orders and receives 10 personal computers for office use for which it signs a note promising to pay $25,000 within three months.

b. A company purchases a new delivery truck that has a list, or sticker, price of $24,000 for $21,000 cash.

c. A women's clothing retailer orders 30 new display stands for $300 each for future delivery.

d. A new company is formed and sells 100 shares for $12 per share to investors.

e. A manufacturing company signs a contract for the construction of a new warehouse for $500,000. At the signing, the company writes a cheque for $50,000 as a deposit on the future construction.

f. A publishing firm purchases the copyright (an intangible asset) to a manuscript for an introductory accounting text from the author for $40,000.

g. A manufacturing firm pays dividends of $100,000 to shareholders in cash.

h. A company purchases 100 shares of BCE Inc. for $5,000 cash.

i. A company purchases a piece of land for $50,000 cash. An appraiser for the buyer valued the land at $52,500.

j. A manufacturing company purchases the patent (an intangible asset) on a new digital satellite system for television reception for $500,000 cash and a note for $400,000, payable in one year at an annual interest of 10 percent.

k. A local company is a sole proprietorship (one owner); its owner buys a car for $10,000 for personal use. Answer from the company's point of view.

l. A company signs a six-month note for a $1,000 loan on June 30, 2007, to be paid back on December 31, 2007, with 10-percent annual interest.

m. A company pays $1,500 principal on its note payable.

Required:

1. Indicate the appropriate elements on the classified balance sheet (use account titles), if any, affected in each of the preceding events. Consider what is given and what is received.

2. At what amount would you record the truck in (b)? The land in (i)? What measurement principle are you applying?

3. What accounting concepts did you apply for situations (c) and (k)?

E2–3 Classifying Accounts and Their Usual Balances

■ **LO3, 5**

Polaroid Corporation

As described in a recent annual report, Polaroid Corporation designs, manufactures, and markets worldwide a variety of products primarily in instant image recording fields, including instant photographic cameras and films, electronic imaging recording devices, conventional films, and light-polarizing filters and lenses.

Required:

For each of the following accounts from Polaroid's recent balance sheet, complete the following chart by indicating whether the account is classified as a current asset (CA), non-current asset (NCA), current liability (CL), non-current liability (NCL), or shareholders' equity (SE), and whether the account usually has a debit or credit balance.

Account	Balance Sheet Classification	Debit or Credit Balance
1. Land		
2. Retained earnings		
3. Notes payable (due in 3 years)		
4. Prepaid expenses		
5. Long-term investments		
6. Share capital		
7. Machinery and equipment		
8. Accounts payable		
9. Short-term investments		
10. Taxes payable		
11. Accounts receivable		
12. Buildings		
13. Cash		
14. Merchandise inventory		
15. Supplies inventory		
16. Wages payable		

E2–4 Identifying Effects on Balance Sheet Elements

■ **LO4**

Complete the following table by entering either the word *increases* or *decreases* in columns (1) and (2), and either the word *debit* or *credit* in columns (3) and (4).

	(1) Debit	(2) Credit	(3) Increases	(4) Decreases
Assets				
Liabilities				
Shareholders' equity				

E2–5 Determining Financial Statement Effects of Several Transactions

■ **LO4**

The following events occurred for Favata Company:

a. Received investment of cash by organizers, $20,000.

b. Borrowed cash from a bank and signed a note for $6,000.

c. Purchased $12,000 in land; paid $1,000 in cash and signed a mortgage note with a local bank for the balance (due in 15 years).

d. Loaned $300 to an employee who signed a note due in three months.

e. Paid the bank the amount borrowed in (b).

f. Purchased $8,000 of equipment, paying $1,000 in cash and signing a note due to the manufacturer.

Required:

For each of the events (a) through (f), perform transaction analysis and indicate the account, amount, and direction of the effects (+ for increase and − for decrease) on the accounting equation. Check that the accounting equation remains in balance after each transaction. Use the following headings:

Event	Assets	=	Liabilities	+	Shareholders' Equity

LO4

Nike Inc.

E2–6 Determining Financial Statement Effects of Several Transactions

Nike, Inc., with headquarters in Beaverton, Oregon, is one of the world's leading manufacturers of athletic shoes and sports apparel. The following activities occurred during a recent year. The amounts are rounded to millions of dollars.

a. Purchased $216.3 in property, plant, and equipment; paid $5 in long-term debt and the rest in cash.

b. Issued $21.1 in additional shares for cash.

c. Declared $100 in dividends; paid $78.8 during the year, with the rest payable in the following year.

d. Several Nike investors sold their own shares to other investors on the stock exchange for $21.

e. Repaid $3.2 in principal on long-term debt obligations.

f. Received cash for sale investments in other companies at their cost of $1.4.

Required:

For each of these events, perform transaction analysis and indicate the account, amount, and direction of the effects on the accounting equation. Check that the accounting equation remains in balance after each transaction. Use the following headings:

Event	Assets	=	Liabilities	+	Shareholders' Equity

LO5

E2–7 Recording Investing and Financing Activities

Refer to E2–5.

Required:

For each of the events in E2–5, prepare journal entries, checking that debits equal credits.

LO5

Nike Inc.

E2–8 Recording Investing and Financing Activities

Refer to E2–6.

Required:

1. For each of the events in E2–6, prepare journal entries, checking that debits equal credits.

2. Explain your response to Transaction (*d*).

LO5

E2–9 Analyzing the Effects of Transactions in T-Accounts

Mulkeen Service Company, Inc., was organized by Conor Mulkeen and five other investors. The following events occurred during the year:

a. Received $60,000 cash from the investors; each was issued 1,000 shares.

b. Purchased equipment for use in the business at a cost of $12,000; one-fourth was paid in cash, and the company signed a note for the balance, payable in six months.

c. Signed an agreement with a cleaning service to pay it $120 per week for cleaning the corporate offices.

d. Lent $2,000 to one of the investors who signed a note due in six months.

e. Issued shares to additional investors who contributed $4,000 in cash and a lot of land valued at $10,000.

f. Paid the amount of the note payable in (*b*).

g. Conor Mulkeen borrowed $10,000 for personal use from a local bank and signed a note payable in one year.

Required:

1. Prepare journal entries for each transaction. If an event does not require a journal entry, explain the reason. Use the account titles listed in requirement 2.

2. Create T-accounts for the following accounts: Cash, Note Receivable, Equipment, Land, Note Payable, and Share Capital. Beginning balances are zero. For each of the preceding transactions, record the effects of the transaction in the appropriate T-accounts. Include good referencing and totals for each T-account.

3. Using the balances in the T-accounts, fill in the following amounts for the accounting equation:

Assets $____ = Liabilities $____ + Shareholders' Equity $____

E2–10 **Inferring Investing and Financing Transactions, and Preparing a Balance Sheet**   ■ LO4, 6

During its first week of operations, January 2–7, 2008, Fullem Fine Furniture Company completed seven transactions with the dollar effects indicated in the following T-accounts:

Cash		Short-Term Note Receivable		Store Fixtures	
(1) 12,000	4,000 (3)	(4) 3,000	2,000 (7)	(5) 7,000	
(2) 50,000	3,000 (4)				
(7) 2,000	7,000 (5)				
	3,000 (6)				

Land		Short-Term Note Payable		Share Capital	
(3) 12,000		(6) 3,000	50,000 (2)		12,000 (1)
			8,000 (3)		

Required:

1. Write a brief explanation of transactions 1 through 7. Explain any assumptions that you made.
2. Compute the ending balance in each account and prepare a classified balance sheet for Fullem Fine Furniture Company on January 7, 2008.

E2–11 **Inferring Investing and Financing Transactions, and Preparing a Balance Sheet**   ■ LO5

During its first month of operations, March 2008, Faye's Fashions, Inc., completed seven transactions with the dollar effects indicated in the following T-accounts:

Cash		Short-Term Investments		Short-Term Note Receivable	
(1) 50,000	4,000 (2)	(4) 6,000	2,000 (6)	(3) 4,000	
(6) 2,000	4,000 (3)				
	6,000 (4)				
	3,000 (5)				

Computer Equipment		Delivery Truck		Long-Term Note Payable	
(7) 4,000		(2) 25,000		(5) 3,000	21,000 (2)

Share Capital	
	50,000 (1)
	4,000 (7)

Required:

1. Write a brief explanation of transactions 1 through 7. Explain any assumptions that you made.
2. Compute the ending balance in each account and prepare a classified balance sheet for Faye's Fashions, Inc., at the end of March 2008.

E2–12 **Recording Journal Entries**   ■ LO5

Boyce Corporation was organized on May 1, 2007. The following transactions occurred during the first month.

a. Received $60,000 cash from the three investors who organized Boyce Corporation.
b. Borrowed $20,000 cash and signed a 12-percent note due in two years.
c. Purchased $10,000 in equipment, paying $1,000 in cash and signing a six-month note for the balance.
d. Ordered $16,000 in store fixtures.
e. Paid the amount of the note signed in (c).
f. Lent $1,000 to an employee who signed a note to repay the loan in three months.
g. Received and paid for the store fixtures ordered in (d).

Required:
Prepare journal entries for each transaction. Be sure to use good referencing and categorize each account as an asset (A), liability (L), or shareholders' equity (SE). If a transaction does not require a journal entry, explain the reason.

■ **LO5**   **E2–13 Recording Journal Entries**

Philippine
Long Distance
Telephone Company

Philippine Long Distance Telephone Company is the leading telecommunications provider in the Philippines. The monetary unit is the Philippine peso (₱). The following transactions were adapted from a recent annual report. Amounts are in millions of pesos.

a. Declared ₱10,970 in dividends to be paid next month.

b. Ordered ₱450 in equipment.

c. Paid ₱10,970 in dividends previously declared in (a).

d. Issued additional shares for ₱334 in cash.

e. Sold land at its cost for cash, ₱912.

f. Received the equipment ordered in transaction (b), paying ₱120 in cash and signing a note for the balance.

g. Purchased temporary investments for ₱1,206.

h. Paid ₱44,323 in principal on long-term debt.

Required:
Prepare journal entries for each transaction. Be sure to use good referencing and categorize each account as an asset (A), liability (L), or shareholders' equity (SE). If a transaction does not require a journal entry, explain the reason.

■ **LO5, 6**   **E2–14 Analyzing the Effects of Transactions Using T-Accounts, Preparing a Balance Sheet, and Interpreting the Debt-to-Equity Ratio as a Manager of the Company**

ANALYSIS

Doane Company has been operating for one year (2007). You are a member of the management team investigating expansion ideas, all of which will require borrowing funds from banks. At the start of 2008, Doane's T-account balances were as follows:

Assets:

Cash	Short-Term Investments	Property and Equipment
5,000	2,000	4,000

Liabilities:

Short-Term Notes Payable	Long-Term Notes Payable
2,100	6,600

Shareholders' Equity:

Share Capital	Retained Earnings
300	2,000

Required:

1. Using the data from these T-accounts, complete the balance sheet equation on January 1, 2008:

    Assets $_____ = Liabilities $_____ + Shareholders' Equity $_____

2. Enter in the T-accounts the following transactions that occurred in 2007:

    (a) Paid one-half of the principal on the long-term note payable.

    (b) Sold $1,500 of the investments for $1,500 cash.

    (c) Paid in full the principal on the short-term notes payable.

    (d) Sold one-fourth of the property and equipment for $1,000 in cash.

    (e) Borrowed $1,600 at 10 percent from the bank (signing a note); the principal and interest are due in three years.

    (f) Paid $600 in dividends to shareholders.

3. Compute ending balances in the T-accounts to complete the balance sheet on December 31, 2008:

   Assets $_____ = Liabilities $_____ + Shareholders' Equity $_____

4. Using the ending balances in the T-accounts, prepare a classified balance sheet at December 31, 2008, in good form.

5. Calculate the debt-to-equity ratio at December 31, 2008. If the industry average for the debt-to-equity ratio is 1.00, what does your computation suggest to you about Doane Company? Would you support expansion by borrowing? Why or why not?

E2–15 Explaining the Effects of Transactions on Balance Sheet Accounts Using T-Accounts   ■ **LO5**

Heavey and Lovas Furniture Repair Service, a company with two shareholders, began operations on June 1, 2008. The following T-accounts indicate the activities for the month of June.

Cash (A)				Notes Receivable (A)				Tools and Equipment (A)			
(a)	17,000	(b)	10,000	(c)	1,500	(d)	500	(a)	3,000	(f)	800
(d)	500	(c)	1,500								
(f)	800	(e)	1,000								

Building (A)				Notes Payable (L)				Share Capital (SE)			
(b)	50,000			(e)	1,000	(b)	40,000			(a)	20,000

Required:

Explain transactions (a) through (f), which resulted in the entries in the T-accounts. That is, what activity made the account increase or decrease?

E2–16 Inferring Typical Investing and Financing Activities in Accounts   ■ **LO5**

The following T-accounts indicate the effects of normal business transactions:

Equipment				Note Receivable				Notes Payable			
1/1	300			1/1	75					130	1/1
	250	?			?	290		?		170	
12/13	450			12/31	50					180	12/31

Required:

1. Describe the typical investing and financing transactions that affect each T-account. That is, what economic events did occur to make these accounts increase or decrease?

2. For each T-account, compute the missing amounts.

E2–17 Identifying Investing and Financing Activities Affecting Cash Flows   ■ **LO7**

The Forzani Group Ltd.

The Forzani Group Ltd. (FGL) is Canada's largest sporting goods retailer, with over 250 company-owned stores under the Forzani's, Sport Chek, Coast Mountain Sports, and Sport Mart banners. FGL also boasts about 200 franchised stores under the Sport Experts, Atmosphere, Intersport, RnR, Econosports, and Tech Shop names. The stores sell name-brand and private-label sports equipment, footwear, and apparel. The following are several of FGL's investing and financing activities that were reflected in a recent annual cash flow statement.

a. Principal repayment of long-term debt.

b. Purchase of investments.

c. Issuance of shares.

d. Addition to capital assets (property, plant, and equipment).

e. Issuance of long-term debt.

f. Repurchase of shares.

g. Disposal of other assets.

Required:

For each of these, indicate whether the activity is investing (I) or financing (F) and the direction of the effect on cash flows (+ = increases cash; − = decreases cash).

E2–18 Preparing the Investing and Financing Section of the Cash Flow Statement   ■ **LO7**

Hilton Hotels Corporation

Hilton Hotels Corporation constructs, operates, and franchises domestic and international hotel and hotel-casino properties. Information from the company's recent annual cash flow statement indicates the following investing and financing activities during that year (simplified):

Payment of bank loans	$439
Purchase of investments	25
Sale of property (assume sold at cost)	279
Issuance of shares	40
Purchase and renovation of properties	202
Additional borrowing from creditors	562
Receipt of payment on a note receivable	5

Required:
Prepare the Investing and Financing sections of the cash flow statement for Hilton hotels. Assume that the company's year-end is December 31, 2007.

■ **LO3, 6, 7**   **E2–19**   **Finding Financial Information as a Potential Investor**

ANALYSIS

You are considering investing the cash you inherited from your grandfather in various company shares. You have received the annual reports of several major companies.

Required:
For each of the following, indicate where you would locate the information in an annual report. (*Hint:* The information may be in more than one location.)

1. Total current assets.
2. Principal amount of debt repaid during the year.
3. Summary of significant accounting policies.
4. Cash received from sales of non-current assets.
5. Amount of dividends paid during the year.
6. Short-term obligations.
7. Date of the statement of financial position.

PROBLEMS

■ **LO1, 3**   **P2–1**   **Identifying Accounts on a Classified Balance Sheet and Their Normal Debit or Credit Balances** (AP2–1)

Petro-Canada

Petro-Canada is a major Canadian integrated oil and gas company that explores, produces, refines, markets, and supplies crude oil and petroleum products. Its operations include refineries in Alberta, Ontario, and Québec and almost 1,600 gas stations across Canada. The following are several of the accounts that appeared on a recent balance sheet of Petro-Canada.

(1) Cash and Short-Term Investments   (7) Inventories
(2) Accounts Receivable   (8) Accounts Payable
(3) Share Capital   (9) Retained Earnings
(4) Long-Term Debt   (10) Property, Plant, and Equipment
(5) Prepaid Expenses   (11) Long-Term Investments
(6) Income Tax Payable

Required:
For each account, indicate how it normally should be categorized on a classified balance sheet. Use CA for current asset, NCA for non-current asset, CL for current liability, NCL for non-current liability, and SE for shareholders' equity. Also indicate whether the account normally has a debit or credit balance.

■ **LO3, 4**   **P2–2**   **Determining Financial Statement Effects of Various Transactions** (AP2–2)

Lester's Home Healthcare Services was organized on January 1, 2008, by four friends. Each organizer invested $10,000 in the company and, in turn, was issued 8,000 shares. To date, they are the only shareholders. During the first month (January 2008), the company completed the following six transactions:

a. Collected a total of $40,000 from the organizers and, in turn, issued the shares.

b. Purchased a building for $65,000, equipment for $16,000, and three acres of land for $12,000; paid $13,000 in cash, and signed a 10-percent mortgage for the balance payable to the local bank in 15 years. (*Hint:* Five different accounts are affected.)

c. One shareholder reported to the company that he sold 500 shares to another shareholder for a cash consideration of $5,000.

d. Purchased short-term investments for $3,000 cash.

e. Sold one acre of land costing $4,000 to another company for $4,000 cash.

f. Loaned one of the shareholders $5,000 for moving costs, in exchange for a signed note due in one year.

Required:

1. Was Lester's Home Healthcare Services organized as a sole proprietorship, a partnership, or a corporation? Explain the basis for your answer.

2. During the first month, the records of the company were inadequate. You were asked to prepare a summary of the preceding transactions. To develop a quick assessment of the transaction effects on Lester's Home Healthcare Services, you have decided to complete the tabulation that follows and to use plus (+) for increases and minus (−) for decreases for each account. The first transaction is used as an example.

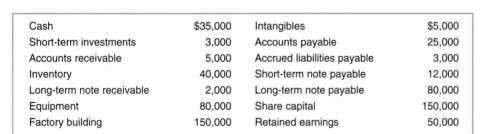

	Assets						=	Liabilities	+	Shareholders' Equity	
Cash	Short-Term Investments	Notes Receivable	Land	Building	Equipment			Notes Payable		Share Capital	Retained Earnings
(a) +40,000							=			+40,000	

3. Did you include all the transactions in the tabulation? If not, which one did you exclude and why?

4. Based only on the completed tabulation, provide the following amounts at January 31, 2008 (show computations):
   a. Total assets.
   b. Total liabilities.
   c. Total shareholders' equity.
   d. Cash balance.
   e. Total current assets.

P2–3 Recording Transactions in T-Accounts, Preparing a Balance Sheet, and Evaluating the Debt-to-Equity Ratio (AP2–3)

■ LO6

Patrie Plastics Company has been operating for three years. At December 31, 2007, the accounting records reflected the following:

Cash	$35,000	Intangibles	$5,000
Short-term investments	3,000	Accounts payable	25,000
Accounts receivable	5,000	Accrued liabilities payable	3,000
Inventory	40,000	Short-term note payable	12,000
Long-term note receivable	2,000	Long-term note payable	80,000
Equipment	80,000	Share capital	150,000
Factory building	150,000	Retained earnings	50,000

During the year 2008, the following summarized transactions were completed:

a. Purchased equipment that cost $30,000; paid $10,000 cash and signed a one-year note for the balance.

b. Issued 2,000 shares for $20,000 cash.

c. Loaned $12,000 to a supplier who signed a two-year note.

d. Purchased $15,000 in investments.

e. Paid $5,000 on the note in transaction (a).

f. Borrowed $20,000 cash on December 31, 2008, from a local bank and signed a note, payable June 30, 2009.

g. Purchased a patent (an intangible asset) for $6,000 cash.

h. Built an addition to the factory for $42,000; paid $15,000 in cash and signed a three-year note for the balance.

i. Hired a new president at the end of the year. The contract was for $125,000 per year plus options to purchase company shares at a set price based on company performance.

j. Returned defective equipment to the manufacturer, receiving a cash refund of $2,000.

Required:

1. Create T-accounts for each of the accounts on the balance sheet and enter the balances at the end of 2007 as beginning balances for 2008.

2. Record each of the transactions for 2008 in T-accounts (including referencing) and determine the ending balances.

3. Explain your response to transaction (*i*).

4. Prepare a classified balance sheet at December 31, 2008.

5. Compute the debt-to-equity ratio for 2008. What does this ratio suggest about Patrie Plastics Company?

■ LO7

ANALYSIS

P2–4 Identifying Effects of Transactions on the Cash Flow Statement (AP2–4)
Refer to P2–3.

Required:
Using the transactions (*a*) through (*j*) in P2–3, indicate whether each transaction is an investing (I) or financing (F) activity for the year and the direction of the effect on cash flows (+ for increase and − for decrease). If there is no effect on cash flows, write NE.

■ LO5, 6

Bayer AG

eXcel

P2–5 Recording Transactions, Preparing Journal Entries, Posting to T-Accounts, Preparing a Balance Sheet, and Evaluating the Debt-to-Equity Ratio (AP2–5)
Bayer AG, with headquarters in Leverkeusen, Germany, is an international research-based group of companies active in health, agriculture, polymers, and chemicals. Popular products include Bayer Aspirin, Alka-Seltzer, and One-A-Day vitamins. The following is Bayer's (simplified) balance sheet from a recent year:

BAYER AG	
Balance Sheet	
At December 31, 2006	
(in millions of euros)	
ASSETS	
Current assets	
Cash and cash equivalents	€ 2,915
Receivables	7,019
Inventories	6,153
Other assets	3,907
	19,994
Non-current assets	
Investments	532
Property, plant, and equipment	8.867
Intangible assets	24,034
Other assets	2,464
	35,897
Total assets	**55,891**
LIABILITIES AND SHAREHOLDERS' EQUITY	
Current liabilities	
Accounts payable	€2 ,639
Other short-term obligations	12,876
	15,515
Long-term liabilities	**27,525**
Shareholders' equity	
Share capital	5,985
Retained earnings	6,866
	12,851
Total liabilities and shareholders' equity	**€55,891**

Assume that the following transactions occurred in 2007:

a. Issued additional shares for €1,200 in cash.

b. Borrowed €3,952 from banks due in two years.

c. Declared and paid €953 in dividends to shareholders.

d. Purchased additional intangibles for €45 cash.

e. Purchased property, plant, and equipment; paid €2,647 in cash and €5,410 with additional long-term bank loans.

f. Acquired additional investments; paid €160 in cash.

g. Lent €250 to an affiliate that signed a six-month note.

h. Sold investments costing €115 for the same amount in cash.

Required:

1. Prepare a journal entry for each transaction.

2. Create T-accounts for each balance sheet account and include the December 31, 2006, balances. Post each journal entry to the appropriate T-accounts.

3. Prepare a balance sheet for Bayer based on the T-account ending balances at December 31, 2007.

4. Compute Bayer's debt-to-equity ratio for 2007. What does this suggest about the company?

P2–6 **Preparing the Investing and Financing Sections of a Cash Flow Statement** (AP2–6)
Refer to P2–5.

■ **LO7**

Bayer AG

Required:
Based on the transactions that occurred in 2007, prepare the Investing and Financing sections of the cash flow statement of Bayer's for 2007.

P2–7 **Using Financial Reports: Preparing a Classified Balance Sheet and Analyzing the Debt-to-Equity Ratio** (AP2–7)
The accounts below, in alphabetical order, are adapted from a recent McDonald's Corporation balance sheet (amounts are in millions of dollars):

■ **LO6**

McDonald's
Corporation

ANALYSIS

	Current Year	Prior Year		Current Year	Prior Year
Accounts and notes			Long-term debt	8,937.4	8,357.3
receivable	795.9	745.5	Notes payable (short term)	544.0	—
Accounts payable	689.4	714.3	Other long-term		
Accrued liabilities	2,344.2	2,144.0	liabilities	1,869.0	1,758.2
Cash and equivalents	4,260.4	1,379.8	Other non-current assets	1,245.0	1,338.4
Current maturities of			Prepaid expenses and		
long-term debt	658.7	862.2	other current assets	646.4	585.0
Intangible assets, net	1,950.7	1,828.3	Property and		
Inventories	147.0	147.5	equipment, net	20,108.0	20,903.1
Investments in and			Retained earnings	12,331.9	11,998.9
advances to affiliates	1,035.4	1,109.9	Share capital	2,814.2	2,202.6

Required:

1. Construct, in good form, a classified balance sheet (with two years reported) for McDonald's Corporation.

2. Compute the company's debt-to-equity ratio for the current year. How do you interpret this ratio for McDonald's?

P2–8 **Preparing Journal Entries, Using T-Accounts, Preparing a Balance Sheet, and Evaluating the Debt-to-Equity Ratio over Time as a Bank Loan Officer**
At the beginning of year 2009, Lee Delivery Company, Inc., which was organized in 2008, applied to your bank for a $100,000 loan to expand the business. The vice-president of the bank asked you to review the information and make a recommendation on lending the

■ **LO5, 6**

ANALYSIS

funds. The following transactions occurred during year 2008 (the company's first year of operations):

(*a*) Received cash from the organizers, $40,000.

(*b*) Purchased land for $12,000 and signed a one-year note (at a 10-percent annual interest rate).

(*c*) Bought two used delivery trucks for operating purposes at the start of the year at a cost of $10,000 each; paid $2,000 cash and signed a promissory note for the balance, payable over the next three years (at an annual interest rate of 11 percent).

(*d*) Sold one-fourth of the land for $3,000 to Birkins Moving, which promised to pay in six months.

(*e*) Paid $2,000 cash to a truck repair shop for a new motor for one of the trucks. (*Hint:* Increase the account you used to record the purchase of the trucks since the usefulness of the truck has been improved.)

(*f*) Traded the other truck and $6,000 cash for a new one. The truck's fair value is $10,000.

(*g*) Shareholder Jonah Lee paid $22,000 cash for a vacant lot (land) for his personal use.

(*h*) Collected the amount of the note due from Birkins Moving in (*d*).

(*i*) Paid one-third of the principal of the note due for the delivery trucks in (*c*).

Required:

1. Set up appropriate T-accounts with beginning balances of $0 for Cash, Short-Term Notes Receivable, Land, Equipment, Short-Term Notes Payable, Long-Term Notes Payable, and Share Capital. Using the T-accounts, record the effects of these transactions on Lee Delivery Company.

2. Prepare a classified balance sheet for Lee Delivery Company at the end of 2008.

3. At the end of the next two years, Lee Delivery Company reported the following amounts on its balance sheets:

	End of 2010	End of 2009
Assets	$120,000	$90,000
Liabilities	70,000	40,000
Shareholders' Equity	50,000	50,000

Compute the company's debt-to-equity ratio for 2009 and 2010. What is the trend and what does this suggest about the company?

4. What recommendation would you make to the bank's vice-president about lending the money to Lee Delivery Company?

ALTERNATE PROBLEMS

LO5, 6   **AP2–1**   **Identifying Accounts on a Classified Balance Sheet and Their Normal Debit or Credit Balances (P2–1)**

Bayer AG

ANALYSIS

According to a recent annual report of Celestica Inc., the company is a "key player in the new technology-driven global economy." The company provides a broad range of services including "design, prototyping, assembly, testing, product assurance, supply chain management, worldwide distribution, and after-sales service." The following are several of the accounts from a recent balance sheet:

(1) Accounts Receivable

(2) Short-Term Borrowings

(3) Share Capital

(4) Long-Term Debt

(5) Prepaid Expenses and Other Assets

(6) Intangible Assets

(7) Property, Plant, and Equipment

(8) Retained Earnings

(9) Accounts Payable

(10) Cash and Short-Term Investments

(11) Accrued Liabilities

(12) Other Long-Term Liabilities

(13) Inventories

(14) Income Taxes Payable

Required:

Indicate how each account normally should be categorized on a classified balance sheet. Use CA for current asset, NCA for non-current asset, CL for current liability, NCL for non-current liability, and SE for shareholders' equity. Also indicate whether the account normally has a debit or credit balance.

AP2–2 Determining Financial Statement Effects of Various Transactions and Interpreting the Debt-to-Equity Ratio (P2–2)

■ LO3, 4

Malamud Incorporated is a small manufacturing company that makes model trains to sell to toy stores. It has a small service department that repairs customers' trains for a fee. The company has been in business for five years. At the end of the most recent year, 2007, the accounting records reflected total assets of $500,000 and total liabilities of $200,000. During the current year, 2008, the following summarized transactions were completed:

a. Issued 10,000 shares for $100,000 cash.

b. Borrowed $120,000 cash from the bank and signed a 10-year, 12-percent note.

c. Built an addition onto the factory for $200,000 and paid cash to the contractor.

d. Purchased equipment for the new addition for $30,000, paying $3,000 in cash and signing a note due in six months for the balance.

e. Purchased $85,000 in long-term investments.

f. Returned a defective piece of the equipment purchased in transaction (d); received a reduction of $3,000 on the note payable.

g. Paid $12,000 of the principal due on the note in (b).

h. Purchased a delivery truck (equipment) for $10,000; paid $5,000 cash and signed a short-term note for the remainder.

i. Loaned the company president, Jennifer Malamud, $2,000 cash. Ms. Malamud promised to pay the amount and annual interest at the rate of 10 percent within one year.

j. A shareholder sold some of her shares in Malamud Incorporated to her neighbour for $5,000.

k. Received $250 cash from Ms. Malamud on the note due, transaction (i).

Required:

1. Prepare a summary of the preceding transactions. To develop a quick assessment of the transaction effects on Malamud Incorporated, you have decided to complete the tabulation that follows and to use plus (+) for increases and minus (−) for decreases for each account. The first transaction is used as an example.

	Assets					=	Liabilities		+	Shareholders' Equity	
Cash	Notes Receivable	Long-Term Investments	Equipment	Building			Short-Term Notes Payable	Long-Term Notes Payable		Share Capital	Retained Earnings
(a) +100,000						=				+100,000	

2. Did you include all transactions in the tabulation? If not, which one did you exclude and why?

3. Based on beginning balances plus the completed tabulation, calculate the following amounts at the end of 2008 (show computations):
   a. Total assets.   b. Total liabilities.   c. Total shareholders' equity.

4. Compute the company's debt-to-equity ratio. What does this ratio suggest to you about Malamud Incorporated?

AP2–3 Recording Transactions in T-Accounts, Preparing a Balance Sheet, and Evaluating the Debt-to-Equity Ratio (P2–3)

■ LO5, 6

Gildan Activewear

Gildan Activewear Inc. specializes in manufacturing and selling T-shirts, sport shirts and sweatshirts. The following is adapted from a recent annual financial report (assume that the fiscal year ends on December 31, 2006). Dollars are in thousands.

Cash and cash equivalents	$ 69,802	Accounts payable and	
Accounts receivable	108,646	accrued expenses	86,843
Inventories	134,861	Other current liabilities	26,045
Prepaid expenses and		Long-term debt	27,288
other current assets	14,529	Other long-term liabilities	36,780
Property, plant, and equipment, net	260,615	Retained earnings	308,539
Other assets	9,063	Share capital	112,021

Assume that the following transactions occurred in the first quarter ended March 31, 2007:

a. Received $630 on accounts receivable from customers.

b. Paid $12,340 in principal on long-term debt.

c. Purchased $3,400 in inventories for cash.

d. Sold equipment at its cost for $4,020 cash.

e. Purchased short-term investments of $2,980.

f. Issued additional shares for $1,020 in cash.

g. Purchased property, plant, and equipment; paid $1,830 in cash and $9,400 with additional long-term bank loans.

h. Sold other assets at cost for $310 cash.

i. Declared and paid $300 in dividends to shareholders.

Required:

1. Create T-accounts for each of the accounts on the balance sheet; enter the balances at December 31, 2006.

2. Record each of the transactions for the first quarter ended March 31, 2007, in the T-accounts (including referencing) and determine the ending balances.

3. Prepare a classified balance sheet at March 31, 2007.

4. Compute the debt-to-equity ratio for the quarter ended March 31, 2007. What does this suggest about Gildan Activewear Inc.?

■ **LO7**   **AP2–4** **Identifying Effects of Transactions on the Cash Flow Statement** (P2–4)

Gildan
Activewear

Refer to AP2–3.

Required:

Using the transactions (*a*) through (*i*) in AP2–3, indicate whether each transaction is an investing (I) or financing (F) activity for the year and the direction of the effect on cash flows (+ for increase and − for decrease). If there is no effect on cash flows related to investing or financing activities, write NE.

■ **LO5, 6**   **AP2–5** **Recording Transactions, Preparing Journal Entries, Posting to T-Accounts, Preparing a Balance Sheet, and Evaluating the Debt-to-Equity Ratio** (P2–5)

Dell Inc.

Dell Inc. is a leading global provider of computer products and services for both the consumer and enterprise markets. Dell offers a full line of desktop and notebook PCs, network servers, workstations, storage systems, printers, handheld computers, digital music players, LCD and plasma televisions, and projectors. The following is Dell's (simplified) balance sheet from a recent year:

DELL Inc.
Balance Sheet
At February 3, 2006
(in millions of US dollars)

ASSETS	
Current assets	
Cash and Cash equivalents	$ 7,042
Short-term investments	2,016
Receivables	5,452
Inventories	576
Other assets	2,620
Total current assets	17,706

(continued)

Non-current assets	
Property, plant, and equipment, net	2,005
Investments	2,691
Other assets	707
Total assets	**$23,109**
LIABILITIES AND SHAREHOLDERS' EQUITY	
Current liabilities	
Accounts payable	$ 9,840
Accured liabilities	6,087
Total current liabilities	15,927
Long-term liabilities	3,053
Total liabilities	**18,980**
Shareholders' equity	**4,129**
Total liabilities and shareholders' equity	**$23,109**

Assume that the following transactions (in millions of dollars) occurred in the remainder of 2006 (ending on February 2, 2007):

a. Issued additional shares for $200 in cash.

b. Borrowed $30 from banks due in two years.

c. Purchased additional investments for $13,000 cash; one-fifth were long term and the rest were short term.

d. Purchased property, plant, and equipment; paid $875 in cash and $1,410 with additional long-term bank loans.

e. Lent $250 to affiliates that signed a six-month note.

f. Sold short-term investments costing $10,000 for $10,000 cash.

Required:

1. Prepare a journal entry for each transaction.

2. Create T-accounts for each balance sheet account and include the February 3, 2006 balances. Post each journal entry to the appropriate T-accounts.

3. Prepare a balance sheet for Dell based on the T-account ending balances at February 2, 2007.

4. Compute Dell's debt-to-equity ratio for 2006. What does this suggest about the company?

AP2–6   Preparing the Investing and Financing Sections of a Cash Flow Statement (P2–6)
Refer to AP2–5.

■ **LO7**

Dell Inc.

Required:
Based on the transactions that occurred in 2006, prepare the Investing and Financing sections of the Dell's cash flow statement for 2006.

AP2–7   Using Financial Reports: Preparing a Classified Balance Sheet and Analyzing the Debt-to-Equity Ratio (P2–7)
The accounts below, in alphabetical order, are adapted from Danier Leather Inc.'s recent balance sheet (amounts in thousands of dollars):

■ **LO7**

Danier Leather

ANALYSIS

	Current Year	Prior Year		Current Year	Prior Year
Accounts payable and					
accrued liabilities	8,170	9,355	Other non-current assets	5,596	6,399
Accounts receivable	594	626	Prepaid expenses and		
Cash	21,193	22,576	other current assets	698	1,894
Income taxes payable	-0-	952	Property & equipment, net	25,314	28,891
Inventories	29,970	29,483	Retained earnings	32,214	36,902
Non-current liabilities	20,258	18,275	Share capital	22,723	24,385

Required:

1. Prepare, in good form, a classified balance sheet (with two years reported) for Danier Leather Inc. Assume the current year ends on June 30, 2007.

2. Compute the company's debt-to-equity ratio for the current year. How do you interpret this ratio for Danier Leather?

CASES AND PROJECTS

FINDING AND INTERPRETING FINANCIAL INFORMATION

LO1, 2, 3, 4, 7

The Forzani Group Ltd.

ANALYSIS

CP2–1 Finding Financial Information

Refer to the financial statements and the accompanying notes of The Forzani Group Ltd., available on the Online Learning Centre Web site at **www.mcgrawhill.ca/olc/libby/student/ resources**.

Required:

1. Is the company a corporation, a partnership, or a proprietorship? How do you know?

2. Use the company's balance sheet to determine the amounts in the accounting equation (A = L + SE).

3. The company shows on the balance sheet that inventories are reported at $278,002,000. Does this amount represent the expected selling price? Why or why not?

4. What is the company's fiscal year-end? Where did you find the exact date?

5. What are the company's long-term obligations?

6. Compute the company's debt-to-equity ratio and explain its meaning.

7. How much cash did the company spend on purchasing property, plant, and equipment each year (capital expenditures)? Where did you find the information?

LO3, 7

The Forzani Group vs. Van Houtte

ANALYSIS

CP2–2 Comparing Companies

Refer to the financial statements and the accompanying notes of The Forzani Group Ltd., available at the Online Learning Centre Web site **www.mcgrawhill.ca/olc/libby/student/ resources**, and of Van Houtte Inc., given in Appendix B.

Required:

1. Which company is larger in terms of total assets?

2. Compute the debt-to-equity ratio for both companies. Which company is assuming more risk? Why do you think that?

3. In the most recent year, what were the net cash flows (that is, the increases in cash minus the decreases in cash) related to the buying and selling of investments for each company?

4. How much did each company pay in dividends for the most recent year?

5. What account title does each company use to report any land, buildings, and equipment it may have?

FINANCIAL REPORTING AND ANALYSIS CASES

LO6

ANALYSIS

CP2–3 Broadening Financial Research Skills: Locating Financial Information on the SEDAR Database

The Securities Commissions regulate companies that issue shares on the stock market. They receive financial reports from public companies electronically under a system called *SEDAR* (System for Electronic Document Analysis and Retrieval). Using the Internet, anyone may search the database for the reports that have been filed. A similar system is available for retrieval of financial information about U.S. public companies. It is known as *EDGAR* (Electronic Data Gathering and Retrieval Service).

Using your Web browser, access the SEDAR database at **www.sedar.com**. To search the database, select "English," then "Company Profiles"; click on the letter V to get a list of all company names that start with V. Select Van Houtte Inc., then click on "View this company's public documents" at the lower left corner of the next screen.

Required:

1. Look at SEDAR filings by clicking on the interim financial statements—English. Then locate the Balance Sheet.

   a. What was the amount of Van Houtte's total assets at the end of the most recent quarter reported?

   b. Did long-term debt increase or decrease for the quarter?

   c. Compute the debt-to-equity ratio. How does it compare to the ratio indicated for Van Houtte in this chapter? What does this suggest about the company?

2. Look at the "Cash Flow Statement" in the interim report.

   a. What amount did Van Houtte spend on capital expenditures for the most recent quarter reported?

   b. What was the total amount of cash flows from (used in) financing activities for the most recent quarter reported?

CP2–4 Interpreting the Financial Press

The December 22, 2003, edition of *Business Week* magazine includes an article entitled "Is Wilbur Ross Crazy?" You can access the article on the Online Learning Centre Web site at **www.mcgrawhill.ca/olc/libby/student/resources.**

■ **LO3, 4**

ANALYSIS

Required:

Read the article and then answer the following questions:

1. What is *distressed investing* according to the article?

2. Mr. Ross usually becomes a bondholder but often swaps debt with equity. Why is this riskier?

3. According to the article, what makes Mr. Ross successful (i.e., what is his approach and attitude toward investing)?

CP2–5 Using Financial Reports: Evaluating the Reliability of a Balance Sheet

Betsey Jordan asked a local bank for a $50,000 loan to expand her small company. The bank asked Betsey to submit a financial statement of the business to supplement the loan application. Betsey prepared the following balance sheet.

■ **LO1, 2**

ANALYSIS

Balance Sheet
June 30, 2007

Assets	
Cash and GICs (investments)	$ 9,000
Inventory	30,000
Equipment	46,000
Personal residence (monthly payments, $2,800)	300,000
Other assets	20,000
Total assets	**$405,000**
Liabilities	
Short-term debt to suppliers	$ 62,000
Long-term debt on equipment	38,000
Total debt	100,000
Shareholders' equity	**305,000**
Total liabilities and shareholders' equity	**$405,000**

Required:

1. The balance sheet has several flaws. However, there is at least one major deficiency. Identify it and explain its significance.

2. As a bank manager, would you lend the company money? Explain.

CP2–6 Using Financial Reports: Analyzing the Balance Sheet

Research In Motion Limited is a Canadian enterprise that designs, manufactures, and markets wireless products for the mobile communications industry. Recent (adapted) balance sheets for the company are presented below.

■ **LO5, 6**

Research In Motion

ANALYSIS

Research In Motion Limited
Consolidated Balance Sheets
(in thousands of US dollars)

	March 4 2006	February 26 2005
Assets		
Current		
Cash and cash equivalents	$ 459,540	$ 610,354
Short-term investments	175,553	315,495
Trade receivables	315,278	227,750
Other receivables	31,861	13,125
Inventory	134,523	92,489
Other current assets	139,824	285,035
	1,256,579	1,544,248
Investments	614,309	753,868
Capital assets	326,313	210,112
Intangible assets	85,929	83,740
Goodwill	29,026	29,026
Total assets	$2,312,156	$2,620,994
Liabilities		
Current		
Accounts payable	$ 94,954	$ 68,464
Accrued liabilities	144,912	87,133
Accured litigation and related expenses	-0-	455,610
Income taxes payable	17,584	3,149
Deferred revenue	20,968	16,235
Current portion of long-term debt	262	223
	278,680	630,814
Long-term debt	6,851	6,504
Other long-term liabilities	27,858	-0-
Total liabilities	313,389	637,318
Shareholders' equity		
Share capital	1,852,713	1,892,266
Retained earnings	146,054	91,410
Total shareholders' equity	1,998,767	1,983,676
Total liabilities and shareholders' equity	$2,312,156	$2,620,994

Required:

1. Is Research In Motion a corporation, sole proprietorship, or partnership? Explain briefly.

2. Use the company's balance sheet to determine the amounts in the accounting equation (A = L + SE) at the end of the fiscal years 2005 and 2006.

3. Calculate the company's debt-to-equity ratio at the end of fiscal 2006. Interpret the ratio that you calculated. What other information would make your interpretation more useful?

4. Prepare the journal entry for the payment of the principal on the long-term debt if it were due at the end of February 2007.

5. Does the company appear to have been generally profitable during its years in business? Explain.

6. Assuming no dividends were declared, how much was the net income (loss) for the fiscal year ended March 4, 2006? How could you verify that no dividends were declared?

■ **LO6**   **CP2–7   Using Financial Reports: Analyzing the Balance Sheet**

ANALYSIS   Smiley Corp. and Tsang Inc. were organized in 2002. Both companies operate in the same line of business. The balance sheets of the two companies at December 31, 2007 are as follows:

<table>
<tr><td colspan="2">Smiley Corp.
Balance Sheet
December 31, 2007</td><td colspan="2">Tsang Inc.
Balance Sheet
December 31, 2007</td></tr>
</table>

Assets		**Assets**	
Cash	$ 17,000	Cash	$ 7,200
Accounts receivable	30,000	Accounts receivable	14,400
Inventory	16,000	Inventory	7,600
Property, plant, and equipment	117,600	Property, plant, and equipment	244,400
Total	$180,600	Total	$273,600

Liabilities and Shareholders' Equity		**Liabilities and Shareholders' Equity**	
Liabilities:		Liabilities:	
Notes payable (short-term)	$ 18,600	Notes payable (short-term)	$ 33,600
Accounts payable	14,400	Accounts payable	64,800
Total liabilities	33,000	Total liabilities	98,400
Shareholders' equity:		Shareholders' equity:	
Share capital	90,000	Share capital	108,000
Retained earnings	57,600	Retained earnings	67,200
Total shareholders' equity	147,600	Total shareholders' equity	175,200
Total	$180,600	Total	$273,600

Required:

1. Eric Frechette wants to invest in one of these two companies by purchasing all of its shares. As a financial adviser to Mr. Frechette, which company would you select as an investment? Provide justification for your selection.

2. Each company applied to Development Bank for a loan of $20,000, payable in four months. As a bank loan officer, would you lend each company the requested amount? Explain.

CRITICAL THINKING CASES

CP2–8 **Making a Decision as a Financial Analyst: Preparing and Analyzing a Balance Sheet**
Your best friend from home writes you a letter about an investment opportunity that has come her way. A company is raising money by issuing shares and wants her to invest $20,000 (her recent inheritance from her great-aunt's estate). Your friend has never invested in a company before and, knowing that you are a financial analyst, asks that you look over the balance sheet and send her some advice. An *unaudited* balance sheet, in only moderately good form, is enclosed with the letter:

■ **LO1, 2, 6**

e**X**cel

ANALYSIS

<table>
<tr><td colspan="2">DEWEY, CHEETUM, AND HOWE, INC.
Balance Sheet
For the Year Ending December 31, 2007</td></tr>
<tr><td>Accounts receivable</td><td>$ 8,000</td></tr>
<tr><td>Cash</td><td>1,000</td></tr>
<tr><td>Inventory</td><td>8,000</td></tr>
<tr><td>Furniture and fixtures</td><td>52,000</td></tr>
<tr><td>Delivery truck</td><td>12,000</td></tr>
<tr><td>Buildings (estimated market value)</td><td>98,000</td></tr>
<tr><td>Total assets</td><td>$179,000</td></tr>
<tr><td>Accounts payable</td><td>$ 16,000</td></tr>
<tr><td>Payroll taxes payable</td><td>13,000</td></tr>
<tr><td>Long-term notes payable</td><td>15,000</td></tr>
<tr><td>Mortgage payable</td><td>50,000</td></tr>
<tr><td>Total liabilities</td><td>$ 94,000</td></tr>
<tr><td>Share capital</td><td>$ 80,000</td></tr>
<tr><td>Retained earnings</td><td>5,000</td></tr>
<tr><td>Total shareholders' equity</td><td>$ 85,000</td></tr>
</table>

There is only one footnote, and it states that the building was purchased for $65,000, has been amortized by $5,000 on the books, and still carries a mortgage (shown in the liability section). The footnote further states that, in the opinion of the company president, the building is "easily worth $98,000."

Required:

1. Draft a new balance sheet for your friend, correcting any errors you note. (If any of the account balances need to be corrected, you may need to adjust the retained earnings balance correspondingly.) If no errors or omissions exist, state so.

2. Write a letter to your friend explaining the changes you made to the balance sheet, if any, and offer your comments on the company's apparent financial condition based only on this information. Suggest other information your friend might want to review before coming to a final decision on whether to invest.

LO3   **CP2–9** **Manipulation of Financial Statements: Ethical Considerations**

ANALYSIS

Technology N Motion is a publicly traded company that is facing financial difficulties. To survive, the company needs large new bank loans. As the chief financial officer of the company you approached several banks, but each has asked for your audited financial statements for 2008, the most recent fiscal year. You called for a meeting with other corporate officers to discuss how the financial statements could be improved. The suggestions made by your colleagues include:

1. We owe $20 million to our suppliers. We could show half this amount as a liability on our balance sheet and report the other half as share capital. This will improve our financial position.

2. We own land that is worth at least $8 million in today's market, but it cost us only $3 million when we bought it. Why not show the land at $8 million on the company's balance sheet, which increases both the total assets and shareholders' equity by $5 million?

3. We owe FirstRate Software $2 million, due in 30 days. I can ask their chief financial officer to let us delay the payment of this debt for a year, and our company could sign him a note that pays 8 percent interest.

Required:

Evaluate each of these three proposals to improve Technology N Motion's financial statements by considering both accounting and ethical issues.

LO3   **CP2–10** **Evaluating an Ethical Dilemma: Analyzing Management Incentives**

Nortel Networks Corporation

ANALYSIS

Nortel Networks Corporation, based in Brampton, Ontario, is a leading global supplier of networking solutions and services. In 2005, the company released the findings of an independent review as a result of continuing problems with its accounting. The review revealed that three former company executives, the chief executive officer, the chief financial officer, and the controller, used accounting practices that increased reported earnings from late 2002 to mid-2003. Through Nortel's internal investigation, several problems had become known, not the least of which was $900 million of inappropriately reported liabilities and approximately $250 million of overstated net income. This mattered to the executives who received a bonus if income before tax exceeded specific levels.

In April 2004, Nortel Networks Corp. (Nortel) issued a news release announcing the appointment of its new chief executive officer (CEO) Mr. William Owens, and the termination of its previous CEO, for cause. The previous CEO resigned his position on April 28 and from the company's board of directors on May 21, 2004. Neither the chairman of the board of directors nor the new CEO would comment on the termination. A month earlier the chief financial officer and the controller had been placed on paid leave of absence and they too were fired. A day later, the U.S. Securities and Exchange Commission announced that it was investigating Nortel, then the Ontario Securities Commission launched its own investigation. But the worst was yet to come.

In May 2004, a U.S. federal grand jury subpoenaed Nortel for accounting records and other documents prepared for the previous four years during which the previous CEO, an accountant, had served as chief financial officer. A few days later the Ontario Public Service Employees Union Pension Trust filed a class action lawsuit to recover losses arising from its investment in Nortel shares between April 2003 and 2005, based on fraudulent financial information. By August 2004, the Royal Canadian Mounted Police began a Canadian criminal investigation into the former CEO's activities. The cost to Nortel so far has been over $2.4 billion in cash awarded to the Ontario pension fund in April 2005 and the company sued the former CEO to recover this money from him personally. Pursuant to the independent review, 12 senior executives agreed to repay a total of $8.6 million in bonuses they received from the company in the past.

Required:

1. Describe the parties that were harmed or helped by this fraud.

2. Explain how greed may have contributed to this fraud.

3. Why do you think the independent auditors failed to catch the fraud?

FINANCIAL REPORTING AND ANALYSIS TEAM PROJECT

CP2–11 Team Project: Analysis of Balance Sheets and Ratios

On an individual basis, each team member should write a short report answering the following questions about the selected company. Discuss any patterns that you as a team observe. Then, as a team, write a short report comparing and contrasting your companies.

LO3, 7

ANALYSIS

1. For the most recent year, what are the top three asset accounts by size? What percentage is each of total assets? (Calculated as Asset A ÷ Total Assets)

2. What are the major investing and financing activities (by dollar size) for the most recent year? (Look at the Cash Flow Statement.)

3. Ratio Analysis:
   a. What does the debt-to-equity ratio measure in general?
   b. Compute the debt-to-equity ratio for the last three years. (You may find prior years' information in the section in the annual report called "Selected Financial Information," or you may search for prior years' annual reports.)
   c. What do your results suggest about the company?
   d. If available, find the industry ratio for the most recent year, compare it to your results, and discuss why you believe your company differs or is similar to the industry ratio.

Operating Decisions and the Income Statement

After studying this chapter, you should be able to:

LEARNING OBJECTIVES

1. Describe a typical business operating cycle and explain the necessity for the periodicity assumption. p. 101

2. Explain how business activities affect the elements of the income statement. p. 103

3. Explain the accrual basis of accounting and apply the revenue and matching principles to measure income. p. 107

4. Apply transaction analysis to examine and record the effects of operating activities on the financial statements. p. 113

5. Prepare an income statement and understand the difference between net income and cash flow from operations. p. 119

6. Compute and interpret the total asset turnover ratio and the return on assets ratio. p. 123

FOCUS COMPANY:

Van Houtte, Inc.

OFFERING COFFEE SERVICE PROGRAMS

TAILORED TO CLIENTS' NEEDS

Van Houtte (**www.vanhoutte.com**) ranks among the most integrated gourmet coffee companies in the North American coffee industry. Van Houtte operates in two significant business segments: the manufacturing and marketing segment, and the coffee services segment. In the manufacturing and marketing segment, Van Houtte purchases green coffee beans, roasts, grinds, packages, distributes, and markets a variety of coffees for home consumption through retail channels such as IGA, A&P, drugstores, and superstores. This business segment also includes café–bistros in Quebec.

Van Houtte also operates one of the largest coffee services networks in North America. This segment focuses on the sale of coffee for consumption in the workplace and other public locations such as businesses, universities, and hospitals. Van Houtte's coffee services network also distributes complementary products such as condiments, snacks, and various beverages. Moreover, this segment includes vending machine operations and food services.

Over the years, Van Houtte expanded its business operations by investing in many companies, including VKI Technologies, which designs and manufactures its own single-cup brewing equipment, and FilterFresh Coffee Service Inc. that carries out Van Houtte's operations in the United States.

By March 31, 2007, Van Houtte's products were offered through roughly 4,400 points of sale in Canada, and approximately 720 outlets in the United States. The company had revenues of $388.2 million in fiscal year 2007 and roasted and distributed roughly 25 million pounds of coffee that year.

Van Houtte exercises a social conscience in the area of coffee production and was one of the first to market Fair Trade coffees, whereby farmers in Africa, Asia, and Central and South America are paid a premium for their product. In a joint initiative with Care Canada it launched a gourmet coffee from Honduras to help producers become self-sufficient. As part of its social responsibility, Van Houtte merchandises a line of organic coffees, the Coffee Lovers brand, and donates a percentage of its revenues from these sales to improve the lives of children of families living in coffee-growing communities.

UNDERSTANDING THE BUSINESS

To become the number-one coffee services company, Van Houtte's executives develop strategies, plans, and measurable indicators of progress toward their goals. In developing operating and growth strategies, companies such as Van Houtte plan their companywide operations in terms of the elements of the income statement (specific revenues and expenses). These strategies are most often disclosed in the Management Discussion and Analysis section of the annual report.

Financial analysts develop their own set of expectations about Van Houtte's future performance. The published income statement provides the primary basis for comparing analysts' projections to the actual results of operations. We discuss these comparisons and the stock market's reactions to Van Houtte's results throughout this chapter as we learn about income recognition and measurement. To understand how business plans and the results of operations are reflected on the income statement, we need to answer the following questions:

1. How do business activities affect the income statement?
2. How are these activities recognized and measured?
3. How are these activities reported on the income statement?

In this chapter we focus on Van Houtte's operating activities, which include sales of roasted coffee beans to retailers; packaged tea and coffee to bistros, hotels, and restaurants; and supplies to franchisees. The results of these activities are reported on the income statement.

ORGANIZATION OF THE CHAPTER

How Do Business Activities Affect the Income Statement?	How Are Operating Activities Recognized and Measured?	The Expanded Transaction Analysis Model	How is the Income Statement Prepared and Analyzed?
• The Operating Cycle • Elements on the Income Statement	• Accrual Accounting • The Revenue Principle • The Matching Principle	• Transaction Analysis Rules • Analyzing Van Houtte's Transactions	• Income Statement • Cash Flow Effects • Total Asset Turnover Ratio • Return on Assets Ratio

HOW DO BUSINESS ACTIVITIES AFFECT THE INCOME STATEMENT?

THE OPERATING CYCLE

The long-term objective for any business is ***to turn cash into more cash***. For companies to stay in business, this excess cash must be generated from operations (that is, from the activities for which the business was established), not from borrowing money or selling long-term assets.

Companies acquire inventory and the services of employees, and then sell inventory or services to customers. The length of time between the payment of cash to suppliers of inventory and to employees, and the collection of cash from customers (known as the **operating (cash-to-cash) cycle**), depends on the nature of the business.

■ **LEARNING OBJECTIVE 1**

Describe a typical business operating cycle and explain the necessity for the periodicity assumption.

The **OPERATING (CASH-TO-CASH) CYCLE** is the time it takes for a company to pay cash to suppliers, sell those goods and services to customers, and collect cash from customers.

The operating cycle for Van Houtte is relatively short. It spends cash to purchase green coffee beans; roasts and packages them according to its own blends and recipes; sells the coffee through distribution channels that reach consumers at home, at work, and at play; and then collects cash from customers. In some companies, inventory is paid for well before it is sold. Toys "R" Us, for example, builds its inventory for months prior to the year-end holiday season. It borrows funds from banks to pay for the inventory and repays the loans with interest when cash is received from customers. In other companies, cash is received from customers well after a sale takes place. For example, car dealerships often sell cars over time, with monthly payments from customers due over several years. Companies attempt to shorten the operating cycle by creating incentives to encourage customers to buy sooner or pay faster in order to improve the company's cash flows.

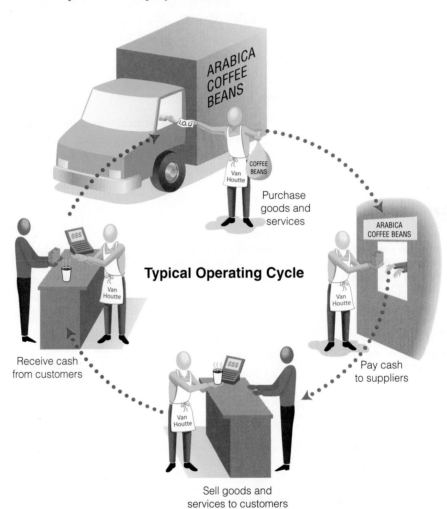

Typical Operating Cycle

Purchase goods and services

Pay cash to suppliers

Sell goods and services to customers

Receive cash from customers

FINANCIAL **ANALYSIS**

SHORT-TERM DEBT FINANCING AND THE OPERATING CYCLE

The timing of the cash outflows and inflows shown in the illustration above indicate that many businesses must pay suppliers and employees before they receive cash from customers, causing them to seek short-term financing. When the companies receive cash from customers, they pay off the liability. In addition, if a company plans to grow—say, to sell twice as many goods as in the prior period—it may not have collected enough cash from the prior period's customers to purchase the quantity of inventory needed in the next period. Sources of financing include suppliers and financial institutions (banks and commercial credit companies).

Managers know that reducing the time needed to turn cash into more cash (that is, shortening the operating cycle) means higher profits and faster growth. With the excess cash, managers may purchase additional inventory or other assets for growth, repay debt, or distribute it to owners.

Until a company ceases activities, the operating cycle is repeated continuously. However, decision makers require periodic information about the financial condition and performance of a business. To measure income for a specific period of time, accountants follow the **periodicity assumption**, which assumes that the long life of a company can be reported in shorter time periods, such as months, quarters, and years.[1] Two types of issues arise in reporting periodic income to users:

1. Recognition issues: **When** should the effects of operating activities be recognized (recorded)?

2. Measurement issues: **What amounts** should be recognized?

Before we examine the rules accountants follow as they resolve these issues, let us review the elements of financial statements that are affected by operating activities.

ELEMENTS ON THE INCOME STATEMENT

Exhibit 3.1 shows a recent income statement for Van Houtte simplified for the purposes of this chapter.[2]

The income statement (also known as statement of earnings or statement of operations)[3] includes up to four major sections:

1. Results of continuing operations

2. Results of discontinued operations

3. Extraordinary items
   Net income (the sum of 1, 2, and 3)

4. Earnings per share

All companies report information for sections 1 and 4, while some companies report information in sections 2 and 3 depending upon their particular circumstances. The bottom line, *Net income,* is the sum of sections 1, 2, and 3. First, we will focus on the most common and most relevant section, *Continuing operations.*

Continuing Operations   This section of the income statement presents the results of continuing operations. It can be presented in one of two common formats:

1. The single-step format, which lists all revenue items followed by all expense items and then shows the difference between revenues and expenses,[4] or

The **PERIODICITY ASSUMPTION** means that the long life of a company can be reported in shorter periods.

■ **LEARNING OBJECTIVE 2**

Explain how business activities affect the elements of the income statement.

---

[1]In addition to the audited annual statements, most businesses prepare quarterly financial statements (also known as *interim reports* covering a three-month period) for external users. The securities commissions require public companies to do so.

[2]For presentation purposes, dollar amounts have been rounded to the nearest one hundred thousand dollars, and several elements in the original statements have been simplified. However, for illustrative purposes one item in the actual statement, Cost of goods sold and net operating expenses, has been separated into three different items: Cost of goods sold, Selling expenses, and General and administrative expenses. Industry information was used in estimating the amounts of these three items. Van Houtte presents income statement information for two consecutive years, but many companies present such details for three years.

[3]A survey of 200 companies showed that 56 companies used the title *Income Statement*, 85 used the title *Statement of Earnings,* 51 used the title *Statement of Operations*, and 8 used other titles in their 2005 annual reports. N. Chlala, A. Lavigne, L. Martel, and C. Byrd, *Financial Reporting in Canada, 2006.* Toronto: CICA 2006, p. 77.

[4]Only three of the 200 companies surveyed in *Financial Reporting in Canada, 2006* used the single-step format. N. Chlala, A. Lavigne, L. Martel, and C. Byrd, *Financial Reporting in Canada, 2006.* Toronto: CICA 2006, p. 76.

EXHIBIT **3.1**

Income Statement

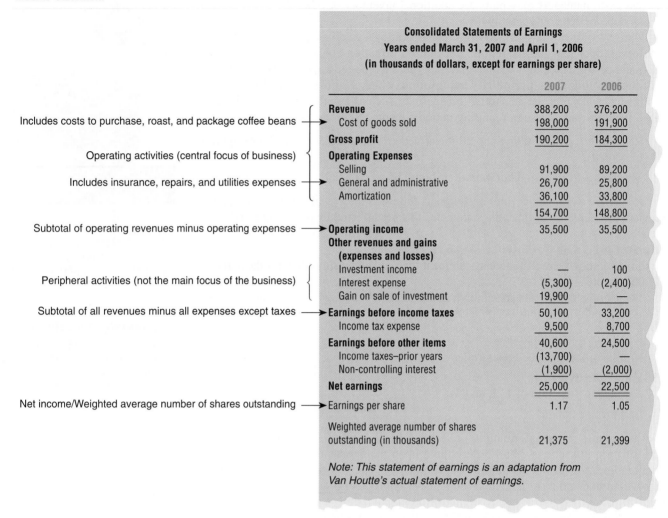

Includes costs to purchase, roast, and package coffee beans

Operating activities (central focus of business)

Includes insurance, repairs, and utilities expenses

Subtotal of operating revenues minus operating expenses

Peripheral activities (not the main focus of the business)

Subtotal of all revenues minus all expenses except taxes

Net income/Weighted average number of shares outstanding

Consolidated Statements of Earnings
Years ended March 31, 2007 and April 1, 2006
(in thousands of dollars, except for earnings per share)

	2007	2006
Revenue	388,200	376,200
Cost of goods sold	198,000	191,900
Gross profit	190,200	184,300
Operating Expenses		
Selling	91,900	89,200
General and administrative	26,700	25,800
Amortization	36,100	33,800
	154,700	148,800
Operating income	35,500	35,500
Other revenues and gains (expenses and losses)		
Investment income	—	100
Interest expense	(5,300)	(2,400)
Gain on sale of investment	19,900	—
Earnings before income taxes	50,100	33,200
Income tax expense	9,500	8,700
Earnings before other items	40,600	24,500
Income taxes–prior years	(13,700)	—
Non-controlling interest	(1,900)	(2,000)
Net earnings	25,000	22,500
Earnings per share	1.17	1.05
Weighted average number of shares outstanding (in thousands)	21,375	21,399

Note: This statement of earnings is an adaptation from Van Houtte's actual statement of earnings.

2. The multiple-step format, with cost of goods sold deducted from sales to present gross margin (or gross profit) as a subtotal. Other operating expenses are then deducted to show operating profit (income) as a second subtotal. Classification of the various income statement items helps financial statement users in assessing the company's operating performance and in predicting the company's future profitability.

Like most companies, Van Houtte uses a multiple-step format in reporting income statement information.

REVENUES are increases in assets or settlements of liabilities from ongoing operations.

Revenues   **Revenues** result from selling goods or services as part of a company's normal ongoing operations. Van Houtte earns revenue when it sells coffee and equipment to customers or earns royalties from franchisees. When revenues are earned, assets, usually cash or receivables, often increase. Sometimes, a company receives cash in exchange for a promise to provide goods or services in the future. At that point, revenue is not earned, but a liability account, either deferred or unearned revenue, is created. When the company provides the promised goods or services to the customer, revenue is recognized and the liability is settled. We can say, then, that revenues are increases in assets or settlements of liabilities from *ongoing operations*.

Like most companies, Van Houtte generates revenues from a variety of sources. Its operating activities are grouped into two main segments:

1. *Manufacturing and Marketing.* This segment encompasses coffee roasting and distribution for home consumption through retail food channels, the production

and distribution of coffeemakers and related equipment, as well as the franchising and operations of café–bistros. Van Houtte's products are available at some 5,200 retail points of sale in Canada and on the East Coast of the United States. This segment contributed 40 percent of Van Houtte's revenues for fiscal year 2007, or $155.3 million.

2. *Coffee Services.* This segment focuses on the sale of coffee for consumption in the workplace and in a variety of public environments such as supermarkets, hospitals, university campuses, and convenience store chains including Chevron in British Columbia, Mac's Milk in Ontario, and Couche-Tard in Quebec. On March 31, 2007, Van Houtte's network was comprised of approximately 2,500 coffee stations in Canada and the United States. The Coffee Services branches operate also vending machines that sell snacks, candies, and hot and cold drinks in major cities in Ontario and Western Canada. In 2007, this segment contributed 60 percent of the company's revenues for a total of $232.9 million.

Expenses Some students confuse the terms *expenditures* and *expenses*. An expenditure is any outflow of money for any purpose, whether to buy equipment or pay off a loan. An expense is more narrowly defined. It results when a cost such as advertising is incurred or an asset such as inventory is used *to generate revenues during a period*. Therefore, not all expenditures are expenses, which are necessary to generate revenues.

Van Houtte pays employees to sell its coffee products and provide services to clients, uses electricity to operate equipment and light facilities, advertises its coffee services, and uses coffee and paper supplies. Without incurring these expenses, Van Houtte could not generate revenues. Although some of the expenses may result from expenditures of cash at the time they are incurred, some may be incurred after cash was paid in the past, and other expenses may be incurred before cash is paid in the future. When an expense occurs, *either* assets (such as supplies inventory and cash) decrease, *or* liabilities (such as salaries or utilities payable) increase. **Expenses** can therefore be defined as decreases in assets or increases in liabilities to generate revenues during the period.

The following are Van Houtte's primary expenses:

1. *Cost of goods sold* is the cost of products sold to customers. When Van Houtte purchases coffee beans from suppliers located in other countries, it pays for import duties, transport, and handling, in addition to the purchase price. All these costs are included in the cost of the asset Inventories. As inventories are used to produce and package the roasted and ground coffee beans, they become an expense, called Cost of Good Sold. This expense also includes the cost of coffee beans, supplies, and equipment, also part of Inventories, that are sold to franchisees. In companies with a manufacturing or merchandising focus, the cost of goods sold (also called cost of sales) is usually the most significant expense. The cost of goods sold for Van Houtte is estimated at $198 million and represents about 51 percent of the revenues for 2007. The difference between sales revenues and cost of goods sold is known as **gross profit** or **gross margin**.

2. *Operating expenses* are the usual expenses, other than cost of goods sold, which are incurred in operating a business during a specific accounting period. The expenses reported will depend on the nature of the company's operations. *Selling expenses* usually include salaries and benefits to employees as well as advertising and promotion expenses. *General and administrative expenses* would include salaries for employees who support the sales effort such as legal counsel, accountants, and computer technicians as well as rent, utilities, and insurance expenses, among others. The *depreciation and amortization expense* refers to the cost of using long-term assets such as buildings and equipment that are used in roasting, grinding, packaging, and distributing the company's coffee products during the period.[5] Another subtotal, **Operating income**, also called Income from Operations, is computed by subtracting operating expenses from gross profit.

---

[5]This expense is discussed in detail in Chapters 4 and 9.

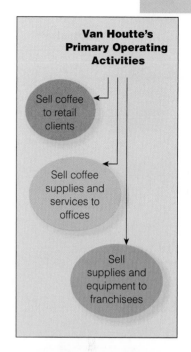

Van Houtte's Primary Operating Activities

Sell coffee to retail clients

Sell coffee supplies and services to offices

Sell supplies and equipment to franchisees

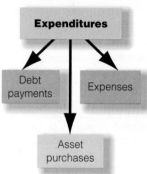

Expenditures

Debt payments

Expenses

Asset purchases

EXPENSES are decreases in assets or increases in liabilities to generate revenues during the period.

GROSS PROFIT (OR GROSS MARGIN) is net sales less cost of goods sold.

OPERATING INCOME (income from operations) equals net sales less cost of goods sold and other operating expenses.

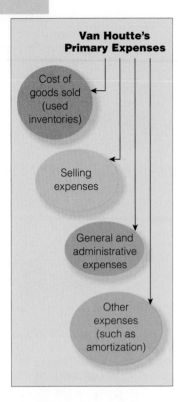

Van Houtte's Primary Expenses

Cost of goods sold (used inventories)

Selling expenses

General and administrative expenses

Other expenses (such as amortization)

GAINS are increases in assets or decreases in liabilities from peripheral transactions.

LOSSES are decreases in assets or increases in liabilities from peripheral transactions.

INCOME BEFORE INCOME TAXES (pretax income) equals revenues minus all expenses except income tax expense.

Non-operating Items   Not all activities affecting an income statement are central to continuing operations. Using excess cash to purchase shares in other companies is an investing activity for Van Houtte. Any interest or dividends earned on the investment is called *investment income*. Likewise, borrowing money is a financing activity. The cost of using that money is called *interest expense*. Except for financial institutions, incurring interest expense or earning investment income are not the central operations of most businesses, including Van Houtte. We say that these are *peripheral* (normal but not central) *transactions*.

Similarly, companies sell property, plant, and equipment occasionally and replace them with new assets to modernize their facilities. Selling land for more than the original purchase price results in a *gain,* not in revenue, because the sale of land is not a central operating focus for the business. The **gain** results in an increase in assets or decrease in liabilities from a peripheral transaction. In contrast, **losses** are decreases in assets or increases in liabilities from peripheral transactions. For example, in June 2006, Van Houtte sold its investment in the shares of Keurig Inc. for $37.4 million and realized a gain of $19.9 million on this transaction. Since the sale of this investment is not central to Van Houtte's ongoing operations, the gain is reported separately as a non-operating item on the company's income statement for fiscal year 2007.

The non-operating items that are subject to income taxes are added or subtracted from operating income to obtain **income before income taxes**, also called *Pretax Income.*

Income Tax Expense   Income Tax Expense is the last expense listed on the income statement. All profit-making corporations are required to compute income taxes owed to federal, provincial, and foreign governments. Income tax expense is calculated as a percentage of the difference between revenues and expenses determined by applying federal and provincial tax rates. Van Houtte's effective tax rate in 2007 was 19 percent (Income Tax Expense $9,500 ÷ Income Before Income Taxes $50,100). This indicates that for every dollar of profit that Van Houtte made in 2007, the company paid $0.19 to taxation authorities.

Nonrecurring Items   Companies may also report one of the following nonrecurring items on their income statements:

1. Discontinued operations
2. Extraordinary items

If any of these two items exists, an additional subtotal is presented for Income from Continuing Operations (or Income before Nonrecurring Items), after which the nonrecurring items are presented. These items are presented separately because they are not useful in predicting the future income of the company given their nonrecurring nature.

When a major component of a business is sold or abandoned, income or loss from that component, as well as any gain or loss on disposal, are included as discontinued operations. Extraordinary items are gains or losses incurred that are unusual, infrequent in occurrence, and not dependent primarily on decisions by management or owners. The Chapter Supplement explains these two nonrecurring items in more detail.

The last item on Van Houtte's income statement is *Non-controlling interest.* Van Houtte has invested in many businesses by purchasing a majority, or in many cases, all of the shares issued by these companies. Purchase of all or a majority of other companies' shares allows Van Houtte to control their operating, investing, and financing decisions. When Van Houtte owns a majority of the shares of another company, it becomes a *controlling* shareholder. The other shareholders are then known as *non-controlling* shareholders, and are entitled to a proportionate share of the earnings of the company in which they invested. Hence, non-controlling interest refers to the portion of the consolidated income that does not belong to Van Houtte, but to the non-controlling shareholders.[6]

---

[6]Intercorporate investments is a complex topic that is covered in advanced accounting courses.

Earnings Per Share Corporations are required to disclose earnings per share on the income statement or in the notes to the financial statements. This ratio is widely used in evaluating the operating performance and profitability of a company. A steady increase in earnings per share is a signal of good management. To compute earnings per share, we divide net income by the weighted average number of shares outstanding during the period. The calculation of the denominator is complex and is presented in advanced accounting courses.

Van Houtte's earnings per share increased from 2006 to 2007. Although this appears to be good news, investors would want to check the historical trend of earnings per share for at minimum a period of five years. More importantly, investors need to compare Van Houtte's performance to its competitors during the same time period. Finally, it should be noted that overreliance on this ratio for investment decisions can lead to inadvisable decisions.

UNDERSTANDING THE MEANING OF ACCOUNT TITLES IN FOREIGN FINANCIAL STATEMENTS

INTERNATIONAL **PERSPECTIVE**

We learned in Chapters 1 and 2 that foreign companies often use different account titles from Canadian companies. For example, the U.K. companies GlaxoSmithKline (pharmaceutical industry) and Diageo (alcoholic beverage industry) use the term "Turnover" to refer to sales revenue. The Australian beer manufacturer Foster's Group Limited, on the other hand, uses "Sales Revenue."

Foreign companies may also use different statement titles. Diageo titles the income statement "Consolidated Profit and Loss Account." Similarly, GlaxoSmithKline uses "Consolidated Statement of Profit and Loss." The Australian beer manufacturer Foster's Group Limited titles its income statement "Statement of Financial Performance."

HOW ARE OPERATING ACTIVITIES RECOGNIZED AND MEASURED?

You probably determine your personal financial position by the cash balance in your bank account. Your financial performance is measured as the difference between your cash balance at the beginning of the period and the balance at the end of the period (that is, whether you end up with more or less cash). If you have a higher cash balance, cash receipts exceeded cash disbursements for the period. Many local retailers, medical offices, and other small businesses use the **cash basis accounting**, in which revenues are recorded when cash is received, and expenses are recorded when cash is paid, regardless of when the revenues are earned or the expenses incurred. This basis is often quite adequate for these organizations that usually do not have to report to external users.

ACCRUAL ACCOUNTING

Net income measured on a cash basis can be misleading. For example, a company using the cash basis can report higher net income in one period simply because (1) a customer paid cash in advance of receiving a good or service or (2) the company postponed the payment of utility bills until the next period. In the first case, the company has not performed the service or exchanged a good to earn a revenue. In the second case, the company has already used gas, electricity, and phone service to generate revenues (creating an expense), but the expense is not recorded because payment occurs in the next period.

Since financial statements created under the cash basis of accounting normally postpone or accelerate recognition of revenues and expenses long before or after goods and services are produced and delivered, they also do not necessarily reflect all assets and liabilities of a company on a particular date. For these reasons, cash basis financial statements are not very useful to external decision makers. Therefore, generally accepted accounting principles require the **accrual basis accounting** for financial reporting purposes.

CASH BASIS Income Measurement

Revenues (= cash receipts)
− Expenses (= cash payments)
Net Income

CASH BASIS ACCOUNTING records revenues when cash is received and expenses when cash is paid.

LEARNING OBJECTIVE 3

Explain the accrual basis of accounting and apply the revenue and matching principles to measure income.

ACCRUAL BASIS ACCOUNTING records revenues when earned and expenses when incurred, regardless of the timing of cash receipts or payments.

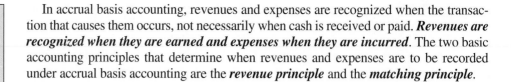

ACCRUAL BASIS
Income Measurement

Revenues (= when earned)
– Expenses (= when incurred)
Net Income

The **REVENUE PRINCIPLE**
states that revenues are
recognized when the earnings
process is complete or nearly
complete, an exchange has
taken place, and collection is
reasonably assured.

In accrual basis accounting, revenues and expenses are recognized when the transaction that causes them occurs, not necessarily when cash is received or paid. ***Revenues are recognized when they are earned and expenses when they are incurred***. The two basic accounting principles that determine when revenues and expenses are to be recorded under accrual basis accounting are the ***revenue principle*** and the ***matching principle***.

THE REVENUE PRINCIPLE

Under the **revenue principle**, three criteria must normally be met for revenue to be recognized (that is, recorded). If *any* of the following conditions is *not* met, revenue normally is *not* recognized and should not be recorded.

1. *The earnings process is complete or nearly complete.* This means that the company has performed or substantially performed the acts promised to the customer by providing goods or services.
2. *An exchange transaction takes place.* In exchange for the company's performance, the customer provides cash or a promise to pay cash (a receivable) that is measureable.
3. *Collection is reasonably assured.* Companies establish credit policies to reduce the risk of extending credit to customers who fail to pay. Since there is always some risk that payment will not be received in the future, normal credit risk is taken into consideration in determining whether collection from customers is reasonably assured.

Van Houtte earns 60 percent of its revenue from contracts with companies that provide brewed coffee by the cup to their employees. A sale is completed when the equipment, coffee, tea, and supplies are delivered to customers. Van Houtte can then recognize revenue if there is reasonable assurance that payment will be received in the future.

The company also sells franchises, although since 1997 it has actively restructured and reorganized its café–bistro network to reduce the number of outlets. When a new franchisee is approved, the franchisee pays Van Houtte a fee *before* obtaining any startup support services or supplies. The company should not record the amount received as revenue because it has not yet performed on any promises. Instead, the company records the amount received as a liability, *unearned or deferred revenue*. This deferred or unearned revenue account represents the amount of goods and services owed to the franchisees. Later, when Van Houtte provides the services or supplies, it earns and records the revenue by reducing the liability account.

Revenue is recorded according to the revenue principle when the three conditions are met, *regardless of when cash is received*. Cash may be received either before or after revenue recognition, each resulting in two transactions—one on the date of cash receipt and one on the date the revenue is earned.

Companies usually disclose their revenue recognition practices in a note to the financial statements. The following excerpt from Van Houtte's note describes how it recognizes its revenue:

REAL WORLD EXCERPT

Van Houtte

ANNUAL REPORT

Van Houtte Inc.
Notes to Consolidated Financial Statements

2. Significant Accounting Policies

k) Revenue recognition
Revenue is recognized when goods are delivered or when services are provided. Rental fees are billed on a periodic or a monthly basis and recognized when services are provided. When clients are invoiced, the portion of unearned revenues is recorded under deferred revenues.

- If cash is received before the company delivers goods or services, the liability account Unearned Revenue is recorded because the company still owes goods or services. Examples include companies that sell magazine subscriptions and companies that sell insurance. Although not corporations, colleges and universities also receive tuition revenue and sell season tickets to sporting events and plays before any revenue is earned.

- If cash is received after goods or services are delivered, the receivable account created when the revenue was recorded is reduced because the customers have paid the company what they owed.

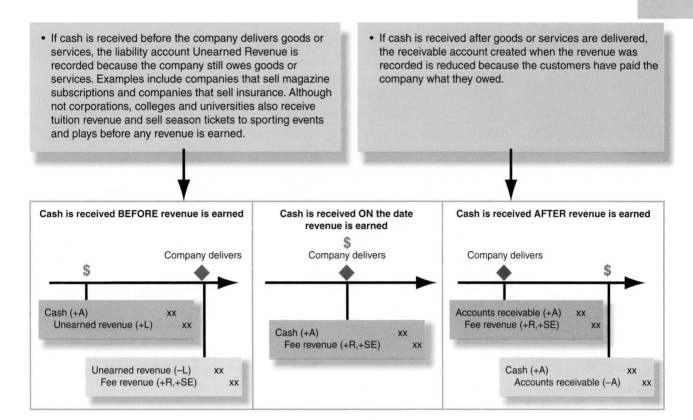

Exhibit 3.2 shows the revenue recognition practices used by other companies that offer different types of products and services. Note that the completion of the earnings process depends on the nature of the products sold and services provided by the company.

EXHIBIT **3.2**

Timing of Revenue Recognition

Company Name	Product or Service	Typical Timing of Revenue Recognition
WestJet Airlines	Air transportation	Guest and charter revenue is recognized when air transportation is provided. Tickets sold but not yet used are included in the consolidated balance sheet as advance ticket sales. The corporation earns revenue under the tri-branded credit card agreement and is included in other revenue. Net retail sales revenue is recognized at the time the transaction occurs. Revenue related to account activations is deferred and not recognized until the credit file issued for the new activation is used or expires.
Research In Motion Inc.	Wireless solutions for the mobile communications market	The company recognizes revenue when it is realized or realizable and earned. The company considers revenue realized or realizable and earned when it has persuasive evidence of an arrangement, the product has been delivered or the services have been provided to the customer, the sales price is fixed or determinable and collectibility is reasonably assured.
CanWest Global Communications Corp.	Radio and television broadcasting, publication of magazines and newspapers, advertisement, sale or licensing of films	Revenue derived from broadcasting activities related to the sale of airtime which is recognized at the time commercials are broadcast, net of any provisions for viewer shortfalls. Circulation and advertising revenue from publishing activities is recognized when the newspaper is delivered. Revenue derived from out-of-home advertising is recognized over the period the advertisement is being displayed. Subscription revenue is recognized on a straight-line basis over the term of the subscription. Revenue from the sale or licensing of film and television programs is recognized when all of the following conditions are met: persuasive evidence of a sale or licensing arrangement exists, the film is complete, the contractual delivery arrangements have been satisfied, the licence period has begun, the fee is fixed or determinable, and collection of the fee is reasonably assured.
Barrick Gold Corporation	Mining (production of quality precious metals)	We record revenue when the following conditions are met: persuasive evidence of an arrangement exists; delivery and transfer of title have occurred under the terms of the arrangement; the price is fixed or determinable; and collectability is reasonably assured.

SELF-STUDY **QUIZ 3-1**

This self-study quiz allows you to practise applying the revenue principle under accrual accounting. We recommend that you refer back to the three *revenue recognition criteria* presented earlier as you answer each question. It is important to complete this quiz now to make sure you can apply this principle.

The following transactions are samples of typical monthly operating activities of Van Houtte.

1. Indicate the account titles that are affected and the type of account for each (A for asset, L for liability, and R for revenue).

2. Identify the amount of revenue that is recognized in April, the revenue that has been earned in March, and the revenue that will be earned in future periods (unearned revenue).

3. Compute the revenue recognized in April and compare it to the amount of cash received in April.

4. Which amount—revenue recognized in April or cash received in April—is a better measure of Van Houtte's operating performance? Explain.

Refer to the Van Houtte chart of accounts presented in Exhibit 3.4 on page 115 for account titles.
Note: All dollar amounts are in thousands.
After you complete the quiz, check your answers with the solutions on page 128.

Activity	Accounts Affected and Type of Account	Cash Received in April	Amount of Revenue Earned in March	April	Unearned Revenue
(a) In April, Van Houtte sold coffee supplies to office services customers for $35,200 cash.					
(b) In April, Van Houtte sold roasted coffee beans to retail outlets for $30,200, of which $20,200 was in cash and the rest was on account.					
(c) In April, franchisees paid Van Houtte $3,450 in cash for royalties, of which $750 related to March sales.					
(d) In April, Van Houtte signed contracts with new clients and received $500 in cash. The company provided $400 in services to these clients during April; the remainder of the services will be provided over the next three months.					
(e) In April, retail outlets paid $1,200 on account to Van Houtte. This amount covers sales of roasted coffee beans in March.					
Totals					

MANAGEMENT'S INCENTIVES TO VIOLATE THE REVENUE PRINCIPLE

A QUESTION OF ETHICS

The decisions of investors in the stock market are based on expectations of future earnings. When companies announce quarterly and annual earnings information, investors evaluate how well the company met expectations and adjust their investing decisions accordingly. Companies that fail to meet expectations often experience a decline in the stock price. Thus, managers are motivated to produce earnings results that meet or exceed expectations to bolster stock prices. Since many executives are given options to purchase company shares as part of their compensation, greed may lead some managers to make unethical accounting and reporting decisions, often involving falsifying revenues and expenses, as described in the April 1, 2002, issue of *Canadian Business*. The article includes two revenue-related frauds involving Livent Inc. and YBM Magnex International Inc.

The Company	What the Company's Management Did
Livent Inc.	Management has been accused by the Securities and Exchange Commission and the Ontario Securities Commission of using false invoices and kickbacks, filing false information, and inflating its earnings.
YBM Magnex International Inc.	The company was investigated by the Ontario Securities Commission for overstating sales by creating fictitious customer lists. At the same time, laundered money poured into the company from Russian gangsters. The company went bankrupt in 1998.

The OSC's investigation of YBM resulted in imposing penalties, totalling $1.2 million, on two brokerage firms and five company officials. The company officials were ordered to resign from their positions and were banned from holding such positions at other companies for periods of three to five years.

At the time of writing this book, none of the senior management or directors of Livent had been convicted of a criminal offence as a result of their actions.

Sources: John Gray, "Home-grown accounting scandals," *Canadian Business*, April 1, 2002, and Peter Fitzpatrick, "OSC hands down YBM penalties," *National Post*, July 3, 2003, FP1, 8.

THE MATCHING PRINCIPLE

The **matching principle** requires that when the period's revenues are properly recognized according to the revenue principle, all of the resources consumed in earning those revenues should be recorded in that same period, *a matching of costs with benefits*. Thus, expenses are "matched" to revenues and recorded in the same period as the related revenues. For example, when Van Houtte provides coffee services to customers, it earns revenue. The costs of generating the revenue include expenses incurred such as:

The **MATCHING PRINCIPLE** requires that expenses be recorded when incurred in earning revenue.

- Salaries to employees who *worked during the period* (Salaries expense)
- Utilities for the electricity *used during the period* (Utilities expense)
- Green coffee beans roasted and *sold during the period* (Cost of goods sold)
- Facilities *rented during the period* (Rent expense)
- *Use* of roasting and packaging equipment *during the period* (Amortization expense)

Some of these expenses are matched directly to sales revenue, such as the cost of goods sold and sales commissions. Other expenses, such as utilities, rent of facilities, insurance, and interest, may not be identifiable with specific sources of revenue but need to be incurred in order to generate revenue during the period.

As with revenues and cash receipts, expenses are recorded as incurred, *regardless of when cash is paid*. Cash may be paid before, during, or after expense recognition, resulting in two transactions: one on the date of the cash payment and one on the date the expense is incurred in generating revenue.

- For example, green coffee beans and packaging supplies are acquired prior to their use. These items are recorded as inventory, an asset, when they are purchased, but are not expensed until they are used. Similarly, companies usually pay for rent in advance of using rental property and record the cash outlay in the asset account, Prepaid Expenses, representing future benefits to the company. This asset is allocated over time to Rent Expense as the property is used. In addition, part of the cost of long-term assets, such as equipment used in operations, needs to be matched with the revenues generated in the period. The portion of the assets that was used up is recognized as Amortization Expense.

- In some cases, resources are used to generate revenues prior to a cash outlay. Van Houtte's payroll expense represents the amount earned by managers and employees who prepare and serve the coffee and tea. It is an expense for that period. While employees are usually paid after they provide their services, Wages Expense and Wages Payable should be recorded when the service is provided by the employees.

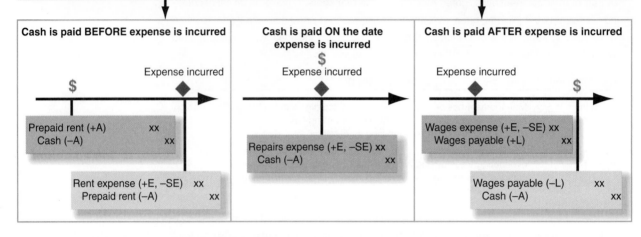

SELF-STUDY **QUIZ 3-2**

This self-study quiz allows you to practise applying the *matching principle* under accrual accounting. It is important to complete this quiz now to make sure you can apply this principle.

The following transactions are samples of typical monthly operating activities of Van Houtte.

1. Indicate the account titles that are affected and the type of account for each (A for asset, L for liability, and E for expense).

2. If an expense is to be recognized in *April,* indicate the amount. If an expense is not to be recognized in April, indicate why.

3. Compute the amount of expenses recognized in April and compare this amount to the cash paid in April.

Refer to the Van Houtte chart of accounts presented in Exhibit 3.4 on page 115 for account titles. *Note:* All dollar amounts are in thousands.

After you complete the quiz, check your answers with the solutions on page 128.

Activity	Accounts Affected and Type of Account	Cash Paid in April	Amount of Expense Incurred in April OR Why an Expense Is Not Recognized
(a) In April, Van Houtte paid $10,000 to suppliers on account for coffee supplies received in March. These supplies were not yet sold to customers.			
(b) In April, the cost of roasting and packaging the beans sold to retail outlets was $14,000.			
(c) On April 5, Van Houtte paid $4,500 for office rent for April, May, and June.			
(d) In April, the cost of coffee supplies sold to coffee services customers was $19,600. These coffee supplies were purchased in previous months.			
(e) In late April, Van Houtte received a utility bill for $500 payable in May for electricity used in April.			
Totals			

THE FEEDBACK VALUE OF ACCOUNTING INFORMATION AND STOCK MARKET REACTION

FINANCIAL ANALYSIS

A company can experience difficulty even if it does not report a net loss. Any unexpected deviation of actual performance from the operating plan, such as lower than expected quarterly earnings, needs to be explained. Stock market analysts and investors use accounting information to make investment decisions. The stock market, which is based on investors' expectations about future company performance, often reacts negatively when a company does not meet previously specified operating results.

On February 15, 2007, Van Houtte announced the results of its third quarter ending January 6, 2007. On the day of the announcement, the price per share closed at $23.59, an increase of $0.39 over the closing price on the previous day.* Van Houtte's quarterly results showed an increase of earnings per share (EPS) by $0.02 compared to the EPS of the third quarter of 2006. The increase in share price suggests that the reported EPS figure is higher than investors' expectations.

This is a clear example of how the release of financial data provides relevant information to investors who revise their expectations about the company performance, causing a change in the price per share. Accounting information has a pervasive effect on the economic decisions that investors and creditors make.

*Van Houtte's Web site: http://investor.vanhoutte.com, accessed June 25, 2007.

THE EXPANDED TRANSACTION ANALYSIS MODEL

Now that we have seen the variety of business activities affecting the income statement and how they are measured, we need to determine how these business activities are recorded in the accounting system and reflected in the financial statements. Chapter 2 covered investing and financing activities affecting assets, liabilities, and share capital. We now expand the transaction analysis model presented in that chapter to include operating activities.

> ■ **LEARNING OBJECTIVE 4**
>
> Apply transaction analysis to examine and record the effects of operating activities on the financial statements.

TRANSACTION ANALYSIS RULES

The complete transaction model presented in Exhibit 3.3 includes all five elements: Assets, Liabilities, Shareholders' Equity, Revenues, and Expenses. Recall that the Retained Earnings account is the accumulation of all past revenues and expenses minus any income distributed as dividends[7] to shareholders (that is, earnings not retained in the business). When net income is positive, Retained Earnings increases; when a net loss occurs, Retained Earnings decreases. These relationships among financial statement elements are summarized in the upper part of Exhibit 3.3.

In constructing this complete model, we maintain the direction rule and the debit-credit framework described in Chapter 2:

- For accounts on the left side of the accounting equation, the increase symbol is written on the left side of the T-account. For accounts on the right side of the accounting equation, the increase symbol is written on the right side.

- Debits (dr) are written on the left side of each T-account and credits (cr) are written on the right.

The expanded transaction analysis model simply replaces net income with two additional elements, revenues and expenses. When revenues increase, both net income and retained earnings increase; hence, the increase in any revenue account is reported on the credit side of the account. Conversely, when expenses increase, both net income and retained earnings decrease. Since the decrease in retained earnings is reported

Assets	
DR +	

Liabilities	
	CR +

Shareholders' Equity Accounts	
	CR +

Revenue and Gains	
	CR +

Expenses and Losses	
DR +	

[7]Instead of reducing Retained Earnings directly when dividends are declared, companies may use the account Dividends Declared, which has a debit balance.

EXHIBIT **3.3**

Transactional Analysis Model

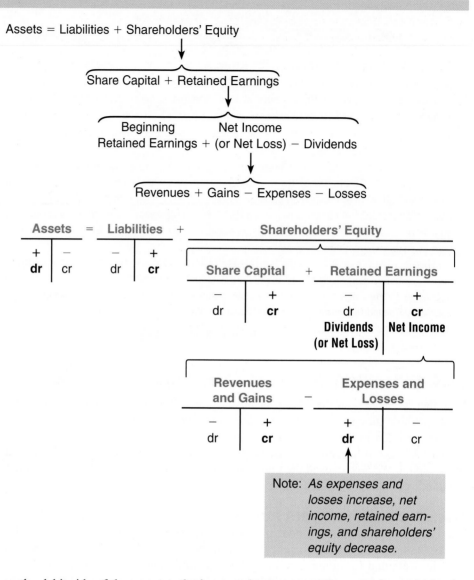

on the debit side of the account, the increase in any expense account is, equivalently, reported on the debit side of the account. Consequently, revenues normally have credit balances and expenses normally have debit balances.

As presented in Chapter 2, every transaction affects at least two accounts. In analyzing transactions:

a. **Identify the accounts affected by title and classify them by type of account**, making sure that at least two accounts change. Ask yourself what is given and what is received. Classifications are an asset (A), a liability (L), a shareholders' equity (SE), a revenue (R), and an expense account (E).

b. **Determine the direction of the effect** (an increase [+] or decrease [−] on each account).

c. **Verify that the accounting equation (A = L + SE) remains in balance.**

Since revenues are defined as inflows of net assets, then, by definition, recording a revenue results in either increasing an asset or decreasing a liability. In like manner, when recording an expense, an asset is decreased or a liability is increased.

You should refer to the transaction analysis model until you can construct it on your own without assistance. Study the following illustration carefully to make sure that you understand the impact of operating activities on both the balance sheet and the income statement.

ANALYZING VAN HOUTTE'S TRANSACTIONS

We begin with Van Houtte's April 30, 2007, balance sheet presented at the end of Chapter 2, which included the effects of the transactions illustrated in that chapter. We use the account titles listed in that balance sheet and those shown on the income statement in Exhibit 3.1 as we analyze a summary of the operating activities. A list of revenue and expense accounts is also provided in Exhibit 3.4.

EXHIBIT **3.4**

Van Houtte's Partial Chart of Accounts

Chart of Accounts (to be used in our Van Houtte example)	To account for
Revenues and Gains (R)	
Sales Revenue—Office Services	— Sales of coffee and other products to office services customers
Sales Revenue—Retail Outlets	— Sales of coffee and other products to retail outlet customers
Franchise-Related Revenue	— Amounts earned from franchises through franchise agreements
Investment Income	— Amounts earned on investments (e.g., dividends and interest)
Expenses and Losses (E)	
Cost of Goods Sold	— Cost of green beans and other products sold to customers
Salaries Expense	— Amount earned by the employees for work performed to generate revenue
Advertising Expense	— Amount incurred for advertising and promotions to generate revenue
Rent Expense	— Amount incurred for renting leased facilities during the period
General and Administrative Expense	— Amount of insurance and utilities used during the period
Amortization Expense	— Estimated cost of buildings and equipment used during the period
Interest Expense	— Cost of using borrowed funds during the period
Income Tax Expense	— Amount of tax related to the income generated during the period

Now let us apply the complete transaction analysis model and rules to our continuing Van Houtte's illustration. All amounts are in thousands of dollars.

(*a*) **Van Houtte sold coffee products to office services clients for $35,200 in cash. The cost of these sales was $19,600. [Note: This requires two entries, one for the revenue earned and one for the expense incurred in generating the revenue.]**

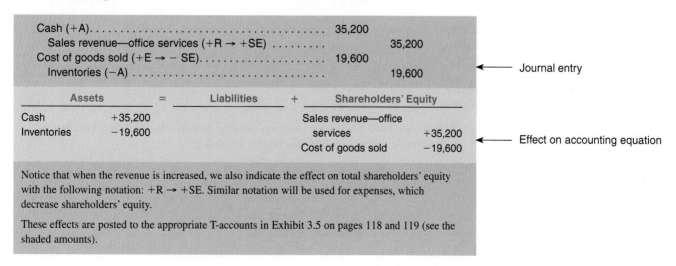

Cash (+A)......................................	35,200	
Sales revenue—office services (+R → +SE).........		35,200
Cost of goods sold (+E → − SE)...................	19,600	
Inventories (−A)...............................		19,600

◄——— Journal entry

Assets		=	Liabilities	+	Shareholders' Equity	
Cash	+35,200				Sales revenue—office	
Inventories	−19,600				services	+35,200
					Cost of goods sold	−19,600

◄——— Effect on accounting equation

Notice that when the revenue is increased, we also indicate the effect on total shareholders' equity with the following notation: +R → +SE. Similar notation will be used for expenses, which decrease shareholders' equity.

These effects are posted to the appropriate T-accounts in Exhibit 3.5 on pages 118 and 119 (see the shaded amounts).

(b) **Van Houtte sold roasted coffee beans to retail outlets for $30,200; $20,200 was received in cash and the rest was due from the outlets. The cost of the beans sold was $14,000.**

Cash (+A).	20,200	
Accounts receivable (+A).	10,000	
Sales revenue—retail outlets (+R → +SE)		30,200
Cost of goods sold (+E → −SE)	14,000	
Inventories (−A)		14,000

Assets		=	Liabilities	+	Shareholders' Equity	
Cash	+20,200				Sales revenue—	
Accounts					retail outlets	+30,200
receivable	+10,000				Cost of goods sold	−14,000
Inventories	−14,000					

(c) **Van Houtte received $3,450 in royalties from franchisees; $750 of the amount was due from franchisees' sales in March and the rest from April sales.**

Cash (+A).	3,450	
Accounts receivable (−A)		750
Franchise-related revenue (+R → +SE)		2,700

Assets		=	Liabilities	+	Shareholders' Equity	
Cash	+3,450				Franchise—related	
Accounts					revenue	+2,700
receivable	−750					

(d) **Van Houtte signed contracts with new office services clients and received $500 cash. The company earned $400 immediately by performing services for these clients; the rest will be earned over the next several months.**

Cash (+A).	500	
Sales revenue—office services (+R → +SE)		400
Unearned revenue (+L)		100

Assets		=	Liabilities		+	Shareholders' Equity	
Cash	+500		Unearned			Sales revenue—	
			revenues	+100		office services	+400

(e) **Van Houtte paid $7,400 for prepaid expenses: $1,600 for insurance for the next four months, $4,500 for rent in shopping centres for the next three months, and $1,300 for advertising in May.**

Prepaid expenses (+A)	7,400	
Cash (−A).		7,400

Assets		=	Liabilities	+	Shareholders' Equity
Cash	−7,400				
Prepaid expenses	+7,400				

(f) **Van Houtte paid $7,310 for utilities, repairs, and fuel for delivery vehicles, all considered general and administrative expenses.**

General and administrative expenses (+E → −SE)	7,310	
Cash (−A).		7,310

Assets		=	Liabilities	+	Shareholders' Equity	
Cash	−7,310				General and administrative	
					expenses	−7,310

(g) **Van Houtte ordered and received $29,000 in supplies inventories; $9,000 was paid in cash and the rest was on account with suppliers.**

Inventories (+A)	29,000	
Cash (−A).		9,000
Accounts payable (+L)		20,000

Assets		=	Liabilities		+	Shareholders' Equity
Cash	− 9,000		Accounts			
Inventories	+29,000		payable	+20,000		

(h) **Van Houtte paid $13,500 in cash to employees for work in April: $9,500 related to sales personnel, and $4,000 for employees in the corporate headquarters, considered general and administrative expenses.**

Salaries expense—sales personnel (+E → −SE)	9,500	
General and administrative expense (+E → −SE)	4,000	
Cash (−A).		13,500

Assets		=	Liabilities		+	Shareholders' Equity	
Cash	−13,500					Salaries expense—	
						sales personnel	−9,500
						General and administrative	
						expenses	−4,000

SELF-STUDY **QUIZ 3-3**

For transactions (i) through (k), fill in the missing information. Be sure to post journal entries to the T-accounts in Exhibit 3.5.

(i) **Van Houtte sold $4,300 in coffee-brewing equipment to retail outlets customers who signed notes due in 18 months. The cost of the equipment was $3,800. (Note: This requires two entries, one for the revenue and one for the expense incurred in generating the revenue.)**

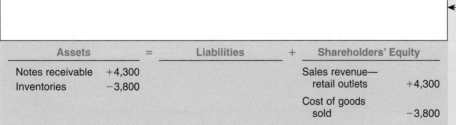

← Write the journal entry; post the effects to the T-accounts

Assets		=	Liabilities	+	Shareholders' Equity	
Notes receivable	+4,300				Sales revenue—	
Inventories	−3,800				retail outlets	+4,300
					Cost of goods	
					sold	−3,800

(j) **Van Houtte paid $10,000 on accounts owed to suppliers.**

← Write the journal entry; post the effects to the T-accounts

Assets	=	Liabilities	+	Shareholders' Equity

← Show the effects on the accounting equation

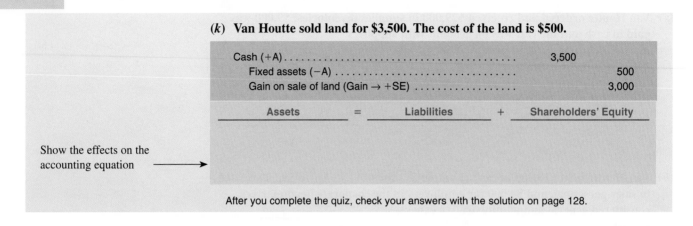

(k) Van Houtte sold land for $3,500. The cost of the land is $500.

Cash (+A)..	3,500
Fixed assets (−A)	500
Gain on sale of land (Gain → +SE)	3,000

Assets	=	Liabilities	+	Shareholders' Equity

Show the effects on the
accounting equation

After you complete the quiz, check your answers with the solution on page 128.

Exhibit 3.5 shows the T-accounts that changed during the period because of trans-actions (*a*) through (*k*). The balances of all other accounts remained the same. The amounts from Van Houtte's balance sheet at the end of Chapter 2 have been included as the beginning balances. At the beginning of every period, income statement accounts have zero beginning balances; therefore, no balances exist in the revenue and expense accounts at the beginning of the month.

You can verify that you posted the entries properly by adding the increase side and subtracting the decrease side and then comparing your answer to the ending balance given in each of the T-accounts.

Based on the April transactions that have been posted in the T-accounts, we can now begin the process of preparing financial statements reflecting the operating, investing, and financing activities recorded in April. This process requires a few additional steps that are covered in Chapter 4.

EXHIBIT **3.5**

T-Accounts

The beginning balances of balance sheet accounts are taken from Exhibit 2.8.

+	Cash (A)	−		+	Accounts Receivable (A)	−		+	Inventories (A)	−
Beg. bal.	1,950			Beg. bal.	56,800			Beg. bal.	29,500	*a* 19,600
a 35,200		*e* 7,400		*b*	10,000	*c* 750				*b* 14,000
b 20,200		*f* 7,310		End. bal.	66,050			*g*	29,000	*i*
c 3,450		*g* 9,000						End. bal.	21,100	
d 500		*h* 13,500								
k 3,500		*j*		+	Prepaid Expenses (A)	−		+	Notes Receivable (A)	−
End. bal.	17,590			Beg. bal.	3,300			Beg. bal.	150	
				e	7,400			*i*		
+	Fixed Assets, net	−		End. bal.	10,700			End. bal.	4,450	
Beg. bal. 118,800		*k* 500								
End. bal. 118,300										

LIABILITIES

−	Unearned Revenue (L)	+		−	Accounts Payable (L)	+
		d 100				Beg. bal. 39,000
		End. bal. 100		*j*		*g* 20,000
						End. bal. 49,000

(continued on next page)

EXHIBIT **3.5**
T-Accounts *(continued)*

REVENUES AND GAINS

− Sales Revenue—Office Services (R) +	
a	35,200
d	400
End. bal.	35,600

− Franchise-Related Revenue (R) +	
c	2,700
End. bal.	2,700

− Sales Revenue—Retail Outlets (R) +	
b	30,200
i	
End. bal.	34,500

− Gain on Sale of Land +	
k	3,000
End. bal.	3,000

EXPENSES

+ Cost of Goods Sold (E) −	
a	19,600
b	14,000
i	
End. bal.	37,400

+ General and Administrative Expenses (E) −	
f	7,310
h	4,000
End. bal.	11,310

+ Salaries Expense—Sales Personnel (E) −	
h	9,500
End. bal.	9,500

HOW IS THE INCOME STATEMENT PREPARED AND ANALYZED?

Based on the April transactions that have just been posted in the T-accounts, we can now prepare an income statement reflecting the operating activities for April.

■ LEARNING OBJECTIVE 5

Prepare an income statement and understand the difference between net income and cash flow from operations.

VAN HOUTTE, INC.
Consolidated Statement of Earnings
For the Month Ended April 30, 2007
(in thousands of dollars)

Revenues	
Sales revenues—office services	$35,600
Sales revenues—retail outlets	34,500
Franchise-related revenues	2,700
Total revenues	72,800
Cost of goods sold	37,400
Gross margin	35,400
Operating expenses	
Selling	9,500
General and administrative	11,310
Operating income	20,810
Other revenues and gains (expenses and losses)	14,590
Gain on sale of land	3,000
Earnings before income taxes	$17,590

This income statement is not yet adjusted for all revenues earned or expenses incurred in April. For example, the account Prepaid Expenses includes rent and insurance used in April, but the expenses are not yet recorded. This is true of the equipment used during the month as well. Also notice that we have not calculated income taxes. The amount of income tax expense is not yet determinable because the income before tax will change as a result of adjustments that affect revenue and expense accounts as discussed in Chapter 4. This income statement does not at this point reflect generally accepted accounting principles based on accrual accounting until we adjust the revenue and expense accounts as illustrated in Chapter 4.

FINANCIAL ANALYSIS

REPORTING FINANCIAL INFORMATION BY GEOGRAPHIC AND OPERATING SEGMENTS

Many companies, especially very large ones, operate in multiple geographic segments. These companies are often called *multinationals*. The Van Houtte income statement presented at the beginning of the chapter is based on aggregated data and may not prove as useful to investors seeking to assess possible risks and returns from companies operating in foreign markets. This is also true if a company operates in more than a single business. For example, a manufacturing operation in a South American country suffering from political unrest is riskier than a manufacturing facility located in Ontario. Therefore, the financial statements show the geographic sources of revenues and operating earnings, as well as Van Houtte's dependence on foreign markets for its revenues and earnings. The annual report of Van Houtte Inc. for the year ended March 31, 2007, included the following details in note 20, Segmented Information.

Extracts from Note 20, Segmented Information

Business Segments

Revenues

Canada	$260,601
United States	125,695
Other countries	1,862
	$388,158

FOCUS ON CASH FLOWS

OPERATING ACTIVITIES

In Chapter 2, we presented Van Houtte's cash flow statement for the investing and financing activities for the month. Recall that investing activities relate primarily to transactions affecting long-term assets; financing activities are those from bank borrowings, issuance of shares, and dividend payments to shareholders.

In this chapter, we focus on cash flows from operating activities, which reflects essentially cash basis accounting. This section of the cash flow statement reports *cash from* operating sources and *cash to* suppliers and others involved in operations. When operating cash inflows and outflows are presented, the company is using the *direct method* of reporting cash flows from operations. However, most companies report cash from operations using the *indirect method* that will be discussed in Chapter 5 and later chapters. The accounts most often associated with operating activities are current assets, such as Accounts Receivable, Inventories, and Prepaid Expenses, and current liabilities, such as Accounts Payable, Salaries Payable, and Unearned Revenue.

When a transaction affects cash, it is included on the cash flow statement. When a transaction does not affect cash, such as acquiring a building with a long-term mortgage note payable or selling goods on account to customers, there is no cash effect to include on the statement.

Effect on Cash Flow Statement

In General

		Effect on Cash Flows
Operating activities		
Cash received from	customers	+
	investments	+
Cash paid	to suppliers	−
	to employees	−
	for interest	−
	for income taxes	−
Investing activities (from Chapter 2)		
Financing activities (from Chapter 2)		

Focus Company Analysis: The Operating Activities section of the cash flow statement for Van Houtte is based on the transactions illustrated in this chapter, while the investing and financing activities relate primarily to transactions from Chapter 2. This section of the statement reports the sources and uses of cash for operating purposes. Remember that only the transactions that affect cash are reported.

VAN HOUTTE INC.
Partial Consolidated Cash Flow Statement
For the Month of April 2007
(in thousands of dollars)

Operating Activities			
Cash received:	from customers (a + b + d)	$55,900	
	from franchisees (c)	3,450	
	Operating cash inflow		$59,350
Cash paid:	to suppliers (g + j)	$19,000	
	to employees (h)	13,500	
	for general and administrative expenses (e + f)	14,710	
	Operating cash outflow		47,210
Net cash flow provided by operating activities			$12,140

($35,200 + 20,200 + 500)

($9,000 + 10,000)

($7,400 + 7,310)

Operating activities contributed $12,140 in cash during April. This cash basis income is different from the operating income of $14,590 that is based on accrual accounting. The difference between these two amounts is due to the fact that revenue is recognized when earned, regardless of when cash is received, and expenses are recognized when incurred, regardless when cash is paid. The difference of $2,450 can be explained as follows:

Cash flow from operating activities.	$12,140
Add: revenue not yet received in cash (amount reflected in the increase in Accounts and Notes Receivable ($9,250 + $4,300).	13,550
Add: prepayment for expenses not yet reported on the income statement	7,400
Deduct: cost of good sold not paid for yet ($37,400 − $19,000)	(18,400)
Deduct: cash received in advance for revenue not yet reported on the income statement (unearned revenue)	(100)
Operating income	$14,590

To remain in business in the long run, companies must generate positive cash flows from operations. Cash is needed to pay suppliers and employees. When cash from operations is negative over a period of time, the only other ways to obtain the necessary funds are to (1) sell long-term assets (which reduces future productivity), (2) borrow from creditors (at increasing rates of interest as risk of default rises), or (3) issue additional shares (where investor expectations about poor future performance drives the stock price down). There are clearly limits on how many of these activities companies can undertake.

Van Houtte has realized positive operating cash flows over the past five years as shown below. This represents a conservative approach to reporting revenues and expenses that builds analysts' confidence as to the reliability of the income information reported.

	2003	2004	2005	2006	2007
Cash flow from operations	$46,892	$45,564	$60,684	$47,811	$57,425
Net earnings	14,728	18,564	21,706	$22,506	$24,961

These operating cash flows are more than double the amount of net income reported by the company during each of the past five years.

SELF-STUDY **QUIZ 3-4**

CANADIAN TIRE CORPORATION LIMITED

Canadian Tire Corporation Limited is a leading hard goods retailer with more than 400 stores across Canada. The transactions below are taken from a recent annual cash flow statement. Indicate whether the transaction affected cash flow as an operating (O), investing (I), or financing (F) activity, and indicate the direction of the effect on cash (+ for increases; − for decreases):

Transactions	Type of Activity (O, I, or F)	Effect on Cash Flows (+ or −)
1. Distribution to shareholders		
2. Receipt of cash from customers		
3. Additions to property		
4. Payment of income taxes		
5. Payment of cash to suppliers		
6. Repayment of long-term debt		
7. Receipt of interest on investments		
8. Borrowings of long-term debt		
9. Issuance of shares		
10. Payment of interest on debt		
11. Payment of cash to employees		
12. Sale of property		

After you complete the schedule, check your solution with the answers on page 129.

KEY RATIO
ANALYSIS

We now introduce two ratios to assess managers' use of assets in total to improve earnings. These two ratios focus on the use of assets to generate revenue and earnings, respectively.

TOTAL ASSET TURNOVER RATIO

ANALYTICAL QUESTION → How effective is management in generating sales from assets (resources)?

RATIO AND COMPARISONS → The total asset turnover ratio is useful in answering this question. It is computed as follows:

$$\text{Total Asset Turnover Ratio} = \frac{\text{Sales (or Operating) Revenues}}{\text{Average Total Assets}}$$

The 2007 ratio for Van Houtte is:

$$\frac{\$388,200}{(\$380,100 + \$370,100)/2} = 1.03$$

> **■ LEARNING OBJECTIVE 6**
> Compute and interpret the total asset turnover ratio and the return on assets ratio.

Comparisons over Time			Comparisons with Competitors*	
Van Houtte Inc.			Starbucks	Green Mountain Coffee Roasters
2005	2006	2007	2006	2006
0.94	1.01	1.03	1.96	1.38

INTERPRETATIONS

In General → The total asset turnover ratio measures the sales generated per dollar of assets. A high asset turnover signifies efficient management of assets and a low asset turnover ratio signifies an inefficient one. A company's products and business strategy contribute significantly to its resulting ratio. However, when competitors are similar, management's ability to control the firm's assets is also vital in determining success. Financial performance improves as the ratio increases.

Creditors and security analysts use this ratio to assess a company's effectiveness at controlling current and non-current assets. In a well-run business, creditors expect fluctuations in the ratio due to seasonal upswings and downturns. For example, as inventory is built up preceding a high sales season, companies need to borrow funds. The asset turnover ratio will decline from the increase in assets. Then the high season sales provide the cash needed to repay the loans. The asset turnover ratio accordingly increases from the increase in sales.

Focus Company Analysis → Van Houtte's total asset turnover ratio increased gradually from 2005 to 2007, suggesting an increase in management effectiveness in using assets to generate sales. Van Houtte's 2007 total asset turnover ratio is lower than those of the competitors listed above. The main reason for the significant differences in these ratios is attributed to the sizable amount of goodwill on Van Houtte's balance sheet compared to the amounts reported for goodwill on the balance sheets of Starbucks and Green Mountain. Goodwill results from Van Houtte's acquisition of other businesses, and is not an asset that is used like equipment and inventories to generate sales. The exclusion of goodwill from Van Houtte's total assets would increase the total asset turnover ratio to 1.62 in 2007 instead of 1.03.

A Few Cautions → The total asset turnover ratio may decrease due to seasonal fluctuation. However, a declining ratio may also be caused by changes in corporate policies, such as more lax collection efforts in accounts receivable, that cause assets to rise. A detailed analysis of the changes in the key components of assets provides additional information on the nature of the change in the asset turnover ratio and thus management's decisions. Remember that any one ratio is not sufficient as a basis for investment decisions.

> **SELECTED FOCUS COMPANY TOTAL ASSET TURNOVER RATIOS**
>
> Forzani Group Ltd. 1.79
> WestJet Airlines 0.68
> Gildan Activewear 1.33

*The ratios for Van Houtte's competitors are shown for 2006 instead of 2007 because the three companies have different fiscal year-ends.

RETURN ON ASSETS (ROA) RATIO

ANALYTICAL QUESTION → How well has management used the total invested capital provided by debtholders and shareholders during the period?

RATIO AND COMPARISONS → Analysts refer to the rate of return on assets (ROA) as a useful measure in addressing this issue. It is computed* as follows:

$$\text{Return on Assets} = \frac{\text{Net Income}}{\text{Average Total Assets **}}$$

Both the total asset turnover ratio (covered earlier in this chapter) and the return on assets measure management's effectiveness in utilizing the company's resources: the first in generating revenue during the period, the second in generating income after expenses are deducted from revenues.

*In more complex return on total asset analyses, interest expense (net of tax) and non-controlling interest are added back to net income in the numerator of the ratio, since the measure assesses return on capital, independent of its source.
**Average Total Assets = (Beginning Total Assets + Ending Total Assets) ÷ 2

The 2007 ratio for Van Houtte is:

$$\frac{\$25,000}{(\$380,100 + \$370,100) \div 2} = 0.067 \ (6.7\%)$$

Comparisons over Time			Comparisons with Competitors*	
Van Houtte Inc.			**Starbucks**	**Green Mountain Coffee Roasters**
2005	2006	2007	2006	2006
5.8%	6.0%	6.7%	14.2%	5.4%

*The ratios for Van Houtte's competitors are shown for 2006 instead of 2007 because the three companies have different fiscal year-ends.

INTERPRETATIONS:

In General → ROA measures how much the firm earned for each dollar of investment. It is the broadest measure of profitability and management effectiveness, independent of financing strategy. ROA allows investors to compare management's investment performance against alternative investment options. Firms with higher ROA are doing a better job of selecting new investments, all other things being equal. Company managers often compute the measure on a division-by-division basis and use it to evaluate division managers' relative performance.

Focus Company Analysis → Van Houtte appears to have done well in fiscal year 2007 (which includes nine months of 2006) compared to both 2005 and 2006. Examination of the company's income statement shown in Exhibit 3.1 indicates that sales increased in 2007 compared to 2006, with corresponding increases in the cost of sales and operating expenses. But the increase in earnings was primarily due to the sale of the investment in Keurig Inc. that generated a net gain of $19.9 million, which was partially offset by additional income taxes of $13.7 million related to prior years. At the same time, the company's total assets did not change significantly during the past two years. All these changes caused ROA to increase in 2007. While Van Houtte achieved a higher ROA than Green Mountain Coffee Roasters, its ROA is much lower than that of Starbucks. Closer examination of Van Houtte's balance sheet indicates that its assets include a significant amount of goodwill (an intangible asset that resulted from past investments in other companies). Goodwill is not an operational asset that generates revenue and income in the same way as roasting equipment. Hence, if this asset is excluded from Van Houtte's balance sheet, total assets would be reduced, which increases ROA to 10.5 percent, bringing it closer to Starbucks' ROA.

A Few Cautions → Effective analysis of ROA requires an understanding of why ROA differs from prior levels and from the ROA of the company's competitors. Analysis of the differences in ROA over time and across companies can be facilitated by a decomposition of this ratio into two other ratios, as shown later in Chapter 13.

SELECTED FOCUS COMPANY COMPARISONS: RETURN ON ASSETS

WestJet Airlines	1.2%
Forzani Group Ltd.	2.2%
Gildan Activewear	15.8%

Sears Canada is one of the biggest Canadian department store retailers. It operates a large number of department stores that sell home fashions, appliances, apparel, home electronics, and garden products. It also sells merchandise online. Selected information about the company's resources and operations are presented below (amounts in millions of dollars).

	2005	2004	2003	2002	2001
Total assets	$3,199	$4,262	$4,139	$4,138	$4,047
Total revenue	6,238	6,230	6,223	6,536	6,726
Net income	771	129	125	44	89

Required:

1. Complete the following table by computing the Total Asset Turnover Ratio and the Return on Assets Ratio for 2003 and 2002.

	2005	2004	2003	2002
Total Asset Turnover Ratio	1.67	1.48		
Return on Assets (ROA)	0.21	0.03		

2. Both ratios increased in 2005 compared to 2004, but the return on assets increased seven-fold. What is the most likely explanation for this significant increase?

3. What conclusion can you draw from these ratios about the company's effectiveness in managing the economic resources under its control?

After you complete the quiz, check your answers with the solution on page 129.

DEMONSTRATION **CASE**

This case is a continuation of the Terrific Lawn Maintenance Corporation introduced in Chapter 2. The company was established with supplies, property, and equipment purchased ready for business. The balance sheet at April 30, 2007, based on investing and financing activities is as follows:

TERRIFIC LAWN MAINTENANCE CORPORATION
Balance Sheet
At April 30, 2007

Assets		Liabilities	
Cash	$ 4,350	Notes payable	$ 3,700
Equipment	4,600		
Land	3,750	**Shareholders' Equity**	
		Share capital	9,000
Total assets	$12,700	Total liabilities and shareholders' equity	$12,700

The following completed activities occurred during April 2007:

a. Purchased and used gasoline for mowers and edgers, paying $90 in cash at a local gas station.

b. In early April, received from the city $1,600 cash in advance for lawn maintenance service for April through July ($400 each month). The entire amount was recorded as Unearned Revenue.

c. In early April, purchased insurance costing $300 covering six months, April through September. The entire payment was recorded as Prepaid Expenses.

d. Mowed lawns for residential customers who are billed every two weeks. A total of $5,200 of service was billed in April.
e. Residential customers paid $3,500 on their accounts.
f. Paid wages every two weeks. Total cash paid in April was $3,900.
g. Received a bill for $320 from the local gas station for additional gasoline purchased on account and used in April.
h. Paid $100 on accounts payable.

Required:

1. On a separate sheet of paper, set up T-accounts for Cash, Accounts Receivable, Equipment, Land, Prepaid Expenses, Accounts Payable, Unearned Revenue (same as deferred revenue), Notes Payable, Share Capital, Retained Earnings, Mowing Revenue, Fuel Expense, and Wages Expense. Beginning balances for balance sheet accounts should be taken from the preceding balance sheet. Beginning balances for operating accounts are $0. Indicate these balances on the T-accounts.
2. Analyze each transaction using the steps outlined in Chapter 2. Please refer to the expanded transaction analysis model presented in this chapter.
3. On a separate sheet of paper, prepare journal entries to record the transactions above in chronological order and indicate their effects on the accounting model (Assets = Liabilities + Shareholders' Equity). Include the equality checks: (1) Debits = Credits and (2) the accounting equation is in balance.
4. Enter the effects of each transaction in the appropriate T-accounts. Identify each amount with its letter in the list of activities.
5. Compute balances in each of the T-accounts.

We strongly recommend that you prepare your own answers to these requirements and then check your answers with the following solution.

SUGGESTED SOLUTION

1. Journal entries, effects on accounting equation, equality checks, and T-accounts:

(a)	Fuel expense (+E → −SE)	90	
	Cash (−A)		90

Assets		=	Liabilities	+	Shareholders' Equity	
Cash	−90				Fuel expense	−90

(b)	Cash (+A)	1,600	
	Unearned revenue (+L)		1,600

Assets		=	Liabilities		+	Shareholders' Equity
Cash	+1,600		Unearned revenue	+1,600		

(c)	Prepaid expenses (+A)	300	
	Cash (−A)		300

Assets		=	Liabilities	+	Shareholders' Equity
Cash	−300				
Prepaid expenses	+300				

(d)	Accounts receivable (+A)	5,200	
	Mowing revenue (+R → +SE)		5,200

Assets		=	Liabilities	+	Shareholders' Equity	
Accounts receivable	+5,200				Mowing revenue	+5,200

(e) Cash (+A)	3,500	
Accounts receivable (−A)		3,500

Assets	=	Liabilities	+	Shareholders' Equity
Cash	+3,500			
Accounts receivable	−3,500			

(f) Wages expense (+E → −SE)	3,900	
Cash (−A)		3,900

Assets	=	Liabilities	+	Shareholders' Equity	
Cash	−3,900			Wages expense	−3,900

(g) Fuel expense (+E → −SE)	320	
Accounts payable (+L)		320

Assets	=	Liabilities		+	Shareholders' Equity	
		Accounts payable	+320		Fuel expense	−320

(h) Accounts payable (−L)	100	
Cash (−A)		100

Assets	=	Liabilities		+	Shareholders' Equity
Cash	−100	Accounts payable	−100		

T-Accounts

The beginning balances of the balance sheet accounts are taken from the solutions to the demonstration case in Chapter 2 (page 76).

ASSETS

+	Cash (A)		−			+	Accounts Receivable (A)		−			+	Prepaid Expenses (A)		−
Beg. bal.	3,800					d	5,200	e	3,500			c	300		
b	1,600	a	90			End. bal.	1,700					End. bal.	300		
e	3,500	c	300												
		f	3,900			+	Equipment (A)		−			+	Land (A)		−
		h	100			Beg. bal.	4,600					Beg. bal.	3,750		
End. bal.	4,510														
						End. bal.	4,600					End. bal.	3,750		

LIABILITIES

−	Accounts Payable (L)		+			−	Unearned Revenue (L)		+			−	Notes Payable (L)		+
h	100	g	320					b	1,600					Beg. bal.	4,400
		End. bal.	220					End. bal.	1,600					End. bal.	4,400

SHAREHOLDERS' EQUITY

−	Share Capital (SE)		+			−	Retained Earnings (SE)		+
		Beg. bal.	9,000						
		End. bal.	9,000						

REVENUES

−	Mowing Revenue (R)		+
		d	5,200
		End. bal.	5,200

EXPENSES

+	Wages Expense (E)		−			+	Fuel Expense (E)		−
f	3,900					a	90		
End. bal.	3,900					g	320		
						End. bal.	410		

SOLUTIONS TO **SELF-STUDY QUIZZES**

Self-Study Quiz 3-1

Accounts Affected and Type of Account	Amount of Cash Received	Amount of Revenue Earned in		Unearned Revenue
		March	April	
(a) Cash (A) Sales Revenue—Office Services (R)	$35,200		$35,200	
(b) Cash (A) Accounts Receivable (A) Sales Revenue—Retail Outlets (R)	20,200		30,200	
(c) Cash (A) Franchise-Related Revenue (R) Accounts Receivable (A)	3,450	$ 750	2,700	
(d) Cash (A) Franchise-Related Revenue (R) Unearned Revenue (L)	500		400	$100
(e) Cash (A) Accounts Receivable (A)	1,200	1,200		
Totals	**$60,550**		**$68,500**	

The total cash received in April, $60,550, is not equal to the amount of revenue recognized for April, $68,500. The cash received in April includes two amounts for revenue recorded for March and $100 for revenue to be recognized in the future. On the other hand, the revenues for April include $10,000 to be collected at a later date. Revenues reflect the efforts made in April, not earlier or later and are therefore a better measure of operating performance than cash receipts.

Self-Study Quiz 3-2

Accounts Affected and Type of Account	Cash Paid in April	Amount of Expense Recognized in April OR Why an Expense Is Not Recognized
(a) Cash (A) Accounts Payable (L)	$10,000	March purchase, paid in April; supplies expensed when used or sold.
(b) Inventories (A) Cost of Goods Sold (E)		$14,000 (of used inventory).
(c) Cash (A) Rent Expense (E) Prepaid Expenses (A)	$ 4,500	$1,500 incurred in April. $3,000 not yet incurred until future months.
(d) Inventories (A) Cost of Goods Sold (E)		$19,600 (of used inventory).
(e) Accounts Payable (L) General and Administrative Expense (E)		$500 incurred in April to be paid in the future.
Totals	**$14,500**	**$35,600 expenses for April.**

The amount of expenses incurred in April provides a better measure of the resources consumed or used in the process of generating revenues in April.

Self-Study Quiz 3-3

(i) Notes receivable (+A)	4,300	
Sales revenue—office services (+R → +SE)		4,300
Cost of goods sold—equipment (+E → −SE)	3,800	
Inventories (−A)		3,800
(j) Accounts payable (−L)	10,000	
Cash (−A)		10,000

Assets	=	Liabilities	+	Shareholders' Equity
Cash −10,000		Accounts payable −10,000		

(k)	Assets		=	Liabilities	+	Shareholders' Equity	
Cash	+3,500					Gain on sale	
Fixed assets	−500					of land	+3,000

Self-Study Quiz 3-4

1. F −   2. O +   3. I −   4. O −   5. O −   6. F −
7. O +   8. F +   9. F +   10. O −   11. O −   12. I +

Self-Study Quiz 3-5

1. Amounts are in millions of dollars.

	2005	2004	2003	2002
Total Asset Turnover Ratio	1.67	1.48	1.50	1.60
Return on Assets (ROA)	0.21	0.03	0.03	0.01

2. The increase in ROA is the net result of a significant increase in net income, from $129 in 2005 to $771 in 2006 along with a decrease in total assets from $4,262 to $3,199. This suggests that Sears Canada sold about one-quarter of its assets and realized a gain on their sale, causing an unusual increase in net income. In fact, the company reported that, on November 15, 2005, it sold the net assets related to its Credit and Financial Services operations, including its Sears Card and Sears MasterCard credit portfolio, to JPMorgan Chase & Co. The sale generated a pre-tax gain of $811.

3. The company grew slowly from 2001 to 2004, from $4,047 to $4,262. But its revenues dropped from $6,726 to $6,230 during the same period. At the same time its net income increased from $89 in 2001 to $129 in 2004. We may conclude that the increase in assets did not result in a corresponding increase in total revenue, but the company was able to manage its expenses and report higher net income figures. The decrease in the total asset turnover ratio and the relative stability of the return on assets may have caused Sears to sell its Credit and Financial Services operations in 2005. Additional information about the company's operations would be needed to support such a conclusion.

Chapter Supplement

Nonrecurring Items

As noted in the chapter, companies may report one of two types of nonrecurring items: discontinued operations and extraordinary items. The income statement of Bombardier Inc., a world-leading manufacturer of innovative transportation solutions, from regional aircraft and business jets to rail transportation equipment, systems and services, includes income from discontinued operations, and is presented in Exhibit 3.6.

Discontinued Operations

Discontinued operations result from either abandoning or selling a major business segment. Information related to operating income (or loss) generated by the discontinued operation and any gain or loss on disposal (the difference between the book value of the net assets and the sale price or the abandonment costs) are included in the financial statements. These amounts are disclosed separately on the income statement with details of the disposal presented in a note to the financial statements. Each amount is reported net of the income tax effects. Separate reporting informs users that the results of discontinued operations are less useful as predictors of the company's future profitability.

During fiscal year 2007, Bombardier continued with its strategy of reducing the former Bombardier Capital segment ("BC") operations by selling its consumer finance operations for cash proceeds of $67 million in May 2006, and its freight car operations for cash proceeds of $94 million in October 2006. Bombardier provides details of these discontinued operations in Note 6 to its financial statements.

DISCONTINUED OPERATIONS result from the disposal of a major segment of the business and are reported net of income tax effects.

EXHIBIT **3.6**

**Income Statements for
Bombardier Inc.**

**REAL WORLD
EXCERPT**

Bombardier Inc.

ANNUAL REPORT

CONSOLIDATED STATEMENTS OF INCOME
(in millions of US dollars, except per share amounts)

For the Fiscal Years Ended January 31	Notes	2007	2006
Revenues			
Manufacturing		**$10,446**	$10,708
Services		**2,697**	2,537
Other		**1,673**	1,481
		14,816	14,726
Cost of sales		**12,685**	12,719
Selling, general and administrative		**863**	842
Research and development		**173**	175
Amortization		**518**	545
Special items	14	**24**	88
		14,263	14,369
Income from continuing operations before the following:		**553**	357
Financing income	15	**(157)**	(156)
Financing expense	15	**375**	363
Income from continuing operations before income taxes		**335**	150
Income taxes	16	**92**	15
Income from continuing operations		**243**	135
Income from discontinued operations, net of tax	6	**25**	114
Net income		**$ 268**	$ 249

Extraordinary Items

**EXTRAORDINARY
ITEMS** are gains
or losses that are
considered unusual in
nature, infrequent in
occurrence, and not
dependent primarily
on decisions by
management or owners.
They are reported net of
income tax effects.

Extraordinary items are gains or losses that are considered unusual in nature, infrequent in occurrence, and not dependent primarily on decisions by management or owners. Examples include losses suffered from natural disasters such as floods and hurricanes in geographic areas where such disasters rarely occur. These items must be reported separately on the income statement, net of income tax effects. Separate reporting informs decision makers that the items are not likely to recur; hence, they are less relevant to predicting the company's future performance. Note disclosure is needed to explain the nature of the extraordinary item. Such items are now reported very rarely. In fact, a recent survey of 200 companies indicated that none of these companies reported extraordinary events in their annual reports for the years 2001 through 2005, except for two companies that reported extraordinary items in 2004.[8]

CHAPTER **TAKE-AWAYS**

1. **Describe a typical business operating cycle and explain the necessity for the periodicity assumption. p. 101**
   - Operating cycle—the cash-to-cash cycle is the time it takes to purchase goods or services from suppliers, sell the goods or services to customers, and collect cash from customers.
   - Periodicity assumption—to measure and report financial information periodically, we assume the long life of the company can be cut into shorter periods.

---

[8]N. Chlala, A. Lavigne, L. Martel, and C. Byrd, *Financial Reporting in Canada, 2006.* Toronto: The Canadian Institute of Chartered Accountants, 2006, p. 484. An example of an extraordinary item was reported by Le Groupe Vidéotron Ltée in the company's 1998 annual report. A note to the financial statements stated: "The Company incurred expenses related to the ice storm that hit the province of Québec in January 1998, for a total of $13,695,000, net of an estimated amount set up for the recovery from the insurers in this matter."

2. **Explain how business activities affect the elements of the income statement. p. 103**
   - Elements on the classified income statement:
     a. Revenues—increases in assets or settlements of liabilities from ongoing operations.
     b. Expenses—decreases in assets or increases in liabilities from ongoing operations.
     c. Gains—increases in assets or settlements of liabilities from peripheral activities.
     d. Losses—decreases in assets or increases in liabilities from peripheral activities.

3. **Explain the accrual basis of accounting and apply the revenue and matching principles to measure income. p. 107**
   When applying accrual accounting concepts, revenues are recognized (recorded) when earned and expenses are recognized when incurred to generate the revenues.
   - Revenue principle—recognize revenues when the earnings process is complete or nearly complete, an exchange has taken place, and collection is probable.
   - Matching principle—recognize expenses when incurred in earning revenue.

4. **Apply transaction analysis to examine and record the effects of operating activities on the financial statements. p. 113**
   The expanded transaction analysis model includes revenues and expenses:

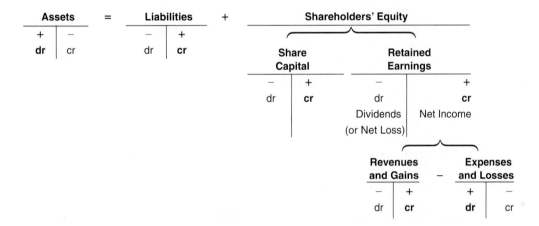

5. **Prepare an income statement and understand the difference between net income and cash flow from operations. p. 119**
   The income statement reports the revenues generated during the period and the related expenses. Net income is the difference between revenues and expenses, whereas cash flow from operations equals the difference between cash receipts and cash payments related to operations. Net income differs from cash flow from operations because the revenue recognition and matching principles result in the recognition of revenues and related expenses that are independent of the timing of cash receipts and payments.

6. **Compute and interpret the total asset turnover ratio and the return on assets ratio. p. 123**
   The total asset turnover ratio (Sales ÷ Average Total Assets) measures the sales generated per dollar of assets. The higher the ratio, the more efficient the company is at managing assets. The return on assets ratio measures how much the company earned for each dollar of assets. It provides information on profitability and management's effectiveness in utilizing assets. An increasing ratio over time suggests increased efficiency. ROA is computed as net income divided by average total assets.

In this chapter, we discussed the operating cycle and accounting concepts relevant to income determination: the periodicity assumption, definitions for the income statement elements (revenues, expenses, gains, and losses), the revenue principle, and the matching principle. These accounting principles are defined in accordance with the accrual basis of accounting, which requires revenues to be recorded when earned and expenses to be recorded when incurred in generating revenues during the period. We expanded the transaction analysis model introduced in Chapter 2 by adding revenues and expenses. In Chapter 4, we discuss the activities at the end of the accounting period: the adjustment process, the preparation of adjusted financial statements, and the closing process.

KEY **RATIOS**

The **total asset turnover ratio** measures the sales generated per dollar of assets. A high ratio suggests that the company is managing its assets (resources used to generate revenues) efficiently. It is computed as follows (p. 123):

$$\text{Total Asset Turnover Ratio} = \frac{\text{Sales (or Operating) Revenues}}{\text{Average Total Assets}^*}$$

The **return on assets ratio** measures how much the company earned for each dollar of assets utilized during the period. A high ratio suggests that the company is managing its assets efficiently. It is computed as follows (p. 124):

$$\text{Return on Assets (ROA)} = \frac{\text{Net Income}}{\text{Average Total Assets}^*}$$

*(Beginning Total Assets + Ending Total Assets) ÷ 2

FINDING **FINANCIAL INFORMATION**

BALANCE SHEET

Current Assets
 Cash
 Accounts and notes
  receivable
 Inventory
 Prepaid expenses
Non-Current Assets
 Long-term
  investments
 Fixed assets
 Intangibles

Current Liabilities
 Accounts payable
 Notes payable
 Accrued liabilities
  payable
Non-Current Liabilities
 Long-term debt
Shareholders' Equity
 Share capital
 Retained earnings

INCOME STATEMENT

Revenues
 Sales (from various operating activities)
 Investment income
Expenses
 Cost of goods sold (sold inventory)
 Rent, wages, interest, amortization,
  insurance, etc.
Pretax Income
 Income tax expense
Net Income

CASH FLOW STATEMENT

Under Operating Activities
 + Cash from customers
 + Cash from interest and dividends
 − Cash to suppliers
 − Cash to employees
 − Cash for interest
 − Cash for income taxes

NOTES

Under Summary of Significant Accounting Policies
 Description of company's revenue
  recognition policy.

KEY **TERMS**

Accrual Basis Accounting p. 107

Cash Basis Accounting p. 107

Discontinued Operations p. 129

Expenses p. 105

Extraordinary Items p. 130

Gains p. 106

Gross Profit (Gross Margin) p. 105

Income before Income Taxes p. 106

Losses p. 106

Matching Principle p. 111

Operating Cycle (Cash-to-Cash) p. 101

Operating Income p. 105

Periodicity Assumption p. 103

Revenues p. 104

Revenue Principle p. 108

QUESTIONS

1. Assume that you have just opened a small gift store that specializes in gift items imported from the Far East. Explain the typical business operating cycle for your store.
2. Explain what the periodicity assumption means in accounting.

3. Indicate the income statement equation and define each element.
4. Explain the difference between
   a. revenues and gains.
   b. expenses and losses.
5. Define *accrual accounting.* Contrast it with cash basis accounting.
6. What three conditions normally must be met for revenue to be recognized under the accrual basis of accounting?
7. Explain the matching principle.
8. Explain why shareholders' equity is increased by revenues and decreased by expenses.
9. Explain why revenues are recorded as credits and expenses as debits.
10. Complete the following matrix by entering either *debit* or *credit* in each cell:

Item	Increase	Decrease
Revenues		
Expenses		
Gains		
Losses		

11. Complete the following matrix by entering either *increase* or *decrease* in each cell:

Item	Debit	Credit
Revenues		
Expenses		
Gains		
Losses		

12. Identify whether each of the following transactions results in a cash flow effect from operating, investing, or financing activities, and indicate the effect on cash (+ for increase and − for decrease). If there is no cash flow effect, write "None":

Transaction	Operating, Investing, or Financing Effect	Direction of the Effect
Cash paid to suppliers		
Sale of goods on account		
Cash received from customers		
Purchase of investments for cash		
Cash paid for interest		
Issuance of shares for cash		

13. State the equation for the total asset turnover ratio, and explain how it is interpreted.
14. State the equation for the return on assets ratio, and explain how it is interpreted.

EXERCISES

E3–1 Inferring Income Statement Values   ■ **LO1**

Supply the missing dollar amounts for the 2008 income statement of Ultimate Style Company for each of the following independent cases:

	Case A	Case B	Case C	Case D	Case E
Sales revenue	$900	$700	$410	$?	$?
Selling expense	?	150	80	400	250
Cost of goods sold	?	380	?	500	310
Income tax expense	?	30	20	40	30
Gross margin	400	?	?	?	440
Income before income tax	200	90	?	190	?
Administrative expense	150	?	60	100	80
Net income	170	?	50	?	80

LO2 **E3–2 Preparing a Multiple-Step Income Statement**

The following data were taken from the records of Village Corporation at December 31, 2008:

Sales revenue	$70,000
Gross profit	24,500
Selling (distribution) expense	8,000
Administrative expense	?
Income before income tax	10,000
Income tax rate	30%
Number of shares outstanding	4,000

Required:

Prepare a complete multiple-step income statement for the company (showing both gross profit and income from operations). Show all computations. (*Hint:* Set up the side captions starting with sales revenue and ending with earnings per share; use the amounts and percentages given to infer missing values.)

LO2 **E3–3 Preparing Single- and Multiple-Step Income Statements**

The following data were taken from the records of Kimberley Appliances, Incorporated, at December 31, 2007:

Sales revenue	$120,000
Administrative expense	12,000
Selling (distribution) expense	18,000
Income tax rate	25%
Gross profit	50,000
Number of shares outstanding	3,000

Required:

1. Prepare a complete single-step income statement for the company. Show all computations. (*Hint:* Set up the side captions or rows starting with sales revenue and ending with earnings per share; use the amounts and percentages given to infer missing values.)

2. Prepare a complete multiple-step income statement for the company (showing both gross profit and income from operations).

LO3 **E3–4 Reporting Cash Basis versus Accrual Basis Income**

Mostert Music Company had the following transactions in March:

a. Sold instruments to customers for $10,000; received $4,000 in cash and the rest on account.

b. Determined that the cost of the instruments sold was $7,000.

c. Purchased $4,000 of new instruments inventory; paid $2,000 in cash and the rest on account.

d. Paid $600 in wages for the month.

e. Received a $200 bill for utilities that will be paid in April.

f. Received $1,000 from customers as deposits on orders of new instruments to be sold to customers in April.

Complete the following statements:

Cash Basis Income Statement		Accrual Basis Income Statement	
Revenues	$.	Revenues	$. . . . .
Cash sales	. . . .	Sales to customers	. . . .
Customer deposits			
Expenses		Expenses	
Inventory purchases	. . . .	Cost of sales	. . . .
Wages paid	. . . .	Wages expense	. . . .
		Utilities expense	. . . .
Net income		Net income	

Does the cash basis or the accrual basis of accounting provide a better indication of the operating performance of Mostert Music Company in March? Explain.

E3–5 Identifying Revenues

LO2, 3

ANALYSIS

Revenues are normally recognized when the earnings process is complete or nearly complete, a transaction has taken place, and collection is reasonably assured. The amount recorded is the cash-equivalent sales price. The following events and transactions occurred in September 2007:

a. A customer orders and receives 10 personal computers from Gateway 2000; the customer promises to pay $20,000 within three months. Answer from Gateway's standpoint.

b. Sam Shell Dodge sells a truck with a list, or sticker, price of $24,000 for $21,000 cash.

c. The Hudson's Bay Company orders 1,000 men's shirts from Gildan Activewear Inc. for $18 each for future delivery. The terms require payment in full within 30 days of delivery. Answer from Gildan's standpoint.

d. Gildan Activewear completes production of the shirts described in (c) and delivers the order. Answer from Gildan's standpoint.

e. Gildan receives payment from the Hudson's Bay Company for the order described in (c). Answer from Gildan's standpoint.

f. A customer purchases a ticket from WestJet for $435 cash to travel the following January. Answer from WestJet's standpoint.

g. General Motors issues $26 million in new shares.

h. Hall Construction Company signs a contract with a customer for the construction of a new $500,000 warehouse. At the signing, Hall receives a cheque for $50,000 as a deposit on the future construction. Answer from Hall's standpoint.

i. On September 1, 2007, a bank lends $10,000 to a company. The loan carries a 12-percent annual interest rate, and the principal and interest are due in a lump sum on August 31, 2008. Answer from the bank's standpoint.

j. A popular ski magazine company receives a total of $1,800 from subscribers on September 30, the last day of its fiscal year. The subscriptions begin in the next fiscal year. Answer from the magazine company's standpoint.

k. Sears Canada, a retail store, sells a $100 lamp to a customer who charges the sale on his store credit card. Answer from the standpoint of Sears.

Required:

For each of the September transactions,

1. Indicate the account titles that are affected and the type of each account (A for asset, L for liability, SE for shareholders' equity, and R for revenue).

2. If a revenue is to be recognized in September, indicate the amount. If a revenue is not to be recognized in September, indicate which of the revenue recognition criteria are not met.

Use the following headings in structuring your solution:

Event or Transaction	Accounts Affected and Type of Account	Amount of Revenue Earned in September OR Revenue Criteria Not Met

E3–6 Identifying Expenses

LO2, 3

ANALYSIS

Revenues are normally recognized when goods or services have been provided and payment or promise of payment has been received. Expense recognition is guided by an attempt to match the costs associated with the generation of those revenues to the same time period. The following events and transactions occurred in January 2008:

a. Gateway 2000 pays its computer service technicians $85,000 in salary for the two weeks ended January 7. Answer from Gateway's standpoint.

b. Turner Construction Company pays $4,500 in workers' compensation insurance for the first three months of the year.

c. McGraw-Hill Ryerson Limited uses $1,200 worth of electricity and natural gas in its headquarters building for which it has not yet been billed.

d. Gildan Activewear Inc. completes production of 500 men's shirts ordered by Bon Ton's Department Store at a cost of $9 each and delivers the order. Answer from Gildan's standpoint.

e. The campus bookstore receives 500 accounting textbooks at a cost of $70 each. The terms indicate that payment is due within 30 days of delivery.

f. During the last week of January, the campus bookstore sold 450 accounting textbooks received in (*e*) at a sales price of $100 each.

g. Sam Shell Dodge pays its salespersons $3,500 in commissions related to December automobile sales. Answer from Sam Shell Dodge's standpoint.

h. On January 31, Sam Shell Dodge determines that it will pay its salespersons $4,200 in commissions related to January sales. The payment will be made in early February. Answer from Sam Shell Dodge's standpoint.

i. A new grill is installed at a McDonald's restaurant. On the same day, payment of $14,000 is made in cash.

j. On January 1, 2008, Carousel Mall had janitorial supplies costing $1,000 in storage. An additional $600 worth of supplies was purchased during January. At the end of January, $900 worth of janitorial supplies remained in storage.

k. A Concordia University employee works eight hours, at $15 per hour, on January 31; however, payday is not until February 3. Answer from the university's point of view.

l. Wang Company paid $3,600 for a fire insurance policy on January 2. The policy covers the current month and the next 11 months. Answer from Wang's point of view.

m. Amber Incorporated has its delivery van repaired in January for $280 and charges the amount on account.

n. Ziegler Company, a farm equipment company, receives its phone bill at the end of January for $230 for January calls. The bill has not been paid to date.

o. Spina Company receives and pays in January a $2,100 invoice from a consulting firm for services received in January.

p. Felicetti's Taxi Company pays a $600 invoice from a consulting firm for services received and recorded in Accounts Payable in December.

Required:
For each of the January transactions:

1. Indicate the account titles that are affected and the type of each account (A for asset, L for liability, SE for shareholders' equity, and E for expense).

2. If an expense is to be recognized in January, indicate the amount. If an expense is not to be recognized in January, indicate why.
Use the following headings in structuring your solution:

Event or Transaction	Accounts Affected and Type of Account	Amount of Expense Incurred in January OR Why an Expense Is Not Recognized

LO2, 3, 5

ANALYSIS

E3–7   **Identifying Revenues and Expenses**

Bob's Bowling, Inc. operates several bowling centres for games and equipment sales. The following transactions occurred in July 2007.

Required:

1. For each transaction, indicate in the appropriate column the account titles that are affected and the type of account (A for asset, L for liability, R for revenue, and E for expense), and the amount of cash received or paid.

2. If a revenue or an expense is to be recognized in July, indicate the amount. If a revenue or expense is not to be recognized in July, indicate why.

3. Explain why the difference between revenues and expenses is not equal to the net cash flow during July 2007.

Activity	Accounts Affected and Type of Account	Cash Received (Paid) in July	Amount of Revenue Earned or Expense Incurred in July OR Why a Revenue or an Expense Is Not Recognized
(a) Bob's collected $10,000 from customers for games played in July.			
(b) Bob's sold bowling equipment inventory for $5,000; received $3,000 in cash and the rest on account. The cost of sales is $2,800.			
(c) Bob's received $1,000 from customers on account who purchased merchandise in June.			
(d) The men's and women's bowling leagues gave Bob's a deposit of $1,500 for the upcoming fall season.			
(e) Bob's paid $2,000 for the June electricity bill and received the July bill for $2,200, which will be paid in August.			
(f) Bob's paid $4,000 to employees for work in July.			
(g) Bob's purchased and paid for $1,200 in insurance for coverage from July 1 to October 1.			
(h) Bob's paid $1,000 to plumbers for repairing a broken pipe in the restrooms.			
Totals			

E3–8 Determining the Financial Statement Effects of Operating Activities   ▨ **LO4**

Bob's Bowling, Inc., operates several bowling centres (for games and equipment sales). For each of the following transactions, complete the tabulation, indicating the amount and effect (+ for increase and − for decrease) of each transaction. (Remember that A = L + SE, R − E = NI, and NI affects SE through Retained Earnings.) Write NE if there is no effect. The first transaction is provided as an example.

Transaction	Balance Sheet			Income Statement		
	Assets	Liabilities	Shareholders' Equity	Revenues	Expenses	Net Income
a. Bob's collected $10,000 from customers for games played in July.	+10,000	NE	+10,000	+10,000	NE	+10,000
b. Bob's sold $5,000 in bowling equipment inventory; received $3,000 in cash and the rest on account. The cost of sales is $2,800.						
c. Bob's received $1,000 from customers on account who purchased merchandise in June.						
d. The men's and women's bowling leagues gave Bob's a deposit of $1,500 for the upcoming fall season.						
e. Bob's paid $2,000 for the June electricity bill and received the July bill for $2,200 to be paid in August.						
f. Bob's paid $4,000 to employees for work in July.						
g. Bob's purchased $1,200 in insurance for coverage from July 1 to October 1.						
h. Bob's paid $1,000 to plumbers for repairing a broken pipe in the restrooms.						

E3–9 Preparing a Simple Income Statement   ▨ **LO4**

Refer to the transactions in E3–8 (including the example) and prepare an income statement for Bob's Bowling, Inc., for the month of July 2008. Use an income tax rate of 40 percent.

E3–10 Determining Financial Statement Effects of Various Transactions   ▨ **LO4**

The following transactions occurred during a recent year:

ANALYSIS

a. Issued shares to organizers for cash (example).
b. Borrowed cash from the local bank.
c. Purchased equipment on credit.
d. Earned revenue, collected cash.
e. Incurred expenses, on credit.
f. Earned revenue, on credit.
g. Paid cash on account.
h. Incurred expenses, paid cash.

i. Earned revenue, collected three-fourths in cash and the rest on credit.
j. Experienced theft of $100 cash.
k. Declared and paid cash dividends.
l. Collected cash from customers on account.
m. Incurred expenses, paid four-fifths in cash and the rest on credit.
n. Paid income tax expense for the period.

Required:

Complete the tabulation below for each of the transactions, indicating the effect (+ for increase and − for decrease) of each transaction. (Remember that A = L + SE, R − E = NI, and NI affects SE through Retained Earnings.) Write NE if there is no effect. The first transaction is provided as an example.

	Balance Sheet			Income Statement		
Transaction	Assets	Liabilities	Shareholders' Equity	Revenues	Expenses	Net Income
(a) (example)	+	NE	+	NE	NE	NE

LO4

Wolverine World Wide Inc.

ANALYSIS

E3–11 Determining Financial Statement Effects of Various Transactions

Wolverine World Wide, Inc., manufactures military, work, sport, and casual footwear and leather accessories under a variety of brand names, such as Hush Puppies, Wolverine, and Bates, to a global market. The following transactions occurred during a recent year. Dollars are in thousands.

a. Issued $1,124 in shares to investors (example).

b. Purchased $677,347 of additional inventory of raw materials on account.

c. Paid $10,730 on long-term notes.

d. Sold $1,060,999 of products to customers on account; the cost of the products sold was $655,800.

e. Declared and paid cash dividends of $14,814.

f. Purchased $19,160 of additional property, plant, and equipment for cash.

g. Incurred $101,891 in selling expenses with two-thirds paid in cash and the rest on account.

h. Earned $1,736 interest on investments, received 90 percent in cash.

i. Incurred $3,647 in interest expense (not yet paid).

Required:

Complete the tabulation below for each of the transactions, indicating the effect (+ for increase and − for decrease) of each transaction. (Remember that A = L + SE, R − E = NI, and NI affects SE through Retained Earnings.) Write NE if there is no effect. The first transaction is provided as an example.

	Balance Sheet			Income Statement		
Transaction	Assets	Liabilities	Shareholders' Equity	Revenues	Expenses	Net Income
(a) (example)	+1,124	NE	+1,124	NE	NE	NE

LO4

Sysco

E3–12 Recording Journal Entries

Sysco, formed in 1969, is the largest U.S. marketer and distributor of food service products, serving nearly 250,000 restaurants, hotels, schools, hospitals, and other institutions. The following summarized transactions are typical of those that occurred in a recent year.

a. Borrowed $80 million from a bank, signing a short-term note.

b. Provided $36.6 billion in service to customers during the year, with $31.2 billion on account and the rest received in cash.

c. Purchased plant and equipment for $514.7 million in cash.

d. Purchased $26.4 billion inventory on account.

e. Paid $2.3 billion in salaries during the year.

f. Received $26.1 billion on account paid by customers.

g. Purchased and used fuel of $637 million in delivery vehicles during the year (paid for in cash).

h. Declared and paid $397.5 million in dividends for the year.

i. Paid $25.6 billion cash on accounts payable.

j. Incurred $47 million in utility usage during the year; paid $30 million in cash and the rest on account.

Required:

Prepare a journal entry to record each of the transactions. Determine whether the accounting equation remains in balance and debits equal credits after each entry.

E3–13   **Recording Journal Entries**

■ **LO4**

Research In Motion

Research In Motion (RIM) designs, manufactures, and markets wireless devices to meet the communication needs of its global market. The company sells its BlackBerry products to customers in 60 countries around the world. RIM also provides communications servers to customers who need secure internal wireless communications. The following hypothetical December transactions are typical of those that occur each month (in thousands of dollars).

a. Borrowed $600 from the bank on December 1 with a six-month note at 8-percent annual interest to finance its operations. The principal and interest are due on the maturity date.

b. Purchased legal software for corporate use for $30 cash on December 1. The software's useful life is estimated at two years with zero residual value.

c. Purchased and received $10,000 of raw materials for use in assembling its wireless products.

d. Incurred $2,200 in routine selling expenses for BlackBerry.

e. Closed a contract of $8,400 to be filled in January and received cash in full payment.

f. Sold products in December for $100,000 in cash.

g. Sold products on account in December for $87,000.

h. Received a $2,000 deposit from a customer in Mexico for delivery of wireless products in January.

i. Paid half of the amount of the transaction in (c).

j. Received $60,000 on account from the customers in (g).

k. Paid $15,000 in wages to manufacturing employees for the month of December.

Required:

1. Prepare a journal entry to record each transaction. (Remember to check that debits equal credits and that the accounting equation is in balance after each transaction.)

2. Assume that RIM had a $12,000 balance in Accounts Receivable at the beginning of the year. Determine the ending balance in the Accounts Receivable account. Show your work in T-account format.

E3–14   **Recording Journal Entries**

■ **LO4**

Rowland & Sons Air Transport Service, Inc., has been in operation for three years. The following transactions occurred in February:

February 1	Paid $1,900 for rent of hangar space in February.
February 2	Purchased fuel costing $450 on account for the next flight to Winnipeg.
February 4	Received customer payment of $950 to ship several items to Montréal next month.
February 7	Flew cargo from Ottawa to Edmonton; the customer paid $1,240 for the air transport.
February 10	Paid pilot $4,000 in wages for flying in January.
February 14	Paid $600 for an advertisement in the local paper to run on February 19.
February 18	Flew cargo for two customers from Regina to Calgary for $1,800; one customer paid $500 cash and the other asked to be billed.
February 25	Purchased spare parts for the planes costing $1,350 on account.
February 27	Declared a $1,300 cash dividend to be paid in March.

Required:

Prepare a journal entry to record each transaction. Be sure to categorize each account as an asset (A), liability (L), shareholders' equity (SE), revenue (R), or expense (E).

E3–15   **Analyzing the Effects of Transactions in T-Accounts, and Computing Cash Basis versus Accrual Basis Net Income**

■ **LO3, 4, 5, 6**

Sbrocchi's Piano Rebuilding Company has been operating for one year (2006). At the start of 2008, its income statement accounts had zero balances and its balance sheet account balances were as follows:

Cash	$ 5,000	Accounts payable	8,000
Accounts receivable	25,000	Deferred revenue (deposits)	3,200
Supplies	1,200	Note payable (due in three years)	40,000
Equipment	8,000	Share capital	8,000
Land	6,000	Retained earnings	18,000
Building	32,000		

Required:

1. Create T-accounts for the balance sheet accounts and for these additional accounts: Rebuilding Fees Revenue, Rent Revenue, Wages Expense, and Utilities Expense. Enter the beginning balances.

2. Enter the following January 2008 transactions in the T-accounts, using the letter of each transaction as the reference:
   a. Received a $500 deposit from a customer who wanted her piano rebuilt.
   b. Rented a part of the building to a bicycle repair shop; received $500 for rent in January.
   c. Delivered 10 rebuilt pianos to customers who paid $16,000 in cash.
   d. Received $8,000 from customers as payment on their accounts.
   e. Received an electric and gas utility bill for $420 to be paid in February.
   f. Ordered $800 in supplies.
   g. Paid $1,900 on account to suppliers.
   h. Received from the home of Ms. Sbrocchi, the major shareholder, an $850 tool (equipment) to use in the business.
   i. Paid $8,500 in wages to employees for work in January.
   j. Declared and paid a cash dividend of $3,000.
   k. Received and paid for the supplies ordered in (f).

3. Using the data from the T-accounts, calculate the amounts for the following on January 31, 2008:

   Revenues, $_____ − Expenses, $_____ = Net Income, $_____

   Assets, $_____ = Liabilities, $_____ + Shareholders' Equity, $_____

4. Calculate the company's net income for January using the cash basis of accounting. Why does this differ from the accrual basis net income (in part 3 above)?

5. Calculate the return on assets ratio for January 2008. If the company had a return on assets ratio of 22 percent in December 2007 and 21 percent in November 2007, what does your computation suggest to you about Sbrocchi's Piano Rebuilding Company? What would you state in your report?

LO4

ANALYSIS

E3–16 Analyzing the Effects of Transactions on the Cash Flow Statement
Refer to E3–15.

Required:
Use the following chart to identify whether each of the transactions in E3–15 results in a cash flow effect from operating (O), investing (I), or financing (F) activities, and indicate the direction and the effect on cash (+ for increase and − for decrease). If there is no cash flow effect, write *none*. The first transaction is provided as an example.

Transaction	Operating, Investing, or Financing Effect	Direction and Amount of the Effect
(a)	O	+ 500

LO4

E3–17 Preparing an Income Statement and a Partial Cash Flow Statement
Refer to E3–15.

Required:

1. Use the ending balances in the T-accounts in E3–15 to prepare the following:
   a. An income statement for January 2008 in good form.
   b. The operating activities section of the cash flow statement for January 2008 in good form.

2. Explain the difference between the net income and the cash flow from operating activities computed in requirement 1.

LO4

E3–18 Analyzing the Effects of Transactions in T-Accounts
Karen Gorewit and Pat Nally had been operating a catering business, Travelling Gourmet, for several years. In March 2009, the partners were planning to expand by opening a retail sales shop and decided to form the business as a corporation called Travelling Gourmet, Inc. The following transactions occurred in March 2009:

a. Received $10,000 cash from each of the two shareholders to form the corporation, in addition to $2,000 in accounts receivable, $5,300 in equipment, a van (equipment) appraised at a fair market value of $14,500, and $1,200 in supplies.

b. Purchased a vacant store in a good location for $60,000 with a $12,000 cash down payment and a mortgage from a local bank for the remainder.

c. Borrowed $25,000 from the local bank on a 10 percent, one-year note.
d. Purchased for cash and used food and paper products costing $8,830.
e. Made and sold food at the retail store for $10,900 in cash.
f. Catered four parties in March for $3,200; $2,000 was billed, and the rest was received in cash.
g. Received a $320 telephone bill for March to be paid in April.
h. Paid $314 for gas to use the van in March.
i. Paid $5,080 for wages of employees who worked in March.
j. Paid a $300 dividend from the corporation to each owner.
k. Paid $15,000 to purchase equipment (refrigerated display cases, cabinets, tables, and chairs), and $9,870 to renovate and decorate the new store (added to the cost of the building).

Required:

1. Set up appropriate T-accounts for Cash, Accounts Receivable, Supplies, Equipment, Building, Accounts Payable, Note Payable, Mortgage Payable, Share Capital, Retained Earnings, Food Sales Revenue, Catering Sales Revenue, Cost of Food and Paper Products, Utilities Expense, Wages Expense, and Gasoline Expense.

2. Record in the T-accounts the effects of each transaction for Travelling Gourmet, Inc., in March. Identify the amounts with the letters starting with (*a*).

E3–19 Analyzing the Effects of Transactions on the Cash Flow Statement

⬛ LO4

Refer to E3–18.

ANALYSIS

Required:

Use the following chart to identify whether each of the transactions in E3–18 results in a cash flow effect from operating (O), investing (I), or financing (F) activities, and indicate the direction and the effect on cash (+ for increase and − for decrease). If there is no cash flow effect, write *none*. The first transaction is provided as an example.

Transaction	Operating, Investing, or Financing Effect	Direction and Amount of the Effect
(a)	F	+ 20,000

E3–20 Preparing an Income Statement and a Partial Cash Flow Statement

⬛ LO4

Refer to E3–18.

Required:

1. Use the ending balances in the T-accounts in E3–18 to prepare the following:
   a. An income statement for March 2009 in good form.
   b. The operating activities section of the cash flow statement for March 2009 in good form.

2. Explain the difference between the net income and the cash flow from operating activities computed in requirement 1.

E3–21 Inferring Operating Transactions and Preparing an Income Statement and a Balance Sheet

⬛ LO2, 3, 4

Kiernan Kite Company (a corporation) sells and repairs kites from manufacturers around the world. Its stores are located in rented space in malls and shopping centres. During its first month of operations ended April 30, 2009, Kiernan Kite Company completed eight transactions with the dollar effects indicated in the following schedule:

Accounts									Ending Balance

Accounts	(a)	(b)	(c)	(d)	(e)	(f)	(g)	(h)	Ending Balance
Cash	$50,000	$(10,000)	$(5,000)	$ 7,000	$(2,000)	$(1,000)		$3,000	
Accounts receivable				3,000					
Inventory			20,000	(3,000)					
Prepaid expenses					1,500				
Store fixtures		10,000							
Accounts payable			15,000				1,200		
Unearned revenue								2,000	
Share capital	50,000								
Sales revenue				10,000				1,000	
Cost of sales				3,000					
Wages expense							1,000		
Rent expense					500				
Utilities expense							1,200		

Table header spanning: **Dollar Effect of Each of the Eight Transactions**

Required:

1. Write a brief explanation of transactions (*a*) through (*h*). Explain any assumptions that you made.

2. Compute the ending balance in each account and prepare an income statement for the company for April 2009 and a classified balance sheet as at April 30, 2009.

■ **LO6**

E3–22 Computing and Explaining the Total Asset Turnover Ratio

The following data are from annual reports of Justin's Jewellery Company:

	2008	2007	2006
Total assets	$ 60,000	$ 50,000	$ 40,000
Total liabilities	12,000	10,000	5,000
Total shareholders' equity	48,000	40,000	35,000
Sales	154,000	144,000	130,000
Net income	5,000	3,800	25,000

Compute Justin's total asset turnover ratio and its return on assets for 2007 and 2008. What do these results suggest to you about Justin's Jewellery Company?

■ **LO4, 6**

E3–23 Analyzing the Effects of Transactions Using T-Accounts and Interpreting the Total Asset Turnover Ratio as a Financial Analyst

Internet Marketing Inc. (IMI), which has been operating for three years, provides marketing consulting services worldwide for dot-com companies. You are a financial analyst assigned to report on the effectiveness of IMI's management team at managing its assets. At the start of 2007 (its fourth year), IMI's T-account balances were as follows. Dollars are in thousands.

ASSETS

Cash		Accounts Receivable		Long-Term Investments	
3,000		10,000		8,000	

LIABILITIES

Accounts Payable		Unearned Revenue		Long-Term Notes Payable	
	3,000		6,000		2,000

SHAREHOLDERS' EQUITY

Share Capital		Retained Earnings	
	6,000		4,000

REVENUES

Consulting Fee Revenue		Investment Income	

EXPENSES

Wages Expense		Travel Expense		Utilities Expense	

Rent Expense	

Required:

1. Using the data from these T-accounts, complete the accounting equation on January 1, 2007.

      Assets $_____ = Liabilities $_____ + Shareholders' Equity $_____

2. Enter the following 2007 transactions in the T-accounts:
   a. Received $7,700 cash from clients on account.
   b. Provided $70,000 in services to clients; received $50,000 in cash and the rest on account.
   c. Received $500 in income on investments.
   d. Paid $20,000 in wages, $21,800 in travel, $12,000 rent, and $2,000 on accounts payable.
   e. Received a utility bill for $1,300 for the current month.
   f. Paid $600 in dividends to shareholders.
   g. Received $2,000 in cash from clients in advance of services that IMI will provide next year.

3. Compute ending balances in the T-accounts to determine the missing amounts on December 31, 2007:

   Revenues $_____ − Expenses $_____ = Net Income $_____

   Assets $_____ = Liabilities $_____ + Shareholders' Equity $_____

4. Calculate the total asset turnover ratio for 2007. If the company had an asset turnover ratio of 2.00 in 2006 and of 1.80 in 2005, what does your computation suggest to you about IMI? What would you state in your report?

E3–24 **Inferring Transactions and Computing Effects Using T-Accounts**　　　■ LO4
A recent annual report of a leading business and financial news company included the following accounts. Dollars are in millions.

Accounts Receivable			Prepaid Expenses			Unearned Revenue		
1/1	313		1/1	25			240	1/1
	2,573	?		43	?	?	328	
12/31	295		12/31	26			253	

Required:

1. Describe the typical transactions that affect each T-account (that is, the economic events that occur to make these accounts increase and decrease).

2. Compute the missing amounts for each T-account.

E3–25 **Computing and Interpreting the Total Asset Turnover Ratio and the Return on Assets Ratio**　　　■ LO6
Bianca Corp. and Uzma, Inc., operate in the same industry. The companies' total assets, revenue, and net income for the years 2006–2009 are provided below. All amounts are in thousands of dollars.

ANALYSIS

Bianca Corp.	2009	2008	2007	2006
Total assets	$ 40,000	$ 50,000	$ 60,000	$ 65,000
Revenue	130,000	144,000	154,000	150,000
Net income	25,000	3,800	5,000	4,800
Uzma, Inc.				
Total assets	$ 65,000	$ 60,000	$ 50,000	$ 40,000
Revenue	150,000	154,000	144,000	130,000
Net income	4,800	5,000	3,800	25,000

Required:

1. Compute the total asset turnover ratio and the return on assets ratio for each company for each of the years 2007, 2008, and 2009.

2. Based on the two sets of ratios that you computed, which company was more efficient in managing its assets during the period 2006–2009? Explain.

PROBLEMS

LO4

P3–1 Recording Non-Quantitative Journal Entries (AP3–1)

The following list includes a series of accounts for Heiss Corporation, which has been operating for three years. These accounts are listed and numbered for identification, and followed by a series of transactions. For each transaction, indicate the account(s) that should be debited and credited by entering the appropriate account number(s) to the right of each transaction. If no journal entry is needed, use number 16. The first transaction is used as an example.

Account No.	Account Title	Account No.	Account Title
1	Cash	9	Wages payable
2	Accounts receivable	10	Income taxes payable
3	Supplies inventory on hand	11	Share capital
4	Prepaid expense	12	Retained earnings
5	Equipment	13	Service revenue
6	Patents	14	Operating expenses
7	Accounts payable	15	Income tax expense
8	Note payable	16	None of the above

Transactions		Debit	Credit
a.	Example: Purchased equipment for use in the business; paid one-third cash and signed a note payable for the balance.	5	1, 8
b.	Issued shares to new investors.	___	___
c.	Paid cash for salaries and wages earned this period.	___	___
d.	Collected cash for services performed this period.	___	___
e.	Collected cash on accounts receivable for services previously performed.	___	___
f.	Performed services this period on credit.	___	___
g.	Paid operating expenses incurred this period.	___	___
h.	Paid cash on accounts payable for expenses previously incurred.	___	___
i.	Incurred operating expenses this period to be paid next period.	___	___
j.	Purchased supplies inventory to be used later; paid cash.	___	___
k.	Used some of the supplies inventory for operations.	___	___
l.	Purchased a patent (an intangible asset); paid cash.	___	___
m.	Made a payment on the equipment note in (a); the payment was part principal and part interest expense.	___	___
n.	Paid three-fourths of the income tax expense for the year; the balance will be paid next year.	___	___
o.	On the last day of the current period, paid cash for an insurance policy covering the next year.	___	___

LO4

P3–2 Recording Journal Entries (AP3–2)

Chad Polovick organized a new company, CollegeCaps, Inc. The company operates a small store in an area mall and specializes in baseball-type caps with logos printed on them. Chad, who is never without a cap, believes that his target market is college students. You have been hired to record the transactions occurring in the first two weeks of operations.

May 1	Issued 1,000 shares for $35 per share.
May 1	Borrowed $40,000 from the bank to provide additional funding to begin operations. The interest rate is 10 percent annually; principal and interest are due in 24 months.
May 1	Paid $1,200 for the current month's rent and another $1,200 for next month's rent.
May 1	Paid $1,800 for a one-year fire insurance policy (recorded as a prepaid expense).
May 3	Purchased furniture and fixtures for the store for $18,000 on account. The amount is due within 30 days.

May 4   Purchased a supply of University of Waterloo, York University, and Saint Mary's University baseball caps for the store for $2,100 cash.

May 5   Placed advertisements in local college newspapers for a total of $360 cash.

May 9   Sold caps totalling $500, half of which was charged on account. The cost of the caps sold was $250.

May 10   Made full payment for the furniture and fixtures purchased on account on May 3.

May 14   Received $100 from a customer on account.

Required:

1. Prepare a journal entry to record each of the transactions. Be sure to categorize each account as an asset (A), liability (L), shareholders' equity (SE), revenue (R), or expense (E).

2. Complete the tabulation below for each of the transactions, indicating the effect (+ for increase and − for decrease) of each transaction. Write NE if there is no effect. The first transaction is provided as an example. (Remember that A = L + SE, R − E = NI, and NI affects SE through Retained Earnings.)

	Balance Sheet			Income Statement		
	Assets	Liabilities	Shareholders' Equity	Revenues	Expenses	Net Income
May 1	+	NE	+	NE	NE	NE

P3–3 Analyzing the Effects of Transactions Using T-Accounts, Preparing an Income Statement, Evaluating the Total Asset Turnover Ratio and the Return on Assets as a Manager (AP3–3)

Paula Abboud, a connoisseur of fine chocolate, opened Paula's Passions Inc. in Collegetown on February 1, 2007. The shop specializes in a selection of gourmet chocolate candies and a line of gourmet ice cream. You have been hired as manager. Your duties include maintaining the store's financial records. The following transactions occurred in February 2008, the first month of operations.

a. Received contributions of $15,000 in total from four shareholders to form the corporation.

b. Paid store rent for three months at $800 per month (recorded as prepaid rent).

c. Purchased supplies for $400 cash.

d. Purchased on account and received candy for $5,000, due in 60 days.

e. Obtained a $10,000 loan at the bank and signed a note at 12-percent annual interest. The principal and interest are due in a lump sum in two years.

f. Used the money from (*e*) to purchase a computer for $2,000 (for recordkeeping and inventory tracking). The rest was used to buy furniture and fixtures for the store.

g. Placed a grand opening advertisement in the local paper for $425 cash.

h. Made sales on Valentine's Day totalling $1,800; $1,525 was in cash and the rest on accounts. The cost of the candy sold was $1,000.

i. Made a $500 payment on accounts payable.

j. Incurred and paid employee wages of $510.

k. Collected accounts receivable of $50 from customers.

l. Made a repair on one of the display cases for $134 cash.

m. Made cash sales of $2,600 during the rest of the month. The cost of the goods sold was $1,400.

Required:

1. Set up appropriate T-accounts for Cash, Accounts Receivable, Supplies, Merchandise Inventory, Prepaid Rent, Equipment, Furniture and Fixtures, Accounts Payable, Notes Payable, Share Capital, Sales Revenue, Cost of Goods Sold (Expense), Advertising Expense, Wages Expense, and Repair Expense. All accounts begin with zero balances.

2. Record in the T-accounts the effects of each transaction for Paula's Passions in February, referencing each transaction in the accounts with the transaction letter. Show the ending balances in the T-accounts.

3. Prepare an income statement for February 2008.

4. Write a short memo to Paula offering your opinion on the results of operations during the first month of business.

5. After three years in business, you are being evaluated for a promotion. One measure is how efficiently you managed the assets of the business. The following data are available:

	2010*	2009	2008
Total assets	$80,000	$45,000	$35,000
Total liabilities	45,000	20,000	15,000
Total shareholders' equity	35,000	25,000	20,000
Total sales	85,000	75,000	50,000
Net income	20,000	10,000	4,000

*At the end of 2010, Paula decided to open a second store, requiring loans and inventory purchases prior to the opening in early 2011.

Compute the total asset turnover ratio and the return on assets for 2009 and 2010 and evaluate the results. Do you think you should be promoted? Why?

LO4

ANALYSIS

P3–4 Analyzing the Effects of Transactions on the Cash Flow Statement (AP3–4)
Refer to P3–3.

Required:
Use the following chart to identify whether each of the transactions in P3–3 results in a cash flow effect from operating (O), investing (I), or financing (F) activities, and indicate the direction and the effect on cash (+ for increase and − for decrease). If there is no cash flow effect, write *none*. The first transaction is provided as an example.

Transaction	Operating, Investing, or Financing Effect	Direction and Amount of the Effect
(a)	F	+15,000

LO4, 5

Canada Post

e**X**cel

P3–5 Analyzing the Effects of Transactions Using T-Accounts, Preparing Financial Statements, and Evaluating the Total Asset Turnover and Return on Assets Ratios (AP3–5)
The following are several March 31, 2008, account balances (in millions of dollars) from a recent annual report of Canada Post Corporation, followed by several typical transactions. The corporation's vision is described in the annual report as follows:

Canada Post will be a world leader in providing innovative physical and electronic delivery solutions, creating value for our customers, employees, and all Canadians.

Account	Balance	Account	Balance
Long-term assets	$1,671	Equity of Canada	$1,394
Accounts payable	400	Receivables	555
Prepaid expenses	207	Other non-current assets	1,467
Accrued expenses payable	554	Cash	474
Long-term debt	76	Investments	230
Deferred revenues	148	Other non-current liabilities	2,032

These accounts are not necessarily in good order and have normal debit or credit balances. The following hypothetical transactions (in millions of dollars) occurred the next month (from April 1, 2008, to April 30, 2008):

a. Provided delivery service to customers, receiving $720 in accounts receivable and $60 in cash.

b. Purchased new equipment costing $816; signed a long-term note.

c. Paid $74 cash to rent equipment, with $64 for rental this month and the rest for rent for the first few days in May.

d. Spent $396 cash to maintain and repair facilities and equipment during the month.

e. Collected $652 from customers on account.

f. Borrowed $90 by signing a long-term note.

g. Paid employees $380 during the month.

h. Purchased for cash and used $49 in supplies.

i. Paid $184 on accounts payable.

j. Ordered $72 in spare parts and supplies.

Required:

1. Set up T-accounts for the preceding list and enter the respective balances. (*Note:* A deficit reflects accumulated losses instead of accumulated profits as in retained earnings.) (You will need additional T-accounts for income statement accounts.)

2. For each transaction, record the effects in the T-accounts. Label each using the letter of the transaction. Compute ending balances.

3. Prepare in good form a multiple-step income statement for April 2008.

4. Prepare in good form a classified balance sheet as at April 30, 2008.

5. Prepare the operating activities section of the cash flow statement for April 2008, and explain the difference between the cash flow from operating activities and the net income computed in requirement 3.

6. Compute the company's total asset turnover ratio and its return on assets ratio. What do these ratios suggest to you about Canada Post?

P3–6 **Determining and Interpreting the Effects of Transactions on Income Statement Categories and Return on Assets (AP3–6)**

Apple Computer popularized both the personal computer and the easy-to-use graphic interface. Today it competes against many companies that rely on Intel microprocessors and the Windows operating system. The company's income statement for a recent year is presented below (in millions of US dollars).

■ **LO4, 6**

Apple Computer

ANALYSIS

Net sales	$13,931
Cost of sales	9,888
Gross margin	4,043
Operating expenses:	
Research and development	534
Selling, general, and administrative	1,859
Total operating expenses	2,393
Operating income	1,650
Other income and expense:	
Interest and other income, net	165
Income before provision for income taxes	1,815
Provision for income taxes	480
Net income	$ 1,335

Required:

Assume that the following hypothetical *additional* transactions occurred during the fiscal year. Complete the following tabulation, indicating the sign of the effect of each additional transaction (+ for increase, − for decrease, and NE for no effect). Consider each item independently and ignore income taxes.

a. Recorded sales on account of $700 and related cost of goods sold of $475.

b. Incurred additional research and development expense of $100, which was paid in cash.

c. Issued additional common shares for $350 cash.

d. Declared and paid dividends of $90.

Transaction	Gross Profit	Operating Income (Loss)	Return on Assets
a.			
b.			
c.			
d.			

LO5, 6

Barrick Gold

Sleeman Breweries

Le Groupe Jean Coutu

ANALYSIS

P3–7 Computing and Analyzing the Total Asset Turnover Ratio and the Return on Assets Ratio (AP3–7)

A summary of selected historical results is presented below for three Canadian companies: Barrick Gold, Sleeman Breweries, and Le Groupe Jean Coutu. Each of these companies has grown in size over time by acquiring assets and investing in other companies. (Amounts are in millions of dollars.)

	2005	2004	2003	2002	2001	2000
Barrick Gold						
Total assets	$6,862	$6,287	$5,358	$5,261	$5,202	$5,393
Total revenue	2,350	1,932	2,035	1,967	1,989	1,936
Net income (loss)	401	248	200	193	96	(1,189)
Operating cash flow	726	509	519	588	588	940
Sleeman Breweries	**2005**	**2004**	**2003**	**2002**	**2001**	**2000**
Total assets	$308	$300	$243	$220	$198	$182
Total revenue	207	213	185	157	142	134
Net income	8	14	12	12	10	9
Operating cash flow	16	14	14	13	19	12
Le Groupe Jean Coutu	**2005**	**2004**	**2003**	**2002**	**2001**	**2000**
Total assets	$5,695	$1,344	$1,723	$1,662	$1,231	$1,033
Total revenue	9,617	3,043	4,052	3,481	2,924	1,578
Net income	104	133	164	140	105	86
Operating cash flow	222	186	214	119	135	89

Required:

1. Complete the following table by computing the total asset turnover ratio and the return on assets ratio for each company for each of the years 2004 and 2005.

	2005	2004	2003	2002	2001
Barrick Gold					
Total Asset Turnover Ratio			0.38	0.38	0.38
Return on Assets (ROA)			3.77%	3.69%	1.81%
Sleeman Breweries					
Total Asset Turnover Ratio			0.80	0.75	0.75
Return on Assets (ROA)			5.18%	5.74%	5.26%
Le Groupe Jean Coutu					
Total Asset Turnover Ratio			2.39	2.41	2.58
Return on Assets (ROA)			9.69%	9.68%	9.28%

2. Based on the computed ratios, rank these companies from most successful to least successful in implementing their growth strategies and in their effectiveness in utilizing their assets.

3. Which of these three companies appears to be is in the best position at the end of 2005 to pay off its short-term liabilities? What additional information would help you provide a more definite answer to this requirement? Explain.

■ **LO4, 6**

Cedar Fair

P3–8 Recording Journal Entries and Identifying Effects on the Total Assets Turnover Ratio

Cedar Fair, L. P. (Limited Partnership), owns and operates four seasonal amusement parks: Cedar Point in Ohio, Valleyfair near Minneapolis/St. Paul, Dorney Park and Wildwater Kingdom near Allentown, Pennsylvania, and Worlds of Fun/Oceans of Fun in Kansas City.

The following are summarized transactions similar to those that occurred in 2007 (amounts in thousands of dollars):

a. Guests at the parks paid $292,408 cash in admissions.

b. The primary operating expenses (such as employee wages, utilities, and repairs and maintenance) for the year 2007 were $243,643, with $231,692 paid in cash and the rest on account.

c. Interest paid on long-term debt was $26,205.

d. The parks sell food and merchandise and operate games. The cash received in 2007 for these combined activities was $219,094.

e. The cost of products sold during the year was $57,606.

f. Cedar Fair purchased and built additional buildings, rides, and equipment during 2007, paying $75,655 in cash.

g. The most significant assets for the company are land, buildings, rides, and equipment. Therefore, a large expense for Cedar Fair is amortization expense (related to the using of these assets to generate revenues during the year). In 2007, the amount was $55,765 (credit Accumulated Amortization).

h. Guests may stay at accommodations owned by the company at the parks. In 2007, Accommodations Revenue was $57,205; $56,045 was paid by the guests in cash and the rest was on account.

i. Cedar Fair paid $2,900 on notes payable.

j. The company purchased $57,652 in food and merchandise inventory for the year, paying $56,500 in cash and the rest on account.

k. The selling, general, and administrative expenses (such as the president's salary and advertising for the parks, those not classified as operating expenses) for 2007 were $73,258; $72,851 was paid in cash and the rest was on account.

l. Cedar Fair paid $10,804 on accounts payable during the year.

Required:

1. Prepare a journal entry to record each of these transactions. Use the letter of each transaction as its reference.

2. Indicate the direction of the effect (increase, decrease, or no effect) of each of the transactions (a) through (l) on the total asset turnover ratio, and provide an explanation for your answer. Cedar Fair's total asset turnover ratio was 0.56 in 2006. For example, transaction (a) increases the ratio. Both sales and total assets would increase. Since the ratio is less than 1.0, the increase in sales (the numerator) is proportionally higher than the increase in total assets (the denominator).

P3–9 Analyzing the Effects of Transactions on Cash Flow Statement

■ **LO6**

Refer to P3–8, and use the following chart to identify whether each transaction in P3–8 results in a cash flow effect from operating (O), investing (I), or financing (F) activities, and indicate the direction and amount of the effect on cash (+ for increase and − for decrease). If there is no cash flow effect, write *none*. The first transaction is provided as an example.

ANALYSIS

Transaction	Operating, Investing, or Financing Effect	Direction and Amount of the Effect
(a)	O	+292,408

ALTERNATE PROBLEMS

AP3–1 Recording Non-Quantitative Journal Entries (P3–1)

■ **LO4**

The following is a series of accounts for Ortiz & Ortiz, Incorporated, which has been operating for two years. The accounts are listed and numbered for identification, followed by a series of transactions. For each transaction, indicate the account(s) that should be debited and credited by entering the appropriate account number(s) to the right of each transaction. If no journal entry is needed, write *none* after the transaction. The first transaction is given as an example.

Account No.	Account Title	Account No.	Account Title
1	Cash	9	Wages payable
2	Accounts receivable	10	Income taxes payable
3	Supplies inventory	11	Share capital
4	Prepaid expense	12	Retained earnings
5	Buildings	13	Service revenue
6	Land	14	Operating expenses
7	Accounts payable	15	Income tax expense
8	Mortgage payable		

Transactions	Debit	Credit
a. Example: Issued shares to new investors.	1	11
b. Performed services this period on credit.		
c. Purchased (but did not use) supplies this period on credit.		
d. Prepaid a fire insurance policy this period to cover the next 12 months.		
e. Purchased a building this period with a 20-percent cash down payment and a mortgage loan for the balance.		
f. Collected cash this year for services rendered and recorded in the prior year.		
g. Paid cash this period for wages earned and recorded last period.		
h. Paid cash for operating expenses charged on accounts payable in the prior period.		
i. Paid cash for operating expenses charged on accounts payable in the current period.		
j. Incurred and recorded operating expenses on credit to be paid next period.		
k. Collected cash at the point of sale for services rendered.		
l. Used supplies from inventory to clean the offices.		
m. Recorded income taxes for this period to be paid at the beginning of the next period.		
n. Declared and paid a cash dividend this period.		
o. Made a payment on the building, which was part principal repayment and part interest.		
p. A shareholder sold some shares this period to another person for an amount above the original issuance price.		

■ LO4   **AP3–2   Recording Journal Entries (P3–2)**

Rhonda Bennett is the president of ServicePro, Inc., a company that provides temporary employees for not-for-profit companies. ServicePro has been operating for five years; its revenues are increasing with each passing year. You have been hired to help Rhonda in analyzing the following transactions for the first two weeks of April:

April	2	Purchased office supplies for $500 on account.
	3	Received the telephone bill for $245.
	5	Billed United Way $1,950 for temporary services provided.
	8	Paid $250 for supplies purchased and recorded on account last period.
	8	Placed an advertisement in the local paper for $400 cash.
	9	Purchased a new computer for the office costing $2,300 cash.
	10	Paid employee wages of $1,200. Of this amount, $200 had been earned and recorded in the prior period.
	11	Received $1,000 on account from United Way.
	12	Purchased land as the site of a future office for $10,000. Paid $2,000 down and signed a note payable for the balance. The note is due in five years and has an annual interest rate of 10 percent.

13   Issued 2,000 additional shares for $40 per share in anticipation of building a new office.

14   Billed Family & Children's Service $2,000 for services rendered.

Required:

1. Prepare a journal entry to record each of the transactions. Be sure to categorize each account as an asset (A), liability (L), shareholders' equity (SE), revenue (R), or expense (E).

2. Complete the tabulation below for each of the transactions, indicating the effect (+ for increase and − for decrease) of each transaction. Write NE if there is no effect. The first transaction is provided as an example. (Remember that A = L + SE, R − E = NI, and NI affects SE through Retained Earnings.)

	Balance Sheet			Income Statement		
	Assets	Liabilities	Shareholders' Equity	Revenues	Expenses	Net Income
April 2	+	+	NE	NE	NE	NE

AP3–3   Analyzing the Effects of Transactions Using T-Accounts, Preparing an Income Statement, Evaluating the Total Asset Turnover Ratio and the Return on Assets as a Manager (P3–3)

■ LO4, 6

Green Stables, Inc., was established on April 1, 2007. The company provides stables, care for animals, and grounds for riding and showing horses. You have been hired as the new assistant controller. The following transactions for April 2007 are provided for your review.

a. Received contributions from five investors of $75,000 in cash ($15,000 each), a barn valued at $100,000, and land valued at $75,000. Each investor received 5,000 shares.

b. Built a small barn for $50,000. The company paid half the amount in cash and signed a three-year note payable for the balance on April 1, 2007.

c. Provided animal care services, all on credit, for $15,260.

d. Rented stables to customers who cared for their own animals and received cash payment of $16,300.

e. Received from a customer $1,800 to board her horse in April, May, and June (record as unearned revenue).

f. Purchased straw (a supply inventory) on account for $4,630.

g. Paid $840 in cash for water utilities expense incurred in the month.

h. Paid $1,700 on accounts payable for previous purchases.

i. Received $3,000 from customers on accounts receivable.

j. Paid $5,600 in wages to employees who worked during the month.

k. Purchased a one-year insurance policy for $1,800 at the end of the month.

l. Received an electric utility bill for $2,130 for usage in April; the bill will be paid next month.

m. Paid $500 cash dividend to each of the investors at the end of the month.

Required:

1. Set up appropriate T-accounts. All accounts begin with zero balances.

2. Record in the T-accounts the effects of each transaction for Green Stables in April, referencing each transaction in the accounts with the transaction letter. Show the ending balances in the T-accounts.

3. Prepare an income statement and a statement of retained earnings at the end of April, 2007, as well as a classified balance sheet as at April 30, 2007.

4. Write a short memo to the five owners offering your opinion on the results of operations during the first month of business.

5. After three years in business, you are being evaluated for a promotion to chief financial officer. One measure is how efficiently you managed the assets of the business. The following data are available:

	2009*	2008	2007
Total assets	$480,000	$320,000	$300,000
Total liabilities	125,000	28,000	30,000
Total shareholders' equity	355,000	292,000	270,000
Total sales	450,000	400,000	360,000
Net income	50,000	30,000	(10,000)

*At the end of 2009, Green Stables decided to build an indoor riding arena for giving lessons year-round. The company borrowed construction funds from a local bank and the arena was opened in early 2010.

Compute the total asset turnover ratio and the return on assets for 2008 and 2009 and evaluate the results. Do you think you should be promoted? Why?

■ **LO4**   **AP3–4** **Analyzing the Effects of Transactions on the Cash Flow Statement (P3–4)**
Refer to AP3–3.

ANALYSIS

Required:
Use the following chart to identify whether each of the transactions in AP3–3 results in a cash flow effect from operating (O), investing (I), or financing (F) activities, and indicate the direction and the effect on cash (+ for increase and − for decrease). If there is no cash flow effect, write *none*. The first transaction is provided as an example.

Transaction	Operating, Investing, or Financing Effect	Direction and Amount of the Effect
(a)	F	+75,000

■ **LO4, 5, 6**   **AP3–5** **Analyzing the Effects of Transactions Using T-Accounts, Preparing Financial Statements, and Evaluating the Total Asset Turnover and Return on Assets Ratios (P3–5)**

Petro-Canada

The following are the summary account balances from a recent balance sheet of Petro-Canada. The accounts are followed by a list of hypothetical transactions for the month of January 2008. The following accounts are shown in millions of dollars.

Cash	$ 635	Accounts payable	$1,822
Long-term debt	2,229	Income tax payable	300
Accounts receivable	1,503	Prepaid expenses	16
Inventories	551	Retained earnings	4,266
Future income taxes (credit)	2,518	Other long-term assets	1,126
Property and equipment, net	10,759	Share capital	3,455

The accounts have normal debit or credit balances, but they are not necessarily listed in good order.

a. Purchased new equipment costing $150 million by issuing long-term debt.

b. Received $900 million on accounts receivable.

c. Received and paid the telephone bills for $1 million.

d. Earned $500 million in sales to customers on account; cost of sales was $300 million.

e. Paid employees $100 million for wages earned in January.

f. Paid half of the income taxes payable.

g. Purchased inventory for $23 million on account.

h. Prepaid rent for February for a warehouse for $12 million.

i. Paid $10 million of long-term debt and $1 million in interest on the debt.

j. Purchased a patent (an intangible asset) for $8 million cash.

Required:

1. Set up T-accounts for the preceding list and enter the respective balances. (You will need additional T-accounts for income statement accounts.)

2. For each transaction, record the effects in the T-accounts. Label each using the letter of the transaction. Compute ending balances.

3. Prepare in good form a multiple-step income statement, and a statement of retained earnings for the month of January 2008, as well as a classified balance sheet as at January 31, 2008.

4. Prepare the operating activities section of the cash flow statement for January 2008, and explain the difference between the cash flow from operating activities and the net income computed in requirement 3.

5. Compute the company's total asset turnover ratio and its return on assets. What do these ratios suggest to you about Petro-Canada?

AP3–6 Determining and Interpreting the Effects of Transactions on Income Statement Categories and Return on Assets (P3–6)

Barnes & Noble, Inc., revolutionized bookselling by making its stores public spaces and community institutions where customers may browse, find a book, relax over a cup of coffee, talk with authors, and join discussion groups. Today it is fighting increasing competition not only from traditional sources but also from online booksellers. Presented here is a recent income statement (in millions).

■ **LO4, 6**

Barnes & Noble, Inc.

ANALYSIS

Net sales	$5,103
Cost of sales	3,533
Gross margin	1,570
Operating expenses:	
Selling and administrative	1,134
Depreciation and amortization	173
Pre-opening expenses	11
Total operating expenses	1,318
Operating profit	252
Other income and expense:	
Interest expense	2
Income before provision for income taxes	250
Provision for income taxes	102
Net income	$ 148

Required:

Assume that the following hypothetical *additional* transactions occurred during the fiscal year. Complete the following tabulation, indicating the sign of the effect of each *additional* transaction (+ for increase, − for decrease, and NE for no effect). Consider each item independently and ignore income taxes.

a. Recorded and received interest income of $14.

b. Purchased $95 of additional inventory on open account.

c. Recorded and paid additional advertising expense of $19.

d. Issued additional common shares for $90 cash.

Transaction	Operating Income (Loss)	Net Income	Return on Assets
a.			
b.			
c.			
d.			

AP3–7 Computing and Analyzing the Total Asset Turnover Ratio and the Return on Assets Ratio (P3–7)

A summary of selected historical results is presented below for three Canadian companies: Canada Post, Research In Motion, and Andrés Wines. Each of these companies has grown in size over time by acquiring assets and investing in other companies. (Amounts are in millions of dollars.)

■ **LO5, 6**

Canada Post
Research In Motion
Andrés Wines

ANALYSIS

	2006	2005	2004	2003	2002
Canada Post					
Total assets	$4,604	$4,314	$4,558	$4,102	$3,677
Total revenue	6,944	6,651	6,344	6,154	4,441
Net income (loss)	199	147	253	71	67
Research In Motion	**2006**	**2005**	**2004**	**2003**	**2002**
Total assets	$2,312	$2,627	$1,937	$ 860	$ 948
Total revenue	2,066	1,350	595	307	294
Net income	382	213	53	(149)	(18)
Andrés Wines	**2006**	**2005**	**2004**	**2003**	**2002**
Total assets	$ 222	$ 162	$ 146	$ 132	$ 69
Total revenue	212	168	156	148	139
Net income	6	8	9	7	5

Required:

1. Complete the following table by computing the total asset turnover ratio and the return on assets ratio for each company for each of the years 2005 and 2006.

	2006	2005	2004	2003
Canada Post				
Total Asset Turnover Ratio			1.47	1.58
Return on Assets (ROA)			5.84%	1.83%
Research In Motion				
Total Asset Turnover Ratio			0.43	0.34
Return on Assets (ROA)			3.79%	−16.48%
Andrés Wines				
Total Asset Turnover Ratio			1.12	1.47
Return on Assets (ROA)			6.47%	6.97%

2. Based on the computed ratios, rank these companies from most successful to least successful in implementing their growth strategies and in their effectiveness in utilizing their assets to generate revenue and net income.

3. Assume that you are interested in investing in one of these three companies, which company would you choose? Write a brief report to justify your choice.

CASES AND PROJECTS

FINDING AND INTERPRETING ACCOUNTING INFORMATION

■ LO2, 4, 6   **CP3–1**   **Finding Financial Information**

The Forzani Group Ltd.

ANALYSIS

Refer to the financial statements and the accompanying notes of The Forzani Group Ltd. (FGL), available on the Online Learning Centre Web site at **www.mcgrawhill.ca/olc/libby/student/resources**.

Required:

1. State the amount of the largest expense on the 2007 income statement and describe the transaction represented by the expense.

2. Prepare the journal entry for interest expense for the year ended January 28, 2007 (for this question, assume that the amount has not yet been paid).

3. Assuming that all net sales are on credit, how much cash did FGL collect from customers? (*Hint:* Use a T-account of accounts receivable to infer collection.)

4. A shareholder has complained that "dividends should be paid because the company had net earnings of $35.22 million. Since this amount is all cash, more of it should go to the owners." Explain why the shareholder's assumption that earnings equal net cash inflow is valid. If you believe that the assumption is not valid, state so and support your position concisely.

5. Describe and contrast the purpose of an income statement versus a balance sheet.

6. Compute the company's total asset turnover ratio and its return on assets for 2007. Explain their meaning.

CP3–2 Comparing Companies

Refer to the financial statements and the accompanying notes of Van Houtte Inc. given in Appendix B, and of The Forzani Group Ltd. on the Online Learning Centre Web site at **www.mcgrawhill.ca/olc/libby/student/resources**.

■ **LO2, 3, 5**

The Forzani Group vs. Van Houtte

ANALYSIS

Required:

1. What title does each company call its income statement? Explain what the term *consolidated* means.

2. Which company had higher net income at the end of its fiscal year?

3. What were the primary causes of the change in sales as reported by the company in the Management Discussion and Analysis section of the annual report?

4. Compute the total asset turnover ratio and the return on assets for each company for the most recent year. Which company is utilizing assets more effectively to generate sales and net income? Explain.

5. How much cash was provided by operating activities by each company during the most recent year? What was the percentage change in operating cash flows for each company during the most recent year? (*Hint*: Percentage Change = [Current Year Amount − Prior Year Amount] ÷ Prior Year Amount.)

6. How much did each company pay in income taxes during the last fiscal year reported in the financial statements? Where did you find this information?

7. What segments does The Forzani Group report in the notes? What does Van Houtte report about segments?

CP3–3 Comparing a Company Over Time

Refer to the annual report for Van Houtte Inc. (in Appendix B).

■ **LO6**

Van Houtte

ANALYSIS

Required:

1. At the beginning of the Management's Discussions and Analysis section of Van Houtte's annual report, the Financial Highlights provide selected financial data for the past three years. Compute the total asset turnover ratio for fiscal years 2006 and 2007.

2. In Chapter 2, we discussed the debt-to-equity ratio. Compute this ratio for fiscal years 2006 and 2007.

3. What do your results from the trends in the two ratios suggest to you about Van Houtte?

FINANCIAL REPORTING AND ANALYSIS CASES

CP3–4 Interpreting the Financial Press

The October 4, 2004 edition of *Business Week* presented an article titled "Fuzzy Numbers" on issues related to accrual accounting and its weaknesses that have led some corporate executives to manipulate estimates in their favour, sometimes fraudulently. You can access the article at **www.mcgrawhill.ca/olc/libby/student/resources**.

■ **LO3**

Business Week

Required:

Read the article and then answer the following questions:

1. What is accrual accounting?

2. What does the article's title "Fuzzy Numbers" mean?

3. What does the article suggest about the reforms adopted by the U.S. Congress and the SEC?

■ **LO4, 6**

Volkswagen

ANALYSIS

CP3–5 Using Financial Reports: Interpreting Challenging International Financial Statements
Your cousin, an engineering major, has inherited some money and wants to invest in an auto company. She has never taken an accounting course and has asked you to help her compare a North American automaker's financial statements to those of German automaker Volkswagen. Find below the (adapted) comparative income statement and balance sheet of the Volkswagen Group for a recent fiscal year.

Required:
Write a letter to your cousin explaining the similarities and differences you would expect to find if you compared Volkswagen's financial statements to those of a company based in North America. Do you think that the underlying accounting principles in Germany and North America would be similar or different? Explain.

Statement of Earnings (adapted) of the Volkswagen Group
for the Fiscal Year Ended December 31
(in millions of €)

	Current Year	Last Year
Sales	87,153	86,948
Cost of sales	76,493	72,950
Gross profit	**+10,660**	**+13,998**
Distribution expenses	7,846	7,560
Administrative expenses	2,724	2,155
Other operating income	4,403	4,137
Other operating expenses	3,163	3,659
Operating profit	**+1,780**	**+4,761**
Share of profit and losses of Group companies	+511	+534
Interest results	+93	−466
Other financial result	−855	−843
Financial result	**−251**	**−775**
Profit before tax	**+1,529**	**+3,986**
Income tax expense	411	1,389
Profit after tax	**+1,118**	**+2,597**
Minority interests	−23	−13
Net profit attributable to shareholders	+1,095	+2,584

Balance sheet (adapted) of the Volkswagen Group
At December 31
(in million of €)

	Current Year	Last Year
Assets		
Fixed assets		
Intangible assets	8,202	7,736
Tangible assets	23,852	22,842
Investment in Group companies	3,360	3,397
Other financial assets	607	588
	36,021	34,563
Leasing and rental assets	8,906	8,445
Current assets		
Inventories	11,670	10,677
Receivables and other assets	50,063	47,314
Securities	3,148	3,192
Cash and cash equivalents	7,536	2,987
	72,417	64,170
Prepayments and deferred charges	1,792	1,718
Total assets	119,136	108,896

(continued)

Equity and liabilities		
Capital and reserves		
Subscribed capital	1,089	1,089
Capital reserve	4,451	4,451
Revenue reserves	14,171	13,905
Accumulated profits	4,719	5,189
	24,430	24,634
Minority interests	104	57
Provisions	22,810	22,349
Deferred tax liabilities	2,472	2,558
Liabilities	68,998	58,965
Deferred income	322	333
Total equity and liabilities	119,136	108,896

CRITICAL THINKING CASES

CP3–6 **Making a Decision as a Bank Loan Officer: Analyzing and Restating Financial Statements That Have Major Deficiencies (A Challenging Case)**

Tom Martinez started and operated a small boat repair service company during 2009. He is interested in obtaining a $100,000 loan from your bank to build a dry dock to store boats for customers in the winter months. At the end of the year, he prepared the following statements based on information stored in a large filing cabinet:

■ **LO3, 6**

ANALYSIS

MARTINEZ COMPANY
Profit for 2009

Service fees collected during 2009		$55,000
Cash dividends received		10,000
Total		$65,000
Expense for operations paid during 2009	$22,000	
Cash stolen	500	
New tools purchased during 2009 (cash paid)	1,000	
Supplies purchased for use on service jobs (cash paid)	3,200	
Total		26,700
Profit		$38,300

Assets Owned at the End of 2009

Cash in chequing account	$ 29,300
Service garage (at current market value)	32,000
Tools and equipment	18,000
Land (at current market value)	30,000
Shares in ABC Industrial	130,000
Total	$239,300

The following is a summary of completed transactions:

(a) Received the following contributions to the business from the owner when it was started in exchange for 1,000 shares in the new company:

Building	$21,000	Land	$20,000
Tools and equipment	17,000	Cash	1,000

(b) Earned service fees during 2009 of $87,000; of the cash collected, $20,000 was for deposits from customers on work to be done by Martinez during 2010.

(c) Received the cash dividends on shares of ABC Industrial purchased by Tom Martinez as a personal investment six years earlier.

(d) Incurred expenses during 2009, $61,000.

(e) Determined amount of supplies on hand (unused) at the end of 2009, $700.

Required:

1. Did Martinez prepare the income statement on a cash basis or an accrual basis? Explain how you can tell. Which basis should be used? Explain why.

2. Reconstruct the correct entries under accrual accounting principles and post the effects to T-accounts.

3. Prepare an accrual-based income statement for 2009 and a balance sheet at the end of 2009. Explain (using footnotes) the reason for each change that you make to the income statement.

4. What additional information would assist you in formulating your decision regarding the loan to Mr. Martinez?

5. Based on the revised statements and additional information needed, write a letter to Mr. Martinez explaining your decision at this time regarding the loan.

■ **LO3**

ANALYSIS

CP3–7 Proper Measurement of Income

Paula Manolakos purchased La Forêt Inc., a bakery, from Gianni Fiori. The purchase agreement included a provision that required Paula to pay Gianni 25 percent of the bakery's net income in each of the next five years. The agreement stated that the bakery's net income would be measured in a "fair and reasonable manner," but did not state that it would be measured in accordance with generally accepted accounting principles. Neither Paula nor Gianni was familiar with accounting concepts.

In measuring net income, Paula used the following accounting policies:

a. Revenue was recognized when cash was received from customers. Because of the nature of the business, most customers paid in cash, but a few customers purchased merchandise on account and were allowed to pay in 30 days.

b. Paula set her annual salary at $60,000, which Gianni has agreed was reasonable. She also paid $30,000 per year to her spouse and to each of her two teenaged children. These family members did not work in the business on a regular basis, but they did help during busy periods.

c. Weekly expenditures for eggs, milk, flour, and other supplies were charged directly to Supplies Expense, as were the weekly groceries for Paula's family.

d. The bakery had modern baking equipment valued at $50,000 at the time Paula purchased the company. The income statement for the first year included a $50,000 equipment expense related to these assets.

e. Income taxes expense included the amount paid by the corporation (which was computed correctly), as well as the personal income taxes paid by various members of Paula's family on the salaries they earned for working in the business.

Gianni was disappointed, however, when Paula reported a net income for the first year that was far below his expectations.

Required:

1. Discuss the fairness and reasonableness of Paula's accounting policies. Identify the accounting principle or assumption that may have been violated.

2. Do you think that the net cash flow from operations (cash receipts minus cash payments) is higher or lower than the net income reported by Paula? Explain.

3. What advice would you give Gianni to ensure that the bakery's net income would be measured properly in future years?

■ **LO3**

CP3–8 Evaluating an Ethical Dilemma

Mike Kruk is the manager of a Vancouver regional office for an insurance company. As the regional manager, his compensation package comprises a base salary, commissions, and a bonus when the region sells new policies in excess of its quota. Mike has been under enormous pressure lately, stemming largely from two factors. First, he is experiencing a mounting personal debt due to a family member's illness. Second, compounding his worries, the region's sales of new policies have dipped below the normal quota for the first time in years.

You have been working for Mike for two years, and like everyone else in the office, you consider yourself lucky to work for such a supportive boss. You also feel great sympathy for his personal problems over the last few months. In your position as accountant for the regional office, you are only too aware of the drop in new policy sales and the impact this will have on the manager's bonus. While you are working late at year-end, Mike stops by your office.

Mike asks you to change the manner in which you have accounted for a new property insurance policy for a large local business. A cheque for the premium, substantial in amount, came in the mail on December 31, the last day of the reporting year. The premium covers a period beginning on January 5. You deposited the cheque and correctly debited cash and credited an *unearned revenue* account. Mike says, "Hey, we have the money this year, so why not count the revenue this year? I never did understand why you accountants are so picky about these things anyway. I'd like you to change the way you have recorded the transaction. I want you to credit a *revenue* account. And anyway, I've done favours for you in the past, and I am asking for such a small thing in return." With that, he leaves for the day.

Required:

1. How should you handle this situation?
2. What are the ethical implications of Mike's request?
3. Who are the parties who would be helped or harmed if you complied with the request?
4. If you fail to comply with his request, how will you explain your position to him in the morning?

FINANCIAL REPORTING AND ANALYSIS TEAM PROJECT

CP3–9 **Team Project: Analysis of Income Statements and Ratios**

As a team, select an industry to analyze. Using a Web browser, each team member should acquire the annual report for one publicly traded company in the industry, with each member selecting a different company.

■ **LO2, 3, 5, 6**

ANALYSIS

Required:

On an individual basis, each team member should write a short report that answers the following questions about the selected company. Discuss any patterns across the companies that you as a team observe. Then, as a team, write a short report comparing and contrasting your companies.

1. For the most recent year, what is/are the major revenue account/s? What percentage is each to total operating revenues? (Computed as Revenue A ÷ Total revenues.)

2. For the most recent year, what is/are the major expense account/s? What percentage is each to total operating expenses? (Computed as Expense A ÷ Total expenses.)

3. Ratio Analysis:
   a. What do the total asset turnover and the return on assets ratios measure in general?
   b. Compute these ratios for the last three years.
   c. What do your results suggest about the company?
   d. If available, find the industry ratio for the most recent year, compare it to your results, and discuss why you believe your company differs or is similar to the industry ratio.

4. Describe the company's revenue recognition policy, if reported. (Usually found in note 2 to the financial statements titled Significant Accounting Policies.)

5. The percentage of cash from operating activities to net income measures how liberal (that is, speeding up revenue recognition or delaying expense recognition) or conservative (that is, taking care not to record revenues too early or expenses too late) a company's management is in choosing among various revenue and expense recognition policies. A ratio above 1.0 suggests more conservative policies and below 1.0, more liberal policies. Compute the percentage for the last three years. What do your results suggest about the company's choice of accounting policies?

Adjustments, Financial Statements, and the Quality of Earnings

4

After studying this chapter, you should be able to:

LEARNING OBJECTIVES

1. Utilize an adjusted trial balance to prepare financial statements. p. 162

2. Analyze the adjustments necessary at the end of the period to update balance sheet and income statement accounts. p. 164

3. Prepare an income statement with earnings per share, a statement of retained earnings,

a balance sheet, and supplemental cash flow information. p. 178

4. Compute and interpret the net profit margin ratio and the return on equity ratio. p. 182

5. Explain the closing process at the end of the period. p. 184

The end of the accounting period is a very busy time for Van Houtte (www.vanhoutte.com). The last day of the fiscal year for Van Houtte falls on the Saturday closest to March 31 of each year.[1] The financial statements are not distributed to users on that day, however. They are only released after management and the external auditors make many critical evaluations.

FOCUS COMPANY:

Van Houtte, Inc.

THE BUSIEST TIME OF THE FISCAL YEAR

■ Management must ensure that the correct amounts are reported on the balance sheet and income statement. This often requires estimations, assumptions, and judgments about the timing of revenue and expense recognition and values for assets and liabilities.

■ The auditors have to (1) assess the strength of the controls established by management to safeguard the company's assets and ensure the accuracy of the financial records, and (2) evaluate the appropriateness of estimates and accounting principles used by management in determining revenues and expenses.

Managers of most companies understand the need to present financial information fairly so as not to mislead users. However, since end-of-period adjustments are the most complex portion of the annual recordkeeping process, they are prone to error. External auditors examine the company's records on a test, or sample, basis. To maximize the chance of detecting any errors significant enough to affect users' decisions, auditors allocate more of their testing to transactions most likely to be in error.

Several accounting research studies have documented the most error-prone transactions for medium size manufacturing companies. End-of-period adjustment errors such as failure to provide adequate product warranty liability, failure to include items that should be expensed, and end-of-period transactions recorded in the wrong period (called *cut-off errors*) are in the top category and thus receive much attention from the auditors.

---

[1]A firm's fiscal year does not have to conform to the calendar year (January 1 to December 31). In a recent survey of 200 companies, 52 (26 percent) did not use a December 31 year-end in 2005, including 15 companies that chose a fiscal year-end defined as, for example, "the last Saturday of the month" or "the Sunday closest to the end of the month," which results in financial information covering 52 weeks in some years and 53 weeks in other years. See N. Chlala, A. Lavigne, L. Martel, and C. Byrd, *Financial Reporting in Canada,* 2006. Toronto: The Canadian Institute of Chartered Accountants, p. 24.

For fiscal year 2007, Van Houtte's estimation and auditing process took until June 5, 2007, the date on which the auditor KPMG LLP completed the audit work and signed its audit opinion. At that point, the financial statements were made available to the public.

UNDERSTANDING THE BUSINESS

Managers are responsible for preparing financial statements that are useful to investors, creditors, and others. Financial information is most useful for analyzing the past and predicting the future when it is considered by users to be of *high quality*. High-quality information is relevant (that is, important in the analysis and available in a timely manner) and reliable (that is, verifiable and unbiased in portraying economic reality).

Users expect revenues and expenses to be reported in the proper period based on the revenue and matching principles discussed in Chapter 3. Revenues must be recorded when earned, and expenses must be recorded when incurred, regardless of when cash is received or paid. Many operating activities take place over one accounting period or over several periods, such as using insurance that has been prepaid or owing salaries to employees for past work. Recording these and similar activities daily is often very costly. Hence, companies wait until the end of the period to record *adjustments* to revenue and expense accounts to reflect the proper amounts in the correct period. These entries update the records and are the focus of this chapter.

Analysts, creditors, and investors assess the quality of financial information by determining how *conservative* the management's estimates and judgments are. When alternative methods to measure and report assets, liabilities, revenues, and expenses are available to management, the choices that produce the lower asset and revenue amounts, or the higher liability or expense amounts, lead to lower net income and are considered to be conservative. Conservative estimates and judgments lead to higher-quality financial information. The information must not mislead the users in anticipating that the company will have a stronger financial position or higher earnings potential than actually exists. The effects of management's choices among alternative accounting methods and the use of estimates are presented throughout the rest of this text.

In this chapter, we emphasize the use of the same analytical tools introduced in Chapters 2 and 3 (T-accounts and journal entries) to help you understand how the necessary adjustments are analyzed and recorded at the end of the accounting period. Then we prepare financial statements using adjusted accounts. Finally, we illustrate the process of "closing the books" to prepare the accounting records for the next accounting period.

ORGANIZATION OF THE CHAPTER

Adjusting Revenues and Expenses	**Preparing and Analyzing Financial Statements**	**Closing the Books**
• Accounting Cycle • Unadjusted Trial Balance • Analysis of Adjusting Entries • Van Houtte's Illustration • Materiality and Adjusting Entries	• Income Statement • Statement of Retained Earnings • Balance Sheet • Net Profit Margin Ratio • Return on Equity Ratio	• End of the Accounting Cycle • Post-closing Trial Balance

ADJUSTING REVENUES AND EXPENSES

ACCOUNTING CYCLE

The **ACCOUNTING CYCLE** is the process used by entities to analyze and record transactions, adjust the records at the end of the period, prepare financial statements, and prepare the records for the next cycle.

The **accounting cycle** is the process used by entities to analyze and record transactions, adjust the records at the end of the period, prepare financial statements, and prepare the records for the next cycle. *During* the accounting period, transactions that result in exchanges between the company and other external parties are analyzed and recorded in the general journal in chronological order (journal entries), and the related accounts are updated in the general ledger (T-accounts), similar to our Van Houtte illustrations in Chapters 2 and 3. In this chapter, we examine the *end-of-period* steps that focus primarily on adjustments to record revenues and expenses in the proper period and to update the balance sheet accounts for reporting purposes. Exhibit 4.1 presents the fundamental steps in the accounting cycle.

UNADJUSTED TRIAL BALANCE

■ LEARNING OBJECTIVE 1

Utilize an adjusted trial balance to prepare financial statements.

The first step normally taken at the end of the accounting period is to create a trial balance, also known as an unadjusted trial balance. A **trial balance** is a list of individual accounts in one column, usually in financial statement order, with their ending debit or credit balances in the next two columns. Debit balances are indicated in the left column and credit balances are indicated in the right column. Then the two columns are totalled to provide a check on the equality of the debits and credits. The trial balance can be prepared as frequently as needed to ensure that, in aggregate, the accounting equation remains in balance after the journal entries have been posted to the appropriate ledger accounts. A trial balance can be produced manually or, more often, generated by computer software. However, errors in a computer-generated trial balance may still exist even though debits equal credits when wrong accounts and/or amounts are used in the journal entries.[2]

A **TRIAL BALANCE** is a list of all accounts with their balances to provide a check on the equality of the debits and credits.

A trial balance is a schedule prepared for internal purposes and is not considered to be a financial statement for external users. Exhibit 4.2 presents an unadjusted trial balance for Van Houtte at April 30, 2007 based on the balances of the T-accounts illustrated in Chapters 2 and 3.

EXHIBIT **4.1**

The Accounting Cycle

DURING THE PERIOD:
- **Analyze** transactions based on source documents.
- **Record** journal entries in the general journal.
- **Post** amounts to the general ledger.

Close revenues, gains, expenses, and losses to Retained Earnings.
Prepare a post-closing trial balance.

AT THE END OF THE PERIOD:
- **Prepare** a trial balance.
- **Analyze** account balances.
- **Record** and post adjustments to revenue, expense, and related balance sheet accounts.
- **Prepare** an adjusted trial balance.

Prepare a complete set of financial statements.
Disseminate statements to users.

---

[2]Errors in a trial balance also may occur in a manual recordkeeping system when wrong accounts and/or amounts are posted from correct journal entries. If the two columns are not equal, errors have occurred in one or more of the following:

- In preparing journal entries when debits do not equal credits.
- In posting the correct dollar effects of transactions from the journal entry to the ledger.
- In computing ending balances in accounts.
- In copying ending balances in the ledger to the trial balance.

These errors can be traced and should be corrected before adjusting the records.

EXHIBIT **4.2**

Trial Balance for
Van Houtte Inc.

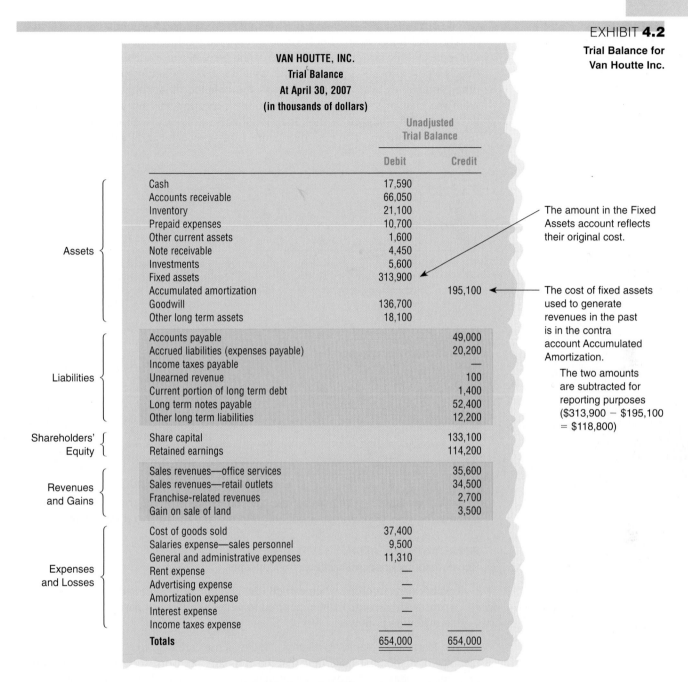

VAN HOUTTE, INC.
Trial Balance
At April 30, 2007
(in thousands of dollars)

	Unadjusted Trial Balance	
	Debit	Credit
Assets		
Cash	17,590	
Accounts receivable	66,050	
Inventory	21,100	
Prepaid expenses	10,700	
Other current assets	1,600	
Note receivable	4,450	
Investments	5,600	
Fixed assets	313,900	
Accumulated amortization		195,100
Goodwill	136,700	
Other long term assets	18,100	
Liabilities		
Accounts payable		49,000
Accrued liabilities (expenses payable)		20,200
Income taxes payable		—
Unearned revenue		100
Current portion of long term debt		1,400
Long term notes payable		52,400
Other long term liabilities		12,200
Shareholders' Equity		
Share capital		133,100
Retained earnings		114,200
Revenues and Gains		
Sales revenues—office services		35,600
Sales revenues—retail outlets		34,500
Franchise-related revenues		2,700
Gain on sale of land		3,500
Expenses and Losses		
Cost of goods sold	37,400	
Salaries expense—sales personnel	9,500	
General and administrative expenses	11,310	
Rent expense	—	
Advertising expense	—	
Amortization expense	—	
Interest expense	—	
Income taxes expense	—	
Totals	654,000	654,000

The amount in the Fixed Assets account reflects their original cost.

The cost of fixed assets used to generate revenues in the past is in the contra account Accumulated Amortization.

The two amounts are subtracted for reporting purposes ($313,900 − $195,100 = $118,800)

Notice that the Fixed Assets account (which is also referred to as Property, Plant and Equipment) is stated at original cost of $313,900 in the trial balance but was stated at $118,800 (original cost minus the portion allocated to past operations) in previous chapters. For long-term assets such as equipment used in operations, individual account balances remain at original cost to preserve the historical information. To reflect the used-up portion of the assets' cost, a **contra account** is created. *Any contra account is directly related to another account but has a balance on the opposite side of the T-account.* As a contra account increases, the net amount (the account balance less the contra account balance) decreases. For fixed assets, the contra asset is called *Accumulated Amortization.*[3] It has a credit balance of $195,100. We will discuss many contra accounts in other chapters and will designate contra accounts with an *X* in front of the type of account to which it is related (e.g., Accumulated Amortization [XA] for contra asset).

A **CONTRA ACCOUNT** is an account that is an offset to, or reduction of, the primary account.

---

[3]The term *amortization* refers to the cost of using up all types of long-term assets, consistent with the recommendations of the *CICA Handbook*. Some companies use the term *depreciation*, which refers to the cost of buildings and equipment used up over time in generating revenues. In this book we use the term amortization, except when actual company statements use the term depreciation.

NET BOOK VALUE (BOOK VALUE, CARRYING VALUE) of an asset is the difference between its acquisition cost and accumulated amortization, its related contra account.

The difference between an asset's acquisition cost and accumulated amortization is called **net book value** (**book value** or **carrying value**). The net book value does *not* represent the current market value of the asset because accounting for amortization is a cost allocation process rather than a market valuation process. As do many other companies, Van Houtte subtracts the balance in Accumulated Amortization from the cost in the Fixed Assets account, reporting the net amount on the balance sheet. The balance of each individual account is disclosed in a footnote to the financial statements. The note disclosure from a recent Van Houtte's annual report follows:

REAL WORLD EXCERPT

Van Houtte Inc.

ANNUAL REPORT

Note 8

Fixed assets

			2007
	Cost	Accumulated depreciation	Net book value
Land	$ 1,571	$ —	$ 1,571
Buildings	15,895	6,049	9,846
Retail equipment	12,273	7,593	4,680
Vending equipment	4,413	2,761	1,652
Coffee service equipment	177,883	117,399	60,484
Machinery and equipment	41,036	21,718	19,318
Furniture, computer equipment and leasehold improvements	31,280	22,952	8,328
Software	4,630	2,374	2,256
Rolling stock	22,680	14,211	8,469
	$311,661	$195,057	$116,604

Adjustments to the balances of many accounts listed on the trial balance are made at the end of the accounting period, before preparing the financial statements.

ANALYSIS OF ADJUSTING ENTRIES

Recall that, under accrual accounting concepts,

LEARNING OBJECTIVE 2

Analyze the adjustments necessary at the end of the period to update balance sheet and income statement accounts.

- Revenues are recorded when earned (the revenue principle) and
- Expenses are recorded when incurred to generate revenues during the same period (the matching principle).

As you learned in Chapter 3, revenues and expenses are easy to measure when cash is received or paid at the same time that the company performs services, delivers goods, or incurs expenses. However, sometimes cash is received before the company performs and earns the revenues; sometimes cash is received after the company performs and earns revenues. The same is true for expenses.

This difference in the timing of recording revenues versus cash receipts requires adjustments to revenue accounts. Similarly, the difference in the timing of recording expenses versus cash payments requires adjustment to expense accounts. Since recording revenues and expenses daily as they are earned or incurred would be too costly in terms of the time and labour needed to make the numerous entries, companies wait until the end of the accounting period to adjust certain accounts. **Adjusting entries** are necessary to report appropriate amounts of revenues, expenses, assets, liabilities, and shareholders' equity. A good tool to help you visualize the impact of the timing difference is a timeline as illustrated in the following discussion.

ADJUSTING ENTRIES are entries necessary at the end of the accounting peiod to identify and record all revenues and expenses of that period.

Recognizing Revenues in the Proper Period When cash is received *prior* to earning a revenue by delivering goods or performing services, the company records a journal entry (❶ on the timeline to the left), debiting Cash and crediting the liability account Unearned Revenue to recognize the obligation to perform services or deliver goods in the future. Unearned Revenue is considered a **deferred revenue** account, since recording revenue is postponed until the company meets its obligation. At the end of the accounting period, Unearned Revenue needs to be reduced and a revenue account needs to be increased by the amount of the revenue earned over time during the period (❷ adjusting entry on the timeline).

When revenues are earned but not yet recorded at the end of the accounting period because cash changes hands *after* the service is performed or goods delivered, we call them **accrued revenues.** They result when services have been provided but not billed or col-

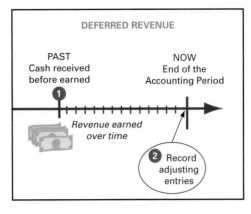

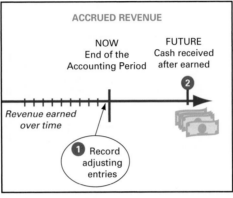

DEFERRED REVENUES are previously recorded liabilities that need to be adjusted at the end of the accounting period to reflect the amount of revenues earned.

EXAMPLES:
• Unearned Ticket Revenue
• Deferred Subscription Revenue

ADJUSTING ENTRY:
↓ Liability and ↑ Revenue

ACCRUED REVENUES are previously unrecorded revenues that need to be recorded at the end of the accounting period to reflect the amount earned and its related receivable account.

EXAMPLES:
• Interest Receivable
• Rent Receivable

ADJUSTING ENTRY:
↑ Asset and ↑ Revenue

lected. Examples include earning interest on loans made to others and earning fees that have not yet been billed. Since no entry was made during the accounting period, an adjusting entry (❶ on the timeline to the right) is necessary to increase a receivable account and its related revenue account to record revenue in the proper period. When the cash is received in the future, the receivable account is reduced (❷ on the timeline).

Exhibit 4.3 summarizes the process involved in adjusting deferred revenues and accrued revenues using unearned fees and interest revenue as examples. AJE in the exhibit refers to *adjusting journal entry*. Note that in both cases, the goal is the same—to record revenues in the proper period. Also note that adjusting entries affect one balance sheet and one income statement account, but cash is never adjusted. Cash was recorded when received prior to the end of the period, or will be collected in a future period.

EXHIBIT **4.3**

Illustration of Adjusting Deferred and Accrued Revenues

		Deferred Revenues	Accrued Revenues
During the period	Entry when **cash is received before** the company performs (earns revenue)	Cash (+A) Unearned fee revenue (+L)	

End of period	**AJE** needed because the company has performed (earned a revenue) during the period	Unearned fee revenue (−L)
		  Fee revenue (+R, +SE)
			Interest receivable (+A)
			  Interest revenue (+R, +SE)

Next period	Entry when **cash is received after** the company performs (earns revenue)		Cash (+A) Interest receivable (−A)

Revenues recorded in the proper period!

Recording Expenses in the Proper Period When cash is paid prior to incurring an expense, the company records a journal entry to debit an asset account and credit Cash (1 on the timeline to the left). Common examples of **deferred expenses** include Supplies; Prepaid Expenses such as rent, advertising, and insurance; Buildings, Equipment, and Intangible Assets such as patents and copyrights. When the assets are used during the period to generate revenues, an adjusting entry is necessary that decreases the asset and increases the related expense account (2 adjusting entry on the timeline).

Numerous expenses are incurred in the current period but not billed or paid for until the next period. Common examples are Interest Expense incurred on debt; Wages Expense owed to employees; and Utilities Expense for water, gas, and electricity used during the period for which the company has not yet received a bill. These unrecorded expenses are called **accrued expenses** that require an adjusting entry (1 on the timeline to the right) to create a payable account along with the related expense account. When cash is paid in the future for these expenses, the payable account is reduced (2 on the timeline).

Exhibit 4.4 summarizes the process involved in adjusting deferred expenses and accrued expenses using prepaid insurance and wages expense as examples. AJE refers again to *adjusting journal entry*. Note that in both cases, the goal is to record expenses in the proper period. In addition, note that the adjusting journal entry involves one balance sheet and one income statement account, and cash is never affected. Cash was recorded when paid prior to the end of the period or will be recorded in a future period.

DEFERRED EXPENSES are previously acquired assets that need to be adjusted at the end of the accounting period to reflect the amount of expense incurred in using the assets to generate revenue.

EXAMPLES:
• Supplies
• Prepaid Expenses (e.g., rent, advertising, insurance)
• Buildings and Equipment

ADJUSTING ENTRY:
↑ Expense and ↓ Asset

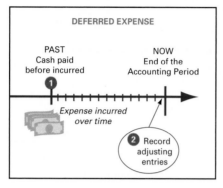

ACCRUED EXPENSES are previously unrecorded expenses that need to be recorded at the end of the accounting period to reflect the amount incurred and its related payable account.

EXAMPLES:
• Interest Payable
• Wages Payable
• Property Taxes Payable

ADJUSTING ENTRY:
↑ Expense and ↑ Liability

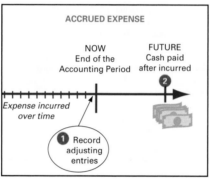

EXHIBIT 4.4

Illustration of Adjusting Deferred and Accrued Expenses

Expenses recorded in the proper period! ⟶

		Deferred Expenses	Accrued Expenses
During the period	Entry when **cash is paid before** the company incurs an expense	Prepaid insurance (+A) Cash (−A)	
End of period	**AJE** needed because the company has incurred an expense during the period	Insurance expense (+E, −SE) Prepaid insurance (−A)	Wages expense (+E, −SE) Wages payable (+L)
Next period	Entry when **cash is paid after** the company incurs an expense		Wages payable (−L) Cash (−A)

The Adjustment Process Throughout the rest of the text, you will discover that nearly every account on a company's balance sheet except cash will need to be adjusted, often requiring management to make judgments and estimates. In this chapter, we will illustrate common adjusting entries. To assist you in identifying and calculating adjusting entries,

• Think about the kinds of transactions that make balance sheet accounts increase and decrease. For example:

+ Supplies (A) −		− Accrued Expenses Payable (L) +	
Beginning bal. *Purchase*	*Use*	*Pay cash*	Beginning bal. *Accrue expense*
Ending Balance			Ending Balance

— Such as wages, interest, and taxes

- Then follow three steps:

> *Step 1.* Identify whether the adjustment is to an existing deferred revenue or expense or an unrecorded accrued revenue or expense. (Ask, "Was cash already received or paid prior to the end of the period—or—will cash be received or paid in the future?") If a deferred account is to be adjusted, write the journal entry that was made when the cash was received or paid.
>
> *Step 2.* Draw a time line to visualize the events related to the amount of revenue earned or expense incurred in the accounting period.
>
> *Step 3.* Record the adjusting journal entry. If you have difficulty determining the accounts to use, usually name the revenue or expense account for what it is, such as Interest Expense or Fee Revenue. The related asset or liability should be similar, such as Interest Payable or Unearned Fee Revenue.

To illustrate the adjustment process, we first apply it to a simplified scenario involving a dental office, and then use the same process to make the necessary adjustments to Van Houtte's accounts at the end of April 2007.

Let us assume that the fiscal year for a dental office ends on December 31. The dentist maintains her accounting records on an accrual basis. Upon reviewing her trial balance at the end of the year, she identified four items that require adjustment:

1. Unearned dental fees representing cash she *received in the past* in advance from local businesses to provide dental care to their employees in the future (insurance coverage and dental services are assumed to occur evenly over time unless otherwise indicated)—a deferred revenue.

2. Interest she will *receive in the future* from a loan made during the year to an employee—an accrued revenue.

3. Professional liability insurance *paid in the past* that provides for insurance coverage in the future—a deferred expense.

4. Wages she will *pay in the future* to employees who worked for her until year-end—an accrued expense.

Deferred Revenues   On December 1, the dental office accepted a $2,400 payment from local businesses to provide dental care to their employees over the next three months. By December 31, the dentist had provided one month of service and thus had earned revenue of $800 ($2,400 ÷ 3 months).

> *Step 1.* On December 1, the amount received represents an obligation to provide future service creating a *deferred revenue account*. The dental office earns revenue over time as it performs the services. The journal entry to record this transaction is:
>
> | | | |
> |---|---|---|
> | Cash (+A). . . . . | 2,400 | |
> | Unearned dental fee revenue (+L) . . . . | | 2,400 |
>
> *Step 2.* As time passes after receiving the fees, a portion of the liability ($800) is settled and revenue is earned.
>
>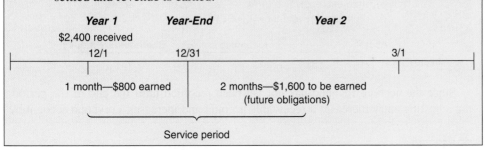

Unearned Dental Fee Revenue (L)

		2,400	12/1
*AJE 800 earned			
		1,600	12/31

Dental Fee Revenue (R)

		0	12/1
		800	AJE
		800	12/31

*AJE = adjusting journal entry

Step 3. The earned portion ($800) of the liability Unearned Dental Fee Revenue is a revenue. The remaining unearned portion ($1,600) is service due in the future. The adjusting journal entry and transaction effects follow:

12/31 AJE— Unearned dental fee revenue (−L).	800	
Dental fee revenue (+R, +SE).		800

Assets	=	Liabilities	+	Shareholders' Equity
		Unearned dental fee revenue −800		Dental fee revenue +800

Accrued Revenues   We assume that the dental office loaned $2,000 to an employee on September 1 for which the employee signed a note to pay the principal and interest at a 6-percent annual rate in six months. Any borrowing or lending of money involves two cash flows: one for the principal and one for the interest. Interest is the cost of borrowing money; it is an expense to the borrower and revenue to the lender. As each day passes until the principal is paid, more interest accumulates.

On September 1, an entry is made to reflect the lending of cash (principal) to the employee, but no interest revenue is recorded since none is earned on the day the note is signed. By the end of the year, however, four months have passed, so the dental office has earned four months of interest revenue that will not be received until March 1.

Step 1. When the money was loaned, the dental office increased the asset Note Receivable and decreased Cash for $2,000. However, no entry was made at that date to recognize interest revenue because interest was not earned yet. Interest is earned over time and will be received in the future, requiring an *accrued revenue*.

Step 2. Interest is calculated by the following formula:

$$\text{Principal} \times \text{Annual Interest Rate} \times \frac{\text{\# of months of interest}[4]}{12}$$

$2,000 \times .06 \times 4/12 = $40 interest earned in the first period.

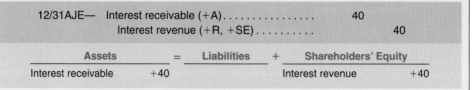

Interest Receivable (A)

AJE	40	
12/31	40	

Interest Revenue (R)

	40	AJE
	40	12/31

T-accounts are not necessary since the amount is computed directly. They are presented here for illustration.

Step 3. To recognize revenues in the period earned, an adjusting journal entry is needed. The effect is an increase in an asset and an increase in a revenue related to interest.

12/31 AJE— Interest receivable (+A).	40	
Interest revenue (+R, +SE).		40

Assets	=	Liabilities	+	Shareholders' Equity
Interest receivable +40				Interest revenue +40

Since the accrued revenue has not yet been recorded until the end of the period, the adjusting entry increases a receivable account and increases a revenue account by

---

[4] In practice, interest calculations are based on the exact number of days, but in this textbook, we use the number of months for convenience.

the computed amount. When the employee pays the principal and interest on March 1 of the next period, the entry is as follows:

March 1	Cash (+A)...........................	2,060	
	Note receivable (−A)................		2,000
	Interest receivable (−A).............		40
	Interest revenue (+R, +SE)...........		20

Assets		=	Liabilities	+	Shareholders' Equity	
Cash	+2,060				Interest revenue	+20
Note receivable	−2,000					
Interest receivable	−40					

The $2,060 received in cash on March 1 includes $2,000 in principal repayment and $60 for interest. Four months of interest were recognized in the preceding year as interest revenue and the other two months of interest ($20) are recognized as interest revenue this year.

Deferred Expenses   Now we consider the second situation when, on November 1, the dentist paid $1,800 for six months of insurance coverage (from November 1 of this year to May 1 of next year). This results in $300 coverage each full month ($1,800 ÷ 6 months). On December 31, two months have passed, and two of the six months of insurance coverage have been used during the year. To reflect incurring this expense in the current period, an adjusting entry is necessary. The process follows:

Step 1. On November 1, the amount paid represents future benefits (insurance coverage) to the dental office, creating a *deferred expense account*. Insurance coverage is partially used in November and December. The journal entry to record this transaction is:

Prepaid insurance (+A).............................	1,800	
Cash (−A)......................................		1,800

Step 2. As time passes after paying for the insurance, a portion of the asset is used during the period representing coverage received by the dentist.

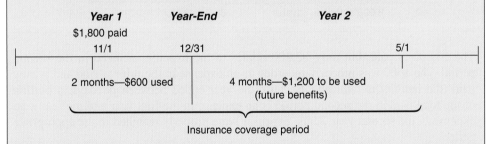

Step 3. The used-up portion ($600) of the asset Prepaid Insurance is an expense. The remaining unused portion ($1,200) provides future benefits into next year. The adjusting entry and transaction effects follow:

12/31 AJE—	Insurance expense (+E, −SE).........	600	
	Prepaid insurance (−A)		600

Assets		=	Liabilities	+	Shareholders' Equity	
Prepaid Insurance	−600				Insurance expense	−600

Prepaid Insurance (A)

11/1	1,800	
		600 used AJE
12/31	1,200	

Insurance Expense (E)

11/1	0	
AJE	600	
12/31	600	

By December 31 (the end of the accounting period), the dentist will have received two months of coverage ($600). Therefore, for the current year, Insurance Expense (E) should be $600 with $1,200 in the Prepaid Insurance (A) account on the balance sheet.

Accrued Expenses   Now assume that all employees are paid a total of $3,000 biweekly. Payment for 10 working days is made on the second Friday. The last payment for the year was on Friday, December 27. The employees continued to work through December 31, the end of the accounting period, but they will not be paid until January 10.

> **Step 1.** Employees worked and generated revenues during December, but will be paid in January, requiring an *accrued expense.*
>
> **Step 2.** The amount of wages owed to employees per day is $300 ($3,000 paid for 10 working days). By December 31, employees are owed $600 for two workdays, December 30 and December 31.

Year 1		Year-End		Year 2
12/27		12/31		1/10

2 working days
$600 incurred

8 working days
$2,400 to be incurred   pay $3,000

Pay period

> **Step 3.** To match expenses in the period when incurred to generate revenue, an adjusting journal entry is needed. The effect is an increase in a liability and an increase in an expense related to wages.

12/31 AJE— Wages expense (+E, −SE)...................... 600
                 Wages payable (+L)............................   600

Assets	=	Liabilities	+	Shareholders' Equity
		Wages payable +600		Wages expense −600

To complete the analysis, consider the entry on the next payday, January 10 in the next period:

January 10   Wages expense (+E, −SE)............. 2,400
                    Wages payable (−L)................. 600
                         Cash (−A)........................   3,000

Assets	=	Liabilities	+	Shareholders' Equity
Cash −3,000		Wages payable −600		Wages expense −2,400

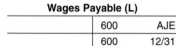

Wages Payable (L)

		600	AJE
		600	12/31

Wages Expense (E)

AJE	600	
12/31	600	

T-accounts are not necessary since the amount is computed directly. They are presented here for illustration.

The $3,000 is paid, but only $2,400 relates to the expense incurred in the second period. The $600 was properly recorded as an expense in the prior period and is now paid (the liability is reduced). Because the year ended between paydays, a portion of the total paid in the second period is an expense in the first year and the rest is an expense in the second year. Thus, expenses were properly matched in the appropriate period.

When adjustments are completed, an adjusted trial balance is prepared and the adjusted balances are used to prepare financial statements, which is the next step of the accounting cycle. Before we illustrate a complete set of financial statements for Van Houtte, we need to adjust the company's accounts at the end of April 2007.[5]

VAN HOUTTE'S ILLUSTRATION

Van Houtte's trial balance is Exhibit 4.2 lists several accounts that suggest adjusting entries are necessary. Note that you can identify them as deferrals or accruals by whether cash is reserved or paid in the past or future.

---

[5]Companies can choose fiscal periods other than actual month-ends, and financial statements can cover different accounting periods (month, quarter, or year). Adjusting entries may be prepared monthly, quarterly, and/or annually to ensure that proper amounts are included on the financial reports presented to external users.

Account	Cash Received or Paid in the Past		Revenue Earned or Expense Incurred (during the month)		Cash to Be Received or Paid in the Future
Unearned Revenue	Deferred revenue (a)	→	All or a portion may have been earned by month-end.		
Accounts Receivable			Franchisees may owe royalties to Van Houtte from weekly sales at the franchises.	→	Accrued revenue (b)
Prepaid Expenses	Deferred expense (c)	→	All or a portion of the prepaid rent, insurance, and advertising may have been used by month-end.		
Property and Equipment	Deferred expense (d)	→	The long-term assets have been used during the month to generate revenues. A portion of their historical cost is recorded as an expense.	→	Accrued expense (e) (f)
Accrued Expenses Payable			Van Houtte owes (1) amounts due for utilities used during the month but not yet billed and (2) wages to employees for work during the last week of April. Neither has yet been recorded as an expense.		
Long-Term Notes Payable			Van Houtte owes interest on borrowed funds.	→	Accrued expense (g)
Income Taxes Payable			Income tax expense needs to be recorded for the period.	→	Accrued expense (h)

We will now use the adjustment process to record adjusting entries for Van Houtte at the end of April. The reference for each adjustment is noted in the preceding chart. Refer to Exhibits 4.3 and 4.4 for the examples of deferred revenues, accrued revenues, deferred expenses, and accrued expenses.

Study the following illustration carefully to understand the steps in the adjustment process, paying close attention to the computation of the amounts in the adjustment and the effects on the account balances. First we adjust the deferred revenues and expenses and then the accrued revenues and expenses utilizing the three-step process previously discussed: (1) identify the original entry, if any, (2) create a time line with relevant dates and amounts, and (3) identify the necessary adjusting entry.

Unearned Revenues

(a) **Van Houtte provided $100 in additional services in April to new office services clients that had previously paid initial fees to Van Houtte.**

Step 1. Office services clients paid fees in cash in the past for future service, creating a *deferred revenue account*. Van Houtte earns revenue over time as it provides the services. The entry made in the past is:

Cash (+A). 100
    Unearned revenue (+L). 100

Step 2. The unadjusted trial balance (Exhibit 4.2) shows that the balance in Unearned Revenue is $100 at April 30. This amount, $100, has been earned in April.

	April	Month-End	May and Beyond
		4/30	
	Revenue earned = $100		To be earned = $0

Unearned Revenue (L)

		100	Ch. 3 bal.
AJE	100		
		0	End.

Sales Revenue— Office Services (R)

		35,600	Ch. 3 bal.
		100	AJE
		35,700	End.

Step 3. Record the adjusting journal entry (AJE).

4/30—Adjusting Journal Entry

Unearned revenue (−L). 100
    Sales revenue—office services (+R, → +SE) 100

Assets	=	Liabilities	+	Shareholders' Equity
		Unearned Revenue −100		Sales revenue—office services +100

Accrued Revenues

(b) Van Houtte's franchisees reported that they owe Van Houtte $900 in additional royalties for sales in the last week of April.

Step 1. Revenue has been earned during April, but cash will be received in the future, requiring an *accrued revenue*. No entry was made in the past.

Step 2. The time line shows that the $900 earned in April will be collected in the future.

	April	Month-End	May and Beyond
	During the last week	4/30	
	$900 Revenue earned		To be collected

Accounts Receivable (A)

Ch. 3 bal.	66,050		
Earned	☐		
End.	66,950		

Step 3. The adjusting entry to recognize the royalties earned in April and the related increase in Record the entry Accounts Receivable follows:

4/30—Adjusting Journal Entry

Franchise-Related Revenue (R)

		2,700	Ch. 3 bal.
		☐	AJE
		3,600	End.

Record the entry →

Assets	=	Liabilities	+	Shareholders' Equity
Accounts receivable +900				Franchise-related revenue +900

After you complete your answers, check them with the solution on page 193.

Deferred Expenses

(c) Prepaid expenses: In April 2007, Van Houtte paid a total of $7,400 for future expenses including insurance ($1,600), rent ($4,500), and advertising ($1,300). The payment for insurance covers four months—one month has passed (April), and three months of future insurance benefits remain. The payment for rent covers three months—one month has passed, and two months of future rent benefits remain. The payment for advertising relates to May 2007 and has not been used yet. In addition to the payment of $7,400 in April, Van Houtte has paid an amount of $3,300 prior to April 2007 to cover future expenses as reflected on its balance sheet at April 1, 2007. For illustrative purposes, we assume that this amount relates entirely to prepaid advertising expenses, and that $2,700 was used in April.

Step 1. Van Houtte prepaid for insurance, rent, and advertising in the past, creating *deferred expense accounts*. The journal entries made in the past to record the prepaid expenses are:

Prepaid expenses (+A)	7,400	
Cash (−A).		7,400

Step 2. As time passes, prepaid expenses are used up during April.

	April		Month-End	May and Beyond
	During the month		4/30	
Insurance expense		$ 400	Insurance to be used	$1,200
Rent expense		$1,500	Rent to be used	$3,000
Advertising expense		$2,700	Advertising to be used ($1,300 + $3,300 − $2,700)	$1,900

Step 3. The used-up portion of the asset Prepaid Expenses is an expense. The unused portion provides benefits in future periods. In this case, three expense accounts are affected by the adjustment—Insurance Expense, Rent Expense, and Advertising Expense, with Insurance Expense categorized as general and administrative expense on the income statement. The adjusting entry and transaction effects follow:

4/30—Adjusting Journal Entry

General and administrative expenses (+E, −SE)........	400	
Rent expense (+E, −SE).............................	1,500	
Advertising expense (+E, −SE).......................	2,700	
Prepaid expenses (−A).........................		4,600

Assets	=	Liabilities	+	Shareholders' Equity	
Prepaid expenses −4,600				General and administrative expenses	−400
				Rent expense	−1,500
				Advertising expense	−2,700

Prepaid Expenses (A)

Beg.	10,700		
Purchased	7,400	4,600	Used
End.	13,500		

General and Administrative Expenses (E)

Bal.	11,310	
AJE	400	
End.	11,710	

Rent Expense (E)

Ch. 3 bal.	0	
AJE	1,500	
End.	1,500	

Advertising Expense (E)

Ch. 3 bal.	0	
AJE	2,700	
End.	2,700	

(d) Fixed Assets (and Accumulated Amortization)

When buildings and equipment are used over time to generate revenue, a part of their cost should be expensed in the same period (the matching principle). Accountants say that buildings and equipment are *amortized* over time as used. The accounting process of amortization involves the systematic and rational allocation of the cost of a long-term asset over its useful life to the company.

A common misconception held by students and others unfamiliar with accounting terminology is that amortization reflects the asset's decline in market value. You may have heard the statement that a new car "depreciates" when it is driven off the dealer's lot. The car's market value has declined; it is now a "used" car. However, until the car is actually used to generate revenues, it has not depreciated from an accounting standpoint. **In accounting, depreciation or amortization is simply a cost allocation concept, not a way of reporting a reduction in market value**. Amortization describes the portion of the asset's historical cost estimated to have been used during the period.

As previously discussed, a contra account, Accumulated Amortization, is used to accumulate the amount of the historical cost allocated to prior periods. It is directly related to the Fixed Assets account but has the opposite balance (a credit balance).

Amortization will be discussed in greater detail in Chapter 9. To simplify matters until we reach that chapter, we assume that long-term assets used in operations provide benefits to the company evenly over time. Therefore, the historical cost is amortized in equal amounts each period. This is known as the *straight-line* method.

Fixed assets have a historical cost of $313,900 at the end of the month. The accumulated amortization of $195,100 is the used-up portion of the historical cost prior to this month. These assets have an average useful life of 10 years and an estimated residual value (the assets' estimated sales prices at the end of their useful lives to the company) of $25,900.

Step 1. Property and equipment (fixed assets) were purchased in the past, creating a *deferred expense account*. The journal entry made in the past to record the purchase of fixed assets is:

Fixed Assets (+A)...........................	(many purchases)
Cash (−A) [or a liability]..................	(many purchases)

Step 2. As time passes, fixed assets are used during the period. The straight-line formula for computing the estimated amount of long-term assets used during the period is as follows:

$$\frac{(\text{Cost} - \text{Residual value})}{\text{Useful life}} = \text{Amortization expense for the period}$$

		May
April	**Month-End**	**and Beyond**
One month used	4/30	
Amortization expense = $2,400		

($313,900 − 25,900) ÷ 10 years = $28,800 per year

$28,800 annual amortization ÷ 12 months = $2,400 per month

Step 3. The adjusting entry to record the amortization expense for April is:

4/30—Adjusting Journal Entry

Amortization expense (+E, −SE)............... 2,400

Accumulated amortization—

fixed assets (+XA→−A).................. 2,400

Assets	=	Liabilities	+	Shareholders' Equity
Accumulated amortization—fixed assets	−2,400			Amortization expense −2,400

Note that increasing the contra-asset account decreases total assets.

Accumulated Amortization—Fixed Assets (XA)

	195,100 Ch. 3 bal.
	2,400 **Used**
	197,500 End.

Amortization Expense (E)

Ch. 3 bal.	0	
AJE	2,400	
End.	2,400	

(e) **Accrued Expenses Payable (Utilities):** On April 30, Van Houtte received a utility bill for $500 for use of natural gas and electricity in the headquarters building during April. The bill will be paid in May.

Step 1. Utilities were used in April but the bill will be paid in May, requiring an *accrued expense*. No entry was made in the past.

Step 2. The time line shows that the $500 expense incurred in April will be paid in the future.

		May
April	**Month-End**	**and Beyond**
During the last week	4/30	
$500 expense incurred		To be paid

Step 3. Since using utilities was necessary for the company to generate revenues in April, the amount should be recorded as an April expense. The adjusting journal entry and transaction effects follow:

4/30—Adjusting Journal Entry

General and administrative expenses (+E, −SE)   500

Accrued expenses payable (+L) 500

Assets	=	Liabilities	+	Shareholders' Equity
		Accrued expenses payable +500		General and administrative expenses −500

Accrued Expenses Payable (L)

	20,200 Ch. 3 bal.
	500 **Incurred**
	20,700 End.

General and Administrative Expenses (E)

Bal. from (c)	11,710	
AJE	500	
End.	12,210	

(f) **Accrued Expenses Payable (Salaries):** Van Houtte owed its employees salaries for the last week in April: $1,500 for salespersons and customer service employees, and $1,600 to administrative employees working at the headquarters. The salaries will be paid during the first week in May.

Step 1. Employees worked and generated revenues during April but will be paid in May, requiring an *accrued expense*. No entry was made in the past.

Step 2. The time line shows that the wages earned by employees in April are payable in the following period.

	April	Month-End	May and Beyond
	During the last week	4/30	
	$3,100 expense incurred		To be paid

Accrued Expenses Payable (L)

	20,700 Bal. from (e)
	3,100 Incurred
	23,800 End.

Step 3. Since the employees worked and generated revenues during April, the amount owed to them should be recorded as an April expense. The adjusting journal entry and transaction effects are:

Salaries Expense—Sales Personnel (E)

Ch. 3 bal.	9,500	
AJE	1,500	
End.	11,000	

4/30—Adjusting Journal Entry

Salaries expense—sales personnel (+E, −SE)	1,500	
General and administrative expenses (+E, −SE)	1,600	
Accrued expenses payable (+L)		3,100

General and Administrative Expenses (E)

Bal. from (e)	12,210	
AJE	1,600	
End.	13,810	

Assets	=	Liabilities	+	Shareholders' Equity
		Accrued expenses payable +3,100		General and administrative expenses −1,600
				Salaries expense— sales personnel −1,500

SELF-STUDY **QUIZ 4-2**

(g) **Notes Payable (Interest):** Van Houtte borrowed $1,000 at the beginning of April from a local bank, signing a note payable in two years with interest of 12 percent payable at the end of each year.

Step 1. Interest is incurred and will be paid in the future, requiring *an accrued expense*. No entry for interest was made in the past.

Step 2. The time line shows that the interest expense incurred in April is payable in the future.

	April	Month-End	May and Beyond
	During the month	4/30	
	$ ☐ expense incurred		To be paid

Step 3. Compute interest using the formula below and record the adjusting journal entry.

Accrued Expenses Payable (L)

	23,800 Bal. from (f)
☐	☐ Incurred
	☐ End.

$$\text{Interest} = \text{Principal} \times \text{Annual Rate} \times \frac{\text{\# of months}}{12}$$

4/30—Adjusting Journal Entry

Record the entry →

Interest Expense (E)

Ch. 3 bal.	0	
AJE	☐	
End.	☐	

Assets	=	Liabilities	+	Shareholders' equity
		Accrued expenses payable + ☐		Interest expense − ☐

After you complete your answers, check them with the solutions on page 193.

(h) **Income Taxes Payable:** The final adjusting journal entry is to record the accrual of income taxes that will be paid in the next quarter (an unrecorded expense). This adjusting entry is recorded last because all other adjustments should be incorporated in computing income before income taxes, which is based on the adjusted balances:

All revenues and gains	$77,300	Unadjusted total $76,300 + 900 + 100
− All expenses	68,820	Unadjusted total $58,210 + 4,600 + 2,400 + 500 + 3,100 + 10
Pretax income	$ 8,480	

(i)   Van Houtte's average income tax rate is 25 percent.

Step 1. Income taxes are computed on April's pretax income but will be paid in the future, requiring an *accrued expense*. No entry was made in the past.

Step 2. The time line indicates that the income tax expense for April is payable in the future.

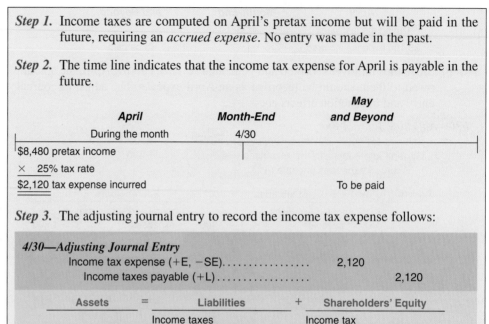

	April	Month-End	**May** and Beyond
	During the month	4/30	
$8,480 pretax income			
× 25% tax rate			
$2,120 tax expense incurred			To be paid

Step 3. The adjusting journal entry to record the income tax expense follows:

Income Taxes Payable (L)		
	0	Ch. 3 bal.
	2,120	**Incurred**
	2,120	End.

Income Tax Expense (E)		
Ch. 3 bal.	0	
AJE	**2,120**	
End.	2,120	

4/30—Adjusting Journal Entry
Income tax expense (+E, −SE).................   2,120
    Income taxes payable (+L).................   2,120

Assets	=	Liabilities	+	Shareholders' Equity
		Income taxes payable +2,120		Income tax expense −2,120

MATERIALITY AND ADJUSTING ENTRIES

MATERIALITY suggests that minor items that would not influence the decisions of financial statement users are to be treated in the easiest and most convenient manner.

The term **materiality** describes the relative significance of financial statement information to influence economic decisions made by financial statement users. An item of information, or an aggregate of items, is material if it is probable that its omission or misstatement would influence or change a decision. It is a practical concept that provides scope for accountants to be cost-effective when they record the effects of transactions and prepare financial disclosure. The concept of materiality allows accountants to estimate amounts and even to ignore specific accounting principles if the results of their actions do not have a material effect on the financial statements. This concept is also of particular importance to the audit process. Auditors use professional judgment to decide if both individual transactions and aggregated small transactions will result in a *material* misstatement of the financial position of the company.

The process of making adjusting entries can be simplified if we account for immaterial items in the easiest and most convenient manner. For example, busi-

nesses purchase many assets that provide benefits for a long period of time. Some of these assets have a very low cost such as pencil sharpeners and wastebaskets. The proper accounting treatment for such assets is to amortize their cost to expense over their useful lives. However, the cost of such assets can be directly charged to expense accounts, rather than to asset accounts in accordance with the materiality concept. Thus, the need for an adjusting entry to record periodic amortization expense is eliminated. Furthermore, adjusting entries to record accrued expenses or revenues may be ignored if the dollar amounts are immaterial.

The accountant's decision to treat a specific item as immaterial depends on a number of considerations and is a matter of professional judgment. Traditional rules of thumb in the auditing profession imply that an item is material if it exceeds 1 to

1.5 percent of total assets or sales, or 5 to 10 percent of net income. Materiality depends upon the nature of the item, as well as its dollar value. If an employee has been stealing small amounts of money systematically, then these amounts should not be judged as immaterial because they indicate a weakness in the company's internal control system that should be corrected.[6] Accountants must also consider the combined effect of numerous immaterial events. While each item may be immaterial when considered by itself, the combined effect of many items may be material.

ADJUSTMENTS AND MANAGEMENT INCENTIVES

A QUESTION OF ETHICS

Owners and managers of companies are most directly affected by the information presented in financial statements. If the financial performance and condition of the company appear strong, the company's share price rises. Shareholders usually receive dividends and the value of their investment increases. Managers often receive bonuses based on the strength of a company's financial performance, and many in top management are compensated with options to buy their company's shares at prices below market.* The higher the market value, the more compensation they earn. When actual performance lags behind expectations, managers and owners may be tempted to manipulate accruals and deferrals to make up part of the difference. For example, managers may record cash received in advance of being earned as revenue in the current period or may fail to accrue certain expenses at year-end.

Evidence from studies of large samples of companies indicates that some do engage in such behaviour. This research is borne out by enforcement actions of the securities commissions against companies and sometimes against their auditors. These enforcement actions most often relate to accrual of revenue and receivables that should be deferred to future periods. In many of these cases, the firms involved, their managers, and their auditors are penalized for such actions. Furthermore, owners suffer because the company's share price is affected negatively by news of an investigation by a securities commission.

For example, in June 2004 the Ontario Securities Commission (OSC) charged four top management personnel of Atlas Cold Storage Income Trust with misleading investors after the warehouse operator restated two years of earnings. The OSC indicated that in preparing Atlas Cold's financial statements the four executives understated some costs and expenses and recorded some expenses in the wrong periods. These errors resulted in overstatements of net income for 2001, 2002, and the second quarter of 2003. The restatement (correction) of the company's financial results erased a total of $42.6 million of earnings in 2001 and 2002, widened the loss for the third quarter of 2003, and caused suspension of payments to investors.

In September 2006, the OSC reached a settlement agreement with Ronald Perryman, the company's vice-president of Finance, who "demonstrated a lack of due diligence that contributed, in part, to the presentation of an improved picture of the financial performance of Atlas for the period including the financial years 2001, 2002, and the first two reporting periods of 2003." Perryman agreed (a) to resign all positions as an officer or director of any issuer, (b) not to become or act as a director or officer of any issuer for ten years, (c) to be reprimanded, and (d) to pay the sum of $20,000 in respect of the costs of the investigation and hearing in this matter.**

* M. Nelson, J. Elliott, and R. Tarpley. "How Are Earnings Managed? Examples from Auditors," *Accounting Horizons*, Supplement 2003, pp. 17–35.

** *In the Matter of the Securities Act, R.S.O. 1990, c. S.5, as Amended and in the Matter of Patrick Gouveia, Andrew Peters, Ronald Perryman and Paul Vickery,* Ontario Securities Commission Web site, accessed January 2, 2007.

---

[6]In fact, a bank employee was able to accumulate a large sum of money by altering a computer program to round off amounts of exchange transactions to the nearest cent and transferring the fractional amounts to a specific account under his control. Even though the amounts involved per transcation were very small, the volume of banking transactions resulted in the accumulation of a relatively large amount. Fortunately, the employee's fraud was detected a few years later and an appropriate penalty was imposed on him.

PREPARING AND ANALYZING FINANCIAL STATEMENTS

■ **LEARNING OBJECTIVE 3**

Prepare an income statement with earnings per share, a statement of retained earnings, a balance sheet, and supplemental cash flow information.

Before we prepare a complete set of financial statements, let us update the trial balance to reflect the adjustments and provide us with adjusted balances for the statements.[7] In Exhibit 4.5, four new columns are added. Two are used to reflect the adjustments in each of the accounts. The other two are the updated balances, determined by adding (or subtracting) across each row. Again, we note that the total debits equal the total

EXHIBIT **4.5**

Adjusted Trial Balance for Van Houtte, Inc.

VAN HOUTTE INC.
Trial Balance
At April 30, 2007
(in thousands of dollars)

	Unadjusted Trial Balance		Adjustments				Adjusted Trial Balance	
	Debit	Credit	Debit		Credit		Debit	Credit
Assets								
Cash	17,590						17,590	
Accounts receivable	66,050		(b)	900			66,950	
Inventory	21,100						21,100	
Prepaid expenses	10,700				(c)	4,600	6,100	
Other current assets	1,600						1,600	
Note receivable	4,450						4,450	
Investments	5,600						5,600	
Fixed assets	313,900						313,900	
Accumulated amortization		195,100			(d)	2,400		197,500
Goodwill	136,700						136,700	
Other long term assets	18,100						18,100	
Liabilities								
Accounts payable		49,000						49,000
Accrued liabilities (expenses payable)		20,200			(e)	500		23,810
					(f)	3,100		
					(g)	10		
Income taxes payable		—			(h)	2,120		2,120
Unearned revenue		100	(a)	100				—
Current portion of long term debt		1,400						1,400
Long term notes payable		52,400						52,400
Other long term liabilities		12,200						12,200
Shareholders' Equity								
Share capital		133,100						133,100
Retained earnings		114,200						114,200
Revenues and Gains								
Sales revenues—office services		35,600			(a)	100		35,700
Sales revenues—retail outlets		34,500						34,500
Franchise-related revenues		2,700			(b)	900		3,600
Gain on sale of land		3,500						3,500
Expenses and Losses								
Cost of goods sold	37,400						37,400	
Salaries expense—sales personnel	9,500		(f)	1,500			11,000	
General and administrative expenses	11,310		(c)	400			13,810	
			(e)	500				
			(f)	1,600				
Rent expense	—		(c)	1,500			1,500	
Advertising expense	—		(c)	2,700			2,700	
Amortization expense	—		(d)	2,400			2,400	
Interest expense	—		(g)	10			10	
Income taxes expense	—		(h)	2,120			2,120	
Totals	654,000	654,000	13,730		13,730		663,030	663,030

Effects of the adjusting entries

---

[7]For a discussion and illustration of the use of a worksheet for end-of-period adjustments, refer to Appendix C on the Online Learning Centre Web site at **www.mcgrawhill.ca/olc/libby/student/resources**.

credits in each of the columns. It is from these adjusted balances that we will prepare an income statement, a statement of retained earnings, and a balance sheet, with supplementary cash flow information to accompany the cash flow statement.

The four financial statements are interrelated. That is, the numbers in one statement flow into the next statement, as illustrated in Exhibit 4.6.

INCOME STATEMENT

The income statement is prepared first because net income is a component of Retained Earnings. The April income statement for Van Houtte is based on transactions in Chapters 2 and 3 and adjustments in this chapter. Note that a few of the expense accounts have been combined into specific categories on the income statement.

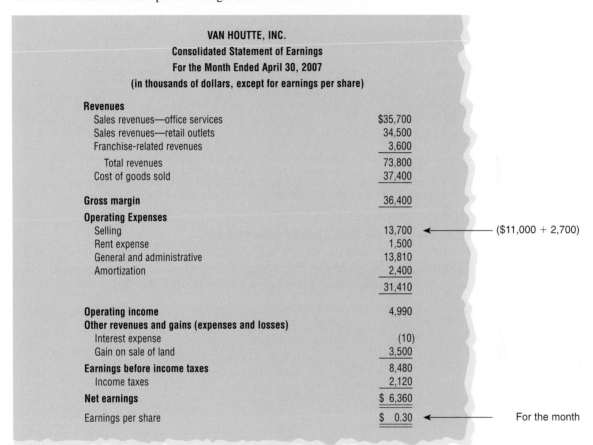

VAN HOUTTE, INC.
Consolidated Statement of Earnings
For the Month Ended April 30, 2007
(in thousands of dollars, except for earnings per share)

Revenues	
Sales revenues—office services	$35,700
Sales revenues—retail outlets	34,500
Franchise-related revenues	3,600
Total revenues	73,800
Cost of goods sold	37,400
Gross margin	36,400
Operating Expenses	
Selling	13,700 ← ($11,000 + 2,700)
Rent expense	1,500
General and administrative	13,810
Amortization	2,400
	31,410
Operating income	4,990
Other revenues and gains (expenses and losses)	
Interest expense	(10)
Gain on sale of land	3,500
Earnings before income taxes	8,480
Income taxes	2,120
Net earnings	$ 6,360
Earnings per share	$ 0.30 ← For the month

You will note that the ratio earnings per share (EPS) is reported on the income statement. It is widely used in evaluating the operating performance and profitability of a company and is the only ratio required to be disclosed on the statement or in the notes to the statements. Earnings per share is computed as follows:

$$\text{Earnings per share} = \frac{\text{Net Income Available to the Common Shareholders}}{\text{Weighted-Average Number of Common Shares Outstanding during the Period}}$$

The calculation of the denominator is complex and is presented in other accounting courses. Based on Van Houtte's actual annual report for 2007, the weighted-average number of common shares outstanding was approximately 21,375,000. For simplicity, we use this same denominator in the computations of the earnings per share shown on the income statement. Additional EPS disclosures will be discussed in Chapter 6.

EPS = $6,360,000 Net Income ÷ 21,375,000 Shares = $0.30

EXHIBIT **4.6**

Relationships of the Financial Statements

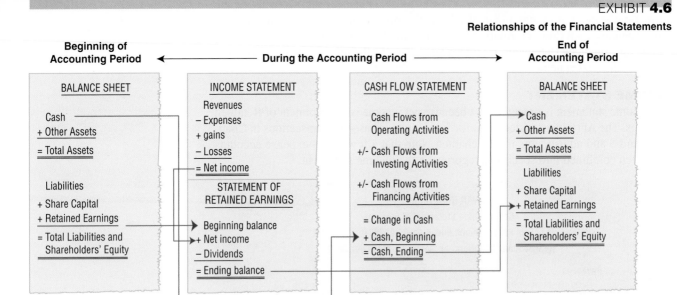

The company starts the accounting period with a set of asset, liability, and shareholders' equity account balances. Its operations during the period are summarized in the income statement and the statement of retained earnings, which are connected by the net income (or loss) for the period. The ending balance of retained earnings is then reported in the shareholders' equity section of the balance sheet at the end of the period. Finally, the cash flow statement provides details of the cash inflows and outflows that explain the change in cash between the two balance sheet dates.

STATEMENT OF RETAINED EARNINGS

The final amount from the income statement, net income, is carried forward to the statement of retained earnings. If dividends had been declared during April 2007, they would be deducted to arrive at the ending balance at April 30, 2007.

VAN HOUTTE, INC.	
Consolidated Statement of Retained Earnings	
For the Month Ended April 30, 2007	
(dollars in thousands)	
Beginning balance, April 1, 2007	$114,200
Net income	6,360
Dividends	-0-
Ending balance, April 30, 2007	**$120,560**

BALANCE SHEET

The balance for retained earnings flows into the balance sheet. You will notice that the contra-asset account, Accumulated Amortization, has been subtracted from the Fixed Assets account to reflect net book value (or carrying value) at month-end for balance sheet purposes. Recall that assets are listed in order of liquidity, while liabilities are listed in order of due date. Current assets are those used or turned into cash within one year. Current liabilities are obligations to be paid with current assets within one year.

In addition to preparing the basic financial statements, companies provide further information about specific elements of these statements in notes that follow these statements. The additional details supporting the reported numbers facilitate analysis of the company's operating performance and financial condition. A closer look at note disclosures related to financial statements is provided in Chapter 6.

VAN HOUTTE INC.
Consolidated Balance Sheet
April 30, 2007
(in thousands of dollars)

Assets
Current assets

Cash	$ 17,590
Accounts receivable	66,950
Inventory	21,100
Prepaid expenses	6,100
Other current assets	1,600
Total current assets	113,340
Notes receivable	4,450
Investments	5,600
Fixed assets (net of accumulated amortization of $197,500)	116,400
Goodwill	136,700
Other long term assets	18,100
Total assets	**$394,590**

Liabilities and shareholders' equity
Current Liabilities

Accounts payable	$ 49,000
Accrued liabilities	23,810
Income taxes payable	2,120
Current portion of long term debt	1,400
Total Current Liabilities	76,330
Long term notes payable	52,400
Other long term liabilities	12,200
Total liabilities	140,930
Shareholders' equity	
Share capital	133,100
Retained earnings	120,560
Total shareholders' equity	253,660
Total liabilities and shareholders' equity	**$394,590**

DISCLOSURE

FOCUS ON
CASH FLOWS

As presented in the previous chapters, the cash flow statement explains the difference between the ending and beginning balances in the Cash account on the balance sheet during the accounting period. Put simply, the cash flow statement is a categorized list of all transactions of the period that affected the Cash account. The three categories are operating, investing, and financing activities. Since the adjustments made in this chapter did not affect cash, the components of the cash flow statement presented in Chapters 2 and 3 have not changed.

For complete disclosure, however, companies are required to provide additional information on the statement itself or in the notes to the statements.

In General → **Disclosure** (on the statement or in the notes): (1) interest paid, (2) income taxes paid, and (3) a schedule of the nature and amounts of significant noncash transactions (e.g., land exchanged for shares, acquisition of a building by signing a long-term mortgage payable).

Focus Company Analysis → For meeting the disclosure requirement using our Van Houtte illustration, no significant noncash transactions and no income taxes or interest were paid during April. In the notes to its actual 2007 financial statements, Van Houtte disclosed $3.75 million in interest paid and $8.10 million in income taxes paid, as well as additions to fixed assets financed by accounts payable ($2.16 million) and by capital lease obligations ($0.61 million).

FINANCIAL ANALYSIS

CASH FLOW FROM OPERATIONS, NET INCOME, AND THE QUALITY OF EARNINGS

Many standard financial analysis texts warn analysts to look for unusual deferrals and accruals when they attempt to predict future periods' earnings. They often suggest that wide disparities between net income and cash flow from operations is a useful warning sign. For example, Wild, et al. suggest that

> Cash flows are often less subject to distortion than is net income. Accounting accruals determining net income rely on estimates, deferrals, allocations, and valuations. These considerations typically admit more subjectivity than factors determining cash flows. For this reason we often relate cash flows from operations to net income in assessing its quality. *Certain users consider earnings of higher quality when the ratio of cash flows from operations divided by net income is greater.* This derives from a concern with revenue recognition or expense accrual criteria yielding high net income but low cash flows (emphasis added).*

*J. Wild, K. Subramanyam, and R. Hasley, *Financial Statement Analysis*. New York, McGraw-Hill/Irwin, 2004, p. 394.

KEY RATIO ANALYSIS

Evaluating company performance is the primary goal of financial statement analysis. Company managers, as well as competitors, use financial statements to better understand and evaluate a company's business strategy. Analysts, investors, and creditors use these same statements to evaluate performance as part of their share valuation and credit evaluation judgments. In Chapter 3, we introduced the return on assets to examine managers' effectiveness at utilizing assets to generate income. We now discuss two other measures of profitability. The net profit margin compares net income to the revenues generated during the period, and the return on equity relates net income to shareholders' investment in the business.

NET PROFIT MARGIN

ANALYTICAL QUESTION → How effective is management in generating profit on every dollar of sales?

RATIO AND COMPARISONS → The net profit margin is useful in answering this question. It is computed as follows:

$$\text{Net profit Margin} = \frac{\text{Net Income}}{\text{Net Sales*}}$$

LEARNING OBJECTIVE 4

Compute and interpret the net profit margin ratio and the return on equity ratio.

The 2007 ratio for Van Houtte:

$$\frac{\$25,000}{\$388,200} = 0.064\ (6.4\%)$$

*Net sales is sales revenue less any returns from customers and other reductions. For companies in the service industry, total operating revenues equal net sales.

Comparisons over Time			Comparisons with Competitors	
Van Houtte Inc.			Starbucks	Green Mountain Coffee Roasters
2005	2006	2007	2006	2006
6.2%	6.0%	6.4%	7.2%	3.3%

INTERPRETATIONS

In General → Net profit margin measures how much profit is earned from every sales dollar generated during the period. A rising net profit margin signals more efficient management of sales and expenses. Differences among industries result from the nature of the products or services provided and the intensity of competition. Differences among competitors in the same industry reflect how each company responds to changes in competition (and demand for the product or service) and changes in managing sales volume, sales price, and costs. Financial analysts expect well-run businesses to maintain or improve their net profit margin over time.

Focus Company Analysis → Van Houtte's net profit margin was relatively stable during the three-year period 2005–2007. Compared to its competitors, Van Houtte has a better performance than Green Mountain, but did not achieve as good a ratio as Starbucks. Despite the improvement in Van Houtte's ratio over the past three years, its management should analyze the various expense items in an effort to better control these costs and continue to improve on its performance.

A Few Cautions → The decisions that management makes to maintain the company's net profit margin in the current period may have negative long-run implications. Analysts should perform additional analysis of the ratio to identify trends in each component of revenues and expenses. This involves dividing each line on the income statement by net sales. Statements presented with these percentages are called *common-sized income statements*; they are discussed more fully in Chapter 13. Changes in the percentages of the individual components of net income provide information on shifts in management's strategies.

SELECTED FOCUS COMPANY NET PROFIT MARGINS	
Forzani Group Ltd.	1.2%
Dell Inc.	6.4%
WestJet Airlines Ltd.	1.7%

RETURN ON EQUITY

ANALYTICAL QUESTION → How well has management used the investment by shareholders during the period?

RATIO AND COMPARISONS → The return on equity (ROE) helps in answering this question. It is computed as follows:

$$\text{Return on Equity} = \frac{\text{Net Income}}{\text{Average Shareholders' Equity*}}$$

*Average Shareholders' Equity = (Beginning Shareholders' Equity + Ending Shareholders' Equity) ÷ 2

The 2007 ratio for Van Houtte is:

$$\frac{\$25,000}{(\$236,600 + \$246,200) \div 2} = 0.103 \,(10.3\%)$$

Comparisons over Time		
Van Houtte		
2005	2006	2007
9.6%	9.6%	10.3%

Comparisons with Competitors	
Starbucks	Green Mountain Coffee Roasters
2006	2006
26.1%	12.5%

INTERPRETATIONS

In General → ROE measures how much the firm earned for each dollar of shareholders' investment. In the long run, firms with higher ROE are expected to have higher share prices than firms with lower ROE, all other things equal. Managers, analysts, and creditors use this ratio to assess the effectiveness of the company's overall business strategy (its operating, investing, and financing strategies).

Van Houtte's ROE increased from 9.6 percent in 2005 to 10.3 percent in 2007, which parallels the increase in its net profit margin over the same period. But it is lower than the ROEs of its competitors. This indicates that Van Houtte's utilization of resources has not generated the level of return on shareholders' investment that the managers of Starbucks and Green Mountain Coffee Roasters were able to achieve. Closer examination of Van Houtte's balance sheet indicates that its assets include a significant amount of goodwill (an intangible asset that resulted from past investments in other companies). Goodwill is not an operational asset; hence it does not generate revenue and income in the same way as roasting equipment. If this asset is excluded from Van Houtte's balance sheet, total assets would be reduced as well as shareholders' equity, which increases ROE to 23.9 percent, making it slightly lower than that of Starbucks, but much higher that the ROE of Green Mountain Coffee Roasters.

A Few Cautions → An increasing ROE can also indicate that a manufacturing company is failing to invest in research and development or modernization of plant and equipment. While such a strategy will decrease expenses and thus increase ROE in the short run, it normally results in future declines in ROE as the company's products and plant and equipment reach the end of their life cycles. As a consequence, experienced decision makers evaluate ROE in the context of a company's business strategy.

More detailed analysis of ROE and its relationship to other financial ratios are covered in Chapter 13.

SELF-STUDY **QUIZ 4-3**

Refer to Exhibit 4.5. Compute the net profit margin for Van Houtte, Inc. based on information disclosed in (1) the unadjusted trial balance, and (2) the adjusted trial balance. Why are the two ratios different? Is the difference between the two ratios material? Explain.

After you complete the quiz, check your answers with the solution on page 193.

CLOSING THE BOOKS

END OF THE ACCOUNTING CYCLE

■ **LEARNING OBJECTIVE 5**

Explain the closing process at the end of the period.

PERMANENT (REAL) ACCOUNTS are the balance sheet accounts whose ending balances are carried into the next accounting period.

TEMPORARY (NOMINAL) ACCOUNTS are income statement (and sometimes dividends declared) accounts that are closed to Retained Earnings at the end of the accounting period.

CLOSING ENTRIES transfer balances in temporary accounts to Retained Earnings and establish zero balances in temporary accounts.

INCOME SUMMARY is a temporary account used only during the closing process to facilitate closing temporary accounts.

The balance sheet accounts are updated continuously throughout the accounting period, and the ending balance for the current period becomes the beginning account balance for the next period. The balances in these accounts, called **permanent** or **real accounts**, are not reduced to zero at the end of the accounting period. For example, the ending Cash balance of one accounting period must be the beginning Cash balance of the next accounting period. The only time a permanent account has a zero balance is when the item represented is no longer owned or owed.

In contrast, revenue, expense, gain, and loss accounts are used to accumulate data for the **current accounting period only**; they are called **temporary or nominal accounts**. At the end of each period, their balances are transferred, or closed, to the Retained Earnings account so that the company starts with zero balances in these accounts at the beginning of the next accounting period. This periodic clearing of the balances of the income statement accounts into Retained Earnings is done by recording closing entries.

The **closing entries** have two purposes:

1. To transfer net income or loss to Retained Earnings.
2. To establish a zero balance in each of the temporary accounts to start the accumulation in the next accounting period.

A special temporary (T) summary account, called **Income Summary**, is used to close the revenue, gain, expense, and loss accounts. Accounts with credit balances are closed by debiting the total amount to Income Summary, and accounts with debit balances are closed by crediting the total amount to Income Summary. The balance of the Income Summary account reflects the net income (or loss) and is then closed to Retained Earnings. In this way, the income statement accounts are again ready for their temporary accumulation function for the next period.

Closing entries are dated the last day of the accounting period, entered in the usual format in the journal, and immediately posted to the ledger (or T-accounts). We illustrate the closing process by preparing the closing entries for Van Houtte at April 30, 2007, although in practice companies close their records only at the end of the fiscal year.

Sales Revenue—Office Services (R)			
Closing	35,700	Sales in April	35,700
		End. Bal	0

Sales revenues—coffee services (−R)..	35,700	
Sales revenues—retail outlets (−R)..	34,500	
Franchise-related revenues (−R)..	3,600	
Gain on sale of land (−R)..	3,500	
Income summary (+T)		77,300
To close the revenue accounts to Income Summary.		

(continued)

Income summary (−T)	70,940	
Cost of goods sold (−E)		37,400
Salaries expense – sales personnel (−E)		11,000
General and administrative expenses (−E)		13,810
Rent expense (−E).		1,500
Advertising expense (−E)		2,700
Amortization expense (−E)		2,400
Interest expense (−E)		10
Income tax expense (−E).		2,120
To close the expense accounts to Income Summary.		
Income summary (−T)	6,360	
Retained earnings (+SE).		6,360
To close the Income Summary account to Retained Earnings.		

Income Summary (T)

Cost of sales in April	37,400	Sales in April	35,700
. . .		. . .	
. . .		. . .	
Closing	6,360		
		End. Bal	0

Cost of Goods Sold (E)

Cost of sales in April	37,400	Closing	37,400
		End. Bal	0

Retained Earnings (SE)

	Beg. bal.	114,200
	Net income	6,360
	End. bal.	120,560

POST-CLOSING TRIAL BALANCE

After the closing process is complete, all of the income statement accounts have a zero balance. These accounts are then ready for recording revenues and expenses in the new accounting period. The ending balance in Retained Earnings now is up to date (matches the amount on the balance sheet) and is carried forward as the beginning balance for the next period. As the last step of the accounting information processing cycle, a **post-closing trial balance** (Exhibit 4.7) should be prepared as a check that debits equal credits and that all temporary accounts have been closed.

POST-CLOSING TRIAL BALANCE should be prepared as the last step of the accounting cycle to check that debits equal credits and all temporary accounts have been closed.

EXHIBIT **4.7**

Post-Closing Trial Balance for Van Houtte, Inc.

VAN HOUTTE INC.
Trial Balance
At April 30, 2007
(in thousands of dollars)

	Adjusted Trial Balance		Post-Closing Trial Balance	
	Debit	Credit	Debit	Credit
Assets				
Cash	17,590		17,590	
Accounts receivable	66,950		66,950	
Inventory	21,100		21,100	
Prepaid expenses	6,100		6,100	
Other current assets	1,600		1,600	
Note receivable	4,450		4,450	
Investments	5,600		5,600	
Fixed assets	313,900		313,900	
Accumulated amortization		197,500		197,500
Goodwill	136,700		136,700	
Other long term assets	18,100		18,100	
Liabilities				
Accounts payable		49,000		49,000
Accrued liabilities (expenses payable)		23,810		23,810
Income taxes payable		2,120		2,120
Unearned revenue		—		—
Current portion of long term debt		1,400		1,400
Long term notes payable		52,400		52,400
Other long term liabilities		12,200		12,200
Shareholders' Equity				
Share capital		133,100		133,100
Retained earnings		114,200		120,560
Revenues and Gains				
Sales revenues—office services		35,700	0	
Sales revenues—retail outlets		34,500	0	
Franchise-related revenues		3,600	0	
Gain on sale of land		3,500	0	

(continued)

Expenses and Losses	Cost of goods sold	37,400		0	
	Salaries expense—sales personnel	11,000		0	
	General and administrative expenses	13,810		0	
	Rent expense	1,500		0	
	Advertising expense	2,700		0	
	Amortization expense	2,400		0	
	Interest expense	10		0	
	Income taxes expense	2,120		0	
	Totals	**663,030**	**663,030**	**592,090**	**592,090**

FINANCIAL ANALYSIS

ACCRUALS AND DEFERRALS: JUDGING EARNINGS QUALITY

The determination of revenues and expenses related to a specific accounting period depends on the assumptions used, such as the useful life and the residual value of equipment, as well as the accounting policies adopted by the company. As we discussed in Chapter 3, the revenue principle requires that revenues be recognized and recorded in the period they are earned regardless of when cash is received, and the matching principle requires that expenses be recognized and recorded in the period they are incurred regardless of when cash is paid. As a result, accrual basis income differs from cash basis income. Hence, management's selection and application of accounting principles influences the level of reported income.

Most of the adjustments discussed in this chapter, such as the allocation of prepaid insurance or the determination of accrued interest revenue, involve direct calculations and require little judgment on the part of the company's management. In later chapters, we will discuss many other adjustments that involve difficult and complex estimates about the future. These include, for example, estimates of customers' ability to make payments to the company for purchases on account, the useful lives of new machines, and future amounts that a company may owe on warranties of products sold in the past. Each of these estimates and many others can have significant effects on the stream of net earnings that companies report over time.

When attempting to value firms based on their balance sheet and income statement data, analysts also evaluate the estimates that form the basis for the adjustments. Those firms that make relatively pessimistic estimates that reduce current income are judged to follow *conservative* financial reporting strategies, and their reports of performance are given more credence. The earnings numbers reported by these companies are often said to be of "higher quality" because they are less influenced by management's natural optimism. Firms that consistently make optimistic estimates that result in reporting higher net income, however, are judged to be *aggressive*. Analysts judge these companies' operating performance to be of lower quality.

DEMONSTRATION **CASE**

We take our final look at the accounting activities of Terrific Lawn Maintenance Corporation by illustrating the activities at the end of the accounting cycle: the adjustment process, financial statement preparation, and the closing process. Chapter 2 presented investing and financing activities, and Chapter 3 presented operating activities. No adjustments had been made to the accounts to reflect all revenues earned and expenses incurred in April, however. The trial balance for Terrific Lawn on April 30, 2007, based on the unadjusted balances in Chapter 3, is as follows:

TERRIFIC LAWN MAINTENANCE CORPORATION
Unadjusted Trial Balance
At April 30, 2007

	Debit	Credit
Cash	5,060	
Accounts receivable	1,700	
Prepaid expenses	300	
Equipment	4,600	
Accumulated amortization		0
Land	3,750	
Accounts payable		220
Unearned revenue		1,600
Notes payable		3,700
Accrued utilities payable		0
Wages payable		0
Interest payable		0
Income tax payable		0
Share capital		9,000
Retained earnings		0
Mowing revenue		5,200
Fuel expense	410	
Wages expense	3,900	
Insurance expense	0	
Utilities expense	0	
Amortization expense	0	
Interest expense	0	
Income tax expense	0	
Totals	19,720	19,720

Additional Information

a. One fourth of the $1,600 cash received from the city at the beginning of April for future mowing service has been earned in April. The $1,600 in Unearned Revenues represents four months of service (April through July).

b. Insurance costing $300 providing coverage for six months (April through September) was paid by Terrific Lawn at the beginning of April and has been partially used in April.

c. Mowers, edgers, rakes, and hand tools (equipment) have been used to generate revenue. They have a total cost of $4,600 and an estimated useful life of 10 years. No residual value is expected. The company uses straight-line amortization.

d. Wages have been paid through April 29. Wages earned in April by the employees but not yet paid accrue at $130 per day.

e. An extra telephone line was installed in April at an estimated cost of $52, including hook-up and usage charges. The bill will be received and paid in May.

f. Interest accrues on the outstanding notes payable at an annual rate of 12 percent. The $3,700 in principal has been outstanding all month.

g. The estimated income tax rate for Terrific Lawn is 35 percent for both federal and provincial income taxes.

Required:

1. Identify deferred revenue, accrued revenue, deferred expense, and accrued expense accounts for items *a* through *g*.
2. Using the process outlined in this chapter, analyze and record adjusting journal entries for April. Include T-accounts for both accruals and deferrals and compute ending balances.
3. Prepare an adjusted trial balance.
4. Use the adjusted account balances from requirement 2 to prepare an income statement and a statement of retained earnings for the month ended April 30, 2007, as well as a balance sheet at April 30, 2007. Include earnings per share on the income statement. The company issued 1,500 shares.
5. Prepare the closing entry for April 30, 2007.
6. Compute the company's net profit margin and the return on equity ratio for the month.

7. For each of the items *a, b,* and *c* above, indicate the effect of omitting the required adjustment on the elements of the balance sheet and income statement. Use O for overstatement, U for understatement, and NE for no effect. Ignore the effects of income taxes on overstatements or understatements of revenues and expenses.

	Balance Sheet			Income Statement		
Transaction	Assets	Liabilities	Shareholders' Equity	Revenues	Expenses	Net Income
a.						
b.						
c.						

We strongly recommend that you prepare your own answers to these requirements and then check your answers with the following solution.

SUGGESTED SOLUTION

1.

Item	Account to be Adjusted	Type of Adjustment	Explanation
a.	Unearned Revenues	Deferred revenue	Cash was received prior to being earned.
b.	Prepaid Expenses	Deferred expense	Cash was paid for insurance prior to being used.
c.	Accumulated Amortization	Deferred expense	Long-term assets were purchased and used.
d.	Accrued Expenses Payable (Wages)	Accrued expense	Cash will be paid to employees in the future.
e.	Accrued Expenses Payable (Utilities)	Accrued expense	Cash will be paid for utilities in the future.
f.	Accrued Expenses Payable (Interest)	Accrued expense	Cash will be paid for interest in the future.
g.	Income Taxes Payable	Accrued expense	Taxes will be paid in the future.

2. Analysis of deferrals and accruals, adjusting entries, and T-accounts:

Deferred Revenue

(a) One fourth of the $1,600 cash received from the city at the beginning of April for future mowing service has been earned in April. The $1,600 in Unearned Revenues represents four months of service (April through July).

Step 1. The city paid cash in the past for future mowing service, creating a *deferred revenue account*. Terrific Lawn earns revenue over time as it performs the services. The journal entry made in the past is:

Cash (+A)......................................	1,600	
Unearned revenue (+L)............................		1,600

Step 2. The amount of revenue that should be recognized in April is $400 ($1,600 ÷ 4 months). The remaining amount will be earned gradually in future periods.

Unearned Revenue (L)

		1,600	Bal.
Earned	400		
		1,200	End.

	April	Month-End	Beyond April
$1,600 received			
	During the month	4/30	
	$400 revenue earned		$1,200 to be earned

Step 3. The adjusting journal entry to recognize the revenue earned in April is:

Mowing Revenue (R)

		5,200	Bal.
		400	AJE
		5,600	End.

4/30—Adjusting Journal Entry

Unearned revenue (−L)........................	400	
Mowing revenue (+R, +SE)................		400

Assets	=	Liabilities	+	Shareholders' Equity	
		Unearned revenue −400		Mowing revenue +400	

Deferred Expenses

(b) **Insurance costing $300 providing coverage for six months (April through September) was paid by Terrific Lawn at the beginning of April and has been partially used in April.**

Step 1. The company paid insurance in the past, creating a *deferred expense account*. Insurance coverage has now been partially used. The journal entry made in the past is:

Prepaid expenses (+A)............................	300	
Cash (−A)...................................		300

Step 2. The amount of insurance expense that should be recognized in April is $50 ($300 ÷ 6 months). The remaining amount, $250, will be recognized as expense gradually over the next five months.

	April	**Month-End**	**Beyond April**
$300 paid			
	During the month	4/30	
	$50 expense incurred		$250 to be incurred

Prepaid Expenses (A)

Bal.	300		
		50	Used
End.	250		

Step 3. The adjusting journal entry to recognize the insurance expense for April is:

4/30—Adjusting Journal Entry

Insurance expense (+E, −SE)................	50	
Prepaid expenses (−A).....................		50

Assets	=	**Liabilities**	+	**Shareholders' Equity**	
Prepaid expenses −50				Insurance expense −50	

Insurance Expense (E)

Bal.	0	
AJE	50	
End.	50	

(c) **Mowers, edgers, rakes, and hand tools (equipment) have been used to generate revenue. They have a total cost of $4,600 and an estimated useful life of 10 years. No residual value is expected. The company uses straight-line amortization.**

Step 1. Equipment was purchased in the past, creating a *deferred expense account*. It has now been used in operations during April. The journal entry made in the past is:

Lawn equipment (+A).............................	4,600	
Cash (−A).......................................		200
Notes Payable (+L).............................		4,400

Step 2. The amortization expense for April 2007 is $38 ($4,600 ÷ 120 months). The remaining amount will be recognized in future periods as the equipment is used.

	April	**Month-End**	**Beyond April**
$4,600 paid			
		4/30	
	$38 expense incurred		The rest incurred in the future when the assets are used.

Accumulated Amortization (XA)

		0	Bal.
		38	Used
		38	End.

Step 3. The adjusting journal entry to record the amortization expense is:

4/30—Adjusting Journal Entry

Amortization expense (+E, −SE)	38	
Accumulated amortization (+XA → −A)		38

Assets	=	**Liabilities**	+	**Shareholders' Equity**	
Accumulated amortization −38				Amortization expense −38	

Amortization Expense (E)

Bal.	0	
AJE	38	
End.	38	

Accrued Expenses

(d) Wages have been paid through April 29. Wages earned in April by the employees but not yet paid accrue at $130 per day.

Step 1. Employees worked and generated revenue during April, but will be paid in May, requiring an *accrued expense*. No entry was made in the past.

Step 2. The amount of wages expense incurred in April will be paid in the next accounting period.

April	Month-End	Beyond April
1 day worked	4/30	
$130 expense incurred		To be paid

Step 3. The adjusting journal entry to record the wages expense is:

Wages Payable (L)

		0	Bal.
		130	Incurred
		130	End.

Wages Expense (E)

Bal.	3,900	
AJE	130	
End.	4,030	

4/30—Adjusting Journal Entry
Wages expense (+E, −SE) 130
    Wages payable (+L) 130

Assets	=	Liabilities	+	Shareholders' Equity
		Wages payable +130		Wages expense −130

(e) An extra telephone line was installed in April at an estimated cost of $52, including hook-up and usage charges. The bill will be received and paid in May.

Step 1. Utilities were installed and used in April, but the bill will be paid in May requiring an *accrued expense*. No entry was made in the past.

Step 2. The amount of the telephone bill should be recognized in April and will be paid in May.

April	Month-End	Beyond April
	4/30	
$52 expense incurred		To be paid

Step 3. The adjusting journal entry to record the utilities expense is:

Utilities Payable (L)

		0	Bal.
		52	Incurred
		52	End.

Utilities Expense (E)

Bal.	0	
AJE	52	
End.	52	

4/30—Adjusting Journal Entry
Utilities expense (+E, −SE) 52
    Utilities payable (+L)......................... 52

Assets	=	Liabilities	+	Shareholders' Equity
		Utilities payable +52		Utilities expense −52

(f) Interest accrued on the outstanding notes payable at an annual rate of 12 percent. The $3,700 in principal has been outstanding all month.

Step 1. The notes payable were recorded when signed. Interest is incurred and will be paid in the future, requiring an accrued expense.

Step 2. The interest expense that should be recognized in April is $37 [$3,700 ×.12 × (1/12)]. This amount is payable in a future period.

April	Month-End	Beyond April
	4/30	
$37 expense incurred		To be paid

Step 3. The adjusting journal entry to record the interest expense is:

Interest Payable (L)

		0	Bal.
		37	Incurred
		37	End.

Interest Expense (E)

Bal.	0	
AJE	37	
End.	37	

4/30—Adjusting Journal Entry
Interest expense (+E, −SE)..................... 37
    Interest payable (+L)......................... 37

Assets	=	Liabilities	+	Shareholders' Equity
		Interest payable +37		Interest expense −37

Income Taxes Payable

(g) The estimated income tax rate for Terrific Lawn is 35 percent for both federal and provincial income taxes.

Step 1. Income taxes are computed on April's pretax income but will be paid in the future, requiring an *accrued expense.* No entry was made in the past.

Step 2. The income tax expense that should be recognized in April is $344, calculated as follows:

Chapter 3 Totals + Adjustments

All revenues	$5,600	= $5,200 + 400
All expenses	−4,617	= 4,310 + 50 + 38 + 130 + 52 + 37
Pretax income	$ 983	× 0.35 tax rate = $344 tax expense (rounded)

April	**Month-End**	**Beyond April**
	4/30	
$344 expense incurred		To be paid

Income Taxes Payable (L)

	0	Bal.
	344	Incurred
	344	End.

Step 3. The adjusting journal entry to record the income tax expense follows:

4/30—Adjusting Journal Entry

Income tax expense (+E, −SE).................   344
   Income taxes payable (+L)   344

Assets	=	Liabilities	+	Shareholders' Equity
		Income taxes payable +344		Income tax expense −344

Income Tax Expense (E)

Bal.	0	
AJE	344	
End.	344	

3. Adjusted trial balance.

TERRIFIC LAWN MAINTENANCE CORPORATION
Trial Balance
At April 30, 2007
(in thousands of dollars)

	Unadjusted Trial Balance		Adjustments		Adjusted Trial Balance	
	Debit	Credit	Debit	Credit	Debit	Credit
Cash	5,060				5,060	
Accounts receivable	1,700				1,700	
Prepaid expenses	300			(b) 50	250	
Equipment	4,600				4,600	
Accumulated amortization		0		(c) 38		38
Land	3,750				3,750	
Accounts payable		220				220
Unearned revenue		1,600	(a) 400			1,200
Notes payable		3,700				3,700
Utilities payable		0		(e) 52		52
Wages payable		0		(d) 130		130
Interest payable		0		(f) 37		37
Income taxes payable		0		(g) 344		344
Share capital		9,000				9,000
Retained earnings		0				—
Mowing revenue		5,200		(a) 400		5,600
Fuel expense	410				410	
Wages expense	3,900		(d) 130		4,030	
Insurance expense	0		(b) 50		50	
Utilities expense	0		(e) 52		52	
Amortization expense	0		(c) 38		38	
Interest expense	0		(f) 37		37	
Income tax expense	0		(g) 344		344	
Totals	19,720	19,720	1,051	1,051	20,321	20,321

4. Financial statements

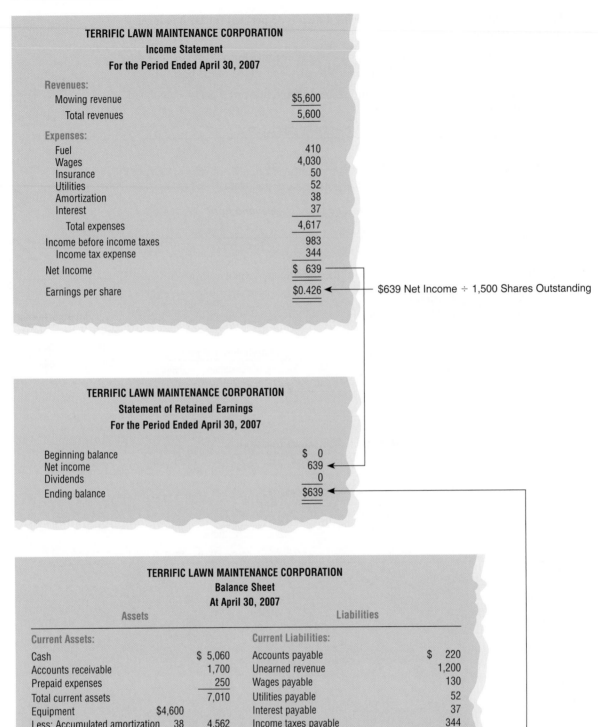

TERRIFIC LAWN MAINTENANCE CORPORATION
Income Statement
For the Period Ended April 30, 2007

Revenues:	
Mowing revenue	$5,600
Total revenues	5,600
Expenses:	
Fuel	410
Wages	4,030
Insurance	50
Utilities	52
Amortization	38
Interest	37
Total expenses	4,617
Income before income taxes	983
Income tax expense	344
Net Income	$ 639
Earnings per share	$0.426

$639 Net Income ÷ 1,500 Shares Outstanding

TERRIFIC LAWN MAINTENANCE CORPORATION
Statement of Retained Earnings
For the Period Ended April 30, 2007

Beginning balance	$ 0
Net income	639
Dividends	0
Ending balance	$639

TERRIFIC LAWN MAINTENANCE CORPORATION
Balance Sheet
At April 30, 2007

Assets			Liabilities	
Current Assets:			Current Liabilities:	
Cash		$ 5,060	Accounts payable	$ 220
Accounts receivable		1,700	Unearned revenue	1,200
Prepaid expenses		250	Wages payable	130
Total current assets		7,010	Utilities payable	52
Equipment	$4,600		Interest payable	37
Less: Accumulated amortization	38	4,562	Income taxes payable	344
Land		3,750	Notes payable	3,700
			Total current liabilities	5,683
			Shareholders' Equity	
			Share capital	9,000
			Retained earnings	639
			Total shareholders' equity	9,639
Total assets		$15,322	Total liabilities and shareholders' equity	$15,322

5. Closing entries

Mowing revenue (−R)	5,600	
Income summary (+T)		5,600
Income summary (−T)	4,961	
Fuel expense (−E)		410
Wages expense (−E)		4,030
Insurance expense (−E)		50
Utilities expense (−E)		52
Amortization expense (−E)		38
Interest expense (−E)		37
Income tax expense (−E)		344
Income summary (−T)	639	
Retained earnings (+SE)		639

6. Net Profit Margin for April:

$$\frac{\text{Net Income}}{\text{Net Sales}} = \$639 \div \$5,600 = 0.1141 \text{ or } 11.41\%$$

Return on Equity for April:

$$\frac{\text{Net Income}}{\text{Average Shareholders' Equity}} = \frac{\$639}{(\$9,000 + \$9,639) \div 2} = 0.0686 \text{ or } 6.86\%$$

7.

	Balance Sheet			Income Statement		
Transaction	Assets	Liabilities	Shareholders' Equity	Revenues	Expenses	Net Income
a.	NE	O, $400	U, $400	U, $400	NE	U, $400
b.	O, $50	NE	O, $50	NE	U, $50	O, $50
c.	O	NE, $38	O, $38	NE	U, $38	O, $38

SOLUTIONS TO **SELF-STUDY QUIZZES**

Self-Study Quiz 4-1

(b) The account to be adjusted is an accrual.

Accounts receivable (+A)	900	
Franchise-related revenue (+R, +SE)		900

Self-Study Quiz 4-2

(g) The principal was recorded when the note was signed. However, the bank's money was used during the month. Using money borrowed from others entails interest expense for the period of use until the principal is repaid.

$1,000 principal × 12% annual interest rate × 1 month/12 = $10 interest expense

Both Accrued Expenses Payable (L) and Interest Expense (E) are increased by $10, resulting in $10 balances for each.

Interest expense (+E, −SE)	10	
Accrued expenses payable (+L)		10

Self-Study Quiz 4-3

Net profit margin based on the unadjusted trial balance:

Income before income taxes = $76,300 − $58,210 = $18,090

Income tax expense = $18,090 × 25% = $4,522; Net income = $18,090 − $4,522 = $13,568

Net profit margin = $13,568 ÷ $72,800 = 0.186 or 18.6%.

Net profit margin based on the adjusted trial balance:

Net profit margin = $6,360 ÷ $73,800 = 0.086 or 8.6%.

The difference between the two ratios is due to the end-of-period adjustments that increased revenues by $1,000 and increased expenses by $8,208, thus lowering net income significantly by $7,208, from $13,568 to $6,360. The difference between the two ratios is 10%. It is certainly a material difference. Clearly, if adjustments to the revenue and expense accounts are not made, the net income will be overstated as well as the net profit margin. Inaccurate information is not useful for decision making. Thus what appears to be a set of very intricate procedures, when properly executed, actually contribute to the decision usefulness of financial statements.

Chapter Supplement

An Optional Recordkeeping Efficiency

In the examples on pages 167 and 168, cash received or paid prior to revenue or expense recognition was recorded in a balance sheet account. This approach is consistent with accrual accounting since, on the cash exchange date, either an asset or a liability exists. Payments or receipts are often recorded, however, as expenses or revenues on the transaction date. This is done to simplify recordkeeping since revenues or expenses are frequently earned or incurred by the end of the accounting period. When the full amount is not completely incurred or earned, an adjustment is necessary in these cases also. Note that, regardless of how the original entry is recorded, the same correct ending balances in the Unearned Dental Fee Revenue and Dental Fee Revenue accounts result after the adjustment. The adjusting entry is different, however, in each case.

For example, for the December 1 illustration, the original entry could have been recorded in a revenue account and adjusted as follows:

Step 1. On December 1, the amount received could have been recorded as revenue.

Cash (+A)	2,400	
Dental fee revenue (+R, +SE)		2,400

Step 2. As time passes after receiving the fees, only a portion of the fees are earned and the rest is due as service in the future.

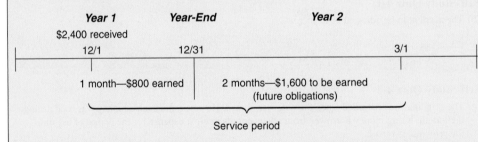

Unearned Dental Fee Revenue (L)

		0	12/1
		1,600	AJE
		1,600	12/31

Dental Fee Revenue (R)

		2,400	12/1
AJE	1,600		
		800	12/31

Step 3. The unearned portion ($1,600) of the revenue is a liability, with service due in the future. The remaining portion ($800) is revenue earned in the current period. The adjusting entry and translation effects follow.

12/31 AJE— Dental fee revenue (−R, −SE)	1,600	
Unearned dental fee revenue (+L)		1,600

Assets	=	Liabilities	+	Shareholders' Equity
		Unearned dental fee revenue +1,600		Dental fee revenue −1,600

CHAPTER **TAKE-AWAYS**

1. **Utilize an adjusted trial balance to prepare financial statements. p. 162**
   A trial balance is a list of all accounts with their debit or credit balances indicated in the appropriate column to provide a check on the equality of the debits and credits. The trial balance may be
   - Unadjusted—before adjustments are made.
   - Adjusted—after adjustments are made.
   - Post-closing—after revenues and expenses are closed to Retained Earnings.

2. **Analyze the adjustments necessary at the end of the period to update balance sheet and income statement accounts. p. 164**
   - Adjusting entries are necessary at the end of the accounting period to measure income properly and provide for appropriate amounts for balance sheet accounts. The analysis involves
     (1) Identifying deferrals (accounts created in the past when cash was received or paid before being earned or incurred) and accruals (revenues earned and expenses incurred before cash is to be received or paid in the future).
     (2) Drawing a time line with relevant dates, amounts, and any computations included for each deferral or accrual.
     (3) Recording the adjusting entry needed to obtain the appropriate ending balances in the accounts.
   The effect is summarized as follows:

   - Recording adjusting entries has no effect on the Cash account.

3. **Prepare an income statement with earnings per share, a statement of retained earnings, a balance sheet, and supplemental cash flow information. p. 178**
   Adjusted account balances are used in preparing the following financial statements:
   - Income Statement → Revenues − Expenses = Net Income (including earnings per share computed as net income available to the common shareholders divided by the weighted-average number of common shares outstanding during the period).
   - Statement of Retained Earnings → Beginning Retained Earnings + Net Income − Dividends = Ending Retained Earnings.
   - Balance Sheet → Assets = Liabilities + Shareholders' Equity.
   - Supplemental cash flow information—Interest paid, income taxes paid, and significant noncash transactions.

4. **Compute and interpret the net profit margin ratio and the return on equity ratio. p. 182**
   The net profit margin ratio (Net Income ÷ Net Sales) measures how much profit each dollar of sales generated during the period. A rising net profit margin signals more efficient management of sales and expenses. The return on equity measures how well management used the investment by shareholders during the period. Managers, analysts, and creditors use this ratio to assess the effectiveness of the overall business strategy (its operating, investing, and financing strategies).

5. **Explain the closing process at the end of the period. p. 184**
   Temporary accounts (revenues, expenses, gains, and losses) are closed to a zero balance at the end of the accounting period to allow for the accumulation of income items in the following period. To close these accounts:
   - Debit each revenue and gain account and credit Retained Earnings.
   - Credit each expense and loss account and debit Retained Earnings.

   Each year, many companies report healthy profits but file for bankruptcy. Some investors consider this situation to be a paradox, but sophisticated analysts understand how this situation can occur. These analysts recognize that the income statement is prepared under the accrual concept (revenue is reported when earned and the related expense is matched with the revenue). The income statement does not report cash collections and cash payments. Troubled companies usually file for bankruptcy because they cannot meet their cash obligations (for example, they cannot pay their suppliers or meet their required interest payments). The income statement does not help analysts assess the cash flows of a company. The cash flow statement discussed in Chapter 5 is designed to help statement users evaluate a company's cash inflows and outflows.

KEY RATIOS

Net profit margin measures how much profit each sales dollar generated during the period. A high or rising ratio suggests that the company is managing its sales and expenses efficiently. It is computed as follows (p. 182):

$$\text{Net Profit Margin} = \frac{\text{Net Income}}{\text{Net Sales}}$$

Return on equity measures how much the firm earned for each dollar of shareholders' investment. It is computed as follows (p. 183):

$$\text{Return on Equity} = \frac{\text{Net Income}}{\text{Average Shareholders' Equity}}$$

FINDING FINANCIAL INFORMATION

BALANCE SHEET

Current Assets
  Accruals include
    Interest receivable
    Rent receivable
  Deferrals include
    Inventory
    Prepaid expenses
Non-Current Assets
  Deferrals include
    Property and equipment
    Intangibles

Current Liabilities
  Accruals include
    Interest payable
    Wages payable
    Utilities payable
    Income tax payable
  Deferrals include
    Unearned revenue

INCOME STATEMENT

Revenues
  Include end-of-period adjustments
Expenses
  Include end-of-period adjustments
Income before Income Taxes
  Income tax expense

Net Income

CASH FLOW STATEMENT

Adjusting Entries Do Not Affect Cash
  Supplemental Disclosure
    Interest paid
    Income taxes paid
    Sgnificant noncash transactions

NOTES

In Various Notes If Not on the Balance Sheet
  Details of accrued expenses payable
  Interest paid, income taxes paid, significant noncash transactions (if not reported on the cash flow statement)

KEY TERMS

Accounting Cycle p. 162
Accrued Expenses p. 165
Accrued Revenues p. 166
Adjusting Entries p. 164
Closing Entries p. 184
Contra Account p. 163
Deferred Expenses p. 166
Deferred Revenues p. 165

Income Summary p. 184
Materiality p. 176
Net Book Value (Book Value, Carrying Value) p. 164
Permanent (Real) Accounts p. 184
Post-Closing Trial Balance p. 185
Temporary (Nominal) Accounts p. 184
Trial Balance p. 162

QUESTIONS

1. Explain the accounting information processing cycle.
2. Identify, in sequence, the phases of the accounting information processing cycle.
3. What is a trial balance? What is its purpose?
4. Briefly explain adjusting entries. List the four types of adjusting entries, and give an example of each type.
5. Explain estimated residual value. Why is it important in measuring amortization expense?
6. What is a contra asset? Give an example of one.
7. Explain why adjusting entries are entered in the journal on the last day of the accounting period and then are posted to the ledger.
8. Explain how the financial statements relate to each other.
9. What is the equation for each of the following statements: (a) income statement, (b) balance sheet, (c) cash flow statement, and (d) statement of retained earnings?
10. Explain the effect of adjusting entries on cash.
11. How is earnings per share computed and interpreted?
12. Contrast an unadjusted trial balance with an adjusted trial balance. What is the purpose of each?
13. Why does net income differ from cash flow from operations? Explain.
14. What is the practical importance of the concept of materiality to preparers, auditors, and users of financial statements?
15. What is meant by the "quality of earnings"?
16. What is the purpose of closing entries? Why are they recorded in the journal and posted to the ledger?
17. Differentiate among (a) permanent, (b) temporary, (c) real, and (d) nominal accounts.
18. Why are the income statement accounts closed but the balance sheet accounts are not?
19. What is a post-closing trial balance? Is it a useful part of the accounting information processing cycle? Explain.
20. How is the net profit margin ratio computed and interpreted?
21. How is the return on equity computed and interpreted?

EXERCISES

E4–1 Preparing a Trial Balance

■ LO1

Swanson Company has the following adjusted accounts and balances at year-end (June 30, 2007):

Accounts payable	200	Cash	120	Land	200
Accounts receivable	400	Cost of sales	820	Long-term debt	1,300
Accrued expenses		Income taxes		Prepaid expenses	40
payable	150	expense	110	Rent expense	400
Accumulated		Income taxes		Retained earnings	170
amortization	250	payable	30	Salaries expense	660
Amortization expense	110	Interest expense	80	Sales revenue	2,400
Buildings and		Interest income	50	Share capital	300
equipment	1,400	Inventories	610	Unearned fees	100

All these accounts have normal debit or credit balances.

Required:
Prepare an adjusted trial balance in good form for the Swanson Company at June 30, 2007.

E4–2 Identifying Adjusting Entries from Unadjusted Trial Balance

■ LO2

As stated in its annual report, Unik Computer Corporation is an information technology company, developing and marketing hardware, software, solutions, and services. Following is a hypothetical trial balance listing account that Unik uses. Assume that the balances are unadjusted at the end of a recent fiscal year ended December 31.

UNIK COMPUTER CORPORATION
Unadjusted Trial Balance
At December 31, 2008
(millions of dollars)

	Debit	Credit
Cash	$ 4,091	
Accounts receivable	6,998	
Inventories	2,005	
Prepaid expenses	624	
Property, plant, and equipment	5,223	
Accumulated amortization		$ 2,321
Intangible assets	3,641	
Other assets	3,414	
Accounts payable		4,237
Accrued liabilities		1,110
Income taxes payable		282
Pension obligations		545
Other liabilities		5,104
Share capital		7,270
Retained earnings		8,633
Product revenue		27,372
Services revenue		3,797
Cost of products sold	21,383	
Cost of services sold	2,597	
Selling, general, and administrative expenses	4,978	
Research and development costs	1,353	
Other operating expenses	4,283	
Income tax expense	81	
	60,671	60,671

Required

1. Based on the information in the unadjusted trial balance, list the balance sheet deferral accounts that may need to be adjusted at December 31 and the related income statement account in each case (no computations are necessary).

2. Based on the information in the unadjusted trial balance, list the balance sheet accrual accounts that may need to be recorded at December 31 and the related income statement account in each case (no computations are necessary).

3. Which accounts should be closed at the end of the year? Why?

LO2

E4–3 Recording Adjusting Entries and Determining Financial Statement Effects (Deferral Accounts)

Consider the following transactions for Liner Company.

a. Collected $1,500 rent for the period December 1, 2007, to March 1, 2008, which was credited to Deferred Rent Revenue on December 1, 2007.

b. Paid $1,800 for a one-year insurance premium on July 1, 2007; debited Prepaid Insurance for that amount.

c. Purchased a machine for $10,000 cash on January 1, 2006; estimated a useful life of five years with a residual value of $2,000.

Required:

1. Prepare the adjusting entries required for the year ended December 31, 2007, using the process illustrated in the chapter.

2. For each of the transactions above, indicate the amounts and direction of effects of the adjusting entry on the elements of the balance sheet and income statement. Using the following format, indicate + for increase, − for decrease, and NE for no effect.

	Balance Sheet			Income Statement		
Transaction	Assets	Liabilities	Shareholders' Equity	Revenues	Expenses	Net Income
a.						
b.						
c.						

E4–4 Recording Adjusting Entries and Determining Financial Statement Effects (Accrual Accounts) ▮ LO2

Consider the following transactions for Liner Company.

a. Received a $220 utility bill for electricity usage in December to be paid in January 2008.

b. Owed wages to 10 employees who worked three days at $150 each per day at the end of December. The company will pay employees at the end of the first week of January 2008.

c. On September 1, 2007, loaned $3,000 to an officer who will repay the loan in one year at an annual interest rate of 12 percent.

Required:

1. Prepare the adjusting entries required for the year ended December 31, 2007, using the process illustrated in the chapter:

2. For each of the transactions above, indicate the amounts and direction of effects of the adjusting entry on the elements of the balance sheet and income statement. Using the following format, indicate + for increase, − for decrease, and NE for no effect.

	Balance Sheet			Income Statement		
Transaction	Assets	Liabilities	Shareholders' Equity	Revenues	Expenses	Net Income
a.						
b.						
c.						

E4–5 Recording Adjusting Entries ▮ LO2

Evans Company completed its first year of operations on December 31, 2008. All of the 2008 entries have been recorded, except for the following:

a. At year-end, employees earned wages of $6,000, which will be paid on the next payroll date, January 6, 2009.

b. At year-end, the company had earned interest revenue of $3,000. The cash will be collected March 1, 2009.

Required

1. What is the annual reporting period for this company?

2. Identify whether each transaction above is a deferral or an accrual. Using the process illustrated in the chapter, prepare the required adjusting entry for transactions (*a*) and (*b*). Include appropriate dates and write a brief explanation of each entry.

3. Why are these adjustments made?

E4–6 Recording Adjusting Entries and Reporting Balances in Financial Statements ▮ LO2

Dion, Ltée is making adjusting entries for the year ended December 31, 2008. In developing information for the adjusting entries, the accountant learned the following:

a. Paid a one-year insurance premium of $3,000 on September 1, 2008, for coverage beginning on that date.

b. At December 31, 2008, obtained the following data relating to shipping supplies from the records and supporting documents. The company uses a large amount of shipping supplies that are purchased in volume, stored, and used as needed.

Shipping supplies on hand, January 1, 2008	$14,000
Purchases of shipping supplies during 2008	72,000
Shipping supplies on hand, per inventory December 31, 2008	11,000

Required

1. What amount should be reported on the 2008 income statement for Insurance Expense? For Shipping Supplies Expense?

2. What amount should be reported on the December 31, 2008, balance sheet for Prepaid Insurance? For Shipping Supplies Inventory?

3. Using the process illustrated in the chapter, record the adjusting entry for insurance at December 31, 2008, assuming that the bookkeeper debited the full amount paid on September 1, 2008, to Prepaid Insurance.

4. Using the process illustrated in the chapter, record the adjusting entry for shipping supplies at December 31, 2008, assuming that the purchases of shipping supplies were debited in full to Shipping Supplies Inventory.

LO2   **E4–7** **Recording Seven Typical Adjusting Entries**

Crawford's Department Store is completing the accounting process for the year just ended, December 31, 2008. The transactions during 2008 have been journalized and posted. The following data with respect to adjusting entries are available:

a. Office supplies inventory at January 1, 2008, was $350. Office supplies purchased and debited to Office Supplies Inventory during the year amounted to $900. The year-end inventory showed $200 of supplies on hand.

b. Wages earned during December 2008, unpaid and unrecorded at December 31, 2008, amounted to $2,700. The last payroll date was December 28; the next pay date will be January 6, 2009.

c. Three-fourths of the basement of the store is rented for $1,200 per month to another merchant, M. Riesman. Riesman sells compatible, but not competitive, merchandise. On November 1, 2008, the store collected six months' rent in the amount of $7,200 in advance from Riesman and credited the amount to Unearned Rent Revenue.

d. The remaining basement space is rented to Rita's Specialty Shop for $500 per month, payable monthly. On December 31, 2008, the rent for November and December 2008 was neither collected nor recorded. Collection is expected on January 10, 2009.

e. The store used delivery equipment that cost $30,000 and was estimated to have a useful life of four years and a residual value of $4,000 at the end of the four years. Assume amortization for a full year for 2008. The asset will be amortized evenly over its useful life.

f. On July 1, 2008, a one-year insurance premium amounting to $1,800 was paid in cash and debited to Prepaid Insurance. Coverage began on July 1, 2008.

g. Crawford's operates an alteration shop to meet its own needs. The shop also does alterations for M. Riesman. At the end of December 31, 2008, Riesman had not paid for alterations completed, amounting to $750. This amount has not yet been recorded as Alteration Shop Revenue. Collection is expected during January 2009.

Required

1. Identify each of these transactions as a deferred revenue, deferred expense, accrued revenue, or accrued expense.

2. Using the process illustrated in the chapter, prepare for each situation the adjusting entry that should be recorded for Crawford's at December 31, 2008.

LO2, 3   **E4–8** **Determining Financial Statement Effects of Seven Typical Adjusting Entries**
Refer to E4–7.

Required:

For each of the transactions in E4–7, indicate the amount and direction of effects of the adjusting entry on the elements of the balance sheet and income statement. Using the following format, indicate + for increase, − for decrease, and NE for no effect.

	Balance Sheet			Income Statement		
Transaction	Assets	Liabilities	Shareholders' Equity	Revenues	Expenses	Net Income
a.						
b.						
c.						
etc.						

E4–9 **Recording Seven Typical Adjusting Entries** ◾ **LO2**

Keanu's Boat Yard, Inc., is completing the accounting process for the year just ended, November 30, 2008. The transactions during 2008 have been journalized and posted. The following data with respect to adjusting entries are available:

a. Keanu cleaned and covered three boats for customers at the end of November, but did not bill the customers $2,100 for the service until December.

b. The Tonga family paid Keanu $2,400 on November 1, 2008, to store their sailboat for the winter until May 1, 2009. Keanu credited the full amount to Unearned Storage Revenue on November 1.

c. Wages earned by employees during November 2008, unpaid and unrecorded at November 30, 2008, amounted to $2,900. The next payroll date will be December 5, 2008.

d. On October 1, 2008, Keanu paid $600 to the local newspaper for an advertisement to run every Thursday for 12 weeks. All ads have been run except for three Thursdays in December to complete the 12-week contract.

e. Keanu used boat-lifting equipment that cost $230,000; the estimated amortization for fiscal year 2008 is $23,000.

f. Boat repair supplies on hand at December 1, 2007 totalled $15,600. Repair supplies purchased and debited to Supplies Inventory during the year amounted to $47,500. The year-end inventory showed $12,200 of the supplies remaining on hand.

g. On April 1, 2008, Keanu borrowed $150,000 at an annual interest rate of 10 percent, to expand boat storage facility. The loan requires Keanu to pay interest quarterly until the note is repaid in three years. Keanu paid quarterly interest on July 1 and October 1, 2008.

Required:

1. Identify each of these transactions as a deferred revenue, deferred expense, accrued revenue, or accrued expense.

2. Using the process illustrated in the chapter, prepare for each situation the adjusting entry that should be recorded for Keanu's at November 30, 2008.

E4–10 **Determining Financial Statement Effects of Seven Typical Adjusting Entries** ◾ **LO2, 3**

Refer to E4–9.

Required:

For each of the transactions in E4–9, indicate the amount and direction of effects of the adjusting entry on the elements of the balance sheet and income statement. Using the following format, indicate + for increase, − for decrease, and NE for no effect.

	Balance Sheet			**Income Statement**		
Transaction	Assets	Liabilities	Shareholders' Equity	Revenues	Expenses	Net Income
a.						
b.						
c.						
etc.						

E4–11 **Determining Financial Statement Effects of Three Adjusting Entries** ◾ **LO2, 3**

Kwan Corp. started operations on January 1, 2008. It is now December 31, 2008, the end of the fiscal year. The part-time bookkeeper needs your help to analyze the following three transactions:

a. On January 1, 2008, the company purchased a special machine for a cash cost of $15,000. The machine has an estimated useful life of 10 years and no residual value.

b. During 2008, the company purchased office supplies that cost $1,800. At the end of 2008, office supplies worth $400 remained on hand.

c. On July 1, 2008, the company paid cash of $900 for a one-year premium on an insurance policy on the machine. Coverage began on July 1, 2008.

Required:

Complete the following schedule of the amounts that should be reported for 2008:

Selected Balance Sheet Amounts at December 31, 2008	Amount to Be Reported
Assets	
Equipment	$ _____
Accumulated amortization	_____
Carrying value of equipment	_____
Office supplies inventory	_____
Prepaid insurance	_____
Selected Income Statement Amounts for the Year Ended December 31, 2008	
Expenses	
Amortization expense	$ _____
Office supplies expense	_____
Insurance expense	_____

■ LO2

Deere & Company

E4–12 Inferring Transactions

Deere & Company is the world's leading producer of agricultural equipment; a leading supplier of a broad range of industrial equipment for construction, forestry, and public works; a producer and marketer of a broad line of lawn and grounds care equipment; and a provider of credit, managed health care plans, and insurance products for businesses and the general public. The following information is taken from an annual report (in millions of dollars):

Income Taxes Payable				Dividends Payable				Interest Payable		
		Beg. bal.	71			Beg. bal.	43			Beg. bal.
(a)	?	(b)	332	(c)	?	(d)	176	(e)	297	(f)
		End. bal.	80			End. bal.	48			End. bal.

Required:

1. Identify the nature of each of the transactions (*a*) through (*f*). Specifically, what activities cause the accounts to increase and decrease?
2. Compute the amounts of transactions (*a*), (*c*), and (*f*).

■ LO2

ANALYSIS

E4–13 Analyzing the Effects of Errors on Financial Statement Items

Scarletti and Long, Inc., publishers of movie and song trivia books, made the following errors in adjusting the accounts at year-end (December 31):

a. Did not record amortization on equipment costing $130,000 with a residual value of $30,000 and a 10-year useful life.

b. Failed to adjust the Unearned Revenue account to reflect that $2,000 was earned by the end of the year.

c. Recorded a full year of accrued interest expense on a $18,000, 10-percent note payable that has been outstanding since November 1 of the current year.

d. Failed to adjust Insurance Expense to reflect that $400 relates to future insurance coverage.

e. Did not accrue $800 owed to the company by another company renting part of the building as a storage facility.

Required:

1. For each error, prepare (a) the adjusting journal entry that was made, if any, (b) the entry that should have been made at year-end, and (c) the entry to correct the error.
2. Using the following headings, indicate the effect of each error and the amount of the effect (that is, the difference between the entry that was or was not made and the entry that should have been made). Use O if the effect overstates the item, U if the effect understates the item, and NE if there is no effect.

	Balance Sheet			Income Statement		
Transaction	Assets	Liabilities	Shareholders' Equity	Revenues	Expenses	Net Income
a.						
b.						
c.						
etc.						

3. Explain the concept of materiality and how it might affect the adjusting entries you prepared in requirement 1.

E4–14   **Analyzing the Effects of Adjusting Entries on the Income Statement and Balance Sheet**

■ **LO2, 3**

ANALYSIS

On December 31, 2007, Cohen and Company prepared an income statement and balance sheet but failed to take into account four adjusting entries. The income statement, prepared on this incorrect basis, reflected pretax income of $30,000. The balance sheet (before the effect of income taxes) reflected total assets, $90,000; total liabilities, $40,000; and shareholders' equity, $50,000. The data for the four adjusting entries follow:

a. Amortization for the year on equipment that cost $75,000 was not recorded. The equipment's useful life is 10 years and its residual value is $5,000.

b. Wages amounting to $17,000 for the last three days of December 2007 were not paid and not recorded (the next pay date is January 10, 2008).

c. An amount of $4,500 was collected on December 1, 2007, for rental of office space for the period December 1, 2007, to February 28, 2008. The $4,500 was credited in full to Unearned Rent Revenue when collected.

d. Income taxes were not recorded. The income tax rate for the company is 30 percent.

Required:
Complete the following tabulation to correct the financial statements for the effects of the four errors (indicate deductions with parentheses):

Items	Net Income	Total Assets	Total Liabilities	Shareholders' Equity
Balances reported	$30,000	$90,000	$40,000	$50,000
Effect of amortization	_____	_____	_____	_____
Effect of wages	_____	_____	_____	_____
Effect of rent revenue	_____	_____	_____	_____
Adjusted balances	_____	_____	_____	_____
Effect of income taxes	_____	_____	_____	_____
Correct balances	======	======	======	======

E4–15   **Reporting a Correct Income Statement with Earnings per Share to Include the Effects of Adjusting Entries and Evaluating the Net Profit Margin as an Auditor**

■ **LO2, 3, 4**

Barton, Inc., completed its first year of operations on December 31, 2008. Because this is the end of the fiscal year, the company bookkeeper prepared the following tentative income statement:

Income Statement, 2008		
Rental revenue		$114,000
Expenses:		
Salaries and wages expense	$28,500	
Maintenance expense	12,000	
Rent expense (on location)	9,000	
Utilities expense	4,000	
Gas and oil expense	3,000	
Miscellaneous expenses (items not listed elsewhere)	1,000	
Total expenses		57,500
Income		$ 56,500

You are an independent accountant hired by the company to audit its accounting systems and review its financial statements. In your audit, you developed additional data as follows:

a. Unpaid wages for the last three days of December amounting to $310 were not recorded.

b. The unpaid $400 telephone bill for December 2008 has not been recorded.

c. Amortization on rental autos, amounting to $23,000 for 2008, was not recorded.

d. Interest on a $20,000, one-year, 10-percent note payable dated October 1, 2008, was not recorded. The full amount of interest is payable on the maturity date of the note.

e. The Unearned Rental Revenue account has a balance of $4,000 as at December 31, 2008 which represents rental revenue for the month of January 2009.

f. Maintenance expense includes $1,000, which is the cost of maintenance supplies still on hand at December 31, 2008. These supplies will be used in 2009.

g. The income tax expense is $7,000. Payment of income tax will be made in 2009.

Required:

1. For each item (*a*) through (*g*) what adjusting entry, if any, do you recommend that Barton should record at December 31, 2008? If none is required, explain why.

2. Prepare a correct income statement for 2008 in good form including earnings per share, assuming that 7,000 shares are outstanding. Show computations.

3. Compute net profit margin based on the corrected information. What does this ratio suggest? If the industry average for net profit margin is 18 percent, what might you infer about Barton?

■ **LO3**

ANALYSIS

E4–16 Evaluating the Effect of Adjusting Unearned Subscriptions on Cash Flows and Performance as a Manager

You are the regional sales manager for Weld News Company. Weld is making adjusting entries for the year ended March 31, 2008. On September 1, 2007, $12,000 cash was received from customers in your region for two-year magazine subscriptions beginning on that date. The magazines are published and mailed to customers monthly. These were the only subscription sales in your region during the year.

Required:

1. What amount should be reported as cash from operations on the 2008 cash flow statement?

2. What amount should be reported on the 2008 income statement for subscriptions revenue?

3. What amount should be reported on the March 31, 2008, balance sheet for unearned subscriptions revenue?

4. Prepare the adjusting entry at March 31, 2008, assuming that the subscriptions received on September 1, 2007, were recorded for the full amount in Unearned Subscriptions Revenue.

5. The company expects your region's annual revenue target to be $4,000.
   a. Evaluate your region's performance, assuming that the revenue target is based on cash sales.
   b. Evaluate your region's performance, assuming that the revenue target is based on accrual accounting.

■ **LO2, 3, 5**

E4–17 Recording Adjusting Entries, Completing a Trial Balance, Preparing Financial Statements, and Recording Closing Entries

Cayuga Ltd. prepared the following trial balance at the end of its first year of operations ending December 31, 2009. To simplify the case, the amounts given are in thousands of dollars. Other data not yet recorded at December 31, 2009:

a. Insurance expired during 2009, $4.

b. Amortization expense for 2009, $4.

c. Wages payable, $8.

d. Income tax expense, $9.

Account Titles	Unadjusted		Adjustments		Adjusted	
	Debit	Credit	Debit	Credit	Debit	Credit
Cash	38					
Accounts receivable	9					
Prepaid insurance	6					
Machinery (20-year life, no residual value)	80					
Accumulated amortization		8				
Accounts payable		9				
Wages payable						
Income taxes payable						
Share capital (4,000 shares)		68				
Retained earnings (deficit)	4					
Revenues (not detailed)		84				
Expenses (not detailed)	32					
Totals	169	169				

Required:

1. Prepare the adjusting entries for 2009.
2. Complete the trial balance Adjustments and Adjusted columns.
3. Using the adjusted balances, complete the following income statement and statement of retained earnings for 2009, and the balance sheet at December 31, 2009.
4. What is the purpose of "closing the books" at the end of the accounting period?
5. Using the adjusted balances, prepare the closing entries for 2009.

Income Statement
For the Year Ended December 31, 2009
(in thousands except for earnings per share)

Revenues (not detailed) $ _____
Expenses (not detailed)   _____
Income before income tax   _____
Income tax expense   _____
Net income $ _____
Earnings per share $ _____

Statement of Retained Earnings
For the Year Ended December 31, 2009
(in thousands)

Beginning balance, January 1, 2009 $ _____
Net income   _____
Dividends declared   _____
Ending balance, December 31, 2009 $ _____

Balance Sheet
December 31, 2009
(in thousands)

Assets		Liabilities	
Cash	$ _____	Accounts payable	$ _____
Accounts receivable	_____	Wages payable	_____
Prepaid insurance	_____	Income taxes payable	_____
Machinery	_____	Total liabilities	_____
Accumulated amortization	_____		
		Shareholders' Equity	
		Share capital	_____
	_____	Retained earnings	_____
		Total liabilities and	
Total assets	$ =======	shareholders' equity	$ =======

■ **LO3, 4**   **E4–18 Preparing Financial Statements and Analyzing Net Profit Margin and Return on Equity**

Liner Company has the following adjusted trial balance at December 31, 2008. No dividends were declared; however, 400 additional shares were issued during the year for $2,000:

	Debit	Credit
Cash	$ 2,700	
Accounts receivable	3,000	
Interest receivable	120	
Prepaid insurance	600	
Notes receivable	3,000	
Equipment	12,000	
Accumulated amortization		$ 2,000
Accounts payable		1,600
Accrued expenses payable		3,820
Income taxes payable		2,900
Deferred rent revenue		600
Share capital (500 shares)		2,400
Retained earnings		1,000
Sales revenue		45,000
Interest revenue		120
Rent revenue		300
Wages expense	20,600	
Amortization expense	2,000	
Utilities expense	1,220	
Insurance expense	600	
Rent expense	10,000	
Income tax expense	3,900	
Total	$59,740	$59,740

Required:

1. Prepare an income statement in good form for 2008. Include earnings per share.
2. Prepare a statement of retained earnings in good form for 2008.
3. Prepare a balance sheet in good form at December 31, 2008.
4. Compute Liner Company's net profit margin for the year. What does this ratio mean?
5. Compute Liner Company's return on equity for the year. What does this ratio mean?

■ **LO4**   **E4–19 Analyzing and Evaluating Return on Equity from a Security Analyst's Perspective**

Papa John's

ANALYSIS

Papa John's is one of the fastest-growing pizza delivery and carry-out restaurant chains. Selected income statement and balance sheet amounts (in thousands) for two recent years are presented below.

	Current Year	Prior Year
Net income	$ 46,056	$ 23,221
Average shareholders' equity	150,251	149,248

Required:

1. Compute the return on equity for the current and prior years and explain the meaning of the change.
2. Would security analysts more likely increase or decrease their estimates of share value on the basis of this change? Explain.

E4–20   Evaluating Profitability Using Net Profit Margin and Return on Equity

Sears Canada is one of the biggest Canadian department store retailers. It operates a large number of department stores that sell home fashions, appliances, apparel, home electronics, and garden products. It also sells merchandise online. Selected information about the company's resources and operations are presented below (amounts in millions of dollars).

■ **LO4**

Sears Canada

ANALYSIS

	2005	2004	2003	2002	2001
Total shareholders' equity	$ 645	$1,877	$1,781	$1,627	$1,608
Total revenue	6,238	6,230	6,223	6,536	6,726
Net income	771	129	125	44	89

Required:

1. Compute the net profit margin and the return on equity for 2002 to 2005.
2. Both ratios increased significantly in 2005 compared to previous years. What are the most likely reasons for the significant increase in both ratios? (Hint: think about the reasons for an increase in net income and a decrease in shareholders' equity.)
3. As a potential investor, how do you interpret these ratios?
4. What additional information would you require before deciding whether or not to invest in Sears' shares?

E4–21   (Chapter Supplement) Recording Adjusting Entries

Consider each of the following independent cases and prepare the adjusting journal entry at year-end.

■ **LO2**

1. On June 30, 2007, Able Ltd. paid $18,000 for a two-year insurance policy. Insurance coverage started on July 1, 2007. The company's bookkeeper debited Insurance Expense and credited Cash, $18,000. Able's fiscal year ends on January 31, 2008.
2. On August 1, 2008, Landlord Inc., received $6,400 from a tenant representing payment of rent in advance for eight months (including August). Landlord's bookkeeper debited Cash and credited Rent Expense for $6,400. Landlord's fiscal year ends on December 31, 2008.
3. The accountant for Jung Corp. computed the income tax expense for the year 2008 to be $12,200. Before recording the journal entry, she noticed that the unadjusted trial balance at December 31, 2008 (the company's fiscal year-end) included Prepaid Income Taxes of $3,400 and a zero balance for Income Tax Expense.
4. On June 1, 2009 the Supplies Inventory account for Katz Ltd. showed a debit balance of $4,400. During June 2009 miscellaneous supplies totalling $1,800 were purchased on account and recorded as follows:

Supplies Expense	1,800	
Accounts Payable		1,800

A physical count of supplies available at June 30, 2009 showed that $2,600 of supplies were still on hand. Katz's fiscal year ends on June 30, 2009.

PROBLEMS

P4–1   Preparing a Trial Balance (AP4–1)

Dell Inc. is the world's largest computer systems company selling directly to customers. Products include desktop computer systems, notebook computers, workstations, network server and storage products, and peripheral hardware and software. The following is a list of accounts and amounts reported in recent financial statements. The accounts have normal debit or credit balances and the dollars are rounded to the nearest million. Assume the year ended on February 1, 2008.

■ **LO1**

Dell Inc.

Accounts payable	$ 7,316	Investments	$ 6,770	Research and development		
Accounts receivable	3,635	Long-term debt	505	expense	$	464
Accrued expenses payable	3,580	Other current assets	1,910	Retained earnings		?
Accumulated amortization	1,133	Other income	180	Sales revenue		41,444
Cash	4,317	Other non-current liabilities	1,630	Selling, general, and		
Cost of sales	33,892	Property, plant, and		administrative expenses		3,544
Income tax expense	1,079	equipment	2,650	Share capital		149
Inventories	327			Short-term investments		835

Required:

Prepare an adjusted trial balance at February 1, 2008. How did you determine the amount for retained earnings?

■ **LO2, 3**   **P4–2 Recording Adjusting Entries** (AP4–2)

McGraw Company's fiscal year ends on December 31. It is December 31, 2007, and all of the 2007 entries have been made, except the following adjusting entries.

a. On September 1, 2007, McGraw collected six months' rent of $7,200 on storage space. At that date, McGraw debited Cash and credited Unearned Rent Revenue for $7,200.

b. The company earned service revenue of $2,000 on a special job that was completed December 29, 2007. Collection will be made during January 2008; no entry has been recorded.

c. On November 1, 2007, McGraw paid a premium of $4,200 for a one-year property insurance policy, for coverage starting on that date. Cash was credited and Prepaid Insurance was debited for this amount.

d. At December 31, 2007, wages earned by employees totalled $14,300. The employees will be paid on the next payroll date, January 15, 2008.

e. Amortization must be recognized on a service truck that cost $12,000 on July 1, 2007 (estimated useful life is six years with no residual value).

f. Cash of $2,400 was collected on November 1, 2007, for services to be rendered evenly over the next year beginning on November 1 (Unearned Service Revenue was credited).

g. On December 27, 2007, the company received a tax bill of $450 from the city for property taxes on land for 2007. The amount is payable during January 2008.

h. On October 1, 2007, the company borrowed $20,000 from a local bank and signed a 8-percent note for that amount. The principal and interest are payable on September 30, 2008.

Required:

1. Indicate whether each transaction relates to a deferred revenue, deferred expense, accrued revenue, or accrued expense.

2. Prepare the adjusting entry required for each transaction at December 31, 2007.

■ **LO2, 3**   **P4–3 Recording Adjusting Entries and Determining Their Financial Statement Effects** (AP4–3)

Handy Haulers Company is at the end of its fiscal year, December 31, 2008. The following data were developed from the company's records and related documents:

a. On July 1, 2008, a one-year insurance premium on equipment in the amount of $1,200 was paid and debited to Prepaid Insurance. Coverage began on July 1.

b. During 2008, office supplies amounting to $800 were purchased for cash and debited in full to Supplies Inventory. At the end of 2007, the inventory of supplies remaining on hand (unused) amounted to $200. The inventory of supplies on hand at December 31, 2008, showed $300.

c. On December 31, 2008, Bert's Garage completed repairs on one of the company's trucks at a cost of $800; the amount is not yet recorded and by agreement will be paid during January 2009.

d. In December 2008, a tax bill for $2,000 on land owned during 2008 was received from the city. The taxes, which have not been recorded, are due on February 15, 2009.

e. On December 31, 2008, the company completed a contract for another company. The bill was for $8,000 payable within 30 days. No journal entry has been made for this transaction.

f. On July 1, 2008, the company purchased a new hauling van at a cash cost of $23,600. The estimated useful life of the van was 10 years, with an estimated residual value of $1,100. No amortization has been recorded for 2008 (compute amortization for six months in 2008).

g. On October 1, 2008, the company borrowed $10,000 from the local bank on a one-year, 9-percent note payable. The principal plus interest is payable on September 30, 2009.

h. The income before any of the adjustments or income taxes was $30,000. The company's income tax rate is 30 percent. Compute the adjusted income after considering the effects of Transactions (*a*) through (*g*) to determine the income tax expense for 2008.

Required:

1. Indicate whether each transaction relates to a deferred revenue, deferred expense, accrued revenue, or accrued expense.

2. Prepare the adjusting entry required for each transaction at December 31, 2008.

3. Using the following headings, indicate the effect of each adjusting entry and the amount of each. Use + for increase, − for decrease, and NE for no effect.

	Balance Sheet			**Income Statement**		
Transaction	**Assets**	**Liabilities**	**Shareholders' Equity**	**Revenues**	**Expenses**	**Net Income**
a.						
b.						
c.						
etc.						

P4–4 **Computing Amounts on Financial Statements and Finding Financial Information** (AP4–4) **LO3**

The following transactions and events are provided by the records of South Hill Apartments (a corporation) at the end of its fiscal year, December 31, 2007:

Revenue	
a. Rent revenue collected in cash during 2007 for occupancy in 2007	$512,000
b. Rent revenue earned for occupancy in December 2007; not collected until 2008	16,000
c. Rent collected in December 2007 in advance of occupancy in January 2008	12,000
Salaries	
d. Cash payment in January 2007 for employee salaries earned in December 2008	4,000
e. Salaries incurred and paid during 2007	62,000
f. Salaries earned by employees during December 2007 that will be paid in January 2008	3,000
g. Cash advance to employees in December 2007 for salaries that will be earned in January 2008	1,500
Supplies	
h. Maintenance supplies inventory on January 1, 2007 (balance on hand)	3,000
i. Maintenance supplies purchased for cash during 2007	8,000
j. Maintenance supplies inventory on December 31, 2007	1,700

Required:

Using T-accounts, compute the amounts that should be reported in South Hill's 2007 financial statements for the following items, and indicate on which financial statement the item is reported. For Cash, create one T-account and label each effect to determine the amounts affecting cash as indicated here (from tenants, to suppliers, to employees):

1. Rent revenue
2. Salary expense
3. Maintenance supplies expense
4. Cash from tenants
5. Rent receivable
6. Cash to suppliers

7. Receivables from employees
8. Maintenance supplies inventory
9. Unearned rent revenue
10. Salaries payable
11. Cash to employees

P4–5 **Inferring Year-End Adjustments, Computing Earnings per Share and Net Profit Margin, and Recording Closing Entry** (AP4–5) **LO1, 2, 4, 5**

Willenborg Company is completing the information processing cycle at its fiscal year-end, December 31, 2009. Following are the correct account balances at December 31, 2009, both before and after the adjusting entries for 2009.

	Trial Balance, December 31, 2009						
	Before Adjusting Entries		Adjustments		After Adjusting Entries		
Items	Debit	Credit	Debit	Credit	Debit	Credit
a. Cash	$ 9,000				$ 9,000	
b. Service revenue receivable					400	
c. Prepaid insurance	600				400	
d. Equipment	120,200				120,200	
e. Accumulated amortization, equipment		$31,500				$ 40,000
f. Accrued advertising payable						4,700
g. Share capital		80,000				80,000
h. Retained earnings, January 1, 2009		14,000				14,000
i. Service revenue		46,000				46,400
j. Salary expense	41,700				41,700	
k. Amortization expense					8,500	
l. Insurance expense					200	
m. Advertising expense					4,700	
	$171,500	$171,500			$185,100	$185,100

Required:

1. Compare the amounts in the columns before and after the adjusting entries to reconstruct the adjusting entries made in 2009. Provide an explanation for each adjustment.

2. Compute the amount of income, assuming that it is based on the amounts (a) before adjusting entries and (b) after adjusting entries. Which income amount is correct? Explain.

3. Compute the earnings per share, assuming that 4,000 shares are outstanding.

4. Compute the net profit margin. What does this suggest to you about the company?

5. Compute the return on equity, assuming that share capital did not change during the year. What does the computed ratio suggest to you about the company?

6. Prepare the closing entries at December 31, 2009.

■ **LO1, 2, 3, 5**   **P4–6**   **Recording Adjusting and Closing Entries and Preparing a Balance Sheet and an Income Statement Including Earnings per Share** (AP4–6)

Mostert, Inc., a small service company, keeps its records without the help of an accountant. After much effort, an outside accountant prepared the following unadjusted trial balance as at the end of the company's fiscal year, December 31, 2008:

Data not yet recorded at December 31, 2008, include:

a. The supplies inventory on December 31, 2008, reflected $200 remaining on hand.

b. Insurance expired during 2008, $400.

c. Amortization expense for 2008, $4,000.

d. Wages earned by employees not yet paid on December 31, 2008, $1,100.

e. Income tax expense was $7,350.

Account Titles	Debit	Credit
Cash	60,000	
Accounts receivable	13,000	
Service supplies inventory	800	
Prepaid insurance	1,000	
Service trucks (5-year life, no residual value)	20,000	
Accumulated amortization, service trucks		12,000
Other assets	11,200	
Accounts payable		3,000
Note payable (3 years; 10% each December 31)		20,000
Share capital (5,000 shares outstanding)		28,200
Retained earnings		7,500
Service revenue		77,000
Other expenses, excluding income tax	41,700	
Totals	147,700	147,700

Required:

1. Prepare the adjusting entries at December 31, 2008.

2. Prepare an income statement for 2008 and a balance sheet at December 31, 2008, including the effects of the preceding five transactions.

3. Assume that you forgot to adjust the balance of the service supplies inventory account. How would this error affect the amount of net income? Does this error lead to a material effect on net income? Explain.

4. Prepare the closing entries at December 31, 2008.

P4–7 Preparing Both an Income Statement and Balance Sheet from a Trial Balance and Closing Entries (AP4–7)   ■ **LO3, 4, 5**

Juan Real Estate Company (organized as a corporation on April 1, 2006) has completed the accounting cycle for the second year, ended March 31, 2008. Juan also has completed a correct trial balance as follows:

JUAN REAL ESTATE COMPANY
Adjusted Trial Balance
At March 31, 2008

Account Titles	Debit	Credit
Cash	$ 53,000	
Accounts receivable	44,800	
Office supplies inventory	300	
Automobiles (company cars)	30,000	
Accumulated amortization, automobiles		$ 10,000
Office equipment	3,000	
Accumulated amortization, office equipment		1,000
Accounts payable		20,250
Salaries and commissions payable		1,500
Note payable, long term		30,000
Share capital (30,000 shares)		35,000
Retained earnings (on April 1, 2007)		7,350
Dividends declared	8,000	
Sales commissions earned		77,000
Management fees earned		13,000
Operating expenses (detail omitted to conserve your time)	48,000	
Amortization expense (including $500 on office equipment)	5,500	
Interest expense	2,500	
Totals	$195,100	$195,100

Required:

1. Prepare an income statement for the reporting year ended March 31, 2008. Include income tax expense, assuming a 30-percent tax rate. Use the following major captions: Revenues, Expenses, Income before Income Taxes, Income Tax, Net Income, and Earnings per Share (list each item under these captions as appropriate).

2. Prepare the journal entry to record income taxes for the year (not yet paid).

3. Prepare a balance sheet at the end of the reporting year, March 31, 2008. Use the following captions (list each item under these captions as appropriate).

Assets

Current Assets
Non-Current Assets

Liabilities

Current Liabilities
Long-Term Liabilities

Shareholders' Equity

Share Capital
Retained Earnings

4. Compute the net profit margin and the return on equity. What do these ratios suggest?

5. Prepare the closing entries at March 31, 2008.

LO1, 2, 3, 4, 5

eXcel

P4–8 **Comprehensive Review Problem: From Recording Transactions (including Adjusting and Closing Entries) to Preparing a Complete Set of Financial Statements and Performing Ratio Analysis (see Chapters 2, 3, and 4) (AP4–8)**

Brothers Hadi and Hamid Gaber began operations of their tool and die shop (H & H Tool, Inc.) on January 1, 2007. The company's fiscal year ends on December 31. The trial balance on January 1, 2008, was as follows (the amounts are rounded to thousands of dollars):

Account No.	Account Titles	Debit	Credit
01	Cash	3	
02	Accounts receivable	5	
03	Service supplies inventory	12	
04	Land		
05	Equipment	60	
06	Accumulated amortization (equipment)		6
07	Other assets (not detailed to simplify)	4	
11	Accounts payable		5
12	Notes payable		
13	Wages payable		
14	Interest payable		
15	Income taxes payable		
21	Share capital (65,000 shares)		65
31	Retained earnings		8
35	Service revenue		
40	Amortization expense		
41	Income tax expense		
42	Interest expense		
43	Other expenses	—	—
	Totals	84	84

Transactions and events during 2008 (summarized in thousands of dollars) follow:

a. Borrowed $10 cash on a 12-percent note payable, dated March 1, 2008.

b. Purchased land for future building site, paid cash, $9.

c. Earned revenues for 2008, $160, including $50 on credit.

d. Sold 3,000 additional shares for $1 cash per share (show dollars in thousands).

e. Recognized other expenses for 2008, $85, including $20 on credit.

f. Collected accounts receivable, $24.

g. Purchased additional assets, $10 cash (debit Other Assets).

h. Paid accounts payable, $13.

i. Purchased service supplies on account, $18 (debit to Account No. 03).

j. Signed a $25 service contract to start February 1, 2009.

k. Declared and paid cash dividend, $15.

Data for adjusting entries:

l. Service supplies inventory on hand at December 31, 2008, $12 (debit Other Expenses).

m. The equipment's useful life is 10 years; no residual or scrap value.

n. Accrued interest on notes payable (to be computed).

o. Wages earned since the December 24 pay date, but not yet paid, $15.

p. Income tax expense payable in 2009, $8.

Required:

1. Set up T-accounts for the accounts on the trial balance and enter their beginning balances.

2. Record Transactions (*a*) through (*k*) and post them to the T-accounts.

3. Record and post the adjusting entries (*l*) through (*p*).

4. Prepare an income statement (including earnings per share) and a statement of retained earnings for 2008, as well as a balance sheet at December 31, 2008.

5. Record and post the closing entries.

6. Prepare a post-closing trial balance.

7. Compute the following ratios for 2008 and explain what they mean:
   a. Debt-to-equity
   b. Total asset turnover
   c. Net profit margin
   d. Return on equity

P4–9 **Using Financial Reports: Evaluating Profitability Using Net Profit Margin and Return on Equity Ratios** (AP4–9)

■ **LO4**

Barrick Gold

Sleeman Breweries

Le Groupe
Jean Coutu

ANALYSIS

A summary of selected historical results is presented below for three Canadia companies: Barrick Gold, Sleeman Breweries, and Le Groupe Jean Coutu. Each of these companies has grown in size over time by acquiring assets and investing in other companies. (Amounts are in millions of dollars.)

	2005	2004	2003	2002	2001	2000
Barrick Gold						
Total shareholders' equity	$3,850	$3,574	$3,481	$3,334	$3,192	$3,190
Total revenue	2,350	1,932	2,035	1,967	1,989	1,936
Net income (loss)	401	248	200	193	96	(1,189)
Operating cash flow	726	509	519	588	588	940
Sleeman Breweries						
Total shareholders' equity	133	122	104	90	73	63
Total revenue	207	213	185	157	142	134
Net income	8	14	12	12	10	9
Operating cash flow	16	14	14	13	19	12
Le Groupe Jean Coutu						
Total shareholders' equity	1,412	853	1,020	946	832	589
Total revenue	9,617	3,043	4,052	3,481	2,924	1,578
Net income	104	133	164	140	105	86
Operating cash flow	222	186	214	119	135	89

Required:

1. Compute the net profit margin and the return on equity for each company for each of the years 2004 and 2005 using the table below.

	2005	2004	2003	2002	2001
Barrick Gold					
Net Profit Margin			9.83%	9.81%	4.83%
Return on Equity (ROE)			5.87%	5.91%	3.01%
Quality of Earnings			2.60	3.05	6.13
Sleeman Breweries					
Net Profit Margin			6.49%	7.64%	7.04%
Return on Equity (ROE)			12.37%	14.72%	14.71%
Quality of Earnings			1.17	1.08	1.90
Le Groupe Jean Coutu					
Net Profit Margin			4.05%	4.02%	3.59%
Return on Equity (ROE)			16.68%	15.75%	14.78%
Quality of Earnings			1.30	0.85	1.29

2. Based on the computed ratios, rank these companies from most successful to least successful in generating net income to shareholders.

3. Assume that you are interested in investing in one of these three companies, which company would you choose? Write a brief report to justify your choice.

4. Analysts examine both the net income and cash flow from operating activities in evaluating a company. One measure that relates these two numbers is the quality of earnings ratio which equals cash flow from operations divided by net income. The higher the ratio, the higher the quality of earnings. Compute this ratio for 2004 and 2005, and rank the three companies from highest to lowest based on the quality of their earnings.

■ **LO2**   **P4–10   Recording Journal Entries and Inferring Adjustments**

Stay'N Shape was started by Jennifer Long several years ago to provide physical fitness services to its customers. The following balances were extracted from the company's general ledger as at the following dates:

	May 31, 2008	April 30, 2008
Unearned revenue	$ 4,500	$ 3,000
Accounts receivable	44,000	59,000
Prepaid rent	?	4,900
Prepaid insurance	?	1,200
Notes payable	20,000	20,000
Supplies inventory	?	7,200
Supplies expense	17,200	

Additional information about several transactions that occurred in May is provided below:

a. Some customers pay for services in advance. The remaining customers are billed for services used and are allowed one month to pay their bills. During May, the company received from customers a total of $62,000 in cash, including an amount of $7,000 which was paid by customers in advance.

b. At the end of April, the company had paid rent for the next five months and recorded the amount as Prepaid rent.

c. The balance of Prepaid insurance at April 30 represents the cost of insuring the company's premises and equipment for one month. In May, the company received an invoice from the insurance company for a renewal of the company's insurance policy for one year. The insurance premium was increased by 10 percent over the amount of the premium of the previous year because the company filed a few insurance claims. The company paid the one-year insurance premium.

d. The note payable carries interest at 6 percent and is due on June 30, 2008 along with accrued interest. The company recognizes interest expense on a monthly basis.

e. An invoice for $780 pertaining to advertising work done during May was received on May 2.

f. Supplies amounting to $17,200 were purchased on account during May and debited to the Supplies expense account. A physical count of supplies on hand on May 31 valued the inventory at $11,500.

Required:

Prepare journal entries to record the following transactions and events:

1. The receipt of cash from customers and the recognition of all revenues earned in May.

2. Rent expense for May.

3. Payment of the premium for the new insurance policy.

4. Interest expense that accrued in May.

5. The invoice for advertising work, received on May 2.

6. The adjustment to the Supplies inventory account.

■ **LO1, 2, 4**   **P4–11   Inferring Adjusting Entries and Information Used in Computations and Recording Closing Entries**

The T-accounts of Longhorn Company at the end of the third year of operations, December 31, 2008, follow. The adjusting entries at December 31 are identified by letters.

Cash			
Bal.	20,000		

Note Payable 8%			
		1/1/2007	10,000

Share Capital (8,000 shares)			
		Bal.	56,000

Inventory, Maintenance Supplies			
Bal.	500	(a)	300

Interest Payable			
		(b)	800

Retained Earnings			
		Bal.	9,000

Service Equipment			
1/1/2006	90,000		

Income Taxes Payable			
		(f)	13,020

Service Revenue			
(c)	6,000	Bal.	220,000

Accumulated Amortization, Service Equipment			
		Bal.	18,000
		(d)	9,000

Wages Payable			
		(e)	500

Expenses			
Bal.	160,000		
(a)	300		
(b)	800		
(d)	9,000		
(e)	500		
(f)	13,020		

Other Assets			
Bal.	42,500		

Unearned Revenue			
		(c)	6,000

Required:

1. Develop three trial balances of Longhorn Company at December 31, 2008, using the following format:

	Unadjusted Trial Balance		Adjusted Trial Balance		Post-Closing Trial Balance	
Account	Debit	Credit	Debit	Credit	Debit	Credit

2. Write an explanation for each adjusting entry for 2008.
3. Prepare the closing journal entries.
4. What was the apparent useful life of the service equipment? What assumptions must you make to answer this question?
5. What was the average income tax rate for 2008?
6. What was the average issue (sale) price per share of the share capital?

ALTERNATE PROBLEMS

AP4–1 Preparing a Trial Balance (P4–1)

■ **LO1**

Starbucks Corporation purchases and roasts high-quality, whole-bean coffees and sells them along with fresh-brewed coffees, Italian-style espresso beverages, a variety of pastries and confections, coffee-related accessories and equipment, and a line of premium teas. In addition to sales through its company-operated retail stores, Starbucks also sells coffee and tea products through other channels of distribution. The following is a simplified list of accounts and amounts reported in financial statements. The accounts have normal debit or credit balances and the dollars are rounded to the nearest million. Assume the year ended on September 29, 2007.

Starbucks Corporation

Accounts payable	$ 169	Income tax expense	$ 168	Other operating expenses	$ 141
Accounts receivable	114	Interest revenue	50	Prepaid expenses	55
Accrued liabilities	440	Inventories	343	Property, plant, and	
Accumulated amortization	1,050	Long-term investments	280	equipment	2,376
Cash	201	Long-term liabilities	38	Retained earnings	?
Cost of sales	1,686	Net sales revenues	4,075	Share capital	998
Amortization expense	239	Other current assets	61	Short-term investments	149
General and administrative		Other long-term assets	140	Store operating expenses	1,379
expenses	244				

Required:

Prepare an adjusted trial balance at September 29, 2007. How did you determine the amount for retained earnings?

■ **LO2, 3**

eXcel

AP4–2 **Recording Adjusting Entries and Determining Their Financial Statement Effects** (P4–2)

Chandra Company's fiscal year ends on June 30. It is June 30, 2008, and all of the 2008 entries have been made, except the following adjusting entries:

 a. On March 30, 2008, Chandra paid $3,200 for a six-month premium for property insurance starting on that date. Cash was credited and Prepaid Insurance was debited for this amount.

 b. At June 30, 2008, wages of $900 were earned by employees but not yet paid. The employees will be paid on the next pay date, July 15, 2008.

 c. On June 1, 2008, Chandra collected maintenance fees of $450 for two months. At that date, Chandra debited Cash and credited Unearned Maintenance Revenue for $450.

 d. Amortization must be recognized on a service truck that cost $19,000 on July 1, 2007. The truck's estimated useful life is four years with a $3,000 residual value.

 e. Cash of $4,200 was collected on May 1, 2008, for services to be rendered evenly over the next year, beginning on May 1 (Unearned Service Revenue was credited).

 f. On February 1, 2008, the company borrowed $16,000 from a local bank and signed a 9-percent note for that amount. The principal and interest are payable on January 31, 2009.

 g. On June 15, 2008, the company received from the city a tax bill for $500 covering property taxes on land for the first half of 2008. The amount is payable during July 2008.

 h. The company earned service revenue of $2,000 on a special job that was completed on June 29, 2008. Collection will be made during July 2009; no entry has been recorded.

Required:

1. Indicate whether each transaction relates to a deferred revenue, deferred expense, accrued revenue, or accrued expense.

2. Prepare the adjusting entry required for each transaction at June 30, 2008.

3. Using the following headings, indicate the effect of each adjusting entry and the amount of the effect. Use + for increase, − for decrease, and NE for no effect.

	Balance Sheet			**Income Statement**		
Transaction	Assets	Liabilities	Shareholders' Equity	Revenues	Expenses	Net Income
a.						
b.						
c.						
etc.						

■ **LO2, 3**

AP4–3 **Recording Adjusting Entries and Determining Their Financial Statement Effects** (P4–3)

Sophie's Catering Company is at its fiscal year-end, December 31, 2008. The following data were developed from the company's records and related documents:

 a. During 2008, office supplies amounting to $1,200 were purchased for cash and debited to Supplies Inventory. At the beginning of 2008, the inventory of supplies on hand (unused) amounted to $350. The inventory of supplies on hand at December 31, 2008, was $400.

 b. On December 31, 2008, the company catered an evening gala for a local celebrity. The $7,500 bill was payable by the end of January 2009. No cash has been collected, and no journal entry has been made for this transaction. (Ignore cost of goods sold.)

 c. On December 15, 2008, repairs on one of the company's delivery vans were completed at a cost of $600; the amount is not yet recorded and will be paid at the beginning of January 2009.

 d. On October 1, 2008, a one-year insurance premium on equipment in the amount of $1,200 was paid and debited to Prepaid Insurance. Coverage began on November 1.

 e. In November 2008, Sophie's signed a lease for a new retail location, providing a down payment of $2,100 for the first three months. The amount was debited to Prepaid Rent. The lease began on December 1, 2008.

 f. On July 1, 2008, the company purchased new refrigerated display counters at a cash cost of $18,000. The estimated useful life of the equipment is five years, with an estimated residual value of $3,000. No amortization has been recorded for 2008 (compute amortization for six months in 2008).

g. On November 1, 2008, the company loaned $6,000 to one of its employees who signed a one-year, 10-percent note. The principal and interest are payable on October 31, 2009.

h. The income before any of the adjustments or income taxes was $22,400. The company's income tax rate is 30 percent. Compute the adjusted income, taking into consideration Transactions (*a*) through (*g*) to determine the income tax expense for 2008.

Required:

1. Indicate whether each transaction relates to a deferred revenue, deferred expense, accrued revenue, or accrued expense.

2. Prepare the adjusting entry required for each transaction at December 31, 2008.

3. Using the following headings, indicate the effect of each adjusting entry and the amount of each. Use + for increase, − for decrease, and NE for no effect.

	Balance Sheet			Income Statement		
Transaction	Assets	Liabilities	Shareholders' Equity	Revenues	Expenses	Net Income
a.						
b.						
c.						
etc.						

AP4–4 Computing Amounts on Financial Statements and Finding Financial Information (P4–4) ■ **LO3**
The following transactions and events are provided by the records of Deerfield Cleaning (a corporation) at the end of its fiscal year, December 31, 2008:

Cash Receipts and Revenue

a. Collected cash in January 2008 for the only cleaning contracts completed in past years that were not yet paid by customers $ 11,000
b. Service revenue collected in cash during 2008 for cleaning contracts in 2008   213,000
c. Service revenue earned for contracts in December 2008 but not collected until 2009   14,000
d. Amount collected in advance in December 2008 for service to be provided in January 2009   19,000

Salaries

e. Cash payment made in January 2008 for employee salaries earned in 2007; no other amounts were due to employees for past periods   1,500
f. Salaries incurred and paid during 2008   78,000
g. Salaries earned by employees during December 2008 that will be paid in January 2009   1,900

Supplies

h. Cleaning supplies inventory on January 1, 2008   1,800
i. Cleaning supplies purchased for cash during 2008   14,500
j. Cleaning supplies inventory on December 31, 2008   2,700

Required:
Using T-accounts, compute the amounts that should be reported in Deerfield's 2008 financial statements for the following items, and indicate on which financial statement the item is reported. For cash, create one T-account and label each effect to determine the amounts affecting cash as indicated here (from customers, to suppliers, to employees):

1. Service revenue
2. Cash to employees
3. Cleaning supplies expense
4. Accounts receivable
5. Cash to suppliers
6. Cleaning supplies inventory
7. Wages expense
8. Cash from customers
9. Unearned revenue
10. Wages payable

AP4–5 Inferring Year-End Adjustments, Computing Earnings per Share and Net Profit Margin, and Recording Closing Entries (P4–5) ■ **LO1, 2, 4, 5**
Gilca Ltd. is completing the information processing cycle at the end of its fiscal year, December 31, 2008. The correct account balances at December 31, 2008, both before and after the adjusting entries for 2008, are shown below:

	Trial Balance, December 31, 2008						
	Before Adjusting Entries		Adjustments		After Adjusting Entries		
Items	Debit	Credit	Debit	Credit	Debit	Credit
a. Cash	$ 18,000				$ 18,000	
b. Service revenue receivable					1,500	
c. Prepaid rent	1,200				800	
d. Property, plant, and equipment	210,000				210,000	
e. Accumulated amortization, PP&E		$52,500				$ 70,000
f. Income taxes payable						6,500
g. Deferred revenue		16,000				8,000
h. Share capital		110,000				110,000
i. Retained earnings, January 1, 2008		21,700				21,700
j. Service revenue		83,000				92,500
k. Salary expense	54,000				54,000	
l. Amortization expense					17,500	
m. Rent expense					400	
n. Income tax expense					6,500	
	$283,200	$283,200			$308,700	$308,700

Required:

1. Compare the amounts in the columns before and after the adjusting entries to reconstruct the adjusting entries made in 2008. Provide an explanation for each adjustment.

2. Compute the amount of income assuming that it is based on the amounts (a) before adjusting entries and (b) after adjusting entries. Which income amount is correct? Explain.

3. Compute the earnings per share, assuming that 5,000 shares are outstanding.

4. Compute the net profit margin. What does this suggest to you about the company?

5. Compute the return on equity, assuming that share capital did not change during the year. What does the computed ratio suggest to you about the company?

6. Prepare the closing entries at December 31, 2008.

■ **LO1, 2, 3, 5 AP4–6   Recording Adjusting and Closing Entries and Preparing a Balance Sheet and an Income Statement Including Earnings per Share (P4–6)**

Vialdi Co., a small service repair company, keeps its records without the help of an accountant. After much effort, an outside accountant prepared the following unadjusted trial balance as at the end of the company's fiscal year, December 31, 2008:

Account Titles	Debit	Credit
Cash	19,600	
Accounts receivable	7,000	
Supplies inventory	1,300	
Prepaid insurance	900	
Equipment (5-year life, no residual value)	27,000	
Accumulated amortization, equipment		12,000
Other assets	5,100	
Accounts payable		2,500
Note payable (2 years; 12% each December 31)		5,000
Share capital (4,000 shares outstanding)		16,000
Retained earnings		10,300
Service revenue		48,000
Other expenses, excluding income tax	32,900	
Totals	93,800	93,800

Data not yet recorded at December 31, 2008, include:

a. Amortization expense for 2008, $3,000.

b. Insurance expired during 2008, $450.

c. Wages earned by employees not yet paid on December 31, 2008, $1,100.

d. The supplies inventory on December 31, 2008, reflected $600 remaining on hand.

e. Income tax expense was $2,950.

Required:

1. Prepare the adjusting entries at December 31, 2008.
2. Prepare an income statement for 2008 and a balance sheet at December 31, 2008. Include the effects of the preceding five transactions.
3. Compute the net income assuming that you did not make an adjustment to the balance of the supplies inventory account. Does this error cause a material change in net income? Explain.
4. Prepare the closing entries at December 31, 2008.

AP4–7 Preparing Both an Income Statement and Balance Sheet from a Trial Balance (P4–7)   ■ **LO3, 4, 5**

ACME Pest Control Services (organized as a corporation on September 1, 2006) has completed the accounting cycle for the second year, ended August 31, 2008. ACME Pest Control also has completed a correct trial balance as follows:

ACME PEST CONTROL SERVICES
Trial Balance
At August 31, 2008

Account Titles	Debit	Credit
Cash	$ 26,000	
Accounts receivable	30,800	
Supplies inventory	1,300	
Service vehicles (company vans)	60,000	
Accumulated amortization, automobiles		$ 20,000
Equipment	14,000	
Accumulated amortization, equipment		4,000
Accounts payable		16,700
Salaries payable		1,100
Note payable, long term		34,000
Share capital (10,000 shares)		40,000
Retained earnings (on September 1, 2007)		4,300
Dividends declared	2,000	
Sales revenue		38,000
Maintenance contract revenue		17,000
Operating expenses (detail omitted to conserve your time)	27,000	
Amortization expense (including $2,000 on equipment)	12,000	
Interest expense	2,000	
Totals	$175,100	$175,100

Required:

1. Prepare an income statement for the reporting year ended August 31, 2008. Include income tax expense, assuming a 30-percent tax rate. Use the following major captions: Revenues, Expenses, Income before Income Tax, Income Tax, Net Income, and Earnings per Share (list each item under these captions as appropriate).
2. Prepare the journal entry to record income taxes for the year (not yet paid).
3. Prepare a balance sheet at the end of the reporting year, August 31, 2008. Use the following captions (list each item under these captions as appropriate).

Assets

Current Assets
Non-Current Assets

Liabilities

Current Liabilities
Long-Term Liabilities

Shareholders' Equity

Share Capital
Retained Earnings

4. Compute the net profit margin and the return on equity. What do these ratios suggest?
5. Prepare the closing entries at August 31, 2008.

■ **LO1, 2, 3,** **AP4–8** **Comprehensive Review Problem: From Recording Transactions (including Adjusting**
4, 5 **and Closing Entries) to Preparing a Complete Set of Financial Statements and**
Performing Ratio Analysis (see Chapters 2, 3, and 4) (P4–8)

Serena and Bill Davis began operations of their furniture repair shop, Rumours Furniture, Inc., on January 1, 2006. The company's fiscal year ends December 31. The trial balance on January 1, 2007, was as follows (the amounts are rounded to thousands of dollars):

Account No.	Account Titles	Debit	Credit
01	Cash	5	
02	Accounts receivable	4	
03	Supplies inventory	2	
04	Small tools inventory	6	
05	Equipment		
06	Accumulated amortization (equipment)		
07	Other assets (not detailed to simplify)	9	
11	Accounts payable		7
12	Notes payable		
13	Wages payable		
14	Interest payable		
15	Income taxes payable		
16	Deferred revenue		
21	Share capital (15,000 shares)		15
31	Retained earnings		4
35	Service revenue		
40	Amortization expense		
41	Income tax expense		
42	Interest expense		
43	Other expenses	—	—
	Totals	26	26

Transactions during 2007 (summarized in thousands of dollars) follow:

a. Borrowed $25 cash on an 8-percent note payable, dated July 1, 2007.

b. Purchased equipment for $18 cash on July 1, 2007.

c. Sold 5,000 additional shares for $1 cash per share (show dollars in thousands).

d. Earned revenues for 2007, $74, including $15 on credit.

e. Recognized other expenses for 2007, $35, including $9 on credit.

f. Purchased additional small tools inventory, $3 cash.

g. Collected accounts receivable, $8.

h. Paid accounts payable, $11.

i. Purchased supplies on account, $10 (debit to Account No. 03).

j. Received a $3 deposit on work to start January 15, 2008.

k. Declared and paid cash dividend, $12.

Data for adjusting entries:

l. Service supplies inventory of $4 and small tools inventory of $9 were on hand at December 31, 2007 (debit Other Expenses).

m. The equipment's useful life is four years and its residual value is $2.

n. Accrued interest on notes payable (to be computed).

o. Wages earned since the December 24 pay date but not yet paid, $4.

p. Income tax expense payable in 2008, $4.

Required:

1. Set up T-accounts for the accounts on the trial balance and enter their beginning balances.

2. Record Transactions (*a*) through (*k*) and post them to the T-accounts.

3. Record and post the adjusting entries (*l*) through (*p*).

4. Prepare an income statement (including earnings per share) and a statement of retained earnings for 2007, as well as a balance sheet at December 31, 2007.

5. Record and post the closing entries.

6. Prepare a post-closing trial balance.

7. Compute the following ratios for 2007 and explain what they mean:
   a. Debt-to-equity
   b. Total asset turnover
   c. Net profit margin
   d. Return on equity

AP4–9   Using Financial Reports: Evaluating Profitability Using Net Profit Margin and Return on Equity Ratios (P4–9)

A summary of selected historical results is presented below for three Canadian companies: WestJet Airlines, Research In Motion, and Andrés Wines. Each of these companies has grown in size over time by acquiring assets and investing in other companies. (Amounts are in millions of dollars.)

■ LO4

WestJet Airlines

Research In Motion

Andrés Wines

eXcel

ANALYSIS

	2005	2004	2003	2002	2001
WestJet Airlines					
Total shareholders' equity	$ 670	$ 590	$ 581	$ 356	$222
Total revenue	1,395	1,058	860	680	478
Net income (loss)	24	−17	61	52	37
Cash flow from operations	248	145	192	162	67
Research In Motion					
Total shareholders' equity	313	637	1,716	705	878
Total revenue	2,066	1,350	595	307	294
Net income (loss)	382	213	52	(149)	(18)
Cash flow from operations	150	278	64	91	40
Andrés Wines					
Total shareholders' equity	90	87	81	73	69
Total revenue	212	168	156	148	139
Net income	6	8	9	7	5
Cash flow from operations	19	7	4	14	5

Required:

1. Compute the net profit margin and the return on equity for each company for each of the years 2004 and 2005 using the table below.

	2005	2004	2003	2002
WestJet Airlines				
Net Profit Margin			7.09%	7.65%
Return on Equity (ROE)			13.02%	17.99%
Quality of Earnings			3.15	3.12
Research In Motion				
Net Profit Margin			8.74%	−48.53%
Return on Equity (ROE)			4.30%	−18.83%
Quality of Earnings			1.23	−0.61
Andrés Wines				
Net Profit Margin			5.77%	4.73%
Return on Equity (ROE)			11.69%	9.86%
Quality of Earnings			0.44	2.00

2. Based on the computed ratios, rank these companies from most successful to least successful in generating net income to shareholders.

3. Assume that you are interested in investing in one of these three companies, which company would you choose? Write a brief report to justify your choice.

4. Analysts examine both the net income and cash flow from operating activities in evaluating a company. One measure that relates these two numbers is the quality of earnings ratio, which equals cash flow from operations divided by net income. The higher the ratio, the higher the quality of earnings. Compute this ratio for 2004 and 2005, and rank the three companies from highest to lowest based on the quality of their earnings.

CASES AND PROJECTS

FINDING AND INTERPRETING FINANCIAL INFORMATION

■ **LO2, 3,**
4, 5

The Forzani Group

ANALYSIS

CP4–1 Finding Financial Information

Refer to the Online Learning Centre Web site at **www.mcgrawhill.ca/olc/libby/student/ resources** for the financial statements of The Forzani Group Ltd. (FGL).

Required:

1. How much is in the Prepaid Expenses account at the end of the 2007 fiscal year?
2. What did the company report for Long-Term Receivables at January 28, 2007? Where did you find this information?
3. How much did the company pay in interest for the 2007 fiscal year? Where did you find this information?
4. To what account is Accumulated Amortization related?
5. What company accounts would not appear on a post-closing trial balance?
6. Prepare the closing entry for Prepaid Expenses.
7. What is the company's basic earnings per share for the two years reported?
8. Compute the company's net profit margin for the six years 2002 to 2007 based on information reported on page 71 of the annual report. What does the trend suggest to you about FGL?

■ **LO2, 5**

The Forzani Group
vs. Van Houtte

ANALYSIS

CP4–2 Comparing Companies Over Time

Refer to the Online Learning Centre Web site at **www.mcgrawhill.ca/olc/libby/student/ resources** for the financial statements of The Forzani Group Ltd. and to Appendix B for the financial statements of Van Houtte, Inc.

Required:

1. What was the Cost of Sales for each company's most recent fiscal year? Where did you find the information? What reasons would a company have for not reporting the cost of sales? Explain.
2. Compute the percentage of Cost of Sales to Sales for each company if possible. Are you able to calculate the same ratios for the previous two fiscal years? If so, show computations. If not, explain why.
3. Compute each company's net profit margin for the years shown in its annual report. What do your results suggest about each company over time and in comparison to each other?
4. Compute each company's return on equity for the most recent year. Which company is more profitable? Explain.

FINANCIAL REPORTING AND ANALYSIS CASES

■ **LO1, 2, 4**

CP4–3 Interpreting the Financial Press

A March 8, 2004, article in *The Wall Street Journal* discusses the underlying cause of accounting scandals and offers a suggestion for improved reporting.* You can access the article on the Online Learning Centre Web site at **www.mcgrawhill.ca/olc/libby/student/resources**.

Required:

Read the brief article and answer the following questions:

1. What did the author suggest as the root cause of accounting scandals?
2. What are the uncertainties referred to in the article and why does the author believe these are problems in current financial reporting?

■ **LO2**

ANALYSIS

CP4–4 Analyzing the Effects of Adjustments

Seneca Land Company, a closely held corporation, invests in commercial rental properties. Seneca's fiscal year ends on December 31. At the end of each year, numerous adjusting entries must be made because many transactions completed during the current and prior years have economic effects on the financial statements of the current and future years. Assume that the current year is 2008.

---

*Alfred Rappaport, "Shareholder Scoreboard (A Special Report): The Best & Worst Performers of the WSJ 1000— Beyond Quarterly Earnings: How to Improve Financial Reporting," *The Wall Street Journal*, March 8, 2004.

Required:
This case concerns four transactions that have been selected for your analysis. Answer the questions for each.

TRANSACTION (*a*): On July 1, 2005, the company purchased office equipment costing $14,000 for use in the business. The company estimates that the equipment will have a useful life of 10 years and no residual value.

1. Over how many accounting periods will this transaction directly affect Seneca's financial statements? Explain.

2. Assuming straight-line amortization, how much amortization expense was reported on the 2005 and 2006 income statements?

3. How should the office equipment be reported on the balance sheet at December 31, 2007?

4. Would Seneca make an adjusting entry at the end of each year during the life of the equipment? Explain your answer.

TRANSACTION (*b*): On September 1, 2008, Seneca collected $24,000 for rent of office space. This amount represented rent for a six-month period, September 1, 2008, through February 28, 2009. Unearned Rent Revenue was increased (credited), and Cash was increased (debited) for $24,000.

1. Over how many accounting periods will this transaction affect Seneca's financial statements? Explain.

2. How much rent revenue on this office space should Seneca report on the 2008 income statement? Explain.

3. Did this transaction create a liability for Seneca as of the end of 2008? Explain. If yes, how much?

4. Should Seneca make an adjusting entry on December 31, 2008? Explain. If your answer is yes, prepare the adjusting entry.

TRANSACTION (*c*): On December 31, 2008, Seneca owed employees wages of $7,500 because the employees worked the last three days in December 2008. The next payroll date is January 5, 2009.

1. Over how many accounting periods does this transaction affect Seneca's financial statements? Explain.

2. How would this $7,500 amount affect Seneca's income statement for 2008 and the balance sheet at December 31, 2008?

3. Should Seneca make an adjusting entry on December 31, 2008? Explain. If your answer is yes, prepare the adjusting entry.

TRANSACTION (*d*): On January 1, 2008, Seneca agreed to supervise the planning and subdivision of a large tract of land for a customer, J. Ray. This service job that Seneca will perform involves four separate phases. By December 31, 2008, three phases had been completed to Ray's satisfaction. The remaining phase will be done during 2009. The total price for the four phases (agreed on in advance by both parties) was $60,000. Each phase involves about the same amount of services. On December 31, 2008, Seneca had not collected any cash for the services already performed.

1. Should Seneca record any service revenue on this job for 2008? Explain. If yes, prepare the adjusting entry to record the revenue.

2. What entry will Seneca make when it completes the last phase, assuming that the full contract price is collected on the completion date, February 15, 2009?

CP4–5 Using Financial Reports: Inferring Adjusting and Closing Entries and Answering Analytical Questions

LO1, 2, 4, 5

Rowland Company was organized on January 1, 2007. At the end of the first year of operations, December 31, 2007, the bookkeeper prepared the following trial balances (amounts in thousands of dollars):

Account No.	Account Titles	Unadjusted Trial Balance		Adjustments		Adjusted Trial Balance	
		Debit	Credit			Debit	Credit
11	Cash	40				40	
12	Accounts receivable	17				17	
13	Prepaid insurance	2				1	
14	Rent receivable					2	
15	Property, plant, and equipment	46				46	
16	Accumulated amortization						11
17	Other assets	6				6	
18	Accounts payable		27				27
19	Wages payable						3
20	Income taxes payable						5
21	Unearned rent revenue						4
22	Note payable (10%; dated January 1, 2007)		20				20
23	Share capital (1,000 shares)		30				30
24	Retained earnings	3				3	
25	Revenues (total)		105				103
26	Expenses (total including interest)	68				83	
27	Income tax expense					5	
	Totals	182	182			203	203

Required:

1. Based on inspection of the two trial balances, prepare the 2007 adjusting entries recorded by the bookkeeper (provide brief explanations).

2. Based on these data, prepare the 2007 closing entries with brief explanations.

3. Answer the following questions (show computations):

   a. How many shares were outstanding at year-end?

   b. What was the estimated useful life of the property, plant, and equipment, assuming a residual value of $2,000 and a purchase date of January 1, 2007?

   c. What was the amount of interest expense included in the total expenses?

   d. What was the balance of Retained Earnings on December 31, 2007?

   e. What was the average income tax rate?

   f. How would the two accounts Rent Receivable and Unearned Rent Revenue be reported on the balance sheet?

   g. Explain why cash increased by $40,000 during the year even though net income was comparatively very low.

   h. What was the amount of earnings per share for 2005?

   i. What was the average selling price of the shares?

   j. When was the insurance premium paid and over what period of time did the coverage extend?

   k. What was the net profit margin for the year?

   l. What was the return on equity for the year?

■ **LO2, 3**   **CP4–6 Using Financial Reports: Analyzing Financial Information in a Sale of a Business— A Challenging Case**

ANALYSIS

Robert Brissette, a local massage therapist, decided to sell his practice and retire. He has had discussions with a therapist from another province who wants to relocate. The discussions are at the complex stage of agreeing on a price. The financial statements of Brissette's practice, Brissette Stress Reduction, played an important role in this process. Brissette's secretary, Kelsey, maintained the records, under his direction. Each year, Kelsey developed a statement of profits on a cash basis from the records she maintained but she did not prepare a balance sheet. Upon request, Brissette provided the other therapist with the following statements for 2008 prepared by Kelsey:

BRISSETTE STRESS REDUCTION		
Statement of Profits		
2008		
Therapy fees collected		$130,000
Expenses paid:		
Rent for office space	$19,500	
Utilities expense	360	
Telephone expense	2,200	
Office salaries expense	22,500	
Office supplies expense	900	
Miscellaneous expenses	2,400	
Total expenses		47,860
Profit for the year		$ 82,140

Upon agreement of the parties, you have been asked to examine the financial figures for 2008. The other therapist said, "I question the figures because, among other things, they appear to be on a 100-percent cash basis." Your investigations revealed the following additional data at December 31, 2008:

a. Of the $130,000 in therapy fees collected in 2008, $30,000 was for services performed prior to 2008.

b. At the end of 2008, therapy fees of $6,000 for services performed during the year were uncollected.

c. Office equipment owned and used by Brissette cost $8,000 and had an estimated useful life of 10 years, with no salvage value.

d. An inventory of office supplies at December 31, 2008, reflected $400 worth of items purchased during the year that were still on hand. Also, the records for 2007 indicate that the supplies on hand at the end of that year were about $250.

e. At the end of 2008, the secretary whose salary is $24,000 per year had not been paid for December because of a long trip that extended to January 15, 2009.

f. The $140 phone bill for December 2008 was not paid until January 11, 2009.

g. The payment for office rent was for 13 months, including January 2009.

Required:

1. Prepare a correct income statement for 2008 based on the information above. Show your computations for any amounts changed from those in the statement prepared by Brissette's secretary. (Suggested solution format—use four-column headings: Items; Cash Basis per Brissette's Statement, $; Explanation of Changes; and Corrected Basis, $.)

2. Write a memo to support your schedule prepared in requirement 1. The purpose should be to explain the reasons for your changes and to suggest other important items that should be considered in the pricing decision.

CP4–7 Using Financial Reports: Preparing Income Statements for Different Periods   ■ LO2, 3
Wong's Insurance Agency adjusts its accounts at the end of each month. The adjusted balances of the revenue and expense accounts at two different dates of the year appear below. The company's fiscal year starts on July 1.

	March 31, 2009	December 31, 2008
Commissions earned	$72,000	$45,000
Salaries expense	18,000	12,000
Rent expense	11,250	7,500
Amortization expense	1,350	900
Advertising expense	14,000	7,500

The company is subject to an income tax rate of 40 percent.

Required:
Prepare income statements for two separate time periods: the quarter ending March 31, 2009, and the 9-month period ending March 31, 2009. Explain how you determined the amounts for each time period and show supporting computations.

■ LO2, 3

WestJet Airlines

ANALYSIS

CP4–8 Using Financial Reports: Analyzing Financial Information from Real Financial Statements

The current liabilities of WestJet Airlines include an account titled Advance Ticket Sales. The company's recent annual reports show the following trend in the balance of this account over a three-year period.

	2005	2004	2003
Advance ticket sales (in thousands)	127,450	81,991	58,086

The first note to the company's financial statements, titled *Significant accounting policies*, includes the following disclosure about revenue recognition:

> Guest and charter revenue is recognized when air transportation is provided. Tickets sold but not yet used are included in the consolidated balance sheet as advance ticket sales.

Required:

1. What does the balance in the account Advance Ticket Sales represent?

2. Why does WestJet recognize guest revenue when transportation is provided, rather than when cash is received?

3. How does WestJet Airlines normally settle this liability?

4. Should WestJet recognize flight expenses, such as jet fuel, salaries of flight crew, and cost of food and beverage, in the period when the flights occur or during the period when tickets are sold? Explain.

5. Explain the most probable reason for the increase in the amount of this liability from 2003 to 2005.

6. Based on the trend in the amount of this liability, would you expect the annual amounts of guest revenue to increase, decrease, or remain stable over the three-year period? Explain.

■ LO2, 3

Andrés Wines

ANALYSIS

CP4–9 Using Financial Reports: Analyzing Financial Information from Real Financial Statements

Andrès Wines Ltd. is a leading producer and marketer of quality wines in Canada. Selected information from the company's financial statements for the year ended March 31, 2005 are provided below (in thousands of dollars).

	March 31, 2005	March 31, 2004
Balance Sheet		
Accounts receivable.....................................	14,132	12,801
Prepaid expenses...	2,531	2,949
Income taxes recoverable (receivable)..............	693	—
Accrued liabilities...	5,795	3,508
Dividends payable...	777	772
Income taxes payable...................................	—	218
Long-term debt...	17,313	19,563
Other information:		
Sales for fiscal year 2005.............................	167,634	
Income taxes paid during the year..................	4,965	

Required:

1. Compute the amount of cash collected from customers during the year. Assume that all sales for fiscal year 2005 were on credit.

2. Prepaid expenses represent the net amount of a number of accounts, including Prepaid Insurance. The company had $935 in prepaid insurance at March 31, 2004 and $1,180 at March 31, 2005. It also paid $2,345 in June 2004 to renew its insurance policies. Prepare the adjusting journal entry on March 31, 2005 to record the amount of insurance expense for fiscal year 2005. The payment of $2,345 was debited to the Prepaid Insurance account.

3. Explain the nature of the account Accrued Liabilities. What would have caused the account balance to increase during the year?

4. The company's board of directors declared dividends of $3,108 during the year. Prepare a summary journal entry to record the amount of dividends paid during the year.

5. The company is required to pay income taxes in advance on a quarterly basis even though the exact amount of income taxes expense is not calculated until the end of the fiscal year. For this reason, the company may overpay the amount of taxes due to taxation authorities. Compute the amount of income taxes expense for 2005 and prepare the related adjusting journal entry at March 31, 2005.

6. The company's long-term debt includes a long-term bank loan for $6,000. The company signed for this loan on October 31, 2004 to be repaid on October 31, 2008. Interest on the loan, at an annual rate 8%, is payable each year on October 31. Prepare the adjusting journal entry that should be made on March 31, 2005 to recognize interest expense for fiscal year 2005.

7. Assume that the company's accountant did not record the journal entry you prepared for requirement 6 above, what would be the effect of this error (overstatement, understatement, no effect) on the following:
   a. total assets at March 31, 2005,
   b. net income for the year 2005, assuming that the company is subject to an income tax rate of 40%,
   c. current liabilities at March 31, 2005.

CRITICAL THINKING CASES

CP4–10 Using Financial Reports: Evaluating Financial Information as a Bank Loan Officer
Magliochetti Moving Corp. has been in operation since January 1, 2008. It is now December 31, 2008, the end of the company's fiscal year. The company has not done well financially during the first year, although revenue has been fairly good. The three shareholders manage the company, but they have not given much attention to recordkeeping. In view of a serious cash shortage, they have applied to your bank for a $20,000 loan. You requested a complete set of financial statements. The following annual financial statements for 2008 were prepared by a clerk and then were given to the bank.

■ **LO2, 3, 4**

e**X**cel
ANALYSIS

MAGLIOCHETTI MOVING CORP.

Income Statement		Balance Sheet	
For the Period Ended December 31, 2008		**At December 31, 2008**	
Transportation revenue	$85,000	**Assets**	
Expenses:		Cash	$ 2,000
Salaries expense	17,000	Receivables	3,000
Maintenance expense	12,000	Inventory of maintenance supplies	6,000
Other expenses	18,000	Equipment	40,000
Total expenses	$47,000	Prepaid insurance	4,000
Net income	$38,000	Other assets	27,000
		Total assets	$82,000
		Liabilities	
		Accounts payable	$ 9,000
		Shareholders' Equity	
		Share capital (10,000 shares outstanding)	35,000
		Retained earnings	38,000
		Total liabilities and shareholders' equity	$82,000

After briefly reviewing the statements and looking into the situation, you requested that the statements be redone (with some expert help) to "incorporate amortization, accruals, inventory counts, income taxes, and so on." As a result of a review of the records and supporting documents, the following additional information was developed:

a. The inventory of maintenance supplies of $6,000 shown on the balance sheet has not been adjusted for supplies used during 2008. An inventory count of the maintenance supplies on hand (unused) on December 31, 2008, showed $1,800. Supplies used should be debited to Maintenance Expense.

b. The insurance premium paid in 2008 was for years 2008 and 2009; therefore, the prepaid insurance at December 31, 2008, amounted to $2,000. The total insurance premium was debited to Prepaid Insurance when paid in 2008.

c. The equipment cost $40,000 when purchased January 1, 2008. It had an estimated useful life of five years (no residual value). No amortization has been recorded for 2008.

d. Unpaid (and unrecorded) salaries at December 31, 2008, amounted to $2,200.

e. At December 31, 2008, transportation revenue collected in advance amounted to $7,000. This amount was credited to Transportation Revenue when the cash was collected.

f. The company is subject to an income tax rate of 30 percent.

Required:

1. Record the six adjusting entries required on December 31, 2008, based on the preceding additional information.

2. Recast the preceding statements after taking into account the adjusting entries. Use the following format for the solution:

Items	Amounts Reported	CHANGES Plus	Minus	Correct Amounts
(List here each item from the two statements)				

3. Omission of the adjusting entries caused:
   a. Net income to be overstated or understated (select one) by $_____.
   b. Total assets to be overstated or understated (select one) by $_____.
   c. Total liabilities to be overstated or understated (select one) by $_____.

4. Use both the unadjusted and adjusted balances to calculate the following ratios for the company: (a) earnings per share, (b) net profit margin, and (c) return on equity. Explain the causes of the differences and the impact of the changes on financial analysis.

5. Write a letter to the company explaining the results of the adjustments, your analysis, and your decision regarding the loan.

CP4–11 Making a Decision as an Auditor: Effects of Errors on Income, Assets, and Liabilities   ■ LO2, 3

ANALYSIS

Megan Company (not a corporation) was careless about its financial records during its first year of operations, 2007. It is December 31, 2007, the end of the company's fiscal year. An external auditor examined the records and discovered numerous errors, all of which are described below. Assume that each error is independent of the others.

	Effect on					
	Net Income		Assets		Liabilities	
Independent Errors	2007	2008	2007	2008	2007	2008
1. Amortization expense for 2007, not recorded in 2007, $950.	O $950	NE	O $950	O $950	NE	NE
2. Wages earned by employees during 2007 not recorded in 2007 but will be paid in 2008, $500.						
3. Revenue earned during 2007 but not colleccted or recorded until 2008, $600; will be collected in 2008.						
4. Amount paid in 2007 and recorded as expense in 2007, but it is not an expense until 2008, $200.						
5. Revenue collected in 2007 and recorded as revenue in 2007, but it is not earned until 2008, $900.						
6. Sale of services for cash in 2007. Recorded as a debit to Cash and as a credit to Accounts Receivable, $300.						
7. On December 31, 2007, bought land on credit for $8,000, but did not record the transaction until payment was made on February 1, 2008.						

Required:

Analyze each error and indicate its effect on 2007 and 2008 income, assets, and liabilities if not corrected. Do not assume any other errors. Use these codes to indicate the effect of each dollar amount: O = overstated, U = understated, and NE = no effect. Write an explanation of your analysis of each transaction to support your response. (The answer for the first item is given as an example.)

A sample explanation of analysis of errors that are not corrected is provided below, using the first error as an example:

1. Failure to record amortization in 2007 caused amortization expense to be too low; therefore, income was overstated by $950. Accumulated amortization also is too low by $950, which causes assets to be overstated by $950 until the error is corrected.

CP4–12 Making Decisions as a Manager: Evaluating the Effects of Business Strategy on Return on Equity   ■ LO4

Sony

ANALYSIS

Sony is a world leader in the manufacture of consumer and commercial electronics as well as the entertainment and insurance industries.

Required:

Using the table below, indicate the most likely effect of each of the following changes in business strategy on Sony's return on equity for the current period and future periods (+ for increase, − for decrease, and NE for no effect), assuming all other things are unchanged. Explain your answer for each. Treat each item independently.

a. Sony decreases its investment in research and development aimed at products to be brought to market in more than one year.

b. Sony begins a new advertising campaign for a movie to be released during the next year.

c. Sony issues additional shares for cash, the proceeds to be used to acquire other high-technology companies in future periods.

Strategy Change	Current Period ROE	Future Periods' ROE
a.		
b.		
c.		

FINANCIAL REPORTING AND ANALYSIS TEAM PROJECT

■ **LO2, 3, 4**   **CP4–13**   **Team Project: Analysis of Accruals, Earnings per Share, Net Profit Margin, and Return on Equity**

ANALYSIS

As a team, select an industry to analyze. Each team member should then use the Internet to obtain the annual report for one Canadian publicly traded company in the industry, with each member selecting a different company.

Required:

On an individual basis, each team member should write a short report answering the following questions about the selected company. Discuss any patterns across the companies that you as a team observe. Then, as a team, write a short report comparing and contrasting your companies.

1. From the income statement, what is the company's earnings per share for the last three years?

2. Ratio analysis:
   a. What does the net profit margin measure in general?
   b. What does the return on equity measure in general?
   c. Compute these ratios for the last three years.
   d. What do your results suggest about the company? (You may refer to Management Discussion and Analysis section of the annual report to learn about the company's stated reasons for any change over time.)
   e. If available, find the industry ratio for the most recent year, compare it to your results, and discuss why you believe the ratio for your company differs or is similar to the industry ratio.

3. List the accounts and amounts of accrued expenses payable on the most recent balance sheet. (You may find the detail in the notes to the statements.) What is the ratio of the total accrued expenses payable to total liabilities?

Reporting and Interpreting Cash Flows

After studying this chapter, you should be able to:

FOCUS COMPANY:

Andrew Peller Limited

MANAGING PRODUCTION AND CASH FLOWS IN A SEASONAL BUSINESS

Andrew Peller, who immigrated to Canada from Hungary in 1927, founded Andrés Wines Ltd. (www.andreswines.com) in 1961 to produce wine using grapes from the fertile Okanagan Valley in British Columbia. Thirty years later, in 1991, the company established Peller Estates as the preeminent premium wine label in Canada, offering a variety of white and red wines produced in the Niagara Peninsula. Over the next 15 years, the company continued to grow and expand its business and markets to become Canada's second largest producer and marketer of wines. By 2006, the company's sales exceeded $200 million, and its name was changed to Andrew Peller Limited, in honour of its founder.

Although it may seem puzzling, growing profitable operations does not always ensure positive cash flow. Also, seasonal fluctuations in sales, purchases of inventory, and advertising expenditures may bring **high profits** and **net cash outflows** in some quarters and **losses** and **net cash inflows** in others. As we have seen in earlier chapters, this occurs because the timing of revenues and expenses does not always match cash inflows and outflows. As a consequence, Andrew Peller Limited (APL) must carefully manage cash flows as well as profits. For the same reasons, financial analysts must consider the information provided in APL's cash flow statement in addition to its income statement and its balance sheet.

UNDERSTANDING THE BUSINESS

Clearly, net income is an important indicator of performance, but cash flow is also critical to a company's success. Cash flow permits a company to expand its operations, replace worn assets, take advantage of new investment opportunities, and pay dividends to its owners. Some financial analysts go as far as saying that "cash flow is king." Both managers and analysts need to understand the various sources and uses of cash that are associated with business activity.

The cash flow statement focuses attention on a firm's ability to generate cash internally, its management of current assets and current liabilities, and the details of its investments and its external financing. It is designed to help both managers and analysts answer important cash-related questions such as these:

- Will the company have enough cash to pay its short-term debts to suppliers, employees, taxation authorities, and other creditors without additional borrowing?
- Is the company adequately managing its accounts receivable, inventory, and other current assets?
- Has the company made necessary investments in new productive capacity?
- Did the company generate enough cash flow internally to finance necessary investments, or did it rely on external financing?
- Is the company changing the proportion of debt and equity in its capital structure?

Andrew Peller Limited (APL) is a particularly good example to illustrate the importance of the cash flow statement. Like all companies in its industry, APL's wine production, inventory purchases, and sales vary with the seasons. This seasonal variation has surprising effects on cash flows and net income.

We begin our discussion with an overview of the cash flow statement. We then use APL's cash flow statement for the second quarter of fiscal year 2007 to provide detailed coverage of the preparation, reporting, and interpretation of information in the cash flow statement.

ORGANIZATION OF THE CHAPTER

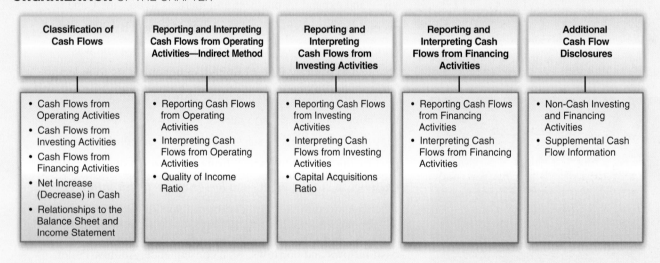

Classification of Cash Flows	Reporting and Interpreting Cash Flows from Operating Activities—Indirect Method	Reporting and Interpreting Cash Flows from Investing Activities	Reporting and Interpreting Cash Flows from Financing Activities	Additional Cash Flow Disclosures
• Cash Flows from Operating Activities • Cash Flows from Investing Activities • Cash Flows from Financing Activities • Net Increase (Decrease) in Cash • Relationships to the Balance Sheet and Income Statement	• Reporting Cash Flows from Operating Activities • Interpreting Cash Flows from Operating Activities • Quality of Income Ratio	• Reporting Cash Flows from Investing Activities • Interpreting Cash Flows from Investing Activities • Capital Acquisitions Ratio	• Reporting Cash Flows from Financing Activities • Interpreting Cash Flows from Financing Activities	• Non-Cash Investing and Financing Activities • Supplemental Cash Flow Information

CLASSIFICATION OF CASH FLOWS

A **CASH EQUIVALENT** is a short-term, highly liquid investment with an original maturity of less than three months.

Basically, the cash flow statement explains how the cash balance at the beginning of the period changed to another cash balance at the end of the period. For purposes of this statement, the definition of *cash* includes cash and cash equivalents. **Cash equivalents** are short-term, highly liquid investments that are both

1. readily convertible to known amounts of cash.
2. so near their maturity that there is little risk that their value will change if interest rates change.

Generally, an investment qualifies as a cash equivalent only when it has an original maturity of three months or less from the date of acquisition. Examples of cash equivalents are Treasury bills (a form of short-term government debt), money market funds, and commercial paper (short-term notes payable issued by large corporations).

As you can see in Exhibit 5.1, the cash flow statement reports cash inflows and outflows based on three broad categories: (1) operating activities, (2) investing activities, and (3) financing activities. To improve comparability, section 1540 of the *CICA Handbook* defines each category included in the required statement. These definitions (with explanations) are presented in the following sections.

■ **LEARNING OBJECTIVE 1**

Classify cash flow statement items as part of net cash flows from operating, investing, and financing activities.

EXHIBIT **5.1**

Consolidated Cash Flow Statement

REAL WORLD EXCERPT

Andrew Peller Limited

QUARTERLY REPORT

ANDREW PELLER LIMITED
Consolidated Statements of Cash Flows—Unaudited
As at September 30, 2006
(in thousands of dollars)

	Three Months Ended September 30, 2006
Cash provided by (used in)	
Operating activities	
Net earnings	2,556
Items not affecting cash:	
Amortization of plant and equipment	1,908
Future income taxes	69
	4,533
Changes in non-cash operating working capital items related to operations	(2,608)*
	1,925
Investing activities	
Purchase of property and equipment	(1,770)
Proceeds from long-term investments	88
	(1,682)
Financing activities	
Repayment of long-term debt	(1,563)
Increase in bank indebtedness	2,098
Payment of dividends	(778)
	(243)
Net cash flow and cash balance, end of period	-0-**

The balances of certain accounts have been adjusted to simplify the presentation.

*Changes in non-cash operating working capital items:	
Increase in accounts receivable	$(6,005)
Increase in inventories	(1,739)
Increase in prepaid expenses	(1,172)
Increase in accounts payable	6,213
Increase in accrued liabilities	565
Decrease in income taxes payable	(470)
	$(2,608)

**Normally, the net cash flow is not equal to zero, and the cash balances at the beginning and end of the period are different from zero. In this specific case, APL did not have any cash either at the beginning or at the end of the period as shown on its balance sheet in Exhibit 5.3. In fact, it borrowed from the bank to cover the shortfall in cash.

CASH FLOWS FROM OPERATING ACTIVITIES are cash inflows and outflows directly related to earnings from normal operations.

The **DIRECT METHOD** of presenting the Operating Activities section of the cash flow statement reports components of cash flows from operating activities as gross receipts and gross payments.

The **INDIRECT METHOD** of presenting the Operating Activities section of the cash flow statement adjusts net income to compute cash flows from operating activities.

CASH FLOWS FROM OPERATING ACTIVITIES

Cash flows from operating activities (cash flows from operations) are the cash inflows and cash outflows that directly relate to revenues and expenses reported on the income statement. These cash flows are not affected by accruals, deferrals, and allocations that result from the timing of revenue and expense recognition. There are two alternative approaches for presenting the operating activities section of the statement:

1. The **direct method** reports the components of cash flows from operating activities listed as gross receipts and gross payments

Inflows	Outflows
Cash received from	*Cash paid for*
Customers	Purchase of goods for resale and
Dividends and interest on investments	services (electricity, etc.)
	Salaries and wages
	Income taxes
	Interest on liablities

The difference between the inflows and outflows is called the ***net cash inflow (outflow) from operating activities***. APL experienced a net cash inflow of $1,925 from its operations for the second quarter of fiscal year 2007.[1] The *CICA Handbook* recommends the direct method, but it is rarely seen in practice. The direct method is the required format in a number of countries. Many financial executives have reported that they do not use it because it is more expensive to implement than the indirect method.

2. The **indirect method** starts with net income and then eliminates non-cash items to arrive at net cash inflow (outflow) from operating activities.

Net income
+/− Adjustments for non-cash items
Net cash inflow (outflow) from operating activities

Notice in Exhibit 5.1 that in the second quarter of 2007, APL reported net income of $2,556 but generated positive cash flows from operating activities of $1,925. Why do net income and cash flow from operating activities differ? Recall that the income statement is prepared under the accrual concept, whereby revenues are recorded when earned without regard to when the related cash is collected. Similarly, expenses are matched with revenues and recorded in the same period as the revenues without regard to when the related cash payments are made.

In this chapter, we present computations of net cash inflow (outflow) from operating activities using the indirect method because of its extensive use in actual financial reporting.[2] In addition, we show in Chapter Supplement B how cash flows from operations can be computed using the direct method.

For now, the most important thing to remember about the two methods is that they are simply alternative ways to compute the same amount. The total amount of **cash flows from operating activities is *always the same*** (an inflow of $1,925 in APL's case), **regardless of whether it is computed using the direct or indirect method**.

---

[1] APL's fiscal year starts on April 1 and ends on March 31 instead of the calendar year (January 1–December 31) that is used by most companies. As a result, APL's first quarter starts on April 1 and ends on June 30, and its second quarter starts on July 1 and ends on September 30.

[2] A recent survey of 200 companies revealed that only one company used the direct method in its 2005 annual report. N. Chlala, L. Martel, A. Lavigne, and C. Byrd, *Financial Reporting in Canada 2006*. Toronto, CICA, 2006, p. 100.

CASH FLOWS FROM INVESTING ACTIVITIES

Cash flows from investing activities are cash inflows and outflows related to the purchase and disposal of long-term productive assets and investments in the securities of other companies. Typical cash flows from investing activities include:

<table>
<tr><td align="center">Inflows</td><td align="center">Outflows</td></tr>
<tr><td>Cash received from</td><td>Cash paid for</td></tr>
<tr><td>Sale or disposal of property, plant and equipment</td><td>Purchase of property, plant and equipment</td></tr>
<tr><td>Sale or maturity of investments in securities</td><td>Purchase of investments in securities</td></tr>
</table>

The difference between these cash inflows and outflows is called *net cash inflow (outflow) from investing activities*.

For APL, this amount was an outflow of $1,682 for the second quarter of 2007. The Investing Activities section of the statement shows APL's long-term investment strategy. The Management Discussion and Analysis (MD&A) section of the report indicates that the company was continuing to invest in expanding its production facilities.

CASH FLOWS FROM FINANCING ACTIVITIES

Cash flows from financing activities include exchanges of cash with external sources (owners and creditors) to finance the enterprise and its operations. Usual cash flows from financing activities include these:

<table>
<tr><td align="center">Inflows</td><td align="center">Outflows</td></tr>
<tr><td>Cash received from</td><td>Cash paid for</td></tr>
<tr><td>Borrowing on notes, mortgages, bonds, etc., from creditors</td><td>Repayment of principal to creditors (excluding interest, which is an operating activity)</td></tr>
<tr><td>Issuing shares to shareholders</td><td>Repurchasing shares from owners</td></tr>
<tr><td></td><td>Dividends to shareholders</td></tr>
</table>

The difference between these cash inflows and outflows is called *net cash inflow (outflow) from financing activities*.

For APL, this amount was an outflow of $243 for the second quarter of 2007. The Financing Activities section of the statement shows that APL repaid $1,563 to its creditors during the period, increased its borrowings from banks by $2,098, and paid $778 in dividends to shareholders.

NET INCREASE (DECREASE) IN CASH

The combination of **the net cash flows from operating activities, investing activities, and financing activities must equal the net increase (decrease) in cash** for the reporting period. For the second quarter of 2007, APL reported a net change of zero in cash. In fact, APL did not report any cash on its balance sheets at June 30, 2006, and September 30, 2006. The cash it generated from operations was not sufficient to pay for the acquisition of property and equipment, and to repay long-term debt, which led APL to borrow from banks to cover the shortfall in cash. Note that significant cash transactions took place during the quarter even though the cash balances were zero at both the beginning and end of this quarter.

	(in thousands)
Net cash provided by operating activities	$1,925
Net cash used in investing activities	(1,682)
Net cash used in financing activities	(243)
Net increase in cash and cash equivalents	0
Cash and cash equivalents at beginning of period	0
Cash and cash equivalents at end of period	$ 0

CASH FLOWS FROM INVESTING ACTIVITIES are cash inflows and outflows related to the acquisition or sale of productive facilities and investments in the securities of other companies.

CASH FLOWS FROM FINANCING ACTIVITIES are cash inflows and outflows related to external sources of financing (owners and creditors) for the enterprise.

SELF-STUDY **QUIZ 5-1**

Canadian Tire Corporation

Canadian Tire Corporation is a network of businesses engaged in retail, financial services, and petroleum. A listing of some of its cash flows follows. Indicate whether each item is disclosed in the Operating Activities (O), Investing Activities (I), or Financing Activities (F) section of the statement. (Refer to Exhibit 5.1 as a guide.)

_____ *a.* Purchase of short-term investments   _____ *f.* Change in inventories

_____ *b.* Net income   _____ *g.* Change in accrued liabilities

_____ *c.* Change in trade accounts receivable   _____ *h.* Depreciation and amortization

_____ *d.* Additions to property and equipment   _____ *i.* Issuance of common shares

_____ *e.* Change in prepaid expenses and other current assets   _____ *j.* Change in trade accounts payable

After you complete your answers, check them with the solutions on page 255.

To give you a better understanding of the cash flow statement, we now discuss in more detail APL's statement and the way that it relates to the balance sheet and income statement. Then we examine the way that each section of the statement describes a set of important decisions that APL's management made. We also discuss the way financial analysts use each section to evaluate the company's performance.

RELATIONSHIPS TO THE BALANCE SHEET AND INCOME STATEMENT

Preparing and interpreting the cash flow statement require analyzing the balance sheet and income statement accounts that relate to the three sections of the cash flow statement. As we discussed in previous chapters, accountants record transactions as journal entries that are posted to specific ledger accounts. The accounts' balances are then used to prepare the income statement and the balance sheet. Companies cannot prepare the cash flow statement by using amounts recorded in the specific accounts because these amounts are based on accrual accounting. Instead, accountants must analyze the amounts recorded under the accrual basis and adjust them to a cash basis. To prepare the cash flow statement, they need the following data:

1. **Comparative balance sheets** that are used in computing the cash flows from all activities (operating, investing, and financing).

2. A **complete income statement,** which is used primarily in identifying cash flows from operating activities.

3. **Additional details** concerning selected accounts that reflect different types of transactions and events. Analysis of individual accounts is necessary because often the net change in an account balance during the year does not reveal the underlying nature of the cash flows.

Our approach to preparing and understanding the cash flow statement focuses on the changes in the balance sheet accounts. It relies on a simple algebraic manipulation of the balance sheet equation

$$\textbf{Assets} = \textbf{Liabilities} + \textbf{Shareholders' Equity}$$

First, assets can be split into cash and non-cash assets:

$$\textbf{Cash} + \textbf{Non-Cash Assets} = \textbf{Liabilities} + \textbf{Shareholders' Equity}$$

If we move the non-cash assets to the right side of the equation, then

$$\textbf{Cash} = \textbf{Liabilities} + \textbf{Shareholders' Equity} - \textbf{Non-Cash Assets}$$

Given this relationship, the change in cash (Δ) between the beginning and end of the period must equal the changes (Δ) in the amounts on the right side of the equation during the same period:

$$\Delta \textbf{ Cash} = \Delta \textbf{ Liabilities} + \Delta \textbf{ Shareholders' Equity} - \Delta \textbf{ Non-Cash Assets}$$

Thus, **any transaction that changes cash must be accompanied by a change in liabilities, shareholders' equity, or non-cash assets.**

In general, increases in cash are associated with decreases in non-cash asset accounts, and increases in liability and shareholders' equity accounts. In contrast, cash decreases when non-cash assets increase, and when liabilities or shareholders' equity decrease. Exhibit 5.2 illustrates this concept along with a sample of cash transactions that affect different asset, liability, and equity accounts.

Decrease in Non-cash Assets
Increase in Liabilities and Shareholders' Equity → **Cash Inflow**

Increase in Non-cash Assets
Decrease in Liabilities and Shareholders' Equity → **Cash Outflow**

EXHIBIT 5.2

Selected Cash Transactions and Their Effects on Other Balance Sheet Accounts

Category	Transaction	Effect on Cash	Other Account Affected
Operating	Collect accounts receivable	+Cash	−Accounts Receivable (A)
	Pay accounts payable	−Cash	−Accounts Payable (L)
	Prepay rent	−Cash	+Prepaid Rent (A)
	Pay interest	−Cash	−Retained Earnings (SE)
	Sell for cash	+Cash	+Retained Earnings (SE)
Investing	Purchase equipment for cash	−Cash	+Equipment (A)
	Sell investment securities for cash	+Cash	−Investments
Financing	Pay back debt to bank	−Cash	−Notes Payable—Bank (L)
	Issue shares for cash	+Cash	+Share Capital (SE)

Next, we will compute the change in each balance sheet account (ending balance − beginning balance) and classify each change as relating to operating (O), investing (I), or financing (F) activities, based on APL's quarterly financial statements.

Exhibit 5.3 shows APL's comparative balance sheets at the end of the first and second quarters of 2007, and its income statement for the second quarter of 2007. **The balance sheet accounts related to earning income (operating items) should be marked with an O.** These accounts include the following:

- most current assets (other than short-term investments which relate to investing activities).[3]

- most current liabilities (other than amounts owed to investors and financial institutions,[4] all of which relate to financing activities).

- retained earnings because it increases by the amount of net income, which is the starting point of the Operating section. (Retained earnings also decreases by the amount of dividends declared and paid, which is a financing outflow noted by an F.)

In Exhibit 5.3, all of the relevant current assets and liabilities have been marked with an O. These items include Accounts receivable, Inventories, Prepaid expenses, Bank indebtedness, Accounts payable, Accrued liabilities, Dividends payable, and Income taxes payable. As we have noted, Retained earnings is also relevant to operations.

The balance sheet accounts related to investing activities should be marked with an I. These include all of the remaining assets on the balance sheet. In Exhibit 5.3, these are Property, plant and equipment, Goodwill, and Other assets.

The balance sheet accounts related to financing activities should be marked with an F. These include all of the remaining liability and shareholders' equity accounts on the balance sheet. In Exhibit 5.3, these are Share capital and Retained earnings (for decreases resulting from dividends declared and paid).

---

[3]Certain noncurrent assets such as long-term receivables from customers and noncurrent liabilities such as post-retirement obligations to employees are considered to be operating items. These items are covered in advanced accounting courses.

[4]Examples of the accounts excluded are Dividends Payable, Short-Term Borrowing (or Bank Indebtedness), and Current Portion of Long-Term Debt (representing long-term debt with an original term longer than one year that is due within one year of the statement date).

In the next sections of this chapter, we use this information to prepare the cash flow statement.

EXHIBIT **5.3**

Andrew Peller Limited: Comparative Balance Sheet and Current Income Statement (In thousands)

ANDREW PELLER LIMITED
Consolidated Balance Sheet—Unaudited
(in thousands of dollars)

Related Cash Flow Section		Sept. 30, 2006	June 30, 2006	Change
	Assets			
	Current assets			
O	Accounts receivable	$ 27,687	$ 21,682	6,005
O	Inventories	71,870	70,131	1,739
O	Prepaid expenses	4,490	3,318	1,172
	Total current assets	104,047	95,131	
I*	Property, plant, and equipment (net)	84,863	85,001	−138
I	Long-term investments	8,131	8,219	−88
I	Goodwill	36,171	36,171	0
	Total assets	$233,212	$224,522	
	Liabilities			
	Current liabilities			
F	Bank indebtedness	$ 44,080	$ 41,982	2,098
O	Accounts payable	18,423	12,210	6,213
O	Accrued liabilities	7,134	6,569	565
F	Dividends payable	917	778	139
O	Income taxes payable	—	470	−470
F	Current portion of long-term debt	5,897	5,892	5
	Total current liabilities	76,451	67,901	
F	Long-term debt	51,430	52,998	−1,568
O	Future income taxes	12,514	12,445	69
	Total liabilities	140,395	133,344	
	Shareholders' Equity			
F	Share capital	7,375	7,375	0
O and F	Retained earnings	85,442	83,803	1,639
	Total shareholders' equity	92,817	91,178	
	Total liabilities and shareholders' equity	$233,212	$224,522	

The balances of certain accounts have been adjusted to simplify the presentation.
*The accumulated amortization account is also related to operations because amortization expense is added back to net income.

ANDREW PELLER LIMITED
Consolidated Statement of Earnings—Unaudited
(in thousands of dollars)

	Quarter ended Sept. 30, 2006
Net Sales	$59,413
Cost of goods sold	34,369
Gross margin	25,044
Selling, general and administrative	17,880
Amortization of plant and equipment	1,908
Operating income	5,256
Interest expense	1,383
Income before income taxes	3,873
Provision for income taxes	1,317
Net income	$ 2,556

REPORTING AND INTERPRETING CASH FLOWS FROM OPERATING ACTIVITIES—INDIRECT METHOD

The operating section can be prepared in one of two formats: the direct method and the indirect method. The next section presents the indirect method and Chapter Supplement B describes the direct method.

Remember that:

1. Cash flow from operating activities is always the same regardless of whether it is computed using the direct or indirect method.

2. The investing and financing sections are always presented in the same manner regardless of the format of the operating section.

REPORTING CASH FLOWS FROM OPERATING ACTIVITIES

We have learned that under accrual accounting, revenues are recognized when earned and expenses are recognized when incurred to generate revenues (the matching principle), regardless of the timing of cash receipts and payments. Consequently, net income includes both cash and non-cash elements related to revenues, expenses, gains, and losses.

> **LEARNING OBJECTIVE 2**
>
> Report and interpret cash flows from operating activities using the indirect method.

> **Net income = Cash elements +/− Non-cash elements**

The direct method focuses on the cash elements of net income by computing cash receipts and cash payments to arrive at net cash flows from operating activities. In contrast, the indirect method starts with net income and eliminates non-cash elements to arrive at the same result.

> **Cash elements = Net income +/− Non-cash elements**

Keeping track of all the additions and subtractions made to convert net income to cash flows from operating activities is facilitated by setting up a schedule to record the computations. We construct such a schedule for APL in Exhibit 5.4 on page 241.

Preparation of the operating section using the indirect method involves the following steps:

Step 1: **Begin the Operating Activities section with net income reported on the income statement.** We begin our schedule presented in Exhibit 5.4 with net income of $2,556 taken from APL's income statement (Exhibit 5.3).

Step 2: **Adjust net income for the effects of items marked O on Exhibit 5.3 that reflect differences in the timing of accrual basis net income and cash flows.** The following adjustments are the ones most frequently encountered:

Income Statement Amounts or Balance Sheet Changes	Impact on the Cash Flow Statement
Net Income	Starting point for computation
Amortization expense	Added
Decreases in current assets	Added
Increases in current liabilities	Added
Increases in current assets	Subtracted
Decreases in current liabilities	Subtracted

This step is completed in two parts:

Step 2a: Adjust net income for amortization expense. Recording amortization expense does not affect the cash account (or any other current asset or liability). It affects a noncurrent asset (such as Equipment, net). **Since amortization expense is subtracted in computing net income, but does not affect cash, we always add it back** to convert net income to cash flow from operating activities.[5] In the case of APL, we need to remove the effect of amortization expense by adding back $1,908 to net income (see Exhibit 5.4).[6]

Step 2b: Adjust net income for changes in current assets and current liabilities marked as operating (O). Each **change** in current assets (other than cash and short-term investments) and current liabilities (other than amounts owed to owners and financial institutions) causes a difference between net income and cash flow from operating activities.[7] When converting net income to cash flow from operating activities, apply the following general rules:

- **Add the change when a current asset decreases or current liability increases.**

- **Subtract the change when a current asset increases or current liability decreases.**

Understanding what makes these current assets and current liabilities increase and decrease is the key to understanding the logic of these additions and subtractions.

Change in Accounts Receivable   We illustrate this logic with the first operating item (O) listed on APL's Balance sheet (Exhibit 5.3), accounts receivable. Remember that the income statement reflects sales revenue, but the cash flow statement must reflect cash collections from customers. As the following accounts receivable T-account illustrates, when sales revenues are recorded, accounts receivable increases, and when cash is collected from customers, accounts receivable decreases.

Accounts Receivable (A)			
Beginning balance	21,682		
Sales revenue (on account)	59,413	Collections from customers	53,408
Ending balance	27,687		

Change +6,005

---

[5]The fact that amortization is added back to net income may lead the reader to conclude that amortization expense is a source of cash. Nothing could be further from the truth! In fact, amortization is a process of allocation of the cost of assets that have been amortized in the past regardless of the timing of payments for the assets.

[6]Gains and losses on sales of equipment and investments are dealt with in a similar manner and are discussed in Chapter Supplement A. Other similar additions and subtractions are discussed in more advanced accounting courses.

[7]Certain noncurrent assets such as long-term receivables from customers and noncurrent liabilities such as post-retirement obligations to employees are considered to be operating items. These items are covered in advanced accounting courses.

EXHIBIT **5.4**

Andrew Peller Limited: Schedule for Net Cash Flow from Operating Activities, Indirect Method (in thousands)

Conversion of net income to net cash flow from operating activities:

Items	Amount	Explanation
Net income, accrual basis	$ 2,556	From income statement.
Add (subtract) to convert to cash basis:		
Depreciation and amortization expense	+1,908	Add because depreciation and amortization expense is a non-cash expense.
Future income tax expense	+69	Add because the future income tax expense is a non-cash expense.
Increase in accounts receivable	−6,005	Subtract because cash collected from customers is less than accrual basis revenues.
Increase in inventories	−1,739	Subtract because cost of goods sold expense is less than purchases.
Increase in prepaid expenses	−1,172	Subtract because accrual basis expenses are less than cash prepayments for expenses.
Increase in accounts payable	+6,213	Add because purchases on account (due to suppliers) are more than cash payments to suppliers.
Increase in accrued liabilities	565	Add because accrual basis expenses are more than the cash payments for expenses.
Decrease in income taxes payable	−470	Subtract because the income tax expense reported on the income statement is less than the income taxes paid.
Net cash inflow from operating activities	$1,925	Reported on the cash flow statement.

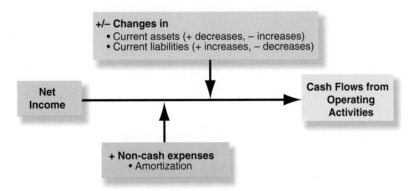

In the APL example, sales revenue on account reported on the income statement is larger than cash collections from customers by $59,413 − $53,408 = $6,005.[8] Since less money was collected from customers, this amount must be subtracted from net income to convert to cash flows from operating activities. Note that this amount is also the same as the **change** in the accounts receivable account:

Ending balance	$27,687
−Beginning balance	21,682
Change	+$ 6,005

---

[8]The amount of cash collected from customers is the same, regardless of the mix of cash sales and credit sales. To make sure, assume that sales are 20 percent cash and 80 percent on account, and calculate the amount of cash collected from customers during the period.

This same underlying logic is used to determine adjustments for the other current assets and liabilities.

To summarize, the income statement reflects revenues of the period, but cash flow from operating activities must reflect cash collections from customers. Sales on account increase the balance in accounts receivable, and collections from customers decrease the balance.

If Accounts Receivable:

Increases ($ is Lower) → Subtract

Decreases ($ is Higher) → Add

Accounts Receivable (A)	
Beg.	21,682
Increase	6,005
End.	27,687

The balance sheet for APL indicates an **increase** in accounts receivable of $6,005 for the period, which means cash collected from customers is lower than revenue. To convert to cash flow from operating activities, the amount of the increase must be **subtracted** from net income in Exhibit 5.4. (A decrease is added to net income.)

Change in Inventory   The income statement reflects merchandise sold for the period, whereas cash flow from operating activities must reflect cash purchases.

Both the change in inventory and the change in accounts payable (borrowing from suppliers) determine the magnitude of this difference. It is easiest to think about the change in inventory in terms of the simple case in which the company pays cash to suppliers of inventory. We address the added complexity involved when purchases are made on account when we discuss the adjustment for the change in accounts payable.

Since purchases of goods increase the balance in inventory and cost of goods sold decreases the balance in inventory, the change in inventory is the difference between purchases and the cost of goods sold.

If Inventory:

Increases ($ is Lower) → Subtract

Decreases ($ is Higher) → Add

Inventories (A)	
Beg.	70,131
Increase	1,739
End.	71,870

APL's balance sheet indicates that inventory **increased** by $1,739, which means that the amount of purchases is larger than the amount of merchandise sold. The increase must be **subtracted** from net income to convert to cash flow from operating activities in Exhibit 5.4. (An increase is subtracted from net income.)

Change in Prepaid Expenses   The income statement reflects expenses of the period, but cash flow from operating activities must reflect the cash payments. Cash prepayments increase the balance in prepaid expenses, and expenses recognized during the period decrease the balance in prepaid expenses.

If Prepaid Expenses:

Increases ($ is Lower) → Subtract

Decreases ($ is Higher) → Add

Prepaid Expenses (A)	
Beg.	3,318
Increase	1,172
End.	4,490

The APL balance sheet indicates an **increase** of $1,172 in prepaid expenses, which means that the amount of expenses is lower than new cash prepayments. The increase (the extra payments) must be **subtracted** from net income in Exhibit 5.4. (A decrease is added to net income.)

Change in Accounts Payable Cash flow from operations must reflect cash purchases, but not all purchases are for cash. Purchases on account increase accounts payable, and cash paid to suppliers decreases accounts payable.

Accounts Payable (L)		
	Beg.	12,210
	Increase	6,213
	End.	18,423

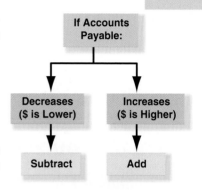

APL's accounts payable **increased** by $6,213, which means that cash payments were lower than purchases on account, and this increase (the lower payments) must be **added** to net income in Exhibit 5.4. (A decrease is subtracted from net income.)

Change in Accrued Liabilities The income statement reflects all accrued expenses, but the cash flow statement must reflect actual payments for those expenses. Recording accrued expenses increases the balance in Accrued liabilities and cash payments for the expenses decrease Accrued liabilities.

Accrued Liabilities (L)		
	Beg.	6,569
	Increase	565
	End.	7,134

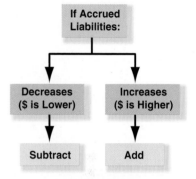

APL's accrued liabilities **increased** by $565, which indicates that accrual-basis expenses are larger than cash paid for the expenses. The increase must be **added** to net income in Exhibit 5.4. (A decrease is subtracted from net income.)

Income Taxes Payable (L)		
	Beg.	470
Decrease	470	
	End.	0

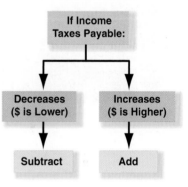

APL's income taxes payable **decreased** by $470, which indicates that accrual-basis expenses are lower than cash paid for the expenses. The decrease must be **subtracted** from net income in Exhibit 5.4. (An increase is added to net income.)

Summary We can summarize the typical additions and subtractions that are required to reconcile net income with cash flow from operating activities as follows:

Item	Additions and Subtractions to Reconcile Net Income to Cash Flow from Operating Activities	
	When Item Increases	When Item Decreases
Amortization	+	NA
Accounts receivable	−	+
Inventory	−	+
Prepaid expenses	−	+
Accounts payable	+	−
Accrued expenses (liabilities)	+	−

Notice in this table that an *increase in an asset or a decrease in a liability* is always *subtracted* to reconcile net income to cash flows from operating activities. A *decrease in an asset or an increase in a liability* is always *added* to reconcile net income to cash flows from operating activities. The cash flow statement for APL (Exhibit 5.1) shows the same additions and subtractions to reconcile net income to cash flows from operating activities described in Exhibit 5.4.

It is important to note again that the net cash inflow or outflow is the same regardless of whether the direct or indirect method of presentation is used (in this case, an inflow of $1,925). The two methods differ only in terms of the details reported on the statement.

A more detailed illustration showing both the direct and indirect methods of computing cash flows from operations is available on the Online Learning Centre Web site at **www.mcgrawhill.ca/olc/libby/student/resources**.

SELF-STUDY **QUIZ 5-2**

Canadian Tire Corporation

Indicate which of the following items taken from Canadian Tire Corporation's cash flow statement would be added (+), subtracted (−), or not included (0) in the reconciliation of net income to cash flow from operations.

_____   *a.* Increase in inventories.

_____   *b.* Net borrowings from bank.

_____   *c.* Depreciation and amortization.

_____   *d.* Decrease in trade accounts receivable.

_____   *e.* Increase in trade accounts payable and accrued expenses.

_____   *f.* Increase in prepaid expenses and other current assets.

After you complete your answers, check them with the solutions on page 255.

INTERPRETING CASH FLOWS FROM OPERATING ACTIVITIES

The Operating Activities section of the cash flow statement focuses attention on the firm's ability to generate cash internally through operations and its management of working capital (current assets minus current liabilities). Many analysts regard this as the most important section of the statement because, in the long run, operations are the only source of cash. Investors should not invest in a company if they believe that it will not be able to pay them dividends or make reinvestments with cash generated from operations. Similarly, creditors should not lend money if they believe that cash generated from operations will not be available to pay back the loan. For example, many Internet-based companies crashed when investors lost faith in their ability to turn business ideas into cash from operations.

A common rule followed by financial and credit analysts is to avoid firms with rising net income but falling cash flow from operations. Rapidly rising inventories require the use of cash until goods are sold. Similarly, rapidly rising accounts receivable also delay the collection of cash. Rising inventories and accounts receivable often predict a future slump in profits as revenues fall. This increases the need for external financing as overall cash inflows from operations decline. In the first quarter of fiscal year 2007, APL exhibited just such a pattern. Is this a sign of troubled waters ahead for APL? Why, as indicated in the following chart, did net income increase slightly in the following quarter, but cash flow from operations showed a significant rebound?

	Net Income		Cash Flows from Operations
1st quarter, 2007	$2,376	>	(892)
2nd quarter, 2007	$2,556	>	$1,925

To answer these questions, we must carefully analyze how APL's operating activities are reported in the cash flow statement. At the same time, we also must learn more about the wine industry to properly interpret this information.

Fluctuating Cash Flows from Operations: A Warning Sign? In the first quarter, APL's net income was $2,376 (in thousands), yet it reported a use of cash for operations of $892. Does this suggest that APL may be facing more difficult times?

Analysts who cover the wine industry know that this is a result of seasonal fluctuations in wine sales to distributors. They recognize that wine sales are low in months of April to June (the first quarter for APL), and that sales are higher during the second quarter (July to September) in anticipation of fall. The higher sales volume in the second quarter requires a buildup of inventories over time to meet demand in the fall months, which leads to cash payments to suppliers and employees exceeding cash collections from customers. The imbalance in cash inflows and outflows increases the need for external financing. However, the use of cash for operations during the first quarter is followed by a net cash inflow from operations in the second quarter, when sales and collections from customers increase. This normal seasonal fluctuation in sales is clearly not a sign of problems for APL.

Managers sometimes attempt to boost declining sales by extending credit terms (for example from 30 to 60 days) or by lowering credit standards (that is, lending to riskier customers). The resulting increase in accounts receivable can cause net income to outpace cash flow from operations. As a consequence, many analysts view this pattern as a warning sign.

Analyzing Inventory Changes An unexpected increase in inventory can be another cause for net income to outpace cash flow from operations. Such inventory growth can be a sign that planned sales growth did not materialize. A decline in inventory can be a sign that the company is anticipating lower sales in the next quarter. Many analysts compute the quality of income (or quality of earnings) ratio as a general warning sign of these and similar problems.

QUALITY OF INCOME RATIO

KEY RATIO
ANALYSIS

ANALYTICAL QUESTION → How much cash does each dollar of net income generate?

RATIO AND COMPARISONS → The quality of income ratio is useful in answering this question. It is computed as follows:

$$\text{Quality of Income Ratio} = \frac{\text{Cash Flow from Operating Activities}}{\text{Net Income}}$$

APL's ratio for the year* 2006 is:

$$\frac{\$18,984}{\$6,054} = 3.14 \ (314\%)$$

■ **LEARNING OBJECTIVE 3**

Analyze and interpret the quality of income ratio.

Comparisons over Time			Comparisons with Competitors	
Andrew Peller (annual)			Constellation Brands	Foster's Group
2004	2005	2006	2006	2006
0.43	0.79	3.14	1.34	0.72

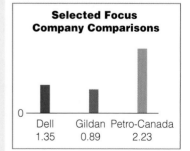

Selected Focus Company Comparisons

Dell	Gildan	Petro-Canada
1.35	0.89	2.23

*We use the ratio for the annual period to eliminate the effects of seasonality.

INTERPRETATIONS

In General → The quality of income ratio measures the portion of income that was generated in cash. All other things being equal, a higher quality of income ratio indicates a greater ability to finance operating and other cash needs from operating cash inflows.[9] A higher ratio also indicates that it is less likely that the company is using aggressive revenue recognition policies to increase net income. When this ratio does not equal 1.0, analysts must establish the source

[9]When a net loss is reported, a more negative ratio indicates greater ability to finance the company from operations.

of the difference to determine the significance of the findings. There are four potential causes of any difference:

1. *The corporate life cycle (growth or decline in sales).* When sales are increasing, receivables and inventory normally increase faster than accounts payable. This often reduces operating cash flows below income, which, in turn, reduces the ratio. When sales are declining, the opposite occurs, and the ratio increases.

2. *Seasonality.* As was the case for APL, seasonal variations in sales and purchases of inventory can cause the ratio to deviate from 1.0.

3. *Changes in revenue and expense recognition.* Aggressive revenue recognition or failure to accrue appropriate expenses will inflate net income and reduce the ratio.

4. *Changes in management of operating assets and liabilities.* Inefficient management will increase operating assets and decrease liabilities, which will reduce operating cash flows and reduce the ratio. More efficient management will have the opposite effect.

Focus Company Analysis → APL's quality of income ratio has increased from 0.43 to 3.14 during the last three years. As we noted earlier, the difference between net income and cash flow from operations in the case of APL for the first quarter of 2007 was not a cause for alarm. It was due to normal seasonal changes in sales and receivables. The increase in the ratio in 2006 is due primarily to changes in inventory levels. Its ratio for 2006 is higher than the quality of income ratio achieved by both Constellation Brands and Foster's Group. The wide variation in APL's ratio would prompt analysts to contact management to determine its causes.

A Few Cautions → The quality of income ratio can be interpreted only based on an understanding of the company's business operations and strategy. For example, a low ratio can be due simply to normal seasonal changes. However, it also can indicate obsolete inventory, slowing sales, or failed expansion plans. Analysts often analyze this ratio in tandem with the accounts receivable turnover and inventory turnover ratios to test for these possibilities.*

*K. G. Palepu, P. M. Healy, and V. L. Bernard, *Business Analysis and Valuation Using Financial Statements,* 2e. Cincinnati, OH: South-Western, 2000.

FINANCIAL ANALYSIS

CLASSIFICATION OF CASH FLOWS

We indicated in Chapter 4 that managers may speed up the recognition of revenues or delay the recognition of expenses in order to increase the reported net income, which would reflect positively on their performance and compensation. For this reason, analysts also examine the cash flow from operations, because cash receipts and payments are less susceptible to manipulation. However, the reported operating cash flow can be influenced by classifying certain operating cash flows as investing cash flows.

Certain companies, such as Nortel Networks Limited, General Motors Corp., and Harley-Davidson Inc., provide loans or other financial assistance (known as vendor financing) to their customers to help them buy the companies' products. These loans reduce cash and increase the amount of receivables. The reduction in cash and corresponding increase in receivables are the result of an operating transaction. But these companies tended to classify such transactions as investing activities rather than operating activities in order to avoid their negative effects on operating cash flows. Recently, the U.S. Securities and Exchange Commission required that cash flows resulting from vendor financing be classified as operating cash flows instead of investing cash flows. This requirement has resulted in significant reductions of operating cash flows for companies that followed this practice. For example, the operating cash flows of General Motors Corp. and Ford Motor Company for the year 2003 declined by US$4.4 billion and US$2.1 billion, respectively. The reclassification of cash flows has implications for a proper evaluation of operating cash flows and related analyses, such as the quality of income ratio discussed below.

Source: Michael Rapoport, "Cash Flow Takes an SEC Hit," *National Post*, March 24, 2005, p. FP15.

FRAUD AND CASH FLOWS FROM OPERATIONS

The cash flow statement often gives outsiders the first hint that financial statements may contain errors and irregularities. The importance of this indicator as a predictor is receiving more attention following corporate scandals in the United States, as *Forbes* reported:

REAL WORLD EXCERPT

Forbes

> From July 1997 to July 2002 the SEC launched 227 investigations of suspected financial misreporting, 126 of them relating to revenue recognition. Improper timing of sales is the biggest offense—borrowing from the next quarter in a desperate effort to make the analysts happy for the quarter. The SEC also found 80 cases of utterly fictitious revenues and 21 cases of improperly valued revenues...
>
> ... How do you protect yourself as an investor? Spend as much time with the cash flow statement as with the profit-and-loss statement that precedes it. If a company is counting dubious transactions in its revenues, in all likelihood the buyers haven't paid yet, and the cash flow from operations will be anemic in relation to reported profit.*

As noted in earlier chapters, unethical managers sometimes attempt to reach earnings targets by manipulating accruals and deferrals of revenues and expenses to inflate income. Since these adjustments do not affect the cash account, they have no effect on the cash flow statement. As a consequence, a growing difference between net income and cash flow from operations can be a sign of such manipulations. This early warning sign has been evident before some famous bankruptcies, such as that of W. T. Grant. This company had inflated income by failing to make adequate accruals of expenses for uncollectable accounts receivable and obsolete inventory. The growing difference between net income and cash flow from operations that resulted was noted by the more astute analysts who recommended selling the stock long before the bankruptcy.

*Source: Andrew T. Gillies, "Is That Revenue for Real," *Forbes*, April 14, 2003, p. 161.

REPORTING AND INTERPRETING CASH FLOWS FROM INVESTING ACTIVITIES

REPORTING CASH FLOWS FROM INVESTING ACTIVITIES

Preparing this section of the cash flow statement requires analyzing the accounts related to property, plant, and equipment; intangible assets; and investments in the securities of other companies, and lending to other than customers. Normally, the relevant balance sheet accounts include short-term investments and long-term asset accounts such as Long-Term Investments and Property, Plant, and Equipment. The following relationships are the ones that you will encounter most frequently:

■ LEARNING OBJECTIVE 4

Report and interpret cash flows from investing activities.

Related Balance Sheet Account(s)	Investing Activity	Cash Flow Effect
Property, plant, and equipment and intangible assets (e.g., patents)	Purchase of property, plant, and equipment or intangible assets for cash	Outflow
	Sale of property, plant, and equipment or intangible assets for cash	Inflow
Short- or long-term investments in shares and bonds issued by other companies	Purchase of investment securities for cash	Outflow
	Sale (maturity) of investment securities for cash	Inflow

Typical investing activities include the following:

1. Cash expenditures that include the acquisition of tangible productive assets such as buildings and equipment or intangible assets such as trademarks and patents. **Only purchases paid for with cash or cash equivalents are included.**

2. Cash proceeds from the sale of productive assets or intangible assets. This is the amount of cash that was received from the sale of assets, regardless of whether the assets were sold at a gain or a loss.

3. Purchase of short- or long-term investments for cash. These investments can include shares or bonds issued by other companies, guaranteed investment certificates, or government securities with maturities of more than three months. (Remember that those with maturities of three months or less are cash equivalents.)

4. Cash proceeds from the sale or maturity of short- or long-term investments. Again, this is the amount of cash that was received from the sale, regardless of whether the assets were sold at a gain or a loss.

In the case of APL, the analysis of changes in the balance sheet (shown in Exhibit 5.3) indicates that two long-term assets (noted with an I) have changed during the period: Property, Plant, and Equipment (net), and Long-Term Investments. To determine the causes of changes in these assets, accountants need to search the related company records.

Property, Plant, and Equipment (net)   The company's Property, Plant, and Equipment (PPE) decreased by an amount of $138, net of accumulated amortization. Typically, the net change in PPE is the result of three main changes: (1) purchase of new assets, (2) disposal of old assets, and (3) periodic amortization of these assets. The purchase of assets increases the balance of PPE, the disposal of assets decreases the balance of PPE by the net book value (original cost − accumulated amortization) of the assets disposed of, and the periodic amortization increases the accumulated amortization, which in turn reduces the balance of PPE.

During the second quarter of 2007, APL purchased new property, plant, and equipment for cash in the amount of $1,770, which is a cash outflow. This amount less the amortization expense of $1,908, which is added to the net income in the Operations section of the cash flow statement, explains the net decrease in PPE of $138.

Property, Plant, and Equipment (net)

Beg.	85,001	Amortization	1,908
Purchases	1,770		
End.	84,863		

Cash purchases and sales of plant and equipment are listed separately on the cash flow statement.

Long-Term Investments   APL's records indicate that it sold long-term investments at book value during the quarter and received $88 in cash. This transaction explains the decrease in the account balance.

Long-Term Investments (A)

Beg.	8,219	Sale	88
End.	8,131		

These investing items are listed in the schedule of investing activities in Exhibit 5.5, and result in a cash outflow of $1,682.

EXHIBIT **5.5**

Andrew Peller Limited: Schedule for Net Cash Flow from Investing Activities (in thousands)

Items from Balance Sheet and Account Analysis	Cash Inflow (Outflows)	Explanation
Additions to property, plant, and equipment	($1,770)	Payment in cash for buildings and equipment.
Proceeds from long-term investments	88	Receipt of cash for sale of investments.
Net cash inflow (outflow) from investing activities	($1,682)	Reported on the cash flow statement.

INTERPRETING CASH FLOWS FROM INVESTING ACTIVITIES

Two common ways of assessing a company's ability to finance its expansion needs from internal sources are the capital acquisitions ratio and free cash flow.

CAPITAL ACQUISITIONS RATIO

KEY RATIO
ANALYSIS

ANALYTICAL QUESTION → To what degree was the company able to finance purchases of property, plant, and equipment with cash provided by operating activities?

RATIO AND COMPARISONS → Since capital expenditures for plant and equipment often vary greatly from year to year, this ratio is often computed over longer periods of time than one year, such as the three-year period used here. It is computed as follows:

■ **LEARNING OBJECTIVE 5**

Analyze and interpret the capital acquisitions ratio.

$$\text{Capital Acquisitions Ratio} = \frac{\text{Cash Flow from Operating Activities}}{\text{Cash Paid for Property, Plant, and Equipment}}$$

The 2004 through 2006* ratio for APL is:

$$\frac{\$29,903}{\$22,732} = 1.32$$

Comparisons over Time		Comparisons with Competitors	
Andrew Peller		Constellation Brands	Foster's Group
2001–2003	2004–2006	2004–2006	2004–2006
1.15	1.32	3.07	2.47

INTERPRETATIONS

In General → The capital acquisitions ratio reflects the portion of purchases of property, plant, and equipment financed from operating activities without the need for outside debt or equity financing or the sale of other investments or fixed assets. A high ratio indicates less need for outside financing for current and future expansion. This provides the company with opportunities for strategic acquisitions, avoids the cost of additional debt, and reduces the risks of bankruptcy that come with additional leverage (see Chapter 11).

Focus Company Analysis → Although APL's ratio has increased from 1.15 to 1.32 in recent years, it is significantly lower than its competitors. To many, the tangible nature of plant and equipment may suggest that it is a low-risk investment. When companies in an industry build more productive capacity than is necessary to meet customer demand, however, the costs of maintaining and financing idle plant can drive a company to ruin. While APL produces and markets its own wine and premium beer, both Constellation Brands and Foster's Group market wine, beer, and other alcoholic beverages produced by other companies, in addition to marketing their own brands. By marketing other brands, these two companies reduce their need to invest in additional productive capacity to expand their operations. These differences in operating strategies are reflected in the companies' capital acquisitions ratio.

Selected Focus Company Comparisons

Dell 8.74

Gildan 1.12

Petro-Canada 1.09

A Few Cautions → Since the needs for investment in plant and equipment differ dramatically across industries (for example, airlines versus pizza delivery restaurants), a particular firm's ratio should be compared only with its prior years' figures or with other firms in the same industry. Also, a high ratio may indicate a failure to update plant and equipment, which can limit a company's ability to compete in the future.

*Since capital expenditures for plant and equipment vary greatly from year to year, this ratio is often computed over longer periods of time than one year, such as three years.

FINANCIAL ANALYSIS

FREE CASH FLOW

FREE CASH FLOW =
Cash Flows from Operating
Activities − Dividends −
Capital Expenditures

Managers and analysts also often calculate **free cash flow** as a measure of the firm's ability to pursue long-term investment opportunities. It is normally calculated as follows:

Free Cash Flow = Cash Flows from Operating Activities −
Dividends − Capital Expenditures

Any positive free cash flow is available for additional capital expenditures, investments in other companies, and mergers and acquisitions, without the need for external financing. While free cash flow is considered a positive sign of financial flexibility, it also can represent a hidden cost to shareholders. Sometimes managers use free cash flow to pursue unprofitable investments just for the sake of growth or for perquisites for management use (such as fancy offices and corporate jets). In these cases, the shareholders would be better off if free cash flow were paid as additional dividends or used to repurchase the company's shares in the open market.

REPORTING AND INTERPRETING CASH FLOWS FROM FINANCING ACTIVITIES

REPORTING CASH FLOWS FROM FINANCING ACTIVITIES

■ LEARNING OBJECTIVE 6

Report and interpret cash flows
from financing activities.

Financing activities are associated with generating capital from creditors and owners. This section reflects changes in two current liabilities, *notes payable to financial institutions* (often called *short-term debt*), *current portion of long-term debt,* as well as changes in *long-term liabilities and shareholders' equity accounts.* These balance sheet accounts relate to the issuance and retirement of debt, repurchase of shares, and the payment of dividends. The following relationships are the ones that you will encounter most frequently:

Related Balance Sheet Account(s)	Cash Flow Financing Activity	Effect
Short-term debt (notes payable)	Borrowing cash from bank or other financial institution	Inflow
	Repayment of loan principal	Outflow
Long-term debt	Issuance of long-term debt for cash	Inflow
	Repayment of principal on long-term debt	Outflow
Share capital	Issuance of shares for cash	Inflow
	Repurchase (retirement) of shares with cash	Outflow
Retained earnings	Payment of cash dividends	Outflow

Financing activities are associated with generating capital from creditors and owners. Typical financing activities include the following:

1. *Proceeds from issuance of short- and long-term debt.* This represents cash received from borrowing from banks and other financial institutions, and issuance of long-term debt (e.g., notes) to the public. **If the debt is issued for other than cash** (for example, issued directly to a supplier of equipment to pay for a purchase), **it is not included on the statement.**

2. *Principal payments on short- and long-term debt.* Cash outflows associated with debt include the periodic repayment of principal as well as interest payments. Cash repayments of principal are listed as cash flows from financing activities. **Interest payments are cash flows from operating activities.**

3. *Proceeds from the issuance of common shares.* This represents cash received from the sale of common shares to investors. If the shares are issued for other than cash (for example, issued directly to an employee as part of salary), the amount is not included in the statement.

4. *Purchase of shares for retirement.* This cash outflow includes cash payments for repurchase of the company's own shares from shareholders.

5. *Cash dividends.* This is the amount of cash dividends paid to shareholders during the year. Some students wonder why cash payments made to creditors (interest) are shown as an operating activity but cash payments to owners (dividends) are shown as a financing activity. Remember that interest is reported on the income statement and is, therefore, directly associated with earning income (it is an operating activity). Dividend payments are not reported on the income statement because they represent a distribution of income. Dividends are more appropriately shown as a financing activity.

To compute cash flows from financing activities, you should review changes in debt and shareholders' equity accounts. In the case of APL, analysis of changes in the balance sheet account balances indicates that bank operating loans, long-term obligations, and retained earnings changed during the period (noted with an F).

Short-Term Debt Company records indicate that the change in bank indebtedness resulted from additional borrowing of $2,098 in cash. This item is listed in Exhibit 5.6.

Bank Indebtedness (L)

	Beg.	41,982
Payment	Additional loans	2,098
	End.	44,080

Long-Term Debt The company's long-term debt, including the current portion, decreased from $58,890 to $57,327. Therefore, APL repaid $1,563 of its long-term debt during the second quarter of 2007, as shown in Exhibit 5.6.

Long-Term Debt (L)

		Beg.	58,890
Payment	1,563		
		End.	57,327

Retained Earnings The change in retained earnings resulted from the addition of net income and the declaration of dividends.

Retained Earnings (SE)

		Beg.	83,803
Dividends declared	917	Net income	2,556
		End.	85,442

Items from Balance Sheet and Account Analysis	Cash Inflow (Outflows)	Explanation
Increase in bank indebtedness	2,098	Additional borrowing from banks
Long-term obligations—principal repayments	(1,563)	Repayment of the principal amount of long-term debt, including the current portion
Payment of dividends	(778)	Payment of cash dividends to shareholders
Net cash outflow for investing activities	($243)	Reported on the cash flow statement

Dividends Payable   The dividends payable at June 30, 2006 were paid during the quarter ended September 30, 2006.

Dividends Payable (L)			
		Beg.	778
Payment	778	Dividends declared	917
		End.	917

INTERPRETING CASH FLOWS FROM FINANCING ACTIVITIES

The long-term growth of a company is normally financed from three sources: internally generated funds (cash from operating activities), the issuance of shares, and money borrowed on a long-term basis. As we discuss in Chapter 11, companies can adopt a number of different capital structures (the balance of debt and equity). The financing sources that management uses to fund growth will have an important impact on the firm's risk and return characteristics. The cash flow statement shows how management has elected to fund its growth. This information is used by analysts who wish to evaluate the capital structure and growth potential of a business.

 **FINANCIAL ANALYSIS**   ## INTERPRETATION OF CASH FLOW PATTERNS

The cash flow statement depicts the relationships among the operating, investing, and financing activities. Throughout this chapter, we have illustrated the reporting and interpretation of APL's cash flows for the second quarter of 2007. These cash flows are specific to one company for a specified time period. To generalize, the table below shows the eight possible patterns of cash flows generated from (used for) operating, investing, and financing activities. A general explanation for each observed pattern is also provided.

TABLE 1
Analysis of Cash Flow Statements: Patterns

	1	2	3	4	5	6	7	8
Cash Flow from Operating	+	+	+	+	−	−	−	−
Cash Flow from Investing	+	−	+	−	+	−	+	−
Cash Flow from Financing	+	−	−	+	+	+	−	−

General explanation of each pattern:

1. The company is using cash generated from operations, from the sale of long-term assets, and from financing to build its cash reserves. This is a very liquid company, possibly looking for acquisitions. This pattern is very unusual.

2. The company is using cash generated from operations to buy long-term assets and to reduce its debt or distribute cash dividends to shareholders. This pattern reflects a mature, successful firm.

3. The company is using cash from operations and from the sale of fixed assets to reduce its debt or distribute cash dividends to shareholders. It is actually downsizing its operations.

4. The company is using cash from operations and from borrowing (or from equity investment) to expand. This pattern is typical of many growing companies.

5. The company's operating cash flow problems are covered by the sale of long-term assets and by borrowing or shareholder contributions. The company is selling its fixed assets to stay in business, and the fact that investors are willing to supply the financing indicates that they apparently expect a turnaround in operating cash flows.

6. The company experiences a shortfall in cash flow from operations and from investing activities. The deficiency in cash is financed by long-term debt or investments by shareholders. This pattern is most typical of a young, fast-growing company.

7. The company is financing operating cash flow shortages, paying its debtholders and/or its shareholders via the sale of long-term assets. The company is actually shrinking.

8. The company is using cash reserves to finance operations, pay long-term creditors and/or investors, and acquire new long-term assets. This unusual scenario is possible only if cash previously accumulated is being used to meet these cash outflows.

Source: Adapted from M. T. Dugan, B. E. Gup, and W. D. Samson, "Teaching the Statement of Cash Flows," *Journal of Accounting Education*, Vol. 9, 1991, pp. 33–52.

Indicate which of the following items taken from Canadian Tire Corporation's cash flow statement would be reported in the Investing section (I) or Financing section (F) and whether the amount would be an inflow (+) or an outflow (−).

_____ *a.* Net payments on borrowings from bank.

_____ *b.* Purchase of property and equipment for cash.

_____ *c.* Purchase of other (intangible) assets for cash.

_____ *d.* Proceeds from sale (issuance) of common shares.

After you complete your answers, check them with the solutions on page 255.

Self-Study Quiz 5-3

Canadian Tire Corporation

ADDITIONAL CASH FLOW DISCLOSURES

The formal cash flow statement for APL is shown in Exhibit 5.1. As you can see, it is a simple matter to construct the statement after the detailed analysis of the accounts and transactions has been completed (shown in Exhibits 5.4, 5.5, 5.6, and 5.7). If the company uses the direct method for computing cash flow from operations, it must present the reconciliation of net income to cash flow from operations (the indirect method as presented in Exhibit 5.4) as a supplemental schedule. Companies also must provide two other disclosures related to the cash flow statement.

■ LEARNING OBJECTIVE 7

Explain the impact of additional cash flow disclosures.

NON-CASH INVESTING AND FINANCING ACTIVITIES

Certain transactions are important investing and financing activities but have no cash flow effects. These are called **non-cash investing and financing activities**. For example, the purchase of a $100,000 building with a $100,000 mortgage given by the former owner does not cause either an inflow or an outflow of cash. As a result, these non-cash activities are not listed in the three main sections of the cash flow statement. Section 1540 of the *CICA Handbook* requires supplemental disclosure of these transactions in either narrative or schedule form. APL's cash flow statement does not list any non-cash investing and financing activities. The following schedule from the 2006 annual report of Gildan Activewear Inc. provides examples of these non-cash transactions.

NON-CASH INVESTING AND FINANCING ACTIVITIES are transactions that do not have direct cash flow effects; they are reported as a supplement to the cash flow statement in narrative or schedule form.

REAL WORLD EXCERPT

Gildan Activewear

ANNUAL REPORT

b) Supplemental cash flow disclosure (in thousands of US dollars)

	2006	2005	2004
Non-cash transactions			
Additions to fixed assets included in accounts payable and accrued liabilities	2,979	740	3,473
Issuance of shares on acquisition of Kentucky Derby	460	—	—

Source: Gildan Activewear Inc., annual report 2006, page 64.

SUPPLEMENTAL CASH FLOW INFORMATION

Companies that use the indirect method of presenting cash flows from operations also must provide two other figures: cash paid for interest and for income taxes. These are normally listed at the bottom of the statement or in the notes.

DEMONSTRATION **CASE**

Redhook Ale Brewery

During the year ended December 31, 2007, Redhook Ale Brewery, a craft brewer, reported net income of $3,182 (all numbers in thousands), and cash and cash equivalents of $472 at the beginning and $24,676 at the end of the year. It also engaged in the following activities:

a. Paid $18,752 in principal on debt.
b. Received $46,202 in cash from initial public offering of common shares.
c. Incurred other non-current accrued operating expenses of $857.
d. Paid $18,193 in cash for purchase of fixed assets.
e. Accounts receivable increased by $881.
f. Borrowed $16,789 from various lenders.
g. Refundable deposits payable increased by $457.
h. Inventories increased by $574.
i. Made cash deposits on equipment of $5,830.
j. Income tax refund receivable decreased by $326.
k. Sold (issued) shares to employees for $13 in cash.
l. Accounts payable decreased by $391.
m. Received $4 from other investing activities.
n. Accrued expenses increased by $241.
o. Prepaid expenses increased by $565.
p. Recorded amortization of $1,324.
q. Paid $5 cash for other financing activities.

Required:

Based on this information, prepare the cash flow statement for the year ended December 31, 2007. Use the indirect method to compute the cash flow from operating activities.

We strongly recommend that you prepare your own answer to this requirement and then check it with the solution below.

SUGGESTED SOLUTION

REDHOOK ALE BREWERY
CASH FLOW STATEMENT
FOR THE YEAR ENDED DECEMBER 31, 2007 (IN THOUSANDS)

Operating activities	
Net income	$3,182
Add (deduct) items not affecting cash:	
Amortization	1,324
Other non-current accrued expenses	857
Increase in accounts receivable	(881)
Increase in inventories	(574)
Decrease in income taxes receivable	326
Increase in prepaid expenses	(565)
Decrease in accounts payable	(391)
Increase in accrued expenses	241
Increase in refundable deposits payable	457
Net cash flow from operating activities	3,976
Investing activities	
Expenditures for fixed assets	(18,193)
Deposits on equipment	(5,830)
Other	4
Net cash flow from investing activities	(24,019)

(continued)

Financing activities	
Proceeds from debt	16,789
Repayment of debt	(18,752)
Proceeds from sale of shares (IPO)	46,202
Proceeds from sale of shares (options)	13
Other	(5)
Net cash flow from financing activities	44,247
Increase in cash and cash equivalents	24,204
Cash and cash equivalents:	
Beginning of year	472
End of year	$24,676

SOLUTIONS TO **SELF-STUDY QUIZZES**

Self-Study Quiz 5-1

a. I, *b.* 0, *c.* 0, *d.* I, *e.* 0, *f.* 0, *g.* 0, *h.* 0, *i.* F, *j.* 0.

Self-Study Quiz 5-2

a. −, *b.* 0, *c.* +, *d.* +, *e.* +, *f.* −.

Self-Study Quiz 5-3

a. F−, *b.* I−, *c.* I−, *d.* F+.

Chapter Supplement A

Adjustment for Gains and Losses: Indirect Method

The operating activities section of the cash flow statement may include an adjustment for gains and losses reported on the income statement. The transactions that cause gains and losses should be classified on the cash flow statement as operating, investing, or financing activities, depending on their dominant characteristics. For example, if the sale of a productive asset (e.g., a delivery truck) produced a gain, it would be classified as an investing activity.

An adjustment must be made in the Operating Activities section to avoid double counting of the gain or loss. To illustrate, consider the following entry for Andrew Peller Limited to record the sale of a delivery truck:[10]

Cash (+A).	8,000	
Accumulated amortization (−XA, +A).	4,000	
Property, plant, and equipment (−A).		10,000
Gain on sale of assets (+Gain, +SE).		2,000

Assets		= Liabilities +	Shareholders' Equity	
Cash	+8,000		Gain on sale of assets	+2,000
Accumulated amortization	+4,000			
Property, plant, and equipment	−10,000			

The $8,000 inflow of cash is an investing cash inflow, but the gain of $2,000 is also reported on the income statement. Because the gain is included in the computation of net income, it is necessary to remove (subtract) the $2,000 gain from the Operating Activities section of the statement to avoid double counting.

---

[10] The disposal of assets and the resulting gains or losses are discussed in detail in Chapter 9.

When a loss is reported on the income statement, it also must be removed from cash flows from operating activities. Consider the following entry to record the sale of assets:

Cash (+A).	41,000	
Accumulated amortization (−XA, +A).	15,000	
Loss on sale of assets (−Loss, −SE).	12,000	
Property, plant, and equipment (−A).		68,000

Assets		=	Liabilities	+	Shareholders' Equity	
Cash	+41,000				Loss on sale of assets	−12,000
Accumulated amortization	+15,000					
Property, plant, and equipment	−68,000					

On the cash flow statement, the loss of $12,000 must be removed (added to net income) in the computation of cash flow from operating activities, and the total cash collected of $41,000 must be shown in the investing activities section of the statement.

Chapter Supplement B

Reporting Cash Flows From Operating Activities—Direct Method

Exhibit 5.3 shows APL's comparative balance sheets at the end of the first and second quarters of 2007, and its income statement for the second quarter of 2007. Recall that the direct method reports gross cash receipts and gross cash payments related to operating activities. It presents a summary of all operating transactions that resulted in either a debit or a credit to cash.

Cash Flows from Operating Activities

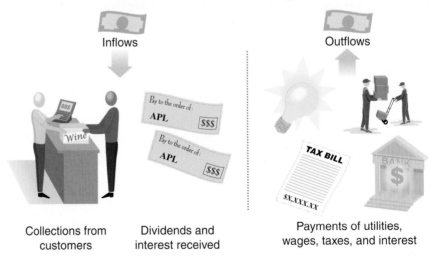

Inflows — Outflows

Collections from customers   Dividends and interest received   Payments of utilities, wages, taxes, and interest

Converting Revenue and Expense Items from an Accrual Basis to a Cash Basis

The computation of cash receipts and payments requires adjusting each item on the income statement from an accrual basis. To facilitate this process, we analyze the change in the balances of each current asset and current liability account by examining the type of transactions that affect the account. This process helps us determine the amount of cash received or paid during the accounting period.

We will use the following relation to analyze the changes in each current asset and liability account:

Beginning Balance	+	Increases	−	Decreases	=	Ending Balance

Converting Revenues to Cash Inflows When sales are recorded, accounts receivable increase, and when cash is collected, accounts receivable decrease. Hence, the change from the beginning balance of Accounts Receivable (AR_B) to the ending balance (AR_E) can be represented as follows:

In general	APL's example
Accounts receivable, beginning (known)	$21,682
+ Sales revenue (known)	+ 59,413
− Cash collections from customers (computed)	− A
= Accounts receivable, ending (known)	=$27,687

The beginning and ending balances of accounts receivable are reported on the balance sheet, and sales revenue is reported on the income statement. However, the amount collected from customers is not reported on either statement, but can be derived from the relation above.

Using information from APL's income statement and balance sheet presented in Exhibit 5.3, we can compute the cash collected from customers as follows:

Cash collections = $21,682 + $59,413 − $27,687 = $53,408[11]

Accounts Receivable

Beg.	21,682		
Sales	59,413	Collections	53,408
End.	27,687		

The beginning balance of accounts receivable increases the cash received from customers on the assumption that all amounts owed to the company at the beginning of the period are collected during the period. In contrast, the ending balance of accounts receivable is deducted from sales revenue because these receivables have already been included in sales revenue, but have not yet been collected from customers.

Converting Cost of Goods Sold to Cash Paid to Suppliers The cost of goods sold during the accounting period may be greater or smaller than the amount of cash paid to suppliers of merchandise during the period. The computation of the cash paid to suppliers is a two-stage process. First, we analyze the change in the Inventory account to determine the amount of merchandise purchases during the period, and then we analyze the change in the Accounts Payable account to compute the amount of cash payments to suppliers using the following relations:

In general	APL's example
Inventories, beginning (known)	$70,131
+ Merchandise purchases (computed)	+ A
− Cost of goods sold (known)	− 34,369
= Inventories, ending (known)	=$71,870

In general	APL's example
Accounts payable, beginning (known)	$12,210
+ Merchandise purchases (computed)	+ A
− Cash payments to suppliers (computed)	− B
= Accounts payable, ending (known)	=$18,423

---

[11]We assume that all scales are made on account. However, the amount of cash collected from customers is the same regardless of the mix of cash and credit sales. To be sure, assume that sales are 20-percent cash and 80-percent on account, and compute the amount of cash collected from customers during the period. You can use other percentages as well.

The beginning and ending balances of inventory and accounts payable are reported on the balance sheet, and the cost of goods sold is reported on the income statement. However, the amount of merchandise purchases and the payments to suppliers are not reported on either statement, but can be derived from the relations above.

Using information from APL's income statement and balance sheet presented in Exhibit 5.3, we can compute the cash paid to suppliers as follows:

Inventory

Beg. 70,131	
	Cost of
Purchases **36,108**	goods sold 34,369
End. 71,870	

Accounts Payable

	Beg. 12,210
Cash	
payments **29,895**	Purchases **36,108**
	End. 18,423

$$\text{Merchandise purchases} = \$34{,}369 + \$71{,}870 - \$70{,}131 = \$36{,}108$$

The ending balance of inventory is added to cost of goods sold to determine the cost of goods that were available for sale during the period. Given that part of the merchandise was available at the beginning of the period, it is deducted from the goods available to determine the amount of purchases during the period.

$$\text{Cash payments to suppliers} = \$36{,}108 + \$12{,}210 - \$18{,}423 = \$29{,}895^{12}$$

The beginning balance of accounts payable is added to merchandise purchases to determine the total amount payable to suppliers. The ending balance of accounts payable is then deducted from that total because this amount has not been paid to suppliers yet.

Converting Other Operating Expenses to a Cash Outflow The total amount of any operating expense on the income statement may differ from the cash payment for that expense during the accounting period. Some expenses are paid before they are recognized as expenses (e.g., prepaid rent). When prepayments are made, the balance in the asset Prepaid Expenses increases; when prepaid expenses are used up and recognized as expenses for the period, the account balance decreases. Other expenses are paid for after they are recognized in the same or previous periods. In this case, when expenses are recorded, the balance in the account Accrued Liabilities increases; when payments are made, the account balance decreases. The computation of the cash paid for operating expenses is therefore a two-stage process. First, we analyze the change in the Prepaid Expenses account to determine the amount of cash paid during the period, and then we analyze the change in the Accrued Liabilities account to compute the amount of cash that was paid during the period for various other expenses, as shown in the following relations:

In general	APL's example
Prepaid expenses, beginning (known)	$3,318
+ Cash payments for future (deferred) expenses (unknown)	+ A
− Prepaid expenses that were used up during the period (unknown)	− B
= Prepaid expenses, ending (known)	=$4,490

In general	APL's example
Accrued liabilities, beginning (known)	$6,569
+ Expenses accrued during the period (unknown)	+ C
− Cash payments for accrued expenses (unknown)	− D
= Accrued liabilities, ending (known)	=$7,134

The beginning and ending balances of prepaid expenses and accrued liabilities are reported on the balance sheet. But, the prepaid expenses (B) that were used up during the period are not reported separately on the income statement. Hence, we cannot compute the amount of cash (A) paid for future expenses. Similarly, the expenses (C)

---

[12]We assume that all purchases are made on account. However, the amount of cash paid to suppliers is the same regardless of the mix of cash and credit purchases. To be sure, assume that purchases are 10-percent cash and 90-percent on account, and compute the amount of cash paid to suppliers during the period. You can use other percentages as well.

that accrued during the period are not reported separately on the income statement, which makes it difficult to compute the amount of cash (D) paid during the period to settle accrued expenses. However, the amounts B and C are reported together on the income statement as operating expenses (or selling, general, and administrative expenses). By combining the two relations, we can then compute the sum of A and D, which represents the payments made for other expenses.

Using information from APL's income statement and balance sheet presented in Exhibit 5.3, we can compute the cash paid for other expenses as follows:

Cash paid for other expenses = $17,880 (general, selling, and administrative expenses, reflecting prepayments that expired during the quarter and accrued expenses)

+ **4,490** (prepaid expenses, end of quarter)

– **3,318** (prepaid expenses, beginning of quarter)

+ **6,569** (accrued liabilities, beginning of quarter)

– **7,134** (accrued liabilities, end of quarter)

= **$18,487**

Similar analysis can be applied to computing the cash payments for interest and income taxes. APL reports interest expense of $1,383. Since there is no balance in Interest Payable, interest paid must be equal to interest expense.

APL's income tax expense equals $1,317. This expense usually consists of two components: an amount that is currently payable to the federal and provincial taxation authorities, and another amount labelled Future Income Taxes. Future income taxes result from temporary differences that exist between the accounting principles that underlie financial reporting and tax rules that govern the preparation of tax returns. These differences relate to the timing of recognition of revenues and expenses for financial reporting (that is based on accrual accounting) compared to taxation rules that essentially use a cash basis of accounting.

The computation of cash paid for income taxes should take into consideration changes in two accounts: Income Taxes Payable and Future Income Taxes. Since there is no balance in Income Taxes Payable, income taxes paid is computed as follows:

Prepaid Expenses

Beg.	3,318	Prepayments that expired unknown
Cash payments unknown		
End.	4,490	

Accrued Liabilities

Cash payments unknown	Beg.	6,569
	Unpaid expenses unknown	
	End.	7,134

Income tax expense	$1,317
+ Income taxes payable, begining	470
– Income taxes payable, ending	0
	1,787
– Increase in future income tax liability	69
Cash payments for income taxes	$1,718

The operating cash inflows and outflows are accumulated in Exhibit 5.7.

EXHIBIT **5.7**

**Andrew Peller Limited:
Schedule of Net Cash Flow
From Operating Activities,
Direct Method (in thousands)**

Cash flows from operating activities		
Cash collected from customers		$53,408
Cash payments		
–to suppliers	$29,895	
–for other operating expenses	18,487	
–for interest	1,383	
–for income taxes	1,718	51,483
Net cash provided by operating activities		$ 1,925

To summarize, the following adjustments must commonly be made to convert income statement items to the related operating cash flow amounts:

Income Statement Account	+/− Change in Balance Sheet Account(s)	= Operating Cash Flow
Sales revenue	+ Beginning accounts receivable − Ending accounts receivable	= Collections from customers
Cost of goods sold	− Beginning inventory + Ending inventory + Beginning accounts payable − Ending accounts payable	= Payments to suppliers of inventory
Other operating expenses	− Beginning prepaid expenses + Ending prepaid expenses + Beginning accrued liabilities − Ending accrued liabilities	= Payments to suppliers of services (e.g., rent, utilities, wages)
Interest expense	+ Beginning interest payable − Ending interest payable	= Payments for interest
Income tax expense	+ Beginning income taxes payable − Ending income taxes payable +/− Changes in future incomes tax assets and liabilities	= Payments for income taxes

INTERNATIONAL PERSPECTIVE — AUSTRALIAN PRACTICES

REAL WORLD EXCERPT

Foster's Brewing

ANNUAL REPORT

Foster's Brewing is the first name in Australian beer and a major player in world beverage markets. Following Australian GAAP, which require use of the direct method of presentation, Foster's cash flow from operations is presented as follows:

STATEMENT OF CASH FLOWS FOR THE YEAR ENDED 30 JUNE 2006
(dollars in million)

Cash Flows from Operating Activities

Receipts from customers	6,841.4
Payments to suppliers, governments, and employees	(5,564.1)
Interest received	41.6
Borrowing costs	(273.8)
Income taxes paid	(210.0)
Net cash flows from operating activities	835.1

Note that Foster's combines payments to suppliers, governments, and employees, but other companies report these items separately. Like Canadian companies that choose the direct method, Foster's reports the indirect presentation in a note to the financial statements.

SELF-STUDY **QUIZ 5-4**

Indicate which of the following items taken from the cash flow statement would be added (+), subtracted (−), or not included (0) in the cash flow from operations section when the direct method is used.

_____ *a.* Increase in inventories.

_____ *b.* Payment of dividends to shareholders.

_____ *c.* Cash collections from customers.

_____ *d.* Purchase of plant and equipment for cash.

_____ *e.* Payment of interest to debtholders.

_____ *f.* Payment of taxes to the taxation authorities.

Answers: *a.* 0, *b.* 0, *c.* +, *d.* 0, *e.* −, *f.* −.

Chapter Supplement C

Spreadsheet Approach—Cash Flow Statement: Indirect Method

As situations become more complex, the analytical approach that we used to prepare the cash flow statement for Andrew Peller Limited becomes cumbersome and inefficient. In actual practice, most companies use a spreadsheet approach to prepare the cash flow statement. The spreadsheet is based on the same logic that we used in our previous illustration. Its primary advantage is that it offers a more systematic way to keep track of data. You may find it useful even in simple situations.

Exhibit 5.8 shows the spreadsheet to prepare APL's cash flow statement. It is organized as follows:

1. Four columns to record dollar amounts are established. The first column is for the beginning balances for items reported on the balance sheet; the next two columns reflect debit and credit changes to those balances; the final column contains the ending balances for the balance sheet accounts.

2. On the left of the top half of the spreadsheet, each account name from the balance sheet is entered.

3. On the left of the bottom half of the spreadsheet, the name of each item that will be reported on the cash flow statement is entered.

Changes in the various balance sheet accounts are analyzed in terms of debits and credits in the top half of the spreadsheet, with the offsetting debits and credits being recorded in the bottom half of the spreadsheet in terms of their impact on cash flows. Each change in the non-cash balance sheet accounts explains part of the change in the Cash account. To illustrate, let us examine each of the entries on the spreadsheet for APL shown in Exhibit 5.8. You will note that they follow each of the items presented in the schedule to prepare the cash flow statement shown in Exhibits 5.4, 5.5, and 5.6.

a. This entry is used to start the reconciliation; net income is shown as an inflow in the Operating Activities section to be reconciled by the non-cash entries. The credit to Retained Earnings reflects the effects of the original closing entry. This is the starting point for the reconciliation.

b. Amortization expense is a non-cash expense. It is added back to net income because this type of expense does not cause a cash outflow when it is recorded. The credit to Accumulated Amortization reflects the effects of the original entry to record amortization.

c. This entry reconciles the accrual of future income tax liabilities with payments for these liabilities. It is added because cash payments for these liabilities were less than new accruals.

d. This entry reconciles the change in accounts receivable during the period with net income. It is added to net income because cash collections from customers exceeded sales revenue.

e. This entry reconciles the purchases of inventory with cost of goods sold. It is subtracted from net income because more inventory was purchased than was sold.

f. This entry reconciles the prepayment of expenses with their expiration. It is subtracted from net income because new cash prepayments exceeded the amounts that expired and were recorded as expenses during the period.

g. This entry reconciles cash paid to suppliers with purchases on account. It is added to net income because less cash was paid than was borrowed during the period.

h. This entry reconciles the accrual of expenses with related payments. It is added to net income because cash payments for these expenses were less than the accrued liabilities.

i. This entry reconciles income taxes expense with related payments. It is subtracted from net income because cash payments exceeded the expense.

EXHIBIT **5.8**

**Spreadsheet to Prepare Cash
Flow Statement, Indirect Method**

ANDREW PELLER LIMITED
Quarter Ended September 30, 2006
(in thousands of dollars)

Items from Balance Sheet	Beginning Balances June 30, 2006	Analysis of Change Debit	Analysis of Change Credit	Ending Balances September 30, 2006
Accounts receivable	21,682	(d) 6,005		27,687
Inventories	70,131	(e) 1,739		71,870
Prepaid expenses	3,318	(f) 1,172		4,490
Property, plant and equipment (net)	85,001	(j) 1,770	(b) 1,908	84,863
Long term investments	8,219		(k) 88	8,131
Goodwill	36,171			36,171
Bank indebtedness	41,982		(l) 2,098	44,080
Accounts payable	12,210		(g) 6,213	18,423
Accrued liabilities	6,569		(h) 565	7,134
Dividends payable	778	(o) 778	(n) 917	917
Income taxes payable	470	(i) 470		—
Current portion of long-term debt	5,892		(m) 5	5,897
Long term debt	52,998	(m) 1,568		51,430
Future income taxes	12,445		(c) 69	12,514
Share capital	7,375			7,375
Retained earnings	83,803	(n) 917	(a) 2,556	85,442

	Inflows	Outflows	Subtotals
Cash Flow Statement			
Cash flows from operating activities			
Net income	(a) 2,556		
Adjustments to reconcile net income to net cash provided by operating activities:			
Amortization of plant and equipment	(b) 1,908		
Future income taxes	(c) 69		
Changes in noncash working capital items			
Accounts receivable		(d) 6,005	
Inventories		(e) 1,739	
Prepaid expenses		(f) 1,172	
Accounts payable	(g) 6,213		
Accrued liabilities	(h) 565		
Income taxes payable		(i) 470	
			1,925
Cash flows from investing activities			
Purchase of property and equipment		(j) 1,770	
Proceeds from long term investments	(k) 88		
			(1,682)
Cash flows from financing activities			
Increase in bank indebtedness	(l) 2,098		
Repayment of long-term debt		(m) 1,563	
Payment of dividends		(o) 778	
			(243)
Net increase (decrease) in cash and cash equivalents	———	———	——
	13,497	13,497	

j. This entry records the purchases of new plant and equipment for cash.

k. This entry records the decrease in long-term investments.

l. This entry records the increase in bank indebtedness.

m. This entry shows the repayment of principal on long-term debt, including the current portion.

n and *o.* These entries show the declaration and payment of cash dividends.

The preceding entries complete the spreadsheet analysis because all accounts are reconciled. The accuracy of the analysis can be checked by adding the two analysis columns to verify that Debits = Credits. You should also note that the debits and credits to the balance sheet accounts directly match those recorded in the T-accounts presented in the body of the chapter. The formal cash flow statement can be prepared directly from the spreadsheet.

The analytical technique that you have learned for preparing the cash flow statement will help you deal with other significant business problems. For example, this type of analysis is useful for developing cash budgets for a business. Many small businesses that experience rapid sales growth get into serious financial difficulties because they did not forecast the cash flow effects associated with credit sales and large increases in inventory.

CHAPTER **TAKE-AWAYS**

1. **Classify cash flow statement items as part of net cash flows from operating, investing, and financing activities. p. 233**

   The statement has three main sections: Cash Flows from Operating Activities, which are related to earning income from normal operations; Cash Flows from Investing Activities, which are related to the acquisition and sale of productive assets; and Cash Flows from Financing Activities, which are related to external financing of the enterprise. The net cash inflow or outflow for the year is the same amount as the increase or decrease in cash and cash equivalents for the year. Cash equivalents are highly liquid investments with original maturities of less than three months.

2. **Report and interpret cash flows from operating activities using the indirect method. p. 239**

   The indirect method for reporting cash flows from operating activities reports a conversion of net income to net cash flow from operating activities. The conversion involves additions and subtractions for (1) non-current accruals including expenses (such as amortization expense) and revenues that do not affect current assets or current liabilities, and (2) changes in each of the individual current assets (other than cash and short-term investments) and current liabilities (other than short-term debt to financial institutions and current portion of long-term debt, which relate to financing), that reflect differences in the timing of accrual basis net income and cash flows.

3. **Analyze and interpret the quality of income ratio. p. 245**

   The quality of income ratio (Cash Flow from Operating Activities ÷ Net Income) measures the portion of income that was generated in cash. A higher quality of income ratio indicates greater ability to finance operating and other cash needs from operating cash inflows. A higher ratio also indicates that it is less likely that the company is using aggressive revenue recognition policies to increase net income.

4. **Report and interpret cash flows from investing activities. p. 247**

   Investing activities reported on the cash flow statement include cash payments to acquire property, plant, and equipment, and short- and long-term investments. They also include cash proceeds from the sale of these assets.

5. **Analyze and interpret the capital acquisitions ratio. p. 249**

   The capital acquisitions ratio (Cash Flow from Operating Activities ÷ Cash Paid for Property, Plant, and Equipment) reflects the portion of purchases of property, plant, and equipment financed from operating activities without the need for outside debt or equity financing or the sale of other investments or other long-term assets. A high ratio is beneficial because it provides the company with opportunities for strategic acquisitions.

6. **Report and interpret cash flows from financing activities. p. 250**

   Cash inflows from financing activities include cash proceeds from issuance of short- and long-term debt and share capital. Cash outflows include principal payments on short- and long-term debt, cash paid for the repurchase of the company's shares, and dividend payments. Cash payments associated with interest relate to operating activities.

7. **Explain the impact of additional cash flow disclosures. p. 253**

   Non-cash investing and financing activities are investing and financing activities that do not involve cash. They include, for example, purchases of long-term assets with long-term debt or shares, exchanges of long-term assets, and exchanges of debt for shares. These transactions are disclosed only as supplemental disclosures to the cash flow statement along with cash paid for taxes and interest under the indirect method.

   The previous four chapters discussed the important steps in the accounting process that lead to the preparation of the four basic financial statements. This end to the internal portions of the accounting process, however, is just the beginning of the process of communicating accounting information to external users.

   In the next chapter, we discuss the important players in this communication process, the many statement format choices available, the additional note disclosures required for both private and public companies, and the process, manner, and timing of the transmission of this information to users. At the same time, we discuss common uses of the information in investment analysis, debt contracts, and management compensation decisions. These discussions will help you consolidate much of what you have learned about the financial reporting process from previous chapters. It will also preview many of the important issues we will address later in the book.

KEY **RATIOS**

The **quality of income ratio** indicates what portion of income was generated in cash. It is computed as follows (p. 245):

$$\text{Quality of Income Ratio} = \frac{\text{Cash Flow from Operating Activities}}{\text{Net Income}}$$

The **capital acquisitions ratio** measures the ability to finance purchases of property, plant, and equipment from operations. It is computed as follows (p. 249):

$$\text{Capital Acquisitions Ratio} = \frac{\text{Cash Flow from Operating Activities}}{\text{Cash Paid for Property, Plant, and Equipment}}$$

FINDING **FINANCIAL INFORMATION**

BALANCE SHEET
Changes in Assets, Liabilities, and Shareholders' Equity

INCOME STATEMENT
Net Income and Accruals

CASH FLOW STATEMENT
Cash Flows from Operating Activities
Cash Flows from Investing Activities
Cash Flows from Financing Activities
Separate Schedule (or note):
   Non-cash investing and financing activities
   Interest and taxes paid

NOTES
Under Summary of Significant Accounting Policies
   Definition of cash equivalents
Under Separate Note
   If not listed on cash flow statement:
      Non-cash investing and financing activities
      Interest and taxes paid

KEY **TERMS**

Cash Equivalent p. 232

Cash Flows from Financing Activities p. 235

Cash Flows from Investing Activities p. 235

Cash Flows from Operating Activities p. 234

Direct Method p. 234

Free Cash Flow p. 250

Indirect Method p. 234

Non-Cash Investing and Financing Activities p. 253

QUESTIONS

1. Compare the purposes of the income statement, the balance sheet, and the cash flow statement.
2. What information does the cash flow statement report that is not reported on the other required financial statements? How do investors and creditors use that information?
3. What are cash equivalents? How are purchases and sales of cash equivalents reported on the cash flow statement?
4. What are the major categories of business activities reported on the cash flow statement? Define each of these activities.
5. What are the typical cash inflows from operating activities? What are the typical cash outflows for operating activities?
6. Under the indirect method, amortization expense is added to net income to compute cash flows from operating activities. Does amortization cause an inflow of cash?
7. Explain why cash paid during the period for purchases and for salaries is not specifically reported as cash outflows on the cash flow statement under the indirect method.
8. Explain why a $50,000 increase in inventory during the year must be included in developing cash flows for operating activities under the indirect method.
9. Compare the two methods of reporting cash flows from operating activities in the cash flow statement.
10. What are the typical cash inflows from investing activities? What are the typical cash outflows for investing activities?
11. What are the typical cash inflows from financing activities? What are the typical cash outflows for financing activities?
12. What are non-cash investing and financing activities? Give two examples. How are they reported on the cash flow statement?
13. A company used cash for both operating and investing activities, but had positive cash flow from financing activities. What does this cash flow pattern suggest about this company?

EXERCISES

E5–1 Determining Cash Flow Statement Effects of Transactions

Leon's Furniture Limited is an Ontario-based retailer of home furnishings. For each of the following first-quarter transactions, indicate whether *net cash inflows (outflows)* from operating activities (O), investing activities (I), or financing activities (F) are affected and whether the effect is an inflow (+) or outflow (−), or (NE) if the transaction has no effect on cash. (*Hint:* Determine the journal entry recorded for the transaction. The transaction affects net cash flows if, and only if, the account Cash is affected.)

____ 1 Paid cash to purchase new equipment.

____ 2. Purchased raw materials inventory on account.

____ 3. Collected cash from customers.

____ 4. Recorded an adjusting entry to record an accrued salaries expense.

■ **LO1**

Leon's Furniture

_____ 5. Recorded and paid interest on debt to creditors.

_____ 6. Repaid principal on revolving credit loan from the bank.

_____ 7. Paid rent for the following period.

_____ 8. Sold used equipment for cash at book value.

_____ 9. Made payment to suppliers.

_____ 10. Declared and paid cash dividends to shareholders.

LO1

Dell Inc.

E5–2 Determining Cash Flow Statement Effects of Transactions

Dell Inc. is a leading manufacturer of personal computers and servers for the business and home markets. For each of the following transactions, indicate whether *net cash inflows (outflows)* from operating activities (O), investing activities (I), or financing activities (F) are affected and whether the effect is an inflow ($+$) or outflow ($-$), or (NE) if the transaction has no effect on cash. (*Hint:* Determine the journal entry recorded for the transaction. The transaction affects net cash flows if, and only if, the account Cash is affected.)

_____ 1. Recorded and paid income taxes to the federal government.

_____ 2. Issued common shares for cash.

_____ 3. Paid rent for the following period.

_____ 4. Recorded an adjusting entry for expiration of a prepaid expense.

_____ 5. Paid cash to purchase new equipment.

_____ 6. Issued long-term debt for cash.

_____ 7. Collected cash from customers.

_____ 8. Purchased raw materials inventory on account.

_____ 9. Recorded and paid salaries to employees.

_____ 10. Purchased new equipment by signing a three-year note.

LO2

ANALYSIS

E5–3 Interpreting Amortization Expense from a Management Perspective

QuickServe, a chain of convenience stores, was experiencing some serious cash flow difficulties because of rapid growth. The company did not generate sufficient cash from operating activities to finance its new stores, and creditors were not willing to lend money because the company had not produced any income for the previous three years. The new controller for QuickServe proposed a reduction in the estimated life of store equipment to increase amortization expense; thus, "we can improve cash flows from operating activities because amortization expense is added back on the cash flow statement." Other executives were not sure that this was a good idea because the increase in amortization would make it more difficult to have positive earnings: "Without income, the bank will never lend us money."

Required:

What action would you recommend for QuickServe? Why?

LO2

E5–4 Reporting and Interpreting Cash Flows from Operating Activities from an Analyst's Perspective (Direct and Indirect Method)

Kane Company completed its income statement and balance sheet for 2009 and provided the following information:

Service revenue		$52,000
Expenses		
Salaries	$42,000	
Amortization	7,300	
Utilities	7,000	
Other	1,700	58,000
Net loss		($ 6,000)
Decrease in accounts receivable	$12,000	
Purchase of a small service machine	5,000	
Increase in salaries payable	9,000	
Decrease in unearned service revenue	4,000	

Required:

1. Prepare the Operating Activities section of the cash flow statement for Kane Company using the indirect method.

2. What were the major reasons that caused Kane to report a net loss but positive cash flow from operations? Why are the reasons for the difference between cash flow from operations and net income important to financial analysts?

E5–5 Reporting and Interpreting Cash Flows from Operating Activities from an Analyst's Perspective (Indirect Method)

■ LO2

Coolbrands
International, Inc.

Coolbrands International, Inc., manufactures and distributes ice cream, sorbet, frozen yogurt, and other frozen dairy-based snacks. The company's annual report for 2005 contained the following information (in thousands):

	2005
Net loss	$(74,070)
Depreciation and amortization	60,567
Decrease in receivables	13,815
Decrease in inventories	4,500
Increase in prepaid expenses	2,207
Increase in accounts payable	5,842
Increase in accrued liabilities	8,744
Increase in income taxes payable	4,935
Reduction of long-term debt	4,007
Additions to equipment	12,409

Required:

1. Based on this information, compute the cash flow from operating activities using the indirect method.
2. What were the major reasons that caused Coolbrands to report a net loss but positive cash flow from operations? Why are the reasons for the difference between cash flow from operations and net income important to financial analysts?

E5–6 Inferring Balance Sheet Changes from the Cash Flow Statement

■ LO2

Colgate-Palmolive

ANALYSIS

A cash flow statement for Colgate-Palmolive reported the following information (in millions):

Operating Activities	Current Year
Net income	$477.0
Amortization	192.5
Cash effect of changes in	
Receivables	(38.0)
Inventories	28.4
Other current assets	10.6
Payables	(10.0)
Other	(117.8)
Net cash provided by operations	$542.7

Required:
Based on the information reported on the cash flow statement for Colgate-Palmolive, determine whether the following accounts increased or decreased during the year: Receivables, Inventories, Other Current Assets, and Payables.

E5–7 Inferring Balance Sheet Changes from the Cash Flow Statement

■ LO2

Apple Computer, Inc.

ANALYSIS

A cash flow statement for Apple Computer contained the following information (in thousands):

Operations	Current Year
Net income	$310,178
Amortization	167,958
Changes in assets and liabilities	
Accounts receivable	(199,401)
Inventories	418,204
Other current assets	33,616
Accounts payable	139,095
Income taxes payable	50,045
Other current liabilities	39,991
Other adjustments	(222,691)
Cash generated by operations	$736,995

Required:
For each of the asset and liability accounts listed on the cash flow statement, determine whether the account balances increased or decreased during the current year.

LO3

PepsiCo

E5–8 Analyzing Cash Flows from Operating Activities; Interpreting the Quality of Income Ratio

An annual report for PepsiCo contained the following information (in millions):

Net income	$4,078
Depreciation and amortization	1,308
Increase in accounts receivable	272
Increase in inventory	132
Decrease in prepaid expenses	56
Increase in accounts payable	220
Increase in taxes payable	609
Decrease in other current liabilities	38
Cash dividends paid	1,642
Repurchase of shares	3,012

Required:

1. Compute the cash flows from operating activities for PepsiCo using the indirect method.
2. Compute the quality of income ratio.
3. What were the major reasons why Pepsi's quality of income ratio did not equal 1.0?

LO4, 6

Pan American
Silver Corp.

E5–9 Reporting Cash Flows from Investing and Financing Activities

Pan American Silver Corp. is a mining company based in British Columbia. In a recent quarter, it reported the following activities:

Net income	$16,355
Purchase of property, plant, and equipment	18,026
Shares issued for cash	698
Repayment of bank loans	2,202
Cash collection from customers	57,608
Depreciation and amortization	4,234
Income taxes paid	1,505
Payments for products and services	39,771
Proceeds from sale of short-term investments	13,714

Required:

Based on this information, present the Investing and Financing Activities sections of the cash flow statement.

LO4, 6

Sobeys

E5–10 Reporting and Interpreting Cash Flows from Investing and Financing Activities with Discussion of Management Strategy

Sobeys Inc. is one of Canada's two national retail grocery and food distributors. The company owns or franchises more than 1,300 corporate and franchised stores in all 10 provinces under retail banners that include Sobeys, Garden Market IGA, IGA, IGA Extra, and Price Chopper. In a recent year, it reported the following activities (in millions):

Net income	$115.9
Purchases of property and equipment	424.2
Decrease in accounts payable and accrued liabilities	77.8
Issue of shares	8.6
Depreciation and amortization	136.1
Proceeds from sale of discontinued operations	412.7
Repayment of long-term debt	147.5
Increase in accounts receivable	2.8
Payment of dividends	15.8

Required:

1. Based on this information, prepare the Investing and Financing Activities sections of the cash flow statement.
2. What do you think was management's plan for the use of the cash generated by the sale of discontinued operations?

E5–11 Analyzing and Interpreting the Capital Acquisitions Ratio

A recent annual report for Boston Beer Company contained the following data for the three most recent years (in millions):

	2006	2005	2004
Cash flow from operating activities	$ 28.8	$19.3	$19.6
Cash flow from investing activities	(13.8)	(13.8)	15.0
Cash flow from financing activities	(9.3)	2.6	(27.4)

Assume that all investing activities involved acquisition of new plant and equipment.

Required:

1. Compute the capital acquisitions ratio for the three-year period in total.

2. What portion of Boston Beer's investing activities was financed from external sources or pre-existing cash balances during the three-year period?

3. What do you think is the likely explanation for the large amount of cash flow from financing activities during 2006?

E5–12 Reporting Non-Cash Transactions on the Cash Flow Statement; Interpreting the Effect on the Capital Acquisitions Ratio

An analysis of Martin Corporation's operational asset accounts provided the following information:

a. Acquired a large machine that cost $26,000, paying for it by signing a $15,000, 12-percent interest-bearing note due at the end of two years, and 500 common shares with a market value of $22 per share.

b. Acquired a small machine that cost $8,700. Full payment was made by transferring a tract of land that had a book value of $8,700.

Required:

1. Show how this information should be reported on the cash flow statement.

2. What would be the effect of these transactions on the capital acquisitions ratio? How might these transactions distort interpretation of the ratio?

E5–13 (Supplement B) Matching Items Reported to Cash Flow Statement Categories (Direct Method)

The Australian company BHP Billiton is one of the world's biggest mining companies. Some of the items included in its annual consolidated cash flow statement presented using the *direct method* are listed below.

Indicate whether each item is disclosed in the Operating Activities (O), Investing Activities (I), or Financing Activities (F) section of the statement or (NA) if the item does not appear on the statement.

_____ 1. Dividends paid

_____ 2. Income taxes paid

_____ 3. Interest received

_____ 4. Net income

_____ 5. Payments for property, plant, and equipment

_____ 6. Payments in the course of operations

_____ 7. Proceeds from ordinary share issues

_____ 8. Proceeds from the sale of property, plant, and equipment

_____ 9. Receipts from customers

_____ 10. Repayment of loans

E5–14 **(Supplement B) Comparing the Direct and Indirect Methods**

To compare the computation of cash flow from operations under the direct and indirect methods, enter check marks to indicate which items are used with each method.

	Method of Computing Cash Flows from Operations	
Cash Flows (and Related Changes)	Direct	Indirect
1. Collections from customers		
2. Increase or decrease in accounts receivable		
3. Payments to suppliers		
4. Increase or decrease in inventory		
5. Increase or decrease in accounts payable		
6. Payments to employees		
7. Increase or decrease in wages payable		
8. Amortization expense		

E5–15 **(Supplement B) Reporting Cash Flows from Operating Activities (Direct Method)**

The following information pertains to Day Company:

Sales		$80,000
Expenses		
Cost of goods sold	$50,000	
Amortization	7,000	
Salaries	11,000	68,000
Net income		$12,000
Increase in accounts receivable	$ 4,000	
Decrease in merchandise inventory	8,000	
Increase in salaries payable	500	

Required:

Prepare the Operating Activities section of the cash flow statement for Day Company using the direct method.

E5–16 **(Supplement C) Preparing a Cash Flow Statement, Indirect Method: Complete Spreadsheet**

An analysis of accounts showed the following:

a. Purchased an operational asset, $20,000, and issued common shares in full payment.

b. Purchased a long-term investment for cash, $15,000.

c. Paid cash dividend, $12,000.

d. Sold operational asset for $2,000 cash (cost, $21,000, accumulated amortization, $19,000).

e. Sold 500 shares at $12 per share cash.

		Analysis of Change		
List of Accounts	Beginning Balances 12/31/2006	Debit	Credit	Ending Balances 12/31/2007
Income statement items				
Sales			$140,000	
Cost of goods sold		$59,000		
Amortization expense		7,000		
Wage expense		28,000		
Income tax expense		9,000		
Interest expense		5,000		
Other expenses		15,800		
Net income		16,200		

Balance sheet items		
Cash	$ 16,500	$ 11,200
Accounts receivable	22,000	22,000
Merchandise inventory	68,000	75,000
Long-term Investments		15,000
Operational assets	114,500	113,500
Total debits	$221,000	$236,700
Accumulated amortization	$ 32,000	$ 20,000
Accounts payable	17,000	14,000
Wages payable	2,500	1,500
Income taxes payable	3,000	4,500
Bonds payable	54,000	54,000
Share capital	100,000	126,000
Retained earnings	12,500	16,700
Total credits	$221,000	$236,700

	Inflows	Outflows
Cash flow statement		
Cash flows from operating activities:		
Cash flows from investing activities:		
Cash flows from financing activities:		
Net increase (decrease) in cash		
Totals		

Required:

1. Complete the spreadsheet for the cash flow statement using the indirect method to compute the cash flows from operating activities.

2. Compute and explain the quality of income ratio and the capital acquisitions ratio.

3. What can you conclude about the company's management of cash?

E5–17 **(Supplement C) Preparing a Cash Flow Statement, Direct Method: Complete Spreadsheet**
Refer to the information in E5–16.

Required:

1. Complete the spreadsheet for the cash flow statement using the direct method to compute the cash flows from operating activities.

2. As the accountant who prepares the company's cash flow statement, would you prefer to use the direct method or the indirect method to report the cash flows from operations? Explain.

PROBLEMS

P5–1 **Preparing the Cash Flow Statement (AP5–1)**
Selected financial information for Frank Corporation is presented below.

LO1, 2, 4, 6, 7

Selected 2007 Transactions:

a. Purchased investment securities for $5,000 cash.

b. Borrowed $15,000 on a two-year, 8-percent interest-bearing note.

c. During 2007, sold machinery for its net book value; received $11,000 in cash.

d. Purchased machinery for $50,000; paid $9,000 in cash and signed a four-year note payable to the dealer for $41,000.

e. At December 31, 2007, declared and paid a cash dividend of $10,000.

Selected account balances at December 31, 2006 and 2007 are as follows:

	December 31	
	2007	2006
Cash	$76,000	$21,000
Accounts receivable	17,000	12,000
Inventory	52,000	60,000
Accounts payable	7,000	10,000
Accrued wages payable	800	1,000
Income taxes payable	5,000	3,000

One-fourth of the sales and one-third of the purchases were made on credit.

FRANK CORPORATION
Income Statement
For the Year Ended December 31, 2007

Sales revenue		$400,000
Cost of goods sold		268,000
Gross profit		132,000
Expenses		
Salaries and wages	$51,000	
Amortization	9,200	
Rent (no accruals)	5,800	
Interest (no accruals)	12,200	
Income tax	$11,800	
Total expenses		90,000
Net income		$ 42,000

Required:

1. Prepare a cash flow statement for the year ended December 31, 2007. Use the indirect method to compute the cash flow from operating activities. Include any additional required note disclosures.

2. Compute and explain the quality of income ratio and the capital acquisitions ratio.

LO2

P5–2 Preparing Cash Flow Statement (Indirect Method)

The comparative balance sheets of Mikos Inc. as at December 31, 2007 and 2008, and its income statement for the year ended December 31, 2008, are presented below.

MIKOS INC.
Comparative Balance Sheets
December 31

	2008	2007
Assets		
Cash	$ 9,000	$ 17,000
Short-term investments	45,000	20,000
Accounts receivable	68,000	26,000
Inventories, at cost	54,000	40,000
Prepaid expenses	4,000	6,000
Land	45,000	70,000
Buildings and equipment, net	280,000	179,000
Intangible assets	24,000	28,000
	$529,000	$386,000
Liabilities and Shareholders' Equity		
Accounts payable	$ 17,000	$ 40,000
Income tax payable	6,000	1,000
Accrued liabilities	10,000	-0-
Long-term notes payable	110,000	150,000
Share capital	200,000	60,000
Retained earnings	186,000	135,000
	$529,000	$386,000

```
                                MIKOS INC.
                             Income Statement
                     For the Year Ended December 31, 2008

Sales                                                                    $850,000
Cost of goods sold                                     $430,000
Amortization expense—intangible assets                    4,000
              —buildings and equipment                   33,000
Operating expenses                                      221,000
Interest expense                                         12,000          700,000
Income before income taxes                                              150,000
Income tax expense                                                        45,000
Net income                                                             $105,000
```

Additional information:

a. Land was sold for cash at book value.

b. The short-term investments will mature in February 2009.

c. Cash dividends were declared and paid in 2008.

d. New equipment with a cost of $166,000 was purchased for cash, and old equipment was sold at book value.

e. Long-term notes of $10,000 were paid in cash, and notes of $30,000 were converted to shares.

f. Accounts payable pertain to merchandise suppliers.

Required:

1. Prepare a cash flow statement for Mikos Inc. for the year ended December 31, 2008. Use the indirect method to report cash flow from operating activities.

2. Assume the role of a bank loan officer who is evaluating this company's cash flow situation. Analyze the cash flow statement you prepared in requirement 1.

3. What additional information does the cash flow statement provide that is not available on either the balance sheet or the income statement? Explain.

P5–3 **Comparing Cash Flows from Operating Activities (Indirect Method)** (AP5–2)   ▧ **LO2**

Beta Company's accountants just completed the financial statements for the year and have provided the following information (in thousands):

```
                        Income Statement for 2007

Sales revenue                                               $20,600
Expenses and losses:
    Cost of goods sold                      $9,000
    Amortization                             2,000
    Salaries                                 5,000
    Rent                                     2,500
    Insurance                                  800
    Utilities                                  700
    Interest                                   600        20,600
Net income                                               $      0
```

```
                  Selected Balance Sheet Accounts

                                          2007         2006

Merchandise inventory                     $ 82         $ 60
Accounts receivable                        380          450
Accounts payable                           240          210
Salaries payable                            29           20
Rent payable                                 2            6
Prepaid rent                                 2            7
Prepaid insurance                           14            5
```

Other Data:

The company signed long-term notes for $20,000 during the year.

Required:

1. Prepare the Operating Activities section of the cash flow statement for 2007 using the indirect method.
2. As a financial analyst, would you prefer to see the cash flow from operations reported using the direct method or the indirect method? Justify your answer.
3. As the accountant who prepares the company's cash flow statement, would you prefer to use the direct or the indirect method to report the cash flow from operations? Explain.

■ LO2, 3, 5   **P5–4**   **(Supplement A) Preparing Cash Flow Statement with Sale of Equipment (Indirect Method)** (AP5–3)

McGregor Corp.'s accountants prepared the balance sheets and income statement to be reported in the company's annual report for 2008, and you have been asked to prepare the company's cash flow statement for 2008 based on the following financial information.

McGREGOR CORP.
Balance Sheets
As at December 31

	2008	2007
Assets		
Cash	$ 16,000	$ 4,000
Accounts receivable	40,000	27,000
Merchandise inventory	28,000	20,000
Prepaid expenses	9,000	5,000
Equipment, at cost	60,000	24,000
Less: Accumulated amortization	(10,000)	(7,000)
Total Assets	$143,000	$73,000
Liabilities and Shareholders' Equity		
Accounts payable	$ 10,000	$ 8,000
Income taxes payable	2,000	5,000
Wages payable	-0-	15,000
Long-term notes payable	60,000	43,000
Common shares	7,000	1,000
Retained earnings	64,000	1,000
Total Liabilities and Shareholders' Equity	$143,000	$73,000

McGREGOR CORP.
Income Statement
For the Year Ended December 31, 2008

Sales revenues		$762,000
Cost of goods sold	$410,000	
Wages expense	122,000	
General expenses	24,000	
Amortization expense	4,000	
Interest expense	5,000	
Gain on sale of equipment	(3,000)	562,000
Income before income taxes		200,000
Income tax expense		60,000
Net income		$140,000

Note: Equipment which originally cost $7,000 was sold for $9,000 cash during 2008. It had a net book value of $6,000 at the date of sale.

Required:

1. Prepare a cash flow statement for McGregor Corp. for the year ended December 31, 2008. Use the indirect method to report cash flows from operating activities.
2. Using the cash flow statement you prepared above, compute and explain each of the following: (a) quality of income ratio, (b) capital acquisitions ratio, and (3) free cash flow.

P5–5 **(Supplements A and B) Preparing Cash Flow Statement with Sale of Equipment (Direct Method) (AP5–4)**
Refer to the information for McGregor Corp. in P5–4.

Required:

1. Compute the following amounts:
   a. Cash collected from customers
   b. Cash paid to suppliers of merchandise
   c. Cash paid for general expenses

2. Prepare a cash flow statement for McGregor Corp. for the year ended December 31, 2008. Use the direct method to report cash flows from operating activities.

3. What additional information does the cash flow statement provide that is not available on either the balance sheet or the income statement?

P5–6 **(Supplement B) Preparing a Cash Flow Statement—Direct Method (AP5-5)**
Refer to the information for Frank Corporation in P5–1.

Required:

1. Prepare a cash flow statement for the year ended December 31, 2007. Use the direct method to compute the cash flow from operating activities. Include any additional required note disclosures.

2. Is the direct method of reporting cash flow from operating activities easier to prepare than the indirect method? Explain.

3. Is the direct method of reporting cash flow from operating activities easier to understand than the indirect method? Explain.

P5–7 **(Supplement C) Preparing Cash Flow Statement Spreadsheet, Cash Flow Statement, and Schedules Using the Indirect Method (AP5–6)**
Hunter Company is developing its annual financial statements at December 31, 2008. The statements are complete except for the cash flow statement. The completed comparative balance sheets and income statement are summarized:

	2008	2007
Balance sheet at December 31		
Cash	$ 44,000	$ 18,000
Accounts receivable	27,000	29,000
Merchandise inventory	30,000	36,000
Property, plant, and equipment (net)	75,000	72,000
	$176,000	$155,000
Accounts payable	$ 25,000	$ 22,000
Wages payable	800	1,000
Note payable, long term	38,000	48,000
Share capital	80,000	60,000
Retained earnings	32,200	24,000
	$176,000	$155,000
Income statement for 2008		
Sales	$100,000	
Cost of goods sold	(61,000)	
Other expenses	(27,000)	
Net income	$ 12,000	

Additional Data:

a. Bought equipment for cash, $9,000.
b. Paid $10,000 on the long-term note payable.
c. Issued common shares for $20,000 cash.
d. Declared and paid a $3,800 cash dividend.
e. Incurred expenses that included amortization, $6,000; wages, $10,000; taxes, $3,000; other, $8,000.

Required:

1. Prepare a cash flow statement spreadsheet using the indirect method to report cash flows from operating activities.

2. Prepare the cash flow statement for the year ended December 31, 2008.

3. Prepare a schedule of non-cash investing and financing activities, if necessary.

4. Evaluate the company's use of the cash flow generated from (or used for) operations.

ALTERNATE PROBLEMS

■ **LO1, 2, 4,**   **AP5–1**   **Preparing the Cash Flow Statement (Direct and Indirect Methods) (P5–1)**
6, 7
Stonewall Company was organized on January 1, 2007. During the year ended December 31, 2007, the company provided the following data:

Income Statement	
Sales revenue	$ 80,000
Cost of goods sold	(35,000)
Amortization expense	(4,000)
Other expenses	(32,000)
Net income	$ 9,000
Balance Sheet	
Cash	$ 48,000
Accounts receivable	18,000
Merchandise inventory	15,000
Machinery (net)	25,000
Total assets	$106,000
Accounts payable	$ 10,000
Accrued expenses (liabilities)	21,000
Dividends payable	2,000
Note payable, short term	15,000
Share capital	54,000
Retained earnings	4,000
Total liabilities and shareholders' equity	$106,000

Analysis of Selected Accounts and Transactions:

a. Issued 3,000 common shares for cash, at $18 per share.

b. Borrowed $15,000 on a one-year, 8-percent interest-bearing note; the note was dated June 1, 2007.

c. Paid $29,000 to purchase machinery.

d. Purchased merchandise for resale at a cost of $50,000; paid $40,000 cash and the balance on account. The company uses a perpetual inventory system.

e. Exchanged plant machinery with a book value of $2,000 for office machines with a market value of $2,000.

f. Declared a cash dividend of $5,000 on December 15, 2007 payable to shareholders on January 15, 2008.

g. Because this is the first year of operations, all account balances are zero at the beginning of the year; therefore, the changes in the account balances are equal to the ending balances.

Required:

1. Prepare a cash flow statement for the year ended December 31, 2007. Use the indirect method to report cash flow from operating activities.

2. Compute and explain the quality of income ratio and the capital acquisitions ratio.

AP5–2 Comparing Cash Flows from Operating Activities (Indirect Method) (P5–3)
The accountants of Pan American Silver Corp. completed the balance sheet at September 30, 2007, and the income statement for the quarter ended on that date and have provided the following information (in thousands):

■ LO2

Pan American
Silver Crop.

Income Statement

Sales revenue		$26,382
Investment income, net		94
Gain on sale of assets		3,523
		29,999
Expenses		
Operating	$28,448	
Depreciation and amortization	3,020	
Reclamation	330	
Exploration	438	
General and administration	1,452	33,688
Net loss		($ 3,689)

Selected Balance Sheet Accounts

	Sept. 30 2007	June 30 2007
Short-term investments	$ 513	$ 13
Accounts receivable	2,067	4,877
Inventories	5,369	7,595
Prepaid expenses	5,615	5,595
Accounts payable	8,414	10,302
Accrued liabilities	5,343	8,793
Current portion of bank loans	1,975	4,209

Required:

1. Prepare the Operating Activities section of the cash flow statement using the indirect method.

2. Companies that use the direct method to report cash flows from operations are also required to disclose in the notes a reconciliation of net income to cash flows from operating activities. What additional information does this disclosure requirement provide to users of financial statements? Explain.

AP5–3 (Supplement A) Preparing Cash Flow Statement with Sale of Equipment (Indirect Method) (P5–4)
Steven Cheng, the sole shareholder and manager of Musical Instruments Ltd. (MIL), has approached you and asked you to prepare a cash flow statement for his company. MIL sells different types of flutes and wind instruments to bands, orchestras and music stores. Steven is presently worried about the meeting that he has scheduled in two weeks with a lending officer of his bank. It is time for a review of the bank loan. This also involves a review of MIL's profitability and financial position.

Steven provided you with the following condensed financial statements for the fiscal years ended December 31, 2007 and 2008. He assures you that the financial statements are free of any omissions or misstatements, and that they conform to generally accepted accounting principles.

■ LO2, 3, 5

MUSICAL INSTRUMENTS LTD.
Balance Sheets as at December 31
(In thousands of dollars)

	2008	2007
Assets		
Current assets		
Cash	$ 500	$ 1,700
Short-term investments	1,000	4,000
Accounts receivable	28,150	5,300
Inventories	5,000	15,000
Total current assets	34,650	26,000
Noncurrent assets		
Furniture and fixtures, at cost	29,500	13,000
Less: accumulated amortization	(12,000)	(6,000)
Investments	1,000	1,500
Total non-current assets	18,500	8,500
Total assets	$53,150	$34,500
Liabilities and Shareholders' Equity		
Current liabilities		
Bank loan	$ 9,000	$ 4,000
Accounts payable	8,500	6,550
Dividends payable	-0-	300
Total current liabilities	17,500	10,850
Noncurrent liabilities		
Mortgage notes payable	14,000	-0-
Total liabilities	31,500	10,850
Shareholders' equity		
Share capital	12,000	11,000
Retained earnings	9,650	12,650
Total shareholders' equity	21,650	23,650
Total liabilities and shareholders' equity	$53,150	$34,500

MUSICAL INSTRUMENTS LTD.
Statements of Income and Retained Earnings
For the Years Ended December 31

	2008	2007
Sales revenue	$245,000	$220,000
Cost of goods sold	(160,000)	(140,000)
Gross profit	85,000	80,000
Operating expenses:		
Amortization	(6,600)	(3,000)
Selling and general	(71,900)	(72,000)
Operating income	6,500	5,000
Interest expense	(2,400)	(800)
Loss on sale of furniture	(300)	-0-
Gain on sale of investments	200	-0-
Income before income taxes	4,000	4,200
Income tax expense (@25%)	(1,000)	(1,050)
Net income	3,000	3,150
Retained earnings—January 1	12,650	9,800
Dividends declared	(6,000)	(300)
Retained earnings—December 31	$ 9,650	$ 12,650

Additional information:

a. In 2008, MIL sold older obsolete furniture with an original cost of $1,000 and $600 of accumulated amortization up to the date of sale.

b. During 2008, one of the noncurrent investments that had cost $500 was sold at a gain of $200.

c. The company considers short-term investments as cash equivalents.

Required:

1. Prepare a cash flow statement for MIL for the year ended December 31, 2008. Use the indirect method to report cash flows from operating activities.

2. Using the cash flow statement you prepared above, compute and explain each of the following: (a) quality of income ratio, (b) capital acquisitions ratio, and (3) free cash flow.

3. In an effort to improve the company's financial performance, Steven Cheng proposed that the furniture and fixtures can be amortized over a longer period. This change will decrease amortization expense by $1,000 in 2007 and by $2,000 in 2008. As a professional accountant, would this proposed change be acceptable to you? Explain.

AP5–4 **(Supplement A) Preparing Cash Flow Statement with Sale of Equipment (Direct Method) (P5–5)**
Refer to the information for Musical Instruments Ltd. (MIL) in AP5–3.

Required:

1. Compute the following amounts:
    a. Cash collected from customers
    b. Cash paid to suppliers of merchandise
    c. Cash received for sale of obsolete furniture
    d. Cash received for sale of non current investments.

2. Prepare a cash flow statement for MIL for the year ended December 31, 2008. Use the direct method to report cash flows from operating activities.

3. Discuss the importance of the cash flow statement to users of financial statements. What additional information does it provide that is not reported in the other financial statements? Explain by referring to the statement that you prepared in requirement 2 above.

AP5–5 **(Supplement B) Preparing a Cash Flow Statement—Direct Method (P5–6)**
Refer to the information for Stonewall Company in AP5–1.

Required:

1. Prepare a cash flow statement for the year ended December 31, 2007. Use the direct method to compute the cash flow from operating activities. Include any additional required note disclosures.

2. Is the direct method of reporting cash flow from operating activities easier to prepare than the indirect method? Explain.

3. Is the direct method of reporting cash flow from operating activities easier to understand than the indirect method? Explain.

AP5–6 **(Supplement C) Preparing Cash Flow Statement Spreadsheet and Cash Flow Statement Using the Indirect Method: Includes Non-Cash Investing and Financing Activity and Sale of an Asset at Book Value (P5–7)**
Choo-Foo Company is developing its 2007 annual report. The following information is provided:

	2007	2006
Cash	$22,400	$21,000
Accounts receivable	21,000	18,000
Inventory	32,000	35,000
Prepaid insurance	1,400	2,400
Long-term investments	9,300	12,500
Property, plant, and equipment (net)	59,600	31,100
Patent	1,500	2,000
Accounts payable	15,000	27,000
Wages payable	1,000	4,000
Income taxes payable	2,200	2,000
Note payable, long term	10,000	20,000
Share capital	86,000	53,000
Retained earnings	33,000	16,000

Other Information:

a. Sold long-term investments at book value for $3,200 cash. Purchased machinery by issuing 3,000 shares that had a market value of $11 per share.

b. Revenues for the year totalled $150,000.

c. Expenses for the year included: amortization, $5,000; insurance, $2,000; wages, $48,500; income taxes, $7,000; and cost of goods sold, $62,000.

Required:

1. Prepare a cash flow statement spreadsheet using the indirect method to report cash flows from operating activities.
2. Prepare the cash flow statement for the year ended December 31, 2007.
3. Prepare a schedule of non-cash investing and financing activities.
4. Evaluate the company's use of the cash flow generated from (or used for) operations.

CASES AND PROJECTS

FINDING AND INTERPRETING FINANCIAL INFORMATION

■ **LO2, 4, 6**   **CP5–1**   **Finding Financial Information**

Van Houtte

ANALYSIS

Refer to the financial statements of Van Houtte Inc. given in Appendix B of this book.

Required:

1. Which of the two basic reporting approaches for the cash flows from operating activities did the company adopt?
2. What amount of cash did the company pay for taxes during the current year?
3. Explain why the gain on disposal of fixed assets was deducted in the reconciliation of net income to net cash provided by operating activities.
4. What was the amount of free cash flow for the year ended March 31, 2007?
5. Has the company paid cash dividends during the last two years? How did you know?

■ **LO2, 4, 6**   **CP5–2**   **Finding Financial Information**

The Forzani Group

ANALYSIS

Refer to the Online Learning Centre Web site at **www.mcgrawhill.ca/olc/libby/student/resources** for the financial statements of The Forzani Group Ltd.

Required:

1. What were the three largest adjustments to reconcile net income to the net cash provided by operating activities? Refer to the cash flow statement and to note 7. Explain the direction of the effect of each adjustment in the reconciliation.
2. What have been The Forzani Group's major uses of cash over the past two years? What have been its major sources of cash for these activities?
3. What was the amount of free cash flow for the year ended January 28, 2007? What does this imply about the company's financial flexibility?

■ **LO3, 5**   **CP5–3**   **Comparing Companies**

Van Houtte

ANALYSIS

Refer to the Online Learning Centre Web site at **www.mcgrawhill.ca/olc/libby/student/resources** for the financial statements of The Forzani Group Ltd. and to Appendix B of this book for the financial statements of Van Houtte Inc.

Required:

1. Compute the quality of income ratio for both companies for the current year. How might the difference in their sales growth rates explain the difference in the ratio? Sales Growth Rate = (Current Year's Sales − Prior Year's Sales) ÷ Prior Year's Sales.
2. Compute the capital acquisitions ratio for both companies for the current year. Compare their abilities to finance purchases of property, plant, and equipment with cash provided by operating activities.

FINANCIAL REPORTING AND ANALYSIS CASES

■ **LO2, 3,**   **CP5–4**   **Using Financial Reports: Analyzing Van Houtte's Cash Flow Statement**
4, 5, 6

Van Houtte

ANALYSIS

Van Houtte Inc. is the largest gourmet coffee roasting organization in Canada, and one of the leading coffee service specialists in North America. Its cash flow statements for fiscal years 2006 and 2005 and the related note are shown below.

Consolidated Statements of Cash Flows
Years ended April 1, 2006 and April 2, 2005
(in thousands of dollars)

	2006	2005
CASH FLOWS FROM OPERATING ACTIVITIES:		
Net earnings:	**$22,506**	$21,706
Adjustments for:		
Depreciation of fixed assets	**30,405**	28,536
Amortization of financial expenses (*note 3*)	**1,405**	271
Amortization of other assets	**3,385**	2,480
Future income taxes (*note 4*)	**356**	1,308
Change in fair value of interest rate swaps	**(2,169)**	—
Non-controlling interest	**1,944**	2,125
Share in net earnings of companies subject to significant influence, net of dividends received	**(13)**	(72)
Increase in value of investment in preferred shares and dividends (*note 7*)	**(1,559)**	—
Stock-based compensation (*note 13*)	**418**	413
Gain on disposal of fixed assets	**(314)**	(254)
Loss (gain) on disposal of businesses	**(921)**	304
Other elements	**(10)**	169
	55,433	56,986
Net change in non-cash balances related to working capital items (*note 17*)	**(7,622)**	3,698
	47,811	60,684
CASH FLOWS FROM INVESTING ACTIVITIES:		
Business acquisitions (*note 18*)	**(9,545)**	(9,330)
Additions to fixed assets	**(29,764)**	(27,986)
Proceeds from disposal of fixed assets	**3,105**	1,043
Acquisition of investments	**(177)**	(944)
Increase in other assets	**(2,012)**	(2,187)
	(38,393)	(39,404)
CASH FLOWS FROM FINANCING ACTIVITIES:		
Issue of subordinate voting shares (*note 13*)	**287**	1,214
Redemption of subordinate voting shares for cancellation (*note 13*)	**(5,200)**	(94)
Increase in long-term debt	**65,197**	43,424
Decrease in long-term debt	**(57,778)**	(59,228)
Dividends	**(9,183)**	(5,176)
Dividends paid to non-controlling shareholders of subsidiaries	**(1,973)**	(1,817)
	(8,650)	(21,677)
Effect of exchange rate changes on cash denominated in foreign currency	**(310)**	(1,606)
Increase (decrease) in cash	**458**	(2,003)
Cash, beginning of year	**5,338**	7,341
Cash, end of year	**$ 5,796**	$ 5,338

See accompanying notes to consolidated financial statements.

NOTE 17
Additional information on cash flows

	2006	2005
Operating activities:		
Changes in non-cash operating working capital items:		
(Increase) decrease in the undernoted items:	**$(1,739)**	$(4,850)
Accounts receivable	**(1,927)**	(1,270)
Inventories	**(671)**	(9)
Prepaid expenses		
(Decrease) increase in the undernoted items:		
Accounts payable and accrued liabilities	**(5,263)**	6,058
Income taxes payable	**346**	2,542
Employee future benefits	**—**	(173)
Working capital acquired	**1,258**	1,400
Consolidation of joint ventures (*note 1b*))	**374**	—
	$(7,622)	$ 3,698
Cash payments of interest and income taxes were as follows:		
Interest paid	**$ 4,754**	$ 3,786
Income taxes paid	**$ 7,691**	$ 3,163
Additions to fixed assets financed by accounts payable	**$ 1,643**	$ 1,147
Additions to fixed assets financed by capital lease obligations	**$ 215**	$ 236

Required:

1. The cash flows from operating activities show that "depreciation of fixed assets" is added to "net earnings." Is depreciation (or amortization) a source of cash? Explain.

2. Was the cash collected from customers during fiscal year 2006 higher or lower than Van Houtte's sales revenue for that year? Explain.

3. Explain why Van Houtte's cash flow from operations decreased in 2006 compared to 2005, while its net earnings increased during the same year?

4. Did Van Houtte expand during 2005 and 2006? If so, how did the company pay for its expansion? Explain.

5. Compute and analyze Van Houtte's quality of income ratio, capital acquisitions ratio, and free cash flow for both years.

▇ LO2, 3, 4, 5, 6

CP5–5 **Using Financial Reports: Analyzing Research In Motion's Cash Flow Statement**

Research In Motion

ANALYSIS

Research In Motion (RIM) is a leading designer, manufacturer, and marketer of innovative wireless solutions for the worldwide mobile communications market. Its products are used around the world and include the BlackBerry® wireless platform, software development tools, and software/hardware licensing agreements. RIM's cash flow statements for fiscal years 2007, 2006, and 2005 are shown below.

RESEARCH IN MOTION LIMITED

Consolidated Statements of Cash Flows

(US dollars, in thousands)

	For the Year Ended		
	March 3, 2007	March 4, 2006	February 26, 2005
		(Restated—note 4)	(Restated—note 4)
Cash flows from operating activities			
Net income	$631,572	$374,656	$ 205,612
Items not requiring an outlay of cash:			
Amortization	126,355	85,873	66,760
Deferred income taxes	101,576	77,154	(144,642)
Share-based payment (note 4)	19,063	2,551	2,899
Other	(315)	507	(137)
Net changes in working capital items (note 18(a))	(142,582)	(390,650)	147,490
Net cash provided by operating activities	735,699	150,091	277,982
Cash flows from financing activities			
Issuance of share capital	44,534	23,269	54,151
Excess tax benefits from share-based compensation (note 12(b))	6,000	—	—
Common shares repurchased pursuant to Common Share Repurchase Program (note 12(a))	(203,933)	(391,212)	—
Repayment of long-term debt	(262)	(229)	(199)
Net cash provided by (used in) financing activities	(153,661)	(368,172)	53,952
Cash flows from investing activities			
Acquisition of investments	(100,080)	(103,179)	(615,098)
Proceeds on sale or maturity of investments	86,583	61,495	18,385
Acquisition of capital assets	(254,041)	(178,732)	(109.363)
Acquisition of intangible assets	(60,303)	(23,702)	(17,061)
Business acquisitions (note 9)	(116,190)	(3,795)	(3,888)
Acquisition of short-term investments	(163,147)	(199,194)	(227,072)
Proceeds on sale or maturity of short-term investments	242,601	514,431	76,022
Net cash provided by (used in) investing activities	(364,577)	67,324	(878,075)
Effect of foreign exchange loss (gain) on cash and cash equivalents	173	(57)	76
Net increase (decrease) in cash and cash equivalents for the year	217,604	(150,814)	(546,065)
Cash and cash equivalents, beginning of year	459,540	610,354	1,156,419
Cash and cash equivalents, end of year	$677,144	$459,540	$ 610,354

See notes to be consolidated financial statements.

18. SUPPLEMENTAL INFORMATION

(a) Cash flows resulting from net changes in working capital items are as follows:

	For the year ended		
	March 3, 2007	March 4, 2006	February 26, 2005
Trade receivables	$(254,370)	$ (87,528)	$(126,177)
Other receivables	(8,300)	(18,727)	(7,326)
Inventory	(121,238)	(42,034)	(49,653)
Other current assets	(16,827)	(11,876)	(1,346)
Accounts payable	47,625	11,031	32,894
Accrued liabilities	119,997	59,398	18,618
Accrued litigation and related expenses	—	(435,610)	351,218
Restricted cash	—	111,978	(75,717)
Income taxes payable	83,310	17,985	5,242
Deferred revenue	7,221	4,733	(263)
	$(142,582)	$(390,650)	$ 147,490

Required

1. Have RIM's trade receivables increased or decreased during fiscal year 2007? By how much have its trade receivables changed during the past three years? Explain.
2. How does the change in inventory during fiscal year 2007 affect cash? Explain.
3. Explain why RIM shows a decrease in cash flow from operations from fiscal year 2005 to 2006 while it reported an increase in net income.
4. How did the company finance the acquisition of long-term assets during fiscal years 2006 and 2007? Explain.
5. What additional information does the cash flow statement provide that is not available on either the balance sheet or the income statement?

CP5–6 Using Financial Reports: Analyzing Celestica's Cash Flow Statement

■ **LO2, 3, 4, 5, 6**

Celestica Inc.

ANALYSIS

Celestica Inc. is a world leader in providing electronics manufacturing services to original equipment manufacturers, communications, and other industries. Celestica provides a wide variety of products and services to its customers, including complex printed circuit board assemblies such as PC motherboards and communication and networking cards. These assemblies end up in servers, workstations, personal computers, peripherals, and communications devices. Celestica also offers supply chain management, as well as design, global distribution, and post-sales repair services. Celestica operates facilities in the Americas, Europe, and Asia. Its cash flow statements for the years 2004 to 2006 are shown below.

CELESTICA INC.
Consolidated Statements of Cash Flows
(in millions of US dollars)

	Year ended December 31		
	2004	2005	2006
Cash provided by (used in):			
Operations:			
Net loss.	$ (854.1)	$ (46.8)	$ (150.6)
Items not affecting cash:			
Depreciation and amortization.	207.7	152.7	134.2
Deferred income taxes.	234.6	(15.6)	55.2
Accretion of convertible debt.	17.6	7.6	—
Non-cash charge for option issuances	7.6	9.0	5.1
Restructuring charges.	35.3	11.0	47.9
Other charges	482.4	(15.3)	34.6
Gain on settlement of principal component of convertible debt (*Note 8*) . .	(32.9)	(13.9)	—
Inventory write-down related to restructuring.	61.2	—	—
Other	1.9	14.5	1.9

(continued)

	2004	2005	2006
Changes in non-cash working capital items:			
Accounts receivable...	(253.0)	42.0	(24.8)
Inventories	85.6	—	(172.0)
Prepaid and other assets....................................	(12.9)	17.3	2.7
Income taxes recoverable	(50.0)	(24.4)	72.1
Accounts payable and accrued liabilities........................	(113.8)	51.2	108.0
Income taxes payable	43.6	29.0	(75.1)
Non-cash working capital changes	(300.5)	115.1	(89.1)
Cash provided by (used in) operations	(139.2)	218.3	39.2
Investing:			
Acquisitions, net of cash acquired/indebtedness assumed (*Note 3*).......	(39.6)	(6.5)	(19.1)
Purchase of capital assets...................................	(142.2)	(158.5)	(189.1)
Proceeds, net of cash divested from sale of operations or assets........	101.3	50.9	1.0
Other..	0.6	2.2	(0.7)
Cash used in investing activities.	(79.9)	(111.9)	(207.9)
Financing:			
Increase in long-term debt (*Note 7*)	500.0	250.0	—
Long-term debt issue costs..................................	(12.0)	(4.2)	—
Repayment of long-term debt	(41.1)	(3.4)	(0.6)
Deferred financing costs	(4.0)	(1.1)	—
Repurchase of convertible debt (*Note 8*)........................	(299.7)	(352.0)	—
Issuance of share capital....................................	14.6	8.0	5.3
Other..	1.3	(3.5)	(1.3)
Cash provided by (used in) financing activities....................	159.1	(106.2)	3.4
Increase (decrease) in cash..................................	(60.0)	0.2	(165.3)
Cash, beginning of year.....................................	1,028.8	968.8	969.0
Cash, end of year..	$ 968.8	$ 969.0	$ 803.7

Cash is comprised of cash and short-term investments.
Supplemental cash flow information (*Note 19*).

See accompanying notes to consolidated financial statements.

Required:

1. The cash flows from operating activities show that "depreciation and amortization" is added to "net loss." Are depreciation and amortization a source of cash? Explain.

2. How does the change in inventory during 2006 affect cash? Explain.

3. Compare the changes in non-cash working capital items across the three years. What conclusions can you draw from this comparison?

4. Compute and analyze Celestica's capital acquisitions ratio and free cash flow for the three years.

5. Has Celestica become more or less risky during 2006? What other financial statement might include information that would help you confirm your answer? Explain.

6. Analyze the company's pattern of cash flows from operating, investing, and financing activities over the three years. What conclusion can you draw from the changing pattern of cash flows? Explain.

7. Obtain a copy of Celestica's cash flow statement for the year 2007 through the company's Web site (www.celestica.com) or the SEDAR service (www.sedar.com). Did the company's cash flow situation in 2007 improve or deteriorate relative to previous years? Explain.

8. As a potential investor in Celestica's shares, what additional information would you need before making your decision whether or not to invest in this company's shares?

■ **LO1, 2**   **CP5–7**   **Using Financial Reports: Analyzing a U.K. Cash Flow Statement**

Geox

ANALYSIS

Geox S.p.A. is an Italy-based company active in the footwear and apparel manufacturing industry, which include classic, casual, and sports footwear, as well as apparel for men, women, and children. The company's products are sold in over 70 countries worldwide through a widespread distribution network. Geox prepares its financial statements in accordance with the International Financial Reporting Standards. Its cash flow statements for the years 2006 and 2005 are shown below.

Cash Flow Statement
(Thousands of Euro)

	Notes	2006	2005
Cash Flow From Operating Activities:			
Net income	22	**97,262**	**75,253**
Adjustments to reconcile net income to net cash provided (used) by operating activities:			
Depreciation and amortization	8	18,564	18,104
Increase in (use of) deferred taxes and other provisions		(1,741)	(1,683)
Provisions for employee severance indemnities, net		663	1,071
Other non-cash items due to adoption of IAS/IFRS		755	(4,601)
		18,241	12,891
Change in current assets /liabilities:			
Accounts receivable		(9,633)	(16,855)
Other assets		(7,217)	(1,358)
Inventories		(23,401)	(27,572)
Accounts payable		13,991	20,001
Other liabilities		3,345	3,680
Taxes payable		(9,477)	5,521
		(32,392)	(16,583)
Other:			
IPO tax benefit cancelled by EU		—	(6,281)
		—	(6,281)
Operating cash flow		**83,111**	**65,280**
CASH FLOW USED IN INVESTING ACTIVITIES:			
Capital expenditure on intangible fixed assets	13	(11,193)	(12,835)
Capital expenditure on tangible fixed assets	14	(16,189)	(18,944)
		(27,382)	(31,779)
Disposals		845	2,415
(Increase) decrease in financial assets		(890)	15,682
Cash flow used in investing activities		**(27,427)**	**(13,682)**
CASH FLOW FROM (USED IN) FINANCING ACTIVITIES:			
Increase (decrease) in short-term bank borrowings, net		9	(3,930)
Loans:			
Proceeds		2,818	11,007
Repayments		(12,474)	(34,229)
Dividends	34	(22,001)	(15,510)
Increase in share capital		—	1,582
Cash flow from financing activities		**(31,648)**	**(41,080)**
Increase in cash and cash equivalents		**24,036**	**10,518**
Cash and cash equivalents, beginning of the period	21	**61,513**	**50,570**
Effect of translation differences on cash and cash equivalents		(623)	425
Cash and cash equivalents, end of the period	21	**84,926**	**61,513**
Supplementary information to the cash flow statement:			
Interest paid during the period		572	1,564
Taxes paid during the period		47,542	29,488

Required:

1. The cash flows from operating activities show that "depreciation and amortization" is added to net income. Are depreciation and amortization a source of cash? Explain.

2. Geox reported sales of €612,258 during 2006. Compute the amount of cash collected from customers during the year, assuming all sales are on account.

3. How does the change in accounts payable during 2006 affect cash?

4. Did Geox expand during 2005 and 2006? If so, how did the company pay for its expansion? Explain.

5. Compute and analyze Geox's quality of income ratio, capital acquisitions ratio, and free cash flow for the two years.

6. As a potential investor in Geox's shares, what additional information would you need before making your decision whether or not to invest in the company's shares?

CP5–8 (Supplements A and B) Using Financial Reports: Analyzing Operating Cash Flows of Foster's Group

Foster's Group

ANALYSIS

Foster's Group is a global multi-beverage Australian company that produces and markets a variety of beer, wine, spirits, cider, and non-alcohol beverages. Foster's reports its cash flows from operating activities using the direct method. Its cash flow statement for 2006 included the following information (in millions of Australian dollars):

	Fiscal Year Ended 30 June	
	2006	2005
Cash flows from operating activities		
Receipts from customers	6,841.4	5,789.8
Payment to suppliers, governments and employees	(5,564.1)	(4,975.0)
Dividends received	0.1	2.9
Interest received	41.6	132.3
Borrowing costs	(273.8)	(241.0)
Income taxes paid	(210.0)	(185.6)
Net cash flows from operating activities	**835.2**	**523.4**

Foster's also presents a reconciliation of net income to cash flow from operating activities in a note to its financial statements. A condensed version of this reconciliation, which is essentially the indirect method of reporting cash flows from operations, is presented below.

	Fiscal Year Ended 30 June	
	2006	2005
Reconciliation of net cash flows from operating activities to profit after income tax		
Profit for the year	1,169.8	925.2
Depreciation and amortization	163.9	149.7
(Profit)/loss on disposal of non-current assets	(10.7)	(14.8)
(Profit)/loss on disposal of intangibles	(733.2)	(57.5)
(Profit)/loss on disposal of discontinued operations	(13.1)	(459.5)
Other non-cash items, net	137.9	211.4
Changes in working capital items		
— receivables	29.7	(14.4)
— inventories	59.8	14.8
— other assets	46.5	3.9
— accounts payable	(7.7)	(84.9)
— accrued liabilities	(7.7)	(150.5)
Net cash flows from operating activities	**835.2**	**523.4**

Required:

1. As a user of financial statements, would you prefer to see the cash flows from operating activities reported using the direct method or the indirect method? Explain.

2. Did Foster's sales to its customers exceed the amount it collected from them during fiscal year 2006? Can you determine Foster's sales during fiscal year 2006? Show computations.

3. Assume for simplicity that Foster's purchases its inventories from trade suppliers. Did Foster's pay its trade suppliers for all the purchases it made during fiscal year 2006? Support your answer with detailed computations.

4. Compute and interpret the quality of income ratios for both years 2005 and 2006.

5. What additional information is reported under the indirect method, but is not reported under the direct method.

CRITICAL THINKING CASE

CP5–9   **Making a Decision as a Financial Analyst: Analyzing Cash Flow for a New Company**
Carlyle Golf, Inc., was formed in September of last year. The company designs, contracts
for the manufacture of, and markets a line of men's golf apparel. A portion of the cash flow
statement for Carlyle follows:

■ **LO2**

Carlyle Golf, Inc.

ANALYSIS

	Current Year
Cash flows from operating activities	
Net income	$(460,089)
Depreciation	3,554
Non-cash compensation (stock)	254,464
Deposits with suppliers	(404,934)
Increase in prepaid assets	(42,260)
Increase in accounts payable	81,765
Increase in accrued liabilities	24,495
Net cash flows	$(543,005)

Management expects a solid increase in sales in the near future. To support the increase
in sales, it plans to add $2.2 million to inventory. The company did not disclose a sales
forecast. At the end of the current year, Carlyle had less than $1,000 in cash. It is not
unusual for a new company to experience a loss and negative cash flows during its
start-up phase.

Required:

As a financial analyst recently hired by a major investment bank, you have been asked to
write a short memo to your supervisor evaluating the problems facing Carlyle. Emphasize
typical sources of financing that may or may not be available to support the expansion.

FINANCIAL REPORTING AND ANALYSIS TEAM PROJECT

CP5–10   **Team Project: Analyzing Cash Flows**
As a team, select an industry to analyze (industry lists can be found at **www.investors.
reuters.com/Industries.aspx** and **www.hoovers.com**; click on Companies & Industries).
Each team member should acquire the annual report for one publicly traded company in the
industry, with each member selecting a different company. (Library files, the SEDAR service
at **www.sedar.com**, or the company itself are good sources.)

■ **LO1, 2, 3, 4, 5, 6**

ANALYSIS

Required:

On an individual basis, each team member should then write a short report answering the
following questions about the selected company. Discuss any patterns across the three
companies that your team observes. Then, as a team, write a short report comparing and
contrasting your companies.

1. Which of the two basic reporting approaches for cash flows from operating activities did
    the company adopt?

2. What is the quality of income ratio for the most current year? What were the major
    causes of differences between net income and cash flow from operations?

3. What is the capital acquisitions ratio for the three-year period presented in total? How is
    the company financing its capital acquisitions?

4. What portion of the cash from operations in the current year is being paid to shareholders
    in the form of dividends?

Communicating and Interpreting Accounting Information

6

After studying this chapter, you should be able to:

LEARNING OBJECTIVES

1. Recognize the people involved in the accounting communication process (regulators, managers, board of directors, auditors, information intermediaries, and users), their roles in the process, and the guidance they receive from legal and professional standards. p. 291

2. Identify the steps in the accounting communication process, including the issuance of press releases, annual reports, quarterly reports, and documents filed with securities commissions, as well as the guiding principles in communicating useful information. p. 299

3. Recognize the different financial statement and disclosure formats used by companies in practice. p. 306

FOCUS COMPANY:

The Forzani Group Ltd.

**COMMUNICATING FINANCIAL INFORMATION AND
CORPORATE STRATEGY**

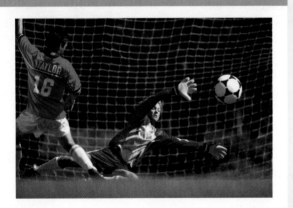

Founded in 1974 by the heralded entrepreneur John Forzani, along with three Calgary Stampeder team-mates, the company that bears his name is Canada's largest retailer of sporting goods. Over the past 30 years, Mr. Forzani took a small retail location in Calgary known as "Forzani's Locker Room" and grew the business steadily allowing the company to expand its initial athletic footwear business to become the industry leader offering a vast assortment of sports related products—from athletic footwear to athletic/leisure apparel to the equipment required to perform a favourite sport.

The growth of the Forzani Group Limited (FGL) (**www.forzanigroup.com**) was the result of numerous acquisitions of other businesses over the years. In August 1993, FGL concluded its initial public offering of shares to investors. This access to capital markets allowed the company to expand further by acquiring other businesses. By 2006, FGL became Canada's largest retailer of sporting goods, offering a comprehensive selection of brand name and private-brand products, operating stores from coast to coast under four corporate banners: Sport Chek, Sports Experts, Coast Mountain Sports, and Sport Mart. In addition, FGL is a franchisor under the names: Sports Experts, Intersport, RnR, Econosports, and Tech Shop/ Pegasus, Nevada Bob's Golf, and Hockey Experts.

As a publicly traded company, FGL is required to provide detailed information in regular filings with the Ontario Securities Commission. As the certifying officers of the company, Bob Sartor, the chief executive officer, and Richard Burnet, vice-president and chief financial officer, are responsible for the accuracy of the filings. The board of directors and auditors monitor the integrity of the system that produces the disclosures. Integrity in communicating with investors and other users of financial statements is a key to maintaining relationship with suppliers of capital. Furthermore, clear and timely communication of the company's financial situation enables FGL to comply with exchange rules and regulations of securities commissions. It also informs FGL's customers, investors, creditors, and other users of financial statements of the company's success in implementing its business strategy.

UNDERSTANDING THE BUSINESS

The Forzani Group Ltd. is a specialty retailer of sporting goods, which includes sports equipment, outdoor technical gear, athletic, leisure, and recreational footwear and apparel. The company operates principally in two business segments: corporately owned and operated retail stores, and as a wholesale business selling to franchisees and others. Franchisees are contractually obligated to pay a royalty based on a percentage of their retail sales. They also pay additional fees for services rendered for buying, distribution, and administration. FGL's operations are influenced by external, market-driven factors such as demand for sporting goods, consumer expectations concerning apparel and sport-inspired fashion, and competition from other companies. These external factors influence management decisions concerning re-investment in existing stores and acquisition of new stores that help grow the business.

Successful companies such as FGL learn to match their financial reporting to their business strategies. Marketing and communication are fundamental to both. As FGL strives to maintain its leading position in the industry, it continues to seek opportunities to innovate in response to its customers' needs. FGL's investments in new stores, the results of operating existing stores, and the company's financial condition are communicated to shareholders, creditors, and other interested parties through press releases, conference calls with shareholders and the media together with financial analysts, and periodic reporting of financial information.

FGL knows that when investors lose faith in the truthfulness of a firm's accounting numbers, they also normally punish the company's stock. The accounting scandals at Enron and WorldCom are the best recent examples.

FGL also invests in **corporate governance**, the procedures designed to ensure that the company is managed in the interests of the shareholders. Much of its corporate governance system consists of practices required by the Toronto Stock Exchange that aim at ensuring integrity in the financial reporting process. Good corporate governance ease's the company's access to capital, lowering both the cost of borrowing (interest rates) and the perceived riskiness of investment in its shares.[1]

CORPORATE GOVERNANCE refers to the procedures designed to ensure that the company is managed in the interests of the shareholders.

In an attempt to restore investor confidence, the U.S. Congress passed the Public Accounting Reform and Investor Protection Act (the Sarbanes-Oxley Act), which strengthens financial reporting and corporate governance for public companies.

---

[1] Examples of accounting research that examine this relationship are R.C. Anderson, S.A. Mansi, D.M. Reeb, "Board Characteristics, Accounting Report Integrity, and the Cost of Debt," *Journal of Accounting and Economics,* September 2004, pp. 315–342; and C.A. Botosan and M.A. Plumlee, "A Re-Examination of Disclosure Level and the Expected Cost of Equity Capital," *Journal of Accounting Research,* March 2002, pp. 21–40.

Compliance with the provisions of this Act has also affected Canadian companies that are publicly traded on U.S. stock exchanges. In light of the U.S. experience, the Canadian Securities Administrators, which coordinates and harmonizes regulation of the Canadian capital markets among the 13 securities regulators of Canada's provinces and territories, has recently imposed new requirements on all publicly traded companies to bolster investors' confidence in financial reporting by Canadian companies. Even with these added safeguards, the wisdom of famed analyst Jack Ciesielski's warning to financial statement users is still evident:

> One usual answer to the question "why does accounting matter?" is that it helps to avoid "blow-ups": the unpleasant outcome when a stock crashes because the firm's management engaged in accounting chicanery that subsequently becomes visible. . . . the analyst who understands accounting matters will know precisely where the "soft spots" are in financial reporting, the ones that can be manipulated in order to meet an expected earnings target or avoid breaking a loan covenant.
>
> Source: Analyst's Accounting Observer, **www.aaopub.com**, August 2000.

Chapters 2 through 5 focused on the mechanics of preparing the four basic financial statements: balance sheet, income statement, statement of retained earnings, and cash flow statement. In these chapters, we explained the importance of generally accepted accounting principles (e.g., historical cost, revenue recognition, and matching) in generating the information disclosed in these statements. We also learned to compute and interpret some financial ratios to analyze and understand how creditors and investors use the information that accountants report to justify financial investment decisions.

In this chapter, we will take a more detailed look at the people involved in the regulations that govern the process that conveys accounting information to statement users in the Internet age. We will also take a look at disclosures provided in financial reports to help you learn how to find relevant information.

ORGANIZATION OF THE CHAPTER

Players in the Accounting Communication Process	The Disclosure Process	A Closer Look at Financial Statements and Notes
• Regulators (CSA, AcSB, AASB, Stock Exchanges) • Managers (CEO, CFO, and Accounting Staff) • Board of Directors (Audit Committee) • Auditors • Information Intermediaries: Analysts and Information Services • Users: Institutional and Private Investors, Creditors, and Others	• Press Releases • Annual Reports • Quarterly Reports • Reports to Securities Commissions • Guiding Principles for Communicating Useful Information • Constraints of Accounting Measurement	• Overview of Forzani's Financial Statements • Notes to Financial Statements • Voluntary Disclosures

PLAYERS IN THE ACCOUNTING COMMUNICATION PROCESS

Exhibit 6.1 summarizes the major actors involved in the integrity of the financial reporting process.

REGULATORS (CSA, AcSB, AASB, STOCK EXCHANGES)

The financial information reported by Canadian companies is subject to strict regulations and standards issued by government regulators and private standard-setting organizations. Canadian publicly traded corporations must comply with provincial securities regulations that are coordinated by the Canadian Securities Administrators (CSA). The CSA is a forum for the 13 securities regulators of Canada's provinces and territories that was established to harmonize regulation of the Canadian capital markets. The CSA's mission is to protect investors from unfair, improper, or fraudulent practices and fosters fair, efficient, and vibrant capital markets. However, provincial or territorial regulators handle all complaints regarding securities violations in their respective jurisdictions and have legal authority to enforce provincial regulations concerning the timeliness and quality of financial disclosure.[2]

Securities regulators work closely with the Accounting Standards Board (AcSB) that is responsible for establishing standards of accounting and reporting by Canadian companies. External auditors ensure that companies prepare their financial reports in accordance with these standards, and their audit work is guided by generally accepted auditing standards that are issued by the Auditing and Assurance Standards Board.

Stock exchanges also provide an essential quality assurance service to listed companies by undertaking ongoing surveillance of their reporting and trading activities. When they suspect non-compliance with accounting standards, the stock exchanges undertake independent investigations, and share information with securities commissions, Canada Customs and Revenue Agency that collects income taxes from corporations, and other law enforcement agencies such as the Royal Canadian Mounted Police (RCMP). As intermediaries, the stock exchanges may also enforce their rules through penalties ranging from temporary cease trade orders to fines and delisting of companies.

> ■ **LEARNING OBJECTIVE 1**
>
> Recognize the people involved in the accounting communication process (regulators, managers, board of directors, auditors, information intermediaries, and users), their roles in the process, and the guidance they receive from legal and professional standards.

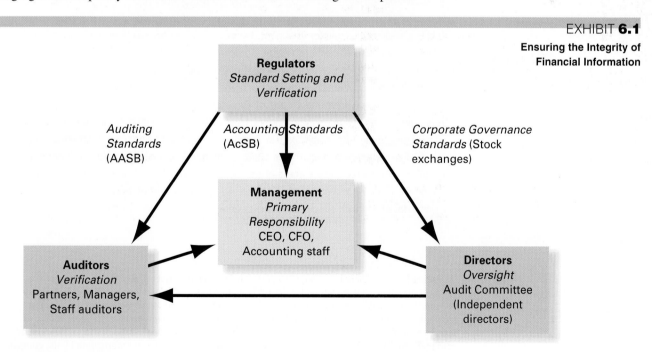

EXHIBIT **6.1**

Ensuring the Integrity of Financial Information

---

[2]The most prominent of these regulators is the Ontario Securities Commission (OSC). The OSC staff review company reports for compliance with their standards, investigate irregularities, and punish violators. Many OSC investigations are reported in the business press such as the *National Post* or the *Globe and Mail*. The OSC also publishes this information online each month at **www.oscbulletin.carswell.com**.

MANAGERS (CEO, CFO, AND ACCOUNTING STAFF)

As noted in Chapter 1, the primary responsibility for the information in FGL's financial statements and related disclosures lies with management as represented by the highest officer in the company, often called the *president and chief executive officer*[3] (CEO) and the highest officer associated with the financial and accounting side of the business, often called the *chief financial officer* (CFO). These two officers must sign the statement of management responsibility that is included in the annual report. For public companies, the same officers are responsible for the principal reports filed with the provincial securities commissions. At FGL, Bob Sartor, CEO, and Richard Burnet, vice-president and CFO, had that responsibility for fiscal year 2006. They were responsible for the conformance of the statements and related disclosures with GAAP.

REAL WORLD EXCERPT

The Forzani Group

ANNUAL REPORT

MANAGEMENT'S RESPONSIBILITIES FOR FINANCIAL REPORTING

The Annual Report, including the consolidated financial statements, is the responsibility of the management of the Company. The consolidated financial statements were prepared by management in accordance with generally accepted accounting principles. The significant accounting policies used are described in Note 2 to the consolidated financial statements. The integrity of the information presented in the financial statements, including estimates and judgments relating to matters not concluded by year-end, is the responsibility of management. Financial information presented elsewhere in this Annual Report has been prepared by management and is consistent with the information in the consolidated financial statements.

Management is responsible for the development and maintenance of systems of internal accounting and administrative controls. Such systems are designed to provide reasonable assurance that the financial information is accurate, relevant and reliable, and that the Company's assets are appropriately accounted for and adequately safeguarded (except as noted on pages 44 and 45 under "internal control over financial reporting"). The Board of Directors is responsible for ensuring that management fulfills its responsibilities for final approval of the annual consolidated financial statements. The Board appoints an Audit Committee consisting of three directors, none of whom is an officer or employee of the Company or its subsidiaries. The Audit Committee meets at least four times each year to discharge its responsibilities under a written mandate from the Board of Directors. The Audit Committee meets with management and with the independent auditors to satisfy itself that they are properly discharging their responsibilities, reviews the consolidated financial statements and the Auditors' Report, and examines other auditing, accounting and financial reporting matters. The consolidated financial statements have been reviewed by the Audit Committee and approved by the Board of Directors of The Forzani Group Ltd. The consolidated financial statements have been examined by the shareholders' auditors,

---

[3] For most U.S. and Canadian companies, the chief executive officer is also the *chairman* of the board of directors. In contrast, in the United Kingdom these two functions should not be held by the same individual in order to ensure that there is a clear division of responsibility for running the company's business. In this regard, the board of directors is likely to be more independent of management if the two functions are held by different individuals. Separation of these two functions could potentially lead to more transparent communication of accounting information by the company. The recent emphasis on corporate governance in both the U.S. and Canada has led a number of Canadian companies to split the two functions. In fact, all the Canadian banks have done so in the past few years.

Ernst & Young, LLP, Chartered Accountants. The Auditors' Report outlines the nature of their examination and their opinion on the consolidated financial statements of the Company. The independent auditors have full and unrestricted access to the Audit Committee, with and without management present.

[signed]   [signed]
Bob Sartor   Richard Burnet, CA
Chief Executive Officer   Vice-President & Chief Financial Officer

The members of the *accounting staff* who actually prepare the details of the reports also have professional responsibility for the accuracy of this information, although their legal responsibility is smaller. Indeed, their future professional success depends heavily on their reputations for honesty and competence.

BOARD OF DIRECTORS (AUDIT COMMITTEE)

As FGL's corporate governance policy indicates, the **board of directors** (elected by the shareholders) is responsible for ensuring that processes are in place for maintaining the integrity of the company's accounting, financial statetment preparation, and financial reporting. The audit committee of the board, which must be composed of nonmanagement (independent) directors with financial knowledge, is responsible for hiring the company's independent auditors. They also meet separately with the auditors to discuss management's compliance with their financial reporting responsibilities.

The **BOARD OF DIRECTORS,** elected by the shareholders to represent their interests, is responsible for maintaining the integrity of the company's financial reports.

Recent changes to securities regulations have increased the burden of responsibility for accurate financial disclosure on company executives and external auditors. If any company listed on a stock exchange is found guilty of knowingly violating any disclosure regulation, not only the company can be sued, but also members of its board of directors and audit committee. If experts such as accountants or financial analysts who relied on the company's financial reports also issued disclosure that misrepresented the company, they too may be individually sued by users who seek to recover some or all of their financial losses, which may have resulted from relying on such misleading information.

AUDITORS

The provincial securities commissions require publicly traded companies to have their statements audited by professional independent accountants following generally accepted auditing standards (GAAS). Many privately owned companies also have their statements audited. By signing an **unqualified** (or **clean**) **audit opinion**, the audit firm assumes part of the financial responsibility for the fairness of the financial statements and related presentations.

UNQUALIFIED (CLEAN) AUDIT OPINION Auditors' statement that the financial statements are fair presentations in all material respects in conformity with GAAP.

AUDITORS' REPORT

To the Shareholders of The Forzani Group Ltd.

We have audited the consolidated balance sheets of The Forzani Group Ltd. as at January 28, 2007 and January 29, 2006 and the consolidated statements of operations and retained earnings and cash flows for the years then ended. These consolidated financial statements are the responsibility of the Company's management. Our responsibility is to express an opinion on these consolidated financial statements based on our audits.

REAL WORLD EXCERPT

The Forzani Group

ANNUAL REPORT

We conducted our audits in accordance with Canadian generally accepted auditing standards. Those standards required that we plan and perform an audit to obtain reasonable assurance whether the financial statements are free of material misstatement. An audit includes examining, on a test basis, evidence supporting the amounts and disclosures in the financial statements. An audit also assessing the accounting principles used and significant estimates made by management, as well as evaluating the overall financial statement presentation.

In our opinion, these consolidated financial statements present fairly, in all material respects, the financial position of the Company as at January 28, 2007 and January 29, 2006 and results of its operations and its cash flows for the years then ended in accordance with Canadian generally accepted accounting principles.

Calgary, Alberta
March 22, 2007
Ernst & Young, LLP
Chartered Accountants

This opinion, which adds credibility to the statements, is also often required by agreements with lenders and private investors.[4] Subjecting the company's statements to independent verification reduces the risk that the company's condition is misrepresented in the statements. As a consequence, rational investors and lenders should lower the rate of return (interest) they charge for providing capital.

Ernst & Young is currently FGL's auditor. KPMG, Deloitte & Touche, Ernst & Young, and PricewaterhouseCoopers are the largest audit firms that employ thousands of professional accountants in offices scattered throughout the world. They audit the great majority of publicly traded companies and many privately held companies. Some public companies and most private companies are audited by audit firms of smaller size. A list of well-known companies and their auditors at the time this chapter was written follows.

Company	Industry	Auditor
Honda Motor Co. Ltd. (Japan)	Automobiles	KPMG
Nortel Networks Corporation	Computer equipment	Deloitte & Touche
Singapore Airlines (Singapore)	Airline	Ernst & Young
Wendy's (United States)	Fast food	PricewaterhouseCoopers

Companies often hire financial managers from their audit firms because of their broad financial experience as well as their specific company knowledge gained during prior years' audits.

---

[4]In some cases, the auditor may not be satisfied that the company's financial statements are in compliance with GAAP. A *qualified* opinion would then be issued if the company's management is not willing to modify the financial reports as per the auditor's recommendation. If the exceptions to GAAP are very serious, then the auditor may issue an *adverse* opinion if the company's management cannot be persuaded to rectify the problems to avoid such an opinion. In extreme cases, the auditor may deny the issuance of an opinion if insufficient information is available to express an opinion. These latter types of opinions are rarely issued by auditors.

WHERE WERE THE AUDITORS?

Most professional accountants act in an honest and ethical manner, abiding by the codes of ethics developed by the professional accounting organizations. Nevertheless, a few accountants act in their own interest and disregard ethical conduct. They even become accomplices in spectacular fraud cases and subsequent company bankruptcies. For example, Enron Corp., a U.S. energy trading company, intentionally inflated its net earnings by hiding assets and related debts from 1997 to 2001. Throughout this period, the auditors of Arthur Andersen LLP, a global accounting services company with revenues in excess of $500 million, should have known that the financial statements issued by Enron's management were fraudulent.[5]

The collapse of Enron, the largest unexpected bankruptcy in U.S. history at that time, caused tremendous losses to the company's shareholders, creditors, employees, and other stakeholders. Furthermore, Enron's bankruptcy in December 2001 caused the collapse of Arthur Andersen. More than 300 clients left the firm within 90 days, taking with them $250 million of potential revenue to other audit firms. This audit failure led to calls for improved accountability by managers and auditors. This generated considerable discussion among securities regulators, financial analysts, investors, and creditors for stricter regulation of the accounting profession.

The Sarbanes-Oxley Act (SOX) approved by the U.S. Congress in July 2002 was a direct response to the Enron and other scandals that occurred in the United States. This law has set higher standards of responsibility on the officers and directors of publicly listed companies as well as auditors. Canadian companies that are listed on U.S. stock exchanges, must also comply with the SOX requirements.

INFORMATION INTERMEDIARIES: ANALYSTS AND INFORMATION SERVICES

Students often view the communication process between companies and financial statement users as a simple process of mailing the report to individual shareholders who read the report and then make investment decisions based on what they have learned. This simple picture is far from today's reality. Now most investors rely on sophisticated financial analysts and information services to gather and analyze information. Exhibit 6.2 summarizes this process.

Financial Analysts Financial analysts receive accounting reports and other information about the company from electronic information services. They also gather information through conversations with company executives and visits to company facilities and competitors. The results of their analyses are combined into analysts' reports.

Analysts' reports normally include forecasts of share price and future quarterly and annual earnings per share; a buy, sell, or hold recommendation for the company shares; and explanations for these judgments.[6] In making these **earnings forecasts**, the analysts rely heavily on their knowledge of how the accounting system translates business events into the numbers on a company's financial statements, which is the

EARNINGS FORECASTS are predictions of earnings for future accounting periods.

---

[5]An overview of the financial and reporting environment in the U.S. and the specific situation faced by Enron's executives and Arthur Anderson's auditors is provided by G. Cunningham and J. Harris, "Enron and Arthur Anderson: The Case of the Crooked E and the Fallen A," *Global Perspectives on Accounting Education*, Vol. 3, 2006, pp. 27–48.

[6]For further discussion of analysts' forecasts, see R. K. Bowen, A. K. Davis, and D. A. Matsumuto, "Do Conference Calls Affect Analysts' Forecasts?" *The Accounting Review*, April 2002, pp. 387–404, and M. Earnes, S. Glover, and J. Kennedy, "The Association between Trading Recommendations and Analysts' Earnings Forecasts," *Journal of Accounting Research*, 2003, 40, 1, pp. 85–104.

EXHIBIT **6.2**

Using Financial Reports

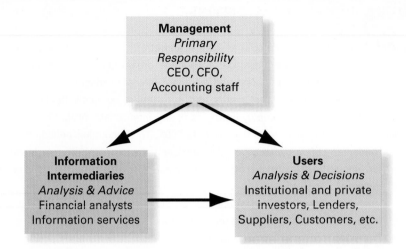

subject matter of this text. Individual analysts often specialize in particular industries (such as sporting goods or energy companies). Analysts are regularly evaluated based on the accuracy of their forecasts, as well as the profitability of their stock picks.[7]

Analysts often work in the research departments of brokerage and investment banking houses such as RBC Dominion Securities, mutual fund companies such as the Investors Group, and investment advisory services such as Standard & Poor's, which sell their advice to others. Through their reports and recommendations, analysts transfer their knowledge of accounting, the company, and the industry to others who lack this expertise. Many believe that decisions made based on analysts' advice cause stock market prices to react quickly to information in financial statements. A quick, unbiased reaction to information is called *market efficiency* in finance. It is highly unlikely that unsophisticated investors can glean more information from financial statements than the sophisticated analysts have already learned. Careful analysis does not lead all analysts to the same conclusions, however. These differences of opinion are reflected in the following earnings (per share) forecasts and stock recommendations made by a number of analysts at the time of writing this chapter.

REAL WORLD EXCERPT

Finance.yahoo.com

THE FORZANI GROUP LTD. EARNINGS FORECASTS		
	For fiscal 2007	For fiscal 2008
Average forecast	$0.97	$1.20
Lowest forecast	0.89	1.01
Highest forecast	1.04	1.31
Number of analysts	11	10

Analysts make recommendations to buy, hold, or sell a company's shares based on their earnings forecasts. In the case of FGL, one analyst recommended "strong buy," eight analysts recommended "buy," and three analysts recommended "hold" at the time of writing this chapter.

In general, financial analysts tend to make optimistic earnings forecasts in order to maintain a good relationship with the company's management. The reason is that managers provide analysts with vital information for their analysis. Optimistic earnings

---

[7]See M. B. Mikhail, B. R. Walther, and R. H. Willis, "Does Forecast Accuracy Matter to Security Analysts?" *The Accounting Review*, April 1999, pp. 185–200.

forecasts, however, put additional pressure on management to meet and even exceed analysts' forecasts in order to please investors. The drive to meet analysts' earnings expectations has led the management of some companies to adopt accounting policies that result in premature recognition of revenue and/or deferral of expenses in order to increase reported earnings.

IT PAYS TO BE A WARY INVESTOR	A QUESTION OF ETHICS

Occasional unethical behaviour on the part of financial analysts and investment advisers suggest that savvy investors should apply a healthy dose of skepticism along with their accounting knowledge when reading or listening to investment advice. Alleged ethical lapses, questionable business practices, and illegal activity by representatives of some of the largest, most highly respected brokerage and investment banking houses occasionally make the news. These activities include the rigging of prices in securities auctions, excess trading of customers' accounts to generate higher commissions, insider trading, the sale of securities without full disclosure of their risks, issuance of flattering research recommendations, and executing trades for some customers at more advantageous prices than others. Most analysts, brokers, and investment bankers act in an honest and ethical fashion; however, they earn profits by charging commissions on securities transactions. When brokers let their need to earn commissions cloud their investment advice, this can lead to questionable or even unethical behaviour.

The information services discussed in the next section allow investors to gather their own information about the company and to monitor the recommendations of a variety of analysts.

Information Services Canadian companies actually can file financial statements and other securities-related forms electronically with SEDAR (System for Electronic Document Analysis and Retrieval), which is the official site for the filing of documents by public companies as required by securities laws in Canada.[8] SEDAR is currently a free service available on the Web at **www.sedar.com**.[9] Many companies also provide access to their financial statements and other information over the Web. FGL's financial information is available at **www.forzanigroup.com**.

Financial analysts and other sophisticated users obtain much of the information they use from the wide variety of commercial online information services. Services such as Lexis-Nexis (**www.lexisnexis.com**), Compustat (**www.compustat.com**), and CanWest Interactive Inc. (**www.fpinfomart.ca**) provide broad access to financial statements and related news information. They also allow users to search the database by keywords, including various financial statement terms.

More general information services include Factiva (**www.factiva.com**) and Bloomberg (**www.bloomberg.com**), as well as the financial sections of national newspapers such as *The Globe and Mail* and *National Post*. Factiva provides access to news stories about companies, and company press releases, including the initial announcements of annual and quarterly financial results. The Bloomberg service also provides the ability to combine these sources of information in sophisticated analyses.

A growing number of other resources offer a mixture of free and fee-based information on many companies on the Web. These include **www.investor.reuters.com**, **www.hoovers.com**, and **finance.yahoo.com**.

---

[8] Canadian companies that have shares traded on U.S. stock exchanges can file SEC forms electronically with EDGAR (Electronic Data Gathering and Retrieval) sponsored by the SEC.

[9] To look at SEDAR, just type the address on your Web browser. Select French or English, depending on your preference, then select Company Profiles followed by the letter of the alphabet that corresponds to the first letter of the company's name. You will then see a list of companies that includes the selected company. Many of the financial statement examples used in this book were downloaded from this Web site.

| FINANCIAL ANALYSIS | INFORMATION SERVICES: USES IN MARKETING, CLASSWORK, AND JOB SEARCHES |

Information services have become the primary tool used not only by sophisticated analysts but also by marketing strategists to analyze competing firms. Sales representatives also use the services to analyze potential customers' needs and creditworthiness. Growing, creditworthy companies are the most profitable targets for the sales representative's efforts.

Information services are an important source of information to students for their term papers and job searches. Potential employers expect top job applicants to demonstrate knowledge about their company during an interview. To learn more about electronic information services, contact the business or reference librarian at your college or university library or explore some of the preceding Websites.

USERS: INSTITUTIONAL AND PRIVATE INVESTORS, CREDITORS, AND OTHERS

INSTITUTIONAL INVESTORS are managers of pension funds, mutual funds, endowment funds, and other funds that invest on behalf of others.

Institutional investors include private pension funds (associated with unions and employees of specific companies); public pension funds (for provincial and municipal employees); mutual funds; and endowment, charitable foundation, and trust funds (such as the endowment of your college or university). These institutional shareholders usually employ their own analysts who also rely on the information intermediaries just discussed. Institutional shareholders control the majority of publicly traded shares of Canadian companies. For example, at the time of writing this book, institutional investors owned approximately 27 percent of FGL's outstanding shares.

PRIVATE INVESTORS include individuals who purchase shares in companies.

Private investors include large individual investors such as John Forzani and some of the company's directors, as well as small retail investors who, like most individuals, buy a small number of shares of publicly traded companies through brokers such as BMO Nesbitt Burns. Retail investors normally lack the expertise to understand financial statements and the resources to gather data efficiently. As a consequence, they often rely on the advice of information intermediaries or turn their money over to the management of mutual and pension funds (institutional investors).

LENDERS (CREDITORS) include suppliers and financial institutions that lend money to companies.

Lenders, or **creditors**, include suppliers, banks, commercial credit companies, and other financial institutions that lend money to companies. Lending officers and financial analysts in these organizations use these same public sources of information. In addition, when companies borrow money from financial institutions, they often agree to provide additional financial information (e.g., monthly statements) as part of the lending contract. Lenders are often the primary external user group for financial statements of private companies. Institutional and private investors also become creditors when they buy a company's publicly traded bonds and debentures.[10]

Financial statements play an important role in the relationships between customers and suppliers. Customers evaluate the financial health of suppliers to determine whether they will be able to provide a reliable, up-to-date source of supply. Suppliers evaluate their customers to estimate their future needs and ability to pay their debts to the suppliers. Competitors also attempt to learn useful information about a company from its statements. The potential loss of competitive advantage is one of the costs to the preparer of public financial disclosures. Accounting regulators consider these costs as well as the direct costs of preparation when they require new disclosures.

---

[10]*Debentures* are debt securities that are not secured with specific collateral (no specific assets are pledged as security for the debt). *Bonds* normally are secured by specific collateral such as investments in shares of other companies. Chapter 11 provides more details about bonds and debentures.

CONFLICTING INTERESTS OF MANAGERS, SHAREHOLDERS, AND CREDITORS

A QUESTION OF ETHICS

The economic interests of managers, shareholders, and creditors often differ. For example, paying dividends to shareholders benefits the shareholders but leaves less money available to pay creditors. Refurnishing the offices occupied by managers benefits them but leaves less money to pay dividends. Ethical conduct and mutual trust play a major role in balancing these differing interests.

Accounting and financial statements also play a major role in enforcing these relationships of trust. Compliance with agreements (contracts) between managers and shareholders and between shareholders and creditors are monitored with financial statement data.*

*Research that examines the use of accounting in contracting is called *agency theory*.

SELF-STUDY **QUIZ 6-1**

Match the players involved in the accounting communication process with their roles or the guiding principles for communicating information with their definitions.

1. Relevant information
2. CEO and CFO
3. Financial analyst
4. External auditor
5. Cost–benefit constraint

a. Management primarily responsible for accounting information.

b. An independent party that provides an opinion that financial statements are presented fairly in accordance to GAAP.

c. Information that influences users' decisions.

d. Only information that provides benefits in excess of costs should be reported.

e. An individual who analyzes financial information and provides advice.

After you complete the quiz, check your answers with those on page 317.

THE DISCLOSURE PROCESS

As noted in our discussion of information services and information intermediaries, the accounting communication process includes more steps and participants than one would envision in a world in which annual and quarterly reports are simply mailed to shareholders.

PRESS RELEASES

To provide timely information to external users and to limit the possibility of selective leakage of information, FGL and most public companies announce quarterly and annual earnings through a **press release** as soon as the audited annual figures (or reviewed quarterly figures) are available. FGL normally issues its earnings press releases within five weeks of the end of the accounting period. The announcements are sent electronically to the major print and electronic news services, which make them immediately available to subscribers. An excerpt of a quarterly press release for FGL is reprinted in Exhibit 6.3. It includes key financial figures and an invitation to interested parties to access a live webcast concerning the company's quarterly results. Attached to the release are condensed income statements and balance sheets (unaudited) that are included in the formal quarterly report to shareholders distributed after the press release.

Press releases related to annual earnings and quarterly earnings often precede the issuance of the quarterly or annual report by 15 to 45 days. This time is necessary to prepare the additional detail and to print and distribute those reports.

Many companies, including FGL, follow these press releases with a conference call at which senior managers answer questions about the quarterly results from analysts. These calls are open to the investing public. Listening to these recordings is a good way to learn about a company's business strategy and its expectations for the future, as well as key factors that analysts consider when they evaluate a company.

> **■ LEARNING OBJECTIVE 2**
>
> Identify the steps in the accounting communication process, including the issuance of press releases, annual reports, quarterly reports, and documents filed with securities commissions, as well as the guiding principles in communicating useful information.

A **PRESS RELEASE** is a written public news announcement normally distributed to major news services.

EXHIBIT **6.3**

Earnings Press Release for The
Forzani Group Ltd.

REAL WORLD EXCERPT

The Forzani Group

PRESS RELEASE

FGL ANNOUNCES SECOND QUARTER RESULTS
SEPT. 1, 2006—07:00 ET

CALGARY, ALBERTA—(CCNMatthews—Sept. 1, 2006)—The Forzani Group Ltd. (TSX: FGL), Canada's largest retailer of sporting goods, today reported fiscal 2007 second quarter results for the 13 weeks ended July 30, 2006.

For the Second Quarter:

Earnings and Earnings Per Share:

Net earnings for the second quarter were $1.9 million, or $0.06 per share, compared to a loss in the prior year's second quarter of $2.3 million, or $0.07 per share. The net earnings were $0.07 before a $0.01 per share, non-recurring, non-cash charge to the Company's future income tax expense resulting from Federal and Provincial income tax rate changes enacted during the quarter. While this change in rates increased the Company's effective tax rate in the second quarter, due to a requirement to recognize the impact of changes in the period in which they occur, it will lower the Company's effective tax rate in future years.

. . .

Sales:

Retail system sales for the quarter were $337.9 million, an increase of $32.8 million, or 10.8% from the comparable 13-week sales of $305.1 million. The increase was due to continued, strong contributions from franchise and corporate stores and the addition, on January 31, 2006, of The Fitness Source Inc. ("Fitness Source"). Exclusive of the acquisition of Fitness Source, retail system sales increased $29.1 million, or 9.5%.

Same store sales in corporate locations were up 5.4% and increased 6.9% in franchise locations, over the fiscal 2006 second quarter, for an overall same store sales increase of 6.0%.

Revenue, consisting of corporate store sales, wholesale sales, service income, equipment rentals, franchise fees and franchise royalties, was $284.0 million, up $40.4 million, or 16.6% over the comparable period last year.

. . .

In conjunction with this release, the Company invites you to listen to its teleconference call / audio web cast that will take place Friday, September 1, 2006 at 10:00 a.m. (Eastern Time).

Teleconference Call: To listen to the teleconference call, please dial the following number approximately five minutes prior to commencement:

Within Toronto: 416-644-3414

Outside Toronto: 800-796-7558

. . .

FOR FURTHER INFORMATION PLEASE CONTACT:

The Forzani Group Ltd., Robert Sartor, C.A., Chief Executive Officer, (403) 717-1342
Website: www.forzanigroup.com

For actively traded shares such as those of FGL, most of the stock market reaction (share price increases and decreases from investor trading) to the news in the press release usually occurs quickly. Recall that a number of analysts follow FGL and regularly predict the company's earnings. When the actual earnings are published, the market reacts *not* to the amount of earnings but to *unexpected earnings*, the difference between actual earnings and expected earnings. For example, FGL's share price decreased slightly from $16.60 to $15.77 on the day of the press release, which implies that the fiscal 2007 second-quarter earnings did not meet analysts' expectations.

The following excerpt from a recent article in *Harvard Business Review* points out the growing importance of meeting or beating the average of analysts' earnings estimates:

REAL WORLD EXCERPT

Harvard Business Review

THE EARNINGS GAME: EVERYONE PLAYS, NOBODY WINS

Quarterly earnings numbers dominate the decisions of executives, analysts, investors, and auditors . . . meeting analysts' expectations that earnings will rise in a smooth, steady, unbroken line has become, at many corporations, a game whose imperatives override even the imperative to deliver the highest possible return to shareholders.

Source: *Harvard Business Review*, June 2001, p. 65.

Companies such as FGL issue press releases concerning other important events including announcement of new services or acquisition of new stores.

ANNUAL REPORTS

For privately held companies, *annual reports* are relatively simple documents photocopied on white paper. They normally include the following:

1. Four basic financial statements: income statement, balance sheet, statement of retained earnings, and cash flow statement.

2. Related notes (footnotes).

3. Report of independent accountants (auditor's opinion).

The annual reports of public companies are significantly more elaborate, both because of additional reporting requirements imposed on these companies by securities commissions and because many companies use their annual reports as public relations tools to communicate non-accounting information to shareholders, customers, the press, and others.

The annual reports of public companies are normally split into two sections: the first, "non-financial," section usually includes a letter to shareholders from the chairman and CEO; descriptions of the company's management philosophy, products, its successes (and occasionally its failures); and exciting prospects and challenges for the future. Beautiful photographs of products, facilities, and personnel often are included. The second, "financial," section includes the core of the report. Securities regulators set minimum disclosure standards for the financial section of the annual reports of public companies. The principal components of the financial section include:

1. Summarized financial data for a 5- or 10-year period.

2. Management's Discussion and Analysis of financial condition and results of operations.

3. The basic financial statements.[11]

4. Notes (Footnotes).

5. Report of Independent Accountants (Auditor's Opinion) and sometimes the Report of Management Responsibility.

6. Recent stock price information.

7. Summaries of the unaudited quarterly financial data (described later).

8. Lists of directors and officers of the company and relevant addresses.

---

[11]The Canadian Accounting Standards Board has recently approved *CICA Handbook* section 1530, "Comprehensive Income," which requires companies to prepare a new Statement of Comprehensive Income. This statement would include all changes in equity during a period except those resulting from investments by shareholders and distributions to shareholders. An introduction to this new statement is available on the Online Learning Centre Web site at **www.mcgrawhill.ca/olc/libby/student/resources**.

Length of MD&A Section	Number of Companies
1–5 pages	1
6–10	15
11–15	23
16–20	56
21–25	25
26 or more pages	79

The order of these components varies.

Most of these components except for Management's Discussion and Analysis (MD&A) have been discussed in earlier chapters. This component includes management's discussion and explanation of key figures in the financial statements and risks the company faces in the future. The MD&A section contains important non-financial and strategic information to help users interpret the financial statements. Many companies devote a sizeable portion of their annual reports to the MD&A section, as the chart in the margin shows.[12] For example, FGL devoted 11 pages of its 2006 annual report for a detailed analysis of its various sources of revenue and related expenses for that year. In addition, management provided non-financial information enabling readers to compare the number of stores and square footage in various regions of Canada, which informs users about the geographic location of the company's operations. FGL's MD&A section also includes a review of the company's liquidity, capital resources, and contractual obligations. A complete annual report from Van Houtte Inc., which includes all of these sections, is reprinted in Appendix B of this textbook. As noted earlier, many companies make their annual reports available on the Web.

QUARTERLY REPORTS

Quarterly reports normally begin with a short letter to shareholders. This is followed by a condensed income statement for the quarter, which often shows less detail than the annual income statement, and a condensed balance sheet dated at the end of the quarter (e.g., March 31 for the first quarter). These condensed financial statements are not audited and so are marked *unaudited*. Often, the cash flow statement, statement of retained earnings, and some notes to the financial statements are omitted. Private companies also normally prepare quarterly reports for lenders. FGL's quarterly reports are issued about five weeks after the end of each quarter.

REPORTS TO SECURITIES COMMISSIONS

Public companies must also file periodic reports with the OSC and other provincial securities commissions. These reports include the annual report, quarterly reports, an annual information form, and an information circular.

The annual information form provides a more detailed description of the business, including such items as the company's corporate structure, the industry in which it operates, the products and services it offers, product and project development, sales and marketing, manufacturing, and competition. The form also lists the properties owned and leased by the company, and significant contracts that the company has signed.

The information circular is a legal document that is forwarded to the company's shareholders prior to the annual general or special meeting of shareholders. It provides information about the items that the shareholders will be asked to consider and vote on during the meeting, including election of new directors, appointment of independent auditors, and other matters of a legal nature. The circular also provides details of the monetary compensation of key management personnel.

In addition to these periodic reports, companies file other types of reports as the need arises. These include a short-form prospectus that provides details of the equity and/or debt securities that they plan to issue to investors, and press releases concerning new developments. The SEDAR Web site **www.sedar.com** lists all of the reports, documents, and news items that FGL and other corporations have filed.[13]

---

[12]C. Byrd, J. Chen, and J. Smith, *Financial Reporting in Canada 2005*. Toronto: Canadian Institute of Chartered Accountants, 2005, p. 52.

[13]U.S., Canadian, and international companies that have shares trading on U.S. securities exchange markets are required to file a number of reports with the SEC. These include Form 10-K, which provides a detailed description of the business, and more detailed schedules concerning various figures reported in the annual financial statements, and Form 10-Q, which is essentially a quarterly report to shareholders.

GUIDING PRINCIPLES FOR COMMUNICATING USEFUL INFORMATION

Information presented in financial reports is useful if it makes a difference in the context of making a decision. Several qualitative characteristics determine the usefulness of accounting information for decision making.[14] These were introduced in Chapter 2 (Exhibit 2.1) and are presented in more detail in Exhibit 6.4.

First of all, information cannot be useful if it is not properly understood. Users of accounting information are assumed to have a reasonable understanding of business and economic activities and accounting, and be willing to study the information with reasonable diligence.[15]

Second, information is useful for decision making if it is both relevant and reliable. **Relevant information** is of little value if it is not reliable, and reliable information is useless if it is not relevant for a specific decision context.

RELEVANT INFORMATION can influence a decision; it is timely and has predictive and/or feedback value.

Relevance Information disclosed in financial statements is relevant if it can influence users' decisions by helping them assess the impact of past activities and/or predict future events. For example, the various elements of an income statement have predictive value if they help users predict future levels of net income or its subcomponents, such as operating income. The *predictive value* of the income statement is enhanced if non-recurring items are presented separately on a multiple-step income statement, because these items are transient in nature. Similarly, information presented on the income statement has *feedback value* if it confirms prior expectations about earnings.

Information that is not available to users in a timely manner loses its relevance because it would not be considered in making decisions. *Timeliness* of accounting information enhances both its predictive and feedback values. The relevance of accounting information for decision making declines as time passes. For this reason, companies produce quarterly reports and issue press releases to convey timely information to investors, creditors, and other user groups.

EXHIBIT **6.4**

Qualitative Characteristics of Accounting Information

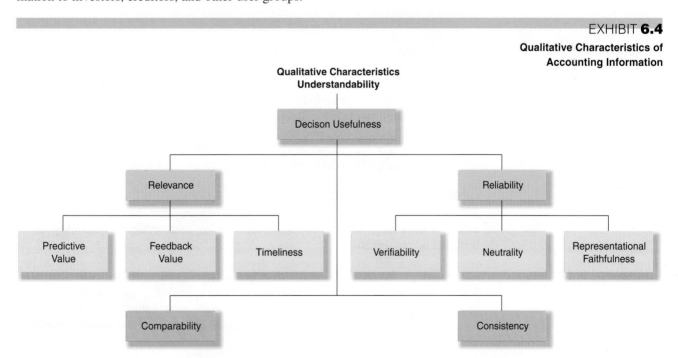

---

[14]Section 1000 "Financial Statement Concepts" of the *CICA Handbook* describes these characteristics.

[15]To help users better understand the contents of its financial reports, IBM includes on its Web site a glossary of terms and provides basic explanations of the information contained in financial statements (**www.ibm.com/investor/tools/financials.phtml**).

RELIABLE INFORMATION
is verifiable, unbiased, and
accurate.

Reliability   Information presented in financial statements is considered **reliable information** when it is verifiable, unbiased, and accurate. *Verifiability, neutrality,* and *representational faithfulness* characterize the reliability of accounting information. Accounting information is verifiable if independent accountants can agree on the nature and amount of the transaction. For example, the historical cost of a piece of land that is reported on FGL's balance sheet on January 29, 2006 is usually highly verifiable. The cost of acquisition is based on the purchase price and related costs that result from actual exchanges with external parties. However, the market value of the land at that date is a subjective estimate that reflects the appraiser's past experience. It is not verifiable because it is not based on an exchange transaction. If FGL is considering the sale of land, its market value would be relevant for that decision even though it is less reliable than the land's historical cost.

Neutrality relates to the measurement and presentation of information. The usefulness of accounting information is enhanced when it is neutral; that is, free from bias in its measurement and presentation. Bias in measurement occurs when the item being measured is consistently understated or overstated. For example, a consistent understatement of amortization expense leads to a biased higher net income. In this context, the development of accounting standards for measurement and reporting of transaction effects should not result in favouring one group of users over others. For example, the measurement and reporting of liabilities should not result in consistent underreporting of liabilities on the balance sheet because this would favour owners over creditors, and may influence investment and credit decisions of financial statement users.

Information provided in financial statements should reflect the substance of the underlying transactions. For instance, the inventory account of a company that sells computer equipment would include items that are held for sale to customers. If inventory included also desktop and laptop computers used by employees in their daily work, then the inventory balance does not faithfully represent the cost of goods available for sale. Similarly, unearned revenue that is recognized prematurely as revenue for the period overstates the amount of revenue reported on the income statement, causing a lack of representational faithfulness.

COMPARABILITY of
accounting information across
businesses is enhanced when
similar accounting methods
have been applied.

**CONSISTENT
INFORMATION** can be
compared over time because
similar accounting methods
have been applied.

Comparability and Consistency   **Comparability** of accounting information enables users to identify similarities and discrepancies between two sets of financial reports produced by two different companies. This quality is also important when comparing information provided by the same company over time.

The comparability of financial reports is enhanced if there is **consistent information** available by using the same accounting methods over time. Changes in accounting methods reduce the comparability of information and necessitate disclosure of the effects of the change in order to maintain comparability.

CONSTRAINTS OF ACCOUNTING MEASUREMENT

Accurate interpretation of financial statements requires that the statement reader be aware of three important constraints of accounting measurement: materiality, cost–benefit, and conservatism.

Materiality   Items and amounts that are of low significance must be accounted for, but they do not have to conform precisely to specified accounting guidelines or be separately reported if they would not influence reasonable decisions. Accountants usually designate such items and amounts as *immaterial*. Determining **material amounts** is often very subjective.

MATERIAL AMOUNTS are
amounts that are large enough
to influence a user's decision.

Cost–Benefit   Companies produce and disseminate accounting information to users with the expectation that the benefits to users from using such information exceed the cost of producing it. The perceived benefits of new information relate to its usefulness in decision making. Such benefits may be difficult to measure, but the costs of producing additional information can be estimated with reasonable accuracy. When standards setters, like the Accounting Standards Board, require companies to disclose specific information, known as *mandatory* disclosure, they would have determined implicitly that the benefits to users exceed the costs that the company will incur to produce the information. For example, a recently introduced regulation by the Canadian Securities Administrators concerning internal control over financial reporting[16] imposed additional costs on companies to evaluate the effectiveness of their internal control procedures in order to discourage corporate fraud by managers. These additional expenditures are expected to lead to improvements in internal control procedures that would curb the misappropriation of assets by managers and other employees. The perceived benefits of this new regulation are increased reliability and decision usefulness of the accounting information disclosed in financial statements. While the cost of improving internal control procedures can be estimated, the related benefits to users of financial statements may be difficult to measure.

In other cases, the company's managers may decide that *voluntary* disclosure of information about specific aspects of the company's operations would be beneficial to users. In such cases, the costs of disclosure should not exceed the expected benefits. In this context, the **cost–benefit constraint** plays an important role in determining whether new information should be produced and communicated to users.

The **COST–BENEFIT CONSTRAINT** suggests that information should be produced only if the perceived benefits of increased decision usefulness exceed the expected costs of providing that information.

Conservatism   **Conservatism** requires that special care be taken to avoid (1) overstating assets and revenues and (2) understating liabilities and expenses. Users of financial statements often want to know about possible sources of trouble for the company. For example, creditors need to know how secure their investments will be if the company's fortunes deteriorate, but they may not be interested in whether the company might do exceptionally well. They care more about the downside risk than the upside potential. For this reason, financial statements that show assets at historical cost, but reduce these amounts when current values are significantly lower, help satisfy the needs of creditors. This lower-of-cost-or-market guideline attempts to offset managers' natural optimism about their business operations, which sometimes creeps into the financial reports that they prepare. More companies have perished through excessive optimism than through excessive caution.

CONSERVATISM suggests that care should be taken not to overstate assets and revenues or understate liabilities and expenses.

INTERNATIONAL ACCOUNTING STANDARDS BOARD AND GLOBAL DIFFERENCES IN ACCOUNTING STANDARDS

INTERNATIONAL **PERSPECTIVE**

Financial accounting standards and disclosure requirements are set by national regulatory agencies and standard-setting bodies. Many countries have already adopted international financial reporting standards (IFRS) issued by the International Accounting Standards Board (IASB). IFRS are similar to Canadian GAAP, but there are several important differences. Two areas of differences at the time of writing this chapter are presented below, along with the chapter in which these issues are addressed:

Difference	Canadian GAAP	IFRS	Chapter
Extraordinary items	Permitted	Prohibited	3
Basis of Property, plant, and equipment	Historical cost	Fair value or historical cost	9

[16]Status of Proposed MI52-111 Reporting on Internal Control over Financial Reporting and Proposed Amended and Restated MI52-109 Certification of Disclosure in Issuers' Annual and Interim Filings, Canadian Securities Administrators, Notice 52-313, March 10, 2006, as posted on CSA's Web site: **www.csa-acvm.ca**, accessed on November 5, 2006.

A CLOSER LOOK AT FINANCIAL STATEMENTS AND NOTES

■ **LEARNING OBJECTIVE 3**

Recognize the different financial statement and disclosure formats used by companies in practice.

To make financial statements more useful to investors, creditors, and analysts, specific *classifications* of information are included in the statements. Various classifications are used in practice. You should not be confused when you notice different formats used by different companies. You will find that each format is consistent with the principles discussed in this text.

OVERVIEW OF FORZANI'S FINANCIAL STATEMENTS

Exhibits 6.5, 6.6, and 6.7 show the financial statements of FGL for fiscal year 2006.

EXHIBIT **6.5**

Balance Sheet of The Forzani Group Ltd.

REAL WORLD EXCERPT

The Forzani Group

ANNUAL REPORT

THE FORZANI GROUP LTD.
Consolidated Balance Sheets
(in thousands)

As at	January 28, 2007	January 29, 2006
ASSETS		
Current		
Cash	$ 22,758	$ 19,266
Accounts receivable	65,543	68,927
Inventory	302,207	278,002
Prepaid expenses	2,688	2,647
	393,196	368,842
Capital assets (Note 3)	191,146	193,594
Goodwill and other intangibles (Note 4)	90,238	75,805
Other assets (Note 5)	8,930	10,080
Future income tax asset (Note 9)	—	4,885
	$683,510	$653,206
LIABILITIES		
Current		
Accounts payable and accrued liabilities	$230,977	$244,293
Current portion of long-term debt (Note 6)	2,082	5,135
	233,059	249,428
Long-term debt (Note 6)	58,303	58,805
Deferred lease inducements	58,543	62,883
Deferred rent liability	5,737	3,810
Future income tax liability (Note 9)	55	—
	355,697	374,926
SHAREHOLDER'S EQUITY		
Share capital (Note 8)	148,424	138,131
Contributed surplus	8,294	4,271
Retained earnings	171,095	135,878
	327,813	278,280
	$683,510	$653,206

See accompanying to the consolidated financial statements.

Approved on behalf of the Board:

[signed]
Roman Doroniuk, CA

[signed]
John M. Forzani

Source: FGL, Annual Report 2007, p. 46.

EXHIBIT **6.6**

Income Statement and
Statement of Retained Earnings
of The Forzani Group Ltd.

REAL WORLD EXCERPT

The Forzani Group

ANNUAL REPORT

THE FORZANI GROUP LTD.
Consolidated Statements of Operations and Retained Earnings
(in thousands, except share data)

	For the 52 weeks ended January 28, 2007	For the 52 weeks ended January 29, 2006
Revenue		
Retail	$ 925,443	$ 856,149
Wholesale	338,512	273,255
	1,263,955	1,129,404
Cost of sale	812,363	746,313
Gross margin	451,592	383,091
Operating and administrative expenses		
Store operating	236,870	225,218
General and administrative	107,462	88,720
	344,332	313,938
Operating earnings before undernoted items	107,260	69,153
Amortization	43,410	41,343
Interest	7,354	6,145
	50,764	47,488
Earnings before income taxes	56,496	21,665
Provision for income taxes (Note 9)		
Current	19,897	8,784
Future	1,382	(876)
	21,279	7,908
Net earnings	35,217	13,757
Retained earnings, opening	135,878	122,121
Retained earnings, closing	$ 171,095	$ 135,878
Earnings per share (note 8(c))	$ 1.06	$ 0.42
Diluted earnings per share (note 8(c))	$ 1.04	$ 0.42

See accompanying notes to the consolidated financial statements.

EXHIBIT **6.7**

Cash Flow Statement of
The Forzani Group Ltd.

REAL WORLD EXCERPT

The Forzani Group

ANNUAL REPORT

THE FORZANI GROUP LTD.
Consolidated Statements of Cash Flows
(in thousands)

	For the 52 weeks ended January 28, 2007	For the 52 weeks ended January 29, 2006
Cash provided by (used in) operating activities		
Net earnings	$ 35,217	$ 13,757
Items not involving cash		
Amortization	43,410	41,343
Amortization of deferred finance charges	580	637
Amortization of deferred lease inducements	(10,549)	(10,661)
Rent expense (Note 7)	2,659	2,281
Stock-based compensation (Note 8(d))	4,730	1,356
Future income tax expense	1,382	(876)
	77,429	47,837
Changes in non-cash elements of working capital (Note 7)	(28,016)	(1,979)
	49,413	45,858
		(continued)

Cash provided by (used in) financing activities		
Net proceeds from issuance of share capital	**9,586**	320
Increase in long-term debt	**(7,429)**	23,573
Debt assumed on acquisition (Note 14)	**(105)**	(17,922)
Proceeds from deferred lease inducements	**6,149**	9,368
	8,201	15,339
Changes in non-cash elements of financing activities (Note 7)	**(927)**	(2,450)
	7,274	12,889
Cash (used in) investing activities		
Net addition of capital assets	**(37,997)**	(50,837)
Net addition of other assets	**(538)**	(3,751)
Acquisition of wholly-owned subsidiaries (Note 14)	**(15,448)**	(12,428)
	(53,983)	(67,016)
Changes in non-cash elements of investing activities (Note 7)	**788**	1,517
	(53,195)	(65,499)
Increase (decrease) in cash	**3,492**	(6,752)
Net cash position, opening	**19,266**	26,018
Net cash position, closing	**$ 22,758**	$ 19,266

See accompanying notes to the consolidated financial statements.

As we have seen in previous chapters, the items presented in these statements are classified in order to provide useful information to users. The assets and liabilities on FGL's balance sheet are split between current and non-current portions. Also, the income statement includes a number of sections and subtotals to aid the user in identifying the company's operating income for the year and to highlight the effect of other items on net income. These classifications will play a major role in our discussions of ratio analysis in later chapters.

The presentation of information in FGL's income statement reflects the nature of the company's business operations. Most manufacturing and merchandising companies use the following basic structure.

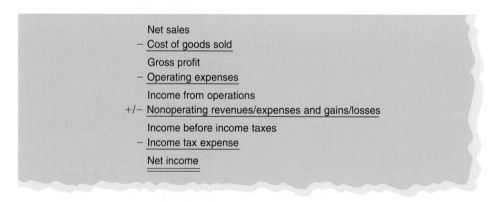

FGL's income statement follows this structure except that amortization expense is shown separately from other operating expenses. This allows FGL's management to highlight the amount of earnings before interest, tax, depreciation, and amortization (known as EBITDA) as a measure of operating performance. FGL has also combined its income statement with the statement of retained earnings instead of presenting two separate, yet related statements.

DIFFERENT EARNINGS FOR DIFFERENT PURPOSES

FINANCIAL
ANALYSIS

In recent years, many companies reported different measures of *earnings* in addition to net income as determined by GAAP. When companies report non-GAAP measures of earnings, they divert investors' attention away from the financial results of continuing operations.

For example, in discussing its annual and quarterly results of operations, FGL's management focuses investors' and analysts' attention on revenues, net income, and EBITA (earnings before interest, income taxes, and amortization). Comparison of the revenue, net income, and EBITA for the years 2003–2006 shows clearly why investors and analysts should be cautious about interpreting this measure of income (amounts in millions of dollars).

	2006	2005	2004	2003
Revenue	$1,129.4	$985.1	$968.1	$923.8
EBITA	69.2	76.5	82.3	82.4
Net income	13.8	21.5	28.1	30.0

While revenue increased by 22 percent over the four-year period, EBITA decreased by 16 percent. However, net income experienced a much steeper decrease of 54 percent over the same period.

Lastly, FGL's cash flow statement shows the sources and uses of cash that resulted from its operating, investing, and financing activities during the past two fiscal years. Such a classification of the cash flows is important, especially those resulting from operating activities. Companies can not survive for a long time without generating positive cash flows from their operations.

The cash flows from operating activities can be reported using either the ***direct*** or ***indirect*** method, as illustrated in Chapter 5. For FGL, the first section is reported using the indirect method, which presents a reconciliation of net income on an accrual basis to cash flows from operations.

OPERATING ACTIVITIES (INDIRECT METHOD)

FOCUS ON
CASH FLOWS

The Operating Activities section prepared using the indirect method helps the analyst understand the ***causes of differences*** between a company's net income and its cash flows. Net income and cash flows from operating activities can be quite different. Remember that the income statement is prepared under the accrual concept. Revenues are recorded when earned without regard to when the related cash flow occurs. Likewise, expenses are matched with revenues and recorded in the same period without regard to when the related cash flows occur.

In the indirect method, the Operating Activities section starts with net income computed under the accrual concept and then eliminates noncash items leaving cash flows from operating activities:

Net income

+/− Adjustments for noncash items

Cash provided by operating acivities

The items listed between net income and cash flow from operations identify the sources of the difference. For example, since no cash is paid during the current period for FGL's amortization expense of $41,410, this amount is added back in the conversion process. Similarly, increases and decreases in current assets and liabilities (also known as noncash elements of working capital) also account for some of the difference between net income and cash flow from operations. As we cover different portions of the income statement and the balance sheet in more detail in Chapters 7 to 12, we will also review the relevant sections of the cash flow statement that is covered in Chapter 5.

FGL's financial statements are condensed reports where each financial statement item is a combination of a number of accounts used in the company's accounting system. While the amounts reported on the various financial statements provide important information, users require additional details to facilitate their analysis. Such details are typically disclosed in notes that follow the financial statements.

NOTES TO FINANCIAL STATEMENTS

Standards-setting organizations, like the Canadian Accounting Standard Board, and securities commissions, such as the Ontario Securities Commission, require public companies to provide a minimum set of detailed information to assist the users of financial statements in making informed investment and credit decisions. In addition, companies may provide other information voluntarily if management believes that such information will reflect positively on the company. In general, management refrains from disclosing information that may have a negative effect on the company's future profitability and financial condition—hence the need for a minimum set of disclosures that are typically provided in notes to financial statements. FGL included 19 notes to its 2006 financial statements covering both mandatory and voluntary disclosures.

Notes to financial statements include three types of information:

1. Description of the key accounting policies (rules) applied to the company's statements.

2. Additional details supporting reported amounts in the financial statements.

3. Relevant financial information not disclosed in the statements.

Excerpts from FGL's notes are illustrated below along with our discussion of selected elements of the company's financial statements.

Accounting Policies Applied in the Company's Statements The first or second note is typically a summary of significant accounting policies. As you will see in your study of subsequent chapters, generally accepted accounting principles (GAAP) permit companies to select from alternative methods for measuring the effects of transactions. The summary of significant accounting policies tells the user which accounting methods the company has adopted.

REAL WORLD EXCERPT

The Forzani Group

ANNUAL REPORT

NOTE 2

SIGNIFICANT ACCOUNTING POLICIES

(h) Revenue recognition

Revenue includes sales to customers through corporate stores operated by the Company and sales to, and service fees from, franchise stores and others. Sales to customers through corporate stores operated by the Company are recognized at the point of sale, net of an estimated allowance for sales returns. Sales of merchandise to franchise stores and others are recognized at the time of shipment. Royalties and administration fees are recognized when earned, in accordance with the terms of the franchise/license agreements.

This note provides information about the timing of recognition of FGL's different types of revenue. Without an understanding of the various accounting methods used, it is impossible to analyze a company's financial results effectively.

ALTERNATIVE ACCOUNTING METHODS AND GAAP

FINANCIAL
ANALYSIS

Many people mistakenly believe that GAAP permit only one accounting method to be used to compute each value in the financial statements (e.g., inventory). Actually, GAAP often allow selection of an accounting method from a menu of acceptable methods. This permits a company to choose the methods that most closely reflect its particular economic circumstances (economic reality). This flexibility complicates the financial statement users' task, however, users must understand how the company's choice of accounting methods affects its financial statement presentations. As renowned financial analysts Gabrielle Napolitano, Michael Moran, and Abby Joseph Cohen of the investment banking firm of Goldman, Sachs & Co. note in a research report,

> Discretionary choices in financial reporting that can ultimately lead to or create future earnings shocks that drive stock prices must be identified; analysts must make adjustments to minimize or eliminate the impacts of these drivers on corporate performance. As a result, financial statement users must (1) develop a keen understanding of the fundamentals underlying each firm's business operations and (2) familiarize themselves with the corporate reporting practices of the companies they are analyzing.*

For example, before analyzing two companies' statements prepared using different accounting methods, one company's statements must be converted to the other's methods to make them comparable. Otherwise, the reader is in a situation similar to comparing distances in kilometres and miles without conversion to a common scale. In Chapters 8 and 9, we discuss alternative accounting methods and their effects on financial statements.

*Gabrielle Napolitano, Michael A. Moran, and Abby Joseph Cohen, "Demand for Forensic Accounting Intensifies," *Global Strategy Research* (New York: Goldman, Sachs & Co., February 11, 2002).

REAL WORLD EXCERPT

*Goldman,
Sachs & Co.*

ANALYSTS' REPORT

Additional Detail Supporting Reported Amounts The second category of notes provides supplemental information concerning the data shown in the financial statements. Among other information, these notes may show revenues broken down by geographic region of business segments describe unusual transactions, and/or offer expanded detail on a specific classification.

For example, in Note 3 that follows, FGL indicates the make up of its capital assets (or property, plant, and equipment) at January 28, 2007. It lists the acquisition costs of six types of long-term assets, their accumulated amortization, and their book values. This helps the financial statement user in estimating the relative age of these assets and whether FGL needs to replace some of its assets in the near future. In addition, Note 2(c) informs the user of the accounting methods and rates that FGL adopted to compute annual amortization for the various types of assets.[17]

REAL WORLD EXCERPT

The Forzani Group

ANNUAL REPORT

NOTES TO CONSOLIDATED FINANCIAL STATEMENTS

3. Capital Assets

	Cost	Accumulated Amortization	Net Book Value
Land	$ 3,173	$ —	$ 3,173
Buildings	20,699	3,943	16,756
Building on leased land	4,583	2,588	1,995
Furniture, fixtures, equipment, software, and automotive	197,993	125,676	72,317
Leasehold improvements	221,043	125,942	95,101
Construction in progress	1,804	—	1,804
	$449,295	**$258,149**	**$191,146**

---

[17]Additional discussion of accounting rules related to property, plant, and equipment is provided in Chapter 9.

312   **CHAPTER 6**   Communicating and Interpreting Accounting Information

Relevant Financial Information Not Disclosed on the Statements   The final category of notes includes information that impacts the company financially but is not shown on the statements. Examples include information on stock option plans, legal matters, and any material event that occurred subsequent to year-end but before the financial statements are published. In Note 10, FGL disclosed the details of its lease commitments.

REAL WORLD EXCERPT

The Forzani Group

ANNUAL REPORT

NOTES TO CONSOLIDATED FINANCIAL STATEMENTS

10. Commitments

(a)   The company is committed, at January 28, 2007 to minimum payments under long-term real property and data processing hardware and software equipment leases, for the next five years, as follows:

	Gross
2008	$87,349
2009	77,312
2010	65,578
2011	62,603
2012	50,721

In addition, the company may be obligated to pay percentage rent under certain of the leases.

(b)   As at January 28, 2007, the company has open letters of credit for purchases of inventory of approximately $6,936,000 (2006—$4,579,000).

VOLUNTARY DISCLOSURES

GAAP and securities regulations set only a minimum level of required financial disclosures. Many companies, including FGL, provide important disclosures beyond those required. Such voluntary disclosures may appear in the annual report, in documents filed with securities commissions, in press releases, or on the company's Web site.

A QUESTION OF ETHICS

ACCOUNTING AND SUSTAINABLE DEVELOPMENT

REAL WORLD EXCERPT

CFO Magazine

A growing area of voluntary disclosures in North America is sustainability reporting as described by *CFO Magazine*:

The idea that a company should conduct its business in ways that benefit not just shareholders but the environment and society, too, is called sustainability, or sustainable development. It's an idea championed by a small but growing number of companies around the globe. One business group, the World Business Council for Sustainable Development, lists some 170 international members, including more than 30 Fortune 500 companies. According to the council's website, these companies share the belief that "the pursuit of sustainable development is good for business and business is good for sustainable development."

To tell stakeholders about that pursuit, companies are issuing sustainability reports. Many, like Suncor, are doing so following the strict guidelines of the Global Reporting Initiative (GRI), an independent institution founded in 1997, to develop a common framework for sustainability reporting. Enter the words "sustainability reporting" into your favourite search engine and you'll find such well-known company names as Alcoa, Alcan, Bristol-Myers Squibb, General Motors, Baxter International and FedEx Kinko's. In all, some 500 organizations publish sustainability reports according to GRI guidelines. Some countries, such as France, South Africa, and the Netherlands, now mandate environmental or social sustainability reporting as a condition to being listed on their stock exchanges.

Such reports are voluntary disclosures in Canada. However, many believe that managing a company in the interests of a wider group of stakeholders and reporting on these efforts is an ethical imperative.

Source: *CFO Magazine*, November 2004, pp. 97–100.

DEMONSTRATION **CASE**

Canadian Tire Corporation is an inter-related network of businesses across Canada that sells home, car, sports, and leisure products, as well as work clothes and casual attire. In addition, Canadian Tire is the country's largest independent gasoline retailer through its Canadian Tire Petroleum subsidiary, which sells fuel and related products at many outlets in most provinces. Canadian Tire's financial statements for the years 2004 and 2005 are shown below.

Consolidated Balance Sheets

As at (Dollars in millions)	December 31, 2005	January 1, 2005
ASSETS		
Current assets		
Cash and cash equivalents (Note 12)	$ 838.0	$ 802.2
Accounts receivable (Note 12)	652.8	370.7
Loans receivable (Note 2)	728.7	592.4
Merchandise inventories	675.5	620.6
Prepaid expenses and deposits	42.4	24.1
Future income taxes (Note 11)	43.6	24.6
Total current assets	2,981.0	2,434.6
Long-term receivables and other assets (Note 3)	132.1	129.7
Goodwill (Note 4)	46.2	41.7
Intangible assets (Note 4)	52.4	52.0
Property and equipment (Note 5)	2,743.9	2,585.2
Total assets	$5,955.6	$5,243.2
LIABILITIES		
Current liabilities		
Accounts payable and other	$1,545.5	$1,437.6
Income taxes payable	71.2	44.2
Current portion of long-term debt (Note 6)	204.3	5.6
Total current liabilities	1,821.0	1,487.4
Long-term debt (Note 6)	1,171.3	1,081.8
Future income taxes (Note 11)	89.0	67.2
Other long-term liabilities (Note 7)	63.2	55.6
Total liabilities	3,144.5	2,692.0
Minority interest (Note 17)	300.0	300.0
SHAREHOLDER'S EQUITY		
Share capital (Note 9)	702.7	709.0
Contributed surplus	1.5	1.3
Accumulated foreign currency translation adjustment	(5.7)	(6.0)
Retained earnings	1,812.6	1,546.9
Total shareholder's equity	2,511.1	2,251.2
Total liabilities, minority interest, and shareholders' equity	$5,955.6	$5,243.2

(Signed)   (Signed)

Gilbert S. Bennett **Maureen J. Sabia**
Director   Director

Consolidated Statements of Earnings and Retained Earnings

For the years ended (Dollars in millions except per share amounts)	December 31, 2005	January 1, 2005
Gross operating revenue	$ 7,774.6	$ 7,153.6
Operating expenses		
Cost of merchandise sold and all other operating expenses except for the undernoted items interest	6,949.1	6,416.9
Long-term debt	79.5	76.0
Short-term debt	4.6	2.4
Depreciation and amortization	185.0	170.6
Employee profit sharing plan (Note 10)	28.7	26.8
Total operating expenses	7,246.9	6,692.7
Earnings before income taxes and minority interest		
Income taxes (Note 11)	527.7	460.9
Current	187.2	150.8
Future	2.8	11.7
Total income taxes	190.0	162.5
Net earnings before minority interest	337.7	298.4
Minority interest (Note 17)	7.6	6.9
Net earnings	$ 330.1	$ 291.5
Basic earnings per share	$ 4.04	$ 3.60
Diluted earnings per share (Note 9)	$ 3.98	$ 3.53
Weighted average number of Common and Class A Non-Voting shares outstanding	81,764,082	80,983,467
Retained earnings, beginning of year	$ 1,546.9	$ 1,318.0
Net earnings	330.1	291.5
Dividends	(47.4)	(40.5)
Repurchase of Class A Non-Voting Shares (Note 9)	(17.0)	(22.1)
Retained earnings, end of year	$ 1,812.6	$ 1,546.9

Consolidated Statements of Cash Flows

For the years ended (Dollars in millions)	December 31, 2005	January 1, 2005
Cash generated from (used for):		
Operating activities		
Net earnings	$ 330.1	$ 291.5
Items not affecting cash		
Net provision for loans receivable	222.1	184.4
Depreciation and amortization of property and equipment	182.0	166.2
Other	9.2	6.5
Amortization of other assets	5.8	7.1
Future income taxes	2.8	11.7
Gain on disposals of property and equipment	(10.9)	(14.4)
Gain on sales of loans receivable (Note 2)	(19.9)	(22.6)
Cash generated from operations	721.2	630.4
Changes in other working capital components (Note 12)	(283.1)	(217.3)
Cash generated from operating activities	438.1	413.1
Investing activities		
Investment in loans receivable	(717.6)	(592.3)
Additions to property and equipment	(391.1)	(340.7)
Long-term receivables and other assets	(24.7)	(16.2)
Purchases of stores	(4.9)	(1.3)

(continued)

Asset retirement obligations	**(1.3)**	(0.3)
Sale of Associate Dealer receivables (Note 12)	**47.8**	321.1
Proceeds on disposition of property and equipment	**78.2**	38.2
Securitization of loans receivable	**395.2**	349.4
Cash used for investing activities	**(618.4)**	(242.1)
Financing activities		
Issuance of long-term debt	**516.4**	201.5
Class A Non-Voting Share transactions, net (Note 9)	**(23.3)**	(13.6)
Dividends	**(45.7)**	(38.5)
Repayment of long-term debt	**(231.3)**	(244.8)
Cash generated from (used for) financing activities	**216.1**	(95.4)
Cash generated in the year	**35.8**	75.6
Cash and cash equivalents, beginning of year	**802.2**	726.6
Cash and cash equivalents, end of the year (Note 12)	**$ 838.0**	$ 802.2

Required:

1. Examine Canadian Tire's balance sheets. Identify the six largest changes in the book value of assets, liabilities, and shareholders' equity between the balance sheet dates. Based on what you have learned so far, what type of transactions could have caused the changes in the book value of these items?

2. Access Note 5 to the financial statements from the company's Web site (**www.canadiantire.ca**), and identify the specific changes to the Property and Equipment account.

3. Compute the following ratios for fiscal years 2004 and 2005: debt-to-equity, total asset turnover, return on assets, return on equity, and net profit margin. Use the results of your computations to comment on the company's financial situation and profitability of its operations in both years. Canadian Tire's total assets and shareholders' equity at the beginning of 2004 amounted to $4,893.1 million and $2,017.1 million, respectively.

4. Canadian Tire's operations generated significant amounts of cash during both the years 2004 and 2005. The company also made significant investments in long-term assets in 2005. How did the company finance the investment in these assets?

5. Compute and interpret the quality of income ratio and the capital acquisitions ratio for both 2004 and 2005.

6. Access Canadian Tire's Web site (**www.canadiantire.ca**) and look up "First Call Earnings Est." under "Investor Relations." What is the average analysts' estimate of Canadian Tire's earnings per share (EPS) for the next two fiscal years. Do analysts expect Canadian Tire's EPS to increase or decrease in the future? What information did the analysts take into consideration in computing their EPS estimates for the next two years?

SUGGESTED SOLUTION

1. The six balance sheet items that had the largest changes in their book values, and the typical reasons for these changes are summarized below (amounts in millions):

Balance sheet item	Change	Typical reasons for change
Accounts receivable	+$282.1	Increase in sales to customers on credit, net of collections.
Loans receivable	+136.3	Increase in the amount of loans to customers, net of collections.
Property and equipment	+158.7	Acquisition of new assets, disposal of old assets, and amortization of assets for the year.
Accounts payable and other	+107.9	Increase in the amounts payable to trade suppliers, and in accrued expenses.
Long-term debt (including current portion)	+282.2	Increase in the long-term notes, net of repayment to creditors.
Retained earnings	+265.7	Net income for the year minus dividends declared during the year.

2. Note 5 to the financial statements shows that Canadian Tire's property and equipment includes Land, Buildings, Fixtures and equipment, Leasehold improvements, Computer software, Assets under capital lease, and Construction in progress. These assets have increased by $308 million during the year. At the same time, accumulated amortization of the Buildings, Fixtures and equipment, Leasehold improvements, Computer software, and Assets under capital lease increased by $149.3 million during the year, which reduces the book value of these assets.

3.

Ratio	2005	2004
Debt to equity = Total liabilities ÷ Total shareholders' equity	1.25	1.20
Total asset turnover = Net sales ÷ Average total assets	1.39	1.41
Return on assets = Net income ÷ Average total assets	5.9%	5.8%
Return on equity = Net income ÷ Average shareholders' equity	13.9%	13.7%
Net profit margin = Net income ÷ Net sales	4.2%	4.1%

Computations:

2005

$D/E = \$3,144.5 \div \$2,511.1 = 1.25$

$TAT/O = \$7,774.6 \div (\$5,243.2 + \$5,955.6)/2 = 1.39$

$ROA = \$330.1 \div (\$5,243.2 + \$5,955.6)/2 = 0.059$

$ROE = \$330.1 \div (\$2,251.2 + 2,511.1)/2 = 0.139$

$NPM = \$330.1 \div \$7,774.6 = 0.042$

2004

$D/E = \$2,692.0 \div \$2,251.2 = 1.20$

$TAT/O = \$7,153.6 \div (\$4,893.1 + \$5,243.2)/2 = 1.41$

$ROA = \$291.5 \div (\$4,893.1 + \$5,243.2)/2 = 0.058$

$ROE = \$291.5 \div (\$2,017.1 + \$2,251.2)/2 = 0.137$

$NPM = \$291.5 \div \$7,153.6 = 0.041$

The debt-to-equity ratio increased from 1.20 to 1.25, suggesting a relative increase in liabilities, and a slight increase in the company's financial risk. The total asset turnover ratio decreased slightly, suggesting a slight deterioration in the utilization of the company's assets to generate revenue. The three profitability ratios—return on assets, return on equity, and net profit margin—increased marginally because the relative increase in net income from 2004 to 2005 was slightly higher than the relative increase in total assets, shareholders' equity and net sales over the same period. This suggests that management has improved on its use of the company's resources in generating net income for 2005.

4. Canadian Tire's cash flow statement shows that the company used a net amount of $618.4 on investing activities during 2005. This amount was partially financed by $438.1 of cash generated from operations, and the rest was financing by the issuance of new long-term debt.

5. Quality of income ratio = Cash Flow from Operating Activities ÷ Net income

    2004: $\$438.1 \div \$330.1 = 1.327$

    2005: $\$413.1 \div \$291.5 = 1.417$

The ratios indicate that cash flows from operations exceeded net income for both years, which suggests to the user that it is less likely that the company is using aggressive revenue recognition policies to increase net income.

$$\text{Capital acquisitions ratio} = \frac{\text{Cash Flow from Operating Activities}}{\text{Cash Paid for Property and Equipment}}$$

    2004: $\$438.1 \div \$391.1 = 1.12$

    2005: $\$413.1 \div \$340.7 = 1.21$

In both years, the company generated enough cash from its operations to cover the payments needed for the additional investments made during these two years.

6. The average analysts' estimate of Canadian Tire's EPS for fiscal year 2006 is $4.26 and $4.88 for fiscal year 2007. These average EPS estimates are based on individual estimates of 7 and 9 analysts, respectively.

    Canadian Tire's basic EPS for fiscal year 2005 is $4.04 as disclosed in its income statement. Analysts expect the company to improve on its performance in the next two years.

    Analysts use a variety of information sources to arrive at their EPS estimates. First, they need to develop a very good understanding of the industry, and Canadian Tire's role in the industry. Their information sources would include examination of the company's financial statements, analysis of population trends and expectations of future demand for the company's products, analysis of the company's strategies and future plans, conversations with company executives, and information about the company's competitors.

SOLUTION TO **SELF-STUDY QUIZ**

Self-Study Quiz 6-1

1. *c*, 2. *a*, 3. *e*, 4. *b*, 5. *d*.

CHAPTER **TAKE-AWAYS**

1. **Recognize the people involved in the accounting communication process (regulators, managers, board of directors, auditors, information intermediaries, and users), their roles in the process, and the guidance they receive from legal and professional standards. p. 291**

   Management of the reporting company must decide on the appropriate format (categories) and level of detail to present in its financial reports. Independent audits increase the credibility of the information. Financial statement announcements from public companies usually are first transmitted to users through electronic information services. The securities commission staff reviews public reports for compliance with legal and professional standards, investigates irregularities, and punishes violators. Analysts play a major role in making financial statements and other information available to average investors through their stock recommendations and earnings forecasts.

2. **Identify the steps in the accounting communication process, including the issuance of press releases, annual reports, quarterly reports, and documents filed with securities commissions, as well as the guiding principles in communicating useful information. p. 299**

   Earnings are first made public in press releases. Companies follow these announcements with annual and quarterly reports containing statements, notes, and additional information. Public companies must also file additional reports with the securities commissions (e.g., OSC, SEC), which contain more details about the company.

3. **Recognize the different financial statement and disclosure formats used by companies in practice. p. 306**

   Most statements are classified and include subtotals that are relevant to analysis. On the balance sheet, the most important distinctions are between current and non-current assets and liabilities. On the income statement and cash flow statement, the separation of operating and non-operating items is most important. The notes to the statements provide descriptions of the accounting rules applied and more information about items disclosed in the statements, as well as information about economic events not disclosed in the statements.

   In Chapter 7, we begin our in-depth discussion of financial statements. We will begin with two of the most liquid assets—cash and accounts receivable—and transactions that involve revenues and certain selling expenses. Accuracy in revenue recognition and the related recognition of cost of goods sold (discussed in Chapter 8) are the most important determinants of the accuracy—and, thus, the usefulness—of financial statement presentations. We will also introduce concepts related to the management and control of cash and receivables, which is a critical business function. A detailed understanding of these topics is crucial to future managers, accountants, and financial analysts.

FINDING **FINANCIAL INFORMATION**

BALANCE SHEET

Key Classifications

   Current and non-current assets and
      liabilities
   Contributed capital and retained earnings

INCOME STATEMENT

Key Subtotals

   Gross profit
   Income from operations
   Net income
   Earnings per share

CASH FLOW STATEMENT

Under Operating Activities (indirect method)

   Net Income
   ± Items Not Affecting Cash
   = Cash Provided by Operating Activities

NOTES

Key Classifications

   Descriptions of accounting rules applied
      in the statements
   Additional detail supporting reported
      numbers
   Relevant financial information not
      disclosed on the statements

KEY **TERMS**

Board of Directors p. 293	**Lenders (Creditors)** p. 298
Comparability p. 304	**Material Amounts** p. 304
Conservatism p. 305	**Press Release** p. 299
Consistent Information p. 304	**Private Investors** p. 298
Corporate Governance p. 289	**Relevant Information** p. 303
Cost–Benefit Constraint p. 305	**Reliable Information** p. 304
Earnings Forecasts p. 295	**Unqualified (Clean) Audit**
Institutional Investors p. 298	**Opinion** p. 293

QUESTIONS

1. Describe the roles and responsibilities of management, the board of directors, and independent auditors in the financial reporting process.
2. Define the following three users of financial accounting disclosures and the relationships among them: *financial analysts, private investors,* and *institutional investors.*
3. Briefly describe the role of information services in the communication of financial information.
4. Explain why information must be relevant and reliable to be useful.
5. Identify the constraints of accounting measurement and their role in the reporting of accounting information.
6. What basis of accounting (accrual or cash) does GAAP require on (a) the income statement, (b) the balance sheet, and (c) the cash flow statement?
7. Briefly explain the normal sequence and form of financial reports produced by private companies in a typical year.
8. Briefly explain the normal sequence and form of financial reports produced by public companies in a typical year.
9. What are the three major subtotals on the income statement, and what purpose do they serve?
10. List the six major classifications reported on a balance sheet.
11. What are the three major classifications on a cash flow statement?
12. What are the three major categories of notes or footnotes presented in annual reports? Cite an example of each.

EXERCISES

LO2

E6–1 Finding Financial Information: Matching Information Items to Financial Reports
Following are information items included in various financial reports. Match each information item with the report(s) where it would most likely be found by entering the appropriate letter(s) in the space provided.

Information Item	Report
_____ (1) Summarized financial data for 5- or 10-year period.	A. Annual report
_____ (2) Initial announcement of quarterly earnings.	B. Annual information form
_____ (3) Complete quarterly income statement, balance sheet, and cash flow statement.	C. Press release
_____ (4) The four basic financial statements for the year.	D. Quarterly report
_____ (5) Detailed discussion of the company's competition.	E. None of the above
_____ (6) Notes to financial statements.	
_____ (7) Identification of those responsible for the financial statements.	
_____ (8) Initial announcement of hiring of new vice-president for sales.	

E6–2 Understanding the Disclosure Process through the Forzani Group Ltd. Web Site

Using your Web browser, contact the Forzani Group Ltd. at its Web site (**www.forzanigroup.com**). Examine the most recent quarterly earnings press release and the related interim report.

Required:

Based on the information provided on the site, answer the following questions.

1. What were the release dates of the quarterly earnings press release and the interim report?

2. What additional information was provided in the interim report that was not reported in the earnings press release?

■ **LO2**

The Forzani Group

E6–3 Information Provided on Company Web Sites

Using your Web browser, contact Van Houtte Inc. at its Web site (**www.vanhoutte.com**).

Required:

Based on the information provided on the site, answer the following questions.

1. Which document(s) provided the most recent information on quarterly earnings?

2. For the most recent quarter, what was the change in sales revenue compared to the same quarter one year earlier? What was management's explanation for the change (if any)?

3. What was the annual earnings per share, stock price per share, and price–earnings ratio (see Chapter 1) on the day of the most recent fourth-quarter earnings press release?

■ **LO2, 3**

Van Houte

E6–4 Earnings per Share and Stock Prices

The following news story appeared in *The Globe and Mail* on September 2, 2006 after the Forzani Group Ltd. released its results of operations for the second quarter of fiscal year 2006.

■ **LO1**

REAL WORLD EXCERPT

The Globe and Mail

ANALYSIS

FORZANI REPORTS PROFIT IN QUARTER, REVERSING LOSS

Sporting goods store operator Forzani Group Ltd. reported yesterday a second-quarter profit of $1.9-million compared with a year-earlier loss of $2.3-million as revenue improved and some stores were revitalized. The retailer said its profit amounted to 6 cents a diluted share, including the effect of a 1-cent-a-share charge against earnings related to income tax expenses, up from a year-earlier loss of 7 cents. Revenue for the three months ended July 30 was $284-million, up from a year-earlier $243.6-million. The group's overall same-store sales increased 6 percent, year over year. FGL (TSX) fell 99 cents to $15.84. *CP*

Source: *The Globe and Mail*, September 2, 2006, p. B7.

Required:

The earnings of Forzani Group Ltd. increased from a loss of 7 cents to a profit of 6 cents per share, but its share price dropped by 99 cents. Explain why the price per share decreased even though the company announced an increase in its earnings per share.

E6–5 Earnings per Share and Share Prices

The following news story appeared in *The Globe and Mail* on July 23, 2004 after Microsoft Corporation released its results of operations for fiscal year 2004.

■ **LO1**

REAL WORLD EXCERPT

The Globe and Mail

ANALYSIS

Microsoft fell 97 cents (U.S.) to $28.03 on the Nasdaq stock exchange after it reported earnings Thursday that missed analyst targets by a penny, although sales topped expectations. Profit at the world's largest software maker climbed to $2.69 billion (U.S.) or 25 cents a share from $1.48 billion or 14 cents a share a year earlier. In addition, Microsoft said it expects to earn 30 cents a share in its first quarter, excluding a 5-cent stock compensation charge, on revenue of between $8.9 billion and $9.0 billion. Analysts were forecasting first-quarter earnings of 32 cents a share on revenue of $8.8 billion.

Source: www.bellzinc.theglobeandmail.com/servlet/story/RTGAM.20040723.wSTOCKS0723/business/Business/businessBN/

Required:

Microsoft's earnings per share increased from 14 cents to 25 cents. Yet its share price dropped by 97 cents. Explain why the price per share decreased even though the company announced an increase in its earnings per share.

LO2

E6–6 Guiding Principles for Communicating Useful Information

Match each qualitative characteristic of useful accounting information with the related definition by entering the appropriate letter in the space provided.

Qualitative Characteristics	Definitions
_____ (1) Relevance	A. Application of the same accounting methods over time.
_____ (2) Timeliness	B. Agreement between what really happened and the disclosed information.
_____ (3) Predictive value	C. The information is available prior to the decision.
_____ (4) Feedback value	D. The accounting information does not favour a particular group.
_____ (5) Reliability	E. The information helps reduce the uncertainty in the future.
_____ (6) Verifiability	F. The information provides input to evaluate previous expectations.
_____ (7) Representational faithfulness	G. The information allows the evaluation of one alternative against another alternative.
_____ (8) Neutrality	H. The information has a bearing on a specific decision.
_____ (9) Comparability	I. The information can be depended upon.
_____ (10) Consistency	J. Implies that qualified persons working independently arrive at similar conclusions.

LO2

ANALYSIS

E6–7 Assessing the Relevance and Reliability of Information

Paula Romanov is the credit manager of Pinnacle Inc. She is considering whether to extend credit to Mak Inc., a new customer. Pinnacle sells most of its goods on credit, but is very careful in extending credit to new customers. Tim Mak, the owner of Mak Inc., provided the following documents to Paula to assist her in her evaluation:

1. A detailed analysis of the sales revenue and net income that Mak Inc. expects to achieve within the next 12 months.
2. Projections of the company's sales during the next five years.
3. The company's monthly bank statements for the past three years.
4. A report of the company's credit history prepared by Mak's employees.
5. A letter signed by all four company officers indicating that they are prepared to personally guarantee the amount of credit that Pinnacle approves.
6. Brief résumés of the four company officers along with descriptions of the functions they perform in the company.
7. Eight letters of reference from close friends and relatives of the four company officers.

Required:

Analyze each of the items above with respect to the characteristics of relevance (predictive value, feedback value, and timeliness) and reliability (verifiability, neutrality, and representational faithfulness). Explain whether or not each item possesses these characteristics.

LO3

E6–8 Finding Financial Information: Matching Financial Statements with the Elements of Financial Statements

Match each financial statement with the items presented in it by entering the appropriate letter in the space provided.

Elements of Financial Statements	Financial Statements
_____ (1) Liabilities	A. Income statement
_____ (2) Cash from operating activities	B. Balance sheet
_____ (3) Losses	C. Cash flow statement
_____ (4) Assets	D. None of the above
_____ (5) Revenues	
_____ (6) Cash from financing activities	
_____ (7) Gains	
_____ (8) Shareholders' equity	
_____ (9) Expenses	
_____ (10) Assets owned by a shareholder	

E6–9 **Ordering the Classifications on a Typical Balance Sheet**

■ **LO3**

A list of classifications on the balance sheet is shown below. Number the classifications in the order in which they normally appear on a balance sheet.

No.	Title
_____	Current liabilities
_____	Long-term liabilities
_____	Long-term investments
_____	Intangible assets
_____	Property, plant, and equipment
_____	Current assets
_____	Retained earnings
_____	Share capital
_____	Other non-current assets

E6–10 **Finding Financial Information as a Potential Investor**

■ **LO3**

You are considering investing the cash gifts you received for graduation in shares of various companies. You visit the Web sites of major companies, searching for relevant information.

Required:

For each of the following, indicate where you would locate the information in an annual report (*Hint:* The information may be in more than one location):

1. The detail on major classifications of long-term assets.
2. The accounting method(s) used for financial reporting purposes.
3. Whether the company has had any capital expenditures for the year.
4. Net amount of property, plant, and equipment.
5. Policies on amortizing intangibles.
6. Amortization expense.
7. Any significant gains or losses on disposals of long-term assets.
8. Accumulated amortization of property, plant, and equipment at the end of the last fiscal year.

E6–11 **Inferring Share Issuances and Cash Dividends from Changes in Shareholders' Equity**

■ **LO3**

Power Corporation recently reported the following December 31 balances in its shareholders' equity accounts (in millions):

Power Corporation

	Current Year	Prior Year
Share capital	$1,249	$ 950
Retained earnings	6,010	5,652
Total shareholders' equity	$7,259	$6,602

During the current year, Power Corp. reported net income of $1,053 million. Assume that the only other transactions that affected shareholders' equity during the current year were the issuance of shares and the declaration and payment of cash dividends.

Required:

Re-create the two journal entries reflecting the issuance of shares and the declaration and payment of dividends.

PROBLEMS

P6–1 **Matching Transactions with Concepts**

■ **LO1, 2**

The concepts of accounting covered in Chapters 2 through 6 are shown below. Match each transaction with its related concept by entering the appropriate letter in the space provided. Use only one letter for each blank space.

Concepts	Transactions
_____ (1) Users of financial statements	A. Recorded a $1,000 sale of merchandise on credit.
_____ (2) Objective of financial statements	B. Counted (inventoried) the unsold items at the end of the period and valued them in dollars.
	C. Acquired a vehicle for use in operating the business.
Qualitative Characteristics	D. Reported the amount of amortization expense because it likely will affect important decisions of statement users.
_____ (3) Relevance	E. Identified as the investors, creditors, and others interested in the business.
_____ (4) Reliability	F. Used special accounting approaches because of the uniqueness of the industry.
Assumptions	G. Issued bonds payable of $1 million.
_____ (5) Separate entity	H. Paid a contractor for an addition to the building with $10,000 cash and $20,000 market value of the company's shares ($30,000 was deemed to be the cash equivalent price).
_____ (6) Continuity	
_____ (7) Unit of measure	I. Engaged an outside independent accountant to audit the financial statements.
_____ (8) Periodicity	J. Sold merchandise and rendered services for cash and on credit during the year; then determined the cost of those goods sold and the cost of rendering those services.
Elements of Financial Statements	
_____ (9) Revenues	K. Established an accounting policy that sales revenue shall be recognized only when ownership of the goods sold passes to the customer.
_____ (10) Expenses	L. To design and prepare the financial statements to assist the users in making decisions.
_____ (11) Gains	
_____ (12) Losses	M. Established a policy not to include in the financial statements the personal financial affairs of the owners of the business.
_____ (13) Assets	
_____ (14) Liabilities	N. Sold an asset at a loss that was a peripheral or incidental transaction.
_____ (15) Accounting equation	O. The value to users of a special financial report exceeds the cost of preparing it.
Principles	P. Valued an asset, such as inventory, at lower than its purchase cost because its market value is lower.
_____ (16) Cost	
_____ (17) Revenue recognition	Q. Dated the income statement "For the Year Ended December 31, 2005."
_____ (18) Matching	R. Used services from outsiders—paid cash for some and the remainder on credit.
_____ (19) Full disclosure	
	S. Acquired an asset (a pencil sharpener that will have a useful life of five years) and recorded it as an expense when purchased for $1.99.
Constraints of Accounting	
_____ (20) Materiality threshold	T. Disclosed in the financial statements all relevant financial information about the business; necessitated the use of notes to the financial statements.
_____ (21) Cost–benefit constraint	
_____ (22) Conservatism constraint	U. Sold an asset at a gain that was a peripheral or incidental transaction.
_____ (23) Industry peculiarities	V. Assets of $500,000 − Liabilities of $300,000 = Shareholders' Equity of $200,000.
	W. Accounting and reporting assume a "going concern."

LO3

P6–2 Matching Definitions with Balance Sheet–Related Terms

Selected terms related to the balance sheet, which were discussed in Chapters 2 through 5, are listed below. Match each definition with its related term by entering the appropriate letter in the space provided.

Terms

____ (1) Retained earnings	____ (10) Book value
____ (2) Current liabilities	____ (11) Contributed surplus
____ (3) Liquidity	____ (12) Liabilities
____ (4) Contra-asset account	____ (13) Long-term assets
____ (5) Accumulated amortization	____ (14) Shareholders' equity
____ (6) Intangible assets	____ (15) Current assets
____ (7) Other assets	____ (16) Assets
____ (8) Shares outstanding	____ (17) Long-term liabilities
____ (9) Normal operating cycle	

Definitions

A. A miscellaneous category of assets.

B. Amount of contributed capital for which shares were not issued.

C. Total assets minus total liabilities.

D. Nearness of assets to cash (in time).

E. Assets expected to be collected in cash within one year or the operating cycle, if longer.

F. Same as carrying value; cost less accumulated amortization to date.

G. Accumulated earnings minus accumulated dividends.

H. Asset offset account (subtracted from asset).

I. Balance of the Common Shares account divided by the issue price per share.

J. Assets that do not have physical substance.

K. Probable future economic benefits owned by the entity from past transactions.

L. Liabilities expected to be paid out of current assets, normally within the next year.

M. The average cash-to-cash time involved in the operations of the business.

N. Sum of the annual amortization expense on an asset from the date of its acquisition to the current date.

O. All liabilities not classified as current liabilities.

P. Property, plant, and equipment.

Q. Debts or obligations from past transactions to be paid with assets or services.

R. None of the above.

P6–3 Preparing a Balance Sheet and Analyzing Some of Its Parts (AP6–1)   ■ LO3

eXcel

King Jewellers Inc. is developing its annual financial statements for 2009. The following amounts were correct at December 31, 2009: cash, $42,000; accounts receivable, $51,300; merchandise inventory, $110,000; prepaid insurance, $800; investment in shares of Z Corporation (long term), $26,000; store equipment, $48,000; used store equipment held for disposal, $7,000; accumulated amortization, store equipment, $9,600; accounts payable, $42,000; long-term note payable, $30,000; income taxes payable, $7,000; retained earnings, $86,500; and common shares, 100,000 shares outstanding (originally issued at $1.10 per share).

Required:

1. Based on these data, prepare the company's balance sheet at December 31, 2009. Use the following major captions (list the individual items under these captions):

   a. Assets: Current Assets; Long-Term Investments; Property, Plant and Equipment; and Other Assets.

   b. Liabilities: Current Liabilities and Long-Term Liabilities.

   c. Shareholders' Equity: Share Capital and Retained Earnings.

2. What is the net book value of the

   a. Inventory?

   b. Accounts receivable?

   c. Store equipment?

   d. Note payable (long term)?

Explain what these values mean.

P6–4 Using Financial Reports: Interpreting Financial Statement Information, Analyzing and Interpreting Ratios (AP6–2)   ■ LO2, 3

WestJet Airlines

WestJet Airlines Ltd. was founded in 1996 by four Calgary entrepreneurs, and has grown from serving Western Canadian destinations to being Canada's largest coast-to-coast low-fare airline.

WestJet's financial statements for 2005 and 2006 and excerpts from selected notes to its financial statements are shown below.

ANALYSIS

CONSOLIDATED BALANCE SHEETS
WestJet Airlines Ltd.
December 31, 2006 and 2005
(Stated in Thousands of Dollars)

	2006	2005
Assets		
Current assets:		
Cash and cash equivalents (note 9)	$ 377,517	$ 259,640
Accounts receivable	12,645	8,022
Income taxes recoverable	13,820	13,909
Assets held for sale (note 2)	13,157	—
Prepaid expenses and deposits (note 1(g))	30,727	31,746
Inventory	8,200	6,259
	456,066	319,576
Property and equipment (note 2)	2,158,746	1,803,497
Other assets (note 3)	111,715	90,019
	$2,726,527	$2,213,092
Liabilities and Shareholders' Equity		
Current liabilities:		
Accounts payable and accrued liabilities	$ 121,157	$ 100,052
Advance ticket sales	148,743	127,450
Non-refundable guest credits	40,508	32,814
Current portion of long-term debt (note 4)	153,720	114,115
Current portion of obligations under capital lease (note 6)	356	2,466
	464,484	376,897
Long-term debt (note 4)	1,291,136	1,044,719
Obligations under capital lease (note 6)	1,483	1,690
Other liabilities (note 5)	14,114	16,982
Future income tax (note 8)	149,283	102,651
	1,920,500	1,542,939
Shareholders' equity:		
Share capital (note 7(b))	431,248	429,613
Contributed surplus (note 7(g))	58,656	39,093
Retained earnings	316,123	201,447
	806,027	670,153
Commitments and contingencies (notes 6 and 10)		
	$2,726,527	$2,213,092

See accompanying notes to consolidated financial statements.

On behalf of the Board:

[signature]   [signature]

Clive Beddoe, Director   Wilmot Matthews, Director

CONSOLIDATED STATEMENTS OF EARNINGS AND RETAINED EARNINGS
WestJet Airlines Ltd.
Years ended December 31, 2006 and 2005
(Stated in Thousands of Dollars, Except Per Share Amounts)

	2006	2005
Revenues:		
Guest revenues	$1,558,471	$1,207,075
Charter and other	201,400	179,379
Interest income	13,815	6,308
	1,773,686	1,392,762
Expenses:		
Aircraft fuel	425,506	354,065
Airport operations	262,310	219,144
Flight operations and navigational charges	229,821	183,463
Sales and marketing	154,734	124,154
Depreciation and amortization	111,442	106,624
General and administration	79,817	71,610
Aircraft leasing (note 11(b))	71,432	65,647
Interest expense	70,196	55,496
Maintenance	69,975	71,397
Inflight	67,220	53,005
Guest services	31,739	27,322
	1,574,192	1,331,927
Earnings from operations	199,494	60,835
Non-operating income (expense):		
Gain (loss) on foreign exchange	32	(2,729)
Gain (loss) on disposal of property and equipment	839	(98)
Non-recurring expenses (note 10(c))	(15,600)	—
	(14,729)	(2,827)
Employee profit shate (note 10(b))	(20,284)	(6,033)
Earnings before income taxes	164,481	51,975
Income tax (expense) recovery (note 8):		
Current	(3,170)	7,367
Future	(46,635)	(35,341)
	(49,805)	(27,974)
Net earnings	114,676	24,001
Retained earnings, beginning of year	201,447	177,446
Retained earnings, end of year	$ 316,123	$ 201,447
Earnings per share (note 7(d)):		
Basic	$ 0.88	$ 0.19
Diluted	$ 0.88	$ 0.19

See accompanying notes to consolidated financial statements.

CONSOLIDATED STATEMENTS OF CASH FLOWS
WestJet Airlines Ltd.
Years ended December 31, 2006 and 2005
(Stated in Thousands of Dollars)

	2006	2005
Cash provided by (used in):		
Operating activities:		
Net earnings	$ 114,676	$ 24,001
Items not involving cash:		
Depreciation and amortization	111,442	106,624
Amortization of other liabilities	(868)	(604)
Amortization of hedge settlements	1,427	1,391
(Gain) loss on disposal of property and equipment	(839)	98
Loss on disposal of aircraft parts (note 2)	(1,233)	(1,126)
Stock-based compensation expense	21,205	17,604
Issued from treasury stock	—	17,705
Future income tax expense	46,635	35,341
Decrease in non-cash working capital (note 9(a))	43,707	46,290
	336,152	247,324
Financing activities:		
Increase in long-term debt	418,581	256,385
Repayment of long-term debt	(132,559)	(100,487)
Increase in other liabilities	—	8,479
Issuance of shares	—	21,094
Share issuance costs	(10)	(215)
Increase in other assets	(28,139)	(14,350)
Decrease in obligations under capital lease	(480)	(5,846)
Increase in non-cash working capital	(1,071)	(837)
	256,322	164,223
Investing activities:		
Aircraft additions	(438,906)	(660,947)
Aircraft disposals	3,822	404,583
Other property and equipment additions	(41,124)	(44,969)
Other property and equipment disposals	1,611	894
	(474,597)	(300,439)
Increase in cash	117,877	111,108
Cash, beginning of year	259,640	148,532
Cash, end of year	$ 377,517	$ 259,640

Cash is defined as cash and cash equivalents. See note 9(b) for additional cash information.
See accompanying notes to consolidated financial statements.

NOTES TO CONSOLIDATED FINANCIAL STATEMENTS

1. Significant accounting policies:

. . .

(c) Revenue recognition:
Guest and charter revenue is recognized when air transportation is provided. Tickets sold but not yet used are included in the consolidated balance sheet as advance ticket sales.

(g) Deferred costs:
Sales and marketing expenses attributed to advance ticket sales are deferred and expensed in the period the related revenue is recognized. Included in prepaid expenses and deposits are $10,878,000 (2004—$13,236,000) of deferred costs.

(i) Maintenance costs:
Maintenance and repairs, including major overhauls, are charged to maintenance expense as they are incurred.

Required:

1. Examine WestJet's balance sheets. The company's assets increased significantly in 2006. Which asset shows the largest increase? How did the company finance the increase in this asset?

2. Compute and interpret the debt-to-equity ratios for 2005 and 2006.

3. WestJet's current liabilities include the account *Advanced ticket sales* with a balance of $148,743. What does this account represent, and what type of transactions would cause an increase or a decrease in the account balance? Explain.

4. Note 1 (g) refers to deferred costs. What is the nature of this item and why is it shown on the balance sheet? What would cause the amount of deferred costs to change over time? Explain.

5. WestJet increased its investment in aircraft during 2006, but its maintenance expense decreased from $71,397 in 2005 to $69,975 in 2006. How does the company account for its maintenance costs, and why has the amount of maintenance expense decreased in 2006? Does the company provide any information on this issue in the Management Discussion and Analysis section of the annual report? (**www.westjet.com/pdffile/ WestJet2006AR.pdf**)

6. Compute the total asset turnover ratio, return on assets, return on equity, and net profit margin for both years 2005 and 2006. Comment on the profitability of WestJet's operations in both years. WestJet's total assets and shareholders' equity at December 31, 2004 amounted to $1,877,354 and $589,892, respectively.

7. WestJet's operations generated significant amounts of cash during both the years 2005 and 2006. The company also made significant investments in new aircraft in 2006. How did the company finance the acquisition of additional aircraft?

8. Compute and interpret the quality of income ratio and the capital acquisitions ratio for both 2005 and 2006.

9. Access **www.investor.reuters.com**, search for WestJet Airlines Ltd. (WJA.TO) under Stocks and Mutual Funds, and choose "estimates" from the list of items below the blank box. What is the average analysts' estimate of WestJet's earnings per share (EPS) for the next two fiscal years? Do analysts expect WestJet's EPS to increase or decrease in the future? What information did the analysts take into consideration in computing their EPS estimates for the next two years?

P6–5 **Using Financial Reports: Interpreting Financial Statement Information, Analyzing and Interpreting Ratios**

Danier Leather Inc. (DL) is one of the largest publicly traded specialty leather apparel retailers in the world. It designs, manufactures, and sells high-quality, fashionable leather clothing and accessories to customers. Its products are sold in stores at shopping malls, through its corporate sales division, and online through its Web site, **www.danier.com**. Since entering the retail business in 1974, the company has produced a strong, long-term track record of growth and profits from continuing operations. DL's financial statements for 2005 and 2006 and Note 11 to its 2006 financial statements are shown on the next few pages.

LO2, 3

Danier Leather

ANALYSIS

Required:

1. Examine Danier Leather's balance sheets. Identify the four largest changes in the book value of assets, liabilities, and shareholders' equity between the balance sheet dates. What type of transactions could have caused the changes in the book value of these items?

2. The company's liabilities include the account *Accrued litigation provision and related expenses* with a balance of $18,000. Note 11 to the 2006 financial statements provides a brief description of the events that led to the recognition of this liability. Review the content of the note and explain the nature of these events. Why did the company disclose such details?

3. Using information from the company's balance sheets and income statement for 2006, can you determine the amount of cash flow generated from operations? If not, where can one find such information?

4. Compute the following ratios for fiscal years 2005 and 2006: debt-to-equity, total asset turnover, return on assets, return on equity, and net profit margin. Use the results of your computations to comment on the company's financial situation and profitability of its operations in both years. DL's total assets and shareholders' equity at June 26, 2004 amounted to $89,689 and $61,287, respectively.

5. Suppose that you are evaluating DL's financial statements for a potential investment in the company's shares. To what extent is the information contained in these financial statements relevant for your decision? What additional information would you require before making your decision?

Danier Leather, Inc.
Consolidated Balance Sheets
(thousands of dollars)

	June 24, 2006	June 25, 2005
Assets		
Current Assets		
Cash	$11,833	$21,193
Accounts receivable	402	594
Income taxes recoverable	2,485	939
Inventories (Note 3)	32,348	29,031
Prepaid expenses	1,026	516
Assets of discontinued operations (Note 2)	—	23
Future income tax asset (Note 10)	529	159
	48,623	52,455
Other Assets		
Property and equipment (Note 4)	27,293	25,314
Goodwill	342	342
Future income taxes asset (Note 10)	5,952	5,254
	$82,210	$83,365
Liabilities		
Current Liabilities		
Accounts payable and accrued liabilities	$10,708	$ 8,170
Current portion of capital lease obligation (Note 6)	911	—
Future income tax liability (Note 10)	624	—
	12,243	8,170
Capital lease obligation (Note 6)	1,829	—
Accured litigation provision and related expenses (Note 11)	18,000	18,000
Deferred lease inducements and rent liability	2,125	1,838
Future income tax liability (Note 10)	57	420
	34,254	28,428
Shareholders' Equity		
Share capital (Note 7)	22,542	22,493
Contributed surplus	275	230
Retained earnings	25,139	32,214
	47,956	54,937
	$82,210	$83,365

See accompanying notes to the consolidated financial statements.

Approved by the Board

(signature)   (signature)

Edwin F. Hawken, Director   **Jeffrey Wortsman**, Director

Danier Leather, Inc.
Consolidated Statements of Earnings (Loss)
(thousands of dollars, except per share amounts)

	For the Years Ended	
	June 24, 2006	June 25, 2005
Revenue	$ 148,351	$ 166,350
Cost of sales (Note 9)	76,953	82,863
Gross profit	71,398	83,487
Selling, general and administrative expenses (Note 9)	78,796	77,215
Interest income	(445)	(340)
Earnings (loss) before undernoted items and income taxes	(6,953)	6,612
Restructuring costs (Note 8 and 9)	1,389	—
Litigation provision and related expenses (Note 11)	—	3,098
Earnings (loss) before discontinued operations and income taxes	(8,342)	3,514
Provision for (recovery of) income taxes (Note 10)		
Current	(2,032)	1,553
Future	(807)	(622)
	(2,839)	931
Net earnings (loss) before discontinued operations	$ (5,503)	$ 2,583
Loss from discontined operations, net of income taxes (Note 2)	—	(2,768)
Net (loss)	$ (5,503)	$ (185)
Net earnings (loss) per share before discontinued operations:		
Basic	($0.84)	$0.38
Diluted	($0.84)	0.38
Net earnings (loss) per share:		
Basic	($0.84)	($0.03)
Diluted	($0.84)	($0.03)
Weighted average number of shares outstanding:		
Basic	6,547,090	6,726,658
Diluted	6,583,540	6,790,056

NOTE 11: LITIGATION PROVISION AND RELATED EXPENSES

	June 24, 2006	June 25, 2005
Provision for damages, costs and interest	$18,000	$18,000
Legal and professional fees	—	—
Accrued litigation provision and related expenses	$18,000	$18,000

In fiscal 1999, the Company and certain of its directors and officers were served with a Statement of Claim under the Class Proceedings Act (Ontario) which made allegations about the accuracy and disclosure of certain information contained in a financial forecast issued by the Company and contained in the Prospectus it issued dated May 6, 1998 for its initial public offering ("IPO") which closed on May 20, 1998. The suit sought damages to be paid equal to the alleged diminution in value of the Subordinate Voting Shares sold under the Prospectus.

In October 2001, a motion to certify the action as a class proceeding was granted. The trail commenced in the Superior Court of Justice (Ontario) in May 2003 and was completed in January 2004. On May 7, 2004, the trial judge issued a judgment against the Company and two of its Senior Officers in favour of the Plaintiffs and awarded damages to Canadian shareholders who purchased Subordinate Voting Shares under the Prospectus. For those shareholders who sold their shares between June 4 and 9, 1998, the trial judge awarded the difference between the IPO price and the price at which they sold their shares. For those shareholders who sold or still held their shares after June 9, 1998, the trial judge awarded $2.35 per share. Although the trial judge concluded that at the date of the Prospectus the forecast was reasonable, and that at the time of closing of the IPO the Company's CEO and CFO had an honest belief that the forecast could still be achieved, and although he held that the forecast was, in fact, substantially achieved, the trial judge decided that management's judgment that the forecast was still achievable at the time of closing was not reasonable and that therefore the Prospectus contained a misrepresentation. Based solely on information available at the time, the Company estimated that the trail judge's award would have totaled approximately $15 million. As noted below, the Company and its Senior Officers have successfully appealed this decision.

In May 2005, the trial judge awarded the Plaintiffs a portion of the costs claimed for the action and referred for assessment the amount of costs to be paid. Based solely on the information available at the time, the Company estimated that these costs would have amounted to approximately $3 million to $4 million.

A hearing to determine the awarding of costs related to the certification and summary judgment motion which was decided in 2000 and 2001 was held in December 2004. In June 2005, partial indemnity costs were awarded to the Plaintiffs for these motions in an amount to assessed. The Company has appealed this decision and the appeal is still waiting to be heard.

In June 2004, a Notice of Appeal was filed by the Company and two of its Senior Officers from the trial judge's decision. The appeal was heard by the Ontario Court of Appeal in June 2005 and in December 2005, the Court of Appeal unanimously allowed the appeal on three separate grounds, set aside the trial decision and dismissed the class proceeding. As a result, the Company and its Senior Officers are not required to pay any of the damages, interest or costs awarded by the trial judge. The Court of Appeal's decision stated that the Company had met its disclosure obligations in the Prospectus and during the IPO process and the trial judge erred in finding that any misrepresentation had occurred. The Court of Appeal will determine the Company's and its Senior Officers' entitlement to costs for the trial and for the appeal at a later date.

In February 2006, the Plaintiffs filed an Application for Leave to Appeal to the Supreme Court of Canada. In June 2006, the Supreme Court of Canada granted the Plaintiff's application. The Company expects the appeal to be heard by the Supreme Court of Canada during March 2007.

Based solely on the information available at the time, if the damages, costs and interest awarded by the trial judge had been paid at the fiscal 2005 year-end, the Company estimated this amount to be approximately $18 million. During the fourth quarter of 2004, the Company recorded an expense and set up a provision of $15 million to reflect the trial judge's decision. This provision was subsequently increased by $3 million to $18 million during the fourth quarter of 2005 to take into account the trial judge's award of costs which was released in May 2005. The provision for recovery of income taxes related to the trial judge's award was based on the entire $18 million provision and the provision did not take into account the potential results of the appeal, any possible insurance recoveries or future tax adjustments. The provision for the damages award, costs and interest and the income tax recovery were based on management's best estimate and is subject to adjustment when all facts are known and all issues are resolved. The possible adjustment could be significant. Although the Court of Appeal has set aside the trial judge's decision, the provision will remain until the Supreme Court of Canada makes a final determination.

ALTERNATE PROBLEMS

AP6–1 **Preparing a Balance Sheet and Analyzing Some of Its Parts** (P6–3)   ■ **LO3**

Carpet Bazaar is developing its annual financial statements for 2008. The following amounts were correct at December 31, 2008: cash, $35,000; investment in shares of ABC Corporation (long term), $32,000; store equipment, $51,000; accounts receivable, $47,500; carpet inventory, $118,000; prepaid insurance, $1,300; used store equipment held for disposal, $3,500; accumulated amortization, store equipment, $10,200; income taxes payable, $6,000; long-term note payable, $26,000; accounts payable, $45,000; retained earnings, $76,100; and common shares, (100,000 shares outstanding, originally sold and issued at $1.25 per share).

Required:

1. Based on these data, prepare the company's balance sheet at December 31, 2008. Use the following major captions (list the individual items under these captions):
   a. Assets: Current Assets; Long-Term Investments; Property, Plant, and Equipment; and Other Assets.
   b. Liabilities: Current Liabilities and Long-Term Liabilities.
   c. Shareholders' Equity: Share Capital and Retained Earnings.

2. What is the net book value of the
   a. Inventory?
   b. Accounts receivable?
   c. Store equipment?
   d. Note payable (long term)?
   Explain what these values mean.

AP6–2 **Using Financial Reports: Interpreting Financial Statement Information, Analyzing and Interpreting Ratios** (P6–4)   ■ **LO2, 3**

RONA Inc. (**www.rona.ca**), founded in 1939, is Canada's leading distributor and retailer of hardware, home improvement, and gardening products. It has a network that exceeds 600 stores across Canada. Its sales grew from $478 million in 1993 to $4,551 million in 2006. Its financial statements for 2005 and 2006 are shown on the next few pages.

RONA Inc.

ANALYSIS

Required:

1. Examine RONA's balance sheets. Why did the company's assets increase significantly in 2006? Which sections of the annual reports would include information that helps the reader answer this question? Which assets show the largest increases, and how did the company finance the increase in these assets?

2. Compute and interpret the debt-to-equity ratios for 2005 and 2006.

3. RONA's current assets include the account *Prepaid expenses* with a balance of $23,454. What does this account represent, and what type of transactions would cause an increase or a decrease in the account balance? Explain.

4. RONA's income statement does not include information related to cost of goods sold and general, selling, and administrative expenses. Why did the company exclude such details from its income statement? Explain.

5. Compute the total asset turnover ratio, return on assets, return on equity, and net profit margin for both years 2005 and 2006. Comment on the profitability of RONA's operations in both years. RONA's total assets and shareholders' equity at December 31, 2004 amounted to $1,336,745 and $610,283, respectively.

6. RONA's operations generated significant amounts of cash during both the years 2005 and 2006. The company also made significant investments in 2006. How did the company finance these investments?

7. Compute and interpret the quality of income ratio for both 2005 and 2006.

8. Access **www.investor.reuters.com**, search for RONA Inc. (RON.TO) under Stocks and Mutual Funds, and choose "estimates" from the list of items below the blank box. What is the average analysts' estimate of RONA's Earnings per share (EPS) for the next two years? Do analysts expect RONA's EPS to increase or decrease in the future? What information did the analysts take into consideration in computing their EPS estimates for the next two years?

RONA Inc.
Consolidated Balance Sheets
December 31, 2006 and December 25, 2005
(in thousands of dollars)

	2006	2005
Assets		
Current assets		
Cash	$ 58,486	$ 4,120
Accounts receivable (Note 7)	205,808	181,707
Inventory	790,496	733,681
Prepaid expenses	23,454	14,083
Future income taxes (Note 4)	10,859	8,513
	1,089,103	942,104
Investments (Note 8)	17,642	18,505
Fixed assets (Note 10)	634,131	415,899
Goodwill	316,558	252,337
Trademarks (Note 11)	1,380	—
Other assets (Note 12)	30,314	17,190
Future income taxes (Note 4)	19,254	21,581
	$2,108,382	$1,667,616
Liabilities		
Current liabilities		
Bank loans (Note 13)	$ 21,221	$ 25,276
Accounts payable and accrued liabilities	394,103	412,964
Income taxes payable	7,242	5,444
Future income taxes (Note 4)	3,314	750
Instalments on long-term debt (Note 14)	29,511	11,789
	455,391	456,223
Long-term debt (Note 14)	455,310	230,300
Other long-term liabilities (Note 15)	20,386	15,736
Future income taxes (Note 4)	19,402	13,792
Non-controlling interest	23,527	15,381
	974,016	731,432
Shareholders' equity		
Capital stock (Note 16)	415,717	410,683
Retained earnings	709,467	518,883
Contributed surplus	9,182	6,618
	1,134,366	936,184
	$2,108,382	$1,667,616

The accompanying notes are an integral part of the consolidated financial statements.

On behalf of the Board,

J. Spencer Lanthier
Director

André H. Gagnon
Director

RONA Inc.
Consolidated Earnings
Years ended December 31, 2006 and December 25, 2005
(in thousands of dollars, except earnings per share)

	2006	2005
Sales[a]	**$4,551,936**	$4,026,424
Earnings before the following items	**383,882**	333,604
Interest on long-term debt	**18,728**	13,052
Interest on bank loans	**3,417**	3,067
Depreciation and amortization (Notes 10, 11 and 12)	**74,545**	55,558
	96,690	71,677
Earnings before income taxes and non-controlling interest	**287,192**	261,927
Income taxes (Note 4)	**92,202**	85,379
Earnings before non-controlling interest	**194,990**	176,548
Non-controlling interest	**4,406**	1,338
Net earnings	**$ 190,584**	$ 175,210
Earnings per share (Note 23)	**$ 1.66**	$ 1.53
Diluted earnings per share (Note 23)	**$ 1.64**	$ 1.51

[a]Refer to Note 2, Changes in accounting policies.

The accompanying notes are an integral part of the consolidated financial statements.

Consolidated Retained Earnings
Consolidated Contributed Surplus
Years ended December 31, 2006 and December 25, 2005
(in thousands of dollars)

	2006	2005
Consolidated Retained Earnings		
Balance, beginning of year	**$518,883**	$343,673
Net earnings	**190,584**	175,210
Balance, end of year	**$709,467**	$518,883
Consolidated Contributed Surplus		
Balance, beginning of year	**$ 6,618**	$ 2,945
Compensation cost relating to stock-based compensation plans	**2,490**	2,408
Exercise of stock options	**(177)**	(69)
Gain on disposal of the company's common shares by joint ventures and a subsidiary, net of income taxes of $59 ($313 in 2005)	**251**	1,334
Balance, end of year	**$ 9,182**	$ 6,618

The accompanying notes are an integral part of the consolidated financial statements.

RONA Inc.
Consolidated Cash Flows
Years ended December 31, 2006 and December 25, 2005
(in thousands of dollars)

	2006	2005
Operating activities		
Net earnings	$ 190,584	$ 175,210
Non-cash items		
Depreciation and amortization	74,545	55,558
Future income taxes	8,933	9,749
Net gain on disposal of assets	(1,594)	(3,357)
Compensation cost relating to stock-based compensation plans	2,490	2,408
Non-controlling interest	4,406	1,338
Other items	3,957	(2,195)
	283,321	238,711
Changes in working capital items (Note 5)	116	(79,999)
Cash flows from operating activities	283,437	158,712
Investing activities		
Business acquisitions (Note 6)	(168,872)	(123,335)
Advances to joint ventures and other advances	(5,295)	926
Other investments	(1,310)	(3,212)
Fixed assets	(232,173)	(143,969)
Other assets	(10,889)	(6,570)
Disposal of assets	6,852	34,499
Cash flows from investing activities	(411,687)	(241,661)
Financing activities		
Bank loans and revolving credit	(199,808)	100,563
Other long-term debt	406,302	5,147
Financing costs	(6,826)	—
Repayment of other long-term debt and redemption of preferred shares	(21,488)	(28,321)
Issue of common shares	4,701	4,149
Issue of equity securities to non-controlling interest	735	1,000
Redemption of equity securities from non-controlling interest	(1,000)	—
Cash flows from financing activities	182,616	82,538
Net increase (decrease) in cash	54,366	(411)
Cash, beginning of year	4,120	4,531
Cash, end of year	$ 58,486	$ 4,120
Supplementary information		
Interest paid	$ 15,791	$ 11,612
Income taxes paid	$ 80,116	$ 81,700

The accompanying notes are an integral part of the consolidated financial statements.

CASES AND PROJECTS

FINDING AND INTERPRETING FINANCIAL INFORMATION

■ LO2, 3

Van Houtte

ANALYSIS

CP6–1 **Finding Financial Information**

Refer to the financial statements of Van Houtte Inc., given in Appendix B at the end of this book. At the bottom of each statement, the company warns readers to "See accompanying notes to consolidated financial statements." The following questions illustrate the types of information that you can find in the financial statements and accompanying notes.

Required:

1. The company spent $32,957,000 on capital expenditures (fixed assets) this year. Were operating activities or financing activities the major source of cash for these expenditures?

2. What was the company's largest asset (net) at the end of the year?

3. What was the amount of interest expense for the most recent year?

CP6–2 Finding Financial Information

■ **LO2, 3**

Refer to the Online Learning Centre at **www.mcgrawhill.ca/olc/libby/student/resources** for the financial statements of The Forzani Group Ltd. (FGL). The following questions illustrate the types of information that you can find in the financial statements and accompanying notes. (*Hint:* Use the notes.)

The Forzani Group

ANALYSIS

Required:

1. What was the highest stock price for the company during the current year?

2. How much land did the company own at the end of the current year?

3. What was the amortization expense for the current year?

4. What amount of goodwill did the company report at the end of the current year?

FINANCIAL REPORTING AND ANALYSIS CASES

CP6–3 Interpreting the Financial Press

■ **LO3**

The Committee of Sponsoring Organizations (COSO) published a research study that examined financial statement fraud occurrences between 1987 and 1997. A summary of the findings by M. S. Beasley, J. V. Carcello, and D. R. Hermanson, "Fraudulent Financial Reporting: 1987–1997: An Analysis of U.S. Public Companies," *The Auditor's Report*, Summer 1999, pp. 15–17, is available on the Online Learning Centre at **www.mcgrawhill. ca/olc/libby/student/resources**.* Read the article and then write a short memo outlining the following:

The Auditor's Report

1. The size of the companies involved.

2. The extent of top management involvement.

3. The specific accounting fraud techniques involved.

4. What might lead managers to introduce misstatements into the income statement near the end of the accounting period.

*Reprinted with permission from *The Auditor's Report*, copyright © 1999 by American Institute of Certified Public Accountants, Inc.

CP6–4 Using Financial Reports: Financial Statement Inferences

■ **LO2, 3**

The following amounts were selected from the annual financial statements for Genesis Corporation at December 31, 2008 (end of the third year of operations):

From the 2008 income statement:	
Sales revenue	$275,000
Cost of goods sold	(170,000)
All other expenses (including income tax)	(95,000)
Net income	10,000
From the December 31, 2008, balance sheet:	
Current assets	$ 90,000
All other assets	212,000
Total assets	302,000
Current liabilities	40,000
Long-term liabilities	66,000
Common shares*	100,000
Contributed surplus	16,000
Retained earnings	80,000
Total liabilities and shareholders' equity	$302,000

*10,000 shares issued and outstanding throughout the year.

Required:

Analyze the data on the 2008 financial statements of Genesis by answering the questions that follow. Show computations.

1. What was the gross margin on sales?
2. What was the amount of earnings per share?
3. If the income tax rate was 25 percent, what was the amount of pretax income?
4. What was the average issuance price per common share?
5. Assuming that no dividends were declared or paid during 2008, what was the beginning balance (January 1, 2008) of retained earnings?

LO3

Geox

CP6–5 Using Financial Reports: Interpreting International Financial Statement Classifications (Challenging)

As the economy becomes more international in scope, users of financial statements may be expected to analyze companies that are not incorporated in Canada. Geox S.p.A. is a major world corporation located in Italy. The company produces and markets classic, casual, and sports footwear and apparel for men, women, and children. It has become the first footwear brand in Italy and ranks third worldwide. Its products are sold in 68 countries.

Required:

Based on the concepts presented in this book, explain the meaning of the various account classifications shown on the portion of the Geox annual report presented here. (*Note:* The notes to the company's financial statements, available at **www.geox.in.com/inglese/index.asp**, provide some insight about these accounts.)

GEOX S.p.A.
Consolidated Balance Sheet
December 31, 2006 and 2005

BALANCE SHEET

(Thousands of Euro)	Notes	Dec. 31, 2006	Dec. 31, 2005
Assets:			
Intangible fixed assets	13	38,057	33,908
Tangible fixed assets	14	32,070	29,029
Deferred tax assets	15	12,466	8,739
Financial fixed assets	20–32	856	—
Other fixed assets	16	5,006	6,833
Total fixed assets		**88,455**	**78,509**
Inventories	17	130,997	107,756
Accounts receivable	18	84,159	74,553
Other current assets	9	20,108	10,828
Financial current assets	20–32	112	2,552
Cash and cash equivalents	21	84,926	61,513
Current assets		**320,302**	**257,202**
Total assets		**408,757**	**335,711**
Liabilities and Shareholders' Equity:			
Share capital	22	25,884	25,884
Reserves	22	153,495	102,663
Net income	22	97,262	75,253
Shareholders' equity	**22**	**276,641**	**203,800**
Employee severance indemnities	23	3,349	2,686
Provisions for liabilities and charges	24	2,294	1,313
Long-term portion of loans	25	1,829	2,475
Other long-term payables	26	1,219	1,144
Total long-term liabilities		**8,691**	**7,618**
Accounts payable	27	96,860	84,665
Other current liabilities	28	14,669	11,249
Taxes payable	29	6,002	15,109
Financial current liabilities	20–32	2,638	932
Bank borrowings and current portion of loans	30	3,256	12,257
Current liabilities		**123,425**	**124,293**
Total liabilities and shareholders' equity		**408,757**	**335,711**

CP6–6 Using Financial Reports: Analyzing Income Statement–Based Executive Bonuses

Callaway Golf believes in tying executives' compensation to the company's performance as measured by accounting numbers. In a recent year, Callaway had agreed to pay its five executive officers bonuses of up to 200 percent of base salary if sales growth and pretax earnings as a percentage of sales (computed here) met or exceeded target amounts. Callaway's income statements for the relevant years are presented here.

(in thousands, except per share data)	Year Ended December 31			
	Current Year		Prior Year	
Net sales	$254,645	100%	$132,058	100%
Cost of goods sold	115,458	45%	62,970	48%
Gross profit	139,187	55%	69,088	52%
Selling expenses	38,485	15%	19,810	15%
General and administrative expenses	28,633	11%	14,990	11%
Research and development costs	3,653	1%	1,585	1%
Income from operations	68,416	27%	32,703	25%
Other income				
Interest income, net	1,024		403	
Other income, net	160	—	69	—
Income before income taxes and cumulative effect of accounting change	69,600	27%	33,175	25%
Provision for income taxes	28,396	—	13,895	—
Income before cumulative effect of accounting change	41,204	16%	19,280	15%
Cumulative effect of accounting change	1,658	—		—
Net income	$ 42,862	17%	$ 19,280	15%

Callaway executives will receive bonuses if *sales growth* and *pretax earnings as a percentage of sales* meet or exceed target amounts (35.1 percent and 21.1 percent, respectively). Meeting these goals in the current year would result in bonuses ranging from $400,000 to $700,000 for each of the five executive officers.

Required:
Use the preceding information to determine whether Callaway executives earned their bonuses in the most recent year presented.

CRITICAL THINKING CASES

CP6–7 Assessing the Relevance and Reliability of Information

Intrawest is a world leader in destination resorts and leisure travel. The company's success formula starts with a resort and then builds an animated village with shops, hotels, conventions facilities, and restaurants. Intrawest's development of real estate properties has resulted in a significant portfolio of real estate holdings.

By June 30, 2005, Intrawest's assets included resort properties with a book value of US$791.8 million, representing the costs incurred by the company to acquire land and build its resort properties. In contrast, financial analysts estimated the market value of these properties at amounts ranging from US$1.12 billion to US$1.70 billion. In fact, analyst Michael Smith of National Bank Financial estimated the market value of Intrawest's real estate at US$1.12 billion compared to an estimate of US$1.45 billion by Pirate Capital. However, both of these estimates were lower than a third estimate by Mark Hill of JMP Securities, which values these properties at US$1.70 billion. (Source: Erik Heinrich, "King of the Hill," *Canadian Business*, April 10–23, 2006, pp. 21–22.)

Required:
1. Assume the role of an auditor of Intrawest's financial statements. Which of these four values would you advise the company's management to report on its balance sheet at June 30, 2005? Justify your reasoning.

2. Assume the role of an investment broker who is advising a client about the purchase of Intrawest's resort properties. Which value would you use as a basis for your recommendation to your client and why?

■ **LO3**

Nortel Networks

CP6–8   **Evaluating an Ethical Dilemma: Management Incentives and Fraudulent Financial Statements**

Nortel Networks is one of the top global makers of telecommunication equipment in North America. It makes core network switching, wireless, and optical systems for customers worldwide. The company grew over time through acquisitions of other companies and reached a peak in 2000, prior to the collapse of the market for telecom equipment. The drastic decline in demand for its products forced management to lay off thousands of employees to cut down on financial losses. The financial losses led top management to manipulate the company's earnings to improve the company's image in the market. In April 2004, Nortel fired its CEO and its CFO amid an accounting scandal. The nature of the accounting manipulation is described in the following excerpts from an article that appeared in the *Wall Street Journal*.

Reversing the Charges: Nortel Board Finds Accounting Tricks Behind '03 Profits; A Telecom Star Manipulated Its Reserves, Hid Losses, An Investigation Discovers; How to Empty the Cookie Jar

Frank Dunn, the chief executive of Nortel Networks Corp., pledged in 2002 to end the giant telecom-equipment maker's years of red ink. At the start of 2003, the company was no closer to that goal. In January, Nortel's executives told its board that the company would lose $112 million in the year's first quarter.

Then the outlook suddenly improved. In mid-February, Nortel's expected quarterly loss—based on the company's own definition of the term—shrunk to $32 million, according to people familiar with the matter. A week later, the projected loss was revised to $20 million. By March 30, when the quarter ended, Nortel had a profit of $40 million, its first positive quarterly result in four years. Based on a bonus plan dubbed "Return to Profitability," nearly every employee received a cash award. After two more profitable quarters, senior executives were given millions of dollars in bonuses.

But the profits turned out to be illusory. According to people familiar with the situation, Nortel's board has determined the company inaccurately employed an accounting maneuver to make it look profitable, when in fact it wasn't. In some cases, the dollar amounts of the many individual moves were so small they were almost impossible to detect.

After making the discovery, Nortel's board fired Mr. Dunn one evening in late April, along with Nortel's chief financial officer and controller. The board debated until 10 p.m. the wording of a press release. The next day, Nortel said the three men had been "terminated for cause." The company didn't provide a detailed explanation of the alleged accounting manipulation.

. . .

Board members don't yet know if any one person instigated the alleged wrongdoing, according to people familiar with their thinking, but they believe it was conducted at "senior levels." The three fired executives, Mr. Dunn, former chief financial officer, Douglas Beatty, and former controller Michael Gollogly, declined both written and oral requests to comment on this account.

. . .

People with knowledge of the board's investigation say the alleged manipulation centred on the misuse of an accounting entry known as accrued liabilities. Accrued liabilities derive from the charges companies often take for matters such as merger costs, write-downs and, in Nortel's case, contractual liabilities.

For example, a company might take a charge if it missed a deadline on a $10-million contract and reasonably believed the error would cost it $1 million in the future—through a customer refund, perhaps. The company would count the $1-million future liability as an expense, which would reduce its earnings in the quarter. It would be entered on the balance sheet as a liability until it was paid. Over time, these liabilities can add up.

Under certain rules, companies can dip into their accrued liabilities and count the withdrawn sum as income. For example, if the company agreed to pay its customer $600,000 for the missed deadline, instead of the $1 million set aside, the company would be able to count the unused $400,000 as profit in the quarter when the customer was paid.

This system can be abused two ways. Companies can exaggerate the liability or hold it on their books too long, in both cases hoping to use the reserves to plump earnings at a later date. This is known in the finance world as "cookie jar" accounting, which is among the most common financial frauds, accounting experts say. "It's probably one of the big three," says Robert Willens, a tax and accounting analyst at Lehman Brothers.

In the first and second quarters of 2003, the board has determined, Nortel emptied the cookie jar. Reserves were inappropriately taken off the balance sheet and added to the company's earnings. The board hasn't found a legitimate trigger for the reserves to be released.

Nortel had also overstated the size of its reserves, a move that gave it a larger pot to dip into. The company said in filings with the SEC in October 2003 that some of its reserves "were recorded in excess of the amounts that now have been determined would have been appropriate at the time of recording." Although taking inflated reserves would initially depress a company's net income, Nortel, like many other companies, dubbed the taking of reserves a "one time" or "special" event, which it encouraged investors to overlook. The "pro forma" earnings Nortel released until recently didn't include these charges.

. . .

Inflating reserve accounts had been a routine end-of-the-quarter game among finance executives at Nortel for years, several former finance executives say. The practice of holding extra reserves was so common that Nortel executives gave it a name: "hardness." In Nortel parlance, having hardness meant having reserves on hand that could be released at some later date to help the company meet Wall Street's profit targets.

Divisional finance chiefs closely guarded their own reserves, which they in turn used to meet internal targets, according to former executives. That meant even the top finance executives didn't have a full grasp of the extent of the reserve provisions.

. . .

Investors used to ignore charges relating to reserves, especially if they occur amid otherwise very good or very bad years. Given that Nortel lost $34 billion from 2000 to 2002, investors didn't pay much attention to several hundred million dollars in reserve-related losses.

But in the summer of 2002, some investors voiced concern to Nortel's executives because the company's accrued liabilities had ballooned to $5 billion. Investors worried Nortel would collapse if they all came due at the same time. To deal with the concerns, Mr. Beatty, the controller at the time, began a review of the company's balance sheet that was continued by Mr. Gollogly when he took the job.

As a result, finance executives found an estimated $303 million of liabilities that were in some way inaccurate, according to people familiar with Nortel. The exercise was not disclosed to investors. It isn't known exactly what was done about those liabilities, but some executives now at Nortel believe some were added to the company's earnings in the third and fourth quarter of 2002. Nortel reported losses in both quarters.

In the first half of 2003, the long-standing practice of dipping into reserves became more significant when it was used to turn losses into profits. Finance executives distributed a document showing the quarter's earnings targets, according to a copy viewed by *The Wall Street Journal*. As the weeks went on, that number kept improving until the expected loss turned into a profit. Each time the profit or loss figure changed, another number on the spreadsheet, labelled "balance sheet," changed too, suggesting that the increase in earnings was funded by Nortel's reserve accounts.

In the first quarter, Nortel made $40 million in what it dubbed pro forma income. Nortel had long used this number—its own measure of profit—in earnings press releases. After investors broadly criticized that formulation for not conforming to standard accounting principles, Nortel, like many other companies, stopped reporting pro forma income in 2003. It still used that number internally for matters including calculating bonuses. At the time, Nortel's reported first-quarter net income was $54 million.

Out of public view, Nortel included in its first-quarter profits about $361 million in reserves. Roughly $160 million of that, the company's board has determined, was inappropriately released. At the time, Nortel identified $80 million of releases in a regulatory filing, saying they were no longer needed. When directors pressed executives at an April 2003 board meeting, they were told the remaining releases related to normal business operations and didn't need to be disclosed, people with knowledge of the meeting said.

Nortel performed an almost identical accounting exercise in the second quarter. Nortel's pro forma profits hit $34 million as a result of the reserve releases. To the public, Nortel actually reported a net loss of $14 million.

The size of the first quarter releases was relatively small compared with Nortel's revenue—the company had sales of $2.3 billion—but they made the difference between a profit and a loss. Under accounting rules, unusual factors leading to such a swing must be disclosed. "If you make [a profit] by doing something that's out of the ordinary you need to tell people about that," says Charles Mulford, an accounting professor at the Georgia Institute of Technology.

Because of that profitable first quarter, most employees received payments equivalent to 10% to 25% of their annual salaries from Nortel's bonus plan. Top managers earned between two and four times their salaries after the company reported four quarters of cumulative pro forma profits. According to bonus plan documents, Mr. Dunn received approximately four times his $900,000 annual salary. Mr. Beatty earned $1.3 million and Mr. Gollogly took home $300,000, according to people familiar with Nortel's compensation.

But in the executive suite, the reserve accounting was causing a rift. Some executives worried the reserves were being released inconsistently, a problem that could make the decisions harder to justify if that was necessary, according to people who have spoken to Mr. Gollogly.

In a decision that ultimately sparked Nortel's unraveling, the board pushed the company's executives to clean up the company's balance sheet and reduce confusion caused by years of accumulated reserve accounting. Mr. Gollogly, the controller, launched the effort in May 2003.

As a result of the house-cleaning, Nortel restated 3 1/2 years of financial results in December 2003. The company announced it had discovered $950 million in faulty reserves; some were inappropriately taken and others should have been released earlier. Nortel retroactively shifted them among past quarterly earnings totals, including the first two quarters of 2003 that are under question.

In the filing that detailed the restatement, Nortel's auditor, Deloitte & Touche, said the company had "material weakness" in its internal controls and specifically cited the balance-sheet-reserve accounts. While Nortel said at the time its reserves were higher than they should have been, it didn't link them to the more elaborate effort to manipulate earnings.

Board members wanted to make sure Nortel didn't make another earnings restatement and hired former SEC enforcement director William McLucas, now a partner at Wilmer Cutler Pickering Hale & Dorr LLP, to figure out how the errors occurred. Mr. McLucas had previously been hired to investigate scandals at both Enron Corp. and WorldCom Inc.

The board's inquiry began in late December. By the spring, it discovered something it wasn't looking for: the alleged manipulation of the company's reserve accounts. Led by Chairman Lynton R. Wilson, who once ran Bell Canada, and Audit Committee Chairman John E. Cleghorn, the former CEO of Royal Bank of Canada, the board suspended Messrs. Beatty and Gollogly in March.

Some former employees and critics say board members, many of whom were former ambassadors and Canadian corporate leaders, should have spotted the accounting problems earlier.

Donald Thain, professor emeritus at Richard Ivey School of Business in London, Ontario, says the board members had impressive credentials but were stretched too thin. Many served on multiple boards. "Unfortunately, they were unwilling, unable or didn't have the time to do the job that was necessary," Mr. Thain says.

People familiar with the board's thinking say the directors feel they were misled by the company's executives. A spokeswoman for Deloitte & Touche, the company's auditors, said confidentiality rules prevented the firm from commenting on client matters.

. . .

Source: Ken Brown and Mark Heinzl. *Wall Street Journal*. (Eastern edition). New York, N.Y.: July 2, 2004, p. A.1.

Copyright © 2004, Dow Jones & Company Inc.

Required:

1. Identify the various stakeholders that are involved in this alleged accounting fraud and the roles that they have played in the accounting communication process that led eventually to the discovery of manipulated earnings.

2. How might executive compensation plans that tied bonuses to accounting earnings motivate unethical conduct in this case?

3. Using more recent news reports through such media as *Factiva, Bloomberg Business News*, or your favourite search engine, identify the main developments that occurred following the discovery of the earnings manipulation?

FINANCIAL REPORTING AND ANALYSIS TEAM PROJECT

LO2, 3   **CP6–9**   **Team Project: Analyzing the Accounting Communication Process**

ANALYSIS

As a team, select an industry to analyze. *Reuters* provides lists of industries and their make-up at **www.investor.reuters.com/Industries.aspx**. Each team member should acquire the annual report for one publicly traded company in the industry, with each member selecting a different company. (Library files, the SEDAR service at **www.sedar.com**, or the company itself are good sources.)

Required:

On an individual basis, each team member should write a short report answering the following questions about the selected company. Discuss any patterns across the companies that you as a team observe. Then, as a team, write a short report comparing and contrasting your companies.

1. What formats are used to present the
   a. Balance Sheets?
   b. Income Statements?
   c. Operating Activities section of the Cash Flow Statements?

2. Find a footnote for each of the following and describe its contents in brief:
   a. An accounting rule applied in the company's statements.
   b. Additional detail about a reported financial statement number.
   c. Relevant financial information but without numbers reported in the financial statements.

3. Using electronic sources, find one article reporting the company's annual earnings announcement. When is it dated and how does that date compare to the balance sheet date?

4. Using electronic sources, find two analysts' reports for your company.
   a. Give the date, name of the analyst, and his/her recommendation from each report.
   b. Discuss why the recommendations are similar or different. Look at the analysts' reasoning for their respective recommendations.

Reporting and Interpreting Sales Revenue, Receivables, and Cash

7

After studying this chapter, you should be able to:

FOCUS COMPANY:

Gildan Activewear Inc.

BUILDING BRANDS TO BUILD GROSS PROFIT:

MANAGING PRODUCT DEVELOPMENT,

PRODUCTION, AND WORKING CAPITAL

Over the past several years, casual wear has become increasingly acceptable in the workplace as employers adopt flexible dress codes. Gildan Activewear Inc., (www.gildan.com) which is based in Montreal, Quebec, took advantage of this trend and became a significant producer and marketer of high-quality casual wear, including T-shirts, sports shirts, and sweatshirts. In 2006, Gildan expanded its product line to include underwear and basic athletic socks. Gildan started as a family operation, and grew to become a publicly traded company in both Canada and the United States.

Gildan's sales grew from US$224 million for fiscal year 1999 to US$773.2 million for fiscal 2006*. Such a growth in sales could not happen if the company did not pursue specific business strategies to produce quality products and market them to its customers. The company's focus on low-cost manufacturing of premium-quality casual wear and its marketing philosophy of controlled distribution have been important factors in its success. The company's management recognized that its dedication to being the lowest-cost producer and leading marketer of branded basic casual wear to wholesale channels of distribution required the adoption of a set of objectives and principles such as (1) nurturing and strengthening the Gildan Activewear brand, (2) remaining price-competitive by constantly reinvesting in state-of-the-art facilities, and (3) maintaining strong relationships with the distributors of the company's products. These objectives and related action plans are aimed at increasing net sales and/or decreasing the cost of sales, thereby increasing gross profit.

*Gildan uses the US dollar as a reporting currency because a significant portion of its revenues, expenses, assets, and liabilities are denominated in US dollars.

UNDERSTANDING THE BUSINESS

The success of each element of Gildan's strategy is seen in the information presented in the income statement excerpt in Exhibit 7.1. Net Sales (Revenue) is reported first, and Cost of Sales (Cost of Goods Sold, Cost of Products Sold) is set out separately from the remaining expenses. Next, the income statement shows *gross profit (gross margin)*, which is net sales revenue minus cost of sales.

Planning Gildan's growth strategy requires careful coordination of sales and production activities, as well as cash collection from customers. Much of this coordination revolves around the use of credit card and sales discounts, managing sales returns and bad debts. These activities affect *net sales revenue* on the income statement and *cash* and *accounts receivable* on the balance sheet, which are the focus of this chapter. We will also introduce the gross profit percentage ratio as a basis for evaluating changes in gross profit, as well as the receivables turnover ratio as a measure of the efficiency of credit-granting and collection activities. Finally, since the cash collected from customers is also a tempting target for frauds and embezzlement, we will discuss how accounting systems commonly include controls to prevent and detect such misdeeds.

Lenders, shareholders, and analysts also carefully monitor these accounts because of their importance as predictors of the future success of companies. Their importance is supported by the fact that the majority of shareholder lawsuits and enforcement actions by securities regulators against companies for misleading financial statements relate to these accounts.

EXHIBIT **7.1**

Net Sales and Gross Profit on the Income Statement

REAL WORLD EXCERPT

Gildan Activewear

ANNUAL REPORT

Consolidated Statements of Earnings
Years ended October 1, 2006, October 2, 2005, and October 3, 2004
(in thousands of US dollars)

	2006	2005	2004
Net sales	$773,190	$653,851	$533,368
Cost of sales	521,095	450,570	378,696
Gross profit	252,095	203,281	154,672

ORGANIZATION OF THE CHAPTER

Accounting for Sales Revenue	Measuring and Reporting Receivables	Reporting and Safeguarding Cash
• Sales to Consumers • Sales Discounts to Businesses • Sales Returns and Allowances • Reporting Net Sales • Gross Profit Percentage	• Classifying Receivables • Accounting for Bad Debts • Reporting Accounts Receivable • Estimating Bad Debts • Internal Control and Management Responsibility • Control over Accounts Receivable	• Cash and Cash Equivalents Defined • Cash Management • Internal Control of Cash • Reconciliation of the Cash Accounts and the Bank Statements

ACCOUNTING FOR SALES REVENUE

As indicated in Chapter 3, the *revenue principle* requires that revenues be recorded when they are earned (delivery has occurred or services have been rendered, the earnings process is complete or nearly complete, and collection is reasonably assured). For sellers of goods, these criteria are most often met and sales revenue is recorded when title and risks of ownership pass to the buyer. The point at which title (ownership) changes hands is determined by the shipping terms in the sales contract. When goods are shipped *FOB (free on board) shipping point*, title changes hands at shipment, and the buyer normally pays for shipment. When they are shipped *FOB destination point*, title changes hands on delivery, and the seller normally pays for shipment. Revenues from goods sold FOB shipping point are normally recognized at shipment. Revenues from goods sold FOB destination point are normally recognized at delivery.

Service companies most often record sales revenue when they have provided services to the buyer. Companies disclose the specific revenue recognition rule they follow in the notes to their financial statements entitled Summary of Significant Accounting Policies. In that note, Gildan reports the following:

> ## NOTES TO CONSOLIDATED FINANCIAL STATEMENTS
>
> ### 1. Summary of significant accounting policies
> *Revenue Recognition*
> Sales are recognized upon shipment of products to customers, since title passes upon shipment. At the time of sale, estimates are made for customer price discounts and rebates based upon existing programs. Accruals required for new programs, which relate to prior sales, are recorded at the time the new program is introduced. Sales are recorded net of these program costs and a provision for estimated sales returns, which is based on historical experience and other known factors, and exclude sales taxes.

> **REAL WORLD EXCERPT**
>
> *Gildan Activewear*
> ANNUAL REPORT

Like Gildan, many manufacturers, wholesalers, and retailers recognize revenue at shipment. This is when title and risks of ownership pass to the buyer. Auditors expend a lot of effort to ensure that revenue recognition rules are applied consistently and revenues are recognized in the proper period.

The appropriate *amount* of revenue to record is the *cash equivalent sales price*. Sales practices differ depending on whether sales are made to businesses or consumers. Gildan sells its products primarily through wholesale distributors, a strategy that enables the company to use a small sales force. Gildan sells its products to a network of more than 200 distributors in over 20 countries, who in turn resell the blank products to garment decorators. Consumers ultimately purchase the company's products in such venues as sports, entertainment and corporate events as well as travel and tourism destinations. In 2005, Gildan decided to enter the retail market and began selling its product line of activewear, underwear, and athletic socks to Canadian and U.S. retailers.

Gildan uses a variety of methods to motivate customers to buy their products and make payment for their purchases. The principal methods include (1) allowing customers to use credit cards to pay for purchases, (2) providing business customers direct credit and discounts for early payment, and (3) allowing returns from all customers under certain circumstances. These methods, in turn, affect the way we compute *net sales revenue*.

SALES TO CONSUMERS

Sales to consumers are for cash or credit card (mainly Visa, MasterCard, and American Express). The seller accepts credit cards as payment for a variety of reasons:

1. Increasing customer traffic at its stores.
2. Avoiding the costs of providing credit directly to customers, including record keeping and bad debts (discussed later).

> **LEARNING OBJECTIVE 1**
>
> Apply the revenue principle to determine the accepted time to record sales revenue for typical retailers, wholesalers, manufacturers, and service companies.

> **LEARNING OBJECTIVE 2**
>
> Analyze the impact of credit card sales, sales discounts, and sales returns on the amounts reported as net sales.

3. Lowering losses due to bad cheques.

4. Avoiding losses from fraudulent credit card sales. (Normally, the credit card company absorbs any losses if the seller follows the credit card company's verification procedure.)

5. Faster receipt of its money. (Since credit card receipts can be directly deposited in its bank account, the seller receives its money faster than it would if it provided credit directly to consumers.)

The credit card company charges a fee for the service it provides. For example, when a seller deposits its credit card receipts in the bank, it might receive credit for an amount equal to only 97 percent of the sales price. The credit card company is charging a 3-percent fee (the **credit card discount**) for its service. If credit card sales were $3,000 on January 2, the seller reports the following:[1]

A **CREDIT CARD DISCOUNT** is the fee charged by the credit card company for services.

Sales revenue	$3,000
Less: Credit card discounts (0.03 × $3,000)	90
Net sales (reported on the income statement)	$2,910

SALES DISCOUNTS TO BUSINESSES

Most of Gildan's sales to businesses are credit sales on open account; that is, there is no formal written promissory note indicating the amount owed to Gildan by the customer. When Gildan sells T-shirts to wholesalers on credit, credit terms are printed on each sales document and invoice (bill) sent to the customer. Often credit terms are abbreviated, using symbols. For example, if the full amount of the invoice is due within 30 days of the invoice date, the credit terms would be noted as *n/30*. Here, the *n* means the sales amount *net* of or less any sales returns.

A **SALES (OR CASH) DISCOUNT** is a cash discount offered to encourage prompt payment of an account receivable.

In other cases, a **sales discount** (often called a **cash discount**) is granted to the purchaser to encourage early payment.[2] For example, Gildan may offer standard credit terms of 2/10, n/30, which means that the customer may deduct 2 percent from the invoice amount if cash payment is made within 10 days from the date of sale. If cash payment is not made within the 10-day discount period, the full invoice amount (less any returns) is due within a maximum of 30 days.

Early Payment Incentive

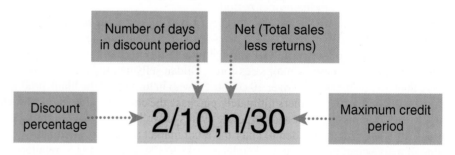

---

[1]Some retail businesses, such as Canadian Tire (CT), issue their own cards, and avoid credit card discounts when customers use CT's credit card to pay for their purchases.

[2]It is important not to confuse a cash discount with a trade discount. Vendors sometimes use a *trade discount* for quoting sales prices; the sales price is the list or printed catalogue price *less* the trade discount. For example, an item may be quoted at $10 per unit subject to a 20-percent trade discount on orders of 100 units or more; thus, the price for the large order is $8 per unit. Similarly, the price on a slow-moving product line can be lowered simply by increasing the trade discount. Sales revenue should always be recorded net of trade discounts. Manufacturers also offer discounts for early order and shipment to help manage production flows.

Gildan offers this sales discount to encourage customers to pay more quickly. This provides two benefits to Gildan:

1. Prompt receipt of cash from customers reduces the necessity to borrow money to meet operating needs.
2. Since customers tend to pay bills providing discounts first, a sales discount also decreases the chances that the customer will run out of funds before Gildan's bill is paid.

Companies commonly record sales discounts taken by subtracting the discount from sales if payment is made *within* the discount period (the usual case).[3] For example, if credit sales are recorded with terms 2/10, n/30 and payment of $980 (= $1,000 × 0.98) is made within the discount period, net sales of the following amount would be reported:

Sales revenue	$1,000
Less: Sales discounts (0.02 × $1,000)	20
Net sales (reported on the income statement)	$ 980

If the payment is made after the discount period, the full $1,000 would be reported as net sales.

Note that both the purpose of and the accounting for sales discounts are very similar to the purpose of and the accounting for credit card discounts. Both sales discounts and credit card discounts provide an attractive service to customers while promoting faster receipt of cash, reducing recordkeeping costs, and minimizing bad debts. Accounting for sales discounts is discussed in more detail in Supplement A.

TO TAKE OR NOT TO TAKE THE DISCOUNT, THAT IS THE QUESTION

FINANCIAL ANALYSIS

Customers usually pay within the discount period because the savings are substantial. With terms 2/10, n/30, 2 percent is saved by paying 20 days early (the 10th day instead of the 30th), which is equivalent to an annual interest rate of 37 percent. This annual interest rate is obtained by first computing the interest rate for the discount period. When the 2-percent discount is taken, the customer pays only 98 percent of the gross sales amount. For example, on a $100 sale with terms 2/10, n/30, $2 would be saved and $98 would be paid 20 days early. The interest rate for the 20-day discount period is

(Amount saved ÷ Amount paid) = Interest rate for 20 days

($2 ÷ $98) = 2.04% for 20 days or 0.102% per day

Given that there are 365 days in a year, the annual interest rate is then computed in the following manner:

Annual interest rate = 0.102% × 365 days = 37.23%

Credit customers would save a lot of money even if they had to borrow cash from a bank at a high rate such as 15 percent to take advantage of cash discounts. Normally, the bank's interest rate is less than the high interest rate associated with failing to take cash discounts.

---

[3]We use the gross method in all examples in this textbook. Some companies use the alternative net method, which records sales revenue after deducting the amount of the cash discount. Since the choice of method has little effect on the financial statements, discussion of this method is left for an advanced course.

A QUESTION OF ETHICS

STRETCHING OUT THE PAYABLES

Hoffa Shoes has been incurring significant interest charges (12 percent) on short-term borrowing from its bank.* Hoffa normally purchases shoes from suppliers on terms 1/10, n/30. The annual rate of interest earned by taking the discount is 18.43 percent computed as follows:

(Amount saved ÷ Amount paid) = Interest rate for 20 days

($1 ÷ $99) = 1.01% for 20 days or 0.0505 per day

Annual interest rate = 0.0505% × 365 days = 18.43%

Hoffa's policy had been to take all purchase discounts even if it had to borrow at 12 percent to make the early payment. Management reasoned that the company earned 6.43 percent more than it paid in interest (18.43 percent − 12 percent).

A new employee suggested a new plan. Records indicated that, even though the terms of Hoffa's agreement with its suppliers (1/10, n/30) required payment of the full amount within a maximum of 30 days, the suppliers would not complain as long as payment was made within 55 days of the purchase date, since they normally did not send out a second bill until 60 days after the purchase date. She reasoned that Hoffa would be better off forgoing the discount and paying on the 55th day after the purchase date. She argued that since Hoffa would now be paying in 55 days instead of 10 days of the purchase, not taking the discount would be borrowing for 45 days, not the 20 days used in the former analysis. The analysis supporting the proposal is as follows:

(Amount saved ÷ Amount paid) = Interest rate for 45 days

($1 ÷ $99) = 1.01% for 45 days or 0.02244%

Annual interest rate = 0.02244% × 365 days = 8.19%

*Hoffa Shoes is a fictitious company, but most companies face this dilemma.

In effect, her plan allows Hoffa to borrow from suppliers at 8.19 percent instead of the bank's rate of 12 percent, saving 3.81 percent. When she presented this plan to the management for discussion, the purchasing manager agreed with the arithmetic presented but objected nonetheless. Since the plan violated its agreement with suppliers, the purchasing manager thought it was unethical. Many ethical dilemmas in business involve trade-offs between monetary benefits and potential violations of moral values.

SALES RETURNS AND ALLOWANCES is a reduction of sales revenues for return of or allowances for unsatisfactory goods.

SALES RETURNS AND ALLOWANCES

For Gildan, prompt delivery of exactly what the customer ordered is a key to maintaining good relations with the customers to whom it sells. Delivery of incorrect or damaged merchandise may cost the customer sales and can destroy these relationships. When this occurs, the customers have a right to return unsatisfactory or damaged merchandise and receive a refund or an adjustment to their bill.

Such returns are often accumulated in a separate account called **Sales Returns and Allowances** and must be deducted from gross sales revenue in determining net sales. This account informs Gildan's management of the volume of returns and allowances providing an important measure of the quality of customer service. Assume that a customer bought 40 dozen T-shirts from Gildan for $2,000 on account. Before paying for the T-shirts, the customer discovered that 10 dozen T-shirts were not the colour ordered and returned them to Gildan.[4] Gildan would compute net sales as follows:

Sales revenue	$2,000
Less: Sales returns (0.25 × $2,000)	500
Net sales (reported on the income statement)	$1,500

The cost of goods sold related to the 10 dozen T-shirts would also be reduced.

REPORTING NET SALES

On the company's books, credit card discounts, sales discounts, and sales returns and allowances are accounted for separately to allow managers to monitor the costs of credit card use, sales discounts, and returns. Using the numbers in the preceding examples, the amount of net sales reported on the income statement is computed in the following manner:[5]

Sales revenue	$6,000
Less: Credit card discounts (a contra revenue)	90
Sales discounts (a contra revenue)	20
Sales returns and allowances (a contra revenue)	500
Net sales (reported on the income statement)	$5,390

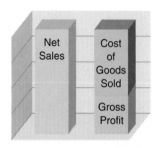

Gildan indicates in its revenue recognition note that its net sales are reported net of appropriate subtractions for these items. Companies rarely disclose the determinants of net sales in the annual report so it often is difficult to determine the effects of these items, even for well-educated external users. As we noted earlier, net sales less cost of goods sold equals the subtotal *gross profit* or *gross margin*. Analysts often examine gross profit as a percentage of net sales, called the gross profit or gross margin percentage.

GROSS PROFIT PERCENTAGE   KEY RATIO ANALYSIS

ANALYTICAL QUESTION → How effective is management in selling goods and services for more than the costs to purchase or produce them?

RATIO AND COMPARISONS → The gross profit percentage is helpful in answering this question. It is computed as follows:

$$\text{Gross Profit Percentage} = \frac{\text{Gross Profit}}{\text{Net Sales}}$$

The 2006 ratio for Gildan is:

$$\frac{\$252,095}{\$773,190} = 0.326 \ (32.6\%)$$

■ LEARNING OBJECTIVE 3

Compute and interpret the gross profit percentage.

Comparisons over Time			Comparisons with Competitors	
Gildan			**Delta Apparel**	**Hanesbrands**
2004	2005	2006	2006	2006
29%	31.1%	32.6%	29.6%	33.2%

---

[4]Alternatively, Gildan might offer the customer a $200 allowance to keep the wrong-colour T-shirts. If the customer accepts the offer Gildan would report $200 as sales returns and allowances.

[5]Sales and credit card discounts may also be reported as expenses on the income statement.

Selected Focus Company Comparisons

Forzani Group 34%

Dell Inc. 18%

Home Depot 34%

INTERPRETATIONS

In General → The gross profit percentage measures how much gross profit is generated from every sales dollar. It reflects the ability to charge premium prices and produce goods and services at low cost. All other things being equal, a higher gross profit results in higher net income.

Business strategy, as well as competition, affects the gross profit percentage. Companies pursuing a product-differentiation strategy use research and development and product promotion activities to convince customers of the superiority or distinctiveness of the company's products. This allows them to charge premium prices, producing higher gross profit percentages. Companies following a low-cost strategy rely on more efficient management of production to reduce costs and increase the gross profit percentage. Managers, analysts, and creditors use this ratio to assess the effectiveness of the company's product development, marketing, and production strategy.

Focus Company Analysis → Gildan's gross profit percentage increased over the three-year period, 2004–2006, surpassing that of Delta Apparel in 2006. At the beginning of the chapter, we discussed key elements of Gildan's business strategy that focused on low-cost manufacturing of premium-quality products and its marketing philosophy of controlled distribution. According to Gildan's annual report for fiscal year 2006, the improvement in the gross profit percentage was due primarily to "manufacturing efficiencies, lower cotton costs, and a favourable product mix." In fact, Gildan continues to concentrate its manufacturing facilities in Central America and the Caribbean Basin to reduce its production costs. Gildan's cost of sales excludes amortization of production facilities, which is an important component of the cost of producing activewear, underwear, and athletic socks. Hence, Gildan's gross margins may not be comparable to those of other companies that include amortization of production facilities in their cost of sales.

A Few Cautions → To assess the company's ability to sustain its gross margins, you must understand the sources of any change in its gross profit percentage. For example, an increase in margin resulting from increases in seasonal sales of high-margin products would be judged to be less sustainable than one resulting from introducing new products. Also, higher prices must often be sustained with higher R&D and advertising costs, which can eat up any increase in gross margin. Finally, be aware that a small change in gross profit percentage can lead to a large change in net income.

SELF-STUDY QUIZ 7-1

1. Assume that Sportswear, Inc. sold $30,000 worth of T-shirts to various retailers with terms 1/10, n30, and half of that amount was paid within the discount period. Gross sales at company-owned stores were $5,000 for the same period, 80 percent being paid using credit cards with a 3-percent discount and the rest in cash. Compute net sales for the period.

_____

_____

2. During the first quarter of fiscal year 2007, the company's net sales were $150,000 and cost of sales was $110,000. Verify that its gross profit percentage was 26.66 percent.

_____

_____

After you have answered the questions, check your answers with the solutions on page 375.

MEASURING AND REPORTING RECEIVABLES

CLASSIFYING RECEIVABLES

ACCOUNTS RECEIVABLE (TRADE RECEIVABLES, RECEIVABLES) are open accounts owed to the business by trade customers.

Receivables may be classified in three common ways. First, the receivable may be either an account receivable or a note receivable. An **account receivable** is created when there is a credit sale. For example, an account receivable is created when

Gildan sells on account to a wholesaler. A **note receivable** is a written promise made by another party (e.g., a customer) to pay the company a specified amount of money, called the *principal*, at a definite future date, known as the *maturity date*. In addition, the company receives *interest* on the principal at one or more future dates. Interest is the amount charged for use of the principal. We discuss the computation of interest when we discuss notes payable in a later chapter.

Second, receivables may be classified as trade or non-trade receivables. A *trade receivable* is created in the normal course of business when there is a sale of merchandise or services on credit. A *non-trade receivable* arises from transactions other than the normal sale of merchandise or services. For example, if Gildan loaned money to key employees to assist them in financing the purchase of their first homes, the loans would be classified as non-trade receivables. Third, in a classified balance sheet, receivables also are classified as either *current* or *non-current* (short term or long term), depending on when the cash is expected to be collected. Like many companies, Gildan reports only one type of receivable account, Accounts Receivable from customers (trade receivables), and classifies the asset as a current asset because the accounts receivable should be collected within one year.

Gildan allows its customers (wholesalers and retailers) to purchase goods on open account because it believes that providing this service will result in more sales. Providing this service to customers also has a cost. Gildan must pay to maintain a credit-granting and collection system, and it must realize that not all customers will pay their debts. Credit policies should be set based on the *trade-off* between profits on additional sales and any additional bad debts. In fact, an extremely low rate of bad debts may not be good because it may indicate a credit policy that is too tight. If the credit policy is too restrictive, the company will turn away many good credit customers, causing a loss of sales volume.

> A **NOTE RECEIVABLE** is a written promise that requires another party to pay the business a specified amount at a specific future date.

FOREIGN CURRENCY RECEIVABLES

INTERNATIONAL PERSPECTIVE

Export (international) sales are a growing part of the Canadian economy. For example, international sales amounted to 93 percent of Gildan's revenues in 2006. As is the case with domestic sales to other businesses, most export sales to businesses are on credit. When the buyer has agreed to pay in its local currency instead of Canadian dollars, Gildan cannot add these accounts receivable, which are denominated in foreign currency, directly to its Canadian-dollar accounts receivable*. Gildan's accountants must first convert them into Canadian dollars using the end-of-period exchange rate between the two currencies. For example, if a European distributor purchased goods from Gildan for €20,000 (euros, the common currency of the European Monetary Union) on August 31, 2006, and each euro was worth $1.20 ($Cdn) on that date, Gildan would add $24,000 to its accounts receivable on that date. If Gildan has not collected the €20,000 by October 1, 2006, the end of its fiscal year, then the receivable should be adjusted for the change in the value of the euro, and an exchange gain or loss would be reported on the income statement.

*Gildan has reported its financial statements in U.S. dollars since 2004. The use of Canadian dollars is for illustrative purposes only.

Selected Foreign Currency Exchange Rates (in C$)

Mexican Peso $0.09

Singapore Dollar $0.66

Euro $1.30

ACCOUNTING FOR BAD DEBTS

For billing and collection purposes, Gildan keeps a separate accounts receivable account (called a *subsidiary account*) for each of the retailers and wholesalers that buy its products. The accounts receivable amount on the balance sheet represents the total of these individual customer accounts. When Gildan extends credit to its customers it knows that a certain amount of credit sales may not be collected in the future. The matching

> ■ **LEARNING OBJECTIVE 4**
>
> Estimate, report, and evaluate the effects of uncollectable accounts receivable (bad debts) on financial statements.

principle requires the recording of bad debt expense in the *same* accounting period in which the related sales are made. This presents an important accounting problem. Gildan may not learn which particular customers will not pay until the *next* accounting period. So, at the end of the period of sale, it normally does not know which customers' accounts receivable are bad debts.

Gildan resolves this problem and satisfies the matching principle by using the **allowance method** to estimate the expected amount of bad debts. There are two primary steps in applying the allowance method: (1) the estimation and recording of bad debts expense and (2) writing off specific accounts determined to be uncollectable during the period.

The **ALLOWANCE METHOD** bases bad debt expense on an estimate of uncollectable accounts.

BAD DEBT EXPENSE (DOUBTFUL ACCOUNTS EXPENSE, UNCOLLECTABLE ACCOUNTS EXPENSE) is the expense associated with estimated uncollectable accounts receivable.

Recording Bad Debt Expense Estimates **Bad debt expense** (also called doubtful accounts expense, uncollectable accounts expense) is the expense associated with estimated uncollectable accounts receivable. It is recorded through an *adjusting journal entry at the end of the accounting period*. Assume that for the year ended October 1, 2006, Gildan estimated bad debt expense to be $2,383 and made the following adjusting entry.[6]

Bad debt expense (E).	2,383	
Allowance for doubtful accounts (XA)		2,383

Assets		=	Liabilities	+	Shareholders' Equity	
Allowance for doubtful accounts	−2,383				Bad debt expense	−2,383

The Bad Debt Expense is included in the category "Selling" expenses on the income statement. It decreases net income and shareholders' equity. Accounts Receivable could not be credited in the journal entry because there is no way to know at that date which customers may not pay in the future. The credit is made, instead, to a contra-asset account called **Allowance for Doubtful Accounts** (also called **Allowance for Bad Debts** or **Allowance for Uncollectable Accounts**). As a contra asset, the balance in Allowance for Doubtful Accounts is always subtracted from the balance of the asset Accounts Receivable. Thus, the entry decreases the net book value of Accounts Receivable and total assets.

ALLOWANCE FOR DOUBTFUL ACCOUNTS (ALLOWANCE FOR BAD DEBTS, ALLOWANCE FOR UNCOLLECTABLE ACCOUNTS) is a contra-asset account containing the estimated uncollectable accounts receivable.

Writing Off Specific Uncollectable Accounts *Throughout the year*, when it is determined that a customer will not pay its debt (e.g., due to bankruptcy), the write-off of that individual debt is recorded through a journal entry. Now that the specific uncollectable account receivable has been identified, it can be removed from Accounts Receivable. At the same time, the related estimate of bad debt is no longer needed and is removed from the Allowance for Doubtful Accounts. The following journal entry summarizes the write-offs of $2,356 during the year 2006:

Allowance for doubtful accounts (XA).	2,356	
Accounts receivable (A).		2,356

Assets		=	Liabilities	+	Shareholders' Equity
Allowance for doubtful accounts	+2,356				
Accounts receivable	−2,356				

Notice that this journal entry *did not affect any income statement accounts*. The estimated bad debt expense was already recorded with an adjusting entry in the period of sale. Also, the entry *did not change the net book value of Accounts Receivable*,

---

[6]Gildan did not disclose in its annual report any information about its bad debt expense or the allowance for doubtful accounts. Hence, the amounts used in this example are for illustration purposes only.

since the decrease in the asset account (Accounts Receivable) was offset by an equal decrease in the contra-asset account (Allowance for Doubtful Accounts). Thus, it did not affect total assets.

Recovery of Accounts Previously Written Off   When a customer makes a payment on an account previously written off, the initial journal entry to write off the account is reversed for the amount that is collected, and another journal entry is made to record the collection of cash. Assume that of the $2,356 receivables that were written off during fiscal year 2006, $48 was recovered from a customer that faced financial difficulties but was able to arrange for long-term financing to restart the business. The journal entries and transaction effects related to the recovery of bad debts are shown below:

Accounts receivable (A)	48	
Allowance for doubtful accounts (XA)		48
Cash (A)	48	
Accounts receivable (A)		48

Assets		=	Liabilities	+	Shareholders' Equity
Accounts receivable	+48				
Allowance for doubtful accounts	−48				
Cash	+48				
Accounts receivable	−48				

Notice that the net effect of the recovered amount on Accounts Receivable is zero. The recovered amount is first recorded in Accounts Receivable in order to show that the customer has honoured its previous commitment to pay Gildan $48.

Summary of the Accounting Process   It is important to remember that accounting for bad debts is a two-step process:

Step	Timing	Accounts Affected	Financial Statement Effects
1. Record estimated bad debts adjustment	End of period in which sales are made	Bad Debt Expense (E) ↑	Net Income ↓
		Allowance for Doubtful Accounts (XA) ↑	Assets (Accounts Receivable, Net) ↓
2. Identify and write off actual bad debts	Throughout period as bad debts become known	Accounts Receivable (A) ↓	Net Income ⎫
		Allowance for Doubtful Accounts (XA) ↓	Assets (Accounts Receivable, Net) ⎭ No effect

The complete accounting process for bad debts can now be summarized in terms of the changes in Accounts Receivable and the Allowance for Doubtful Accounts (in thousands):[7]

Accounts Receivable (A)			
Beginning balance	108,646	Collections on account	673,610
Sales on account	733,190	Write-offs	2,356
Ending balance	165,870		

Allowance for Doubtful Accounts (XA)			
		Beginning balance	1,742
Write-offs	2,356	Bad debt expense adjustment	2,383
		Ending balance	1,769

[7]This assumes that all sales are on account.

REPORTING ACCOUNTS RECEIVABLE

Analysts who want information on Gildan's receivables will find Accounts Receivable, net of allowance for doubtful accounts, of $165,870 and $108,646 for fiscal years 2006 and 2005, respectively, reported on the balance sheet (Exhibit 7.2).

EXHIBIT **7.2**

Accounts Receivable on the Balance Sheet

REAL WORLD EXCERPT

Gildan Activewear

ANNUAL REPORT

Consolidated Balance Sheets
October 1, 2006 and October 2, 2005
(in thousands of US dollars)

	2006	2005
Assets		
Current assets:		
Cash and cash equivalents	$ 29,007	$ 69,802
Accounts receivable	165,870	108,646
Inventories	200,653	134,861
Prepaid expenses and deposits	5,757	4,394
Future income taxes (note 14)	5,298	10,135

Accounts Receivable (Gross) includes the total accounts receivable, both collectible and uncollectible. The balance in the Allowance for Doubtful Accounts is the portion of the accounts receivable balance the company estimates to be uncollectible. Accounts Receivable (Net) reported on the balance sheet is the portion of the accounts the company expects to collect (or its estimated net realizable value).

Gildan did not disclose any information about its Allowance for Doubtful Accounts.[8] *Financial Reporting in Canada 2006* indicates that the majority of companies (164 out of 200) did not disclose or refer to an allowance for doubtful accounts in their 2005 annual reports. In contrast, many U.S. companies disclose in their annual reports information about their bad debt expense and the related allowance for doubtful accounts.

SELF-STUDY **QUIZ 7-2**

In a recent year, Delta Apparel Inc, a Gildan competitor, had a beginning credit balance in the Allowance for Doubtful Accounts of $1,290 (all numbers in thousands of dollars). It wrote off accounts receivable totalling $1,160 during the year and made a bad debt expense adjustment of $1,230 for the year.

1. Prepare the adjusting journal entry that Delta made to record bad debt expense at the end of the year.

2. Prepare the journal entry summarizing Delta's total write-offs of bad debts during the year.

3. Compute the balance in the Allowance for Doubtful Accounts at the end of the year.

After you complete your answers, check them with the solutions on page 375.

ESTIMATING BAD DEBTS

The bad debt expense amount recorded in the end-of-period adjusting entry often is estimated based on either (1) a percentage of the total credit sales for the period or (2) an aging of accounts receivable. Both methods are acceptable under GAAP and are widely used in practice, but do not produce the same estimate of bad debts. The percentage of credit sales method is simpler to apply, but the aging method is generally more accurate. Many companies use the simpler method on a weekly or monthly basis and use the more accurate method on a monthly or quarterly basis to check the accuracy of the earlier estimates.

---

[8]Canadian companies are not required to disclose such information. The *CICA Handbook* (section 3020.01) states: "Since it is to be assumed that adequate allowance for doubtful accounts has been made if no statement is made to the contrary, it is not considered necessary to refer to such an allowance."

Percentage of Credit Sales Method Many companies make their estimates using the **percentage of credit sales method**, which bases bad debt expense on the historical percentage of credit sales that result in bad debts. This method is also called the *income statement method* because it involves the direct computation of the income statement number, *bad debt expense,* based on the income statement number *credit sales.*

The average percentage of credit sales that result in bad debts can be computed by dividing total bad debts by total *credit* sales. A company that has been operating for some years has sufficient experience to estimate probable future bad debts. For example, assume that Amar and Ciero (a hypothetical company) had experienced the following in three recent years:

PERCENTAGE OF CREDIT SALES METHOD bases bad debt expense on the historical perspective of credit sales that result in bad debts.

Year	Bad Debts	Credit Sales
2006	$ 900	$190,000
2007	1,200	220,000
2008	1,400	290,000
Total	$3,500	$700,000

The average bad debt rate equals 0.005 ($3,500 ÷ $700,000) or 0.5% for the three-year period 2006–2008.

If net credit sales in the current year were approximately $268,000 and the company used this method, then the bad debt expense is $1,340, computed as follows:

$$\textbf{Bad debt expense} = \textbf{Credit sales} \times \textbf{Bad debt rate}$$
$$= \$268,000 \times 0.5\% = \$1,340$$

This amount is directly recorded as Bad Debt Expense in the current year, with a corresponding increase in Allowance for Doubtful Accounts. New companies often rely on the experience of similar companies that have been operating for a number of years. A company usually adjusts the historical average bad debt rate to reflect future expectations. For example, if retail sales were rising, the company might decrease its rate to 0.4 percent, reasoning that fewer of its business customers (retailers) will become bankrupt.

Allowance for Doubtful Accounts (XA)

	Beginning balance	1,455
Write-offs (throughout the year) 1,267		
	Unadjusted balance	188
	Bad debt expense (adjustment)	1,340 ← Based on percentage of credit sales
	Ending balance	1,528

Aging of Accounts Receivable Method As an alternative to the percentage of credit sales method, many companies estimate bad debt expense by examining the age of accounts receivable that are outstanding. The **aging of accounts receivable method** relies on the fact that, as accounts receivable become older and overdue, they usually are less likely to be collectable. For example, a receivable that is due in 30 days but has not been paid after 60 days is more likely to be collected, on average, than a similar receivable that still remains unpaid after 120 days. Based on its prior experience, the company could estimate the percentage of receivables of different ages that may not be paid.

AGING OF ACCOUNTS RECEIVABLE METHOD estimates uncollectable accounts based on the age of each account receivable.

This method is also called the ***balance sheet method*** because it involves the direct computation of the balance of the ***allowance for doubtful accounts*** based on the ending balance of ***accounts receivable.*** Suppose that Amer and Ciero split its receivables into five age categories, as presented in Exhibit 7.3. Management of the company might then *estimate* the following probable bad debt rates: 1 percent of receivables not yet due; 3 percent of receivables that are past due by 1 to 30 days; 6 percent of receivables

EXHIBIT **7.3**

Trial Balance for
Van Houtte Inc.

AMER AND CIERO **Aging Anaysis of Accounts Receivable,** **December 31, 2007**						
Customer	**Not Yet Due**	**1–30 Days Past Due**	**31–60 Days Past Due**	**61–90 Days Past Due**	**Over 90 Days Past Due**	**Total**
Adams, Inc.	$ 600					$ 600
Baker Stores	300	$ 900	$ 100			1,300
Cox Co.			400	$ 900	$ 100	1,400
Zoe Stores	2,000		1,000			3,000
Total	$17,200	$12,000	$8,000	$1,200	$1,600	$40,000
Estimated % uncollectable	1%	3%	6%	10%	25%	
Estimated uncollectable accounts	$ 172	$ 360	$ 480	$ 120	$ 400	$ 1,532

that are past due by 31 to 60 days; and so on. The total of the amounts estimated to be uncollectable under the aging method is the balance that ***should be*** in the allowance for doubtful accounts at the end of the period. This is called the ***estimated balance***.

The approach to recording bad debt expense using the aging method is different from that for the percentage of credit sales method. Recall that, using the percentage of credit sales, we ***directly computed*** the amount to be recorded as bad debt expense on the income statement for the period. Alternatively, when using the aging method, we are computing the ***final ending balance*** in the allowance for doubtful accounts. Thus, the amount of bad debt expense for the period is the ***difference*** between the estimated uncollectable accounts (just calculated) and the balance of the allowance for doubtful accounts at the end of the period ***before the adjusting entry*** has been made.

Computation	
Estimated balance (from aging schedule)	$1,532
Less: Current balance (preadjustment balance from ledger account)	188
Bad debt expense to be recorded for the current year	$1,344

This computation also can be illustrated in T-account form. The current credit balance in the allowance account, before the end-of-period adjustment, is $188. We insert the new ending balance from the aging schedule and then solve for the current amount of bad debt expense.

Allowance for Doubtful Accounts (XA)

		Beginning balance	1,455
Write-offs (throughout the year)	1,267		
		Unadjusted balance	188
Step 2: Adjustment inferred ⟶		Bad debt expense (adjustment)	1,344
Step 1: Ending balance estimated ⟶ from aging of accounts receivable		Estimated balance (from aging)	1,532

The end-of-period adjusting entry to Bad Debt Expense and Allowance for Doubtful Accounts is made on December 31 for $1,344.

The amount written off throughout the year may sometimes exceed the beginning balance of the Allowance in Doubtful Accounts, which indicates that the company underestimated the amount that is potentially uncollectable. If the total amount written off equals $1,567, the Allowance account will have an unadjusted *debit* balance of $112, and the bad debt expense would equal $1,644.

The percentage of credit sales method focuses on an income statement valuation (bad debt expense matched to the period's credit sales), whereas the aging method focuses on a balance sheet valuation (estimated net realizable value of accounts receivable). In both cases, the objective is to estimate the amount of bad debt expense related to the period's credit sales. The balance sheet method takes into consideration the unadjusted balance of the Allowance account, whereas the income statement method does not.

The computation of bad debt expense under the two methods are contrasted below, where the computed amounts are highlighted.

Percentage of Credit Sales	Aging of Accounts Receivable
Beginning balance of Allowance account	Beginning balance of Allowance account
− Write-offs throughout the year	− Write-offs throughout the year
+ **Bad debt expense (computed)**	+ Bad debt expense (inferred)
= Ending balance of Allowance account (inferred)	= **Ending balance of Allowance account (computed)**

Actual Write-Offs Compared with Estimates The amount of uncollectable accounts actually written off seldom equals the estimated amount previously recorded. This error in estimating bad debts is taken into consideration in determining the bad debt expense at the end of the next accounting period. *When estimates are found to be incorrect, financial statement values for* **prior** *annual accounting periods are* **not** *corrected*.

SALES VERSUS COLLECTIONS—THE MARKETING/ FINANCIAL MANAGEMENT CONFLICT	FINANCIAL ANALYSIS

Company managers often forget that extending credit increases sales volume but it may also increase the volume of bad debts if proper credit checks of the customers are not made or if the company relaxes its credit policy. Marketing-oriented companies that emphasize sales without monitoring the collection of credit sales will soon find much of their current assets tied up in accounts receivable. On the other hand, the absence of bad debts may be the result of a very tight credit policy that reduces both sales and net income.

In the late 1990s, the leading telecommunications companies, such as Nortel Networks Corporation, Cisco Systems Inc., and Lucent Technologies Inc., contributed to sales growth by providing short- and medium-term financing to their telecommunications equipment customers in order to encourage them to purchase such equipment. Financing of sales by the seller, called *vendor financing*, had become common industry practice until the risks of vendor financing came to light when demand for telecommunications equipment and services weakened. Customers started to default on their debts and vendors were forced to absorb credit losses and increase their allowances for doubtful accounts.

When credit losses are relatively high because of vendor financing, financial analysts should be cautious in their analysis of companies' sales growth.

Conservatism in the Valuation of Accounts Receivable Creditors and analysts prefer that companies follow *conservative* financial strategies that result in reporting lower amounts for net income and assets and higher amounts for liabilities. Accountants and auditors are also cautious about reporting optimistic values that overstate the company's operating performance and its financial position. For accounts receivable, the amount reported on the balance sheet should reflect the amount expected to be collected from customers. In this context, conservatism suggests that the allowance for doubtful accounts be commensurate with the creditworthiness of the company's customers. A conservative measure of accounts receivable means a larger amount of bad debt expense and a larger allowance for doubtful accounts. However, it is better to err on the side of having a larger allowance than having a smaller one that may not be adequate to cover future bad debts.

FOCUS ON CASH FLOWS

ACCOUNTS RECEIVABLE

The change in accounts receivable can be a major determinant of a company's cash flow from operations. The income statement reflects the revenues earned during the period, whereas the cash flow from operating activities reflects the cash collections from customers for the same period. Since sales on account increase the balance in accounts receivable, and cash collections from customers decrease the balance in accounts receivable, the change in accounts receivable from the beginning to the end of the period is the difference between sales and cash collections.

EFFECT ON CASH FLOW STATEMENT

IN GENERAL → When a net *decrease in accounts receivable* for the period occurs, the amount of cash collected from customers exceeds revenue; thus, the decrease must be *added* to revenue or to net income (since revenue is a component of net income) in computing cash flows from operations. When a net *increase in accounts receivable* occurs, cash collected from customers is less than revenue; thus, the increase must be *subtracted* from net income in computing cash flows from operations.

	Effect on Cash Flows
Operating activities (indirect method)	
Net income	$xxx
Adjusted for	
Decrease in accounts receivable	+
or	
Increase in accounts receivable	–

FOCUS COMPANY ANALYSIS → Exhibit 7.4 is the Operating Activities section of Gildan's cash flow statement. When the accounts receivable balance increases during the period, as was the case at Gildan in all three years, the company records more net sales than it collects in cash from customers during the period. Thus, the increase is subtracted from net earnings in the computation of Gildan's cash flow from operations. In fiscal year 2006, Gildan's sales totalled US$773 million. Accounts receivable also increased during the same period, indicating that the company did not collect this whole amount in 2006. For this reason, the increase in accounts receivable is subtracted from sales revenue (hence, net income) in computing the cash received from operating activities.

EXHIBIT **7.4**

Accounts Receivable on the Cash Flow Statement

REAL WORLD EXCERPT

Gildan Activewear

ANNUAL REPORT

GILDAN ACTIVEWEAR, INC. Consolidated Statements of Cash Flows Years ended October 1, 2006, October 2, 2005, and October 3, 2004 (in thousands of US dollars)			
	2006	2005	2004
Cash flows from (used in) operating activities:			
Net earnings	$ 106,829	$ 86,043	$ 60,251
Adjustments for:			
Depreciation and amortization	32,383	25,615	22,275
Impairment loss (note 16(a))	15,149	—	—
Loss on disposal and writedown of fixed assets	1,197	7,373	1,949
Stock-based compensation costs	908	1,050	477
Future income taxes	1,764	176	2,947
Non-controlling interest	260	34	—
Unrealized foreign exchange loss	843	2,552	586
Changes in non-cash working capital balances:			
Accounts receivable	(41,058)	(22,694)	(20,236)
Inventories	(35,435)	(17,790)	(13,112)
Prepaid expenses and deposits	95	(1,082)	440
Accounts payable and accrued liabilities	11,046	11,979	5,416
Income taxes payable	740	(6)	(2,073)
	94,721	93,250	58,920

To assess the effectiveness of overall credit granting and collection activities, managers and analysts often compute the receivables turnover ratio.

RECEIVABLES TURNOVER

KEY RATIO
ANALYSIS

ANALYTICAL QUESTION → How effective are credit-granting and collection activities?
RATIO AND COMPARISONS → An answer to this question is provided by the receivables turnover ratio, which is computed as follows:

$$\text{Receivables Turnover} = \frac{\text{Net Sales}^*}{\text{Average Net Trade Accounts Receivable}^\dagger}$$

*Since the amount of net credit sales is normally not reported separately, most analysts use net sales in this equation.
†Average Net Trade Accounts Receivable = (Beginning Net Trade Accounts Receivable + Ending Net Trade Accounts Receivable) ÷ 2

The 2006 ratio for Gildan is:

$$\frac{\$773,190}{(\$108,646 + \$165,870) \div 2} = 5.63$$

This ratio can be stated in a more intuitive manner by dividing the average trade accounts receivable by the average credit sales per day:

$$\text{Average Collection Period} = \frac{\text{Average Trade Accounts Receivable}}{\text{Credit Sales} / 365}$$

The 2006 average collection period for Gildan is:

$$\text{Average Collection Period} = \frac{\$137,258}{\$773,190 \div 365} = 64.8 \text{ days}$$

An equivalent computation is

$$\text{Average Collection Period} = \frac{365}{\text{Receivables Turnover}} = \frac{365}{5.63} = 64.8 \text{ days}$$

> ■ **LEARNING OBJECTIVE 5**
> Compute and interpret the accounts receivable turnover ratio and the effects of accounts receivable on cash flows.

Comparisons over Time			Comparisons with Competitors	
Gildan			Delta Apparel	Hanesbrands
2004	2005	2006	2006	2006
7.13	6.74	5.63	6.66	8.14

INTERPRETATIONS

In General → The receivables turnover ratio reflects how many times average trade receivables were recorded and collected during the period. The higher the ratio, the faster the collection of receivables. A higher ratio benefits the company because it can invest the cash collected to earning interest income or reduce borrowings to reduce interest expense. Overly generous payment schedules and ineffective collection methods keep the receivables turnover low. Analysts and creditors watch this ratio because a sudden decline may mean that a company is extending payment deadlines in an attempt to prop up lagging sales or is even recording sales that will later be returned by customers. Many managers and analysts compute the average collection period, which indicates the average time it takes a customer to pay the amounts due.

Focus Company Analysis → Gildan's receivables turnover decreased from 7.13 in 2004 to 5.63 in 2006. Its ratio is lower than both of its competitors. Gildan's sales increased from $533 million in 2004 to $773 million in 2006. This significant increase in sales was accompanied by an increase in the average collection period, from 51 days in 2004 to 64 days in 2006. Thus, it appears that Gildan loosened its credit policy as it achieved this sizeable increase in sales. Selling products at the retail level in 2006 may have contributed to the decrease in receivables turnover.

A Few Cautions → Since differences across industries and between firms in the manner in which customer purchases are financed can cause dramatic differences in the ratio, a particular firm's ratio should be compared only with its prior years' figures or with other firms in the same industry following the same financing practices.

> **Selected Industry Comparisons: Receivables Turnover Ratio**
>
> Variety stores 98.6
>
>
> Malt beverages 14.9
>
> Lumber and building materials 12.7

SELF-STUDY **QUIZ 7-3**

1. Assume that Kleer Company reported beginning and ending balances in the Allowance for Doubtful Accounts of $723 and $904, respectively. It also reported that write-offs of bad debts amounted to $648 (all numbers in thousands). Assuming that the company did not collect any amounts that were written off previously, what amount did the company record as bad debt expense for the period? (**Solution approach**: Use the Allowance for Doubtful Accounts T-account to solve for the missing value.)

Allowance for Doubtful Accounts (XA)

2. Kleer Company reported an increase in accounts receivable for the period. Was that increase added to or subtracted from net income in the computation of cash flow from operations? Explain your answer.

3. Indicate whether **granting longer payment deadlines** (e.g., 60 days instead of 30 days) will most likely **increase** or **decrease** the accounts receivable turnover ratio. Explain.

After you complete your work, check your answers with the solution on page 375.

INTERNAL CONTROL AND MANAGEMENT RESPONSIBILITY

INTERNAL CONTROLS are the processes by which the company's board of directors, management, and other personnel provide reasonable assurance regarding the reliability of the company's financial reporting, the effectiveness and efficiency of its operations, and its compliance with applicable laws and regulations.

The term **internal control** refers to the process by which a company's board of directors, audit committee, management, and other personnel provide reasonable assurance regarding the reliability of the company's financial reporting, the effectiveness and efficiency of its operations, and its compliance with applicable laws and regulations.[9] Internal control procedures should extend to all aspects of the company's financial reporting process. A well-designed system of internal controls prevents inadvertent errors and removes opportunities for individuals to steal, misrepresent, defraud, or embezzle assets from a company.

Recent high-profile scandals in the United States, such as Enron and WorldCom, led the U.S. Congress to approve the Sarbanes-Oxley Act in July 2002. This Act, commonly known as SOX, requires public companies to take measures that are intended to provide better protection for investors by improving the accuracy and reliability of financial reporting. Specifically, the new legislation requires top executives to certify the accuracy of the financial statements released by their companies. It also places greater emphasis on internal control systems and procedures to prevent, detect, and remediate fraud and misconduct by management and other employees. The Sarbanes-Oxley Act also requires that external auditors vouch for the accuracy of management's statements concerning the company's financial results. Furthermore, auditors are required to audit the company's internal controls.

As indicated in Chapter 1, SOX's requirements apply to large Canadian corporations that are listed on U.S. stock exchanges. Gildan's management has complied with these requirements as indicated in the following excerpt from the company's Management Discussion and Analysis section of its annual report:

REAL WORLD EXCERPT

Gildan Activewear

ANNUAL REPORT

Internal Control Over Financial Reporting

Management's Annual Report on Internal Control Over Financial Reporting

Our management is responsible for establishing and maintaining adequate internal control over financial reporting, as such term is defined in Rules 13a-15(f) and 15d-15(f) under the U.S. *Securities Exchange Act of 1934*.

---

[9]According to the *CICA Handbook* (section 5200.05), "internal control comprises the plan of organization and all the co-ordinate systems established by the management of an enterprise to assist in achieving management's objective of ensuring, as far as practical, the orderly and efficient conduct of its business, including the safeguarding of assets, the reliability of accounting records and the timely preparation of reliable financial information."

> Our internal control over financial reporting includes those policies and procedures that: (1) pertain to the maintenance of records that, in reasonable detail, accurately and fairly reflect the transactions and dispositions of our assets; (2) provide reasonable assurance that transactions are recorded as necessary to permit preparation of financial statements in accordance with generally accepted accounting principles, and that our receipts and expenditures are being made only in accordance with authorizations of our management and directors; and (3) provide reasonable assurance regarding prevention or timely detection of unauthorized acquisition, use or disposition of our assets that could have a material effect on the financial statements.
>
> Under the supervision and with the participation of our Chief Executive Officer and our Chief Financial Officer, management conducted an evaluation of the effectiveness of our internal control over financial reporting, as of October 1, 2006, based on the framework set forth in *Internal Control-Integrated Framework* issued by the Committee of Sponsoring Organizations of the Treadway Commission (COSO). Based on its evaluation under this framework, management concluded that our internal control over financial reporting was effective as of that date.

Because of the interdependence between the U.S. and Canadian financial markets, and the listing of major Canadian companies on U.S. stock exchanges, the Canadian Securities Administrators require all publicly traded companies in Canada to report on the effectiveness of their internal controls over financial reporting, as of December 31, 2007.[10] In this regard, Canada differs significantly from the United States where public companies have been required since 2002 to have an *audit* of internal control over financial reporting. The cost of compliance with SOX's requirement has been higher than anticipated. This led the U.S. legislators to exempt from this requirement any public company with a market capitalization[11] not exceeding US$500 million, including Canadian companies that are listed on U.S. stock exchanges. In Canada, the CSA does not require an external audit of internal control over financial reporting, which saves substantial audit fees for approximately 3,400 Canadian public companies.

Compliance with SOX's requirements has cost companies billions of dollars, which prompted the top executives of many companies to question whether the expected benefits from implementing the new requirements are worth the additional costs of compliance. Furthermore, some have questioned whether such measures will effectively prevent future corporate scandals.[12] Complaints about the excessive cost of compliance with section 404 of the SOX regulation caused the SEC and the Public Company Accounting Oversight Board to revise SOX's requirements for smaller companies. Nevertheless, the initial Sarbanes-Oxley Act restored authority to the accounting profession and raised the profile of the auditing function in ensuring that information conveyed in financial reports has a high degree of reliability. It also helped companies identify material weaknesses and significant deficiencies in their internal control procedures. For example, Revlon Inc., which provides cosmetics and personal care products, reported that review of its internal control procedures, as required by Sarbox, revealed that a US$1.2-million error was made in estimating the allowance for sales returns.[13]

---

[10]Canadian Securities Administrators Notice 52-313, Status of Proposed Multilateral Instrument 52-111 *Reporting on Internal Control over Financial Reporting* and Proposed Amended and Restated Multilateral Instrument 52-109 *Certification of Disclosure in Issuers' Annual and Interim Filings,* March 10, 2006.

[11]Market capitalization is calculated by multiplying the number of issued and outstanding shares of a corporation by its share price.

[12]See, for example, J. Gray, "Down the Drain? The Costs of Regulatory Compliance are Soaring" *Canadian Business*, July 19–August 15, 2004, pp. 67–68, and T. Tedesco, "Audit Rules Called No Cure for Fraud" *National Post*, May 31, 2004, FP1, 9.

[13]The company's stock declined by 2.7 percent pursuant to the company's announcement of this error. *National Post*, March 11, 2005, FP13.

A QUESTION OF ETHICS   ETHICS AND THE NEED FOR INTERNAL CONTROL

Some people are bothered by the recommendation that all well-run companies should have strong internal control procedures. These people believe that control procedures suggest that the company's management does not trust its employees. Although the vast majority of employees are trustworthy, employee theft costs businesses billions of dollars each year. Interviews with convicted felons indicate that, in many cases, they stole from their employers because they thought that it was easy and that no one cared (internal control procedures were not present).

A recent survey of actual fraud committed by company employees, managers, and executives revealed that internal controls were not effective in detecting the fraud.[14] In fact, internal control procedures were identified as the primary source of fraud detection in fewer than 20 percent of the cases. The reported weaknesses in internal control systems explain why the Sarbanes-Oxley Act requires companies to strengthen their internal controls.

Many companies have a formal code of ethics that requires high standards of behaviour in dealing with customers, suppliers, fellow employees, and the company's assets. Although each employee is ultimately responsible for his or her own ethical behaviour, internal control procedures can be thought of as important value statements from management. Preventing theft through strong internal controls prevents people from destroying their lives if they steal and are subsequently caught and penalized for their unethical behaviour.

CONTROL OVER ACCOUNTS RECEIVABLE

Many managers forget that extending credit will increase sales volume but unless the related receivables are collected they do not increase net income. Companies that emphasize sales without monitoring the collection of credit sales will soon find much of their current assets tied up in accounts receivable. To guard against extending credit to non-worthy customers, the following practices can help minimize bad debts:

1. Require approval of customers' credit history by a person independent of the sales and collection functions.

2. Monitor the age of accounts receivable periodically and contact customers with overdue payments.

3. Reward both sales and collection personnel for speedy collections so that they work as a team.

REPORTING AND SAFEGUARDING CASH

CASH AND CASH EQUIVALENTS DEFINED

Cash is defined as money or any instrument that banks will accept for deposit and immediate credit to the company's account, such as a cheque, money order, or bank draft. Cash usually is divided into three categories: cash on hand, cash deposited in banks, and other instruments that meet the definition of cash.

Section 1540 of the *CICA Handbook* defines **cash equivalents** as short-term, highly liquid investments that are readily convertible to known amounts of cash and which are subject to an insignificant risk of change in value. Typical instruments included as cash equivalents are bank certificates of deposit and treasury bills issued by the government to finance its activities.

Even though a company may have several bank accounts and several types of cash equivalents, all cash accounts and cash equivalents are usually combined as one amount for financial reporting purposes. Gildan reports a single account, Cash and

LEARNING OBJECTIVE 6

Report, control, and safeguard cash.

CASH is money or any instrument that banks will accept for deposit and immediate credit to the company's account, such as a cheque, money order, or bank draft.

CASH EQUIVALENTS are short-term, highly liquid investments that are readily convertible to known amounts of cash and which are subject to an insignificant risk of change in value.

---

[14]*2006 Report to the Nation on Occupational Fraud and Abuse.* Certified Fraud Examiners, Austin: USA, 2006.

Cash Equivalents. The company treats as cash equivalents all liquid investments with maturities of three months or less from the date of acquisition.

CASH MANAGEMENT

Many businesses receive a large amount of cash, cheques, and credit card receipts from their customers each day. Anyone can spend cash, so management must develop procedures to safeguard the cash it uses in the business. Effective cash management involves more than protecting cash from theft, fraud, or loss through carelessness. Other cash management responsibilities include the following:

1. Accurate accounting so that reports of cash flows and balances may be prepared.
2. Controls to ensure that enough cash is on hand to meet (a) current operating needs, (b) maturing liabilities, and (c) unexpected emergencies.
3. Prevention of the accumulation of excess amounts of idle cash. Idle cash earns no revenue; therefore, it is often invested in securities to earn revenue (return) until it is needed for operations.[15]

INTERNAL CONTROL OF CASH

Because cash is the asset most vulnerable to theft and fraud, a significant number of internal control procedures should focus on cash. You have already observed internal control procedures for cash, although you may not have known it at the time. At most movie theatres, one employee sells tickets and another employee collects them. It would be less expensive to have one employee do both jobs, but it would also be easier for that single employee to steal cash and admit a patron without issuing a ticket. If different employees perform the tasks, a successful theft requires participation of both.

Effective internal control of cash should include the following:

1. *Separation of duties related to cash handling and record keeping*
   a. Complete separation of the tasks of receiving cash and disbursing cash ensures that the individual responsible for depositing cash has no authority to sign cheques.
   b. Complete separation of the procedures of accounting for cash receipts and cash disbursements ensures, for example, that those handling sales returns do not create fictitious returns to conceal cash shortages.
   c. Complete separation of the physical handling of cash and all phases of the accounting function ensures that those either receiving or paying cash have no authority to make accounting entries.

The following diagram illustrates how the separation of duties contributes to strong internal control:

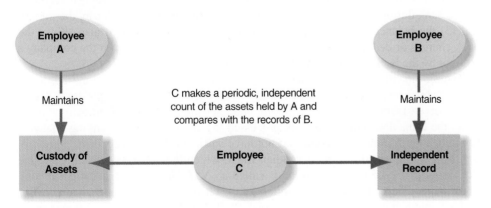

---

[15]An introduction to accounting for short-term investment in securities is available on the Online Learning Centre at **www.mcgrawhill.ca/olc/libby/student/resources**.

The separation of individual responsibilities deters theft because the collusion of two or more persons is needed to steal cash and then conceal the theft in the accounting records.

2. *Prescribed policies and procedures*

   Specific policies and procedures should be established so that the work done by one individual is compared to the results reported by other individuals. Exhibit 7.5 provides a summary of typical policies and procedures to control cash.

EXHIBIT **7.5**

Typical Internal Controls for Cash

Internal Control Component	Prescribed Policies or Procedures
Cash budget	Prepare a monthly forecast of cash receipts, disbursements, and balances for the year and require that managers document and justify any deviations from the budget each month.
Cash receipts	Prepare a listing of cash receipts on a daily basis. In practice this often takes the form of cash register receipts, or a descriptive list of incoming cheques. Require that all cash receipts be deposited in a bank daily. Keep any cash on hand under strict control.
Cash payments	Require separate approval of the purchases and other expenditures and separate approval of the actual cash payments. Assign the cash payment approval and the actual cheque-signing responsibilities to different individuals. Use pre-numbered cheques and pay special attention to payments by electronic funds transfers since the bank does not process controlled documents (cheques).
Independent internal verification	Require comparison of cash receipts to bank deposits, and cheques issued to invoices by an independent supervisor. Require monthly reconciliation of bank accounts with the cash accounts on the company's books (discussed in detail in the next section).
Rotation of duties	Require employees to take vacations, and rotate their duties.

When procedures similar to those described in Exhibit 7.5 are followed, concealing a fraudulent cash disbursement is difficult without the collusion of two or more persons. Reconciliation of cash accounts with bank statements provides an additional control on disbursements. The level of internal control, which is reviewed by the outside independent auditor, increases the reliability of the financial statements of the business.

RECONCILIATION OF THE CASH ACCOUNTS AND THE BANK STATEMENTS

Content of a Bank Statement   Proper use of the bank accounts of a business can be an important internal control procedure for cash. Each month, the bank provides the company (the depositor) with a **bank statement** that lists (1) each deposit recorded by the bank during the period, (2) each cheque cleared by the bank during the period, and (3) the balance in the company's account. The bank statement also shows the bank charges or deductions (such as service charges) made directly to the company's account by the bank. A typical bank statement is shown in Exhibit 7.6.

Exhibit 7.6 lists three items that need explanation. Notice that on June 20, listed under Debits, there is a deduction for $204.76 coded *NSF*.[16] A cheque for $204.76 was received from a customer, R. Smith, and deposited by J. Doe Company with its bank, the Canadian Bank. The bank processed the cheque through banking channels to Smith's bank. Smith's account did not have sufficient funds to cover it; therefore, Smith's bank returned it to the Canadian Bank, which then charged it back to J. Doe Company. This type of cheque often is called an *NSF cheque* (not sufficient funds). The company needs to collect the amount of the cheque again from the customer. The NSF cheque is now a receivable; consequently, J. Doe Company must make an entry to debit Receivables (R. Smith) and credit Cash for the $204.76.

A **BANK STATEMENT** is a monthly report from a bank that shows deposits recorded, cheques cleared, other debits and credits, and a running bank balance.

---

[16]These codes vary among banks.

EXHIBIT **7.6**

Example of a Bank Statement

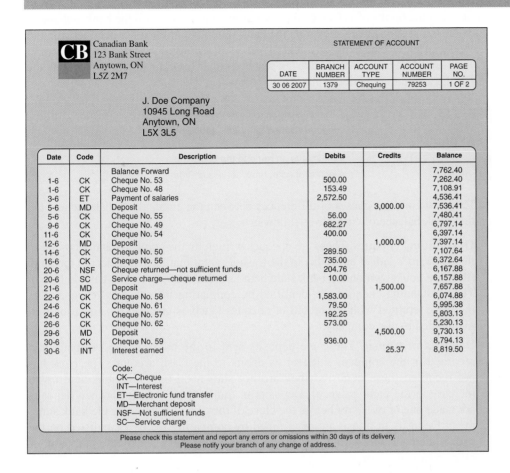

Notice the $10 listed on June 20 under Debits and coded *SC*. This is the code for bank service charges. The bank statement included a memo by the bank explaining this service charge (which was not documented by a cheque). J. Doe Company must make an entry to reflect the $10 decrease in the bank balance as a debit to a relevant expense account, such as Bank Service Expense, and a credit to Cash.

Notice the $25.37 listed on June 30 under Credits and the code INT for interest earned. The bank pays interest on chequing account balances, which increased J. Doe Company's account for interest earned during the period. The Company must record the interest by making an entry to debit Cash and credit Interest Revenue for the $25.37.

Need for Reconciliation A **bank reconciliation** is the process of comparing (reconciling) the ending cash balance in the company's records and the ending cash balance reported by the bank on the monthly bank statement. A bank reconciliation should be completed for each separate chequing account (i.e., for each bank statement received from each bank) at the end of each month.

Usually, the ending cash balance as shown on the bank statement does not agree with the ending cash balance shown by the related Cash ledger account on the books of the company. For example, the Cash ledger account of J. Doe Company showed the following at the end of June (Doe has only one chequing account):

A **BANK RECONCILIATION** is the process of verifying the accuracy of both the bank statement and the cash accounts of a business.

Cash			
June 1 balance	6,637.14	Cheques written in June	8,714.45
June deposits	11,800.00		
Ending balance	9,722.69		

The $8,819.50 ending cash balance shown on the bank statement (Exhibit 7.6) is different from the $9,722.69 ending balance of cash shown on the books of J. Doe

Company. This difference exists because (1) some transactions affecting cash were recorded in the books of J. Doe Company but were not shown on the bank statement, (2) some transactions were shown on the bank statement but had not been recorded in the books of the J. Doe Company, and (3) errors in recording transactions.

The flow of documents that have not reached either the company or the bank by the end of the accounting period is illustrated below:

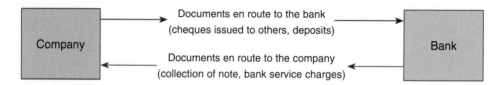

The most common causes of differences between the ending bank balance and the ending book balance of cash are as follows:

1. **Outstanding cheques.** These are cheques written by the company and recorded in the company's ledger as credits to the Cash account that have not cleared the bank (they are not shown on the bank statement as a deduction from the bank balance). The outstanding cheques are identified by comparing the cancelled cheques that the bank returned with the record of cheques (such as cheque stubs or a journal) maintained by the company.

2. **Deposits in transit.** These are deposits sent to the bank by the company and recorded in the company's ledger as debits to the Cash account. The bank has not recorded these deposits (they are not shown on the bank statement as an increase in the bank balance). Deposits in transit usually happen when deposits are made one or two days before the close of the period covered by the bank statement. Deposits in transit are determined by comparing the deposits listed on the bank statement with the copies of the deposit slips retained by the company or other company records.

3. **Bank service charges.** An expense for bank services listed on the bank statement. This expense is not recorded on the company's books.

4. **NSF cheques.** A "bad cheque" or "bounced cheque" that was deposited but must be deducted from the company's cash account and recorded as an account receivable.

5. **Interest.** The interest paid by the bank to the company on its bank balance.

6. **Errors.** Both the bank and the company may make errors, especially when the volume of cash transactions is large.

Bank Reconciliation Illustrated   The company should make a bank reconciliation immediately after receiving each bank statement. The general format for the bank reconciliation follows:

Ending cash balance per books	$xxx	Ending cash balance per bank statement	$xxx
+ Collections by bank	xx	+ Deposits in transit	xx
− NSF cheques/Service charges	xx	− Outstanding cheques	xx
± Company errors	xx	± Bank errors	xx
Ending correct cash balances	$xxx	Ending correct cash balance	$xxx

Exhibit 7.7 shows the bank reconciliation prepared by J. Doe Company for the month of June to reconcile the ending bank balance ($8,819.50) with the ending book balance ($9,722.69). On the completed reconciliation, the correct cash balance is $9,542.30. This balance is different from both the reported bank and book balances before the reconciliation with the bank statement. This correct balance is the amount that should be shown in the Cash account after the reconciliation. In this example, it

EXHIBIT **7.7**
Bank Reconciliation Illustrated

J. DOE COMPANY
Bank Reconciliation
June 30, 2007

Company's Books		Bank Statement	
Ending cash balance per books	$9,722.69	Ending cash balance per bank statement	$ 8,819.50
Additions		Additions	
Interest earned	25.37	Deposit in transit	1,800.00
Error in recording cheque No. 55	9.00		
	9,757.06		10,619.50
Deductions		Deductions	
NSF cheque of R. Smith	204.76	Outstanding cheques	1,077.20
Bank service charges	10.00		
Ending correct cash balance	$9,542.30	Ending correct cash balance	$ 9,542.30

is also the correct amount of cash that should be reported on the balance sheet (J. Doe Company has only one chequing account and no cash on hand). J. Doe Company followed these steps in preparing the bank reconciliation:

1. **Identify the outstanding cheques.** A comparison of the cancelled cheques returned by the bank with the company's records of all cheques drawn showed the following cheques still outstanding (not cleared) at the end of June:

Cheque No.	Amount
60	$ 145.00
63	815.00
64	117.20
Total	$1,077.20

This total was entered on the reconciliation as a deduction from the bank account. These cheques will be deducted by the bank when they clear the bank.

2. **Identify the deposits in transit.** A comparison of the deposit slips on hand with those listed on the bank statement revealed that a deposit of $1,800 made on June 30 was not listed on the bank statement. This amount was entered on the reconciliation as an addition to the bank account. It will be added by the bank when it records the deposit.

3. **Record bank charges and credits:**
   a. Interest received from the bank, $25.37—entered on the bank reconciliation as an addition to the book balance; it already has been included in the bank balance.
   b. NSF cheque of R. Smith, $204.76—entered on the bank reconciliation as a deduction from the book balance; it has been deducted from the bank statement balance.
   c. Bank service charges, $10—entered on the bank reconciliation as a deduction from the book balance; it has been deducted from the bank balance.

4. **Determine the impact of errors.** At this point, J. Doe Company found that the reconciliation did not balance by $9. Because this amount is divisible by 9, a transposition of numbers was suspected. (A transposition, such as writing 27 for 72, always will cause an error that is exactly divisible by 9.) Upon checking the journal entries made during the month, a cheque written for $56 to pay an account

payable was found. The cheque was recorded in the company's accounts as $65. The incorrect entry made was a debit to Accounts Payable and a credit to Cash for $65 (instead of $56). Therefore, $9 (i.e., $65 − $56) must be added to the book cash balance on the reconciliation; the bank cleared the cheque for the correct amount, $56.

Note that in Exhibit 7.7, the two sections of the bank reconciliation now show a correct cash balance of $9,542.30. This amount will be reported as cash on a balance sheet prepared at June 30, 2007.

A bank reconciliation as shown in Exhibit 7.7 accomplishes two major objectives:

1. Checks the accuracy of the bank balance and the company cash records, which involves developing the correct cash balance. The correct cash balance (plus cash on hand, if any) is the amount of cash that is reported on the balance sheet.

2. Identifies any previously unrecorded transactions or changes that are necessary to cause the company's Cash account(s) to show the correct cash balance. Any transactions or changes on the *Company's Books side* of the bank reconciliation need journal entries. Therefore, the following journal entries based on the Company's Books side of the bank reconciliation (Exhibit 7.7) must be entered into the company's records.

Accounts of J. Doe Company

(a) Cash (A)	25.37	
Interest revenue (R)		25.37
To record interest from bank.		
(b) Accounts receivable (A)	204.76	
Cash (A)		204.76
To record NSF cheque.		
(c) Bank service expense (E)	10.00	
Cash (A)		10.00
To record service fees charged by bank.		
(d) Cash (A)	9.00	
Accounts payable (L)		9.00
To correct error made in recording a cheque payable to a creditor.		

Assets		=	Liabilities		+	Shareholders' Equity	
Cash (+25.37 − 204.76			Accounts			Bank service	
− 10.00 + 9.00)	−180.39		payable	+9.00		expense	−10.00
Accounts receivable	+204.76					Interest earned	+25.37

Cash Account of J. Doe Company

The Cash account prior to reconciliation was given earlier in this chapter. After the preceding journal entries are posted, the Cash account is as follows:

Cash					
June 1	Balance	6,637.14	June	Cheques written	8,714.45
June	Deposits	11,800.00	June 30	NSF cheque*	204.76
June 30	Interest earned*	25.37	June 30	Bank service charge*	10.00
June 30	Correcting entry*	9.00			
	Correct cash balance	9,542.30			

*Based on the bank reconciliation.

Notice that all of the additions and deductions on the Company's Books side of the reconciliation need journal entries to update the Cash account. The additions and deductions on the Bank Statement side do not need journal entries because they will work out automatically when they clear the bank.

SELF-STUDY **QUIZ 7-4**

Indicate which of the following items discovered while preparing a company's bank reconciliation will result in adjustment of the cash balance on the balance sheet.

1. Outstanding cheques.

2. Deposits in transit.

3. Bank service charges.

4. NSF cheques that were deposited.

After you complete your answers, check them with the solutions on page 375.

DEMONSTRATION **CASE A**

Wholesale Warehouse Stores sold $950,000 in merchandise during 2008, $400,000 of which was on credit with terms 2/10, n/30 (75 percent of these amounts were paid within the discount period), $500,000 was paid with credit cards (there was a 3-percent credit card discount), and the rest was paid in cash. On December 31, 2008, the Accounts Receivable balance was $80,000, and the Allowance for Doubtful Accounts was $3,000 (credit balance).

Required:
1. Compute net sales for 2008, assuming that sales and credit card discounts are treated as contra-revenue accounts.
2. Assume that Wholesale uses the percentage of sales method for estimating bad debt expense and that it estimates that 2 percent of credit sales will produce bad debts. Record bad debt expense for 2008.
3. Assume that Wholesale uses the aging of accounts receivable method and that it estimates that $10,000 worth of current accounts are uncollectable. Record bad debt expense for 2008.

We strongly recommend that you prepare your own answers to these requirements and then check your answers with the following suggested solution.

SUGGESTED SOLUTION

1. Both sales discounts and credit card discounts should be subtracted from sales revenues in the computation of net sales.

Sales Revenue	$950,000
Less: Sales discounts (0.02 × 0.75 × $400,000)	6,000
Credit card discounts (0.03 × $500,000)	15,000
Net sales	$929,000

2. The percentage estimate of bad debts should be applied to credit sales. Cash sales never produce bad debts.

Bad debt expense (E) (0.02 × $400,000).	8,000	
Allowance for doubtful accounts (XA)		8,000

Assets		=	Liabilities	+	Shareholders' Equity	
Allowance for doubtful					Bad debt	
accounts	−8,000				expense	−8,000

3. The entry made when using the aging of accounts receivable method is the estimated balance minus the unadjusted balance.

Bad debt expense (E) ($10,000 − $3,000).		7,000	
Allowance for doubtful accounts (XA)			7,000

Assets	=	Liabilities	+	Shareholders' Equity	
Allowance for doubtful accounts	−7,000			Bad debt expense	−7,000

DEMONSTRATION **CASE B**

Heather Ann Long, a first-year university student, has just received her first chequing account statement. This was her first chance to attempt a bank reconciliation. She had the following information to work with:

Bank balance, September 1	$1,150
Deposits during September	650
Cheques cleared during September	900
Bank service charge	5
Bank balance, October 1	895

Heather was surprised that the deposit of $50 she made on September 29 had not been posted to her account and was pleased that her rent cheque of $200 had not cleared her account. Her chequebook balance was $750.

Required:
1. Complete Heather's bank reconciliation.
2. Why is it important for individuals such as Heather and businesses to do a bank reconciliation each month?

We strongly recommend that you prepare your own answers to these requirements and then check your answers with the following suggested solution.

SUGGESTED SOLUTION

1. Heather's bank reconciliation:

Heather's Books		Bank Statement	
October 1 cash balance	$750	October 1 cash balance	$895
Additions		Additions	
None		Deposit in transit	50
Deductions		Deductions	
Bank service charge	(5)	Outstanding cheque	(200)
Correct cash balance	$745	Correct cash balance	$745

2. Bank statements, whether personal or business, should be reconciled each month. This process helps ensure that a correct balance is reflected in the customer's books. Failure to reconcile a bank statement increases the chance that an error will not be discovered and may result in bad cheques being written. Businesses must reconcile their bank statements for an additional reason: the correct balance that is calculated during reconciliation is recorded on the balance sheet. A bank reconciliation is an important internal control measure.

Chapter Supplement A

Recording Discounts and Returns

In the chapter, both *credit card discounts* and *cash discounts* have been recorded as contra revenues. For example, if the credit card company is charging a 3-percent fee for its service and credit card sales were $3,000 at a factory store for January 2, the sales transaction is recorded as follows:

Cash (A)	2,910
Credit card discount (XR or E)	90
Sales revenue (R)	3,000

Assets		=	Liabilities	+	Shareholders' Equity	
Cash	+2,910				Sales revenue	+3,000
					Credit card discount	−90

Similarly, if credit sales are recorded with terms 2/10, n/30 ($1,000 × 0.98 = $980), and payment is made within the discount period, the selling company would record the following:

Accounts receivable (A)	1,000
Sales revenue (R)	1,000

Assets		=	Liabilities	+	Shareholders' Equity	
Accounts receivable	+1,000				Sales revenue	+1,000

Cash (A)	980
Sales discount (XR or E)	20
Accounts receivable (A).	1,000

Assets		=	Liabilities	+	Shareholders' Equity	
Cash	+980				Sales discount	−20
Accounts receivable	−1,000					

Sales returns and allowances should always be treated as a contra-revenue account. Assume that the T-shirt company bought 1,000 T-shirts for $6,000 on account. On the date of sale, the selling company makes the following journal entry:

Accounts receivable (A)	6,000
Sales revenue (R)	6,000

Assets		=	Liabilities	+	Shareholders' Equity	
Accounts receivable	+6,000				Sales revenue	+6,000

Before paying for the T-shirts, the T-shirt company discovered that 50 T-shirts were not the colour ordered and returned them to the seller. On that date, the seller records:

Sales returns and allowances (XR).	300
Accounts receivable (A).	300

Assets		=	Liabilities	+	Shareholders' Equity	
Accounts receivable	−300				Sales returns and allowances	+300

In addition, the related cost of goods sold entry for the 50 T-shirts would be reversed.

Chapter Supplement B

Applying the Revenue Principle in Special Circumstances

The revenue principle was introduced in Chapter 3. As noted earlier, application of this principle in the case of Gildan and similar companies was fairly straightforward. Such companies record revenue when goods or services are shipped or delivered. We now expand our discussion of the revenue principle and see how it is applied in business practice by companies other than typical manufacturers, wholesalers, and retailers.

DELAYED REVENUE RECOGNITION: INSTALMENT METHOD

The **INSTALMENT METHOD** recognizes revenue on the basis of cash collection after the delivery of goods.

Recall that to record revenue (1) an exchange must take place, (2) the earnings process must be nearly complete, and (3) collection must be probable. Failure to meet the third revenue recognition criterion (collection must be probable) requires that revenue recognition be delayed until after an initial exchange. When a high level of uncertainty concerning the collectability of the sales price exists, revenue recognition is postponed until *cash is collected from the customer*. This revenue recognition method, called the **instalment method**, is considered to be a very conservative method since it postpones revenue recognition, sometimes until long after goods have been delivered. The most common applications are in certain types of *retail* and *real estate transactions* in which payment is made over a multi-year period and a large proportion of customers stop making payments long before the final payment is due. Certain types of expensive equipment, such as supercomputers, are sometimes sold under contracts calling for payment to be made over a multi-year period and giving the customers the right to return the equipment and cease making payments if they are dissatisfied. The instalment method also is required here. Application of this specialized revenue recognition method is discussed in intermediate accounting courses.

REVENUE RECOGNITION BEFORE THE EARNINGS PROCESS IS COMPLETE: LONG-TERM CONSTRUCTION CONTRACTS

The **PERCENTAGE OF COMPLETION METHOD** records revenue based on the percentage of work completed during the accounting period.

The **COMPLETED CONTRACT METHOD** records revenue when the completed product is delivered to the customer.

An important exception to the usual criteria exists for companies involved in long-term construction projects such as building an office complex for a large corporation. These projects may take a number of years to complete. As a result, if the company recorded no revenue or expenses directly related to the project during the years that it worked on the project and then recorded a massive amount of revenue in the year that it delivered the product to the customer, the financial statements would not accurately represent the company's economic activities. This method of accounting is often referred to as the *completed contract method*.

To deal with this unique problem for long-term construction projects, many companies use the **percentage of completion method**, which records revenue based on the percentage of work completed during the accounting period, instead of the **completed contract method**, which records revenue when the completed product is delivered to the customer.

Under the percentage of completion method, revenues are based on the amount of work done each year. Typically, the amount of work accomplished each year is measured by the *percentage of total cost* that was incurred during the year. For example, assume that the total contract price was $50 million and the total cost for construction was $40 million. In 2007, the construction company spent $10 million, which was 25 percent of the contract cost ($10 million ÷ $40 million).[17] This percentage of completion is then multiplied by the total contract revenue to determine the amount of revenue to be reported in 2007 (25% × $50,000,000 = $12,500,000).

---

[17]The difference between the expected cost and the actual cost of construction, which did not occur in this simple example, creates additional accounting problems.

The amount of expense reported each year is the actual cost incurred ($10,000,000 in 2007), and the amount of income is simply the difference between revenue and expense ($12,500,000 − $10,000,000 = $2,500,000 in 2007). It is important to note that the total revenue, expenses, and income for the two methods over the life of the contract are exactly the same. The methods differ only in terms of the accounting periods in which the various revenues and expenses are reported (their timing). The percentage of completion method recognizes income throughout the contract period; the completed contract method recognizes income only in the year of completion.

Notice that the percentage of completion method does not completely satisfy the second revenue recognition criterion because revenue is reported before the earnings process is complete. It is the preferred method, however, in cases such as this because the completed contract method makes it appear that the contractor was not able to generate any profits for the initial years of the contract but then became very profitable in the final year. In reality, the company was active in all years. Thus, the percentage of completion method better represents this type of underlying economic activity.

Companies may use the percentage of completion method when progress toward completion and costs to complete the contract can be reasonably estimated and they have a firm contract that guarantees payment to satisfy the cash collectability criterion.

REVENUE RECOGNITION FOR SERVICE CONTRACTS

Companies that provide services over more than one accounting period often follow revenue recognition policies similar to those followed for long-term construction contracts. They may record revenue after all services have been provided (after the contract is completed) or may recognize revenue from the completed portion of the services. Since the individual size of the contracts involved often is small (compared to construction contracts) and companies often are engaged in many service contracts with different beginning and ending dates, the distortion caused by the completed contract method is usually smaller than that of long-term construction contracts. Yet many service companies, such as Federal Express, which provides air delivery service, employ the percentage of completion revenue recognition policy as indicated in the following note:

REAL WORLD EXCERPT

Federal Express
ANNUAL REPORT

FEDERAL EXPRESS CORPORATION AND SUBSIDIARIES

Notes to Consolidated Financial Statements
NOTE 1. SUMMARY OF SIGNIFICANT ACCOUNTING POLICIES
Revenue recognition. Revenue is generally recognized upon delivery of shipments. For shipments in transit, revenue is recorded based on the percentage of service completed.

For the services in progress at the end of the accounting period, Federal Express uses the percentage of completion method for revenue recognition, recognizing only a percentage of the revenues and related costs of providing the services based on the degree of completion of the service. This method is also called the *proportional performance* method. This form of revenue recognition is very similar to CanWest Global's accounting for its TV cable contracts and SNC-Lavalin's accounting for its construction contracts. Each company recognizes revenues and expenses related to the *completed portion* of its contract with the customer. The major difference is that CanWest Global is paid for the cable subscriptions in advance, SNC-Lavalin receives progress payments throughout the contract period, and Federal Express receives payment from its business customers after it provides the service.

FINANCIAL ANALYSIS

REVENUE RECOGNITION AND FINANCIAL STATEMENT ANALYSIS

Financial analysts cannot evaluate the income earned by a company if they do not understand how it applied the revenue recognition criteria. As a result, all companies disclose any special revenue recognition issues in the notes to their financial statements. For example, CAE, Inc., a provider of flight simulators and training to the aviation and marine transport industries, states the following in its annual report:

> Revenue from long-term contracts for building simulators and controls systems is recognized using the percentage-of-completion method, where revenue, earnings and unbilled accounts receivable are recorded as related costs are incurred on the basis of the percentage of actual costs incurred to date on a contract, relative to the estimated total costs to complete that contract. Revision in cost and earnings estimates during the term of the contract are reflected in the period in which the need for revision becomes known. Losses, if any, are recognized fully when first anticipated. Generally, the terms of long-term contracts provide for progress billings based on completion of certain phases of work. Warranty provisions are recorded at the time revenue is recognized, based on past experience. No right of return or complimentary upgrades are provided to customers. Post-delivery customer support is billed separately, and revenue is recorded ratably over the support period.

This succinct explanation of the percentage of completion method is an adequate explanation for someone who has read this chapter, but it is doubtful that someone who has not studied accounting would understand its meaning. This is an excellent example of the importance of careful study of accounting even if you do not major in accounting.

DEMONSTRATION CASE C

Assume that (1) Canada Post had shipments in transit involving fees totalling $20 million on December 31 of the current year, (2) none of the fees had been collected, and (3) on average, the shipments in transit were 60-percent completed.

Required:

1. Determine what amount related to the shipments in transit is recognized as revenue in the current year using the revenue recognition rule indicated in the Federal Express note that is shown in the prior section.

2. Indicate what asset(s) is(are) affected by recording revenue from the shipments in transit (accounts and amounts).

We strongly recommend that you prepare your own answers to these requirements and then check your answers with the suggested solution below.

SUGGESTED SOLUTION

1. Delivery revenue is recorded for $12,000,000 ($20,000,000 × 60%).

2. Accounts Receivable increases by $12,000,000.

SOLUTIONS TO **SELF-STUDY QUIZZES**

Self-Study Quiz 7-1

1.

Gross Sales	$35,000
Less: Sales discounts ($0.01 \times 1/2 \times \$30,000$)	150
Credit card discounts ($0.03 \times 0.8 \times \$5,000$)	120
Net Sales	$34,730

2. Gross profit = $150,000 - $110,000 = $40,000

Gross profit percentage = $40,000 \div $150,000 = 26.66\%$

Self-Study Quiz 7-2

1.

Bad debt expense (+E)...	1,230	
Allowance for doubtful accounts (+XA)...........................		1,230

2.

Allowance for doubtful accounts (−XA).............................	1,160	
Accounts receivable (−A)...		1,160

3. Ending balance = Beginning balance + Bad debt expense − Write-offs
   = $1,290 + $1,230 − $1,160 = $1,360

Self-Study Quiz 7-3

1.

Allowance for Doubtful Accounts (XA)			
		Beginning balance	723
Write-offs	648	Bad debt expense (solve)	829
		Ending balance	904

Beginning + Bad debt expense − Write-offs = Ending; $723 + X − 648 = $904; X = $829

2. The amount would be subtracted from net income because an increase in the Accounts Receivable account indicates that sales revenue was in excess of cash collected from customers for the period.

3. Granting longer payment deadlines will most likely *decrease* the accounts receivable turnover ratio because later collections from customers will increase the average accounts receivable balance (the denominator of the ratio), thus decreasing the ratio.

Self-Study Quiz 7-4

3. Bank service charges are deducted from the company's account; thus, cash must be reduced and an expense must be recorded.

4. NSF cheques that were deposited were recorded on the books as increases in the Cash account; thus, cash must be decreased and the related account receivable increased.

CHAPTER **TAKE-AWAYS**

1. **Apply the revenue principle to determine the accepted time to record sales revenue for typical retailers, wholesalers, manufacturers, and service companies. p. 345**
   Revenue recognition policies are widely recognized as one of the most important determinants of the fair presentation of financial statements. For most merchandisers and manufacturers, the required revenue recognition point is the time of shipment or delivery of goods. For service companies, it is the time at which services are provided.

2. **Analyze the impact of credit card sales, sales discounts, and sales returns on the amounts reported as net sales. p. 345**
   Both *credit card discounts* and *cash discounts* can be recorded either as contra revenues or as expenses. When recorded as contra revenues, they reduce net sales. *Sales returns and allowances,* which should always be treated as contra revenues, also reduce net sales.

3. **Compute and interpret the gross profit percentage. p. 349**
   The gross profit percentage measures the ability to charge premium prices and produce goods and services at lower cost. Managers, analysts, and creditors use this ratio to assess the effectiveness of the company's product development, marketing, and production strategy.

4. **Estimate, report, and evaluate the effects of uncollectable accounts receivable (bad debts) on financial statements. p. 351**

   When receivables are material, companies must employ the allowance method to account for uncollectables. The steps in the process are

   1. Preparing the end-of-period adjusting entry to record an estimate of bad debt expense.

   2. Writing off specific accounts determined to be uncollectable during the period, and recovery of amounts written off.

   The adjusting entry reduces net income as well as net accounts receivable. The write-off of accounts receivable affects neither.

5. **Compute and interpret the accounts receivable turnover ratio and the effects of accounts receivable on cash flows. p. 359**

   Accounts receivable turnover ratio—Measures the effectiveness of credit granting and collection activities. It reflects how many times average trade receivables were recorded and collected during the period. Analysts and creditors watch this ratio because a sudden decline in it may mean that a company is extending collection deadlines in an attempt to prop up lagging sales or even is recording sales that later will be returned by customers. Alternatively, the average age of receivables indicates the average number of days it takes to collect from customers.

   Effects on cash flows—When a net decrease in accounts receivable for the period occurs, cash collected from customers exceeds revenue, and cash flows from operations increases. When a net increase in accounts receivable occurs, cash collected from customers is less than revenue; thus, the cash flow from operations declines.

6. **Report, control, and safeguard cash. p. 362**

   Cash is the most liquid of all assets, flowing continually into and out of a business. As a result, a number of critical control procedures, including the reconciliation of bank accounts, should be applied. Also, management of cash may be critically important to decision makers who must have cash available to meet current needs yet must avoid excess amounts of idle cash that produce no revenue.

   Closely related to recording revenue is recording the cost of what was sold. Chapter 8 will focus on transactions related to inventory and cost of goods sold. This topic is important because cost of goods sold has a major impact on a company's gross profit and net income, which are watched closely by investors, analysts, and other users of financial statements. Increasing emphasis on quality, productivity, and costs has further focused production managers' attention on cost of goods sold and inventory. Since inventory cost figures play a major role in product introduction and pricing decisions, they also are important to marketing and general managers. Finally, since inventory accounting has a major effect on many companies' tax liabilities, this is an important place to introduce the effect of taxation on management decision making and financial reporting.

KEY **RATIOS**

The gross profit percentage measures the excess of sales prices over the costs to purchase or produce the goods or services sold as a percentage. It is computed as follows (p. 349):

$$\text{Gross Profit Percentage} = \frac{\text{Gross Profit}}{\text{Net Sales}}$$

The receivables turnover ratio measures the effectiveness of credit-granting and collection activities. It is computed as follows (p. 359):

$$\text{Receivables Turnover} = \frac{\text{Net Sales}}{\text{Average Net Trade Accounts Receivable}}$$

BALANCE SHEET
Under Current Assets
    Accounts receivable (net of allowance for
        doubtful accounts)

INCOME STATEMENT
Revenues
    Net sales (sales revenue less discounts if
        treated as contra revenues and sales
        returns and allowances)
Expenses
    Selling expenses (including bad debt
        expense and discounts if treated
        as expenses)

CASH FLOW STATEMENT
Under Operating Activities (indirect method)
    Net income
    + decrease in accounts receivable (net)
    − increase in accounts receivable (net)

NOTES
*Under Summary of Significant Accounting
Policies*
    Revenue recognition policy

KEY **TERMS**

Accounts Receivable (Trade Receivables or
    Receivables) p. 350
Aging of Accounts Receivable Method
    p. 355
**Allowance for Doubtful Accounts
    (Allowance for Bad Debts** or **Allowance
    for Uncollectable Accounts)** p. 352
Allowance Method p. 352
**Bad Debt Expense (Doubtful Accounts
    Expense, Uncollectable Accounts
    Expense)** p. 352
Bank Reconciliation p. 365
Bank Statement p. 364

Cash p. 362
Cash Equivalents p. 362
Completed Contract Method p. 372
Credit Card Discount p. 346
Instalment Method p. 372
Internal Controls p. 360
Note Receivable p. 351
Percentage of Completion Method p. 372
Percentage of Credit Sales Method
    p. 355
Sales (or Cash) Discount p. 346
Sales Returns and Allowances p. 348

QUESTIONS

1. Explain the difference between sales revenue and net sales.
2. What is gross profit or gross margin on sales? How is the gross profit ratio computed?
   In your explanation, assume that net sales revenue is $100,000 and cost of goods sold is
   $60,000.
3. What is a credit card discount? How does it affect amounts reported on the income
   statement?
4. What is a sales discount? Use credit terms 1/10, n/30 in your explanation.
5. What is the distinction between *sales allowances* and *sales discounts*?
6. Differentiate accounts receivable from notes receivable.
7. Which basic accounting principle is satisfied by using the allowance method of accounting
   for bad debts?
8. Using the allowance method, is bad debt expense recognized in (a) the period in which
   sales related to the uncollectable were made or (b) the period in which the seller learns that
   the customer is unable to pay?
9. What is the effect of the write-off of bad debts (using the allowance method) on (a) net
   income and (b) accounts receivable, net?
10. Does an increase in the receivables turnover ratio generally indicate faster or slower
    collection of receivables? Explain.
11. Define *cash* and *cash equivalents* in the context of accounting. Indicate the types of items
    that should be included.

12. Summarize the primary characteristics of an effective internal control system for cash.
13. Why should cash-handling and cash-recording activities be separated? How is this separation accomplished?
14. What are the purposes of a bank reconciliation? What balances are reconciled?
15. Briefly explain how the total amount of cash reported on the balance sheet is computed.
16. (Chapter Supplement A) Under the gross method of recording sales discounts, is the amount of sales discount taken recorded (a) at the time the sale is recorded or (b) at the time the collection of the account is recorded?
17. (Chapter Supplement B) When is it acceptable to use the percentage of completion method?

EXERCISES

LO1

E7–1 Interpreting the Revenue Principle

Identify the *most likely* point in time when sales revenue should be recorded for each of the listed transactions.

Transaction	Point A	Point B
a. Airline tickets sold by an airline on a credit card	____ Point of sale	____ Completion of flight
b. Computer sold by mail-order company on a credit card	____ Shipment	____ Delivery to customer
c. Sale of inventory to a business customer on open account	____ Shipment	____ Collection from customers

LO2

E7–2 Reporting Net Sales with Credit Sales and Sales Discounts

During the months of January and February, Bronze Corporation sold goods to three customers. The sequence of events was as follows:

Jan. 6   Sold goods for $2,000 to S. Green and billed that amount subject to terms 2/10, n/30.
      9   Sold goods to M. Munoz for $800 and billed that amount subject to terms 2/10, n/30.
     14   Collected cash due from S. Green.
Feb. 8   Collected cash due from M. Munoz.
     28   Sold goods for $1,000 to R. Reynolds and billed that amount subject to terms 2/10, n/45.

Required:

1. Assuming that sales discounts are treated as contra revenues, compute net sales for the two months ended February 28.
2. Prepare the journal entries to record the transactions that occurred on January 6 and 14.

LO2

E7–3 Reporting Net Sales with Credit Sales, Sales Discounts, and Credit Card Sales

The following transactions were selected from the records of Evergreen Company:

July 12   Sold merchandise to Rami, who charged the $1,000 purchase on his Visa credit card. Visa charges Evergreen a 2-percent credit card fee.
July 15   Sold merchandise to Steven at an invoice price of $6,000; terms 2/10, n/30.
      20   Sold merchandise to Tania at an invoice price of $2,000; terms 2/10, n/30.
      23   Collected payment from Steven from July 15 sale.
Aug. 25   Collected payment from Tania from July 20 sale.

Required:

1. Assuming that sales discounts are treated as contra revenues, compute net sales for the two months ended August 31.
2. Prepare the journal entries to record the transactions that occurred on July 12, 15, and 23.

LO2

E7–4 Reporting Net Sales with Credit Sales, Sales Discounts, Sales Returns, and Credit Card Sales

The following transactions were selected from among those completed by Gunzo Wholesalers in 2008:

Nov. 20   Sold two items of merchandise to Brigitte, who charged the $600 sales amount on her Visa credit card. Visa charges Gunzo a 2-percent credit card fee.

    25   Sold 20 items of merchandise to Clara for $5,000; terms 3/10, n/30.
    28   Sold 10 identical items of merchandise to David for $6,000; terms 3/10, n/30.
Nov. 30   David returned one of the items purchased on the 28th; the item was defective, and credit was given to the customer.
Dec. 6   David paid the account balance in full.
   30   Clara paid in full the amount due for the purchase on November 25, 2008.

Required:

1. Assume that sales discounts and credit card discounts are treated as contra revenues; compute net sales for the two months ended December 31, 2008.

2. Prepare the journal entries to record the transactions that occurred on November 20, 25, and December 30.

E7–5 Determining the Effects of Credit Sales, Sales Discounts, Credit Card Sales, and Sales Returns and Allowances on Income Statement Categories

■ LO2

Rockland Shoe Company records sales returns and allowances as contra revenues, and sales discounts and credit card discounts as selling expenses. Complete the following tabulation, indicating the effect (+ for increase, − for decrease, and NE for no effect) of each transaction. Do not record the related cost of goods sold.

July 12   Sold merchandise to Rosa, who charged the $300 purchase on her American Express card. American Express charges a 3-percent credit card fee.
July 15   Sold merchandise to Thomas for $5,000; terms 2/10, n/30.
July 20   Collected the amount due from Thomas.
July 21   Lee returned shoes with an invoice price of $1,000, before paying for them.

Transaction	Net Sales	Gross Profit	Income from Operations
July 12			
July 15			
July 20			
July 21			

E7–6 Evaluating the Effects of Sales Returns and Allowances on Sales

■ LO2

ANALYSIS

Teen World, Inc. sells a wide selection of clothing items for teenage girls. The company imports merchandise from various international suppliers, and distributes its merchandise to retail stores in major shopping areas. The company sells merchandise on credit, allows retailers to return incorrect or damaged merchandise within a period of two months, and grants them sales allowances under certain circumstances. The company is currently reviewing its sales returns policy and provided you with the following information for the past six quarters:

Quarter	Gross Sales	Cost of Sales	Sales Returns and Allowances
Jan. 1–March 31, 2008	$1,346,300	$ 942,400	$ 53,852
April 1–June 30, 2008	1,474,500	1,042,100	76,674
July 1–Sept. 30, 2008	1,529,100	1,080,300	94,804
Oct. 1–Dec. 31, 2008	1,671,400	1,101,200	140,397
Jan. 1–March 31, 2009	1,708,800	1,103,600	153,792
April 1–June 30, 2009	1,992,700	1,317,500	219,197

Required:

1. Compute the following percentages for each of the six quarters: (1) cost of sales to net sales, and (2) sales return and allowances to gross sales.

2. Comment on the ratios computed in requirement 1 and identify possible reasons for the increase in the amount of sales returns and allowances as well as your recommendations for controlling the amount of sales returns and allowances.

■ **LO3**

ANALYSIS

E7–7 Analyzing Gross Profit Percentage on the Basis of a Multiple-Step Income Statement

The following summarized data were provided by the records of Slate, Inc., for the year ended December 31, 2008:

Sales of merchandise for cash	$220,000
Sales of merchandise on credit	32,000
Cost of goods sold	147,000
Selling expense	40,200
Administrative expense	19,000
Sales returns and allowances	7,000
Items not included in the above amounts:	
Estimated bad debt, 2.5% of credit sales	
Average income tax rate, 30%	
Number of common shares outstanding, 5,000	

Required:

1. Based on these data, prepare a multiple-step income statement (showing both gross profit and income from operations).

2. What was the amount of gross profit? What was the gross profit percentage? Explain what these two numbers mean.

■ **LO3**

Brown Shoe

Payless Shoesource

ANALYSIS

E7–8 Analyzing Gross Profit Percentage on the Basis of a Multiple-Step Income Statement and Within-Industry Comparison

Brown Shoe Company, Inc. and Payless Shoesource, Inc. are two leading footwear companies in the United States and Canada. The following data were taken from the 2005 annual reports of both companies (amounts in millions of US dollars):

	Brown	Payless
Sales of merchandise	$2,292.1	$2,667.3
Income taxes	30.1	30.8
Cash dividends declared	7.3	3.5
Selling and administrative expense	809.7	770.8
Cost of products sold	1,293.7	1,778.9
Interest expense	18.8	7.4
Other expenses (income)	(1.3)	13.0
Number of common shares outstanding	27.7	67.2

Required:

1. Based on these data, prepare a multiple-step income statement for each company for the year ending December 31, 2005 (showing both gross profit and income from operations).

2. Compute the gross profit and the gross profit percentage for each company. Explain what these two numbers mean. What do you believe accounts for the difference between the gross profit percentages of both companies?

■ **LO4**

E7–9 Comparing Two Methods of Estimating Bad Debts

Kwan Ltd. earned $328,000 in credit sales during its first year of operation. At year end, it had $79,636 in accounts receivable and estimated that 2.5 percent of its credit sales may not be collectable in the future.

Required:

1. Prepare the adjusting journal entry to record bad debt expense, and compute the balance of the Allowance for Doubtful Accounts at year end.

2. Assume that the company's estimate of uncollectible accounts was based on the balance of accounts receivable at a rate of 10 percent. Compute the balance of the Allowance for Doubtful Accounts at year end, and prepare the adjusting journal entry to record bad debt expense.

3. What are the main differences between the two methods of estimating bad debt expense?

E7–10 **Recording and Determining the Effects of Bad Debt Transactions on Income Statement Categories Using the Percentage of Credit Sales Method**   ■ **LO4**

During 2007, Choi and Goldstein Furniture recorded credit sales of $600,000. Based on prior experience, the company estimates that the bad debt rate is 2 percent of credit sales.

Required:

1. Prepare journal entries to record the following transactions:
   a. The appropriate bad debt expense adjustment that was recorded for the year 2007.
   b. On December 31, 2007, an account receivable for $1,600 from a prior year was determined to be uncollectable and was written off.

2. Complete the following tabulation, indicating the amount and effect (+ for increase, − for decrease, and NE for no effect) of each transaction.

Transaction	Net Sales	Gross Profit	Income from Operations
a.			
b.			

E7–11 **Computing Bad Debt Expense Using Aging Analysis**   ■ **LO4**

Brown Cow Dairy uses the aging approach to estimate bad debt expense. The balance of each account receivable is aged on the basis of three time periods as follows: (1) not yet due, $24,000; (2) up to 120 days past due, $10,000; and (3) more than 120 days past due, $6,000. Experience has shown that for each age group, the average bad debt rates on the amount of the receivable at year-end due to uncollectability are (1) 2 percent, (2) 10 percent, and (3) 30 percent, respectively. At December 31, 2008 (end of the current year), the Allowance for Doubtful Accounts balance was $600 (credit) before the end-of-period adjusting entry is made.

Required:

What amount should be recorded as bad debt expense for the current year?

E7–12 **Recording, Reporting, and Evaluating a Bad Debt Estimate**   ■ **LO4**

Connor Company started business on January 1, 2007. During the year, the company's records indicated the following:

Sales on cash basis	$500,000
Sales on credit basis	250,000
Collections on accounts receivable	200,000

The company's manager is concerned about accounting for bad debts. At December 31, 2007, although no accounts were considered bad, several customers were considerably late in paying their accounts. A friend of the manager suggested a 1-percent bad debt rate on sales, which the manager decided to use at the start.

Required:

1. You have been employed on a part-time basis to assist with the company's record keeping. The manager told you to set up bad debt expense of $7,500. Prepare the required journal entry.

2. You are concerned about how the $7,500 was determined. The manager told you the figure was provided by another manager "who knew his business" and used 1 percent of sales. Do you agree with the estimate of bad debts? If you disagree, prepare the correct journal entry and explain the basis for your disagreement.

3. Show how the various accounts related to credit sales should be shown on the company's income statement for 2007 and its balance sheet at December 31, 2007.

E7–13 **Recording, Reporting, and Evaluating a Bad Debt Estimate**   ■ **LO4**

During 2009, Gauthier's Camera Shop had sales revenue of $170,000, of which $85,000 was on credit. At the start of 2009, Accounts Receivable showed a $10,000 debit balance, and the Allowance for Doubtful Accounts showed a credit balance of $800. Collections of accounts receivable during 2009 amounted to $68,000. On December 31, 2009, an Account Receivable (J. Doe) of $1,500 from a prior year was determined to be uncollectable; therefore, it was written off immediately as a bad debt. On the basis of experience, a decision was made to continue the accounting policy of basing estimated bad debt at 2 percent of credit sales for the year.

Required:

1. Prepare the required journal entries on December 31, 2009 (end of the accounting period).

2. Show how the amounts related to Bad Debt Expense and Accounts Receivable would be reported on the income statement for 2009 and the balance sheet at December 31, 2009. Disregard income tax considerations.

3. On the basis of the data available, does the 2-percent rate appear to be reasonable? Explain.

4. There are two alternative methods that can be used to determine the amount of bad debt expense for the year. Do you have a preference for either of these methods? Explain.

▪ LO4

DaimlerChrysler AG

E7–14 Interpreting Bad Debt Disclosures

DaimlerChrysler is the largest industrial group headquartered in Germany. Best known as the manufacturer of Mercedes-Benz and Chrysler cars and trucks, it also manufactures products in the fields of rail systems, aerospace, propulsion, defence, and information technology. In a recent filing pursuant to its listing on the New York Stock Exchange, it disclosed the following information concerning its allowance for doubtful accounts (in millions of euros, denoted €):

Balance at Beginning of Period	Charged to Costs and Expenses	Amounts Written Off	Balance at End of Period
591	41	(92)	540

Required:

1. Record summary journal entries related to bad debts for the current year.

2. If DaimlerChrysler had written off an additional €10 million of accounts receivable during the period, how would net receivables and net income have been affected? Explain.

▪ LO4

Microsoft

ANALYSIS

E7–15 Inferring Bad Debt Write-Offs and Cash Collections from Customers

Microsoft develops, produces, and markets a wide range of computer software including the Windows operating system. On a recent balance sheet, Microsoft reported the following information about accounts receivable and net sales revenue.

	Year 2	Year 1
Accounts receivable, net of allowances of $142 and $171	$ 9,316	$ 7,180
Net revenues	44,282	39,788

According to its annual report, Microsoft recorded bad debt expense of $120 and did not reinstate any previously written-off accounts during year 2.

Required:

1. What amount of bad debts was written off during year 2?

2. Assuming that all of Microsoft's sales during the period were on open account, compute the amount of cash collected from customers for year 2.

▪ LO4

Bombardier

ANALYSIS

E7–16 Determining the Impact of Uncollectable Accounts on Income and Working Capital

An annual report for Bombardier, Inc. contained the following information at the end of its fiscal year (in millions of dollars):

	Year 2	Year 1
Credit card receivable	$1,418	1,129
Allowance for uncollectable accounts	(101)	(74)
	1,684	1,513

A footnote to the financial statements disclosed that uncollectable accounts amounting to $13 million were written off as bad during year 1 and $21 million during year 2. Assume that the tax rate for Bombardier was 30 percent.

Required:

1. Determine the bad debt expense for year 2 based on the preceding facts.

2. *Working capital* is defined as current assets minus current liabilities. How was Bombardier's working capital affected by the write-off of $21 million in uncollectable accounts during year 2? What impact did the recording of bad debt expense have on working capital in year 2?

3. How was net income affected by the $21 million write-off during year 2? What impact did recording bad debt expense have on net income for year 2?

E7–17 Analyzing and Interpreting the Receivables Turnover Ratio

An annual report for Federal Express contained the following data:

■ **LO5**

Federal Express

ANALYSIS

	(in millions)	
	Current Year	Previous Year
Accounts receivable	$ 3,178	$2,776
Less: Allowance for doubtful accounts	151	149
Net accounts receivable	$ 3,027	$2,627
Net sales (assume all on credit)	$24,710	

Required:

1. Determine the accounts receivable turnover ratio and average age of receivables for the current year.

2. Explain the meaning of the number that you calculated in requirement 1.

E7–18 Comparing Receivables Turnover Ratios of Two Companies

The net sales and average balances of accounts receivable for ACE Aviation and WestJet Airlines for a recent fiscal year are shown below (in millions of dollars):

■ **LO5**

ACE Aviation
WestJet Airlines

ANALYSIS

	Average Accounts Receivable	Sales
ACE Aviation	$592	$9,830
WestJet Airlines	10	1,395

Required:

1. Compute the following for each company:
   a. The receivable turnover ratio.
   b. The average collection period.

2. Based on your computations for requirement 1, which company's accounts receivable appear to be the more "liquid" asset? Explain.

E7–19 Interpreting the Effects of Sales Growth and Changes in Receivables on Cash Flow from Operations

Apple Computer, Inc. is best known for its iMac and iPod product lines. Three recent years produced a combination of dramatic increases in sales revenue and net income. Cash flows from operations declined during the period, however. Contributing to that declining cash flow was the change in accounts receivable. The current and prior year balance sheets reported the following:

■ **LO5**

Apple

ANALYSIS

	(in millions)	
	Current Year	Previous Year
Accounts receivable, less allowance for doubtful accounts	$1,252	$895

Required:

1. How would the change in accounts receivable affect cash flow from operations for the current year? Explain why it would have this effect.

2. Explain how increasing sales revenue often leads to (a) increasing accounts receivable and (b) an excess of sales revenue over collections from customers.

■ **LO6**   **E7–20   Identifying Strengths and Weaknesses of Internal Control**

You have been engaged to review the internal control procedures used by Data Flow Inc. During the course of your review, you note the following practices:

a. The credit manager maintains the accounts receivable records and handles all collections from customers, because the accounting department personnel are not authorized to handle cash receipts.

b. All cash received from customers is deposited daily in the company's bank account.

c. Employees who handle cash receipts are not permitted to write off accounts receivable as uncollectable.

d. Invoices that require payment are first verified by the accounting personnel for accuracy. An accounting clerk stamps them "paid" if they are cleared for payment and sends them to the treasurer, who issues and signs the cheques.

e. The cheques issued by the company treasurer are not pre-numbered.

f. After preparing the bank reconciliation, any difference between the adjusted cash balance per the company's books and the adjusted balance per the bank statement is debited (or credited) to the Cash account.

Required:
Indicate whether each of these six practices reflects a strength or a weakness of the internal control system. Provide justification for your answer.

■ **LO6**   **E7–21   Internal Control Over Cash**

Organic Growers, Inc. is a successful grower of summer fruits and vegetables. The company has a seasonal business that starts in June and ends in October. The owners use a vast agricultural terrain to grow a variety of vegetables and fruits. They employ four workers during peak periods to help during the planting season and to pick the vegetables and fruits as they become ready for consumption. To save on the cost of harvesting the produce, the owners allow customers to pick the produce they like from the field and then collect the cash for the goods sold. They also have a small store where they keep small quantities of produce for sale to customers who do not wish to pick the produce themselves. Receipts for the purchased goods are only given to those who ask for them. During the summer, the owners accumulate enough cash to pay for farm supplies at the time they are delivered. They do so to avoid wasting time to prepare cheques and to balance the chequebook.

Required:
How can Organic Growers strengthen its internal control over cash and improve on its overall cash management?

■ **LO6**   **E7–22   Reporting Cash and Cash Equivalents When There Are Several Bank Accounts**

Singh Corporation has manufacturing facilities in several cities and has cash on hand at several locations as well as in several bank accounts. The general ledger at the end of 2007 showed the following accounts:

Cash on Hand—Home Office	$ 700	Cash on Hand—Location C	200
City Bank—Home Office	58,600	National Bank—Location C	965
Cash on Hand—Location A	100	Petty Cash Fund	300
National Bank—Location A	3,350	Credit Suisse—3-month Certificate	
Cash on Hand—Location B	200	of Deposit	5,800
National Bank—Location B	785	FransaBank—6-month Certificate	
		of Deposit	4,500

The bank balances given represent the current cash balances as reflected on the bank reconciliations.

Required:

What amount of cash and cash equivalents should be reported on the company's 2007 balance sheet? Explain the basis for your decisions on any questionable items.

E7–23 Preparing Bank Reconciliation, Entries, and Reporting   ■ **LO6**

The June 30, 2008, bank statement for Zoltan Company and the June ledger accounts for cash are summarized below:

Bank Statement			
	Cheques	**Deposits**	**Balance**
Balance, June 1, 2008			$ 7,200
Deposits during June		$17,000	24,200
Cheques cleared through June	$18,100		6,100
Bank service charges	50		6,050
Balance, June 30, 2008			6,050

Cash in Bank				
June 1	Balance	6,800	June	Cheques written	18,400
June	Deposits	19,000			

Cash on hand	
June 30 Balance	300

Required:

1. Reconcile the bank balance to the book balance at June 30, 2008. A comparison of the cheques written with the cheques that have cleared the bank shows outstanding cheques of $700. Some of the cheques that cleared in June were written prior to June. No deposits in transit were carried over from May, but a deposit is in transit at the end of June.

2. Prepare any journal entries that should be made as a result of the bank reconciliation.

3. What is the balance in the Cash account after the reconciliation entries?

4. What is the total amount of cash that should be reported on the balance sheet at June 30, 2008?

E7–24 Preparing Bank Reconciliation, Entries, and Reporting   ■ **LO6**

The September 30, 2009, bank statement for Russell Company and the September ledger accounts for cash are summarized here:

Bank Statement			
	Cheques	**Deposits**	**Balance**
Balance, September 1, 2009			$ 6,300
Deposits recorded during September		$27,000	33,300
Cheques cleared during September	$28,500		4,800
NSF cheque—Betty Brown	150		4,650
Bank service charges	50		4,600
Balance, September 30, 2009			4,600

Cash				
Sept 1	Balance	6,300	Sept.	Cheques written	28,600
Sept.	Deposits	28,000			

Cash on hand	
Sept 30 Balance	400

No outstanding cheques and no deposits in transit were carried over from August; however, there are deposits in transit and cheques outstanding at the end of September.

Required:

1. Reconcile the balance in the bank account with the cash balance in the books at September 30, 2009.

2. Prepare any journal entries that should be made as a result of the bank reconciliation.

3. What should be the balance in the Cash account after the reconciliation entries?

4. What total amount of cash should the company report on the balance sheet at September 30, 2009?

■ LO6 **E7–25 Preparing Bank Reconciliation, Entries, and Reporting**

The bank statement for the Mini Mart Corporation shows a balance of $1,330 on June 30, but the company's Cash in Bank account had a balance of $499 on the same date. Comparison of the amounts reported on the bank statement with the company's records indicates that (1) deposits of $160, representing cash receipts of June 30, which did not appear on the bank statement, (2) there were outstanding cheques totalling $240, (3) bank service charges for June amounted to $9, (4) collection of a note receivable by the bank on behalf of the company for $800 plus $40 in interest revenue, and (5) a cheque for $80 from a customer was returned with the bank statement and marked NSF.

Required:

1. Prepare a bank reconciliation statement for Mini Mart Corporation as at June 30.

2. Prepare any journal entries that should be made as a result of the bank reconciliation.

3. Why is it important to reconcile the balance in the bank statement with the cash balance in the company's records?

4. What is the amount of cash that the company should report on its balance sheet at June 30?

E7–26 Recording Credit Sales, Sales Discounts, Sales Returns, and Credit Card Sales (Supplement A)

The following transactions were selected from among those completed by Hailey Retailers in 2008:

Nov. 20 Sold two items of merchandise to Baja, who charged the $400 sales amount on her Visa credit card. Visa charges Hailey a 2-percent credit card fee.

25 Sold 20 items of merchandise to Christine for $4,000; terms 2/10, n/30.

28 Sold 10 identical items of merchandise to Daoud for $6,000; terms 2/10, n/30.

30 Daoud returned one of the items purchased on the 28th; the item was defective, and credit was given to the customer.

Dec. 6 Daoud paid the account balance in full.

30 Christine paid in full the amount due for the purchase on November 25, 2008.

Required:

Prepare the appropriate journal entry for each of these transactions, assuming the company uses the gross method to record sales revenue. Do not record the cost of goods sold.

E7–27 Determining Income Using the Percentage of Completion Method (Supplement B)

Blanchard Construction Company entered into a long-term construction contract with the government to build a special landing strip at an Air Force base in Saint Hubert, Québec. The project took three years and cost the government $12 million. Blanchard spent the following amounts each year: 2007, $2 million; 2008, $5 million; 2009, $3 million. The company uses the percentage of completion method. Cost estimates equalled actual costs.

Required:

Determine the amount of net income that Blanchard can report each year for this project. Ignore income taxes.

PROBLEMS

■ LO1 **P7–1 Applying the Revenue Principle (AP7–1)**

At what point should revenue be recognized in each of the following independent cases? Explain your answers.

Case A. For December holiday presents, a fast-food restaurant sells coupon books for $10. Each of the $1 coupons may be used in the restaurant at any time during the following 12 months. The customer must pay cash when purchasing the coupon book.

Case B. Howard Land Development Corporation sold a lot to Quality Builders to construct a new home. The price of the lot was $50,000. Quality made a down payment of $10,000 and agreed to pay the balance in six months. After making the sale, Howard learned that Quality Builders often entered into these agreements but refused to pay the balance if it did not find a customer who wanted a house built on the lot.

Case C. Driscoll Corporation has always recorded revenue at the point of sale of its refrigerators. Recently, it has extended its warranties to cover all repairs for a period of seven years. One young accountant with the company now questions whether Driscoll has completed its earning process when it sells the refrigerators. She suggests that the warranty obligation for seven years means that a significant amount of additional work must be performed in the future.

P7–2   Reporting Net Sales and Expenses with Discounts, Returns, and Bad Debts (AP7–2)   ■ **LO2, 4**
The following data were selected from the records of May Company for the year ended December 31, 2009.

Balances January 1, 2009	
Accounts receivable (various customers)	$110,000
Allowance for doubtful accounts	5,000

The company sells merchandise for cash and on open account with credit terms 2/10, n/30. Assume a unit sales price of $500 in all transactions, and use the gross method to record sales revenue.

Transactions during 2009

a. Sold merchandise for cash, $226,000.

b. Sold merchandise to R. Agostino; invoice amount, $12,000.

c. Sold merchandise to K. Black; invoice amount, $30,000.

d. Two days after purchase, R. Agostino returned one of the units purchased in (b) and received account credit.

e. Sold merchandise to B. Assaf; invoice amount, $24,000.

f. R. Agostino paid his account in full within the discount period.

g. Collected $98,000 cash from customers for credit sales made in 2008, all within the discount periods.

h. K. Black paid the invoice in (c) within the discount period.

i. Sold merchandise to R. Fong; invoice amount, $17,000.

j. Three days after paying the account in full, K. Black returned seven defective units and received a cash refund.

k. After the discount period, collected $8,000 cash on an account receivable on sales made in 2006.

l. Wrote off an old account of $2,900 after deciding that the amount would never be collected.

m. The estimated bad debt rate used by the company was 1 percent of credit sales net of returns.

Required:

1. Using the following categories, indicate the dollar effect (increase, decrease, no effect) of each listed transaction, including the write-off of the uncollectable account and the adjusting entry for estimated bad debts (ignore cost of goods sold).

Sales Revenue	Sales Discounts (taken)	Sales Returns and Allowances	Bad Debt Expense

2. Show how the accounts related to the preceding sale and collection activities should be reported on the income statement for 2009. (Treat sales discounts as contra revenues.)

■ **LO3**

P7–3 **Understanding the Income Statement Based on the Gross Profit Percentage** (AP7–3)

The following data were taken from the year-end records of Nomura Export Company.

Income Statement Items	Year 1	Year 2
Gross sales revenue	$160,000	$232,000
Sales returns and allowances	?	18,000
Net sales revenue	?	?
Cost of goods sold	68%	?
Gross profit	?	30%
Operating expenses	18,500	?
Income before income taxes	?	20,000
Income tax expense (20%)	?	?
Income before extraordinary items	?	?
Extraordinary items, net of tax	8,000 (gain)	1,600 (loss)
Net income	?	?
EPS (10,000 shares outstanding)	3.00	?

Required:
Fill in all of the missing amounts. Show computations.

■ **LO4**

Kimberly-Clark

P7–4 **Interpreting Disclosure of Allowance for Doubtful Accounts** (AP7–4)

Kimberly-Clark manufactures and markets a variety of paper and synthetic fibre products, including well-known Kleenex tissues. It recently disclosed the following information concerning the allowance for doubtful accounts in its annual report.

SCHEDULE II
Valuation and Qualifying Accounts
For the Years Ended December 31, 2006, 2005, and 2004
(millions of dollars)

Description: Allowances for Doubtful Accounts	Balance at Beginning of Period	Charged to Costs and Expenses	Charged to Other Accounts*	Write-Offs	Balance at End of Period
December 31, 2006	$35.8	$11.7	$3.2	$11.8	$38.9
December 31, 2005	42.5	8.9	0	?	35.8
December 31, 2004	47.9	?	4.0	18.2	42.5

*These are primarily bad debt recoveries. *Hint:* These require a reversal of the previous entry made when they were written off.

Required:

1. Record summary journal entries related to bad debts for 2006.
2. Supply the missing dollar amounts noted by (?) for 2004 and 2005.

■ **LO4**

P7–5 **Determining Bad Debt Expense Based on Aging Analysis** (AP7–5)

Green Pastures Equipment Company uses the aging approach to estimate bad debt expense at the end of each accounting year. Credit sales occur frequently on terms n/60. The balance of each account receivable is aged on the basis of three time periods as follows: (1) not yet due, (2) up to one year past due, and (3) more than one year past due. Experience has shown that for each age group, the average bad debt rate on the amounts receivable at year-end due to uncollectability are (a) 1 percent, (b) 5 percent, and (c) 30 percent, respectively.

At December 31, 2008 (end of the current accounting year), the Accounts Receivable balance was $41,000, and the unadjusted balance of the Allowance for Doubtful Accounts was $1,020 (credit). To simplify, the accounts of only five customers are used; the details of each follow:

B. Brown—Account Receivable

Date	Explanation	Debit	Credit	Balance
3/11/2007	Sale	14,000		14,000
6/30/2007	Collection		5,000	9,000
1/31/2008	Collection		4,000	5,000

D. Di Lella—Account Receivable

2/28/2008	Sale	22,000		22,000
4/15/2008	Collection		10,000	12,000
11/30/2008	Collection		8,000	4,000

N. Gidda—Account Receivable

11/30/2008	Sale	9,000		9,000
12/15/2008	Collection		2,000	7,000

S. Kavouris—Account Receivable

3/2/2006	Sale	5,000		5,000
4/15/2006	Collection		5,000	0
9/1/2007	Sale	10,000		10,000
10/15/2007	Collection		8,000	2,000
2/1/2008	Sale	19,000		21,000
3/1/2008	Collection		5,000	16,000
12/31/2008	Sale	3,000		19,000

T. Patel—Account Receivable

12/30/2008	Sale	6,000		6,000

Required:

1. Prepare an aging analysis schedule and complete it.

2. Compute the estimated uncollectable amount for each age category and in total.

3. Prepare the adjusting entry for bad debt expense at December 31, 2008.

4. Show how the amounts related to accounts receivable should be presented on the income statement for 2008 and the balance sheet at December 31, 2008.

P7–6 Determining Bad Debts and Reporting Accounts Receivable (AP7–6)

■ **LO4**

The bookkeeper of Vital Inc. has asked you to assist him with the preparation of information about the company's accounts receivable for presentation in the financial statements at December 31, 2008, the end of the company's fiscal year. The following details have been extracted from the company's files.

	Debit	Credit
Accounts Receivable, January 1, 2008	$500,000	
Allowance for Doubtful Accounts, January 1, 2008		$35,000

Sales for 2008 totalled $1,300,000; $300,000 were in cash and the rest on account. The company collected $800,000 from credit customers during 2008, and wrote off $40,000 of accounts receivable as uncollectable.

Required:

1. Determine the balance of Accounts Receivable at December 31, 2008.

2. Vital uses the balance sheet method to estimate the net realizable value of accounts receivable at year end, and estimates that 6 percent of the ending balance of its accounts receivable may not be collected in the future. Prepare the journal entries to record the write-off of accounts receivable and the bad debt expense for 2008.

3. Show how the information related to accounts receivable is presented on the company's balance sheet as at December 31, 2008.

4. After you finished helping the bookkeeper with the journal entries and the balance sheet presentation, he said: "These calculations seem to be complicated. Would it not be simpler

to treat the $40,000 as bad debt expense when the company is certain that the customers are not able to pay the amount owed? That way, you record the exact amount of bad debt when it happens, and you do not have to estimate an amount of doubtful accounts and risk being incorrect." Prepare a response to the bookkeeper.

■ **LO2, 3, 4**

P7–7 **Preparing a Multiple-Step Income Statement and Computing the Gross Profit Percentage with Discounts, Returns, and Bad Debts** (AP7–7)

Builders Company, Inc., sells heavy construction equipment. It has 10,000 common shares outstanding and its fiscal year ends on December 31. The adjusted trial balance was taken from the general ledger on December 31, 2009.

Account Titles	Debit	Credit
Cash	$ 42,000	
Accounts receivable (net)	18,000	
Inventory, ending	65,000	
Long-term assets	51,000	
Accumulated amortization		$ 21,000
Liabilities		30,000
Common shares		90,000
Retained earnings, January 1, 2009		11,600
Sales revenue		182,000
Sales returns and allowances	5,000	
Cost of goods sold	98,000	
Selling expenses	17,000	
Administrative expenses	18,000	
Bad debt expense	3,000	
Sales discounts	8,000	
Income tax expense	9,600	
Totals	$334,600	$334,600

Required:

1. Beginning with net sales, prepare a multiple-step income statement (showing both gross profit and income from operations). Treat sales discounts as contra revenues.

2. The beginning balance of Accounts Receivable (net) was $16,000. Compute the gross profit percentage and accounts receivable turnover ratio and explain their meaning.

■ **LO6**

P7–8 **Evaluating Internal Controls** (AP7–8)

Cripple Creek Company has one trusted employee who, as the owner said, "handles all of the bookkeeping and paperwork for the company." This employee is responsible for counting, verifying, and recording cash receipts and payments, making the weekly bank deposit, preparing cheques for major expenditures (signed by the owner), making small expenditures from the cash register for daily expenses, and collecting accounts receivable. The owner asked the local bank for a $20,000 loan. The bank asked that an audit be performed covering the year just ended. The independent auditor, in a private conference with the owner, presented some evidence of the following activities of the trusted employee during the past year:

a. Cash sales sometimes were not entered in the cash register, and the trusted employee pocketed approximately $50 per month.

b. Cash taken from the cash register (and pocketed by the trusted employee) was replaced with expense memos with fictitious signatures (approximately $12 per day). Cripple Creek is open five days per week throughout the year.

c. A $300 collection on an account receivable of a valued out-of-town customer was pocketed by the trusted employee and was covered by making a $300 entry as a debit to Sales Returns and a credit to Accounts Receivable.

d. An $800 collection on an account receivable from a local customer was pocketed by the trusted employee and was covered by making an $800 entry as a debit to Allowance for Doubtful Accounts and a credit to Accounts Receivable.

Required:

1. What was the approximate amount stolen during the past year?

2. What would be your recommendations to the owner about the company's internal controls?

P7–9 **Preparing a Bank Reconciliation** (AP7–9)

■ **LO6**

Sergio Lucas worked long hours during the summer and saved enough money to pay his tuition and living expenses to continue his studies at the local university. On September 1, he downloaded from the bank's website his bank statement for August to make sure that the bank has not made any errors related to his bank account. Sergio has developed a habit of verifying all the entries in his bank account ever since he discovered that the bank had charged him a service fee for a transaction that was unrelated to his account. After comparing the bank statement with the entries he has made in his chequebook, Sergio found that the bank statement showed a balance of $12,506.60 but his chequebook showed a balance of $12,651.65 on August 31, a difference of $145.05. He decided to compare the entries in his chequebook with those in the bank statement, hoping that the bank owes him this difference.

Sergio's review of the bank statement showed the following:

a. Three cheques (#124, #125, and #126) that he made in late August have not been withdrawn from his bank account yet. They totalled $619.35.

b. An automatic deduction of $44.10 was made to pay the hydro bill for August.

c. Another automatic deduction of $55.30 was made to pay for telecommunication services from Telus Corp.

d. He forgot to record in his chequebook two withdrawals from instant teller machines for a total of $300.

e. A cheque for $385 he deposited in the bank the night of August 31 did not appear on the bank statement.

f. Sergio discovered that he recorded cheque #123 as $96.25 but the correct amount that cleared his bank account was $69.25.

g. The bank charged him a service fee of $7 for August transactions.

Required:

1. Assume the role of Sergio and prepare a bank reconciliation at August 31.

2. Which amounts should Sergio enter into his chequebook to avoid making any errors in reconciling his chequebook with the bank statement for September?

P7–10 **Preparing a Bank Reconciliation and Related Journal Entries** (AP7–10)

■ **LO6**

The bookkeeper at Hopkins Company has not reconciled the bank statement with the Cash account, saying, "I don't have time." You have been asked to prepare a reconciliation and review the procedures with the bookkeeper.

The April 30, 2009, bank statement and the April ledger accounts for cash showed the following (summarized):

Bank Statement			
	Cheques	Deposits	Balance
Balance, April 1, 2009			$25,850
Deposits during April		$36,000	61,850
Notes collected for company (including $70 interest)		1,070	62,920
Cheques cleared during April	$44,200		18,720
NSF cheque—A. B. Wright	140		18,580
Bank service charges	50		18,530
Balance, April 30, 2009			18,530

Cash in Bank					
Apr. 1	Balance	23,250	Apr.	Cheques written	43,800
Apr.	Deposits	42,000			

Cash on hand		
Apr. 30	Balance	100

A comparison of cheques written before and during April with the cheques cleared through the bank showed that cheques of $2,200 are still outstanding at April 30. No deposits in transit were carried over from March, but a deposit was in transit at April 30.

Required:

1. Prepare a detailed bank reconciliation at April 30, 2009.
2. Prepare any required journal entries as a result of the reconciliation. Why are they necessary?
3. What were the balances in the cash accounts in the ledger on May 1, 2009?
4. What total amount of cash should be reported on the balance sheet at April 30, 2009?

ALTERNATE PROBLEMS

■ LO1

AP7–1 Applying the Revenue Principle (P7–1)

Review the revenue recognition practices of the following companies, and indicate at what point in time revenue should be recognized in each of these independent cases. Explain your answer.

Case A. The sales representatives of Computec Corporation are under intense pressure to achieve very high sales levels. To achieve their specific objectives, the sales representatives ask customers to order computer equipment in advance with payment to be made later. In many cases, the company records sales on the basis of customers' orders, even though the ordered equipment may have not been manufactured yet.

Case B. Scenic Trails, Inc. is a campground operator that sells annual memberships to interested campers. Members are allowed to pay the annual memberships fees over a period of six months. The company records revenue from membership fees as soon as a new member signs the membership agreement. Members are allowed 10 days to cancel their memberships and many members cancel their memberships within days of signing.

Case C. Educational Toys, Inc. sells a wide variety of toys to distributors and allows them to return unsold merchandise within a period of three months. The company's policy encourages distributors to buy products and keep them for three months knowing they could return any unsold merchandise during this period. The company recognizes revenue as soon as it delivers its products to distributors.

■ LO2, 4

AP7–2 Reporting Net Sales and Expenses with Discounts, Returns, and Bad Debts (P7–2)

The following data were selected from the records of Fluwars Company for the year ended December 31, 2009.

Balances January 1, 2009:	
Accounts receivable (various customers)	$103,000
Allowance for doubtful accounts	6,000

The company sold merchandise for cash and on open account with credit terms 1/10, n/30. Assume a unit sales price of $400 in all transactions and use the gross method to record sales revenue.

Transactions during 2008

a. Sold merchandise for cash, $118,000.
b. Sold merchandise to Abbey Corp; invoice amount, $7,600.
c. Sold merchandise to Brown Company; invoice amount, $14,000.
d. Abbey paid the invoice in (b) within the discount period.
e. Sold merchandise to Cavendish Inc; invoice amount, $9,200.
f. Two days after paying the account in full, Abbey returned four defective units and received a cash refund.
g. Collected $99,000 cash from customers for credit sales made in 2008, all within the discount periods.
h. Three days after the purchase date, Brown returned three of the units purchased in (c) and received account credit.
i. Brown paid its account in full within the discount period.
j. Sold merchandise to Decca Corporation; invoice amount, $9,000.

k. Cavendish paid its account in full after the discount period.

l. Wrote off an old account of $1,400 after deciding that the amount would never be collected.

m. The estimated bad debt rate used by the company was 2 percent of credit sales net of returns.

Required:

1. Using the following categories, indicate the dollar effect (increase, decrease, no effect) of each listed transaction, including the write-off of the uncollectable account and the adjusting entry for estimated bad debts (ignore the cost of goods sold).

Sales Revenue	Sales Discounts (taken)	Sales Returns and Allowances	Bad Debt Expense

2. Show how the accounts related to the preceding sale and collection activities should be reported on the income statement for 2009. (Treat sales discounts as contra revenues.)

AP7–3 Understanding the Income Statement Based on the Gross Profit Percentage (P7–3)   ■ **LO3**
The following data were taken from the year-end records of Glare Import Company.

Income Statement Items	Year 1	Year 2
Gross sales revenue	$210,000	$255,000
Sales discounts	?	5,000
Net sales revenue	207,000	?
Cost of goods sold	?	60%
Gross profit	40%	?
Operating expenses	42,800	?
Income before income taxes	?	70,000
Income tax expense (30%)	?	?
Income before discontinued operations	?	?
Discontinued operations, net of tax	10,000 (loss)	2,500 (gain)
Net income	?	?
EPS (8,000 shares outstanding)	?	?

Required:
Fill in all of the missing amounts. Show computations.

AP7–4 Interpreting Disclosure of Allowance for Doubtful Accounts (P7–4)   ■ **LO4**
Dell Computer Corporation is the leading direct-sales computer systems company and a provider of products and services for customers to build their information technology and Internet infrastructures. Dell recently disclosed the following information concerning the allowance for doubtful accounts in its annual report:

Dell Computer

	SCHEDULE II Valuation and Qualifying Accounts (dollars in millions)				
Fiscal Year	Description	Balance at Beginning of Period	Charged to Bad Debt Expense	Write-Offs Charged to Allowance	Balance at End of Period
Year 3	Allowance for doubtful accounts	$84	$31	$37	?
Year 2	Allowance for doubtful accounts	71	?	35	$84
Year 1	Allowance for doubtful accounts	68	39	?	71

Required:

1. Record summary journal entries related to bad debts for year 1.
2. Supply the missing dollar amounts noted by (?) for year 1, year 2, and year 3.

■ **LO4**

AP7–5   Determining Bad Debt Expense Based on Aging Analysis (P7–5)

Briggs & Stratton Engines Inc. uses the aging approach to estimate bad debt expense at the end of each fiscal year. Credit sales occur frequently on terms n/45. The balance of each account receivable is aged on the basis of four time periods as follows: (1) not yet due, (2) up to 6 months past due, (3) 6 to 12 months past due, and (4) more than one year past due. Experience has shown that for each age group, the average bad debt rate on the amounts receivable at year-end due to uncollectability is (a) 1 percent, (b) 5 percent, (c) 20 percent, and (d) 50 percent, respectively.

At December 31, 2008 (end of the current fiscal year), the Accounts Receivable balance was $39,500, and the Allowance for Doubtful Accounts balance was $1,550 (debit). To simplify, the accounts of only five customers are used; the details of each follow:

Date	Explanation	Debit	Credit	Balance
\multicolumn{5}{c}{**R. Aouad—Account Receivable**}
3/13/2008	Sale	19,000		19,000
5/12/2008	Collection		10,000	9,000
9/30/2008	Collection		7,000	2,000
\multicolumn{5}{c}{**C. Chronis—Account Receivable**}
06/01/2007	Sale	31,000		31,000
11/01/2007	Collection		20,000	11,000
12/01/2008	Collection		5,000	6,000
\multicolumn{5}{c}{**D. McClain—Account Receivable**}
10/31/2008	Sale	12,000		12,000
12/10/2008	Collection		8,000	4,000
\multicolumn{5}{c}{**T. Skibinski—Account Receivable**}
05/02/2008	Sale	15,000		15,000
06/01/2008	Sale	10,000		25,000
06/15/2008	Collection		15,000	10,000
07/15/2008	Collection		10,000	0
10/01/2008	Sale	26,000		26,000
11/15/2008	Collection		16,000	10,000
12/15/2008	Sale	4,500		14,500
\multicolumn{5}{c}{**H. Wu—Account Receivable**}
12/30/2008	Sale	13,000		13,000

Required:

1. Set up an aging analysis schedule and complete it.
2. Compute the estimated uncollectable amount for each age category and in total.
3. Prepare the adjusting entry for bad debt expense at December 31, 2008.
4. Show how the amounts related to accounts receivable should be presented on the income statement for 2008 and the balance sheet at December 31, 2008.

■ **LO4**

AP7–6   Determining Bad Debts and Reporting Accounts Receivable (P7–6)

Les Belles Cuisines Ltée. (LBC) is a Montreal-based company that sells imported fancy kitchenware to retailers. Selected account balances as at November 30, 2008 are shown below.

	Debit	Credit
Accounts receivable	$54,500	
Allowance for doubtful accounts		$1,500

During December 2008, the following transactions occurred:

a. The company sold merchandise on account to various retailers for a total amount of $38,000, terms 1/10, n/30. A few retailers who purchased merchandise for a gross amount of $20,000 paid the amount due within 10 days. A total of $8,000 of the December sales remained unpaid at December 31, 2008.

b. Customers paid the company $25,000 for merchandise they purchased prior to November 30, 2008. These customers did not pay within the discount period.

c. Two of LBC's customers owed the company a total of $2,500 and were facing financial difficulties during December due to increased competition. They were forced to close their businesses before the end of the year. LBC does not expect to receive any money from these two customers and considered their accounts uncollectable.

d. The company received new kitchenware from a Korean supplier, Kim & Sons, Ltd., for $20,000. The invoice indicated that the supplier would allow a cash discount of 1% if the invoice were paid before the end of December 2008. LBC paid the supplier on January 10, 2009.

LBC estimates that 4 percent of its accounts receivable at December 31, 2008 will not be collected in the future.

Required:

1. Prepare the journal entries to record the transactions that occurred in December 2008, and any related adjusting journal entries at December 31, 2008, the end of LBC's fiscal year.

2. Show how the information related to accounts receivable is presented on the company's balance sheet at December 31, 2008.

3. The major shareholder of LBC, Michel Beauregard, was reading through the company's balance sheet and noticed the account *Allowance for doubtful accounts*. He called Carol, LBC's accountant, and made the following statement: "Carol, I don't think we need to make a provision for doubtful accounts as it will reduce the amount of accounts receivable unnecessarily. I think we should wait until we are certain that we cannot collect from our customers before showing a reduction in the accounts receivable on the balance sheet. This way, the accounts receivable balance will be more accurate. I would like you to make the necessary change to the financial statements before they are distributed to the other shareholders." Assume the role of Carol and prepare a response to Mr. Beauregard.

4. LBC had an opportunity to get a loan from the Bank of International Trade (BIT) to pay the amount due to Kim & Sons, Ltd. The loan would have cost LBC $150 in interest charges. Should LBC have obtained the loan from BIT to pay its debt to Kim & Sons, Ltd. before December 31, 2008?

AP7–7 Preparing a Multiple-Step Income Statement and Computing the Gross Profit Percentage with Discounts, Returns, and Bad Debts (P7–7)

■ **LO2, 3, 4**

Big Tommy Corporation is a local grocery store organized seven years ago as a corporation. At that time, 6,000 common shares were issued to the three organizers. The store is in an excellent location, and sales have increased each year. At the end of 2009, the bookkeeper prepared the following statement (assume that all amounts are correct; note the incorrect terminology and format):

BIG TOMMY CORPORATION
Profit and Loss
December 31, 2009

	Debit	Credit
Sales		$420,000
Cost of goods sold	$279,000	
Sales returns and allowances	8,000	
Selling expenses	58,000	
Administrative and general expenses	16,000	
Bad debt expense	3,000	
Sales discounts	6,000	
Income tax expense	15,000	
Net profit	35,000	
Totals	$420,000	$420,000

Required:

1. Beginning with net sales, prepare a multiple-step income statement (showing both gross profit and income from operations). Treat sales discounts as an expense.

2. The beginning and ending balances of Accounts Receivable were $38,000 and $42,000, respectively. Compute the gross profit percentage and receivables turnover ratio and explain their meaning.

■ **LO6**   **AP7–8   Evaluating Internal Controls**

ANALYSIS

Cory Magnum has been working for Matrix Products Inc. for five years and has gained the respect of his peers for his exemplary behaviour and work ethic. His job includes receiving cash and cheques from customers, depositing the cash receipts in the company's account at the local bank, and recording the transactions in the company's computerized accounting program. Cory was faced with personal financial problems and decided to make use of $2,000 of the company's available cash to solve them. He planned to return the money as soon as his financial situation improved. The $2,000 he took was part of the total cash sales to customers during the previous two business days. At the same time, Cory had received a cheque for $2,000 from PLC, Ltd. as a partial payment on its account receivable.

To hide his theft, Cory deposited the cheque in the company's bank account instead of the cash, and made the following journal entry:

Cash in Bank.	2,000	
Cash on Hand		2,000

In addition, he recorded the following journal entry to credit the account of PLC, Ltd. to avoid any questions from that company in the future.

Sales Returns and Allowances.	2,000	
Accounts Receivable—PLC, Ltd..		2,000

Required:

1. Assume that Matrix Products prepares financial statements on a monthly basis. Would any items on the income statement or the balance sheet be incorrect? Explain.

2. Identify the weaknesses that exist in the company's internal control system. What changes should be made to strengthen internal control over cash receipts?

■ **LO6**   **AP7–9   Preparing a Bank Reconciliation and Related Journal Entries (P7–9)**

The president of Kostas Fashions Ltd., Joan Kostas, has just received the monthly bank statement for June, which shows a balance of $10,517. She remembers seeing a different balance for Cash at June 30 when the company accountant, Peter Wong, presented to her the monthly balance sheet. She checks the balance sheet and finds a Cash balance of $6,518. She is not sure which amount is correct. She calls Peter and asks him why the two amounts are different. Peter takes the bank statement and related documents and promises to provide his boss with an explanation within a few hours. He then proceeds to prepare a bank reconciliation report for the month of June.

A review of the documents that accompanied the bank statement shows the following:

a. A credit memorandum for the collection of a note for $2,080, including $80 of interest on the note. The bank charged the company a collection fee of $25.

b. A debit memorandum for an NSF cheque for $286 from customer Rami Cossette.

c. Total service charges for June amounting to $39.

When comparing the bank statement with the company's records, Peter discovers the following discrepancies:

d. A deposit of $1,145 was not recorded on the bank statement.

e. Three cheques had not been presented to the bank for payment yet. The amounts of these cheques are $1,573, $679, and $1,252.

f. A deposit of $2,340 was recorded incorrectly in the books at $2,430.

Required:

1. Explain to Joan Kostas why the two balances for cash are not equal, and why it is important to prepare a bank reconciliation statement.

2. Prepare a bank reconciliation statement at June 30 and the related journal entries.

■ **LO6**   **AP7–10   Computing Outstanding Cheques and Deposits in Transit and Preparing a Bank Reconciliation and Journal Entries (P7–10)**

The August 2009 bank statement for Martha Company and the August 2009 ledger accounts for cash follow:

PB Provincial Bank 594 Water Street Faubourg, ON L2G 4S6			STATEMENT OF ACCOUNT		

DATE	BRANCH NUMBER	ACCOUNT TYPE	ACCOUNT NUMBER	PAGE NO.
31 08 2009	815	Chequing	85157	1 OF 1

Martha Company
2784, 7th Avenue
Faubourg, ON
L3G 3B5

Date	Description	Debits	Credits	Balance
Aug. 1	Balance Forward			17,470
2	Cheque No. 103	300		17,170
3	Deposit		12,000	29,170
4	Cheque No. 101	400		28,770
5	Cheque No. 105	250		28,520
9	Cheque No. 102	900		27,620
10	Cheque No. 104	300		27,320
15	Deposit		4,000	31,320
21	Cheque No. 106	400		30,920
24	Cheque No. 108	21,000		9,920
25	Deposit		7,000	16,920
30	Cheque No. 109	800		16,120
30	Collection of note		2,180	18,300
30	Service charge	10		18,290
31	Interest earned		80	18,370

The amount collected on August 30 includes interest of $180.

Cash in Bank

Aug. 1 Balance	16,520	Cheques written	
Deposits		Aug. 2	300
Aug. 2	12,000	4	900
12	4,000	15	290
24	7,000	17	550
31	5,000	18	800
		20	400
		23	21,000

Cash on hand

Aug. 31 Balance	200	

Outstanding cheques at the end of July were for $250, $400, and $300. No deposits were in transit at the end of July.

Required:

1. Compute the amount of deposits in transit at August 31, 2009.

2. Compute the amount of outstanding cheques at August 31, 2009.

3. Prepare a bank reconciliation at August 31, 2009.

4. Prepare any journal entries that the company should make as a result of the bank reconciliation. Why are they necessary?

5. After the reconciliation journal entries are posted, what balances would be reflected in the cash accounts in the ledger?

6. What total amount of cash should be reported on the August 31, 2009, balance sheet?

CASES AND PROJECTS

FINDING AND INTERPRETING FINANCIAL INFORMATION

CP7–1 **Finding Financial Information**

Refer to the financial statements of Van Houtte Inc. given in Appendix B of this book.

Required:

1. How much cash and cash equivalents does the company hold at the end of the current year?

2. Does the company report an allowance for doubtful accounts on the balance sheet or in the notes? Explain why it does or does not.

■ **LO1, 3, 4, 6**

Van Houtte

ANALYSIS

3. Compute the company's gross profit percentage for the most recent two years. Has it risen or fallen? Explain the meaning of the change.

4. Does the company disclose its revenue recognition policy? What point in time does it use to recognize revenue?

■ LO2, 5, 6   CP7–2 Finding Financial Information

The Forzani Group

ANALYSIS

Refer to the Online Learning Centre Web site at **www.mcgrawhill.ca/olc/libby/student/ resources** for the financial statements of The Forzani Group Ltd.

Required:

1. The company sells to both consumers and business customers. What items would you expect to be subtracted from sales revenue in the computation of net sales?

2. What expenses does The Forzani Group subtract from net sales in the computation of income before income taxes? How does this differ from Van Houtte's practice?

3. Compute The Forzani Group's receivables turnover ratio for the year ended January 30, 2005. What characteristics of its business might cause it to be so high?

4. What was the change in accounts receivable and how did it affect the cash provided by operating activities for the current year?

■ LO3, 5   CP7–3 Comparing Companies

Van Houtte vs.
The Forzani Group

ANALYSIS

Refer to the Online Learning Centre Web site at **www.mcgrawhill.ca/olc/libby/student/ resources** for the financial statements of The Forzani Group Ltd. and to Appendix B for the financial statements of Van Houtte Inc.

Required:

1. Compute the gross profit percentage for both companies for the current year. Does The Forzani Group comment on the company's gross profit percentage in its Management's Discussion and Analysis?

2. Compute the accounts receivable turnover ratio for both companies for fiscal years 2006 and 2007. The Forzani Group had $54,651,000 in accounts receivable (net) at January 30, 2005, and Van Houtte had $41,298,000 in accounts receivable (net) at April 2, 2005. What accounts for the change in these ratios?

FINANCIAL REPORTING AND ANALYSIS CASES

■ LO4, 5   CP7–4 Using Financial Reports: International Bad Debt Disclosure

Foster's Brewing

Foster's Brewing controls more than 50 percent of the beer market in Australia. As an Australian company, it follows Australian GAAP and uses Australian accounting terminology. In the footnotes to a recent annual report, it discloses information on receivables (all numbers are reported in millions of Australian dollars).

Note 11: Receivables	Year 2	Year 1
Current		
Trade debtors	837.9	553.9
Provision for doubtful debts	(15.7)	(12.6)
Other debtors	171.2	152.6
Provision for doubtful debts	(4.1)	(1.8)
Non-current		
Trade debtors	0.6	0.5
Other debtors	80.1	82.3
Note 3: Profit from ordinary activities	Year 2	Year 1
Amounts to provisions for		
Doubtful debts—trade debtors	(3.2)	(1.7)
Doubtful debts—other debtors	(2.4)	(0)

Required:

1. The account titles used by Foster's are different from those normally used by Canadian companies. What account titles does it use in place of Allowance for Doubtful Accounts and Bad Debt Expense?

2. Sales on account for year 2 were $3,972.3. Compute the accounts receivable (trade debtors) turnover ratio for year 2 (ignore uncollectable accounts).

3. Compute the provision for doubtful debts as a percentage of current receivables separately for receivables from trade debtors and receivables from others. Explain why these percentages might be different.

4. What was the total amount of receivables written off in year 2, net of recoveries?

CP7–5   Canadian Banks   ■ LO4

In June 2001, the shares of Toronto-Dominion Bank lost 8 percent of their market value in two days after the bank increased its provisions for credit losses on loans to companies operating in the telecommunications industry. The telecom companies were facing weak demand for their products and services, and a number of companies in this sector were facing financial difficulties. In fact, the other major Canadian banks were similarly affected by the downturn of activity in the telecom industry, as they had loaned sizeable amounts of money to companies in this sector.

ANALYSIS

Using your Web browser, contact the Web sites and consult the latest annual reports of three of the following banks: Bank of Montreal, Scotiabank, Canadian Imperial Bank of Commerce, National Bank of Canada, Royal Bank of Canada, and Toronto-Dominion Bank.

Required:

1. How much did each bank report as "provision for credit losses"?

2. Compute the following percentage: Provision for credit losses/Net interest income. Which bank has the largest ratio?

3. How much did each bank report as "allowance for credit losses"?

4. Compute the following percentage: Allowance for credit losses/Total loans receivable. Which bank has the largest ratio? Is it the same bank identified in requirement 2 above? Identify reasons why this bank has a higher ratio than the other two. (*Hint*: The notes to the financial statements and Management's Discussion and Analysis are useful sources of information.)

CRITICAL THINKING CASES

CP7–6   Making Decisions as an Independent Accountant   ■ LO6

Lane Manufacturing Company is a relatively small local business that specializes in the repair and renovation of antique furniture. The owner is an expert craftsperson. Although a number of skilled workers are employed, there is always a large backlog of work to be done. A long-time employee who serves as clerk-bookkeeper handles cash receipts, keeps the records, and writes cheques for disbursements. The owner signs the cheques. The clerk-bookkeeper pays small amounts in cash, subject to a month-end review by the owner. Approximately 80 regular customers are extended credit that typically amounts to less than $1,000. Although credit losses are small, in recent years the bookkeeper had established an allowance for doubtful accounts, and all write-offs were made at year-end. During January 2008 (the current year), the owner decided to start as soon as possible the construction of a building for the business that would provide many advantages over the currently rented space and would allow space to expand facilities. As a part of the considerations in financing, the financing institution asked for 2007 audited financial statements. The company statements had never been audited. Early in the audit, the independent accountant found numerous errors and one combination of amounts, in particular, that caused concern.

There was some evidence that a $2,500 job completed by Lane had been recorded as a receivable (from a new customer) on July 15, 2007. The receivable was credited for a $2,500 cash collection a few days later. The new account was never active again. The auditor also observed that shortly thereafter, three write-offs of accounts receivable balances had been made to Allowance for Doubtful Accounts as follows: Jones, $800; Blake, $750; and Sellers, $950—all of whom were known as regular customers. These write-offs drew the attention of the auditor.

Required:

1. Explain what caused the auditor to be concerned. Should the auditor report the suspicions to the owner?

2. What recommendations would you make with respect to internal control procedures for this company?

■ **LO1**   **CP7–7**   **Making a Decision as a Manager: Choosing among Alternative Recognition Points**

UPS, Federal Express, and Airborne

UPS, Federal Express, and Airborne are three of the major players in the highly competitive package delivery industry. Comparability is a key qualitative characteristic of accounting information that allows analysts to compare similar companies. The revenue recognition footnotes of the three competitors reveal three different revenue recognition points for package delivery revenue: package delivery, percentage of service completed, and package pick-up. These points correspond to the end, continuous recognition, and the beginning of the earnings process, respectively.

> **UNITED PARCEL SERVICE OF AMERICA, INC.**
>
> Revenue is recognized upon delivery of a package.

> **FEDERAL EXPRESS CORPORATION**
>
> Revenue is generally recognized upon delivery of shipments. For shipments in transit, revenue is recorded based on the percentage of service completed.

> **AIRBORNE FREIGHT CORP.**
>
> Domestic revenues and most domestic operating expenses are recognized when shipments are picked up from the customer . . .

The Airborne footnote goes on to say, however: "The net revenue resulting from existing recognition policies does not materially differ from that which would be recognized on a delivery date basis."

Required:

1. Do you believe that the difference between Airborne's and UPS's revenue recognition policies materially affects their reported earnings? Why or why not?

2. Assume that all three companies pick up packages from customers and receive payment of $1 million for services each day of the year and that each package is delivered the next day. What would be each company's service revenue for a year, given its stated revenue recognition policy?

3. Given your answer to requirement 2, under what conditions would that answer change?

4. Which revenue recognition rule would you prefer as a manager? Why?

■ **LO1**   **CP7–8**   **Evaluating an Ethical Dilemma: Management Incentives, Revenue Recognition, and Sales with the Right of Return**

Symbol Technologies

ANALYSIS

Symbol Technologies, Inc. was a fast-growing maker of bar-code scanners. According to the federal charges, Symbol's CEO, Tomo Razmilovic, was obsessed with meeting the stock market's expectation for continued growth. His executive team responded by improperly recording revenue and allowances for returns, manipulating inventory levels and accounts receivable data to conceal the adverse side effects of the revenue recognition schemes, as well as a variety of other tricks, to overstate revenues by $230 million and pretax earnings by $530 million. What makes this fraud nearly unique is that virtually the whole senior management team is charged with participating in the six-year fraud. At the time this case was written, the former CEO has fled the United States to avoid prosecution, and six other former Symbol executives pleaded guilty to various charges. The exact nature of the fraud is described in the following excerpt dealing with the guilty plea of the former vice-president of finance:

Ex-Official at Symbol Pleads Guilty

By Kara Scannel

26 March 2003

The Wall Street Journal

(Copyright © 2003, Dow Jones & Company, Inc.)

A former finance executive at Symbol Technologies, Inc. pleaded guilty to participating in a vast accounting fraud that inflated revenue at the maker of bar-code scanners by roughly 10%, or $100 million a year, from 1999 to 2001.

The criminal information and civil complaint filed yesterday accuse Mr. Asti and other high-level executives of stuffing the firm's distribution channel with phony orders at the end of each quarter to meet revenue and earnings targets. Under generally accepted accounting practices, revenue can be booked only when the products are shipped to a customer. Symbol's customers include delivery services and grocery stores.

Investigators alleged that Mr. Asti and others engaged in "candy" deals, where Symbol bribed resellers with a 1% fee to "buy" products from a distributor at the end of a quarter, which Symbol would later buy back. Symbol would then allegedly convince the distributor to order more products from the company to satisfy the newly created inventory void.

The SEC said the inflated inventory figures helped boost Symbol's stock price, as well as enriching Mr. Asti. He allegedly sold thousands of shares of Symbol stock, which he received from exercising stock options, when the stock was trading at inflated prices.

Copyright 2003, *The Wall Street Journal.* Reprinted by permission.

Required:

1. What facts, if any, presented in the article suggest that Symbol violated the revenue principle?

2. Assuming that Symbol did recognize revenue when goods were shipped, how could it have properly accounted for the fact that customers had a right to cancel the contracts (make an analogy with accounting for bad debts)?

3. What do you think may have motivated management to falsify the statements? Why was management concerned with reporting continued growth in net income?

4. Explain who was hurt by management's unethical conduct.

5. Assume that you are the auditor for other firms. After reading about the fraud, to what types of transactions would you pay special attention in the audit of your clients in this industry? What ratio might provide warnings about channel stuffing?

CP7–9 Evaluating the Effects of Credit Policy Changes on the Receivables Turnover Ratio and Cash Flows from Operating Activities

■ **LO5**

V. R. Rao and Company has been operating for five years as a software consulting firm specializing in the installation of industry standard products. During this period, it has experienced rapid growth in sales revenue and in accounts receivable. Ms. Rao and her associates all have computer science backgrounds. This year, the company hired you as its first corporate controller. You have put into place new credit-granting and collection

ANALYSIS

procedures that are expected to reduce receivables by approximately one-third by year-end. You have gathered the following data related to the changes:

	(in thousands)	
	Beginning of Year	End of Year (projected)
Accounts receivable	$1,000,608	$660,495
Less: Allowance for doubtful accounts	36,800	10,225
Net accounts receivable	$ 963,808	$650,270
		Current Year (projected)
Net sales (assume all on credit)		$7,015,069

Required:

1. Compute the accounts receivable turnover ratio based on two different assumptions:
   a. Those presented in the preceding table (a decrease in the balance in accounts receivable, net).
   b. No change in the balance of net accounts receivable; the balance was $963,808 at year-end.

2. Compute the effect (sign and amount) of the projected change in net accounts receivable on cash flow from operating activities for the year.

3. On the basis of your findings in requirements 1 and 2, write a brief memo explaining how an increase in the accounts receivable turnover ratio can result in an increase in cash flow from operating activities. Also explain how this increase can benefit the company.

FINANCIAL REPORTING AND ANALYSIS TEAM PROJECT

ANALYSIS

LO1, 4, 5 CP7–10 Team Project: Analyzing Revenues and Receivables

As a team, select an industry to analyze (industry lists can be found at **www.investor. reuters.com/Industries.aspx** and **www.hoovers.com**; click on "Companies and Industries"). Each team member should acquire the annual report for one publicly traded company in the industry, with each member selecting a different company. (Library files, the SEDAR service at **www.sedar.com**, the SEC EDGAR service at **www.freeedgar.com**, or the company Web sites are good sources.)

Required:

On an individual basis, each team member should then write a short report answering the following questions about the selected company. Discuss any patterns across the companies that you as a team observe. Then, as a group, write a short report comparing and contrasting your companies.

1. If your company lists receivables on its balance sheet, what percentage is this asset of total assets for each of the last three years? If your company does not list receivables, discuss why this is so.

2. Ratio analysis:
   a. What does the accounts receivable turnover ratio measure in general?
   b. If your company lists receivables, compute the ratio for the last three years.
   c. What do your results suggest about the company?
   d. If available, find the industry ratio for the most recent year, compare it to your results, and discuss why you believe your company differs or is similar to the industry ratio.

3. If your company lists receivables, determine what additional disclosure is available concerning the allowance for doubtful accounts. If the necessary information is provided, what is bad debt expense as a percentage of sales for the last three years?

4. What is the effect of the change in accounts receivable on cash flows from operations for the most recent year, that is, did the change increase or decrease operating cash flows? Explain your answer.

Reporting and Interpreting Cost of Goods Sold and Inventory

8

After studying this chapter, you should be able to:

LEARNING OBJECTIVES

1. Apply the cost principle to identify the amounts that should be included in inventory and the matching principle to determine the cost of goods sold for typical retailers, wholesalers, and manufacturers. p. 406

2. Compare methods for controlling and keeping track of inventory, and analyze the effects of inventory errors on financial statements. p. 410

3. Report inventory and cost of goods sold using three inventory costing methods. p. 415

4. Decide when the use of different inventory costing methods is beneficial to a company. p. 421

5. Report inventory at the lower of cost and net realizable value. p. 423

6. Evaluate inventory management using the inventory turnover ratio and the effects of inventory on cash flows. p. 425

FOCUS COMPANY:

Dell Inc.

SELLING DIRECTLY TO THE CUSTOMER

If you shopped for a personal computer recently, you probably considered buying one of the well-known and long-standing brand names in the computer industry such as Apple, Hewlett-Packard, or IBM. You also may have considered buying a desktop computer or a notebook computer directly from Dell Inc. (**www.dell.com**) through the Internet.

Dell Inc. was founded in 1984 by Michael Dell on a simple concept: selling personal computer systems directly to customers. The company designs, develops, manufactures, markets, and sells a wide range of computer systems, including desktop and notebook computers, servers, workstations, networking products, and printing and imaging systems. It also offers software, peripherals, and service and support programs. The company sells its products and services directly to large corporate, government, health care, and education customers, as well as to individuals. In 2006, Dell was the leading direct-seller of computer systems worldwide.

Dell uses a direct business model, which is based on the principle that delivering custom-built computer systems is the best way to provide relevant solutions that meet the needs of end-users. This model eliminates the need to support an extensive network of wholesale and retail dealers, thereby avoiding dealer mark-ups. It also avoids the higher inventory costs associated with the wholesale and retail channels, and the competition for retail shelf space. In addition, Dell's build-to-order manufacturing process is designed to allow the company to quickly produce customized computer systems and to reduce the high risk of obsolescence associated with products in a rapidly changing technological market.

Selling directly to the customer is only part of Dell's strategy. Introducing new and improved products to stay ahead of the competition, controlling inventory quality and cost, establishing mutually beneficial relationships with its suppliers, and developing accounting information systems that provide real-time inventory and order information are keys to Dell's continued success. Furthermore, selection of appropriate accounting methods for inventory can affect the amount Dell pays in income taxes. Continuous improvement in product development, manufacturing, inventory management, and information system design will be necessary for Dell to maintain its leading position in the computer industry.

UNDERSTANDING THE BUSINESS

Concerns about the cost and quality of inventory face all modern manufacturers and merchandisers and turn our attention to *cost of goods sold* (cost of sales, cost of products sold) on the income statement and *inventory* on the balance sheet. Exhibit 8.1 presents the relevant excerpts from Dell's financial statements that include these accounts. The Cost of Goods Sold is subtracted from net sales revenue to produce gross profit on its income statement. Inventory is a current asset on the balance sheet; it is reported below Cash, Short-term Investments, and Accounts Receivable because it is less liquid than those three current assets.

EXHIBIT **8.1**

Income Statement and Balance Sheet Excerpts

REAL WORLD EXCERPT

Dell Inc.

ANNUAL REPORT

DELL INC.
CONSOLIDATED STATEMENTS OF INCOME
Fiscal Years Ended February 3, 2006, January 28, 2005, and January 30, 2004
(in millions, except per share amounts)

	Fiscal Year Ended		
	February 3, 2006	January 28, 2005	January 30, 2004
Net revenue	$55,908	$49,205	$41,444
Cost of revenue (cost of goods sold)	45,958	40,190	33,892
Gross margin	9,950	9,015	7,552

DELL INC.
CONSOLIDATED STATEMENTS OF FINANCIAL POSITION
February 3, 2006 and January 28, 2005
(in millions, except per share amounts)

	February 3, 2006	January 28, 2005
ASSETS		
Current assets:		
Cash and cash equivalents	$ 7,042	$ 4,747
Short-term investments	2,016	5,060
Accounts receivable, net	5,452	4,548
Inventories	576	459
Other	2,620	2,083
Total current assets	17,706	16,897

Dell's successful expansion of production and management of cost of goods sold and inventory require a combined effort by human resource managers, engineers, production managers, marketing managers, and accounting and financial managers. It is truly a multidisciplinary task. The primary goals of inventory management are to have sufficient quantities of high-quality inventory available to serve customers' needs while minimizing the costs of carrying inventory (production, storage, obsolescence, and financing). Low quality leads to customer dissatisfaction, returns, and a decline in future sales. Also, purchasing or producing too few units of a hot-selling item causes stock-outs that mean lost sales revenue and potential customer dissatisfaction. Conversely, purchasing or producing too many units of a slow-selling item increases the storage costs and interest costs on short-term borrowings to finance the production or purchases. It may even lead to losses if the merchandise cannot be sold at normal prices.

To meet these inventory management goals, managers from many departments must work together to forecast customer demand for different computer models or peripheral items and provide feedback so that production or purchasing adjustments can be made. Production, human resource, and purchasing managers also must work to control the cost of goods sold to improve gross profit. Because both cost of goods sold and inventory are such important determinants of a company's success, managers, investors, and financial analysts pay close attention to these financial statement items.

The accounting system plays three roles in the inventory management process. First, the system must provide accurate information necessary for preparation of periodic financial statements and reports to tax authorities.[1] Second, it must provide up-to-date information on inventory quantities and costs to facilitate ordering and manufacturing decisions. Third, since inventories are subject to theft and other forms of misuse, the system also must provide the information necessary to help protect and control these important assets.

First we discuss the makeup of inventory, the important choices management must make in the financial and tax reporting process, and how these choices affect taxes paid. Then we will briefly discuss how accounting systems are organized to keep track of inventory quantities and costs for decision making and control. This topic will be the principal subject matter of your managerial accounting course. Finally, we discuss how managers and analysts evaluate the efficiency of inventory management.

ORGANIZATION OF THE CHAPTER

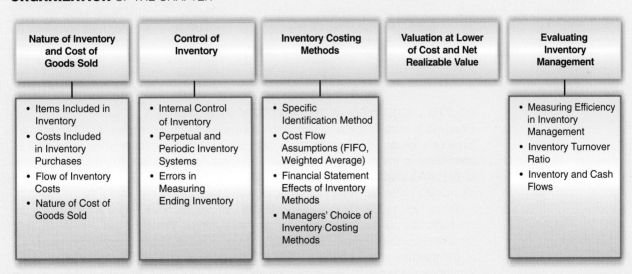

Nature of Inventory and Cost of Goods Sold	Control of Inventory	Inventory Costing Methods	Valuation at Lower of Cost and Net Realizable Value	Evaluating Inventory Management
• Items Included in Inventory • Costs Included in Inventory Purchases • Flow of Inventory Costs • Nature of Cost of Goods Sold	• Internal Control of Inventory • Perpetual and Periodic Inventory Systems • Errors in Measuring Ending Inventory	• Specific Identification Method • Cost Flow Assumptions (FIFO, Weighted Average) • Financial Statement Effects of Inventory Methods • Managers' Choice of Inventory Costing Methods		• Measuring Efficiency in Inventory Management • Inventory Turnover Ratio • Inventory and Cash Flows

---

[1]Tax reports often differ from the statements prepared for shareholders and other external users.

NATURE OF INVENTORY AND COST OF GOODS SOLD

ITEMS INCLUDED IN INVENTORY

■ **LEARNING OBJECTIVE 1**

Apply the cost principle to identify the amounts that should be included in inventory and the matching principle to determine the cost of goods sold for typical retailers, wholesalers, and manufacturers.

INVENTORY is tangible property held for sale in the normal course of business or used in producing goods or services for sale.

MERCHANDISE INVENTORY includes goods held for resale in the ordinary course of business.

RAW MATERIALS INVENTORY includes items acquired for the purpose of processing into finished goods.

WORK-IN-PROCESS INVENTORY includes goods in the process of being manufactured.

FINISHED GOODS INVENTORY includes manufactured goods that are complete and available for sale.

REAL WORLD EXCERPT

Dell Inc.

ANNUAL REPORT

Inventory is tangible property that is (1) held for sale in the normal course of business or (2) used to produce goods for sale. Inventory is reported on the balance sheet as a current asset because it normally is used or converted into cash within one year or within the next operating cycle of the business, whichever is longer. The types of inventory normally held depend on the characteristics of the business.

Merchandisers (wholesale or retail businesses) hold the following:

Merchandise inventory Goods (or merchandise) held for resale in the normal course of business. The goods usually are acquired in a finished condition and are ready for sale without further processing.

Dell manufactures most of the products it sells, but it also purchases products from other manufacturers and resells them to customers.

Manufacturing businesses hold the following types of inventory:

Raw materials inventory Items acquired by purchase, growth (such as food products), or extraction (natural resources) for processing into finished goods. Such items are included in raw materials inventory until used, at which point they become part of work-in-process inventory.

Work-in-process inventory Goods in the process of being manufactured but not yet complete. When complete, work-in-process inventory becomes finished goods inventory.

Finished goods inventory Manufactured goods that are complete and available for sale.

Inventories related to Dell's manufacturing operations are recorded in these accounts. Dell's recent inventory note reports the following:

NOTE 10—Supplemental Consolidated Financial Information		
	February 3, 2006	January 28, 2005
	(in millions)	
Inventories:		
Production materials	$329	$228
Work-in-process	78	58
Finished goods	169	173
	$576	$459

COSTS INCLUDED IN INVENTORY PURCHASES

Goods in inventory are recorded in conformity with the *cost principle*. The primary basis of accounting for inventory is cash equivalent cost, which is the price paid or consideration given to acquire an asset. Inventory cost includes, in principle, the sum of the applicable expenditures and charges directly or indirectly incurred in bringing an article to a usable or saleable condition and location.

When Dell purchases raw materials (e.g., microprocessor chips) for the computer products line and software (e.g., Microsoft Windows Vista) for resale to customers, the amount recorded should include the invoice price and indirect expenditures related to the purchase, such as import duties or freight charges to deliver the items to its warehouses (freight-in) and inspection and preparation costs. In general, the company should cease accumulating purchase costs when the raw materials are *ready for use* or when the merchandise inventory is *ready for shipment* to customers. Any additional costs related to selling the merchandise inventory to customers, such as salaries of marketing personnel, should be included in Selling, General, and Administrative

Expenses of the period of sale since they are incurred after the inventory is ready for use. Direct sales to customers, by telephone or through the Internet, have reduced the need to stock inventory for long periods and help reduce inventory storage costs and the cost of obsolescence.

APPLYING THE MATERIALITY CONSTRAINT IN PRACTICE

FINANCIAL ANALYSIS

Incidental costs such as inspection and preparation costs often are not material in amount (see the discussion of the materiality constraint in Chapter 4) and do not have to be assigned to the inventory cost. Thus, for practical reasons, many companies use the invoice price, less returns and discounts, to assign a unit cost to raw materials or merchandise and record other indirect expenditures as a separate cost that is reported as an expense. Invoice price may or may not include transportation charges (freight-in) for shipment to the warehouse.

FLOW OF INVENTORY COSTS

The flow of inventory costs for merchandisers (wholesalers and retailers) is relatively simple, as shown in Exhibit 8.2A. When merchandise is purchased, the Merchandise Inventory account is increased. When the goods are sold, the merchandise inventory is decreased and the cost of goods sold is increased.

The flow of inventory costs in a manufacturing environment is more complex, as diagrammed in Exhibit 8.2B. First *raw materials* (also called *direct materials*) must be purchased. For Dell, these raw materials include memory chips, processors, hard disks, and graphic cards, among others. When they are used, the cost of each material is removed from the raw materials inventory and added to the work-in-process inventory.

EXHIBIT 8.2

Flow of Inventory Costs

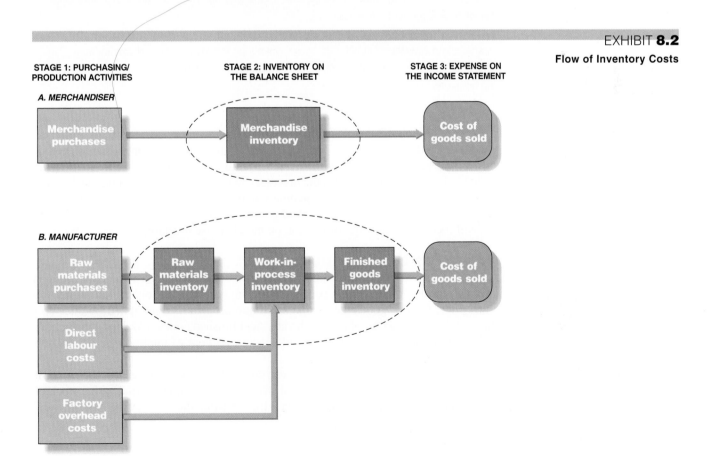

STAGE 1: PURCHASING/ PRODUCTION ACTIVITIES — STAGE 2: INVENTORY ON THE BALANCE SHEET — STAGE 3: EXPENSE ON THE INCOME STATEMENT

A. MERCHANDISER

Merchandise purchases → Merchandise inventory → Cost of goods sold

B. MANUFACTURER

Raw materials purchases → Raw materials inventory → Work-in-process inventory → Finished goods inventory → Cost of goods sold

Direct labour costs

Factory overhead costs

Two other components of manufacturing costs, direct labour and factory overhead, are also added to the work-in-process inventory when incurred in the manufacturing process. **Direct labour** cost represents the earnings of employees who work directly on the products being manufactured. **Factory overhead** costs include all other manufacturing costs. For example, the salary of the factory supervisor and the cost of utilities, security, and material handling are included in factory overhead. When the computers are completed and ready for sale, the related amounts in work-in-process inventory are transferred to finished goods inventory. When the finished goods are sold, cost of goods sold increases and the finished goods inventory decreases.

DIRECT LABOUR refers to the earnings of employees who work directly on the products being manufactured.

FACTORY OVERHEAD comprises manufacturing costs that are not raw material or direct labour costs.

FINANCIAL
ANALYSIS

MODERN MANUFACTURING TECHNIQUES AND INVENTORY COSTS

The flows of inventory costs diagrammed in Exhibit 8.2B represent the keys to manufacturing cost and quality control. Since the company must pay to finance and store raw materials and purchased parts, minimizing the size of these inventories in keeping with projected manufacturing demand is the first key to the process. This requires that Dell work closely with its suppliers in design, production, and delivery of raw materials and/or manufactured parts. (This approach to inventory management is called *just-in-time*.) To reduce the costs of work-in-process and finished goods, companies redesign and simplify manufacturing processes and retrain their manufacturing personnel to minimize both the direct labour and factory overhead costs. Simplified product design and production processes often lead to higher product quality and reduced scrap and rework costs. Dell's build-to-order manufacturing process is designed to allow it to quickly produce customized computer systems and to achieve rapid inventory turnover and reduce inventory levels, which reduces the company's exposure to the risk of declining inventory values.

Dell's management accounting system is designed to monitor the success of these changes and provide information to allow continuous improvements in manufacturing. The design of such systems is the subject matter of management accounting and cost accounting courses.

Note in Exhibit 8.2 that there are three stages to inventory cost flows for both merchandisers and manufacturers. The first involves purchasing and/or production activities. In the second, these activities result in additions to inventory accounts on the balance sheet. At the third stage, the inventory items are sold and the amounts become cost of goods sold expense on the income statement. Since the flow of inventory costs for merchandise inventory and finished goods to cost of goods sold are very similar, we will focus the rest of our discussion on merchandise inventory.

NATURE OF COST OF GOODS SOLD

Cost of goods sold (CGS) is directly related to sales revenue. The amount of sales revenue during an accounting period is the number of units sold multiplied by the sales price. Cost of goods sold is the same number of units multiplied by their unit costs; it includes the cost of all merchandise and finished goods sold during the period. The measurement of cost of goods sold is an excellent example of the application of the matching principle.

Let us examine the relationship between cost of goods sold on the income statement and inventory on the balance sheet. Dell starts each accounting period with a stock of inventory called *begining inventory* (BI). During the accounting period, new *purchases* (P) are added to inventory. The sum of the cost of beginning inventory and the cost of purchases is the **cost of goods available for sale** during that period. What remains unsold at the end of the period becomes *ending inventory* (EI) on the balance sheet. The portion of the cost of goods available for sale that are actually sold becomes *cost of goods sold* on the income statement. The ending inventory for one accounting period then becomes the beginning inventory for the next period. The relationships between these various amounts are brought together in the **cost of goods sold equation**.

To illustrate the relationships represented by this equation, assume that Dell began the period with $40 million of software in beginning inventory, purchased additional software during the period for $55 million, and had $35 million in inventory at the end of the period. These amounts are combined as follows to compute the cost of goods sold of $60 million:

Beginning inventory	$40 million
Add: Purchases of merchandise during the year	+55 million
Cost of goods available for sale	$95 million
Deduct: Ending inventory	−35 million
Cost of goods sold	$60 million

These same relationships are illustrated in Exhibit 8.3 and can be represented in the merchandise inventory T-account as follows (amounts in millions):

Merchandise Inventory (A)			
Beginning inventory	40		
Purchases of inventory	55	Cost of goods sold	60
Ending inventory	35		

If three of these four amounts are known, either the cost of goods sold equation or the inventory T-account can be used to solve for the fourth amount.

The **COST OF GOODS AVAILABLE FOR SALE** refers to the sum of the cost of beginning inventory and the cost of purchases (or transfers to finished goods) for the period.

COST OF GOODS SOLD EQUATION:
BI + P − EI = CGS

EXHIBIT **8.3**

Nature of Cost of Goods Sold for Merchandise Inventory

*Last period's ending inventory

SELF-STUDY **QUIZ 8-1**

Assume the following facts for computer monitor model 1707FP that Dell purchased and sold to customers during the year:

> Beginning inventory: 500 units at unit cost of $200.
>
> Ending inventory: 600 units at unit cost of $200.
>
> Sales: 1,100 units at a sales price of $300 (cost per unit $200).

1. Using the cost of goods sold equation, compute the dollar amount of purchases of model 1707FP for the period.

> Beginning inventory
> +Purchases of merchandise during the year
> _____
> Cost of goods available for sale
> −Ending inventory
> _____
> Cost of goods sold
> _____

2. Prepare the first three lines of a multiple-step income statement (showing gross profit) for the 1707FP monitor for the year.

After you complete your answers, check them with the solutions presented on page 435.

CONTROL OF INVENTORY

INTERNAL CONTROL OF INVENTORY

■ **LEARNING OBJECTIVE 2**

Compare methods of controlling and keeping track of inventory, and analyze the effects of inventory errors on financial statements.

After cash, inventory is the asset second most vulnerable to theft. Efficient management of inventory to avoid cost of stock-outs and overstock situations is also crucial to the profitability of most companies. Consequently, a number of control features focus on safeguarding inventories and providing up-to-date information for management decisions. The most important control features are:

1. Separation of responsibilities for inventory accounting and physical handling of inventory.
2. Storage of inventory in a manner that protects it from theft and damage.
3. Limiting access to inventory to authorized employees.
4. Maintaining perpetual inventory records (described below).
5. Comparing perpetual records to periodic physical counts of inventory.

PERPETUAL AND PERIODIC INVENTORY SYSTEMS

To compute cost of goods sold, three amounts must be known: (1) beginning inventory, (2) purchases of merchandise (or transfers to finished goods) during the period, and (3) ending inventory. The amount of purchases for the period is always accumulated in the accounting system. The amounts of cost of goods sold and ending inventory can be determined by using one of two different inventory systems: perpetual or periodic. To simplify the discussion of how accounting systems keep track of these amounts, we will focus this discussion on the monitors that Dell sells. Although the same general principles apply, the more complex details of manufacturing accounting systems are discussed in management accounting and cost accounting courses.

In a **PERPETUAL INVENTORY SYSTEM**, a detailed inventory record is maintained, recording each purchase and sale during the accounting period.

Perpetual Inventory System   In a **perpetual inventory system**, a detailed record is maintained for each type of merchandise stocked, showing (1) units and cost of the beginning inventory, (2) units and cost of each purchase, (3) units and cost of the goods for each sale, and (4) the units and cost of the goods on hand at any point in time. This up-to-date record is maintained on a transaction-by-transaction basis throughout the period. In a complete perpetual inventory system, the inventory record gives both the amount of ending inventory and the cost of goods sold amount at any point in time. Under this system, a physical count must be performed from time to time to ensure that records are accurate in case errors or theft of inventory occur.

All journal entries for purchase and sale transactions discussed in the text so far have been recorded using a perpetual inventory system. In a perpetual inventory system, purchase transactions are directly recorded in an inventory account. In addition, when each sale is recorded, a companion cost of goods sold entry is made, decreasing inventory and recording cost of goods sold. As a result, information on cost of goods sold and ending inventory is available on a continuous (perpetual) basis.

Whether the accounting system is manual or computerized, the data that are recorded and reported are the same. The maintenance of a separate inventory record for each type of good stocked on a transaction-by-transaction basis usually is necessary for purchasing, manufacturing, and distribution decisions. Most companies rely heavily on this system and may even share some of this information electronically with their suppliers or customers.[2]

Periodic Inventory System   Under the **periodic inventory system,** companies do not maintain up-to-date records of inventory during the year. An actual physical count of the goods remaining on hand is required at the *end of each period*. The number of units of each type of merchandise on hand is multiplied by their unit cost to compute the dollar amount of the ending inventory. Cost of goods sold is calculated using the cost of goods sold equation.

In a **PERIODIC INVENTORY SYSTEM**, ending inventory and cost of goods sold are determined at the end of the accounting period based on a physical count.

Because the amount of inventory is not known until the end of the period when the physical inventory count is taken, the amount of cost of goods sold cannot be determined reliably until the inventory count is completed. Inventory purchases are debited to a temporary account called *Purchases*. Revenues are recorded at the time of each sale. However, cost of goods sold is not recorded until after the inventory count is completed. At other times, companies using a periodic system must estimate the amount of inventory on hand. We briefly discuss the estimation of inventory amounts later in the chapter.

Before affordable computers and bar code readers were available, the primary reason for using the periodic inventory system was its low cost. The primary disadvantage of a periodic inventory system is the lack of inventory information. Managers are not informed about low stock or overstocked situations. Most modern companies could not survive without this information. As noted at the beginning of the chapter, cost and quality pressures from increasing competition, combined with dramatic declines in the cost of computers, have made sophisticated perpetual inventory systems a minimum requirement at all but the smallest companies.

Comparison of Perpetual and Periodic Systems   The differences between the perpetual and periodic inventory systems are highlighted in italics in Exhibit 8.4.

EXHIBIT **8.4**

Comparison of Perpetual and Periodic Inventory Systems

Perpetual	Periodic
Beginning inventory (carried over from prior period)	Beginning inventory (carried over from prior period)
+ Purchases for the period (accumulated in an *Inventory* account	+ Purchases for the period (accumulated in *Purchases* account)
= Cost of goods available for sale	= Cost of goods available for sale
− *Cost of goods sold (measured at every sale, based on perpetual record)*	− *Ending inventory (measured at end of period, based on physical inventory count)*
= *Ending inventory (perpetual record updated at every sale)*	= *Cost of goods sold (computed as a residual amount)*

Assume, for this illustration only, that Dell stocks and sells only one item, its 1707FP Flat Panel LCD monitor, and that only the following events occur in 2007:

[2]Many companies, such as Gildan Activewear Inc., the focus company in Chapter 7, provide product information to their current and potential customers. The Web site www.gildanfinder.com allows Gildan's customers to find out how many units of each product are available at each location that distributes its products in Canada, the United States, or Europe.

Jan. 1: Beginning inventory: 800 units, at unit cost of $200.

April 14: Purchased 1,100 additional units, at unit cost of $200.

Nov. 30: Sold 1,300 units, at unit sales price of $279.

In the two types of inventory systems, the following sequential steps would take place:

Perpetual Records	Periodic Records

1. Record all purchases in the *Inventory* account and in a detailed perpetual inventory record.
April 14, 2007:
 	
Inventory (A) (1,100 units at $200)* 220,000
   Accounts payable (L) (or Cash)   220,000
 	
*Also entered in the detailed perpetual inventory record as 1,100 units at $200 each.
	1. Record all purchases in an account called *Purchases.*
	April 14, 2007:
	
	Purchases* (T) (1,100 units at $200) . . . 220,000
	   Accounts payable (L) (or Cash). 220,000
	
	*Purchases is a temporary account (T) closed to cost of goods sold at the end of the period.

2. Record all sales in the Sales Revenue account and record the cost of goods sold.
November 30, 2007:
 	
Accounts receivable (A) (or Cash) 362,700
   Sales revenue (R) (1,300 units at $279)   362,700
Cost of goods sold (E). 260,000
   Inventory (A) (1,300 units at $200)* . .   260,000
 	
*Also entered in the perpetual inventory record as a reduction of 1,300 units at $200 each.
	2. Record all sales in a Sales Revenue account.
	November 30, 2007:
	
	Accounts receivable (A) (or Cash) 362,700
	   Sales revenue (R) (1,300 units at $279) . . . 362,700

3. At end of period:
   Use the cost of goods sold and inventory amounts. It is not necessary to compute the cost of goods sold because, under the perpetual inventory system, the Cost of Goods Sold account is up to date. The balance in the Cost of Goods Sold account is reported on the income statement. Also, the Inventory account shows the ending inventory amount reported on the balance sheet. A physical inventory count is still necessary to assess the accuracy of the perpetual records and to assess theft and other forms of misuse (called *shrinkage*).
 	
December 31, 2007:
 	
  No entry
	3. At end of period:
	   a. Count the number of units on hand.
	   b. Compute the dollar value of the ending inventory.
	   c. Compute and record the cost of goods sold.
	
	Beginning inventory (last period's ending inventory) $160,000
	Add purchases (balance in the Purchases account) *220,000*
	Cost of goods available for sale 380,000
	Deduct ending inventory
	  (physical count—600 units at $200) $120,000
	Cost of goods sold $260,000
	
	December 31, 2007:
	Transfer beginning inventory and purchases to the Cost of Goods Sold account:
	
	Cost of goods sold (E) 380,000
	   Inventory (A) (beginning) 160,000
	   Purchases (T) 220,000
	
	Transfer the ending inventory amount from the Cost of Goods Sold account to determine the cost of goods sold and establish the ending inventory balance:
	
	Inventory (A) (ending) 120,000
	   Cost of goods sold (E) 120,000

Assets	=	Liabilities	+	Shareholders' Equity	Assets	=	Liabilities	+	Shareholders' Equity
Inventory +220,000		Accounts		Sales	Purchases +220,000		Accounts		Sales
Accts. Rec. +362,700		Payable +220,000		Revenue +362,700	Accts. Rec. +362,700		Payable +220,000		Revenue +362,700
Inventory −260,000				Cost of Goods	Inventory −160,000				Cost of Goods
				Sold −260,000	Purchases −220,000				Sold −380,000
					Inventory +120,000				Cost of Goods
									Sold +120,000

Note that the effects of the entries on the accounting equation are the same under both systems. Only the timing of the recording of amounts changes.

Perpetual Inventory Records in Practice   The decision to use a perpetual versus a periodic inventory system is based primarily on management's need for timely information for use in operating decisions and on the cost of the perpetual system. Further, the specific manner in which the perpetual system is designed will also be determined with these trade-offs in mind. Many inventory ordering and production decisions require accurate information on inventory quantities but not costs. Quantities on hand provide the information necessary for efficient management of inventory, providing delivery information to dealers, and quality control.

METHODS FOR ESTIMATING INVENTORY

FINANCIAL
ANALYSIS

When a periodic inventory system is used and detailed perpetual inventory records are not kept, the cost of goods sold and the amount of ending inventory can be directly computed only when a physical inventory count is taken. Because taking a physical inventory is expensive, it is normally done only once each year. In these circumstances, managers who wish to prepare monthly or quarterly financial statements for internal use often estimate the cost of goods sold and ending inventory using the **gross profit method**. The gross profit method uses the historical gross profit percentage (introduced in Chapter 7) to estimate cost of goods sold.

For example, if Dell's historical gross profit percentage on monitors is 30 percent and $500,000 worth of monitors were sold in January, it would estimate the cost of goods sold to be $350,000 ($500,000 × [100% − 30%]) for the month. If Dell keeps track of purchases and other additions to inventory, it could then use the cost of goods sold equation to solve for an estimate of ending inventory. Retailers often take their physical inventory counts based on the retail price instead of cost and then use a similar method (called the **retail method**) to estimate cost. Methods for estimating inventory and cost of goods sold are discussed in detail in intermediate accounting courses.

ERRORS IN MEASURING ENDING INVENTORY

As the cost of goods sold equation indicates, a direct relationship exists between the cost of ending inventory and cost of goods sold because items not in the ending inventory are assumed to have been sold. Thus, the measurement of ending inventory quantities and costs affects both the balance sheet (assets) and the income statement (cost of goods sold, gross profit, and net income). The measurement of ending inventory affects not only the net income for that period but also the net income for the next accounting period. This two-period effect occurs because the ending inventory for one period is the beginning inventory for the next accounting period.

Greeting card maker Gibson Greetings had overstated its current year profits by 20 percent because one division had overstated ending inventory for the year. You can compute the effects of the error on both the current year's and next year's income before taxes using the cost of goods sold equation. Assume that the ending inventory was inadvertently overstated by $10,000 due to a clerical error that was not discovered. This would have the following effects in the current year and next year:

Current Year	
Beginning inventory	
+ Purchases of merchandise during the year	
− Ending inventory	**Overstated by $10,000**
Cost of goods sold	**Understated by $10,000**

Next Year	
Beginning inventory	**Overstated by $10,000**
+ Purchases of merchandise during the year	
− Ending inventory	
Cost of goods sold	**Overstated by $10,000**

Because the cost of goods sold was understated, *income before taxes would be overstated* by $10,000 in the *current year*. In addition, since the current year's ending inventory becomes next year's beginning inventory, it would have the following effects: the cost of goods sold would be overstated, and *income before taxes would be understated* by the same amount in the *next year*.

Each of these errors would flow into retained earnings so that at the end of the current year, retained earnings would be overstated by $10,000 (less the related income tax expense). This error would be offset in the next year, and retained earnings and inventory at the end of next year would be correct.

Exhibit 8.5 shows how an error that understates the cost of ending inventory affects other elements of financial statements during the year of the error and the following year.

An error that overstates ending inventory would have exactly the opposite effects on the financial statement items shown in Exhibit 8.5.

EXHIBIT **8.5**

Effect of Understatement in Ending Inventory on Selected Financial Statement Items

ERROR: UNDERSTATEMENT OF ENDING INVENTORY

	Year of the Error	Following Year
Beginning inventory	NE*	U
Ending inventory	U	NE
Cost of goods sold	O	U
Gross profit	U	O
Income before income tax	U	O
Income tax expense	U	O
Net income	U	O
Retained earnings, end of year	U	NE

*U = Understated; O = Overstated; NE = No Effect

SELF-STUDY **QUIZ 8-2**

Sarlos Ltd. provided the following summary income statements for fiscal years 2006 and 2007. Assume that an error in the inventory count at December 31, 2006, resulted in an overstatement of ending inventory by $10,000.

SARLOS LTD.
INCOME STATEMENTS
For the Years Ended December 31

	With Inventory Error		Without Inventory Error	
	2007	2006	2007	2006
Sales	$600,000	$500,000	$600,000	$500,000
Cost of goods sold	350,000	300,000	?	?
Gross profit	250,000	200,000	?	?
Selling, general, and administrative expenses	120,000	100,000	?	?
Income before income tax	130,000	100,000	?	?
Income tax expense (at 40%)	52,000	40,000	?	?
Net income	$ 78,000	$ 60,000	?	?

1. Complete the income statements above for 2006 and 2007 assuming that the inventory error was discovered at the end of 2007.

2. Compute the combined net income for both years 2006 and 2007. Would the inventory error at December 31, 2006, affect the financial statements for year 2008? Explain.

After you complete your answers, check them with the solutions provided on page 435.

INVENTORY COSTING METHODS

In the example presented earlier, the cost of all units of computer monitor model 1707FP was the same—$200. If inventory costs do not change, this would be the end of our discussion. As we are all aware, the prices of most goods do change. In recent years, the costs of many manufactured items such as automobiles and motorcycles have risen gradually. In other industries, such as computers, however, costs of production have dropped dramatically along with retail prices.

When inventory costs change, the determination of the cost of goods sold and the cost of ending inventory can turn profits into losses (and vice versa) and cause companies to pay or save hundreds of millions of dollars in taxes. A simple example will illustrate these dramatic effects. Do not let the simplicity of our example mislead you. It applies broadly to actual company practices.

The example is based on the following data for Dell during the first quarter of the current year, assuming for simplicity that Dell buys and sells only computer monitor model 1707FP.

Date	Transaction or Event	Number of Monitors	Number of Monitors on Hand	Cost per Monitor	Sale Price Per Monitor
January 1	Beginning inventory	800	800	$200	
January 31	Sale to customers	(600)	200		$279
February 5	Purchase from supplier	800	1,000	210	
February 28	Sale to customers	(900)	100		$295
March 10	Purchase from supplier	900	1,000	220	
March 31	Sale to customers	(200)	800		$299

Total number of monitors sold = 600 + 900 + 200 = 1,700
Ending inventory = 800 monitors

Given the rising cost of model 1707FP, the challenge for the accountant is to determine the cost of goods sold and the gross profit from the three sale transactions. Which unit cost should the accountant use? ***The answer depends on which specific goods we assume are sold***. Three generally accepted inventory costing methods are available for doing so:[3]

1. Specific identification.
2. First-in, first-out (FIFO).
3. Weighted average.

The three inventory costing methods are alternative ways to assign the total cost of goods available for sale between (1) ending inventory and (2) cost of goods sold. Generally accepted accounting principles (GAAP) require only that the inventory costing method used be rational and systematic. The selected inventory costing method should be the method that provides the best matching of expenses with revenues. The first method identifies individual items that remain in inventory or are sold. The remaining two methods assume that inventory items follow a certain physical flow.

SPECIFIC IDENTIFICATION METHOD

When the **specific identification method** is used, the cost of each item sold is individually identified and recorded as cost of goods sold. This method requires keeping track of the purchase cost of each item. This is done by either (1) coding the purchase cost on each unit before placing it in stock or (2) keeping a separate record of the unit and identifying it with a serial number. The technology of bar code scanning and radio frequency identification is a simple and cost-effective method to keep track of inventory items at all times, even for items with low unit costs. The scanner transmits cost and quantity information to

■ **LEARNING OBJECTIVE 3**

Report inventory and cost of goods sold using three inventory costing methods.

The **SPECIFIC IDENTIFICATION METHOD** identifies the cost of the specific item that was sold.

[3]A fourth method, last-in, first-out (LIFO) is accepted in the U.S. and is covered in Supplement B. LIFO was also an acceptable method under Canadian GAAP until the recent introduction of *CICA Handbook*, Section 3031, "Inventories," which prohibits its use.

a company's central database, thereby creating a perpetual record of inventory costs. This affects the computation of the cost of goods sold and the cost of ending inventory. To compute the cost of goods sold, the bar code identifies the specific monitor that is sold and matches it to the recorded cost through the scanning process. The recorded cost of all monitors that remain unsold at March 31 represents the cost of ending inventory.

The specific identification method is appropriate when dealing with expensive items such as houses or fine jewellery because each item tends to differ from the other items. The method may be manipulated when the units are identical because one can affect the cost of goods sold and the ending inventory accounts by picking and choosing from among the several available unit costs. For example, the manager of a textbook store could either increase or decrease the store's net income by choosing from among the identical textbooks that have been sold. For this reason, Canadian GAAP prohibits the use of the specific identification method when there are large numbers of items of inventory that are interchangeable, such as the computer monitors. As a consequence, most inventory items are accounted for using one of two cost flow assumptions.

COST FLOW ASSUMPTIONS

The *choice of an inventory costing method is NOT based on the physical flow of goods* on and off the shelves. That is why the methods are called *cost flow assumptions*. A useful visual learning tool for representing inventory cost flows is a stack of inventory units such as computer monitors at Dell. The different inventory costing methods then can be visualized as flows of inventory in and out of the stack. We use this concept to illustrate inventory flow throughout the following sections. We assume first that Dell uses a periodic inventory system, where the costs of goods sold and ending inventory are determined at the end of the accounting period.[4] Next, we illustrate the computation of cost of goods sold and ending inventory using the more realistic perpetual inventory system.

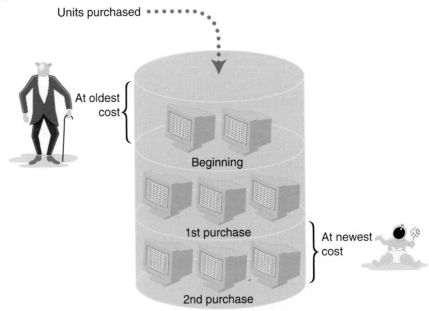

The oldest monitors are placed at the top of the stack because they are typically sold first.

FIRST-IN, FIRST-OUT METHOD

The **first-in, first-out method,** frequently called **FIFO,** assumes that the earliest goods purchased (the first ones in) are the first units sold (the first ones out) and the last goods purchased are left in ending inventory. First, each purchase is treated as if it

The **FIRST-IN, FIRST-OUT (FIFO) METHOD** assumes that the oldest units (the first costs in) are the first units sold.

---

[4]This assumption, though unrealistic, allows us to focus our attention on the fundamental differences between the two inventory costing methods.

were added to the stack in sequence (800 monitors at $200 each, 800 monitors at $210 each, and 900 monitors at $220 each). The 1,700 monitors sold are then removed from the stack in the same sequence they were added (800 units at $200, 800 units at $210, and 100 units at $220); *first in is first out*. FIFO allocated the *oldest* unit costs to *cost of goods sold* and the *newest* unit costs to *ending inventory*.

Periodic Inventory System When a periodic inventory system is used, the cost of goods and ending inventory are computed at the end of the accounting period. Exhibit 8.6 summarizes the flow of goods.

Perpetual Inventory System Would the computation of cost of goods sold and ending inventory change if Dell used a perpetual inventory system? When a perpetual inventory system is used, the inventory records are updated after every purchase and sale transaction in order to keep track of the number of inventory items on hand. This process of continuous updating of the inventory records requires computation of the cost of goods sold for each sales transaction. Hence, the computation of the cost of goods sold is done throughout the accounting period, but it is done only once at the end of the accounting period if a periodic inventory system is used.

In Exhibit 8.7, the cost of goods sold is computed after each sales transaction. The 600 monitors sold on January 31 are taken from the beginning inventory of 800 monitors at a cost of $200 per monitor. When Dell sold 900 monitors on February 28, the company shipped to customers the remaining 200 monitors at a cost of $200 each, plus 700 monitors from the 800 units purchased on February 5 at a cost of $210 each. The remaining 100 monitors were then sold on March 31 in addition to 100 monitors that were purchased earlier on March 10 at a cost of $220 each. The total cost of goods sold is $350,000, the same amount computed under a periodic inventory system. This is not surprising because the old units that are in inventory at any date are assumed to be sold first before the new units are sold. Under both the periodic and perpetual systems, the 800 units in the beginning inventory, the 800 units purchased on February 5, and 100 of the 900 units purchased on March 10 are assumed to be sold.

EXHIBIT 8.6

FIFO Inventory Flows—Periodic Inventory System

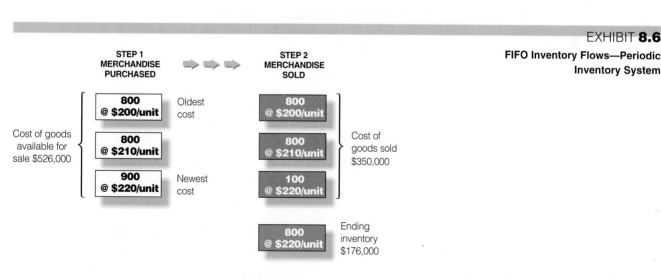

Cost of Goods Sold Calculation (FIFO Periodic)

Beginning inventory	(800 units at $200 each)	$160,000
+Purchases	(800 units at $210 each)	168,000
	(900 units at $220 each)	198,000
Cost of goods available for sale		526,000
−Ending inventory	(800 units at $220 each)	176,000
Cost of goods sold	(800 units at $200 each plus 800 units at $210 each plus 100 units at $220 each)	$350,000

EXHIBIT **8.7**

FIFO Inventory Flows—
Perpetual Inventory System

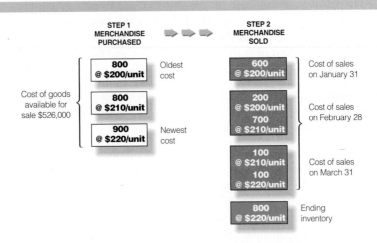

Cost of Goods Sold Calculation (FIFO Perpetual)

Beginning inventory	(800 units at $200 each)	$160,000
− Sales (January 31)	(600 units at $200 each)	(120,000)
+ Purchases (February 5)	(800 units at $210 each)	168,000
Cost of goods available for sale	(200 units at $200 each and 800 units at $210 each)	208,000
− Sales (February 28)	(200 units at $200 each and 700 units at $210 each)	(187,000)
+ Purchases (March 10)	(900 units at $220 each)	198,000
Cost of goods available for sale	(100 units at $210 each and 900 units at $220 each)	219,000
− Sales (March 31)	(100 units at $210 each and 100 units at $220 each)	(43,000)
Ending inventory	(800 units at $220 each)	$176,000

The **WEIGHTED-AVERAGE COST METHOD** uses the weighted-average unit cost of the goods available for sale for both cost of goods sold and ending inventory.

WEIGHTED-AVERAGE COST METHOD

The **weighted-average cost method** requires computation of the weighted-average unit cost of the goods available for sale.

Periodic Inventory System   When a periodic inventory system is used, the cost of goods and ending inventory are computed at the end of the accounting period. For our example, the weighted-average unit cost is computed as follows:

Number of Monitors	×	Unit Cost	=	Total Cost
800	×	$200	=	$160,000
800	×	$210	=	168,000
900	×	$220	=	198,000
2,500				$526,000

$$\text{Average Cost} = \frac{\text{Cost of Goods Available for Sale}}{\text{Number of Monitors Available for Sale}}$$

$$\text{Average Cost} = \frac{\$526,000}{2,500 \text{ Monitors}} = \$210.40^5 \text{ per Monitor}$$

In these circumstances, the cost of goods sold and the ending inventory are assigned the same weighted-average cost of $210.40 per monitor. The cost of goods sold is $357,680 (1,700 monitors at $210.40 each) and the cost of the ending inventory is $168,320 (800 monitors at $210.40 each).

---

[5]Notice that the simple average of the unit costs is $210 [($200 + $210 + $220)/3], but the weighted-average is $210.40 because the latter considers the number of monitors purchased at each unit cost. Beware of using a simple average.

Cost of Goods Sold Calculation (Weighted-Average Periodic)

Beginning inventory	(800 units at $200 each)	$160,000
+ Purchases	(800 units at $210 each)	168,000
	(900 units at $220 each)	198,000
Cost of goods available for sale		526,000
− Ending inventory	(800 units at $210.40 each)	168,320
Cost of good sold	(1,700 units at $210.40 each)	$357,680

Perpetual Inventory System Would the computation of cost of goods sold and ending inventory change if Dell used a perpetual inventory system? As indicated before, when a perpetual inventory system is used, the inventory records are updated after every purchase and sale transaction in order to keep track of the number of inventory items on hand. The 600 monitors sold on January 31 are taken from the beginning inventory of 800 monitors at cost of $200 per monitor, for a total cost of $120,000. The cost of the remaining 200 monitors is then added to the cost of the 800 monitors purchased on February 5 to compute a new weighted-average unit cost as follows:

$$\text{Weighted-Average Cost} = \frac{200 \text{ units} \times \$200 + 800 \text{ units} \times \$210}{1,000 \text{ units}} = \$208$$

This average cost is then used to compute the cost of the 900 monitors sold on February 28; that is, $900 \times \$208$ or $187,200. The cost of the remaining 100 monitors is then added to the cost of the 900 monitors purchased on March 10 to compute another weighted-average unit cost as follows:

$$\text{Weighted-Average Cost} = \frac{100 \text{ units} \times \$208 + 900 \text{ units} \times \$220}{1,000 \text{ units}} = \$218.80$$

This average cost is then used to compute the cost of the 200 monitors sold on March 31; that is $200 \times \$218.80$, or $43,760. Since the average cost changed three times, this method is called the *moving weighted-average cost* method.

Cost of Goods Sold Calculation (Moving Weighted-Average Cost)

Beginning inventory	(800 units at $200 each)	$160,000
− Sales (January 31)	(600 units at $200 each)	(120,000)
+ Purchases (February 5)	(800 units at $210 each)	168,000
Cost of goods available for sale	(200 units at $200 each and (800 units at $210 each)	208,000
− Sales (February 28)	(900 units at $208 each and (900 units at $208 each)	(187,200)
+ Purchases (March 10)	(900 units at $220 each)	198,000
Cost of goods available for sale	(100 units at $208 each and 900 units at $220 each)	218,800
− Sales (March 31)	(200 units at $218.80 each)	(43,760)
Ending inventory	(800 units at $218.80 each)	$175,040

The total cost of goods sold during the quarter is $350,960 ($120,000 + $187,200 + $43,760) compared to $357,880 under the periodic inventory system. The periodic average cost is always higher than the perpetual average cost in a period of rising prices because the periodic average cost per unit includes the cost of all units available for sale during the accounting period, whereas the perpetual average cost method considers only the cost of units available for sale at different dates in the accounting period.

FINANCIAL STATEMENT EFFECTS OF INVENTORY METHODS

Each of the three alternative inventory costing methods is in conformity with Canadian GAAP. To understand why managers choose different methods in different circumstances, we must first understand their effects on the income statement and balance sheet. Exhibit 8.8 summarizes the financial statement effects of FIFO and weighted-average methods using either the periodic or perpetual inventory system.

Remember that the methods differ only in the portion of goods available for sale allocated to cost of goods sold versus ending inventory. For that reason, the method that gives the highest ending inventory amount also gives the lowest cost of goods sold and the highest gross profit, income tax expense, and income amounts, and vice versa.

Notice in Exhibit 8.8 that the cost of goods sold under FIFO is the same whether Dell uses either a periodic or a perpetual inventory system, as previously illustrated. Furthermore, the weighted-average cost of goods sold is closer to FIFO cost when a perpetual inventory system is used because the moving average cost increased with each new purchase of monitors, thus approaching FIFO cost.

In the comparison in Exhibit 8.8, unit costs were increasing. *When unit costs are rising, the weighted-average cost method produces lower income and a lower inventory valuation than FIFO.* Even in inflationary times, some companies' costs decline. *When unit costs are declining, the weighted-average cost method produces higher income and a higher inventory valuation than FIFO.* These effects are summarized in the following table:

| | Normal Financial Statement Effects of | | | |
| | Rising Costs | | Declining Costs | |
	FIFO	Weighted Average	FIFO	Weighted Average
Cost of goods sold	Lower	Higher	Higher	Lower
Gross profit	Higher	Lower	Lower	Higher
Net income	Higher	Lower	Lower	Higher
Ending inventory	Higher	Lower	Lower	Higher

These effects occur because the weighted-average cost method causes the newer unit costs to be reflected in cost of goods sold on the income statement; FIFO causes the older unit costs to be reflected in cost of goods sold on the income statement. In contrast, on the balance sheet, the ending inventory amount under the weighted-average cost method reflects a mix of unit costs, which may be an unrealistic valuation, whereas FIFO ending inventory is based on the newest costs, thus assisting the user in predicting the amount of cash needed to replace the inventory.

EXHIBIT **8.8**

Financial Statement Effects of Inventory Costing Methods

| | Periodic Inventory System | | Perpetual Inventory System | |
	FIFO	Weighted Average	FIFO	Weighted Average
Cost of Goods Sold Calculation				
Beginning inventory	$160,000	$160,000	$160,000	$160,000
Add: Purchases	366,000	366,000	366,000	366,000
Cost of goods available for sale	526,000	526,000	526,000	526,000
Deduct: Ending inventory (to balance sheet)	176,000	168,320	176,000	175,040
Cost of goods sold (to income statement)	$350,000	$357,680	$350,000	$350,960
Effect on the Income Statement				
Sales	$492,700*	$492,700	$492,700	$492,700
Cost of goods sold	350,000	357,680	350,000	350,960
Gross profit	$142,700	$135,020	$142,700	141,740
Effect on the Balance Sheet				
Inventory	$176,000	$168,320	$176,000	$175,040

*600 × $279 + 900 × $295 + 200 × $299

Consistency in Use of Inventory Costing Methods It is important to remember that regardless of the physical flow of goods, a company can use either the weighted average or FIFO inventory costing methods. Furthermore, a company is not required to use the same inventory costing method for all inventory items, and no particular justification is needed for the selection of one or more of the acceptable methods. *Financial Reporting in Canada* shows that 48 of the companies surveyed used different inventory costing methods for different inventory items.[6] For example, in a recent annual report, Finning International Inc., which sells Caterpillar equipment, disclosed that it used specific identification to account for the cost of equipment it sells to customers, but it used FIFO for two-thirds of parts and supplies, and average cost for the remainder of its inventory.

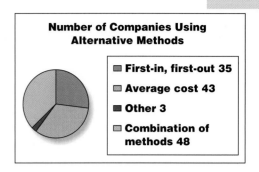

Number of Companies Using Alternative Methods

- First-in, first-out 35
- Average cost 43
- Other 3
- Combination of methods 48

To enhance comparability, accounting rules require companies to apply their accounting methods on a consistent basis. A company is not permitted to use FIFO one period, weighted average the next, and then go back to FIFO. A change in method is allowed only if the change will improve the measurement of financial results and financial position. Changing from one inventory costing method to another is a significant event. Such a change requires full disclosure about the reason for the change and the accounting effects.

DIFFERENT INVENTORY COSTING METHODS AND INTERNATIONAL COMPARISONS

INTERNATIONAL PERSPECTIVE

In recent years, accounting standard-setting organizations in many countries either adopted (or declared their intentions to adopt) International Financial Reporting Standards (IFRS) issued by the International Accounting Standards Board. This harmonization of accounting standards across countries enhances the comparability of financial statements issued by companies operating in different countries. In this regard, the international standard related to inventories (currently IAS 2) permits the use of specific identification, FIFO, and weighted-average cost methods. In the United States, however, the last-in, first-out (LIFO) method, which assumes that items that are purchased last are sold first, is permitted for financial reporting and for tax purposes to reduce income taxes. The use of LIFO by U.S. companies for some or all of their inventories creates comparability problems when one attempts to compare companies across international borders. For example, Honda (of Japan) uses FIFO for all inventories, while General Motors uses LIFO to value most of its U.S. inventories, and either average cost or FIFO for non-U.S. inventories.

MANAGERS' CHOICE OF INVENTORY COSTING METHODS

Financial Reporting in Canada reported that 43 of the surveyed companies used weighted-average cost in 2005, compared to 35 companies that used FIFO. This raises one important question: What motivates companies to choose different inventory costing methods? Our discussion in Chapter 6 suggests that management should choose the method allowed by GAAP that most reflects its economic circumstances for financial reporting purposes. Management must also make a second choice of inventory costing method to use on its tax return (tax purposes). In general, the choice from among the acceptable methods for use on the company's tax return should be the one that allows payment of the least amount of taxes as late as possible—the "least-latest rule."

The income tax effects associated with FIFO and weighted average for companies facing rising costs can be illustrated by continuing our simple Dell example. Using the

> **■ LEARNING OBJECTIVE 4**
>
> Decide when the use of different inventory costing methods is beneficial to a company.

---

[6]N. Chlala, L. Martel, A. Lavigne, and C. Byrd, *Financial Reporting in Canada 2006*. Toronto: Canadian Institute of Chartered Accountants, 2006, p. 216.

data from Exhibit 8.8 and assuming that expenses other than cost of goods sold were $42,700 and a tax rate of 25 percent, the following differences in taxes result:

	Periodic Inventory System		Perpetual Inventory System	
	FIFO	Weighted Average	FIFO	Weighted Average
Sales	$492,700*	$492,700	$492,700	$492,700
Cost of goods sold	350,000	357,680	350,000	350,960
Gross profit	142,700	135,020	142,700	141,740
Other expenses	42,700	42,700	42,700	42,700
Income before income taxes	100,000	92,320	100,000	99,040
Income tax expense (at 25%)	25,000	23,080	25,000	24,760
Net income	$ 75,000	$ 69,240	$ 75,000	$ 74,280

*600 × $279 + 900 × $295 + 200 × $299

For this illustration, the use of weighted average produces a lower amount of incomes taxes than FIFO, but the difference in income taxes under the perpetual inventory system are not material. While the lowest amount of income taxes results from the use of weighted average and a periodic inventory system, other important considerations should be taken into account when choosing between a periodic and a perpetual inventory system, such as the cost savings that may result from better control of the inventory flows throughout the year.

Many high-technology companies are facing declining costs. In such circumstances, the FIFO method, in which the oldest, most expensive goods become cost of goods sold, produces the largest cost of goods sold, the lowest gross profit, and thus the lowest income tax liability. Dell and its competitor, Apple Computer Inc., account for inventories using FIFO.

As indicated earlier, most Canadian companies use either FIFO or weighted-average cost for inventory costing. The choice of either method affects both the reported value on the balance sheet as well as net income and cash flows. The reported amounts also affect the calculation of several financial ratios. When prices are rising, companies that wish to minimize their income taxes would logically choose weighted-average cost rather than FIFO because the weighted-average cost method produces lower income before income taxes. The lower net income reduces profitability and other ratios. However, management may be interested in maximizing net income and the reported inventory value to satisfy restrictions imposed by creditors in lending agreements. While companies are expected to adopt the inventory costing method that provides the best matching of costs to revenues, the choice of a specific accounting method is influenced, in some cases, by management's objectives and the effects of the chosen method on the reported results.

A QUESTION OF ETHICS

INVENTORY COSTING AND CONFLICTS BETWEEN MANAGERS' AND OWNERS' INTERESTS

We have seen that the selection of an inventory method can have significant effects on financial statements. Company managers may have an incentive to select a particular method that may not be consistent with the objectives of the owners. For example, the use of weighted-average cost during a period of rising prices may be in the best interests of the owners because the weighted-average cost method often reduces the company's tax liability. If managers' compensation is tied to reported income, they may prefer FIFO, which typically results in higher income.

A well-designed compensation plan should reward managers for acting in the best interests of the owners, but unfortunately, this is not always the case. Clearly, a manager who selects an accounting method that is not optimal for the company solely to increase his or her compensation has engaged in questionable ethical behaviour.

SELF-STUDY **QUIZ 8-3**

Assume that a company began operations this year. Its purchases for the year included:

January	10 units @ $ 6 each
May	5 units @ $11 each
November	5 units @ $13 each

During the year, 15 units were sold for $20 each and other operating expenses totalled $100.

1. Compute cost of goods sold and pretax income for the year under FIFO and weighted-average cost methods, assuming the use of a periodic inventory system.

2. Which method would you recommend that the company adopt? Why?

_____

_____

After you complete your answers, check them with the solutions presented on page 435.

INVENTORY COSTING METHODS AND FINANCIAL STATEMENT ANALYSIS

FINANCIAL
ANALYSIS

Critics of GAAP argue that the existence of alternative accounting methods is inconsistent with the *comparability* characteristic of useful information. This quality is needed so that analysts can compare information for a company with that of other companies for the same period. These types of comparisons are more difficult if companies use different accounting methods, since one company's statements must be converted to a comparable basis before meaningful comparisons can be made.

Users of financial statements must be certain that their decisions are based on real differences, not artificial differences created by alternative accounting methods. For this reason, users must be knowledgeable about alternative accounting methods and how they affect statements.

VALUATION AT LOWER OF COST AND NET REALIZABLE VALUE

Inventories should be measured at their acquisition cost in conformity with the cost principle. When the market value of ending inventory drops below cost, the lower amount should be used as the inventory valuation. This is consistent with conservatism, which suggests that care should be taken not to overstate inventory values. Market value refers to a number of alternative measures, depending on whether the company is considering the cost of replacing an asset in its present condition or selling it to another party. For the purpose of inventory valuation, market value usually refers to the **net realizable value** of the inventory, which is essentially an estimate of the amount that a company expects to receive for selling its inventory on a specific date. An alternative measure of market value is **replacement cost**, which reflects the current purchase price for identical inventory items. *Financial Reporting in Canada 2006* indicates that 74 of the 200 companies included in the survey used net realizable value, 11 companies used replacement cost, while 53 companies used a combination of valuation methods.[7] In 2007, the Canadian Accounting Standards Board revised the accounting standards related to inventories and issued Section 3031, "Inventories," as part of its project to align Canadian accounting standards with international accounting standards. As a result, only net realizable value was retained as a measure of market value. This rule is known as measuring inventories at the **lower of cost and net realizable value (LCNRV)**.

This departure from the cost principle is particularly important for two types of companies: (1) high-technology companies such as Dell that manufacture goods for

■ **LEARNING OBJECTIVE 5**
Report inventory at the lower of cost and net realizable value (NRV).

NET REALIZABLE VALUE
is the expected sales price less selling costs (e.g., repair and disposal costs).

REPLACEMENT COST is the current purchase price for identical goods.

LOWER OF COST AND NET REALIZABLE VALUE (LCNRV) is a valuation method departing from the cost principle; it serves to recognize a loss when the net realizable value drops below cost.

[7]N. Chlala, L. Martel, A. Lavigne, and C. Byrd, *Financial Reporting in Canada 2006*. Toronto: Canadian Institute of Chartered Accountants, 2006, p. 218.

which the cost of production and the selling price are declining and (2) companies such as The Gap that sell seasonal goods such as clothing, the value of which drops dramatically at the end of each selling season (fall or spring).

Under LCNRV, companies recognize a loss in the period in which the net realizable value of an item drops rather than in the period in which the item is sold. The loss is the difference between the purchase cost and the net realizable value, and is added to the cost of goods sold of the period. To illustrate, assume that Dell had the following in the current period's ending inventory:

Item	Quantity	Cost per Item	Net Realizable Value (NRV) per Item	Lower of Cost and NRV per Item	Total Lower of Cost and NRV
Pentium chips	1,000	$250	$200	$200	1,000 × $200 = $200,000
Disk drives	400	100	110	100	400 × $100 = 40,000

The 1,000 Pentium chips should be recorded in the ending inventory at the net realizable value ($200), which is lower than the cost ($250). Dell makes the following journal entry to record the write-down:[8]

Cost of goods sold (E) (1,000 × $50)......................	50,000	
Inventory (A)		50,000

Assets		=	Liabilities	+	Shareholders' Equity	
Inventory	−50,000				Cost of Goods Sold	−50,000

Since the net realizable value of the disk drives ($110) is higher than the original cost ($100), no write-down is necessary. The drives remain on the books at their cost of $100 per unit ($40,000 in total). Recognition of holding gains on inventory is not permitted by GAAP.

The write-down of the Pentium chips to net realizable value produces the following financial statement effects:

Effects of LCNRV Write-Down	Current Period	Period of Sale
Cost of goods sold	Increase $50,000	Decrease $50,000
Pretax income	Decrease $50,000	Increase $50,000
Ending inventory on balance sheet	Decrease $50,000	Unaffected

The LCNRV rule accounts for the added expense in the current period, not in the period of sale. Consequently, pretax income is reduced by $50,000 in the period in which the net realizable value drops rather than in the next period when the chips will be used in the production of computers that are sold. Since the cost of goods sold for the current period *increases* by $50,000 and the cost of goods sold for the next period *decreases* by $50,000, the total cost of goods sold (and income before taxes) for the two periods combined does not change. On the balance sheet, the $50,000 loss in the current period reduces the amount of inventory reported at year-end.

If the net realizable value of the inventory items that were written down increases in a subsequent accounting period because of changed economic circumstances, then the amount of the write-down is reversed up to the original write-down. Normally, a reversal of a previous write-down occurs when an inventory item that is carried at net realizable value is still on hand in a subsequent period when its selling price has increased.

---

[8]The loss could be debited to a separate account, such as Loss Due to Write-Down of Inventory, which is closed to Cost of Goods Sold at the end of the accounting period.

Under generally accepted accounting principles, the LCNRV rule can be applied to inventories the cost of which is determined using any of the acceptable inventory costing methods. For example, in the excerpt below, Dell reports the use of the lower of cost (FIFO) and market rule for financial statement purposes.

REAL WORLD EXCERPT

Dell Inc.

ANNUAL REPORT

DELL COMPUTER CORPORATION
NOTES TO CONSOLIDATED FINANCIAL STATEMENTS

NOTE 1—Description of Business and Summary of Significant Accounting Policies
Inventories—Inventories are stated at the lower of cost or market, with cost being determined on a first-in, first-out basis.

EVALUATING INVENTORY MANAGEMENT

MEASURING EFFICIENCY IN INVENTORY MANAGEMENT

As noted at the beginning of the chapter, the primary goals of inventory management are to have sufficient quantities of high-quality inventory available to serve customers' needs while minimizing the costs of carrying inventory (production, storage, obsolescence, and financing). The inventory turnover ratio is an important measure of the company's success in balancing these conflicting goals.

> **■ LEARNING OBJECTIVE 6**
>
> Evaluate inventory management using the inventory turnover ratio and the effects of inventory on cash flows.

INVENTORY TURNOVER

KEY RATIO ANALYSIS

ANALYTICAL QUESTION → How efficient are inventory management activities?

RATIO AND COMPARISONS → The answer to this question is facilitated by the computation of the inventory turnover ratio as follows:

$$\text{Inventory Turnover} = \frac{\text{Cost of Goods Sold}}{\text{Average Inventory*}}$$

*Average Inventory = (Beginning Inventory + Ending Inventory) ÷ 2

The 2005 inventory turnover ratio for Dell is:

$$\frac{\$45,958}{(\$459 + \$576) \div 2} = 88.8$$

Comparisons over Time			Comparisons with Competitors	
Dell			Gateway	IBM
2003	2004	2005	2005	2005
108.1	102.8	88.8	16.9	17.7

Dell's fiscal year ends in late January/early February, so its financial statements essentially cover Dell's activities during the previous calendar year.

INTERPRETATIONS

In General → The inventory turnover ratio reflects how many times the average inventory was produced and sold during the period. A higher ratio indicates that inventory moves more quickly through the production process to the ultimate customer, reducing storage and obsolescence costs. Because less money is tied up in inventory, the excess can be invested to earn interest income or to reduce borrowings, which reduces interest expense. More efficient purchasing and production techniques such as just-in-time inventory, as well as high product demand, cause this ratio to be high. Inefficient purchasing and production techniques and declining product demand cause this ratio to be low. Analysts and creditors watch this ratio because a sudden decline may mean that a company is facing an unexpected decline in demand for its products or is becoming sloppy in its production management. Many managers and analysts compute the related number of average days to sell inventory, which is equal to average inventory ÷ (cost of goods sold ÷ 365 days), or 4.11 days for Dell. It indicates the average time it takes the company to produce and deliver inventory to customers.

Focus Company Analysis → Dell has maintained a relatively high inventory turnover during the period 2003–2005. This high turnover is the result of the company's direct business model, which enables it to operate with reduced levels of components and finished goods inventories. Dell's inventory turnover is much higher than that of its competitors: Gateway, a Dell competitor that has adopted the direct business model of sales to customers, and IBM, which continues to rely on wholesalers and retailers to sell its products and services to customers. As indicated earlier, comparisons may not be appropriate if companies use different accounting methods. Both Dell and Gateway use the FIFO method of inventory costing, but IBM uses the weighted-average cost method. Given that the computer industry has faced declining prices in the past few years, the average cost method would produce lower cost of goods sold and higher inventory values than FIFO. Consequently, IBM's inventory turnover would be higher under FIFO compared to average cost, but this difference in inventory costing methods would not account for the sizeable difference between Dell's and IBM's ratios.

Dell's impressive inventory turnover ratio is greatly influenced by its method of classifying product shipments that are in transit to customers at year-end. Dell includes these in-transit shipments in Other Current Assets instead of Inventories, whereas its competitors treat them as inventory. If in-transit shipments ($420 and $430 million as of February 3, 2006 and January 28, 2005, respectively) were added to Dell's ending inventory, its inventory turnover ratio for 2005 would decrease to 48.8, about half the initial computation. Careful reading of the notes to financial statements is often essential for proper analysis.

A Few Cautions → Differences across industries in purchasing, production, and sales processes cause dramatic differences in the ratio. For example, restaurants such as Pizza Hut, which must turn over their perishable inventory very quickly, tend to have much higher inventory turnover than automakers such as Toyota. A particular firm's ratio should be compared only with its prior years' figures or with other firms in the same industry.

SELECTED FOCUS COMPANY INVENTORY TURNOVER	
Andrew Peller Ltd.	1.9
Home Depot	5.0
Van Houtte	6.6

INVENTORY AND CASH FLOWS

When companies expand production to meet increases in demand, this increases the amount of inventory reported on the balance sheet. However, when companies overestimate demand for a product, they usually produce too many units of the slow-moving item. This increases storage costs as well as the interest costs on short-term borrowings that finance the inventory. It may even lead to losses if the excess inventory cannot be sold at normal prices. The cash flow statement often provides the first sign of such problems.

FOCUS ON CASH FLOWS   INVENTORY

As with the change in accounts receivable, the change in inventories can be a major determinant of a company's cash flow from operations. The income statement reflects the cost of goods sold during the period, whereas the cash flow statement should reflect the cash payments to suppliers for the same period. Cost of goods sold may be more or less than the amount of cash paid to suppliers during the period. Since most inventory is purchased on open credit (the borrowing from a supplier is normally called *accounts payable*), reconciling cost of goods sold with cash paid to suppliers requires consideration of the changes in both the Inventory and Accounts Payable accounts.

The simplest way to think about the effects of changes in inventory is that buying (increasing) inventory eventually decreases cash, and selling (decreasing) inventory eventually increases cash. Similarly, borrowing from suppliers, which increases accounts payable, increases cash; paying suppliers, which decreases accounts payable, decreases cash.

EFFECT ON CASH FLOW STATEMENT

IN GENERAL → A *decrease in inventory* for the period indicates that the cost of goods sold exceeded the cost of goods purchased; thus, the decrease in inventory must be *added* to net income to reflect the cost of goods purchased.

An *increase in inventory* for the period indicates that the cost of goods purchased exceeded the cost of goods sold; thus, the increase in inventory must be *subtracted* from net income to reflect the cost of goods purchased.

A *decrease in accounts payable* for the period indicates that the payments to suppliers exceeded the cost of goods purchased; thus, the decrease in accounts payable must be *subtracted* from net income in computing cash flows from operations.

An *increase in accounts payable* for the period indicates that the cost of goods purchased exceeded the payments to suppliers; thus, the increase in accounts payable must be *added* to net income in computing cash flows from operations.

	Effect on Cash Flows
Operating activities (indirect method)	
Net income	$xxx
Adjusted for	
Add inventory *decrease*	+
or	
Subtract inventory *increase*	–
Add accounts payable *increase*	+
or	
Subtract accounts payable *decrease*	–

FOCUS COMPANY ANALYSIS → Exhibit 8.9 is the Operating Activities section of Dell's cash flow statement. When the inventory balance increases during the period, as was the case at Dell in fiscal years 2003, 2004, and 2005, the company purchased or produced more inventory than it sold during the period. Thus, the increase is subtracted from net

EXHIBIT 8.9

Inventories on the Cash Flow Statement

REAL WORLD EXCERPT

Dell Inc.

ANNUAL REPORT

DELL INC.
CONSOLIDATED STATEMENT OF CASH FLOWS
Fiscal Years Ended February 3, 2006, January 28, 2005, and January 30, 2004
(in millions)

	Fiscal Year Ended		
	February 3, 2006	January 28, 2005	January 30, 2004
Cash flows from operating activities:			
Net income	$3,572	$3,043	$2,645
Adjustments to reconcile net income to net cash provided by operating activities:			
Depreciation and amortization	393	334	263
Tax benefits of employee stock plans	261	249	181
Effects of exchange rate changes on monetary assets and liabilities denominated in foreign currencies	70	(602)	(677)
Other	188	78	113
Changes in:			
Operating working capital	(67)	1,755	872
Non-current assets and liabilities	422	453	273
Net cash provided by operating activities	4,839	5,310	3,670

NOTE 10: Supplemental Consolidated Financial Information

Supplemental Consolidated Statement of Cash Flows Information

	Fiscal Year Ended		
	February 3, 2006	January 28, 2005	January 30, 2004
Changes in operating working capital accounts:			
Accounts receivable, net	$(1,029)	$ (824)	$ (932)
Inventories	(119)	(130)	(53)
Accounts payable	1,004	1,595	1,283
Accrued and other liabilities	799	1,538	867
Other, net	(722)	(424)	(293)
	$ (67)	$1,755	$ 872
Income taxes paid	$ 996	$ 575	$ 699
Interest paid	$ 39	$ 31	$ 30

income in the computation of cash flow from operations. When the accounts payable balance increased during these periods, the company borrowed more from its suppliers than it paid back during the period. Thus, the increase is added to net income in the computation of cash flow from operations.*

When sales rise quickly, as they have at Dell in fiscal years 2004 and 2005, inventories usually rise, decreasing cash flow from operations. However, the highlighted section of Exhibit 8.9 indicates that increases in borrowing from suppliers have more than offset the inventory increases.

_____

*For companies with foreign currency or business acquisitions/dispositions, the amount of the change reported on the cash flow statement will not equal the change in the accounts reported on the balance sheet.

SELF-STUDY **QUIZ 8-4**

Research In Motion (RIM) is best known for its popular BlackBerry, a small wireless product that offers multiple services: mobile phone, e-mail device, Web browser, and organizer. RIM's sales increased significantly over time, which is reflected in the following cost of goods sold and ending inventory for a recent six-year period (amounts in thousands of dollars).

	2006	2005	2004	2003	2002	2001
Cost of goods sold	$925,215	$635,914	$323,365	$187,289	$195,493	$133,852
Ending inventory	134,523	92,489	42,836	31,275	37,477	68,044

1. Compute the inventory turnover ratios for 2002 through 2006. Is RIM managing its inventory efficiently?

2. If RIM had been able to manage its inventory more efficiently and *decreased* purchases and ending inventory by $10,000 in 2006, would its inventory turnover ratio for 2006 increase or decrease? Explain.

3. If RIM had been able to manage its inventory more efficiently and *decreased* ending inventory, would its cash flow from operations increase or decrease?

After you complete your answers, check them with the solutions on page 435.

DEMONSTRATION CASE A

This case reviews the application of the inventory costing methods and the inventory turnover ratio.

Balent Appliances distributes a number of high-cost household appliances. One product, microwave ovens, has been selected for case purposes. Assume that the following summarized transactions were completed during the accounting period in the order given:

	Units	Unit Cost
a. Beginning inventory	11	$200
b. Inventory purchases	9	220
c. Sales (at $420 per unit)	8	?
d. Inventory purchases	10	210
e. Sales (at $420 per unit)	11	?

Required:
1. Compute the following amounts in accordance with each of the inventory costing methods, assuming that a periodic inventory system is used.

	Ending Inventory		Cost of Goods Sold	
	Units	Dollars	Units	Dollars
1. FIFO				
2. Weighted Average				

2. Compute the inventory turnover ratio for the current period using each of the inventory costing methods. What does this ratio mean? Which inventory costing method provides the higher ratio? Is this true in all situations? Explain.
3. Will the choice of inventory costing method affect cash flow from operations? Explain.

We strongly recommend that you prepare your own answers to these requirements and then check your answers with the suggested solution.

SUGGESTED SOLUTION

1.

	Ending Inventory		Cost of Goods Sold	
	Units	Dollars	Units	Dollars
1. FIFO	11	$2,320	19	$3,960
2. Weighted Average	11	2,303	19	3,977

Computations
Cost of goods available for sale = Beginning Inventory + Purchases
    = (11 units × $200)   + (9 units × $220 + 10 units × $210)
    = $6,280

FIFO Cost
    Ending inventory = (10 units × $210 + 1 unit × $220) = $2,320
    Cost of goods sold = $6,280 − $2,320 = $3,960

Weighted-Average Cost
    Average cost   = $6,280/30 units   = $209.33
    Ending inventory = 11 units × $209.33 = $2,303
    Cost of goods sold = $6,280 − $2,303   = $3,977

2. Inventory turnover ratio   = Cost of Goods Sold ÷ Average Inventory
    FIFO $3,960 ÷ [($2,200 + $2,320) ÷ 2] = 1.75
    Weighted Average $3,977 ÷ [($2,200 + $2,303) ÷ 2] = 1.77

The inventory turnover ratio reflects how many times the average inventory was purchased and sold during the period. Thus, Balent Appliances purchased and sold its average inventory less than two times during the period.

The weighted-average costing method provides the higher inventory turnover ratio. This is generally true when the prices of inventory items increase over time, because the cost of goods sold reflects more recent, higher prices and ending inventory includes older, lower prices, than FIFO.

3. The choice of an inventory costing method does not affect the total amount of purchases and the amount paid to suppliers. It simply allocates the purchases differently between cost of goods sold and ending inventory. However, the method chosen affects the computation of cost of goods sold, gross profit, and income before income taxes. Hence, the amount of income taxes payable is affected by the inventory costing method.

DEMONSTRATION **CASE B**

Metal Products, Incorporated, has been operating for three years as a distributor of a line of metal products. It is now the end of 2008, and for the first time, the company will undergo an audit by an external auditor. The company uses a *periodic* inventory system. The annual income statements prepared by the company are as follows:

	For the Year Ended December 31			
	2008		2007	
Sales revenue		$800,000		$750,000
Cost of goods sold				
Beginning inventory	$ 40,000		$ 45,000	
Add purchases	484,000		460,000	
Cost of goods available for sale	524,000		505,000	
Less ending inventory	60,000		40,000	
Cost of goods sold		464,000		465,000
Gross margin on sales		336,000		285,000
Operating expenses		306,000		275,000
Pretax income		30,000		10,000
Income tax expense (20%)		6,000		2,000
Net income		$ 24,000		$ 8,000

During the early stages of the audit, the external auditor discovered that the ending inventory for 2007 was understated by $15,000.

Required:

1. Based on the preceding income statement amounts, compute the gross profit percentage on sales for each year. Do the results suggest an inventory error? Explain.
2. Correct and reconstruct the two income statements.
3. Answer the following questions:

   a. What are the correct gross profit percentages?

   b. What effect did the $15,000 understatement of the ending inventory have on the pretax income for 2007? Explain.

   c. What effect did the inventory error have on the pretax income for 2008? Explain.

   d. How did the inventory error affect the income tax expense?

We strongly recommend that you prepare your own answers to these requirements and then check your answers with the suggested solution.

SUGGESTED SOLUTION

1. The gross profit percentages as reported are:

   2007: $285,000 ÷ $750,000 = 0.38

   2008: $336,000 ÷ $800,000 = 0.42

   The change in the gross profit percentage from 0.38 to 0.42 suggests the possibility of an inventory error in the absence of any other explanation.

2. The corrected income statements follow:

	For the Year Ended December 31			
	2008		**2007**	
Sales revenue		$800,000		$750,000
Cost of goods sold				
Beginning inventory	$ 55,000*		$ 45,000	
Add purchases	484,000		460,000	
Cost of goods available for sale	539,000		505,000	
Less ending inventory	60,000		55,000*	
Cost of goods sold		479,000		450,000
Gross margin on sales		321,000		300,000
Operating expenses		306,000		275,000
Pretax income		15,000		25,000
Income tax expense (20%)		3,000		5,000
Net income		$ 12,000		$ 20,000

*Increased by $15,000.

3. *a.* The correct gross profit percentages are:
   2007: $300,000 ÷ $750,000 = 0.400
   2008: $321,000 ÷ $800,000 = 0.401
   The inventory error of $15,000 was responsible for the difference in the gross profit percentages reflected in requirement 1. The error in the 2007 ending inventory affected the gross margin for both years 2007 and 2008 by the same amount, $15,000, but in the opposite direction.

   b. Effect on pretax income in 2007: The *understatement* ($15,000) of ending inventory caused an *understatement* of pretax income by the same amount.

   c. Effect on pretax income in 2008: The *understatement* of beginning inventory (by the same $15,000 since the inventory amount is carried over from the prior period) caused an *overstatement* of pretax income by the same amount.

   d. The total income tax expense for 2007 and 2008 combined was the same ($8,000) regardless of the error. However, there was a shift of $3,000 ($15,000 × 20%) in income tax expense from 2007 to 2008.

OBSERVATION An ending inventory error in one year affects pretax income by the amount of the error and in the same direction. It affects pretax income again in the following year by the same amount but in the opposite direction.

Chapter Supplement A

Additional Issues in Measuring Purchases

PURCHASE RETURNS AND ALLOWANCES

Goods purchased may be returned to the vendor if they do not meet specifications, arrive in damaged condition, or otherwise are unsatisfactory. When the goods are returned or when the vendor makes an allowance because of the circumstances, the effect on the cost of purchases must be measured. The purchaser normally receives a cash refund or a reduction in the liability to the vendor. Assume that Dell returned to a supplier unsatisfactory monitors that cost $1,000. The return would be recorded by Dell as follows:

Accounts payable (L) (or Cash)	1,000	
Inventory* (A)		1,000

Assets		=	Liabilities		+	Shareholders' Equity
Inventory	−1,000		Accounts Payable	−1,000		

*Purchase Returns and Allowances (T) may be credited when the periodic inventory system is used. It is subtracted in the calculation of cost of goods sold.

PURCHASE RETURNS AND ALLOWANCES are a reduction in the cost of purchases associated with unsatisfactory goods.

Purchase returns and allowances are treated as a reduction in the cost of inventory purchases associated with unsatisfactory goods.

PURCHASE DISCOUNTS

A **PURCHASE DISCOUNT** is a cash discount received for prompt payment of an account.

Cash discounts must be accounted for by both the seller and the buyer (accounting by the seller was discussed in Chapter 7). When merchandise is bought on credit, terms such as 2/10, n/30 are sometimes specified. This means that if payment is made within 10 days from date of purchase, a 2-percent cash discount known as the **purchase discount** is granted. If payment is not made within the discount period, the full invoice cost is due 30 days after the date of purchase. Assume that on January 17, Dell bought goods that had a $1,000 invoice price with terms 2/10, n/30. Assuming that the company uses the *gross method*, the purchase should be recorded as follows:

Date of Purchase

| Jan. 17 | Inventory* (A) .... | 1,000 | |
| | Accounts payable (L) .... | | 1,000 |

	Assets	=	Liabilities	+	Shareholders' Equity
Inventory	+1,000		Accounts Payable +1,000		

*Purchases (T) is debited when a periodic inventory system is used.

Date of Payment, within the Discount Period

Jan. 26	Accounts payable (L)	1,000	
	Inventory* (A)		20
	Cash (A)		980

	Assets	=	Liabilities	+	Shareholders' Equity
Inventory	−20		Accounts Payable −1,000		
Cash	−980				

*Purchase Discounts (T) is credited when a periodic inventory system is used. Purchase Discounts would be reported as a deduction from the cost of purchases in the calculation of cost of goods sold.

If for any reason Dell did not pay within the 10-day discount period, the following try would be needed:

| Feb. 1 | Accounts payable (L) .... | 1,000 | |
| | Cash (A) .... | | 1,000 |

	Assets	=	Liabilities	+	Shareholders' Equity
Cash	−1,000		Accounts Payable −1,000		

Chapter Supplement B

Last-in, First-out Method

The **LAST-IN, FIRST-OUT (LIFO) METHOD** assumes that the most recently acquired units are sold first.

The computations of cost of goods sold and ending inventory in the chapter focused primarily on the weighted average and FIFO inventory costing methods. Another method, used mainly by U.S. companies, is the **last-in, first-out method**, often called **LIFO**. How does this method differ from FIFO? Let us use the example shown on p. 415 to illustrate the computation of cost of goods sold and ending inventory under LIFO.

Date	Transaction or Event	Number of Monitors	Number of Monitors in Store	Cost per Monitor	Sale Price Per Monitor
January 1	Beginning inventory	800	800	$200	
January 31	Sale to customers	(600)	200		$279
February 5	Purchase from supplier	800	1,000	210	
February 28	Sale to customers	(900)	100		$295
March 10	Purchase from supplier	900	1,000	220	
March 31	Sale to customers	(200)	800		$299

Total number of monitors sold = 600 + 900 + 200 = 1,700
Ending inventory = 800 *monitors*

LIFO assumes that the most recently acquired goods (the last ones in) are sold first and the oldest units are left in ending inventory. LIFO allocates the **newest** unit costs to **cost of goods sold** and the **oldest** unit costs to **ending inventory**. The LIFO flow assumption is the exact opposite of the FIFO flow assumption. These relationships are summarized as follows:

	FIFO	LIFO
Cost of goods sold on income statement	Oldest unit costs	Most recent unit costs
Inventory on balance sheet	Most recent unit costs	Oldest unit costs

Periodic Inventory System   When a periodic inventory system is used, the cost of goods and ending inventory are computed at the end of the accounting period. The flow of goods is summarized in Exhibit 8.10. Unlike the FIFO method, the monitors sold are removed in the following sequence (900 units at $220 and 800 units at $210); *last in is first out.*

EXHIBIT **8.10**

LIFO Inventory Flows—Periodic Inventory System

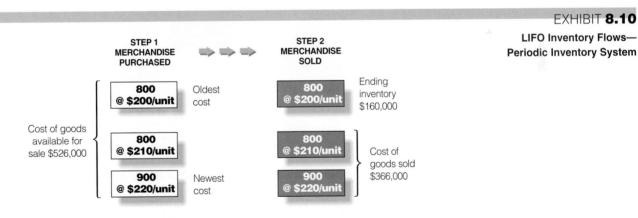

Cost of Goods Sold Calculation (LIFO Periodic)

Beginning inventory	(800 units at $200 each)	$160,000
+ Purchases	(800 units at $210 each)	168,000
	(900 units at $220 each)	198,000
Cost of goods available for sale		526,000
− Ending inventory	(800 units at $200 each)	160,000
Cost of goods sold	(900 units at $220 each plus 800 units at $210 each)	$366,000

Perpetual Inventory System   Would the computation of cost of goods sold and ending inventory change if Dell used a perpetual inventory system? When a perpetual inventory system is used, the inventory records are updated after every purchase and sale transaction in order to keep track of the number of inventory items on hand. This process of continuous updating of the inventory records requires computation of the cost of goods sold for each sales transaction. Hence, the computation of the cost of goods sold is done throughout the accounting period, but it is done only once at the end of the accounting period if a periodic inventory system is used.

In Exhibit 8.11, the monitors purchased last are assumed to be removed from the stack when a sale occurs. The 600 monitors sold on January 31 are taken from the beginning inventory of 800 monitors at a cost of $200 per monitor, the 900 monitors sold on February 28 are taken first from the 800 monitors purchased on February 5 at a cost of $210 each, and an additional 100 monitors are taken from the remaining inventory at $200 each. The 200 monitors sold on March 31 are taken from the 900 monitors that were purchased on March 10 at a cost of $220 each. The 800 monitors left in ending inventory consist of two layers of units purchased on different dates at different costs per unit.

EXHIBIT 8.11

LIFO Inventory Flows—Perpetual Inventory System

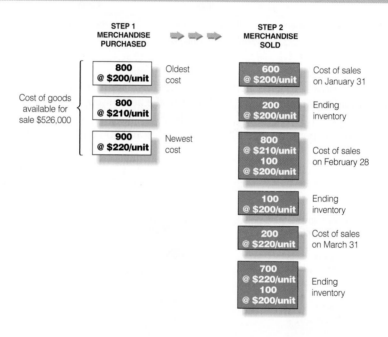

Cost of Goods Sold Calculation (LIFO Perpetual)

Beginning inventory	(800 units at $200 each)	$160,000
− Sales (January 31)	(600 units at $200 each)	(120,000)
+ Purchases (February 5)	(800 units at $210 each)	168,000
Cost of goods available for sale	*(200 units at $200 each and 800 units at $210 each)*	*208,000*
− Sales (February 28)	(800 units at $210 each and 100 units at $210 each)	(188,000)
+ Purchases (March 10)	(900 units at $220 each)	198,000
Cost of goods available for sale	*(100 units at $200 each and 900 units at $220 each)*	*218,000*
− Sales (March 31)	(200 units at $220 each)	(44,000)
Ending inventory	*(100 units at $200 each and 700 units at $220 each)*	$174,000

The total cost of goods sold is $352,000 ($120,000 + $188,000 + $44,000), compared to $366,000 under the periodic inventory system. When unit costs increase over time, periodic LIFO produces a higher cost of goods sold than does perpetual LIFO, and vice versa. Perpetual records are rarely kept on a LIFO basis because of the complexity and cost of such systems.

SOLUTIONS TO **SELF-STUDY QUIZZES**

Self-Study Quiz 8-1

1. BI = 500 × $200 = $100,000   BI   + P − EI   = CGS
    EI = 600 × $200 = $120,000   100,000 + P − 120,000 = 220,000
    CGS = 1,100 × $200 = $220,000   P = 240,000

2. Net sales $330,000
    Cost of goods sold   220,000
    Gross profit $110,000

Self-Study Quiz 8-2

1.

SARLOS LTD.
INCOME STATEMENTS
For the Years Ended December 31

	With Inventory Error		Without Inventory Error	
	2007	2006	2007	2006
Sales	$600,000	$500,000	$600,000	$500,000
Cost of goods sold	350,000	300,000	340,000	310,000
Gross profit	250,000	200,000	260,000	190,000
Selling, general, and administrative expenses	120,000	100,000	120,000	100,000
Income before income tax	130,000	100,000	140,000	90,000
Income tax expense (at 40%)	52,000	40,000	56,000	36,000
Net income	$ 78,000	$ 60,000	$ 84,000	$ 54,000

2. The combined net income for each of the years 2006 and 2007 is $138,000. The effects of the inventory error at the end of 2006 cancel out after two years. The 2006 error would not affect the financial statements for 2008.

Self-Study Quiz 8-3

1. FIFO cost of goods sold = (10 × $6) + (5 × $11) = $115

$$\text{Average cost} = \frac{\$60 + \$55 + \$65}{10 + 5 + 5} = \$9$$

Weighted average cost of goods sold = 15 × $9 = $135

	FIFO	Weighted Average
Sales revenue (15 × $20)	$300	$300
Cost of goods sold	115	135
Gross profit	185	165
Other expenses	100	100
Pretax income	85	65

2. The weighted-average cost would be recommended because it produces lower pretax income and lower taxes. The FIFO method would be recommended if the company's objective is to report higher income.

Self-Study Quiz 8-4

1.

Year	2006	2005	2004	2003	2002
Inventory turnover ratio	8.15	9.40	8.73	5.45	3.71

These ratios show improved efficiency in managing inventory from 2002 to 2005 with a slight decrease in 2006.

2. Inventory turnover will increase because the denominator of the ratio will decrease by $5,000.
    Inventory turnover ratio = $925,215 / [($92,489 + $124,524)/2] = 8.52

3. The decrease in inventory does not affect cash flows. What matters is the payment made to suppliers.

CHAPTER **TAKE-AWAYS**

1. **Apply the cost principle to identify the amounts that should be included in inventory and the matching principle to determine the cost of goods sold for typical retailers, wholesalers, and manufacturers. p. 406**

   Inventory should include all of the items held for resale that the entity owns. Costs flow into inventory when goods are purchased or manufactured, and they flow out (as an expense) when the goods are sold or otherwise disposed of. In conformity with the matching principle, the total cost of the goods sold during the period must be matched with the sales revenue earned during the period.

2. **Compare methods for controlling and keeping track of inventory, and analyze the effects of inventory errors on financial statements. p. 410**

   A company can keep track of the ending inventory and cost of goods sold for the period using: (1) the perpetual inventory system, which is based on the maintenance of detailed and continuous inventory records for each kind of inventory stocked, and (2) the periodic inventory system, which is based on a physical inventory count of ending inventory and the costing of those goods to determine the proper amounts for cost of goods sold and ending inventory. An error in the measurement of ending inventory affects the cost of goods sold on the current period's income statement and ending inventory on the balance sheet. It also affects the cost of goods sold in the following period by the same amount, but in the opposite direction, because this year's ending inventory becomes next year's beginning inventory. These relationships can be seen through the cost of goods sold equation (BI + P − EI = CGS).

3. **Report inventory and cost of goods sold using three inventory costing methods. p. 415**

   The chapter discussed three different inventory costing methods and their applications in different economic circumstances. The methods discussed were FIFO, weighted-average cost, and specific identification. Each of the inventory costing methods is in conformity with Canadian GAAP. Remember that the cost flow assumption need not match the physical flow of inventory.

4. **Decide when the use of different inventory costing methods is beneficial to a company. p. 421**

   The selection of a method of inventory costing is important because it will affect reported income, income tax expense (and, hence, cash flow), and the inventory valuation reported on the balance sheet. In a period of rising prices, FIFO normally results in a higher income than does weighted-average cost; in a period of falling prices, the opposite result occurs.

5. **Report inventory at the lower of cost and net realizable value (NRV). p. 423**

   Ending inventory should be measured based on the lower of actual cost or market value (LCNRV basis). This practice can have a major effect on the statements of companies facing declining costs. Damaged, obsolete, and out-of-season inventory also should be written down to their current estimated net realizable value if that is below cost. The LCNRV adjustment increases cost of goods sold, decreases income, and decreases reported inventory.

6. **Evaluate inventory management using the inventory turnover ratio and the effects of inventory on cash flows. p. 425**

   The inventory turnover ratio measures the efficiency of inventory management. It reflects how many times the average inventory was produced and sold during the period. Analysts and creditors watch this ratio because a sudden decline in this ratio may mean that a company is facing an unexpected decline in demand for its products or is becoming sloppy in its production management. When a net *decrease in inventory* for the period occurs, sales are more than purchases; thus, the decrease must be *added* to net income in computing cash flows from operations. When a net *increase in inventory* for the period occurs, sales are less than purchases; thus, the increase must be *subtracted* from net income in computing cash flows from operations.

In this and previous chapters, we discussed the current assets of a business. These assets are critical for the operations of a business, but many of them do not directly produce value. In Chapter 9, we will discuss the noncurrent assets property, plant, and equipment; natural resources; and intangibles that are the elements of productive capacity. Many of the noncurrent assets produce value, such as a factory that manufactures cars. These assets present some interesting accounting problems because they benefit a number of accounting periods.

KEY **RATIO**

Inventory turnover ratio measures the efficiency of inventory management. It reflects how many times the average inventory was produced and sold during the period (p. 425):

$$\text{Inventory Turnover} = \frac{\text{Cost of Goods Sold}}{\text{Average Inventory}}$$

FINDING **FINANCIAL INFORMATION**

BALANCE SHEET
Under Current Assets
   Inventories

INCOME STATEMENT
Expenses
   Cost of goods sold

CASH FLOW STATEMENT
Under Operating Activities (indirect method):
   + decreases in inventory
   − increases in inventory
   + increases in accounts payable
   − decreases in accounts payable

NOTES
Under Summary of Significant Accounting Policies:
   Description of management's choice of inventory accounting policy (FIFO, Average cost, LCNRV, etc)
Under a Separate Note
   If not listed on the balance sheet, components of inventory (merchandise, raw materials, work-in-process, finished goods)

KEY **TERMS**

Cost of Goods Available for Sale p. 409
Cost of Goods Sold Equation p. 409
Direct Labour p. 408
Factory Overhead p. 408
Finished Goods Inventory p. 406
First-In, First-Out (FIFO) Method p. 416
Inventory p. 406
Last-In, First-Out (LIFO) Method p. 432
Lower of Cost and Net Realizable Value (LCNRV) p. 423
Merchandise Inventory p. 406

Net Realizable Value p. 423
Periodic Inventory System p. 411
Perpetual Inventory System p. 410
Purchase Discount p. 432
Purchase Returns and Allowances p. 432
Raw Materials Inventory p. 406
Replacement Cost p. 423
Specific Identification Method p. 415
Weighted-Average Cost Method p. 418
Work-in-Process Inventory p. 406

QUESTIONS

1. Why is inventory an important item to both internal (management) and external users of financial statements?
2. What are the general guidelines for deciding which items should be included in inventory?
3. Explain the application of the cost principle to an item in the ending inventory.
4. Define *cost of goods available for sale*. How does it differ from cost of goods sold?
5. Define *beginning inventory* and *ending inventory*.
6. When a perpetual inventory system is used, unit costs of the items sold are known at the date of each sale. In contrast, when a periodic inventory system is used, unit costs are known only at the end of the accounting period. Why are these statements correct?
7. The periodic inventory calculation is BI + P − EI = CGS. The perpetual inventory calculation is BI + P − CGS = EI. Explain the significance of the difference between these two calculations.

8. The chapter discussed three inventory costing methods. List the three methods and briefly explain each.
9. Explain how income can be manipulated when the specific identification inventory costing method is used.
10. Contrast the effects of weighted average versus FIFO on reported assets (i.e., the ending inventory) when (a) prices are rising and (b) prices are falling.
11. Contrast the income statement effect of weighted average versus FIFO (i.e., on income before income taxes) when (a) prices are rising and (b) prices are falling.
12. Contrast the effects of weighted average versus FIFO on cash outflow and inflow.
13. Explain briefly the application of the LCNRV concept to the ending inventory and its effect on the income statement and balance sheet when the net realizable value of inventory is lower than its cost.

EXERCISES

■ LO1

E8–1   Recording the Cost of Purchases for a Merchandiser

Elite Apparel purchased 80 new shirts for cash and recorded a total cost of $3,140 determined as follows:

Invoice amount	$2,600
Shipping charges	165
Import taxes and duties	115
Interest paid in advance (10%) on $2,600 borrowed to finance the purchase	260
	$3,140

Required:

Make the needed corrections in this calculation. Prepare the journal entry(ies) to record this purchase in the correct amount, assuming a perpetual inventory system. Show computations.

■ LO1

E8–2   Analyzing Items to Be Included in Inventory

Boilard, Inc. planned to report inventory of $50,000 based on its physical count of inventory in its warehouse at year-end, December 31, 2008. During the audit, the auditor developed the following additional information:

a. Goods from a supplier costing $300 are in transit with Canada Post on December 31, 2008. The terms are F.O.B. shipping point (explained in the "Required" section). Because these goods had not arrived, they were excluded from the physical inventory count.

b. Boilard delivered samples costing $400 to a customer on December 27, 2008, with the understanding that they would be returned to Boilard on January 18, 2009. Because these goods were not on hand, they were excluded from the physical inventory count.

c. On December 31, 2008, goods in transit to customers, with terms F.O.B. shipping point, amounted to $2,000 (the expected delivery date was January 10, 2009). Because the goods had been shipped, they were excluded from the physical inventory count.

d. On December 31, 2008, goods in transit to a customer, F.O.B. destination, amounted to $1,000 and are not expected to arrive at their destination before January 10, 2009. Because the goods had been shipped, they were not included in the physical inventory count.

Required:

Boilard's accounting policy requires including in inventory all goods for which it has title. Note that the point where title (ownership) changes hands is determined by the shipping terms in the sales contract. When goods are shipped "F.O.B. shipping point," title changes hands at shipment and the buyer normally pays for shipping. When they are shipped "F.O.B. destination," title changes hands on delivery, and the seller normally pays for shipping. Begin with the $50,000 inventory amount and compute the correct amount for the ending inventory. Explain the basis for your treatment of each of the preceding items. (*Hint:* Set up three columns: Item, Amount, and Explanation.)

E8–3 Inferring Missing Amounts Based on Income Statement Relationships

LO1

Supply the missing dollar amounts for the 2008 income statement of Laurin Retailers for each of the following independent cases:

Cases	Sales Revenue	Beginning Inventory	Purchases	Total Available	Ending Inventory	Cost of Goods Sold	Gross Profit	Operating Expenses	Pretax Income or (Loss)
A	$ 650	$100	$700	$?	$500	$?	$?	$200	$?
B	900	200	800	?	?	?	?	150	0
C	?	150	?	?	300	200	400	100	?
D	800	?	600	?	250	?	?	250	100
E	1,000	?	900	1,100	?	?	500	?	(50)

E8–4 Inferring Missing Amounts Based on Income Statement Relationships

LO1

Supply the missing dollar amounts for the 2010 income statement of Kwan Company for each of the following independent cases:

	Case A	Case B	Case C
Sales revenue	$ 8,000	$ 6,000	$?
Sales returns and allowances	150	?	275
Net sales revenue	?	?	5,920
Beginning inventory	11,000	6,500	4,000
Purchases	5,000	?	9,420
Transportation-in	?	120	170
Purchase returns	350	600	?
Cost of goods available for sale	?	14,790	13,370
Ending inventory	10,000	10,740	?
Cost of goods sold	?	?	5,400
Gross profit	?	1,450	?
Expenses (operating)	1,300	?	520
Pretax income (loss)	$ 800	$ (500)	$ 0

E8–5 Inferring Merchandise Purchases

LO1

The Gap Inc.

The Gap, Inc., is a specialty retailer that operates stores selling clothes under the trade names Gap, GapKids, BabyGap, and Banana Republic. Assume that you are employed as a stock analyst and your boss has just completed a review of the new Gap annual report. She provided you with her notes, but they are missing some information that you need. Her notes show that the ending inventory for Gap in the current year was $243,482,000 and in the previous year was $193,268,000. Net sales for the current year were $1,586,596,000. Gross profit was $540,360,000; net income was $97,628,000. For your analysis, you determine that you need to know the amount of purchases and the cost of goods sold for the year.

Required:
Do you need to ask your boss for her copy of the annual report, or can you develop the information from her notes? Explain and show calculations.

E8–6 Analyzing the Effects of an Error in Recording Purchases

LO2

ANALYSIS

Garraway Ski Company mistakenly recorded purchases of inventory on account received during the last week of December 2007 as purchases during January of 2008 (this is called a *purchases cut-off error*). Garraway uses a periodic inventory system, and ending inventory was correctly counted and reported each year. Assuming that no correction was made in 2007 or 2008, indicate whether each of the following financial statement amounts will be understated, overstated, or correct.

1. Net Income for 2007.
2. Net Income for 2008.
3. Retained Earnings at December 31, 2007.
4. Retained Earnings at December 31, 2008.

LO2

E8–7 Recording Purchases and Sales Using a Perpetual and Periodic Inventory System

Demski Company reported beginning inventory of 100 units at a unit cost of $25. It engaged in the following purchase and sale transactions during 2007:

Jan. 14 Sold 25 units at unit sales price of $40 on open account.

April 9 Purchased 15 additional units at unit cost of $25 on open account.

Sept. 2 Sold 50 units at sales price of $45 on open account.

At the end of the 2007, a physical count showed that Demski Company had 40 units of inventory still on hand.

Required:

Record each transaction, assuming that Demski Company uses (a) a perpetual inventory system and (b) a periodic inventory system (including any necessary entries at December 31, the end of the accounting period).

LO2

Gibson Greeting Cards

E8–8 Analyzing the Effect of an Inventory Error Disclosed in an Actual Note to a Financial Statement

Several years ago, the financial statements of Gibson Greeting Cards contained the following note:

> On July 1, the Company announced that it had determined that the ending inventory . . . had been overstated. . . . The overstatement of inventory . . . was $8,806,000.

Gibson reported an incorrect net income amount of $25,852,000 for the year in which the error occurred and the income tax rate was 39.3 percent.

Required:

1. Compute the amount of net income that Gibson reported after correcting the inventory error. Show computations.

2. Assume that the inventory error was not discovered. Identify the financial statement accounts that would have been incorrect for the year the error occurred and for the subsequent year. State whether each account was understated or overstated.

LO2

E8–9 Analyzing and Interpreting the Impact of an Inventory Error

Dalez Corporation prepared the following two income statements (simplified for illustrative purposes):

	Second Quarter 2008		First Quarter 2008	
Sales revenue		$18,000		$17,000
Cost of goods sold				
Beginning inventory	$ 4,000		$ 3,000	
Purchases	12,000		7,000	
Cost of goods available for sale	16,000		10,000	
Ending inventory	9,000		4,000	
Cost of goods sold		7,000		6,000
Gross profit		11,000		11,000
Expenses (operating)		6,000		5,000
Pretax income		$ 5,000		$ 6,000

During the third quarter, it was discovered that the ending inventory for the first quarter should have been $4,400.

Required:

1. What effect did this error have on the combined pretax income of the two quarters? Explain.

2. Did this error affect the EPS amounts for each quarter? (See the discussion of EPS in Chapter 6.) Explain.

3. Prepare corrected income statements for each quarter.

4. Set up a schedule with the following headings to reflect the comparative effects of the correct and incorrect amounts on the income statement:

	2nd Quarter			1st Quarter		
Income Statement Item	Incorrect Amount	Correct Amount	Error (if any)	Incorrect Amount	Correct Amount	Error (if any)

E8–10 **Calculating Ending Inventory and Cost of Goods Sold Under FIFO and Weighted Average Cost Methods**   ■ **LO2**

Clor Company uses a periodic inventory system. At the end of its accounting period, December 31, 2009, the accounting records provided the following information for Product 1:

	Units	Unit Cost
Inventory, December 31, 2008	3,000	$8
For the year 2009:		
Purchases, March 31	5,000	9
Purchases, August 1	2,000	7
Inventory, December 31, 2009	4,000	

Required:

Compute the cost of goods sold and the ending inventory under the FIFO and weighted-average costing methods. (*Hint:* Set adjacent columns for each case.)

E8–11 **Analyzing and Interpreting the Financial Statement Effects of FIFO and Weighted Average Cost Methods**   ■ **LO2**

Lunar Company uses a periodic inventory system. The company's accounting records provided the following information for Product 2:

Transactions	Units	Unit Cost
a. Inventory, December 31, 2007	3,000	$12
For the year 2008:		
b. Purchase, April 11	9,000	10
c. Sale, May 1 ($30 each)	5,000	
d. Purchase, June 1	8,000	13
e. Sale, July 3 ($30 each)	6,000	
f. Operating expenses (excluding income tax expense), $85,000		

Required:

1. Prepare an income statement for 2008 through pretax income, showing the detailed computation of cost of goods sold for
   a. Case A: FIFO.
   b. Case B: Weighted average.
   For each case, show the computation of the ending inventory. (*Hint:* Set up adjacent columns, one for each case.)

2. Compare the pretax income and the ending inventory amounts between the two cases. Explain the similarities and differences.

3. Which inventory costing method may be preferred for income tax purposes? Explain.

4. Prepare journal entries to record transactions (*b*) through (*e*), as well as the cost of goods sold at December 31, 2008, assuming that Lunar uses FIFO for inventory costing.

■ **LO3**

E8–12   Analyzing and Interpreting the Financial Statement Effects of FIFO and Weighted Average Cost Methods

Scoresby Inc. uses a perpetual inventory system. At December 31, 2009, the end of the company's annual accounting period, its accounting records provided the following information for Product B:

Transactions		Units	Unit Cost
a.	Inventory, December 31, 2008	7,000	$8
	For the year 2009:		
b.	Purchase, March 5	19,000	9
c.	Sale, June 15 ($29 each)	10,000	
d.	Purchase, September 19	8,000	11
e.	Sale, November 20 ($31 each)	16,000	
f.	Operating expenses (excluding income tax expense), $500,000		

Required:

1. Prepare an income statement for 2009 through pretax income, showing the detailed computation of cost of goods sold for
   a. Case A: FIFO.
   b. Case B: Weighted average.
   For each case, show the computation of the ending inventory. (*Hint:* Set up adjacent columns, one for each case.)

2. Compare the two cases with regard to the pretax income and the ending inventory amounts. Explain the similarities and differences.

3. Which inventory costing method may be preferred for income tax purposes? Explain.

4. Prepare journal entries to record transactions (*b*) through (*e*), assuming that Scoresby uses FIFO for inventory costing.

■ **LO3, 4**

E8–13   Evaluating the Choice between Two Alternative Inventory Costing Methods Based on Cash Flow and Income Effects

Courtney Company uses a periodic inventory system. Data for 2008: beginning merchandise inventory (December 31, 2007), 2,000 units at $35; purchases, 8,000 units at $38; operating expenses (excluding income taxes), $142,000; ending inventory per physical count at December 31, 2008, 1,800 units; sales price per unit, $70; and average income tax rate, 30 percent.

Required:

1. Prepare income statements under the FIFO and weighted-average costing methods. Use a format similar to the following:

		Inventory Costing Method	
Income Statement	Units	FIFO	Weighted Average
Sales revenue	_____	$_____	$_____
Cost of goods sold	_____	_____	_____
Beginning inventory	_____	_____	_____
Purchases	_____	_____	_____
Cost of goods available for sale	_____	_____	_____
Ending inventory	_____	_____	_____
Cost of goods sold	_____	_____	_____
Gross profit		_____	_____
Expenses (operating)		_____	_____
Pretax income		_____	_____
Income tax expense		_____	_____
Net income		_____	_____

2. Which method, FIFO or weighted-average cost, is preferable in terms of (a) net income and (b) cash flow? Explain.

3. What would be your answer to requirement 2, assuming that prices were falling? Explain.

E8–14 **Evaluating the Choice between Two Alternative Inventory Costing Methods Based on Cash Flow Effects**

■ **LO3, 4**

Following is partial information for the income statement of Timber Company under three different inventory costing methods, assuming the use of a periodic inventory system:

	FIFO	Weighted Average
Unit sales price, $50		
Cost of goods sold		
Beginning inventory (330 units)	$11,220	$11,220
Purchases (475 units)	17,100	17,100
Cost of goods available for sale		
Ending inventory (510 units)		
Cost of goods sold		
Operating expenses, $1,600		

Required:

1. Compute the cost of goods sold under the FIFO and weighted-average inventory costing methods.

2. Prepare an income statement through pretax income for each method.

3. Compare the two methods with regard to favourable cash flow and explain the basis for your ranking.

E8–15 **Reporting Inventory at Lower of Cost and Net Realizable Value**

■ **LO5**

Peterson Company is preparing the annual financial statements dated December 31, 2008. Ending inventory information about the five major items stocked for regular sale follows:

	Ending Inventory, 2008		
Item	Quantity on Hand	Unit Cost When Acquired (FIFO)	Net Realizable Value at Year-End
A	50	$15	$13
B	75	40	40
C	10	50	52
D	30	30	30
E	400	8	6

Required:

1. Compute the valuation that should be used for the 2008 ending inventory using the LCNRV rule applied on an item-by-item basis. (*Hint:* Set up columns for Item, Quantity, Total Cost, Total Market, and LCNRV Valuation.)

2. What will be the effect of the write-down of inventory to lower of cost and net realizable value on cost of goods sold for the year 2008?

3. Assume that 20 units of Item E had not been sold by December 31, 2009, and that the net realizable value of that item increased to $7.50 per unit. How would this information be reflected in Peterson's income statement for 2009 and its balance sheet at year-end? Explain.

E8–16 **Reporting Inventory at Lower of Cost and Net Realizable Value**

■ **LO5**

Research In Motion, Inc. (RIM), which is best known for its wireless communication product, the Blackberry, disclosed the following information in Note 5 to its annual report for fiscal year 2006.

Inventory is comprised as follows:

	March 4, 2006
Raw materials	$107,049
Work in process	31,848
Finished goods	3,905
Provision for excess and obsolete inventory	(8,279)
	$134,523

The provision for excess and obsolete inventory is essentially a write-down of specific inventory items to their net realizable values.

Required:

1. Assume that the write-down relates to the values of specific items of raw materials. Prepare the journal entry to record the write-down of inventory costs. RIM uses a perpetual inventory system.

2. Assume that some of the raw materials that were written down on March 4, 2006 were not used for production purposes by March 3, 2007, the end of its 2007 fiscal year. The inventory items that were written down had an original cost of $9,347 and their net realizable value was $7,634. Changes in market conditions increased the net realizable values of these items to $9,563, which exceeded their original cost. How would this information be reflected in RIM's income statement for fiscal 2007 and its balance sheet at March 3, 2007? Explain.

■ **LO6**   **E8–17** **Analyzing and Interpreting the Inventory Turnover Ratio**

Gateway, Inc.

ANALYSIS

Gateway, Inc., competes with Dell in manufacturing and selling personal computers directly to customers. In recent years, it reported the following amounts (in millions).

Net sales revenue	$6,079
Cost of sales	5,241
Beginning inventory	315
Ending inventory	120

Required:

1. Determine the inventory turnover ratio and average days to sell inventory for the current year.

2. Explain the meaning of each of the amounts computed in requirement 1.

■ **LO6**   **E8–18** **Analyzing and Interpreting the Effects of the FIFO/Weighted Average Choice on Inventory Turnover Ratio**

ANALYSIS

The records at the end of January 2009 for All Star Company showed the following for a particular kind of merchandise:

Inventory, December 31, 2008, at FIFO: 19 units @ $12 = $228

Inventory, December 31, 2008, at weighted average: 19 units @ $10 = $190

Transactions	Units	Unit Cost	Total Cost
Purchase, January 9, 2009	25	15	$375
Purchase, January 20, 2009	50	16	800
Sale, January 11, 2009 (at $38 per unit)	40		
Sale, January 27, 2009 (at $39 per unit)	28		

Required:

Compute the inventory turnover ratio under the FIFO and weighted average inventory costing methods and a periodic inventory system (show computations and round to the nearest dollar). Explain which method you believe is the better indicator of the efficiency of inventory management?

E8–19 **Interpreting the Effect of Changes in Inventories and Accounts Payable on Cash Flow from Operations**

■ **LO6**

First Team Sports, Inc.

First Team Sports, Inc., is engaged in the manufacture (through independent contractors) and distribution of in-line roller skates, ice skates, street hockey equipment, and related accessory products. Its recent annual report included the following on its balance sheet:

ANALYSIS

CONSOLIDATED BALANCE SHEETS
February 29, 2008, and February 28, 2007

	2008	2007
. . . .		
Inventory (Note 3)	22,813,850	20,838,171
. . . .		
Trade accounts payable	9,462,883	9,015,376

Required:

Explain the effects of the changes in inventory and trade accounts payable in 2008 on cash flow from operating activities for 2008.

E8–20 **(Supplement A) Recording Sales and Purchases with Cash Discounts**

A. The Cycle Shop sells merchandise on credit terms of 2/10, n/30. Merchandise that cost $500 was sold to Claudette Labelle on February 1, 2009, at $800. The company uses the gross method of recording sales discounts.

Required:

1. Prepare the journal entry to record the credit sale. Assume that the company uses the perpetual inventory system.

2. Prepare the journal entry to record the collection of cash from C. Labelle. Assume that the cash was received on (a) February 9, 2009, and (b) March 2, 2009.

B. On March 4, 2009, the Cycle Shop purchased bicycles and accessories from a supplier on credit for $8,000; the terms were 1/15, n/30. The company uses the gross method to record purchases.

Required:

3. Prepare the journal entry to record the purchase on credit. Assume that the company uses the perpetual inventory system.

4. Prepare the journal entry to record the payment of the invoice, assuming that the cash was paid on (a) March 12, 2009, and (b) March 28, 2009.

E8–21 **(Supplement B) Analyzing the Financial Statement Effects of Inventory Costing Methods in a Perpetual Inventory System**

Refer to the information related to Product 2 in E8–11. Assume that Lunar Company uses a perpetual inventory system.

Required:

1. Prepare an income statement for 2008 through pretax income, showing the detailed computation of cost of goods sold under each of the following inventory costing methods:

   a. Case A: FIFO.

   b. Case B: LIFO.

   c. Case C: Moving average.

   For each case, show the computation of the ending inventory. (*Hint:* Set up adjacent columns, one for each case.)

2. Compare the pretax income and the ending inventory amounts among the three cases. Explain the similarities and differences.

3. Which inventory costing method may be preferred for income tax purposes? Explain.

4. Prepare journal entries to record transactions (*b*) through (*e*), as well as the cost of goods sold at December 31, 2008, assuming that Lunar uses LIFO for inventory costing.

■ **LO4**

Ford Motor Company

E8–22 (Supplement B) Analyzing Notes to Adjust Inventory from LIFO to FIFO

The following note was contained in a Ford Motor Company annual report:

> **Inventory Valuation—Automotive.** Inventories are stated at the lower of cost or market. The cost of most U.S. inventories is determined by the last-in, first-out ("LIFO") method. The cost of the remaining inventories is determined substantially by the first-in, first-out ("FIFO") method.
>
> If FIFO were the only method of inventory accounting used by the company, inventories would have been $1,235 million higher than reported this year and $1,246 million higher than reported last year.

The major classes of inventory for the company's automotive business segment at December 31 were as follows:

	Inventory (in $ millions)	
	Current Year	Previous Year
Finished products	$3,413.8	$3,226.7
Raw material and work in process	2,983.9	2,981.6
Supplies	419.1	429.9
Total	$6,816.8	$6,638.2

Required:

1. Determine the ending inventory that would have been reported in the current year if Ford had used only FIFO.

2. The cost of goods sold reported by Ford for the current year was $74,315 million. Determine the cost of goods sold that would have been reported if Ford had used only FIFO for both years.

PROBLEMS

■ **LO1**

P8–1 Analyzing Items to Be Included in Inventory

Reggie Company has just completed a physical inventory count at year-end, December 31, 2009. Only the items on the shelves, in storage, and in the receiving area were counted and costed on a FIFO basis. The inventory amounted to $55,000. During the audit, the auditor developed the following additional information:

a. Goods costing $500 were being used by a customer on a trial basis and were excluded from the inventory count at December 31, 2009.

b. Goods costing $600 were in transit on December 31, 2009, with terms F.O.B. destination. Because these goods had not arrived, they were excluded from the physical inventory count.

c. On December 31, 2009, goods in transit to customers, with terms F.O.B. shipping point, amounted to $1,000 (the expected delivery date was January 10, 2010). Because the goods had been shipped, they were excluded from the physical inventory count.

d. On December 28, 2009, a customer purchased goods for $2,000 cash and left them "for pick-up on January 3, 2010." The cost of goods sold totalled $1,200 and was included in the physical inventory count because the goods were still on hand.

e. On the date of the inventory count, the company received notice from a supplier that goods ordered earlier at a cost of $2,200 had been delivered to the transportation company on December 27, 2009; the terms were F.O.B. shipping point. Because the shipment had not arrived by December 31, 2009, it was excluded from the physical inventory count.

f. On December 31, 2009, the company shipped goods to a customer, F.O.B. destination. The goods, which cost $950, are not expected to arrive at their destination before January 8,

2010. Because the goods were not on hand, they were not included in the physical inventory count.

g. One of the items sold by the company has such a low volume that the management planned to drop it last year. To induce Reggie Company to continue carrying the item, the manufacturer-supplier provided the item on a "consignment basis." This means that the manufacturer-supplier retains ownership of the item, and Reggie Company (the consignee) has no responsibility to pay for the items until they are sold to customers. Each month, Reggie Company sends a report to the manufacturer on the number sold and remits cash for the cost. At the end of December 2009, Reggie Company had five of these items on hand; therefore, they were included in the physical inventory count at $1,000 each.

Required:
Assume that Reggie's accounting policy requires including in inventory all goods for which it has title. Note that the point where title (ownership) changes hands is determined by the shipping terms in the sales contract. When goods are shipped "F.O.B. shipping point," title changes hands at shipment and the buyer normally pays for shipping. When they are shipped "F.O.B. destination," title changes hands on delivery, and the seller normally pays for shipping. Begin with the $55,000 inventory amount and compute the correct amount for the ending inventory. Explain the basis for your treatment of each of the preceding items. (*Hint:* Set up three columns: Item, Amount, and Explanation.)

P8–2   Analyzing and Interpreting the Effects of Inventory Errors (AP8–1)

The income statements for four consecutive years for Clement Company reflected the following summarized amounts:

■ LO2

	2011	2010	2009	2008
Sales revenue	$58,000	$62,000	$51,000	$50,000
Cost of goods sold	37,000	43,000	35,000	32,500
Gross profit	21,000	19,000	16,000	17,500
Operating expenses	12,000	14,000	12,000	10,000
Pretax income	$ 9,000	$ 5,000	$ 4,000	$ 7,500

Subsequent to the development of these amounts, it has been determined that the physical inventory taken on December 31, 2009, was understated by $3,000.

Required:

1. Revise the income statements to reflect the correct amounts, taking into consideration the inventory error.

2. Compute the gross profit percentage for each year (a) before the correction and (b) after the correction. Do the results lend confidence to your corrected amounts? Explain.

3. What effect would the error have had on the income tax expense, assuming an average tax rate of 30 percent?

P8–3   Analyzing the Effects of Three Alternative Inventory Methods (AP8–2)

Allsigns Company uses a periodic inventory system. The company's accounting records for the most popular item in inventory showed the following details:

■ LO3

Transactions	Units	Unit Cost
Beginning inventory, January 1, 2010	400	$30
Transactions during 2010:		
a. Purchase, February 20	600	32
b. Sale, April 1 ($46 each)	(700)	
c. Purchase, June 30	500	36
d. Sale, August 1 ($46 each)	(100)	
e. Sales return, August 5 (related to Transaction [d])	20	

Required:
Compute (a) the cost of goods available for sale during 2010, (b) the cost of ending inventory at December 31, 2010, and (c) the cost of goods sold for 2010, under each of the following inventory costing methods (show computations and round to the nearest dollar):

1. Weighted-average cost.
2. First-in, first-out.
3. Specific identification, assuming that the company is permitted to use it and that one-fifth of the units sold on April 1, 2010 was selected from the beginning inventory and four-fifths were taken from the purchase of February 20, 2010. Assume that the sale of August 1, 2010 was selected from the purchase of June 30, 2010.

As a shareholder, which of these three methods would you prefer?

■ **LO2**

P8–4   Evaluating Three Alternative Inventory Methods Based on Income and Cash Flow

At the end of January 2008, the records of Regina Company showed the following for a particular item that sold at $18 per unit:

Transactions	Units	Amount
Inventory, January 1, 2008	500	$2,500
Sale, January 10	(400)	
Purchase, January 12	600	3,600
Sale, January 17	(300)	
Purchase, January 26	160	1,280

Required:

1. Assuming the use of a perpetual inventory system, prepare a summarized income statement through gross profit on sales under each of the following inventory costing methods: (a) weighted-average cost, (b) FIFO, and (c) specific identification. For specific identification, assume that the first sale was out of the beginning inventory and the second sale was out of the January 12 purchase. Show the inventory computations in detail.
2. Which method would result in:
   a. the highest pretax income?
   b. the lowest income tax expense?
   c. the more favourable cash flow? Explain.
3. Prepare journal entries to record the transactions that occurred in January 2008, assuming that FIFO is used for inventory costing.

■ **LO2**

P8–5   Evaluating the FIFO/Weighted Average Choice When Costs Are Rising and Falling

Income is to be evaluated under four different situations as follows:

a. Prices are rising:
   1. Situation A: FIFO is used.   2. Situation B: Weighted average is used.
b. Prices are falling:
   1. Situation C: FIFO is used.   2. Situation D: Weighted average is used.

The basic data common to all four situations are sales, 500 units for $12,500; beginning inventory, 300 units; purchases, 400 units; ending inventory, 200 units; and operating expenses, $4,000. The following tabulated income statements for each situation have been set up for analytical purposes:

	Prices Rising		Prices Falling	
	Situation A FIFO	Situation B Weighted Average	Situation C FIFO	Situation D Weighted Average
Sales revenue	$12,500	$12,500	$12,500	$12,500
Cost of goods sold				
Beginning inventory	3,600	?	?	?
Purchases	5,200	?	?	?
Cost of goods available for sale	8,800	?	?	?
Ending inventory	2,600	?	?	?
Cost of goods sold	6,200	?	?	?
Gross profit	6,300	?	?	?
Operating expenses	4,000	4,000	4,000	4,000
Pretax income	2,300	?	?	?
Income tax expense (30%)	690	?	?	?
Net income	$ 1,610			

Required:

1. Complete the preceding tabulation for each situation. In Situations A and B (prices rising), assume the following: beginning inventory, 300 units at $12 = $3,600; purchases, 400 units at $13 = $5,200. In Situations C and D (prices falling), assume the opposite; that is, beginning inventory, 300 units at $13 = $3,900; purchases, 400 units at $12 = $4,800. Use periodic inventory procedures.

2. Analyze and discuss the relative effects on pretax income and on net income as demonstrated by requirement 1 when prices are rising and when prices are falling.

3. Discuss the relative effects, if any, on the cash position for each situation.

4. Would you recommend FIFO or weighted average? Explain.

P8–6 Evaluating the Effects of Inventory Costing Methods on Financial Statement Elements ■ **LO4**
(AP8–3)

Neverstop Corporation sells item A as part of its product line. Information about the beginning inventory, purchases, and sales of item A are given in the following table for the first six months of 2009. The company uses a periodic inventory system.

	Purchases		Sales	
Date	Number of Units	Unit Cost	Number of Units	Sales Price
January 1 (beginning inventory)	500	$2.50		
January 24			300	$4.00
February 8	600	$2.60		
March 16			560	$4.20
June 11	300	$2.75		

Required:

1. Compute the cost of ending inventory using the weighted-average costing method.

2. Compute the gross profit for the first six months of 2009 using the FIFO costing method.

3. Would the gross profit be higher, lower, or the same if Neverstop used the weighted-average costing method rather than the FIFO method? Explain. No calculations are required.

4. Prepare journal entries to record the purchase and sale transactions, as well as the cost of goods sold assuming that the weighted-average method is used.

5. Assume that due to a clerical error, the ending inventory is reported to be 440 units rather than the actual number of units (540) on hand. If FIFO is used, calculate the amount of the understatement or overstatement in
   a. the cost of goods sold for the first six months of 2009.
   b. the current assets at June 30, 2009.

P8–7 Evaluating the Income Statement and Cash Flow Effects of Lower of Cost and Net Realizable Value ■ **LO5**

Smart Company prepared its annual financial statements dated December 31, 2008. The company applies the FIFO inventory costing method; however, the company neglected to apply LCNRV to the ending inventory. The preliminary 2008 income statement follows:

Sales revenue		$280,000
Cost of goods sold		
Beginning inventory	$ 30,000	
Purchases	182,000	
Cost of goods available for sale	212,000	
Ending inventory (FIFO cost)	44,000	
Cost of goods sold		168,000
Gross profit		112,000
Operating expenses		61,000
Pretax income		51,000
Income tax expense (30%)		15,300
Net income		$ 35,700

Assume that you have been asked to restate the 2008 financial statements to incorporate the LCNRV inventory valuation rule. You have developed the following data relating to the ending inventory at December 31, 2008:

Item	Quantity	Acquisition Cost Unit	Acquisition Cost Total	Net Realizable Value (Market)
A	3,000	$3	$ 9,000	$4
B	1,500	4	6,000	2
C	7,000	2	14,000	4
D	3,000	5	15,000	3
			$44,000	

Required:

1. Restate the income statement to reflect the valuation of the ending inventory on December 31, 2008, at the lower of cost and net realizable value. Apply the LCNRV rule on an item-by-item basis and show computations.

2. Compare and explain the LCNRV effect on each amount that was changed in requirement 1.

3. What is the conceptual basis for applying LCNRV to merchandise inventories?

4. What effect (increase, decrease, no effect) did the LCNRV rule have on the cash flow for 2008? What will be the long-term effect on cash flow (increase, decrease, no effect)? Computations are not necessary.

■ **LO5**

ANALYSIS

P8–8 Evaluating the Effects of Manufacturing Changes on Inventory Turnover Ratio and Cash Flows from Operating Activities (AP8–4)

H.–T. Tan and Company has been operating for five years as an electronics component manufacturer specializing in cellular phone components. During this period, it has experienced rapid growth in sales revenue and in inventory. Mr. Tan and his associates have hired you as the company's first corporate controller. You have put into place new purchasing and manufacturing procedures that are expected to reduce inventories by approximately one-third by year-end. You have gathered the following data related to the changes:

	(in thousands) Beginning of Year	(in thousands) End of Year (projected)
Inventory	$463,808	$310,270
		Current Year (projected)
Cost of goods sold		$7,015,069

Required:

1. Compute the inventory turnover ratio based on two different assumptions:

   a. Those presented in the preceding table (a decrease in the balance in inventory).

   b. No change from the beginning of the year in the inventory balance.

2. Compute the effect of the projected change in the balance in inventory on cash flow from operating activities for the year (show the sign and amount of the effect).

3. On the basis of the preceding analysis, write a brief memo explaining how an increase in inventory turnover can result in an increase in cash flow from operating activities. Also explain how this increase can benefit the company.

P8–9 **(Supplement A) Recording Sales and Purchases with Cash Discounts and Returns**
(AP8–5)

Campus Stop, Incorporated, is a student co-op. On January 1, 2009, the beginning inventory was $150,000, the Accounts Receivable balance was $4,000, and the Allowance for Doubtful Accounts had a credit balance of $800. Campus Stop uses a perpetual inventory system and records inventory purchases using the gross method.

The following transactions (summarized) occurred during 2009:

a.	Sold merchandise for cash (cost of sales $137,500)	$275,000
b.	Received merchandise returned by customers as unsatisfactory and paid a cash refund (cost of sales $800)	1,600
c.	Purchased merchandise from vendors on credit; terms 3/10, n/30 as follows:	
	(*i*) August Supply Company invoice price before deduction of cash discount	5,000
	(*ii*) Other vendors, invoice price before deduction of cash discount	120,000
d.	Purchased equipment for use in store; paid cash	2,200
e.	Purchased office supplies for future use in the store; paid cash	700
f.	Freight on merchandise purchased; paid cash	400
g.	Paid accounts payable in full during the period as follows:	
	(*i*) Paid August Supply Company after the discount period	5,000
	(*ii*) Paid other vendors within the 3% discount period	116,400

Required:
Prepare journal entries for each of the preceding transactions.

P8–10 **(Supplement B) Analyzing and Interpreting Income Manipulation Under the LIFO Inventory Method**

LO3, 4

ANALYSIS

Pacific Company sells electronic test equipment that it acquires from a foreign source. During the year 2009, the inventory records reflected the following:

	Units	Unit Cost	Total Cost
Beginning inventory	15	$12,000	$180,000
Purchases	40	13,000	520,000
Sales (45 units at $25,000 each)			

Inventory is valued at cost using the LIFO inventory method. On December 28, 2009, the unit cost of the test equipment increased to $14,000. The cost will increase again during the first quarter of the next year.

Required:

1. Complete the following income statement summary and ending inventory using the LIFO method and the periodic inventory system (show computations):

Sales revenue	$_____
Cost of goods sold	_____
Gross profit	_____
Operating expenses	300,000
Pretax income	$_____
Ending inventory	$_____

2. Pacific's management is considering the purchase of 20 additional units before December 31, 2009, at $14,000 each. Restate the income statement for the year, assuming the purchase of these 20 units.

3. Assume that you are the manager responsible for purchasing these 20 additional units, and that your annual bonus is based on Pacific's net income for the year. Would you purchase these 20 units before the end of 2009? Explain.

4. Assume that Pacific did not purchase additional test equipment, and that the market price per unit dropped suddenly to $12,500 because of oversupply. At what amount would the ending inventory be shown on the company's balance sheet? Would this amount be different if Pacific used FIFO instead of LIFO? Explain.

■ **LO4**

P8–11 **(Supplement B) Evaluating the FIFO to LIFO Change from a Shareholder's Perspective**

Allendale Corporation reported the following summarized annual data at the end of 2010:

	(millions)
Sales revenue	$850
Cost of goods sold*	400
Gross profit	450
Operating expenses	310
Pretax income	$140

*Based on ending FIFO inventory of $120 million. On a LIFO basis, this ending inventory would have been $75 million.

Before issuing the preceding statement, the company decided to change from FIFO to LIFO for 2010 because "it better reflects our operating results." The company has always used FIFO.

Required:

1. Restate the summary income statement on a LIFO basis.

2. How much did pretax income change due to the LIFO decision for 2010? What caused the change in pretax income?

3. If you were a shareholder, what would be your reaction to this change? Explain.

P8–12 **(Supplement B) Evaluating the Effects of Perpetual Inventory Costing Methods on Financial Statement Elements**

This problem is an extension of P8–6. Neverstop Corporation sells item A as part of its product line. Information about the beginning inventory, purchases, and sales of item A are given in the following table for the first six months of 2009. The company uses a perpetual inventory system.

Date	Purchases		Sales	
	Number of Units	Unit Cost	Number of Units	Sales Price
January 1 (beginning inventory)	500	$2.50		
January 24			300	$4.00
February 8	600	$2.60		
March 16			560	$4.20
June 11	300	$2.75		

Required:

1. Compute the cost of ending inventory using the moving average costing method.

2. Compute the gross profit for the first six months of 2009 using the FIFO costing method.

3. Would the gross profit be higher, lower, or the same if Neverstop used the LIFO costing method rather than the FIFO method? Explain. No calculations are required.

4. Prepare journal entries to record the purchase and sale transactions, assuming that the FIFO method is used.

5. Compare your answers to the requirements above to your answers to the corresponding requirements in P8-6 and comment on the differences, if any. Explain why the gross profit under perpetual LIFO differs from the gross profit under periodic LIFO.

ALTERNATE PROBLEMS

AP8–1 **Analyzing and Interpreting the Effects of Inventory Errors (P8–2)**

■ **LO2**

The income statement for Sherwood Company summarized for a four-year period shows the following:

	2010	2009	2008	2007
Sales revenue	$3,000,000	$2,500,000	$2,400,000	$2,000,000
Cost of goods sold	2,100,000	1,780,000	1,630,000	1,400,000
Gross profit	900,000	720,000	770,000	600,000
Operating expenses	550,000	520,000	500,000	450,000
Pretax income	350,000	200,000	270,000	150,000
Income tax expense (30%)	105,000	60,000	81,000	45,000
Net income	$ 245,000	$ 140,000	$ 189,000	$ 105,000

An audit revealed that in determining these amounts, the ending inventory for 2008 was overstated by $20,000. The company uses a periodic inventory system.

Required:

1. Revise these income statements to reflect the correct amounts.

2. Did the error affect the cumulative net income for the four-year period? Explain.

3. What effect would the error have had on the income tax expense, assuming a 30-percent tax rate?

AP8–2 **Analyzing the Effects of Four Alternative Inventory Methods (P8–3)**

■ **LO3**

Yared Company uses a periodic inventory system. The company's accounting records for the most popular item in inventory showed the following details:

Transactions	Units	Unit Cost
Beginning inventory, January 1, 2009	1,800	$2.50
Transactions during 2009:		
a. Purchase, January 30	2,500	3.10
b. Sale, March 14 ($5 each)	(1,450)	
c. Purchase, May 1	1,200	4.00
d. Sale, August 31 ($5 each)	(1,900)	

Required:

Compute (a) the cost of goods available for sale during 2009, (b) the cost of ending inventory at December 31, 2009, and (c) the cost of goods sold for 2009, under each of the following inventory costing methods (show computations and round to the nearest dollar):

1. Weighted-average cost.

2. First-in, first-out.

3. Specific identification, assuming that the company is permitted to use it and that two-fifths of the units sold on March 14, 2009 were selected from the beginning inventory and three-fifths from the purchase of January 30, 2009. Assume that the sale of August 31, 2009 was selected from the remainder of the beginning inventory, with the balance from the purchase of May 1, 2009.

4. As a shareholder, which of these three methods would you prefer?

■ **LO4**   **AP8–3 Evaluating the Effects of Inventory Costing Methods on Financial Statement Elements**
(P8–6)

The Sportex Company, a diversified distribution outlet for sporting goods, purchases cartons of tennis balls from the Ball Corporation and markets the balls under the Sportex name. Purchases and sales data for January 2008, the first month of operations, are provided below.

	Date	Number of Cartons	Total Cost	Amount of Invoice
Purchases:	January 2	800	$16,000	
	January 19	600	13,200	
	January 29	500	11,000	
Sales:	January 5	500		$20,000
	January 21	700		29,200

Sportex uses a perpetual inventory system.

Required:

1. Compute the cost of goods sold in January 2008 using FIFO.

2. Compute the cost of ending inventory at January 31, 2008, assuming that Sportex uses the weighted-average cost method. (Round your calculation of the average cost to the nearest cent.)

3. Would the computation you made in requirements 1 and 2 change if the company used a periodic inventory system? Explain.

■ **LO6**   **AP8–4 Evaluating the Effects of Failed Expansion Plans on Inventory Turnover Ratio and**

Arctic Enterprises

ANALYSIS

Cash Flows from Operating Activities (P8–8)

Arctic Enterprises, Inc., was the world's second-largest manufacturer of snowmobiles and had experienced exceptional growth in recent years. It planned for a major increase in sales in the following period by increasing production dramatically. Unfortunately, North America experienced less snow that year than in any of the preceding 20 years. As a consequence, sales remained flat, and Arctic reported a small profit of $1.9 million. However, its inventory balance increased by $24 million. Based on the following information, answer the questions that follow:

	(in thousands)	
	Beginning of Year	End of Year
Inventory	$23,808	$47,270
		Current Year
Cost of goods sold		$161,069

Required:

1. Compute the inventory turnover ratio based on two different assumptions:
   a. Those presented in the preceding table.
   b. No change from the beginning of the year in the inventory balance.

2. Compute the effect of the change in the balance in inventory on cash flow from operating activities for the year (show the sign and amount of the effect).

3. On the basis of your analysis, write a brief memo explaining how a decrease in inventory turnover can result in a decrease in cash flow from operating activities.

AP8–5 (Supplement A) Recording Sales and Purchases with Cash Discounts and Returns
(P8–9)

The following transactions were selected from those occurring during the month of January 2010 for Dan's Store, Incorporated. A wide line of goods is offered for sale. Credit sales are extended to a few select customers; the usual credit terms are n/EOM. The cost of sales is always one-half of the gross sales price.

a. Sales to customers:

Cash	$228,000
On credit	72,000

b. Unsatisfactory merchandise returned by customers:

Cash	3,000
Credit	2,000

c. Purchased merchandise from vendors on credit; terms 2/10, n/30:

(*i*) Amount billed by Amy Supply Company	4,000
(*ii*) Amount billed by other vendors	68,000

d. Freight on merchandise purchased; paid cash	1,500
e. Collections on accounts receivable	36,000

f. Paid accounts payable in full during the period as follows:

(*i*) Amy Supply Company after the discount period	4,000
(*ii*) Paid other vendors within the discount period	66,640

g. Purchased two new typewriters for the office; paid cash	1,000

Required:
Prepare journal entries for these transactions, assuming that a perpetual inventory system is used. Record inventory purchases using the gross method.

CASES AND PROJECTS

FINDING AND INTERPRETING FINANCIAL INFORMATION

CP8–1 Finding Financial Information

Refer to the Online Learning Centre Web site at **www.mcgrawhill.ca/olc/libby/student/ resources** for the financial statements of The Forzani Group Ltd. (FGL).

1. How much inventory does the company own at the end of the current year?
2. Estimate the amount of inventory that the company purchased and produced during the current year. (*Hint:* Use the cost of goods sold equation.)
3. What method does the company use to determine the cost of its inventory?
4. What was the change in inventory? How did it affect net cash provided by operating activities for the current year?

■ LO1, 3

The Forzani Group

ANALYSIS

CP8–2 Finding Financial Information

Refer to the financial statements of Van Houtte Inc. given in Appendix B at the end of this book.

1. What method does the company use to determine the cost of its inventory?
2. What are the components of the company's inventory balance? What aspects of its operations might determine why the last component is the largest?
3. Compute Van Houtte's inventory turnover ratio for the year ended March 31, 2007. Assume that Van Houtte's cost of sales is $198 million.

■ LO1, 3, 6

Van Houtte

ANALYSIS

CP8–3 Comparing Companies

Refer to the Online Learning Centre Web site at **www.mcgrawhill.ca/olc/libby/student/ resources** for the financial statements of The Forzani Group Ltd. and to Appendix B of this book for the financial statements of Van Houtte Inc.

Required:

1. Compute the inventory turnover ratio for both companies for the current year. What would you infer from the difference? Assume that Van Houtte's cost of sales is $198 million.
2. Both companies measure inventory at the lower of cost or market. However, one of the companies determines cost of inventory using the average cost method while the other uses FIFO. Would you expect the different methods to cause a large difference in cost of goods sold? Why?

■ LO6

Van Houtte vs.
The Forzani Group

ANALYSIS

FINANCIAL REPORTING AND ANALYSIS CASES

■ LO2   **CP8–4   Interpreting the Financial Press**

The Wall Street Journal

In an article entitled "Convenient Fiction: Inventory Chicanery Tempts More Firms, Fools More Auditors," *The Wall Street Journal* outlined a series of cases in which companies used inventory fraud to overstate earnings. The article is available on the Online Learning Centre Web site at **www.mcgrawhill.ca/olc/libby/student/resources**. Read the article and then write a short memo outlining the cases involved and how each of the inventory misstatements inflated earnings. Each case involved inflating ending inventory quantities or values. Indicate how doing so increases earnings. Also discuss the steps the author suggests that auditors should take to avoid such misstatements in the future.

■ LO2, 3, 6   CP8–5   Using Financial Reports: Analyzing Reported Information

Alimentation
Couche-Tard

ANALYSIS

Alimentation Couche-Tard is the third-largest convenience store operator in North America. It has more than 5,000 outlets: Couche-Tard in eastern Canada; Mac's in central and western Canada; and Circle K in the U.S. The following table includes selected information from its financial statements (amounts in millions of US dollars).

	Year Ended April 29, 2007	Year Ended April 30, 2006	Year Ended April 24, 2005
Revenues	12,087.4	10,157.3	8,036.8
Cost of goods sold	10,082.9	8,365.8	6,479.0
Earnings before income taxes	310.3	297.7	228.5
Income tax expense	113.9	101.5	73.3
Accounts receivable	199.0	153.0	109.7
Inventories	382.1	322.3	295.4
Accounts payable	537.0	494.1	435.4

Required:

1. Compute the following amounts for each of the fiscal years 2006 and 2007:
   a. Collections from customers.
   b. Purchases of merchandise from suppliers.
   c. Payments to suppliers.
   d. The accounts receivable turnover ratio and the average collection period.
   e. The inventory turnover ratio and the average period to sell inventory.
   f. The average period for conversion of inventories into cash.

2. The company uses the indirect method to report its cash flows from operations. How would the changes in accounts receivable, inventory, and accounts payable be reported in the operating activities section of its cash flow statement for 2007?

3. In the notes to its financial statements, the company states that the cost of merchandise is determined according to the first-in first-out method. Would you expect the company's net income to increase or decrease if it used the weighted-average costing method instead of FIFO? Explain.

4. Assume that the company purchased canned products from a local supplier on April 29, 2007 with terms F.O.B. Shipping point. The merchandise, at a cost of $1,400, had not arrived at the company's warehouse until May 1, and was not included in the inventory count at year-end. What effect would this error have on the company's net income for 2007? Show calculations.

■ LO 2, 3, 6   CP8–6   Using Financial Reports: Analyzing Reported Information

ANALYSIS

Geox S.p.A. is an Italy-based company active in the footwear and apparel manufacturing industry, which includes classic, casual, and sports footwear, as well as apparel for men, women, and children. The company's products are sold in over 70 countries worldwide through a widespread distribution network. Geox prepares its financial statements in accordance with the International Financial Reporting Standards. The following table includes selected information from its financial statements (amounts in millions of euros).

	2006	2005	2004
Net sales	612.3	454.9	340.1
Cost of sales	302.0	214.5	156.8
Earnings before income taxes	133.9	106.1	68.4
Income tax expense	36.7	30.9	15.7
Accounts receivable	84.2	74.5	57.5
Inventories	131.0	107.8	77.9
Accounts payable	96.9	84.7	61.9

Required:

1. Compute the following amounts for each of the fiscal years 2005 and 2006:
   a. Collections from customers.
   b. Purchases of merchandise from suppliers. Assume for simplicity that the company buys its products from other manufacturers.
   c. Payments to suppliers.
   d. Accounts receivable turnover ratio and the average collection period.
   e. Inventory turnover ratio and the average period to sell inventory.
   f. Average period for conversion of inventories into cash.

2. The company uses the indirect method to report its cash flows from operations. How would the changes in accounts receivable, inventory, and accounts payable be reported in the operating activities section of its cash flow statement for 2006?

3. In the notes to its financial statements, the company states that the cost of merchandise is determined by using the weighted-average costing method. Would you expect the company's net income to increase or decrease if it used FIFO instead of weighted-average cost? Explain.

4. Assume that the company purchased goods from a supplier in the Far East with terms F.O.B. Destination point. These goods, which cost €1.2 million, were shipped on December 24, 2006 but had not arrived by December 31. The company's accountant included the cost of these goods in inventory at year-end. Is that an error? If so, what effect would this error have on the company's net income for 2006? Show calculations.

CP8–7 Analyzing and Interpreting the Inventory Turnover Ratio

■ **LO6**

Loblaw Companies Ltd. and Shoppers Drug Mart Corporation are two companies operating in the same industry. Starting in 2004, Loblaw expanded the scope of the goods it sold from primarily food to include pharmaceutical items, cosmetics, appliances, home entertainment products, and items for use at home. At the same time, Shoppers expanded the scope of the goods it sold from primarily items for use at home, pharmaceutical products, and electronic goods such as digital cameras to include food items, excluding fresh fruit and vegetables. These changes affected the type of inventory items carried by both companies.

ANALYSIS

Selected financial statement information over the five-year period 2002–2006 is presented below.

	2006	2005	2004	2003	2002
Loblaw Companies Ltd.					
Sales	$28,640	$27,801	$26,209	$25,220	$23,082
Cost of sales, selling and administrative expenses	26,917	25,716	24,084	23,360	21,425
Inventory	2,037	2,020	1,821	1,746	1,702
Shoppers Drug Mart Corp.					
Revenue	$ 7,786	$ 7,151	$ 6,566	$ 4,415	$ 4,019
Cost of goods sold and Other operating expenses	6,958	6,431	5,928	3,847	3,518
Inventory	1,372	1,217	1,136	293	268

Neither company disclosed its cost of sales separately. However, the industry average indicates that the cost of sales represents 77 percent of revenue, on average.

Required:

1. Compute the inventory turnover ratio and the average number of days to sell inventory for each company for the years 2003–2006.

2. In your opinion, which of these two companies was more efficient in managing its inventory subsequent to the change in the line of products they sell? Explain.

CRITICAL THINKING CASES

▪ LO2

ANALYSIS

CP8–8   Evaluating the Use of a Perpetual Inventory System to Control Theft

The president of National Wholesalers suspected that employees are stealing several items of merchandise, particularly items that are sufficiently small enough to hide in clothing. The president's suspicions resulted from complaints made in April by several retailers who claimed that shortages were frequently found when orders of financial and programmable calculators were inspected upon receipt.

The assistant controller was asked to provide whatever information might prove helpful in identifying the extent of any problem that might have developed since the end of the previous fiscal year on December 31. The following report was submitted on May 1.

	Financial Calculators	Programmable Calculators
Number of units in inventory on December 31 per physical count....	19,600	7,600
Cost per unit..	$ 8.40	$29.25
Number of units purchased since January 1:		
January..	4,200	1,400
February...	2,600	3,100
March...	5,100	2,700
April..	2,700	1,800
Total..	15,600	9,000
Average cost per unit of purchases since January 1......................	$8.40	30.00
Average gross profit percentage on merchandise billed to retailers...	30%	25%
Sales recorded from January 1 to April 30.................................	$343,200	$496,400
Number of units physically counted in the warehouse on April 30.....	6,400	3,900

Required:

1. Compute the number of units of each type of merchandise that are unaccounted for on May 1. The company uses a periodic inventory system and the weighted average inventory costing method.

2. Determine the monetary value of the apparent loss.

3. Assuming that the apparent loss realized during the period January 1–April 30 is representative of the loss that might be realized on these two items during an entire year, would you recommend that: (a) a new inventory system be installed in the warehouse at an annual cost of $4,000 to maintain perpetual inventory records of these two items of merchandise, and (b) a quarterly physical inventory count of these items be implemented at an additional cost of $1,000 per quarterly count? Show supporting computations.

▪ LO2

Micro Warehouse

ANALYSIS

CP8–9   Evaluating an Ethical Dilemma: Earnings, Inventory Purchases, and Management Bonuses

Micro Warehouse is a computer software and hardware online and catalogue sales company. A *Wall Street Journal* article disclosed the following:

MICRO WAREHOUSE IS REORGANIZING TOP MANAGEMENT

Micro Warehouse Inc. announced a "significant reorganization" of its management, including the resignation of three senior executives.

The move comes just a few weeks after the Norwalk, Conn., computer catalogue sales company said it overstated earnings by $28 million since 1992 as a result of accounting irregularities. That previous disclosure prompted a flurry of shareholder lawsuits against the company. In addition, Micro Warehouse said it is cooperating with an "informal inquiry" by the Securities and Exchange Commission.

Source: Stephan E. Frank, *The Wall Street Journal,* November 21, 1996, p. B2.

Its quarterly report filed with the Securities and Exchange Commission two days before indicated that inaccuracies involving understatement of purchases and accounts payable in current and prior periods amounted to $47.3 million. It also indicated that, as a result, $2.2 million of executive bonuses for 1995 would be cancelled. Micro Warehouse's effective tax rate is approximately 40.4 percent. Both cost of goods sold and executive bonuses are fully deductible for tax purposes.

Required:
As a new staff member at Micro Warehouse's auditing firm, you are assigned to write a memo outlining the effects of the understatement of purchases and the cancellation of the bonuses. In your report, be sure to include the following:

1. The total effect on pretax and after-tax earnings of the understatement of purchases.

2. The total effect on pretax and after-tax earnings of the cancellation of the bonuses.

3. An estimate of the percentage of after-tax earnings that management is receiving in bonuses.

4. A discussion of why Micro Warehouse's board of directors may have decided to tie managers' compensation to reported earnings and the possible relationship between this type of bonus scheme and the accounting errors.

CP8–10 (Supplement B) Making a Decision as a Financial Analyst: Analysis of the Effect of a Change to LIFO

An annual report for Quaker Oats included the following information:

■ **LO4**

Quaker Oats

ANALYSIS

The company adopted the LIFO cost flow assumption for valuing the majority of remaining U.S. Grocery Products inventories. The Company believes that the use of the LIFO method better matches current costs with current revenues. The cumulative effect of this change on retained earnings at the beginning of the year is not determinable, nor are the pro forma effects of retroactive application of LIFO to prior years. The effect of this change on the current year was to decrease net income by $16.0 million, or $0.20 per share.

Required:
As a new financial analyst at a leading investment banking firm, you are assigned to write a memo outlining the effects of the accounting change on Quaker's financial statements. Assume a 34-percent tax rate. In your report, be sure to discuss the following issues:

1. In addition to the reason that was cited, why did management adopt LIFO?

2. As an analyst, how would you react to the $0.20 per share decrease in income caused by the adoption of LIFO?

FINANCIAL REPORTING AND ANALYSIS TEAM PROJECT

ANALYSIS

■ **LO4**

CP8–11 **Team Project: Analyzing Inventories**

As a team, select an industry to analyze (industry lists can be found at **www.investor.reuters.com** and **www.hoovers.com**; click on "Companies and Industries"). Each team member should acquire the annual report for one publicly traded company in the industry, with each member selecting a different company. (Library files, the SEDAR service at **www.sedar.com**, or the company Web sites are good sources.)

Required:

On an individual basis, each team member should then write a short report answering the following questions about the selected company. Discuss any patterns across the companies that you as a team observe. Then, as a group, write a short report comparing and contrasting your companies.

1. If your company lists inventories on its balance sheet, what percentage is this asset of total assets for each of the last three years? If your company does not list inventories, discuss why this is so.

2. If your company lists inventories, what inventory costing method does it use? What do you think motivated this choice?

3. Ratio analysis:
   a. What does the inventory turnover ratio measure in general?
   b. If your company reports inventories, compute the ratio for the last three years.
   c. What do your results suggest about the company?
   d. If available, find the industry ratio for the most recent year, compare it to your results, and discuss why you believe your company differs or is similar to the industry ratio.

4. What is the effect of the change in inventories on cash flows from operations for the most recent year, that is, did the change increase or decrease operating cash flows? Explain your answer.

Reporting and Interpreting Property, Plant, and Equipment; Natural Resources; and Intangibles

9

After studying this chapter, you should be able to:

1. Define, classify, and explain the nature of long-term assets and interpret the fixed asset turnover ratio. p. 463

2. Apply the cost principle to measure the acquisition and maintenance of property, plant, and equipment. p. 465

3. Apply various amortization methods as assets are held and used over time. p. 470

4. Explain the effect of asset impairment on the financial statements. p. 482

5. Analyze the disposal of property, plant, and equipment. p. 483

6. Apply measurement and reporting concepts for natural resources and intangible assets. p. 486

7. Explain the impact on cash flows of the acquisition, use, and disposal of long-term assets. p. 491

FOCUS COMPANY:

WestJet Airlines

MANAGING PROFITS THROUGH

CONTROL OF PRODUCTIVE CAPACITY

WestJet Airlines, (www.westjet.com) Canada's second largest airline, provides low-fare, friendly service to 34 North American cities. Clive Beddoe, along with a small team of Calgary entrepreneurs, started up WestJet in 1996 with three Boeing 737-200 aircraft. In 1999, the company completed its initial public offering on the Toronto Stock Exchange. By the end of 2003, the company's fleet had grown to 44 aircraft, its property and equipment reached a value of $1.14 billion, and it had captured 25 percent of the travellers (or guests, as the company prefers to call its passengers) in the markets it serves. As the company purchases new aircraft it increases the number of available seat miles,[1] or capacity to serve its customers' travel requirements.

WestJet is a capital-intensive company with more than $2.1 billion in property and equipment reported on its balance sheet at December 31, 2006, representing over 75 percent of its total assets. In fiscal years 2004, 2005, and 2006, WestJet spent over $1.5 billion on aircraft and other flight equipment as it replaced old aircraft with newer, quieter, more fuel-efficient Boeing 737 aircraft. WestJet's expansion plan is part of a long-term strategy of controlled growth, financed by a combination of debt, equity, and cash generated from its operations.

Since the demand for air travel is seasonal, with peak demand occurring during the summer months, planning for optimal productive capacity in the airline industry is very difficult. WestJet's managers must determine how many aircraft are needed in which cities at what points in time to fill all seats demanded. Otherwise, the company loses revenue (not enough seats) or has higher costs (too many seats).

---

[1] An available seat mile is the number of miles a seat travels in a given period of time, whether or not it contains a passenger.

UNDERSTANDING THE BUSINESS

Running a business such as an airline, a resource extraction and processing organization, or a pharmaceuticals company means acquiring adequate property, plant facilities, and equipment that will provide the capacity to serve the customers' current and future needs. Airlines require aircraft, spare engines and parts, flight simulators, buildings, and equipment. Resource extraction, processing, and distribution companies such as Petro-Canada, the focus company in Chapters 10 and 11, require the property from which they extract raw resources, the plant facilities to process raw materials into refined products, and a distribution system to bring the refined products to the point of sale.

In contrast, pharmaceutical and biotechnology companies require the property, plant, and equipment to conduct research and manufacture their products, but more importantly, they require the know-how to discover and apply scientific information. The most prominent assets on a pharmaceutical company's balance sheet are usually intangible assets such as licences, brand names, and patents.

One of the major challenges facing managers of most businesses is forecasting the level of long-term productive capacity (that is, the size of the company's plant and equipment) it will need to produce specified revenue streams. If managers underestimate the level of capacity needed in the future, the company will not be able to produce goods or services that are in demand and will miss the opportunity to earn revenue. On the other hand, if managers overestimate the productive capacity needed, the company will incur excessive costs that will reduce its profitability.

The airline industry provides an outstanding example of the difficulty associated with planning for and analyzing its capacity to produce revenue. If an airline takes off from Calgary to Toronto with empty seats, the economic value associated with these seats is lost for that flight. There is obviously no way to sell the seat to a customer after the airplane has left the gate. Unlike a manufacturer, an airline cannot place seats in inventory for use on future flights.

Likewise, if a large number of people want to board a flight, the airline must turn away some customers if seats are not available. You might be willing to buy a television set from Future Shop even if you are told that it is out of stock and there will be a one-week delay in delivery. But you probably won't fly home for a holiday on an airline that would have you wait one week because no seats were available on its flights when you wanted to fly. You would simply pick another airline or use a different mode of transportation.

Much of the battle for passengers in the airline industry is fought in terms of property, plant, and equipment. Passengers want convenient schedules (which require a large number of aircraft) and they want to fly in new, modern airplanes. Because airlines have such a large investment in equipment with no opportunity to hold unused seats in inventory, they work hard to fill aircraft to capacity for each flight. The importance of filling aircraft with passengers is highlighted in the following excerpt from WestJet's annual report for 2005 (page 16).

REAL WORLD EXCERPT

WestJet Airlines

ANNUAL REPORT

MANAGEMENT'S DISCUSSION AND ANALYSIS OF FINANCIAL RESULTS
Revenues

In 2005, we increased capacity, as measured by available seat miles, by 19.1% and increased the number of revenue passenger miles ("RPMs") by 26.8% to 10.7 billion and 8.0 billion respectively compared to 9.0 billion and 6.3 billion in 2004. This performance resulted in an increased annual load factor from 70.0% in 2004 to 74.6% in 2005—a level not seen since 2001.[2]

Each flight not only generates revenue but also creates wear and tear on the equipment, no matter how many seats are filled. In pricing an airline ticket for a specific flight, WestJet's management includes an amount to cover this daily wear and tear that is part

---

[2]The load factor is a measure of total capacity utilization, calculated as the proportion of total available seats occupied by revenue passengers.

of the cost of operating an aircraft. The wear and tear is estimated and recorded as annual amortization expense. Industry practice is to assume that the lifetime of an aircraft is 20 years, during which companies like WestJet recover the acquisition cost of the aircraft and the related maintenance, operating, and financing costs, and turn a profit.

As you can see from this brief discussion, issues related to property, plant, and equipment have a pervasive impact on a company in terms of strategy, pricing decisions, and profitability. Business managers devote considerable time planning optimal levels of productive capacity adequate to meet expected future demand. Accountants estimate and report the cost of using these assets throughout their productive lives, taking into consideration applicable income tax laws and regulations, and financial analysts closely review financial statements to determine the impact of management decisions on the company's profitability and financial condition.

This chapter is organized according to the life cycle of long-term assets—acquisition, use, and disposal. First we will discuss the measuring and reporting issues related to land, buildings, and equipment. Then we will discuss the measurement and reporting issues for natural resources and intangible assets. Among the issues we will discuss are maintaining, using, and disposing of property and equipment over time and measuring and reporting assets considered impaired in their ability to generate future cash flows.

ORGANIZATION OF THE CHAPTER

Acquisition and Maintenance of Plant and Equipment	**Use, Impairment, and Disposal of Plant and Equipment**	**Natural Resources and Intangible Assets**
• Classification of Long-Term Assets • Fixed Asset Turnover Ratio • Measuring and Recording Acquisition Cost • Various Acquisition Methods • Repairs, Maintenance, and Betterments	• Amortization Concepts • Alternative Amortization Methods • Changes in Amortization Estimates • Managers' Selection Among Accounting Alternatives • Measuring Asset Impairment • Disposal of Property, Plant, and Equipment	• Acquisition and Depletion of Natural Resources • Acquisition and Amortization of Intangible Assets • Examples of Intangible Assets

ACQUISITION AND MAINTENANCE OF PLANT AND EQUIPMENT

Exhibit 9.1 shows the asset section of WestJet's balance sheet at December 31, 2005. Nearly 77 percent of WestJet's total assets are property and equipment. The company's annual report contains additional information about the cost of property, plant, and equipment owned or controlled by WestJet and related amortization; the amount of new investment in equipment during the year; and the amount of equipment that was sold or retired, as well as details of other long-term assets with probable long-term benefits. Let us begin by classifying these long-term assets.

CLASSIFICATION OF LONG-TERM ASSETS

Accountants use the terms **long-term assets, long-lived assets, or capital assets** to identify property, plant, equipment, and intangible properties held for production, rental to others, or administrative purposes, or for the development, construction, maintenance, or repair of other assets. Long-term assets are acquired, constructed, or developed for long-term use on a continuing basis. They are not normally sold to generate revenue, although the normal course of business for real estate companies is

Plant and Equipment as a Percentage of Total Assets for Selected Focus Companies

Dell Inc. 8.7%

Forzani Group 29.7%

BCE Inc. 54.3%

■ **LEARNING OBJECTIVE 1**

Define, classify, and explain the nature of long-term assets and interpret the fixed asset turnover ratio.

LONG-TERM (OR LONG-LIVED OR CAPITAL) ASSETS are tangible and intangible resources owned by a business and used in its operations over several years.

EXHIBIT **9.1**

WestJet Airlines Asset Section of the Balance Sheet

REAL WORLD EXCERPT

WestJet Airlines

ANNUAL REPORT

WESTJET AIRLINES LTD.
CONSOLIDATED BALANCE SHEETS
December 31, 2006 and 2005
(in thousands of dollars)

	2006	2005
Assets		
Current assets:		
Cash and cash equivalents [note 9]	$ 377,517	$ 259,640
Accounts receivable	12,645	8,022
Income taxes recoverable	13,820	13,909
Assets held for sale [note 2]	13,157	—
Prepaid expenses and deposits [note 1[g]]	30,727	31,746
Inventory	8,200	6,259
	456,066	319,576
Property and equipment [note 2]	2,158,746	1,803,497
Other assets [note 3]	111,715	90,019
	$2,726,527	$2,213,092

the purchase and sale of long-term assets such as land and buildings. Long-term assets can be tangible or intangible, and have the following characteristics:

TANGIBLE ASSETS (or fixed assets) have physical substance.

1. **Tangible assets** can be touched because they have physical substance. This classification is most often called *property, plant, and equipment*. The three kinds of tangible assets held for use in operations are:

   a. *Land*, which is reported on the balance sheet as a separate item if it has a material value. Unlike aircraft or patents on pharmaceutical products, land does not become obsolete; therefore, it is never amortized.

   b. *Buildings, fixtures, and equipment* that are reported as a separate item on the balance sheet or in the notes. WestJet reports the details of such assets in Note 2, separating buildings from computer hardware, equipment, aircraft, and spare engines and parts.

   c. *Natural resources*, which include mineral deposits such as gold or iron ore, oil wells and reserves, and timber tracts. Corporations such as Barrick Gold, Suncor Energy Inc., and Noranda Mining and Exploration extract natural resources.

INTANGIBLE ASSETS have property ownership rights but not physical substance.

2. **Intangible assets** have no physical substance. Historically, they were called *Intangibles and Other Nothings*. Often, intangible assets arise from intellectual effort and are known as *intellectual property*. Examples include copyrights, patents, licences, trademarks, software, franchises, and subscription lists.

KEY RATIO ANALYSIS

FIXED ASSET TURNOVER

ANALYTICAL QUESTION → How effectively is management utilizing its property, plant, and equipment or fixed assets to generate revenues?

RATIO AND COMPARISONS → The fixed asset turnover ratio is useful in answering this question. It is computed as follows:

$$\text{Fixed Asset Turnover} = \frac{\text{Net Sales (or operating revenues)}}{\text{Average Net Fixed Assets*}}$$

*[Beginning + Ending Fixed Asset Balance (net of accumulated amortization)] ÷ 2

The 2006 ratio for WestJet is:

$$\$1,773,686 \div [(\$1,803,497 + \$2,158,746) \div 2] = 0.90 \text{ times}$$

Comparisons over Time			Comparisons with Competitors	
WestJet Airlines			Southwest	Jet Blue
2004	2005	2006	2006	2006
0.77	0.77	0.90	0.94	0.74

INTERPRETATIONS

In General → The fixed asset turnover ratio measures the sales dollars generated by each dollar of fixed assets used. A high rate normally suggests effective management. An increasing rate over time signals more efficient fixed asset use. Creditors and security analysts use this ratio to assess a company's effectiveness in generating sales from its long-term assets.

Focus Company Analysis → WestJet's fixed assets turnover ratio has increased over the last three years, suggesting that there might be an improvement in asset efficiency. Net fixed assets increased by $355 million during 2006, but net sales increased by a larger amount, $380 million, during 2006. The new fleet of aircraft that WestJet acquired during 2005 and 2006 helped the company improve on its service to passengers and increased its net sales. When compared to two other companies in the industry, WestJet appears to be more efficient in utilizing its fixed assets than Jet Blue, but less efficient than Southwest Airlines. WestJet can further improve on its ratio by continuing to dispose of older aircraft and by increasing its revenues from flights, either by increasing the number of flights, increasing the number of paying passengers for existing flights, or increasing the revenue per paying passenger.

A Few Cautions → A lower or declining rate may indicate that a company is expanding (by acquiring additional productive assets) in anticipation of higher sales in the future. An increasing ratio could also signal that a firm has cut back on capital expenditures due to anticipation of a downturn in business. As a consequence, appropriate interpretation of the fixed asset turnover ratio requires an investigation of related activities.

> **Selected Focus Companies' Fixed Asset Turnover Ratios for 2006**
>
> Petro-Canada 1.08
>
> Gildan Activewear 2.75
>
> Dell 30.3

MEASURING AND RECORDING ACQUISITION COST

The *cost principle* requires that all reasonable and necessary costs incurred in acquiring a long-term asset, placing it in its operational setting, and preparing it for use should be recorded in a designated asset account. We say that the costs are *capitalized* when they are recorded as assets instead of as expenses in the current period. These costs, including any sales taxes, legal fees, transportation costs, and installation costs, are added to the purchase price of the asset. Special discounts and interest charges associated with the purchase should not, however, be included in the cost of the asset. Interest charges should be reported as interest expense.

In addition to purchasing buildings and equipment, a company may acquire undeveloped land, typically with the intent to build a new factory or office building. When a company purchases land, all of the incidental costs paid by the purchaser, such as title fees, sales commissions, legal fees, title insurance, delinquent taxes, and surveying fees, should be included in its cost. Because land is not subject to amortization, it must be recorded as a separate asset.

Sometimes a company purchases an old building or used machinery for use in its business operations. Renovation and repair costs incurred by the purchaser prior to the asset's use should be included as a part of its cost.

The cash flow statement of WestJet for fiscal year 2006 shows that WestJet acquired additional aircraft for $438.9 million. However, details of these purchases are not publicly available. For the sake of illustration, let us assume that WestJet purchased a new 737 aircraft from Boeing on January 1, 2008 (the beginning of WestJet's fiscal year), for a list price of $62 million. Let us also assume that Boeing offered WestJet a discount of $3 million for signing the purchase agreement. This means that the price of a new airplane to WestJet is $59 million. In addition WestJet paid $500,000 to have the airplane delivered and $1,000,000 to prepare the airplane for use. The amount recorded for the purchase, called the **acquisition cost**, is the net cash amount paid or, when noncash assets are used up as payment, the fair market value of the asset given

LEARNING OBJECTIVE 2

Apply the cost principle to measure the acquisition and maintenance of property, plant, and equipment.

The **ACQUISITION COST** is the net cash equivalent amount paid or to be paid for the asset.

or asset received, whichever can be more clearly determined (called the ***cash equivalent price***). WestJet would calculate the acquisition cost of the aircraft as follows:

Invoice price	$62,000,000
Less: Discount from Boeing	3,000,000
Net cash invoice price	59,000,000
Add: Transportation charges paid by WestJet	500,000
Preparation costs paid by WestJet	1,000,000
Cost of the aircraft (added to the asset account)	$60,500,000

VARIOUS ACQUISITION METHODS

For Cash   Assuming that WestJet paid cash for the aircraft and related transportation and preparation costs, the transaction is recorded as follows:

Aircraft (A).	60,500,000	
Cash (A).		60,500,000

Assets		=	Liabilities	+	Shareholders' Equity
Aircraft	+60,500,000				
Cash	−60,500,000				

It might seem unusual for WestJet to pay cash to purchase new assets that cost $60.5 million, but this is often the case. When it acquires productive assets, a company may pay with cash that was generated from operations or cash that was recently borrowed. Notice that WestJet's cash balance at December 31, 2006 exceeds $377.5 million. It also is possible for the seller to finance the purchase on credit.

For Debt   Now let us assume that WestJet signed a note payable for the aircraft and paid cash for the transportation and preparation costs. WestJet would record the following journal entry:

Aircraft (A).	60,500,000	
Cash (A).		1,500,000
Note payable (L)		59,000,000

Assets		=	Liabilities		+	Shareholders' Equity
Aircraft	+60,500,000		Note payable	+59,000,000		
Cash	−1,500,000					

For Equity (or Other Non-Cash Consideration)   A non-cash consideration, such as a company's common shares or a right given by the company to the seller to purchase the company's goods or services at a special price, might be part of the transaction. When a non-cash consideration is included in the purchase of an asset, the cash-equivalent cost (fair market value of the asset given or received) is determined.

Assume that WestJet gave Boeing 2,000,000 of its common shares, with a market value of $25 per share (the approximate stock price on the date of the transaction), and paid the balance in cash, including cash for the transportation and preparation costs. The journal entry and transaction effects follow:

Aircraft (A).	60,500,000	
Cash (A).		10,500,000
Common shares (SE)		50,000,000

Assets		=	Liabilities	+	Shareholders' Equity	
Aircraft	+60,500,000				Common shares	+50,000,000
Cash	−10,500,000					

By Construction   In some cases, a company may construct an asset for its own use instead of buying it from a manufacturer. For example, in 2005, WestJet expanded a hangar facility in Calgary to shelter its aircraft. Because the company expanded the asset for its own use, the hangar's cost includes necessary costs of construction such as labour and materials, as well as overhead costs directly attributable to the construction activity. The costs also include the interest expense incurred during the construction period, based on the amount of funds invested in the construction of the hangar. WestJet can add the interest incurred to the other construction costs of the hangar until it is ready for use in operations. The amount of interest that is included in the cost of the hangar is called **capitalized interest**, which reduces the company's total interest expense every year until the hanger is in use. The complex computation of interest capitalization is discussed in other accounting courses.

CAPITALIZED INTEREST represents interest on borrowed funds directly attibutable to construction until the asset is substantially complete.

Capitalizing labour, materials, and a portion of interest expense increases assets, decreases expenses, and increases net income. Let us assume the new hangar cost WestJet $600,000 in labour costs, $1,300,000 in materials and supplies, as well as interest expense of $100,000 incurred during the construction project:

| Building (A). . . . . | 2,000,000 | |
| Cash (A). . . . . | | 2,000,000 |

Assets		=	Liabilities	+	Shareholders' Equity
Building	+2,000,000				
Cash	−2,000,000				

WestJet described its policy on capitalized interest in note 1 to its financial statements:

NOTES TO CONSOLIDATED FINANCIAL STATEMENTS

1. Significant Accounting Policies

. . .

(j) Capitalized costs:

Costs associated with assets under development which have probable future economic benefit, which can be clearly defined and measured and are costs incurred for the development of new products or technologies are capitalized. These costs are not amortized until the assets are substantially complete and ready for their intended use, at which time they are amortized over five to 10 years. Interest attributable to funds used to finance property and equipment is capitalized to the related asset. Legal and financing costs for the loan facilities are capitalized to other assets on the balance sheet and amortized on a straight-line basis over the term of the related loan.

Costs of new route development are expensed as incurred.

REAL WORLD EXCERPT

WestJet Airlines

ANNUAL REPORT

As a Basket Purchase of Assets   When several long-term assets, such as land, building, and equipment, are acquired in a single transaction and for a single lump sum, known as a **basket purchase**, the cost of each asset must be measured and recorded separately. This is true because land is not amortized, but buildings

BASKET PURCHASE is an acquisition of two or more assets in a single transaction for a single lump sum.

and equipment are, although at different rates. The purchase price must be apportioned among the land, the building, and the equipment on a rational basis.

Accountants use relative market values of the acquired assets on the date of acquisition to apportion the single lump sum to the various assets in the basket. Assume that WestJet paid $300,000 cash to purchase a building and the land on which the building is located. Since the current market values of the building and land were not known, a professional appraisal was obtained. This appraisal, totalling $315,000, showed the following estimated market values: $189,000 for the building and $126,000 for the land. The total purchase price is then apportioned on the basis of relative market values as follows:

Building	Land
$\dfrac{\text{Market Value}}{\text{Total Market Value}} = \dfrac{\$189,000}{\$315,000} = 60\%$	$\dfrac{\text{Market Value}}{\text{Total Market Value}} = \dfrac{\$126,000}{\$315,000} = 40\%$
$60\% \times \$300,000 \text{ Total Cost} = \$180,000$	$40\% \times \$300,000 \text{ Total Cost} = \$120,000$

The cost of the building is determined by multiplying the total cost of $300,000 by the ratio of the market value of the building to the total market value ($189,000 ÷ $315,000 = 60 percent). Similarly, the cost of the land is determined by multiplying the total cost by the ratio of the market value of the land to the total market value ($126,000 ÷ $315,000 = 40 percent). Assuming that WestJet purchases the assets with cash, the journal entry and effects are as follows:

Land (A)	120,000	
Building (A)	180,000	
Cash (A)		300,000

Assets		=	Liabilities	+	Shareholders' Equity
Land	+120,000				
Building	+180,000				
Cash	−300,000				

SELF-STUDY **QUIZ 9-1**

McDonald's Corporation

In a recent year, McDonald's Corporation purchased property, plant, and equipment priced at $1.8 billion. Assume that the company also paid $70 million for sales tax; $8 million for transportation costs; $1.3 million for installation and preparation of the property, plant, and equipment before use; and $100,000 in maintenance contracts to cover repairs to the property, plant, and equipment during use.

1. Compute the acquisition cost for the buildings and equipment.

2. For each situation below, indicate the effects of this acquisition on the following financial statement categories. Use + for increase and − for decrease and indicate the accounts and amounts:

	Assets	Liabilities	Shareholders' Equity
a. Paid 30% in cash and signed a note payable for the balance.			
b. Issued 10 million shares at a market price of $45 per share and paid the balance in cash.			

After you complete your answers, check them with the solutions presented on page 495.

REPAIRS, MAINTENANCE, AND BETTERMENTS

Most assets require substantial expenditures during their useful lives to maintain or enhance their productive capacity. These expenditures include cash outlays for ordinary repairs and maintenance, major repairs, replacements, and additions. Remember that the terms *expenditure* and *expense* are not synonymous. An expenditure is the payment of money to acquire goods or services. These goods and services may be recorded as either assets or expenses, depending on whether they benefit future periods or only the current period. Expenditures that are made after an asset is acquired are classified as follows:

1. **Ordinary repairs and maintenance**—expenditures that maintain the productive capacity of the asset during the current accounting period only. These cash outlays are recorded as *expenses* in the current period. Ordinary repairs and maintenance, also called **revenue expenditures**, are expenditures for the normal maintenance and upkeep of long-term assets. These expenditures are recurring in nature, involve relatively small amounts at each occurrence, and do not directly lengthen the useful life of the asset.

   In the case of WestJet, examples of ordinary repairs include changing oil in aircraft engines, replacing the lights in the control panels, and fixing torn fabric on passenger seats. Although the cost of individual ordinary repairs is relatively small, in the aggregate these expenditures can be substantial. In the year 2005, WestJet incurred more than $75.7 million for aircraft maintenance and repairs. This amount was reported as an expense on its income statement.

2. **Extraordinary repairs** and **betterments**—expenditures that increase the productive life, operating efficiency, or capacity of the asset. These **capital expenditures**, which provide benefits to the company over a number of accounting periods, are added to the appropriate *asset* accounts. They occur infrequently, involve large amounts of money, and increase an asset's economic usefulness in the future through either increased efficiency or longer life. Examples include additions, major overhauls, complete reconditioning, and major replacements and improvements, such as the complete replacement of an engine on an aircraft.

An example of an extraordinary repair has also arisen in the airline industry from a change in Transport Canada's regulation to reduce the acceptable level of engine noise. WestJet had to undertake an unplanned, very expensive, one-time repair that extended the economic life of its aircraft. It installed hushkits on all of its old aircraft engines that did not meet new noise-abatement regulations. Without hushkits, WestJet would not be able to fly these planes. This extraordinary repair is a one-time cost that certainly increased the aircraft's future economic usefulness.

An example of a betterment is WestJet's installation of blended winglets on its aircraft to improve the aerodynamic performance and handling design of the 737-700s. From a maintenance perspective, winglets help aircraft achieve better climb performance that allows lower thrust settings, which extends engine life and reduces costs.

In many cases, no clear line distinguishes capital expenditures (assets) from revenue expenditures (expenses). In these situations, accountants must exercise professional judgment and make subjective decisions. Many managers prefer to classify an item as a capital expenditure for financial reporting because it reduces expenses and increases net income for the period. Of course, most managers prefer to classify the expenditure as a deductible expense on the income tax return to pay lower taxes in the current period. Because the decision to capitalize or expense is subjective, auditors closely review the items reported as capital and revenue expenditures.

To avoid spending too much time on classifying capital and revenue expenditures, some companies develop simple policies that govern the accounting for these expenditures. For example, one large computer company expenses all individual items that cost less than $1,000. These policies are acceptable because immaterial (relatively small dollar) amounts will not affect users' decisions when analyzing financial statements.

ORDINARY REPAIRS AND MAINTENANCE are expenditures for normal operating upkeep of long-term assets.

REVENUE EXPENDITURES maintain the productive capacity of the asset during the current accounting period only and are recorded as expenses.

EXTRAORDINARY REPAIRS are infrequent expenditures that increase the asset's economic usefulness in the future.

BETTERMENTS are costs incurred to enhance the productive or service potential of a long-term asset.

CAPITAL EXPENDITURES increase the productive life, operating efficiency, or capacity of the asset and are recorded as increases in asset accounts, not as expenses.

FINANCIAL ANALYSIS

WORLDCOM: HIDING BILLIONS IN EXPENSES THROUGH CAPITALIZATION

When expenditures that should be recorded as current period expenses are improperly capitalized as part of the cost of an asset, the effects on the financial statements can be enormous. In one of the largest accounting frauds in history, WorldCom inflated its income and cash flows from operations by billions of dollars in just such a scheme. This fraud turned WorldCom's actual losses into profits.

Over five quarters in 2001 and 2002, the company initially announced that it had capitalized $3.8 billion that should have been recorded as operating expenses. By early 2004, auditors discovered $74.4 billion in necessary restatements (reduction to previously reported pretax income) for 2000 and 2001.

Accounting for expenses as capital expenditures increases current income because it spreads a single period's operating expenses over many future periods as amortization expense. It increases cash flows from operations by moving cash outflows from the operating section to the investing section of the cash flow statement.

In 2005, Bernard Ebbers, the co-founder and former CEO of WorldCom, was found guilty of securities fraud, conspiracy, and filing false documents with regulators. His actions caused investors in WorldCom shares to lose billions of dollars. He has been serving a jail sentence of 25 years at a U.S. prison.

SELF-STUDY **QUIZ 9-2**

A building that originally cost $400,000 has been used over the past 10 years and needs continuous maintenance and repairs. For each of the following expenditures, indicate whether it should be expensed in the current period or capitalized as part of **the cost of the asset**.

	EXPENSE OR CAPITALIZE?
1. Replacing electrical wiring throughout the building.	_____
2. Repairs to the front door of the building.	_____
3. Annual cleaning of the filters on the building's air conditioning system.	_____
4. Significant repairs due to damage from an unusual and infrequent flood.	_____

After you have completed your answers, check them with the solutions on page 495.

USE, IMPAIRMENT, AND DISPOSAL OF PLANT AND EQUIPMENT

AMORTIZATION CONCEPTS

LEARNING OBJECTIVE 3

Apply various amortization methods as assets are held and used over time.

All long-term assets, except land, have limited useful lives (such as aircraft purchased by WestJet). They represent the prepaid cost of a bundle of future services or benefits. The ***matching principle*** requires that a portion of an asset's cost be allocated as an expense to the periods in which revenue is earned as a result of its use. Thus, the cost of long-term assets is matched in a systematic and rational manner with the revenues that are earned by using them. WestJet earns revenue when it provides air travel service and incurs an expense when using its aircraft to generate the revenue.

The term used to identify the matching of the cost of using buildings and equipment with revenues generated by the assets is **amortization**.

AMORTIZATION is the process of allocating the acquisition cost of property, plant, and equipment (but not land) over their useful lives using a systematic and rational method.

> **Amortization:** The process of *allocating the acquisition cost* of property, plant, and equipment, other than land, over their productive lives using a systematic and rational method. Amortization is sometimes referred to as depreciation.

Students are often confused about the concept of amortization as accountants define it. In accounting, amortization is a process of ***cost allocation***, not a process of determining an asset's current market value or worth. When an asset is amortized, the remaining balance sheet amount ***does not represent its current market value***. Under the cost principle, the cost of a long-term asset is recorded at its current market value only on the acquisition date. At subsequent balance sheet dates, the unamortized cost is not measured on a market value basis. WestJet reported in its income statement an amortization expense of $111.4 million for the year 2006. The journal entry and transaction effects, including the contra-asset account (XA) follow:

Amortization expense (E) 111,400,000		
Accumulated amortization (XA)		111,400,000

Assets	=	Liabilities	+	Shareholders' Equity
Accumulated				Amortization
amortization (+XA) −111,400,000				expense (+E) −111,400,000

The periodic amortization expenses throughout the asset's useful life are accumulated in the contra-asset account, Accumulated Amortization, and deducted from the related asset's cost. The acquisition cost minus accumulated amortization is called **net book value or net carrying value** and appears on the balance sheet. In addition, companies like WestJet disclose, in a note to the financial statements for 2006, information about the long-term assets they own or control and the related accumulated amortization.

NET BOOK (OR NET CARRYING) VALUE is the acquisition cost of an asset less accumulated amortization.

REAL WORLD EXCERPT

WestJet Airlines

ANNUAL REPORT

NOTES TO CONSOLIDATED FINANCIAL STATEMENTS

2. Property and Equipment

2006	Cost	Accumulated depreciation	Net book value
Aircraft—Next-Generation	$2,086,301	$185,526	$1,900,775
Ground property and equipment	153,896	65,854	88,042
Spare engines and parts—Next-Generation	70,459	10,145	60,314
Buildings	40,028	4,825	35,203
Leasehold improvements	6,914	4,579	2,335
Other assets under capital lease	2,481	694	1,787
	2,360,079	271,623	2,088,456
Deposits on aircraft	38,011	—	38,011
Assets under development	32,279	—	32,279
	$2,430,369	$271,623	$2,158,746

NET BOOK VALUE AS AN APPROXIMATION OF REMAINING LIFE

FINANCIAL ANALYSIS

Some analysts compare the net book value of assets to their original cost as an approximation of their remaining life. If the net book value of an asset is 100 percent of its cost, it is a new asset; if the net book value is 25 percent of its cost, the asset has about 25 percent of its estimated life remaining. In WestJet's case, the net book value of its aircraft is 90 percent of its original cost. This compares with 73 percent for Southwest Airlines and 93 percent for ACE Holdings. This comparison suggests that the aircraft used by WestJet may have more of its estimated life remaining than those of some other major airlines.

Book Value/ Original Cost

WestJet 90%

Southwest 73%

ACE Holdings 93%

Based on the information WestJet provided in its note 1 (h) and note 2, the net book value can be used to estimate the asset's remaining useful life. You simply calculate the ratio of net book value to acquisition cost and multiply it by the asset's estimated useful life. Consider, for example, WestJet's spare engines and parts—Next-Generation.

$$\frac{\text{Net book value}}{\text{Acquisition cost}} \times \text{Estimated useful life} = \frac{\$60,314,000}{\$70,459,000} \times 20 = 17.1 \text{ years}$$

The useful life of WestJet's important assets can be analyzed in this manner and comparisons can be made to other companies in the industry. This is, however, only a rough approximation because the net book value of long-term assets depends on the estimates of useful life and residual value, as well as the specific amortization method used.

The calculation of amortization expense requires three amounts for each amortizable asset:

1. Acquisition cost.
2. *Estimated* useful life to the company.
3. *Estimated* residual (or salvage) value at the end of the asset's useful life to the company.

Two of these three amounts are estimates. Therefore, ***amortization expense is an estimate.***

ESTIMATED USEFUL LIFE is the expected service life of an asset to the present owner.

Estimated useful life represents management's estimate of the asset's useful *economic life* to the company rather than the total economic life to all potential users. For example, WestJet has estimated the useful life of a typical 737-200 at 17,500 flight hours and that of a typical 737-700 at 86,500 flight hours. Furthermore, let us assume that WestJet estimates the number of flight hours per year at 2,500 for the 737-200 and at 3,460 hours for the 737-700. The older 737-200 must be repaired more frequently than the newer 737-700 and therefore will not fly as many hours each year. Dividing the total estimated useful life by the annual use provides an estimate of 7 years for the 737-200 and 25 years for the new 737-700.

The determination of estimated useful life of a long-term asset must conform to the *continuity assumption.* This assumption holds that the business will continue to pursue its commercial objectives and will not liquidate in the foreseeable future.

WestJet, similar to other companies, discloses in note 1 to its financial statements the useful lives of its long-term assets and the methods used to amortize them. We will use the same estimates in our illustrations, where appropriate.

REAL WORLD EXCERPT

WestJet Airlines

ANNUAL REPORT

NOTES TO CONSOLIDATED FINANCIAL STATEMENTS

1. Significant Accounting Policies

(h) Property and equipment:

Property and equipment are recorded at cost and depreciated to their estimated residual values. Aircraft under capital lease are initially recorded at the present value of minimum lease payments at the inception of the lease.

Asset	Basis	Rate
Aircraft net of estimated residual value—Next-Generation	Cycles	Cycles flown
Live satellite television included aircraft—Next-Generation	Straight-line	10 years/lease term
Aircraft net of estimated residual value—200-series	Flight hours	Hours flown
Ground property and equipment	Straight-line	5 to 25 years
Spare engines and parts net of estimated residual value—Next-Generation	Straight-line	20 years
Spare engines and parts net of estimated residual value—200-series	Flight hours	Fleet hours flown
Aircraft under capital lease	Straight-line	Term of lease
Other assets under capital lease	Straight-line	Term of lease
Buildings	Straight-line	40 years
Leasehold improvements	Straight-line	Term of lease

Residual (or salvage) value represents management's estimate of the amount the company expects to recover upon disposal of the asset at the end of its estimated useful life. The residual value may be the estimated value of the asset as salvage or scrap or its expected value if sold to another user.

Residual value is the estimated amount to be recovered less any estimated costs of dismantling, disposal, and sale. In many cases, disposal costs may approximately equal the gross residual value. Therefore, many amortizable assets are assumed to have no residual value.

In the case of aircraft owned by WestJet, the company uses a conservative approach by estimating only the residual value of the aircraft's engines, which is approximately $1,400,000. Other companies such as Delta Air Lines estimate the residual value at 5 percent of the acquisition cost, which is greater than $1,400,000.

RESIDUAL (OR SALVAGE) VALUE is the estimated amount to be recovered, less disposal costs, at the end of the estimated useful life of an asset.

DIFFERENCES IN ESTIMATED LIVES WITHIN A SINGLE INDUSTRY

FINANCIAL **ANALYSIS**

Notes to actual financial statements of companies in the airline industry reveal the following estimates for lives of flight equipment:

Company	Estimated Life (in years)
WestJet Airlines	7 to 25
Delta Air Lines	20 to 25
US Airways	11 to 30
Singapore Airlines	15
Southwest Airlines	20 to 25

The differences in estimated lives may be attributable to a number of factors such as type of aircraft used by each company, equipment replacement plans, differences in operations, and the degree of management conservatism. In addition, given the same type of aircraft, companies that plan to use the equipment over fewer years may estimate higher residual values than do companies that plan to use the equipment longer. For example, Singapore Airlines uses a residual value of 20 percent over a relatively short useful life, as compared to 5 percent for Delta Air Lines over a 25-year useful life.

Differences in estimated lives and residual values of assets used by specific companies can have a significant impact on the comparison of the profitability of the companies. Analysts must be certain that they identify the causes for the differences in amortizable lives.

ALTERNATIVE AMORTIZATION METHODS

Accountants have not been able to agree on a single, best method of amortization because matching the cost of using long-term assets to the revenue they generate differs significantly among companies. As a result, managers may choose from several different acceptable amortization methods, basing their decision on how they believe the asset will generate revenues over time. Once selected, the method should be applied consistently over time to enhance comparability of financial information to users. We will discuss the three most common amortization methods:

1. Straight-line.
2. Units-of-production.
3. Declining-balance.

The facts shown in Exhibit 9.2 will be used to illustrate each of the three methods of calculating amortization expense for one 737-700 aircraft purchased on January 1, 2008.[3]

---

[3]Most of the examples that we discuss in this chapter assume that assets were acquired on the first day of the year and amortized for the entire year. In practice, assets are purchased at various times during the year. Most companies adopt a policy to cover partial-year amortization, such as "to the nearest full month" or "half year in the year of acquisition."

EXHIBIT **9.2**

Illustrative Data for Computing Amortization under Alternative Methods

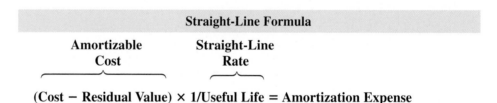

WESTJET AIRLINES

Acquisition cost of aircraft, purchased on January 1, 2008	$45,000,000
Estimated life (in years)	25
Estimated residual value	$1,400,000
Estimated life in flight hours	86,500 flight hours
Actual flight hours in: Year 2008	3,460 flight hours
Year 2009	3,600 flight hours
Year 2010	3,350 flight hours

STRAIGHT-LINE AMORTIZATION is the method that allocates the cost of an asset in equal periodic amounts over its useful life.

Straight-Line Method   More companies, including WestJet, use **straight-line amortization** in their financial statements than all other methods combined. Under the straight-line method, an equal portion of an asset's amortizable cost is allocated to each accounting period over its estimated useful life. The formula to estimate annual amortization expense follows:

Straight-Line Formula

$$\underbrace{\text{Amortizable Cost}}\qquad\underbrace{\text{Straight-Line Rate}}$$

(Cost − Residual Value) × 1/Useful Life = Amortization Expense

In this formula, "cost minus residual value" is the amount to be amortized, also called amortizable cost. "1 ÷ Useful life" is the straight-line rate. Using the data provided in Exhibit 9.2, the amortization expense is computed as follows:

($45,000,000 − $1,400,000) × 1/25 = $1,744,000

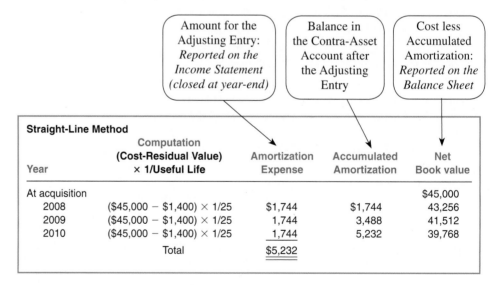

	Amount for the Adjusting Entry: *Reported on the Income Statement (closed at year-end)*	Balance in the Contra-Asset Account after the Adjusting Entry	Cost less Accumulated Amortization: *Reported on the Balance Sheet*

Straight-Line Method

Year	Computation (Cost−Residual Value) × 1/Useful Life	Amortization Expense	Accumulated Amortization	Net Book value
At acquisition				$45,000
2008	($45,000 − $1,400) × 1/25	$1,744	$1,744	43,256
2009	($45,000 − $1,400) × 1/25	1,744	3,488	41,512
2010	($45,000 − $1,400) × 1/25	1,744	5,232	39,768
	Total	$5,232		

Notice that

■ Amortization expense is a constant amount for each year.

■ Accumulated amortization increases by an equal amount each year.

■ Net book value decreases by the same amount each year until it equals the estimated residual value.

This is the reason for the name ***straight-line method***. Notice, too, that the adjusting entry can be prepared from this schedule and the effects on the income statement and ending balance on the balance sheet are known. WestJet uses the straight-line method for all of its long-term assets, except for aircraft and spare engines and parts. WestJet reported amortization expense in the amount of $111,442,000 for 2006. Most companies in the airline industry use the straight-line method.

Units-of-Production (Activity) Method   WestJet uses the **units-of-production amortization** method to relate amortizable cost to the total estimated productive output. The formula to estimate annual amortization expense under this method follows:

UNITS-OF-PRODUCTION AMORTIZATION is the method that allocates the cost of a long-term asset over its useful life based on the relation of its periodic output to its total estimated output.

Units-of-Production Formula

$$\underbrace{\frac{(\text{Cost} - \text{Residual Value})}{\text{Estimated Total Production}}}_{\substack{\text{Amortization Rate} \\ \text{per Unit}}} \times \frac{\text{Actual}}{\text{Production}} = \text{Amortization Expense}$$

Dividing the amortizable amount by the estimated total production yields the amortization rate per unit of production (or activity), which then is multiplied by the actual annual production (or activity) to determine amortization expense. Using the information in Exhibit 9.2, the computation of the amortization rate per unit follows:

$$\frac{\$45,000,000 - \$1,400,000}{86,500 \text{ flight hours}} = \$504 \text{ per Flight Hour}$$

For every flight hour that the aircraft flies, WestJet records amortization expense of $504. The amortization schedule for the years 2008, 2009, and 2010 under the units-of-production method follows (amounts in thousands of dollars):

Year	Computations	Amortization Expense	Accumulated Amortization	Net Book Value
At acquisition				$45,000
2008	$504 × 3,460 flight hours	$1,744	$1,744	43,256
2009	504 × 3,600 flight hours	1,814	3,558	41,442
2010	504 × 3,350 flight hours	1,688	5,246	39,754
	Total	$5,246		

Notice that amortization expense, accumulated amortization, and net book value vary from period to period directly with the number of flight hours. When the units-of-production method is used, amortization expense is said to be a *variable expense* because it varies directly with production or use.

You might wonder what happens if the total estimated productive output differs from actual output. Remember that the estimate is management's best guess of total output. If any difference occurs at the end of the asset's life, the final adjusting entry to amortization expense should be for the amount needed to bring the asset's net book value to equal the asset's estimated residual value.

The units-of-production method is based on an estimate of an asset's total productive capacity or output that is difficult to estimate. This is another example of the degree of subjectivity that is inherent in accounting.

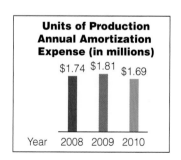

Units of Production Annual Amortization Expense (in millions)

$1.74 $1.81 $1.69

Year   2008 2009 2010

Declining-Balance Method   If the asset is considered to be more efficient or productive when it is newer, managers might choose the **declining-balance amortization method** to match a higher amortization expense with higher revenues in the early

DECLINING-BALANCE AMORTIZATION is the method that allocates the cost of an asset over its useful life based on a multiple of the straight-line rate (often two times).

EXHIBIT **9.3**

The Relationship among
Amortization Expense, Repair
Expense, and Total Expense

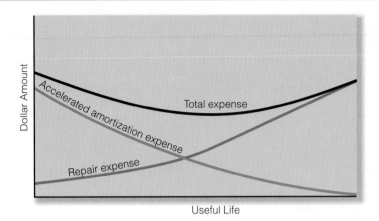

years of an asset's life and lower in the later years. This method results in accelerated amortization of the asset's cost over time. As repair costs increase in the later years, the decreasing amortization expense offsets the increasing repair expense over time.

The relationship between accelerated amortization expense, repair expense, and the total expense of using the asset is shown in Exhibit 9.3 above. Although accelerated methods are seldom used for financial reporting purposes, the method that is used more frequently than accelerated methods is the declining-balance method.

Declining-balance amortization is based on multiplying the asset's net book value by a fixed rate that exceeds the straight-line (SL) rate. The rate is often double (two times) the straight-line rate and is called the ***double-declining-balance rate***. For example, if the estimated useful life of an asset is 10 years, the straight-line rate is 10 percent (1 ÷ 10), then the declining-balance rate is 20 percent (2 × the straight-line rate of 10 percent). Other typical acceleration rates are 1.5 times and 1.75 times. The double-declining-balance (DDB) rate is adopted most frequently by companies utilizing the accelerated method and will be used in our illustration.

To calculate amortization expense under the double-declining-balance method, the net book value of the asset is multiplied by the DDB rate as follows:

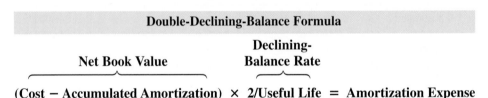

There are two important differences between this method and the others described previously:

- Notice that accumulated amortization, not residual value, is included in the formula. Since accumulated amortization increases each year, net book value (cost − accumulated amortization) decreases. The double-declining rate is applied to a lower net book value each year, resulting in a decline in amortization expense over time.
- An asset's net book value cannot be amortized below residual value. Therefore, if the annual computation reduces net book value below residual value, a lower amount of amortization expense must be recorded so that net book value equals residual value. No additional amortization expense is computed in subsequent years.

Computation of DDB amortization expense is illustrated using the data given in Exhibit 9.2 (amounts in thousands of dollars):

Year	Computations	Amortization Expense	Accumulated Amortization	Net Book Value
At acquisition				$45,000
2008	($45,000 − $0) × 2/25	$3,600	$3,600	41,400
2009	($45,000 − $3,600) × 2/25	3,312	6,912	38,088
2010	($45,000 − $6,912) × 2/25	3,047	9,959	35,041
	Total	$9,959		

Double-Declining-Balance Annual Amortization Expense

The calculated amortization expense for this asset differs depending upon the amortization method used. Using the straight-line method, the annual expense is $1,744,000 each year of the aircraft's 25-year useful life. Using the units-of-production method, annual amortization expense varies each year from a low of $1,688,400 in year 2010 to a high of $1,814,400 in year 2009. Finally, using the DDB method, amortization expense declines every year from $3,600,000 in 2008 to $3,047,000 in year 2010. This, in part, explains why an analyst must be careful when using net book value to estimate the remaining useful life of an asset. Using our example, we obtain different estimates for the remaining useful life for the same aircraft after three years, depending on the amortization method used:

Amortization Method	Estimated Remaining Useful Life
Straight line	($39,768/$45,000) × 25 = 22.24 years or approximately 22 years
Units of production	($39,754/$45,000) × 25 = 22.09 years or approximately 22 years
Double-declining balance	($35,041/$45,000) × 25 = 19.47 years or approximately 20 years

This example illustrates why care must be taken to read the notes to the financial statements of any company and identify the accounting policies it uses before comparing its financial results to those of other companies.

Companies in industries that expect fairly rapid obsolescence of their equipment use the declining-balance method. Sony is one of the companies that uses this method.

2. Summary of significant accounting policies:

Property, plant, and equipment and depreciation

Property, plant, and equipment are stated at cost. Depreciation of property, plant, and equipment is primarily computed on the declining-balance method for Sony Corporation and Japanese subsidiaries . . . and on the straight-line method for foreign subsidiaries at rates based on estimated useful lives of the assets, principally, ranging from 15 years up to 50 years for buildings and from 2 years up to 10 years for machinery and equipment.

REAL WORLD EXCERPT

Sony

ANNUAL REPORT

As this note indicates, companies may use different amortization methods for different classes of assets. Under the consistency principle, they are expected to apply the same methods to those assets over time.

In the previous illustration, we assumed that the aircraft was purchased at the beginning of the year. In reality, however, companies purchase assets at any date during the year, which complicates the computation of amortization expense for the first year of acquisition. For practical purposes, acquisitions made during the year are amortized in a convenient manner during the asset's first year of operation. Amortization expense can be computed for the number of months the asset is actually in use, or it can be computed for half a year using the half-year convention.

For example, if WestJet acquired the aircraft on May 1, 2008 instead of January 1, 2008, the annual straight-line amortization expense could be prorated by determining the monthly amortization expense and multiplying the monthly amortization by the number of months WestJet flew this aircraft during 2008 (eight months in this case):

$$\text{Amortization expense} = (\$1,744,000 \div 12) \times 8 \text{ months} = \$1,162,667$$

Alternatively, companies that acquire many long-term assets during the year may use the half-year rule, which implies that similar long-term assets, such as office equipment, that are acquired at different dates throughout the year can be assumed to have been purchased around the middle of the year. Thus, all the office equipment acquired during the fiscal year is amortized for half a year at the end of the year of acquisition. This practical rule is acceptable as long as the amount of amortization expense for the year is not materially misstated.

In Summary   The following table summarizes the three amortization methods and computations for each method. Exhibit 9.4 shows graphically the differences in amortization expense over time for each method.

Method	Computation	Amortization Expense
Straight-line	(Cost − Residual Value) × 1/Useful Life	Equal amounts each year
Units-of-production	(Cost − Residual Value)/Estimated Total Production × Annual Production	Varying amounts based on production level
Double-declining-balance	(Cost − Accumulated Amortization) × 2/Useful Life	Declining amounts over time

EXHIBIT **9.4**

**Differences in Amortization
Methods over Time**

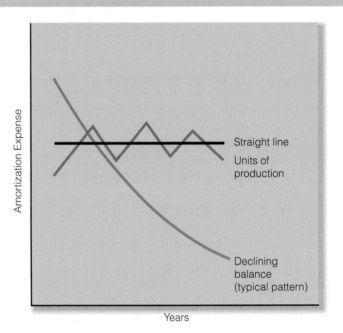

FINANCIAL
ANALYSIS    **IMPACT OF ALTERNATIVE AMORTIZATION METHODS**

Assume that you are analyzing two companies that are exactly the same except for the fact that one uses accelerated amortization and the other uses the straight-line method. Which company would you expect to report higher net income? Actually, the question is a bit tricky. The answer is that you cannot say for certain which company's income would be higher.

The accelerated methods report higher amortization and therefore lower net income during the early years of the life of an asset. As the age of the asset increases, this effect reverses. Therefore, companies that use accelerated amortization report lower amortization expense and higher net income during the later years of an asset's life. The preceding graph shows the pattern of amortization over the life of an asset for the straight-line and declining-balance methods discussed in this chapter. When the curve for the accelerated method falls below the curve for the straight-line method, the accelerated method produces a higher net income than the straight-line method. However, the total amortization of the asset over its useful life should be the same for each method.

Users of financial statements must understand the impact of alternative amortization methods used over time. Differences in amortization methods rather than real economic differences can cause significant variations in reported net incomes.

SELF-STUDY **QUIZ 9-3**

Assume that WestJet acquired new computer equipment at a cost of $240,000. The equipment has an estimated life of six years (and an estimated operating life of 50,000 hours) with an estimated residual value of $30,000. Determine the amortization expense for the first full year under each of the following methods:

1. Straight-line

2. Double-declining-balance

3. Units-of-production (assuming the equipment ran for 8,000 hours in the first year)

After you complete your answers, check them with the solutions presented on page 495.

INCREASED PROFITABILITY DUE TO AN ACCOUNTING ADJUSTMENT? READING THE NOTES

FINANCIAL **ANALYSIS**

Financial analysts are particularly interested in changes in accounting estimates because they can have a large impact on a company's before-tax operating income. As an example, in its news release, TransAlta Power, a power transmission limited partnership headquartered in Calgary, Alberta, announced first quarter earnings of $4.9 million for 2001, up from $3.6 million in the first quarter of 2000. Naturally, the president and director of TransAlta is "very pleased with the first quarter results ... " and notes that "our operating performance continues at industry leading levels ..."

However, in examining the information presented in the notes to the financial statements, the following disclosure is found: "Effective January 1, 2001, the estimated useful life of the power plant has increased to 27 years from 17 years." This change in estimate—a 59 percent increase in the estimated useful life of the plant—had the effect of increasing TransAlta's net income by $1.35 million.

Therefore, if the change in estimate had not been made, TransAlta's results for the first quarter of 2001 would be $3.55 million, a slight decrease from the first quarter of 2000. TransAlta may still be operating at industry leading levels, but without a convenient change in estimates, its bottom line would not have improved from the prior year.

Source: "TransAlta Power, L.P. announces first quarter results," CNN Newswire, April 19, 2001.

CHANGES IN AMORTIZATION ESTIMATES

Amortization is based on two estimates—useful life and residual value. These estimates are made at the time an amortizable asset is acquired. As experience with the asset accumulates, one or both of these initial estimates may have to be revised. In addition, extraordinary repairs and betterments may be added to the original acquisition cost at some time during the asset's use. When it is clear that either estimate should be revised to a material degree or the asset's cost has been changed, the unamortized asset balance (less any residual value at that date) should be apportioned over the remaining estimated life from the current year into the future. This is called a *change in estimate.*

To compute the new amortization expense due to a change in estimate for any of the amortization methods described in this chapter, substitute the net book value for the original acquisition cost, the new residual value for the original amount, and the estimated remaining life in place of the original estimated life. As an illustration, the computation using the straight-line method is as follows.

Assume the following for an aircraft owned by WestJet:

Cost of aircraft when acquired	$45,000,000
Estimated useful life	20 years
Estimated residual value	$ 1,400,000
Accumulated amortization through year 5	
($45,000,000 − $1,400,000) × 1/20 =	$ 2,180,000 per year
	× 5 years
	= $10,900,000

Shortly after the start of year 6, WestJet changed the initial estimated life to 25 years and lowered the estimated residual value to $750,000. At the end of year 6, the computation of the new amount for amortization expense is as follows:

Acquisition cost	$45,000,000
Less: Accumulated amortization (years 1–5)	10,900,000
Net book value	$34,100,000
Less: New residual value	750,000
New amortizable amount	$33,350,000
Annual amortization based on remaining life:	
$33,350,000 ÷ 20 years (25 − 5 years) =	$ 1,667,500 per year

Companies may also change amortization methods (for example, from declining-balance to straight-line), although such change requires significantly more disclosure since the consistency principle is violated. Under GAAP, changes in accounting estimates and amortization methods should be made only when the new estimate or accounting method "better measures" the periodic income of the business.

SELF-STUDY **QUIZ 9-4**

Assume that WestJet Airlines owned a service truck that originally cost $100,000. When purchased, the truck had an estimated useful life of 10 years, with no residual value. After operating the truck for five years, WestJet determined that the remaining life was only two more years. Based on this change in estimate, what amount of annual amortization should be recorded over the remaining life of the asset? WestJet uses the straight-line method.

After you complete your answer, check it with the solution presented on page 495.

MANAGERS' SELECTION AMONG ACCOUNTING ALTERNATIVES

Financial Reporting For financial reporting purposes, corporate managers must select the amortization method that provides the best matching of revenues and expenses for any given asset. If the asset is expected to provide benefits evenly over time, then the straight-line method is preferred. Managers also find this method to be easy to use and to explain. If no other method is more systematic or rational, then the straight-line method is selected. Also, during the early years of an asset's life, the straight-line method reports higher income than the accelerated methods do. For these reasons, the straight-line method is by far the most common.

On the other hand, certain assets produce more revenue in their early lives because they are more efficient than in later years. In this case, managers select an accelerated method to allocate cost. In addition, as the asset ages, repair costs are likely to increase. Thus, the total of the amortization expense and repair expense for any given period is likely to provide a nearly constant amount charged to income each period.

The 2006 edition of *Financial Reporting in Canada* reported the amortization methods used by 200 companies in 2005.[4] More than 50 percent of the companies surveyed used a single amortization method. The majority of companies (105) used the straight-line method, followed by eight companies that used the units-of-production method. In addition, 83 companies used at least two different amortization methods. Most of these companies used straight-line amortization and either the units-of-production method or the declining-balance method.

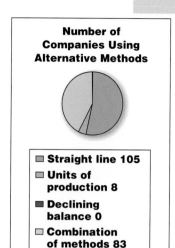

Number of Companies Using Alternative Methods

- ☐ **Straight line 105**
- ☐ **Units of production 8**
- ■ **Declining balance 0**
- ☐ **Combination of methods 83**

Tax Reporting   WestJet Airlines, like most public companies, must prepare two sets of reports. One set of reports is prepared under GAAP for reporting to shareholders. The other set is prepared to determine the company's tax obligation under the Income Tax Act. When they first learn that companies prepare two sets of reports, some people question the ethics or the legality of the practice. In reality, ***it is both legal and ethical to prepare separate reports for tax and financial reporting purposes*** because the objectives of GAAP and the Income Tax Act differ.

Financial Reporting (GAAP)	Tax Reporting
The primary objective of financial reporting is to provide economic information about a business that is useful in projecting the future cash flows of that business. Financial accounting rules follow generally accepted accounting principles.	The objective of the Income Tax Act is to raise sufficient revenues to pay for the expenditures of the federal government, with many provisions designed to encourage certain behaviours that are thought to benefit society (e.g., contributions to charities are tax-deductible to encourage people to support worthy programs).

It is easy to understand why two sets of accounting reports are permitted, but perhaps the more interesting aspect concerns the reason why managers incur the extra cost of preparing two sets of reports. In some cases, differences between the Income Tax Act and GAAP leave the manager no choice but to have separate reports. In other cases, the explanation is an economic one, called the ***least and the latest rule***. All taxpayers want to pay the lowest amount of tax that is legally permitted at the latest possible date. If you had the choice of paying $100,000 to the federal government at the end of this year or at the end of next year, you would choose the end of next year. By doing so, you would be able to invest the money for an extra year and earn a return on the investment.

By complying with the requirements of the Income Tax Act, corporations can defer (delay) paying millions and sometimes billions of dollars in taxes. The following companies reported significant gross future income tax obligations in a recent year. Much of these deferrals was due to differences in amortization methods:

Company	Future Tax Liabilities Due to Applying Different Amortization Methods
WestJet Airlines	$ 251,347,000
Potash Corp.	833,600,000
Petro-Canada	3,114,000,000

[4]N. Chlala, L. Martel, A. Lavigne, and C. Byrd, *Financial Reporting in Canada 2006*. Toronto: Canadian Institute of Chartered Accountants, 2006, p. 262.

The amortization methods discussed in the previous section are not acceptable for federal income tax reporting. Corporations that are subject to taxation in Canada must apply Capital Cost Allowance (CCA) to tangible assets, as determined by the schedules provided by the tax authorities. These schedules are used to calculate the maximum annual expense that is used in computing taxable income according to the tax rules and regulations. CCA schedules classify capital assets into different classes and stipulate the maximum CCA rate (a declining-balance rate) for each class. For example, aircraft is currently Class 9, with a CCA rate of 25 percent per year.

CCA does not attempt to match the cost of an asset with the revenue it produces over its useful life in conformity with the matching principle. Instead, CCA provides for accelerated amortization of an asset over a period that is usually much shorter than the asset's estimated useful life. The intent of CCA is to provide an incentive for corporations to invest in modern property, plant, and equipment to be competitive in world markets. The high amortization expense reported under CCA reduces a corporation's taxable income and therefore the amount it must pay in taxes.

INTERNATIONAL PERSPECTIVE   AMORTIZATION METHODS IN OTHER COUNTRIES

The various amortization methods discussed in this chapter are widely used by corporations in most countries. As the International Financial Reporting Standards become more widely accepted in many countries, some methods that are currently used in some countries will not be used in the future.

Many countries permit the revaluation of property, plant, and equipment to their current cost as of the balance sheet date. The primary argument in favour of such revaluation is that the historical cost of an asset purchased 15 or 20 years ago is not meaningful because of the impact of inflation. For example, most people would not compare the original price of a 1965 Ford to the original price of a 2008 Ford because the purchasing power of the dollar changed dramatically during the intervening period. Revaluation to current cost is prohibited (under GAAP) in Canada and the United States. A primary argument against restatement is the lack of objectivity involved in estimating the current cost of an asset.

MEASURING ASSET IMPAIRMENT

LEARNING OBJECTIVE 4

Explain the effect of asset impairment on the financial statements.

Canadian corporations are required to review the net book value of their long-term assets for possible impairment. *Impairment* occurs when events or changed circumstances cause the book value of these assets to exceed their fair value, such as a significant decrease in its market price.

If net book value > fair value, then the asset is impaired.

Fair value represents the amount at which an asset can be bought or sold between two willing parties. Fair values can be determined based on quoted market prices. If these are not available, fair values can be based on prices of similar assets or by using specific valuation techniques.

For any asset that is impaired, companies recognize a loss for the difference between the asset's book value and its fair value.

Impairment Loss = Net Book Value − Fair Value

That is, the asset is *written down* to fair value. If the fair value of the assets increases subsequent to the write down, the reduced book value of the asset should not be increased and the previous impairment loss should not be reversed. Total impairment losses and the methods used to calculate impairments should be disclosed in the financial statements and related notes.

As part of its significant accounting policies, Gildan Activewear, Inc. stated its impairment policy in note 2(f) to its financial statements. A write-down may occur whenever events or conditions indicate that the net carrying (book) value of a long-term asset may not be recoverable from estimated future cash flows. If it is determined that the estimated net recoverable amount of the asset is less than its net carrying value, then the asset is written down and a loss is recognized. In note 16 to its consolidated financial statements, Gildan reported an asset impairment loss of $ 15,149,000.

REAL WORLD EXCERPT

Gildan Activewear

ANNUAL REPORT

Note 16

Restructuring and Other Charges

The following table summarizes the components of restructuring and other charges.

	2006	2005	2004
Canadian textile manufacturing restructuring (a)	$18,930	$ —	$ —
Restructuring of yarn-spinning facilities (b)	—	10,726	—
Charge to comply with employment contract (c)	1,456	1,050	4,614
	$20,386	$11,776	$4,614

(a) In September 2006, the Company announced a restructuring of its Canadian manufacturing operations to take effect in December 2006, involving the closure of its textile manufacturing facility in Valleyfield, Quebec and the downsizing of its Montreal, Quebec knitting facility. The Company has recorded a charge of $18,930 relating to this restructuring and the concurrent re-assessment of the recoverability of the carrying values of its remaining Canadian textile manufacturing and related assets. Under the Company's business model, there are essentially no tax recoveries with respect to this charge. The components of this charge include . . . an asset impairment loss of $15,149 relating to all of the Canadian textile and related manufacturing fixed assets . . . . The Company was required to recognize asset impairment charges to reduce the carrying value of the fixed assets to fair value because the carrying value of the assets exceeded the future cash flows which they were projected to generate during the balance of their estimated economic lives.

WestJet did not report any impairment loss on its long-term assets. However, let us assume that a review of WestJet's aircraft indicated that aircraft with a net book value of $132 million had an estimated amount of $100 million in future cash flows. These aircraft are therefore impaired because they are not expected to generate future benefits equal to their net book value. To compute the amount of the impairment loss, *fair value* should be determined. For WestJet, that process includes using published sources and third-party bids to obtain the value of these aircraft. If the aircraft's fair value is $90 million, then the loss is calculated as $42 million ($132 million net book value less $90 million fair value). The following journal entry would be recorded:

Loss due to impairment of assets (+Loss, −SE)	42,000,000	
Aircraft (A)		42,000,000

Assets	=	Liabilities	+	Shareholders' Equity
Aircraft −42,000,000				Loss due to impairment −42,000,000

DISPOSAL OF PROPERTY, PLANT, AND EQUIPMENT

In some cases, a business may *voluntarily* decide not to hold a long-term asset for its entire life. The company may drop a product from its line and no longer need the equipment that was used to produce the product, or managers may want to replace a machine with a more efficient one. These disposals include sale, trade-in, or retirement. When WestJet disposes of an old aircraft, it may sell it to a cargo airline or

■ LEARNING OBJECTIVE 5

Analyze the disposal of property, plant, and equipment.

regional airline. A business may also dispose of an asset ***involuntarily*** as a result of a casualty, such as a storm, fire, or accident.

Disposals of long-term assets seldom occur on the last day of the accounting period. Therefore, amortization must be updated to the date of disposal. The disposal of an amortizable asset usually requires two entries:

(1) an adjusting entry to update the amortization expense and accumulated amortization accounts and

(2) an entry to record the disposal. Then the cost of the asset and any accumulated amortization at the date of disposal must be removed from the accounts. The difference between any resources received on disposal of an asset and its net book value at the date of disposal is a gain or loss on disposal of the asset. This gain (or loss) is revenue (or expense) from "peripheral or incidental" activities rather than from normal operations. Gains and losses from disposals are usually shown separately on the income statement after income from operations.

Assume that at the end of year 2006, WestJet sold an aircraft that was no longer needed because of the elimination of service to a small city. The original cost of the aircraft was $2.6 million, with an estimated useful life of 17,500 flight hours and no residual value. The unrecorded amortization expense for the year was $371,000.[5] The aircraft was sold for $1.6 million in cash and had accumulated amortization of $224,000 at the beginning of 2006. The loss on the sale of this aircraft is $405,000, calculated as follows:

Cash received		$1,600,000
Original cost	$2,600,000	
Less: Accumulated amortization	595,000	
Net book value		2,005,000
Loss on disposal		$ (405,000)

The entries and effects of the transaction on the date of the sale follow:

① Amortization expense (E)	371,000	
Accumulated amortization—Aircraft (XA)		371,000
② Cash (A)	1,600,000	
Accumulated amortization—Aircraft (XA)	595,000	
Loss on sale of asset (+Loss, −SE).	405,000	
Aircraft (A)		2,600,000

Assets		=	Liabilities	+	Shareholders' Equity	
① Accumulated amortization	− 371,000				① Amortization expense	−371,000
② Cash	+1,600,000				② Loss on sale of asset	−405,000
Accumulated amortization	+ 595,000					
Aircraft	−2,600,000					

A gain or loss on disposal occurs because (1) amortization expense is based on estimates that may differ from actual experience and (2) amortization is based on original cost, not current market value. Because the gain or loss on disposal is not part of the continuing operating activities of a company, it usually is shown as a separate line item on the income statement. In 2006, for example, WestJet sold property and equipment and reported a net gain of $63,000 as a separate item on its income statement.

---

[5]Sale of the aircraft during the year requires updating the accumulated amortization account to the date of sale by computing amortization for a fraction of the year. The amortization expense could be based on the number of months of amortization or 50 percent of the annual amortization if the company uses the half-year rule.

SELF-STUDY **QUIZ 9-5**

Now let us assume the same facts as above except that the asset was sold for $2,300,000 cash. Prepare the two entries on the date of the sale.

1. Update the amortization expense for the year.

2. Record the sale.

After you have completed your answers, check them with the solutions on page 496.

Companies may also trade in an old asset in exchange for a new asset and pay cash to cover the difference in the assets' values. Let us assume that an old vehicle, originally acquired at $20,000 with $16,000 of accumulated amortization, has a fair market value of $3,000. The company exchanges this vehicle in partial payment for computer hardware, and pays an additional amount of $1,600 in cash. This trade-in transaction includes a non-cash consideration. Hence, the computer hardware is recorded at its fair market value, unless the fair market value of the old vehicle is more objectively determinable. Notice that the net book value of the vehicle is $4,000 and the total payment for the computer hardware is $4,600, which is equal to the fair market value of the vehicle plus the cash consideration. Assuming that the fair market value of the vehicle is more objectively determinable, the journal entry and effects of the trade-in transaction would be as follows:[6]

Computer hardware (A)........................	4,600	
Accumulated amortization—Delivery van (XA).......	16,000	
Loss on disposal of assets (Loss, −SE)............	1,000	
Delivery van (A).............................		20,000
Cash (A)....................................		1,600

In certain situations, the company may dispose of an old, unusable asset if it cannot sell it to another party. The abandonment or retirement of an asset results in a loss that is equal to the asset's net book value. The journal entry to record the retirement of an asset is similar to the case of a sale or a trade-in, except that the cash account is not affected.

TAKING A DIFFERENT STRATEGY

A QUESTION OF ETHICS

Singapore Airlines, formed in 1972, has shown continued profitability as one of the world's largest operators of the most technologically advanced "jumbo jets," the Boeing 747-400. Unlike the rest of the airline industry with an average fleet age of more than 12 years, Singapore Airlines uses its aircraft for an average of just under six years. This strategy has a dual effect. Amortization expense is significantly higher due to the shorter estimated useful life, thus reducing net income. Singapore Airlines sells its used aircraft, however—an activity that has resulted in gains reported on the income statement. The choice of estimated useful lives and the timing of asset sales provide management with the flexibility to ***manage earnings***.

For example, Singapore Airlines' 2006 annual report shows a gain on disposal of aircraft spares and spare engines of $237.9 million, representing 10.4 percent of pretax income. This is compared to $115.7 million in 2005 or 14.7 percent of pretax income. These gains on disposals increase the company's normal operating profits.

How can this lead to earnings management? Singapore Airlines amortizes its aircraft faster than most other airlines. Therefore, when it sells its aircraft, the book value used to record the sale is quite low relative to the actual proceeds from the sale, resulting in a gain. When ordinary earnings are low, management can retire more aircraft, recognize the gains, and increase net income.

---

[6]The same analysis applies when a company exchanges an old asset for a new asset of the same kind, such as an old vehicle for a newer model.

In general, the practice of using conservative accounting policies (in this case, high amortization from conservative useful life estimates) to increase subsequent net income is called creating a "cookie jar." These "cookies" (aircraft whose sale will result in a large gain) are available as needed to boost net income. However, use of cookie jar reserves to manage earnings is under increasing scrutiny from auditors and regulators and is not desirable.

NATURAL RESOURCES AND INTANGIBLE ASSETS

ACQUISITION AND DEPLETION OF NATURAL RESOURCES

■ **LEARNING OBJECTIVE 6**

Apply measurement and reporting concepts for natural resources and intangible assets.

NATURAL RESOURCES are assets that occur in nature, such as mineral deposits, timber tracts, oil, and gas.

You are probably most familiar with large companies that are involved in manufacturing goods (Bombardier, Dell), distribution of goods (Sears Canada, Home Depot), or performing a service (Canada Post, Holiday Inn). A number of large companies, some of which are less well known, develop raw materials and products from **natural resources**, which include mineral deposits such as gold or iron ore (Barrick Gold), oil wells (Suncor Energy), and timber tracts (Timber West). These resources are often called *wasting assets* because they are depleted (i.e., physically used up). Companies that develop natural resources are critical to the economy because they produce such essential items as lumber for construction, fuel for heating and transportation, and food for consumption. Such companies attract considerable public attention because of the significant effect they can have on the environment. Concerned citizens often read financial statements from companies involved in exploration for oil, coal, and various ores to determine the amount of money spent to protect the environment.

DEPLETION is the systematic and rational allocation of the cost of a natural resource over the period of exploitation.

When natural resources are acquired or developed, they are recorded in conformity with the *cost principle*. As a natural resource is used up, its acquisition cost must be apportioned among the periods in which revenues are earned, in conformity with the *matching principle*. The term **depletion** refers to the systematic and rational allocation of the acquisition cost of natural resources to future periods in which their use contributes to revenue.[7] The units-of-production method is often applied to compute depletion.

To illustrate, Suncor Energy Inc. is a Canadian integrated petroleum explorer, developer, and refiner. The company depletes the acquisition cost of its natural gas reserves based on engineering estimates of the proven quantity of natural gas in the reserve, known as *proved reserves*. Proved reserves are considered to be recoverable under current technology and existing economic conditions. Suncor also explores and develops its own reserves and produces natural gas primarily from three areas in western Alberta and northeastern British Columbia. Its summary of significant accounting policies included the following:

REAL WORLD EXCERPT

Suncor Energy Inc.

ANNUAL REPORT

Depreciation, depletion and amortization

Natural Gas:

. . . Acquisition costs of proved properties are depleted using the unit of production method based on proved reserves. Capitalized exploratory drilling costs and development costs are depleted on the basis of proved developed reserves. For purposes of the depletion calculation, production and reserves volumes for oil and natural gas are converted to a common unit of measure on the basis of their approximate relative energy content. Gas plants, support facilities and equipment are depreciated on a straight-line basis over their useful lives, which average 12 years.

---

[7]Consistent with the procedure for recording amortization, an accumulated depletion account may be used. In practice, most companies credit the asset account directly for the periodic depletion. This procedure is also typically used for intangible assets, which are discussed in the next section.

For example, assume that the depletion of Suncor's proved and proved developed reserves is $6,000,000 for the current year. The journal entry to record the depletion of reserves and the transaction effects are:

Natural gas inventory (A) 6,000,000		
Natural gas reserves (A)		6,000,000
(or Accumulated depletion XA)		

Assets	=	Liabilities	+	Shareholders' Equity
Natural gas inventory	+6,000,000			
Natural gas reserves	−6,000,000			
(or Accumulated depletion)				

Note that the amount of the natural resource that is depleted is capitalized as inventory, not expensed. When the inventory is sold, the cost of goods sold is then included as an expense on the income statement.

A *depletion rate* is computed by dividing the total acquisition and development cost (less any estimated residual value, which is rare) by the estimated units that can be withdrawn economically from the resource. The depletion rate is multiplied each period by the actual number of units withdrawn during the accounting period. This procedure is the same as the units-of-production method of calculating amortization.

When buildings and similar improvements are acquired for the development and exploitation of a natural resource, they should be recorded in separate asset accounts and amortized—not depleted. Their estimated useful lives cannot be longer than the time needed to exploit the natural resource unless they have a significant use after the source is depleted.

ACQUISITION AND AMORTIZATION OF INTANGIBLE ASSETS

Intangible assets are increasingly important resources for organizations. An intangible asset, like any other asset, has value because of certain rights and privileges conferred by law on its owner. An intangible asset has no material or physical substance as do tangible assets such as land and buildings. Examples of intangible assets include patents, trademarks, and licences. Most intangible assets usually are evidenced by a legal document. The growth in the importance of intangible assets has resulted from the tremendous expansion in computer information systems and web technologies and the frenzy of companies purchasing other companies at high prices, with the expectation that the intangible resources will provide significant future benefits to the purchasing companies.

Intangible assets are recorded *at historical cost only if they are purchased*. If an intangible asset is developed internally, the cost of development normally is recorded as an expense. Upon acquisition of intangible assets, managers determine whether the separate intangibles have definite or indefinite lives.

Definite Life: The cost of an intangible with a definite life is allocated on a straight-line basis each period over its useful life in a process similar to amortization of long-term assets. However, most companies do not estimate a residual value for their intangible assets. Let us assume a company purchases a patent for $800,000 and intends to uses it for 20 years. The adjusting entry to record $40,000 in patent amortization expense ($800,000 ÷ 20 years) is as follows:

Patent amortization expense (E) 40,000		
Patent (A) (or Accumulated amortization XA)		40,000

Amortization expense is included on the income statement each period and the intangible assets are reported at cost less accumulated amortization on the balance sheet.

Indefinite Life: Intangible assets with indefinite lives are ***not amortized***. Instead, these assets are to be tested at least annually for possible impairment, and the asset's book value is written down (decreased) to its fair value if impaired. The two-step process is similar to that used for other long-term assets including intangibles with definite lives.

Let us assume a company purchases for $120,000 cash a copyright that is expected to have an indefinite life. At the end of the current year, management determines that the fair value of the copyright is $90,000. The $30,000 loss ($120,000 book value less $90,000 fair value) is recorded as follows:

Loss due to impairment (+Loss, −SE)	30,000	
Copyright (A)		30,000

EXAMPLES OF INTANGIBLE ASSETS

The 2006 edition of *Financial Reporting in Canada* reported that 133 of the 200 companies included in the survey disclosed information about goodwill in their 2005 annual reports. This compares to 74 companies that disclosed information about intangibles other than goodwill.[8] These intangibles include broadcast rights, publishing rights, trademarks, patents, licences, customer lists, franchises, and purchased research and development.

For example, CAE Inc., a Canadian provider of flight simulators and training, provided the followings details about its intangible assets (other than goodwill) in a note to its financial statements for 2006.

REAL WORLD EXCERPT

CAE Inc.

ANNUAL REPORT

NOTE 8—INTANGIBLE ASSETS

(amounts in millions)	Cost	Accumulated Amortization	Net Book Value 2006
Trade names	$12.2	$0.9	$11.3
Customer relations	1.2	0.2	1.0
Customer contractual agreements	7.7	3.0	4.7
Enterprise resources planning—software (ERP)	3.3	—	3.3
Other intangibles assets	4.0	1.0	3.0
	$28.4	$5.1	$23.3

For accounting purposes, **GOODWILL** is the excess of the purchase price of a business over the market value of the business's identifiable assets and liabilities.

Goodwill   By far, the most frequently reported intangible asset is **goodwill**. The term goodwill, as used by most businesspeople, means the favourable reputation that a company has with its customers. Goodwill arises from factors such as customer confidence, reputation for good service and quality products, and financial standing. For example, WestJet's promise to deliver no-frills, friendly, reliable transportation combines factors that produce customer loyalty and repeated travel. From its first day of operations, a successful business continually builds its own goodwill through a combination of factors that cannot be sold separately. In this context, goodwill is said to be ***internally generated*** and is not reported as an asset.

[8]N. Chlala, L. Martel, A. Lavigne, and C. Byrd, *Financial Reporting in Canada 2006*. Toronto: Canadian Institute of Chartered Accountants, 2006, pp. 273, 275.

The only way to report goodwill as an asset is to purchase another business. Often, the purchase price of a business exceeds the fair market value of all of the identifiable assets owned by the business minus all of the identifiable liabilities owed to others. Why would a company pay more to acquire a business as a whole than it would pay if it bought the assets individually? The answer is to obtain the acquired company's goodwill. It may be easy for the acquiring company to buy a fleet of aircraft, but a new business would not generate the same level of revenue flying the same routes as if it acquired WestJet's goodwill.

For accounting purposes, goodwill is defined as the difference between the purchase price of a company as a whole and the fair market value of its net assets (all identifiable assets minus all identifiable liabilities).

```
  Purchase price
- Fair market value of identifiable assets and liabilities
  Goodwill to be reported
```

Both parties to the sale estimate an acceptable amount for the goodwill of the business and add it to the appraised fair value of the business's assets and liabilities. Then the sale price of the business is negotiated. The resulting amount of goodwill is recorded as an intangible asset only when it actually is purchased at a measurable cost, in conformity with the *cost principle*.

Companies that reported goodwill related to acquisitions prior to July 1, 2001, were required to amortize it over an estimated useful life (not to exceed 40 years) using the straight-line method. Revised Canadian and U.S. accounting standards consider goodwill arising from acquisitions after January 1, 2002 to have an indefinite life, but any subsequent impairment in its value should be written down. This leads to the recognition of a loss that is reported as a separate item on the income statement in the year the impairment occurs.

Trademarks A **trademark** is a special name, image, or slogan identified with a product or a company. For example, banks such as the Bank of Montreal, auto manufacturers such as Toyota and General Motors, and fast-food restaurant chains such as Pizza Hut have familiar trademarks. Trademarks are protected by law when they are registered at the Canadian Intellectual Property Office of Industry Canada. The protection of a trademark provides the registered holder with exclusive rights to the trademark and can be renewed every 15 years throughout its life. Trademarks are often some of the most valuable assets that a company can own, but they are rarely seen on balance sheets. The reason is simple: intangible assets are not recorded unless they are purchased. Companies often spend millions of dollars developing trademarks, but these expenditures are recorded as expenses and not capitalized. Purchased trademarks that have definite lives are amortized on a straight-line basis over their estimated useful life, up to a maximum period of 40 years.

A **TRADEMARK** is an exclusive legal right to use a special name, image, or slogan.

Patents A **patent** is an exclusive right granted by the Canadian Intellectual Property Office of Industry Canada for a period of 20 years. It is typically granted to a person who invents a new product or discovers a new process. The patent enables the owner to use, manufacture, and sell both the subject of the patent and the patent itself. Without the protection of a patent, inventors likely would be unwilling to search for new products. The patent prevents a competitor from simply copying a new invention or discovery until the inventor has had a period of time to earn an economic return on the new product.

A patent that is *purchased* is recorded at cost. An ***internally developed*** patent is recorded at only its registration and legal cost because GAAP require the immediate expensing of research and development costs. In conformity with the matching principle, the cost of a patent must be amortized over the shorter of its economic life or its remaining legal life.

A **PATENT** is granted by the federal government for an invention; it is an exclusive right given to the owner to use, manufacture, and sell the subject of the patent.

A **COPYRIGHT** is the exclusive right to publish, use, and sell a literary, musical, or artistic work.

Copyrights **Copyright** protection is granted by the Canadian Intellectual Property Office. It gives the owner the exclusive right to publish, use, and sell a literary, musical, or artistic piece of work for a period not exceeding 50 years after the author's death. The book that you are reading has a copyright to protect the publisher and the authors. It would be against the law, for example, for an instructor were to copy several chapters from this book and hand them out in class. The same principles, guidelines, and procedures used in accounting for the cost of patents also are used for copyrights.

A **FRANCHISE** is a contractual right to sell certain products or services, use certain trademarks, or perform activities in a geographical region.

Franchises **Franchises** may be granted by either the government or other businesses for a specified period and purpose. A city may grant one company a franchise to distribute gas to homes for heating purposes, or a company may sell franchises, such as the right for a local outlet to operate a Mikes restaurant. Franchise agreements are contracts that can have a variety of provisions. They usually require an investment by the franchisee; therefore, they should be accounted for as intangible assets. The life of the franchise agreement depends on the contract. It may be for a single year or an indefinite period. Blockbuster Video is a popular company in the home video rental business. Its franchise agreement covers a period of 20 years. Blockbuster has more than 900 stores under franchise agreements.

TECHNOLOGY includes costs for computer software and Web development.

Technology The number of companies reporting a **technology** intangible asset has increased significantly in recent years. Computer software and Web development costs are becoming increasingly significant as companies modernize their processes and make greater use of advances in information and communication technology. In 2005, IBM Corporation reported a net amount of $113 million in *completed technology* in a note to its balance sheet and disclosed the following in its accounting policies:

REAL WORLD EXCERPT

International Business Machines Corporation

ANNUAL REPORT

The company capitalizes certain costs that are incurred to purchase or to create and implement internal-use computer software, which includes software coding, installation, testing, and data conversion. Capitalized costs are amortized on a straight-line basis over two years.

LICENCES AND OPERATING RIGHTS, obtained through agreements with governmental units and agencies, permit owners to use public property in performing their services.

Licences and Operating Rights **Licences and operating rights** are typically obtained through agreements with governmental units or agencies, and permit the holders to use public property in performing their services. For airline companies, the operating rights are authorized landing slots that are regulated by the government and are in limited supply at many airports. They are intangible assets that can be bought and sold by the airlines. Other types of licences that grant permission to companies include air waves for radio and television broadcasts, and land for cable and telephone lines.

Research and Development Expense—*Not an Intangible Asset* If an intangible asset is developed internally, the cost of development normally is recorded as *research and development expense*. For example, QLT, Inc. (a manufacturer of pharmaceutical products) recently spent more than $56.4 million on research to discover new products. This amount was reported as an expense, not an asset, because research and development expenditures typically do not possess sufficient probability of resulting in measurable future cash flows. If QLT had spent an equivalent amount to purchase patents for new products from other drug companies, it would have recorded the expenditure as an asset.

Under specific circumstances, development costs can be deferred to future accounting periods, recorded as assets, and then amortized over time, if the company can demonstrate that it is technically and commercially feasible to produce and market the product or process, that adequate resources are available or can be obtained to complete the project, and that future benefits are reasonably certain.

Leaseholds A **leasehold** is the right granted in a contract called a *lease* to use a specific asset. Leasing is a common type of business contract. For a consideration called *rent,* the owner (lessor) extends to another party (lessee) certain rights to use specified property. Leases may vary from simple arrangements, such as the month-to-month (*operating*) lease of an office or the daily rental of an automobile, to long-term (*capital*) leases having complex contractual arrangements.

Lessees sometimes make significant improvements to a leased property when they enter into a long-term lease agreement. A company that agrees to lease office space on a 15-year lease may install new fixtures or move walls to make the space more useful. These improvements are called *leasehold improvements* and are recorded as an asset by the lessee despite the fact that the lessor usually owns the leasehold improvements at the end of the lease term. The cost of leasehold improvements should be amortized over the estimated useful life of the related improvements or the remaining life of the lease, whichever is shorter.

WestJet has made leasehold improvements to the administrative building, two training centres, warehousing buildings, and numerous airport stations and maintenance facilities across Canada. These leasehold improvements had a net book value of $2,310,000 at December 31, 2005, as reported in note 2 to WestJet's financial statements. WestJet amortizes this intangible asset on a straight-line basis over the term of the lease.

LEASEHOLDS are rights granted to a lessee under a lease contract.

EFFECT ON CASH FLOW STATEMENT

FOCUS ON
CASH FLOWS

The indirect method for preparing the operating activities section of the cash flow statement involves reconciling net income (reported on the income statement) to cash flows from operations. This means that (1) revenues and expenses that do not affect cash and (2) gains and losses that relate to investing or financing activities (not operations) should be eliminated. When amortization is recorded, no cash payment is made (i.e., there is no credit to Cash). Since amortization expense (a non-cash expense) is subtracted from revenues in calculating net income, it must be added back to net income to eliminate its effect.

Gains and losses on disposal of long-term assets represent the difference between cash proceeds and the book value of the assets disposed of. Hence, gains and losses are non-cash amounts that do not relate to operating activities, but they are included in the computation of net income. Therefore, gains are subtracted from net income and losses are added to net income in the computation of cash flow from operations.

■ **LEARNING OBJECTIVE 7**

Explain the impact on cash flows of the acquisition, use, and disposal of long-term assets.

EFFECT ON CASH FLOW STATEMENT

IN GENERAL → Acquiring, selling, and amortizing long-term assets affect a company's cash flows as indicated in the following table:

	Effect on Cash Flows
Operating activities (indirect method)	
Net income	$xxx
Adjusted for: Amortization expense	+
Gains on disposal of long-term assets	−
Losses on disposal of long-term assets	+
Losses due to asset impairment write-downs	+
Investing activities	
Purchase of long-term assets	−
Sale of long-term assets	+

FOCUS COMPANY ANALYSIS → Exhibit 9.5 shows a condensed version of WestJet's cash flow statements prepared using the indirect method. Buying and selling long-term assets are investing activities. In 2006, WestJet used $480 million in cash to purchase

SELECTED FOCUS COMPANY COMPARISONS: PERCENTAGE OF AMORTIZATION TO CASH FLOWS FROM OPERATIONS

WestJet Airlines	33%
Van Houtte	78%
Forzani Group	88%

EXHIBIT **9.5**

WestJet Cash Flow Statements

REAL WORLD EXCERPT

WestJet Airlines

ANNUAL REPORT

WESTJET AIRLINES LTD.
CONSOLIDATED STATEMENT OF CASH FLOWS
Years ended December 31, 2006 and 2005
(in thousands of dollars)

	2006	2005
Cash provided by (used in):		
Operating activities:		
Net earnings	$ 114,676	$ 24,001
Items not involving cash:		
Amortization	111,442	106,624
(Gain) loss on disposal of property and equipment	(839)	98
(Gain) loss on disposal of aircraft parts (note 2)	(1,233)	(1,126)
Other (summarized)	112,106	117,727
	336,152	247,324
Investing activities:		
Aircraft additions	(438,906)	(660,947)
Aircraft disposals	3,822	404,583
Other property and equipment additions	(41,124)	(44,969)
Other property and equipment disposals	1,611	894
	(474,597)	(300,439)

aircraft and other property and equipment. WestJet completed the sale of its fleet of 737-200 aircraft during 2006 and received $3.8 million in cash. Since selling long-term assets is not an operating activity, any gains (losses) on sales of long-term assets that are included in net income are deducted from (added to) net income in the operating activities section to eliminate the effect of the sale. Unless they are large, these gain and loss adjustments are normally not specifically highlighted on the cash flow statement. WestJet lists a gain of $2,072,000 in its cash flow statement for 2006.

Finally, in capital-intensive industries such as airlines, amortization is a significant non-cash expense included in net income. In WestJet's case, amortization expense is the single largest adjustment to net income in determining cash flows from operations. It was 33 percent of operating cash flows in 2006 and reached 43 percent in 2005.

FINANCIAL
ANALYSIS

A MISINTERPRETATION

Some analysts misinterpret the meaning of a non-cash expense and often say that "cash is provided by amortization." Although amortization is added in the operating section of the cash flow statement, **amortization is not a source of cash**. Cash from operations can be provided only by selling goods and services. A company with a large amount of amortization expense does not generate more cash compared with a company that reports a small amount of amortization expense, assuming that they are exactly the same in every other respect. Amortization expense reduces the amount of reported net income for a company, but it does not reduce the amount of cash generated by the company because it is a non-cash expense. Remember that the effects of recording amortization are a reduction in shareholders' equity and in long-term assets, not in cash. That is why, on the cash flow statement, amortization expense is added back to net income (on an accrual basis) to compute cash flows from operations (income on a cash basis). Note that the amortization expense on WestJet's cash flow statement is listed under the subtitle "Items not involving cash."

Although amortization is a non-cash expense, the **amortization method used for tax purposes can affect a company's cash flows**. Amortization, in the form of Capital Cost Allowance (CCA), is a deductible expense for income tax purposes. The higher the amount of CCA reported by a company for tax purposes, the lower the taxable income and the taxes it must pay. Because taxes must be paid in cash, a reduction in the tax obligation of a company reduces the company's cash outflows.

The maximum deduction for CCA for each class of assets is based on rates specified by Canada Revenue Agency, but corporations may choose to deduct lower amounts for CCA during periods of losses or low income before taxes and postpone CCA deductions to future years to minimize their tax obligations.

DEMONSTRATION **CASE**

Diversified Industries has been operating for a number of years. It started as a residential construction company. In recent years, it expanded into heavy construction, ready-mix concrete, sand and gravel, construction supplies, and earth-moving services.

The following transactions were selected from those completed during year 2008. They focus on the primary issues discussed in this chapter. Amounts have been simplified for case purposes.

2008

Jan. 1   The management decided to buy a building that was about 10 years old. The location was excellent, and there was adequate parking space. The company bought the building and the land on which it was situated for $305,000. It paid $100,000 in cash and signed a mortgage note payable for the rest. A reliable appraiser provided the following market values: land, $132,300; and building, $182,700.

Jan. 12   Paid renovation costs on the building of $38,100 prior to use.

June 19   Bought a third location for a gravel pit (designated No. 3) for $50,000 cash. The location had been carefully surveyed. It was estimated that 100,000 cubic yards of gravel could be removed from the deposit.

July 10   Paid $1,200 for ordinary repairs on the building.

Aug. 1   Paid $10,000 for costs of preparing the new gravel pit for exploitation.

Dec. 31   Year-end adjustments:

   a. The building will be amortized on a straight-line basis over an estimated useful life of 30 years. The estimated residual value is $35,000.

   b. During 2008, 12,000 cubic yards of gravel were removed from gravel pit No. 3 and sold.

   c. The company owns a patent right that is used in operations. On January 1, 2008, the patent account had a balance of $3,300. The patent has an estimated remaining useful life of six years (including 2008).

   d. At the beginning of the year, the company owned equipment with a cost of $650,000 and a book value of $500,000. The equipment is being amortized using the double-declining-balance method, with a useful life of 20 years with no residual value.

   e. At year-end, the company identified a piece of old excavation equipment with a cost of $156,000 and remaining book value of $120,000. Due to its smaller size and lack of safety features, the old equipment has limited use. The company reviewed the asset for possible impairment of value. The equipment has a fair value of $40,000.

Required:

1. Indicate the accounts affected and the amount and direction (+ for increase and − for decrease) of the effect for each of the preceding events on the balance sheet equation. Use the following headings:

Date	Assets	=	Liabilities	+	Shareholders' Equity

2. Record the adjusting journal entries based on the information for December 31([*a*] and [*b*] only).
3. Show the December 31, 2008, balance sheet classifications and amount for each of the following items:

   Fixed assets—land, building, equipment, and gravel pit

   Intangible asset—patent

4. Assuming that the company had sales of $1,000,000 for the year and a net book value of $500,000 for fixed assets at the beginning of the year, compute the fixed asset turnover ratio. Explain its meaning.

We strongly recommend that you attempt to answer the requirements on your own and then check your answers with the suggested solution.

SUGGESTED SOLUTION

1. Effects of events (with computations):

Date	Assets		Liabilities		Shareholders' Equity	
Jan. 1 (1)	Cash Land Building	−100,000 +128,100 +176,900	Note payable	+205,000		
Jan. 12 (2)	Cash Building	−38,100 +38,100				
June 19 (3)	Cash Gravel pit No. 3	−50,000 +50,000				
July 10 (4)	Cash	−1,200			Repairs expense	−1,200
Aug. 1 (5)	Cash Gravel pit No. 3	−10,000 +10,000				
Dec. 31 *a* (6)	Accumulated amortization	−6,000			Amortization expense	−6,000
Dec. 31 *b* (7)	Gravel pit No. 3 Gravel inventory	−7,200 +7,200				
Dec. 31 *c* (8)	Patent	−550			Amortization expense	−550
Dec. 31 *d* (9)	Accumulated amortization	−50,000			Amortization expense	−50,000
Dec. 31 *e* (10)	Accumulated amortization	−80,000			Loss due to asset impairment	−80,000

(1)

	Land		Building		Total
Market	$132,300	+	$182,700	=	$315,000
Percentage of total	42%	+	58%	=	100%
Cost	$128,100	+	$176,900	=	$305,000

(2) Capitalize the expenditure of $38,100 because it is necessary to prepare the asset for use.

(3) This is a natural resource.

(4) This is an ordinary repair (revenue expenditure) that should be expensed.

(5) Capitalize the expenditure of $10,000 because it is necessary to prepare the asset for use.

(6) **Cost of building**

Initial payment	$176,900
Repairs prior to use	38,100
Acquisition cost	$215,000

Straight-line amortization

($215,000 cost − $35,000 residual value) ×
1/30 years = $6,000 annual amortization

(7) **Cost of gravel pit**

Initial payment	$50,000
Preparation costs	10,000
Acquisition cost	$60,000

Units-of-production depletion

($60,000 cost/100,000 estimated production) ×
12,000 actual production = $7,200 annual depletion

(8) **Straight-line amortization**

Unamortized cost of patent	$3,300
÷Remaining useful life	÷ 6 years
	$ 550

(9) **Double-declining-balance amortization**

$500,000 (net book value) × 2/20 = $50,000 annual amortization

(10) **Asset impairment**

Book value of old equipment	$120,000
Fair value	40,000
Loss due to impairment	$ 80,000

2. Adjusting entries Dec. 31, 2008:

a. Amortization expense, building (E)	6,000	
Accumulated amortization (XA).		6,000
b. Gravel inventory (A)	7,200	
Gravel pit No. 3 (A)		7,200

3. Balance sheet, December 31, 2008:

Assets		
Fixed assets		
Land		$128,100
Building	$215,000	
Less: Accumulated amortization	6,000	209,000
Equipment	650,000	
Less: Accumulated amortization ($150,000 + 50,000 + 80,000)	280,000	370,000
Gravel pit		52,800
Total fixed assets		$759,900
Intangible asset		
Patent ($3,300 − $550)		$ 2,750

4. Fixed asset turnover ratio:

$$\frac{\text{Net Sales}}{\text{Average Net Fixed Assets}} = \frac{\$1,000,000}{(\$500,000 + \$759,900) \div 2} = 1.59$$

This construction company is capital-intensive. The fixed asset turnover ratio measures the company's efficiency at using its investment in property, plant, and equipment to generate sales.

SOLUTIONS TO **SELF-STUDY QUIZZES**

Self-Study Quiz 9-1

1.

Property, Plant, and Equipment (PPE)	
Acquisition cost	$1,800,000,000
Sales tax	70,000,000
Transportation	8,000,000
Installation	1,300,000
Total	$1,879,300,000

The maintenance contracts are not necessary for making the assets ready for use and therefore are not included in the acquisition cost.

2.

	Assets		Liabilities		Shareholders' Equity	
a. PPE	+1,879,300,000	Note payable	+1,315,510,000			
Cash	−563,790,000					
b. PPE	+1,879,300,000				Share capital	+450,000,000
Cash	−1,429,300,000					

Self-Study Quiz 9-2

1. Capitalize   2. Expense   3. Expense   4. Capitalize

Self-Study Quiz 9-3

1. ($240,000 − $30,000) × $\frac{1}{6}$ = $35,000

2. ($240,000 − 0) × $\frac{2}{6}$ = $80,000

3. [($240,000 − $30,000) ÷ 50,000] × 8,000 = $33,600

Self-Study Quiz 9-4

$50,000 (book value after 5 years) ÷ 2 years (remaining life) = $25,000 amortization expense per year.

Self-Study Quiz 9-5

1. Amortization expense (E)	371,000		
Accumulated amortization—aircraft (XA)		371,000	
2. Cash (A)	2,300,000		
Accumulated amortization—aircraft (XA)	595,000		
Gain on sale of asset (+Gain, +SE)		295,000	
Aircraft (A)		2,600,000	

CHAPTER **TAKE-AWAYS**

1. **Define, classify, and explain the nature of long-term assets and interpret the fixed asset turnover ratio. p. 463**
   a. Noncurrent assets are those that a business retains for long periods of time for use in the course of normal operations rather than for sale. They may be divided into tangible assets (land, buildings, equipment, natural resources) and intangible assets (including goodwill, patents, and franchises).
   b. The cost allocation method utilized affects the amount of net property, plant, and equipment that is used in the computation of the fixed asset turnover ratio. Accelerated methods reduce book value and increase the turnover ratio.

2. **Apply the cost principle to measure the acquisition and maintenance of property, plant, and equipment. p. 465**
   Acquisition cost of property, plant, and equipment is the cash-equivalent purchase price plus all reasonable and necessary expenditures made to acquire and prepare the asset for its intended use. These assets may be acquired using cash, debt, equity, or through self-construction. Expenditures made after the asset is in use are either capital expenditures or revenue expenditures:
   a. **Capital expenditures** provide benefits for one or more accounting periods beyond the current period. Amounts are debited to the appropriate asset accounts and amortized or depleted over their useful lives.
   b. **Revenue expenditures** provide benefits during the current accounting period only. Amounts are debited to appropriate current expense accounts when the expenses are incurred.

3. **Apply various amortization methods as assets are held and used over time. p. 470**
   Cost allocation methods: In conformity with the matching principle, cost (less any estimated residual value) is allocated to periodic expense over the periods benefited. Because of amortization, the net book value of an asset declines over time and net income is reduced by the amount of the expense. Common amortization methods include straight-line (a constant amount over time), units-of-production (a variable amount over time), and double-declining-balance (a decreasing amount over time).
   • Amortization—buildings and equipment, intangibles.
   • Depletion—natural resources.

4. **Explain the effect of asset impairment on the financial statements. p. 482**
   When events or changes in circumstances reduce the estimated future cash flows of long-term assets below their book value, the book values should be written down (by recording a loss) to the fair value of the assets.

5. **Analyze the disposal of property, plant, and equipment. p. 483**
   When assets are disposed of through sale or abandonment,
   • Record additional amortization since the last adjustment was made.
   • Remove the cost of the old asset and its related accumulated amortization, or depletion.
   • Recognize the cash proceeds.
   • Recognize any gains or losses when the asset's net book value is not equal to the cash received.

6. **Apply measurement and reporting concepts for natural resources and intangible assets. p. 486**
   The cost principle should be applied in recording the acquisition of natural resources and intangible assets. Natural resources should be depleted (usually by the units-of-production

method) usually with the amount of the depletion expense capitalized to an inventory account. Intangibles with definite useful lives are amortized using the straight-line method. Intangibles with indefinite useful lives, including goodwill, are not amortized, but are reviewed at least annually for impairment. Report intangibles at net book value on the balance sheet.

7. **Explain the impact on cash flows of the acquisition, use, and disposal of long-term assets. p. 491**
   Amortization expense is a noncash expense that has no effect on cash. It is added back to net income on the cash flow statement to determine cash from operations. Acquiring and disposing of long-term assets are investing activities.

In the previous chapters, we discussed business and accounting issues related to the assets a company holds. In Chapters 10, 11, and 12, we shift our focus to the other side of the balance sheet to see how managers finance the operations of their business and the acquisition of productive assets. We discuss various types of liabilities in Chapters 10 and 11 and examine owners' equity in Chapter 12.

KEY **RATIO**

The **fixed asset turnover ratio** measures how efficiently a company utilizes its investment in property, plant, and equipment over time. Its ratio can be compared to the ratio of its competitors. It is computed as follows (p. 464):

$$\text{Fixed Asset Turnover} = \frac{\text{Net Sales (or operating revenues)}}{\text{Average Net Fixed Assets}}$$

FINDING **FINANCIAL INFORMATION**

BALANCE SHEET
Under Non-Current Assets
  Property, plant, and equipment (net of accumulated amortization)
  Natural resources (net of accumulated depletion)
  Intangibles (net of accumulated amortization)

INCOME STATEMENT
Under Operating Expenses
  Amortization and depletion expense or as part of
  Selling, general, and administrative expenses and
  Cost of goods sold (with the amount of amortization expense disclosed in a note)

CASH FLOW STATEMENT
Under Operating Activities (indirect method)
  Net income
  + Amortization expense
  − Gains on sales of assets
  + Losses on sales of assets
Under Investing Activities
  + Sales of assets for cash
  − Purchases of assets for cash

NOTES
Under Summary of Significant Accounting Policies
  Description of management's choice for amortization methods, including useful lives, and the amount of annual amortization expense, if not listed on the income statement.
Under a Separate Footnote
  If not specified on the balance sheet, a listing of the major classifications of long-term assets at cost and the balance in accumulated amortization and depletion.

KEY **TERMS**

Acquisition Cost p. 465	**Licences and Operating Rights** p. 490
Amortization p. 470	**Long-Term (or Long-Lived or Capital) Assets** p. 463
Basket Purchase p. 467	**Natural Resources** p. 486
Betterments p. 469	**Net Book (or Net Carrying) Value** p. 471
Capital Expenditures p. 469	**Ordinary Repairs and Maintenance** p. 469
Capitalized Interest p. 467	
Copyright p. 490	**Patent** p. 489
Declining-Balance Amortization p. 475	**Residual (or Salvage) Value** p. 473
Depletion p. 486	**Revenue Expenditures** p. 469
Estimated Useful Life p. 472	**Straight-Line Amortization** p. 474
Extraordinary Repairs p. 469	**Tangible Assets** p. 464
Franchise p. 490	**Technology** p. 490
Goodwill p. 488	**Trademark** p. 489
Intangible Assets p. 464	**Units-of-Production Amortization** p. 475
Leaseholds p. 491	

QUESTIONS

1. Define *long-term assets*. Why are they considered a "bundle of future services"?
2. How is the fixed asset turnover ratio computed? Explain its meaning.
3. What are the classifications of long-term assets? Explain each.
4. Relate the cost principle to accounting for long-term assets. Under the cost principle, what amounts usually should be included in the acquisition cost of a long-term asset?
5. Describe the relationship between the matching principle and accounting for long-term assets.
6. What is a basket purchase? What measurement problem does it pose?
7. Distinguish between
   a. Capital expenditures and revenue expenditures. How is each accounted for?
   b. Ordinary and extraordinary repairs. How is each accounted for?
8. Distinguish between amortization and depletion.
9. In computing amortization, three values must be known or estimated; identify and explain the nature of each.
10. Estimated useful life and residual value of a long-term asset relate to the current owner or user rather than all potential users. Explain this statement.
11. What type of amortization expense pattern is provided under each of the following methods? When is the use of each method appropriate?
   a. Straight line.
   b. Units of production.
   c. Double declining balance.
12. Over what period should an addition to an existing long-term asset be amortized? Explain.
13. What is an *asset impairment?* How is it accounted for?
14. Define *intangible asset*. What period should be used to amortize an intangible asset?
15. Define *goodwill*. When is it appropriate to record goodwill as an intangible asset?
16. Distinguish between a leasehold and a leasehold improvement. Over what period should a leasehold improvement be amortized? Explain.
17. Why is amortization expense added to net income on the cash flow statement when using the indirect method of reporting cash flow from operations?

EXERCISES

LO1   **E9–1**   **Classifying Long-Term Assets and Related Cost Allocation Concepts**
For each of the following long-term assets, indicate its nature and related cost allocation concept. Use the following symbols:

Nature		Cost Allocation Concept	
L	Land	DP	Depletion
B	Building	A	Amortization
E	Equipment	NO	No cost allocation
NR	Natural resource	O	Other
I	Intangible		
O	Other		

Asset	Nature	Cost Allocation	Asset	Nature	Cost Allocation
(1) Copyright	_____	_____	(6) Operating licence	_____	_____
(2) Land held for use	_____	_____	(7) Land held for sale	_____	_____
(3) Warehouse	_____	_____	(8) Delivery vans	_____	_____
(4) Oil well	_____	_____	(9) Timber tract	_____	_____
(5) New engine for old machine	_____	_____	(10) Production plant	_____	_____

E9–2 Preparing a Partial Classified Balance Sheet

The following is a list of account titles and amounts (in thousands) reported by Ballard Power Systems Inc., a leading developer and manufacturer of fuel cells, an alternative power source for automobiles:

■ LO1

Ballard Power Systems Inc.

Materials	$ 8,872	System and subsystem technology	$ 47,189
Leasehold improvements	16,077	Accumulated amortization—Intangibles	59,469
Prepaid expenses	1,409	Fuel cell technology	41,869
Trade names	7,997	Work in progress	2,557
Accounts receivable	14,666	Cash and cash equivalents	148,919
Finished goods	2,418	Computer equipment	19,557
Furniture and fixtures	5,325	Building	13,037
Land	4,803	Short-term investments	84,114
Investments	8,962	Production and test equipment	71,775
Goodwill	155,324	Accumulated amortization— Property, plant, and equipment	70,259

Required:

Prepare the asset section of the balance sheet for Ballard Power Systems Inc., classifying the assets into Current Assets; Property, Plant, and Equipment (net); and Intangible Assets.

E9–3 Identifying Capital and Revenue Expenditures

For each of the following items, enter the correct letter to the left to show the type of expenditure. Use the following:

■ LO2

Type of Expenditure

C Capital expenditure   **R** Revenue expenditure   **N** Neither

Transactions

_____ (1) Paid $400 for ordinary repairs.
_____ (2) Paid $6,000 for extraordinary repairs.
_____ (3) Paid cash, $20,000, for addition to old building.
_____ (4) Paid for routine maintenance, $200, on credit.
_____ (5) Purchased a machine, $7,000; signed a long-term note.
_____ (6) Paid $2,000 for organization costs.
_____ (7) Paid one-year insurance premium in advance, $900.
_____ (8) Purchased a patent, $4,300 cash.
_____ (9) Paid $10,000 for monthly salaries.
_____ (10) Paid cash dividends, $20,000.

LO1

ANALYSIS

E9–4   Computing and Evaluating the Fixed Asset Turnover Ratio

The following information was reported by Cutter's Air Cargo Service for 2006:

Net fixed assets (beginning of year)	$1,450,000
Net fixed assets (end of year)	2,250,000
Net sales for the year	3,250,000
Net income for the year	1,700,000

Compute the company's fixed asset turnover ratio for the year. What can you say about Cutter's ratio when compared to WestJet's ratio for 2006, as computed in the chapter?

LO1

QLT Inc.

ANALYSIS

E9–5   Computing and Interpreting the Fixed Asset Turnover Ratio from a Financial Analyst's Perspective

The following data were disclosed in the annual reports of QLT Inc., a Canadian biotechnology company that has recently developed a product to treat macular degeneration of the eyes. If left untreated, this medical condition causes blindness.

(in thousands of dollars)	2006	2005	2004	2003	2002
Net sales	$175,090	$241,973	$186,072	$146,750	$110,513
Net property, plant, and equipment	50,497	$75,497	81,674	43,262	35,281

Required:

1. Compute QLT's fixed asset turnover ratio for the four years 2003 through 2006.

2. How might a financial analyst interpret the results?

LO2

E9–6   Determining Financial Statement Effects of Acquisition of Several Assets in a Basket Purchase

Kline Corporation acquired additional land and a building that included several pieces of equipment for $600,000. The acquisition was settled as follows: cash, $120,000; issuance of Kline's common shares, $120,000; and signing a long-term note for $360,000. An appraiser estimated the market values to be $200,000 for the land, $500,000 for the building, and $100,000 for the equipment. Indicate the accounts affected and the amount and direction (+ for increase and − for decrease) of the effect of this acquisition on the balance sheet equation. Use the following headings:

Assets	=	Liabilities	+	Shareholders' Equity

LO2, 3

E9–7   Computing and Recording Cost and Amortization of Assets in a Basket Purchase (Straight-Line Amortization)

Zeidler Company bought a building and the land on which the building is located for a total cash price of $178,000. The company paid transfer costs of $2,000. Renovation costs on the building were $23,000. An independent appraiser provided market values for the land, $50,000, and building, $150,000 before renovation.

Required:

1. Apportion the cost of the property on the basis of the appraised values. Show computations.

2. Prepare the journal entry to record the purchase of the building and land, including all expenditures. Assume that all transactions were for cash and that all purchases occurred at the start of the year.

3. Compute amortization of the building at the end of one year, using the straight-line method. Assume an estimated useful life of 12 years and an estimated residual value of $14,000.

4. What would be the book value of the property (building and land) at the end of year 2?

LO2, 3

E9–8   Determining Financial Statement Effects of an Asset Acquisition and Amortization (Straight-Line Amortization)

Vicario Company purchased a machine on March 1, 2009, at an invoice price of $20,000. On the date of delivery, March 2, 2009, the company paid $8,000 on the machine, and signed a note for the balance at 12-percent interest. On March 3, 2009, it paid $250 for freight on the machine. On March 5, Vicario paid installation costs of $1,200 relating to the machine. On October 1, 2009, the company paid the balance due on the machine plus the interest. On December 31, 2009 (the end of the accounting period), Vicario recorded straight-line amortization on the machine based on an estimated useful life of 10 years and an estimated residual value of $3,450.

Required (round all amounts to the nearest dollar):

1. Indicate the accounts affected and the amount and direction (+ for increase and − for decrease) of the effect of each transaction (on March 1, 2, 3, 5, and October 1) on the accounting equation. Use the following headings:

Date	Assets	=	Liabilities	+	Shareholders' Equity

2. Compute the acquisition cost of the machine.

3. Compute the amortization expense to be reported for 2009.

4. What is the impact on the cost of the machine of the interest paid on the 12-percent note? Under what circumstances can interest expense be included in an asset's cost?

5. What would be the net book value of the machine at the end of 2010?

E9–9 Evaluating the Impact of Capitalized Interest on Cash Flows and Fixed Asset Turnover from an Analyst's Perspective

■ **LO1, 2**

ACE Aviation Holdings

ANALYSIS

You are a financial analyst charged with evaluating the asset efficiency of companies in the airline industry. The financial statements for ACE Aviation Holdings Inc. include the following note:

> **(l) Interest Capitalized**
>
> Interest on funds used to finance the acquisition of new flight equipment and other property and equipment is capitalized for periods preceding the dates the assets are available for service.

Required:

1. Assume that ACE Aviation followed this policy for a major construction project this year. What is the sign of the effect of ACE Aviation's policy on the following? Use + for increase, − for decrease, and NE for no effect.
   a. Cash flows.
   b. Fixed asset turnover ratio.

2. Normally, how would your answer to requirement 1(*b*) affect your evaluation of ACE Aviation's effectiveness in utilizing property, plant, and equipment?

3. If the fixed asset turnover ratio changes due to interest capitalization, does this change indicate a real change in efficiency? Why or why not?

E9–10 Recording Amortization and Repairs (Straight-Line Amortization) and Determining Financial Statement Effects

■ **LO3**

Stacey Company operates a small manufacturing facility as a supplement to its regular service activities. At the beginning of 2009, an asset account for the company showed the following balances:

Manufacturing equipment	$80,000
Accumulated amortization through 2008	55,000

In early January 2009, the following expenditures were incurred for repairs and maintenance:

Routine maintenance and repairs on the equipment	$ 850
Major overhaul of the equipment	10,500

The equipment is being amortized on a straight-line basis over an estimated life of 15 years with a $5,000 estimated residual value. The company's fiscal year ends on December 31.

Required:

1. Prepare the adjusting entry to record the amortization of the manufacturing equipment on December 31, 2008.

2. Prepare the journal entries to record the two expenditures that occured during 2009.

3. Prepare the adjusting entry at December 31, 2009, to record the amortization of the manufacturing equipment, assuming no change in the estimated life or residual value of the equipment. Show computations.

4. Indicate the accounts affected and the amount and direction (+ for increase and − for decrease) of the balance sheet effects of the journal entries you prepared for requirements 1 to 3. Use the following headings:

Date	Assets	=	Liabilities	+	Shareholders' Equity

LO3

E9–11 Computing Amortization under Alternative Methods

Rita's Pita Company bought a new dough machine at the beginning of the year at a cost of $7,600. The estimated useful life was four years, and the residual value was $800. Assume that the estimated productive life of the machine is 10,000 hours. Annual usage was 3,500 hours in year 1; 3,200 hours in year 2; 2,200 hours in year 3; and 1,100 hours in year 4.

Required:

1. Complete a separate amortization schedule for each of the alternative methods. Round your computations to the nearest dollar.
   a. Straight line.
   b. Units of production.
   c. Double-declining balance.

Method: _____

Year	Computation	Amortization Expense	Accumulated Amortization	Net Book Value
At acquisition				
1				
2				
Etc.				

2. Assuming that the machine was used directly in the production of one of the products that the company manufactures and sells, what factors might management consider in selecting a preferable amortization method in conformity with the matching principle?

LO3

E9–12 Computing Amortization under Alternative Methods

Alexa Plastics Company purchased a new stamping machine at the beginning of the year at a cost of $125,000. The estimated residual value was $15,000. Assume that estimated useful life was five years, and the estimated productive life of the machine was 250,000 units. Actual annual production was as follows:

Year	1	2	3	4	5
Units	75,000	60,000	30,000	45,000	40,000

Required:

1. Complete a separate amortization schedule for each of the alternative methods. Round your computations to the nearest dollar.
   a. Straight line.
   b. Units of production.
   c. Double-declining balance.

Method: _____				
Year	Computation	Amortization Expense	Accumulated Amortization	Net Book Value
At acquisition				
1				
2				
Etc.				

2. Assuming that the machine was used directly in the production of one of the products that the company manufactures and sells, what factors might management consider in selecting a preferable amortization method in conformity with the matching principle?

E9–13 Explaining Depreciation Policy

An annual report for Ford Motor Company contained the following note:

> **Significant Accounting Policies**
>
> **Amortization of Property, Plant, and Equipment.** Property and equipment are stated at cost and depreciated primarily using the straight-line method over the estimated useful life of the asset. Useful lives range from 3 years to 36 years. The estimated useful lives generally are 14.5 years for machinery and equipment and 30 years for buildings and land improvements. Special tools placed in service beginning in 1999 are amortized using the units-of-production method over the expected vehicle model cycle life. Maintenance, repairs, and rearrangement costs are expensed as incurred.

Required:

Why do you think the company changed its amortization method for special tools acquired in 1992 and subsequent years? What impact did the change have on net income?

■ LO3

Ford Motor Company

ANALYSIS

E9–14 Interpreting Management's Choice of Different Depreciation Methods for Tax and Financial Reporting

An annual report for Federal Express Corporation included the following information:

> For financial reporting purposes, depreciation and amortization of property and equipment is provided on a straight-line basis over the asset's service life. For income tax purposes, depreciation is generally computed using accelerated methods.

Required:

Explain why Federal Express uses different methods of depreciation for financial reporting and tax purposes.

■ LO3

Federal Express

ANALYSIS

E9–15 Computing Amortization and Book Value for Two Years Using Alternative Amortization Methods, and Interpreting the Impact on Cash Flows

Cotton Company bought a machine for $65,000 cash. The estimated useful life was five years, and the estimated residual value was $5,000. Assume that the estimated useful life is 150,000 units. Units actually produced were 40,000 in year 1 and 45,000 in year 2.

■ LO3, 7

ANALYSIS

Required:

1. Determine the appropriate amounts to complete the following schedule. Show computations, and round to the nearest dollar.

	Amortization Expense for		Book Value at the End of	
Method of Amortization	Year 1	Year 2	Year 1	Year 2
Straight line				
Units of production				
Double-declining balance				

2. Which method would result in the lowest earnings per share for year 1? For year 2?

3. Which method would result in the highest amount of cash outflows in year 1? Why?

4. Indicate the effects of (a) acquiring the machine and (b) recording annual amortization on the operating and investing activities on the cash flow statement for year 1. Assume that straight-line amortization is used.

LO4   **E9–16 Identifying Asset Impairment**

For each of the following scenarios, indicate whether an asset has been impaired (Y for yes and N for no) and, if so, the amount of loss that should be recorded.

	Book Value	Estimated Future Cash Flows	Fair Value	Is Asset Impaired?	If so, Amount of Loss
a. Machine	$ 16,000	$ 10,000	$ 9,000		
b. Copyright	40,000	41,000	39,000		
c. Factory building	50,000	35,000	30,000		
d. Building	230,000	230,000	210,000		

LO4   **E9–17 Inferring Asset Impairment and Disposal of Assets**

United Parcel Service Inc.

ANALYSIS

United Parcel Service is the world's largest package delivery company and a leading global provider of specialized transportation and logistics services. The following note and information were reported in a recent annual report:

Note 1—SUMMARY OF ACCOUNTING POLICIES

Impairment of Long-Lived Assets

. . . We review long-lived assets for impairment when circumstances indicate the carrying amount of an asset may not be recoverable based on the undiscounted future cash flows of the asset. If the carrying amount of the asset is determined not to be recoverable, a write down to fair value is recorded. Fair values are determined based on quoted market values, discounted cash flows, or external appraisals, as applicable . . . In December (of a recent year), we permanently removed from service a number of Boeing 727, 747, and McDonnell Douglas DC-8 aircraft. As a result, we conducted an impairment evaluation, which resulted in an impairment charge of . . .

	Dollars in millions
Cost of property and equipment (beginning of year)	$26,444
Cost of property and equipment (end of year)	27,478
Capital expenditures during the year	2,127
Accumulated amortization (beginning of year)	12,516
Accumulated amortization (end of year)	13,505
Amortization expense during the year	1,543
Cost of property and equipment sold during the year	983
Accumulated amortization on property and equipment sold	554
Cash received on property and equipment sold	75

Required:

1. Reconstruct the journal entry for the disposal of property and equipment during the year.

2. Compute the amount of property and equipment that United Parcel wrote off as impaired during the year. (*Hint:* Set up T-accounts.)

LO4   **E9–18 Inferring Asset Impairment and Disposal of Assets**

ANALYSIS

Saputo Inc., the largest dairy processor in Canada, makes Italian and European-style cheeses for sale to retail, foodservice, and industrial customers in Canada, the U.S., and Argentina. It also produces milk, cultured dairy products, and distributes imported cheeses for the Canadian consumer retail market. The following note and information were reported in a recent annual report:

Note 1—SIGNIFICANT ACCOUNTING POLICIES

Impairment of Long-Lived Assets

In the event indications exist that the carrying amount of long-lived assets may not be recoverable, undiscounted estimated cash flows are projected over their remaining term, and compared to the carrying amount. To the extent such projections indicate that future undiscounted cash flows are not sufficient to recover the carrying amounts of related assets, a charge is recorded to reduce the carrying amount to equal projected future discounted cash flows.

	Dollars in millions
Cost of property and equipment (beginning of year)	$ 997.6
Cost of property and equipment (end of year)	1,074.2
Capital expenditures during the year	96.2
Accumulated amortization (beginning of year)	349.0
Accumulated amortization (end of year)	399.6
Amortization expense during the year	69.4
Cost of property and equipment sold during the year	13.8
Accumulated amortization on property and equipment sold	13.0
Cash received on property and equipment sold	3.3

During the year, Saputo wrote down certain buildings, machinery and equipment to their fair value. The impairment loss was included in the reported amortization expense for the year.

Required:

1. Reconstruct the journal entry for the disposal of property and equipment during the year.
2. Compute the amount of property and equipment that Saputo wrote off as impaired during the year. (*Hint:* Set up T-accounts.)

E9–19 **Recording the Disposal of an Asset and Financial Statement Effects**   ■ LO5

Sears Canada Inc. has developed a consolidated distribution network in Vaughan, Ontario, and in Calgary, Alberta. As part of its distribution service, Sears trucks transport inventory to its various department, furniture, appliance, automotive, and outlet stores, as well as to individual customers. Assume that Sears sold a small delivery truck that had been used in the business for three years. The records of the company reflect the following:

Sears Canada Inc.

Delivery truck	$28,000
Accumulated amortization	23,000

Required:

1. Prepare the journal entry to record the disposal of the truck and the related transaction effects, assuming that the sales price was: (a) $5,000; (b) $5,600; or (c) $4,600.
2. Based on the three preceding situations explain the effects of the disposal of an asset on financial statements.

E9–20 **Inferring Asset Age and Recording Accidental Loss on a Long-Term Asset (Straight-Line Amortization)**   ■ LO5

On January 1, 2009, the records of Barken Corporation showed the following:

Truck (estimated residual value, $3,000)	$18,000
Accumulated amortization (straight line, two years)	6,000

On September 30, 2009, the delivery truck was a total loss as a result of an accident. As the truck was insured, the company collected $5,600 cash from the insurance company on October 5, 2009.

Required:

1. Based on the data given, compute the estimated useful life of the truck.

2. Prepare all journal entries to record the events that occurred on September 30 and October 5, 2009, and the related adjustments to the accounts. Show computations.

■ LO6

Freeport-McMoRan Copper & Gold Inc.

E9–21 Computing the Acquisition and Depletion of a Natural Resource

Freeport-McMoRan Copper & Gold Inc. is a natural resources company involved in the exploration, development, and extraction of natural resources with the majority of its resources in Indonesia. Annual revenues exceed $4 billion. Assume that in February 2008, Freeport-McMoRan paid $700,000 for a mineral deposit in Bali. During March, it spent $65,000 in preparing the deposit for exploitation. It was estimated that 900,000 total cubic yards could be extracted economically. During 2008, 60,000 cubic yards were extracted and sold. During January 2009, the company spent another $6,000 for additional developmental work. After conclusion of the latest work, the estimated remaining recovery was increased to 1,200,000 cubic yards over the remaining life. During 2009, 50,000 cubic yards were extracted.

Required:

1. Compute the acquisition cost of the deposit in 2008.

2. Compute the depletion expense for 2008.

3. Compute the net book value of the deposit after payment of the January 2009 developmental costs.

4. Compute the depletion expense for 2009.

5. Prepare the journal entries to record the acquisition of the deposit in 2008 and the depletion expense for 2008.

■ LO6

E9–22 Computing Goodwill and Patents

Elizabeth Pie Company has been in business for 30 years and has developed a large group of loyal restaurant customers. Vaclav's Foods made an offer to buy Elizabeth Pie Company for $5,000,000. The book value of Elizabeth Pie's recorded assets and liabilities on the date of the offer is $4,400,000, with a market value of $4,600,000. Elizabeth Pie holds a patent for a piecrust fluting machine that the company invented (the patent, with a market value of $200,000, was never recorded by Elizabeth Pie because it was developed internally). The company estimates goodwill from loyal customers to be $300,000 (also never recorded by the company). Should Elizabeth Pie Company management accept Vaclav's Foods' offer of $5,000,000? If so, compute the amount of goodwill that Vaclav's Foods should record on the date of the purchase.

■ LO6

E9–23 Computing and Reporting the Acquisition and Amortization of Three Different Intangible Assets

Wyatt Company had three intangible assets at the end of 2009 (end of the fiscal year):

a. A patent purchased from R. Jay on January 1, 2009, for a cash cost of $7,670. Jay had registered the patent with the Canadian Intellectual Property Office seven years earlier on January 1, 2002. The cost of the patent is amortized over its legal life.

b. A franchise acquired from the local community to provide certain services for five years starting January 1, 2009. The franchise cost $25,000 cash.

c. A lease on some property for a five-year term beginning January 1, 2009. The company immediately spent $7,800 cash for long-term improvements (estimated useful life, eight years; no residual value). At the termination of the lease, there will be no recovery of these improvements.

d. A trademark that was purchased for $16,000. Management decided that the trademark has an indefinite life.

Required:

1. What is the acquisition cost of each intangible asset?

2. Compute the amortization of each intangible asset at December 31, 2009. The company does not use contra accounts.

3. Show how these assets and any related expenses should be reported on the balance sheet at December 31, 2009, and on the income statement for 2009.

E9–24 **Recording Rent Paid in Advance, Leasehold Improvements, Periodic Rent, and Related Amortization**

■ **LO6**

Starbucks Coffee
Company

Starbucks Coffee Company is a rapidly expanding retailer of specialty coffee with more than 12,000 coffee shops worldwide. Assume that Starbucks planned to open a new store on St. George Street near the University of Toronto and obtained a 15-year lease starting January 1, 2009. Although a serviceable building was on the property, the company had to build an additional structure for storage. The 15-year lease required a $18,000 cash advance payment plus cash payments of $5,000 per month during occupancy. During January 2009, the company spent $90,000 cash building the structure. The new structure has an estimated life of 18 years with no residual value.

Required:

1. Prepare the journal entries for the company to record the payment of the $18,000 advance on January 1, 2009, and the first monthly rental.

2. Prepare the journal entry to record the construction of the new structure.

3. Prepare any adjusting entries required at December 31, 2009, the end of the company's fiscal year, with respect to (a) the advance payment and (b) the new structure. Assume that straight-line amortization is used. Show computations.

4. Compute the total expense resulting from the lease for 2009.

E9–25 **Finding Financial Information as a Potential Investor**

■ **LO1–7**

You are considering investing the cash gifts you received for graduation in shares of various companies. You visit the Web sites of major companies, searching for relevant information.

Required:

For each of the following, indicate where you would locate the information in an annual report (*Hint:* The information may be in more than one location):

1. The detail on major classifications of long-term assets.

2. The accounting method(s) used for financial reporting purposes.

3. Whether the company has had any capital expenditures for the year.

4. Net amount of property, plant, and equipment.

5. Policies on amortizing intangibles.

6. Amortization expense.

7. Any significant gains or losses on disposals of long-term assets.

8. Accumulated amortization of property, plant, and equipment at the end of the last fiscal year.

9. The amount of assets written off as impaired during the year.

E9–26 **Recording and Explaining Amortization, Extraordinary Repairs, and Changes in Estimated Useful Life and Residual Value (Straight-Line Amortization)**

■ **LO2**

The records of Luci Company reflected the following details for Machine A at December 31, 2009, the end of the company's fiscal year.

Cost when acquired	$28,000
Accumulated amortization	10,000

During January 2010, the machine was renovated at a cost of $11,000. As a result, the estimated life increased from five years to eight years, and the residual value increased from $3,000 to $5,000. The company uses straight-line amortization.

Required:

1. Prepare the journal entry to record the renovation.

2. How old was the machine at the end of 2009?

3. Prepare the adjusting entry at the end of 2010 to record straight-line amortization for the year.

4. Explain the rationale for your entries in requirements 1 and 3.

■ **LO3**

E9–27 Computing the Effect of a Change in Useful Life and Residual Value on Financial Statements and Cash Flows (Straight-Line Amortization)

Dustin Company owns the office building occupied by its administrative office. The office building was reflected in the accounts at the end of last year as follows:

Acquisition cost	$450,000
Accumulated amortization (based on straight-line amortization, an estimated life of 30 years, and residual value of $30,000)	196,000

Following a careful study, management decided in January of this year that the total estimated useful life should be changed to 25 years (instead of 30) and the residual value reduced to $23,000 (from $30,000). The amortization method will not change.

Required:

1. Compute the annual amortization expense prior to the change in estimates.

2. Compute the annual amortization expense after the change in estimates.

3. What will be the net effect of changing the estimates on the balance sheet, net income, and cash flows for the year?

PROBLEMS

■ **LO3, 5**

P9–1 Understanding the Nature of Amortization

At the beginning of his first year at university, Georgio Labos bought a used combination colour television and stereo system for $960. He estimates that these two items will be almost worthless by the time he graduates in four years, and plans to abandon them then.

Required:

1. Assume that Georgio expects to receive four years of entertainment services for the $960. What is the book value of these items after one year? Use straight-line amortization with no residual value.

2. The university's academic year lasts a total of 30 weeks, from early September to late April. Georgio does not take the TV and stereo system with him on vacations. During the academic year, he participates in many activities, so he averages three hours per week of television viewing and listening to music. What is the average cost per hour of use? (Ignore costs of electricity and repairs.)

3. Georgio is disturbed by the answer to requirement 2. He complains to a friend that this amount exceeds the hourly cost of going to the movies on specific days of the week. His friend suggests that he could lower the average cost by leaving the TV set on whenever he goes to class. Georgio attends classes for 12 hours per week. Comment on this suggestion.

4. After owning the TV set and stereo system for one year, Georgio became curious about the price he could get for selling these items. He discovered that the most he could receive is $600. He does not plan to sell them but the information distresses him. What amount should he associate with the TV set and stereo system after one year? Explain.

■ **LO1, 2, 3, 5**

P9–2 Determining the Acquisition Cost and the Financial Statement Effects of Amortization, Extraordinary Repairs, and Asset Disposal (AP9–1)

On January 2, 2006, Athol Company bought a machine for use in operations. The machine has an estimated useful life of eight years and an estimated residual value of $1,500. The company provided the following information:

a. Invoice price of the machine, $70,000.

b. Freight paid by the vendor per sales agreement, $800.

c. Installation costs, $2,000 cash.

d. Payment of the machine's price was made as follows:

   January 2:

   • Issued 1,000 common shares of Athol Company at $5 per share.

   • Signed a $40,000 note payable due April 16, 2006, plus 12-percent interest.

   • Balance of the invoice price to be paid in cash. The invoice allows for a 2-percent cash discount if the cash payment is made by January 11.

January 15: Paid the balance of the invoice price in cash.

April 16: Paid the note payable and interest in cash.

e. On June 30, 2008, the company completed the replacement of a major part of the machine that cost $12,375. This expenditure is expected to reduce the machine's operating costs, increase its estimated useful life by two years, and its estimated residual value to $2,000.

f. Assume that on October 1, 2013, the company decided to replace the machine with a newer, more efficient model. It then sold the machine to Sako Ltd. on that date for $17,000 cash.

Required:

1. Compute the acquisition cost of the machine, and explain the basis for including certain costs in the determination of the machine's acquisition cost.

2. Indicate the accounts affected and the amounts and direction (+ for increase and − for decrease) of the effects of the purchase and subsequent cash payment on the accounting equation. Use the following headings:

Date	Assets	=	Liabilities	+	Shareholders' Equity

3. Prepare the journal entries to record the purchase of the machine and subsequent cash payments on January 15 and April 16, 2006.

4. Compute the amortization expense for each of the years 2006, 2007, and 2008, assuming the company's fiscal year ends on December 31. Use the straight-line amortization method.

5. Prepare the journal entry to record the sale of the machine on October 1, 2013. (*Hint:* First determine the balance of the account Accumulated Amortization on that date.)

P9–3 Analyzing the Effects of Repairs, a Betterment, and Amortization (AP9–2)

Assume that Sears Canada Inc. made extensive repairs on an existing office building and added a new wing. The existing building originally cost $75 million when it was purchased at the beginning of 1989, and was amortized on a straight-line basis over a 40-year useful life, with no residual value. During the year 2008, the following expenditures related to the building were made:

a. Ordinary repairs and maintenance expenditures for the year, $585,000 paid in cash.

b. Extensive and major repairs to the roof of the building, $850,000 paid in cash. These repairs were completed on December 31, 2008.

c. The new wing was completed on December 31, 2008 at a cash cost of $26 million, has an estimated useful life of 20 years, and no residual value.

■ LO2, 3

Sears Canada Inc.

Required:

1. Applying the policies of Sears Canada Inc., complete the following schedule, indicating the effects of the preceding expenditures. If there is no effect on an account, write NE on the line (amounts in thousands):

	Building	Accumulated Amortization	Amortization Expense	Repairs Expense	Cash
Balance January 1, 2008	$75,000	$35,625			
Amortization for 2008		_____	_____		_____
Balance prior to expenditures	75,000	_____	_____		
Expenditure a	_____	_____	_____	_____	_____
Expenditure b	_____	_____	_____	_____	_____
Expenditure c	_____	_____	_____	_____	_____
Balance December 31, 2008	_____	_____	_____	_____	_____

2. What was the book value of the building at December 31, 2008?

3. Compute the amortization expense for 2009, assuming no additional capital expenditures on this building in 2009.

4. Explain the effect of amortization on cash flows.

LO 2, 3

eXcel

P9–4 Computing a Basket Purchase Allocation and Recording Amortization under Three Alternative Methods (AP9–3)

At the beginning of the year, Wong's Martial Arts Centre bought three used fitness machines from Hangar, Inc., for a total cash price of $38,000. Transportation costs on the machines were $2,000. The machines immediately were overhauled, installed, and started operating. The machines were different; therefore, each had to be recorded separately in the accounts. An appraiser was requested to estimate their market value at date of purchase (prior to the overhaul and installation). The net book values shown on Hangar's books also are available. The book values, appraisal results, installation costs, and renovation expenditures follow:

	Machine A	Machine B	Machine C
Net book value—Hangar	$8,000	$12,000	$6,000
Appraisal value	9,500	32,000	8,500
Installation costs	300	500	200
Renovation costs prior to use	2,000	400	600

By the end of the first year, each machine had been operating 8,000 hours.

Required:

1. Compute the cost of each machine by making a supportable allocation of the total cost to the three machines. Explain the rationale for the allocation basis used.

2. Prepare the entry to record amortization expense at the end of year 1, assuming the following:

	Estimates		
Machine	Life	Residual Value	Amortization Method
A	5	$1,500	Straight line
B	40,000 hours	900	Units of production
C	4	2,000	Double-declining balance

LO1, 3

REX Stores
Corporation

ANALYSIS

P9–5 Inferring Amortization Amounts and Determining the Effects of an Amortization Error on Key Ratios (AP9–4)

REX Stores Corporation, headquartered in Dayton, Ohio, is one of the leading consumer electronics retailers in the United States, operating more than 200 stores in 37 states. The following is a note from a recent annual report:

(1) SUMMARY OF SIGNIFICANT ACCOUNTING POLICIES—

Property and Equipment—Property and equipment is recorded at cost. Depreciation is computed using the straight-line method. Estimated useful lives are 15 to 40 years for buildings and improvements and 3 to 12 years for fixtures and equipment. Leasehold improvements are depreciated over the initial lease term and one renewal term when exercise of the renewal term is assured. The components of property and equipment at January 31, 2006 and 2005, are as follows:

	2006	2005
	(in thousands)	
Land	$ 38,269	$ 38,598
Buildings and improvements	103,525	102,210
Fixtures and equipment	17,431	17,979
Leasehold improvements	8,886	8,886
	167,521	167,673
Less: Accumulated depreciation	(42,276)	(39,023)
	$125,245	$128,650

Required:

1. Assuming that REX Stores did not sell any property, plant, and equipment in 2006, what was the amount of amortization expense recorded in 2006?

2. Assume that REX Stores failed to record amortization in 2006. Indicate the effect of the error (i.e., overstated or understated) on the following ratios: (*a*) earnings per share, (*b*) fixed asset turnover, and (*c*) return on equity. Computations are not required.

P9–6 Evaluating the Effect of Alternative Amortization Methods on Key Ratios from an Analyst's Perspective

■ **LO1, 3**

Bombardier

ANALYSIS

Bombardier Inc. is one of the largest manufacturers of planes and trains in the world. The company's assets exceed $17 billion. As a result, amortization is a significant item on Bombardier's income statement. You are a financial analyst for Bombardier and have been asked to determine the impact of alternative amortization methods. For your analysis, you have been asked to compare methods based on a machine that cost $90,225. The estimated useful life is 10 years, and the estimated residual value is $2,225. The machine has an estimated useful life in productive output of 88,000 units. Actual output was 10,000 in year 1 and 8,000 in year 2.

Required:

1. For years 1 and 2 only, prepare a separate amortization schedule for each of the following alternative methods. Round your computations to the nearest dollar.
   a. Straight line.
   b. Units of production.
   c. Double-declining balance.

Method: _____				
Year	Computation	Amortization Expense	Accumulated Amortization	Net Book Value
At acquisition				
1				
2				

2. Evaluate each method in terms of its effect on cash flow, fixed asset turnover, and earnings per share (EPS). Assuming that Bombardier is most interested in reducing taxes and maintaining a high EPS for year 1, which method of amortization would you recommend to management? Would your recommendation change for year 2? Why or why not?

P9–7 Inferring Asset Age and Determining Financial Statement Effects of a Long-Term Asset Disposal (Challenging) (AP9–5)

■ **LO5, 7**

Mattel Inc.

Mattel Inc. is the leading toy maker in the world. The company's revenues exceed $5 billion. In the toy business, it is very difficult to determine the life expectancy of a product. Products that children love one year may sit on the shelf the following year. As a result, companies in the toy business often sell productive assets that are no longer needed. Assume that on December 31, 2008, the end of the company's fiscal year, Mattel's records showed the following data about a machine that was no longer needed to make a toy that was popular last year:

Machine, original cost	$52,000
Accumulated amortization	27,500*

*Based on an estimated useful life of eight years, a residual value of $8,000, and straight-line amortization.

On April 1, 2009, the machine was sold for $26,000 cash.

Required:

1. How old was the machine on January 1, 2009? Show computations.

2. Indicate the effect (i.e., the amount and direction—increase or decrease) of the sale of the machine on April 1, 2009, on
   a. Total assets.
   b. Net income.
   c. Cash flows (by each section of the statement: Operating, Investing, and Financing Activities).

■ **LO5, 7**

Singapore Airlines

ANALYSIS

P9–8 Inferring Activities Affecting Fixed Assets from Notes to the Financial Statements and Analyzing the Impact of Amortization on Cash Flows (AP9–6)

Singapore Airlines reported the following information in the notes to a recent annual report (in Singapore dollars):

SINGAPORE AIRLINES
Notes to the Accounts
17. **Fixed Assets** (in $ Million)
The Company

	Beginning of Year	Additions	Disposals/ Transfers	End of Year
Cost				
Aircraft	17,256.5	1,834.5	2,030.5	17,060.5
Other fixed assets (summarized)	6,373.9	2,236.8	2,224.7	6,386.0
	23,630.4	4,071.3	4,255.2	23,446.5
Accumulated amortization				
Aircraft	5,672.2	923.1	1,279.2	5,316.1
Other fixed assets (summarized)	2,735.3	285.5	194.9	2,825.9
	8,407.5	1,208.6	1,474.1	8,142.0

Singapore Airlines also reported the following cash flow details:

Cash Flow from Operating Activities (in $ Million)	The Company	
	Current Year	Prior Year
Operating Profit	1,829.4	820.9
Adjustments for:		
Amortization of fixed assets	1,208.6	1,180.2
Gain on disposal of fixed assets	(223.9)	(108.2)
Other adjustments (summarized)	(27.5)	(132.4)
Net Cash Provided by Operating Activities	2,786.6	1,760.5

Required:

1. Reconstruct the information in Note 17 into T-accounts for Fixed Assets and Accumulated Amortization:

Fixed Assets			**Accumulated Amortization**	
Beg. balance				Beg. balance
Acquisitions	Disposals/transfers		Disposals/transfers	Amortization expense
End. balance				End. balance

2. Compute the amount of cash the company received for disposals and transfers. Show computations.

3. Compute the percentage of amortization expense to cash flows from operations. How do you interpret this percentage?

■ **LO5**

P9–9 Recording and Interpreting the Disposal of Three Long-Term Assets (AP9–7)

During 2009, Coté Company disposed of three different assets. On January 1, 2009, prior to their disposal, the accounts reflected the following:

Asset	Original Cost	Residual Value	Estimated Life	Accumulated Amortization (straight line)
Machine A	$20,000	$3,000	8 years	$12,750 (6 years)
Machine B	42,600	4,000	20 years	15,440 (8 years)
Machine C	76,200	4,200	15 years	57,600 (12 years)

The machines were disposed of in the following ways:

a. Machine A: Sold on January 1, 2009, for $8,200 cash.

b. Machine B: Sold on April 1, 2009, for $27,000; received cash, $23,000, and a $4,000 interest-bearing (12%) note receivable due at the end of 12 months.

c. Machine C: Suffered irreparable damage from an accident on July 2, 2009. On July 10, 2009, a salvage company removed the machine immediately at no cost. The machine was insured, and $18,000 cash was collected from the insurance company.

Required:

1. Prepare all journal entries related to the disposal of each machine in 2009.

2. Explain the accounting rationale for the way that you recorded each disposal.

P9–10 Determining Financial Statement Effects of Activities Related to Various Long-Term Assets (AP9–8)   ■ **LO6**

During the 2010 fiscal year, Boyd Company completed the following transactions:

a. On January 10, 2010, paid $7,000 for a complete reconditioning of each of the following machines acquired on January 1, 2006 (total cost, $14,000). Although the reconditioning of the machines was necessary, it did not extend their useful lives.
   (1) Machine A: Original cost, $26,000; accumulated amortization (straight line) to December 31, 2009, $18,400 (residual value, $3,000).
   (2) Machine B: Original cost, $32,000; accumulated amortization (straight line) $13,000 (residual value, $6,000).

b. On July 1, 2010, purchased a patent for $19,600 cash (estimated useful life, seven years).

c. On January 1, 2010, purchased another business for cash $160,000, including $46,000 for goodwill. The company assumed no liabilities. The company follows the new Canadian accounting standards for goodwill.

d. On September 1, 2010, constructed a storage shed on land leased from A. Kumar. The cost was $10,800, paid in cash; the estimated useful life was five years with no residual value. The company uses straight-line amortization. The lease will expire in three years.

e. Total expenditures during 2010 for ordinary repairs and maintenance were $6,800.

f. On July 1, 2010, sold Machine A for $6,500 cash.

Required:

1. Indicate the accounts, amounts, and direction of the effects of each transaction on the accounting equation. Use the following structure:

Date	Assets	=	Liabilities	+	Shareholders' Equity

2. For each of the long-term assets, compute the amortization expense for 2010 to the nearest month.

P9–11 Computing Goodwill from the Purchase of a Business and Related Amortization (AP9–9)   ■ **LO6**

RONA Inc.

RONA is the largest Canadian distributor and retailer of hardware, home renovation, and gardening products. RONA operates a large network of franchised, affiliated, and corporate stores of various sizes and formats. The notes to the company's financial statements for the year 2005 indicate that it acquired the outstanding shares of TOTEM Building Supplies Ltd. (TOTEM) on April 1, 2005. The purchase price was $96,400,000 and the fair market value of identifiable assets acquired and liabilities assumed are as follows (in thousands of dollars):

Current assets	$ 55,547
Property, plant, and equipment	22,910
Current liabilities	(43,448)
Future income tax liability	(657)
Long-term debt	(15,109)

Required:

1. Compute the amount of goodwill resulting from the purchase.

2. Compute the adjustments that RONA would make at the end of its fiscal year, December 31, 2005, for amortization of all long-term assets (straight line), assuming an estimated remaining useful life of 10 years and no residual value. The company does not amortize goodwill.

LO6

P9–12 Determining the Financial Statement Effects of the Acquisition and Amortization of Intangibles

Figg Company, with a fiscal year ending December 31, acquired three intangible assets during 2009. For each of the following transactions, indicate the accounts and amounts affected and the direction of the effect (+ for increase, − for decrease, and NE for no effect). Use the following headings:

Date	Assets	=	Liabilities	+	Shareholders' Equity

a. On January 1, 2009, the company purchased a patent from Ullrich Ltd. for $6,000 cash. Ullrich had developed the patent and registered it with the Canadian Intellectual Property Office on January 1, 2004.

b. On January 1, 2009, the company purchased a copyright for a total cash cost of $12,000; the remaining legal life was 25 years. Company executives estimated that the copyright would have no value by the end of 20 years.

c. The company purchased another company in January 2009 at a cash cost of $130,000. Included in the purchase price was $30,000 for goodwill; the balance was for plant, equipment, and fixtures (no liabilities were assumed).

d. On December 31, 2009, amortized the patent over its remaining legal life.

e. On December 31, 2009, amortized the copyright over the appropriate period.

LO4, 6

P9–13 Computing Amortization, Net Book Value, and Asset Impairment Related to Different Intangible Assets (AP9–10)

Havel Company has five different intangible assets to be accounted for and reported on the financial statements. The management is concerned about the amortization of the cost of each of these intangibles. Facts about each intangible follow:

a. *Patent.* The company purchased a patent at a cash cost of $54,600 on January 1, 2008. The patent had a legal life of 20 years from the date of registration with the Canadian Intellectual Property Office, which was January 1, 2004. It is amortized over its remaining legal life.

b. *Copyright.* On January 1, 2008, the company purchased a copyright for $22,500 cash. The legal life remaining from that date is 30 years. It is estimated that the copyrighted item will have no value by the end of 25 years.

c. *Franchise.* The company obtained a franchise from McKerma Company to make and distribute a special item. It obtained the franchise on January 1, 2008, at a cash cost of $14,400 for a 12-year period.

d. *Licence.* On January 1, 2007, the company secured a licence from the city to operate a special service for a period of five years. Total cash expended to obtain the licence was $14,000.

e. *Goodwill.* The company started business in January 2006 by purchasing another business for a cash lump sum of $400,000. Included in the purchase price was "Goodwill, $60,000." Company executives stated that "the goodwill is an important long-term asset to us." It has an indefinite life.

Required:

1. Compute the amount of amortization that should be recorded for each intangible asset at the end of the fiscal year, December 31, 2008.

2. Compute the net book value of each intangible asset on *December 31, 2009.*

3. Assume that on January 2, 2010, the copyrighted item was impaired in its ability to continue to produce strong revenues. The other intangible assets were not affected. Havel estimated that the copyright will be able to produce future cash flows of $18,000. The fair value of the copyright is determined to be $16,000. Compute the amount, if any, of the impairment loss to be recorded.

P9–14 **Analyzing and Recording Entries Related to a Change in Estimated Life and Residual Value**

■ **LO3**

Reader's Digest

Reader's Digest is a global publisher of magazines, books, and music and video collections, and is one of the world's leading direct-mail marketers. Many direct-mail marketers use high-speed Didde press equipment to print their advertisements. These presses can cost more than $1 million. Assume that Reader's Digest owns a Didde press acquired at an original cost of $400,000. It is being amortized on a straight-line basis over a 20-year estimated useful life and has a $50,000 estimated residual value. At the end of 2009, the press had been amortized for eight years. In January 2010, a decision was made, on the basis of improved maintenance procedures, that a total estimated useful life of 25 years and a residual value of $73,000 would be more realistic. The fiscal year ends December 31.

Required:

1. Compute (a) the amount of amortization expense recorded in 2009 and (b) the net book value of the printing press at the end of 2009.

2. Compute the amount of amortization that should be recorded in 2010. Show computations.

3. Prepare the adjusting entry to record amortization expense at December 31, 2010.

ALTERNATE PROBLEMS

AP9–1 **Explaining the Nature of a Long-Term Asset and Determining the Financial Statement Effects of Its Purchase** (P9–2)

■ **LO1, 2, 3, 5**

On July 1, 2006, the Fitzgerald Corp. bought a machine for use in operations. The machine has an estimated useful life of six years and an estimated residual value of $2,500. The company provided the following information:

a. Invoice price of the machine, $60,000.

b. Freight paid by the vendor per sales agreement, $650.

c. Installation costs, $2,500 cash.

d. Payment of the machine's price was made as follows:

July 1:

• Fitzgerald Corp. issued 2,000 common shares at $5 per share.

• Signed an interest-bearing note for the balance of the invoice price, payable on September 1, 2006, plus 9-percent interest.

October 1: Paid the note payable and related interest in cash.

e. On June 30, 2009, the company completed the replacement of a major part of the machine that cost $11,500. This expenditure is expected to reduce the machine's operating costs and increase its estimated useful life by two years. At the same time, the machine's estimated residual value was reduced to $2,000.

f. Assume that on July 1, 2012, the company decided to dispose of the machine by selling it to Ayad, Inc. on that date for $16,000 cash.

Required:

1. Compute the acquisition cost of the machine, and explain the basis for including certain costs in the determination of the machine's acquisition cost.

2. Indicate the accounts affected and the amounts and direction (+ for increase and − for decrease) of the effects of the purchase and subsequent cash payment on the accounting equation. Use the following headings:

Date	Assets	=	Liabilities	+	Shareholders' Equity

3. Prepare the journal entries to record the purchase of the machine and subsequent cash payments on October 1, 2006.

4. Compute the amortization expense for each of the years 2006 and 2009, assuming the company's fiscal year ends on December 31. Use the straight-line amortization method.

5. Prepare the journal entry to record the sale of the machine on July 1, 2012. (*Hint:* First determine the balance of the account Accumulated Amortization on that date.)

■ **LO2, 3**

AP9–2   Analyzing the Effects of Repairs, a Betterment, and Amortization (P9–3)

AMERCO

A recent annual report for AMERCO, the holding company for U-Haul International, Inc., included the following note:

Property, Plant, and Equipment

Property, plant, and equipment are stated at cost. Interest costs incurred during the initial construction of buildings or rental equipment are considered part of the cost. Depreciation is computed for financial reporting purposes principally using the straight-line method over the following estimated useful lives: rental equipment 2–20 years, building and non-rental equipment 3–55 years. Major overhauls to rental equipment are capitalized and are amortized over the estimated period benefited. Routine maintenance costs are charged to operating expense as they are incurred.

AMERCO subsidiaries own property, plant, and equipment that are utilized in the manufacture, repair, and rental of U-Haul equipment and that provide offices for U-Haul. Assume that AMERCO made extensive repairs on an existing building and added a new wing. The building is a garage and repair facility for rental trucks that serve the Seattle area. The existing building originally cost $230,000, and by the end of 2008 (5 years), it was one-quarter amortized on the basis of a 20-year estimated useful life and no residual value. Assume straight-line amortization computed to the nearest month. During 2009, the following expenditures related to the building were made:

a. Ordinary repairs and maintenance expenditures for the year, $5,000 paid in cash.

b. Extensive and major repairs to the roof of the building, $17,000 paid in cash. These repairs were completed on June 30, 2009.

c. The new wing was completed on June 30, 2009, at a cash cost of $86,500. By itself, the wing had an estimated useful life of 15 years and no residual value. The company intends to sell the building and wing at the end of the building's useful life (in 14 1/2 years from June 30, 2009).

Required:

1. Applying the policies of AMERCO, complete the following schedule, indicating the effects of the preceding expenditures. If there is no effect on an account, write NE on the line:

	Building	Accumulated Amortization	Amortization Expense	Repairs Expense	Cash
Balance January 1, 2009	$230,000	$57,500			
Amortization Jan. 1–June 30		_____	_____		_____
Balance prior to expenditures	230,000	_____	_____		
Expenditure a	_____	_____	_____	_____	_____
Expenditure b	_____	_____	_____	_____	_____
Expenditure c	_____	_____	_____	_____	_____
Amortization July 1–December 31:					
Existing building		_____	_____	_____	_____
Major repairs and betterments		_____	_____	_____	_____
Balance December 31, 2009	_____	_____	_____	_____	

2. What was the net book value of the building on December 31, 2009?

3. Explain the effect of amortization on cash flows.

■ **LO2, 3**

AP9–3   Computing a Basket Purchase Allocation, and Recording Amortization under Three Alternative Methods (P9–4)

At the beginning of the year, Labinski Inc. bought three used machines from Dumas Corporation, for a total cash price of $62,000. Transportation costs on the machines were $3,000. The machines immediately were overhauled, installed, and started operating. The machines were different; therefore, each had to be recorded separately in the accounts. An appraiser was requested to estimate their market value at the date of purchase (prior to the overhaul and installation). The net book values shown on Dumas's books also are available. The net book values, appraisal results, installation costs, and renovation expenditures follow:

	Machine A	Machine B	Machine C
Net Book value—Lucas	$10,500	$22,000	$16,000
Appraisal value	11,500	32,000	28,500
Installation costs	800	1,100	1,100
Renovation costs prior to use	600	1,400	1,600

By the end of the first year, each machine had been operating 7,000 hours.

Required:

1. Compute the cost of each machine by making a supportable allocation of the total cost to the three machines (round your calculations to two decimal places). Explain the rationale for the allocation basis used.

2. Prepare the entry to record amortization expense at the end of year 1, assuming the following:

	ESTIMATES		
Machine	Life	Residual Value	Amortization Method
A	4	$1,000	Straight line
B	35,000 hours	2,000	Units of production
C	5	1,500	Double-declining balance

AP9–4 Inferring Amortization Amounts and Determining the Effects of an Amortization Error on Key Ratios (P9–5)

■ **LO1, 3**

The Forzani Group Ltd. (FGL) franchises several specialty sports retail clothing and sports equipment stores. Its stores include SportChek, Coast Mountain Sports, Sport Mart, and National Sports. Its franchises are Intersport, RnR, Atmosphere, and Sports Experts. As at January 28, 2007, its fiscal year-end, the company operated 270 corporate stores and sold merchandise to 209 franchises. Its retail and franchise operations network spans Canada. The following is a note from a recent annual report:

The Forzani
Group Ltd.

ANALYSIS

1. Significant Accounting Policies

(c) Capital Assets

Capital assets are recorded at cost and are amortized using the following methods and ratios:

Building	—4% declining-balance basis
Building on leased land	—straight-line basis over the lesser of the length of the lease and estimated useful life of the building, not exceeding 20 years
Furniture, fixtures, equipment, and automotive	—straight line over 3–5 years
Leasehold improvements	—straight-line over the lesser of the length of the lease and estimated useful life of the improvements, not exceeding 10 years

Capital assets at January 28, 2007, and January 29, 2006, are as follows (in thousands of dollars):

	2007	2006
Land	$ 3,173	$ 3,173
Building	20,699	20,007
Building on leased land	4,583	4,564
Furniture, fixtures, equipment, software, and automotive	197,993	173,868
Leasehold improvements	221,043	204,595
Construction in progress	1,804	3,763
	$449,295	$409,970
Less accumulated amortization	258,149	216,376
Net book value	$191,146	$193,594

Required:

1. Assuming that FGL did not have any asset impairment write-offs and did not sell any property, plant, and equipment in fiscal year 2007, what was the amount of amortization expense recorded in 2007?

2. Assume that FGL failed to record amortization in 2007. Indicate the effect of the error (i.e., overstated or understated) on the following ratios: (*a*) earnings per share, (*b*) fixed asset turnover, and (*c*) return on equity. Computations are not required.

▌ **LO5, 7   AP9–5   Inferring Asset Age and Determining Financial Statement Effects of a Long-Term Asset Disposal (Challenging) (P9–7)**

Hasbro, Inc.

Hasbro, Inc., designs, manufactures, and markets high-quality toys, games, and infant products. The company's revenues exceed $3.0 billion. In the toy business, it is very difficult to determine the life expectancy of a product. Products that children love one year may sit on the shelf the following year. As a result, companies in the toy business often sell productive assets that are no longer needed. Assume that on December 31, 2008, the end of the company's fiscal year, Hasbro's records showed the following data about a machine that was no longer needed to make a toy that was popular last year:

Machine, original cost	$107,000
Accumulated amortization	64,000*

*Based on an estimated useful life of six years, a residual value of $11,000, and straight-line amortization.

On July 1, 2009, the machine was sold for $38,000 cash.

Required:

1. How old was the machine on January 1, 2009? Show computations.

2. Indicate the effect (i.e., the amount and direction—increase or decrease) of the sale of the machine on July 1, 2009, on
   a. Total assets.
   b. Net income.
   c. Cash flows (by each section of the statement: Operating, Investing, and Financing Activities).

▌ **LO5, 7   AP9–6   Inferring Activities Affecting Fixed Assets from Notes to the Financial Statements and Analyzing the Impact of Amortization on Cash Flows (P9–8)**

Cathay Pacific Airways

Cathay Pacific Airways reported the following information in the notes to a recent annual report (in Hong Kong dollars):

ANALYSIS

CATHAY PACIFIC AIRWAYS

Notes to the Accounts

8. Fixed Assets (in millions of HK dollars)

	Acquisition Cost	Accumulated Amortization
Balance, beginning of year	$80,111	$29,852
Additional acquisitions	4,008	
Amortization expense		3,965
Disposals	(341)	(195)
Balance, end of year	$83,778	$33,622

Cathay Pacific also reported the following cash flow details:

Cash Flow from Operating Activities (in millions of HK dollars)

	Current Year	Prior Year
Operating Profit	$4,143	$ 5,247
Adjustments for:		
Amortization of fixed assets	3,965	3,764
Loss on disposal of fixed assets	54	29
Other adjustments (summarized)	544	1,555
Cash generated from operations	$8,706	$10,595

Required:

1. Reconstruct the information in Note 8 into T-accounts for Fixed Assets and Accumulated Amortization:

Fixed Assets		**Accumulated Amortization**	
Beg. balance			Beg. balance
Acquisitions	Disposals	Disposals	Amortization expense
End. balance			End. balance

2. Compute the amount of cash the company received for disposals during the current year. Show computations.

3. Compute the percentage of amortization expense to cash flows from operations. How do you interpret this percentage?

AP9–7 **Recording and Interpreting the Disposal of Three Long-Term Assets** (P9–9)   ■ **LO5**

During 2009, Callaway Company disposed of three different assets. On January 1, 2009, prior to their disposal, the accounts reflected the following:

Asset	Original Cost	Residual Value	Estimated Life	Accumulated Amortization (straight line)
Machine A	$24,000	$2,000	5 years	$17,600 (4 years)
Machine B	16,500	5,000	10 years	8,050 (7 years)
Machine C	59,200	3,200	14 years	48,000 (12 years)

The machines were disposed of in the following ways:

a. Machine A: Sold on January 1, 2009, for $6,250 cash.

b. Machine B: Sold on July 1, 2009, for $9,500; received cash, $4,500, and a $5,000 interest-bearing (10%) note receivable due at the end of 12 months.

c. Machine C: Suffered irreparable damage from an accident on October 2, 2009. On October 10, 2009, a salvage company removed the machine immediately at a cost of $500. The machine was insured, and $11,500 cash was collected from the insurance company.

Required:

1. Prepare all journal entries related to the disposal of each machine.

2. Explain the accounting rationale for the way that you recorded each disposal.

■ LO6

AP9–8 Determining Financial Statement Effects of Activities Related to Various Long-Term Assets (P9–10)

During the 2010 fiscal year, Zhou Corporation completed the following transactions:

a. On January 1, 2010, paid $8,000 for a complete reconditioning of each of the following machines acquired on January 1, 2007 (total cost, $16,000). Although the reconditioning of the machines was necessary, it did not extend their useful lives.
   (1) Machine A: Original cost, $21,500; accumulated amortization (straight line) to December 31, 2009, $13,500 (residual value, $3,500).
   (2) Machine B: Original cost, $18,000; accumulated amortization (straight line) to December 31, 2009, $10,200 (residual value, $1,000).

b. On July 1, 2010, purchased a licence for $6,300 cash (estimated useful life, three years).

c. On July 1, 2010, purchased another business for cash $120,000, including $29,000 for goodwill. The company assumed $24,000 of liabilities from the other business. The company does not amortize goodwill.

d. On July 1, 2010, sold Machine A for $11,000 cash.

e. On October 1, 2010, repaved the parking lot of the building leased from J. Caldwell. The cost was $7,800, paid in cash; the estimated useful life was five years with no residual value. The company uses straight-line amortization. The lease will expire on December 31, 2013.

f. Total expenditures during 2010 for ordinary repairs and maintenance were $6,700.

Required:

1. For each of these transactions, indicate the accounts, amounts, and direction of the effects (+ for increase and − for decrease) on the accounting equation. Use the following structure:

2. For each of the long-term assets, compute the amortization expense for 2010 to the nearest amount.

Date	Assets	=	Liabilities	+	Shareholders' Equity

■ LO6

AP9–9 Computing Goodwill from the Purchase of a Business and Related Amortization (P9–11)

The notes to a recent annual report from Weebok Corporation included the following:

Business Acquisitions

During the current year, the company acquired the assets of Sport Shoes, Inc.

Assume that Weebok acquired Sport Shoes on January 2, 2008. Weebok acquired the name of the company and all of its assets, except cash, for $450,000 cash. Weebok did not assume the liabilities. On January 2, 2008, the balance sheet of Sport Shoes reflected the following book values and an independent appraiser estimated the following market values for the assets:

January 2, 2008	Book Value	Market Value
Accounts receivable, net	$ 45,000	$ 45,000
Inventory	220,000	210,000
Property, plant, and equipment, net	32,000	60,000
Other assets	3,000	10,000
Total assets	$300,000	
Liabilities	$ 60,000	
Shareholders' equity	240,000	
Total liabilities and shareholders' equity	$300,000	

Required:

1. Compute the amount of goodwill resulting from the purchase. (*Hint:* Assets are purchased at market value, which is their cost at the date of acquisition.)

2. Compute the adjustments that Weebok would make at the end of its fiscal year, December 31, 2008, for amortization of all long-term assets (straight line), assuming an estimated remaining useful life of 15 years and no residual value. The company does not amortize goodwill.

AP9–10 Computing Amortization, Net Book Value, and Asset Impairment Related to Different Intangible Assets (P9–13) ■ LO4, 6

Theriault Corporation has five different intangible assets to be accounted for and reported on the financial statements. The management is concerned about the amortization of the cost of each of these intangibles. Facts about each intangible follow:

a. *Patent.* The company purchased a patent at a cash cost of $18,600 on January 1, 2009. The patent had a legal life of 20 years from date of registration with the Canadian Intellectual Property Office, which was January 1, 2007. It is amortized over its remaining legal life.

b. *Copyright.* On January 1, 2009, the company purchased a copyright for $24,750 cash. The legal life remaining from that date is 30 years. It is estimated that the copyrighted item will have no value by the end of 15 years.

c. *Franchise.* The company obtained a franchise from Farrell Company to make and distribute a special item. It obtained the franchise on January 1, 2009, at a cash cost of $19,200 for a 12-year period.

d. *Licence.* On January 1, 2008, the company secured a licence from the city to operate a special service for a period of seven years. Total cash expended to obtain the licence was $21,000.

e. *Goodwill.* The company started business in January 2007 by purchasing another business for a cash lump sum of $650,000. Included in the purchase price was "Goodwill, $75,000." Company executives stated that "the goodwill is an important long-term asset to us." It has an indefinite life.

Required:

1. Compute the amount of amortization expense that should be recorded for each intangible asset at the end of the fiscal year, December 31, 2009.

2. Compute the net book value of each intangible asset on *January 1, 2012.*

3. Assume that on January 2, 2011, the franchise was impaired in its ability to continue to produce strong revenues. The other intangible assets were not affected. Theriault estimated that the franchise will be able to produce future cash flows of $16,500, with a fair value of $15,000. Compute the amount, if any, of the impairment loss to be recorded.

CASES AND PROJECTS

FINDING AND INTERPRETING FINANCIAL INFORMATION

LO1, 3   **CP9–1 Finding Financial Information**

Van Houtte

Refer to the financial statements and accompanying notes of Van Houtte Inc. given in Appendix B at the end of this book.

Required:

1. What method of depreciation and amortization does the company use?
2. What is the amount of accumulated depreciation and amortization at the end of the current year?
3. For depreciation purposes, what is the estimated useful life of the coffee-service equipment?
4. What amount of depreciation and amortization was reported as expense for the current year?
5. What is the fixed asset turnover ratio for the current year? What does it suggest?
6. For each of the preceding questions, for the current year where did you locate the information?

LO1, 3   **CP9–2 Comparing Companies within an Industry**

WestJet Airlines vs.
Southwest Airlines

Southwest Airlines is an exuberant, no-frills airline that was started more than 30 years ago. WestJet Airlines has followed Southwest's successful corporate strategy, which is based on "keeping airplanes in the air." Selected data from Southwest's annual reports appear below (in millions of dollars):

	December 31	
	2006	2005
Property and equipment, at cost	$13,859	$12,508
Less allowance for depreciation	3,765	3,296
	10,094	9,212
Total assets	13,460	14,003
Total operating revenues for the year	9,086	7,584
Southwest uses the straight-line amortization method.		

Similar data for WestJet Airlines for fiscal year 2006 were provided earlier in this chapter.

Required:

1. Compute the percentage of net capital assets to total assets for both companies each year. Why might the two ratios differ?
2. Compute the percentage of the capital assets that has been amortized for each company for the most recent year. Why do you think the percentages differ?
3. Compute the fixed asset turnover ratio for the most recent year presented for both companies. Which has the higher efficiency in using assets? Why?
4. Would you expect Southwest's ratios to increase or decrease over time? Why? What about WestJet's ratios?

FINANCIAL REPORTING AND ANALYSIS CASES

CP9–3 Broadening Financial Research Skills: Identifying Competitors in an Industry

Reuters provides lists of industries and the competitors in each at **www.investor.reuters.com/Industries.aspx**.

Required:

Using your Web browser, contact Reuters and identify three competitors for the following industries:

1. Airline.
2. Hotels and motels.
3. Footwear.
4. Computer hardware.

CP9–4 Interpreting the Financial Press

■ **LO4**

The October 5, 1998, edition of *Business Week* includes the article, "Earnings Hocus-Pocus." You can access the article on the Online Learning Centre Web site at **www.mcgrawhill.ca/olc/libby/student/resources**.

Required:

Read pages 1 through 9 of the article (stopping at the paragraph beginning with "Meanwhile, the SEC...." Then answer the following questions:

1. What is meant by the concept that many companies take a "big bath"?

2. List several companies mentioned in the article that have taken a big bath by writing down fixed assets or intangibles. Indicate for each the nature of the earnings manipulation.

CP9–5 Using Financial Reports: Analyzing the Age of Assets

■ **LO3**

A note to a recent annual report for PapaJohn's International contained the following information (in thousands of dollars):

Papa John's
International

ANALYSIS

	Current Year	Previous Year
Land	$ 30,449	$ 25,798
Buildings and improvements	78,970	66,494
Leasehold improvements	70,838	60,763
Equipment and other	136,410	121,414
Construction in progress	12,642	23,089
	329,309	297,558
Less accumulated depreciation and amortization	(83,435)	(69,745)
Net property and equipment	$245,874	$227,813

Depreciation and amortization expense (in thousands of dollars) charged to operations was $34,172 in the current year and $24,827 in the previous year. Depreciation generally is computed using the straight-line method for financial reporting purposes.

Required:

1. What is your best estimate of the average expected life for PapaJohn's depreciable assets?

2. What is your best estimate of the average age of PapaJohn's depreciable assets?

CP9–6 Using Financial Reports: Analyzing Fixed Asset Turnover Ratio and Cash Flows

■ **LO1, 3, 6, 7**

CanWest Global Communications Corp., with headquarters in Winnipeg, Manitoba, is one of Canada's largest media conglomerates and the owner of many Canadian newspapers, television stations, and cable channels, as well as several stations in Australia, Ireland, and New Zealand. During 2001, CanWest acquired additional companies, adding more than $2 billion to its intangible assets. Selected data from a recent annual report are as follows (in thousands of dollars):

CanWest Global
Communications
Corp.

ANALYSIS

Property and equipment, and intangibles	Current Year	Prior Year
From the consolidated balance sheet and notes		
Property and equipment, net	$ 692,698	$ 705,339
Intangible assets with indefinite lives	1,096,655	1,054,037
Intangible assets with finite lives, net	77,301	88,081
From the consolidated income statement		
Revenue	2,878,625	3,032,485
From the consolidated statement of cash flows		
Net earnings for the year	178,672	10,205
Adjustments:		
Amortization of property, plant, and equipment	94,171	90,943
Amortization of intangible assets	12,423	20,341
Other adjustments, net	(168,332)	415,319
Cash provided by operations	$ 116,934	$ 536,808
From the notes to the financial statements		
Accumulated amortization on property and equipment	$ 600,737	$ 536,702

Required:

1. Compute the cost of the property and equipment at the end of the current year. Explain your answer.

2. What is your best estimate of the average expected life of CanWest's property and equipment? What was the approximate age of the property and equipment at the end of the current year? Assume that CanWest uses straight-line amortization.

3. Compute the fixed asset turnover ratio for the current year. Explain your results.

4. Compute an estimate of the amortization expense of intangible assets with finite lives for the next year.

5. On the consolidated cash flow statement, why are the amortization amounts added to net earnings for the year?

■ **LO5**   **CP9–7**   **Using Financial Reports: Inferring the Sale of Assets**

Eastman Kodak   An annual report for Eastman Kodak reported that the balance of property, plant, and equipment at the end of the current year was $11,379 million. At the end of the previous year, it had been $12,694 million. During the current year, the company bought $1,472 million worth of new equipment. The balance of accumulated amortization at the end of the current year was $7,601 million and at the end of the previous year was $8,182 million. Amortization expense for the current year was $1,402 million. The annual report did not disclose any gain or loss on the disposition of property, plant, and equipment, so you may assume that the amount was zero.

Required:

What amount of proceeds did Eastman Kodak receive when it sold property, plant, and equipment during the current year? (*Hint:* Set up T-accounts.)

CRITICAL THINKING CASES

■ **LO3**   **CP9–8**   **Making a Decision as a Financial Analyst: Interpreting the Impact of the Capitalization of Interest on an Accounting Ratio**

WestJet Airlines   The capitalization of interest associated with self-constructed assets was discussed in this chapter. A recent annual report for WestJet Airlines disclosed the following information concerning capitalization of interest:

ANALYSIS

> **1. Significant accounting policies (continued):**
>
> (i) Capitalized interest costs:
> Costs associated with the introduction of new aircraft and other assets under construction are capitalized from inception through to commencement of commercial operations. Interest attributable to funds used to finance the acquisition of new aircraft and construction of major ground facilities is capitalized as an additional cost of the asset.

Assume that WestJet capitalized interest in the amount of $500,000 and disclosed $2.2 million of interest expense in its income statement for the year. One useful accounting ratio is the interest coverage ratio (Income before interest and taxes divided by Interest Expense).

Required:

1. Explain why an analyst would calculate this ratio.

2. Did WestJet include the $500,000 in the reported interest expense of $2.2 million? If not, should an analyst include it when calculating the interest coverage ratio? Explain.

■ **LO3, 7**   **CP9–9**   **Evaluating an Ethical Dilemma: Analyzing an Accounting Change**

Ford Motor Company   An annual report for Ford Motor Company included the following information:

ANALYSIS

Note 6. Net Property, Amortization and Amortization—Automotive

Assets placed in service before January 1, 1993, are depreciated using an accelerated method. Assets placed in service beginning in 1993 will be depreciated using the straight-line method of amortization. This change in accounting principle is being made to reflect improvements in the design and flexibility of manufacturing machinery and equipment and improvements in maintenance practices. These improvements have resulted in more uniform productive capacities and maintenance costs over the useful life of an asset. Straight-line is preferable in these circumstances. The change is expected to improve 1993 after-tax results by $80 to $100 million.

Required:

1. What was the stated reason for the change in method? What other factors do you think management considered when it decided to make this accounting change?

2. Do you think this is an ethical decision?

3. Who were affected by the change and how were they benefited or harmed?

4. What impact did this change have on cash flows for Ford?

5. As an investor, how would you react to the fact that Ford's net income will increase by $80 to $100 million as the result of this change?

FINANCIAL REPORTING AND ANALYSIS TEAM PROJECT

CP9–10 **Team Project: Analysis of Long-Term Assets**

As a team, select an industry to analyze. Reuters provides lists of industries and their makeup at **www.investor.reuters.com/Industries.aspx**. Another source is **www.hoovers.com**; click on "Companies and Industries"). Each team member should acquire the annual report for one publicly traded company in the industry, with each member selecting a different company. (Library files, the SEDAR service at **www.sedar.com**, the SEC EDGAR service at **www.freeedgar.com**, or the company Web sites are good sources.)

■ **LO3, 7**

ANALYSIS

Required:

On an individual basis, each team member should then write a short report answering the following questions about the selected company. Discuss any patterns across the companies that you as a team observe. Then, as a group, write a short report comparing and contrasting your companies.

1. List the accounts and amounts of the company's long-term assets (land, buildings, equipment, intangible assets, natural resources, and other).
    a. What is the percentage of each to total assets?
    b. What do the results of your analysis suggest about the strategy your company has followed with respect to investing in long-term assets?

2. What cost allocation method(s) and estimates does the company use for each type of long-term asset?

3. Compute the approximate average life of property, plant, and equipment overall.

4. Ratio analysis:
    a. What does the fixed asset turnover ratio measure in general?
    b. Compute the ratio for the last three years.
    c. What do your results suggest about the company?
    d. If available, find the industry ratio for the most recent year, compare it to your results, and discuss why you believe your company differs or is similar to the industry ratio.

5. What was the effect of amortization expense on cash flows from operating activities? Compute the percentage of amortization expense to cash flows from operating activities for each of the past three years.

6. Refer to the cash flow statement and identify the capital expenditures that the company made over the last three years. Did the company sell any long-term assets?

Reporting and Interpreting Current Liabilities

FOCUS COMPANY:

Petro-Canada

MANAGING CAPITAL STRUCTURE

Petro-Canada (**www.petrocanada.ca**) was established in 1975 by the Government of Canada to create a strong Canadian presence in the oil industry and identify new Canadian energy sources. In 2004, the Government of Canada sold its remaining ownership of Petro-Canada to other investors. Petro-Canada is an integrated oil and gas company, a leader in the Canadian petroleum industry, with a portfolio of businesses spanning both the upstream and downstream sectors of the industry. In the upstream businesses, the company explores for, develops, produces, and markets crude oil, natural gas liquids (NGL), and natural gas in Canada and internationally. The downstream business refines crude oil and other feedstocks and markets petroleum products and related goods and services, primarily in Canada. It also offers services such as convenience stores, car washes, and automotive repair and maintenance services through a network of more than 1,500 wholesale and retail outlets across Canada. For 2007, it planned to spend $4.0 billion on a number of projects including modification of refineries to produce cleaner-burning diesel fuels, exploration activities, and establishing new ventures for the long run. Achieving these plans requires the investment of large amounts of capital, some of which will be borrowed from creditors.

In addition to operating activities, management must focus on a number of critical financing activities to ensure that the company remains profitable and is able to generate sufficient resources to eventually meet its goals. The financing activities for Petro-Canada serve two important purposes. They generate funds (1) to finance the current operating activities of the business and (2) to acquire long-term assets that permit the company to grow in the future.

UNDERSTANDING THE BUSINESS

Businesses finance the acquisition of their assets from two sources: funds supplied by creditors (debt) and funds provided by owners (equity). The mixture of debt and equity used by a business is called its **capital structure**. In addition to selecting a capital structure, management can select from a variety of sources from which to borrow money. The liabilities and shareholders' equity of Petro-Canada's balance sheet (Exhibit 10.1) shows that its capital structure at December 31, 2006, was composed of approximately 54 percent debt and 46 percent equity. This proportional mix of debt and equity reflects management's financing strategy to achieve the company's goals.

In deciding how best to finance its projects, Petro-Canada's management must consider two key factors: the risk associated with the source of financing, and the return to shareholders on their investment in the company. From the firm's perspective, debt capital is riskier than equity because interest payments on debt are legal obligations that must be paid. If a company cannot meet a required debt payment (either principal or interest) because of a temporary cash shortage, creditors may force the company

CAPITAL STRUCTURE is the mixture of debt and equity that finances the short- and long-term operating requirements of a company.

EXHIBIT **10.1**

Petro-Canada's Balance Sheet

PETRO-CANADA
CONSOLIDATED BALANCE SHEETS
(stated in millions of Canadian dollars)

As at December 31,	2006	2005
Assets		
Current assets		
Cash and cash equivalents *(Note 13)*	$ 499	$ 721
Accounts receivable *(Note 10)*	1,600	1,617
Inventories *(Note 14)*	632	596
Future income taxes *(Note 7)*	95	—
Assets of discontinued operations *(Note 4)*	—	237
	2,826	3,171
Property, plant and equipment, net *(Note 15)*	18,577	15,921
Goodwill *(Note 16)*	801	737
Deferred charges and other assets *(Note 17)*	442	415
Assets of discontinued operations *(Note 4)*	—	411
	$22,646	$20,655
Liabilities and Shareholders' Equity		
Current liabilities		
Accounts payable and accrued liabilities	$ 3,319	$ 2,895
Income taxes payable	22	82
Liabilities of discontinued operations *(Note 4)*	—	102
Current portion of long-term debt	7	7
	3,348	3,086
Long-term debt *(Note 18)*	2,887	2,906
Other liabilities *(Note 19)*	1,826	1,888
Asset retirement obligations *(Note 20)*	1,170	882
Future income taxes *(Note 7)*	2,974	2,405
Commitments and contingent liabilities *(Note 25)*		
Shareholders' equity		
Common shares *(Note 21)*	1,366	1,362
Contributed surplus *(Note 21)*	469	1,422
Retained earnings	8,557	7,018
Foreign currency translation adjustment	49	(314)
	10,441	9,488
	$22,646	$20,655

REAL WORLD EXCERPT

Petro-Canada

ANNUAL REPORT

into bankruptcy and require the sale of assets to satisfy the debt obligations. In contrast, dividend payments to shareholders are not legal obligations until declared by the board of directors; thus, equity offers lower financial risk to the issuing corporation. As with any business transaction, borrowers and lenders attempt to negotiate the most favourable terms possible. Managers devote considerable effort to analyzing alternative borrowing arrangements.

Companies that include debt in their capital structure also must make strategic decisions concerning the proper balance between short-term debt and long-term debt. To evaluate a company's capital structure, financial analysts calculate a number of accounting ratios. In this chapter, we discuss primarily short-term liabilities as well as some important accounting ratios. In the next chapter, we discuss long-term liabilities, including a special category of long-term debt, bonds payable.

ORGANIZATION OF THE CHAPTER

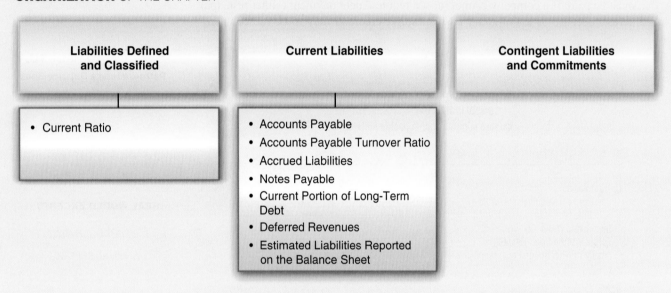

Liabilities Defined and Classified	Current Liabilities	Contingent Liabilities and Commitments
• Current Ratio	• Accounts Payable • Accounts Payable Turnover Ratio • Accrued Liabilities • Notes Payable • Current Portion of Long-Term Debt • Deferred Revenues • Estimated Liabilities Reported on the Balance Sheet	

LIABILITIES DEFINED AND CLASSIFIED

■ **LEARNING OBJECTIVE 1**

Define, measure, and report current liabilities.

LIABILITIES are debts or obligations arising from past transactions that will be paid with assets or services.

CURRENT LIABILITIES are short-term obligations that will be paid within the normal operating cycle or one year, whichever is longer.

Most people have a reasonable understanding of the definition of the word *liability*. Accountants formally define **liabilities** as debts or obligations arising from an entity's past transactions that will be paid with assets or services. As Exhibit 10.1 shows, Petro-Canada reported short-term and long-term liabilities amounting to $12,205 million at December 31, Petro-Canada has borrowed money in the past from creditors and purchased goods and services on credit (past transactions), promising its creditors to pay cash (an asset) at some point in the future, based on the terms of its debt agreements.

When a liability is first recorded, it is measured in terms of its current cash equivalent, which is the cash amount that a creditor would accept to settle the liability immediately. Petro-Canada's long-term debt is $2,887 million, but it will repay much more than that because the company must also pay interest on the debt. Interest that will be paid in the future is not included in the amount of the liability because it accrues and becomes a liability with the passage of time. For fiscal year 2006, the company reported $165 million of interest expense on its income statement.

Like most businesses, Petro-Canada has several kinds of liabilities and a wide range of creditors. The list of liabilities on the balance sheet differs from one company to the next because different operating activities result in different types of liabilities. The liability section of Petro-Canada's balance sheet begins with the caption Current Liabilities. **Current liabilities** are defined as short-term obligations that will be paid within the current operating cycle of the business or within one year of the balance sheet date, whichever is longer. Because most companies have an operating cycle that is shorter than one year, normally, current liabilities can be defined simply as liabilities that are due within one year. Non-current liabilities include all other liabilities.

Information about current liabilities is very important to managers and analysts because these obligations must be paid in the near future. Analysts say that a company has **liquidity** if it has the ability to meet its current obligations. A number of financial ratios are useful in evaluating liquidity, including the current ratio.

LIQUIDITY is the ability to pay current obligations.

CURRENT RATIO

KEY RATIO **ANALYSIS**

ANALYTICAL QUESTION → Does the company currently have the resources to pay its short-term debt?

RATIO AND COMPARISONS → Analysts use the *current ratio* as an indicator of the amount of current assets available to satisfy current liabilities. It is computed as follows:

Current Ratio = Current Assets ÷ Current Liabilities

The 2006 ratio for Petro-Canada is:

$$\$2,826 \div 3,348 = 0.84$$

■ **LEARNING OBJECTIVE 2**

Compute and interpret the current ratio.

Comparisons over Time			Comparisons with Competitors	
Petro-Canada			Suncor Energy	Imperial Oil
2004	2005	2006	2006	2006
0.69	1.03	0.84	1.07	0.99

INTERPRETATIONS

In General → A high ratio normally suggests good liquidity, but too high a ratio suggests inefficient use of resources. An old guideline was that companies should have a current ratio between 1 and 2. Today, many strong companies use sophisticated management techniques to minimize funds invested in current assets, and, as a result, have current ratios below 1.

Focus Company Analysis → Petro-Canada's current ratio for 2006 indicates that the company has $0.84 to pay each $1.00 in current liabilities. The decrease in Petro-Canada's current ratio from 2005 to 2006 signals that Petro-Canada's liquidity position is deteriorating. However, in the notes to its financial statements, Petro-Canada discloses that it has $2,200 million available in various short-term credit facilities, enough to repay more than half of its current liabilities in full if they suddenly become due. The industry comparison indicates that Petro-Canada's current ratio in 2006 was lower than those of Suncor and Imperial Oil.

A Few Cautions → The current ratio may be a misleading measure of liquidity if significant funds are tied up in assets that will not be easily converted into cash. A company with a high current ratio might still have liquidity problems if the majority of its current assets comprised slow-moving inventory. Analysts recognize that managers can manipulate the current ratio by engaging in certain transactions just before the close of the fiscal year. In most cases, for example, the current ratio can be improved by paying creditors immediately prior to the preparation of financial statements.

BALANCE SHEET RATIOS AND DEBT CONTRACTS

FINANCIAL **ANALYSIS**

When firms borrow money, they agree to make specific payments of interest and principal in the future. To provide protection for the creditors, they also often agree to other restrictions on their activities. For example, Petro-Canada has issued long-term notes for US$600 million payable in the year 2035, along with semi-annual interest payments. The agreement between the company and the creditors puts some limitations on the company's issuance of additional debt. Other types of debt contracts require companies to maintain a minimum specified current ratio and a maximum debt-to-equity ratio.

Maintaining a specified level of the current ratio assures creditors that the company has sufficient *liquidity* (liquid assets, after the payment of other current liabilities) to pay its current debts. The debt-to-equity ratio measures the portion of the company that is financed with debt as opposed to equity. By limiting the debt-to-equity ratio, the company agrees to limit the amount of its additional borrowing, which limits additional demands by these new creditors on the company's cash.

SELF-STUDY **QUIZ 10-1**

Refer to the balance sheet of Petro-Canada presented in Exhibit 10.1. Assume that the long-term debt contracts require Petro-Canada to maintain a minimum current ratio of 0.75 and a maximum debt-to-equity ratio of 1.50.

1. Compute the current ratio and the debt-to-equity ratio at December 31, 2005 and December 31, 2006, to verify if Petro-Canada violated these conditions of its lending agreement.

2. Should the company's management be concerned about the level of these two ratios? Explain.

After you complete the quiz, check your answers with the solution on page 545.

WORKING CAPITAL is the dollar difference between total current assets and total current liabilities.

The current ratio relates current assets to current liabilities, which are also related through another concept called **working capital**. Working capital is defined as the dollar amount of the difference between current assets and current liabilities. It is important to both managers and financial analysts because it has a significant impact on the health and profitability of a company.

The working capital accounts are actively managed to achieve a balance between costs and benefits. If a business has too little working capital, it runs the risk of not being able to meet its obligations to creditors. On the other hand, too much working capital may tie up resources in unproductive assets and incur additional costs. Excess inventory, for example, ties up dollars that could be invested more profitably elsewhere in the business and incur additional costs associated with storage and deterioration.

The current ratio and working capital are measures of a company's liquidity. Petro-Canada's negative working capital of $522 million confirms that if all current liabilities had to be repaid immediately, the company would have a cash shortage of $522 million, assuming that all current assets can be readily converted into cash at their book value.

SELF-STUDY **QUIZ 10-2**

The current ratio for Petro-Canada is 0.84. For each of the following events, indicate whether the current ratio and working capital will increase or decrease:

1. Petro-Canada incurs an account payable of $250,000, with no change in current assets.

2. The company borrows $1,000,000 in long-term debt.

3. The company pays taxes payable in the amount of $750,000.

4. The company finances a new building with long-term debt.

After you complete your answers, check them with the solutions on page 545.

Liabilities are very important from an analytical perspective because they affect a company's future cash flows and risk characteristics. Current liabilities are usually grouped according to type of creditor, separating liabilities owed to suppliers and other trade creditors (accounts payable) from those owed to banks (short-term borrowings), providers of services (accrued liabilities), governments (taxes payable), and others. For many types of liabilities, the amount of the debt is determined based on contractual agreements between the company and suppliers of goods, services, or funds. Most of these liabilities are recorded as they occur during the accounting period, as in the case of trade payables for merchandise purchases, loans from banks, and notes payable to creditors. However, specific liabilities that can be determined with accuracy, such as salaries payable and interest payable, require accrual through adjusting entries at the end of the accounting period prior to the preparation of financial statements.

For other types of liabilities, the exact amount will not be known with certainty until a future event, but they must be estimated and recorded if they relate to transactions that occurred during the accounting period. For example, a liability for product warranty will not be known until the repair work is carried out in the future. But the matching principle requires that warranty costs be matched to the related sales revenue that is recorded in the period of sale. As these costs and the related liability are not known, they must be estimated based on past experience or some reasonable basis and recorded through adjusting entries.

In certain cases, it may not be possible to provide a reasonable estimate of a potential future liability that is contingent on a future event. Relevant information about contingent liabilities must therefore be disclosed in notes to the financial statements.

CURRENT LIABILITIES

Many current liabilities have a direct relationship to the operating activities of a business. In other words, specific operating activities are financed, in part, by a related current liability. By understanding the relationship between operating activities and current liabilities, an analyst can easily explain changes in the various current liability accounts.

We will now discuss the current liability accounts that are found on most balance sheets.

ACCOUNTS PAYABLE

Most companies do not produce all the goods and services that they use in their basic operations. Instead, they purchase goods and services from other businesses. Typically, these transactions are made on credit with cash payments occurring after the goods and services have been provided. As a result, these transactions create accounts payable, also called *trade accounts payable*.

For many companies, trade credit is a relatively inexpensive way to finance the purchase of inventory, because interest does not normally accrue on accounts payable. As an incentive to encourage more sales, some vendors may offer very generous credit terms that may allow the buyer to resell merchandise and collect cash before payment must be made to the original vendor. For example, Dell Inc. reported the following details in its annual report for fiscal year 2006:

	2006	2005	2004
Average age of receivables (days)	29	27	27
Average age of payables (days)	77	73	70

Dell maintains an efficient cash management system as it collects from customers within one month of the sale, but pays its suppliers 77 days after the date of purchase.

Some managers may be tempted to delay payment to suppliers for as long as possible to conserve cash. This strategy normally is not advisable. Most successful companies develop positive working relationships with their suppliers to ensure that they receive quality goods and services. Managers can destroy good supplier relationships if they are slow to pay. In addition, financial analysts become concerned if a business does not meet its obligations to trade creditors on a timely basis because such slowness often indicates that the company is experiencing financial difficulties. Both managers and analysts use the accounts payable turnover ratio to evaluate effectiveness in managing payables.

ACCOUNTS PAYABLE TURNOVER RATIO

KEY RATIO ANALYSIS

ANALYTICAL QUESTION → How efficient is management in meeting its obligations to suppliers?

RATIO AND COMPARISONS → The *accounts payable turnover ratio* is a measure of how quickly management is paying trade creditors. Analysts use this ratio as a measure of liquidity. It is computed as follows:

Accounts Payable Turnover = Cost of Goods Sold ÷ Average Accounts Payable

■ **LEARNING OBJECTIVE 3**

Compute and interpret the accounts payable turnover ratio.

The 2006 ratio for Petro-Canada is:

$$\$9,649 \div \$3,107 = 3.11$$

*($2,895 + $3,319) ÷ 2 = $3,107

In the oil and gas industry, companies report the cost of purchases of crude oil and products instead of cost of goods sold. In addition, the company reported its accounts payable along with accrued liabilities without a separate disclosure of accounts payable. Consequently, the denominator of the computed ratio overstates the average accounts payable, and understates the computed ratio. This observation applies to the ratios computed for Petro-Canada over time and its two competitors, Suncor Energy Inc. and Imperial Oil Limited.

Comparisons over Time				Comparisons with Competitors	
Petro-Canada				Suncor Energy	Imperial Oil
2004	2005	2006		2006	2006
3.33	3.51	3.11		2.40	4.70

INTERPRETATIONS

In General → A high ratio normally suggests that a company is paying its suppliers in a timely manner. The ratio can be stated in a more intuitive manner by dividing average accounts payable by the cost of goods sold per day:

Average Age of Payables = Average Accounts Payable ÷ (Cost of Goods Sold ÷ 365)

The 2006 ratio for Petro-Canada is:

$$\$3,107 \div (\$9,649 \div 365) = 117.5 \text{ Days}$$

Alternatively, the average age of payables can be computed by dividing the accounts payable turnover into 365 (365 ÷ 3.11 = 117.5 days).

Focus Company Analysis → The accounts payable turnover for Petro-Canada has decreased over the past three years, from 3.33 in 2004 to 3.11 in 2006. Petro-Canada's 2006 ratio is lower than that of Imperial Oil, which may indicate that Petro-Canada is more aggressive than Imperial Oil in its cash management policy. By conserving cash (with slower payments to suppliers), the company is able to minimize the amount of money it must borrow and pay back with interest.

A Few Cautions → The accounts payable turnover ratio is an average associated with all accounts payable. The ratio might not reflect reality if a company pays some creditors on time but is late with others. The ratio is also subject to manipulation. Managers could be late with payments to creditors during the entire year but catch up at year-end so that the ratio is at an acceptable level. As our focus company analysis indicates, a low ratio can indicate either liquidity problems (i.e., the company is not able to generate sufficient cash to meet its obligations) or aggressive cash management (i.e., the company maintains only the minimum amount of cash necessary to support its operating activities). The first is a problem; the second is a strength. Analysts would have to study other factors (such as the current ratio and the amount of cash flows generated from operating activities) to determine which is the case.

ACCRUED LIABILITIES

ACCRUED LIABILITIES are expenses that have been incurred but have not been paid at the end of the accounting period.

In many situations, a business incurs an expense in one accounting period and makes cash payment for the expense in a subsequent period. **Accrued liabilities** are expenses that have been incurred before the end of an accounting period but have not yet been paid. These expenses include such items as employee salaries and wages, rent, interest, and income taxes. They are recorded as adjusting entries at year-end.

Income Taxes Payable   Like individuals, corporations must pay tax at the appropriate federal and provincial rates on income from active business operations, property income, and capital gains arising from the sale of assets. Based on data from the 200 corporations that participated in the survey for *Financial Reporting in Canada 2006*, combined statutory tax rates ranged from a low combined federal and provincial rate of 32 percent to a high of 41 percent.[1] Petro-Canada reported a combined statutory tax rate of 38 percent in the year 2006, and discloses its income tax expense for 2006 in note 7 to its financial statements:

REAL WORLD EXCERPT

Petro-Canada

ANNUAL REPORT

PETRO-CANADA INCOME STATEMENT for the years ended December 31			
	2006	2005	2004
Earnings from continuing operations before income taxes	3,972	3,402	3,090
Provision for income taxes *(Note 7)*			
Current	2,073	1,794	1,365
Future	311	(85)	27
	2,384	1,709	1,392
Net earnings from continuing operations	1,588	1,693	1,698
Net earnings from discontinued operations *(Note 4)*	152	98	59
Net earnings	$1,740	$1,791	$1,757

Notice that the income taxes expense is composed of two components: (1) a current portion of $2,073 million and (2) a future portion of $311 million. The current portion is payable within prescribed time limits, but the future portion increases the balance of future income tax liabilities. The basic reason for dividing the income tax expense into current and future portions is explained in Chapter Supplement A.

Taxes Other than Income Taxes In addition to paying taxes on income, companies are often required to pay other types of taxes and fees, depending on the specific industry in which they operate. These taxes add to the cost of producing and selling goods and services, and are eventually passed on to customers through higher sales prices.[2] Companies serve as agents of the federal and provincial governments in collecting taxes that are charged to customers for their purchases of goods and services. Sales of most goods and services in Canada are subject to sales taxes at both the federal and provincial levels. Typically, the prices of goods and services are increased by the federal Goods and Services Tax (GST), which is currently set at 5 percent, and a Provincial Sales Tax (PST) that varies between zero and 10 percent, depending on the province.

The GST and PST amounts are added to the sales price, collected from customers, and then remitted to the federal and provincial governments. In this respect, the seller acts as an intermediary between the customer and the government and facilitates the collection of sales taxes from customers. When a company sells goods and services, the applicable sales taxes, if any, are added to the sales price, but they are not revenue for the seller. The sales taxes collected from customers represent liabilities that are remitted periodically (monthly or quarterly) to the respective governments. For example, when a Petro-Canada gas station sells gasoline to a customer for $40, the total cash paid by the customer would include a GST of $2.00 ($40 × 5%) and another

---

[1] N. Chlala, L. Martel, A. Lavigne, and C. Byrd, *Financial Reporting in Canada 2006*. Toronto: Canadian Institute of Chartered Accountants, 2006, pp. 453–466.

[2] To highlight the relative significance of the taxes and fees imposed on the airlines industry, WestJet Airlines offered to sell one-way tickets for $3 on flights between Calgary and Edmonton on June 30, 2002. However, the price of a $6 return ticket quickly rose to $89.27 when all of the applicable fees and taxes were added! See P. Fitzpatrick, "WestJet Launches $3 Ticket Protest." *National Post* (*Financial Post*), June 21, 2002, p. FP1.

amount for PST, for example, $3.20 ($40 × 8%). The journal entry to record this transaction and the transaction effects would be:

Cash	45.20	
Sales revenue		40.00
GST payable		2.00
PST payable.		3.20

Assets		=	Liabilities		+	Shareholders' Equity	
Cash	+45.20		GST payable	+2.00		Sales revenue	+40.00
			PST payable	+3.20			

All of the GST and PST collected from customers are accumulated in these two liability accounts. The balance of the account GST payable is reduced by the amount of GST that the company pays on its own purchases of goods and services, and the net amount is then remitted to the federal government. Provincial governments follow different practices for collecting provincial sales taxes from companies, and for reimbursing them for the PST they pay on their purchases. The unpaid amounts at year-end are included in current liabilities. The following note to the 2006 financial statements of Imperial Oil Limited shows an assortment of taxes that Imperial Oil pays to the federal, provincial, and local governments:

REAL WORLD EXCERPT

Imperial Oil Limited

ANNUAL REPORT

Notes to the Consolidated Financial Statements

16. Net payments/payables to governments

millions of dollars	2006	2005	2004
Current income tax expense (note 4)	776	1,361	1,103
Federal excise tax	1,274	1,278	1,264
Property taxes included in expenses	100	99	85
Payroll and other taxes included in expenses	46	52	50
GST/QST/HST collected (a)	2,715	2,703	2,297
GST/QST/HST input tax credits (a)	(2,293)	(2,344)	(1,948)
Other consumer taxes collected for governments	1,667	1,613	1,670
Crown royalties	904	620	472
Total paid or payable to governments	5,189	5,382	4,993
Less investment tax credits and other receipts	11	9	14
Net paid or payable to governments	5,178	5,373	4,979
Net payments to:			
Federal government	2,352	2,736	2,472
Provincial governments	2,726	2,538	2,422
Local governments	100	99	85
Net paid or payable to governments	5,178	5,373	4,979

(a) The abbreviations refer to the federal goods and services tax, the Quebec sales tax and the federal/provincial harmonized sales tax, respectively. The HST is applicable in the provinces of Nova Scotia, New Brunswick and Newfoundland and Labrador.

Note that the provincial sales tax in Quebec is referred to as Quebec Sales Tax, and that the Atlantic Provinces have combined the GST and PST into one Harmonized Sales Tax of 13 percent.

Payroll Liabilities   At the end of each accounting period, employees usually will have earned salaries that have not been paid. Unpaid salaries may be reported as a separate item or as part of accrued liabilities, as is the case with Petro-Canada. In addition to reporting salaries that have been earned but unpaid, companies also must report the cost of unpaid benefits, which include retirement programs, vacation time, employment insurance, health insurance, and many others. In addition to the current liability arising directly from wages and salaries payable, employers must also remit income tax and other social benefit contributions on behalf of their employees to the appropriate government agencies.

Employee Deductions   Employee income tax is usually the largest amount withheld from wages and salaries by the employer. Federal and provincial laws require the employer to deduct an appropriate amount of income tax each period from the gross earnings of each employee. The amount of income tax withheld from the employee's salary is recorded by the employer as a current liability between the date of deduction and the date on which the amount held is remitted to the government.

If you have been employed and received a pay cheque, you would have noticed that additional amounts were deducted from your gross earnings for employment insurance (EI), contributions to the Canada Pension Plan (CPP) for future retirement benefits, health insurance, and other contributions that you and your employer must remit to the appropriate agencies. In general, employers match the employee's CPP remittance, but pay $1.40 for every $1.00 remitted by the employee for employment insurance. Other deductions such as union dues and workers' compensation will depend on the terms of employment and will result in a future obligation for the employer to remit these amounts to the legal recipient. In total, the employer's share of contributions remitted by a corporation on behalf of its employees to other parties can add up to 20 percent of the employee's gross earnings. This is one reason why corporations prefer to have existing employees work overtime rather than hire new ones.

Compensation expense for employee services includes all funds earned by the employee as well as funds that must be paid to others on behalf of employees (i.e., benefits). To illustrate, let us assume that Petro-Canada accumulated the following information in its detailed payroll records for the first two weeks of January 2008:

Salaries and wages earned	$1,800,000
Income taxes withheld	450,000
CPP contributions	71,000
EI contributions	35,000

Remember that the employer must also contribute an equal amount of CPP contributions and 1.40 times the employees' contributions to employment insurance. As a result, the total liability associated with CPP and EI contributions is $226,000 ($71,000 + $71,000 + $35,000 + $49,000). The entry to record the payroll and employee deductions, and the related transaction effects, follow:

Compensation expense (E)...........................	1,920,000	
Liability for income taxes withheld (L)		450,000
CPP payable (L).....................................		142,000
EI payable (L)......................................		84,000
Cash (A)...		1,244,000

Assets		=	Liabilities	+	Shareholders' Equity
Cash	−1,244,000		Liability for income		Compensation
			taxes withheld +450,000		expense −1,920,000
			CPP payable +142,000		
			EI payable +84,000		

The compensation expense ($1,800,000 + $120,000) includes salaries and wages earned, as well as the employer's share of CPP and EI contributions because these are fringe benefits earned by the employees. The cash paid to employees ($1,244,000) is less than the total amount earned ($1,800,000) because the employer must withhold both income taxes ($450,000) and the employees' share of CPP and EI contributions ($106,000). The CPP and EI payable reflect both the employees' share and the employer's share.

■ **LEARNING OBJECTIVE 4**

Report notes payable and
explain the time value of money.

The **TIME VALUE OF
MONEY** is interest that is
associated with the use of
money over time.

NOTES PAYABLE

Most companies need to borrow money to finance their operations. When a company
borrows money, a formal written contract is usually prepared. Obligations supported
by these written notes are typically called *notes payable*. A note payable specifies the
amount borrowed, the date by which it must be paid, and the interest rate associated
with the borrowing.

Creditors are willing to lend cash because they will earn interest to compensate
them for giving up the use of their money for a period. This simple concept is called
the **time value of money**. The longer borrowed money is held, the larger is the total
dollar amount of interest expense. Interest at a given interest rate on a two-year loan is
more than interest on a one-year loan. To the *borrower*, interest is an expense; to the
creditor, interest is a revenue.

To calculate interest, three variables must be considered: (1) the principal (i.e., the
cash that was borrowed), (2) the annual interest rate, and (3) the time period for
the loan. The interest formula is

$$\text{Interest} = \text{Principal} \times \text{Annual Interest Rate} \times \text{Time}$$

To illustrate the accounting for a note payable, assume that on November 1, 2007, Petro-
Canada borrowed $100,000 cash on a one-year, 12-percent note payable. The interest is
payable on April 30, 2008, and October 31, 2008. The principal is payable at the maturity date of the note, October 31, 2008. The note is recorded in the accounts as follows:

Cash (A)	100,000	
Note payable, short term (L)		100,000

Assets		=	Liabilities		+	Shareholders' Equity
Cash	+100,000		Notes payable	+100,000		

Interest on this note is incurred as long as the debt is outstanding. Under the matching
concept, interest expense is recorded when it is incurred rather than when the cash actually is paid. Because the company uses the money for two months during 2007, it records
interest expense in 2007 for two months, even though cash is not paid until April 30.

The computation of interest expense for 2007 is as follows:

$$\text{Interest} = \text{Principal} \times \text{Annual Interest Rate} \times \text{Time}$$

$$\text{Interest} = \$100,000 \times 12\% \times 2/12 = \$2,000$$

Note that interest expense is calculated for a specific accounting period, which varies
from one month up to one year. The entry to record interest expense on December 31,
2007, is

Interest expense (E)	2,000	
Interest payable (L)		2,000

Assets	=	Liabilities		+	Shareholders' Equity	
		Interest payable	+2,000		Interest expense	−2,000

On April 30, 2008, Petro-Canada would pay $6,000 in interest, which includes the
$2,000 accrued and reported in 2007 plus the $4,000 interest accrued in the first four
months of 2008. The following journal entry would be made:

Interest expense (E)	4,000	
Interest payable (L)	2,000	
Cash (A)		6,000

Assets		=	Liabilities		+	Shareholders' Equity	
Cash	−6,000		Interest payable	−2,000		Interest expense	−4,000

SELF-STUDY **QUIZ 10-3**

In the previous example, we assumed that the $100,000 note payable by Petro-Canada required payment of interest on April 30 and October 31. Assume that the note required the payment of interest on January 31 and July 31.

1. What adjusting entry should Petro-Canada make at December 31, 2007, the end of its fiscal year?

2. What entry should the company make on January 31, 2008?

3. What entry should the company make on July 31, 2008?

After you complete your answers, check them with the solutions on page 546.

CURRENT PORTION OF LONG-TERM DEBT

The distinction between current and long-term debt is important for both managers and analysts. Because current debt must be paid within the next year, companies must have sufficient cash to repay currently maturing debt. To provide accurate information concerning current liabilities, a company must reclassify long-term debt within a year of its maturity date as a current liability. Assume that Petro-Canada signed a note payable of $5 million on January 1, 2007. Repayment is required on December 1, 2009. The December 31, 2008 and 2009 balance sheets report the following:

December 31, 2008

Long-term liabilities	
Note payable	$5,000,000

December 31, 2009

Current liabilities	
Current portion of long-term note	5,000,000

An example of this type of disclosure can be seen in Exhibit 10.1. Notice that Petro-Canada reported $7 million as the current portion of long-term debt at December 2006 that is payable in full during 2007. In some cases, companies will refinance debt when it comes due rather than pay out cash currently on hand.

REFINANCED DEBT: CURRENT OR NONCURRENT?

FINANCIAL ANALYSIS

Instead of repaying a debt from current cash, a company may refinance it either by negotiating a new loan agreement with a new maturity date or by borrowing money from a new creditor and repaying the original creditor. If a company intends to refinance a currently maturing debt and has the ability to do so, should the debt be classified as a current or as a long-term liability? Remember that analysts are interested in a company's current liabilities because those liabilities will generate cash outflows in the next accounting period. If a liability will not generate a cash outflow in the next accounting period, GAAP requires that it not be classified as current. This rule is illustrated by a note from the General Mills annual report.

We have a revolving credit agreement expiring in January 2006 that provides us with the ability to refinance short-term borrowing on a long-term basis. Therefore we have reclassified a portion of our notes payable to long-term debt.

REAL WORLD EXCERPT

General Mills

ANNUAL REPORT

DEFERRED REVENUES

In most business transactions, cash is paid after the product or service has been delivered. In some cases, cash is paid before delivery. You have probably paid for magazines that you will receive at some time in the future. The publisher collects money

DEFERRED REVENUES
are revenues that have been collected but not earned; they are liabilities until the goods or services are provided.

for your subscription in advance, before publishing the magazine. When a company collects cash before the related revenue has been earned, this cash is called **deferred revenues** (or *unearned revenues* or *revenues collected in advance*).

For example, Starbucks Corporation, which is the world's leading retailer of specialty coffee, has introduced the popular Starbucks card that permits customers to pay in advance for their coffee. The advantage for the customer is convenience at the point of sale. The advantage for the company is that Starbucks is able to collect and use cash before customers actually buy the product. The cash that Starbucks collects from customers prior to providing them with coffee is included in Deferred revenue as explained in the following note:

REAL WORLD EXCERPT

Starbucks Corporation

ANNUAL REPORT

Revenues from the company's stored value cards, such as the Starbucks Card, are recognized when tendered for payment, or upon redemption. Outstanding customer balances are included in "Deferred revenue" on the consolidated balance sheets.

Deferred revenues are reported as a liability because cash has been collected but the related revenue has not been earned by the end of the accounting period. The obligation to provide the services or goods in the future still exists. These obligations are classified as current or long-term, depending on when they must be satisfied.

ESTIMATED LIABILITIES REPORTED ON THE BALANCE SHEET

Some recorded liabilities are based on estimates because the exact amount will not be known until a future date. For example, an estimated liability is created when a company offers a warranty with the products it sells. The cost of providing repair work must be estimated and recorded as a liability (and expense) in the period in which the product is sold. Most companies quickly refund money for any defective products that they sell. To illustrate, Dell Inc., which sells computer products, has included the following in a recent annual report:

REAL WORLD EXCERPT

Dell Inc.

ANNUAL REPORT

NOTE 7—Deferred Revenue and Warranty Liability

Revenue from extended warranty and service contracts, for which Dell is obligated to perform, is recorded as deferred revenue and subsequently recognized over the term of the contract or when the service is completed. Dell records warranty liabilities at the time of sale for the estimated costs that may be incurred under its basic limited warranty. Changes in Dell's aggregate deferred revenue and warranty liability (basic and extended warranties), which are included in other current and non-current liabilities on Dell's consolidated statement of financial position, are presented in the following table:

	Fiscal Year Ended	
	February 3, 2006	January 28, 2005
	(in millions)	
Aggregate deferred revenue and warranty liability at beginning of period	$3,594	$2,694
Revenue deferred and costs accrued for new warranties	4,603	3,435
Service obligations honoured	(1,651)	(1,176)
Amortization of deferred revenue	(1,974)	(1,359)
Aggregate deferred revenue and warranty liability at end of period	$4,572	$3,594
Current portion	$2,478	$1,893
Non-current portion	2,094	1,701
Aggregate deferred revenue and warranty liability at end of period	$4,572	$3,594

Dell determines its warranty liability based on the number of units sold, historical and anticipated rates of warranty claims on those units, and the cost per claim to satisfy Dell's warranty obligation. Assuming that Dell's costs of new warranties is $1,000 million, the journal entry to record the estimated liability at year end follows:

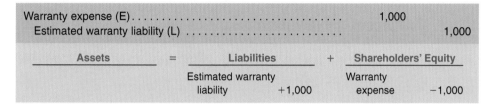

| Warranty expense (E)...................................... | 1,000 | |
| Estimated warranty liability (L) .... | | 1,000 |

Assets	=	Liabilities	+	Shareholders' Equity
		Estimated warranty		Warranty
		liability +1,000		expense −1,000

When the company receives units that require repair under the warranty, its computer technicians repair the defective product, replace component parts as needed, and return the units to customers. If repairs during the year total $983 million, the entry to record the repairs would be:

| Estimated warranty liability (L) .... | 983 | |
| Inventories (A), Wages payable (L) .... | | 983 |

The cost of repairs affects two accounts: Inventories for the cost of parts replaced, and Wages Payable for the cost of labour needed to replace or repair the defective products. If Dell paid cash to satisfy the warranty, then the cash account would be credited instead of Inventories. The warranty expense is not affected by the costs incurred under the warranty because the expense was recognized in the same period of sale of the products, which is consistent with the matching principle.

OVERSTATEMENT OF LIABILITIES AND MANAGEMENT INCENTIVES

A QUESTION OF ETHICS

The amount of liabilities that companies are expected to pay in the future is not always known with certainty. As we indicated above, estimates of potential liabilities are often made when companies accrue expenses associated with specific accounting periods. The methods of estimating such expenses and liabilities often lead to imprecise amounts of future payments. The imprecise nature of the estimation process leads to either an overstatement or an understatement of the correct amount of the liability. An overstatement of expenses leads to an understatement of net income in the estimation period, and a subsequent overstatement of net income in the next accounting period. Occasionally, managers may rely on the inaccurate nature of estimated liabilities to manipulate net income in ways that serve their self-interests. For example, the key executives of Nortel, which is one of the top global makers of telecommunication equipment in North America, overstated accrued liabilities during the years 2000 to 2002. In the first quarter of 2003, Nortel's executives reduced the overstated accrued liabilities, which had the effect of turning a net loss for that quarter into a net income figure. Since the compensation of key executives was related to the company's financial performance, the key executives, who decided to reduce the balance of accrued liabilities in order to reduce net income, received bonus payments from the company because the reported net income was sufficiently large to cause a distribution of bonuses to key management personnel. When such an action was later uncovered by auditors the company's board of directors fired the three top executives who were responsible for this manipulation of the company's net income.

CONTINGENT LIABILITIES AND COMMITMENTS

Each of the liabilities that we have discussed is reported on the balance sheet with a specific dollar amount because each involves the *probable* future sacrifice of economic benefits. Some transactions or events create only a *potential* (but not probable)

■ **LEARNING OBJECTIVE 5**
Report contingent liabilities and commitments.

A **CONTINGENT LIABILITY** is a potential liability that is created as a result of a past event; it is not an effective liability until some future event occurs.

future sacrifice of economic benefits. These situations create **contingent liabilities**, which are potential liabilities that are created as a result of a past event. A contingent liability may or may not become a recorded liability depending on future events. A situation that produces a contingent liability also causes a contingent loss.

Contingent Liability Examples

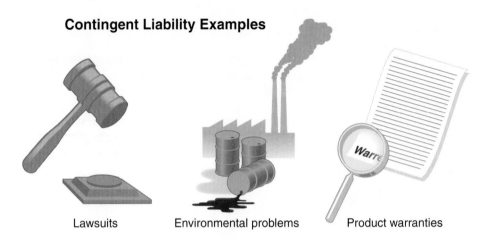

Lawsuits   Environmental problems   Product warranties

Whether a situation produces a recorded or a contingent liability depends on two factors: the probability of the future economic sacrifice and the ability of management to estimate the amount of the liability. The following table illustrates the various possibilities:

	Likely	Unlikely	Not Currently Determinable
Subject to reasonable estimate	Record as liability	Disclosure not required	Disclose in note
Not subject to estimate	Disclose in note	Disclosure not required	Disclose in note

The probabilities of occurrence are defined in the following manner:

1. Likely—the chance that the future event or events will occur is high.
2. Unlikely—the chance that the future event or events will occur is low.
3. Not currently determinable—the chance that the future event or events will (or will not) occur cannot be determined.

When recording liabilities, a company must determine whether the amount of any liability can be reasonably estimated. The general accounting guidelines are (1) a liability that is *both* likely and can be reasonably estimated must be recorded and reported on the balance sheet, (2) a liability that is reasonably possible (whether it can be estimated or not) must be disclosed in a note in the financial statements if the occurrence of the confirming event is not determinable, or if the event is likely to occur but the amount of the loss cannot be reasonably estimated, and (3) disclosure of unlikely contingencies is desirable but not required.

The notes to Petro-Canada's 2006 annual report include the following:

REAL WORLD EXCERPT

Petro-Canada

ANNUAL REPORT

Notes to the Consolidated Financial Statements
25. COMMITMENTS AND CONTINGENT LIABILITIES

Commitments	2007	2008	2009	2010	2011	Thereafter	Total
Transportation agreements	$215	$213	$145	$129	$109	$ 930	$1,741
Exploration work commitments	88	18	18	7	1	—	132
Operating leases	492	140	106	99	75	237	1,149
	$795	$371	$269	$235	$185	$1,167	$3,022

(continued)

Contingent Liabilities

The Company is involved in litigation and claims in the normal course of operations. In addition, the Company may provide indemnifications, in the normal course of operations, that are often standard contractual terms to counterparties in certain transactions, such as purchase and sale agreements. The terms of these indemnifications will vary based upon the contract, the nature of which prevents the Company from making a reasonable estimate of the maximum potential amounts that may be required to be paid. Management is of the opinion that any resulting settlements relating to the litigation matters or indemnifications would not materially affect the financial position or results of operations of the Company.

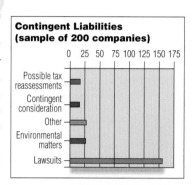

Contingent Liabilities (sample of 200 companies)

Petro-Canada reported not only its contingencies, but also its commitments to pay specific amounts in the future. Commitments reflect contractual agreements to enter into a transaction with another party. Commitments to buy or sell goods and services or to make specific payments are not normally recorded in the accounting system as long as there is no exchange transaction. Commitments to pay or receive cash are relevant to financial statement users and help them in predicting the company's future cash flows.

Financial Reporting in Canada surveyed the financial statements of 200 companies and found that litigation was the most common type of contingent liability in 2005.

CURRENT LIABILITIES AND CASH FLOWS

FOCUS ON CASH FLOWS

The changes in current liabilities can be a major determinant of a company's cash flow from operations. While the income statement reflects the expenses of the period, the cash flow from operating activities reflects cash payments to suppliers of goods and services.

■ **LEARNING OBJECTIVE 6**

Explain the impact of changes in current liabilities on cash flows.

EFFECT ON THE CASH FLOW STATEMENT

IN GENERAL → When there is a net *increase in a current liability* for the period, cash paid to suppliers is less than the expense reported on the income statement; thus, the increase must be *added* to net income in computing cash flow from operations.

When there is a net *decrease in a current liability* for the period, cash paid to suppliers is more than the related expense; thus, the decrease must be *subtracted* from net income in computing cash flow from operations.

	Effect on Cash Flows
Operating activities (indirect method)	
Net income	$xxx
Adjusted for:	
Add increase in any current liability	+
Subtract decrease in any current liability	−

FOCUS COMPANY ANALYSIS → A segment of Petro-Canada's cash flow statement for 2006 and related note 10 follow.

REAL WORLD EXCERPT

Petro-Canada

ANNUAL REPORT

PETRO-CANADA
CONSOLIDATED STATEMENT OF CASH FLOWS
(stated in millions of Canadian dollars)
For the years ended December 31

For the years ended December 31,	2006	2005	2004
OPERATING ACTIVITIES			
Net earnings	**$1,740**	$1,791	$1,757
Less: Net earnings from discontinued operations	**152**	98	59
Net earnings from continuing operations	**1,588**	1,693	1,698
	(continued)		

Items not affecting cash flow from continuing operating activities:			
Depreciation, depletion and amortization	**1,365**	1,222	1,256
Future income taxes	**311**	(85)	27
Accretion of asset retirement obligations *(Note 20)*	**54**	50	50
Unrealized gain on translation of foreign currency denominated long-term debt	**(1)**	(88)	(77)
Gain on disposal of assets *(Note 5)*	**(30)**	(48)	(12)
Unrealized loss associated with the Buzzard derivative contracts *(Note 24)*	**259**	889	333
Other	**18**	14	33
Exploration expenses *(Note 15)*	**123**	140	117
Proceeds from sale of accounts receivable *(Note 10)*	**—**	80	399
(Increase) decrease in non-cash working capital related to continuing operating activities *(Note 9)*	**(79)**	(84)	104
Cash flow from continuing operating activities	**3,608**	3,783	3,928
Cash flow from discontinued operating activities *(Note 4)*	**15**	204	233
Cash flow from operating activities	**3,623**	3,987	4,161

Note 10 Changes in non-cash working capital

	2006	2005	2004
Operating activities from continuing operations			
Accounts receivable	$ 17	$(563)	$(131)
Inventories	(36)	(18)	4
Accounts payable and accrued liabilities	365	662	266
Income taxes payable	(60)	(190)	96
Current portion of long-term liabilities and other	(365)	25	(131)
	$ (79)	$ (84)	$ 104
Investing activities			
Accounts payable and accrued liabilities	$ 59	$ (12)	$ 10
Financing activities			
Accounts payable and accrued liabilities	$ —	$ —	$ (26)

Recall from our previous discussions of the cash flow statement that revenues and expenses reported on the income statement include both cash and non-cash components, and that changes in working capital accounts (other than cash and cash equivalents) reflect non-cash revenues and expenses during the accounting period. The disclosed information shows that changes in non-cash working capital items reduced cash flows from operating activities by $79 million. Petro-Canada's note 9 shows further that changes in current liabilities during 2006 increased cash flows from operations by $365 million simply because of delayed payments related to operating activities. Notice that changes in accounts payable and accrued liabilities resulted not only from operating activities, but from investing and financing activities as well, which is uncommon.

Chapter Supplement A

Future Income Tax Assets and Liabilities

In previous chapters, we made simplifying assumptions concerning income tax expense. We often provided the amount of income tax expense (e.g., $100,000) and prepared a journal entry similar to the following:

Income tax expense (E)	100,000	
Income tax payable (L)		100,000

Assets	=	Liabilities	+	Shareholders' Equity
		Income tax payable +100,000		Income tax expense −100,000

However, separate rules govern the preparation of financial statements (GAAP) and tax returns (Income Tax Act). Specifically, some types of revenue are exempt from tax while other types of expenses are not deductible in computing taxable income. These *permanent differences* do not cause much complication in accounting for income taxes. Examples of such permanent differences appear in the upper part of Exhibit 10.2. However, *temporary differences* of the following types result in complex accounting:

1. Revenue that is recognized in financial statements (e.g., rent revenue) when the goods are sold or the services are rendered, but is taxable only when the cash is received.

2. Product warranty costs that are recognized as a liability and an expense for financial reporting purposes when the related products are sold, but are deductible for tax purposes only when payments under the warranty are made.

3. Long-term assets, including development costs, that are usually amortized using the straight-line method for financial reporting purposes, but are amortized on an accelerated basis (Capital Cost Allowance) for tax purposes.

EXHIBIT **10.2**

Disclosure Made by Petro-Canada

REAL WORLD EXCERPT

Petro-Canada

ANNUAL REPORT

Note 7 Income Taxes

The computation of the provision for income taxes is as follows:

	2006	2005	2004
Earnings from continuing operations before income taxes	**$3,972**	$3,402	$3,090
Add (deduct):			
Non-deductible royalties and other payments to provincial governments, net	61	393	352
Resource allowance	(158)	(413)	(512)
Non-taxable foreign exchange	(1)	(45)	(40)
Other	(24)	5	(10)
Earnings from continuing operations as adjusted before income taxes	**$3,850**	$3,342	$2,880
Canadian federal income tax rate	**38.0%**	38.0%	38.0%
Income tax on earnings from continuing operations as adjusted at Canadian federal income tax rate	**$1,463**	$1,270	$1,094
Provincial income taxes	295	325	271
Federal—abatement and other credits	(262)	(378)	(274)
Current income tax increase due to provincial reassessments	70	—	—
Future income tax increase (decrease) due to Canadian federal and provincial rate changes	(63)	6	(13)
Future income tax increase due to foreign rate changes	242	—	—
Higher foreign income tax rates	627	482	320
Income tax credits and other	12	4	(6)
Provision for income taxes	**$2,384**	$1,709	$1,392
Effective income tax rate on earnings from continuing operations before income taxes	**60.0%**	50.2%	45.0%

The following table summarizes the temporary differences that give rise to the net future income tax asset and liability:

	2006	2005
Future income tax liabilities		
Property, plant and equipment	**$3,919**	$3,114
Partnership income[1]	367	532
Deferred charges and other assets	75	58
Future income tax assets		
Asset retirement obligations and other liabilities	(1,010)	(906)
Inventories	(212)	(230)
Other	(260)	(163)
Net future income tax liability	2,879	2,405
Add: Current future income tax asset	95	—
Future income tax liability	**$2,974**	$2,405

[1]Taxable income for certain Canadian upstream activities are generated by a partnership and the related taxes will be included in current income taxes in the next year.

The differences between amortization expense and CCA are by far the most common source of temporary differences, which disappear over the long run. Assuming the corporation is a going concern, a specific long-term asset will eventually be unable to generate further benefits to the corporation and will be fully amortized. Similarly, the cost of this asset would have been deducted over the years as CCA for tax purposes. So the main issue is timing of the recognition of revenues and expenses for financial reporting versus tax purposes. These temporary differences cause the income tax expense (which is based on the income before taxes reported on the income statement) to be different from the income tax payable (which is based on the taxable income computed on the income tax return).

This difference creates an interesting accounting problem: Should the tax liability reported on the balance sheet be the amount of income taxes currently payable based on the tax return or should the liability include future tax effects that exist because of differences between GAAP and the income tax rules? Accountants have resolved this issue by recording the "economic" liability, which includes income taxes currently payable adjusted for the effects of temporary differences between GAAP and the income tax rules.

The difference between the amounts of income tax expense and income taxes payable is called *Future Income Taxes*. Future income tax items exist because of temporary differences caused by reporting revenues and expenses on a company's income statement in conformity with GAAP and on the tax return in accordance with the Income Tax Act. In practice, future income taxes can be either assets (such as taxes related to cash collected from a customer, which is taxable before it is reported as a revenue on the income statement) or liabilities (such as taxes related to amortization, reported on the tax return on an accelerated basis and on the income statement on a straight-line basis).

To illustrate, let us consider one item that gives rise to future income taxes. Petro-Canada uses straight-line amortization for its financial statements and the capital cost allowance (CCA) for its tax return. As a result, it reports lower income on its tax return than on its income statement because of the higher amount of amortization expense (CCA) on the tax return. Assume that Petro-Canada computed income taxes payable of $8,000,000 based on the numbers reported on the tax return, and income tax expense of $10,000,000 based on the income statement. The company records its tax obligation as follows:

Income tax expense (E)	10,000,000	
Future income taxes (L).................................		2,000,000
Income tax payable (L)		8,000,000

Assets	=	Liabilities		+	Shareholders' Equity	
		Future income			Income tax	
		taxes	+2,000,000		expense	−10,000,000
		Income tax				
		payable	+8,000,000			

The future income tax amount is settled when amortization expense "reverses" in the future. This happens when the CCA recorded on the tax return becomes lower than the straight-line amortization reported on the income statement (remember from Chapter 9 that accelerated amortization, such as CCA, causes higher amortization expense than straight-line amortization in the early years of an asset's life and lower amortization in the later years). When a temporary difference reverses, the future income tax amount is reduced.

In reality, although temporary differences reverse in theory, new temporary differences are created and offset the reversing differences. As a result, the future income tax liabilities reported by most companies may not result in significant cash outflows in the foreseeable future. For Petro-Canada, its future income tax liability actually increased by $569 million during 2006, indicating that new originating temporary differences exceeded the reversing temporary differences.

As indicated earlier, the future income tax liability arises primarily from differences between amortization expense and CCA. What if companies used CCA for reporting purposes instead of straight-line amortization? In this case, most of the temporary differences would disappear and the future income tax asset or liability would be reduced to a relatively small amount, thus reducing the significance of this item on the balance sheets of most companies. However, the use of CCA for financial reporting purposes increases the amortization expense, thus reducing income before taxes and net income. Managers may not favour this outcome if it affects their remuneration and the market value of the company's shares, even though the use of CCA instead of straight-line amortization does not affect cash outflows for income tax purposes.

CURRENT INCOME TAX REPORTING REQUIREMENTS

The *CICA Handbook,* section 3465, describes in considerable detail the concepts and principles that are the foundation of accounting standards for the recognition, measurement, presentation, and disclosure of income taxes. This *Handbook* section affects all audited corporate financial disclosure beginning January 2001 and amends previous Canadian accounting disclosure practices to match those in effect in the U.S. since 1992. The approach currently recommended is called the Future Income Tax Asset/Liability (FITAL) approach.

Using the FITAL approach, the accountant must identify and disclose the sources of the temporary differences that give rise to probable future income tax benefits (i.e., reduction of future income taxes) or liabilities (taxes that are deferred to some future period). In general, the accountant must measure, record, and disclose these future assets and liabilities, as well as their cause in a format that informs the readers about the type of transactions that resulted in temporary differences and the related future tax effects.

Exhibit 10.2 shows the disclosures made by Petro-Canada in the notes to its financial statements for 2006. The disclosures include a detailed account of the components of the income tax expense (or provision for income taxes) for 2006, as well as a listing of the items that caused temporary differences between financial reporting and income tax reporting. Note that the temporary difference between amortization expense and CCA resulted in the largest effect on the future income tax liabilities reported on Petro-Canada's balance sheet.

The computation of future income taxes involves some complexities that are discussed in advanced accounting courses.

SOLUTIONS TO **SELF-STUDY QUIZZES**

Self-Study Quiz 10-1

1.

	December 31, 2005	December 31, 2006
Current ratio	$\dfrac{\$3,171}{\$3,086} = 1.03$	$\dfrac{\$2,826}{\$3,348} = 0.84$
Debt-to-equity ratio	$\dfrac{\$11,167}{\$9,488} = 1.18$	$\dfrac{\$12,205}{\$10,441} = 1.17$

The current ratio is above the minimum level required at both dates, but the debt-to-equity ratio is below 1.50 at both dates.

2. Management should be concerned about the decrease in the current ratio and must take the necessary steps to increase this ratio in the future.

Self-Study Quiz 10-2

Current ratio	Working capital
1. Decrease	Decrease
2. Increase	Increase
3. Decrease	No change
4. No change	No change

Self-Study Quiz 10-3

1. Interest expense...............	2,000	
Interest payable..............		2,000
2. Interest expense...............	1,000	
Interest payable...............	2,000	
Cash......................		3,000
3. Interest expense...............	6,000	
Cash.....................		6,000

CHAPTER **TAKE-AWAYS**

1. **Define, measure, and report current liabilities. p. 528**
   Strictly speaking, accountants define liabilities as obligations arising from past transactions that will be settled in the future by some transfer or use of assets or provision of a service. They are classified on the balance sheet as either current or long term. Current liabilities are short-term obligations that will be paid within the normal operating cycle of the business or within one year of the balance sheet date, whichever is longer. Long-term liabilities are all obligations not classified as current.

2. **Compute and interpret the current ratio. p. 529**
   The current ratio is a comparison of current assets to current liabilities. Analysts use this ratio to assess the liquidity of a company.

3. **Compute and interpret the accounts payable turnover ratio. p. 531**
   This ratio is computed by dividing cost of goods sold by accounts payable. It shows how quickly management is paying its trade creditors and is considered to be a measure of liquidity.

4. **Report notes payable and explain the time value of money. p. 536**
   A note payable specifies the amount borrowed, when it must be repaid, and the interest rate associated with the debt. Accountants must report the debt and the interest as it accrues. The time value of money refers to the fact that interest accrues on borrowed money with the passage of time.

5. **Report contingent liabilities and commitments. p. 539**
   A contingent liability is a potential liability that has arisen as a result of a past event. Such liabilities are disclosed in a note if the obligation is reasonably possible but not currently determinable. A commitment is a contractual agreement to enter into a transaction with another party in the future.

6. **Explain the impact of changes in current liabilities on cash flows. p. 541**
   Changes in accounts payable and accrued liabilities affect cash flows from operating activities. Cash flows are increased by increases in accounts payable and accrued liabilities, and vice versa.

   In this chapter, we focused on current liabilities. In the next chapter, we will discuss long-term liabilities in the context of the capital structure of the company, and use present value concepts to measure long-term debt.

KEY **RATIOS**

Current ratio measures the ability of a company to pay its current obligations. It is computed as follows (p. 529):

$$\text{Current Ratio} = \frac{\text{Current Assets}}{\text{Current Liabilities}}$$

Accounts payable turnover and its companion **average age of payables** are measures of how quickly a company pays its creditors. They are computed as follows (p. 531):

$$\text{Accounts Payable Turnover} = \frac{\text{Cost of Goods Sold}}{\text{Average Accounts Payable}}$$

$$\text{Average Age of Payables} = \frac{\text{Average Accounts Payable}}{\text{Cost of Goods Sold} \div 365}$$

BALANCE SHEET
Under Current Liabilities
Liabilities listed by account title, such as
Accounts payable
Accrued liabilities
Notes payable
Future income taxes
Under Non-Current Liabilities
Liabilities listed by account title, such as
Long-term debt
Future income taxes

INCOME STATEMENT
Liabilities are shown only on the balance sheet, never on the income statement. Transactions affecting liabilities often affect an income statement account. For example, accrued salary compensation affects an income statement account (compensation expense) and a balance sheet account (salaries payable).

FINDING
FINANCIAL INFORMATION

CASH FLOW STATEMENT
Under Operating Activities (indirect method)
Net income
+ Increases in most current liabilities
− Decreases in most current liabilities
Under Financing Activities
+ Increases in long-term liabilities
− Decreases in long-term liabilities

NOTES
Under Summary of Significant Accounting Policies
Description of pertinent information concerning the accounting treatment of liabilities. Normally, there is minimal information.
Under a Separate Note
If not listed on the balance sheet, a listing of the major classifications of liabilities with information about maturities and interest rates appears in a note. Information about contingent liabilities is reported in the notes.

KEY **TERMS**

Accrued Liabilities p. 532
Capital Structure p. 527
Contingent Liability p. 540
Current Liabilities p. 528
Deferred Revenues p. 538

Liabilities p. 528
Liquidity p. 529
Time Value of Money p. 536
Working Capital p. 530

QUESTIONS

1. Define *liability*. Differentiate between a current liability and a long-term liability.
2. How can external parties be informed about the liabilities of a business?
3. Liabilities are measured and reported at their current cash equivalent amount. Explain.
4. A *liability* is a known obligation of either a definite or an estimated amount. Explain.
5. Define *working capital*. How is it computed?
6. What is the current ratio? How is it related to the classification of liabilities?
7. Define *accrued liability*. What type of entry usually reflects an accrued liability?
8. Define *deferred revenue*. Why is it a liability?
9. Define *note payable*. What other liability is associated with a note payable? Explain.
10. What is a contingent liability? How is a contingent liability reported?
11. Compute interest expense for the following note: face, $4,000; 12-percent interest; date of note, April 1, 2008. Assume that the fiscal year ends on December 31, 2008.
12. Explain the concept of the time value of money.

EXERCISES

E10–1   **Identifying Current Liabilities**

■ **LO1**

A current liability is a short-term obligation that is expected to be settled normally within one year. For each of the following events and transactions that occurred in November 2008, indicate the title of the current liability account that is affected and the amount that would be reported on a balance sheet prepared on December 31, 2008. If an event does not result in a current liability, explain why.

a. A customer purchases a ticket from WestJet Airlines for $470 cash to travel in January 2009. Answer from WestJet's standpoint.

b. Hall Construction Company signs a contract with a customer for the construction of a new $500,000 warehouse. At the signing, Hall receives a cheque for $50,000 as a deposit on the future construction. Answer from Hall's standpoint.

c. On November 1, 2008, a bank lends $10,000 to a company. The loan carries a 9-percent annual interest rate, and the principal and interest are due in a lump sum on October 31, 2009. Answer from the company's standpoint.

d. A popular ski magazine company receives a total of $1,800 from subscribers on November 30, the last day of its fiscal year. The subscriptions begin in the next fiscal year. Answer from the magazine company's standpoint.

e. On November 20, the campus bookstore receives 500 accounting textbooks at a cost of $70 each. The terms indicate that payment is due within 30 days of delivery. Answer from the bookstore's standpoint.

f. Ziegler Company, a farm equipment company, receives its phone bill at the end of January 2009 for $230 for January calls. The bill has not been paid to date.

LO1, 2

E10–2 Computing Shareholders' Equity and Working Capital; Explaining the Current Ratio and Working Capital

Flair Corporation is preparing its 2008 balance sheet. The company records show the following related amounts at the end of the fiscal year, December 31, 2008:

Total assets	$295,100
Total non-current assets	125,000
Liabilities:	
Notes payable (8%, due in 5 years)	18,000
Accounts payable	60,000
Income taxes payable	12,000
Liability for withholding taxes	3,000
Rent revenue collected in advance	14,000
Bonds payable (due in 15 years)	68,000
Wages payable	7,800
Property taxes payable	2,000
Note payable (10%; due in 6 months)	10,000
Interest payable	300
Shareholders' equity	100,000

Required:

1. Compute (a) the amount of working capital and (b) the current ratio (show computations). Why is working capital important to management? How do financial analysts use the current ratio?

2. Would your computations be different if the company reported $250,000 worth of contingent liabilities in the notes to its financial statements? Explain.

LO2

ANALYSIS

E10–3 Analyzing the Impact of Transactions on Liquidity

API Ltd. has a current ratio of 2.0 and working capital in the amount of $1,240,000. For each of the following transactions, determine whether the current ratio and working capital will increase, decrease, or remain the same.

a. Paid accounts payable in the amount of $50,000.

b. Recorded accrued salaries in the amount of $100,000.

c. Borrowed $250,000 from a local bank, to be repaid in 90 days.

d. Purchased $20,000 of new inventory on credit.

LO1

E10–4 Recording Payroll Costs with Discussion

Matyas Company completed the salary and wage payroll for March 2007. The payroll provided the following details:

Salaries and wages earned	$224,000
Employee income taxes withheld	46,000
Union dues withheld	3,000
Insurance premiums withheld	1,000
CPP contibutions*	16,445
EI contributions†	9,611

*$16,445 each for employer and employees.
†Employment insurance, employees' share.

Required:

1. Prepare the journal entry to record the payroll for March, including employee deductions.

2. Prepare the journal entry to record the employer's additional payroll expenses.

3. Prepare a combined journal entry to show the payment of amounts owed to governmental agencies and other organizations.

4. What was the total compensation expense for the company? Explain. What percentage of the payroll was take-home pay? From the employers' perspective, does an economic difference between the cost of salaries and the cost of fringe benefits exist? From the employees' perspective, does a difference exist?

E10–5 Computing Payroll Costs; Discussion of Labour Costs　　　　　　　　　　　　■ **LO1**

Town Lake Company has completed the payroll for January 2008, reflecting the following data:

Salaries and wages earned	$79,000
Employee income taxes withheld	8,900
Union dues withheld	1,200
CPP contibutions*	6,013
EI contributions†	3,514

*$6,013 each for employer and employee.
†Employment insurance, employees' share.

Required:

1. What amount of additional compensation expense must be paid by the company? What was the amount of the employees' take-home pay?

2. List the liabilities that are reported on the company's January 31, 2008, balance sheet. The employees' take-home pay was paid on that day.

3. Would employers react differently to a 10-percent increase in the employer's share of CPP than to a 10-percent increase in the basic level of salaries? Would financial analysts react differently?

E10–6 Recording a Note Payable through Its Time to Maturity with Discussion of Management Strategy　　　　　　　　　　　■ **LO1, 4**

Many businesses borrow money during periods of increased business activity to finance inventory and accounts receivable. Hudson's Bay is one of Canada's largest general merchandise retailers. Each year, Hudson's Bay builds up its inventory to meet the needs of December holiday shoppers. A large portion of these holiday sales are on credit. As a result, Hudson's Bay often collects cash from the sales several months after the December holidays. Assume that on November 1, 2007, Hudson's Bay borrowed $4.5 million cash from Provincial Bank for working capital purposes and signed an interest-bearing note due in six months. The interest rate was 8 percent per annum, payable at maturity. Assume that the Hudson's Bay fiscal year ends on December 31.

Hudson's Bay

Required:

1. Prepare the journal entry to record the note on November 1, 2007.

2. Prepare any adjusting entry required at December 31, 2007.

3. Prepare the journal entry to record payment of the note and interest on the maturity date, April 30, 2008.

4. If Hudson's Bay needs extra cash for every December holiday season, should management borrow money on a long-term basis to avoid the necessity of negotiating a new short-term loan each year?

LO1, 4   **E10–7   Determining Financial Statement Effects of Transactions Involving Notes Payable**

Hudson's Bay

Using the data from the previous exercise, complete the following:

Required:

Determine the financial statement effects for each of the following: (a) issuance of the note on November 1, 2007, (b) impact of the adjusting entry at December 31, 2007, and (c) the payment of the note and interest on April 30, 2008. Indicate the accounts, amounts, and direction of the effects (+ for increases and − for decreases) on the balance sheet equation. Use the following headings:

Date	Assets	Liabilities	Shareholders' Equity

LO1   **E10–8   Reporting Short-Term Borrowings**

PepsiCo. Inc

PepsiCo, Inc., engages in a number of businesses that include Pepsi-Cola, Slice, Mountain Dew, and Fritos. The company's annual revenues exceed $25 billion. A recent PepsiCo annual report contained the following information:

> At the end of the current year, $3.6 billion of short-term borrowings were classified as long term, reflecting PepsiCo's intent and ability to refinance these borrowings on a long-term basis, through either long-term debt issuances or rollover of existing short-term borrowings. The significant amount of short-term borrowings classified as long term, as compared to the end of the previous year when no such amounts were reclassified, primarily reflects the large commercial paper issuances in the current year, but also resulted from a refined analysis of amounts expected to be refinanced beyond one year.

Required:

As an analyst, comment on the company's classification of short-term borrowings as long-term liabilities. What conditions should exist to permit a company to make this type of classification?

LO1   **E10–9   Reporting Warranty Liability**

Gonzales Co. provides warranties for many of its products. Its Estimated Warranty Liability account had a balance of $35,200 at January 1, 2008. Based on an analysis of warranty claims during the past several years, the warranty expense for 2008 was established at 0.4 percent of sales. During 2008, the actual cost of servicing products under warranty was $15,600, and sales were $3,600,000.

Required:

1. Compute the warranty expense that should appear on the company's income statement for the year ended December 31, 2008.

2. What amount will be reported in the Estimated Warranty Liability account on the balance sheet as at December 31, 2008?

LO1   **E10–10   Reporting Warranty Liabilities**

Amster Corp. produces and sells a single product that requires considerable servicing and adjustment during the first two years after sale. The company offers a warranty for two years covering most service requirements. The product's price ranges from $900 to $1,200 depending on the particular model produced. Warranty work costs $100 per product, regardless of the model. This amount has been quite stable for several years. Most of the warranty work occurs between the 6th and the 18th month after sale. The company's sales have been expanding, from approximately 9,000 units in 2003 to approximately 12,000 units in 2007.

Required:

How should Amber Corp. account for warranty costs, and how should the information be reported in its financial statements?

LO1, 2, 6   **E10–11   Determining the Impact of Transactions, Including Analysis of Cash Flows**

ANALYSIS

Mawani Company sells a wide range of goods through two retail stores operated in adjoining cities. Most purchases of goods for resale are on account. Occasionally, a short-term note payable is used to obtain cash for current use. The following transactions were selected from those occurring during 2008:

a. On January 10, 2008, purchased merchandise on credit, $18,000; the company uses a perpetual inventory system.

b. On March 1, 2008, borrowed $100,000 cash from Local Bank and signed an interest-bearing note payable: face amount, $100,000, due at the end of one year, with an annual interest rate of 8 percent payable at maturity.

c. On April 5, 2008, sold merchandise on credit, $33,900; this amount included GST of $1,500 and PST of $2,400. The cost of goods sold represents 70 percent of the sales invoice.

Required:

1. Describe the impact of each transaction on the balance sheet equation. Indicate the accounts, amounts, and direction of the effects (+ for increases and − for decreases) on the balance sheet equation. Use the following headings:

Date	Assets	Liabilities	Shareholders' Equity

2. What amount of cash is paid on the maturity date of the note?

3. Discuss the impact of each transaction on Mawani's cash flows.

4. Discuss the impact of each transaction on the current ratio. Assume that the current ratio is greater than 1 before considering each transaction.

E10–12 Reporting Contingent Liabilities ▇ LO5

Buzz Coffee Shops is famous for its large servings of hot coffee. After a famous case involving McDonald's, the lawyer for Buzz warned management (during 2005) that it could be sued if someone were to spill hot coffee and be burned: "With the temperature of your coffee, I can guarantee it's just a matter of time before you're sued for $1,000,000." Unfortunately, in 2007, the prediction came true when a customer filed suit. The case went to trial in 2008, and the jury awarded the customer $400,000 in damages, which the company immediately appealed. During 2009, the customer and the company settled their dispute for $150,000. What is the proper reporting each year of the events related to this liability?

E10–13 (Supplement A) Computing Future Income Tax: One Temporary Difference, with Discussion ▇ LO1

The comparative income statements of Martin Corporation at December 31, 2009, showed the following summarized pretax data:

	Year 2008	Year 2009
Sales revenue	$65,000	$72,000
Expenses (excluding income tax)	50,000	54,000
Pretax income	$15,000	$18,000

The expenses for 2009 included an amount of $2,800 that was deductible only in the 2008 income tax return (rather than in 2009). The average income tax rate was 40 percent. Taxable income from the income tax returns was $12,200 for 2008, and $20,800 for 2009.

Required:

1. For each year compute (a) the income taxes payable and (b) the future income tax. Is the future income tax a liability or an asset? Explain.

2. Show what amounts related to income taxes should be reported each year on the income statement and the balance sheet. Assume that the income tax is paid on March 1 of the next year.

3. Explain why tax expense is not simply the amount of cash paid during the year.

E10–14 (Supplement A) Recording Future Income Tax: One Temporary Difference; Discussion of Management Strategy ▇ LO1

The comparative income statement for Chung Corporation at the end of December 31, 2008, provided the following summarized pretax data:

	Year 2007	Year 2008
Revenue	$80,000	$88,000
Expenses (excluding income tax)	65,000	69,000
Pretax income	$15,000	$19,000

The revenue for 2008 included an amount of $5,000 that was taxable only in the 2007 income tax return. The average income tax rate was 35 percent. Taxable income shown in the tax returns was $20,000 for 2007, and $14,000 for 2008.

Required:

1. For each year compute (a) the income taxes payable and (b) the future income tax. Is the future income tax a liability or an asset? Explain.

2. Prepare the journal entry for each year to record income taxes payable, the future income tax, and the income tax expense.

3. Show the tax-related amounts that should be reported each year on the income statement and the balance sheet. Assume that income tax is paid on March 1 of the next year.

4. Why would management want to incur the cost of preparing separate tax and financial accounting reports to defer the payment of taxes?

LO1 **E10–15** (Supplement A) Computing and Reporting Future Income Tax: Amortization

Amber Corporation reported the following summarized pretax data at the end of each year:

Income Statement at December 31	2007	2008	2009
Revenues	$170,000	$182,000	$195,000
Expenses (including amortization)*	122,000	126,000	130,000
Pretax income	$ 48,000	$ 56,000	$ 65,000

*Straight-line amortization expense on a machine purchased January 1, 2007, for $75,000. The machine has a three-year estimated life and no residual value. The company used accelerated amortization on the income tax return as follows: 2007, $37,500; 2008, $25,000; and 2009, $12,500. The average income tax rate is 28 percent for each of the three years.

Taxable income from the income tax return was as follows: 2007, $32,000; 2008, $56,000; and 2009, $85,000.

Required:

1. For each year, compute (a) the income taxes payable and (b) the future income tax. Is the future income tax a liability or an asset? Explain.

2. Show the tax-related amounts that should be reported each year on the income statement and the balance sheet.

PROBLEMS

LO1 **P10–1** **Recording and Reporting Current Liabilities**

Valdir Company completed the following transactions during 2008. The company's fiscal year ends on December 31.

Jan. 15   Purchased and paid for merchandise for resale at an invoice cost of $13,580; assume a periodic inventory system.

April 1   Borrowed $500,000 from Summit Bank for general use; signed an 11-month, 8-percent interest-bearing note payable.

June 14   Received a deposit of $10,000 from customer Marina Malek for services to be performed in the future.

July 15   Performed services to Marina Malek for $2,500.

Dec. 12   Received electricity bill for $540. The company will pay it in early January.

31   Determined that wages of $12,000 were earned but not yet paid on December 31 (disregard payroll taxes).

Required:

1. Prepare journal entries for each of these transactions.

2. Prepare all adjusting entries required on December 31, 2008.

3. What is the effect of each transaction on working capital and on the current ratio (increase, decrease, no effect)? Assume that the current ratio is 1.40 at January 1, 2008.

LO1, 2 **P10–2** **Recording and Reporting Current Liabilities with Discussion of Effects on Current Ratio (AP10–1)**

Uzma Company completed the following transactions during 2008. The company's fiscal year ends on December 31, 2008.

ANALYSIS

Jan. 8 Purchased merchandise for resale at a cost of $12,420. The company uses a periodic inventory system.

17 Paid the invoice received on January 8.

Mar. 10 Sold merchandise on credit for a total amount of $11,300, which included GST at 5 percent and PST at 8 percent.

Apr. 1 Borrowed $40,000 from National Bank for general use; signed a 12-month, 12-percent interest-bearing note payable.

June 3 Purchased merchandise for resale at a cost of $17,820.

July 5 Paid the invoice received on June 3.

Aug. 1 Rented a small office in a building owned by the company and collected $5,400 for six months' rent in advance. (Record the collection in a way that will not require an adjusting entry at year-end.)

Dec. 20 Received a $100 deposit from a customer as a guarantee to return a large trailer "borrowed" for 30 days.

31 Determined that wages earned but not yet paid on December 31 amounted to $7,200. Ignore payroll taxes.

Required:

1. Prepare journal entries for each of these transactions.

2. Prepare the adjusting entry (entries) required on December 31, 2008.

3. Show how all of the liabilities arising from these transactions are reported on the balance sheet at December 31, 2008.

4. For each transaction and related adjusting entry, state whether the current ratio is increased, decreased, or remains the same. Assume that the current ratio is greater than 1 before considering each transaction.

P10–3 Determining Financial Effects of Transactions Affecting Current Liabilities with Discussion of Cash Flow Effects (AP10–2)

▇ **LO1, 6**

Using data from the previous problem, complete the following requirements.

Required:

1. For each transaction (including adjusting entries) listed in the previous problem, indicate the accounts, amounts, and direction of the effects (+ for increases and − for decreases) on the balance sheet equation. Use the following headings:

Date	Assets	Liabilities	Shareholders' Equity

2. For each transaction and related adjusting entry, state whether cash flow from operating activities is increased, decreased, or remains unchanged.

P10–4 Recording and Reporting Accrued Liabilities and Deferred Revenue, Financial Statement Effects with Discussion

▇ **LO1**

During 2009, Riverside Company completed the following two transactions. The company's fiscal year ends on December 31.

a. Paid and recorded wages of $130,000 during 2009; however, at the end of December 2009, wages of $5,100 for three days are unpaid and unrecorded because the next weekly pay day is January 6, 2010.

b. Rented office space to another party and collected $3,000 on December 10, 2009. The rent collected was for 30 days from December 12, 2009, through January 10, 2010, and was credited in full to Rent Revenue.

Required:

1. Prepare (a) the adjusting entry required on December 31, 2009, and (b) the journal entry on January 6, 2010, to record the payment of any unpaid wages from December 2009.

2. Prepare (a) the journal entry for the collection of rent on December 10, 2009, and (b) the adjusting entry on December 31, 2009.

3. Determine the financial statement effects for each of the journal entries you prepared in requirements 1 and 2. Indicate the accounts, the amounts, and direction of the effects (+ for increases and − for decreases) on the balance sheet equation. Use the following headings:

Date	Assets	Liabilities	Shareholders' Equity

4. Show how any liabilities related to these transactions should be reported on the company's balance sheet at December 31, 2009.

5. Explain why the accrual method of accounting provides more relevant information to financial analysts than the cash method.

■ **LO1, 4**   **P10–5** **Determining Financial Statement Effects of Various Liabilities** (AP10–3)

Polaroid

1. Polaroid designs, manufactures, and markets products primarily in instant image recording. Its annual report contained the following note:

> **Product Warranty**
>
> Estimated product warranty costs are accrued at the time products are sold.

Required:

Assume that estimated warranty costs for 2007 were $2 million and that the warranty work was performed during 2008. Describe the financial statement effects for each year.

Reader's Digest Association

2. Reader's Digest Association is a publisher of magazines, books, and music collections. The following note is from its annual report:

> **Revenues**
>
> Sales of subscriptions to magazines are recorded as unearned revenue at the time the order is received. Proportional shares of the subscription price are recognized as revenues when the subscription is fulfilled.

Required:

Assume that Reader's Digest collected $10 million in 2007 for magazines that will be delivered in future years. During 2008, the company delivered $8 million worth of magazines on those subscriptions. Describe the financial statement effects for each year.

Brunswick Corporation

3. Brunswick Corporation is a multinational company that manufactures and sells marine and recreational products. Its annual report contained the following information:

> **Litigation**
>
> A jury awarded $44.4 million in damages in a suit brought by Independent Boat Builders, Inc., a buying group of boat manufacturers and its 22 members. Under the antitrust laws, the damage award has been trebled, and the plaintiffs will be entitled to their attorney's fees and interest.
>   The Company has filed an appeal contending the verdict was erroneous as a matter of law, both as to liability and damages.

Required:

How should Brunswick report this litigation in its financial statements?

The Coca-Cola Company

4. A recent annual report for The Coca-Cola Company reported current assets of $4,247,677 and current liabilities of $5,303,222 (dollars in thousands). Based on the current ratio, do you think that Coca-Cola is experiencing financial difficulty?

Alcoa

5. Alcoa is involved in the mining and manufacturing of aluminum. Its products can become an advanced alloy for the wing of a Boeing 777 or a common recyclable Coca-Cola can. The annual report for Alcoa stated the following:

> **Environmental Expenditures**
>
> Liabilities are recorded when remedial efforts are probable and the costs can be reasonably estimated.

Required:

In your own words, explain Alcoa's accounting policy for environmental expenditures. What is the justification for this policy?

P10–6 Recording and Reporting Product Warranties (AP10–4)

■ **LO1**

Bombardier Inc. specializes in manufacturing transportation products (aircraft, railway equipment, snowmobiles, and watercraft). The company offers warranties on all of its products. Note 9 to Bombardier's financial statements for fiscal year 2006 stated the following:

> Product warranties typically range from one to five years, except for aircraft structural warranties that extend up to 20 years.

Selected information from Bombardier's annual reports follows (amounts in millions of US dollars).

	2006	2005	2004
Revenues	14,726	15,546	15,508
Estimated warranty liability at year end	970	1,055	932

During fiscal year 2006, Bombardier paid $469 million to customers in exchange for returned products under the warranty.

Required:

1. Compute the amount of warranty expense for 2006.

2. Prepare journal entries to record both the warranty expense for the year and the payments made under the warranty.

3. Compute the ratio of the warranty liability to revenues for the three years. Has the ratio increased or decreased during the three-year period?

4. Based on the limited information available about the warranty expense and payments in 2006, should Bombardier reduce the balance of the warranty liability in future years? Explain.

P10–7 Determining Financial Statement Effects of Deferred (Unearned) Revenues

■ **LO1**

A. Unearned revenues—customer deposits

Eastern Brewing Company (EBC) distributes its products in an aluminium keg. Customers are charged a deposit of $25 per keg, and deposits received from customers are recorded in the Keg Deposits account.

Required:

1. Where on the balance sheet will the Keg Deposits account be found? Explain.

2. A production specialist who works for EBC estimates that 50 kegs for which deposits were received during the year will never be returned. How would the deposits related to these 50 kegs be reflected in the company's financial statements?

B. Unearned revenues—rent

On September 1, 2008, Noreen Ltd. collected $9,000 in cash from its tenant as an advance rent payment on its store location. The six-month lease period ends on February 28, 2009, at which time the lease contract may be renewed. Noreen's fiscal year ends on December 31.

Required:

1. Prepare journal entries to record the collection of rent on September 1, 2008, and the related adjustment for the amount of rent earned during 2008.

2. If the amount received on September 1, 2008, had covered a period of 18 months, how should Noreen report the unearned rent amount on its balance sheet as at December 31, 2008?

C. Unearned revenues—subscription fees

Tremblay Inc. publishes a monthly newsletter for retail marketing managers and requires its subscribers to pay $60 in advance for a one-year subscription. During the month of April 2009, Tremblay Inc. sold 150 one-year subscriptions and received payments in advance from all new subscribers. Only 70 of the new subscribers paid their fees in time to receive the April newsletter. The other subscribers received the newsletter in May.

Required:

Prepare journal entries to record the subscription fees received in advance during April 2009, and the related adjusting entry to recognize the subscription revenue earned during April 2009.

■ **LO2**

PepsiCo

ANALYSIS

P10–8 Analyzing the Reclassification of Debt (AP10–5)

PepsiCo, Inc. is a $25-billion company in the beverage, snack food, and restaurant businesses. PepsiCo's annual report included the following note:

> At year-end, $3.5 billion of short-term borrowings were reclassified as long-term, reflecting PepsiCo's intent and ability to refinance these borrowings on a long-term basis, through either long-term debt issuances or rollover of existing short-term borrowings.

As a result of this reclassification, PepsiCo's current ratio improved from 0.51 to 0.79. Do you think the reclassification was appropriate? Why do you think management made the reclassification? As a financial analyst, would you use the current ratio before the reclassification or after the reclassification to evaluate PepsiCo's liquidity?

■ **LO1**

CHC
Helicopter

P10–9 Defining and Analyzing Changes in Current Liabilities (AP10–6)

CHC Helicopter Corporation is the world's largest provider of helicopter services to the global offshore oil and gas industry, with aircraft operating in more than 30 countries around the world. The company reported the following items in its balance sheet dated December 31, 2006 (in thousands of Canadian dollars):

	Dec. 31, 2006	Dec. 31, 2005
Current liabilities		
Payables and accruals	$221,861	$229,925
Deferred revenue	2,608	3,180
Dividends payable	8,548	6,404
Income taxes payable	8,361	25,126
Future income tax liabilities	8,852	705
Current portion of debt obligations	25,694	26,812

Required:

1. Define each of the current liabilities and identify the type of transactions that cause each liability to change (increase, decrease).

2. The company reported that $23,957 of deferred revenue was earned during 2006. Determine the amount that was collected in advance from customers during 2006 and prepare the related journal entry.

3. The company's board of directors declared dividends of $17,083 during 2006. Prepare the journal entries to record the declaration and payment of dividends during 2006.

■ **LO1, 5**

P10–10 Making a Decision as an Auditor: Contingent Liabilities

For each of the following situations, determine whether the company should (a) report a liability on the balance sheet, (b) disclose a contingent liability, or (c) not report the situation. Justify and explain your conclusions.

1. An automobile company introduces a new car. Past experience demonstrates that lawsuits will be filed as soon as the new model is involved in any accidents. The company can be certain that at least one jury will award damages to people injured in an accident.

2. A research scientist determines that your company's best-selling product may infringe on another company's patent. If the other company discovers the infringement and files suit, your company could lose millions.

3. As part of land development for a new housing project, your company has polluted a natural lake. Under provincial law, you must clean up the lake once you complete the development. The development project will take five to eight years to complete. Current estimates indicate that it will cost $2 to $3 million to clean up the lake.

4. Your company has just been notified that it lost a product liability lawsuit for $1 million that it plans to appeal. Management is confident that the company will win on appeal, but the lawyers believe that it will lose.

5. A key customer is unhappy with the quality of a major construction project. The company believes that the customer is being unreasonable but, to maintain goodwill, has decided to do $250,000 in repairs next year.

P10–11 Analyzing and Interpreting the Current Ratio and the Accounts Payable Turnover Ratio (AP10–7)

■ **LO2, 3**

Suncor Energy Inc. is an integrated energy company, with corporate headquarters in Calgary, Alberta. The company focuses on developing one of the world's largest petroleum resource basins—Canada's Athabasca oil sands. It also explores for, acquires, develops, produces, and markets crude oil and natural gas, transports and refines crude oil and market petroleum and petrochemical products. Selected financial statement information for the company over the six-year period 2001–2006 is presented below (amounts in millions of dollars).

Financial statement item	2006	2005	2004	2003	2002	2001
Current assets	$2,302	$1,916	$1,195	$1,279	$ 722	$ 622
Current liabilities	2,158	1,935	1,409	1,060	797	773
Cost of purchases	4,723	4,184	2,867	1,570	1,156	1,510
Accounts payable	2,111	1,830	1,306	972	716	672
Inventory	589	523				

Required:

1. Compute the current ratio for each of the six years, and comment on the six-year trend of the ratio.

2. Compute the accounts payable turnover ratio and the average age of payables for the years 2002–2006. Did the company's management of its accounts payable improve over time? Explain.

3. Suncor uses the LIFO (Last-In, First-Out) method of inventory costing, whereby the cost of the most recent purchases (or costs of production) is included in the computation of the cost of goods sold. The company reported in a note to its financial statements that the replacement cost of its inventory exceeded the LIFO cost by $243 million at December 31, 2006, and by $202 million at December 31, 2005. Assume that the replacement cost of the inventory approximates FIFO cost. Would the current ratio and the accounts payable turnover ratio for 2006 change if the company used the FIFO inventory costing method instead of LIFO. Show your computations. Which method, FIFO or LIFO, provides a more accurate indication of the company's liquidity and its efficiency in managing its payables? Explain.

P10–12 Determining Cash Flow Effects (AP10–8)

■ **LO6**

For each of the following transactions, determine whether cash flows from operating activities will increase, decrease, or remain the same:

a. Purchased merchandise on credit.

b. Paid an account payable.

c. Accrued payroll for the month but did not pay it.

d. Borrowed money from the bank. The term of the note is 90 days.

e. Reclassified a long-term note as a current liability.

f. Paid accrued interest expense.

g. Recorded a contingent liability based on a pending lawsuit.

h. Paid back the bank for money borrowed in d, along with related interest.

i. Collected cash from a customer for services that will be performed in the next accounting period.

j. Paid GST to the federal government. The amount was previously collected from customers.

■ **LO1, 5**   **P10–13**   **(Supplement A) Recording and Reporting Future Income Tax: Amortization** (AP10–9)

At December 31, 2007, the records of Pearson Corporation provided the following information:

Income statement	
Revenues	$160,000
Amortization expense (straight line)	(11,000)
Other expenses (excluding income tax)	(90,000)
Income before income taxes	$ 59,000

Additional information:

a. Revenues include $20,000 interest on tax-free municipal bonds.

b. Amortization expense relates to equipment acquired on January 1, 2007, at a cost of $44,000, with no salvage value and an estimated useful life of four years.

c. The accelerated amortization (capital cost allowance) used on the tax return is as follows: 2007, $17,600; 2008, $13,200; 2009, $8,800: and 2010, $4,400.

d. The company is subject to an income tax rate of 30 percent. Assume that 85 percent of the income tax liability is paid in the year incurred.

e. The income tax return for 2007 shows a taxable income of $32,400.

Required:

1. Compute the income taxes payable and the future income tax for 2007. Is the future income tax a liability or an asset? Explain.

2. Prepare the journal entry to record income taxes for 2007.

3. Show how the tax-related amounts should be reported on the income statement for 2007 and the balance sheet at December 31, 2007.

ALTERNATE PROBLEMS

■ **LO1, 6**   **AP10–1**   **Recording and Reporting Current Liabilities, with Discussion of Effects on the Current Ratio** (P10–2)

ANALYSIS

Fontaine Company completed the following transactions during 2008. The company's fiscal year ends on December 31, 2008.

Jan.	2	Paid accrued interest in the amount of $52,000.
Apr.	30	Borrowed $550,000 from Commerce Bank; signed a 12-month, 10-percent interest-bearing note payable.
May	20	Sold merchandise for $5,000 cash plus Harmonized Sales Tax at 14 percent.
June	3	Purchased merchandise for resale at a cost of $75,800, terms 2/10, n/30.
July	5	Paid the invoice received on June 3.
Aug.	31	Signed a contract to provide security service to a small apartment complex and collected $9,000 of fees for six months in advance. (Record the collection in a way that will not require an adjusting entry at year-end.)
Dec.	31	Reclassified a long-term liability in the amount of $100,000 to a current liability.
	31	Determined that salary and wages earned but not yet paid on December 31 totalled $85,000. Ignore payroll taxes.
	31	Recorded income tax expense for the year in the amount of $125,000. The current income taxes payable were $93,000.

Required:

1. Prepare journal entries to record each of these transactions.

2. Prepare all adjusting and reclassification entries required on December 31, 2008.

3. Show how all of the current liabilities arising from these transactions are reported on the balance sheet at December 31, 2008.

4. For each transaction and entry, state whether the current ratio is increased, decreased, or remains unchanged. Assume that the current ratio is less than 1 prior to each transaction/entry.

AP10–2 **Determining Financial Effects of Transactions Affecting Current Liabilities, with Discussion of Cash Flow Effects (P10–3)**

■ **LO1, 6**

Using data from the previous problem, complete the following requirements.

Required:

1. For each transaction (including adjusting and reclassification entries) listed in the previous problem, indicate the accounts, amounts, and direction of the effects (+ for increases and − for decreases) on the balance sheet equation. Use the following headings:

Date	Assets	Liabilities	Shareholders' Equity

2. For each transaction, state whether cash flow from operating activities is increased, decreased, or remains unchanged.

AP10–3 **Determining Financial Statement Effects of Various Liabilities (P10–5)**

■ **LO1, 4**

1. Pulte Corporation is a national builder of homes, doing more than $2 billion in business each year. Its annual report contained the following note:

Pulte

> **Allowance for Warranties**
>
> Home purchasers are provided with warranties against certain building defects. Estimated warranty cost is provided in the period in which the sale is recorded.

Required:

Assume that estimated warranty costs for 2007 were $8.5 million and that the warranty work was performed during 2008. Describe the financial statement effects for each year.

2. Carnival Cruise Lines operates cruise ships in Alaska, the Caribbean, the South Pacific, and the Mediterranean. Some cruises are brief; others can last for several weeks. The company does more than $1 billion in cruise business each year. The following note is from its annual report:

Carnival Cruise Lines

> **Revenues**
>
> Customer cruise deposits, which represent unearned revenue, are included in the balance sheet when received and are recognized as cruise revenue upon completion of voyages of a duration of 10 days or less and on a pro rata basis computed using the number of days completed for voyages in excess of 10 days.

Required:

In your own words, explain how unearned revenue is reported on the balance sheet for Carnival. Assume that Carnival collected $19 million in 2008 for cruises that will be completed in the following year. Of that amount, $4 million was related to cruises of 10 or fewer days that were not complete; $8 million to cruises of more than 10 days that, on average, were 60 percent complete; and $7 million was related to cruises that had not yet begun. What is the amount of unearned revenue that should be reported on the 2008 balance sheet?

3. Sunbeam Corporation is a consumer products company that manufactures and markets a number of familiar brands, including Mr. Coffee, Osterizer, First Alert, and Coleman. Annual revenues for the company exceed $2 billion. Its annual report contained the following information:

Sunbeam

> **Litigation**
>
> The Company and its subsidiaries are involved in various lawsuits arising from time to time that the Company considers to be ordinary routine litigation incidental to its business. In the opinion of the Company, the resolution of these routine matters will not have a material adverse effect upon the financial position, results of operations, or cash flows of the Company. At the end of the current year, the Company had established accruals for litigation matters of $31.2 million.
>
>   The Company recorded a $12.0 million charge related to a case for which an adverse development arose. In the fourth quarter of this year, the case was favorably resolved and, as a result, $8.1 million of the charge was reversed into income.

Required:

Explain the meaning of this note in your own words. Describe how litigation has affected the financial statements for Sunbeam.

Exxon

4. An annual report for Exxon reported a current ratio of 0.90. For the previous year, the ratio was 1.08. Based on this information, do you think that Exxon is experiencing financial difficulty? What other information would you want to consider in making this evaluation?

Brunswick

5. Brunswick Corporation is a multinational company that manufactures and sells marine and recreational products. Its annual report contained the following information:

Legal and Environmental

The company is involved in numerous environmental remediation and clean-up projects with an aggregate estimated exposure of approximately $21 million to $42 million. The Company accrues for environmental remediation-related activities for which commitments or clean-up plans have been developed and for which costs can be reasonably estimated.

Required:

In your own words, explain Brunswick's accounting policy for environmental expenditures. What is the justification for this policy?

■ **LO1**   **AP10–4** **Recording and Reporting Warranty Liabilities** (P10–6)

Gateway Inc. makes desktop and portable PCs and network servers for individual and enterprise customers. The company also offers third-party peripherals including printers, as well as consumer electronics such as digital music players and plasma televisions. Gateway provides standard warranties with the sale of its products. The company's note on significant accounting policies states:

The estimated cost of providing the product warranty is recorded at the time revenue is recognized. Gateway maintains product quality programs and processes including monitoring and evaluating the quality of its suppliers. Estimated warranty costs are affected by ongoing product failure rates, specific product class failures outside of experience and material usage and service delivery costs incurred in correcting a product failure or in providing customer support.

In addition, Gateway offers its customers an option to purchase extended warranties. Revenue related to sales of extended warranties sold on behalf of third parties is recognized at the time of sale. Revenue from sales of extended warranties where Gateway is the legal obligor is deferred and recognized on a straight-line basis over the warranty service period.

Selected information related to warranties provided by Gateway follows (in thousands of dollars):

	2006	2005	2004
Net sales	3,980,803	3,854,061	3,649,734
Accrued warranty, end of year	64,839	37,040	19,291
Settlements made during the year	64,898	40,997	62,984
Extended warranty deferred revenue, end of year	40,039	87,806	178,381
Additions to extended warranty deferred revenue during the year	10,885	23,193	93,839

Required:

1. Compute the amount of warranty expense for 2005 and 2006.

2. Prepare journal entries to record both the warranty expense for 2006 and the payments made under the warranty during the year.

3. Compute the ratio of the warranty expense to net sales for the three years. Assume that the warranty expense is $55,378 for 2004. Has the ratio increased or decreased during the three-year period? Provide possible reasons for the changes in the ratio.

4. Based on the limited information available about the warranty expense and settlements during these three years, should Gateway reduce the ratio of the warranty expense to net sales in future years? Explain.

5. Compute the extended warranty revenue recognized during 2005 and 2006, and prepare the journal entry to record the revenue recognized in 2006.

AP10–5 Analyzing the Reclassification of Debt (P10–8)

■ LO2

General Mills

General Mills is a multi-billion dollar company that makes and sells products used in the kitchens of most homes. The company's annual report included the following note:

> We have a revolving credit agreement expiring in two years that provides for a credit line (which permits us to borrow money when needed). This agreement provides us with the opportunity to refinance short-term borrowings on a long-term basis.

Should General Mills classify the short-term borrowings as current or noncurrent debt based on this ability to borrow money to refinance the debt if needed? If you were a member of the management team, explain what you would want to do and why? If you were a financial analyst, would your answer be different?

AP10–6 Defining and Analyzing Changes in Current Liabilities (P10–9)

■ LO1

Leon's Furniture

Leon's Furniture is one of Canada's largest retailers of home furnishings. The company reported the following items in its balance sheet dated December 31, 2006 (in thousands of Canadian dollars):

	Dec. 31, 2006	Dec. 31, 2005
Current liabilities		
Accounts payables and accrued liabilities	$54,820	$75,485
Customers' deposits	9,145	9,496
Dividends payable	4,424	3,844
Deferred warranty plan revenue	9,971	10,299
Income taxes payable	49	—
Future income tax liabilities	3	455

The company's annual report included the following information:

> Warranty revenues are deferred and taken into income on a straight-line basis over the life of the warranty period. Warranty revenues included in sales for fiscal year 2006 are $9,818,000 compared to $9,450,000 in 2005. Warranty expenses deducted through cost of goods sold for the year 2006 are $3,841,000 compared to $3,336,000 in 2005.

Required:

1. Define each of the current liabilities and identify the type of transactions that cause each liability to change (increase, decrease).

2. Determine the amount that the company received from customers to purchase deferred warranty plans during fiscal year 2006, and prepare the related journal entries to record the transactions that affected this account.

3. The company's board of directors declared dividends of $14,725 during 2006. Prepare the journal entries to record the declaration and payment of dividends during the year.

AP10–7 Analyzing and Interpreting the Current Ratio and the Accounts Payable Turnover Ratio (P10–11)

■ LO2, 3

eXcel
ANALYSIS

Imperial Oil Limited is one of the largest producers of crude oil in Canada and a major producer of natural gas, as well as the largest refiner and marketer of petroleum products and a significant presence in the petrochemical industry. Selected financial statement information for each company over the six-year period 2001–2006 is presented below (amounts in millions of dollars).

Financial statement item	2006	2005	2004	2003	2002	2001
Current assets	$ 5,309	$ 4,999	$ 3,897	$ 2,628	$ 2,980	$ 2,685
Current liabilities	5,348	5,145	4,658	3,390	2,743	3,025
Cost of purchases	13,793	17,168	13,094	11,580	10,155	10,134
Accounts payable	3,080	3,170	2,525	2,222	2,114	1,791
Inventory	556	481	432	407	433	478

Required:

1. Compute the current ratio for each of the six years, and comment on the six-year trend of the ratio.

2. Compute the accounts payable turnover ratio and the average age of payables for the years 2002–2006. Did the company improve on its management of accounts payable? Explain.

3. Imperial Oil is one of the few Canadian companies that use the LIFO (Last-In, First-Out) method of inventory costing, whereby the cost of the most recent purchases (or costs of production) is included in the computation of the cost of goods sold. The company reported in a note to its financial statements that the replacement cost of its inventory exceeded the LIFO cost by $506, $941, $797, $1,013, $1,429, and $1,509, for the years 2001–2006, respectively. Assume that the replacement cost of the inventory approximates FIFO cost. Would the current ratio and the accounts payable turnover ratio for the years 2002–2006 change if the company had used the FIFO inventory costing method instead of LIFO? Show your computations. Which method, FIFO or LIFO, provides a more accurate indication of the company's liquidity and its efficiency in managing its payables? Explain.

LO4

AP10–8 Determining Cash Flow Effects (P10–12)

For each of the following transactions, determine whether cash flows from operating activities will increase, decrease, or remain the same:

a. Purchased merchandise for cash.

b. Paid salaries and wages for the last month of the previous accounting period.

c. Paid PST to the provincial government, based on collections from customers.

d. Borrowed money from the bank. The term of the note is two years.

e. Withheld CPP contributions from employees' paycheques and immediately paid them to the government.

f. Recorded accrued interest expense.

g. Paid cash as a result of losing a lawsuit. A contingent liability associated with the liability had been recorded.

h. Paid salaries and wages for the current month.

i. Performed services for a customer who had paid for them in the previous accounting period.

LO1, 5

AP10–9 (Supplement A) Recording and Reporting Future Income Taxes: Two Temporary Differences (P10–13)

The records of Calib Corporation provided the following summarized data for 2007 and 2008:

Year-End December 31		
	2007	2008
Income statement		
Revenues	$210,000	$218,000
Expenses (excluding income tax)	130,000	133,000
Income before income taxes	$ 80,000	$ 85,000

a. Calib is subject to an income tax rate of 35 percent. Assume that 80 percent of the income taxes payable are paid in the current year and 20 percent on February 28 of the next year.

b. The temporary differences resulted from the following:
   (1) The 2008 expenses include an amount of $8,000 that must be deducted only in the 2007 tax return.
   (2) The 2008 revenues include an amount of $6,000 that was taxable only in 2009.

c. The taxable income shown in the tax returns was $72,000 for 2007, and $87,000 for 2008.

Required:

1. For each year compute (a) the income taxes payable and (b) the future income taxes. Identify whether the future income tax amounts are assets or liabilities. Explain.

2. Prepare the journal entry for each year to record income taxes payable, future income taxes, and income tax expense.

3. Show the tax-related amounts that should be reported each year on the income statement and the balance sheet.

4. As a financial analyst, would you evaluate differently a future income tax liability compared with income taxes currently payable?

CASES AND PROJECTS

FINDING AND INTERPRETING FINANCIAL INFORMATION

CP10–1 Finding Financial Information
Refer to the financial statements of Van Houtte Inc. in Appendix B of this book.

■ **LO1, 3, 4**

Van Houtte

Required:

1. Does Van Houtte report income taxes payable as a separate account on its balance sheet at the end of the current year? If not, where would this account be included on Van Houtte's balance sheet?

2. How did changes in accounts payable and accrued liabilities affect cash flows from operating activities in the current year?

3. What is the amount of long-term debt at the end of the current year?

4. What amounts of future income tax assets and liabilities are reported on the balance sheet at the end of the current year?

5. Does the company have a post-retirement or a defined benefit pension program?

CP10–2 Finding Financial Information
Refer to the Online Learning Centre Web site at **www.mcgrawhill.ca/olc/libby/student/ resources** for the financial statements of The Forzani Group Ltd.

■ **LO1, 4**

The Forzani Group

Required:

1. What is the amount of accounts payable and accrued liabilities at the end of the current year?

2. How did changes in accounts payable and accrued liabilities affect cash flows from operating activities in the current year?

3. What is the amount of long-term debt at the end of the current year?

4. Does the company have any contingent liabilities?

CP10–3 Comparing Companies within an Industry
Refer to the Online Learning Centre Web site at **www.mcgrawhill.ca/olc/libby/student/ resources** for the financial statements of The Forzani Group Ltd. and to Appendix B of this book for the financial statements of Van Houtte Inc.

■ **LO2, 3**

Van Houtte Inc. vs. The Forzani Group

ANALYSIS

Required:

1. Compute the current ratio for each company for each year shown in the financial statements.

2. Compute the accounts payable turnover ratio for each company for each year. Assume that Van Houtte's cost of sales for the current year is $198,000.

3. Using this information and any other data from the annual report, write a brief assessment of the liquidity of the two companies.

FINANCIAL REPORTING AND ANALYSIS CASES

■ **LO1** **CP10–4** **Explaining a Note: Accrued Liability for a Frequent Flyer Program**

Southwest Airlines

Most major airlines have frequent flyer programs that permit passengers to earn free tickets based on the number of reward miles they have flown. A Southwest Airlines annual report contained the following note:

> **Frequent Flyer Awards**
>
> The Company accrues the estimated incremental cost to provide transportation for travel awards when earned under its Company Club frequent flyer program.

The phrase *incremental cost* refers to additional expense associated with an extra passenger taking the flight (e.g., the cost of a soft drink and a snack).

Required:

1. What cost measures other than incremental cost could Southwest use?

2. What account should Southwest debit when it accrues this liability?

ANALYSIS

■ **LO2, 3** **CP10–5** **Using Financial Reports: Evaluating Cash Management**

Starbucks

Starbucks is a leading retailer of specialty coffee. It purchases and roasts high-quality whole bean coffees and sells them, along with Italian style espresso beverages, a variety of pastries and confections, and coffee-related accessories and equipment, primarily through its company-operated retail stores. Selected financial information is presented below for the period 2002–2006 (amounts are in millions of dollars).

	2006	2005	2004	2003	2002
Net sales	$7,787	$6,369	$5,294	$4,076	$3,289
Cost of goods sold	3,179	2,605	2,191	1,686	1,350
Accounts receivable	224	191	131	114	97
Inventory	636	546	423	343	263
Accounts payable	341	221	192	169	136

Required:

1. Compute the following ratios for each of the years 2003–2006:
   a. Accounts payable turnover
   b. Inventory turnover
   c. Accounts receivable turnover

2. One of the measures of a company's effectiveness in utilizing cash resources is the cash conversion cycle, which is computed as the difference between the average number of days needed to convert inventory to cash and the average number of days to pay trade suppliers. Compute the cash conversion cycle for each of the years 2003–2006. Did Starbucks improve on its management of cash? Explain.

■ **LO4** **CP10–6** **Interpreting the Financial Press**

Increasingly, companies are becoming sensitive to environmental issues surrounding their business operations. They recognize that some of their actions can have detrimental impacts on the environment in ways that may not be fully understood for years or even decades. Environmental issues present complex problems for companies that must report contingent liabilities. A related article, Munter, Sacasas, and Garcia, "Accounting and Disclosure of

Environmental Contingencies," January 1996, pp. 36–37, 50–52, from the *CPA Journal* (www.cpaj.com) is available on the Web site at **www.mcgrawhill.ca/olc/libby/student/ resources**. Read the article and prepare a brief memo concerning how companies should report environment issues on their financial statements.

CP10–7 **Interpreting Contingent Liabilities: Litigation**

Research In Motion (RIM) is a leading designer, manufacturer, and marketer of innovative wireless solutions for the worldwide mobile communications market. RIM's products include the BlackBerry wireless platform, software development tools, and software/hardware licensing agreements.

■ **LO5**

Research In Motion

The following excerpt from the company's balance sheet as at February 26, 2005 shows Accrued litigation and related expenses for US$455,610,000. Note 15 to the company's financial statements provides an explanation for the nature of this liability (refer to **http://www.rim.com/investors/pdf/2006 rim_ar.pdf**).

Consolidated Balance Sheets

As at	March 4, 2006	February 26, 2005
	(in thousands of US dollars)	
Liabilities		
Current		
Accounts payable	$ 94,954	$ 68,464
Accrued liabilities (notes 13 and 18(c))	144,912	87,133
Accrued litigation and related expenses (note 15)	—	455,610
Income taxes payable (note 9)	17,584	3,149
Deferred revenue	20,968	16,235
Current portion of long-term debt (note 10)	262	223
	278,680	630,814
Long-term debt (note 10)	6,851	6,504
	$285,531	637,318

Required:

1. Review note 15 to RIM's financial statements and identify the main reason for the reported liability as well as the specific amounts that the company recorded as liabilities during each of the fiscal years 2003–2006.

2. Reconstruct the journal entry to record the payment of $612.5 million in settlement of the NTP lawsuit, as disclosed in Note 15 to RIM's financial statements.

3. Does the company's annual report include information about other litigation during the past few years? If so, has the company provided an estimate of the liabilities that it may have to pay in the future? Explain.

CRITICAL THINKING CASES

CP10–8 **Making Decisions as a Manager: Liquidity**

In some cases, a manager can engage in transactions that improve the appearance of financial reports without affecting the underlying economic reality. In this chapter, we discussed the importance of liquidity as measured by the current ratio and working capital. For each of the following transactions, (a) determine whether reported liquidity (as measured by the current ratio and working capital) is improved and (b) state whether you believe that the fundamental liquidity of the company has been improved. Assume that the company has positive working capital and a current ratio of 2 immediately prior to each transaction event.

■ **LO1, 2**

a. Borrowed $1 million from the bank, payable in 90 days.

b. Borrowed $10 million with a long-term note, payable in five years.

c. Reclassified the current portion of long-term debt as long term as a result of a new agreement with the bank that guarantees the company's ability to refinance the debt when it matures.

d. Paid $100,000 of the company's accounts payable.

e. Entered into a borrowing agreement that allows the company to borrow up to $10 million when needed.

f. Required all employees to take accrued vacation to reduce its liability for vacation compensation.

LO2

CP10–9 **Evaluating an Ethical Dilemma: Managing Reported Results**

The president of a regional wholesale distribution company planned to borrow a significant amount of money from a local bank at the beginning of the next fiscal year. He knew that the bank placed a heavy emphasis on the liquidity of potential borrowers. To improve the company's current ratio, the president told his employees to stop shipping new merchandise to customers and to stop accepting merchandise from suppliers for the last three weeks of the fiscal year. Is this behaviour ethical? Would your answer be different if the president had been concerned about reported profits and asked all of the employees to work overtime to ship out merchandise that had been ordered at the end of the year?

LO2

CP10–10 **Making a Decision as a Financial Analyst: Cash Flows**

As a young analyst at a large mutual fund, you have found two companies that meet the basic investment criteria of the fund. One company has a very high current ratio but a relatively low amount of cash flow from operating activities reported on the cash flow statement. The other company has a very low current ratio but very significant cash flows from operating activities. Which company would you tend to prefer?

LO4

CP10–11 **Assessing Contingent Liabilities**

If a liability is both likely and subject to reasonable estimate, it must be recorded as a liability on the balance sheet. The *CICA Handbook* has defined *likely* as "the chance of the occurrence (or non-occurrence) of the future event(s) is high." Working in a small group, decide on a specific probability that is appropriate for this standard. (For example, is an 80 percent chance of occurrence likely?) Be prepared to justify your determination.

FINANCIAL REPORTING AND ANALYSIS TEAM PROJECT

LO1–4

ANALYSIS

CP10–12 **Team Project: Examining an Annual Report**

As a team, select an industry to analyze. Reuters provides lists of industries and their make up at **www.investor.reuters.com/Industries.aspx**. Each team member should acquire the annual report for one publicly traded company in the industry, with each member selecting a different company. (Library files, the SEDAR service at **www.sedar.com**, or the company itself are good sources.)

Required:

1. List the accounts and amounts of the company's current liabilities for the last three years.
   a. What is the percentage of each to the respective year's total liabilities?
   b. What do the results of your analysis suggest about the strategy your company has followed with respect to borrowed funds overall and over time?

2. What, if any, contingent liabilities are reported by the company for the most recent year and what is your assessment of the risk of each after reading the footnote(s)?

3. Ratio analysis:
   a. What does the current ratio measure in general?
   b. Compute the ratio for the last three years.
   c. What do your results suggest about the company?
   d. If available, find the industry ratio for the most recent year, compare it to your results, and discuss why you believe the ratio for your company differs or is similar to the industry ratio.

4. Ratio analysis:
   a. What does the accounts payable turnover ratio measure in general?
   b. Compute the ratio for the last three years.
   c. What do your results suggest about the company?
   d. If available, find the industry ratio for the most recent year, compare it to your results, and discuss why you believe the ratio for your company differs or is similar to the industry ratio.

5. What is the effect of the change in accounts payable on cash flows from operating activities for the most recent year, that is, did the change increase or decrease operating cash flows? Explain your answer.

Reporting and Interpreting Long-term Liabilities

After studying this chapter, you should be able to:

LEARNING OBJECTIVES

1. Describe the characteristics of long-term notes and bonds payable. p. 571

2. Report bonds payable and interest expense for bonds sold at par, at a discount, and at a premium. p. 575

3. Compute and interpret the times interest earned ratio. p. 586

4. Report the early retirement of bonds. p. 587

5. Describe other long-term liabilities. p. 589

6. Compute and interpret the financial leverage ratio. p. 593

7. Explain how financing activities are reported on the cash flow statement. p. 594

Canada is rich in natural resources, such as oil, gas, mineral deposits, and timberland. In the oil and gas industry, Petro-Canada (**www.petro-canada.ca**) and its competitors spend hundreds of millions of dollars to develop existing sources of oil and gas, and to explore for new sources.

FOCUS COMPANY:

Petro-Canada

FINANCING GROWTH WITH LONG-TERM DEBT

In 2006, Petro-Canada spent $3.4 billion to upgrade its production facilities and expand on its operations. Over the next few years, the company plans to bring on five major projects: the Edmonton refinery conversion project (2008), the Montreal refinery coker (2009), the Syria gas project (2010), the MacKay River expansion (2010), and the Fort Hills project (2011).

Achieving these plans requires Petro-Canada to invest in large amounts of new capital in addition to retaining much of its income. Some of this capital will be borrowed from creditors through long-term notes and bonds. For example, in May 2005, Petro-Canada raised US$600 million by selling long-term notes to financial intermediaries, and will likely finance its investment program in the future by selling long-term notes and bonds. By December 31, 2006, Petro-Canada had raised almost $2.9 billion of funds through long-term debt.

In this chapter, we will study Petro-Canada's sale of long-term debt and understand how its value is measured and reported in financial statements.

UNDERSTANDING THE BUSINESS

Long-term liabilities include all of the entity's obligations that are not classified as current liabilities, such as long-term notes and bonds payable. Typically, a long-term liability will require payment more than one year in the future. These obligations may be created by borrowing money, or they may result from other activities.

Long-term liabilities are reported on the balance sheet immediately following current liabilities, as shown in Exhibit 11.1 for Petro-Canada. The accounts Long-term debt, Other liabilities, Asset retirement obligations, and Future income taxes are disclosed separately and explained in notes.

In Chapter 10, we introduced the term *capital structure*, the mix of debt and equity that is used to finance a company's growth. Almost all companies employ some debt in their capital structure. In this chapter, we focus on long-term debt, which simply reflects a contractual obligation whereby the borrower receives cash or other assets in exchange for a promise to pay the lender a fixed or determinable amount of money at a specific date in the future.

The use of long-term debt offers significant advantages to companies such as Petro-Canada:

1. Debt does not dilute ownership and control of the company because debtholders participate neither in the management of operations nor in the distribution of accumulated earnings that are eventually distributed to shareholders.

2. Cash payments to the debtholders are limited to the scheduled payments of interest and the repayment of the principal amount of the debt.

3. Interest expense is deductible for tax purposes but dividends paid to shareholders are not. The deductibility of interest for tax purposes reduces the net cost of borrowing, as shown in the following simplified example where net income is calculated under two scenarios: (1) a company that uses 100-percent equity financing ($600,000) and (2) a similar company that uses a mix of 50-percent debt ($300,000) and 50-percent equity ($300,000). Assume that both companies earned $100,000 of income before interest and taxes, that the interest rate on the debt is 10 percent, and that both companies are subject to a tax rate of 40 percent.

LONG-TERM LIABILITIES are all of the entity's obligations not classified as current liabilities.

EXHIBIT **11.1**

The Accounting Cycle

REAL WORLD EXCERPT

Petro-Canada

ANNUAL REPORT

PETRO-CANADA
Consolidated Balance Sheets
(in millions of Canadian dollars)

	Dec. 31, 2006	Dec. 31, 2005
Liabilities and Shareholders' Equity		
Current liabilities		
Accounts payable and accrued liabilities	$3,319	$2,895
Income taxes payable	22	82
Liabilities of discontinued operations *(Note 4)*	—	102
Current portion of long-term debt	7	7
	3,348	3,086
Long-term debt *(Note 18)*	2,887	2,906
Other liabilities *(Note 19)*	1,826	1,888
Asset retirement obligations *(Note 20)*	1,170	882
Future income taxes *(Note 7)*	2,974	2,405

	Capital Structure	
	100% Equity	50% Debt 50% Equity
Income before interest and income taxes	$100,000	$100,000
Interest expense	0	30,000
	100,000	70,000
Income tax expense (at 40%)	40,000	28,000
Net income	$ 60,000	$ 42,000
Owners' equity	$600,000	$300,000
Return on equity (Net income/Owners' equity)	10%	14%

FINANCIAL LEVERAGE is the use of borrowed funds to increase the rate of return on owners' equity; it occurs when the interest rate on debt is lower than the rate of return on total assets.

It is evident from this simplified illustration that borrowing reduces net income but the deductibility of interest expense for tax purposes increases the return on the owners' investment. This example also illustrates the use of positive **financial leverage**, whereby a company borrows funds at a specified interest rate and invests them in productive assets. Shareholders benefit from borrowing when the rate of return on assets exceeds the after-tax interest rate on the debt.

However, the issuance of long-term debt has some disadvantages. The primary disadvantage is that the required interest and principal payments must be made at specific dates in the future, whether the corporation earns income or incurs a loss. These payments, which are legally enforceable, increase the financial risk of the company. In contrast, dividends are usually paid to shareholders only if the corporation has generated earnings from its past operations. Each year, some companies go bankrupt because of their inability to make required debt payments to their creditors.[1] Sound business practice requires maintaining an appropriate balance between debt and equity capital.

In this chapter, we will examine Petro-Canada's issuance of various types of long-term debt and describe other typical long-term liabilities. We will study the accounting rules that govern the recording of long-term notes and bonds payable, and examine the related financial statement disclosures. We will also examine the reasons for which management raises money through long-term debt, and how the reported debt and supplementary disclosures are used by financial statement analysts to make informed judgments about investment and/or credit risk.

ORGANIZATION OF THE CHAPTER

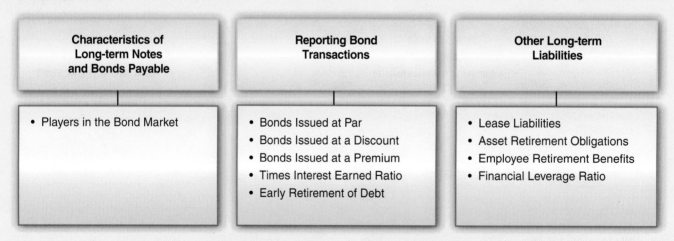

Characteristics of Long-term Notes and Bonds Payable	Reporting Bond Transactions	Other Long-term Liabilities
• Players in the Bond Market	• Bonds Issued at Par • Bonds Issued at a Discount • Bonds Issued at a Premium • Times Interest Earned Ratio • Early Retirement of Debt	• Lease Liabilities • Asset Retirement Obligations • Employee Retirement Benefits • Financial Leverage Ratio

---

[1]Recent examples include Enron Corp. and WorldCom Inc., which received extensive coverage in the financial press because they used aggressive accounting methods and stretched the interpretation and application of GAAP to hide their poor financial performances. These companies were unable to repay sizeable amounts of debt to their creditors and could not overcome their financial difficulties, which led to their inevitable collapse.

CHARACTERISTICS OF LONG-TERM NOTES AND BONDS PAYABLE

Companies can raise long-term debt directly from a number of financial service organizations, including banks, insurance companies, and pension fund companies. Raising debt from one of these organizations is known as *private placement*. This type of debt often is called a *note payable*, which is a written promise to pay a stated sum at one or more specified future dates, called the *maturity date(s)*.

In many cases, a company's need for debt capital exceeds the financial ability of any single creditor. In these situations, the company may issue publicly traded debt called *bonds*. The bonds can be traded in established markets that provide bondholders with liquidity (i.e., the ability to sell the bond and receive cash quickly). They can sell their bonds to other investors prior to maturity if they have an immediate need for cash.

Petro-Canada borrows billions of dollars in long-term debt to explore for oil and natural gas and bring these natural resources to the market. In exchange for the borrowed money, Petro-Canada signs debt agreements in the form of a loan, a note, or a mortgage note with banks and other institutional lenders. Loans and notes are often for terms of five years or less while mortgage terms can exceed 25 years.

Lenders often protect their interests by requesting that the debt be secured rather than unsecured. If you have a credit card, a student loan, or perhaps an automobile loan, you may have read the terms of the debt contract, which indicates if the debt is secured or not. In the case of a personal credit card the debt is unsecured, which means if a debtor fails to make the required payment, or *defaults,* the lender cannot repossess any specific asset of the cardholder.

In the case of a large, personal, long-term loan such as an automobile loan, lenders will insist on the right to repossess the automobile in the event of default. Repossession allows the lender to sell the automobile and recover all or part of the unpaid loan. Corporations such as Petro-Canada can secure their notes and bonds payable using revenue, inventory, property, equipment, and buildings. Secured debt provides the creditor with the right to foreclose on the debt and repossess the assets, or collateral, pledged by the company as security should the company violate the terms of its debt contract.

Exhibit 11.2 shows note 18 to Petro-Canada's financial statements, which lists the different types of long-term debt that the company has issued in the past—mostly unsecured notes and debentures that are denominated in US dollars. After studying this chapter, you will understand the terms used in the note, particularly the accounting and financial issues associated with bonds and debentures.

A bond usually requires the payment of interest over its life, with the repayment of principal on the maturity date. The **bond principal** is (1) the amount payable at the maturity date and (2) the basis for computing periodic cash interest payments. The principal also is called the **par value, face amount,** and *maturity value*. All bonds have a par value, which is the amount that will be paid when the bond matures. For most bonds the par value is $1,000, but it can be any amount.

A bond always specifies a **stated rate** of interest and the timing of periodic cash interest payments, usually annually or semi-annually. Each periodic interest payment is equal to the principal times the stated interest rate. The selling price of a bond does not affect the periodic cash payment of interest. For example, a $1,000, 8 percent bond always pays cash interest of (1) $80 on an annual basis or (2) $40 on a semi-annual basis.

Different types of bonds have different characteristics for good economic reasons. Different types of creditors have different types of risk and return preferences. A retired person, for example, may be willing to receive a lower interest rate in return for greater security. This type of creditor might want a mortgage bond that pledges a specific asset as security if the company is unable to repay the bond. Another creditor might be willing to accept a low interest rate and an unsecured status if the company provides the opportunity to convert the bond into common shares at some point in the future. Companies try to design bond features that are attractive to different groups of

■ **LEARNING OBJECTIVE 1**

Describe the characteristics of long-term notes and bonds payable.

The **BOND PRINCIPAL** is the amount payable at the maturity of the bond. It is also the basis for computing periodic cash interest payments.

PAR VALUE and **FACE AMOUNT** are other names for bond principal or the maturity value of a bond.

The **STATED RATE** is the rate of cash interest per period specified in the bond contract.

EXHIBIT **11.2**

Long-term Debt

REAL WORLD EXCERPT

Petro-Canada

ANNUAL REPORT

Note 18 Long-term debt

	Maturity	2006	2005
Debentures and notes			
5.95% unsecured senior notes ($600 million US)[1]	2035	$ 699	$ 700
5.35% unsecured senior notes ($300 million US)[2]	2033	349	350
7.00% unsecured debentures ($250 million US)	2028	291	292
7.875% unsecured debentures ($275 million US)	2026	321	321
9.25% unsecured debentures ($300 million US)	2021	349	350
5.00% unsecured senior notes ($400 million US)	2014	466	466
4.00% unsecured senior notes ($300 million US)[2]	2013	349	350
Capital leases (*Note 15*)[3]	2007–2017	70	77
Retail licensee trust loans		—	7
		2,894	2,913
Current portion		(7)	(7)
		$2,887	$2,906

[1]In May 2005, the Company issued $600 million US 5.95% notes due May 15, 2035. The proceeds were used primarily to repay existing short-term notes payable.
[2]In anticipation of issuing these senior notes, the Company entered into interest rate derivatives, which resulted in effective interest rates of 6.073% for the 5.35% notes due in 2033 and 4.838% for the 4.00% notes due in 2013.
[3]The Company is party to one transportation and one time charter agreement that are accounted for as capital leases and have implicit rates of interest of 14.65% and 11.90%, respectively. The aggregate remaining repayments under the transportation and time charter agreements are $70 million, including the following amounts in the next five years: 2007—$7 million; 2008—$2 million; 2009—$3 million; 2010—$3 million; and 2011—$4 million.

creditors, just as automobile manufacturers try to design cars that appeal to different groups of consumers. Some key types of bonds are shown below.

A **DEBENTURE** is an unsecured bond; no assets are specifically pledged to guarantee repayment.

CALLABLE BONDS may be called for early retirement at the option of the issuer.

CONVERTIBLE BONDS may be converted to other securities of the issuer (usually common shares).

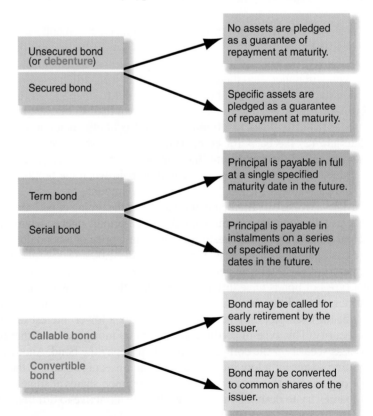

Companies like Petro-Canada often need to undertake massive mining projects to explore for and produce gold. One possibility is for Petro-Canada to finance the project by issuing bonds that are secured by the assets that will be in place once the project is finished. Another possibility is to issue bonds secured by the amount of revenues expected from the completed project. The company could also issue debentures that are unsecured, depending on how much risk the debenture holders are willing to take.

When a company decides to issue new bonds, it prepares a bond **indenture** (bond contract) that specifies the legal provisions of the bonds. These provisions include the maturity date, rate of interest to be paid, date of each interest payment, and any conversion privileges. The indenture also contains covenants designed to protect the creditors. These include limitations on new debt that the company might issue in the future. Other typical covenants include limitations on the payment of dividends, and required minimum levels of certain accounting ratios, such as the current ratio. Managers prefer covenants that are least restrictive because they may limit the company's future actions. Creditors, however, prefer more restrictive covenants that reduce the risk of losing their investment. As with any business transaction, the final result is achieved through a process of negotiation.

An **INDENTURE** is a bond contract that specifies the legal provisions of a bond issue.

Bond covenants are usually reported in the notes to the financial statements. For example, CHC Helicopter Corporation, which is the world's largest provider of helicopter services to the global offshore oil and gas industry, disclosed the following information in Note 13 to its financial statements:

REAL WORLD EXCERPT

CHC Helicopter Corporation

ANNUAL REPORT

Notes to the Consolidated Financial Statements

13. Debt obligations

. . .

The terms of certain of the Company's debt agreements and helicopter lease agreements impose operating and financial limitations on the Company. Such agreements limit the extent to which the Company may, among other things, incur additional indebtedness, create liens, make capital expenditures, sell or sublease assets, engage in mergers or acquisitions and make dividend and other payments. During the years ended April 30, 2006 and 2005 the Company was in compliance with all material covenants and other conditions imposed by its debt and helicopter lease agreements.

The bond issuer also prepares a prospectus, which is a legal document that is given to potential bond investors. The prospectus describes the company, the bond, and how the proceeds of the bonds will be used. For example, the 7.00% unsecured debentures shown in Exhibit 11.2 were issued by Petro-Canada in November 1998. At that time, the company filed a prospectus with the securities commissions to sell US$250 million of 7.00% debentures due November 15, 2028. The prospectus specified the dates of interest payments, the covenants that apply to this debt, and that the net proceeds from these debentures will be used to repay long-term debt that matured in December 1998.[2]

When a bond is issued, the investor receives a **bond certificate**. All of the bond certificates for a single bond issue are identical. The face of each certificate shows the same maturity date, interest rate, interest dates, and other provisions. An independent party, called the **trustee**, is usually appointed to represent the bondholders. A trustee's duties are to ascertain whether the issuing company fulfils all of the provisions of the bond indenture.

A **BOND CERTIFICATE** is the bond document that each bondholder receives.

A **TRUSTEE** is an independent party appointed to represent the bondholders.

---

[2]A copy of this prospectus is available on the SEDAR system (**www.sedar.com**). Access the Web site, search for Petro-Canada under the letter P, view the documents filed by the company, and select Supplemented short-form PREP prospectus – English, dated November 19, 1998.

PLAYERS IN THE BOND MARKET

Most companies work with an underwriter, who either buys the entire issue of bonds and then resells them to individual creditors (called a *firm commitment underwriter*), or simply sells the bonds or notes without any obligation to purchase them (called a *best efforts underwriter*). It is not uncommon for companies to use several underwriters to sell a large bond issue. For example, Petro-Canada deals with underwriters like CIBC World Markets Inc., Scotia Capital Inc., HSBC Securities (USA) Inc., J. P. Morgan Securities Inc., and RBC Capital Markets Corporation.

Bonds dealers sell bonds typically to institutional investors such as banks, insurance companies, and mutual and pension funds. They also create a secondary market for bonds by trading them for their own account in response to supply and demand by institutional investors. Almost all trades occur by telephone, known as an over the counter (OTC) market, not through a formal bond exchange. The market in bonds exceeds by far the value of stocks traded on a typical day because of the high value of each trade. A bond trade of $200 million would not be unusual in this market.[3]

Because of the complexities associated with bonds, several agencies exist to evaluate the probability that a bond issuer will not be able to meet the requirements specified in the indenture. This risk is called ***default risk***. In general, the higher the risk of default, the higher will be the interest rate required to successfully persuade investors to purchase the bond and the more restrictive will be the covenants protecting the bondholder. Dominion Bond Rating Service (DBRS), Moody's Investor Services Inc. (Moody's), and Standard and Poor's Rating Services (S&P) each assess the default risk for every issue of corporate debentures and bonds.[4] Their ratings range from investment grade to extremely speculative junk bonds. If it becomes apparent that there has been a change in default risk for any debt already issued, each rating service will issue a public bulletin that upgrades or downgrades the credit rating, along with reasons for the change.[5]

Companies such as Petro-Canada, which rely on bonds to expand their operations, publish the debt ratings in the prospectus of the debt issue.

REAL WORLD EXCERPT

Petro-Canada

PROSPECTUS SUPPLEMENT

Credit ratings

Credit ratings are intended to provide investors with an independent measure of the credit quality of any issue of securities. The following table discloses the ratings of our unsecured long-term debt securities by the rating agencies indicated:

Rating Agency Rating

Moody's Investors Service, Inc. ("Moody's")	Baa2
Standard & Poor's Rating Services, a division of the McGraw-Hill Companies, Inc. ("S&P")	BBB
Dominion Bond Rating Services ("DBRS")	A (low)

Bond prices change for two main reasons: the creditworthiness of the bond issuer and changes in interest rates. The company's creditworthiness depends on the operating, investing and financing decisions made by management. However, interest rates are not within the control of corporations, but depend on the supply and demand for money. The most important interest rate is the rate at which the federal government

---

[3]Further details about the bond market are available at **www.investinginbonds.com**.

[4]Standard & Poor's (S&P) has a useful Web site at **www.standardandpoors.com** for those interested in learning about the credit ratings used by this credit rating agency.

[5]The details of how default risk is rated vary slightly from one agency to another. You can view a sample of these descriptions in detail at **www.dbrs.com**.

can borrow money for the long term. This is the benchmark, risk-free rate of return on bonds because purchasers believe that the federal government will never fail to repay, or default on its debts. The interest rates of all other debt instruments are established relative to this risk-free rate. The difference between the interest rate on debt instruments and the risk-free rate is called the spread. The size of the spread depends upon the perceived additional risk that the company will default on either its interest or principal payments on the debt.

REPORTING BOND TRANSACTIONS

Exhibit 11.2 shows that Petro-Canada has issued unsecured bonds for a total face value of $963 million as at December 31, 2005. Each bond indenture specifies two types of cash payments:

1. *Principal.* This is usually a single payment made when the bond matures. It is also called the *par,* or *face, value.*
2. *Cash interest payments.* These payments are computed by multiplying the principal amount times the interest rate, called the **contract, stated,** or **coupon rate** of interest stated in the bond contract. The bond contract specifies whether these payments are made quarterly, semi-annually, or annually.

Neither the company nor the underwriter determines the price at which the bonds sell. Instead, the market determines the current cash equivalent of future interest and principal payments using present value concepts.[6] To determine the present value of the bond, you compute the present value of the principal (a single payment) and the present value of the interest payments (an annuity) and add the two amounts.

Creditors demand a certain rate of interest to compensate them for the risks related to bonds, called the **market interest rate** (also known as the **yield,** or **effective interest rate**). Because the market rate is the interest rate on a debt when it is incurred, it should be used in computing the present value of the bond.

The present value of a bond may be the same as par, above par (**bond premium**), or below par (**bond discount**). If the stated and the market interest rates are the same, a bond sells at par. If a bond pays a stated interest rate that is lower than the market rate that creditors demand, they will not buy it unless its price is reduced (i.e., a discount must be provided). If a bond pays a stated rate that is higher than the market rate that creditors demand, they will be willing to pay a premium to buy it.

This relationship can be shown graphically as follows:[7]

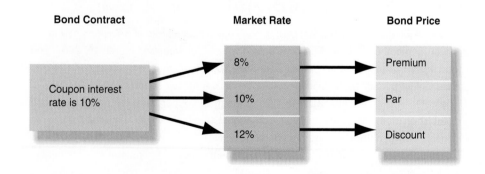

Bond Contract	Market Rate	Bond Price
	8%	Premium
Coupon interest rate is 10%	10%	Par
	12%	Discount

■ LEARNING OBJECTIVE 2
Report bonds payable and interest expense for bonds sold at par, at a discount, and at a premium.

The **COUPON RATE** is the stated rate of interest on bonds.

MARKET INTEREST RATE is the current rate of interest on a debt when incurred; also called the **YIELD,** or **EFFECTIVE-INTEREST RATE.**

BOND PREMIUM is the difference between the selling price and par when the bond is sold for more than par.

BOND DISCOUNT is the difference between the selling price and par when the bond is sold for less than par.

---

[6]Students who have not been exposed to present value concepts in previous courses are strongly advised to read Chapter Supplement A before continuing with the rest of this chapter.

[7]The difference between the coupon interest rate and the market interest rate is often very small, usually a fraction of 1 percent, when the bonds are sold. Companies try to sell their bonds at prices close to their par value. However, the market rate of interest continually changes as a result of such factors as inflation expectations and the level of business activity. It is therefore virtually impossible to issue a bond at a point when the coupon rate and the market rate are exactly the same.

Basically, corporations and creditors are indifferent to whether a bond is issued at par, at a discount, or at a premium because bonds are always priced to provide the market rate of interest. To illustrate, consider a corporation that issues three separate bonds on the same day. The bonds are exactly the same except that one has a stated interest rate of 6 percent, another 7 percent, and a third 8 percent. If the market rate of interest was 7 percent, the first would be issued at a discount, the second at par, and the third at a premium, but a creditor who bought any one of the bonds would earn the market interest rate of 7 percent.

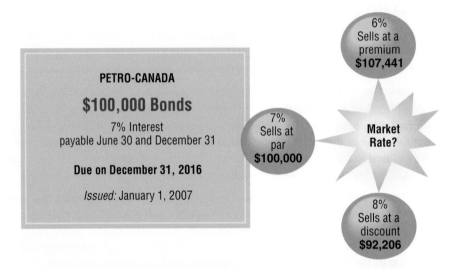

PETRO-CANADA

$100,000 Bonds

7% Interest
payable June 30 and December 31

Due on December 31, 2016

Issued: January 1, 2007

6%
Sells at a
premium
$107,441

7%
Sells at
par
$100,000

**Market
Rate?**

8%
Sells at a
discount
$92,206

FINANCIAL ANALYSIS

BOND INFORMATION FROM THE BUSINESS PRESS

Bond prices are reported each day in the business press based on transactions that occurred in the market on the previous trading day. The following is typical of the information that you will find:

Bond	Coupon	Mat. Date	March 16, 2007		August 16, 2007	
			Bid $	Yld	Bid $	Yld
CIBC	3.75	Sept. 9/10	98.37	4.26	96.67	4.94
Domtar	10.00	Apr. 15/11	112.51	6.45	109.70	6.94

The highlighted listing means that CIBC's bond has a coupon rate of 3.75 percent and will mature on September 9, 2010. The bond's yield was 4.26 percent on March 16, 2007, and its price was 98.37 percent of its par value, or $983.70. Market conditions caused the yield to increase to 4.94 percent by August 16, 2007, but notice that the coupon rate remains fixed at 3.75 percent. As the yield increased relative to the fixed coupon rate, the price decreased from $98.37 on March 16, 2007, to $96.67 on August 16, 2007, which illustrates the inverse relationship between the yield and the bond price.

CIBC's bond sold on March 16, 2007, at a discount because the market rate demanded by buyers is higher than the coupon rate offered by the company. By comparison, Domtar's bond sold at a premium of 12.51 percent of its face value on the same date because it offers a 10-percent coupon rate that exceeded by far the market interest rate of 6.45 percent.

Although analysts may study the daily price changes of bonds, remember that these changes do not affect the company's financial statements. For financial reporting purposes, the company uses the interest rates that existed when the bonds were first sold to the public in conformity with the historical cost principle. Subsequent changes do not affect the company's accounting for the bonds.

SELF-STUDY **QUIZ 11-1**

Your study of bonds will be easier if you understand the terminology that has been introduced in this chapter. Let us review some of those terms. Define the following:

1. Market interest rate. Identify synonyms for *market interest rate*.

2. Coupon interest rate. Identify synonyms for *coupon interest rate*.

3. Bond discount.

4. Bond premium.

After you complete your work, check your answers with the solution on page 603.

BONDS ISSUED AT PAR

Bonds sell at their par value when buyers are willing to invest in them at the interest rate stated on the bond. To illustrate, let us assume that on January 1, 2007, Petro-Canada issued 10 percent bonds with a par value of $400,000 and received $400,000 in cash (which means that the bonds sold at par). The bonds were dated to start interest on January 1, 2007, and will pay interest each June 30 and December 31. The bonds mature in 10 years on December 31, 2016.

The amount of money a corporation receives when it sells bonds is the present value of the future cash flows associated with them. When Petro-Canada issued its bonds, it agreed to make two types of payments in the future: a single payment of $400,000 when the bond matures in 10 years and an annuity of $20,000 payable twice each year for 10 years. The bond payments can be shown graphically as follows:

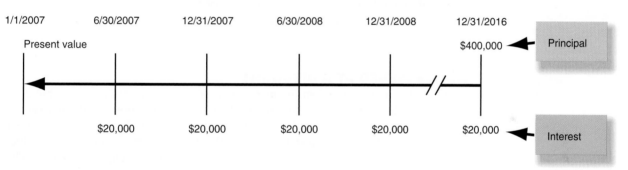

The present value of the bond payments can be computed with the tables contained in Appendix A using the factor for 20 periods and an interest rate of 5 percent (10 percent ÷ 2):

	Present Value
a. Single payment: $400,000 × 0.3769	$150,760
b. Annuity: $20,000 × 12.4622	249,240*
Issue price of Petro-Canada's bonds	$400,000
*Rounded.	

When the effective rate of interest equals the stated rate of interest, the present value of the future cash flows associated with a bond always equals the bond's par value. Remember that a bond's selling price is determined by the present value of its future cash flows, not the par value. On the date of issue, bond liabilities are recorded at the present value of future cash flows as follows:

Cash (A)   400,000
  Bonds payable (L)   400,000

Assets		=	Liabilities		+	Shareholders' Equity
Cash	+400,000		Bonds payable	+400,000		

Reporting Interest Expense on Bonds Issued at Par   The creditors who bought the bonds did so with the expectation that they would earn interest over the life of the bond. Petro-Canada will pay interest at 5 percent (i.e., 10 percent per year) on the par value of the bonds each June 30 and December 31 until the bond's maturity date. The amount of interest each period will be $20,000 (5% × $400,000). The entry to record the interest payments follows:

Bond interest expense (E)........................	20,000
Cash (A)......................................	20,000

Assets		=	Liabilities	+	Shareholders' Equity	
Cash	−20,000				Bond interest expense	−20,000

Bond interest payment dates rarely coincide with the last day of a company's fiscal year. Under the matching concept, interest expense that has been incurred but not paid must be accrued with an adjusting entry. If Petro-Canada's fiscal year ended on May 31, the company would accrue interest for five months and record interest expense and interest payable.

SELF-STUDY QUIZ 11-2

Assume that Petro-Canada issued $100,000 bonds that will mature in 10 years. The bonds pay interest at the end of each year at an annual rate of 9 percent. They were sold when the market rate was 9 percent. Determine the selling price of the bonds.

After you complete your work, check your answer with the solution on page 604.

BONDS ISSUED AT A DISCOUNT

Bonds sell at a discount when the market rate of interest demanded by the buyers is higher than the stated interest rate offered by the issuer. Assume that the market rate of interest was 12 percent when Petro-Canada sold its bonds (which have a par value of $400,000). The bonds have a stated rate of 10 percent, payable semi-annually, which is less than the market rate on that date. Therefore, the bonds sold at a *discount*. This usually occurs when the market rate of interest increases after the company determines the coupon rate on the bonds.

To compute the issue price of the bonds, we need to compute the present value of the future cash flows specified on the bond. As in the previous example, the number of periods is 20, but we must use an interest rate of 6 percent (12 percent ÷ 2), which is the market rate of interest. Thus, the issue price of Petro-Canada's bonds is computed as follows:

	Present Value
a. Principal: $400,000 × 0.3118	$124,720
b. Interest: $20,000 × 11.4699	229,398
Issue (sale) price of Petro-Canada's bonds	$354,118*
*Discount: $400,000 − $354,118 = $45,882.	

The cash price of the bonds issued by Petro-Canada is $354,118. Some people refer to this price as 88.5, which means that the bonds were sold at 88.5 percent of their par value ($354,118 ÷ $400,000).

When a bond is sold at a discount, the Bonds Payable account is credited for the par value, and the discount is recorded as a debit to Discount on Bonds Payable. The issuance of Petro-Canada's bonds at a discount is recorded as follows:

Cash (A)	354,118	
Discount on bonds payable (XL)	45,882	
Bonds payable (L)		400,000

Assets		=	Liabilities		+	Shareholders' Equity
Cash	+354,118		Bonds payable	+400,000		
			Discount on bonds payable	−45,882		

Note that the discount is recorded in a separate contra-liability account (Discount on Bonds Payable) as a debit. The balance sheet reports the bonds payable at their book value, which is their maturity amount less any unamortized discount. Petro-Canada, like most companies, does not separately disclose the amount of unamortized discount (or premium) when the amount is small relative to other balance sheet amounts.

Although Petro-Canada received only $354,118 when it sold the bonds, it must repay $400,000 when the bonds mature. This extra cash that must be paid is an adjustment to the interest payments to ensure that creditors earn the market rate of interest on the bonds. To compute the interest expense, the borrower apportions or amortizes the bond discount to each semi-annual interest period as an increase to the interest payment. Therefore, the amortization of bond discount is an increase in bond interest expense. Two amortization methods are often used by companies: (1) straight line and (2) effective interest. Many companies use straight-line amortization because it is easy to compute the required numbers. However, the effective-interest method is theoretically correct. You may wonder why companies are permitted to use a method that is not theoretically correct. The answer is *materiality*. Companies are permitted to use the straight-line method because the results are normally not materially different from the effective-interest method. We will first discuss the straight-line method and then the effective-interest method.

Part A: Reporting Interest Expense on Bonds Issued at a Discount Using Straight-Line Amortization To amortize the $45,882 bond discount over the life of Petro-Canada's bonds using **straight-line amortization**, an equal dollar amount is allocated to each interest period. Petro-Canada's bonds have 20 six-month interest periods. Therefore, the amount amortized on each semi-annual interest date is $2,294 ($45,882 ÷ 20 periods). This amount is added to the interest paid ($20,000) to compute interest expense for the period ($22,294). The interest payments on Petro-Canada's bonds each period are as follows:

STRAIGHT-LINE AMORTIZATION of a bond discount or premium is a simplified method that allocates an equal dollar amount to each interest period.

Bond interest expense (E)	22,294	
Discount on bonds payable (XL)		2,294
Cash (A)		20,000

Assets		=	Liabilities		+	Shareholders' Equity
Cash	−20,000		Discount on bonds payable (−XL)	+2,294		Bond interest expense	−22,294

Bonds payable are reported on the balance sheet at their book value; that is, the maturity amount less any unamortized bond discount (or plus any unamortized bond premium). At June 30, 2007, the book value of Petro-Canada's bonds is more than the original issue price. The book value increases to $356,412 ($354,118 + $2,294) because of the amortization of the discount. In each interest period, the book value of the bonds increases by $2,294 because the unamortized discount decreases by $2,294. At the maturity date of the bonds, the unamortized discount (i.e., the balance in the Discount on Bonds Payable account) is zero. At that time, the maturity amount of the bonds and the book value are the same (i.e., $400,000). The process can be seen in the following amortization schedule, which shows the first two years and the last year of the bond's life.

Amortization Schedule: Bond Discount (straight line)				
Date	(a) Interest to Be Paid ($400,000 × 5%)	(b) Interest Expense (a) + (c)	(c) Amortization [$45,882 ÷ 20 periods]	(d) Book Value Beginning Book Value + (c)
1/1/2007				$354,118
6/30/2007	$20,000	$22,294	$2,294	356,412
12/31/2007	20,000	22,294	2,294	358,706
6/30/2008	20,000	22,294	2,294	361,000
12/31/2008	20,000	22,294	2,294	363,294
.	.	.	.	.
.	.	.	.	.
6/30/2016	20,000	22,294	2,294	397,706
12/31/2016	20,000	22,294	2,294	400,000

SELF-STUDY **QUIZ 11-3**

Assume that Petro-Canada issued $100,000 bonds that will mature in 10 years. The bonds pay interest twice each year at an annual rate of 7 percent. They were sold when the market rate was 8 percent.

1. Determine the selling price of the bonds.

2. What amount of interest was paid at the end of the first year?

3. What amount of interest expense would be reported at the end of the first year using straight-line amortization of bond discount?

After you complete your work, check your answer with the solution on page 604.

The **EFFECTIVE-INTEREST METHOD** amortizes a bond discount or premium on the basis of the effective-interest rate; it is the theoretically preferred method.

Part B: Reporting Interest Expense on Bonds Issued at a Discount Using Effective-Interest Amortization   Under the **effective-interest method**, interest expense for a bond is computed by multiplying the current unpaid balance (i.e., the amount that was actually borrowed) times the market rate of interest that existed on the date the bonds were sold. The periodic amortization of a bond premium or discount is then calculated as the difference between interest expense and the amount of cash paid or accrued. This process can be summarized as follows:

Step 1: Compute interest expense.

Unpaid Balance × Effective Interest Rate × n/12
n = Number of Months in Each Interest Period

Step 2: Compute amortization amount.

Amortization of Bond Discount = Interest Expense − Interest Paid (or Accrued)

The first interest payment on Petro-Canada's bonds is on June 30, 2007. Interest expense at the end of the first six months is calculated by multiplying the unpaid balance of the debt by the market rate of interest for six months ($354,118 × 12% × $^6/_{12}$ = $21,247). The amount of cash paid is calculated by multiplying the principal by the stated rate of interest for six months ($400,000 × 10% × $^6/_{12}$ = $20,000). The difference between the interest expense and the cash paid (or accrued) is the amount of discount that has been amortized ($21,247 − $20,000 = $1,247). The journal entry to record interest expense is basically the same as the one shown earlier under the straight-line method. The only difference is the amount of discount amortized.

Bond interest expense (E).....	21,247	
Discount on bonds payable (XL).....		1,247
Cash (A).....		20,000

Effective-interest amortization causes these amounts to change each period.

Assets	=	Liabilities	+	Shareholders' Equity
Cash −20,000		Discount on bonds +1,247		Bond interest expense −21,247

Each period, the amortization of the bond discount increases the bond's book value (or unpaid balance). The amortization of bond discount can be thought of as interest that was earned by the bondholders but not paid to them. During the first six months of 2007, the bondholders earned interest of $21,247 but received only $20,000 in cash. The additional $1,247 was added to the principal of the bond and will be paid when the bond matures.

Interest expense for the second half of 2007 is calculated by multiplying the unpaid balance on June 30, 2007, by the market rate of interest for six months ($355,365 \times 12\% \times \frac{6}{12} = \$21,322$). The amortization of the bond discount in the second period is $1,322.

Bond interest expense (E).....	21,322	
Discount on bonds payable (XL).....		1,322
Cash (A).....		20,000

Assets	=	Liabilities	+	Shareholders' Equity
Cash −20,000		Discount on bonds +1,322		Bond interest expense −21,322

Notice that interest expense for the second half of 2007 is more than the amount for the first six months of 2007. This is logical because Petro-Canada effectively borrowed more money during the second half of the year (i.e., the $1,247 unpaid interest). Interest expense increases each year during the life of the bond because the amortized bond discount reflects unpaid interest on an increasing amount. This process can be illustrated with the following amortization schedule for the first two years and the last year of the bond's life. Compare it to the amortization schedule based on the straight-line method.

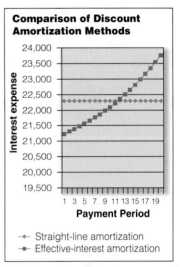

Comparison of Discount Amortization Methods

Interest expense / Payment Period

→ Straight-line amortization
→ Effective-interest amortization

Amortization Schedule: Bond Discount (effective interest)				
Date	(a) Interest to Be Paid ($400,000 × 5%)	(b) Interest Expense (6% × (d) Book Value, Beginning of Period)	(c) Amortization (b) − (a)	(d) Book Value Beginning Book Value + (c)
1/1/2007				$354,118
6/30/2007	$20,000	$21,247	$1,247	355,365
12/31/2007	20,000	21,322	1,322	356,687
6/30/2008	20,000	21,401	1,401	358,088
12/31/2008	20,000	21,485	1,485	359,573
.	.	.	.	.
.	.	.	.	.
6/30/2016	20,000	23,560	3,560	396,226
12/31/2016	20,000	23,774	3,774	400,000

Interest expense (column b) is computed by multiplying the market rate of interest by the book value at the beginning of the period (column d). Amortization is computed by subtracting interest paid (column a) from interest expense (column b). The book value (column d) is computed by adding amortization of bond discount (column c) to the book value at the beginning of the period.

In summary, under the effective-interest method, interest expense changes each accounting period as the effective amount of the liability changes. Under the straight-line method, interest expense remains constant over the life of the bond. The graph in the margin illustrates these differences. The effective-interest method produces a book value that reflects the present value of remaining payments using the effective interest rate at the date of issue. However, both methods amortize the same historic discount and do not reflect current market values.

SELF-STUDY **QUIZ 11-4**

Refer to Self-Study Quiz 11-3. Assume that Petro-Canada uses the effective-interest method to amortize the discount.

1. What amount of interest expense would be reported at the end of the first year?

2. What is the book value of the bonds at the end of the first year?

After you complete your work, check your answer with the solution on page 604.

A note from an annual report for Ames Department Stores effectively summarizes our discussion of this point:

REAL WORLD EXCERPT

Ames Department Stores

ANNUAL REPORT

Debt

Debt obligations that carried face interest rates significantly less than market were discounted to their present values using estimated market rates. The discount amount will be amortized to interest expense over the term of the related obligation. The determination of appropriate interest rates was based upon evaluation of Ames' credit standing, the nature of the collateral, if any, and other terms pertaining to the debt, and the prevailing rates for similar instruments or issues with similar credit rating.

Bonds are recorded at the present value of their future cash flows using an interest rate determined by the market on the date the bonds were sold. The accounting for the bonds is not affected by subsequent changes in the market rate of interest. This interest rate is based on the terms of the debt issue and the risk characteristics of the debt.[8]

BONDS ISSUED AT A PREMIUM

Bonds sell at a premium when the market rate of interest is lower than the stated interest rate. Assume that the market rate of interest was 8 percent while Petro-Canada's bonds paid interest of 10 percent. In this case, the bonds sell at a premium. The issue price for Petro-Canada's bonds is computed as follows:

	Present Value
a. Principal: $400,000 × 0.4564	$182,560
b. Interest: $20,000 × 13,5903	271,806
Issue (sale) price of Petro-Canada's bonds	$454,366

When a bond is sold at a premium, the Bonds Payable account is credited for the par value, and the premium is recorded as a credit to Premium on Bonds Payable, an adjunct-liability account. The issuance of Petro-Canada's bonds at a premium is recorded as follows:

---

[8]While most companies issue bonds that pay interest on a semi-annual basis, certain bond issues do not pay interest on a regular basis. These bonds are often called *zero coupon bonds* because the coupon interest rate is zero. Why would an investor buy a bond that does not pay interest? Our discussion of bond discounts has probably given you a good idea of the right answer. The coupon interest rate on a bond can be virtually any amount and the price of the bond will be adjusted so that investors earn the market rate of interest. A bond with a zero coupon interest rate is a *deep discount bond* that will sell for substantially less than its maturity value.

Cash (A)	454,366
Premium on bonds payable (L)	54,366
Bonds payable (L)	400,000

Assets	=	Liabilities	+	Shareholders' Equity
Cash +454,366		Premium on bonds		
		payable +54,366		
		Bonds payable +400,000		

The book value of the bond is the sum of the two accounts, Premium on Bonds Payable and Bonds Payable, or $454,366.

Part A: Reporting Interest Expense on Bonds Issued at a Premium Using Straight-line Amortization   The premium of $54,366 recorded by Petro-Canada must be apportioned to each of the 20 interest periods. Using the straight-line method, the premium that is amortized in each semi-annual interest period is $2,718 ($54,366 ÷ 20 periods). This amount is subtracted from the interest payment ($20,000) to calculate the interest expense ($17,282). Thus, amortization of the bond premium decreases interest expense.

The payment of interest on the bonds is recorded as follows:

Bond Interest expense (E)	17,282
Premium on bonds payable (L).	2,718
Cash (A).	20,000

Assets	=	Liabilities	+	Shareholders' Equity
Cash −20,000		Premium on bonds		Bond interest
		payable −2,718		expense −17,282

Notice that the $20,000 cash paid each period includes $17,282 interest expense and $2,718 premium amortization. Thus, the cash payment to the investors includes the current interest they have earned plus a return of part of the premium they paid when they bought the bonds.

The book value of the bonds is the amount in the Bonds Payable account plus any unamortized premium. On June 30, 2007, the book value of the bonds is $451,648 ($400,000 + $54,366 − $2,718). A partial amortization schedule follows:

Amortization Schedule: Bond Premium (straight line)				
Date	(a) Interest to Be Paid ($400,000 × 5%)	(b) Interest Expense (a) + (c)	(c) Amortization [$54,366 ÷ 20 periods]	(d) Book Value Beginning Book Value − (c)
1/1/2007				$454,336
6/30/2007	$20,000	$17,282	$2,718	451,618
12/31/2007	20,000	17,282	2,718	448,900
6/30/2008	20,000	17,282	2,718	446,182
12/31/2008	20,000	17,282	2,718	443,464
.	.	.	.	.
.	.	.	.	.
6/30/2016	20,000	17,282	2,718	402,718
12/31/2016	20,000	17,282	2,718	400,000

At the maturity date, after the last interest payment, the bond premium is fully amortized, and the maturity amount equals the book value of the bonds. When the bonds are paid off in full, the same entry whether the bond was originally sold at par, at a discount, or at a premium. Exhibit 11.3 compares the effects of the amortization of bond discount and bond premium on a $1,000 bond.

SELF-STUDY **QUIZ 11-5**

Assume that Petro-Canada issued $100,000 bonds that will mature in 10 years. The bonds pay interest twice each year at an annual rate of 9 percent. They were sold when the market rate was 8 percent.

1. Determine the selling price of the bonds.

2. What amount of interest was paid at the end of the first year?

3. What amount of interest expense would be reported at the end of the first year using straight-line amortization?

After you complete your work, check your answer with the solution on page 604.

EXHIBIT **11.3**

Amortization of Bond Discount and Premium Compared— Straight-Line Amortization

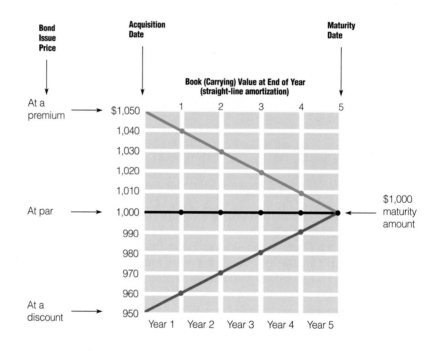

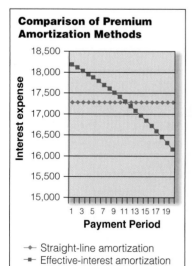

Comparison of Premium Amortization Methods

- Straight-line amortization
- Effective-interest amortization

Part B: Reporting Interest Expense on Bonds Issued at a Premium Using Effective-Interest Amortization The effective-interest method is basically the same for a discount or a premium. In either case, interest expense for a bond is computed by multiplying the book value (i.e., the unpaid balance) by the market rate of interest on the date the bonds were sold. The periodic amortization of a bond premium or discount is then calculated as the difference between interest expense and the amount of cash paid or accrued.

The first interest payment on Petro-Canada's bonds is made on June 30, 2007. The interest expense at the end of the first six months is calculated by multiplying the unpaid balance of the debt by the market rate of interest for six months ($454,366 \times 8\% \times ^6/_{12} = \$18,175$). The amount of cash paid is calculated by multiplying the principal by the stated rate of interest for six months ($400,000 × 10% × $^6/_{12}$ = $20,000). The difference between the interest expense and the cash paid (or accrued) is the amount of premium that has been amortized ($20,000 − $18,175 = $1,825).

Bond interest expense (E)............................	18,175	
Premium on bonds payable (L)......................	1,825	
Cash (A)...		20,000

Assets		=	Liabilities		+	Shareholders' Equity	
Cash	−20,000		Premium on bonds	−1,825		Bond interest expense	−18,175

The basic difference between effective-interest amortization of a bond discount and a bond premium is that the amortization of a discount *increases* the book value of the liability and the amortization of a premium *reduces* it. The following schedule illustrates amortization of the bond premium for the first two years and the last year of the bond's life. Compare it to the amortization schedule based on the straight-line method.

Amortization Schedule: Bond Premium (effective interest)				
Date	(a) Interest to Be Paid ($400,000 × 5%)	(b) Interest Expense (4% × (d) Book Value, Beginning of Period)	(c) Amortization (b) − (a)	(d) Book Value Beginning Book Value − (c)
1/1/2007				$454,366
6/30/2007	$20,000	$18,175	$1,825	452,541
12/31/2007	20,000	18,102	1,898	450,643
6/30/2008	20,000	18,026	1,974	448,669
12/31/2008	20,000	17,947	2,053	446,616
.	.	.	.	.
.	.	.	.	.
6/30/2016	20,000	16,444	3,556	403,846
12/31/2016	20,000	16,154	3,846	400,000

SELF-STUDY **QUIZ 11-6**

Refer to the amortization schedule above and answer the following requirements:

1. Complete the schedule for three additional semi-annual payments of interest until June 30, 2010.

2. Compute the unpaid balance of the bonds at June 30, 2010. Can you think of another way of computing this balance? If so, show your computations.

After you complete your work, check your answers with the solution on page 604.

Interest expense is reported on the income statement. Because interest is related to financing activities rather than operating activities, it is normally not included in operating expenses on the income statement. Instead, interest expense is reported as a deduction from "income from operations." Petro-Canada reports interest expense on its income statement as the last item among its expenses as shown in Exhibit 11-4.

Because interest payments are legal obligations for the borrower, financial analysts want to be certain that a business is generating sufficient resources to meet its obligations. The times interest earned ratio is useful when making this assessment.

EXHIBIT **11.4**

Reporting of Interest Expense

REAL WORLD EXCERPT

Petro-Canada

ANNUAL REPORT

PETRO-CANADA
CONSOLIDATED STATEMENT OF EARNINGS
(stated in millions of Canadian dollars, except per share amounts)

For the years ended December 31,	2006	2005	2004
Revenue			
Operating	$18,911	$17,585	$14,270
Investment and other income (expense) *(Note 5)*	(242)	(806)	(312)
	18,669	16,779	13,958
Expenses			
Crude oil and product purchases	9,649	8,846	6,740
Operating, marketing and general *(Note 6)*	3,180	2,962	2,572
Exploration *(Note 15)*	339	271	235
Depreciation, depletion and amortization *(Notes 6 and 15)*	1,365	1,222	1,256
Unrealized gain on translation of foreign currency denominated long-term debt	(1)	(88)	(77)
Interest	165	164	142
	14,697	13,377	10,868
Earnings from continuing operations before income taxes	3,972	3,402	3,090
Provision for income taxes *(Note 7)*			
Current	2,073	1,794	1,365
Future	311	(85)	27
	2,384	1,709	1,392
Net earnings from continuing operations	1,588	1,693	1,698
Net earnings from discontinued operations *(Note 4)*	152	98	59
Net earnings	$ 1,740	$ 1,791	$ 1,757

KEY RATIO
ANALYSIS   TIMES INTEREST EARNED

ANALYTICAL QUESTION → Is the company generating sufficient resources (added value) from its profit-making activities to meet its current obligations associated with debt?

RATIO AND COMPARISONS → The *times interest earned ratio* is helpful in answering this question. It is computed as follows:

LEARNING OBJECTIVE 3

Compute and interpret the times interest earned ratio.

$$\text{Times Interest Earned Ratio} = \frac{\text{Net Income} + \text{Interest Expense} + \text{Income Tax Expense}}{\text{Interest Expense}}$$

The 2006 ratio for Petro-Canada is:

($1,740 + $165 + $2,384) ÷ $165 = 26.0

Comparisons over Time			Comparisons with Competitors	
Petro-Canada			Suncor Energy	Imperial Oil
2004	2005	2006	2006	2006
23.2	22.3	26.0	26.4	66.1

INTERPRETATIONS

In General → A high ratio is viewed more favourably than a low ratio. Basically, the ratio shows the amount of income before interest and income tax that is generated for each dollar of interest expense. A high ratio shows an extra margin of protection in case profitability deteriorates.

Analysts are particularly interested in a company's ability to meet its required interest payments because failure to do so could result in bankruptcy.

Focus Company Analysis → Petro-Canada's profit-making activities generated $26.0 for each dollar of interest in 2006. Petro-Canada's income could fall substantially before the company would appear to have trouble meeting its interest obligations with resources generated by normal operations. Petro-Canada's ability to repay its creditors has strengthened steadily over the last three years, but it fell short of that of Imperial Oil. This is consistent with the fact that Petro-Canada uses proportionally more debt than Imperial Oil.

A Few Cautions → The times interest earned ratio is often misleading for new or rapidly growing companies that tend to invest considerable resources to build capacity for future operations. In such cases, the times interest earned ratio will reflect significant amounts of interest expense associated with the new capacity but not the income that will be earned with the new capacity. Analysts should consider the company's long-term strategy when using this ratio. While this ratio is widely used, some analysts prefer to compare interest expense to the amount of cash that a company can generate, because creditors cannot be paid with "income" that is generated. The cash coverage ratio addresses this concern and is discussed in Chapter 13.

EARLY RETIREMENT OF DEBT

Bonds are normally issued for long periods, such as 20 or 30 years. As mentioned earlier, bondholders who need cash prior to the maturity date can simply sell the bonds to another investor. This transaction does not affect the books of the company that issued the bonds.

As mentioned earlier, each bond issue has characteristics that are specified in the bond indenture. The issuing company often adds special characteristics to a bond to make it more attractive to investors, who normally have a large number of investment alternatives from which to select.

Bonds sometimes offer different features with respect to early retirement. **Redeemable (callable) bonds** may be called for early retirement at the option of the issuer. **Retractable bonds** may be turned in for early retirement at the option of the bondholder. *Convertible bonds* may be converted to other securities of the issuer (usually common shares) at the option of the bondholder. These features are normally present for debt issues that are marketable. Of 127 companies that reported marketable debt in their 2005 annual reports, 52 companies disclosed details of the redemption features and 23 companies provided details of the conversion features of their bonds.[9]

Petro-Canada's notes and debentures are redeemable. Typically, the bond indenture includes a call premium for bonds retired before the maturity date. For example, the prospectus for Petro-Canada's 7.00% debentures included the following:

> The debentures will be redeemable, in whole or in part, at the option of the Corporation, at any time at a redemption price equal to the greater of (i) 100% of their principal amount and (ii) the sum of the present values of the remaining scheduled payments of principal and interest thereon discounted to the redemption date on a semi-annual basis (assuming a 360-day year consisting of twelve 30-day months) at the Treasury Rate plus 25 basis points plus, in each case, accrued interest thereon to the redemption date.

■ LEARNING OBJECTIVE 4
Report the early retirement of bonds.

REDEEMABLE (CALLABLE) BONDS may be called for early retirement at the option of the issuer.

RETRACTABLE BONDS may be turned in for early retirement at the option of the bondholder.

REAL WORLD EXCERPT

Petro-Canada
ANNUAL REPORT

Assume that the $400,000 face-value bonds that were issued by Petro-Canada on January 1, 2007 were sold for $354,118 as shown on page 578, and that the company called the bonds on December 31, 2012 at 102 percent of par, four years before their maturity. The company's decision to call these bonds is typically made when the market rate of interest decreases below the coupon rate of the bonds. Petro-Canada would issue new bonds that pay a lower interest rate than the outstanding bonds, thus saving on interest payments.

If the market rate of interest drops to 8 percent, then Petro-Canada can issue new bonds that pay interest of 8 percent instead of 10 percent. Semi-annual interest payments would then be reduced from $20,000 to $16,000 ($400,000 × 0.04). The cash savings of $4,000 every six months are equivalent to $26,930.80 ($4000 × 6.7327)

[9]N. Chlala, L. Martel, A. Lavigne, and C. Byrd, *Financial Reporting in Canada 2006*. Toronto: Canadian Institute of Chartered Accountants, 2006, p. 336.

at December 31, 2012. Redemption of the bonds requires Petro-Canada to pay a premium of $8,000 ($400,000 × 0.02), but it saves the company $26,930.80. It is therefore a sound economic decision.

However, the early retirement of these bonds would result in an accounting loss. The loss equals the difference between the redemption amount and the book value of the bonds. At December 31, 2012, the unamortized bond discount is $18,352 ($2,294 × 8 semi-annual periods), assuming that straight-line amortization is used. The book value of $381,648 ($400,000 − $18,352) is then compared to the redemption amount of $408,000 ($400,000 × 1.02), resulting in a loss of $26,352. The company's accountants would make the following journal entry to record the bond redemption:

Bonds payable (L).	400,000	
Loss on redemption of bonds (Loss).	26,352	
Discount on bonds payable (XL).		18,352
Cash (A).		408,000

Assets		=	Liabilities		+	Shareholders' Equity	
Cash	−408,000		Bonds payable	−400,000		Loss	−26,352
			Discount on bonds	+18,352			

The bond redemption results in an economic gain but in an accounting loss because the book value of the bonds is not adjusted over time to reflect changes in the market value of these bonds.

In some cases, a company may elect to retire debt early by purchasing it on the open market, just as an investor would. This approach is necessary when the bonds do not have a call feature. It might also be an attractive approach if the price of the bonds fell after the date of issue. What could cause the price of a bond to fall? The most common cause is a rise in interest rates. As you may have noticed during our discussion of present value concepts, bond prices move in the opposite direction of interest rates. If interest rates go up, bond prices fall, and vice versa. When interest rates go up, a company that wants to retire a bond before maturity may find buying the bond on the open market to be less expensive than paying a call premium.

When interest rates increase, the market value of the bonds would decrease, and the redemption or repurchase of the bonds in the open market would result in a gain. The gain increases the company's net income, which reflects positively on the performance of management. However, if the company needs to reissue bonds at a higher interest rate, then the gain on redemption or repurchase of the bonds is misleading, because the company will need to make higher interest payments on the refinanced debt. In contrast, when interest rates decrease the refinancing of long-term debt by retiring old debt and issuing new debt will result in a loss on debt retirement, but will reduce the amount of periodic interest payments. Hence, management may be inclined to retire debt prematurely in order to show improved financial performance, but this decision may affect cash flows negatively in the future.

INTERNATIONAL PERSPECTIVE   BORROWING IN FOREIGN CURRENCIES

Many corporations with foreign operations elect to finance those operations with foreign debt to lessen the exchange rate risk. This type of risk exists because the relative value of each nation's currency varies virtually on a daily basis due to various economic factors. As this book is being written, the euro is worth approximately $1.55. A year earlier, it was worth $1.40. A Canadian company that owed debt denominated in euros would experience a loss from this decrease in the value of the euro.

A Canadian corporation that conducts business operations in Europe might decide to borrow euros to finance its operations. The profits from the business will be in euros, which can be used to pay off the debt, which is in euros. If the business earned profits in euros but paid off debt in Canadian dollars, it would be exposed to exchange rate risk because the value of the Canadian dollar fluctuates relative to the euro.

Foreign corporations face this same problem. A note to an annual report from Toyota, a Japanese company that does significant business in North America, stated:

> Earnings declined in the current year ended, as the appreciation of the yen aggravated the adverse effects of sluggish demand. . . . The movement in exchange rates reduced operating income of the company. Losses on currency exchange thus offset most of the cost savings we achieved.

REAL WORLD EXCERPT

Toyota
ANNUAL REPORT

Even if a company does not have international operations, it may elect to borrow in foreign markets. When a country is experiencing a recession, interest rates often are low. These situations give corporations the opportunity to borrow money at a lower cost.

For reporting purposes, accountants must convert, or translate, foreign debt into Canadian dollars. Conversion rates for all major currencies are published in most newspapers and on the Internet. To illustrate foreign currency translation, assume that Petro-Canada borrowed 1 million US dollars. For the Petro-Canada annual report, the accountant must use the conversion rate as of the balance sheet date, which we assume was $1.00 ($US) = $1.15 ($Cdn). The dollar equivalent of the debt is $1,150,000 ($Cdn) ($1,000,000 [$US] × 1.15). As you can see, the dollar equivalent of foreign debt may change if the conversion rate changes even when no additional borrowings or repayments occur. The changes in conversion rates result in foreign exchange gains or losses that are covered in advanced accounting courses.

The notes to the balance sheet for Petro-Canada indicate that the company has borrowed money primarily in Canada and the United States. In contrast, consider the following excerpt from the 2006 annual report of CanWest Global Communications Corp. Inc. (in thousands):

REAL WORLD EXCERPT

*CanWest Global
Communications*
ANNUAL REPORT

Long-term Debt	Interest Rate	Amount
Term bank loan NZ$185,000 (2005—NZ$187,802)	7.5%	133,977
Unsecured bank loan AUS$170,000 (2005—AUS$180,000)	6.6%	143,514
Senior unsecured notes US$125,000 (2005—US$125,000)	7.2%	138,320
Senior notes AUS$150,000	6.8%	126,630

CanWest Global Communications Corp. is Canada's largest media company. It owns and operates television networks, radio stations, and networks in Canada, New Zealand, Australia, the United States, and many other countries. The company has borrowed in New Zealand (NZ), Australian (AUS), and US dollars to minimize the risk associated with variations in exchange rates. This is typical for most large corporations and is further justification for business executives to develop an understanding of international markets.

OTHER LONG-TERM LIABILITIES

In addition to long-term debt, companies report a number of other long-term liabilities that result from their operating, investing, and financing activities. Typical long-term liabilities include lease obligations, asset retirement obligations, accrued retirement benefits liability, and future income taxes (which are covered in Supplement A to Chapter 10).[10]

■ LEARNING OBJECTIVE 5
Describe other long-term liabilities.

---

[10] One additional topic commonly encountered in accounting for long-term debt is the reporting of financial instruments and related disclosures. This topic is discussed in the Online Learning Centre Web site at **www.mcgrawhill.ca/olc/libby/student/resources**.

An **OPERATING LEASE** does not meet any of the four criteria established by GAAP and does not cause the recording of an asset and liability.

A **CAPITAL LEASE** meets at least one of the four criteria established by GAAP and results in the recording of an asset and liability.

LEASE LIABILITIES

Companies often lease assets rather than purchasing them. For example, renting extra delivery trucks during a busy period is more economical than owning them if they are not needed during the rest of the year. When a company leases an asset on a short-term basis, the agreement is called an **operating lease**. No liability is recorded when an operating lease is created. Instead, a company records rent expense as it uses the asset. Assume that on December 15, 2008, Petro-Canada signed an operating lease contract to rent five large trucks during January 2009. No liability is recorded in 2008. Rent expense is recorded during January 2009 as the trucks are actually used.

For a number of reasons, a company may prefer to lease an asset on a long-term basis rather than purchase it. This type of lease is called a **capital lease**. In essence, a capital lease contract represents the purchase and financing of an asset even though it is legally a lease agreement. Unlike an operating lease, capital leases are accounted for as if an asset has been purchased by recording an asset and a liability. Because of the significant differences between operating and capital leases, GAAP have specified criteria to distinguish between them. If a lease meets any of the following criteria, it is considered a capital lease:

• The lease term is 75 percent or more of the asset's expected economic life.

• Ownership of the asset is transferred to the lessee at the end of the lease term.

• The lease contract permits the lessee to purchase the asset at a price that is lower than its fair market value.

• The present value of the lease payments is 90 percent or more of the fair market value of the asset when the lease is signed.

Note 18 to Petro-Canada's 2006 annual report indicates that the balance sheet includes $70 million in long-term debt associated with capital leases. The recorded value of debt associated with a capital lease is the present value of the required lease payments.

The accounting for leases as capital leases reflects the substance of the transaction, which is in essence a purchase of an asset with long-term financing, rather than the legal form of the commitment to make specific payments in the future. In the absence of accounting rules governing the distinction between operating and capital leases, companies would prefer to report all lease contracts as operating leases because the commitment to make future payments on the lease contract would not be reported as liabilities on the balance sheet (a form of off–balance sheet financing). In contrast, the accounting for capital leases requires the reporting of a long-term liability, thereby increasing the debt-to-equity ratio. Furthermore, the current portion of the lease liability increases current liabilities, reduces working capital and lowers the current ratio. Companies would avoid these undesirable consequences if capital leases are accounted for as operating leases. It is important to note, however, that the cash outflows would not be affected by the classification of leases.

Many financial analysts are concerned that companies can avoid reporting debt associated with capital leases by structuring the lease agreement in a manner that meets the requirements for recording it as an operating lease.

ASSET RETIREMENT OBLIGATIONS

In recent years, concern about the adverse impact of business activities on the environment and the effects of environmental obligations on companies' financial positions and profitability led to new accounting standards that require the reporting of such obligations. These reporting requirements are particularly important for companies that operate in industries that result in environmental pollution, such as the chemical and petrochemical industries. Companies in these industry sectors incur significant obligations associated with the environmental impact of their operations.

For example, if Petro-Canada completes construction of and places into service an offshore oil platform on June 1, 2008, it would be legally required to dismantle and remove the platform at the end of its useful life. Petro-Canada should then recognize a liability for an asset retirement obligation and capitalize an amount for an asset retirement cost. The fair value of the asset retirement obligation is determined using the present value concept. In this regard, Petro-Canada's liabilities include an Asset Retirement Obligation of $1,170 million as at December 31, 2006, representing 13 percent of its long-term liabilities. This liability reflects legal obligations to retire long-term assets and restoration of sites such as producing well sites, offshore production platforms, and natural gas processing plants and marketing sites.

REAL WORLD EXCERPT

Petro-Canada

ANNUAL REPORT

Notes to Consolidated Financial Statements

Note 20   Asset retirement obligations

Asset retirement obligations are recorded for obligations where the Company will be required to retire tangible long-lived assets such as well sites, offshore production platforms, natural gas processing plants and marketing sites.

The following table summarizes the changes in the asset retirement obligations:

	2006	2005
Asset retirement obligations at beginning of year	$ 962	$873
Obligations incurred	95	92
Changes in estimates	138	104
Abandonment expenditures	(55)	(98)
Accretion expense	54	50
Foreign exchange	43	(59)
Asset retirement obligations at end of year	1,237	962
Less: Current portion	(67)	(80)
	$1,170	$882

In determining the fair value of the asset retirement obligations, the estimated cash flows of new obligations incurred during the year have been discounted at 5.5% (2005—5.5%). The total undiscounted amount of the estimated cash flows required to settle the obligations is $3,481 million (2005—$2,839 million). The obligations will be settled on an ongoing basis over the useful lives of the operating assets, which extend up to 50 years in the future. The current portion of asset retirement obligations is included in accounts payable and accrued liabilities.

Liabilities associated with future service obligations are often based on estimates that are very difficult to develop accurately. The future cost of cleaning up pollution depends on a number of factors, including changing technology and legal standards. Many companies have faced bankruptcy because they underestimated the cost of environmental regulations. Managers and analysts must be very cautious in evaluating potential costs associated with activities that impact the environment.

EMPLOYEE RETIREMENT BENEFITS

Most employers provide retirement programs for their employees. In a ***defined contribution*** program, the employer makes cash payments to an investment fund. When employees retire, they are entitled to a portion of the fund. If the investment strategy of the fund is successful, the retirement income for the employees will be larger. If the strategy is not successful, it will be lower. In other words, the employees bear the risk associated with the investments in the plan. The employer's only obligation is to make the required annual payments to the fund, which are recorded as pension expense.

Other employers offer ***defined benefit*** programs. Under these programs, an employee's retirement benefits are based on a percentage of his or her pay at retirement or a certain number of dollars for each year of employment. In these cases, the amount of pension expense that must be accrued each year is the change in the current cash value of the employee's retirement package. The current cash value changes each year for a variety of reasons. For example, it changes (1) as employees get closer to receiving benefits, (2) as employees' retirement benefits increase because of higher pay or longer service, or (3) if the employees' life expectancies change. The company must report a pension liability based on any portion of the current cash value of the retirement program that has not actually been funded. For example, if the company transferred $8 million to the pension fund manager but the current cash value of the pension program was $10 million, the company would report a $2-million pension liability on its balance sheet.

For many corporations, especially those with unionized work forces, the financial obligation associated with defined benefit retirement programs can be very large because the risk associated with investments in the pension plan is borne by the employer, which must cover any shortfall between the investment earnings and the payments to retirees. For this reason, companies are moving away from defined benefit pension plans in favour of defined contribution pension plans.[11]

Petro-Canada has set up both a defined benefit pension plan and a defined contribution pension plan for its eligible employees. In addition, Petro-Canada provides post-retirement benefits, including certain health and life insurance benefits for its retired employees and eligible surviving dependants.

REAL WORLD EXCERPT

Petro-Canada

ANNUAL REPORT

Notes to the Consolidated Financial Statements

Note 22. EMPLOYEE FUTURE BENEFITS

The Company maintains pension plans with defined benefit and defined contribution provisions, and provides certain health care and life insurance benefits to its qualifying retirees. The actuarially determined cost of these benefits is accrued over the estimated service life of employees. The defined benefit provisions are generally based upon years of service and average salary during the final years of employment. Certain defined benefit options require employee contributions and the balance of the funding for the registered plans is provided by the Company, based upon the advice of an independent actuary. The accrued benefit obligations and the fair value of plan assets are measured for accounting purposes at December 31 of each year. The most recent actuarial valuation of the pension plan for funding purposes was as of December 31, 2004 and the next required valuation will be as of December 31, 2007.

The defined contribution option provides for an annual contribution of 5% to 8% of each participating employee's pensionable earnings.

Petro-Canada's obligations under these various plans totalled $1,786 million as at December 31, 2006. The company has set aside funds that had a fair value of $1,486 million at that date. The shortfall of $300 million is important to analysts who forecast Petro-Canada's future cash flows, and to employees who may be concerned about the availability of money in the pension fund to pay them cash during their retirement. However, Petro-Canada disclosed in note 23 to its financial statements an accrued benefit asset of $128 million, which does not reflect the net unfunded obligation. The computation of the pension asset or liability is complex and covered in advanced accounting courses.

In recent years, employer-provided health care benefits have been the subject of much discussion. Many large companies pay for a portion of their employees' health insurance costs. The payments are recorded as an expense in the current accounting period. Some employers agree to continue to pay for health care costs after employees retire. The cost of these future benefits must be estimated and recorded as an expense in the periods when the employees perform services. The recording of future health care costs for retired employees is an excellent example of the use of estimates in accounting. Imagine the difficulty of estimating future health care costs when you do not know how long employees will live, how healthy they will be during their lives, and how much doctors and hospitals will charge for their services in the future.

Accounting for retirement benefits is a complex topic that is discussed in detail in subsequent accounting courses. We introduce this topic at this point as another example

---

[11]For example, Sears Canada Inc, one of Canada's biggest department store chains, announced in February 2007 that it has redesigned its employee retirement plan by introducing a defined contribution plan, effective July 1, 2008.

of the application of the matching concept, which requires that expenses be recorded in the year in which the benefit is received. The benefit in this case is the work performed by the employees, and all costs incurred to compensate employees for their work, must be recorded regardless of the timing of pension payments. This accounting procedure also avoids creating improper incentives for managers. If the future cost of retirement benefits was not included in the period in which work was performed, managers might have the incentive to offer employees increases in their retirement benefits instead of increases in their salaries. In this manner, managers could understate the true cost of employee services and make their companies appear more profitable. Many economists argue that the local, provincial, and federal governments have fallen into this trap. Government officials can give large pensions to current workers without the cost being recognized until the employee retires. By doing this, governments can appear to be very efficient when in reality they are simply deferring costs to the future.

FINANCIAL LEVERAGE RATIO

KEY RATIO
ANALYSIS

ANALYTICAL QUESTION → How is management using debt to increase the amount of assets the company employs to earn income for shareholders?

RATIO AND COMPARISONS → The financial leverage ratio is useful in addressing this issue. It is computed as follows:

$$\text{Financial Leverage Ratio} = \frac{\text{Average Total Assets}}{\text{Average Shareholders' Equity}}$$

■ LEARNING OBJECTIVE 6

Compute and Interpret the financial leverage ratio.

The 2006 ratio for Petro-Canada is:

$$\frac{(\$20,655 + \$22,646)/2}{(\$9,488 + \$10,441)/2} = 2.17$$

Comparisons over Time			Comparisons with Competitors	
Petro-Canada			Suncor Energy	Imperial Oil
2004	2005	2006	2006	2006
2.01	2.13	2.17	2.27	2.26

INTERPRETATIONS

In General → The financial leverage ratio measures the relationship between total assets and the shareholders' equity that finances the assets. As noted, companies finance their assets with shareholders' equity and debt. The higher the proportion of assets financed by debt, the higher the financial leverage ratio. Conversely, the higher the proportion of assets financed with shareholders' equity, the lower the ratio. Increasing debt (and the leverage ratio) increases the amount of assets the company employs to earn income for shareholders, which increases the chances of earning higher income. However, it also increases *risk*. Debt financing is riskier than financing with shareholders' equity because the interest payments on debt must be made every period (they are legal obligations), whereas dividends on shares can be postponed. An increasing ratio over time signals more reliance on debt financing and more risk.

Creditors and security analysts use this ratio to assess a company's risk level, while managers use the ratio in deciding whether to expand by adding debt. As long as the interest on borrowing is less than the additional earnings generated, utilizing debt will enhance the shareholders' earnings.

Focus Company Analysis → Petro-Canada's financial leverage has been increased slightly over the three-year period 2004–2006. For every $1 of equity, the company had $1.17 of debt during 2006. The company's financial leverage for 2006 is lower than those of its competitors. This suggests that Petro-Canada is following a less riskier (more conservative) financing strategy than are other companies in the gold-mining industry. Petro-Canada's use of debt has been beneficial to its shareholders as the company's return on equity for both 2005 and 2006 reached 17 percent.

SELECTED FOCUS COMPANY LEVERAGE RATIOS	
WestJet Airlines	3.35
Gildan Activewear	1.39
Dell Inc.	4.37

A Few Cautions → A financial leverage ratio near 1:1 indicates a company that is choosing not to utilize debt to expand. This suggests the company has lower risk but is not enhancing the return to shareholders. When comparing competitors, the ratio may be influenced by differences in business strategies, such as whether the company rents or buys facilities.

SELF-STUDY QUIZ 11-7

Petro-Canada's annual report for 2006 indicates that the unfunded benefits obligation equals $378 and $300 million at December 31, 2005 and December 31, 2006, respectively. Assume that the unfunded benefit obligation is reported on Petro-Canada's balance sheet as a long-term liability with an equal decrease in shareholders' equity. Compute the financial leverage ratio using the adjusted balance sheet amounts. Do you think companies would favour the reporting of the unfunded benefits obligation on their balance sheets? Explain.

After you complete your work, check your answers with the solution on page 604.

FOCUS ON CASH FLOWS   FINANCING ACTIVITIES ON THE CASH FLOW STATEMENT

BONDS PAYABLE

■ LEARNING OBJECTIVE 7

Explain how financing activities are reported on the cash flow statement.

The *Financing Activities* section of the cash flow statement reports both cash inflows and outflows that relate to how cash was obtained from external sources (owners and creditors) to finance the enterprise and its operations. The issuance of long-term debt is reported as a cash inflow from financing activities. The repayment of principal is reported as an outflow from financing activities. Many students are surprised to learn that the payment of interest is *not* reported in the Financing Activities section of the cash flow statement. Interest payments are directly related to earning income and are therefore reported in the *Cash Flows from Operating Activities* section of the statement. In addition, companies are required to report the amount of cash paid for interest each accounting period. *Financial Reporting in Canada 2006* shows that companies reported this information in a variety of locations in their 2005 annual reports.

Disclosure of Interest Payments (sample of 200 companies)

```
        0  25  50  75  100
Not disclosed ─■■■■■
Bottom of CFS ─■■■■■■■■
Notes to CFS ─■■■■■■
       Other ─■
```

EFFECT ON CASH FLOW STATEMENT

IN GENERAL → As we saw in Chapter 10, transactions involving short-term creditors (e.g., accounts payable) affect working capital, and are therefore reported in the operating activities section of the cash flow statement. Cash received from long-term creditors is reported as an inflow from financing activities. Cash payments made to long-term creditors (with the exception of interest expense) are reported as outflows from financing activities. Examples are shown in the following table:

	Effect on Cash Flows
Financing activities	
Issuance of bonds	+
Debt retirement	−
Repayment of bond principal upon maturity	−

SELECTED FOCUS COMPANY COMPARISONS: CASH FLOWS FROM FINANCING ACTIVITIES (IN MILLIONS)

WestJet Airlines	256
Forzani Group	13
Gildan Activewear	−39

FOCUS COMPANY ANALYSIS → A segment of Petro-Canada's cash flow statements for the years 2004, 2005, and 2006 follows. Only two of the items listed pertain to the issues discussed in this chapter. Other items will be discussed in Chapter 12.

In 2005, the company raised a substantial amount of long-term debt ($762 million) to finance its operating and investing activities. It reduced its long-term debt by $299 million in 2004. Repayments of long-term debt are made when the debt matures or when a company decides to redeem the outstanding debt prematurely in order to take advantage of lower interest rates.

Analysts are particularly interested in the Financing Activities section of the cash flow statement because it provides important insights about the future capital structure for the company. Rapidly growing companies typically report significant amounts of funds in this section of the cash flow statement.

REAL WORLD EXCERPT

Petro-Canada

ANNUAL REPORT

CONSOLIDATED STATEMENTS OF CASH FLOWS
For the Year ended December 31

(in millions of United States dollars)	2006	2005	2004
Financing activities			
Increase (decrease) in short-term notes payable	—	(303)	314
Proceeds from issue of long-term debt	—	762	533
Repayment of long-term debt	**(7)**	(6)	(299)
Proceeds from issue of common shares	**44**	64	39
Purchase of common shares	**(1,011)**	(346)	(447)
Dividends on common shares	**(201)**	(181)	(159)

DEMONSTRATION **CASE**

To raise funds to build a new plant, Reed Company management issued bonds. The bond indenture specified the following:

Par value of the bonds ($1,000 bonds): $600,000.

Date of issue: February 1, 2008; due in 10 years on January 31, 2018.

Interest: 10 percent per annum, payable 5 percent on each July 31 and January 31.

All of the bonds were sold on February 1, 2008, at 102.5. The fiscal year for Reed Company ends on December 31.

Required:
1. How much cash did Reed Company receive from the sale of the bonds on February 1, 2008? Show your computations.
2. What was the amount of premium on the bonds payable? Over how many months should it be amortized?
3. Compute the amount of amortization of the premium per month and for each six-month interest period; use straight-line amortization. Round to the nearest dollar.
4. Prepare the journal entry on February 1, 2008, to record the sale and issuance of the bonds payable.
5. Prepare the journal entry for the payment of interest and amortization of the premium for the first interest payment on July 31, 2008.
6. Prepare the adjusting entry required on December 31, 2008, at the end of the fiscal year.
7. Prepare the journal entry to record the second interest payment and the amortization of the premium on January 31, 2008.
8. Show how bond interest expense and bonds payable are reported on the financial statements at December 31, 2008.

We highly recommend that you attempt to answer the requirements on your own before consulting the suggested solution below.

SUGGESTED SOLUTION

1. Sale price of the bonds: $600,000 × 102.5% = $615,000.
2. Premium on the bonds payable: $600,000 × 2.5% = $15,000.
   Months of amortization: From date of sale, February 1, 2008, to maturity date, January 31, 2018 = 120 months.
3. Premium amortization: $15,000 ÷ 120 months = $125 per month, or $750 each six-month interest period (straight line).

4. February 1, 2008 (issuance date):

Cash (A)	615,000	
Premium on bonds payable (L)		15,000
Bonds payable (L)		600,000
To record sale of bonds payable at 102.5.		

5. July 31, 2008 (first interest payment date):

Bond interest expense (E) ($30,000 − $750)	29,250	
Premium on bonds payable (L).	750	
Cash (A) ($600,000 × 5%)		30,000
To record payment of semi-annual interest.		

6. December 31, 2008 (end of the accounting period):

Bond interest expense (E).	24,375	
Premium on bonds payable (L) ($125 × 5 months)	625	
Bond interest payable (L) ($600,000 × 10% × ⁵⁄₁₂)		25,000
Adjusting entry for five months' interest accrued plus amortization of the premium, August 1 to December 31, 2008.		

7. January 31, 2009 (second interest date):

Bond interest payable (L)	25,000	
Premium on bonds payable (L).	125	
Bond interest expense (E)	4,875	
Cash (A).		30,000
To record payment of semi-annual interest.		

8. Interest expense reported on the 2008 income statement should be for the period outstanding during the year (i.e., for 11 months, February 1 through December 31). Interest expense, per these entries, is $29,250 + $24,375 = $53,625; alternatively ($600,000 × 10% × ¹¹⁄₁₂ = $55,000) − ($125 × 11 months = $1,375) = $53,625.

Income statement for 2008:

Interest expense	$ 53,625

Balance sheet, December 31, 2008:

Long-term liabilities:

Bonds payable, 10% (due January 31, 2018)	600,000
Add unamortized premium*	13,625
	$613,625

*$15,000 − ($750 + $625) = $13,625.

Chapter Supplement A

Present Value Concepts

PRESENT VALUE is the current cash equivalent of an amount to be received in the future; a future amount discounted for compound interest.

The concept of **present value** (PV) is based on the time value of money. It provides a foundation for measuring and reporting long-term notes and bonds. Quite simply, money received today is worth more than money to be received one year from today (or at any other future date) because it can be used to earn interest. If you invest $1,000 today at 10 percent, you will have $1,100 in one year. In contrast, if you receive $1,000 one year from today, you will lose the opportunity to earn the $100 interest revenue. The difference between the $1,000 and the $1,100 is interest that can be earned during the year.

In one of your math courses, you have probably already solved some problems involving the time value of money. In the typical problem, you were told a certain dollar amount had been deposited in a savings account earning a specific rate of interest. You were asked to determine the dollar amount that would be in the savings account after a certain number of years. In this supplement, we will show you how to solve problems that are the opposite of the ones you have worked with. In present value problems, you will be told a dollar amount to be received in the future (such as the balance of a savings account after five years) and will be asked to determine the present value of the amount (which is the amount that must be deposited in the savings account today).

The value of money changes over time because money can earn interest. A present value problem is one when you know the dollar amount of a cash flow that will occur in the future and need to determine its value now. The opposite situation occurs when you know the dollar amount of a cash flow that occurs today and need to determine its value at some point in the future. These problems are called **future value** problems. The following illustrates the basic difference between present value and future value problems:

FUTURE VALUE is the sum to which an amount will increase as a result of compound interest.

	Now	Future
Present value	?	$1,000
Future value	$1,000	?

Present and future value problems may involve two types of cash flow: a single payment or an annuity (a series of cash payments).[12] Thus, four different situations are related to the time value of money:

1. Present value of a single payment.
2. Future value of a single payment.
3. Present value of an annuity.
4. Future value of an annuity.

Present value problems involving single amounts and annuities are discussed below. Future value problems are covered in an online supplement to this chapter available at **www.mcgrawhill.ca/olc/libby/student/resources.**

PRESENT VALUE OF A SINGLE AMOUNT

The present value of a single amount is the amount of cash that you are willing to accept today in lieu of a cash receipt at some date in the future. You might be offered the opportunity to invest in a debt instrument that would pay you $10,000 in 10 years. Before you decided whether to invest, you would want to determine the present value of the instrument. Graphically, the present value of $1 due at the end of the third period with an interest rate of 10 percent can be represented as follows:

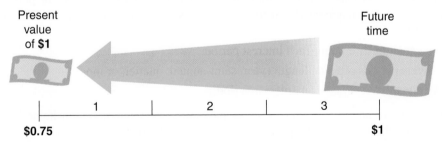

To compute the present value of an amount to be received in the future, we subtract interest that is earned over time from the amount to be received in the future. For example, if you place $100 in a savings account that earns 5 percent, you will have $105 at the end of a year. In a present value problem, you will be told that you have $105 at the end of the year and must compute the amount to be deposited at the beginning of the year. To solve this type of problem, you must discount the amount to be received in the future at interest rate i for n periods. The formula to compute the present value of a single amount is

$$\text{Present Value} = \frac{1}{(1+i)^n} \times \text{Amount}$$

---

[12] Present value and future value problems involve cash flows. The basic concepts are the same for cash inflows (receipts) and cash outflows (payments). No fundamental differences exist between present value and future value calculations for cash payments versus cash receipts.

The formula is not difficult to use, but most analysts use calculators, Excel, or present value tables for computations. We will illustrate how to use present value tables. Assume that today is January 1, 2008, and you have the opportunity to receive $1,000 cash on December 31, 2010. At an interest rate of 10 percent per year, how much is the $1,000 payment worth to you on January 1, 2008? You could discount the amount year by year,[13] but it is easier to use Table A.1 in Appendix A, Present Value of $1. For $i = 10\%$, $n = 3$, we find that the present value of $1 is 0.7513. The present value of $1,000 to be received at the end of three years can be computed as follows:

$$\$1,000 \times 0.7513 = \$751.30$$

> From Table A.1,
> Interest rate = 10%
> N = 3

Learning how to compute a present value amount is not difficult, but it is more important that you understand what it means. The $751.30 is the amount that you would pay to have the right to receive $1,000 at the end of three years, assuming an interest rate of 10 percent. Conceptually, you would be indifferent about having $751.30 today and receiving $1,000 in three years, because you can use financial institutions to convert dollars from the present to the future and vice versa. If you had $751.30 today but preferred $1,000 in three years, you could simply deposit the money into a savings account that paid annual interest at 10% and it would grow to $1,000 in three years. Alternatively, if you had a contract that promised you $1,000 in three years, you could sell it to an investor for $751.30 cash today because it would permit the investor to earn the difference in interest.

SELF-STUDY **QUIZ 11-8**

1. If the interest rate in a present value problem increases from 10 percent to 11 percent, will the present value increase or decrease? Explain.

2. What is the present value of $10,000 to be received 10 years from now if the interest rate is 5 percent compounded annually?

Check your answers with those in footnote 14.

> An **ANNUITY** is a series of equal amounts of cash that are paid or received at equally distant points in time.

PRESENT VALUE OF AN ANNUITY

Many business problems involve multiple cash payments over a number of periods instead of a single payment. An **annuity** is a series of consecutive payments characterized by

1. An equal dollar amount each interest period.

2. Interest periods of equal length (year, semi-annual, quarter, or month).

3. An equal interest rate each interest period.

Examples of annuities include monthly payments on an automobile or home loan, annual contributions to a savings account, and monthly retirement benefits.

---

[13] The detailed discounting is as follows:

Periods	Interest for the Year	Present Value*
1	$ 1,000 − ($1,000 × 1/1.10) = $90.91	$ 1,000 − $90.91 = $909.09
2	$909.09 − ($909.09 × 1/1.10) = $82.65	$909.09 − $82.65 = $826.44
3	$826.44 − ($826.44 × 1/1.10) = $75.14[†]	$826.44 − $75.14 = $751.30

*Verifiable in Table A.1.   [†]Adjusted for rounding.

[14] 1. The present value will decrease. With a higher interest rate, more interest will accumulate over time, so the initial amount needed at the start would be smaller because the interest component will be larger.

2. $10,000 × 0.6139 = $6,139

The present value of an annuity is the value now of a series of equal amounts to be received (or paid) each period for some specified number of periods in the future. It is computed by discounting each of the equal periodic amounts. A good example of this type of problem is a retirement program that offers the retiree a monthly income after retirement. The present value of an annuity of $1 for three periods at 10 percent may be represented graphically as follows:

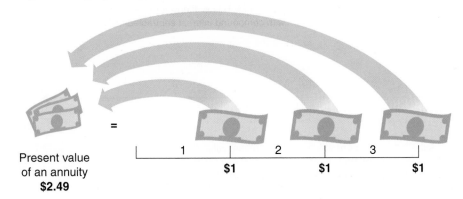

We can compute the present value more easily however, by using Table A.2, Appendix A, as follows:

Present value
of an annuity
$2.49

Assume you are to receive $1,000 cash on each December 31, 2008, 2009, and 2010. How much would the sum of these three $1,000 future amounts be worth on January 1, 2008, assuming an interest rate of 10 percent per year? We could use Table A.1 in Appendix A to calculate the present value as follows:

Year	Amount		Factor from Table A.1, Appendix A, *I* 10%		Present Value
1	$1,000	×	0.9091 ($n = 1$)	=	$ 909.10
2	$1,000	×	0.8264 ($n = 2$)	=	826.40
3	$1,000	×	0.7513 ($n = 3$)	=	751.30
			Total present value	=	$2,486.80

We can compute the present value of this annuity more easily however, by using Table A.2, Appendix A, as follows:

$$\$1{,}000 \times 2.4869 = \$2{,}487 \text{ (rounded)}$$

From Table A.2,
Interest rate = 10%
N = 3

Exhibit 11.5 provides a graphical illustration of the present value computations discussed above.

INTEREST RATES AND INTEREST PERIODS The preceding illustrations assumed annual periods for compounding and discounting. Although interest rates almost always are quoted on an annual basis, most interest-compounding periods encountered in business are less than one year (such as semi-annually or quarterly). When interest periods are less than a year, the values of n and i must be restated to be consistent with the length of the interest period.

To illustrate, 12-percent interest compounded annually for five years requires use of $n = 5$ and $i = 12\%$. If compounding is quarterly, the interest period is one-quarter of a year (i.e., four periods per year), and the quarterly interest rate is one-quarter of the annual rate (i.e., 3 percent per quarter). Therefore, 12-percent interest compounded quarterly for five years requires use of $n = 20$ and $i = 3\%$.

EXHIBIT **11.5**

Overview of Present Value
Computations

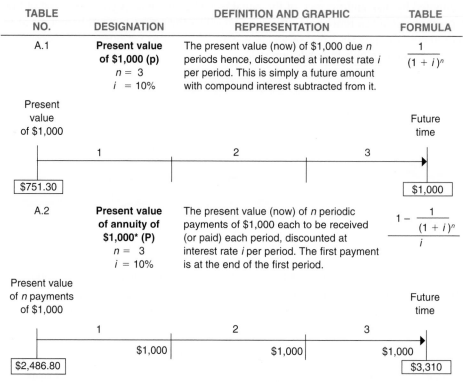

TABLE NO.	DESIGNATION	DEFINITION AND GRAPHIC REPRESENTATION	TABLE FORMULA
A.1	**Present value of $1,000 (p)** $n = 3$ $i = 10\%$	The present value (now) of $1,000 due n periods hence, discounted at interest rate i per period. This is simply a future amount with compound interest subtracted from it.	$\dfrac{1}{(1 + i)^n}$

Present
value
of $1,000   Future
                                                                                                 time

| 1   2   3
$751.30 $1,000

| A.2 | **Present value of annuity of $1,000* (P)** $n = 3$ $i = 10\%$ | The present value (now) of n periodic payments of $1,000 each to be received (or paid) each period, discounted at interest rate i per period. The first payment is at the end of the first period. | $\dfrac{1 - \dfrac{1}{(1 + i)^n}}{i}$ |

Present value
of n payments   Future
of $1,000   time

| 1   2   3
               $1,000 $1,000 $1,000
$2,486.80 $3,310

*Notice that these are ordinary annuities; that is, they are often called *end-of-period annuities*. Thus, the table values for P, the present value, are at the beginning of the period of the first payment. Annuities due assume the opposite; that is, they are *beginning-of-period annuities*. Ordinary annuity values can be converted into annuities due simply by multiplication of $(1 + i)$.

A QUESTION OF ETHICS

TRUTH IN ADVERTISING

A number of advertisements in newspapers and magazines and on television easily can be misinterpreted if the consumer does not understand present value concepts. We discuss two examples.

Most car companies offer seasonal promotions with special financing incentives. A car dealer may advertise 1.9-percent interest on car loans when banks are charging 10 percent. Typically, the lower interest rate is not a special incentive because the dealer simply charges a higher price for cars that the dealership finances. It may be better to borrow from the bank and "pay cash" at the dealership to negotiate a lower price. Customers should use the present value concepts illustrated in this chapter to compare financing alternatives.

Another misleading advertisement is seen every January and promises a chance to become an instant millionaire. The fine print discloses that the winner will receive $25,000 for 40 years, which is $1,000,000 (40 × $25,000), but the present value of this annuity at 8 percent is only $298,000. Most winners are happy to get the money, but they are not really millionaires.

Some consumer advocates criticize businesses that use these types of advertisements. They argue that consumers should not have to study present value concepts to understand advertisements. Some of these criticisms may be valid, but the quality of information contained in advertisements that include interest rates has improved during the past few years.

ACCOUNTING APPLICATIONS OF PRESENT VALUES

Many business transactions require the use of present value concepts. We illustrate two such cases so that you can test your understanding of these concepts:

CASE A On January 1, 2008, Petro-Canada bought some new equipment. The company signed a note and agreed to pay $200,000 for the equipment on December 31, 2009. The market interest rate for this note was 12 percent. The $200,000 represents the cash equivalent price of the equipment and the interest that will be earned for two years.

1. How should the accountant record the purchase?

Answer: This case requires application of the present value of a single amount. In conformity with the cost principle, the cost of the equipment is its current cash equivalent price, which is the present value of the future payment. The problem can be shown graphically as follows:

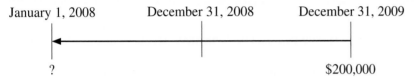

January 1, 2008	December 31, 2008	December 31, 2009
?		$200,000

The present value of the $200,000 is computed as follows:

$$\$200,000 \times 0.7972 = \$159,440$$

From Table A.1,
Interest rate = 12%
N = 2

Therefore, the journal entry is as follows:

| Equipment (A)................................... | 159,440 | |
| Note payable (L) .... | | 159,440 |

Assets	=	Liabilities	+	Shareholders' Equity
Equipment +159,440		Note payable +159,440		

Some companies prefer to record the following journal entry:

Equipment (A)...................................	159,440	
Discount on notes payable (XL)	40,560	
Note payable (L)		200,000

Assets	=	Liabilities	+	Shareholders' Equity
Equipment +159,440		Note payable +200,000		
		Discount −40,560		

The discount account is a contra-liability account that represents the interest that will accrue on the note over its life.

2. What journal entry should be made at the end of the first and second years for interest expense?

Answer: The following schedule shows the computation of interest expense for the two years.

Date	Interest Expense Unpaid Balance × 12%	Unpaid Balance of Note payable
January 1, 2008		$159,440
December 31, 2008	$159,440 × 12% = $19,132	178,572
December 31, 2009	178,573 × 12% = 21,428	200,000

Each year's interest expense is recorded in an adjusting entry as follows:

| Dec. 31, 2008 | Interest expense (E) .... | 19,132 | |
| | Note payable (L)....................... | | 19,132 |

Assets	=	Liabilities	+	Shareholders' Equity
		Note payable +19,132		Interest expense −19,132

| Dec. 31, 2009 | Interest expense (E) .... | 21,428 | |
| | Note payable (L)....................... | | 21,428 |

Assets	=	Liabilities	+	Shareholders' Equity
		Note payable +21,428		Interest expense −21,428

Notice that interest of $19,132 accrued during 2008, but was not paid. It is therefore added to the balance of the note payable account. This interest amount has itself earned interest during 2009.

3. What journal entry should be made on December 31, 2009, to record the payment of the debt?

Answer: At this date, the amount to be paid is the balance of Note Payable, which is the same as the maturity amount on the due date. The journal entry to record full payment of the debt follows:

| Note payable (L).. | 200,000 | |
| Cash (A).. | | 200,000 |

Assets	=	Liabilities	+	Shareholders' Equity
Cash −200,000		Note payable −200,000		

CASE B   On January 1, 2008, Petro-Canada bought new drilling equipment. The company elected to finance the purchase with a note payable to be paid in three equal annual instalments of $163,686. Each instalment includes principal plus interest on the unpaid balance at 11 percent per year. The annual instalments are due on December 31, 2008, 2009, and 2010. This problem can be shown graphically as follows:

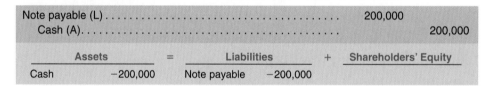

January 1, 2008	December 31, 2008	December 31, 2009	December 31, 2010
?	$163,686	$163,686	$163,686

1. What is the amount of the note?

Answer: The note is the present value of each instalment payment, $i = 11\%$ and $n = 3$. This is an annuity because payment is made in three equal instalments. The amount of the note is computed as follows:

$$\textbf{\$163,686} \times \textbf{2.4437} = \textbf{\$400,000}$$

> From Table A.2,
> Interest rate = 11%
> N = 3

The acquisition is recorded as follows:

| Drilling equipment (A)..................................... | 400,000 | |
| Note payable (L) .... | | 400,000 |

Assets	=	Liabilities	+	Shareholders' Equity
Drilling equipment +400,000		Note payable +400,000		

2. What was the total amount of interest expense in dollars?

Answer:

$$\$163,686 \times 3 \ (= \$491,058) - \$400,000 = \$91,058$$

3. Prepare a debt payment schedule that shows the entry for each payment and the effect on interest expense and the unpaid amount of principal each period.

Answer:

Debt Payment Schedule

Date	Cash Payment (Credit)	Interest Expense (Unpaid Principal × 11%) (Debit)	Decrease in Principal (Debit)	Unpaid Principal
1/1/2008				$400,000
12/31/2008	$163,686	$400,000 × 11% = $44,000	$119,686[a]	280,314[b]
12/31/2009	163,686	280,314 × 11% = $30,835	132,851	147,463
12/31/2010	163,686	147,463 × 11% = $16,223*	147,463	0
Total	$491,058	$91,058*	$400,000	

*To accommodate rounding error.
Computations:
[a]$163,686 − $44,000 = $119,686   [b]$400,000 − $119,686 = $280,314

Notice in the debt payment schedule that for each successive payment, the payment on principal increases and interest expense decreases. This effect occurs because the interest each period is based on a lower amount of the unpaid principal. When an annuity is involved, schedules such as this one often are useful analytical tools.

4. What journal entry should be made at the end of each year to record the payments on this note?

Answer:

Dec. 31, 2008 Note payable (L) 119,686
               Interest expense (E) 44,000
                   Cash (A)   163,686

Assets		=	Liabilities		+	Shareholders' Equity	
Cash	−163,686		Note payable	−119,686		Interest expense	−44,000

Dec. 31, 2009 Note payable (L) 132,851
               Interest expense (E) 30,835
                   Cash (A)   163,686

Assets		=	Liabilities		+	Shareholders' Equity	
Cash	−163,686		Note payable	−132,851		Interest expense	−30,835

Dec. 31, 2010 Note payable (L) 147,463
               Interest expense (E) 16,223
                   Cash (A)   163,686

Assets		=	Liabilities		+	Shareholders' Equity	
Cash	−163,686		Note payable	−147,463		Interest expense	−16,223

SOLUTIONS TO **SELF-STUDY QUIZZES**

Self-Study Quiz 11-1

1. The market rate is the interest rate demanded by creditors. It is the rate used in the present value computations to discount future cash flows. The market interest rate is also called *yield* or *effective-interest rate.*

2. The coupon interest rate is the stated rate on the bonds. It is also called *stated rate* and *contract rate.*

3. A bond that sells for less than par is sold at a discount. This occurs when the stated rate is lower than the market rate.

4. A bond that sells for more than par is sold at a premium. This occurs when the coupon rate is higher than the market rate.

Self-Study Quiz 11-2

Principal: $100,000 $\times$ 0.4224 = $ 42,240
Interest: 9,000 $\times$ 6.4177 = $\underline{\quad 57,760}$
$\qquad\qquad\qquad\qquad\qquad\quad$ $\overline{\$100,000}$

Self-Study Quiz 11-3

1. Principal: $100,000 $\times$ 0.4565 = $45,650
    Interest: 3,500 $\times$ 13.5903 = $\underline{\quad 47,566}$
    $\qquad\qquad\qquad\qquad\qquad\quad$ $\overline{\$93,216}$

2. Interest paid = $100,000 $\times$ 0.07 = $7,000

3. Interest expense = Interest payment + Amortization of bond discount
    $\qquad\qquad\qquad$ = $7,000 + $6,784 / 10 = $7,678.40

Self-Study Quiz 11-4

1. Interest expense, first semi-annual period = $93,216 $\times$ (0.08 / 2) = $3,729
    Amortization of bond discount = $3,729 − $3,500 = $229
    Book value, end of first semi-annual period = $93,216 + $229 = $93,445
    Interest expense, second semi-annual period = $93,445 $\times$ (0.08 / 2) = $3,738
    Interest expense for the first year = $3,729 + $3,738 = $7,467

2. Book value, end of second semi-annual period = $93,445 + $238 = $93,683

Self-Study Quiz 11-5

1. Principal: $100,000 $\times$ 0.4565 = $ 45,650
    Interest: 4,500 $\times$ 13.5903 = $\underline{\quad 61,156}$
    $\qquad\qquad\qquad\qquad\qquad\quad$ $\overline{\$106,806}$

2. Interest paid = $100,000 $\times$ 0.09 = $9,000

3. Interest expense = Interest payment + Amortization of bond premium
    $\qquad\qquad\qquad$ = $9,000 − $6,806 / 10 = $8,319.40

Self-Study Quiz 11-6

1.

	(a) Interest to Be Paid ($400,000 × 5%)	(b) Interest Expense (4% × Book Value, Beginning of Period)	(c) Amortization (b) − (a)	(d) Book Value
Amortization Schedule: Bond Premium (effective interest)				
Date				
12/31/2008				$446,616
6/30/2009	$20,000	$17,865	$2,135	444,481
12/31/2009	20,000	17,779	2,221	442,260
6/30/2010	20,000	17,690	2,310	439,950

2. The book value at June 30, 2010, is $439,949. This amount is the unpaid balance of the bonds, and represents the present value of the remaining payments using the market rate of interest when the bonds were issued. At June 30, 2010, there are 13 interest payments remaining and the principal of the bonds. Their present value is:

    Present value = $400,000 $\times$ 0.6006 (Table A.1, Appendix A)
    $\qquad\qquad\qquad$ + $20,000 $\times$ 9.9856 (Table A.2, Appendix A)
    $\qquad\qquad\qquad$ = $539,952 (The difference of $3 is due to rounding.)

Self-Study Quiz 11-7

Financial leverage ratio = Average total assets / Average shareholders' equity
$\qquad\qquad\qquad\qquad$ = [($20,655 + $22,646) / 2] / [($9,488 − $378 + $10,441 − $300) /2] = 2.25

The ratio has increased from 2.17 to 2.25 indicating that Petro-Canada's financial risk has increased. An increase in financial risk causes debtholders to require a higher interest rate to compensate them for the additional risk. Companies try to avoid reporting liabilities on their balance sheets, whenever possible, because of their negative impact of the credit rating on their debts.

CHAPTER **TAKE-AWAYS**

1. **Describe the characteristics of long-term notes and bonds payable. p. 571**
   Long-term notes and bonds payable have a number of characteristics designed to meet the needs of the issuing corporation and the creditor.

   Corporations use debt to raise long-term capital. Long-term debt offers a number of advantages compared to equity, including financial leverage, the tax deductibility of interest, and the fact that control of the company is not diluted. Long-term debt carries additional risk because interest and principal payments are not discretionary.

2. **Report bonds payable and interest expense for bonds sold at par, at a discount, and at a premium. p. 575**
   Three types of events must be recorded over the life of a typical bond: (1) the receipt of cash when the bond is first sold, (2) the periodic payment of cash interest, and (3) the repayment of principal upon the maturity of the bond.

   Bonds are sold at a discount whenever the coupon interest rate is less than the market rate of interest. A discount is the difference between the par value of the bond and its selling price. The discount is recorded as a contra liability when the bond is sold and is amortized over the life of the bond as an adjustment to interest expense.

   Bonds are sold at a premium whenever the coupon interest rate is higher than the market rate of interest. A premium is the difference between the selling price of the bond and its par value. The premium is recorded as a liability when the bond is sold and is amortized over the life of the bond as an adjustment to interest expense.

3. **Compute and interpret the times interest earned ratio. p. 586**
   This ratio measures the ability of a company to meet its interest obligations with resources from its profit-making activities. The ratio is computed by comparing interest expense to income before interest expense and income taxes.

4. **Report the early retirement of bonds. p. 587**
   A corporation may retire bonds before their maturity date. The difference between the book value and the amount paid to retire the bonds is reported as a gain or loss, depending on the circumstances.

5. **Describe other long-term liabilities. p. 589**
   In addition to long-term debt, companies report a number of other long-term liabilities that result from their operating, investing and financing activities. Typical long-term liabilities include lease obligations, asset retirement obligations, accrued retirement benefits liability, and future income taxes.

6. **Compute and interpret the financial leverage ratio. p. 593**
   The financial leverage ratio compares the amount of capital supplied by creditors to the amount supplied by owners. It is a measure of a company's debt capacity. It is an important ratio because high risk is associated with debt capital because of obligatory payments.

7. **Explain how financing activities are reported on the cash flow statement. p. 594**
   Cash flows associated with transactions involving long-term creditors are reported in the Financing Activities section of the cash flow statement. Interest expense is reported in the Operating Activities section.

   The capital structure of a business is made up of funds supplied by both the creditors and the owners. In this chapter, we discussed the role of bonds payable in the capital structure of a business. In the next chapter, we will discuss shareholders' equity.

KEY **RATIOS**

Times interest earned ratio measures a company's ability to generate resources from current operations to meet its interest obligations. The computation of this ratio follows (p. 586):

$$\text{Times Interest Earned} = \frac{\text{Net Income} + \text{Interest Expense} + \text{Income Tax Expense}}{\text{Interest Expense}}$$

The financial leverage ratio measures the relationship between total assets and the shareholders' equity that finances the assets. The ratio is computed as follows (p. 593):

$$\text{Financial Leverage} = \frac{\text{Average Total Assets}}{\text{Average Shareholders' Equity}}$$

FINDING FINANCIAL INFORMATION

BALANCE SHEET

Under Current Liabilities

Notes, bonds, and debentures are normally listed as long-term liabilities. An exception occurs when these liabilities are within one year of maturity. Such debts are reported as current liabilities with the following title:

Current portion of long-term debt

Under Non-Current Liabilities

Notes, bonds, and debentures are listed under a variety of titles, depending on the characteristics of the debt. Titles include

Notes payable

Bonds payable

Debentures

INCOME STATEMENT

Interest expense associated with long-term debt is reported on the income statement. Most companies report interest expense in a separate category on the income statement.

CASH FLOW STATEMENT

Under Financing Activities

+ Cash inflows from long-term creditors

− Cash outflows to long-term creditors

Under Operating Activities

The cash outflow associated with interest expense is reported as an operating activity.

NOTES

Under Summary of Significant Accounting Policies

Description of pertinent information concerning accounting treatment of liabilities. Normally, there is minimal information. Some companies report the method used to amortize bond discounts and premiums.

Under a Separate Note

Most companies include a separate note called "Long-Term Debt" that reports information about each major debt issue, including amount and interest rate. The note may also provide detail concerning debt covenants.

KEY **TERMS**

Annuity p. 598

Bond Certificate p. 573

Bond Discount p. 575

Bond Premium p. 575

Bond Principal p. 571

Callable Bonds p. 572

Capital Lease p. 590

Convertible Bonds p. 572

Coupon Rate p. 575

Debenture p. 572

Effective-Interest Method p. 580

Effective-Interest Rate p. 575

Face Amount p. 571

Financial Leverage p. 570

Future Value p. 597

Indenture p. 573

Long-term Liabilities p. 569

Market Interest Rate p. 575

Operating Lease p. 590

Par Value p. 571

Present Value p. 596

Redeemable (Callable) Bonds p. 587

Retractable Bonds p. 587

Stated Rate p. 571

Straight-Line Amortization p. 579

Trustee p. 573

Yield p. 575

QUESTIONS

1. What are the primary characteristics of a bond? For what purposes are bonds usually issued?
2. What is the difference between a bond indenture and a bond certificate?
3. Differentiate secured debt from unsecured debt.
4. Differentiate among redeemable, retractable, and convertible bonds.
5. From the perspective of the issuer, what are some advantages of using debt instead of issuing shares?
6. As the tax rate increases, the net cost of borrowing money decreases. Explain.
7. Explain financial leverage. Can it be negative?
8. At the date of issuance, bonds are recorded at their current cash equivalent amount. Explain.
9. What is the nature of the discount and premium on bonds payable? Explain.
10. What is the difference between the stated interest rate and the effective-interest rate on a bond?
11. Differentiate between the stated and effective rates of interest on a bond sold (a) at par, (b) at a discount, and (c) at a premium.
12. What is the book value of a bond payable?
13. Explain the basic difference between straight-line amortization and effective-interest methods of amortizing bond discount or premium. Explain when each method should or may be used.
14. If a company issues a bond at a discount, will interest expense each period be more or less than the cash payment for interest? If another company issues a bond at a premium, will interest expense be more or less than the cash payment for interest? Is your answer to either question affected by the method used to amortize the discount or premium?
15. (Supplement A) Explain the basic difference between future value and present value.
16. (Supplement A) What does an annuity mean?

EXERCISES

E11–1 Recording Bonds Based on an Annual Report

LO1, 2

Lennar Corporation

Lennar Corporation is a builder of new homes that has constructed more than 140,000 single-family residences since its founding in 1954. Lennar's annual report contained the following information (in thousands):

	2006	2005	2004
Interest expense	$ 241,066	$ 187,154	$ 134,193
Bonds payable	2,613,503	2,592,772	2,021,014

Required:

1. Record interest expense using a single journal entry for each year.
2. Record the issuance of bonds payable during 2006, assuming that they were issued at par and no repayment of bonds issued in prior years.
3. Recognizing that Lennar is a home builder, why do you think that the amounts of bonds payable increased so much during this period?

E11–2 Determining Financial Statement Effects for Long-term Note and First Interest Payment, with Premium

LO1, 2

Grocery Corporation sold $500,000, 11-percent notes on January 1, 2008, at a market rate of 8 percent. The notes were dated January 1, 2008, with interest to be paid each December 31; they mature 10 years from January 1, 2008. Use straight-line amortization.

Required:

1. How are the financial statements affected by the issuance of the notes? Describe the impact on the financial leverage and times interest earned ratios, if any.
2. How are the financial statements affected by the payment of interest on December 31? Describe the impact on the financial leverage and times interest earned ratios, if any.
3. Show how the interest expense, interest payment, and the notes payable should be reported on the December 31, 2008, annual financial statements.

■ **LO1**

Apple Computer

E11–3   Explaining Why Debt Is Sold at a Discount

The annual report of Apple Computer, Inc., contained the following note:

> **Long-Term Debt**
>
> On February 10, 2004, the Company issued $300 million aggregate principal amount of its 6.5% unsecured notes. The notes were sold at 99.925% of par, for an effective yield of 6.51%. The notes pay interest semi-annually and mature on February 15, 2014.

After reading this note, one student asked why Apple didn't simply sell the notes for an effective yield of 6.5 percent and avoid having to account for a very small discount over the next 10 years. Prepare a written response to this question.

■ **LO2**

Carnival Cruise Lines

E11–4   Explaining Bond Terminology

The balance sheet for Carnival Cruise Lines includes "zero coupon convertible subordinated notes." In your own words, explain the features of this debt. The balance sheet does not report a premium or a discount associated with this debt. Do you think it is recorded at par?

■ **LO1**

Bell Canada Inc.

ANALYSIS

E11–5   Interpreting Information Reported in the Business Press

The business press reported the following information concerning a bond issued by Bell Canada Inc.:

Bonds	Coupon	Maturity	Bid	Yield
Bell	6.55	May 01/29	111.29	5.68

Required:

Explain the meaning of the reported information. If you bought Bell Canada Inc. bonds with $10,000 face value, how much would you pay (based on the preceding information reported)? Assume that the bond was originally sold at par. What impact would the increase in value have on the financial statements for Bell Canada Inc.?

■ **LO1**

PepsiCo, Inc.

The Walt Disney Company

ANALYSIS

E11–6   Evaluating Bond Features

You are a personal financial planner working with a married couple in their early 40s who have decided to invest $100,000 in corporate bonds. You have found two bonds that you think will interest your clients. One is a zero coupon bond issued by PepsiCo with an effective interest rate of 9 percent and a maturity date of 2015. It is callable at par. The other is a Walt Disney bond that matures in 2093. It has an effective interest rate of 9.5 percent and is callable at 105 percent of par. Which bond would you recommend and why? Would your answer be different if you expected interest rates to fall significantly over the next few years? Would you prefer a different bond if the couple's ages were in the late 60s and they were retired?

■ **LO1, 2**

E11–7   Computing the Issue Price of a Bond, with Discussion

Charger Corporation issued a $250,000 bond that matures in five years. The bond has a stated interest rate of 8 percent and pays interest on February 1, May 1, August 1, and November 1. When the bond was issued, the market rate of interest was 12 percent. Record the issuance of the bond on February 1. Also record the payment of interest on May 1 and August 1. Use the straight-line method for amortization of any discount or premium. Explain why someone would buy a bond that did not pay the market rate of interest.

■ **LO1, 2**

The Walt Disney Company

E11–8   Explaining an International Transaction

A Walt Disney annual reported contained the following note:

> The Company issued Yen 100 billion (approximately $920 million) of Japanese yen bonds through a public offering in Japan. The bonds are senior, unsecured debt obligations of the Company, which mature in June 1999. Interest on the bonds is payable semi-annually at a fixed interest rate of 5% per year through maturity. The bonds provide for principal payments in dollars and interest payment in Japanese yen.

Required:

1. Describe how this bond would be reported on the balance sheet.

2. Explain why you think management borrowed money in this manner.

E11–9 Analyzing Financial Ratios

You have just started your first job as a financial analyst for a large investment company. Your boss, a senior analyst, has finished a detailed report evaluating bonds issued by two different companies. She stopped by your desk and asked for help: "I have compared two ratios for the companies and found something interesting." She went on to explain that the financial leverage ratio for Applied Technologies, Inc., is much lower than the industry average and that the one for Innovative Solutions, Inc., is much higher. On the other hand, the times interest earned ratio for Applied Technologies is much higher than the industry average, and the ratio for Innovative Solutions is much lower. Your boss then asked you to think about what the ratios indicate about the two companies so that she could include the explanation in her report. How would you respond to your boss?

■ LO1, 3, 6

ANALYSIS

E11–10 Computing the Issue Price of a Note Payable

On January 1, 2008, Kaizen Corporation issued a $500,000 note that matures in 10 years. The note has a stated interest rate of 10 percent. When the note was issued, the market rate was 10 percent. The note pays interest twice per year on June 30 and December 31. At what price was the note issued?

■ LO2

E11–11 Computing the Issue Price of a Bond with Analysis of Income and Cash Flow Effects

Imai Company issued a $1-million bond that matures in five years. The bond has a 9-percent coupon rate. When the bond was issued, the market rate was 8 percent. The bond pays interest twice per year on June 30 and December 31. Record the issuance of the bond on June 30. Was the bond issued at a discount or at a premium? How will the discount or premium affect future income and future cash flows?

■ LO2, 7

E11–12 Computing Issue Prices of Bonds for Three Cases

Thompson Corporation is planning to issue $100,000, five-year, 8-percent bonds. Interest is payable semi-annually each June 30 and December 31. All of the bonds will be sold on July 1, 2008; they mature on June 30, 2013.

■ LO2

Required:

Compute the issue (sale) price on July 1, 2008, if the yield is: (a) 8 percent, (b) 7.5 percent, and (c) 8.5 percent. Show computations.

E11–13 Recording Bond Issue and First Interest Payment with Discount (Straight-Line Amortization)

On January 1, 2009, Seton Corporation sold a $1,000,000, 8.5-percent bond issue. The bonds were dated January 1, 2009, had a yield of 9 percent, pay interest each December 31, and mature 10 years from January 1, 2009.

■ LO2

Required:

1. Prepare the journal entry to record the issuance of the bonds.

2. Prepare the journal entry to record the interest payment on December 31, 2009. Use straight-line amortization.

3. Show how the bond interest expense and the bonds payable should be reported on the annual financial statements for 2009.

E11–14 Recording Bond Issue and First Interest Payment with Premium (Effective-Interest Amortization)

On January 1, 2009, Bochini Corporation sold a $10-million, 9.25-percent bond issue. The bonds were dated January 1, 2009, had a yield of 9 percent, pay interest each December 31, and mature 10 years from that date.

■ LO2

Required:

1. Prepare the journal entry to record the issuance of the bonds.

2. Prepare the journal entry to record the interest payment on December 31, 2009. Use effective-interest amortization.

3. Show how the bond interest expense and the bonds payable should be reported on the annual financial statements for 2009.

■ LO2   **E11–15 Recording Bond Issue: Entries for Issuance and Interest**
Northland Corporation had $400,000, 10-year bonds outstanding on December 31, 2008 (end of the fiscal year). Interest is payable each December 31. The bonds were issued (sold) on January 1, 2008. The 2008 annual financial statements showed the following:

Income statement	
Bond interest expense (straight-line amortization)	$ 33,200
Balance sheet	
Bonds payable (net liability)	389,200

Required (show computations):

1. What was the issue price of the bonds? Prepare the journal entry to record the issuance of the bonds on January 1, 2008.

2. What was the coupon rate on the bonds? Prepare the entry to record interest expense for 2008.

■ LO3   **E11–16 Determining Financial Statement Balance with the Straight-Line Amortization of a Bond Discount**
Eagle Corporation issued $10,000,000, 6.5 percent bonds dated April 1, 2009. The market rate of interest was 7 percent, with interest paid each March 31. The bonds mature in three years on March 31, 2012. Eagle's fiscal year ends on December 31.

Required:

1. What was the issue price of these bonds?

2. Compute the bond interest expense for fiscal year 2009. The company uses the straight-line method of amortization.

3. Show how the bonds should be reported on the balance sheet at December 31, 2009.

4. What amount of interest expense will be recorded on March 31, 2010? Is this amount different from the amount of cash that is paid? If so, why?

■ LO2   **E11–17 Analyzing a Bond Amortization Schedule: Reporting Bonds Payable**
Stein Corporation issued a $1,000 bond on January 1, 2008. The bond specified an interest rate of 9 percent payable at the end of each year. The bond matures at the end of 2010. It was sold at a market rate of 11 percent per year. The following schedule was completed:

	Cash	Interest	Amortization	Balance
January 1, 2008 (issuance)				$ 951
End of year 2008	?	$105	$15	966
End of year 2009	?	106	16	982
End of year 2010	?	108	18	1,000

Required:

1. What was the bond's issue price?

2. Did the bond sell at a discount or a premium? How much was the premium or discount?

3. What amount of cash was paid each year for bond interest?

4. What amount of interest expense should be shown each year on the income statement?

5. What amount(s) should be shown on the balance sheet for bonds payable at each year-end? (For year 2010, show the balance just before repayment of the bond.)

6. What method of amortization was used?

7. Show how the following amounts were computed for year 2009: (a) $106, (b) $16, and (c) $982.

8. Is the method of amortization that was used preferable? Explain why.

■ LO2   **E11–18 Preparing a Debt Payment Schedule with Effective-Interest Method of Amortization and Determining Reported Amounts**
Shuttle Company issued $1,000,000, three-year 10-percent bonds on January 1, 2007. The bond interest is paid each December 31. The bond was sold to yield 9 percent.

Required:

1. Complete a bond payment schedule. Use the effective interest method.

2. What amounts will be reported on the financial statements (balance sheet, income statement and cash flow statement) for the years 2007, 2008, and 2009?

E11–19 Determining Financial Statement Effects of Long-Term Debt and Related Interest

Chamandy Corporation issued a $250,000, 7-percent note on July 1, 2008, at a market rate of 6 percent. The note was dated July 1, 2008, with interest to be paid each June 30. The note matures in 10 years. The company's fiscal year ends on December 31.

■ **LO2, 3, 6**

ANALYSIS

Required:

1. How are the financial statements affected by the issuance of the note? Describe the impact on the financial leverage and the times interest earned ratios, if any.

2. How are the financial statements affected by the payment of interest on June 30, 2009? Describe the impact on the financial leverage and the times interest earned ratios, if any.

3. Show how the interest expense and the note payable should be reported on the December 31, 2009 annual financial statements. Use the straight line method to amortize any discount or premium.

E11–20 Reporting the Retirement of a Bond with Discount

The Nair Company issued a $5 million bond at a discount five years ago. The current book value of the bond is $4.75 million. The company now has excess cash and decides to retire the bond. The bond is callable at 101 percent of its face value.

■ **LO4**

Required:

Prepare the journal entry to record the retirement of the bond.

E11–21 Determining Effects on the Cash Flow Statement

A number of events over the life of a bond have effects that are reported on the cash flow statement. Determine whether each of the following events affects the cash flow statement. If so, describe the impact and specify where the effect is reported on the statement.

■ **LO7**

1. A $1,000,000 bond is issued at a discount in 2007. The book value of the bond reported on the balance sheet on that date is $985,000, before any amortization of bond discount.

2. At year-end, accrued interest amounted to $50,000 and $1,000 of the bond discount is amortized using the straight-line method.

3. Early in 2008, the accrued interest is paid. At the same time, $8,000 of interest that accrued in 2008 is paid.

E11–22 Evaluating Lease Alternatives

As the new vice-president for consumer products at Acme Manufacturing, you are attending a meeting to discuss a serious problem associated with delivering merchandise to customers. Bob Vargas, director of logistics, summarized the problem: "It's easy to understand, we just don't have enough delivery trucks given our recent growth." Barb Belini from the accounting department responded: "Maybe it's easy to understand but it's impossible to do anything. Because of Bay Street's concern about the amount of debt on our balance sheet, we're under a freeze and can't borrow money to acquire new assets. There's nothing we can do."

On the way back to your office after the meeting, your assistant offers a suggestion: "Why don't we just lease the trucks we need? That way we can get the assets we want without having to record a liability on the balance sheet."

How would you respond to this suggestion?

■ **LO5**

E11–23 Reporting a Liability

Carnival Cruise Lines provides exotic vacations on board luxurious passenger ships. In 1998, the company moved its offices and included the following note in its current annual report:

■ **LO5**

Carnival Cruise Lines

ANALYSIS

Leases

On March 27, 1998, the Company entered into a 10-year lease for 230,000 square feet of office space located in Miami, Florida. The Company moved its operation to this location in October 1998. The total rent payable over the 10-year term of the lease is approximately $24 million.

Required:

Based on these facts, do you think the company should report this obligation on its balance sheet? Explain. If the obligation should be reported as a liability, how should the amount be measured?

■ **LO5, 6**   **E11–24** **Reporting Retirement Benefits and Effect on Financial Leverage Ratio**

Sears Canada

ANALYSIS

Sears Canada Inc. offers Canadian consumers a diverse array of shopping options, with department and specialty stores, a comprehensive Web site, and a broad range of home-related services. At December 31, 2006, Sears had approximately 37,000 associates (or employees) helping customers through their personal shopping and catalogue ordering. On February 5, 2007, the company made the following announcement about its employee retirement program.

Sears Canada Announces Re-design of its Retirement Program

TORONTO, Feb. 5, 2007 (Canada NewsWire via COMTEX News Network)—Changes effective in 2008 Sears Canada Inc. (TSX: SCC) today announced a re-design of its retirement program for associates that will come into effect in 2008. This will affect some, but not all, active associates . . .

The Company will amend its pension plan effective July 1, 2008 by introducing a defined contribution component to the plan on that date . . .

Under the new defined contribution component of the plan, associates who are members of the pension plan will be able to contribute a percentage of their eligible earnings within defined limits: the more they contribute, the more the Company will contribute.

The company's annual report for 2006 includes the following information (in millions of dollars):

	2006	2005
Total assets	$3,093.3	$3,290.8
Shareholders' equity	785.0	645.3
Accrued benefit asset (liability)	30.9	33.2

In addition, a note to the company's financial statements shows that Sears had unfunded benefit obligations of $369.4 million and $220.1 million at December 31, 2005 and at December 31, 2006, respectively.

Required:

1. Compare and contrast defined benefit and defined contribution pension plans.

2. What change did Sears introduce to its employee retirement program? What is the main reason for this change? Explain.

3. Compute and interpret the financial leverage ratio for 2006.

4. Assume that the unfunded benefit obligation was reported on Sears's balance sheet for 2005 and 2006 as a long-term liability with an equal decrease in shareholders' equity. Compute the financial leverage ratio using the adjusted balance sheet amounts. Do you think Sears's management would favour the reporting of the unfunded benefits obligation on the company's balance sheet? Explain.

■ **LO5**   **E11–25** **Reporting a Liability, with Discussion**

ACE Aviation
Holdings

An annual report for ACE Aviation Holdings Inc., contained the following information:

---

9. PENSION AND OTHER BENEFIT LIABILITIES

Air Canada maintains several defined benefit and defined contribution plans providing pension, other retirement and post-employment benefits to its employees…

The other employee benefits consist of health, life and disability. These benefits consist of both post-employment and post-retirement benefits. The post-employment benefits relate to disability benefits available to eligible active employees, while the post-retirement benefits are comprised of health care and life insurance benefits available to eligible retired employees.

Required:

Should ACE Aviation report a liability for these benefits on its balance sheet? Explain.

E11–26 **(Supplement A) Computing Value of an Asset Based on Present Value**

Quetario Company is considering purchasing a machine that would save the company $13,500 in cash per year for six years, at the end of which the machine would be retired with no salvage value. The firm wishes to earn a minimum of 12 percent interest, compounded annually, on any such investment. Assume that the cash savings occur at year-end and ignore taxes.

Required:

1. What is the maximum amount that the firm should be willing to pay for this machine? Show your computations.

2. Would the maximum amount be different if the machine is expected to have a salvage value of $4,000 at the end of six years? Explain.

3. As an alternative to the scenario in requirement 2, the company could buy a machine that had no salvage value and offered no cost savings for the first five years, but this machine would offer cost savings of $113,561 at the end of the sixth year. If the company can buy only one machine, which one should it be? Defend your answer.

E11–27 **(Supplement A) Reporting a Mortgage Note**

On January 1, 2009, Wong Corporation signed a mortgage note for $5,000,000 at 8 percent for a term of 5 years. Mortgage payments are made semi-annually on June 30 and on December 31. Each mortgage payment is a blend of interest on the unpaid amount and a partial repayment of the principal loan.

Required:

1. Compute the amount of each mortgage payment.

2. Record the mortgage payments on June 30, 2009 and on December 31, 2009.

3. What is the current portion of the mortgage at December 31, 2009? What portion of the mortgage would appear as long-term debt on the balance sheet at that same date?

PROBLEMS

P11–1 **Recording Issuance of Note and Computation of Interest** (AP11–1)   ■ **LO1, 2**

On October 20, 2006, RONA Inc, the Quebec-based retailer and distributor of hardware, home improvement and gardening products, sold debentures with the following specifications:

Principal amount:	$400 million
Maturity date:	October 20, 2016
Issue price:	99.792% of principal amount
Coupon rate:	5.40%
Interest payment dates:	Annually on January 20

The underwriters (Scotia Capital Inc., RBC Dominion Securities Inc., BMO Nesbitt Burns Inc., National Bank Financial Inc., and Desjardins Securities Inc.) that sold these debentures to investors received an underwriting fee of $3,000,000 and remitted to the company the net proceeds of $396,168,000 from the sale of these debentures. The effective interest rate on these debentures is 5.429 percent.

Required:

1. Prepare a journal entry to record the sale of these debentures on October 20, 2006.

2. Compute the interest expense that accrued from October 20, 2006 to December 31, 2006, the end of RONA's fiscal year, and prepare the adjusting journal entry on December 31, 2006 to record amortization of the discount on the debentures. Assume that the company uses the straight-line method of amortization.

3. Prepare the journal entry to record the payment of interest on January 20, 2007.

4. Show the amounts that should be reported on RONA's financial statements for the year 2006.

5. Compute the total amount of interest expense over the life of the debentures.

6. Assume that RONA uses the effective interest method of amortization. Would the bond interest expense for 2006 be different from the amount computed in requirement 2? If so, is the difference in interest expense computations a material amount? Explain.

7. After looking at the issue price, a student asked why RONA did not simply sell the debentures at 100 percent of the principal amount instead of selling them at a discount. How would you respond to this question?

■ LO1, 2

P11–2 Comparing Bonds Issued at Par, Discount, and Premium

Sikes Corporation, whose fiscal year ends on December 31, issued the following bonds:

Date of bonds: January 1, 2009.
Maturity amount and date: $10 million due in 10 years (December 31, 2018).
Interest: 10 percent per annum payable each December 31.
Date of sale: January 1, 2009.

Required:

1. Provide the following amounts to be reported on the 2009 financial statements (use straight-line amortization and show amounts in thousands):

	Issued at Par Case A	at 96 Case B	at 102 Case C
a. Interest expense	$	$	$
b. Bonds payable			
c. Unamortized premium or discount			
d. Net book value of bonds			
e. Stated rate of interest			
f. Cash paid for interest			

2. Explain why items (*a*) and (*f*) in requirement 1 are different for cases B and C.

3. Assume that you are an investment adviser and a retired person has written to you asking, "Why should I buy a bond at a premium when I can find one at a discount? Isn't that stupid? It's like paying the list price for a car instead of negotiating a discount." Write a brief letter in response to the question.

■ LO2, 3, 6

P11–3 Recording Bond Issuance and Interest Payment with Discussion of Management Strategy (AP11–2)

On March 1, 2008, Chung Corporation issued $40 million in bonds that mature in 10 years. The bonds have a stated interest rate of 8.2 percent and pay interest on March 1 and September 1. When the bonds were sold, the market rate of interest was 8 percent. Chung uses the effective-interest method. By December 31, 2008, the market interest rate had increased to 10 percent.

Required:

1. Record the issuance of the bond on March 1, 2008.

2. Record the payment of interest on September 1, 2008.

3. Record the adjusting entry for accrued interest on December 31, 2008.

4. As a manager of a company, would you prefer the straight-line method or the effective-interest method to amortize the bond discount or premium?

5. Determine the impact of these transactions at year-end on the financial leverage ratio and the times interest earned ratio.

■ LO2

P11–4 Completing Schedule Comparing Bonds Issued at Par, Discount, and Premium (AP11–3)

Quartz Corporation sold a $50 million, 7-percent bond issue on January 1, 2009. The bonds pay interest each December 31 and mature 10 years from January 1, 2009. For comparative study and analysis, assume three independent selling scenarios: Case A, bonds sold at par; Case B, bonds sold at 98; Case C, bonds sold at 102. Use straight-line amortization and disregard income tax unless specifically required.

Required:

1. Complete the following schedule to analyze the differences among the three cases.

	Case A (Par)	Case B (at 98)	Case C (at 102)

   a. Cash inflow at the date of issue (sale).
   b. Total cash outflow through the maturity date.
   c. Net cash outflow—total interest expense over
      the life of the bonds.
   d. Total interest expense, net of income tax
      (25 percent).

Income statement for 2009
   e. Bond interest expense.

Balance sheet at December 31, 2009, long-term liabilities
   f. Bonds payable, 7 percent.
   g. Unamortized discount.
   h. Unamortized premium.
   i. Net liability.

  2. For each case, explain why the amounts in items (*c*), (*d*), and (*e*) of requirement 1 are the same or different.

P11–5   Recording Bond Issuance and Interest Payments (Straight-Line Method) (AP11–4)   ■ **LO2**
West Company issued bonds with the following provisions:

Maturity value: $60,000,000.
Interest: 9 percent per annum payable semi-annually each June 30 and December 31.
Terms: Bonds dated January 1, 2008, due five years from that date.

The company's fiscal year ends on December 31. The bonds were sold on January 1, 2008, at a yield of 8 percent.

Required:

1. Compute the issue (sale) price of the bonds (show computations).

2. Prepare the journal entry to record the issuance of the bonds.

3. Prepare the journal entries at the following dates: June 30, 2008; December 31, 2008; and June 30, 2009. Use the straight-line method to amortize bond discount or premium.

4. How much interest expense would be reported on the income statement for 2008? Show how the liability related to the bonds should be reported on the balance sheet at December 31, 2008.

P11–6   Completing an Amortization Schedule (Effective-Interest Amortization)   ■ **LO2**
Berj Corporation issued bonds and received cash in full for the issue price. The bonds were dated and issued on January 1, 2007. The coupon rate was payable at the end of each year. The bonds mature at the end of four years. The following schedule has been partially completed (amounts in thousands):

Date	Cash	Interest	Amortization	Balance
January 1, 2007				$6,101
End of year 2007	$450	$427	$23	6,078
End of year 2008	450	?	?	6,053
End of year 2009	450	?	?	?
End of year 2010	450	?	?	6,000

Required:

1. Complete the amortization schedule.

2. What was the maturity amount of the bonds?

3. How much cash was received at the date of issuance (sale) of the bonds?

4. What was the amount of discount or premium on the bond?

5. How much cash will be disbursed for interest each period and in total for the full life of the bond issue?

6. What method of amortization is being used? Explain.

7. What is the coupon rate of interest?

8. What is the effective rate of interest?

9. What amount of interest expense should be reported on the income statement each year?

10. Show how the bonds should be reported on the balance sheet at the end of each year (show the last year immediately before repayment of the bonds).

11. Why is the method of amortization being used preferable to other methods? When must it be used?

■ **LO2**

P11–7 Computing Amounts for Bond Issue and Comparing Amortization Methods (AP11–5)

Dektronik Corporation manufactures electrical test equipment. The company's board of directors authorized a bond issue on January 1, 2007, with the following terms:

Maturity (par) value: $800,000.
Interest: 7.5 percent per annum payable each December 31.
Maturity date: December 31, 2011.
Effective-interest rate when sold: 8 percent.

Required:

1. Compute the bond issue price. Explain why both the stated and effective-interest rates are used in this computation.

2. Assume that the company used the straight-line method to amortize the discount or premium on the bond issue. Compute the following amounts for each year (2007–2011):
   a. Cash payment for bond interest.
   b. Amortization of bond discount or premium.
   c. Bond interest expense.
   d. Net book value of the bond.
   e. Interest expense as a percentage of net book value (item [*c*] ÷ item [*d*]).
   f. The straight-line method is theoretically deficient when interest expense is related to the net book value of the debt. Explain.

3. Assume instead that the company used the effective-interest method to amortize the discount or premium. Prepare an effective-interest bond amortization schedule similar to the one in the text (see p. 581). The effective-interest method provides a constant interest rate when interest expense is related to the net book value (unpaid balance). Explain by referring to the bond amortization schedule.

4. Which method should the company use to amortize the bond discount or premium? As a financial analyst, would you prefer one method over the other? If so, why?

■ **LO1, 2**

P11–8 Recording Issuance of Bonds and Related Interest Expense

Rothmans, Benson and Hedges (RBH), is a Canadian company that produces tobacco products. The company's annual report for 2005 included the following information in a note to its financial statements.

REAL WORLD EXCERPT

Rothmans Inc.

ANNUAL REPORT

7. Long-term debt

During the fiscal year 2005, RBH issued a total of $150.0 million of senior, unsecured bonds through a private placement. On December 21, 2004, $97.0 million of bonds carrying a coupon rate of 5.552% payable semi-annually were issued. Under the same terms and conditions as the December 21, 2004 debt issue, an additional $53.0 million of bonds at a discount of $0.3 million to their face value were issued on January 13, 2005. The proceeds from the issuance of these bonds were used to fully repay the Company's floating rate credit facility.

These bonds mature on December 21, 2011 and their principal is repayable in full at maturity without amortization... Under this debt obligation, RBH is subject to certain covenants, including a maximum debt to EBITDA ratio of 3.0 times on a consolidated basis. RBH has the right to repay the bonds at any time in whole or in part, subject to certain "make-whole" provisions.

Required:

1. Prepare the journal entries to record the issuance of the two bonds on December 21, 2004, and January 13, 2005.

2. Compute the interest that accrued on these bonds from the date of issuance until March 31, 2005, the end of RBH's fiscal year.

3. Prepare the journal entries at March 31, 2005 to record the accrued interest expense and the related amortization of bond discount using the straight-line method of amortization.

4. Like most bond issues, RBH's debt obligation is subject to certain covenants. Explain what bond covenants mean and the purpose they serve in lending agreements?

P11–9 Understanding the Early Retirement of Debt (AP11–6)

AMC Entertainment Inc., owns and operates movie theatres. The company sold $11\frac{7}{8}$ percent bonds for $52,750,000 and used the cash proceeds to retire bonds with a face value of $50,000,000 with a coupon rate of 13.6 percent. At that time, the old bonds had a book value of $49,547,000.

Required:

1. Why did the company issue new bonds to retire the old bonds?

2. Prepare the journal entries to record the issuance of the new bonds and the early retirement of the old bonds.

3. How should AMC report the gain or loss on retirement of the old bonds?

P11–10 (Supplement A) Comparing Options Using Present Value Concepts (AP11–7)

After hearing a knock at your front door, you are surprised to see the Prize Patrol from a large, well-known magazine subscription company. It has arrived with the good news that you are the big winner, having won $20 million. Later, after consulting with a lawyer, you discover that you have three options: (1) you can receive $1 million per year for the next 20 years (starting one year from now), (2) you can have $8 million today, or (3) you can have $2 million today and receive $700,000 for each of the next 20 years. Your investment adviser tells you that it is reasonable to expect to earn 10 percent compound interest on investments. Which option do you prefer? What factors influence your decision?

P11–11 (Supplement A) Computing Equal Periodic Debt Payments and Completing a Schedule (AP11–8)

On January 1, 2008, you bought a new Toyota Corolla automobile for $24,000. You made a $5,000 cash down payment and signed a $19,000 note, payable in four equal instalments on each December 31; the first payment to be made on December 31, 2008. The interest rate is 12 percent per year on the unpaid balance. Each payment will include payment on principal plus the interest.

Required:

1. Compute the amount of the equal payments that you must make.

2. What is the total amount of interest that you will pay during the four years?

3. Complete the following schedule:

Debt Payment Schedule				
Date	Cash Payment	Interest Expense	Decrease in Principal	Unpaid Principal
1/1/2008				
12/31/2008				
12/31/2009				
12/31/2010				
12/31/2011				
Totals				

4. Explain why the amount of interest expense decreases each year.

5. To reduce the total amount of interest paid on this note, you considered the possibility of making equal payments every three months (four payments per year). Compute the amount of the equal payments that you must make, and the amount of interest that will be saved over the life of the note.

P11–12 (Supplement A) Computing Amounts for a Debt Fund with Journal Entries

On December 31, 2007, Post Company set aside in a fund the cash to pay the principal amount of a $160,000 debt due on December 31, 2010. The company will make four equal annual deposits on December 31 of the years 2007 through 2010. The fund will earn 7 percent compound annual interest, which will be added to the balance at each year-end. The fund trustee will pay the loan principal (to the creditor) upon receipt of the last fund deposit. The company's fiscal year ends on December 31.

Required (show computations and round to the nearest dollar):

1. How much cash must be deposited each December 31?

2. What amount of interest will be earned on the four deposits until December 31, 2010?

3. How much interest revenue will the fund earn each year?

4. Prepare journal entries for the company to record the following transactions:
   a. The first deposit on December 31, 2007.
   b. The deposit at December 31, 2008 and interest revenue for 2008.
   c. The payment of the debt on December 31, 2010.

5. Show how the effect of the fund will be reported on the income statement for 2008 and the balance sheet at December 31, 2008.

ALTERNATE PROBLEMS

■ **LO1, 2** **AP11–1 Recording Issuance of Note and Computation of Interest** (P11–1)

Shaw Communications Inc., is a diversified Canadian communications company that provides cable television, Internet, digital phone, telecommunications and satellite direct-to-home services to more than 3 million customers. On March 1, 2007, the company sold long-term notes with the following specifications:

Principal amount:	$400 million
Maturity date:	March 1, 2017
Issue price:	99.767% of principal amount
Coupon rate:	5.70%
Interest payment dates:	March 1 and September 1

The underwriters (TD Securities Inc., RBC Dominion Securities Inc., CIBC World Markets Inc., Scotia Capital Inc., GMP Securities L.P., Merrill Lynch Canada Inc., and National Bank Financial Inc.) that sold these notes to investors received an underwriting fee of $3,812,500 and remitted to the company the net proceeds of $395,255,500 from the sale of these notes. The effective interest rate on these notes is 5.731 percent.

Required:

1. Prepare the journal entries to record the payment of interest on September 1, 2007, and the amortization of the discount on the notes. The company uses the straight-line method to amortize the discount.

2. Compute the interest expense that accrued from September 1, 2007 to December 31, 2007, the end of Shaw's fiscal year, and prepare the adjusting journal entries on December 31, 2007 to record amortization of the discount on the notes.

3. Prepare the journal entry to record the payment of interest on March 1, 2008.

4. Show the amounts that should be reported on Shaw's financial statements for the year 2007.

5. Compute the total amount of interest expense over the life of the notes.

6. Assume that Shaw uses the effective interest method of amortization. Would the interest expense for 2007 be different from the amount computed in requirement 4? Show your calculations. Is the difference in interest expense computations a material amount? Explain.

7. As a manager of a company, would you prefer the straight-line method or the effective-interest method to amortize the bond discount or premium?

8. After looking at the issue price, a student asked why the management of Shaw Communications did not simply sell the notes at 100 percent of the principal amount instead of selling them at a discount. How would you respond to this question?

■ **LO2** **AP11–2 Using the Effective-Interest Method with Discussion of Management Strategy** (P11–3)

On March 1, 2009, Carter Corporation issued $5,000,000 in bonds that mature in 10 years. The bonds have a coupon rate of 6.3 percent and pay interest on March 1 and September 1.

When the bonds were sold, the market rate of interest was 6 percent. Carter uses the effective-interest method to amortize bond discount or premium. By December 31, 2009, the market interest rate of interest had increased to 7 percent.

Required:

1. Record the issuance of the bond on March 1, 2009.

2. Record the payment of interest on September 1, 2009.

3. Record the adjusting entry for accrued interest on December 31, 2009.

4. As a manager of a company, would you prefer the straight-line or the effective-interest method of amortization?

5. Determine the impact of these transactions at year-end on the financial leverage ratio and the times interest earned ratio.

AP11–3 **Completing a Schedule That Involves a Comprehensive Review of the Issuance of Bonds at Par, Discount, and Premium, Including Cash Flows (P11–4)**

■ LO2, 7

On January 1, 2007, Ontec Corporation sold and issued $100 million, five-year, 10-percent bonds. The bond interest is payable annually each December 31. Assume three separate and independent selling scenarios: Case A, bonds sold at par; Case B, bonds sold at 90; and Case C, bonds sold at 110.

Required:

1. Complete a schedule similar to the following for each separate case, assuming straight-line amortization of discount and premium. Disregard income tax. Show all dollar amounts in millions.

						At End of 2011	
	At Start of 2007	At End of 2007	At End of 2008	At End of 2009	At End of 2010	Prior to Payment of Principal	Payment of Principal
Case A: sold at par (100)	$	$	$	$	$	$	$
Cash inflow							
Cash outflow							
Interest expense on income statement							
Net book value on balance sheet							
Case B: sold at a discount (90)							
Cash inflow							
Cash outflow							
Interest expense on income statement							
Net book value on balance sheet							
Case C: sold at a premium (110)							
Cash inflow							
Cash outflow							
Interest expense on income statement							
Net book value on balance sheet							

2. For each separate case, calculate each of the following:

   a. Total cash outflow.

   b. Total cash inflow.

   c. Net cash outflow.

   d. Total interest expense over the life of the bonds.

3. *a.* Explain why the net cash outflows differ among the three cases.

   b. For each case, explain why the net cash outflow is the same as total interest expense.

■ **LO2**

AP11–4 Computing Issue Price of Bonds and Recording Issuance and Interest Payments (P11–5)

Jaymar Company issued bonds with the following provisions:

> **Maturity value: $100,000,000.**
> Interest: 9 percent per annum payable semi-annually each June 30 and December 31.
> Terms: Bonds dated January 1, 2009, due 10 years from that date.

The company's fiscal year ends on December 31. The bonds were sold on January 1, 2009, at a yield of 10 percent.

Required:

1. Compute the issue (sale) price of the bonds (show computations).
2. Prepare the journal entry to record the issuance of the bonds.
3. Prepare the journal entries at the following dates: June 30, 2009; December 31, 2009; and June 30, 2010. Use the straight-line method to amortize bond discount or premium.
4. How much interest expense would be reported on the income statement for 2009? Show how the liability related to the bonds should be reported on the balance sheet at December 31, 2009.

■ **LO2**

AP11–5 Straight-Line versus Effective-Interest Methods of Amortizing Bond Discount, with Discussion (P11–7)

Canadian Products Corporation manufactures office equipment and supplies. The company authorized a bond issue on January 1, 2007, with the following terms:

> **Maturity (par) value: $120,000,000.**
> Interest: 7.9 percent per annum payable each December 31.
> Maturity date: December 31, 2011.
> Effective-interest rate when sold: 8 percent.

Required:

1. Compute the bond issue price. Explain why both the stated and effective-interest rates are used in this computation.
2. Prepare the entry to record this bond issue.
3. Assume that the company used the straight-line method to amortize the discount or premium on the bond issue. Compute the following amounts for each year (2007–2011):
   a. Interest paid.
   b. Amortization of bond discount or premium.
   c. Bond interest expense.
   d. Net book value of the bond.
   e. Interest expense as a percentage of the net book value (item [*c*] ÷ item [*d*]).
   f. The straight-line method is theoretically deficient when interest expense is related to the net book value of the debt. Explain.
4. Assume instead that the company used the effective-interest method to amortize the discount or premium. Prepare an effective-interest bond amortization schedule similar to the one in the text (see p. 581). The effective-interest method provides a constant interest rate when interest expense is related to the net liability. Explain by referring to the bond amortization schedule.
5. Which method should the company use to amortize the bond discount or premium? As a financial analyst, would you prefer one method over the other? If so, why?

■ **LO1, 4**

AP11–6 Understanding the Difference between Carrying Value and Market Value (P11–9)

Quaker Oats is a well-known name at most breakfast tables. The company does more than $6 billion in sales revenue each year. The Quaker annual report contained the following information concerning long-term debt:

REAL WORLD EXCERPT

Quaker Oats

ANNUAL REPORT

Long-Term Debt

The fair value of long-term debt was $779.7 million at the end of the current fiscal year, which was based on market prices for the same or similar issues or on the current rates offered to the Company for similar debt of the same maturities. The carrying value of long-term debt as of the same date was $759.5 million.

Required:

What is meant by "fair value"? Explain why there is a difference between the carrying value and the fair value of the long-term debt for Quaker Oats. Assume that Quaker Oats decided to retire all of its long-term debt for cash (a very unlikely event). Prepare the journal entry to record the transaction.

AP11–7 (Supplement A) Comparing Options Using Present Value Concepts (P11–10)

After completing a long and successful career as senior vice-president for a large bank, you are preparing for retirement. After visiting the human resources office, you have found that you have several retirement options: (1) you can receive an immediate cash payment of $600,000, (2) you can receive $60,000 per year for life (you have a life expectancy of 20 years), or (3) you can receive $50,000 per year for 10 years and then $70,000 per year for life (this option is intended to give you some protection against inflation). You have determined that you can earn 8 percent compounded annually on your investments. Which option do you prefer and why?

AP11–8 (Supplement A) Computing Equal Periodic Debt Payments and Completing a Schedule with Journal Entries (P11–11)

On January 1, 2008, Ontario Company sold a new machine to Canada Company for $80,000. Canada Company made a cash down payment of $20,000 and signed a $60,000, 8-percent note for the balance due. The note is payable in three equal instalments due on December 31, 2008, 2009, and 2010. Each payment includes principal plus interest on the unpaid balance. Canada Company recorded the purchase as follows:

Jan.1, 2008

Machinery	80,000
Cash	20,000
Note payable	60,000

Required (show computations and round to the nearest dollar):

1. What is the amount of the equal annual payments that Canada Company must make?
2. What is the total interest on the note over the three years?
3. Complete the following debt payment schedule:

Date	Cash Payment	Interest Expense	Decrease in Principal	Unpaid Principal
1/1/2008				
12/31/2008				
12/31/2009				
12/31/2010				
Total				

4. Prepare the journal entries for each of the three payments.
5. Explain why interest expense decreased in amount each year.

CASES AND PROJECTS

FINDING AND INTERPRETING FINANCIAL INFORMATION

CP11–1 Finding Financial Information

Refer to the financial statements of Van Houtte Inc. given in Appendix B of this book.

LO2, 7

Van Houtte

Required:

1. How much cash was paid for interest during the fiscal year ended March 31, 2007?
2. Review the company's note on long-term debt and identify the characteristics of each debt issue.
3. Describe the company's established arrangements, if any, that permit it to borrow money if needed.
4. Does the company report other long-term liabilities? If so, identify these liabilities.

■ **LO2, 7**   **CP11–2**   **Finding Financial Information**

The Forzani
Group Ltd.

Refer to the financial statements of The Forzani Group Limited provided on the Web site **www.mcgrawhill.ca/olc/libby/student/resources**.

Required:

1. How much cash was paid for interest during the fiscal year ended January 28, 2007?

2. Review the company's note on long-term debt and identify the characteristics of each debt issue.

3. Describe the company's established arrangements, if any, that permit it to borrow money if needed.

■ **LO1, 3, 6**   **CP11–3**   **Comparing Companies**

Van Houtte vs.
The Forzani
Group Ltd.

ANALYSIS

Refer to the Online Learning Centre Web site at **www.mcgrawhill.ca/olc/libby/student/resources** for the financial statements of The Forzani Group Ltd. and to Appendix B of this textbook for the financial statements of Van Houtte Inc.

Required:

1. Examine the cash flow statements for both companies. What are the primary sources of cash flow for both companies?

2. Two financial ratios (the financial leverage ratio and the times interest earned ratio) are discussed in this chapter. Are they relevant for these companies? Explain.

FINANCIAL REPORTING AND ANALYSIS CASES

■ **LO1**   **CP11–4**   **Analyzing Financial Leverage**

ANALYSIS

Cricket Corporation's financial statements for 2008 showed the following:

Income Statement	
Revenues	$300,000
Expenses	(198,000)
Interest expense	(2,000)
Pretax income	100,000
Income tax (30%)	(30,000)
Net income	$ 70,000
Balance Sheet	
Assets	$300,000
Liabilities (average interest rate, 10%)	$ 20,000
Share capital	200,000
Retained earnings	80,000
	$300,000

Notice that the company had a debt of only $20,000 compared with share capital of $200,000. A consultant recommended the following: debt, $100,000 (at 10 percent) instead of $20,000 and share capital of $120,000 (12,000 shares) instead of $200,000 (20,000 shares). That is, the company should finance the business with more debt and less owner contribution.

Required (round to nearest percent):

1. You have been asked to develop a comparison between (a) the actual results and (b) the results based on the consultant's recommendation. To do this, you decided to develop the following schedule:

Item	Actual Results for 2008	Results with an $80,000 Increase in Debt

    a. Total debt.
    b. Total assets.
    c. Total shareholders' equity.
    d. Interest expense.
    e. Net income.
    f. Return on total assets.
    g. Earnings available to shareholders:
        (1) Amount.
        (2) Per share.
        (3) Return on shareholders' equity.

2. Based on the completed schedule in requirement 1, provide a comparative analysis and interpretation of the actual results and the consultant's recommendation.

CP11–5 Analyzing Zero Coupon Bonds from an Actual Company

In July 2001, Shaw Communications issued a convertible zero coupon debt and raised $790 million. The debt is called a *liquid yield option note* or LYON. The LYONs were issued at $639.23 per $1,000 and the maturity date is May 1, 2021. The yield to maturity is 2.25 percent over 20 years. The LYONs are both redeemable after May 1, 2007, and convertible by the holders at any time into 8.82988 common shares per LYON. When this debt was issued, the yield ranged between 6 and 7 percent. A magazine article has noted, "It's easy to see why corporations like to issue debt that does not pay interest. But why would anybody want to buy that kind of paper?"

■ LO1

Shaw Communications Inc.

ANALYSIS

Required:
Explain why an investor would buy a LYON with a zero interest rate.

CP11–6 Explaining Bond Premiums and Effective-Interest Rate Amortization

Times Company issued a $100-million bond with a stated interest rate of 6.3 percent. When the bond was issued, the market rate was 6 percent. The bond matures in 10 years and pays interest on December 31 each year. The bond was issued on January 1, 2007.

■ LO2

Required:

1. Compute the present value of the difference between the interest paid each year ($6.3 million) and the interest demanded by the market ($100 million × 6% = $6 million). Use the market rate of interest and the 10-year life of the bond in your present value computation. What does this amount represent? Explain.

2. Why does interest expense change each year when the effective-interest method is used?

3. Compute the present value of the Times Company bonds, assuming that they had a 7-year life instead of 10-year life. Compare this amount to the net book value of the bond at the end of year 2009. What does this comparison demonstrate?

CP11–7 Interpreting the Financial Press

In this chapter, we talked about bonds primarily from the perspective of the issuing corporation. To understand bonds, it is also necessary to develop an understanding of why investors buy bonds. An article on this topic is available on the Web site at **www.mcgrawhill.ca/olc/libby/student/resources**. You should read the article, "It's Time for Bonds to Get Some Respect,"* and then write a short memo summarizing the article in your own words. What type of investors are interested in buying bonds? Describe the impact of inflation on bonds.

■ LO1

CP11–8 International Financing

Access the Web site of Bombardier Inc. at **www.bombardier.ca** and retrieve the most recent annual report. The note related to long-term debt discloses that Bombardier has borrowed money in a currency other than the dollar. Write a brief memo explaining why the company borrowed money in a foreign currency.

■ LO1

---

*"It's Time for Bonds to Get Some Respect," Reprinted from January 19, 1998 issue of *BusinessWeek* by special permission, copyright © 1998 by The McGraw Hill Companies, Inc.

CRITICAL THINKING CASES

LO1   **CP11–9 Making a Decision as a Financial Analyst**

You are working for a large mutual fund company as a financial analyst. You have been asked to review two competitive companies in the same industry. Both have similar cash flows and net income, but one has no debt in its capital structure and the other has a financial leverage ratio of 3.2. Based on this limited information, which would you prefer? Justify your conclusion. Would your preference be influenced by the companies' industry?

LO1   **CP11–10 Evaluating an Ethical Dilemma**

You work for a small company considering investing in a new Internet business. Financial projections suggest that the company will be able to earn in excess of $40 million per year on an investment of $100 million. The company president suggests borrowing the money by issuing bonds that will carry a 7-percent interest rate. He says, "This is better than printing money! We won't have to invest a penny of our own money, and we get to keep $33 million per year after we pay interest to the bondholders." As you think about the proposed transaction, you feel a little uncomfortable about taking advantage of the creditors in this fashion. You feel that it must be wrong to earn such a high return by using money that belongs to other people. Is this an ethical business transaction?

LO1   **CP11–11 Evaluating an Ethical Dilemma**

Many retired people invest a significant portion of their money in bonds of corporations because of their relatively low level of risk. During the 1980s, significant inflation caused some interest rates to rise to as high as 15 percent. Retired people who bought bonds that paid only 6 percent continued to earn at the lower rate. During the 1990s, inflation subsided and interest rates declined. Many corporations took advantage of call options on bonds and refinanced high interest rate debt with low interest rate debt. In your judgment, is it ethical for corporations to continue paying low interest rates when rates increase but to call bonds when rates decrease?

LO1   **CP11–12 Evaluating an Ethical Dilemma**

Assume that you are a portfolio manager for a large insurance company. The majority of the money you manage is from retired school teachers who depend on the income you earn on their investments. You have invested a significant amount of money in the bonds of a large corporation and have just received a call from the company's president explaining that it is unable to meet its current interest obligations because of deteriorating business operations related to increased international competition. The president has a recovery plan that will take at least two years. During that time, the company will not be able to pay interest on the bonds and, she admits, if the plan does not work, bondholders will probably lose more than half of their money. As a creditor, you can force the company into immediate bankruptcy and probably get back at least 90 percent of the bondholders' money. You also know that your decision will cause at least 10,000 people to lose their jobs if the company ceases operations. Given only these two options, what should you do?

CP11–13 (Supplement A) Computing the Present Value of Lease Obligations

Petro-Canada

The 2006 annual report for Petro-Canada indicated that the company has made the following commitments in relation to non-cancellable operating leases during the next five years:

Years	Minimum Payments (in millions)
2007	492
2008	140
2009	100
2010	90
2011	75

You are a lending officer for a large commercial bank and for comparative purposes want to compute the present values of these leases.

Required:

Determine the present value of the lease payments shown as of December 31, 2006. You may assume an interest rate of 7 percent.

CP11–14 (Supplement A) Evaluating an Ethical Dilemma: Fair Advertising

The New York State Lottery Commission ran the following advertisement in a number of New York newspapers:

> The Lotto jackpot for Wednesday, August 25, 1999, will be $3 million including interest earned over a 20-year payment period. Constant payments will be made each year.

Explain the meaning of this advertisement in your own words. Evaluate the "fairness" of this advertisement. Could anyone be misled? Do you agree that the lottery winner has won $3 million? If not, what amount is more accurate? State any assumptions that you make.

FINANCIAL REPORTING AND ANALYSIS TEAM PROJECT

CP11–15 Team Project: Examining an Annual Report

As a team, select an industry to analyze. Each group member should acquire the annual report for one publicly traded company in the industry, with each member selecting a different company. (Library files, the SEDAR service at **www.sedar.com**, and the company itself are good sources.)

■ **LO1, 2, 3, 6, 7**

ANALYSIS

Required:

On an individual basis, each team member should then write a short report answering the following questions about the selected company. Discuss any patterns across the companies that you as a team observe. Then, as a group, write a short report comparing and contrasting your companies.

1. Has your company issued any long-term bonds or notes? If so, read the related note and list any unusual features (e.g., callable, convertible, secured by specific collateral).

2. If your company issued any bonds, were they issued at either a premium or a discount? If so, does the company use the straight-line or effective-interest amortization method?

3. Ratio analysis:
   a. What does the times interest earned ratio measure in general?
   b. Compute the ratio for the last three years.
   c. What do your results suggest about the company?
   d. If available, find the industry ratio for the most recent year, compare it to your results, and discuss why you believe your company differs or is similar to the industry ratio.

4. Ratio analysis:
   a. What does the financial leverage ratio measure in general?
   b. Compute the ratio for the last three years.
   c. What do your results suggest about the company?
   d. If available, find the industry ratio for the most recent year, compare it to your results, and discuss why you believe your company differs or is similar to the industry ratio.

5. During the recent year, how much cash did the company receive on issuing debt? How much did it pay on debt principal? What does management suggest were the reasons for issuing and/or repaying debt during the year?

Reporting and Interpreting Owners' Equity

12

After studying this chapter, you should be able to:

FOCUS COMPANY:

Sun Life Financial Inc.

FINANCING CORPORATE GROWTH WITH CAPITAL SUPPLIED BY OWNERS

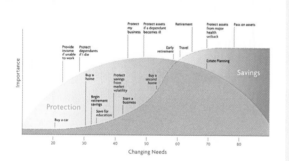

un Life Financial (**www.sunlife.com**) is a leading international financial services organization providing a diverse range of protection and wealth accumulation products and services to individuals and corporate customers. Chartered in 1865, Sun Life Financial and its partners have operations in key markets worldwide, including Canada, the United States, the United Kingdom, Ireland, Hong Kong, the Philippines, Japan, Indonesia, India, China, and Bermuda.

Expansion of the company's activities over the years led to an initial public offering of its shares in 2000. Investors who bought the company's common shares when it first went public have benefited from its rapid growth. To achieve this level of success, Sun Life's management needed to develop and execute a sound business strategy. Equally important, however, is management's ability to develop a solid capital structure with which to finance the company's growth. In this chapter, we study the role that shareholders' equity plays in building a successful business.

UNDERSTANDING THE BUSINESS

To some people, the words *corporation* and *business* are almost synonymous. You have probably heard friends refer to a career in business as "the corporate world." Equating business and corporations is understandable because corporations are the dominant form of business organization in terms of volume of operations. If you were to write the names of 50 familiar companies on a piece of paper, probably all of them would be corporations.

The popularity of the corporate form can be attributed to a critical advantage that corporations have over sole proprietorships and partnerships. They can raise large amounts of capital because both large and small investors can easily participate in their ownership. This ease of participation is related to three important factors:

- Shares can be purchased in small amounts. You could buy a single share of Sun Life for approximately $50 and become one of the owners of this company.

- Ownership interest can easily be transferred through the sale of shares on established markets such as the Toronto Stock Exchange.

- Stock ownership provides investors with limited liability.[1]

Many Canadians own shares, either directly or indirectly through a mutual fund or pension program. Share ownership offers them the opportunity to earn higher returns than they could on deposits to bank accounts or investments in corporate bonds. Unfortunately, share ownership also involves higher risk. The proper balance between risk and the expected return on an investment depends on individual preferences.

Exhibit 12.1 presents the shareholders' equity section of Sun Life's balance sheet, as well as consolidated statements of retained earnings. We use this exhibit to illustrate our discussion of shareholders' equity.

EXHIBIT **12.1**

Shareholders' Equity Sections of Consolidated Balance Sheets and Statements of Retained Earnings

REAL WORLD EXCERPT

Sun Life Financial Inc.

ANNUAL REPORT

PARTIAL CONSOLIDATED BALANCE SHEETS
At December 31, 2006 and 2005

($ millions)	2006	2005
Shareholders' Equity		
Preferred shares (Note 15)	1,250	712
Common shares (Note 18)	7,082	7,173
Contributed surplus (Note 18)	72	66
Retained earnings	10,117	9,095
Currency translation adjustment (Note 22)	(1,337)	(1,500)
Total shareholders' equity	17,184	15,546

This excerpt is adapted from the company's actual balance sheets.

CONSOLIDATED STATEMENTS OF RETAINED EARNINGS
For the year ended December 31

(in $ millions)	2006	2005
Balance, beginning of year	9,095	8,204
Net income	2,144	1,876
Dividends on common shares	(663)	(581)
Dividends on preferred shares	(48)	(24)
Common shares purchased for cancellation	(411)	(380)
Balance, end of year	10,117	9,095

This excerpt is adapted from the company's actual statement of retained earnings.

---

[1] If a corporation becomes insolvent, creditors have recourse for their claims only to the corporation's assets. Thus, shareholders stand to lose only their equity in the corporation. In the case of a partnership or sole proprietorship, creditors have recourse to the owners' personal assets if the assets of the business are insufficient to meet its debts.

The shareholders' equity section of Sun Life's balance sheet reports five different accounts, as shown in Exhibit 12.1. These accounts represent the two primary sources of shareholders' equity:

1. *Contributed capital*, which reflects the amount invested by shareholders. Contributed capital has two distinct components: (a) amounts initially received from the sale of shares, and (b) contributed surplus that reflects contributions made by shareholders in excess of the amounts credited to share capital accounts. The contributed capital accounts for Sun Life are preferred shares, common shares, and contributed surplus. (The account *currency translation adjustment* relates to transactions involving foreign currencies, which are discussed in advanced accounting courses.)

2. *Retained earnings* generated by the profit-making activities of the company. This is the *cumulative* amount of net income earned since the organization of the corporation less the cumulative amount of dividends paid by the corporation since organization.

Most companies generate a significant part of their shareholders' equity from retained earnings rather than from capital raised through the sale of shares. In the case of Sun Life, its retained earnings exceeded its contributed capital at December 31, 2006.

ORGANIZATION OF THE CHAPTER

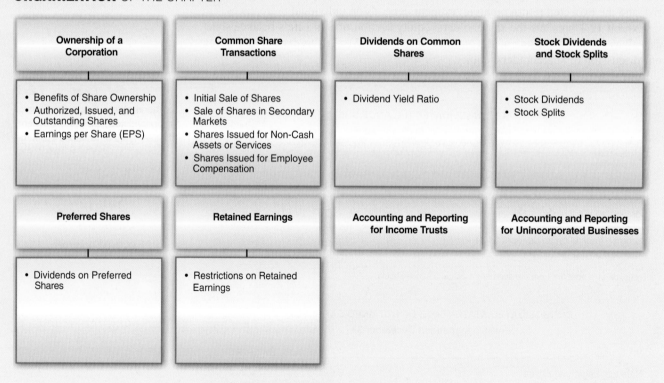

Ownership of a Corporation	Common Share Transactions	Dividends on Common Shares	Stock Dividends and Stock Splits
• Benefits of Share Ownership • Authorized, Issued, and Outstanding Shares • Earnings per Share (EPS)	• Initial Sale of Shares • Sale of Shares in Secondary Markets • Shares Issued for Non-Cash Assets or Services • Shares Issued for Employee Compensation	• Dividend Yield Ratio	• Stock Dividends • Stock Splits

Preferred Shares	Retained Earnings	Accounting and Reporting for Income Trusts	Accounting and Reporting for Unincorporated Businesses
• Dividends on Preferred Shares	• Restrictions on Retained Earnings		

OWNERSHIP OF A CORPORATION

The corporation is the only business form that the law recognizes as a separate entity. As a distinct entity, the corporation enjoys a continuous existence separate and apart from its owners. It may own assets, incur liabilities, expand and contract in size, sue others, be sued, and enter into contracts independently of the shareholders.

To protect everyone's rights, the creation and governance of corporations are tightly regulated by law. Corporations are created by making application to the federal government or a specific provincial government. The Canada Business Corporations

Act (CBCA) outlines all of the legal requirements of federal incorporation (**www.laws. justice.gc.ca**).

To create a corporation, an application for a charter must be submitted to the appropriate government authorities. The application must specify the name of the corporation, the purpose (type of business), the types and number of shares authorized, and a minimum amount of capital that the owners must invest at the date of organization. Upon approval of the application, the government issues a charter, sometimes called the *articles of incorporation*. Each corporation is governed by a board of directors elected by the shareholders.

BENEFITS OF SHARE OWNERSHIP

When you invest in a corporation, you are known as a *shareholder* or *stockholder*. As a shareholder, you receive shares that you can subsequently sell on established stock exchanges without affecting the corporation. The share certificate states the name of the shareholder, date of purchase, type of shares, number of shares represented, and their characteristics. The back of the certificate has instructions and a form to be completed when the shares are sold or transferred to another party.

Owners of common shares receive the following benefits:

1. **A voice in management.** You may vote at the shareholders' meeting (or by proxy) on major issues concerning management of the corporation.[2]

2. **Dividends.** You receive a proportionate share of the distribution of the corporation's profits.

3. **Residual claim.** You may receive a proportionate share of the distribution of remaining assets upon the liquidation of the company.

Owners, unlike creditors, are able to vote at the annual shareholders' meeting. The following notice of annual and special meeting of shareholders was sent to all shareholders of Sun Life in May 2007.

> **SUN LIFE FINANCIAL INC**
> **Notice of Annual Meeting**
> **May 9, 2007**
>
> The Annual meeting of Common Shareholders of Sun Life Financial Inc. will be held at The Carlu, 444 Yonge Street (at College Street), 7th Floor, Toronto, Ontario, Canada on Wednesday, May 9, 2007 at 10:00 a.m. (Toronto time), for the following purposes:
>
> 1. to receive the consolidated financial statements of Sun Life Financial Inc. for the year ended December 31, 2006, together with the reports of the auditor and the actuary on those statements;
> 2. to elect directors;
> 3. to appoint an auditor;
> 4. to consider a proposal submitted by a shareholder as set out in Schedule C of the attached Management Information Circular; and
> 5. to transact such other business as may properly be brought before the meeting or any continuation of the meeting after an adjournment.
>
> The meeting will be held at the same time in the same place as the annual meeting of Sun Life Assurance Company of Canada. The Management Information Circular, which follows this Notice of Annual Meeting, is your guide to understanding the business that will be dealt with at the meeting.
>
> The number of eligible votes that may be cast at the meeting as of March 16, 2007 is 572,181,386. If you were a shareholder of record at the close of business on March 16, 2007 you are entitled to receive notice of and to vote at the meeting. If you cannot attend the meeting, please vote by completing the form of proxy and returning

LEARNING OBJECTIVE 1

Explain the role of share capital in the capital structure of a corporation.

REAL WORLD EXCERPT

Sun Life Financial Inc.

NOTICE OF SHAREHOLDERS' ANNUAL AND SPECIAL MEETING

---

[2]A voting proxy is written authority given by a shareholder that gives another party the right to vote the shareholder's shares in the annual meeting of the shareholders. Typically, proxies are solicited by, and given to, the president of the corporation.

it in the envelope provided or faxing it to 416-368-2502. For your vote to be recorded your proxy form must be received no later than 5:00 p.m. (Toronto time) on Monday, May 7, 2007 by our transfer agent, CIBC Mellon Trust Company, or its co-agents. For further information please see the section entitled How to Vote Your Shares in the accompanying Management Information Circular.

If the meeting is adjourned, your proxy form must be received as described above no later than 5:00 p.m. (Toronto time) on the second business day before the meeting is reconvened.

By order of the Board of Directors

Signed
Joan M. Wilson
Vice-President and Corporate Secretary
March 16, 2007

The notice of the annual meeting was accompanied by a *management information circular* that contained several pages of information concerning the people who were nominated to be members of the board of directors. Since most owners do not actually attend the annual meeting, the notice included a proxy card, which is similar to an absentee ballot. Each owner may complete the proxy and mail it to the company, which will include it in the votes at the annual meeting.

Shareholders have ultimate authority in a corporation, as shown in Exhibit 12.2. The board of directors and, indirectly, all the employees are accountable to the shareholders. The organizational structure shown in Exhibit 12.2 is typical of most corporations, but the specific structure depends on the nature of the company's business.

AUTHORIZED, ISSUED, AND OUTSTANDING SHARES

When a corporation is created, its corporate charter specifies the type and maximum number of shares that it can sell to the public. This maximum is called the **authorized number of shares**. Typically, the corporate charter authorizes a larger number of shares than the corporation expects to issue initially. This strategy provides future flexibility for the issuance of additional shares without the need to amend the charter. In the case of Sun Life, the number of authorized common shares is unlimited.[3]

The number of **issued shares** and the number of **outstanding shares** are determined by the corporation's equity transactions. For Sun Life, the number of issued shares and of outstanding shares is the same; at December 31, 2006, this number was 577 million. The number of issued shares may differ from the number of outstanding shares if the company has bought back some of its shares from shareholders. If a corporation needs to sell more shares than its charter authorizes, it must seek permission from the current shareholders to modify the charter.

Exhibit 12.3 defines and illustrates the terms usually used in relation to corporate shares.

The **AUTHORIZED NUMBER OF SHARES** is the maximum number of shares that a corporation can issue, as specified in the charter.

The term **ISSUED SHARES** refers to the number of shares that have been issued.

The term **OUTSTANDING SHARES** refers to the total number of shares that are owned by shareholders on any particular date.

---

[3]Of the 200 companies surveyed in *Financial Reporting in Canada 2006,* 174 corporations have charters that authorize them to issue an unlimited number of shares. N. Chlala, A. Lavigne, L. Martel, and C. Byrd, *Financial Reporting in Canada 2006.* Toronto: Canadian Institute of Chartered Accountants, 2006, p. 353.

EXHIBIT **12.2**

Typical Organizational Structure of a Corporation

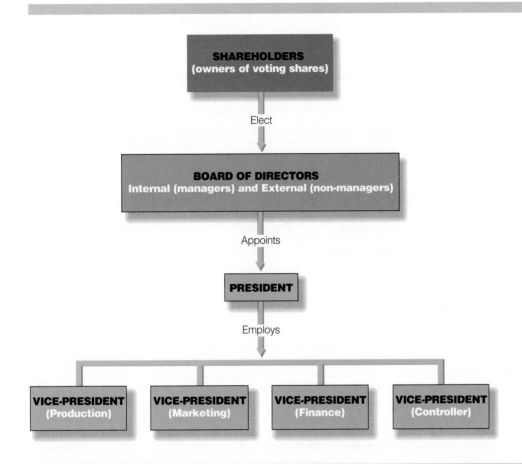

EXHIBIT **12.3**

Authorized, Issued, and Outstanding Shares

Definitions	Illustrations
Authorized number of shares: The maximum number of shares that can be issued, as specified in the charter of the corporation.	The charter specifies "an unlimited number of common shares."
Issued number of shares: The total number of shares that the corporation has issued to date.	To date, XYZ Corporation has sold and issued 30,000 common shares.

Unissued number of shares: The number of authorized shares that have never been issued to date.		
	Authorized shares	100,000
	Issued shares	30,000
	Unissued shares	70,000

Treasury shares:* Shares that have been issued to investors and then reacquired by the issuing corporation.	To date, XYZ Corporation has repurchased 1,000 previously issued shares.	

Outstanding number of shares: The number of shares currently owned by shareholders; that is, the number of shares authorized minus the total number of unissued shares and minus the number of treasury shares.		
	Authorized shares	100,000
	Treasury shares	(1,000)
	Unissued shares	(70,000)
	Outstanding shares	29,000

*Treasury shares will be discussed later. Notice that when treasury shares are held, the number of shares issued and the number outstanding differ by the number of treasury shares held (treasury shares are included in "issued" but not in "outstanding").

KEY RATIO ANALYSIS

EARNINGS PER SHARE

■ LEARNING OBJECTIVE 2

Analyze the earnings per share ratio.

ANALYTICAL QUESTION → How profitable is a company?

RATIO AND COMPARISONS → The *earnings per share* is a measure of the investment that is based on the number of shares outstanding instead of the dollar amounts reported on the balance sheet. In simple situations, it is computed as follows:

$$\text{Basic Earnings per Share} = \text{Net Income Available to Common Shareholders} \div \text{Average Number of Common Shares Outstanding}$$

The 2006 ratio for Sun Life Financial is:

$$\$2{,}089 \div 577 = \$3.62$$

Comparisons over Time			Comparisons with Competitors	
Sun Life Financial			Great-West Lifeco	Fairfax Financial
2004	2005	2006	2006	2006
$2.81	$3.14	$3.62	$2.10	$12.17

INTERPRETATIONS

In General → All analysts and investors are interested in a company's earnings. You have probably seen newspaper headlines announcing a company's earnings. Notice that those news stories normally report basic earnings on a per share (EPS) basis. The reason is simple. Numbers are much easier to compare on a per share basis. For example, in 2006, Sun Life earned income of $2,089 million compared to $1,843 million in the previous year, reflecting an increase of 13.3 percent. If we make that comparison on a per share basis, EPS increased from $3.14 to $3.62, an increase of 15.3 percent that takes into consideration the change in the number of common shares outstanding during the year.

Focus Company Analysis → Sun Life's basic EPS has increased steadily from $1.84 in 2002 to $3.62 in 2006, reflecting a strategy of growth and reinvestment of earnings. Sun Life's EPS is greater than that of Great-West Lifeco, but much lower that Fairfax's ratio. Comparison of Sun Life's EPS to those of its competitors may not be very informative as a measure of profitability of shareholders' investments in these companies. The reason is simple. Shares of different companies are likely to have different prices, which makes EPS comparisons less meaningful than other measures of profitability.

A Few Cautions → While EPS is an effective and widely used measure of profitability, it can be misleading if there are significant differences in the market values of the shares being compared. Two companies earning $1.50 per share might appear to be comparable, but if shares in one company cost $10 while shares of the other cost $175, they are not comparable.

COMMON SHARE TRANSACTIONS

■ LEARNING OBJECTIVE 3

Describe the characteristics of common shares and analyze transactions affecting common shares.

Corporations issue two types of shares, common shares and preferred shares. All corporations issue common shares, while only some issue preferred shares, which grant preferences that the common shares do not have. In this section, we discuss common shares and in a subsequent section, we discuss preferred shares.

In Chapter 11, we mentioned that corporations issue many different types of bonds to appeal to the risk and return preferences of individual creditors. The same is true of shares. In this chapter, we introduce you to many features that are used to encourage investors to buy shares.

Common shares are the basic voting shares issued by a corporation. They are often called the *residual equity* because they rank after the preferred shares for dividend and asset distribution upon liquidation of the corporation. The dividend rate for common shares is determined by the board of directors based on the company's profitability, unlike the dividend rate on preferred shares, which is determined by contract. When the company is not profitable, the board may cut or eliminate dividends on common shares, but in most cases it cannot reduce preferred dividends.

COMMON SHARES are the basic, normal, voting shares issued by a corporation; called *residual equity* because they rank after preferred shares for dividend and liquidation distributions.

The fact that dividends on common shares may increase with increases in the company's profitability helps explain why investors can make money on the stock market. Basically, you can think of the price of a share as the present value of all of its future dividends. If a company's profitability improves so that it can pay out higher dividends, the present value of its common share will increase. In this situation, you would not expect the value of the preferred share to change significantly because preferred dividends may change only if the share contract provides for some flexibility.

No Par Value and Par Value Shares **Par value** is the nominal value per share established in the charter of a corporation. It has no relationship to the market value per share. The Canada Business Corporations Act (CBCA) and most provincial corporations Acts prohibit the issuance of par value shares. The few Canadian companies that still have par value shares outstanding issued them before the CBCA was amended in 1985. According to *Financial Reporting in Canada 2006*, only 4 of the 200 companies surveyed have reported use of par value shares, 91 companies issued shares without par value, and 105 companies made no reference to par value of their shares.[4] For this reason, the remainder of this chapter focuses on **no par value shares**, which do not have an amount per share specified in the corporate charter. In contrast, most U.S. corporations issue par value shares.

> **PAR VALUE** is the nominal value per share specified in the charter; it serves as the basis for legal capital.

The original purpose of requiring corporations to specify a par value per share was to establish a minimum permanent amount of capital that the owners could not withdraw as long as the corporation existed. Thus, owners could not withdraw all of their capital in anticipation of a bankruptcy, which would leave creditors with an empty corporate shell. This permanent amount of capital is called **legal capital**. The requirement that shares not be issued for less than their par value often resulted in par values that were too small to be effectively meaningful. This notion of legal capital has lost its significance over time because the par values of shares have been set at very low amounts by issuing corporations. In contrast, when a corporation issues no par value shares, the legal capital is the initial amount received from shareholders.

> **NO PAR VALUE SHARES** are shares that have no par value specified in the corporate charter.

BCE's corporate charter authorizes the issue of no par value common shares. However, its preferred shares have a stated value upon which the dividend payments are based. This stated value has no relationship to the market value of the preferred shares.

> **LEGAL CAPITAL** is the permanent amount of capital, defined by law, that must remain invested in the business; it serves as a cushion for creditors.

INITIAL SALE OF SHARES

Two names are applied to transactions involving the initial sale of a company's shares to the public. An *initial public offering*, or *IPO*, involves the very first sale of a company's shares to the public (i.e., when the company first "goes public"). You have probably heard stories of Internet companies that had their shares increase dramatically in value the day of their IPO. While investors sometimes earn significant returns on IPOs, they also take significant risks. Once the shares of a company are traded on established markets, additional sales of new shares to the public are called *seasoned new issues*.

As was the case with debt (discussed in Chapter 11), most companies use an underwriter to assist in the sale of shares. The underwriter is usually an investment bank that acts as an intermediary between the corporation and the investors. The underwriter advises the corporation on matters concerning the sale and is directly involved in the sale of shares to the public.

Most sales of shares to the public are cash transactions. To illustrate accounting for an initial sale of shares, assume that Sun Life sold 100,000 common shares for $22 per share. The company records the following journal entry:

SELECTED FOCUS COMPANY COMPARISONS: RETAINED EARNINGS AS A PERCENTAGE OF SHAREHOLDER'S EQUITY	
Gildan Activewear	78.3%
WestJet Airlines	30.1%
Petro-Canada	73.9%

---

[4]N. Chlala, A. Lavigne, L. Martel, and C. Byrd, *Financial Reporting in Canada 2006*. Toronto: Canadian Institute of Chartered Accountants, 2006, p. 354.

| Cash (A) (100,000 × $22)............................... | 2,200,000 | |
| Common shares...................................... | | 2,200,000 |

Assets		=	Liabilities	+	Shareholders' Equity	
Cash	+2,200,000				Common shares	+2,200,000

The sale of common shares is reported on the balance sheet in the format shown in Exhibit 12.1.

SALE OF SHARES IN SECONDARY MARKETS

When a company sells shares to the public, the transaction is between the issuing corporation and the buyer. Subsequent to the initial sale, investors can sell shares to other investors without directly affecting the corporation. For example, if investor Jon Drago sold 1,000 of Sun Life's common shares to Jennifer Lea, Sun Life does not record a journal entry on its books. Mr. Drago received cash for the shares he sold, and Ms. Lea received shares for the cash she paid. Sun Life itself did not receive or pay anything because of this transaction.

Each business day, the *National Post* and other newspapers report the results of thousands of transactions between investors in the secondary markets, where trading of shares among investors takes place. These markets include the Toronto Stock Exchange (TSX) and TSX Venture Exchange (in Canada), the New York Stock Exchange, the American Stock Exchange, and NASDAQ (in the United States), and similar markets in other countries.

Managers of corporations follow very closely the movements in the price of their company's shares. Shareholders expect to earn money on their investment from both dividends and increases in the share (or stock) price. In many instances, senior management has been replaced because of poor performance of the shares in the secondary markets. Although managers watch the share price on a daily basis, it is important to remember that the transactions between investors do not directly affect the company's financial statements.

FINANCIAL ANALYSIS

GOING PUBLIC

As noted earlier, an initial public offering (IPO) is the first sale of shares to the public. Prior to that sale, the company is a private company. A company might want to go public for two common reasons. For it to grow and meet consumer demand, it must expand its productive capacity. The need for new capital may be beyond the capability of the private owners. By going public, the company can raise the funds needed to expand.

In some cases, the company may not need significant funds, but the current owners may want to create a market for its shares. Often, selling shares is difficult if the company is not listed on a major stock exchange. By going public, a company can increase the marketability of its shares.

Initial public offerings often create a lot of interest among investors. Some good opportunities are available to earn excellent returns by investing in growing companies. Substantial risk also is associated with many IPOs.

In recent years, much interest has surrounded Internet companies that have gone public. Virtually any company with ".com" in its name has received significant attention from investors. Recently, Google Inc., which operates one of the most popular search engines, had an initial public offering of its shares at an initial price of $85. Since the IPO in August 2004, Google's share price increased significantly, reaching $482 by April 2007 due to investors' expectations of the company's future profitability.

There are countless stories of people in their twenties and thirties who have become instant millionaires after the IPO of a new Internet company. Less well publicized, however, are the stories of individuals who have lost money investing in new and unproven businesses.

SHARES ISSUED FOR NON-CASH ASSETS OR SERVICES

Small companies are playing an increasingly important role in the North American economy. They account for a large percentage of the new jobs that have been created in the past decade. Many of today's corporate giants were small start-up companies just a few years ago. Companies such as Dell, Microsoft, and Amazon.com began literally as basement operations in the homes of their founders.

One feature common to all start-up companies is a shortage of cash. Because these companies often cannot afford to pay cash for needed assets and services, they sometimes issue shares to people who can supply these assets and services. Many executives, for instance, will join start-up companies for very low salaries because they also earn compensation in the form of common shares. An executive who was granted BCE shares during its early days would be very wealthy today.

When a company issues shares to acquire assets or services, the acquired items are recorded at the ***market value*** of the shares issued at the date of the transaction in accordance with the ***cost principle***. If the market value of the shares issued cannot be determined, the market value of the consideration received should be used.

To illustrate, assume that during its early years of operations, Sun Life was unable to pay cash for needed legal services. The company issued 10,000 shares to a law firm when the share was selling for $15. At that time, the company recorded the following journal entry:

Legal fees (E)	150,000	
Common shares.		150,000

Assets	=	Liabilities	+	Shareholders' Equity	
				Legal fees	−150,000
				Common shares	+150,000

Notice that the value of the legal services received is assumed to be the same as the value of the shares that were issued. This assumption is reasonable because two independent parties usually keep negotiating a deal until the value of what is given up equals the value of what is received.

SHARES ISSUED FOR EMPLOYEE COMPENSATION

One of the advantages of the corporate form is the possibility to separate the management of a business from its ownership. This separation can also be a disadvantage because some managers may not act in the shareholders' best interests. This problem can be overcome in a number of ways. Compensation packages can be developed to reward managers for meeting goals that are important to shareholders. Another strategy is to offer managers *stock options,* which permit them to buy shares at a fixed price.

The holder of a stock option has an interest in a company's performance in the same manner as a shareholder. Stock option plans have become an increasingly common form of compensation over the past years. Indeed, 194 of the 200 companies surveyed by *Financial Reporting in Canada 2006* reported stock option plans for their employees.[5] However, the excessive use of stock options as a form of compensating key executives led the executives of some companies to manipulate reported financial information in an effort to increase the share price so they can benefit by buying shares at a fixed price and selling them at a higher price for a profit.

[5]N. Chlala, A. Lavigne, L. Martel, and C. Byrd, *Financial Reporting in Canada 2006.* Toronto: Canadian Institute of Chartered Accountants, 2006, p. 621.

The Sun Life annual report provides the following disclosures:

REAL WORLD EXCERPT

*Sun Life
Financial Inc.*

ANNUAL REPORT

Note 18. Stock-based compensation from Sun Life Annual Report.

The stock options outstanding and exercisable as at December 31, 2006, by exercise price are as follows:

	Options Outstanding			Options Exercisable		
Range of exercise prices	Number of stock-options (thousands)	Weighted average remaining contractual life (years)	Weighted average exercise price	Number of stock-options (thousands)	Weighted average remaining contractual life (years)	Weighted average exercise price
$19.05 to $24.28	2,213	5.27	$22.20	1,831	5.09	$22.43
$25.28 to $30.91	2,751	5.05	28.45	2,310	4.86	28.57
$31.00 to $33.20	1,433	5.16	32.82	1,396	5.10	32.83
$36.50 to $44.73	1,345	7.98	40.46	370	7.62	39.87
$46.80 to $49.90	1,396	9.15	49.38	2	9.15	49.40
	9,138	6.19	$32.58	5,909	5.17	$28.39

The options issued by Sun Life specify that shares could be bought at a predetermined exercise price. Granting a stock option is a form of compensation even if the exercise price and the current share price are the same. If someone gives you a stock option, you could think of it as a risk-free investment. If you hold a stock option when the share price declines, you have lost nothing. If the share price increases, you can exercise your option at the specified price and sell the shares at a higher price for a profit.

Stock options are a widely used form of executive compensation. Most companies offer them with an exercise price equal to the current market price per share.

For example, in 2006 Sun Life granted its key employees options to purchase a total of 1,460,000 common shares in the future at an average price of $49.29, which equals the market price per share on the date of the grant. The option holders would benefit from the stock option in a few years if the market price per share exceeds $49.29, presumably because the increase in Sun Life's market value is partially attributed to their managerial skills. Undoubtedly, the difference between the increased market price and the exercise price of $49.29 is a form of compensation to the key employees. When the options are exercised, Sun Life receives $49.29 per common share, while it could obtain a higher price if it sold the same shares in the market to other investors. Clearly, the exercise of employee stock options entails a cost to Sun Life that should be measured and reported. The more interesting issue, however, is whether Sun Life incurs a cost at the time of granting the options, even if the exercise price equals the market price at the grant date. In general, a fair value of the options can be estimated using complex mathematical formulae, and then compared to the exercise price to determine the additional compensation expense for the period.

The measurement and reporting of the cost of stock options has been hotly debated by accounting standard setters and company executives. Many companies rely on stock options to compensate their employees and key executives, especially in the technology, energy, and gold mining sectors. Companies in these sectors have lobbied against reporting the cost of stock options as an expense on the income statement because it would lower their net income, and may even turn the net income into a net loss.

Recent changes in Canadian accounting standards require Canadian companies to measure the cost of their stock option plans using a conventional but complex present value calculation, then include the result as a compensation expense in the computation of net income. The specific procedures to compute the compensation expense are covered in intermediate accounting courses.

DIVIDENDS ON COMMON SHARES

Investors buy common shares because they expect a return on their investment. This return can come in two forms: appreciation of the share price and dividends. Some investors prefer to buy shares that pay little or no dividends because companies that reinvest the majority of their earnings tend to increase their future earnings potential, along with their stock price. Wealthy investors in high tax brackets prefer to receive their return on equity investments in the form of higher stock prices because capital gains may be taxed at a lower rate than dividend income. Other investors, such as retired people who need a steady income, prefer to receive their return on an investment in the form of dividends. These people often seek shares that will pay very high dividends, such as shares of utility companies.

A corporation does not have a legal obligation to pay dividends. While creditors can force a company into bankruptcy if it does not meet required interest payments on debt, shareholders do not have a similar right if a corporation is unable to pay dividends.

Without a qualifier, the term *dividend* means a cash dividend, but dividends can also be paid in assets other than cash or by issuing additional shares. The most common type of dividend is a cash dividend.

Although a corporation does not have a legal obligation to pay a dividend, a liability is created when the board of directors approves (i.e., declares) a dividend.

Sun Life pays cash dividends on its outstanding common shares on a quarterly basis. The company provides details of the quarterly dividends on its preferred and common shares on its Web site. For example, the cash dividends on common shares for the last quarter of 2006 follows.

Type of Share	Amount of Dividend	Declaration Date	Date of Record	Payment Date
Common share	$0.30	Oct. 22, 2006	Nov. 22, 2006	Jan. 2, 2007

A dividend declaration includes three important dates:

1. **Declaration date.** The **declaration date** is the date on which the board of directors officially approved the dividend. As soon as it makes the declaration, it creates a dividend liability.

2. **Date of record.** The **date of record** follows the declaration; it is the date on which the corporation prepares the list of current shareholders, based on its shareholder records. The dividend is payable only to those names listed on the record date. No journal entry is made on this date.

3. **Payment date.** The **payment date** is the date on which the cash is disbursed to pay the dividend liability. It follows the date of record as specified in the dividend announcement.

For instructional purposes, the time lag between the date of declaration and the date of payment may be ignored because it does not pose any substantive issues. When all three dates fall in the same accounting period, a single entry on the date of payment may be made in practice for purely practical reasons.

Assume, for simplicity, that Sun Life had 10 million common shares outstanding on the declaration date. The amount of cash dividends is therefore $3,000,000.

The declaration of dividends creates a liability on October 22, 2006, that is recorded as follows:

Retained earnings (SE).....................................	3,000,000	
Dividend payable—Common (L)		3,000,000

Assets	=	Liabilities	+	Shareholders' Equity
		Dividends payable—C +3,000,000		Retained earnings −3,000,000

LEARNING OBJECTIVE 4
Discuss dividends and analyze related transactions.

REAL WORLD EXCERPT

Sun Life Financial Inc.

DIVIDEND INFORMATION

The **DECLARATION DATE** is the date on which the board of directors officially approves a dividend.

The **DATE OF RECORD** is the date on which the corporation prepares the list of current shareholders as shown on its records; dividends can be paid only to the shareholders who own shares on that date.

The **PAYMENT DATE** is the date on which a cash dividend is paid to the shareholders of record.

The payment of the dividends on common shares on January 2, 2007 is recorded as follows:

| Dividend payable—Common (L)........................ | 3,000,000 | |
| Cash (A)... | | 3,000,000 |

Assets		=	Liabilities		+	Shareholders' Equity
Cash	−3,000,000		Dividends payable—C	−3,000,000		

Notice that the declaration and payment of a cash dividend have two impacts: they reduce assets (cash) and shareholders' equity (retained earnings) by the same amount. This observation explains the two fundamental requirements for the payment of a cash dividend:

1. ***Sufficient retained earnings***. The corporation must have accumulated a sufficient amount of retained earnings to cover the amount of the dividend. Incorporation laws often limit cash dividends to the balance in the Retained Earnings account.

2. ***Sufficient cash***. The corporation must have access to sufficient cash to pay the dividend and to meet the operating needs of the business. The mere fact that the Retained Earnings account has a large credit balance does not mean that the board of directors can declare and pay a cash dividend. The cash generated in the past by earnings represented in the Retained Earnings account may have been expended to acquire inventory, buy operational assets, and pay liabilities. Consequently, no necessary relationship exists between the balance of retained earnings and the balance of cash on any particular date. Quite simply, retained earnings is not cash.

FINANCIAL ANALYSIS   **IMPACT OF DIVIDENDS ON SHARE PRICE**

Another date that is important in understanding dividends has no accounting implications. The date two business days before the date of record is known as the ***ex-dividend date***. This date is established by the stock exchanges to make certain that dividend cheques are sent to the right people. If you buy shares before the ex-dividend date, you receive the dividend. If you buy the shares on the ex-dividend date or later, the previous shareholder receives the dividend.

If you follow share prices, you will notice that the price of a company's common share often falls on the ex-dividend date. The reason is simple. On that date, the share is worth less because it no longer includes the right to receive the next dividend.

SELF-STUDY **QUIZ 12-1**

The board of directors of Sun Life Financial Inc. declared dividends of $0.32 per common share, payable on July 3, 2007 to shareholders of record on May 23, 2007. Assume that Sun Life had 573,463,000 common shares outstanding on the declaration date. Answer the following questions concerning this dividend:

1. On which date is a liability created?

2. On which date does a cash outflow occur?

3. Prepare the journal entry to record the payment of the dividend

4. What are the three fundamental requirements for the payment of a dividend?

After you complete your answers, check them with the solutions on page 655.

Because of the importance of dividends to many investors, analysts often compute the dividend yield ratio to evaluate a corporation's dividend policy.

DIVIDEND YIELD

KEY RATIO
ANALYSIS

■ **LEARNING OBJECTIVE 5**
Analyze the dividend yield ratio.

ANALYTICAL QUESTION → Investors in common shares expect to earn a return on their investment. A portion of this return comes in the form of dividends. How much do investors earn on their investment based on dividends?

RATIO AND COMPARISONS → The *dividend yield ratio* is a measure of the percentage return that shareholders earn from the dividends they receive. Potential investors often use this ratio to help select from alternative investment opportunities. It is computed as follows:

Dividend Yield Ratio = Dividends per Share ÷ Market Price per Share

The 2006 ratio for Sun Life is:

$$\$1.15 \div \$49.30 = 2.3\%$$

Comparisons over Time			Comparisons with Competitors	
Sun Life Financial			Great-West Lifeco	Fairfax Financial
2004	2005	2006	2006	2006
2.1%	2.1%	2.3%	1.7%	1.2%

INTERPRETATIONS

In General → Investors in common shares earn a return from dividends and capital appreciation (increases in the market price of the shares they own). Growth-oriented companies often pay out very small amounts of dividends and rely on increases in their market price to provide a return to investors. Others pay out large dividends but have more stable market prices. Each type of share appeals to different types of investors with different risk and return preferences.

Focus Company Analysis → During the three years 2004, 2005, and 2006, Sun Life distributed increasing annual dividends of $0.86, $0.99, and $1.15 per share, respectively; yet its dividend yield remained relatively stable. This is because the market price of Sun Life's common shares increased as well to reflect the increase in the dividend per share. In comparison with Sun Life, both Great-West Lifeco and Fairfax Financial paid a low dividend per share relative to their share prices; hence, their lower dividend yields.

A Few Cautions → Remember that the dividend yield ratio tells only part of the return on investment story. Often, potential capital appreciation is a much more important consideration. When analyzing changes in the ratio, it is important to understand the cause. For example, a company might pay out $2 per share in dividends each year. If the market price of its shares is $100 per share, the yield is 2 percent. If the market price per share falls to $25 the following year and the company continues to pay out $2 per share in dividends, the dividend yield ratio will "improve" to 8 percent. Most analysts would not interpret this change as being favourable.

STOCK DIVIDENDS AND STOCK SPLITS

STOCK DIVIDENDS

A **stock dividend** is a distribution of additional shares of a corporation's own share capital to its shareholders on a pro rata basis at no cost to the shareholder. Stock dividends usually consist of additional common shares issued to the holders of common shares. The phrase ***pro rata basis*** means that each shareholder receives additional shares equal to the percentage of shares already held. A shareholder with 10 percent of the outstanding shares receives 10 percent of any additional shares issued as a stock dividend.

The term ***stock dividend*** is sometimes misused in annual reports and news articles. A recent *Wall Street Journal* headline announced that a particular company had just declared a "stock dividend." A close reading of the article revealed that the company had declared a cash dividend on the shares.

The value of a stock dividend is the subject of much debate. In reality, a stock dividend has no economic value. All shareholders receive a pro rata distribution of shares, which means that each shareholder owns exactly the same portion of the company as before. The value of an investment is determined by the percentage of the company that is owned, not the number of shares that are held. If you get change for a dollar, you

■ **LEARNING OBJECTIVE 6**
Discuss the purpose of stock dividends, stock splits, and report transactions.

A **STOCK DIVIDEND** is a distribution of additional shares of a corporation's own equity.

are not wealthier because you hold *four* quarters instead of only *one* dollar. Similarly, if you own 10 percent of a company, you are not wealthier simply because the company declares a stock dividend and gives you (and all other shareholders) more shares.

At this point, you may still wonder why having extra shares does not make an investor wealthier. The reason is simple: the stock market reacts immediately when a stock dividend is issued, and the share price falls proportionally. Theoretically, if the share price was $60 before a stock dividend, normally (in the absence of events affecting the company) the price falls to $30 if the number of shares is doubled. Thus, an investor could own 100 shares worth $6,000 before the stock dividend (100 × $60) and 200 shares worth $6,000 after the stock dividend (200 × $30).

In reality, the fall in price is not exactly proportional to the number of new shares that are issued. In some cases, the stock dividend makes the stock more attractive to new investors. Many investors prefer to buy shares in round lots, which are multiples of 100 shares. An investor with $10,000 might not buy a share selling for $150 because she cannot afford to buy 100 shares. She might buy the share, however, if the price is less than $100 as a result of a stock dividend. In other cases, stock dividends are accompanied by an announcement of increases in cash dividends, which are attractive to some investors.

When a common stock dividend occurs, the company must transfer an additional amount into the Common Shares account to reflect the additional shares that have been issued. The amount transferred should reflect the fair market value per share at the declaration date, as recommended in the Canada Business Corporations Act.

For small stock dividends that are less than 20–25 percent of the outstanding shares, the amount transferred from the Retained Earnings account to the Common Shares account is based on the market price per share at the date of declaration. If the company declared a cash dividend instead of a stock dividend and the shareholders used the cash they receive to buy additional shares, the shareholders would be paying the market price to acquire additional shares. This assumption is valid if the stock dividend is relatively small, so that it will not cause a significant change in the market price. For larger stock dividends, the market price per share will drop significantly, so it will not be an appropriate basis for transferring an amount from Retained Earnings to Common Shares. In this case, the amount transferred is based on the average issue price per share. In either situation, the stock dividend does not change total shareholders' equity. It changes only the balances of specific shareholders' equity accounts.

Let us assume that a company declared on July 25, 2008, a 10-percent stock dividend on common shares to be issued on August 25, 2008, to shareholders of record on August 10, 2008. The company had 100,000 shares outstanding and the market price per share was $20 on the date of declaration. The declaration of the stock dividend requires the following journal entry on July 25, 2008:

Retained earnings (SE) (100,000 × 10% × $20).	200,000	
Stock dividend to be issued (SE).		200,000

Assets	=	Liabilities	+	Shareholders' Equity	
				Retained earnings	−200,000
				Stock dividend to be issued	+200,000

The equity account, Stock Dividend To Be Issued, is credited, instead of Common Shares, until the shares are issued. The issuance and distribution of the additional shares on August 25, 2008 is recorded as follows:

Stock dividend to be issued (SE)	200,000	
Common shares (SE).		200,000

Assets	=	Liabilities	+	Shareholders' Equity	
				Stock dividend to be issued	−200,000
				Common shares	+200,000

If the company had declared a 50-percent stock dividend, the average price received for issuing all of the common shares would be used instead of the market price per share as a basis for the reduction of retained earnings. If the average issue price per share is $15,[6] the Retained Earnings account would be reduced by $750,000 (100,000 × 50% × $15) and the Common Shares account would be increased by the same amount.

STOCK SPLITS

Stock splits are *not* dividends. They are similar to a stock dividend but are quite different in terms of their impact on the shareholders' equity accounts. In a **stock split**, the *total* number of authorized shares is increased by a specified number, such as a 2-for-1 split. In this instance, each share held is called in, and two new shares are issued in its place.

A **STOCK SPLIT** is an increase in the total number of authorized shares by a specified ratio; it does not decrease retained earnings.

Sun Life did not have any stock splits. In contrast, Bell Canada Enterprises (BCE) has three stock splits over the years. A 4-for-1 split occurred on October 4, 1948, followed by a second 3-for-1 split on April 26, 1979. The last split was a 2-for-1, executed on May 14, 1997. In summary, a common share issued prior to October 4, 1948, has already split into 24 shares. If these stock splits did not occur, BCE's share price would have been $792 at the time of writing this book.

In both a stock dividend and a stock split, the shareholder receives more shares but does not pay to acquire the additional shares. A stock dividend requires a journal entry; a stock split does not require one but is disclosed in the notes to the financial statements. The comparative effects of a stock dividend versus a stock split may be summarized as follows:

Shareholders' Equity	Before	After a 100% Stock Dividend	After a Two-for-One Stock Split
Contributed capital			
Number of shares outstanding	30,000	60,000	60,000
Issue price per share	$ 10	$ 10	$ 5
Common shares	300,000	600,000	300,000
Retained earnings	650,000	350,000	650,000
Total shareholders' equity	$950,000	$950,000	$950,000

Self-Study **Quiz 12-2**

Barton Corporation issued 100,000 new common shares as a result of a stock dividend when the market value was $30 per share. The average issue price is $10 per share.

1. Record this transaction, assuming that it was a small stock dividend.

2. Record this transaction, assuming that it was a large stock dividend.

3. What journal entry is required if the transaction is a stock split?

After you complete your answers, check them with the solutions on page 655.

PREFERRED SHARES

In addition to common shares, some corporations issue **preferred shares**. Preferred shares differ from common shares because of a number of rights granted to the preferred shareholders. The most significant differences are:

■ **LEARNING OBJECTIVE 7**

Describe the characteristics of preferred shares and analyze transactions affecting preferred shares.

- **Preferred shares do not grant voting rights.** As a result, they do not appeal to investors who want some control over the operations of the corporation. Indeed, this is one of the main reasons why some corporations issue preferred shares to raise equity capital. Preferred shares permit them to raise funds without diluting

PREFERRED SHARES are shares that have specified rights over common shares.

---

[6]The average issue price per share equals the balance of the Common Shares account divided by the number of common shares outstanding.

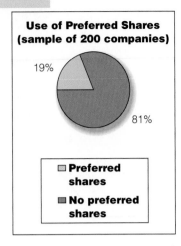

Use of Preferred Shares (sample of 200 companies)

19%

81%

☐ **Preferred shares**

■ **No preferred shares**

CONVERTIBLE PREFERRED SHARES are preferred shares that are convertible to common shares at the option of the holder.

common shareholders' control of the company. The chart in the margin shows the percentage of companies surveyed by *Financial Reporting in Canada 2006* that include preferred shares in their capital structure.

- **Preferred shares are less risky than common shares.** Preferred shareholders have a priority over common shareholders for the receipt of dividends and in the distribution of assets if the corporation goes out of business. Usually a specified amount per share must be paid to preferred shareholders upon dissolution before any remaining assets can be distributed to the common shareholders.

- **Preferred shares typically have a fixed dividend rate.** Preferred shares typically have no par value but, unlike common shares, they often carry a nominal value called the *stated value*. Sun Life's preferred shares have a stated value of $25 per share. Most preferred shares have fixed dividend rates or amounts per share. For example, Sun Life's Preferred Shares, Class A Series 4, pay an annual dividend of $1.112 per share.

Special Features of Preferred Shares Some corporations issue **convertible preferred shares**, which provide preferred shareholders the option to exchange their preferred shares for a different series of preferred shares or common shares of the corporation. The terms of the conversion specify the conversion dates and a conversion ratio.

The classification of preferred shares as equity or debt depends upon the terms of the preferred equity issue. Preferred shares may be *redeemable* or *callable* at some future date at the option of the issuing corporation. Corporations are unlikely to redeem preferred shares if conditions are financially unfavourable to the company. Such redeemable shares are classified as equity because the issuing corporation can choose to not redeem the shares. However, preferred shares that have fixed redemption dates are classified as debt because the issuing corporation has a future financial liability. Moreover, dividends on these shares are treated as expenses, much like the interest expense related to long-term debt.

Some preferred share issues are *retractable* at the option of the shareholder. In that case, preferred shareholders have the right to receive the redemption price from the corporation at a specific future date. Thus, retractable preferred shares represent a contractual obligation to deliver cash or another financial asset at a future date under conditions that may be unfavourable to the issuing corporation. Consequently, retractable preferred shares are classified as debt.

The notes to Sun Life's consolidated financial statements for the year 2006 provide details regarding its preferred shares.

REAL WORLD EXCERPT

Sun Life Financial Inc.

ANNUAL REPORT

15. Share capital and normal course issuer bid

A) Share Capital

The authorized share capital of Sun Life Financial Inc. consists of the following:

- An unlimited number of common shares without nominal or par value. Each common share is entitled to one vote at meetings of the shareholders of Sun Life Financial Inc. There are no pre-emptive, redemption, purchase or conversion rights attached to the common shares.

- An unlimited number of Class A and Class B non-voting preferred shares, issuable in series. The Board is authorized before issuing the shares, to fix the number, the consideration per share, the designation of, and the rights and restrictions of the Class A and Class B shares of each series, subject to the special rights and restrictions attached to all the Class A and Class B shares. The Board has authorized four series of Class A non-voting preferred shares.

The changes and the number of shares issued and outstanding are as follows:

	2006		2005	
	Number of shares	Amount	Numbers of shares	Amount
Preferred shares (in millions of shares)				
Balance, January 1	29	$ 712	—	$ —
Preferred shares issued, Class A, Series 1	—	—	16	400
Preferred shares issued, Class A, Series 2	—	—	13	325
Preferred shares issued, Class A, Series 3	10	250	—	—
Preferred shares issued, Class A, Series 4	12	300	—	—
Issuance costs, net of taxes	—	(12)	—	(13)
Balance, December 31	51	$1,250	29	$712

On October 10, 2006, Sun Life Financial Inc. issued $300 Class A Non-cumulative Preferred Shares Series 4 at $25 per share. Holders are entitled to receive non-cumulative quarterly dividends of $0.278 per share, yielding 4.45% annually. Subject to regulatory approval, on or after December 31, 2011, Sun Life Financial Inc. may redeem these shares in whole or in part at a declining premium. On January 13, 2006, Sun Life Financial Inc. issued $250 Class A Non-cumulative preferred Shares Series 3 At 25 per share. Holders are entitled to receive non-cumulative quarterly dividends of $0.278 per share, yielding 4.45% annually. Subject to regulatory approval, on or after March 31, 2011, Sun Life Financial Inc. may redeem these shares in whole or in part at a declining premium. Underwriting commissions of $12 (net taxes of $6) related to the 2006 preferred share issuances were deducted from preferred shares in the consolidated statements of equity.

Self-Study **Quiz 12-3**

Refer to the previous table showing a summary of Sun Life's preferred shares, and answer the following questions related to Preferred Shares, Class A Series 4.

1. How much did Sun Life receive per share when it sold the Series 4 shares to investors?

2. What is the total amount of dividends payable on Series 4 per year?

3. What is meant by redemption date?

4. What is the earliest date when Sun Life can redeem its Series 4 shares?

After you complete your answers, check them with the solutions on page 655.

DIVIDENDS ON PREFERRED SHARES

Investors who purchase preferred shares give up certain advantages that are available to investors in common shares. Generally, preferred shareholders do not have the right to vote at the annual meeting, nor do they share in increased earnings if the company becomes more profitable. To compensate these investors, preferred shares offer some advantages not available to common shareholders. Perhaps the most important advantage is dividend preference. The two most common dividend preferences are:

1. Current dividend preference.
2. Cumulative dividend preference.

Current Dividend Preference   Preferred shares always carry a **current dividend preference**, which requires that the current preferred dividend be paid before any dividends are paid on the common shares. When the current dividend preference has been met and there are no other preferences, dividends can then be paid to the common shareholders.

CURRENT DIVIDEND PREFERENCE is the feature of preferred shares that grants preferred shareholders priority for dividends over common shareholders.

Declared dividends must be allocated between the preferred and common shares. First, dividends are allocated to the preferred shares, and then the remainder of the total dividend is allocated to the common shares. Exhibit 12.4, Case A, illustrates the allocation of the current dividend preference under three different assumptions concerning the total amount of dividends to be paid.

CUMULATIVE DIVIDEND PREFERENCE is the feature of preferred shares that requires specified current dividends not paid in full to accumulate for every year in which they are not paid. These cumulative preferred dividends must be paid before any common dividends can be paid.

DIVIDENDS IN ARREARS are dividends on cumulative preferred shares that have not been declared in prior years.

Cumulative Dividend Preference   The **cumulative dividend preference** states that if all or a part of the current dividend is not paid in full, the unpaid amount, known as **dividends in arrears**, must be paid before any common dividends can be paid. Of course, if the preferred shares are non-cumulative, dividends cannot be in arrears; any dividends that are not declared are lost permanently by the preferred shareholders. Because preferred shareholders are not willing to accept this unfavourable feature, preferred shares are usually cumulative.

The allocation of dividends between cumulative preferred shares and common shares is illustrated in Exhibit 12.4, Case B, under four different assumptions concerning the total amount of dividends to be paid. Notice that the dividends in arrears are paid first, then the current dividend preference is paid, and, finally, the remainder is paid to the common shareholders.

EXHIBIT **12.4**

Dividends on Preferred Shares

Case A—Current dividend preference only

Preferred shares outstanding, $1.20; 2,000 shares.

Common shares outstanding, 5,000 shares.

Allocation of dividends between preferred and common shares assuming current dividend preference only:

Assumptions	Total Dividends Paid	$1.20 Preferred Shares (2,000 shares)*	Common Shares (5,000 shares)
No. 1	$ 2,000	$2,000	0
No. 2	3,000	2,400	$ 600
No. 3	18,000	2,400	15,600

*Preferred dividends = 2,000 × $1.20 = $2,400.

Case B—Cumulative dividend preference

Preferred and common shares outstanding—same as in Case A. Dividends in arrears for the two preceding years.

Allocation of dividends between preferred and common shares, assuming cumulative preference:

Assumptions (dividends in arrears, 2 years)	Total Dividends Paid	$1.20 Preferred Shares (2,000 shares)*	Common Shares (5,000 shares)
No. 1	$ 2,400	$2,400	0
No. 2	7,200	7,200	0
No. 3	8,000	7,200	$ 800
No. 4	30,000	7,200	22,800

*Current dividend preference, 2,000 × $1.20 = $2,400; dividends in arrears preference, $2,400 × 2 years = $4,800; and current dividend preference plus dividends in arrears = $7,200.

FINANCIAL **ANALYSIS**

IMPACT OF DIVIDENDS IN ARREARS

The existence of dividends in arrears is important information because they limit a company's ability to pay dividends to its common shareholders and has implications for the company's future cash flows. Dividends are never an actual liability until the board of directors declares them. Hence, dividends in arrears are not reported on the balance sheet but are disclosed in the notes to the statements. The following note from Lone Star Industries is typical if a company has dividends in arrears:

The total of dividends in arrears on the $13.50 preferred shares at the end of the year was $11,670,000. The aggregate amount of such dividend must be paid before any dividends are paid on common shares.

Remember that various issues of preferred shares can offer different features. Most preferred shares have the cumulative dividend preference to provide shareholders with extra security. Companies can offer additional features to provide even more security. Many companies offer the feature described in the following note from Bally Manufacturing:

The holders of preferred shares do not have voting rights except that the holders would have the right to elect two additional directors of Bally if dividends on the preferred shares are in arrears in an amount equal to at least six quarterly dividends.

By electing two members of the board of directors, preferred shareholders have specific individuals to represent their interests. Bally included this feature with its preferred shares to make the shares more attractive to potential shareholders.

REAL WORLD EXCERPT

Lone Star Industries
ANNUAL REPORT

REAL WORLD EXCERPT

Bally Manufacturing
ANNUAL REPORT

RETAINED EARNINGS

Retained earnings represent income that has been earned less dividends that have been declared since the first day of the company's operations. By December 31, 2006, Sun Life's retained earnings reached $10 billion, exceeding the amount of capital contributed by shareholders.

Under rare circumstances, you may see a statement that includes an adjustment to the beginning balance of retained earnings as a result of the correction of a material accounting error that occurred in the financial statements of a prior period.

If an accounting error from a previous period is corrected by making an adjustment to the current income statement, net income for the current period would be improperly measured. To avoid this problem, the financial statements of the prior period in which the error occurred are restated to reflect the correction of the error. The nature of the prior period error should be disclosed along with the effect of the correction on each financial statement item that is affected by the error. To the extent that prior period errors affect income statement items, then retained earnings of prior period will also be affected.

Adjustments to the financial statements of prior periods should also be made if the entity changes its accounting policies, such as a change from the FIFO method of inventory valuation to the Weighted Average Cost method, or when companies are required to adopt new accounting standards. In these cases, the entity shall adjust the opening balance of each affected component of equity, including retained earnings. This was the cause, for example, of the prior period adjustment made by Forzani Group Ltd. in 2003 to its retained earnings.

■ LEARNING OBJECTIVE 8
Measure and report retained earnings.

Notes to Consolidated Financial Statements

3. Adoption of New Accounting Policies

Effective February 3, 2003, the Company changed its accounting policy on accounting for stock-based compensation. In accordance with the Canadian Institute of Chartered Accountants ("CICA") standard on "Stock-based Compensation and Other Stock-based Payments," the Company has changed its accounting policy to account for stock-based compensation using the fair value method. This change in accounting policy has been adopted retroactively to January 28, 2002. In accordance with the CICA handbook, section 3870, only stock options issued on, or after, the initial adoption date of section 3870 are recognized in the financial statements. ...The net impact of the change in accounting policy created a $546,000 decrease to retained earnings as at February 2, 2003.

REAL WORLD EXCERPT

Forzani Group Ltd.
ANNUAL REPORT 2004

RESTRICTIONS ON RETAINED EARNINGS

Several types of business transactions may cause restrictions to be placed on retained earnings that limit a company's ability to pay dividends. The most typical example is borrowing money from a bank. For additional security, some banks include a loan covenant that limits the amount of dividends that a corporation can pay.[7] In addition, debt covenants often include a limit on borrowing and required minimum balances of cash or working capital. If debt covenants are violated, the creditor can demand immediate repayment of the debt.

The full-disclosure principle requires that restrictions on retained earnings be reported on the financial statements or in a separate note to the financial statements.

Most companies report restrictions on retained earnings in the notes to the statements. An example of such a note from an annual report of the May Department Store follows:

REAL WORLD EXCERPT

May Department Store

ANNUAL REPORT

> Under the most restrictive covenants of long-term debt agreements, $1.2 billion of retained earnings was restricted as to the payment of dividends and/or common share repurchase.

Analysts are particularly interested in information concerning these restrictions because of the impact they have on the company's dividend policy.

FOCUS ON CASH FLOWS

FINANCING ACTIVITIES

LEARNING OBJECTIVE 9

Discuss the impact of share capital transactions on cash flows.

Transactions involving share capital have a direct impact on the capital structure of a business. Because of the importance of these transactions, they are reported in a separate section of the statement called *Cash Flows from Financing Activities*. Examples of cash flows associated with share capital are included in the cash flow statement for Sun Life shown in Exhibit 12.5.

EXHIBIT 12.5

Excerpt from Statements of Cash Flows for Sun Life Financial Inc.

REAL WORLD EXCERPT

Sun Life Financial Inc.

ANNUAL REPORT

CONSOLIDATED STATEMENTS OF CASH FLOWS
For the Year Ended December 31

($ million)	2006	2005
Cash flows provided by (used in) financing activities		
Debentures and borrowed funds	1,028	516
Payments to underwriters	(18)	(20)
Redemption of subordinated debt	—	—
Issuance of preferred shares	550	725
Issuance of common shares on exercise of stock options	61	78
Common shares purchased for cancellation	(575)	(544)
Dividends paid on common shares	(633)	(450)
Dividends paid on preferred shares	(57)	(15)
Net cash provided by (used in) financing activities	356	290

---

[7]In 2005, only nine of the 200 companies surveyed in *Financial Reporting in Canada 2006* indicated that there were conditions that affected their ability to pay dividends.

EFFECT ON CASH FLOW STATEMENT

IN GENERAL → Cash received from owners is reported as an inflow. Cash paid to owners is reported as an outflow. Examples are shown in the following table:

	Effect on Cash Flows
Financing activities	
Issuance of shares	+
Repurchase of shares	−
Payment of cash dividends	−

FOCUS COMPANY ANALYSIS → During the last two years, Sun Life issued preferred shares. At the same time, it repurchased common shares for cancellation, and paid dividends on both common and preferred shares.

In both 2005 and 2006, Sun Life's equity transactions resulted in net cash outflows; the payment of dividends offset the relatively smaller net increases in share capital.

SELECTED FOCUS COMPANY COMPARISONS: CASH FLOWS FROM FINANCING ACTIVITIES (IN MILLIONS)	
WestJet Airlines	$256
Petro-Canada	−1,175
Van Houtte	−8.6

ACCOUNTING AND REPORTING FOR INCOME TRUSTS

In recent years, many Canadian corporations have converted to income trusts. In its basic form, an income trust issues units of securities to the public in exchange for funds that are used to purchase the equity and debt of an operating business. The cash generated from the investment in the debt and equity securities issued by the operating business flows to the income trust, and most of the cash is then distributed to unit-holders. By distributing most of the cash received to unitholders, income trusts avoid paying income taxes, which has been the main reason for corporations that converted into income trusts. For example, Big Rock Brewery Ltd., which produces and markets its own brands of specialty draught and bottled beer for sale across Canada and in the United States, converted the common shares to trust units in January 2003, and became know as Big Rock Brewery Income Trust. Its share capital became trust unitholders' capital, and its retained earnings were renamed undistributed income.

The tax savings that resulted from converting common shares to trust units prompted many companies to seek conversion of their businesses to income trusts simply to avoid paying income taxes. The potential loss of sizable amounts of taxes prompted the Canadian government to introduce in late 2006 a new form of tax on cash distributions by income trust to their unitholders. This new tax, which is effective in 2011 for existing income trusts, and in 2007 for corporations that were considering conversion of their businesses to income trusts, has effectively put an end to the flurry of conversions. Two large corporations, Telus Corporation and Bell Canada Enterprises Inc., which had planned to convert to income trusts, ended up scrapping their plans subsequent to the new rules.

The practices that some income trusts used in computing distributable cash to unitholders raised concerns by accountants, investors and regulators about the viability of specific income trusts. The complexities related to issues affecting income trusts are covered in advanced accounting courses.[8]

ACCOUNTING AND REPORTING FOR UNINCORPORATED BUSINESSES

In this book, we emphasize the corporate form of business because it plays a dominant role in our economy. In fact, there are three forms of business organizations: corporations, sole proprietorships, and partnerships. As we have seen in this chapter, a *corporation* is a legal entity, separate and distinct from its owners. It can enter into contracts in its own name, be sued, and is taxed as a separate entity. A *sole proprietorship* is an unincorporated business owned by one individual. If you started a lawn care

---

[8]For more information on income trusts, see, for example, *Demystifying Income Trusts,* Certified General Accountants Association of Canada, January 2006. This study is accessible at www.cga-online.org.

business in the summer by yourself, it would have been a sole proprietorship. It is not necessary to file any legal papers to create a proprietorship. A *partnership* is a business owned by two or more people. Again, it is not necessary to file legal papers to create a partnership, but it is certainly a good idea to have a lawyer draw up a contract between the partners.

Neither partnerships nor proprietorships are separate legal entities. As a result, owners may be directly sued and are individually taxed on the earnings of the business.

The fundamentals of accounting and reporting for unincorporated businesses are the same as for a corporation, except for owners' equity. Typical account structures for the three forms of business organizations are outlined in Exhibit 12.6.

EXHIBIT **12.6**

Comparative Account Structure among Types of Business Entities

Typical Account Structure		
Corporation (Shareholders' Equity)	Sole Proprietorship (Owner's Equity)	Partnership (Partners' Equity)
Share Capital Contributed Surplus	Doe, Capital	Able, Capital Baker, Capital
Retained Earnings	Not used	Not used
Dividends Paid	Doe, Drawings	Able, Drawings Baker, Drawings
Revenues, expenses, gains, and losses	Same	Same
Assets and liabilities	Same	Same

Accounting for sole proprietorships and partnerships is discussed in Chapter Supplement B.

DEMONSTRATION **CASE**

This case focuses on the organization and operations for the first year of Mera Corporation, which was organized on January 2, 2008. The laws specify that the legal capital for no par value shares is the full amount of the shares. The corporation was organized by 10 local entrepreneurs for the purpose of operating a business to sell various supplies to hotels. The charter authorized the following share capital:

Common shares, no par value, unlimited number of shares.

Preferred shares, 5 percent, $25 par value, 10,000 shares (cumulative, non-convertible, and non-voting; liquidation value, $26).

The following summarized transactions, selected from 2008, were completed during the months indicated:

a. Jan.   Sold a total of 7,500 shares of no par value common shares to the 10 entrepreneurs for cash at $52 per share. Credit the Common Shares account for the total issue amount.

b. Feb.   Sold 7,560 preferred shares at $25 per share; cash collected in full.

c. Mar.   Purchased land for a store site and made full payment by issuing 400 preferred shares. Early construction of the store is planned. Debit Land (store site). The preferred share is selling at $25 per share.

d. Apr.   Paid $2,000 cash for organization costs. Debit the intangible asset account Organization Costs.

e. May   Issued 40 preferred shares to A.B. Cain in full payment of legal services rendered in connection with organization of the corporation. Assume that the preferred share is selling regularly at $25 per share. Debit Organization Costs.

f. June   Sold 500 no par value common shares for cash to C.B. Abel at $54 per share.

g. Nov. 30 The company's board of directors declared the annual dividends on the preferred shares, and a dividend of $0.50 per common share. The dividends are payable on December 20 to shareholders on record at December 15.

h. Dec. 20 Paid the declared dividends on preferred and common shares.

i. Dec. 31 Purchased equipment for $600,000; paid cash. No amortization expense should be recorded in 2008.

j. Dec. 31 Borrowed $20,000 cash from the City Bank on a one-year, interest-bearing note. Interest is payable at a 12-percent rate at maturity.

k. Dec. 31   Calculated the following for the year: gross revenues, $129,300; expenses, including corporation income tax but excluding amortization of organization costs, $98,000. Assume that these summarized revenue and expense transactions involved cash. Because the equipment and the bank loan transactions were on December 31, no related adjusting entries at the end of 2008 are needed.

l. Dec. 31   Decided that a reasonable amortization period for organization costs, starting as of January 1, 2008, is 10 years. This intangible asset must be amortized to expense.

Required:

1. Prepare appropriate journal entries, with a brief explanation for each of these transactions.

2. Prepare the required adjusting entry for 2008 to amortize organization costs.

3. Prepare appropriate closing entries at December 31, 2008.

4. Prepare a balance sheet for Mera Corporation at December 31, 2008. Emphasize full disclosure of shareholders' equity.

5. Assume that, instead of issuing common shares in January for $390,000, the company issued shares for $260,000 and borrowed an amount of $130,000 from its bank and signed a note, payable on December 31, 2010. Interest on the note is 10 percent, payable on December 31 of each year. Is borrowing from the bank more beneficial to the common shareholders compared to issuing additional common shares? Explain. For the purpose of this analysis, use an income tax rate of 40 percent.

We strongly recommend that you prepare your own answers to these requirements and then check your answers with the suggested solution.

SUGGESTED SOLUTION

1. Journal entries:

a.	Jan.	Cash (A).	390,000	
		Common shares (7,500 shares) (SE)		390,000
		Sale of no par value common shares		
		($52 × 7,500 shares = $390,000).		
b.	Feb.	Cash (A).	189,000	
		Preferred shares, 5% (par $25, 7,560 shares) (SE)		189,000
		Sale of preferred shares ($25 × 7,560 shares = $189,000).		
c.	Mar.	Land (A).	10,000	
		Preferred shares, 5% (par $25, 400 shares) (SE).		10,000
		Purchased land for future store site; paid in full by issuance		
		of 100 preferred shares ($25 × 400 shares = $10,000.)		
d.	Apr.	Organization costs (A)	2,000	
		Cash (A).		2,000
		Paid organization costs.		
e.	May	Organization costs (A)	1,000	
		Preferred shares 5% (par $25, 40 shares) (SE)		1,000
		Organization costs (legal services) paid by issuance of		
		40 preferred shares. The implied market value is		
		$25 × 40 shares = $1,000.		
f.	June	Cash (A).	27,000	
		Common shares (500 shares) (SE).		27,000
		Sold 500 no par value common shares		
		($54 × 500 shares = $27,000).		
g.	Nov. 30	Retained earnings (SE).	14,000	
		Dividends payable—Preferred (8,000 × $25 × 0.05). . . .		10,000
		Dividends payable—Common.		4,000
		Declaration of the annual dividend on preferred		
		shares and a dividend of $0.50 per common share		
h.	Dec. 20	Dividends payable—Preferred	10,000	
		Dividends payable—Common	4,000	
		Cash		14,000
		Payment of the declared dividends		

i.	Dec. 31	Equipment (A)	600,000	
		Cash (A).		600,000
		Purchased equipment.		
j.	Dec. 31	Cash (A).	20,000	
		Note payable (L)		20,000
		Borrowed cash and signed a one-year, 12 percent		
		interest-bearing note.		
k.	Dec. 31	Cash (A).	129,300	
		Revenues (E).		129,300
		Expenses (E)	98,000	
		Cash (A).		98,000
		To record summarized revenues and expenses.		
2.	Dec. 31	Expenses (E)	300	
		Organization costs (A).		300
		Adjusting entry to amortize organization cost for one year		
		[($2,000 + $1,000) ÷ 10 years = $300].		

3. Closing entries:

	Dec. 31	Revenues (R).	129,300	
		Retained earnings		129,300
		Retained earnings	98,300	
		Expenses ($98,000 + $300) (E)		98,300

4. Balance sheet:

MERA CORPORATION
Balance Sheet
At December 31, 2008

Assets			
Current assets			
Cash			$ 41,300
Tangible assets			
Land		$ 10,000	
Equipment (no depreciation assumed in the problem)		600,000	610,000
Intangible assets			
Organization cost (cost, $3,000 less amortization, $300)			2,700
Total assets			$654,000
Liabilities			
Current liabilities			
Note payable, 12%			$ 20,000
Shareholders' Equity			
Contributed capital			
Preferred shares, 5% (par value $25; authorized 10,000 shares, issued and outstanding 8,000 shares)		$200,000	
Common shares (no par value; authorized unlimited, issued and outstanding 8,000 shares)		417,000	
Total contributed capital		$617,000	
Retained earnings		17,000	
Total shareholders' equity			$634,000
Total liabilities and shareholders' equity			$654,000

5. Interest on the loan equals $13,000 ($130,000 × 10%) for 2008. This expense will reduce the income tax expense by $5,200 ($13,000 × 40%). The net income of $31,000 will then be reduced by $7,800 ($13,000 − $5,200) for a revised net income of $23,200. Income available to common shareholders equals $13,200 after deducting $10,000 of dividends on preferred shares. The return on *common* shareholders' equity would therefore equal 4.7 percent [$13,200 / $278,100, average common shareholders' equity = ($260,000 + $296,200)/2].

Without the $130,000 loan, the return on *common* shareholders' equity is 5.1 percent [($31,000 − $10,000) / $412,500]. This shows that borrowing an amount of $130,000 at 10 percent is not preferable to issuing additional common shares in this particular case.

Chapter Supplement A

Repurchase of Shares

A corporation may want to purchase its own shares from existing shareholders for a number of strategic reasons. A common reason is the existence of an employee bonus plan that provides workers with the company's shares as part of their compensation. Because of provincial securities regulations concerning newly issued shares, most companies find that it is less costly to give their employees shares that were purchased from shareholders than to issue new shares. Shares that were issued to shareholders and then subsequently reacquired and held by that corporation are called **treasury shares**. While these shares are held by the issuing corporation, they have no voting, dividend, or other shareholder rights.

Most Canadian companies cancel their shares when they buy them back from shareholders, as indicated in *Financial Reporting in Canada 2006*.[9] When shares are cancelled, the appropriate share capital account is reduced by an amount that reflects the average issuance price per share. If the purchase price is less than the average issuance price, the difference is credited to Contributed Surplus. For example, if Sun Life purchased 100,000 common shares in the open market at $15 per share and the average price of all of the previously issued common shares is $17, the journal entry and the transaction effects would be as follows:

TREASURY SHARES are a corporation's own shares that have been issued but were subsequently reacquired and held by that corporation.

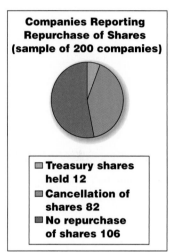

Companies Reporting Repurchase of Shares (sample of 200 companies)

- ■ Treasury shares held 12
- ■ Cancellation of shares 82
- ■ No repurchase of shares 106

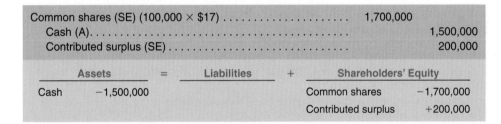

```
Common shares (SE) (100,000 × $17) .................   1,700,000
   Cash (A)..........................................              1,500,000
   Contributed surplus (SE).........................                200,000
```

Assets	=	Liabilities	+	Shareholders' Equity	
Cash −1,500,000				Common shares	−1,700,000
				Contributed surplus	+200,000

Assume further that Sun Life subsequently purchased 50,000 of its own common shares when the price per share was $23. In this case, the excess of the purchase price over the issuance price is $6 per share for a total of $300,000. This difference is debited first to Contributed Surplus to the extent of $200,000 (the account balance) and the remaining amount, $100,000, is debited to Retained Earnings. The Retained Earnings account is reduced because the excess of the purchase price over the contribution made previously by shareholders reflects the company's profitable operations, which resulted in net income and increased retained earnings; hence, the debit to Retained Earnings. The journal entry and the transaction effects follow:

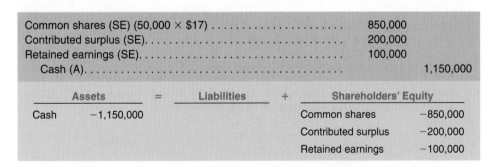

```
Common shares (SE) (50,000 × $17) .................   850,000
Contributed surplus (SE)............................   200,000
Retained earnings (SE)..............................   100,000
   Cash (A).........................................            1,150,000
```

Assets	=	Liabilities	+	Shareholders' Equity	
Cash −1,150,000				Common shares	−850,000
				Contributed surplus	−200,000
				Retained earnings	−100,000

[9]N. Chlala, A. Lavigne, L. Martel, and C. Byrd, *Financial Reporting in Canada 2006*. Toronto: Canadian Institute of Chartered Accountants, 2006, p. 355.

Chapter Supplement B

Accounting for Owners' Equity for Sole Proprietorships and Partnerships

OWNER'S EQUITY FOR A SOLE PROPRIETORSHIP

A sole proprietorship is an unincorporated business owned by one person. Only two owner's equity accounts are needed: (1) a capital account for the proprietor (J. Doe, Capital), and (2) a drawing (or withdrawal) account for the proprietor (J. Doe, Drawings).

The capital account of a sole proprietorship serves two purposes: to record investments by the owner and to accumulate periodic income or loss. The drawing account is used to record the owner's withdrawals of cash or other assets from the business. The drawing account is closed to the capital account at the end of each accounting period. The capital account reflects the cumulative total of all investments by the owner plus all earnings of the entity less all withdrawals of resources from the entity by the owner.

In most respects, the accounting for a sole proprietorship is the same as for a corporation. Exhibit 12.7 presents the recording of selected transactions and the owner's equity section of the balance sheet of Doe Retail Store to illustrate the accounting for owner's equity for a sole proprietorship.

EXHIBIT 12.7

Accounting for Owner's Equity for a Sole Proprietorship

Selected Transactions during 2008

January 1, 2008

J. Doe started a retail store by investing $150,000 of personal savings. The journal entry for the business is as follows:

Cash (A)	150,000	
J. Doe, capital (OE)		150,000

Assets		=	Liabilities	+	Shareholders' Equity	
Cash	+150,000				J. Doe, capital	+150,000

During 2008

Each month during the year, Doe withdrew $1,000 cash from the business for personal living expenses. Accordingly, the following journal entry was made each month:

J. Doe, drawings (OE)	1,000	
Cash (A).		1,000

Assets		=	Liabilities	+	Shareholders' Equity	
Cash	−1,000				J. Doe, drawings	−1,000

Note: At December 31, 2008, after the last withdrawal, the drawings account will reflect a debit balance of $12,000.

December 31, 2008

The store's operations for the year resulted in revenues of $128,000 and expenses of $110,000. The revenue and expense accounts are closed to the capital account at the end of the year. The closing entry follows:

Individual revenue accounts (R)	128,000	
Individual expense account (E)		110,000
J. Doe, capital (OE)		18,000

Assets	=	Liabilities	+	Shareholders' Equity	
				Revenues	−128,000
				Expenses	+110,000
				J. Doe, capital	+18,000

December 31, 2008

The journal entry required to close the drawings account follows:

J. Doe, capital (OE)	12,000	
J. Doe, drawings (OE)		12,000

Assets	=	Liabilities	+	Shareholders' Equity	
				J. Doe, capital	−12,000
				J. Doe, drawings	+12,000

Balance Sheet December 31, 2008 (partial)

Owner's equity	
J. Doe, capital, January 1, 2008	$150,000
Add: Net income for 2008	18,000
Total	168,000
Less: Withdrawals for 2008	(12,000)
J. Doe, capital, December 31, 2008	$156,000

A sole proprietorship does not pay income taxes. Therefore, its financial statements do not reflect income tax expense or income taxes payable. Instead, the net income of a sole proprietorship is taxed when it is included on the owner's personal income tax return. Because an employer/employee contractual relationship cannot exist with only one party involved, a "salary" to the owner is not recognized as an expense of a sole proprietorship. The owner's salary is accounted for as a distribution of profits (i.e., a withdrawal).

OWNERS' EQUITY FOR A PARTNERSHIP

Small businesses and professionals such as accountants, doctors, and lawyers use the partnership form of business. It is formed by two or more persons reaching mutual agreement about the terms of the partnership. The law does not require an application for a charter as it does in the case of a corporation. Instead, the agreement between the partners constitutes a partnership contract. The agreement should specify matters such as division of periodic income, management responsibilities, transfer or sale of partnership interests, disposition of assets upon liquidation, and procedures to be followed in case of the death of a partner. If the partnership agreement does not specify these matters, the applicable provincial laws are binding.

The primary advantages of a partnership are (1) ease of formation, (2) complete control by the partners, and (3) lack of income taxes on the business itself. The primary disadvantage is the unlimited liability of each partner for the partnership's liabilities. If the partnership does not have sufficient assets to satisfy outstanding debt, its creditors can seize the partners' personal assets.

As with a sole proprietorship, accounting for a partnership follows the same underlying fundamentals of accounting as any other form of business organization, except for those entries that directly affect owners' equity. Accounting for partners' equity follows the same pattern as illustrated earlier for a sole proprietorship, except that separate partner capital and drawings accounts must be established for each partner. Investments by each partner are credited to the partner's capital account, and withdrawals from the partnership by each partner are debited to the respective drawings account. The net income for a partnership is divided between the partners in the profit ratio specified in the partnership agreement and credited to each partner's account. The respective drawings accounts also are closed to the partner capital accounts. After the closing process, each partner's capital account reflects the cumulative total of all investments of that individual partner plus the partner's share of all partnership earnings less all the partner's withdrawals.

Exhibit 12.8 presents selected journal entries and partial financial statements for AB Partnership to illustrate the accounting for the distribution of income and partners' equity.

EXHIBIT **12.8**

Accounting for Partners' Equity

Selected Transactions during 2008

January 1, 2008

A. Able and B. Baker organized AB Partnership on this date. Able contributed $60,000 and Baker $40,000 cash to the partnership and agreed to divide net income (and net loss) 60% and 40%, respectively. The journal entry for the business to record the investment follows:

Cash (A)	100,000	
A. Able, capital (OE)		60,000
B. Baker, capital (OE)		40,000

Assets		=	Liabilities	+	Shareholders' Equity	
Cash	+100,000				A. Able, capital	+60,000
					B. Baker, capital	+40,000

During 2008

The partners agreed that Able would withdraw $1,000 and Baker $650 per month in cash. Accordingly, the following journal entry for the withdrawals was made each month:

A. Able, drawings (OE)...........................	1,000	
B. Baker, drawings (OE)...........................	650	
Cash (A)..		1,650

Assets		=	Liabilities	+	Shareholders' Equity	
Cash	−1,650				A. Able, drawings	−1,000
					B. Baker, drawings	−650

December 31, 2008

Assume that the normal closing entries for the revenue and expense accounts resulted in a net income of $30,000 that was distributed between the two partners. The closing entry is as follows:

Individual revenue accounts (R)	150,000	
Individual expense accounts (E)		120,000
A. Able, capital (OE)		18,000
B. Baker, capital (OE)		12,000

Assets	=	Liabilities	+	Shareholders' Equity	
				Revenues	−150,000
				Expenses	+120,000
				A. Able, capital	+18,000
				B. Baker, capital	+12,000

Net income is divided as follows:

A. Able, $30,000 × 60%	$18,000
B. Baker, $30,000 × 40%	12,000
Total	$30,000

December 31, 2008

The journal entry required to close the drawings accounts follows:

A. Able, capital (OE)...........................	12,000	
B. Baker, capital (OE)...........................	7,800	
A. Able, drawings (OE)		12,000
B. Baker, drawings (OE)		7,800

Assets	=	Liabilities	+	Shareholders' Equity	
				A. Able, capital	−12,000
				B. Baker, capital	−7,800
				A. Able, drawings	+12,000
				B. Baker, drawings	+7,800

A separate statement of partners' capital similar to the following is customarily prepared to supplement the balance sheet:

AB PARTNERSHIP
Statement of Partners' Capital
For the Year Ended December 31, 2008

	A. Able	B. Baker	Total
Investment, January 1, 2008	$60,000	$40,000	$100,000
Add: Additional investments during the year	0	0	0
Net income for the year	18,000	12,000	30,000
Totals	78,000	52,000	130,000
Less: Drawings during the year	(12,000)	(7,800)	(19,800)
Partners' equity, December 31, 2008	$66,000	$44,200	$110,200

The financial statements of a partnership follow the same format as those for a corporation except that (1) the income statement includes an additional section entitled Distribution of Net Income, (2) the partners' equity section of the balance sheet is detailed for each partner, (3) a partnership has no income tax expense because partnerships do not pay income tax (each partner must report his or her share of the partnership profits on his or her individual tax return), and (4) salaries paid to partners are not recorded as expense but are treated as a distribution of earnings (withdrawals).

SOLUTIONS TO **SELF-STUDY QUIZZES**

Self-Study Quiz 12-1

1. The liability is created on the declaration date.
2. The cash outflow occurs on the payment date, July 3, 2007.
3. Dividends payable   183,508,160
      Cash   18,350,720
4. The fundamental requirements are: availability of retained earnings, declaration by the board of directors, and availability of cash.

Self-Study Quiz 12-2

1. Retained earnings   3,000,000
      Common shares   3,000,000
2. Retained earnings   1,000,000
      Common shares   1,000,000
3. No journal entry is required in the case of a stock split.

Self-Study Quiz 12-3

1. Amount received per share = Stated capital / Number of shares issued and outstanding
   = $300,000,000/12,000,000 = $25
2. Total annual dividends = Number of shares $\times$ Dividend per share
   = 12,000,000 $\times$ ($0.278 $\times$ 4) = $13,344,000.
3. The redemption date is the earliest date when Sun Life can call Class A Series 4 back from shareholders and pay them $25.00 per share.
4. The earliest redemption date is December 31, 2011.

CHAPTER **TAKE-AWAYS**

1. **Explain the role of share capital in the capital structure of a corporation. p. 629**
   The law recognizes corporations as separate legal entities. Owners invest in a corporation and receive shares that can be traded on established stock exchanges. Shares provide a number of rights, including the right to receive dividends.

2. **Analyze the earnings per share ratio. p. 632**
   The earnings per share ratio facilitates the comparison of a company's earnings over time or with other companies' at a single point in time. By expressing earnings on a per share basis, differences in the size of companies become less important.

3. **Describe the characteristics of common shares and analyze transactions affecting common shares. p. 632**

    A common share is the basic voting share issued by a corporation. Usually it has no par value, but par value shares also can be issued. Preferred shares are issued by some corporations. These shares contain some special rights and may appeal to certain investors.

    A number of key transactions involve share capital: (1) initial sale of shares, (2) cash dividends, and (3) stock dividends and stock splits. Each is illustrated in this chapter.

4. **Discuss dividends and analyze related transactions. p. 637**

    The return associated with an investment in shares comes from two sources: appreciation of share price and dividends. Dividends are recorded as a liability when they are declared by the board of directors (i.e., on the date of declaration). The liability is satisfied when the dividends are paid (i.e., the date of payment).

5. **Analyze the dividend yield ratio. p. 639**

    The dividend yield ratio measures the percentage of return on investment from dividends. For most companies, the return associated with dividends is very small.

6. **Discuss the purpose of stock dividends, stock splits, and report transactions. p. 639**

    Stock dividends are distributions of a company's shares to existing shareholders on a pro rata basis. The transaction involves transferring an additional amount into the Common Shares account from the Retained Earnings account. A stock split also involves the distribution of additional shares to shareholders but no additional amount is transferred into the Common Shares account from the Retained Earnings account.

7. **Describe the characteristics of preferred shares and analyze transactions affecting preferred shares. p. 641**

    Preferred shares provide investors certain advantages including dividend preferences and a preference on asset distributions in the event the corporation is liquidated.

8. **Measure and report retained earnings. p. 645**

    The Retained Earnings account includes income that has been earned since a company began its operations minus any dividends that have been distributed to shareholders. The amount of retained earnings is important because dividends normally can be paid only if there is a sufficient balance in this account (and in the cash account).

9. **Discuss the impact of share capital transactions on cash flows. p. 646**

    Both inflows (e.g., issuance of share capital) and outflows (e.g., repurchase of shares) are reported in the Financing Activities section of the cash flow statement. The payment of dividends is reported as an outflow in this section.

Throughout the preceding chapters, we emphasized the conceptual basis of accounting. An understanding of the rationale underlying accounting is important for both preparers and users of financial statements. In Chapter 13, we bring together our discussion of the major users of financial statements and how they analyze and use them. We discuss and illustrate many widely used analytical techniques discussed in earlier chapters, as well as additional techniques. As you study Chapter 13, you will see that an understanding of accounting rules and concepts is essential for effective analysis of financial statements.

KEY **RATIOS**

The **earnings per share** ratio states the net income of a corporation on a per common share basis. The ratio is computed as follows (p. 632):

$$\text{Earnings per Share} = \frac{\text{Net Income}}{\text{Average Number of Common Shares Outstanding}}$$

The **dividend yield ratio** measures the dividend return on the current share price. The ratio is computed as follows (p. 639):

$$\text{Dividend Yield Ratio} = \frac{\text{Dividends per Share}}{\text{Market Price per Share}}$$

FINDING FINANCIAL INFORMATION

BALANCE SHEET

Under Current Liabilities
Dividends, once declared by the board of directors, are reported as a liability (usually current).

Under Non-Current Liabilities
Transactions involving share capital do not usually generate non-current liabilities.

Under Shareholders' Equity
Typical accounts include
  Preferred shares
  Common shares
  Contributed surplus
  Retained earnings

STATEMENT OF SHAREHOLDERS' EQUITY

This statement reports detailed information concerning shareholders' equity, including
(1) amounts in each equity account,
(2) number of shares outstanding,
(3) impact of transactions such as earning income, declaration of dividends, and repurchase of shares.

INCOME STATEMENT

Share capital is never shown on the income statement. Dividends are not an expense. They are a distribution of income and are, therefore, not reported on the income statement.

CASH FLOW STATEMENT

Under financing activities:
  +Cash inflows from initial sale of shares
  −Cash outflows for dividends
  −Cash outflows for repurchase of shares

NOTES

Under Summary of Significant Accounting Policies:
Usually, very little information concerning share capital is provided in this summary.

Under a separate note:
Most companies report information about their stock option plans and information about major transactions such as stock dividends. A historical summary of dividends paid per share is typically provided.

KEY TERMS

Authorized Number of Shares p. 630

Common Shares p. 632

Convertible Preferred Shares p. 642

Cumulative Dividend Preference p. 644

Current Dividend Preference p. 643

Date of Record p. 637

Declaration Date p. 637

Dividends in Arrears p. 644

Issued Shares p. 630

Legal Capital p. 633

No Par Value Shares p. 633

Outstanding Shares p. 630

Par Value p. 633

Payment Date p. 637

Preferred Shares p. 641

Stock Dividend p. 639

Stock Split p. 641

Treasury Shares p. 651

QUESTIONS

1. Define *corporation* and identify its primary advantages.
2. What is the charter of a corporation?
3. Explain each of the following terms: (a) *authorized capital shares,* (b) *issued capital shares,* and (c) *outstanding capital shares.*
4. Name three rights of shareholders. Which of these is most important in your mind? Why?
5. Differentiate between common shares and preferred shares.
6. Explain the distinction between par value shares and no par value shares.
7. What are the usual characteristics of preferred shares?
8. What are the two basic sources of shareholders' equity? Explain each.
9. Owners' equity is accounted for by source. What does *source* mean?
10. What are the two basic requirements to support a cash dividend? What are the effects of a cash dividend on assets and shareholders' equity?
11. Differentiate between cumulative and non-cumulative preferred shares.
12. Define *stock dividend.* How does it differ from a cash dividend?
13. What are the primary purposes of issuing a stock dividend?

14. Identify and explain the three important dates with respect to dividends.

15. Define *retained earnings*. What are the primary components of retained earnings at the end of each period?

16. Define *prior period adjustments*. How are they reported?

17. What does the term *restrictions on retained earnings* mean?

18. Your parents have just retired and have asked you for some financial advice. They have decided to invest $100,000 in a company very similar to Sun Life Financial Inc. The company has issued both common and preferred shares. What factors would you consider in giving them advice? Which type of shares would you recommend?

EXERCISES

LO1, 3, 7   **E12–1** **Determining the Effects of the Issuance of Common and Preferred Shares**

Kelly, Incorporated, was issued a charter on January 15, 2008, that authorized the following share capital:

Common shares, no par value, 100,000 shares.
Preferred shares, $1.50, no par value, 5,000 shares. (*Note*: $1.50 is the dividend rate.)

During 2008, the following selected transactions occurred:

a. Issued 20,000 common shares at $18 cash per share.

b. Issued 2,000 preferred shares at $22 cash per share.

At the end of 2008, the company's net income equalled $42,000.

Required:

1. Prepare the shareholders' equity section of the balance sheet at December 31, 2008.

2. Assume that you are a common shareholder. If Kelly needed additional capital, would you prefer to have it issue additional common or preferred shares? Explain.

LO1, 2   **E12–2** **Reporting Shareholders' Equity**

The financial statements of Sun Media Inc. included the following selected information at December 31, 2009:

Common shares	$6,000,000
Retained earnings	850,000
Net income	1,200,000
Dividends declared	800,000

The common shares were sold at $20 per share.

Required:

1. What was the amount of retained earnings at the beginning of 2009?

2. Compute earnings per share.

3. Prepare the shareholders' equity section of the company's balance sheet at December 31, 2009.

LO1, 3   **E12–3** **Reporting Shareholders' Equity and Determining Dividend Policy**

Sampson Corporation was organized in 2008 to operate a financial consulting business. The charter authorized the issue of 12,000 common shares. During the first year, the following selected transactions were completed:

a. Issued 5,000 common shares for cash at $22 per share.

b. Issued 600 common shares for a piece of land to be used for a facilities site; construction began immediately. Assume that the market price per share was $22 on the date of issuance. Debit Land.

c. Issued 2,000 common shares for cash at $23 per share.

d. At year-end, the accounts reflected a loss of $7,000. Because a loss was incurred, no income tax expense was recorded.

Required:

1. Prepare the journal entry required for each of these transactions.

2. Prepare the shareholders' equity section as it should be reported on the balance sheet at year-end, December 31, 2008.

3. Can Sampson pay dividends at year-end? Explain.

E12–4 Determining the Effects of Transactions on Shareholders' Equity

LO1, 3, 7

Nguyen Corporation was organized in January 2009 by 10 shareholders to operate an air-conditioning sales and service business. The charter issued by the government authorized the following no par value shares:

Common shares, 200,000 shares.

Preferred shares, 50,000 shares.

During January and February 2009, the following transactions were completed:

a. Collected $50,000 cash from each of the 10 organizers and issued 2,500 common shares to each of them.

b. Issued 10,000 preferred shares at $25 per share; collected the cash.

c. Issued 500 common shares to an outsider at $25 per share; collected the cash.

The company's operations resulted in net income of $40,000 for 2009. The board of directors declared cash dividends of $25,000 that were paid in December 2009. The preferred shares have a dividend rate of $1 per share.

Required:

1. Prepare the shareholders' equity section of the balance sheet at December 31, 2009.

2. Why would an investor prefer to buy a preferred share rather than a common share?

3. Is it ethical to sell shares to outsiders at a higher price than the amount paid by the organizers?

E12–5 Recording Shareholders' Equity Transactions, Including Non-Cash Consideration: Write a Brief Memo

LO1, 3

Teacher Corporation obtained a charter at the start of 2007 that authorized 50,000 no par value common shares and 20,000, $2, no par value preferred shares. The corporation was organized by four individuals who "reserved" 51 percent of the common shares for themselves. The remaining shares were to be sold to other individuals at $40 per share on a cash basis. During 2008, the following selected transactions occurred:

a. Collected $25 per share cash from three of the organizers and received two adjoining lots of land from the fourth organizer. Issued 3,000 common shares to each of the four organizers and received title to the land.

b. Issued 6,000 common shares to an outsider at $40 cash per share.

c. Issued 8,000 preferred shares at $25 cash per share.

d. At the end of 2008, the accounts reflected net income of $42,000.

Required:

1. Prepare the journal entries to record each of these transactions.

2. Write a brief memo to explain the basis that you used to determine the cost of the land.

3. Is it ethical to sell shares to outsiders at a higher price than the amount paid by the organizers?

E12–6 Preparing a Statement of Retained Earnings and Evaluating Dividend Policy

LO1, 4

The following account balances were selected from the records of Blake Corporation at December 31, 2008, after all adjusting entries were completed:

Common shares (no par value; authorized 100,000 shares, issued 36,000 shares)	$540,000
Contributed surplus	150,000
Dividends declared and paid in 2008	18,000
Retained earnings, January 1, 2008	67,000
Correction of prior period accounting error (a debit, net of income tax)	8,000
Income summary for 2008 (credit balance)	28,000

The stock price was $22.43 per share on that date.

Required:

1. Prepare the statement of retained earnings for 2008.

2. Prepare the shareholders' equity section of the balance sheet at December 31, 2008.

3. Compute and evaluate the dividend yield ratio.

■ **LO4, 6**   **E12–7**   **Analyzing the Impact of Dividend Policy**

McDonald and Associates is a small manufacturer of electronic connections for local area networks. Consider three independent situations.

Case 1: McDonald increases its cash dividends by 50 percent, but no other changes occur in the company's operations.

Case 2: The company's income and cash flows increase by 50 percent but this does not change its dividends.

Case 3: McDonald issues a 50-percent stock dividend, but no other changes occur.

Required:

1. How do you think each situation would affect the company's stock price?

2. If the company changed its accounting policies and reported higher net income, would the change have an impact on the stock price?

■ **LO4**   **E12–8**   **Computing Dividends on Preferred Shares and Analyzing Differences**

The records of Hoffman Company reflected the following balances in the shareholders' equity accounts at December 31, 2008:

Common shares, no par value, 40,000 shares outstanding	$800,000
Preferred shares, $2, no par value, 6,000 shares outstanding	$150,000
Retained earnings	$235,000

On September 1, 2009, the board of directors was considering the distribution of a $62,000 cash dividend. No dividends were paid during 2007 and 2008. You have been asked to determine dividend amounts under two independent assumptions (show computations):

a. The preferred shares are non-cumulative.

b. The preferred shares are cumulative.

Required:

1. Determine the total amounts that would be paid to the preferred shareholders and to the common shareholders under the two independent assumptions.

2. Write a brief memo to explain why the dividend per common share was less under the second assumption.

3. Why would an investor buy Hoffman's common shares instead of its preferred shares if they pay a lower dividend per a share? Explain. The market prices of the preferred and common shares were $25 and $40, respectively, on September 1, 2009.

■ **LO4**   **E12–9**   **Determining the Impact of Dividends**

Average Corporation has the following shares outstanding at the end of 2008:

Preferred shares, $4, no par value; 8,000 outstanding shares.

Common shares, no par value; 30,000 outstanding shares.

On October 1, 2008, the board of directors declared dividends as follows:

Preferred shares: Full dividend amount, payable December 20, 2008.

Common shares: 10 percent common stock dividend (i.e., one additional share for each 10 held), issuable December 20, 2008.

On December 20, 2008, the market prices were $50 per preferred share and $32 per common share.

Required:

Explain the effect of each of the dividends on the assets, liabilities, and shareholders' equity of the company at each of the specified dates.

■ **LO4**   **E12–10**   **Recording the Payment of Dividends**

Sun Life Financial Inc. disclosed the following information in a press release:

Sun Life
Financial Inc.

> **(TORONTO)—May 1, 2007**—The Board of Directors of Sun Life Financial Inc. (TSX/ NYSE: SLF) today announced a quarterly shareholder dividend of $0.32 per common share, payable July 3, 2007 to shareholders of record at the close of business on May 23, 2007. This is the same amount as paid in the previous quarter.
>
> The Board of Directors of Sun Life Financial Inc. also announced quarterly dividends of $0.296875 per Class A Non-Cumulative Preferred Share Series 1; $0.30 per Class A Non-Cumulative Preferred Share Series 2; $0.278125 per Class A Non-Cumulative Preferred Share Series 3; $0.278125 per Class A Non-Cumulative Preferred Share Series 4; and $0.28125 per Class A Non-Cumulative Preferred Share Series 5, payable June 29, 2007 to shareholders of record at the close of business on May 23, 2007.

Assume that Sun Life has the following number of shares outstanding at the date of dividend declaration: Common shares, 572 million; Preferred shares, Series 1—16 million, Series 2—13 million, Series 3—10 million, Series 4—12 million, Series 5—10 million.

Required:

1. Prepare the journal entries to record the declaration and payment of dividends to common shareholders.

2. Prepare the journal entries to record the declaration and payment of dividends to preferred shareholders.

E12–11 Analyzing Stock Dividends   ■ **LO6**

On December 31, 2009, the shareholders' equity section of the balance sheet of R & B Corporation reflected the following:

Common shares (no par value, authorized 60,000 shares, outstanding 25,000 shares)	$250,000
Contributed surplus	12,000
Retained earnings	75,000

On February 1, 2010, the board of directors declared a 12-percent stock dividend to be issued April 30, 2010. The market value per share was $18 on the declaration date.

Required:

1. For comparative purposes, prepare the shareholders' equity section of the balance sheet (a) before the stock dividend and (b) after the stock dividend. (*Hint:* Use two columns for this requirement.)

2. Explain the effects of this stock dividend on the company's assets, liabilities, and shareholders' equity.

E12–12 Analyzing Stock Dividends   ■ **LO1, 6**

At the beginning of the year 2009, the shareholders' equity of the balance sheet of R & B Corporation reflected the following:

Common shares, authorized 60,000 shares, issued and outstanding 36,000 shares	$360,000
Retained earnings	750,000

On February 1, 2009, the board of directors declared a 100-percent stock dividend to be issued on April 30, 2009. The price per common share was $18 on February 1.

Required:

1. For comparative purposes, prepare the Shareholders' Equity section of the balance sheet (a) immediately before the stock dividend, and (b) immediately after the stock dividend. (*Hint:* use two columns to shows amounts for this requirement.)

2. Explain the effects of this stock dividend on assets, liabilities, and shareholders' equity.

E12–13 Determining the Impact of Stock Dividends and Stock Splits   ■ **LO6**

Milano Tools, Inc., announced a 100-percent stock dividend. Determine the impact (increase, decrease, no change) of this dividend on the following:

1. Total assets.

2. Total liabilities.

3. Common shares.

4. Total shareholders' equity.

5. Market value per common share.

Now assume that the company announced a 2-for-1 stock split. Determine the impact of the stock split on the five items above. Explain why the accounting for stock dividends differs from that of the stock split.

E12–14 Evaluating Dividend Policy   ■ **LO4**

H&R Block is a well-known name, especially during income tax time each year. The company serves more than 18 million taxpayers in more than 10,000 offices in Canada, Australia, England, and the United States. A 2005 press release contained the following information:

H & R Block

> H&R Block Inc. (NYSE:HRB) today reported a net loss of $72.2 million, or 22 cents per share, for the second quarter of fiscal 2006 compared with a loss of $49.9 million, or 15 cents per share, in the year-ago quarter. Revenues in the quarter rose 14 percent to $620.4 million from $542.0 million in the prior-year period, with all business segments contributing to top-line growth.
>
> . . .
>
> H&R Block's board of directors declared a quarterly cash dividend of 12.5 cents per share, payable Jan. 3, 2006, to shareholders of record Dec. 13, 2005. The payment will be the company's 173rd consecutive quarterly dividend.

Required:

1. Explain why H&R Block can pay dividends despite its loss.

2. What factors did the board of directors consider when it declared the dividends?

E12–15 **(Chapter Supplement A) Analyzing the Repurchase of Shares**

Winnebago

Winnebago is a familiar name on vehicles travelling North American highways. The company manufactures and sells large motor homes for vacation travel. These motor homes can be quickly recognized because of the company's "flying W" trademark. A news article contained the following information:

> The Company's profits have been running double a year ago, revenues were up 27 percent in the May quarter and order backlog stands at 2,229 units. Those are the kind of growth statistics that build confidence in the boardroom. The Company has announced plans to spend $3.6 million to expand its manufacturing facilities and it recently authorized repurchase of $15 million worth of its own shares, the third buyback in two years. The Company's stock is now selling for $25 per share.

Required:

1. Determine the impact of this transaction on the financial statements.

2. Why do you think the board decided to repurchase the company's shares?

3. What impact will this purchase have on Winnebago's future dividend obligations?

E12–16 **(Chapter Supplement A) Repurchase of Shares**

Danier Leather

Danier Leather Inc. manufactures and retails leather products, earning international recognition as a leader in leather and suede design. The company's annual report for the fiscal year ended June 30, 2005, included the following (all amounts are in thousands):

> (c) Normal course issuer bid
>
> On February 2, 2005, the Company received approval from the Toronto Stock Exchange to renew its Normal Course Issuer Bid. The bid permits the Company to acquire up to 421,061 Subordinate Voting Shares, representing approximately 10% of the public float of the Subordinate Voting Shares, during the period from February 7, 2005 to February 6, 2006. During the year ended June 25, 2005, 402,400 Subordinate Voting Shares were purchased for cancellation at prevailing market prices for cash consideration of $4,583. The excess of $2,883 over the average paid-in value of the shares was charged to retained earnings.

Required:

1. What was the average price that the company paid to repurchase these shares?

2. Prepare the journal entry to record a summary of the 2005 repurchase transactions.

PROBLEMS

■ **LO1–4, 6** **P12–1** **Finding Missing Amounts** (AP12–1)

At December 31, 2008, the records of Nortech Corporation provided the following selected and incomplete data:

> Common shares, no par value
>
>   Shares authorized, 200,000.
>
>   Shares issued, ____?___; issue price $17 per share; cash collected in full, $2,125,000.
>
> Net income for 2008, $118,000.
>
> Dividends declared and paid during 2008, $75,000.
>
> Prior period adjustment, correction of 2007 accounting error, $9,000 (a credit, net of income tax).
>
> Retained earnings balance, January 1, 2008, $155,000.

Required:

1. Complete the following tabulation:
   Shares authorized _____.
   Shares issued _____.
   Shares outstanding _____.

2. Earnings per share is $ _____.

3. Dividend paid per common share is $ _____.

4. The prior period adjustment should be reported on the _____ as an addition
   to _____ (or a deduction from _____).

5. The amount of retained earnings available for dividends on January 1, 2008, was
   $_____.

6. Assume that the board of directors voted a 100-percent stock split (the number of shares
   will double). After the stock split, the average issue price per share will be $_____,
   and the number of outstanding shares will be _____.

7. Assume that the company declared a 100-percent stock dividend instead of the
   100-percent stock split. Compare and contrast the stock dividend and the stock split with
   regard to their effects on shareholders' equity components.

P12–2 Recording Transactions Affecting Shareholders' Equity (AP12–2)   ■ **LO1, 3**

Pappas Corporation began operations in January 2009. The charter authorized the following
share capital:

  Preferred shares: 9 percent, $25 par value, authorized 40,000 shares.

  Common shares: no par value, authorized 80,000 shares.

During 2009, the following transactions occurred in the order given:

a. Issued 20,000 common shares to each of the three organizers. Collected $9 cash per share
from two of the organizers and received a plot of land with a small building on it in full
payment for the shares of the third organizer and issued the shares immediately. Assume
that 30 percent of the non-cash payment received applies to the building.

b. Sold 2,400 preferred shares at $25 per share. Collected the cash and issued the shares
immediately.

c. Sold 2,000 preferred shares at $25 and 1,000 common shares at $12 per share. Collected
the cash and issued the shares immediately.

d. The operating results at the end of 2009 were as follows:

Revenues	$220,000
Expenses, including income taxes	160,000

Required:

1. Prepare the journal entries to record each of these transactions and to close the accounts.

2. Write a brief memo explaining how you determined the cost of the land and the building
   in the first journal entry.

3. Prepare the shareholders' equity section of the balance sheet for Pappas Corporation as at
   December 31, 2009.

P12–3 Preparing the Shareholders' Equity Section after Selected Transactions (AP12–3)   ■ **LO1, 3, 4**

Eddie Edwards Limited, a public company, was formed on January 2, 2008 with the
following authorized capital structure:

  Preferred shares: No par value, $1.00 per share quarterly cumulative dividend,
callable at 103, 100,000 shares authorized.

Common shares: Unlimited number of shares authorized.

The following selected transactions occurred during the first six months of operations:

January 2: Issued 100,000 common shares in exchange for land and building with a combined appraised value of $2,200,000. Sixty percent of the acquisition cost is attributable to the building.

January 3 Issued 50,000 preferred shares for $1,250,000 cash.

April 1 Declared the quarterly cash dividend on the preferred shares, payable on April 25.

April 10 Declared and distributed a 5-percent common stock dividend on all outstanding common shares as of March 31. The market price of the common shares on March 31 was $24 per share.

April 25 Paid the preferred dividend that was declared on April 1.

Required:

1. Prepare journal entries to record the above transactions.

2. Prepare the shareholders' equity section of the balance sheet for Eddie Edwards Limited as at June 30, 2008. Assume that the company recorded net income of $500,000 for its first six months.

■ LO5, 6   **P12–4 Comparing Stock and Cash Dividends** (AP12–4)

*e***X***cel*

Water Tower Company had the following shares outstanding and retained earnings at December 31, 2008:

Preferred shares, 7% (par value $25; outstanding, 2,400 shares)	$ 60,000
Common shares (outstanding, 30,000 shares)	240,000
Retained earnings	280,000

The board of directors is considering the distribution of a cash dividend to the two groups of shareholders. No dividends were declared during 2006 or 2007. Three independent cases are assumed:

Case A: The preferred shares are non-cumulative; the total amount of dividends is $30,000.

Case B: The preferred shares are cumulative; the total amount of dividends is $12,600.

Case C: Same as Case B, except the amount is $66,000.

Required:

1. Compute the amount of dividends, in total and per share, that would be payable to each class of shareholders for each case. Show computations.

2. Assume that the company issued a 10-percent common stock dividend on the outstanding common shares when the market value per share was $24. Complete the following comparative schedule, including explanation of the differences.

	Amount of Dollar Increase (decrease)	
	Cash Dividend—	
Item	Case C	Stock Dividend
Assets	$_____	$_____
Liabilities	$_____	$_____
Shareholders' equity	$_____	$_____

■ LO4   **P12–5 Analyzing Dividend Policy**

Dana and David, two young financial analysts, were reviewing financial statements for Compaq, a manufacturer of personal computers. Dana noted that the company did not report any dividends in the financing activity section of the cash flow statement and said, "Just a few years ago, *Forbes* magazine named that company as one of the best-performing companies. If it's so good, I wonder why it isn't paying any dividends." David wasn't convinced that Dana was looking in the right place for dividends but didn't say anything.

Dana continued the discussion by noting, "When *Forbes* selected it as a best-performing company, its sales doubled over the previous two years, just as they doubled over the prior two years. Its income was only $789 million that year, compared with $867 million the previous year, but cash flow from operating activities was $943 million, compared to an outflow of $101 million the prior year."

At that point, David noted that the cash flow statement reported that the company had invested $703 million in new property this year, compared with $408 million the prior year. He also was surprised to see that inventory and accounts receivable had increased by $1 billion and nearly $2 billion, respectively, the previous year. "No wonder it can't pay dividends; it generated less than $1 billion from operating activities and had to put it all back into accounts receivable and inventory."

Required:
1. Correct any misstatements that either Dana or David made. Explain.
2. Which of the factors presented in the case help you understand the company's dividend policy?

P12–6 Determining the Financial Statement Effects of Dividends ■ **LO4**
Legrand Company has outstanding 45,000 common shares and 25,000, $4, preferred shares. On December 1, 2008, the board of directors voted to distribute a $4 cash dividend per preferred share and a 5 percent common stock dividend on the common shares. At the date of declaration, the common share was selling at $40 and the preferred share at $50. The dividends are to be paid, or issued, on February 15, 2009. The company's fiscal year ends on December 31.

Required:
Explain the comparative effects of the two dividends on the assets, liabilities, and shareholders' equity (a) through December 31, 2008, (b) on February 15, 2009, and (c) the overall effects from December 1, 2008, through February 15, 2009. A schedule similar to the following might be helpful:

	Comparative Effects Explained	
Item	Cash Dividend on Preferred	Stock Dividend on Common
1. Through December 31, 2008: Assets, etc.		

P12–7 Recording Dividends ■ **LO5, 6**
RBC Financial Group provides personal and commercial banking, wealth management services, insurance, corporate and investment banking and transaction processing services on a global basis. On March 3, 2006 a press release announced the following:

RBC Financial Group

> Royal Bank of Canada (RY: TSX, NYSE, SWX) today announced that its Board of Directors has declared a stock dividend, which has the same effect as a two-for-one split of its common shares.
>
> RBC's last stock dividend was paid on October 5, 2000.
>
> The Board of Directors today also declared a quarterly common share cash dividend of $0.72 per share, which represents $0.36 per share on a post-stock dividend basis. This dividend of $0.36 per share is payable on May 24, 2006, to common shareholders of record on April 25, 2006.

Required:
1. Prepare any journal entries that RBC Financial should make as the result of information in the preceding report. Assume that the company has 1.3 million shares outstanding with a market value of $47 per share and an average issue price of $5.60.
2. What do you think happened to the company's stock price after the March 3 announcement?
3. What factors did the board of directors consider in making this decision?

P12–8 Preparing the Statement of Retained Earnings and the Shareholders' Equity Section ■ **LO8**
(AP12–5)
The annual report of Andrew Peller Ltd. for fiscal year 2006 included the financial statements for fiscal year 2005, which were restated to reflect the effects of a fraudulent action by a former employee. The restated financial statements included the following items and their account balances:

Andrew Peller

Share capital	$ 7,375	
Retained earnings, beginning of year	79,260	
Net income	6,054	
Dividends declared	3,109	
Effect of prior period adjustment	593	Debit balance

Required:

1. Prepare the statement of retained earnings for the year ending March 31, 2005, and the shareholders' equity section of the balance sheet as at March 31, 2005.

2. The company provided the following explanation for the prior period adjustment. Use the amounts shown in the "Adjustment" column below to reconstruct the journal entry that was prepared to record the effect of the alleged fraud on the identified income statement and balance sheet accounts.

PRIOR PERIOD ADJUSTMENT

During fiscal 2006, management uncovered evidence of a misappropriation of certain assets (related to an alleged fraud by a former nonexecutive employee). As a result, management determined that certain costs, which previously had been included in the cost of inventories, should have been expensed. In addition, certain costs previously included in cost of goods sold have been reclassified as unusual items. Accordingly, the consolidated financial statements for the fiscal year ended March 31, 2005 have been restated as follows from the amounts previously reported:

	As previously reported	Adjustment	As restated
Cost of goods sold	$ 96,660	$ (1,058)	$ 95,602
Unusual items	—	1,173	1,173
Income tax expense	4,730	(44)	4,686
Net earnings	8,538	(71)	8,467
Inventories	62,045	(1,072)	60,973
Income taxes recoverable	693	408	1,101
Retained earnings as at March 31, 2005	79,924	(664)	79,260
Retained earnings as at March 31, 2004	74,494	(593)	73,901

P12–9 (Chapter Supplement A) Analyzing the Repurchase of Shares

Petro-Canada

Petro-Canada is one of the largest integrated oil and gas companies in Canada, offering a variety of petroleum products and services. Its annual report for fiscal year 2006 included the following (amounts are in millions of dollars):

Changes in common shares and contributed surplus were as follows:

			2006
	Shares	Amount	Contributed Surplus
Balance at beginning of year	515,138,904	$1,362	$1,422
Issued for cash under employee stock option and share purchase plans	2,177,881	57	5
Repurchases of common shares	(19,778,400)	(53)	(958)
Balance at end of year	497,538,385	$1,366	$ 469

In June 2006, the Company renewed its normal course issuer bid to repurchase up to 25 million of its common shares during the period from June 22, 2006 to June 21, 2007, subject to certain conditions. During 2006, the Company purchased 19,778,400 common shares at an average price of $51.10 per common share for a total cost of $1,011 million (2005—8,333,400 common shares at an average price of $41.54 per common share for a total cost of $346 million). The excess of the purchase price over the carrying amount of the shares purchased, which totalled $958 million in 2006 (2005—$324 million), was recorded as a reduction of contributed surplus.

Required:

1. Why do you think Petro-Canada's board of directors decided to repurchase the company's shares?

2. Prepare the journal entry to record a summary of the repurchase transactions.

3. Compute the average issuance price per common share, and explain why Petro-Canada paid a much higher price for repurchasing its own shares.

4. What impact will this transaction have on Petro-Canada's future dividend obligations?

P12–10 (Chapter Supplement B) Comparing Owners' Equity Sections for Alternative Forms of Organization

■ **LO1**

Assume for each of the following independent cases that the accounting period for NewBiz ends on December 31, 2009, and that the Income Summary account at that date reflected a debit balance (loss) of $20,000.

Case A: Assume that NewBiz is a *sole proprietorship* owned by Proprietor A. Prior to the closing entries, the capital account reflected a credit balance of $50,000 and the drawings account a balance of $8,000.

Case B: Assume that NewBiz is a *partnership* owned by Partner A and Partner B. Prior to the closing entries, the owners' equity accounts reflected the following balances: A, Capital, $40,000; B, Capital, $38,000; A, Drawings, $5,000; and B, Drawings, $9,000. Profits and losses are divided equally.

Case C: Assume that NewBiz is a *corporation.* Prior to the closing entries, the shareholders' equity accounts showed the following: Share Capital, authorized 30,000 shares, outstanding 15,000 shares, $150,000; Contributed Surplus, $5,000; Retained Earnings, $65,000.

Required:

1. Prepare all of the closing entries indicated at December 31, 2009, for each of the three separate cases.

2. Show for each case how the owners' equity section of the balance sheet would appear at December 31, 2009.

ALTERNATE PROBLEMS

AP12–1 Finding Missing Amounts (P12–1)

■ **LO1, 3, 4, 5**

At December 31, 2009, the records of Kozmetsky Corporation provided the following selected and incomplete data:

> Common shares, no par value.
>   Shares authorized, unlimited.
>   Shares issued, ____?___; issue price $75 per share.
> Net income for 2009, $4,800,000.
>   Common shares account $1,500,000.
> Dividends declared and paid during 2009, $2 per share.
> Retained earnings balance, January 1, 2009, $82,900,000.

Required:

1. Complete the following tabulation:

   Shares issued _____.

   Shares outstanding _____.

2. Earnings per share is $_____.

3. Total dividends paid on common shares during 2009 equal $_____.

4. Assume that the board of directors voted a 100-percent stock split (the number of shares will double). After the stock split, the average issue price per share will be $_____, and the number of outstanding shares will be _____.

5. Disregard the stock split (assumed in requirement 4). Assume instead that a 10-percent stock dividend was declared and issued when the market price of the common shares was $91. Explain how the shareholders' equity will change.

AP12–2 Recording Transactions Affecting Shareholders' Equity (P12–2)

■ **LO1, 3**

Arnold Company was granted a charter that authorized the following share capital:

Preferred shares: 8 percent, par value $25, 20,000 shares.

Common shares: No par value, 100,000 shares.

During the first year, 2008, the following selected transactions occurred in the order given:

a. Sold 20,000 common shares at $35 cash per share and 5,000 preferred shares at $25 per share. Collected cash and issued the shares immediately.

b. Issued 2,500 preferred shares as full payment for a plot of land to be used as a future plant site. Assume that the share was selling at $25.

c. Declared and paid the quarterly cash dividend on the preferred shares.

d. At December 31, 2008, the accounts reflected net income of $33,500.

Required:

1. Prepare the journal entries to record each of these transactions.

2. Explain the economic difference between acquiring an asset for cash compared with acquiring it by issuing shares. Is it "better" to acquire a new asset without having to give up another asset?

■ **LO1, 3, 4** **AP12–3** **Preparing the Shareholders' Equity Section After Selected Transactions** (P12–3)
The shareholders' equity accounts of Freeman Inc. at January 2, 2008, are as follows:

Preferred shares, no par value, cumulative, 6,000 shares issued	$300,000
Common shares, no par value, 250,000 shares issued	500,000
Retained earnings	600,000

The following transactions occurred during the year:

March 10	Purchased a building for $500,000. The seller agreed to receive 7,000 preferred shares and 15,000 common shares of Freeman in exchange for the building. The preferred shares were trading in the market at $50 per share on that day.
July 1	Declared a semi-annual cash dividend of $0.50 per common share and the required amount of dividends on preferred shares, payable on August 1, 2008 to shareholders of record on July 21, 2008. The annual dividend of $4 per preferred share had not been paid in either 2007 or 2008.
August 1	Paid the cash dividend declared on July 1 to both common and preferred shareholders.
December 31	Determined that net income for the year was $385,000.

Required:

1. Prepare journal entries to record the above transactions.

2. Prepare the shareholders' equity section of Freeman's balance sheet as at December 31, 2008.

■ **LO5, 6** **AP12–4** **Comparing Stock and Cash Dividends** (P12–4)
Ritz Company had the following shares outstanding and retained earnings at December 31, 2009:

Preferred shares, 8% (par value $25; outstanding, 8,400 shares)	$210,000
Common shares (outstanding, 50,000 shares)	500,000
Retained earnings	900,000

The board of directors is considering the distribution of a cash dividend to the two groups of shareholders. No dividends were declared during 2007 or 2008. Three independent cases are assumed:

Case A: The preferred shares are non-cumulative; the total amount of dividends is $25,000.

Case B: The preferred shares are cumulative; the total amount of dividends is $25,000.

Case C: Same as Case B, except the amount is $75,000.

Required:

1. Compute the amount of dividends, in total and per share, payable to each class of shareholders for each case. Show computations.

2. Assume that the company issued a 15-percent common stock dividend on the outstanding common shares when the market value per share was $50. Complete the following comparative schedule, including explanation of the differences.

	Amount of Dollar Increase (decrease)	
Item	Cash Dividend— Case C	Stock Dividend
Assets	$_____	$_____
Liabilities	$_____	$_____
Shareholders' equity	$_____	$_____

AP12–5 **Preparing the Statement of Retained Earnings and the Shareholders' Equity Section** (P12–8)

■ **LO8**

Van Houtte

The annual report of Van Houtte Inc. for fiscal year 2005 included the following items and their account balances:

Share capital	$128,250	
Contributed surplus	2,043	
Cumulative translation adjustment	13,519	Debit balance
Retained earnings, beginning of year	99,757	
Net income	21,706	
Dividends declared	5,132	
Change in accounting policy— stock-based compensation	1,630	Debit balance

Required:

1. Prepare the statement of retained earnings for the year ending April 2, 2005.
2. Prepare the shareholders' equity section of the balance sheet at April 2, 2005.

CASES AND PROJECTS

FINDING AND INTERPRETING FINANCIAL INFORMATION

CP12–1 **Finding Financial Information**

■ **LO1, 3, 4**

Van Houtte

Refer to the financial statements of Van Houtte given in Appendix B of this book.

Required:

1. Identify the types of shares that Van Houtte is authorized to issue and their characteristics. Do all types of shares have the same voting rights? If not, explain why.
2. What is the number of shares outstanding on March 31, 2007?
3. Did the company pay dividends during fiscal year 2007? If so, how much per share?
4. Has the company ever issued a stock dividend or declared a stock split? If so, describe.
5. What is the average price received per each class of shares?

CP12–2 **Finding Financial Information**

■ **LO1, 3, 4**

The Forzani Group Ltd.

Refer to the Online Learning Centre Web site at **www.mcgrawhill.ca/olc/libby/student/ resources** for the financial statements of The Forzani Group Ltd. (FGL).

Required:

1. Identify the types of shares that FGL is authorized to issue and their characteristics.
2. What was the highest price for the company's Class A shares during the past 12 years?
3. Did the company purchase any of its own shares during the period covered by the financial statements?
4. Describe the company's dividend policy, if any.

FINANCIAL REPORTING AND ANALYSIS CASES

CP12–3 **Finding Information Missing from an Annual Report**

■ **LO1, 2, 3, 4**

Procter & Gamble

Procter & Gamble is a multi-billion dollar company that sells a variety of consumer products such as Mr. Clean, Cheer, Crest, Vicks, Scope, Pringles, Folgers, Vidal Sassoon, and Zest. The company's annual report contained the following information:

a. Retained earnings at June 30, 2006 totalled $35,666.
b. Net income for the year ended June 30, 2006 was $8,684 million.

c. The number of common shares outstanding at June 30, 2006 was 3,178,841 shares with a total book value of $61,832 million.

d. Dividends declared on common shares equaled $1.15 per share.

Required:

1. Compute the total amount of dividends declared by the company.

2. A shareholder observed that P&G has a sizeable amount of retained earnings, and wondered why the company accumulated this amount instead of distributing it to its shareholders. Write a brief memo to explain why earnings have been retained by the company.

3. Compute the amount of retained earnings at July 1, 2005, the beginning of P&G's fiscal year.

4. Compute the company's earnings per share. Is EPS a useful measure of performance? Explain.

■ LO3, 4   **CP12–4** **Financial Reporting and Analysis Cases**

Andrew Peller

ANALYSIS

Andrew Peller Ltd. is a leading producer and marketer of quality wines in Canada. With wineries located in British Columbia, Ontario, and Nova Scotia, the Company markets wines produced from grapes grown in British Columbia's Okanagan Valley, Ontario's Niagara Peninsula, and vineyards around the world. Andrew Peller sells its ultra-premium wines and icewines throughout the United States, Asia, and Europe.

The company's annual report for fiscal year 2006 includes the following details about its share capital (amounts in thousands of dollars):

9   Capital stock

		2006		2005	
		Issued		Issued	
	Authorized	Shares	Amounts	Shares	Amounts
Class A shares, non-voting	Unlimited	3,962,547	$6,975	3,954,302	$6,844
Class B shares, voting	Unlimited	1,001,547	400	1,001,772	400
		4,964,094	$7,375	4,956,074	$7,244

Class A shares are non-voting and are entitled to a dividend in an amount equal to 115% of any dividend paid or declared on Class B shares. Class B shares are voting and convertible into Class A shares on a one-for-one basis. During 2006, 225 (2005—200) Class B shares were converted into Class A shares.

Selected information about the company's net income, dividends, and retained earnings for the five-year period 2002–2006 has been extracted from its annual reports:

	3/31/2006	3/31/2005	3/31/2004	3/31/2003	3/31/2002
Net income	$ 6,054	$ 8,538	$ 9,570	$ 6,929	$ 5,325
Dividends on Class A and Class B shares	3,109	3,108	3,086	2,971	2,967
Retained earnings, end of year	82,205	79,260	74,494	69,010	64,052

Required:

1. The note indicates that 225 Class B shares were converted into Class A shares. What is the apparent reason for the share conversion? Explain.

2. Prepare the journal entry to record the conversion. (Note that the book value of the shares is rounded to the nearest thousand).

3. How much of the dividends for 2006 were paid to Class A shareholders?

■ LO3   **CP12–5** **Characteristics of Preferred Shares**

Power Financial Corporation

ANALYSIS

Power Financial Corporation is a Canadian diversified international management company that holds interests, directly or indirectly, in companies that are active in the financial services industry in Canada, the United States, and Europe. The company's 2006 annual report included the following information about specific issues of preferred shares:

15. Share Capital

The 5.20% Non-Cumulative First Preferred Shares, Series C are entitled to fixed non-cumulative preferential cash dividends at a rate equal to $1.30 per share per annum. On and after October 31, 2007, the Corporation may redeem for cash the Series C First Preferred Shares in whole or in part, at the Corporation's option, at $26.00 per share if redeemed within the twelve months commencing October 31, 2007, declining by $0.20 per share for each subsequent twelve-month period thereafter to October 31, 2011, 25.20 if redeemed on or after October 31, 2011 and before July 31, 2012, and $25.00 if redeemed on or after July 31, 2012, in each case together with all declared and unpaid dividends to the date of redemption.

On or after July 31, 2012, the Corporation may convert each Series C First Preferred Share into that number of common shares determined by dividing $25.00 together with all declared and unpaid dividends to the date of conversion by the greater of $3.00 and 95% of the weighted average trading price of the common shares for the 20 trading days ending on the last trading day occurring on or before the fourth day immediately prior to the date of conversion.

On or after October 31, 2012, subject to the right of the Corporation to offer the right to convert into a further series of preferred shares, to redeem for cash or to find substitute purchasers for such shares, each Series C First Preferred Share will be convertible at the option of the holder, on the last day of January, April, July and October of each year into that number of common shares determined by dividing $25.00 together with all declared and unpaid dividends to the date of conversion by the greater of $3.00 and 95% of the weighted average trading price of the common shares for the 20 trading days ending on the last trading day occurring on or before the fourth day immediately prior to the date of conversion.

Required:

1. Identify the various characteristics of these preferred shares.
2. Based on the characteristics of these shares, should they be classified as debt or equity? Explain.

CP12–6 Analyzing Dividend Policy

■ **LO5, 6**

Wal-Mart has been one of the most successful retail companies in history with steady growth in earnings over the past eight years. The following information was extracted from the company's annual reports. The market price is an average of the highest and lowest price for the year.

Wal-Mart

	2007	2006	2005	2004	2003	2002	2001	2000
Dividends	$ 2,802	$ 2,511	$ 2,214	$1,569	$1,328	$1,249	$1,070	$ 890
Net income	11,284	11,231	10,267	9,054	7,955	6,592	6,235	5,377
Dividends per share	0.67	0.60	0.52	0.36	0.30	0.28	0.24	0.20
Market price per share	47.23	48.00	56.19	53.41	54.18	51.93	53.41	54.82
Dividend yield	1.42%	1.25%	0.93%	0.67%	0.55%	0.54%	0.45%	0.36%

Assume that you are a financial analyst preparing a forecast of Wal-Mart's operating results for fiscal year 2008. Due to a number of factors, you believe that net income for next year will be in the range of $12,000 to $12,500 million. To complete your financial forecast, you now need to estimate the total amount of dividends that Wal-Mart will pay.

Required:

1. Based on the information above, describe the dividend policy of Wal-Mart, and estimate the dividends that the company will pay in 2008. (*Hint:* the ratio of dividends to net income, called dividend payout ratio, may provide useful information about the company's dividend policy.)
2. Wal-Mart's board of directors has increased dividends per share continuously over the past eight years. What would be your expectation of dividends per share for 2008? Justify your answer.
3. The dividend yield has also increased steadily over the past eight years. What should be the market price per share for the dividend yield to reach 1.50 percent? Explain.

CP12–7 (Chapter Supplement A) Interpreting the Financial Press

■ **LO3, 4**

As discussed in this chapter, companies buy back their own shares for a number of reasons. An article on this topic is available on the Web site **www.mcgrawhill.ca/olc/libby/student/ resources**. Read the article, "Stock market time bomb,"[10] November 15, 1999, and then write a short memo summarizing is contents. In general, do you think large stock buy-backs are good for investors?

---

[10]Reprinted from November 15, 1999 issue of *BusinessWeek* by special permission, copyright © 1999 by the McGraw-Hill Companies, Inc.

CRITICAL THINKING CASES

■ LO5, 6 **CP12–8** **Evaluating an Ethical Dilemma**

You are a member of the board of directors of a large company that has been in business for more than 100 years. The company is proud of the fact that it has paid dividends every year that it has been in business. Because of this stability, many retired people have invested large portions of their savings in the company's common stock. Unfortunately, the company has struggled for the past few years as it tries to introduce new products and is considering not paying a dividend this year. The president wants to skip the dividend in order to have more cash to invest in product development: "If we don't invest this money now, we won't get these products to market in time to save the company. I don't want to risk thousands of jobs." One of the most senior board members speaks next: "If we don't pay the dividend, thousands of retirees will be thrown into financial distress. Even if you don't care about them, you have to recognize our stock price will crash when they all sell." The company treasurer proposes an alternative: "Let's skip the cash dividend and pay a stock dividend. We can still say we've had a dividend every year." The entire board now turns to you for your opinion. What should the company do?

■ LO4 **CP12–9** **Evaluating an Ethical Dilemma**

You are the president of a very successful Internet company that has had a remarkably profitable year. You have determined that the company has more than $10 million in cash generated by operating activities not needed in the business. You are thinking about paying it out to shareholders as a special dividend. You discuss the idea with your vice-president, who reacts angrily to your suggestion: "Our stock price has gone up by 200 percent in the last year alone. What more do we have to do for the owners? The people who really earned that money are the employees who have been working 12 hours a day, six or seven days a week to make the company successful. Most of them didn't even take vacations last year. I say we have to pay out bonuses and nothing extra for the shareholders." As president, you know that you are hired by the board of directors, which is elected by the shareholders. What is your responsibility to both groups? To which group would you give the $10 million?

FINANCIAL REPORTING AND ANALYSIS TEAM PROJECT

■ LO1, 3, 4, 7 **CP12–10** **Team Project: Examining an Annual Report**

As a team, select an industry to analyze. Each team member should acquire the annual report for one publicly traded company in the industry, with each member selecting a different company. (Library files, the SEDAR service at **www.sedar.com**, or the company itself are good resources.)

Required:

On an individual basis, each team member should then write a short report answering the following questions about the selected company. Discuss any patterns across the companies that you as a team observe. Then, as a team, write a short report comparing and contrasting your companies.

1. *a.* List the accounts and amounts of the company's shareholders' equity.
   b. From the notes to financial statements, identify any unusual features in the contributed capital accounts (e.g., convertible preferred, nonvoting common), if any.

2. Identify the cash flows related to share capital transactions. You will need to refer to the cash flow statement.
   a. If new shares were issued during the year, what was the average price per share at the time of issuance?
   b. Reconstruct the journal entry for the issuance of shares.

3. What type of dividends did the company declare during the year? How much was paid in cash?

Analyzing Financial Statements

After studying this chapter, you should be able to:

FOCUS COMPANY:

Home Depot

FINANCIAL ANALYSIS:

BRINGING IT ALL TOGETHER

The history of Home Depot (**www.homedepot.com**) is an unusual success story. Founded in 1978 in Atlanta, Home Depot has grown to be the world's largest home improvement retailer. Its stores are located in major cities in Canada, the United States, Mexico, and Puerto Rico. Home Depot's financial statements are presented in Exhibit 13.1.

Home Depot operates more than 2,200 stores and design centres that sell building materials, decor, lawn and garden products, and home remodelling services. In Canada, Home Depot has 155 stores employing over 27,000 people. During the previous 10 years, Home Depot's revenues grew at an average rate of 16.6 percent per year and its earnings grew at an average annual rate of 19.9 percent.

Financial analysts evaluate Home Depot's historical performance to determine if they should recommend that their clients purchase its shares. The analysts want to have some reasonable assurance that the company will continue to thrive, causing the company's share price to increase and thereby benefit their clients. However, two analysts looking at the same company may arrive at different conclusions, and this depends in part on investors' objectives for their investments: growth or safety. Some analysts may reject Home Depot because it is too risky relative to other investment opportunities, whereas others may recommend investment because Home Depot is growing quickly relative to the risk in its business.

EXHIBIT **13.1**

Home Depot Financial
Statements

REAL WORLD EXCERPT

Home Depot

ANNUAL REPORT

THE HOME DEPOT, INC., AND SUBSIDIARIES
Consolidated Balance Sheets
(in millions of US dollars, except per share data)

	January 28, 2007	January 29, 2006
Assets		
Current Assets:		
Cash and Cash Equivalents	$ 600	$ 793
Short-Term Investments	14	14
Receivables, net	3,223	2,396
Merchandise Inventories	12,822	11,401
Other Current Assets	1,341	665
Total Current Assets	18,000	15,269
Property and Equipment, at cost:		
Land	8,355	7,924
Buildings	15,215	14,056
Furniture, Fixtures and Equipment	7,799	7,073
Leasehold Improvements	1,391	1,207
Construction in Progress	1,123	843
Capital Leases	475	427
	34,358	31,530
Less Accumulated Depreciation and Amortization	7,753	6,629
Net Property and Equipment	26,605	24,901
Notes Receivable	343	348
Goodwill	6,314	3,286
Other Assets	1,001	601
Total Assets	$52,263	$44,405
Liabilities and Stockholders' Equity		
Current Liabilities:		
Short-Term Debt	$ —	$ 900
Accounts Payable	7,356	6,032
Accrued Salaries and Related Expenses	1,295	1,068
Sales Taxes Payable	475	488
Deferred Revenue	1,634	1,757
Income Taxes Payable	217	388
Current Instalments of Long-Term Debt	18	513
Other Accrued Expenses	1,936	1,560
Total Current Liabilities	12,931	12,706
Long-Term Debt, excluding current instalments	11,643	2,672
Other Long-Term Liabilities	1,243	1,172
Deferred Income Taxes	1,416	946
Stockholders' Equity		
Common Stock, par value $0.05; authorized: 10,000 shares; issued 2,421 shares at January 28, 2007 and 2,401 shares at January 29, 2006; outstanding 1,970 shares at January 28, 2007 and 2,124 shares at January 29, 2006	121	120
Paid-In Capital	7,930	7,149
Retained Earnings	33,052	28,943
Accumulated Other Comprehensive Income	310	409
Treasury Stock, at cost, 451 shares at January 28, 2007 and 277 shares at January 29, 2006	(16,383)	(9,712)
Total Stockholders' Equity	25,030	26,909
Total Liabilities and Stockholders' Equity	$52,263	$44,405

See accompanying Notes to Consolidated Financial Statements.

EXHIBIT **13.1**
(continued)

THE HOME DEPOT, INC., AND SUBSIDIARIES
Consolidated Statements of Earnings
(in millions of US dollars, except per share data)

	January 28, 2007	January 29, 2006	January 30, 2005
Net Sales	$90,837	$81,511	$73,094
Cost of Sales	61,054	54,191	48,664
Gross Profit	29,783	27,320	24,430
Operating Expenses:			
Selling, General and Administrative	18,348	16,485	15,256
Depreciation and Amortization	1,762	1,472	1,248
Total Operating Expenses	20,110	17,957	16,504
Operating Income	9,673	9,363	7,926
Interest Income (Expense):			
Interest and Investment Income	27	62	56
Interest Expense	(392)	(143)	(70)
Interest, net	(365)	(81)	(14)
Earnings Before Provision for Income Taxes	9,308	9,282	7,912
Provision for Income Taxes	3,547	3,444	2,911
Net Earnings	$ 5,761	$ 5,838	$ 5,001
Weighted Average Common Shares	2,054	2,138	2,207
Basic Earnings Per Share	$ 2.80	$ 2.73	$ 2.27
Diluted Weighted Average Common Shares	2,062	2,147	2,216
Diluted Earnings Per Share	$ 2.79	$ 2.72	$ 2.26

[1]Fiscal years ended January 28, 2007, January 29, 2006, and January 30, 2005 include 52 weeks.
See accompanying Notes to Consolidated Financial Statements.

THE HOME DEPOT, INC., AND SUBSIDIARIES
Consolidated Statements of Cash Flows
(amounts in millions of US dollars)

	January 28, 2007	January 29, 2006	January 30, 2005
Cash Flows from Operating Activities:			
Net Earnings	$5,761	$5,838	$5,001
Reconciliation of Net Earnings to Net Cash Provided by Operating Activities:			
Depreciation and Amortization	1,886	1,579	1,319
Impairment Related to Disposition of EXPO Real Estate	—	78	—
Stock-Based Compensation Expense	297	175	125
Changes in Assets and Liabilities, net of the effects of acquisitions:			
Decrease (Increase) in Receivables, net	96	(358)	(266)
Increase in Merchandise Inventories	(563)	(971)	(849)
(Increase) Decrease in Other Current Assets	(225)	16	29
Increase in Accounts Payable and Accrued Liabilities	531	148	645
(Decrease) Increase in Deferred Revenue	(123)	209	263
(Decrease) Increase in Income Taxes Payable	(172)	175	2
Increase (Decrease) in Deferred Income Taxes	46	(609)	319
(Decrease) Increase in Other Long-Term Liabilities	(51)	151	119
Other	178	189	(75)
Net Cash Provided by Operating Activities	7,661	6,620	6,632

(continued)

EXHIBIT **13.1**
(concluded)

	Fiscal Year Ended[1]		
	January 28, 2007	January 29, 2006	January 30, 2005
Cash Flows from Investing Activities:			
Capital Expenditures, net of $49, $51 and $38 of non-cash capital expenditures in fiscal 2006, 2005 and 2004, respectively	(3,542)	(3,881)	(3,948)
Payments for Businesses Acquired, net	(4,268)	(2,546)	(727)
Proceeds from Sales of Property and Equipment	138	164	96
Purchases of Investments	(5,409)	(18,230)	(25,890)
Proceeds from Sales and Maturities of Investments	5,434	19,907	25,990
Net Cash Used in Investing Activities	(7,647)	(4,586)	(4,479)
Cash Flows from Financing Activities:			
(Repayments of) Proceeds from Short-Term Borrowings, net	(900)	900	—
Proceeds from Long-Term Borrowings, net of discount	8,935	995	995
Repayments of Long-Term Debt	(509)	(24)	(510)
Repurchase of Common Stock	(6,684)	(3,040)	(3,106)
Proceeds from Sale of Common Stock	381	414	285
Cash Dividends Paid to Stockholders	(1,395)	(857)	(719)
Other Financial Activities	(31)	(136)	272
Net Cash Used in Financing Activities	(203)	(1,748)	(2,783)
(Decrease) Increase in Cash and Cash Equivalents	(189)	286	(630)
Effect of Exchange Rate Changes on Cash and Cash Equivalents	(4)	1	33
Cash and Cash Equivalents at Beginning of Year	793	506	1,103
Cash and Cash Equivalents at End of Year	$ 600	$ 793	$ 506
Supplemental Disclosure of Cash Payments Made For:			
Interest, net of interest capitalized	$ 270	$ 114	$ 78
Income Taxes	$3,963	$3,860	$2,793

[1]Fiscal years ended January 28, 2007, January 29, 2006, and January 30, 2005 include 52 weeks.
See accompanying Notes to Consolidated Financial Statements.

As you analyze Home Depot's financial results, it is important to remember that any analysis is understood in the context of what an investor wants to accomplish. Your analysis, in itself, will present neither a good nor a bad picture of Home Depot's performance. This assessment must be made in the context not only of the investor's goals but also of the industry's performance and the economic environment.

Would you want to buy shares in Home Depot? To make a rational decision, you would want to consider more factors than just the company's rapid growth in profitability and the recommendation of a financial analyst. The information contained in Home Depot's financial statements and the analytical tools discussed in this chapter provide an important basis to help you decide whether to invest in Home Depot shares.

UNDERSTANDING THE BUSINESS

In Canada and the United States, companies spend billions of dollars each year preparing, auditing, and publishing their financial statements. These statements are then mailed to current and prospective investors. Most companies also make financial information available on the Internet. Home Depot has a particularly interesting Web site (**www.homedepot.ca**) that contains current financial statements, recent news articles about the company, and a variety of relevant information.

The reason that Home Depot and other companies spend so much money to provide information to investors is simple: Financial statements help people make better economic decisions. Two broad groups of people use financial statements. One group is the management of the business; it relies on accounting data to make important operating decisions, such as the pricing of products or expansion of productive capacity. The second group comprises external decision makers. In fact, published financial statements are designed primarily to meet the needs of external decision makers, including present and potential owners, investment analysts, and creditors.

Users of financial statements are interested in three types of information:

1. *Information about past performance.* Information concerning items such as income, sales volume, cash flows, and return earned on the investment helps people assess the success of the business and the effectiveness of its management. Such information also helps the decision maker compare one company with others.

2. *Information about the present condition of a business.* This type of information helps answer questions such as: What types of assets are owned? How much debt does the business owe, and when is it due? What is its cash position? What are its EPS, return on investment, and debt-to-equity ratios? What is the inventory position? Answers to these and similar questions help people assess the successes and failures of the past; more importantly, they provide information useful in assessing the cash flow and profit potentials of the business.

3. *Information about the future performance of the business.* Decision makers select from among several alternative courses of action. Because all decisions are future-oriented, financial statements based on historical cost are not an ideal basis upon which to forecast future performance. Investors are most interested in risk and the potential rewards for accepting risk. In general, as risk in the business environment increases, investors demand a higher future return on their investments to compensate them for the increased riskiness of their investments. Investors prefer to earn maximum return for minimum risk when choosing companies in which to invest.

Reliable accounting measures of past performance are one source of information upon which investors base their assessments of risk and potential return. Analysis of reliable measures that indicate financial trends for each company is therefore very important. If investors can reasonably assume that important business factors will be very similar in future to the current situation, then a reliable historical trend is often a satisfactory basis upon which to predict future financial performance. For example, the recent sales and earnings trends of a business are usually good indicators of what might be expected in the future. In other words, investors must know where the company has been in order to predict where it is likely to go.

ORGANIZATION OF THE CHAPTER

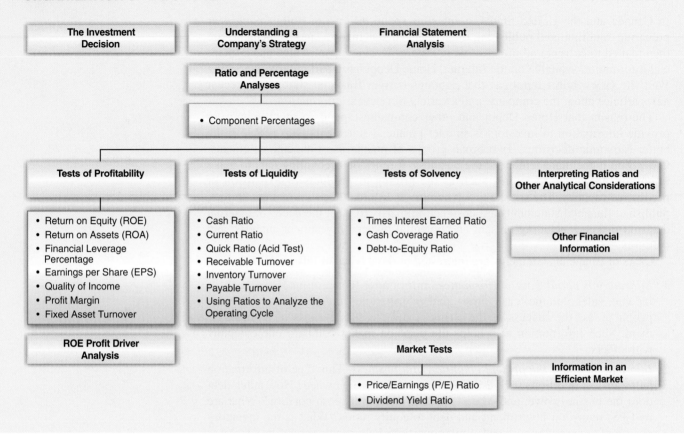

THE INVESTMENT DECISION

Of the people who use financial statements, current and potential investors are perhaps the single largest group. They often rely on the advice of professional analysts, who develop recommendations on widely held stocks such as Home Depot. Most individual investors use analysts' reports and track their recommendations. As this book was being written, professional analysts issued the following investment recommendations for Home Depot:

Analyst Ratings: Home Depot	Current Month	Last Month	Two Months Ago	Three Months Ago
1—Strong Buy	7	6	6	6
2—Buy	5	6	6	6
3—Hold	10	10	10	10
4—Sell	1	1	2	2
5—Strong Sell	0	0	0	0

Source: Thomson/First Call.

Perhaps the most important observation about this summary of investment recommendations is the degree of disagreement. While seven analysts strongly recommended the purchase of Home Depot's shares, 10 other analysts recommended holding the company's shares if they already owned them. One analyst recommended that shareholders sell the shares they already own. This level of disagreement shows that financial analysis is part art and part science.

When considering an investment in shares, the investor should evaluate the future income and growth potential of the business on the basis of three factors:

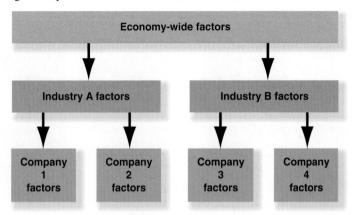

1. *Economy-wide factors*. Often the overall health of the economy has a direct impact on the performance of an individual business. Investors should consider data such as the unemployment rate, general inflation rate, and changes in interest rates. For example, increases in interest rates often slow economic growth because consumers are less willing to buy merchandise on credit when interest rates are high. Furthermore, companies that wish to expand their operations will find it too expensive to borrow funds.

2. *Industry factors*. Certain events have a major impact on each company within an industry, but have only a minor impact on other companies outside the industry. For example, a major drought may be devastating for food-related industries but may have no effect on the electronics industry.

3. *Individual company factors*. To properly analyze a company, you should learn as much as you can about it. Good analysts do not rely only on the information contained in the financial statements. They visit the company, buy its products, and read about it in the business press. For example, if you evaluate McDonald's, it is equally important to assess the quality of its balance sheet and the quality of its McChicken® sandwich.

Besides considering these factors, investors should understand a company's business strategy when evaluating its financial statements. Before discussing analytical techniques, we will show you how business strategy affects financial statement analysis.

UNDERSTANDING A COMPANY'S STRATEGY

Financial statement analysis involves more than just "crunching numbers." Before you start looking at numbers, you should know what you are looking for. While financial statements report on transactions, each of these transactions is the result of a company's operating decisions as it implements its business strategy.

■ **LEARNING OBJECTIVE 1**

Explain how a company's business strategy affects financial analysis.

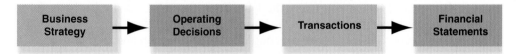

A useful starting point for financial statement analysis is the return on equity (ROE) profit driver analysis (also called *ROE decomposition* or *DuPont analysis*), which shows a logical relationship among the three ratios presented in Exhibit 13.2. These ratios are based on financial statement elements that are often called *profit drivers* or *profit levers* because they describe the three ways that management can improve ROE. The DuPont model helps us understand that a number of business strategies affect the profitability of a business. The model follows:

EXHIBIT **13.2**
ROE Profit Driver Analysis

Businesses can earn a high rate of return for the owners (i.e., a high ROE) by following different strategies. Two fundamental strategies follow:

1. *Product differentiation.* Under this strategy, companies offer products with unique benefits, such as being of high quality or offering unusual features or style. These unique benefits allow a company to charge higher prices. In general, higher prices result in higher profit margins, which lead to higher returns on equity (as shown in the ROE model).

2. *Cost advantage.* Under this strategy, companies attempt to operate more efficiently than their competitors, which permit them to offer lower prices to attract customers. The efficient use of resources is captured in the asset turnover ratio, and as the ROE model illustrates, a high asset turnover ratio leads to higher return on investment.

You can probably think of a number of companies that have followed one of these two basic strategies.

Differentiation on Quality	**Differentiation on Cost**
Cars:	**Cars:**
Cadillac	Hyundai Accent
Mercedes	Dodge Neon
Lincoln	Toyota Echo
Retail Stores:	**Retail Stores:**
Cartier	Zellers
Holt Renfrew	Wal-Mart

The best place to start your analysis is with a solid understanding of a company's business strategy. To evaluate how a company is doing, you must know what managers are trying to do. You can learn a lot about a company's strategy by reading its complete annual report, especially the letter from the president. It also is useful to read articles about the company in the business press.

Home Depot's business strategy is described in its annual report as follows:

REAL WORLD EXCERPT

Home Depot

ANNUAL REPORT

OPERATING STRATEGY. The operating strategy for Home Depot stores is to offer a broad assortment of high-quality merchandise and services at competitive prices using knowledgeable, service-oriented personnel and strong marketing and credit promotions. We believe that our associates' knowledge of products and home improvement techniques and applications is very important in our marketing approach and our ability to maintain and enhance customer satisfaction.

This strategy has several implications for our analysis of Home Depot:

1. Cost control is critical. Home Depot must be able to purchase merchandise at low prices to beat competitors.

2. To cover the cost of operating large stores, Home Depot must be able to generate high volume of business.

3. To offer a high level of service, Home Depot must incur employee compensation and training costs that are higher than competitors' costs. This puts pressure on Home Depot to control costs in other areas.

With these implications in mind, we can attach more meaning to the information contained in Home Depot's financial statements.

As the preceding discussion indicates, a company can take different actions to try to affect each of its profit drivers. To understand the impact of these actions, financial analysts disaggregate each of the profit drivers into more detailed ratios. For example, the asset turnover ratio is further disaggregated into turnover ratios for specific assets such as accounts receivable, inventory, and fixed assets. We have developed our understanding of these ratios in previous chapters but we will bring them together in the next few sections as part of a comprehensive review of ratio analysis.

FINANCIAL STATEMENT ANALYSIS

Analyzing financial data without a basis of comparison is impossible. For example, would you be impressed with a company that earned $1 million last year? You are probably thinking, "It depends." A $1-million profit might be very good for a company that lost money the year before but not good for a company that made $500 million during the previous year. It might be good for a small company but not good for a very large company. And, it might be good if all the other companies in the industry lost money but not good if they all earned much larger profits.

> ■ **LEARNING OBJECTIVE 2**
> Discuss how analysts use financial statements.

As you can see from this simple example, financial results cannot be evaluated in isolation. To properly analyze the information reported in financial statements, you must develop appropriate comparisons. The task of finding appropriate benchmarks requires judgment and is not always an easy task. For this reason, financial analysis is a sophisticated skill, not a mechanical process.

There are two types of benchmarks for making financial comparisons, time series and comparisons with other companies.

1. *Time series analysis.* In this type of analysis, information for a single company is compared over time. For example, a key measure of performance for a retail company is the change in sales volume each year for its existing stores. The following time series chart shows that Home Depot was able to achieve sales growth in existing stores in 2003–2005, but failed to do so in 2006.[1]

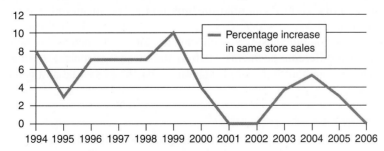

[1]The percentage change in sales for existing stores is computed as follows:

$$\text{Percentage change} = \left[\frac{\text{Sales}_{\text{Current Year}} - \text{Sales}_{\text{Previous Year}}}{\text{Sales}_{\text{Previous Year}}} \times 100 \right]$$

Similar percentage changes can be computed for various elements of financial statements.

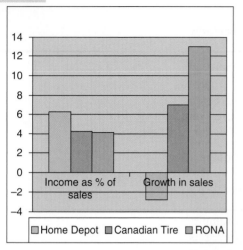

2. *Comparison with similar companies.* Financial results are often affected by industry and economy-wide factors. By comparing a company with another one in the same line of business, an analyst can obtain better insight into its performance. For example, the comparison of profit margin (income as a percentage of sales) for 2006, and growth in 2006 sales over 2005 sales for Home Depot, Canadian Tire, and RONA, shows that RONA had the highest increase in sales in 2006. However, Home Depot achieved a higher profit margin than RONA, which highlights its operating strength.

Finding comparable companies often is very difficult. Magna International Inc. is a well-known company that supplies automotive components and owns a subsidiary that is the largest operator of thoroughbred race tracks in North America. No other company sells exactly that group of products. Care must be exercised when selecting comparable companies from the same basic industry. Days Inn, Hilton, Holiday Inn, Marriott, and Intrawest are all in the hotel industry but not all could be considered comparable companies for purposes of financial analysis. These hotels offer different levels of quality and appeal to different types of customers.

The governments of the United States, Canada, and Mexico developed the North American Industry Classification System for use in reporting economic data. The system assigns a specific industry code to each corporation based on its business operations. Analysts often use these six-digit codes to identify companies that have similar business operations. Financial information services, such as Standard & Poor's, provide averages for many common accounting ratios for various industries as defined by the industrial classification codes. Because of the diversity of companies included in each industry classification, these data should be used with great care. For this reason, some analysts prefer to compare two companies that are very similar instead of using industry-wide comparisons.

RATIO AND PERCENTAGE ANALYSES

RATIO (PERCENTAGE) ANALYSIS is an analytical tool designed to identify significant relationships; it measures the proportional relationship between two financial statement amounts.

All financial analysts use **ratio analysis**, or **percentage analysis**, when they review companies. A ratio or percentage expresses the proportionate relationship between two different amounts, allowing for easy comparisons. Assessing a company's profitability is difficult if you know only that it earned a net income of $500,000. Comparing income to other numbers, such as shareholders' equity, provides additional insights. If shareholders' equity is $5 million, the relationship of earnings to shareholder investment is $500,000 ÷ $5,000,000 = 10 percent. This measure indicates a different level of performance than would be the case if shareholders' equity were $50 million. Ratio analysis condenses the large volume of raw financial data and helps decision makers to identify significant relationships and make meaningful comparisons between companies.

Ratios may be computed using amounts in one statement, such as the income statement, or in two different statements, such as the income statement and the balance sheet. In addition, amounts on a single statement may be expressed as a percentage of a base amount.

COMPONENT PERCENTAGES

LEARNING OBJECTIVE 3

Compute and interpret component percentages.

A **COMPONENT PERCENTAGE** expresses each item on a particular financial statement as a percentage of a single base amount.

Analysts often compute **component percentages**, which express each item on a financial statement as a percentage of a single *base amount*, the denominator of the ratio. To compute component percentages for the income statement, the base amount is net sales revenue. Each expense is expressed as a percentage of net sales revenue. On the balance sheet, the base amount is total assets; each balance sheet account is divided by total assets. This is also known as creating a common-size financial statement.

Discerning important relationships and trends in the Home Depot income statement shown in Exhibit 13.1 is difficult without using component percentages. Income increased by more than 15.2 percent between 2004 and 2006,[2] which appears to be good, but it is difficult for an analyst to evaluate the operating efficiency of Home Depot based on the reported numbers on the income statement.

Exhibit 13.3 shows a component percentage analysis for Home Depot's income statement (from Exhibit 13.1). If you simply reviewed the dollar amounts on the income statement, you might be concerned about several significant differences. For example, cost of goods sold increased by almost $7 billion between 2005 and 2006. Is this increase reasonable? Should you be concerned as an analyst? The component percentage indicates that cost of goods sold actually increased as a percentage of sales revenue during that period. In other words, cost of goods sold has increased primarily because of the increase in sales revenue.

The component analysis for Home Depot (in Exhibit 13.3) helps highlight several additional issues:

1. Income increased by $760 million between January 30, 2005, and January 28, 2007. This increase is attributed to an increase in sales revenue. It could have been a larger amount if it were not for the decreased efficiency in operations. In fact, the cost of goods sold as a percentage of sales increased during the period, and the gross profit decreased from 33.4 percent to 32.8 percent.

2. Some of the changes in percentages may seem immaterial, but they involve very significant amounts of money. The decrease in the ratio of selling, general and administrative expenses as a percentage of sales from 20.9 percent in 2005 to 20.2 percent in 2006 increased earnings before taxes by $636 million [$90,837 × (20.9% − 20.2%)].

3. The gross profit as a percentage of sales declined between 2004 and 2006. The company attributes this decrease to a higher penetration of the lower margin HD Supply segment of its business, which sells products to its business customers, including home builders, professional contractors, and maintenance professionals.

4. Significant stability in all of the income statement relationships indicates a well-run company. Notice that most of the individual income statement items changed by approximately one percentage point over a three-year period.

EXHIBIT **13.3**

Component Percentages for Home Depot

Income Statement	Component Percentages		
	2006	2005	2004
Net sales	100.0%	100.0%	100.0%
Cost of merchandise sold	67.2	66.5	66.6
Gross profit	32.8	33.5	33.4
Operating expenses:			
Selling, general and administrative	20.2	20.2	20.9
Depreciation and amortization	1.9	1.8	1.7
Total operating expenses	22.1	22.0	22.6
Operating income	10.7	11.5	10.8
Interest Income (Expense):			
Interest and investment income	0.0	0.1	0.1
Interest expense	(0.4)	(0.2)	(0.1)
Interest, net	(0.4)	(0.1)	—
Earnings, before taxes	10.3	11.4	10.8
Income taxes	(4.0)	(4.2)	(4.0)
Net earnings	6.3	7.2	6.8

[2]The fiscal year of Home Depot ends in January, so its income statement covers essentially the results of the previous calendar year.

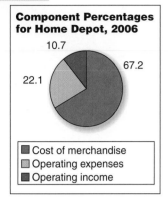

Component Percentages for Home Depot, 2006

10.7

22.1

67.2

- ■ Cost of merchandise
- □ Operating expenses
- ■ Operating income

Many analysts use graphics software in their study of financial results. Graphic representation is especially useful when communicating findings during meetings or in printed form. A graphic summary of key 2006 data from Exhibit 13.3 is shown in the chart in the margin.

In addition to component percentages, analysts use ratios to compare related items from the financial statements. Of the many ratios that can be computed from a single set of financial statements, analysts use only those that can be helpful in a given situation. Comparing cost of goods sold to property, plant, and equipment is never useful because these items have no natural relationship. Instead, an analyst will often compute certain widely used ratios and then decide which additional ratios are relevant to the particular decision. For example, research and development costs as a percentage of sales is not a commonly used ratio, but it is useful when analyzing companies that depend on new products, such as pharmaceutical or technology firms.

When you compute ratios, remember a basic fact about financial statements: Balance sheet amounts relate to an instant in time, and income statement amounts relate to a specified period. Therefore, when an income statement account is compared with a balance sheet amount, you should express the balance sheet amount as an average of the beginning and ending balances. In practice, many analysts simply use the ending balance sheet amount. This approach is appropriate only if no significant changes have occurred in balance sheet amounts. For consistency, we always use average amounts.

Financial statement analysis is a judgmental process. Not all ratios are helpful in a given situation. We will discuss several ratios that are appropriate to most situations. They can be grouped into the five categories shown in Exhibit 13.4.

TESTS OF PROFITABILITY

■ LEARNING OBJECTIVE 4

Compute and interpret profitability ratios.

TESTS OF PROFITABILITY compare income with one or more primary activities

Profitability is a primary measure of the overall success of a company. Indeed, it is necessary for a company's survival. Investors and creditors prefer a single measure of profitability that is meaningful in all situations. Unfortunately, no single measure can be devised to meet this comprehensive need. Several **tests of profitability** focus on measuring the adequacy of income by comparing it to other items reported on the financial statements.

1. RETURN ON EQUITY (ROE)

Return on equity (also called *return on owners' investment*) relates income to the investment made by the owners. It reflects the simple fact that investors expect to earn more money if they invest more money. Two investments that offer a return of $10,000 are not comparable if one requires an investment of $100,000 and the other requires an investment of $250,000. The return on equity ratio is computed as follows:[3]

$$\text{Return on Equity} = \frac{\text{Income}^*}{\text{Average Shareholders' Equity}}$$

$$\text{Home Depot, 2006} = \frac{\$5,761}{\$25,969^\dagger} = 22.2\%$$

*Income **before** extraordinary items should be used.

$\dagger$($26,909 + $25,030) ÷ 2

---

[3]The figures for Home Depot used throughout the following ratio examples are taken from the financial statements in Exhibit 13.1.

EXHIBIT **13.4**

Widely Used Accounting Ratios

Ratio	Basic Computation

Tests of Profitability

1. Return on equity (ROE)
   (Chapter 4)

$$\frac{\text{Income}}{\text{Average Shareholders' Equity}}$$

2. Return on assets (ROA)
   (Chapter 3)

$$\frac{\text{Income} + \text{Interest Expense (net of tax)}}{\text{Average Total Assets}}$$

3. Financial leverage percentage
   (Chapter 11)

$$\text{Return on Equity} - \text{Return on Assets}$$

4. Earnings per share
   (Chapter 12)

$$\frac{\text{Income Available to Common Shareholders}}{\text{Weighted-Average Number of Common Shares Outstanding}}$$

5. Quality of income
   (Chapter 5)

$$\frac{\text{Cash Flows from Operating Activities}}{\text{Net Income}}$$

6. Profit margin
   (Chapter 4)

$$\frac{\text{Income (before extraordinary items)}}{\text{Net Sales Revenue}}$$

7. Fixed asset turnover
   (Chapter 9)

$$\frac{\text{Net Sales Revenue}}{\text{Average Net Fixed Assets}}$$

Tests of Liquidity

8. Cash ratio
   (Chapter 13)

$$\frac{\text{Cash} + \text{Cash Equivalent}}{\text{Current Liabilities}}$$

9. Current ratio
   (Chapter 10)

$$\frac{\text{Current Assets}}{\text{Current Liabilities}}$$

10. Quick ratio
    (Chapter 13)

$$\frac{\text{Quick Assets}}{\text{Current Liabilities}}$$

11. Receivable turnover
    (Chapter 7)

$$\frac{\text{Net Credit Sales}}{\text{Average Net Trade Receivables}}$$

12. Inventory turnover
    (Chapter 8)

$$\frac{\text{Cost of Goods Sold}}{\text{Average Inventory}}$$

13. Payable turnover
    (Chapter 10)

$$\frac{\text{Net Credit Purchases}}{\text{Average Net Trade Payables}}$$

Tests of Solvency

14. Times interest earned
    (Chapter 11)

$$\frac{\text{Net Income} + \text{Interest Expense} + \text{Tax Expen}}{\text{Interest Expense}}$$

15. Cash coverage
    (Chapter 13)

$$\frac{\text{Cash Flow from Operating Activities (before interest and tax paid)}}{\text{Interest Paid}}$$

16. Debt-to-equity
    (Chapter 2)

$$\frac{\text{Total Liabilities}}{\text{Shareholders' Equity}}$$

Market Tests

17. Price/earnings ratio
    (Chapter 1)

$$\frac{\text{Current Market Price per Share}}{\text{Earnings per Share}}$$

18. Dividend yield
    (Chapter 12)

$$\frac{\text{Dividends per Share}}{\text{Market Price per Share}}$$

Note: Most of these ratios have been discussed in previous chapters. The specific chapter appears below the ratio.

Home Depot earned 22.2 percent on the owners' investment. Was that return high or low? We can answer this question by comparing Home Depot's return on equity with the ratios of similar companies. The return on equity for two of Home Depot's competitors follows:

Canadian Tire	13.4%
RONA	18.5
Home Depot	22.2

<table>
<tr><td colspan="4" align="center">RETURN ON EQUITY
FOR SELECTED
INDUSTRIES, 2005</td></tr>
<tr><td>Retailing</td><td>16.32%</td></tr>
<tr><td>Telecommunication
  Services</td><td>15.49%</td></tr>
<tr><td>Paper and Forest
  Products</td><td>5.50%</td></tr>
<tr><td>Gold</td><td>−13.50%</td></tr>
</table>

Clearly, Home Depot produced a better return than its competitors.

We gain additional insight by examining Home Depot's ROE over time:

	2006	2005	2004
ROE	22.2	22.9	21.5

This comparison shows that Home Depot's performance as measured by ROE improved over the three-year period. In the annual report, management attributes this increase to changing customer preferences and continuing benefits from the company's centralized purchasing approach, which improved inventory management.

2. RETURN ON ASSETS (ROA)

Another test of profitability compares income to the total assets (i.e., total investment) used to earn the income. Many analysts consider the *return on assets ratio* to be a better measure of management's ability to utilize assets effectively because it is not affected by the way in which the assets were financed. For example, the return on equity could be very large for a company that has borrowed a large amount of debt compared to a company that earned the same return based on the same amount of assets but borrowed less money. The return on equity measures profitability from the perspective of the shareholders, whereas the return on assets takes into consideration the resources contributed by both shareholders and creditors. For this reason, the return to shareholders, net income, is augmented by the return to creditors, which is interest expense. Interest expense is measured net of income tax because it represents the net cost of the funds provided by the creditors to the corporation.[4]

The return on assets is computed as follows:

$$\text{Return on Assets} = \frac{\text{Income}^* + \text{Interest Expense (net of tax)}}{\text{Average Total Assets}^\dagger}$$

$$\text{Home Depot, 2006} = \frac{\$5{,}761 + (\$392 \times 62\%)}{\$48{,}334} = 12.4\%$$

*Income before extraordinary items should be used. This illustration uses a corporate tax rate of 38 percent.
†($44,405 + $52,263) ÷ 2

---

[4]To illustrate the net cost of using debt, assume that a company earned $100 in revenue and incurred $70 in operating expenses. Consider two scenarios: (1) the company uses long-term debt that cost $10 in interest expense, and (2) the company does not use debt.

	Debt Financing	Equity Financing
Income before interest and taxes	$30	$30
Interest expense	(10)	0
Income before income taxes	$20	$30
Income tax expense (@40 percent)	(8)	(12)
Net income	$12	$18

The deduction of interest expense from income reduced the income tax expense from $12 to $8, and net income decreased by only $6. Therefore, the net cost of using debt in this case is $6, or $10 × (1 − 0.4, the tax rate).

Home Depot earned 12.4 percent on the total resources it used during the year. The return on assets for Home Depot's competitors is shown below. This comparison indicates that Home Depot utilizes its assets more effectively than its competitors.

Canadian Tire	6.5%
RONA	10.9
Home Depot	12.4

3. FINANCIAL LEVERAGE PERCENTAGE

The *financial leverage percentage* measures the advantage or disadvantage that occurs when a company's return on equity differs from its return on assets (i.e., ROE − ROA). In the ROE profit driver analysis discussed earlier in this chapter, financial leverage was defined as the proportion of assets acquired with funds supplied by owners. The *financial leverage percentage* measures a related but different concept. It describes the relationship between the return on equity and the return on assets. Leverage is positive when the rate of return on a company's assets exceeds the average after-tax interest rate on its borrowed funds. Basically, the company borrows at one rate and earns a higher rate of return on its investments. Most companies have positive leverage.

Financial leverage percentage can be measured by comparing the two return on investment ratios as follows:

Financial Leverage Percentage = Return on Equity − Return on Assets
$$\text{Home Depot, 2006} = \quad 22.2\% \quad - \quad 12.4\% \quad = 9.8\%$$

When a company is able to borrow funds at an after-tax interest rate and invest those funds to earn a higher after-tax rate of return, the difference benefits the owners. The notes to Home Depot's annual report indicate that the company has borrowed money at rates ranging from 3.75 percent to 5.875 percent and invested this money in assets earning 12.4 percent. The difference between the income earned on the money it borrows and the interest it paid to creditors is available for the owners of Home Depot. This benefit of financial leverage is the primary reason that most companies obtain a significant amount of their resources from creditors rather than from the sale of shares. Notice that financial leverage can be enhanced either by investing effectively (i.e., earning a high return on investment) or borrowing effectively (i.e., paying a low rate of interest).

A negative financial leverage percentage means that ROE has decreased relative to ROA or that ROA has increased relative to ROE. The return on equity decreases when net income decreases, which signals a deterioration in the company's profitability, or when equity increases through the issuance of additional shares. An inflow of cash from a new equity issue may indicate that the company is entering a growth phase that is expected to increase profits. Without careful interpretation of all of the reliable and relevant information available on a specific company, investors cannot accurately interpret a decrease in ROE as either good news or bad news.

The second possibility is that the return on assets may have increased substantially relative to the return on equity. Again, an increase in ROA may reflect an increase in after-tax interest expense and in the cost of debt financing.

In general, if a decrease in ROE signals future growth despite a temporarily negative financial leverage percentage, investors may not be too alarmed by negative leverage. If, however, an increase in ROA is the result of borrowing at high interest rates, investors could well interpret negative leverage as reflecting bad news. It is therefore important for investors to be cautious when interpreting any increase or decrease in ratios.

Home Depot's financial leverage ratio is higher than those of Canadian Tire (8.9%) and RONA (7.6%).

4. EARNINGS PER SHARE (EPS)

Earnings per share is a measure of the return on investment that is based on the number of shares outstanding instead of the dollar amounts reported on the balance sheet. In simple situations, EPS is computed as follows:

$$\text{Earnings per Share} = \frac{\text{Income Available to Common Shareholders}}{\text{Weighted-Average Number of Common Shares Outstanding}}$$

$$\text{Home Depot, 2006} = \frac{\$5,761}{2,054^*} = \$2.80 \text{ per share}$$

*Reported on the income statement.

This computation of EPS is based on information provided in note 7 of the company's consolidated financial statements. The additional complexities in the computation of EPS are discussed in advanced accounting courses.

Earnings per share is probably the single most widely watched ratio. Companies' announcements of their net earnings each quarter during the fiscal year are normally reported in the business press. The following news story by Associated Press concerning Home Depot's earnings results for the second quarter of 2006 illustrates the importance of earnings per share.

REAL WORLD EXCERPT

Home Depot

EARNINGS ANNOUNCEMENT
BY *THE WALL STREET JOURNAL*

Home Depot Posts 5.3% Profit Rise, Tames Forecast

Feeling the downdraft of a slowing U.S. housing market, home-improvement retailer Home Depot Inc. reported second-quarter net rose 5.3% and cautioned that profit and sales for the year would fall at the low end of its forecasts.

. . .

The chain reported net income of $1.86 billion, or 90 cents a share, compared with $1.77 billion, or 82 cents a share, in the year-ago quarter. Excluding a three-cents-a-share retroactive tax bill, results exceeded Wall Street estimates by a penny a share.

Sales for the quarter ended July 30 rose 17% to $26.03 billion from $22.31 billion in the year-ago period. Same-store sales, or sales at stores open at least a year, fell by two-tenths of one percent, the first such decline in more than three years.

. . .

In 4 p.m. composite trading on the New York Stock Exchange, Home Depot shares were up $1.18, or 3.6%, to $34.44 amid a strong advance in stock prices. Some analysts also said the company's forecast slowdown was less severe than they had expected.

Source: Gary McWilliams, *Wall Street Journal* (Eastern edition) New York, N.Y.: August 16, 2006, p. A.2. © 2006 Dow Jones & Company, Inc. Reproduced with permission of copyright owner.

5. QUALITY OF INCOME

Most financial analysts are concerned about the quality of a company's earnings because some accounting procedures can be used to report higher income. For example, a company that uses short estimated lives for long-term assets will report lower earnings than a similar company that uses longer estimated lives. One method of evaluating the quality of a company's earnings is to compare its reported earnings to its cash flows from operating activities, as follows:

$$\text{Quality of Income} = \frac{\text{Cash Flows from Operating Activities}}{\text{Net Income}}$$

$$\text{Home Depot, 2006} = \frac{\$7,661}{\$5,761} = 1.33$$

A quality of income ratio higher than 1 is considered to indicate higher-quality earnings because each dollar of income is supported by at least one dollar of cash flow. A ratio below 1 represents lower-quality earnings.

6. PROFIT MARGIN

The *profit margin* measures the percentage of each sales dollar, on average, that represents profit. It is computed as follows:

$$\text{Profit Margin} = \frac{\text{Income (before Extraordinary Items)}}{\text{Net Sales Revenue}}$$

$$\text{Home Depot, 2006} = \frac{\$5,761}{\$90,837} = 6.3\%$$

During 2006, each dollar of Home Depot's sales generated 6.3 cents of profit. Care must be used in analyzing the profit margin because it does not consider the amount of resources employed (i.e., total investment) to earn income. For example, the hypothetical income statements of Home Depot and Canadian Tire might show the following:

	Home Depot	Canadian Tire
a. Sales revenue	$500,000	$150,000
b. Income	$ 25,000	$ 7,500
c. Profit margin (b ÷ a)	5%	5%
d. Total investment	$250,000	$125,000
e. Return on total investment* (b ÷ d)	10%	6%

*Assuming no interest expense.

In this example, both companies reported the same profit margin (5 percent). Home Depot, however, appears to be performing much better because it is earning a 10 percent return on the total investment versus the 6 percent earned by Canadian Tire. The profit margin percentages do not reflect the effect of the $250,000 total investment in Home Depot compared to the $125,000 total investment in Canadian Tire. Thus, the profit margin omits one of the two important factors that should be used in evaluating return on the investment.

It is very difficult to compare profit margins for companies in different industries. For example, profit margins are low in the food industry, but they are high in the jewellery business. Both types of businesses can be quite profitable, however, because a high sales volume can compensate for a low profit margin. Grocery stores have low profit margins, but generate a large sales volume from their relatively inexpensive stores and inventory. Although jewellery stores earn more profit from each sales dollar, they require a large investment in luxury stores and very expensive inventory.

The trade-off between profit margin and sales volume can be stated in very simple terms: Would you prefer to have 5 percent of $1,000,000 or 10 percent of $100,000? As you can see, a larger percentage is not always better.

The operating strength of Home Depot comes more clearly into focus when you compare its profit margin with that of major competitors:

Canadian Tire	4.2%
RONA	4.1
Home Depot	6.3

7. FIXED ASSET TURNOVER

Another measure of operating efficiency is the fixed asset turnover ratio, which compares sales volume with a company's investment in fixed assets. The term *fixed assets* is synonymous with *property, plant, and equipment*. The ratio is computed as follows:

$$\text{Fixed Asset Turnover} = \frac{\text{Net Sales Revenue}}{\text{Average Net Fixed Assets}}$$

$$\text{Home Depot, 2006} = \frac{\$90,837}{\$25,753^*} = 3.53$$

*($24,901 + $26,605) ÷ 2

The fixed asset turnover ratio for Home Depot is lower than RONA's (8.67) but higher than Canadian Tire's (2.94). In simple terms, this means that Home Depot has a competitive advantage over Canadian Tire in terms of its ability to effectively utilize its fixed assets to generate revenue. For each dollar that Home Depot invested in property, plant, and equipment, it was able to earn $3.53 in sales revenue while RONA earned $8.67 and Canadian Tire earned only $2.94. This comparison is extremely important because it indicates that management of Home Depot is able to operate more efficiently than Canadian Tire's, but not RONA's.

The fixed asset turnover ratio is widely used to analyze capital-intensive companies such as airlines and electric utilities. For companies that have large amounts of inventory and accounts receivable, analysts often prefer to use the asset turnover ratio, which is based on total assets rather than fixed assets:

$$\text{Asset Turnover} = \frac{\text{Net Sales Revenue}}{\text{Average Total Assets}}$$

$$\text{Home Depot, 2006} = \frac{\$90,837}{\$48,334^*} = 1.88$$

*($44,405 + $52,263) ÷ 2

In 2006, Home Depot was able to generate $1.88 in revenue for each dollar invested in the company's assets. This ratio does not compare favourably to RONA's ratio of 2.41 but exceeds Canadian Tire's ratio of 1.41. Both turnover ratios show that Home Depot was able to operate more efficiently than Canadian Tire, but less efficiently than RONA.

As we showed with the ROE model earlier in this chapter, one strategy to improve return on equity is to generate more sales dollars from the company's assets. Many analysts consider this type of improvement to be an important indication of the quality of the company's management.

SELF-STUDY **QUIZ 13-1**

Canadian Tire Corporation Ltd. reported the following data in a recent annual report (in millions of dollars):

	Current Year	Last Year
Net income	$ 148	
Sales	5,207	
Interest expense (net of tax)	58	
Shareholders' equity	1,459	$1,345
Total assets	3,748	3,871

The company did not report any extraordinary items in the current year.

Compute the following ratios:

1. Return on equity.
2. Return on assets.
3. Profit margin.

After you complete your work, check your answers with the solutions on page 703.

ROE PROFIT DRIVER ANALYSIS

Exhibit 13.5 shows a decomposition of Home Depot's ROE profit driver analysis that was presented earlier in Exhibit 13.2. This analysis shows the sources of the change in ROE and can provide useful insights into Home Depot's business strategy.

EXHIBIT **13.5**

Home Depot ROE Profit Driver Analysis

	Fiscal Year Ending		
	Jan. 28, 2007	Jan. 29, 2006	Jan. 30, 2005
ROE Profit Drivers			
Net income	$ 5,761	$ 5,838	$ 5,001
Net sales	90,837	81,511	73,094
Average total assets	48,334	41,713	36,672
Average shareholders' equity	25,969	25,534	23,283
ROE Profit Driver Analysis			
Net income / Net sales	0.063	0.072	0.068
× Net sales / Avg. total assets	1.879	1.954	1.993
× Avg. total assets / Avg. shareholders' equity	1.861	1.634	1.575
= Net income / Avg. shareholders' equity	0.222	0.229	0.215

Exhibit 13.5 shows an increase in profit margin in fiscal year 2006 followed by a decline in fiscal year 2007. The component percentages (see Exhibit 13.3) suggest that this decrease was caused mainly by the increase in the cost of goods sold relative to net sales. The analysis also shows a steady decline in asset turnover, indicating that Home Depot utilized increasing amounts of assets to generate each dollar of sales. Home Depot can increase asset turnover by increasing sales volume or by decreasing less-productive assets. Home Depot's balance sheet at January 28, 2007, reported an increase of $3 billion in goodwill, a non-productive asset, which contributed to the decrease in the asset turnover. Home Depot financed the increase in its assets by issuing $9 billion of additional long-term debt, which increased its financial leverage. Furthermore, the company repurchased its own shares, which reduced shareholders' equity, thus increasing both financial leverage and return on equity.

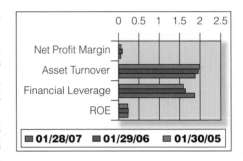

In summary, the improvement in Home Depot's return on equity during the fiscal years 2004–2006 was essentially due to an increasing financial leverage, suggesting that Home Depot's use of additional debt to finance its operations and investments benefited the company's shareholders.[5] The decline in the asset turnover was not significant enough to offset the effects of the other components of the DuPont model.

SELF-STUDY **QUIZ 13-2**

We used ROE analysis in Exhibit 13.5 to understand why Home Depot's ROE had changed over the fiscal years 2003–2005. This type of analysis is often called *time series analysis*. ROE analysis can also be used to explain why a company has an ROE different from its competitors at a single point in time. This type of analysis is called *cross-sectional analysis*. Dell Inc. and Gateway Inc. are the largest computer manufacturers that employ mail-order/Internet distribution. Both of these companies have followed a low-cost strategy, developing reputations for good products and service at low prices. The following is an analysis of their ROEs for the year 2005. Dell produced higher ROE in the previous two years, and its shareholders were amply rewarded with a significant increase in the value of their shares, whereas Gateway's share price declined during the same period because of net losses. Using ROE analysis, explain how Dell produced its higher ROE.

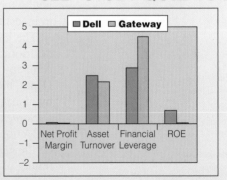

ROE Profit Drivers	Dell	Gateway
Net Income/Net Sales	0.064	0.002
× Net Sales/Average Total Assets	2.41	2.09
× Avg. Total Assets/Average Shareholders' Equity	2.79	4.33
= Net Income/Average Shareholders' Equity	0.67	0.025

After you complete your analysis, check your answers with the solutions on page 703.

[5] An expanded version of the ROE profit driver analysis is provided by the Scott formula. Interested readers are referred to the Online Learning Centre Web site at **www.mcgrawhill.ca/olc/libby/student/resources** for a detailed application of the Scott formula to the financial statements of Home Depot, Inc.

TESTS OF LIQUIDITY

■ **LEARNING OBJECTIVE 5**
Compute and interpret liquidity ratios.

TESTS OF LIQUIDITY are ratios that measure a company's ability to meet its currently maturing obligations.

Liquidity refers to a company's ability to meet its currently maturing debts. **Tests of liquidity** focus on the relationship between current assets and current liabilities. A company's ability to pay its current liabilities is an important factor in evaluating its short-term financial strength. For example, a company that does not have cash available to pay for purchases on a timely basis will lose its cash discounts and run the risk of having its credit discontinued by vendors. Three ratios are used to measure liquidity: the cash ratio, the current ratio, and the quick ratio.

8. CASH RATIO

Cash is the lifeblood of a business. Without cash, a company cannot pay its employees or meet obligations to its creditors. Even a profitable business will fail without sufficient cash. One measure of the adequacy of available cash, called the *cash ratio*, is computed as follows:

$$\text{Cash Ratio} = \frac{\text{Cash} + \text{Cash Equivalents}}{\text{Current Liabilities}}$$

$$\text{Home Depot, 2006} = \frac{\$600}{\$12,931} = 0.05$$

Analysts often use this ratio to compare similar companies. The cash ratios for Canadian Tire and RONA indicate that Canadian Tire has a larger cash reserve compared to its current liabilities.

Canadian Tire	0.44
RONA	0.13
Home Depot	0.05

Would analysts be concerned about the lower ratio for Home Depot? Probably not, because there are other factors to consider. The cash flow statement for Home Depot shows that the company generates a very large amount of cash from operating activities each year. As a result, it does not have to keep a large amount of cash on reserve to meet unexpected needs. Indeed, most analysts believe that the cash ratio should not be too high, because holding excess cash usually is uneconomical. It is far better to invest the cash in productive assets or reduce debt.

The cash ratio for Home Depot has decreased in recent years. In most cases, a deteriorating ratio might be a cause for concern. It could be an early warning that the company is experiencing financial difficulty. Given the strong performance of Home Depot, the deterioration in the cash ratio is more likely the result of aggressive efforts by managers to minimize the amount of cash used to operate the business.

Some analysts do not use this ratio because it is very sensitive to small events. The collection of a large account receivable, for example, may have a significant impact on the cash ratio. The current ratio and the quick ratio are much less sensitive to the timing of such transactions.

9. CURRENT RATIO

The *current ratio* measures the relationship between current assets and current liabilities at a specific date. It is computed as follows:

$$\text{Current Ratio} = \frac{\text{Current Assets}}{\text{Current Liabilites}}$$

$$\text{Home Depot, 2006} = \frac{\$18,000}{\$12,931} = 1.39$$

The current ratio measures the cushion of working capital that companies maintain to allow for the inevitable unevenness in the flow of funds through the working capital accounts. At the end of 2006, Home Depot had $1.39 in current assets for each $1 of liabilities. Most analysts would judge the ratio to be very strong, given Home Depot's ability to generate cash. By comparison, both Canadian Tire and RONA have higher current ratios than Home Depot.

Canadian Tire	1.53
RONA	2.39
Home Depot	1.39

To properly use the current ratio, analysts must understand the nature of a company's business. Many manufacturing companies have developed sophisticated systems to minimize the amount of inventory they must hold. These systems, called *just-in-time inventory*, are designed to have an inventory item arrive just as it is needed. While these systems work well in manufacturing processes, they do not work as well in retailing. Customers expect to find merchandise when they want it, and it has proven difficult to precisely forecast consumer behaviour. As a result, most retailers have comparatively large current ratios because they must carry large inventories. To illustrate this issue, Home Depot maintains an inventory of 50,000 different products in each store.

Analysts consider a current ratio of 2 to be financially conservative. Indeed, most companies have current ratios that are below 2. The optimal level for a current ratio depends on the business environment in which a company operates. If cash flows are predictable and stable (as they are for a utility company), the current ratio can even be lower than 1. For a business with highly variable cash flows (such as an airline), a ratio exceeding 1 may be desirable.

Analysts become concerned if a company's current ratio is high compared to that of other companies. A firm is operating inefficiently when it ties up too much money in inventory or accounts receivable. There is no reason, for instance, for a Home Depot store to hold 1,000 hammers in stock if it sells only 100 hammers a month.

CURRENT RATIO FOR SELECTED INDUSTRIES, 2006	
Metals and Mining	5.19
Pharmaceuticals	4.53
Biotechnology	3.34
Software	1.98
Paper and Forest Products	1.60
Telecommunication Services	0.57

10. QUICK RATIO (ACID TEST)

The *quick ratio* is a more stringent test of short-term liquidity than the current ratio. The quick ratio compares quick assets, defined as **cash and near-cash assets**, to current liabilities. Quick assets include cash, short-term investments, and accounts receivable (net of the allowance for doubtful accounts). Inventories are omitted from quick assets because of the uncertainty of the timing of cash flows from their sale. Prepaid expenses are also excluded from quick assets. Thus, the quick, or acid test, ratio is a more severe test of liquidity than is the current ratio. It is computed as follows:

$$\text{Quick Ratio} = \frac{\text{Quick Assets}}{\text{Current Liabilites}}$$

$$\text{Home Depot, 2006} = \frac{\$3,837}{\$12,931} = 0.30$$

The quick ratio is a measure of the safety margin that is available to meet a company's current liabilities. Home Depot has 30 cents in cash and near-cash assets for every $1 in current liabilities. This ratio is below the threshold of 0.40 that is considered appropriate for this ratio. Analysts should not be concerned about the magnitude of this ratio because of the large amount of cash that Home Depot generates from operating activities. By comparison, the quick ratios for Canadian Tire and RONA are 1.07 and 0.58, respectively.

SELF-STUDY **QUIZ 13-3**

The current ratios for six industries appear in the margin on page 693. The following quick ratios, presented in a random order, pertain to the same six industries:

	Industries					
	1	2	3	4	5	6
Quick ratio	2.97	0.93	0.37	1.68	4.59	3.95

Two of these six industries are software, and metals and mining. Identify the ratio associated with each of these two industries. On average, the quick assets for the software industry represent 85 percent of the industry's current assets.

After you complete your work, check your answers with the solutions on page 703.

11. RECEIVABLE TURNOVER

Accounts receivable are closely related to both short-term liquidity and operating efficiency. A company that can quickly collect cash from its customers has good liquidity and does not needlessly tie up funds in unproductive assets. The receivable turnover ratio is computed as follows:

$$\text{Receivable Turnover} = \frac{\text{Net Credit Sales}^*}{\text{Average Net Trade Receivables}}$$

$$\text{Home Depot, 2006} = \frac{\$90,837}{\$2,809^\dagger} = 32.3 \text{ Times}$$

*When the amount of credit sales is not known, total sales may be used as a rough approximation.
†($2,396 + $3,223) ÷ 2

This ratio is called a *turnover* because it reflects how many times the trade receivables were recorded, collected, and then recorded again during the period (i.e., "turnover"). Receivable turnover expresses the relationship of the average balance in Accounts Receivable to the transactions (i.e., credit sales) that created those receivables. This ratio measures the effectiveness of the company's credit-granting and collection activities. A high receivable turnover ratio suggests effective collection activities. Granting credit to poor credit risks and making ineffective collection efforts cause this ratio to be low. A very low ratio obviously is a problem, but a very high ratio also can be troublesome because it suggests an overly stringent credit policy that could cause lost sales and profits.

The receivable turnover ratio often is converted to a time basis known as the *average age of trade receivables*. The computation is as follows:

$$\text{Average Age of Trade Receivables} = \frac{\text{Days in a Year}}{\text{Receivable Turnover}}$$

$$\text{Home Depot, 2006} = \frac{365}{32.3} = 11.3 \text{ Average Days to Collect}$$

This computation is equivalent to dividing the average net trade receivables by the average net credit sales per day; that is:

Average Collection Period = $2,809 ÷ ($90,837 ÷ 365) = 11.3 days

The effectiveness of credit and collection activities sometimes is judged by the general rule that the average collection period should not exceed 1.5 times the credit terms. For example, if the credit terms require payment in 30 days, the average collection period should not exceed 45 days (i.e., not more than 15 days past due). Like all rules, this one has many exceptions.

When you evaluate financial statements, you should always think about the reasonableness of the numbers you compute. We computed the average age of receivables for Home Depot as 11.3 days. Is that number reasonable? Probably not. It is very unlikely that Home Depot collects cash from its credit customers on average in just 11 days. Because we did not know the amount of Home Depot's credit sales, we used total sales as an approximation. Think about the last time you watched a customer buying merchandise on credit in a retail store. Most customers use a bank credit card such as MasterCard or Visa. From the seller's perspective, a sales transaction involving a bank credit card is recorded in virtually the same manner as a cash sale. A credit sale involving a credit card does not create an account receivable on the seller's books. Instead, the account receivable is recorded on the books of the credit card company. In practice, the majority of Home Depot's credit sales involve bank credit cards. As a result, Home Depot's accounts receivable turnover ratio is not meaningful.

12. INVENTORY TURNOVER

Like the receivable turnover, *inventory turnover* is a measure of both liquidity and operating efficiency. It reflects the relationship of inventory to the volume of goods sold during the period. It is computed as follows:

$$\text{Inventory Turnover} = \frac{\text{Cost of Goods Sold}}{\text{Average Inventory}}$$

$$\text{Home Depot, 2006} = \frac{\$61,054}{\$12,111^*} = 5.0 \text{ Times}$$

*($11,401 + $12,822) ÷ 2

Because a company normally realizes a profit each time the inventory is sold, an increase in the ratio is usually favourable. If the ratio is too high, however, it may be an indication that sales were lost because desired items were not in stock. The cost of a lost sale is often much higher than the lost profit. When a business is out of stock on a item desired by a customer, the individual will often go to a competitor to find it. That visit may help the competitor establish a business relationship with the customer. Thus, the cost of being out of stock may be all future profits to a lost customer.

On average, Home Depot's inventory was acquired and sold to customers five times during the year.[6] The inventory turnover ratio is critical for companies that have adopted the Home Depot strategy. They want to be able to offer the customer the right product when it is needed at a price that beats the competition. If Home Depot does not effectively manage its inventory levels, it will incur extra costs that must be passed on to the customer.

Turnover ratios vary significantly from one industry to the next. Companies in the food industry (grocery stores and restaurants) have high inventory turnover ratios because their inventory is subject to rapid deterioration in quality. Companies that sell expensive merchandise (automobiles and high-fashion clothes) have much lower ratios because sales of these items are infrequent but customers want to have a selection to choose from when they do buy.

The turnover ratio often is converted to a time basis called *the average days' supply in inventory*. The computation is

$$\text{Average Days' Supply in Inventory} = \frac{\text{Days in Year}}{\text{Inventory Turnover}}$$

$$\text{Home Depot, 2006} = \frac{365}{5.0} = 73 \text{ Average Days' Supply in Inventory}$$

---

[6]The inventory turnover ratios for both RONA and Canadian Tire cannot be computed because neither company disclosed its cost of goods sold on its income statement.

Equivalently, the average days' supply in inventory can be computed by dividing the average inventory by the cost of goods sold per day; that is:

Average Days' Supply in Inventory = \$12,111 ÷ (\$61,054 ÷ 365) = 73 days

13. PAYABLE TURNOVER

The payable turnover ratio evaluates the company's effectiveness in managing payables to trade creditors. It is computed as follows:

$$\textbf{Payable Turnover} = \frac{\textbf{Net Credit Purchases}}{\textbf{Average Net Trade Payables}}$$

Credit purchases are not usually reported in financial statements; hence, we use total purchases of merchandise inventory as a rough approximation. However, purchases are usually not reported separately in financial statements, but can be calculated by adjusting the cost of goods sold for the change in inventory during the period.

Purchases = Cost of Goods Sold + Ending Inventory − Beginning Inventory

The computation of the payable turnover for Home Depot follows:[7]

$$\textbf{Home Depot, 2006} = \frac{\$61,054 + \$12,822 - 11,401}{\$6,694^{*}} = \textbf{9.33 Times}$$

*(\$6,032 + \$7,356) ÷ 2

This ratio reflects how many times the trade payables were recorded, paid, and then recorded again during the period. The payable turnover expresses the relationship of the average balance in accounts payable to the purchase transactions that created those payables. Usually, a low ratio raises questions concerning a company's liquidity. It could also reflect aggressive cash management. By conserving cash with slow payment to trade suppliers, the company minimizes the amount of money it must borrow, and the related interest.

The payable turnover ratio is often converted to a time basis known as the ***average age of payables***. The computation is:

$$\textbf{Average Age of Payables} = \frac{\textbf{Days in a Year}}{\textbf{Payable Turnover}}$$

$$\textbf{Home Depot, 2006} = \frac{365}{9.33} = \textbf{39 Average Days to Pay}$$

This computation is equivalent to dividing the average net trade payables by the average net credit purchases per day.

The payable turnover can be subject to manipulation. Managers may delay payment to creditors during the entire year, but catch up at year end so that the ratio is at an acceptable level.

USING RATIOS TO ANALYZE THE OPERATING CYCLE

In Chapter 3, we introduced the concept of the operating cycle, which is the time it takes for a company to pay cash to its suppliers, sell goods to its customers, and collect cash from its customers. Analysts are interested in the operating cycle because it helps them evaluate a company's cash needs and is a good indicator of management efficiency.

The operating cycle for most companies involves three distinct phases: the acquisition of inventory, the sale of the inventory, and the collection of cash from the customer. We have discussed three ratios that are helpful in evaluating a company's operating cycle. They are the accounts payable turnover ratio, the inventory turnover ratio, and the accounts receivable turnover ratio. Each of these ratios measures the number of days it takes to complete an operating activity. The length of the component parts for Home Depot's operating cycle are:

---

[7]The payable turnover ratios for both RONA and Canadian Tire cannot be computed because neither company disclosed its cost of goods sold on its income statement.

Ratio	Operating Activity	Time
Accounts payable turnover ratio	Purchase of inventory	39.0 days
Inventory turnover ratio	Sale of inventory	73.0 days
Accounts receivable turnover ratio	Collection of cash from customers	11.3 days

The component parts of the operating cycle help us understand the cash needs of the company. Home Depot on average pays for its inventory 39 days after it receives it. It takes, on average, 84.3 days (73.0 + 11.3) for Home Depot to sell the inventory and collect cash from customers. Therefore, Home Depot must invest cash in its operating activities for nearly 46 days between the time it pays its vendors and the time it collects from its customers. Companies prefer to minimize the time between paying vendors and collecting cash from customers because it frees up cash for other productive purposes. Home Depot could reduce this time by slowing payments to creditors or by increasing the inventory turnover.

Companies that sell products through the Internet may not need to stock merchandise for long periods. In fact, Dell Inc. disclosed in its annual report for fiscal 2006 that its cash conversion cycle was −44 days during that year, indicating that Dell paid suppliers, on average, 44 days after it sold its products and collected from customers. While Home Depot needs money to finance the purchase of inventory, Dell has relied on suppliers to provide the necessary financing.

SELF-STUDY **QUIZ 13-4**

Canadian Tire Corporation Ltd. reported the following data in a recent annual report (in millions of dollars):

Net income	$ 148
Cash and short-term investments	131
Accounts receivable	515
Credit card receivables	453
Current liabilities	1,128
Cash flows from operating activities	502

Compute the following ratios:
1. Quality of income.
2. Quick ratio.
3. Cash ratio.

After you complete your work, check your answers with the solutions on page 703.

TESTS OF SOLVENCY

Solvency refers to a company's ability to meet its long-term obligations. **Tests of solvency**, which are measures of a company's ability to meet these obligations, include the times interest earned, cash coverage, and debt-to-equity ratios.

■ **LEARNING OBJECTIVE 6**

Compute and interpret solvency ratios.

14. TIMES INTEREST EARNED RATIO

Interest payments are a fixed obligation of the borrowing company. If a company fails to make required interest payments, creditors may force it into bankruptcy. Because of the importance of interest payments, analysts often compute a ratio called *times interest earned:*

TESTS OF SOLVENCY are ratios that measure a company's ability to meet its long-term obligations.

$$\text{Times Interest Earned} = \frac{\text{Net Income} + \text{Interest Expense} + \text{Income Tax Expense}}{\text{Interest Expense}}$$

$$\text{Home Depot, 2006} = \frac{\$5,761 + \$392 + \$3,547}{\$392} = 24.7 \text{ Times}$$

This ratio compares the income that a company generated during one period to its interest obligation for the same period. It represents a margin of protection for the creditors. In 2006, Home Depot generated more than $24.7 in income for each $1 of interest expense, a high ratio that indicates a secure position for creditors.

Some analysts prefer to calculate this ratio based on all contractually required payments, including principal payments and rent obligations under lease contracts. Other analysts believe that this ratio is flawed because interest expense and other obligations are paid in cash, not with net income. These analysts prefer to use the cash coverage ratio.

15. CASH COVERAGE RATIO

Given the importance of cash flows and required interest payments, it is easy to understand why many analysts use the *cash coverage ratio*. It is computed as follows:

$$\text{Cash Coverage} = \frac{\text{Cash Flows from Operating Activities before Interest and Taxes}}{\text{Interest Paid (from cash flow statement)}}$$

$$\text{Home Depot, 2006} = \frac{\$7,661 + \$270 + \$3,963}{\$270} = 44 \text{ Times}$$

The cash coverage ratio compares the cash generated with the cash obligations of the period. Analysts are concerned about a company's ability to make required interest payments. The cash coverage ratio for Home Depot shows that the company generated $44 in cash from operations for every $1 of interest paid, which is very strong coverage. Note that the numerator and the denominator of the cash coverage ratio use *interest paid and income taxes paid* from the cash flow statement instead of *interest expense and income taxes expense* from the income statement. Accrued interest and interest payments are normally similar in amount, but not always the same.

16. DEBT-TO-EQUITY RATIO

The *debt-to-equity ratio* expresses a company's debt as a proportion of its owners' equity.[8] It is computed as follows:

$$\text{Debt-to-Equity Ratio} = \frac{\text{Total Liabilities}}{\text{Shareholders' Equity}}$$

$$\text{Home Depot, 2006} = \frac{\$27,233}{\$25,030} = 1.09 \text{ (or 109\%)}$$

In 2006, for each $1 of shareholders' equity, Home Depot had $1.09 of liabilities. By comparison, RONA and Canadian Tire's debt-to-equity ratios were 0.86 and 1.08, respectively.

Debt is risky for a company because specific interest payments must be made even if the company has not earned sufficient income to pay them. In contrast, dividends are always at the company's discretion and are not legally enforceable until they are declared by the board of directors. Thus, equity capital is usually considered much less risky than debt.

Despite the risk associated with debt, most companies obtain significant amounts of resources from creditors because of the advantages of financial leverage discussed earlier. In addition, interest expense is a deductible expense on the corporate income tax return. In selecting a capital structure, a company must balance the higher returns available through leverage against the higher risk associated with debt. Because of the importance of this risk–return relationship, most analysts consider the debt-to-equity ratio to be a key part of any company evaluation.

DEBT-TO-EQUITY RATIO FOR SELECTED INDUSTRIES, 2006	
Paper and Forest Products	1.34
Telecommunication Services	0.82
Software	0.71
Gold	0.27
Retailing	0.18

---

[8]The relationship between debt and owners' equity alternatively may be calculated with the following ratio:

$$\text{Total Liabilities to Total Equities} = \frac{\text{Total Liabilities}}{\text{Total Liabilities and Shareholders' Equity}}$$

$$\text{Home Depot, 2006} = \frac{\$27,233}{\$52,263} = 52.1\%$$

MARKET TESTS

Several ratios, often called **market tests**, relate the current market price per share to the return that accrues to investors. Many analysts prefer these ratios because they are based on the current value of an owner's investment in a company.

■ **LEARNING OBJECTIVE 7**
Compute and interpret market test ratios.

17. PRICE/EARNINGS (P/E) RATIO

The *price/earnings (P/E) ratio* measures the relationship between the current market price per share and its earnings per share. Recently, when the price of a Home Depot common share was $43.95, EPS was $2.80, as calculated earlier. The P/E ratio for the company is computed as follows:

MARKET TESTS are ratios that tend to measure the market worth of a common share.

$$\text{Price/Earnings Ratio} = \frac{\text{Current Market Price per Share}}{\text{Earnings per Share}}$$

$$\text{Home Depot, 2006} = \frac{\$43.95}{\$2.80} = 15.7$$

The P/E ratio indicates that Home Depot's shares were selling at a price that was 15.7 times its earning per share. The P/E ratio reflects the stock market's assessment of the company's future business performance. A high ratio indicates that the market expects earnings to grow rapidly. Home Depot's P/E ratio is reasonable and comparable to the ratios of its competitors.

Canadian Tire	16.1
RONA	12.5
Home Depot	15.7

Sometimes the components of the P/E ratio are inverted, giving the *capitalization rate*, a rate at which the stock market apparently is capitalizing the current earnings. The capitalization rate for Home Depot is $2.80 ÷ $43.95 = 6.3 percent.

In economic terms, the share price is related to the present value of the company's future earnings. Thus, a company that expects to increase its earnings in the future is worth more than one that cannot grow its earnings (assuming other factors are the same). But while a high P/E ratio and good growth prospects are considered favourable, there are risks. When a company with a high P/E ratio does not meet the level of earnings expected by the market, the negative impact on its share price can be dramatic.

AVERAGE P/E RATIO FOR SELECTED INDUSTRIES, 2006

Gold	29.6
Software	19.2
Retailing	17.9
Telecommunications	15.3
Transportation	10.8

18. DIVIDEND YIELD RATIO

When investors buy shares, they expect returns from two sources: price appreciation and dividend income. The *dividend yield ratio* measures the relationship between the dividends per share paid to shareholders and the current market price per share. Home Depot paid dividends of 75 cents per share when the market price per share was $43.95. Its dividend yield ratio is computed as follows:

$$\text{Dividend Yield Ratio} = \frac{\text{Dividend per Share}}{\text{Market Price per Share}}$$

$$\text{Home Depot, 2006} = \frac{\$0.75}{\$43.95} = 1.7\%$$

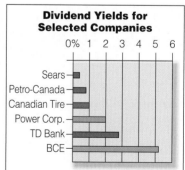

Dividend Yields for Selected Companies

It might seem surprising that Home Depot's dividend yield was below 1 percent, given that an investor could earn higher returns on alternative investments. In fact, the dividend yield for shares of most companies is not high compared to returns on alternative investments. Investors may accept low dividend yields if they expect that the price of a company's shares will increase while they own it. Clearly, investors who bought Home Depot's common shares did so with the expectation that their price would increase. In contrast, companies with low growth potential tend to offer much higher dividend yields than do companies with high growth potential. These latter companies usually appeal to retired investors who need current income rather than future growth potential. The chart in the margin shows dividend yields for a selection of companies.

SELF-STUDY **QUIZ 13-5**

Canadian Tire Corporation Ltd. reported the following data in a recent annual report (in millions of dollars):

	Current Year	Last Year
Current assets	$1,528	
Current liabilities	1,128	
Cost of goods sold (assumed)	3,645	
Inventory	412	$473
Earnings per share	1.89	
Share price at year-end	19	

Compute the following ratios:

1. Current ratio.
2. Inventory turnover.
3. Price/earnings ratio.

After you complete your work, check your answers with the solutions on page 703.

INTERPRETING RATIOS AND OTHER ANALYTICAL CONSIDERATIONS

Except for earnings per share, the computation of financial ratios has not been standardized by the accounting profession or security analysts. Thus, users of financial statements should compute the various ratios in accordance with their decision objectives. Before using ratios computed by others, the analyst should determine the computational approach that was used.

Ratios can best be interpreted only by comparing them to other ratios or to some threshold value. For example, a very low current ratio may indicate an inability to meet maturing debts, and a very high current ratio may indicate an unprofitable use of funds. Furthermore, an optimal ratio for one company may not be optimal for another. Comparisons of ratios for different companies are appropriate only if the companies are indeed comparable in terms of industry, nature of operations, size, and accounting policies.

Because ratios are based on the aggregation of information, they may obscure underlying factors that are of interest to the analyst. To illustrate, a current ratio that is considered optimal may obscure a short-term liquidity problem if the company has a very large amount of inventory but a minimal amount of cash with which to pay debts as they mature. Careful analysis can uncover this type of problem.

In other cases, analysis cannot uncover obscured problems. For example, consolidated statements include financial information about the parent and its subsidiaries. The parent company may have a high current ratio and the subsidiary a low ratio. When the statements are consolidated, the current ratio may fall within an acceptable range. The fact that the subsidiary could have a serious liquidity problem is obscured in this case.

Despite limitations, ratio analysis is a useful analytical tool. For instance, financial ratios are effective for predicting bankruptcy. Exhibit 13.6 gives the current and debt-to-equity ratios for Braniff International Corporation for each year before it filed for bankruptcy. Notice the deterioration of these ratios each year. Analysts who studied the financial ratios probably were not surprised by Braniff's bankruptcy. After selling many of its assets and undergoing a complete financial restructuring, Braniff was able to resume limited flight operations but was forced to file for bankruptcy for a second time after additional financial difficulty.

EXHIBIT **13.6**

Selected Financial Ratios for Braniff International

	Years before Bankruptcy				
	5	4	3	2	1
Current ratio	1.20	0.91	0.74	0.60	0.49
Debt-to-equity ratio	2.03	2.45	4.88	15.67	N/A*

*In the year before bankruptcy, Braniff reported negative owners' equity as a result of a large net loss that produced a negative balance in retained earnings. Total liabilities exceeded total assets.

Financial statements provide information to all investors, both sophisticated and unsophisticated. However, users who understand basic accounting principles and terminology are able to more effectively analyze the information contained in financial statements. For example, some unsophisticated users who do not understand the cost principle believe that assets are reported on the balance sheet at their fair market value. Interpreting accounting numbers without an understanding of the concepts that were used to develop them is impossible.

In analyzing different companies, you will find that they rarely use exactly the same accounting policies. Comparisons among companies are appropriate only if the analyst who is making them understands the impact of various accounting alternatives. For example, one company may use conservative accounting alternatives such as accelerated amortization, while another may use income-maximizing alternatives such as straight-line amortization. Those who do not understand the different effects of accounting methods are very likely to misinterpret financial results. Perhaps the most important first step in analyzing financial statements is a review of the company's accounting policies, which are disclosed in a note to the statements.

OTHER FINANCIAL INFORMATION

The ratios we have discussed are useful for most analytical purposes. Because each company is different, you must exercise professional judgment when you conduct each financial analysis. To illustrate, let us look at some special factors that might affect our analysis of Home Depot.

1. *Rapid growth.* Growth in total sales volume does not always indicate that a company is successful. Sales volume from new stores may obscure the fact that existing stores are not meeting customer needs and are experiencing declining sales. The family pizza chain Chuck-E-Cheese appeared to be a success when it reported rapid growth in total sales revenue by opening new restaurants. Unfortunately, the novelty of the Chuck-E-Cheese stores proved to be a short-lived fad, and same-store sales volume fell quickly. Because its older restaurants were unprofitable, the company was forced to reorganize. In contrast, the Home Depot's annual report shows that the company posted same-store sales increases ranging from zero percent to 10 percent during the previous 10 years, which indicates that it is able to generate increases in sales volume from both new and existing stores.

2. *Uneconomical expansion.* Some growth-oriented companies open stores in less desirable locations if good locations cannot be found. These poor locations can cause the company's average productivity to decline. One measure of productivity in the retail industry is sales volume per square foot of selling space. For Home Depot, productivity has increased steadily since 2002, but declined in 2006. Management explains the slowdown in growth as the direct result of its strategy.

Year	Sales per Square Foot
2006	$358
2005	377
2004	375
2003	371
2002	370

In order to meet our customer service objectives, we strategically open stores near market areas served by existing stores ("cannibalize") to enhance service levels, gain incremental sales, and increase market penetration. Our new stores cannibalized approximately 13.5% of our existing stores during fiscal 2006, which had a negative impact to retail comparable store sales of approximately 1.9%.

REAL WORLD EXCERPT

Home Depot

ANNUAL REPORT

3. *Subjective factors.* Remember that vital information about a company is not contained in the annual report. The best way to evaluate Home Depot's strategy of being a price leader, for instance, is to visit its stores and those of competitors. An analyst who studied Home Depot for Salomon Smith Barney did exactly that:

REAL WORLD EXCERPT

Home Depot

SALOMON SMITH BARNEY
RESEARCH REPORT

> On July 15, we surveyed the Boca Raton, Florida, market. The Home Depot store is about two years old and was particularly impressive with respect to its in-stock position, customer service and total store presentation. We were able to compare Home Depot's pricing on 20 sample items. Our price analysis revealed that Home Depot is the price leader in the market by an average of 11 percent below the average total price of our 20-item market basket. Given the Home Depot's low cost structure, we believe that it will remain the price leader in this important market.

As these examples illustrate, no single approach can be used to analyze all companies. Furthermore, an effective analyst will look beyond the information contained in an annual report.

A QUESTION OF ETHICS

INSIDER INFORMATION

Financial statements are an important source of information for investors. Announcement of an unexpected earnings increase or decrease can cause a substantial movement in the price of a company's shares.

A company's accountants are often aware of important financial information before it is made available to the public. This type of data is called *insider information*. Some people may be tempted to buy or sell shares based on insider information, but to do so is a serious criminal offence. Securities commissions have brought charges against a number of individuals who traded on insider information. Their conviction resulted in large fines and time served in jail. Recent examples include key executives at Enron and WorldCom.

In some cases, it may be difficult to determine whether something is insider information. For example, an individual may simply overhear a comment made in the company elevator by two executives. A well-respected Wall Street investment banker gave good advice when dealing with such situations: "If you are not sure if something is right or wrong, apply the newspaper headline test. Ask yourself how you would feel to have your family and friends read about what you had done in the newspaper." Interestingly, many people who spent time in jail and lost small fortunes in fines because of insider trading convictions say that the most difficult part of the process was telling their families.

To uphold the highest ethical standard, many public accounting firms have rules that prevent members of their professional staff from investing in companies that the firm audits. These rules are designed to ensure that the company's auditors cannot be tempted to engage in insider trading and to maintain independence from the audited firm.

INFORMATION IN AN EFFICIENT MARKET

Considerable research has been performed on the way in which stock markets react to new information. Much of this evidence supports the view that the markets react very quickly to new information in an unbiased manner (that is, the market does not systematically overreact or underreact to new information). A market that reacts to information in this manner is called an **efficient market**. In an efficient market, the price of a security fully reflects all publicly available information.

It is not surprising that the stock markets react quickly to new information. Many professional investors manage stock portfolios valued in the hundreds of millions of dollars. These investors have a large financial incentive to discover new information about a company and to trade quickly based on that information.

EFFICIENT MARKETS are securities markets in which prices fully reflect all publicly available information.

The research on efficient markets has important implications for financial analysis. It probably is not beneficial to study old information (for example, an annual report that was released six months earlier) in an effort to identify an undervalued stock. In an efficient market, the price of the stock reflects all of the information contained in the report shortly after it was released. Furthermore, a company cannot manipulate the price of its stock by manipulating its accounting policy. The market should be able to differentiate between a company with increasing earnings due to improved productivity and one that has increased its earnings by changing from conservative to liberal accounting policies.

SOLUTIONS TO **SELF-STUDY QUIZZES**

Self-Study Quiz 13-1

1. $\text{ROE} = \dfrac{\text{Income}}{\text{Average Shareholders' Equity}} = \dfrac{\$148}{(\$1,459 + \$1,345)/2} = 0.106$, or 10.6%

2. $\text{ROE} = \dfrac{\text{Income} + \text{Interest Expense (net of tax)}}{\text{Average Total Assets}} = \dfrac{\$148 + \$58}{(\$3,748 + \$3,871)/2} = 0.054$, or 5.4%

3. $\text{Profit margin} = \dfrac{\text{Income (before extraordinary items)}}{\text{Net Sales Revenue}} = \dfrac{\$148}{\$5,207} = 0.028$, or 2.8%

Self-Study Quiz 13-2

Dell has an edge over Gateway in the efficiency of its operations, as reflected in its high asset turnover ratio. Dell's major edge is its significantly higher net profit margin. This reflects Dell's success with its primary market segment, business customers. They often purchase in large quantities, which decreases order processing and production costs. They also often purchase higher-end, higher–net profit margin machines than customers in Gateway's primary market segment, individuals.

Self-Study Quiz 13-3

The quick ratio should be lower than the current ratio because the numerator of the quick ratio includes only part of the current assets. The quick ratio of 4.59 is greater than the current ratios of five of the six industries, so it cannot be associated with any of these five industries. Consequently, this quick ratio must be associated with the metals and mining industry. Since the quick assets for the software industry equal 85 percent of its current assets, the quick ratio of this industry must equal 1.98 × 85 percent, or 1.68.

Self-Study Quiz 13-4

1. $\dfrac{\text{Cash Flows from Operating Activities}}{\text{Net Income}} = \dfrac{\$502}{\$148} = 3.39$

2. $\dfrac{\text{Quick Assets}}{\text{Current Liabilities}} = \dfrac{\$131 + \$515 + \$453}{\$1,128} = 0.97$

3. $\dfrac{\text{Cash} + \text{Cash Equivalents}}{\text{Current Laibilities}} = \dfrac{\$131}{\$1,128} = 0.12$

Self-Study Quiz 13-5

1. $\dfrac{\text{Current Assets}}{\text{Current Liabilities}} = \dfrac{\$1,528}{\$1,128} = 1.35$

2. $\dfrac{\text{Cost of Goods Sold}}{\text{Average Inventory}} = \dfrac{\$3,645}{(\$412 + \$473)/2} = 8.24$

3. $\dfrac{\text{Current Market Price per Share}}{\text{Earnings per Share}} = \dfrac{\$19}{\$1.89} = 10.1$

CHAPTER **TAKE-AWAYS**

1. **Explain how a company's business strategy affects financial analysis. p. 679**
   In simple terms, a business strategy establishes the objectives a business is trying to achieve. Performance is best evaluated by comparing the financial results to the objectives that the business was working to achieve. In other words, an understanding of a company's strategy provides the context for conducting financial statement analysis.

2. Discuss how analysts use financial statements. p. 681

Analysts use financial statements to understand present conditions and past performance as well as to predict future performance. Financial statements provide important information to help users understand and evaluate corporate strategy. The data reported on statements can be used for either time-series analysis (evaluating a single company over time) or in comparison with similar companies at a single point in time. Most analysts compute component percentages and ratios when using statements.

3. Compute and interpret component percentages. p. 682

To compute component percentages for the income statement, the base amount is net sales revenue. Each expense is expressed as a percentage of net sales revenue. On the balance sheet, the base amount is total assets; each balance sheet account is divided by total assets. Component percentages are evaluated by comparing them over time for a single company or by comparing them with percentages for similar companies.

4. Compute and interpret profitability ratios. p. 684

Several tests of profitability focus on measuring the adequacy of income by comparing it to other items reported on the financial statements. Exhibit 13.4 lists these ratios and shows how to compute them. Profitability ratios are evaluated by comparing them over time for a single company or by comparing them with ratios for similar companies.

5. Compute and interpret liquidity ratios. p. 692

Tests of liquidity measure a company's ability to meet its current maturing debt. Exhibit 13.4 lists these ratios and shows how to compute them. Liquidity ratios are evaluated by comparing them over time for a single company or by comparing them with ratios for similar companies.

6. Compute and interpret solvency ratios. p. 697

Solvency ratios measure a company's ability to meet its long-term obligations. Exhibit 13.4 lists these ratios and shows how to compute them. Solvency ratios are evaluated by comparing them over time for a single company or by comparing them with ratios for similar companies.

7. Compute and interpret market test ratios. p. 699

Market test ratios relate the current price per share to the return that accrues to investors. Exhibit 13.4 lists these ratios and shows how to compute them. Market test ratios are evaluated by comparing them over time for a single company or by comparing them with ratios for similar companies.

FINDING FINANCIAL INFORMATION

BALANCE SHEET

Ratios are not reported on the balance sheet, but analysts use balance sheet information to compute many ratios. Most analysts use an average of the beginning and ending amounts for balance sheet accounts when comparing the account to an income statement account.

INCOME STATEMENT

Earnings per share is the only ratio that is required to be reported on the financial statements. It is usually reported at the bottom of the income statement.

CASH FLOW STATEMENT

Ratios are not reported on this statement, but some ratios use amounts from this statement.

STATEMENT OF RETAINED EARNINGS

Ratios are not reported on this statement.

NOTES

Under Summary of Significant Accounting Policies

This note has no information pertaining directly to ratios, but it is important to understand accounting differences if you are comparing two companies.

Under a Separate Note

Most companies include a 5-year or a 10-year financial summary as a separate note. These summaries include data for significant accounts, some accounting ratios, and non-accounting information.

KEY **TERMS**

Component Percentage p. 682   **Tests of Liquidity** p. 692

Efficient Markets p. 702   **Tests of Profitability** p. 684

Market Tests p. 699   **Tests of Solvency** p. 697

Ratio (Percentage) Analysis p. 682

QUESTIONS

1. What are three fundamental uses of external financial statements by decision makers?
2. What are some of the primary items on financial statements about which creditors usually are concerned?
3. Why are the notes to the financial statements important to decision makers?
4. What is the primary purpose of comparative financial statements?
5. Why are statement users interested in financial summaries covering several years? What is the primary limitation of long-term summaries?
6. What is *ratio analysis?* Why is it useful?
7. What are *component percentages?* Why are they useful?
8. Explain the two concepts of return on investment.
9. What is *financial leverage?* How is it measured as a percentage?
10. Is profit margin a useful measure of profitability? Explain.
11. Compare and contrast the current ratio and the quick ratio.
12. What does the debt-to-equity ratio reflect?
13. What are market tests?
14. Identify two factors that limit the effectiveness of ratio analysis.
15. Doritos Company has prepared draft financial results now being reviewed by the accountants. You notice that the financial leverage percentage is negative. You also note that the current ratio is 2.4 and the quick ratio is 3.7. You remember that these financial relationships are unusual. Does either imply that a mistake has been made? Explain.

EXERCISES

E13–1 Preparing a Schedule Using Component Percentages

Le Groupe Jean Coutu is one of the fastest-growing retailers in North America. It claims to lead the Canadian chain drugstore industry in sales and profits. Complete the component percentage analysis on the company's income statement that follows. Discuss the insights provided by this analysis.

Le Groupe Jean Coutu	2006	2005
Income Statement (amounts in millions)		
Net sales	$11,143	$9,617
Cost of sales	8,401	7,290
Operating expenses	2,477	2,074
Interest expense	205	162
Income tax expense (recovery)	(44)	(13)
Net income	104	104

■ **LO3**

Le Groupe
Jean Coutu

ANALYSIS

E13–2 Analyzing the Impact of Selected Transactions on the Current Ratio

Current assets totalled $54,000, and the current ratio was 1.8. Assume that the following transactions were completed: (1) purchased merchandise for $6,000 on short-term credit and (2) purchased a delivery truck for $20,000, paid $4,000 cash, and signed a two-year interest-bearing note for the balance.

Required:

Compute the current ratio after each transaction.

■ **LO5**

E13–3 Analyzing the Impact of Selected Transactions on Accounts Receivable and Inventory Turnover

Procter & Gamble is a multinational corporation that manufactures and markets many products that are probably in your home. Last year, sales for the company were $51,407

■ **LO5**

Procter & Gamble

(all amounts in millions). The annual report did not disclose the amount of credit sales, so we will assume that 30 percent of sales was on credit. The average gross margin rate was 45 percent on sales. Account balances follow:

	Beginning	Ending
Accounts receivable (net)	$4,185	$5,725
Inventory	5,006	6,291

Required:
Compute the turnover for the accounts receivable and inventory, the average age of receivables, and the average days' supply of inventory.

LO4, 5

ANALYSIS

E13–4   Analyzing the Impact of Specific Events on Selected Ratios
Consider the following two independent situations:

1. A manufacturer reported an inventory turnover ratio of 8.6 during 2007. During 2008, management introduced a new inventory control system that was expected to reduce average inventory levels by 25 percent without affecting sales volume. Given these circumstances, would you expect the inventory turnover ratio to increase or decrease during 2008? Explain.

2. Lexis Corporation is considering changing its inventory method from FIFO to weighted average and wants to determine the impact on selected accounting ratios. In general, what would be the impact of this change on the following ratios, assuming that prices have been increasing over time: profit margin, fixed asset turnover, current ratio, and quick ratio?

LO4

Motorola

E13–5   Computing Financial Leverage
Motorola is a global leader in providing integrated communications and electronic solutions for businesses. Its financial statements reported the following at year-end (in millions):

Total assets	$38,593
Total debt (average 7% interest)	21,451
Net income (average tax rate 30%)	3,661

Required:
Compute the financial leverage percentage. Was it positive or negative?

LO5

E13–6   Analyzing the Impact of Selected Transactions on the Current Ratio
Current assets totalled $100,000, and the current ratio was 1.5. Assume that the following transactions were completed: (1) paid $6,000 for merchandise purchased on short-term credit, (2) purchased a delivery truck for $20,000 cash, (3) wrote off a bad account receivable for $1,000, and (4) paid previously declared dividends in the amount of $20,000.

Required:
Compute the current ratio after each transaction.

LO3

Dollar General
Corporation

E13–7   Inferring Financial Information
Dollar General Corporation operates general merchandise stores that feature quality merchandise at low prices. All stores are located predominantly in small towns. In a recent year, the company reported average inventories of $1,276 million and an inventory turnover of 4.2. Average total fixed assets were $1,019 million, and the fixed asset turnover ratio was 7.6. Determine the gross margin for Dollar General.

LO5

E13–8   Computing Selected Ratios
Sales for the year were $600,000, of which one-half was on credit. The average gross margin rate was 40 percent on sales. Account balances follow:

	Beginning	Ending
Accounts receivable (net)	$50,000	$70,000
Inventory	50,000	30,000

Required:
Compute and comment on the turnover for the accounts receivable and inventory, the average age of receivables, and the average days' supply of inventory.

E13–9 **Analyzing the Impact of Selected Transactions on the Current Ratio**
Current assets totalled $500,000, the current ratio was 2.0, and the company uses the periodic inventory method. Assume that the following transactions were completed: (1) sold $13,000 in merchandise on short-term credit, (2) declared but did not pay dividends of $20,000, (3) paid prepaid rent in the amount of $12,000, (4) paid previously declared dividends in the amount of $20,000, (5) collected an account receivable in the amount of $10,000, and (6) reclassified $45,000 of long-term debt as a short-term liability.

Required:
Compute the current ratio after each transaction.

LO5

E13–10 **Computing Liquidity Ratios**
Cintas designs, manufactures, and implements corporate identity uniform programs that it rents or sells to customers throughout the United States and Canada. The company's stock is traded on the NASDAQ and has provided investors with significant returns over the past few years. Selected information from the company's balance sheet follows. The company reported revenue of $2,568,776 and cost of goods sold of $1,406,829 for fiscal year 2006.

LO5

Cintas

ANALYSIS

Cintas	2006	2005
Balance Sheet (amounts in thousands)		
Cash and cash equivalents	$ 38,914	$ 43,196
Marketable securities	202,539	266,232
Accounts receivable, less allowance of $15,519 ($9,891)	389,905	326,896
Inventories, net	198,000	216,412
Prepaid expenses	11,163	8,358
Accounts payable	71,635	69,296
Accrued compensation and related liabilities	51,615	38,710
Future income taxes, current	43,694	32,864
Long-term debt due within one year	4,288	7,300

Required:
Compute the current ratio, quick ratio, inventory turnover, and accounts receivable turnover (assuming that 60 percent of sales was on credit), and comment on the liquidity position of the company.

E13–11 **Determining the Impact of Selected Transactions on Measures of Solvency**
Three commonly used measures of solvency are the debt-to-equity ratio, the times interest earned ratio, and the cash coverage ratio. For each of the following transactions, determine whether the measure will increase, decrease, or not change. Assume that all ratios are higher than 1.
a. Issued shares in exchange for equipment for $500,000.
b. Issued bonds at par for $1 million cash.
c. Previously declared dividends are paid in cash.
d. Accrued interest expense is recorded.
e. A customer pays money on his account receivable.

LO5

ANALYSIS

E13–12 **Using Financial Information to Identify Mystery Companies**
The following selected financial data pertain to four unidentified companies:

LO3, 5, 6

	Companies			
	1	2	3	4
Balance Sheet Data (component percentage)				
Cash	3.5	4.7	8.2	11.7
Accounts receivable	16.9	28.9	16.8	51.9
Inventory	46.8	35.6	57.3	4.8
Property and equipment	18.3	21.7	7.6	18.7
Income Statement Data (component percentage)				
Gross profit	22.0	22.5	44.8	N/A*
Profit before taxes	2.1	0.7	1.2	3.2
Selected Ratios				
Current ratio	1.3	1.5	1.6	1.2
Inventory turnover	3.6	9.8	1.5	N/A
Debt to equity	2.6	2.6	3.2	3.2

*N/A = Not applicable

This financial information pertains to the following companies:

a. Retail fur store.

b. Advertising agency.

c. Wholesale candy company.

d. Car manufacturer.

Required:

Match each company with its financial information. Support your choices.

■ LO3, 5, 6   **E13–13**   **Using Financial Information to Identify Mystery Companies**

The following selected financial data pertain to four unidentified companies:

	Companies			
	1	2	3	4
Balance Sheet Data (component percentage)				
Cash	7.3	21.6	6.1	11.3
Accounts receivable	28.2	39.7	3.2	22.9
Inventory	21.6	0.6	1.8	27.5
Property and equipment	32.1	18.0	74.6	25.1
Income Statement Data (component percentage)				
Gross profit	15.3	N/A*	N/A	43.4
Profit before taxes	1.7	3.2	2.4	6.9
Selected Ratios				
Current ratio	1.5	1.2	0.6	1.9
Inventory turnover	27.4	N/A	N/A	3.3
Debt to equity	1.7	2.2	5.7	1.3
*N/A = Not applicable				

This financial information pertains to the following companies:

a. Travel agency.

b. Hotel.

c. Meat packer.

d. Drug company.

Required:

Match each company with its financial information. Support your choices.

■ LO3, 5, 6   **E13–14**   **Using Financial Information to Identify Mystery Companies**

The following selected financial data pertain to four unidentified companies:

	Companies			
	1	2	3	4
Balance Sheet Data (component percentage)				
Cash	5.1	8.8	6.3	10.4
Accounts receivable	13.1	41.5	13.8	4.9
Inventory	4.6	3.6	65.1	35.8
Property and equipment	53.1	23.0	8.8	35.7
Income Statement Data (component percentage)				
Gross profit	N/A*	N/A	45.2	22.5
Profit before taxes	0.3	16.0	3.9	1.5
Selected Ratios				
Current ratio	0.7	2.2	1.9	1.4
Inventory turnover	N/A	N/A	1.4	15.5
Debt to equity	2.5	0.9	1.7	2.3
*N/A = Not applicable				

This financial information pertains to the following companies:

a. Cable TV company.

b. Grocery store.

c. Accounting firm.

d. Retail jewellery store.

Required:
Match each company with its financial information. Support your choices.

E13–15 Using Financial Information to Identify Mystery Companies   ■ **LO3, 5, 6**
The following selected financial data pertain to four unidentified companies:

a. Full-line department store.

b. Wholesale fish company.

c. Automobile dealer (both new and used cars).

d. Restaurant.

	Companies			
	1	**2**	**3**	**4**
Balance Sheet Data (component percentage)				
Cash	11.6	6.6	5.4	7.1
Accounts receivable	4.6	18.9	8.8	35.6
Inventory	7.0	45.8	65.7	26.0
Property and equipment	56.0	20.3	10.1	21.9
Income Statement Data (component percentage)				
Gross profit	56.7	36.4	14.1	15.8
Profit before taxes	2.7	1.4	1.1	0.9
Selected Ratios				
Current ratio	0.7	2.1	1.2	1.3
Inventory turnover	30.0	3.5	5.6	16.7
Debt to equity	3.3	1.8	3.8	3.1

Required:
Match each company with its financial information. Support your choices.

E13–16 Inferring Information from the ROE Model   ■ **LO1**
In this chapter, we discussed the ROE profit driver (or DuPont) model. Using that framework, find the missing amount in each case below:

Case 1: ROE is 10 percent, net income is $200,000; asset turnover is 5, and net sales are $1,000,000. What is the amount of average shareholders' equity?

Case 2: Net income is $1,500,000; net sales are $8,000,000; average shareholders' equity is $12,000,000; ROE is 22 percent and asset turnover is 8. What is the amount of average total assets?

Case 3: ROE is 15 percent; net profit margin is 10 percent; asset turnover is 5; and average total assets are $1,000,000. What is the amount of average shareholders' equity?

Case 4: Net income is $500,000; ROE is 15 percent; asset turnover is 5; net sales are $1,000,000; and financial leverage is 2. What is the amount of average total assets?

PROBLEMS

P13–1 Analyzing Comparative Financial Statements Using Percentages (AP13–1)   ■ **LO3**
The comparative financial statements prepared at December 31, 2008, for Goldfish Company showed the following summarized data:

	2008	2007
Income Statement		
Sales revenue	$195,000*	$165,000
Cost of goods sold	120,000	100,000
Gross margin	75,000	65,000
Operating expenses and interest expense	60,000	53,000
Pretax income	15,000	12,000
Income tax	4,000	3,000
Net income	$ 11,000	$ 9,000
Balance Sheet		
Cash	$ 4,000	$ 8,000
Accounts receivable (net)	15,000	18,000
Inventory	40,000	35,000
Property, plant, and equipment (net)	45,000	38,000
	$104,000	$ 99,000
Current liabilities (no interest)	$ 16,000	$ 19,000
Long-term liabilities (10% interest)	45,000	39,000
Common shares (6,000 shares)	30,000	30,000
Retained earnings†	13,000	11,000
	$104,000	$ 99,000

*One-third was credit sales.
†During 2008, cash dividends amounting to $9,000 were declared and paid.

Required:

1. Complete the following columns for each item in the preceding comparative financial statements:

Increase (Decrease) 2008 over 2007	
Amount	Percent

2. Answer the following:
   a. By what amount did working capital change?
   b. What was the percentage change in the average income tax rate?
   c. What was the amount of cash inflow from revenues for 2008?
   d. What was the percentage change for the average mark-up realized on goods sold?

■ **LO3, 4, 5, 6, 7** **P13–2** **Analyzing Comparative Financial Statements Using Percentages and Selected Ratios (AP13–2)**

Use the data given in P13–1 for Goldfish Company.

Required:

1. Present component percentages for 2008 only.

ANALYSIS

2. Answer the following for 2008:
   a. What was the average percentage mark-up on sales?
   b. What was the average income tax rate?
   c. Compute the profit margin. Was it a good or poor indicator of performance? Explain.
   d. What percentage of total resources was invested in property, plant, and equipment?
   e. Compute the debt to equity ratio. Does it look good or bad? Explain.
   f. What was the return on assets?
   g. What was the return on equity?
   h. Compute the financial leverage percentage. Did borrowing from creditors benefit shareholders? Explain.

■ **LO3, 4, 5, 6, 7** **P13–3** **Analyzing Ratios (AP13–3)**

Sears Canada Inc. and Canadian Tire Corporation

Sears Canada Inc. and Canadian Tire Corporation are two giants of the Canadian retail industry. Both offer full lines of moderately priced merchandise. Annual sales for Sears total $5.9 billion. Canadian Tire is somewhat larger, with $8.3 billion in revenues. Compare the two companies as a potential investment based on the following ratios:

ANALYSIS

Ratio	Sears Canada	Canadian Tire
P/E	12.8	14.4
Profit margin	2.6%	0.4%
Quick ratio	0.6	1.1
Current ratio	1.2	1.5
Debt to equity	2.9	1.1
Return on equity	21.3%	13.4%
Return on assets	5.7%	6.9%
Dividend yield	0.7%	1.1%
Earnings per share	$ 1.42	$4.35
Price per share at year end	$18.10	$62.5
Dividends per share	$ 0.12	$0.66

P13–4 Analyzing a Financial Statement Using Several Ratios

Summer Corporation has just completed its comparative statements for the year ended December 31, 2009. At this point, certain analytical and interpretive procedures are to be undertaken. The completed statements (summarized) are as follows:

■ LO3, 4, 5, 6, 7

eXcel

ANALYSIS

	2009	2008
Income Statement		
Sales revenue	$480,000ᵃ	$420,000ᵃ
Cost of goods sold	270,000	230,000
Gross margin	210,000	190,000
Operating expenses		
(including interest on bonds)	171,000	168,000
Pretax income	39,000	22,000
Income tax	12,000	6,000
Net income	$ 27,000	$ 16,000
Balance Sheet		
Cash	$ 6,800	$ 3,900
Accounts receivable (net)	42,000	28,000
Merchandise inventory	25,000	20,000
Prepaid expenses	200	100
Property, plant, and equipment (net)	130,000	120,000
	$204,000	$172,000
Accounts payable	$ 17,000	$ 18,000
Income taxes payable	1,000	2,000
Bonds payable (10% interest rate)	70,000ᵇ	50,000
Common shares (20,000 shares)	100,000ᶜ	100,000
Retained earnings	16,000ᵈ	2,000
	$204,000	$172,000

ᵃCredit sales totalled 40 percent of total sales.
ᵇ$20,000 of bonds were issued on January 2, 2009.
ᶜThe market price of the stock at the end of 2009 was $18 per share.
ᵈDuring 2009, the company declared and paid a cash dividend of $13,000.

Required:

1. Compute appropriate ratios for 2009 and explain the meaning of each.

2. Answer the following for 2009:

   a. Evaluate the financial leverage. Explain its meaning using the computed amount(s).

   b. Evaluate the profit margin ratio and explain how a shareholder might use it.

   c. Explain to a shareholder why the current ratio and the quick ratio are different. Do you observe any liquidity problems? Explain.

   d. Assuming that credit terms are 1/10, n/30, do you perceive an unfavourable situation for the company related to credit sales? Explain.

   e. By how much should the balance of Accounts Receivable decrease if the company wishes to reduce its average collection period to 30 days?

■ **LO3, 4, 5,**   **P13–5**   **Comparing Alternative Investment Opportunities (AP13–4)**
6, 7

The 2008 financial statements for Armstrong and Blair companies are summarized below:

	Armstrong Company	Blair Company
Balance Sheet		
Cash	$ 35,000	$ 22,000
Accounts receivable (net)	40,000	30,000
Inventory	100,000	40,000
Property, plant, and equipment (net)	140,000	400,000
Other assets	85,000	308,000
Total assets	$400,000	$800,000
Current liabilities	$100,000	$50,000
Long-term debt (10%)	60,000	70,000
Share capital	150,000	500,000
Contributed surplus	30,000	110,000
Retained earnings	60,000	70,000
Total liabilities and shareholders' equity	$400,000	$800,000
Income Statement		
Sales revenue (1/3 on credit)	$450,000	$810,000
Cost of goods sold	(245,000)	(405,000)
Expenses (including interest and income tax)	(160,000)	(315,000)
Net income	$ 45,000	$ 90,000

Selected data from the 2007 statements:

Accounts receivable (net)	$20,000	$ 40,000
Inventory	92,000	48,000
Long-term debt	60,000	70,000

Other data:

Share price at end of 2008	$ 18	$ 15
Income tax rate	30%	30%
Dividends declared and paid in 2008	$36,000	$150,000
Number of common shares during 2008	15,000	50,000

The companies are in the same line of business and are direct competitors in a large metropolitan area. Both have been in business approximately 10 years, and each has had steady growth. The management of each has a different viewpoint in many respects. Blair is more conservative, and as its president said, "We avoid what we consider to be undue risk." Neither company is publicly held. Armstrong Company has an annual audit by an independent auditor but Blair Company does not.

Required:

1. Complete a schedule that reflects a ratio analysis of each company. Compute the ratios discussed in the chapter. Use ending balances if average balances are not available.

2. A client of yours has the opportunity to buy 10 percent of the shares in one or the other company at the share prices given and has decided to invest in one of the companies. Based on the data given, prepare a comparative written evaluation of the ratio analyses (and any other available information) and give your recommended choice with the supporting explanation.

■ **LO4, 5**   **P13–6**   **Analyzing the Impact of Alternative Inventory Methods on Selected Ratios**

Company A uses the FIFO method to cost inventory, and Company B uses the weighted average method. The two companies are exactly alike except for the difference in inventory costing methods. Costs of inventory items for both companies have been rising steadily in recent years, and each company has increased its inventory each year. Each company has paid its tax liability in full for the current year (and all previous years), and each company uses the same accounting methods for both financial reporting and income tax reporting, except for inventory valuation.

Required:

Identify which company will report the higher amount for each of the following ratios. If it is not possible, explain why.

1. Current ratio.

2. Quick ratio.

3. Debt-to-equity ratio.

4. Return on equity.

5. Earnings per share.

P13–7 **Analyzing Financial Statements Using Appropriate Ratios (AP13–5)**

Sears Canada Inc. offers Canadian consumers a diverse array of shopping options through department and specialty stores, catalogues, and the Internet. The following information was reported in a recent annual report.

■ **LO3, 4, 5, 6, 7**

Sears Canada Inc.

ANALYSIS

Required:

1. Compute the ratios discussed in this chapter for the last two years. If there is not sufficient information, describe what is missing and explain what you would do.

2. Assume that you work in the loan department of the Provincial Bank, and you are evaluating an application from Sears for a two-year loan of $200 million that would be used to purchase the shares of another competing company. What specific ratios would you consider in your evaluation, and would you lend Sears the requested amount?

SEARS CANADA INC.
Consolidated Statements of Earnings
(in millions, except per share amounts)

	52 Weeks Ended Dec. 30, 2006	52 Weeks Ended Dec. 31, 2005	52 Weeks Ended January 1, 2005
Total Revenues	$5,932.8	$6,237.6	$6,230.5
Cost of merchandise sold, operating, administrative and selling expenses	5,468.3	5,814.6	5,816.9
Depreciation and amortization	152.1	164.2	166.0
Interest expense, net	48.0	48.9	55.0
Unusual items—expense (gain)	25.2	(747.7)	3.2
Earnings before income taxes	239.2	957.6	189.4
Income taxes expense (recovery)			
Current	35.5	202.5	41.3
Future	51.1	(15.7)	19.4
	86.6	186.8	60.7
Net earnings	$ 152.6	$ 770.8	$ 128.7
Earnings per share	$ 1.42	$ 7.22	$ 1.21
Diluted earnings per share	$ 1.42	$ 7.19	$ 1.20

SEARS CANADA INC.
Consolidated Statements of Retained Earnings
(in millions)

	52 Weeks Ended Dec. 30, 2006	52 Weeks Ended Dec. 31, 2005	52 Weeks Ended January. 1, 2005
Opening Balance	$631.6	$1,417.9	$1,321.7
Net earnings	152.6	770.8	128.7
Dividends declared	(12.9)	(1,557.1)	(25.6)
Notional dividends	(2.0)	—	—
Repurchase of shares (Note 10)	—	—	(6.9)
Closing Balance	$769.3	$ 631.6	$1,417.9

SEARS CANADA INC.

Consolidated Statements of Financial Position

(in millions)	As at Dec. 30, 2006	As at Dec. 31, 2005	As at Jan. 1, 2005
ASSETS			
Current Assets			
Cash and short-term investments	$ 746.8	$ 771.7	$ 78.0
Restricted cash	10.1	3.4	—
Accounts receivable	145.0	146.5	1,526.3
Income taxes recoverable	0.6	7.9	—
Inventories	804.5	788.2	789.8
Prepaid expenses and other assets	120.0	128.3	132.4
Current portion of future income tax assets	121.2	130.3	85.0
	1,948.2	1,976.3	2,611.5
Investments and other assets			83.9
Capital assets	874.3	980.9	1,065.8
Deferred charges	220.2	243.8	270.5
Future income tax assets	15.2	54.1	79.3
Other long-term assets	35.4	35.7	115.4
	$3,093.3	$3,290.8	$4,226.4
LIABILITIES			
Current liabilities			
Accounts payable	$ 834.0	$ 696.6	$ 735.2
Accrued liabilities	489.1	522.3	434.7
Income and other taxes payable	105.1	322.5	101.7
Principal payments on long-term obligations due within one year	146.7	216.1	21.3
Future income tax liabilities	0.1	—	—
	1,575.0	1,757.5	1,292.9
Long-term obligations	395.6	533.2	734.6
Accrued benefit liability	167.7	188.3	180.5
Other long-term liabilities	170.0	166.5	141.0
	2,308.3	2,645.5	2,349.0
SHAREHOLDERS' EQUITY			
Capital stock	15.7	13.7	459.5
Retained earnings	769.3	631.6	1,417.9
	785.0	645.3	1,877.4
	$3,093.3	$3,290.8	$4,226.4

■ **LO5, 6, 7**   **P13–8** **Analyzing an Investment by Comparing Selected Ratios** (AP13–6)

You have the opportunity to invest $10,000 in one of two companies from a single industry. The only information you have follows. The word *high* refers to the top third of the industry; *average* is the middle third; *low* is the bottom third. Which company would you select? Write a brief report justifying your recommendation.

Ratio	Company A	Company B
Current	High	Average
Quick	Low	Average
Debt to equity	High	Average
Inventory turnover	Low	Average
Price/earnings	Low	Average
Dividend yield	High	Average

P13–9 Analyzing an Investment by Comparing Selected Ratios (AP13–7)

■ **LO5, 6, 7**

You have the opportunity to invest $10,000 in one of two companies from a single industry. The only information you have is shown below. The word *high* refers to the top third of the industry; *average* is the middle third; *low* is the bottom third. Which company would you select? Write a brief report justifying your recommendation.

Ratio	Company A	Company B
Current	Low	Average
Quick	Average	Average
Debt to equity	Low	Average
Inventory turnover	High	Average
Price/earnings	High	Average
Dividend yield	Low	Average

P13–10 Analyzing Financial Statements Using Appropriate Ratios

■ **LO3, 4, 5, 6, 7**

ANALYSIS

Morksen Corp. has enjoyed modest success in penetrating the personal electronic devices market since it began operations a few years ago. A new line of devices introduced recently has been received well by customers. However, the company president who is knowledgeable about electronics but not in accounting is concerned about the future of the company.

Although the company has a line of credit with the local bank, it currently needs cash to continue operations. The bank wants more information before it extends the company's credit line. The president has asked you, as the company's chief accountant, to evaluate the company's performance using appropriate financial statement analysis, and to recommend possible courses of action for the company. In particular, the president wants to know how the company can obtain additional cash. Summary financial statements are available to you for the past three years.

Required:

1. Evaluate the company's performance and its financial condition for the past two years. Select six appropriate ratios to analyze the company's profitability, liquidity, and solvency for 2007 and 2008, and explain to the company's president the meaning of each ratio you calculate.

2. Based on your analysis of the ratios that you computed in part 1, what recommendation would you make to the president to obtain additional cash?

MORKSEN CORP.
Consolidated Statements of Earnings and Retained Earnings
For the Years Ended December 31
(in thousands of dollars)

	2008	2007	2006
Sales	$32,000	$28,000	$23,400
Cost of goods sold	25,000	21,500	18,000
Gross profit	7,000	6,500	5,400
Operating expenses before interest and income taxes	4,000	3,700	3,310
Interest expense	890	610	0
Income before income taxes	2,110	2,190	2,090
Income tax expense	950	1,020	970
Net earnings	1,160	1,170	1,120
Retained earnings, beginning of year	1,950	1,480	960
	3,110	2,650	2,080
Dividends	800	700	600
Retained earnings, end of year	$ 2,310	$ 1,950	$ 1,480

MORKSEN CORP.
Consolidated Balance Sheets
At December 31
(in thousands of dollars)

	2008	2007	2006
Assets			
Current assets			
Cash	$ 190	$ 240	$ 500
Marketable securities	370	370	370
Accounts receivable—trade	5,440	4,200	2,570
Merchandise inventory	8,330	5,030	3,610
Total current assets	14,330	9,840	7,050
Capital assets			
Land	2,000	2,000	1,000
Buildings and equipment	13,000	13,000	9,000
	15,000	15,000	10,000
Less: accumulated amortization	4,470	3,720	2,880
Net capital assets	10,530	11,280	7,120
Total Assets	$24,860	$21,120	$14,170
Liabilities and Shareholders' Equity			
Current liabilities			
Bank loan	8,250	5,700	0
Accounts payable—trade	3,000	2,150	1,440
Other liabilities	820	800	750
Income tax payable	480	520	500
Total current liabilities	12,550	9,170	2,690
Shareholders' equity			
Common shares	10,000	10,000	10,000
Retained earnings	2,310	1,950	1,480
Total shareholders' equity	12,310	11,950	11,480
Total Liabilities and Shareholders' Equity	$24,860	$21,120	$14,170

ALTERNATE PROBLEMS

LO3, 4, 5, 6, 7 **AP13–1** **Analyzing Financial Statements Using Ratios and Percentage Changes** (P13–1)

Taber Company has just prepared the following comparative annual financial statements for 2009:

ANALYSIS

TABER COMPANY
Comparative Income Statement
For the Years Ended December 31, 2009 and 2008

	2009	2008
Sales revenue (one-half on credit)	$110,000	$100,000
Cost of goods sold	52,000	49,000
Gross margin	58,000	51,000
Expenses (including $4,000 interest expense each year)	40,000	37,000
Pretax income	18,000	14,000
Income tax on operations (30%)	5,400	4,200
Income before extraordinary items	12,600	9,800
Extraordinary loss (net of tax)	1,400	
Extraordinary gain (net of tax)		2,100
Net income	$ 11,200	$ 11,900

TABER COMPANY
Comparative Balance Sheet
At December 31, 2009 and 2008

	2009	2008
Assets		
Cash	$ 49,500	$ 18,000
Accounts receivable (net; terms 1/10, n/30)	37,000	32,000
Inventory	25,000	38,000
Property, plant, and equipment (net)	95,000	105,000
Total assets	$206,500	$193,000
Liabilities		
Accounts payable	$ 42,000	$ 35,000
Income taxes payable	1,000	500
Note payable, long term	40,000	40,000
Shareholders' equity		
Share capital (9,000 shares)	90,000	90,000
Retained earnings	33,500	27,500
Total liabilities and shareholders' equity	$206,500	$193,000

Required (round percentage and ratios to two decimal places):

1. For 2009, compute the tests of (a) profitability, (b) liquidity, (c) solvency, and (d) market. Assume that the quoted price of the stock was $23 per share for 2009. Dividends declared and paid during 2009 were $5,200.

2. Answer the following for 2009:

   a. Compute the percentage changes in sales, income before extraordinary items, net income, cash, inventory, and debt.

   b. What appears to be the pretax interest rate on the note payable?

3. Identify at least two problems facing the company that are suggested by your responses to requirements 1 and 2.

AP13–2 Using Ratios to Analyze Several Years of Financial Data (P13–2)

The following information was contained in the annual financial statements of Pine Company, which started business January 1, 2007 (assume account balances only in Cash and Share Capital on this date; all amounts are in thousands of dollars).

■ **LO3, 4, 5**

ANALYSIS

	2007	2008	2009	2010
Accounts receivable (net; terms n/30)	$11	$12	$18	$ 24
Merchandise inventory	12	14	20	30
Net sales (¾ on credit)	44	66	80	100
Cost of goods sold	28	40	55	62
Net income (loss)	(8)	5	12	11

Required (show computations and round to two decimal places):

1. Complete the following tabulation:

Items	2007	2008	2009	2010
a. Profit margin—percentage				
b. Gross margin—ratio				
c. Expenses as percentage of sales, excluding cost of goods sold				
d. Inventory turnover				
e. Days' supply in inventory				
f. Receivable turnover				
g. Average collection period				

2. Evaluate the results of the related ratios *a, b,* and *c* to identify the favourable or unfavourable factors. Give your recommendations to improve the company's operations.

3. Evaluate the results of the last four ratios (*d, e, f,* and *g*) and identify any favourable or unfavourable factors. Give your recommendations to improve the company's operations.

LO3, 4   AP13–3 Analyzing Ratios (P13–3)

Coca-Cola and PepsiCo

ANALYSIS

Coke and Pepsi are well-known international brands. Coca-Cola sells more than $24 billion worth of beverages each year, while annual sales of Pepsi products exceed $35 billion. Compare the two companies as a potential investment based on the following ratios:

Ratio	Coca-Cola	PepsiCo
P/E	65.0	26.5
Gross profit margin	69.3	58.4
Profit margin	12.2%	8.8%
Quick ratio	0.4	0.7
Current ratio	0.6	1.1
Debt to equity	0.7	0.4
Return on equity	27.4%	29.1%
Return on assets	28.0%	16.6%
Dividend yield	1.0%	1.6%

LO3, 4   AP13–4 Comparing Loan Requests from Two Companies Using Several Ratios (P13–5)

e**X**cel

ANALYSIS

The 2008 financial statements for Rand and Tand companies are summarized below:

	Rand Company	Tand Company
Balance Sheet		
Cash	$ 25,000	$ 45,000
Accounts receivable (net)	55,000	5,000
Inventory	110,000	25,000
Property, plant, and equipment (net)	550,000	160,000
Other assets	140,000	57,000
Total assets	$880,000	$292,000
Current liabilities	$120,000	$ 15,000
Long-term debt (12%)	190,000	55,000
Share capital	480,000	210,000
Contributed surplus	50,000	4,000
Retained earnings	40,000	8,000
Total liabilities and shareholders' equity	$880,000	$292,000
Income Statement		
Sales revenue (on credit)	(½) $800,000	(¼) $280,000
Cost of goods sold	(480,000)	(150,000)
Expenses (including interest and income tax)	(240,000)	(95,000)
Net income	$ 80,000	$ 35,000
Selected Data from the 2007 Statements		
Accounts receivable, net	$ 47,000	$ 11,000
Long-term debt (12%)	190,000	55,000
Inventory	95,000	38,000
Other Data		
Share price at end of 2008	$ 14.00	$ 11.00
Income tax rate	30%	30%
Dividends declared and paid in 2008	$ 20,000	$ 9,000
Number of common shares during 2008	24,000	10,500

These two companies are in the same line of business and in the same province but in different cities. Each company has been in operation for about 10 years. Rand Company is audited by one of the national accounting firms; Tand Company is audited by a local accounting firm. Both companies received an unqualified opinion (i.e., the independent auditors found nothing wrong) on the financial statements. Rand Company wants to borrow $75,000 cash, and Tand Company needs $30,000. The loans will be for a two-year period and are needed for "working capital purposes."

Required:

1. Complete a schedule that reflects a ratio analysis of each company. Compute the ratios discussed in the chapter.

2. Assume that you work in the loan department of a local bank. You have been asked to analyze the situation and recommend which loan is preferable. Based on the data given, your analysis prepared in requirement 1, and any other information, give your choice and provide a supporting explanation.

AP13–5 **Analyzing Financial Statements Using Appropriate Ratios (P13–7)**

Canadian Tire Corporation provides Canadians with a wide selection of goods and services through its retail channels. The following information was reported in recent annual reports.

Required:

1. Compute the ratios discussed in this chapter for the last two years. If there is not sufficient information, describe what is missing and explain what you would do.

2. Assume the role of an investment adviser. A client of yours has the opportunity to invest $1 million in shares of Canadian companies. Prepare a written evaluation of relevant ratios and indicate whether you would recommend to your client that the $1 million be invested in the shares of Canadian Tire.

CANADIAN TIRE CORPORATION

Consolidated Statements of Earnings and Retained Earnings

For the years ended (Dollars in millions except per share amounts)	Dec. 30, 2006	Dec. 31, 2005	Jan. 1, 2005
Gross Operating revenue	$ 8,269.1	$ 7,721.6	$ 7,153.6
Operating expenses			
Cost of merchandise sold and all operating expenses except for the undernoted items Interest	7,415.7	6,896.1	6,416.9
Long-term debt	71.2	79.5	76.0
Short-term debt	4.5	4.6	2.4
Depreciation and amortization	191.7	185.0	170.6
Employee Profit Sharing Plan	28.2	28.7	26.8
Total operating expenses	7,711.3	7,193.9	6,692.7
Earnings before income taxes and minority interest	557.8	527.7	460.9
Income taxes			
Current	222.7	187.2	150.8
Future	(21.9)	2.8	11.7
Total income taxes	200.8	190.0	162.5
Net earnings before minority interest	357.0	337.7	298.4
Minority interest	2.4	7.6	6.9
Net earnings	$ 354.6	$ 330.1	$ 291.5
Basic earnings per share	$ 4.35	$ 4.04	$ 3.60
Diluted earnings per share	$ 4.31	$ 3.98	$ 3.53
Retained earnings, beginning of year	$ 1,812.6	$ 1,546.9	$ 1,318.0
Net earnings	354.6	330.1	291.5
Dividends	(53.8)	(47.4)	(40.5)
Repurchase of Class A Non-Voting Shares	(25.3)	(17.0)	(22.1)
Retained earnings, end of year	$ 2,088.1	$ 1,812.6	$ 1,546.9
Weighted average number of Common and Class A Non-Voting Shares outstanding	81,575,556	81,764,082	80,983,467

CANADIAN TIRE CORPORATION

Consolidated Balance Sheets

As at (Dollars in millions)	Dec. 30, 2006	Dec. 31, 2005	Jan. 1, 2005
ASSETS			
Current assets			
Cash and cash equivalents (Note 12)	$ 741.3	$ 838.0	$ 802.2
Accounts receivable (Note 12)	340.5	652.8	370.7
Loans receivable (Note 2)	694.2	720.8	592.4
Merchandise inventories	667.3	675.5	620.6
Prepaid expenses and deposits	46.2	42.4	24.1
Future income taxes (Note 11)	51.5	43.6	24.6
Total current assets	2,541.0	2,973.1	2,434.6

(continued)

CANADIAN TIRE CORPORATION

Consolidated Balance Sheets *(continued)*

As at (Dollars in millions)	Dec. 30, 2006	Dec. 31, 2005	Jan. 1, 2005
Long-term receivable and other assets (Note 3)	283.5	140.0	129.7
Goodwill (Note 4)	46.4	46.2	41.7
Intangible assets (Note 4)	52.4	52.4	52.0
Property and equipment (Note 5)	2,881.3	2,743.9	2,585.2
Total assets	$5,804.6	$5,955.6	$5,243.2
LIABILITIES			
Current liabilities			
Accounts payable and other	$1,579.5	$1,545.5	$1,437.6
Income taxes payable	81.1	71.2	44.2
Current portion of long-term debt (Note 6)	3.0	204.3	5.6
Total current liabilities	1,663.6	1,821.0	1,487.4
Long-term debt (Note 6)	1,168.4	1,171.3	1,081.8
Future income taxes (Note 11)	75.0	89.0	67.2
Other long-term liabilities (Note 7)	112.4	63.2	55.6
Total liabilities	3,019.4	3,144.5	2,692.0
Minority interest (Note 17)	—	300.0	300.0
SHAREHOLDERS' EQUITY			
Share capital (Note 9)	702.7	702.7	709.0
Contributed surplus	0.1	1.5	1.3
Accumulated foreign currency translation adjustment	(5.7)	(5.7)	(6.0)
Retained earnings	2,088.1	1,812.6	1,546.9
Total shareholders' equity	2,785.2	2,511.1	2,251.2
Total liabilities, minority interest and shareholders' equity	$5,804.6	$5,955.6	$5,243.2

LO4, 5   **AP13–6** **Analyzing an Investment by Comparing Selected Ratios** (P13–8)

You have the opportunity to invest $10,000 in one of two companies from a single industry. The only information you have is shown below. The word *high* refers to the top third of the industry; *average* is the middle third; *low* is the bottom third. Which company would you select? Write a brief report justifying your recommendation.

Ratio	Company A	Company B
EPS	High	Low
ROA	Low	High
Debt to equity	High	Average
Current	Low	Average
Price/earnings	Low	High
Dividend yield	High	Average

LO4, 5,   **AP13–7** **Analyzing an Investment by Comparing Selected Ratios** (P13–9)
6, 7

You have the opportunity to invest $10,000 in one of two companies from a single industry. The only information you have is shown below. The word *high* refers to the top third of the industry; *average* is the middle third; *low* is the bottom third. Which company would you select? Write a brief report justifying your recommendation.

Ratio	Company A	Company B
ROA	High	Average
Profit margin	High	Low
Financial leverage	High	Low
Current	Low	High
Price/earnings	High	Average
Debt to equity	High	Low

CASES AND PROJECTS

FINDING AND INTERPRETING FINANCIAL INFORMATION

CP13–1 Analyzing Financial Statements
Refer to the financial statements of Van Houtte Inc. given in Appendix B of this book. From the list of ratios that were discussed in this chapter, select and compute the ratios that help you evaluate the company's operations for fiscal year 2007. Assume a market price of $24.90 per share.

■ **LO4, 5, 6, 7**
Van Houtte

CP13–2 Analyzing Financial Statements
Refer to the Online Learning Centre Web site at **www.mcgrawhill.ca/olc/libby/student/ resources** for the financial statements of The Forzani Group Ltd. From the list of ratios that were discussed in this chapter, select and compute the ratios that help you evaluate the company's operations for fiscal year 2007.

■ **LO4, 5, 6, 7**
The Forzani
Group Ltd.

FINANCIAL REPORTING AND ANALYSIS CASES

CP13–3 Interpreting Financial Results Based on Corporate Strategy
In this chapter, we discussed the importance of analyzing financial results based on an understanding of the company's business strategy. Using the ROE model, we illustrated how different strategies could earn high returns for investors. Assume that two companies in the same industry adopt fundamentally different strategies. One manufactures high-quality consumer electronics. Its products employ state-of-the-art technology, and the company offers a high level of customer service both before and after the sale. The other company emphasizes low cost with good performance. Its products utilize well-established technology but are never innovative. Customers buy these products at large, self-service warehouses and are expected to install the products using information contained in printed brochures. Which of the ratios discussed in this chapter would you expect to differ for these companies as a result of their different business strategies?

■ **LO1**

CP13–4 Interpreting Financial Results Based on Corporate Strategy
In this chapter, we discussed the importance of analyzing financial results based on an understanding of the company's business strategy. Using the ROE model, we illustrated how different strategies could earn high returns for investors. Both Nordstrom and JCPenney are in the retail industry. Nordstrom is a specialty apparel retailer operating in 23 states. Annual revenues exceed $5 billion. The store is well known for high-quality merchandise and a high level of customer service. JCPenney is a full-line retailer appealing to middle-income shoppers. Its merchandise is moderately priced, and customers receive a lower level of service. The following are several ratios from each company. Identify which company is Nordstrom and which is JCPenney. Which of these ratios do you think are affected by the different strategies? Explain.

■ **LO4, 5, 6, 7**
Nordstrom and
JCPenney

ANALYSIS

Ratio	Company A	Company B
Gross margin	34.4%	23.1%
Profit margin	4.0%	1.7%
Current ratio	1.8	1.6
Debt to equity	0.8	1.4
Return on equity	15.9%	7.5%
Return on assets	6.5%	2.3%
Dividend payout	22.1	117.0
Price/earnings	15.3	9.3

CRITICAL THINKING CASES

CP13–5 Analyzing the Impact of Alternative Amortization Methods on Ratio Analysis
Speedy Company uses the double-declining-balance method to amortize its property, plant, and equipment, and Turtle Company uses the straight-line method. Both companies use declining-balance amortization for income tax purposes. The two companies are exactly alike except for the difference in amortization methods.

■ **LO4, 5, 6, 7**

Required:

1. Identify the financial ratios discussed in this chapter that are likely to be affected by the difference in amortization methods.

2. Which company will report the higher amount for each ratio that you have identified? If you cannot be certain, explain why.

ANALYSIS

LO4, 5   **CP13–6**   **Analyzing the Impact of Alternative Accounting Methods on Ratios**

The ratios computed for Home Depot in this chapter are compared to those of RONA Inc., and Canadian Tire Corporation. The comparison of ratios across these three companies assumes that they use the same accounting methods in reporting the various elements of their financial statements.

Required:

1. Access the annual reports of the three companies through their respective websites and identify the method(s) each company uses
   a. to amortize its long-term assets, and
   b. to value its inventory at year end.

2. Are the methods used by these companies similar or different? Explain.

3. If two of these companies use different accounting methods, what impact would the different methods have on the following ratios:
   a. Profit margin
   b. Return on equity
   c. Current ratio
   d. Debt-to-equity ratio

LO4   **CP13–7**   **Evaluating an Ethical Dilemma**

Almost Short Company requested a sizeable loan from Provincial Bank to acquire a large tract of land for future expansion. Almost Short reported current assets of $1,900,000 ($430,000 in cash) and current liabilities of $1,075,000. Provincial denied the loan request for a number of reasons, including the fact that the current ratio was below 2. When Almost Short was informed of the loan denial, the comptroller of the company immediately paid $420,000 that was owed to several trade creditors. The comptroller then asked Provincial to reconsider the loan application. Based on these abbreviated facts, would you recommend that Provincial approve the loan request? Why? Are the comptroller's actions ethical?

FINANCIAL REPORTING AND ANALYSIS TEAM PROJECT

LO3, 4,   **CP13–8**   **Team Project: Examining an Annual Report**
5, 6, 7

ANALYSIS

As a team, select an industry to analyze. Each team member should acquire the annual report for one publicly traded company in the industry, with each member selecting a different company. (Library files, the SEDAR service at **www.sedar.com**, or the company itself are good resources.)

Required:

On an individual basis, each team member should write a brief report that shows computations of each of the ratios discussed in this chapter, and provides interpretations of the computed ratios. The most frequently used sections will be the financial statements. Also, you may want to review notes, the summary of financial information (usually for the past five to 10 years, and management's discussion and analysis.

Discuss any patterns across the companies that you as a team observe. Then, as a team, write a short report comparing and contrasting your companies.

Appendix A—Present Value Tables

TABLE A.1

Present Value of $1, p = 1/(1 + i)^n$

Periods	2%	3%	3.75%	4%	4.25%	5%	6%	7%	8%
1	0.9804	0.9709	0.9639	0.9615	0.9592	0.9524	0.9434	0.9346	0.9259
2	0.9612	0.9426	0.9290	0.9246	0.9201	0.9070	0.8900	0.8734	0.8573
3	0.9423	0.9151	0.8954	0.8890	0.8826	0.8638	0.8396	0.8163	0.7938
4	0.9238	0.8885	0.8631	0.8548	0.8466	0.8227	0.7921	0.7629	0.7350
5	0.9057	0.8626	0.8319	0.8219	0.8121	0.7835	0.7473	0.7130	0.6806
6	0.8880	0.8375	0.8018	0.7903	0.7790	0.7462	0.7050	0.6663	0.6302
7	0.8706	0.8131	0.7728	0.7599	0.7473	0.7107	0.6651	0.6227	0.5835
8	0.8535	0.7894	0.7449	0.7307	0.7168	0.6768	0.6274	0.5820	0.5403
9	0.8368	0.7664	0.7180	0.7026	0.6876	0.6446	0.5919	0.5439	0.5002
10	0.8203	0.7441	0.6920	0.6756	0.6595	0.6139	0.5584	0.5083	0.4632
20	0.6730	0.5534	0.4789	0.4564	0.4350	0.3769	0.3118	0.2584	0.2145

Periods	9%	10%	11%	12%	13%	14%	15%	20%	25%
1	0.9174	0.9091	0.9009	0.8929	0.8850	0.8772	0.8696	0.8333	0.8000
2	0.8417	0.8264	0.8116	0.7972	0.7831	0.7695	0.7561	0.6944	0.6400
3	0.7722	0.7513	0.7312	0.7118	0.6931	0.6750	0.6575	0.5787	0.5120
4	0.7084	0.6830	0.6587	0.6355	0.6133	0.5921	0.5718	0.4823	0.4096
5	0.6499	0.6209	0.5935	0.5674	0.5428	0.5194	0.4972	0.4019	0.3277
6	0.5963	0.5645	0.5346	0.5066	0.4803	0.4556	0.4323	0.3349	0.2621
7	0.5470	0.5132	0.4817	0.4523	0.4251	0.3996	0.3759	0.2791	0.2097
8	0.5019	0.4665	0.4339	0.4039	0.3762	0.3506	0.3269	0.2326	0.1678
9	0.4604	0.4241	0.3909	0.3606	0.3329	0.3075	0.2843	0.1938	0.1342
10	0.4224	0.3855	0.3522	0.3220	0.2946	0.2697	0.2472	0.1615	0.1074
20	0.1784	0.1486	0.1240	0.1037	0.0868	0.0728	0.0611	0.0261	0.0115

TABLE A.2

Present Value of Annuity of $1, P = [1 - 1/(1 + i)^n]/i$

Periods*	2%	3%	3.75%	4%	4.25%	5%	6%	7%	8%
1	0.9804	0.9709	0.9639	0.9615	0.9592	0.9524	0.9434	0.9346	0.9259
2	1.9416	1.9135	1.8929	1.8861	1.8794	1.8594	1.8334	1.8080	1.7833
3	2.8839	2.8286	2.7883	2.7751	2.7620	2.7232	2.6730	2.6243	2.5771
4	3.8077	3.7171	3.6514	3.6299	3.6086	3.5460	3.4651	3.3872	3.3121
5	4.7135	4.5797	4.4833	4.4518	4.4207	4.3295	4.2124	4.1002	3.9927
6	5.6014	5.4172	5.2851	5.2421	5.1997	5.0757	4.9173	4.7665	4.6229
7	6.4720	6.2303	6.0579	6.0021	5.9470	5.7864	5.5824	5.3893	5.2064
8	7.3255	7.0197	6.8028	6.7327	6.6638	6.4632	6.2098	5.9713	5.7466
9	8.1622	7.7861	7.5208	7.4353	7.3513	7.1078	6.8017	6.5152	6.2469
10	8.9826	8.5302	8.2128	8.1109	8.0109	7.7217	7.3601	7.0236	6.7101
20	16.3514	14.8775	13.8962	13.5903	13.2944	12.4622	11.4699	10.5940	9.8181

Periods*	9%	10%	11%	12%	13%	14%	15%	20%	25%
1	0.9174	0.9091	0.9009	0.8929	0.8550	0.8772	0.8696	0.8333	0.8000
2	1.7591	1.7355	1.7125	1.6901	1.6681	1.6467	1.6257	1.5278	1.4400
3	2.5313	2.4869	2.4437	2.4018	2.3612	2.3216	2.2832	2.1065	1.9520
4	3.2397	3.1699	3.1024	3.0373	2.9745	2.9137	2.8550	2.5887	2.3616
5	3.8897	3.7908	3.6959	3.6048	3.5172	3.4331	3.3522	2.9906	2.6893
6	4.4859	4.3553	4.2305	4.1114	3.9975	3.8887	3.7845	3.3255	2.9514
7	5.0330	4.8684	4.7122	4.5638	4.4226	4.2883	4.1604	3.6046	3.1611
8	5.5348	5.3349	5.1461	4.9676	4.7988	4.6389	4.4873	3.8372	3.3289
9	5.9952	5.7590	5.5370	5.3282	4.1317	4.9464	4.7716	4.0310	3.4631
10	6.4177	6.1446	5.8892	5.6502	5.4262	5.2161	5.0188	4.1925	3.5705
20	9.1285	8.5136	7.9633	7.4694	7.0248	6.6231	6.2593	4.8696	3.9539

*There is one payment each period.

Le goût de **L'EUROPE** dans votre tasse
A taste of **EUROPE** in your cup

Annual Report
2007

Van Houtte Inc.
Annual Report 2007

MANAGEMENT'S DISCUSSION AND ANALYSIS

Company profile

Van Houtte Inc. ("Van Houtte," the "Company," "we") is the most integrated gourmet coffee roaster and distributor in North America. By "integrated roaster and distributor" we mean that our business activities, carried out directly or through our subsidiaries, affiliates or franchisees cover just about the entire supply chain, starting with the purchase of green coffee, followed by roasting, retail marketing and distribution to food and other retail stores, to total coffee solutions that include the coffee, the brewer, condiments and other related products, designed for wherever the drink is consumed: the workplace, commercial spaces, institutions, hotels and restaurants.

Our beginnings date back to 1919 when Albert-Louis Van Houtte launched an imported coffee and fine grocery store in Montreal.

On March 31, 2007, Van Houtte and its subsidiaries employed 1,900 people, mostly full-time employees.

Additional information

This MD&A was prepared on June 7, 2007. Additional information relating to the Company, including its Annual Information Form, is available on the Company's Web site at www.vanhoutte.com as well as on the SEDAR Web site at www.sedar.com.

Unless otherwise indicated, the information contained herein is current as at June 7, 2007.

Fiscal year

Van Houtte's fiscal year ends on the Saturday closest to March 31 of each year. Rather than 365 days, it therefore comprises full weeks, usually 52 but sometimes 53. Thus, fiscal 2004 had 53 weeks, one more week than 2005 and 2006. The last year before 2004 with 53 weeks was fiscal 1999.

The additional week in fiscal 2004 was added to the fourth quarter, which therefore had 13 rather than 12 weeks.

In this analysis, unless otherwise indicated, "2007" means the 52-week fiscal year ended March 31, 2007, "2006" means the 52-week fiscal year ended April 1, 2006, "2005" means the fiscal year ended April 2, 2005, and "2004" means the 53-week fiscal year ended April 3, 2004.

Main activities

The Company groups its activities into two broad categories: Manufacturing and Marketing and Coffee Services.

Manufacturing and Marketing

The Manufacturing and Marketing segment encompasses coffee roasting and distribution for home consumption through retail food channels, the production and distribution of coffeemakers and related equipment as well as the franchising and operation of café bistros. Canadian and American consumers can also buy our products online at www.vanhoutte.com.

Coffee roasting and distribution

Van Houtte is Canada's leading gourmet coffee roaster. We purchase our green coffee—almost always Arabica—from the main producing countries located in the equatorial areas of Latin America, Africa and

Asia. Because we buy gourmet coffee beans, we pay a premium over the prices published on the coffee exchange. And although we deal primarily with Canadian brokers, we pay for our purchases in U.S. dollars.

We operate three roasting plants: two in Montreal, Quebec, and one in Vancouver, British Columbia. The main plant in Montreal is a state-of-the-art facility with equipment that carefully controls the roasting process according to the specific profile required for each recipe. To ensure superior roasting worthy of the best hand-mixed blends, we roast the coffee in small batches of 450 lbs. (204 kg). And thanks to our cutting-edge technology, this hand-mixed quality is carefully reproduced in each batch. For its ground coffees, Van Houtte has developed a cold-grinding technique that preserves the aroma and ensures uniform grain size.

Van Houtte coffees are available in some 5,150 retail points of sale across Canada and on the East Coast of the United States, compared with 4,700 a year ago.

Although sold mainly under the Van Houtte name, our coffees are also marketed under the Orient Express and other labels. We offer more than 100 blends along with a variety of roasting profiles and packaging to suit the discriminating tastes of fine coffee lovers and connoisseurs everywhere. The Company is constantly developing new blends, roasting profiles and packaging in response to a changing market. For example, in 2005 we launched JAVANATION™, a line of single origin coffees and espresso blends designed to meet the expectations of young, demanding consumers. In 2006 we restructured our fair trade and organic coffee offer by replacing the CoffeeLovers™ line with organic fair trade-certified coffees bearing the Van Houtte label.

Finally, we roast and package our coffees under private labels for supermarkets that also carry the Van Houtte brand.

TABLE 1
Breakdown of retail points of sale carrying Van Houtte products 2006 and 2007 (at year-end)

	Number of Points of Sale	
	2007	**2006**
Canada	4,426	3,983
United States	720	700
Total	**5,146**	**4,683**

We usually negotiate directly with our supermarket accounts and design, set up and stock the gourmet coffee department in most of their stores. A distributor under contract with Van Houtte then handles replenishment and inventory management.

Coffeemaker production

Through our subsidiary VKI Technologies Inc. ("VKI"), we design, manufacture and market hopper-based, single-cup coffeemakers that prepare coffee one cup at a time. At its plant in the Montreal suburb of Longueuil, VKI produces several models of single-cup coffeemakers adapted to various purposes and intensity of use. These machines can be equipped with an electronic control system, a microprocessor, a liquid crystal display, a coffee/hot chocolate option and a paperless brewer.

In addition to the hopper-based coffeemaker, VKI has designed and produces the Espresso Café™, a coffeemaker that uses pre-packaged doses of coffee to prepare a consistently high-quality espresso, cappuccino, latte or americano in just 45 seconds.

VKI also manufactures a single-cup tea machine for an American account and in 2006, added a hot chocolate unit to its product line.

VKI also markets the Scalehammer™, a hard water treatment system for residential and institutional use for which it holds exclusive international marketing rights. Distributed by two Canadian hardware chains, the Scalehammer is also used in our Coffee Services network in areas where it is required.

Until January 2007, VKI was also licensed to produce a coffeemaker that does not use its own hopper-based technology but rather a coffee pod system called K-Cup® which contains a hermetically sealed individual portion of coffee and a single filter. This system was developed by Keurig Inc. ("Keurig"), a Massachusetts-based company. Although we sold our stake in Keurig on June 16, 2006 (See Sale of Our Interest in Keurig, page 8), the company remains a strategic partner. In the normal course of its business, VKI actively prospects potential customers to maintain and increase its sales volume.

VKI sells its coffeemakers to our Coffee Services network (see next section) and to vending machine manufacturers in North America. It also exports components to Japan and Europe.

Café bistros

Van Houtte operates 62 café bistros in Quebec and in the Ottawa region, of which 58 are franchised.

Bistros represent a very small portion of our consolidated revenues. But they help promote our brand image to consumers. Measuring from 70 to 200 square metres, the café bistros offer their clientele an extensive range of regular and specialty coffees as well as light meals and snacks.

Coffee Services

Coffee Services is our other major sphere of activity. It focuses on the sale of coffee for consumption away from home, e.g. at work and other public places. This segment also operates vending machines in four cities in Ontario and Western Canada.

Thanks to its turn-key "Total Coffee Solutions," coffee lovers are guaranteed a fresh cup of brew in any number of public locations.

Although its customer base consists mainly of people in the workplace, Coffee Services is diversifying its offer and serving a growing number of public places, for example, through our coffee bar concept. Located in high-traffic areas such as supermarkets, hospitals and university campuses across Canada and some U.S. regions, and offering the same ambiance as café bistros, coffee bars are smaller and carry a more limited range of products. On March 31, 2007, we had 3,366 coffee bars in Canada and the U.S.

With this service, a company or operator typically leases the type and quantity of coffeemakers it requires and for which we supply the coffee, condiments, drinks and snacks. Van Houtte has a broad range of brewers and coffees priced for every budget and designed to suit every taste. Our flexibility and size therefore allow us to meet the needs of any company, large or small.

As the largest Coffee Services network in North America, we have branches and franchised establishments in 75 cities across most of Canada and the U.S. We jointly own three of our Canadian branches and own the remainder outright. In the U.S., our Coffee Services operations are carried out through our subsidiary Filterfresh Coffee Services Inc. ("Filterfresh"). Headquartered in the metro Boston, Massachusetts area, Filterfresh has wholly-owned and franchised branches, as well as branches that are jointly-owned with local partners.

TABLE 2
Breakdown of Coffee Services branches in Canada and the U.S. by method of ownership and operation

	Wholly- or Jointly-Owned Branches	Franchised Branches	Total
Canada	32	–	32
United States	30	13	43
Total	**62**	**13**	**75**

We built this network primarily through acquisitions, driving most of the consolidation in the Canadian coffee services market. However, in the U.S. the market remains highly fragmented with many founder-led businesses in search of a successor and therefore offering strong consolidation potential. Our strategy involves acquiring businesses or forming joint ventures with local entrepreneurs in regions where we already

have a footprint. In most cases we incorporate these acquisitions into our existing network. Thus, these acquisitions help densify our network, enabling us to offer better service at a lower cost.

Thus, in 2007 we completed 11 coffee services acquisitions representing $2.5 million in annual sales. Moreover, we bought out the interests of several minority joint venture partners. Following these transactions the branches in Columbus, Cleveland, Cincinnati, Detroit and Louisville have become the exclusive property of Van Houtte. This simplified ownership structure allows us to deploy the necessary resources to step up the growth of these branches and boost the Van Houtte brand.

Thanks to our network – the only one of its kind in North America – we can service continental accounts with points of sale in Canada and the U.S. For example, our coffeemakers or coffee bars can be found in the Couche-Tard (Quebec), Mac's Milk (Ontario), and Chevron on the West Coast of Canada and the U.S. In the U.S., we operate Caffé Mio™ coffeemakers in more than 1,100 Lowe's stores, America's second largest hardware and home improvement chain.

Our Coffee Services branches operate vending machines that sell snacks, candies and hot and cold drinks in four cities in Ontario and Western Canada. We have spent the last four years streamlining this aspect of our business, selling the vending business units in 12 cities where the current or projected profitability no longer justified the investment. These units accounted for $14.7 million in annual sales.

Impact of currency fluctuations

The U.S. dollar's volatility over the past two years has had a major impact on Van Houtte's sales and operating results. The U.S. currency fell 6.6% against the Canadian dollar between 2005 and 2006, and 4.6% between 2006 and 2007. These decreases have a negative impact on U.S. sales and operating income when converted to Canadian dollars. Our analysis indicates this impact whenever possible. However, while difficult to measure accurately, the effect of currency fluctuations on consolidated net earnings is minimal since some of the Canadian operating costs, notably, the procurement of green coffee, as well as a portion of the depreciation and financial expenses are incurred in U.S. dollars and are also sensitive to currency variations.

Non-GAAP financial measures

Van Houtte's consolidated financial statements are prepared according to generally accepted accounting principles in Canada (GAAP) and are stated in Canadian dollars. Unless otherwise mentioned, additional financial data appearing in this MD&A are also stated in Canadian dollars.

The Company defines EBITDA as earnings before amortization and depreciation, financial expenses and tax on earnings and unusual items such as gains realized on the sale of an investment, income tax on past earnings, asset write-down and strategy review fees of value enhancement. Equity in net earnings of companies subject to significant influence, non-controlling interests and discontinued activities are not considered in the computation of EBITDA. The Company defines operating cash flows as cash flow from operating activities before changes in non-cash operating working capital.

EBITDA and operating cash flows as defined above are not measures of results that are consistent with generally accepted accounting principles in Canada, nor are they intended to be regarded as an alternative to other financial operating performance measures or to the statement of cash flows as a measure of liquidity. They are not intended to represent funds available for debt service, dividend payments, reinvestment or other discretionary uses, and should not be considered separately or as a substitute for measures of performance prepared in accordance with generally accepted accounting principles in Canada. EBITDA and operating cash flows are used by the Company because management believes they are meaningful measures of performance. EBITDA and operating cash flows are commonly used in investment circles to analyze and compare the performance of companies in the industries in which the Company is active. The Company's definition of EBITDA and operating cash flows may differ from similarly titled measures reported by other companies.

Moreover, in the first and last quarters, we reported "earnings before unusual items," which measure the Company's performance excluding two unusual items not associated with operations that occurred in the first quarter, namely, a gain realized on the sale of an investment, net of taxes, and tax on past earnings; and unusual items recorded in the fourth quarter to reflect the current status of negotiations with the Quebec government as regards tax on past earnings (See "Amendment to the Taxation Act," p. 7).

The following tables reconcile EBITDA, earnings before unusual items and operating cash flows with GAAP measures.

TABLE 3

Reconciliation of EBITDA, net earnings before unusual items and net earnings, 2006 and 2007
(In thousands of $ except per share amounts)

	2007	2006
EBITDA	72,878	69,256
Depreciation and amortization	(36,105)	(33,790)
Financial expenses	(4,271)	(2,382)
Income tax on current earnings, before unusual items	(10,284)	(8,665)
Share in net earnings of companies subject to significant influence	-	31
Non-controlling interest	(1,921)	(1,944)
Net earnings, before unusual items	20,296	22,506
Per share ($)	0.95	1.05
Gain realized on sale of an investment	19,948	-
Tax on past earnings	(13,712)	-
Strategy review fees of value enhancement, net of $312 in taxes	(663)	-
Write-down of the value of certain assets, net of $428 in taxes	(909)	-
Net earnings	24,961	22,506
Per share ($)	1.17	1.05

TABLE 4

Reconciliation of operating cash flow before unusual items as reported (total and per share) and cash flows from operating activities (total and per share), 2007 and 2006
(In thousands of $, except per share amounts)

	2007 Total	2007 Per share	2006 Total	2006 Per share
Operating cash flow as reported	46,933	2.20	55,433	2.59
Tax on past earnings	13,712	0.64	-	-
Strategy review fees of value enhancement	663	0.03	-	-
Asset write-down, net of $428 in taxes	909	0.04	-	-
Operating cash flow before unusual items	62,217	2.92	-	-
Net change in non-cash operating working capital [1]	2,525	0.12$	(7,622)	(0.36)
Cash flow from operating activities	64,742	3.03$	47,811	2.23

(1) Excluding unusual items

Unusual items

Fiscal 2007 was characterized by four unusual items: the sale of our interest in Keurig, which gave rise to an unusual gain; an amendment to the Taxation Act of Quebec, which resulted in a provision for taxes on past earnings; write-down of certain assets; and strategy review fees of value enhancement. Since these four unusual items are referred to throughout this analysis, they are described below.

Sale of our interest in Keurig

On June 16, 2006, we completed the sale of our interest in Keurig to Green Mountain Coffee Roasters Inc. ("Green Mountain") for US$34.1 million (C$37.4 million on the date of the transaction). Of this amount, US$7.4 million (C$8.3 million on the date of the transaction) will be held in escrow until June 15, 2007 to guarantee the vendor's usual representations. There is no indication that the Company will not collect the full amount. This transaction gave rise to a $19.9 million gain. No taxes will be due on this gain as it was offset by tax losses not recorded as tax benefits. These tax losses pertain to translation variances on investments made in the U.S. when the Canadian dollar was much weaker.

Van Houtte and Keurig will remain partners after the transaction, and the Company will continue to use Keurig coffeemakers and sell its coffees in K-Cups in its Coffee Services network throughout North America. Through selected retailers, Van Houtte will also offer the coffeemakers and the required coffees to consumers for home use.

For its part, Keurig will continue to market its technology through roasters. In a joint press release announcing the transaction, Keurig and Green Mountain affirmed that they will "remain committed to Keurig's multi-brand strategy" in terms of its coffee offering. Keurig will also continue to sell Van Houtte coffees on its Web site.

Amendment to the Taxation Act

On May 9, 2006, the Quebec Minister of Revenue tabled a bill in the National Assembly entitled the *Act to amend the Taxation Act and other legislative provisions* (the "Act"), which came into force on June 13, 2006.

The impact of the Act is to retroactively increase taxable earnings in Quebec for prior years with the result that Van Houtte recorded a provision of $15.8 million in the first quarter of 2007. In the second and third quarters, we paid the Quebec government a sum of $7.3 million in this regard. However, we have filed a notice of objection to the assessment and are exploring various ways to reduce this retroactive charge. In the fourth quarter, we reduced our estimate of income tax on past earnings to $13.7 million to reflect the current status of our discussions with the Quebec government.

This Act prospectively reconciles our effective tax rate with the combined regulatory rate of the various jurisdictions in which we are taxable. It therefore increases the tax expense on current earnings.

To facilitate comparison between this and last fiscal year, we calculated what net earnings per share would have been for 2006 and for each of its quarters had our income tax been calculated according to the amended Act.

TABLE 5

CALCULATION OF NET EARNINGS AND EARNINGS PER SHARE FOR 2006 GIVING PRO FORMA EFFECT TO THE PROVISIONS OF THE ACT TO AMEND THE TAXATION ACT AND OTHER LEGISLATIVE PROVISIONS IN FORCE SINCE JUNE 13, 2006.

	Total Fiscal 2006	Q4	Q3	Q2	Q1
Actual net earnings (thousands of $)	22,506	6,464	5,948	5,097	4,998
Pro forma net earnings (thousands of $)	19,834	5,632	5,496	4,391	4,316
Actual earnings per share ($)	1.05	0.30	0.28	0.24	0.23
Pro forma earnings per share ($)	0.93	0.26	0.26	0.21	0.20

Write-down of certain assets

The Company adopted stricter rules as regards recording certain asset items and other assets, including allowance for inventory obsolescence. We made a non-recurring adjustment to give effect to these new measures, resulting in devaluations and write-downs of $1.3 million ($0.9 million after taxes).

Strategy review fees of value enhancement

In the second quarter, we began examining various value-creating strategies. This review entailed non-recurring expenses of $1.0 million ($0.7 million after tax). Additional costs in the order of approximately $3.5 million ($2.4 million after tax) incurred after year-end will be recorded in the next quarter.

Three-year highlights

For the year ended March 31, 2007, Van Houtte achieved net earnings, before unusual items, of $20.3 million or $0.95 per share (basic and diluted), a decrease from the $22.5 million or $1.05 per share recorded in 2006.

The comparison is more significant when made with the earnings that give pro forma effect to Quebec's new tax rules, shown in table 5, page 7. This comparison translates into a 2.3% increase on pro forma earnings for 2006, i.e., $19.8 million ($0.93 per share).

TABLE 6

Key figures, 2005, 2006, 2007
(In thousands of dollars, except per share amounts and coffee shipments)

	Year ended:		
	March 31, 2007	April 1, 2006	April 2, 2005
Revenue	388,158	376,173	348,755
Earnings before unusual items	20,296	22,506	21,706
Net earnings	24,961	22,506	21,706
Net earnings per share ($)			
Before unusual items (basic and diluted)	0.95	1.05	1.01
Net earnings (basic and diluted)	1.17	1.05	1.01
Total assets	370,120	380,119	370,682
Long-term liabilities[1]	64,712	106,448	97,712
Dividend per share ($)	0.25 + 0.32[2]	0.28 + 0.15[2]	0.24
Coffee shipments *(millions of lbs)*	25.9	25.0	25.3

[1] Including the short-term portion of long-term debt and non-controlling interests.
[2] Van Houtte paid an annual dividend until November 2005. Thus, on October 28, 2005 Van Houtte paid an annual dividend of $0.28 per share. Since then, the Company has paid a quarterly dividend. In 2006, Van Houtte paid out two quarterly dividends of $0.075 per share, equivalent to an annual rate of $0.30 per share. In 2007, the Company paid out four quarterly dividends of $0.08 per share for an annual rate of $0.32 per share. Van Houtte also declared a special dividend of $0.50 per share payable in two instalments of $0.25, the first of which was paid on September 15, 2006, the second will be paid in June, 2007.

Revenues reached $388.2 million in 2007, up 3.2% from the previous year.

The following factors explain the year's performance, excluding the unusual items:

- Shipments of the Van Houtte brand increased to both the retail and Coffee Services networks.
- Improved operating profitability, both in the Manufacturing and Marketing and Coffee Services segments. EBITDA advanced 5.2%.
- The EBITDA increase was particularly strong in the U.S.
- However, net earnings decreased due to higher depreciation expense and the cost of Quebec's new tax legislation.

The year's results were also characterized by an unusual gain of $19.9 million following the sale of our stake in Keurig and an unusual expense of $13.7 million for income taxes on past earnings following an amendment to Quebec's tax laws.

For the year ended April 1, 2006, Van Houtte recorded net earnings of $22.5 million or $1.05 per share (basic and diluted), up 3.7% over the $21.7 million and $1.01 (basic and diluted) recorded for the year ended April 2, 2005.

Revenues in 2006 were $376.2 million or 7.9% more than in 2005, mainly due to:

- A solid performance by VKI in terms of sales and earnings;
- Improved operating profitability, particularly in the Canadian Coffee Services segment;
- A decrease in financial expenses.

However, these results were adversely affected by the following factors:

- A sharp increase in the cost price of our main raw material, green coffee;
- A disappointing performance by Coffee Services in the U.S.;
- Changes in equipment depreciation policies that will cause amortization expense to increase as of 2006.

A reclassification of certain intangible assets created when acquisitions are made. Specifically, a portion of the $9.9 million of the non-depreciable goodwill has been reclassified as *Customer Relations and Non-compete Clauses*, both depreciable.

Review of operations – 2007

Van Houtte has filed its 2007 audited consolidated financial statements with Canadian securities regulators. These statements may be accessed through www.sedar.com or on the Van Houtte Web site at www.vanhoutte.com. This Management's Discussion and Analysis ("MD&A") should be read in conjunction with these financial statements and related notes. In addition, once filed, Van Houtte's Annual Information Form for the year ended March 31, 2007 will be available through www.sedar.com.

Sales up 3.2%

For the year ended March 31, 2007, Van Houtte achieved consolidated sales of $388.2 million, compared to $376.2 million in 2006. The 3.2% increase is attributable to the following factors:

- Organic growth. Coffee Services sales per active account (excluding vending operations and on a constant exchange rate basis) rose more than 6.4% in 2007. At the retail level, increased sales were recorded as a result of the penetration of a new network of retailers. Coffee shipments moved ahead 3.6%.

- Acquisitions. Van Houtte uses a consolidation strategy in the fragmented coffee services market, and acquisitions still account for a good part of our growth, particularly in the U.S. However, in 2007, the new chief executive of Van Houtte USA decided to focus on optimizing operations before resuming the company's historical acquisition pace.

- The change in sales also reflects the negative impact of currency fluctuations and the divestiture of vending operations in 2006. Adjusted for these two factors, sales would have advanced 5.1%.

TABLE 7
Sources of revenue growth, 2007 (in thousands of dollars)
(In thousands of dollars)

Revenues, 2006	376,173
Organic growth	16,062
Impact of acquisitions made in 2006 and 2007	5,141
Impact of sale of vending operations	(4,594)
Impact of coffee price increases	963
Impact of currency fluctuations	(5,588)
Revenues, 2007	**388,158**

Consolidated EBITDA was $72.9 million in 2007, compared to $69.3 million a year earlier. Growth was 5.2%.

The operating margin (EBITDA/sales) was 18.8%, against 18.4% last year. This increase is largely the result of a slight improvement in the gross margin rate, which recovered in 2007 following price adjustments made in 2006, and a slight improvement in operating efficiency as operating expenses accounted for a smaller proportion of gross profit than in 2006.

Amortization and depreciation was $36.1 million, compared to $33.8 million in the prior year. The shortened amortization period for some Coffee Services equipment in 2006 continues to negatively affect amortization expense.

Financial expenses amounted to $4.3 million or $1.9 million more than the $2.4 million recorded in 2006. The increase stems in part from changes in the fair value of interest rate swaps and from the $1.6 million gain on Keurig's cumulative preferred shares recorded against financial expenses in 2006.

In 2007, we recorded a $1.0 million expense ($0.7 million after tax) as *Strategy review fees of value enhancement* (See "Enhancing shareholder value", p. 17).

On June 16, 2006, we completed the sale of our interest in Keurig for US$34.1 million (C$37.4 million). Of this amount, US$7.4 million (C$8.3 million on the date of the transaction) will be held in escrow until June 15, 2007 to guarantee the vendor's usual representations. There is no indication that the Company will not collect the full amount. This transaction gave rise to a $19.9 million gain.

Taxes for the year, excluding unusual items, were $10.3 million, for an effective tax rate of 31.6%. This compares with $8.7 million and 26.2% in 2006 (See "'Amendment to the Taxation Act'" p. 7).

Segment analysis

TABLE 8
Segment analysis
(In thousands of dollars, except % change)

	Year ended March 31, 2007	Year ended April 1, 2006	Change (%)
Sales			
Manufacturing and Marketing	175,603	172,680	1.7
Coffee Services	278,766	267,469	4.2
Intersegment	(66,211)	(63,976)	3.5
Total sales	**388,158**	**376,173**	**3.2**
EBITDA			
Manufacturing and Marketing	35,754	32,944	8.5
Coffee Services	44,125	41,748	5.7
General expenses	(7,001)	(5,436)	28.8
Total EBITDA	**72,878**	**69,256**	**5.2**

Manufacturing and Marketing

Manufacturing and Marketing sales reached $175.6 million in 2007, up 1.7% from the $172.7 million recorded in 2006. Currency fluctuations have only a minor impact on sales in this segment.

TABLE 9
Coffee shipments by distribution channel and brand, 2006 and 2007
(In thousands of lbs.)

	2007	(%)	2006	(%)	Change (000 lbs)	Change (%)
Retail channels						
Van Houtte brand	7,709	29.8	7,270	29.1	439	6.0
Other brands	8,382	32.4	8,537	34.2	(155)	(1.8)
Sub-total	16,091	62.2	15,807	63.3	284	1.8
Coffee Services						
Van Houtte brand	6,909	26.7	6,397	25.6	512	8.0
Other brands	2,868	11.1	2,762	11.1	106	3.8
Sub-total	9,777	37.8	9,159	36.7	618	6.7
TOTAL	**25,868**	**100.0**	**24,966**	**100.0**	**902**	**3.6**
All channels						
Van Houtte brand	14,618	56.5	13,667	54.7	951	7.0
Other brands	11,250	43.5	11,299	45.3	49	(0.4)

The sales growth in the Manufacturing and Marketing segment is explained by the following factors:

- Coffee shipments to both the retail and Coffee Services networks increased, bolstered by among other things, the agreement signed with the A&P Canada supermarket chain, which introduced our merchandising concepts and coffees into their stores. A&P operates some 250 stores in Ontario under the A&P, Dominion and Food Basics banner.

Growth was particularly strong for the Van Houtte brand, whose sales are a determining factor for EBITDA. Thus, shipments of our brand advanced 6.0% on the retail side, 8.0% on the Coffee Services side and 7.0% for all the networks combined.

Manufacturing and Marketing growth was held back by a significant decrease in VKI sales, especially in the first half of the year. This slowdown is a consequence of the rationalization operated in active coffee services accounts declined, which freed up brewers that were subsequently refurbished and redeployed in the network.

Manufacturing and Marketing EBITDA rose 8.5% from $32.9 million in 2006 to $35.8 million in 2007. The EBITDA margin improved from 19.1% to 20.4%, fuelled by volume growth and restored gross margins on coffee, which suffered early last year as a result of higher green coffee prices. Our selling prices have since been adjusted.

Coffee Services

Coffee Services sales advanced 4.2% from the $267.5 million recorded last year to $278.8 million or 6.5% on a constant exchange rate basis.

- Sales advanced 10.1% in Canada, driven by all the regions but especially by the East and the Prairies.

- U.S. sales grew 4.8% after conversion to Canadian dollars or 9.8% on a constant exchange rate basis. About half of this growth was organic; the remainder stems from acquisitions made in 2006 and 2007.

- Following the streamlining of our vending machine network, sales in this segment declined $4.6 million from the same period last year.

- Active accounts expanded by 1,111 in one year to 75,216 at year-end. Sales per active account (on a constant exchange rate basis, excluding vending operations) picked up 8.2%.

Coffee Services EBITDA rose 5.7% to $44.1 million, reflecting the measures taken in the second quarter to offset the gross margin pressures in the first quarter.

- Coffee Services EBITDA advanced 4.1% in Canada. Thanks to sales growth, gross profit improved despite a slight reduction in the gross margin rate in most regions.

- In the U.S., EBITDA climbed 17.1% or 23.4% on a constant exchange rate basis. This excellent performance stems from sales growth and its leverage effect on operating profit. Beyond the usual leverage effect, operating expenses decreased in absolute terms.

The Coffee Services operating margin was 15.8% in 2007, compared to 15.6% a year ago.

TABLE 10
Number of active coffee services accounts

March 31, 2007	January 6, 2007	October 14, 2006	July 22, 2006	April 1, 2006
75,216	75,167	73,667	73,437	74,105

TABLE 11
Installed base of single-cup coffeemakers in Van Houtte's Coffee Services network

	March 31, 2007	January 6, 2007	October 14, 2006	July 22, 2006	April 1, 2006
Canada	26,659	26,318	25,982	26,763	25,572
United States	23,145	22,903	22,692	22,697	22,515
Total	49,804	49,221	48,498	49,460	48,087

The number of single-cup coffeemakers installed in our Coffee Services network rose 3.6% during the year to 49,804 units as at March 31, 2007.

As part of our agreement concluded in the first quarter with Chevron, we are continuing to install coffee bars in Chevron's corporate ExtraMile convenience stores on the U.S. West Coast, supplying the

coffeemakers, Van Houtte brand coffee and other hot beverages. At the time of writing, coffee bars had been installed in 140 stores.

We began executing our new agreement with Cincinnati-based Kroger Supermarkets. Under this agreement, signed in the second quarter, the coffee program will be enhanced as we will supply Van Houtte freshly brewed coffee to over 1,000 stores across the U.S. Each store will have a Van Houtte branded coffee station, which in over 80% of cases, will be equipped with our Suprema™ system. Thus, Kroger shoppers will be able to pick up a fresh cup of coffee brewed "one cup at a time" in either one of two Columbian blends or a steaming cup of Swiss Miss premium hot chocolate and in some stores, even a French vanilla cappuccino. As of the date of this report, the points of service have been upgraded to the new standards in about 290 of the 1,000 stores covered by the agreement.

Launched in the second quarter, our Source H2O system of filtered purified water for the workplace is doing well.

Van Houtte was awarded the tender for supplying coffee and refreshment services to a major company headquartered in Calgary with 166 coffee stations. We believe that this account will develop into the biggest office coffee services contract in our history. We have finished installing all the brewers required to serve this new customer.

Under an agreement with Culligan®, a company that delivers innovative water treatment solutions for commercial and residential customers, Corporate Coffee Systems, our New York-based joint venture, added more than 500 accounts in Culligan's Manhattan premises.

Intersegment sales and unallocated general expenses

Intersegment sales moved ahead 3.5% while unallocated general expenses increased $1.6 million as a result of changes to senior management's pension plan, as well as new governance and disclosure requirements for companies subject to Ontario securities regulations.

Capital resources, financial position and outlook

Liquidity
Van Houtte generates strong cash flows. For 2007 we recorded operating cash flows before unusual items of $62.2 million before unusual items, compared to $55.4 million a year earlier.

Operating cash flow per share stood at $2.91 ($2.90 diluted) against $2.59 ($2.58 diluted) in 2006.

Excluding unusual items, changes in non-cash working capital generated $2.5 million in 2007, whereas they used $7.6 million in 2006.

We invest primarily in the purchase of coffeemakers and rolling stock, in our roasting plants and in information technology, as well as in designing and building the gourmet coffee departments in supermarkets where we implement our concepts. Thus, the Company spent $32.9 million on fixed asset acquisition in 2007, compared to $30.6 million a year earlier. This temporary increase is associated mostly with the implementing of the gourmet coffee departments in some 250 A&P supermarkets in Ontario, the completion of a new K-Cup production line and the installation of coffee equipment required for the Kroger contract.

Acquisitions and divestitures resulted in net disbursements of $0.4 million in 2007, compared to $9.5 million in the prior year. The divestiture involves our vending business units. With regards to acquisitions, most of them were made in the U.S. More specifically, we concluded agreements with some minority joint venture partners to buy back their interests. Following these transactions the branches in Columbus, Cleveland, Cincinnati, Detroit and Louisville have become the exclusive property of Van Houtte.

The sale of our stake in Keurig produced inflows of $29.1 million (see "Sale of our interest in Keurig," p. 6).

Quarterly information

As is typical in our industry, particularly in the Coffee Services segment, business flows in the summer which overlaps Van Houtte's first and second quarters. However, this fluctuation is tempered by the fact that the first quarter has 16 weeks whereas each of the other three has 12. Consequently, we record the strongest sales of the year in the first quarter but not necessarily the highest earnings.

TABLE 14
Quarterly results (unaudited)
(In thousands of dollars, except for per share amounts)

	2007				2006			
	Q4	Q3	Q2	Q1	Q4	Q3	Q2	Q1
Sales	94,542	95,971	86,439	111,206	91,556	91,309	84,383	110,386
EBITDA	18,597	19,989	16,572	17,810	17,941	17,605	15,483	18,228
Net earnings, before unusual items ($)	5,868	6,323	4,263	3,842	6,464	5,948	5,097	4,998
Net earnings	10,340	6,323	4,263	4,034	6,464	5,948	5,097	4,998
Earnings per share, before unusual items($)	0.28	0.30	0.20	0.18	0.30	0.28	0.24	0.23
Earnings per share ($)	0.48	0.30	0.20	0.19	0.30	0.28	0.24	0.23

Q1 of each year has 16 weeks; the others have 12 each.

The first few weeks of 2006 began on the heels of the increases in the cost price of green coffee which occurred at the end of fiscal year 2005. Because our own adjustments could only be completed in the middle of the first quarter, Q1 profitability suffered. However, the situation stabilized and second and third quarter performance was more in line with our expectations.

The first quarter of 2007 was characterized by an increase in coffee shipments, particularly of the Van Houtte brand. The Manufacturing and Marketing segment saw its EBITDA jump 17.8%. However, Coffee Services fared poorly, particularly in the U.S. as a result of gross margin pressures. Moreover, the increase in depreciation expense and the fact that we were subject to Quebec's new tax legislation shaved $0.06 from the quarter's earnings per share.

In the second quarter, we implemented measures to boost sales and improve the operating margin, which we successfully did in both segments. Coffee Services saw sales grow both in Canada and in the U.S. while Manufacturing and Marketing saw coffee shipments increase. However, this segment's sales were adversely affected by the slowdown at VKI. Once again, the net quarterly results were impacted by the increase in depreciation and income tax.

Third quarter sales and operating margins in both segments improved considerably, so much so that net earnings increased year-over-year despite the depreciation and income tax impact.

Fourth quarter 2007

Before unusual items, fourth quarter net earnings were $5.9 million or $0.28 per share ($0.27 diluted), compared with $6.5 million and $0.30 per share (basic and diluted) in the same period last year.

The proceeds of this sale combined with our strong operating cash flows allowed us to reduce our long-term debt by a net amount of $42.7 million despite paying an unprecedented amount in dividends.

We paid out $12.2 million in dividends during the year, broken down as follows: $6.9 million for the four regular quarterly dividends and $5.3 million for the first instalment of the special dividend announced following the sale of our interest in Keurig.

Financial position and cash requirements

Working capital (excluding the short-term portion of long-term debt and dividends payable in the amount of $5.4 million) stood at $42.3 million as at March 31, 2007, against $47.0 million a year earlier. This decrease stems largely from the increase in payables.

Among the short-term assets, the Note receivable of $8.3 million represents the balance of the sale of our interest in Keurig.

With regards to short-term liabilities, income taxes payable represent, in addition to current income taxes, the unpaid portion of the allowance recorded for taxes on past earnings.

Long-term assets consist of investments, fixed assets, goodwill, other assets and future income taxes (long term). The net value of fixed assets declined slightly. In fact, depreciation of fixed assets was slightly higher than the net additions to capital stock. The book value of our investments decreased by $17.5 million, following the sale of our interest in Keurig.

The Company will continue its strict investment policy. The capital budget for 2008 has been set at approximately $28.3 million, a figure closer to its historical level.

Van Houtte's debt (including the short-term portion of long-term debt) declined considerably since the beginning of the year, from $95.1 million on April 1, 2006 to $52.5 million on March 31, 2007. The decrease is attributable to the partial payment of the sale price of our investment in Keurig and to our rigorous cash management. The debt/capital employed ratio was 16.8%, compared to 27.7% as at April 1, 2006.

As at March 31, 2007, we had authorized unused credit facilities of $100.3 million.

TABLE 12
Contractual obligations by term, as at March 31, 2007

Contractual obligations	Total	Payments due by term (in thousands of $)			
		Less than 1 year	1–2 years	3–4 years	5 and more
Long-term debt	52,480	1,407	657	579	49,837
Net capital leases	20,376	5,931	4,612	5,808	4,025
Purchasing contracts – green coffee	8,207	8,207	-	-	-
Total	81,063	15,545	5,269	6,387	53,862

TABLE 13

Outstanding shares as at May 25, 2007	
Multiple voting shares (five votes per share)	5,300,000
Subordinate voting shares (one vote per share)	16,202,831
Unexercised options (entitling the holder to the same number of subordinate voting shares)	630,146

Van Houtte's operations generate substantial cash flows. Depreciation for 2008 is projected at $37 million.

In management's opinion, the Company has the necessary financial resources to pursue its operations and implement its development plan. Moreover, it has the financial flexibility to seize attractive acquisition opportunities that are consistent with its business plan.

TABLE 15
Reconciliation of EBITDA, net earnings before unusual items and net earnings, fourth quarter 2006 and 2007
(In thousands of $ except for per share amounts)

	2007	2006
EBITDA	18,597	17,941
Depreciation and amortization	(9,007)	(8,622)
Financial expenses	(743)	574
Income tax on current earnings, before unusual items	(2,445)	(3,082)
Share in net earnings of companies subject to significant influence	--	31
Non-controlling interest	(534)	(346)
Net earnings, before unusual items	**5,868**	**6,464**
Per share ($)	**0.28**	**0.30**
Reversal of provision for income tax on gain on sale of an investment	3,985	-
Strategy review fees of value enhancement, net of $312 in taxes	(663)	-
Write-down of certain assets, net of $428 in taxes	(909)	-
Adjustment to prior year income taxes	2,060	-
Net earnings	**10,341**	**6,464**
Per share ($)	**0.48**	**0.30**

Quarterly sales advanced 3.8% to $94.5 million.

Bucking the general trend of the last few years, the U.S. dollar rose 1.5% in the fourth quarter year-over-year. At a constant exchange rate basis, sales would have advanced 2.9%. Most of this growth was organic.

Quarterly EBITDA was up 3.7% to $18.6 million.

Amortization and depreciation was $9.0 million in the fourth quarter, against $8.6 million at the same time last year. The shortening of the amortization period of certain coffee service equipment in 2006 still has an impact on the depreciation expense.

During the fourth quarter, Van Houtte standardized its method of recording lease revenues, thus correcting the imbalance caused by the deployment of the Enterprise Resource Planning system ("ERP") across the Coffee Services network in the last three years. Moreover, the Company adopted stricter rules as regards recording certain assets, including allowance for inventory obsolescence. We made a non-recurring adjustment to give effect to these new measures. We therefore proceeded with devaluations and write-downs of $1.3 million ($0.9 million after tax).

Tax on current earnings, excluding unusual items, was $2.5 million. The effective rate was 28.3%, compared to 31.1% a year earlier. This decrease is due to adjustments made at quarter-end. Van Houtte's prospective effective tax rates should be around the same as for 2007, i.e., 31.6%.

The allowance for prior year income taxes was adjusted based on the status of our discussions with the Quebec government (See "Amendment to the Taxation Act," p. 7). This downward adjustment resulted in an unusual gain of $2.1 million for the quarter.

TABLE 16
Quarterly segment results
(In thousands of dollars, except percent change)

	Quarter ended March 31, 2007	Quarter ended April 1, 2006	Change (%)
Sales			
Manufacturing and Marketing	41,642	40,330	3.3
Coffee Services	70,465	66,307	6.4
Intersegment	(17,564)	(15,515)	13.2
Total	**94,542**	**91,122**	**3.9**
EBITDA			
Manufacturing and Marketing	7,569	8,121	(6.9)
Coffee Services	12,942	10,908	18.7
General expenses	(1,914)	(1,089)	75.8
Total EBITDA	**18,597**	**17,940**	**3.7**

Manufacturing and Marketing

Manufacturing and Marketing sales were up 3.3% in the fourth quarter to $41.6 million, an improvement in line with our expectations. Currency fluctuations have only a minor impact on sales in this segment.

TABLE 17
Coffee shipments by distribution channel and brand, fourth quarter and 2006 and 2007
(In thousands of lbs.)

	Quarter ended March 31, 2007	(%)	Quarter ended April 1, 2006	(%)	Change (000 lb)	Change (%)
Retail channels						
Van Houtte brand	1,721	28.9	1,723	29.6	(2)	(0.1)
Other brands	1,835	30.8	1,789	30.7	46	2.6
Sub-total	3,556	59.7	3,512	60.3	44	1.3
Coffee Services						
Van Houtte brand	1,721	28.9	1,640	28.2	81	4.9
Other brands	677	11.4	669	11.5	8	1.2
Sub-total	2,398	40.3	2,309	39.7	89	3.9
Total	5,954	100.0	5,821	100.0	133	2.3
All networks						
Van Houtte brand	3,442	57.8	3,363	57.8	79	2.3
Other brands	2,512	42.2	2,458	42.2	54	2.2

The quarter's performance is explained by the following factors:

· Coffee shipments advanced 2.3%.

· Shipments of the Van Houtte brand, all networks combined, moved ahead 2.3%. The increase was 4.9% in the Coffee Services segment. The substitution of other brands by Van Houtte coffees had a positive effect on the average selling price and on gross margin.

· Manufacturing and Marketing EBITDA was $7.6 million compared to $8.1 million at the same time last year. Consequently, the segment's operating ratio was 18.2% in the last quarter of 2007, against 20.1% in the same quarter a year earlier.

· The price of green coffee rose in the fourth quarter, adversely affecting gross margin. Selling prices were revised upward on April 1, 2007.

· Operating expenses rose as a result of a surge in shipping costs following the increase in gas prices.

Coffee Services

Coffee Services sales reached $70.5 million in the fourth quarter, up 6.3% from the $66.3 million recorded a year earlier.

- The segment advanced 11.9% in Canada, fuelled by all the regions but especially by the East and the Prairies.

- U.S. sales were up 11.3% after conversion to Canadian dollars and 9.6% on a constant exchange rate basis. Most of this growth was organic.

- As a result of the decision to streamline our vending network by selling some operations, sales in this segment fell $2.6 million from the corresponding year-ago period.

- The number of active accounts increased by 49 from the third quarter, to 75,216 at quarter-end.

- Sales per active account (excluding vending sales) rose 9.5% or 8.8% on a constant exchange rate basis.

- The installed base of single-cup coffeemakers expanded by 583 units during the quarter.

Subsequent events

Enhancing shareholder value

As a result of a strategic review process initiated in October 2006 and announced on January 12, 2007 (the "Announcement Date"), Van Houtte announced on May 7, 2007 the signature of a definitive acquisition agreement (the "Agreement") to be acquired and taken private by a Company controlled by Littlejohn & Co. LLC. ("Littlejohn"), a Greenwich, Connecticut-based private equity firm.

Under the terms of the Agreement, Littlejohn will acquire all of the issued and outstanding shares of the Company for a consideration of $25.00 per share. The total enterprise value of the transaction is approximately $600 million, including the assumption of existing indebtedness. The $25.00 per share consideration represents a 44% premium over the volume-weighted average price of $17.36 for the 20-day period ending prior to the Announcement Date.

In addition, the $0.25 per share special dividend payable on June 15, 2007 to shareholders of record on June 7, 2007 will be maintained. However, the regular quarterly dividend of $0.08 per share will not be declared.

The strategic review process was led by the Strategic Orientation Committee, with the assistance of CIBC World Markets. This committee is composed of six non-management Board members: Paul-André Guillotte, Pierre Brodeur, Roger Desrosiers, Robert Parizeau, Christian Pouliot and Pierre-Luc Van Houtte.

Van Houtte spent five months seeking interest from a wide variety of parties with respect to a potential sale of the Company. Through a broad and thorough sale process, the Company contacted approximately 50 potential strategic and financial buyers from across the United States, Canada, Europe and Asia. Extensive discussions took place with several buyers who had previously executed confidentiality and standstill agreements. The transaction with Littlejohn is the culmination of this extensive process.

Van Houtte's founding and principal shareholders, Famille Pierre Van Houtte Inc., Société Agro-Alimentaire Sogal Inc., Les Placements Michel Ouellet (1986) Inc. and Les Placements Christian Pouliot (1986) Inc., have agreed, pursuant to the support and voting agreement, to irrevocably support and vote in favour of the transaction. Pursuant to the support and voting agreement, such shareholders cannot agree to or contemplate any competing transaction until January 1, 2008. These shareholders collectively hold approximately 36% of the outstanding Van Houtte shares representing 68% of voting rights, consisting of 5.3 million or 100% of the multiple voting shares, and approximately 2.5 million or 16% of the subordinate voting shares of the Company.

The Board of Directors unanimously approved the transaction (with interested directors abstaining) upon a unanimous recommendation of its Strategic Orientation Committee and also resolved to inform the Company's shareholders that they were in favour of the transaction.

In reviewing the proposed transaction, Van Houtte's Strategic Orientation Committee received an opinion from both National Bank Financial and CIBC World Markets that the consideration offered to the Van Houtte shareholders is fair from a financial point of view.

The transaction will be implemented by way of a plan of arrangement under the Canada Business Corporations Act and will have to be approved by Van Houtte shareholders at a Special Meeting to be held on July 9, 2007. The plan of arrangement will be subject to approval by at least two thirds of the votes cast by the holders of subordinate voting shares and multiple voting shares, each voting separately as a class, and by a majority of the votes cast by the holders of subordinate voting shares (other than interested shareholders). Once approved by the shareholders, the plan of arrangement will then have to be sanctioned by the Superior Court of Quebec.

The transaction will also be subject to certain other customary conditions described in the Agreement, including receipt of a limited number of regulatory approvals and no material adverse change in the Company's business. The transaction is not subject to any financing condition. It is anticipated that the plan of arrangement, if approved by the Company's shareholders, will be completed shortly after the Special Meeting.

The Agreement also provides for, among other things, a non-solicitation covenant on the part of Van Houtte, a right in favour of Littlejohn to match any superior proposal and the payment of a termination fee to Littlejohn in the amount of $10 million under certain circumstances.

Outlook and guidance

For the past few years, Van Houtte has been executing a three-pronged strategy while developing the Van Houtte brand in North America: 1) accelerate sales growth in the retail and Coffee Services networks in order to improve profitability; 2) exercise strict cost management; and 3) optimize capital management.

While this strategy remains the cornerstone of our development, each aspect has its own issues.

Accelerate sales growth

Energizing sales growth calls for combining the complementary strengths of our Coffee Services network and coffee distribution through supermarket chains. We believe that depending on the markets, our brand image in each network flows to the other and vice versa. That said, the growth challenges are different for coffee services and coffee sold for home consumption.

On the coffee services side, competitive pressures are affecting margins, particularly in the U.S. market, which is far less consolidated than Canada's. However, there are opportunities for growth in the development of regional, national and continental multi-location accounts. The fact that we are one of the few companies that can manage and serve such accounts gives us an enduring competitive edge. Expanding our product line (for example, hot chocolate, and water) and coffeemaker line is another excellent way to grow.

We will also continue opening coffee bars in high-traffic public areas. Not only does this initiative stimulate coffee sales, it also boosts our visibility and enhances our brand image at little cost. For instance, the coffee bars set up in Chevron stores on the U.S. West Coast and in Florida will enrich our brand equity in regions experiencing strong population growth.

To this end, we will continue to deploy a variety of marketing tools—advertising, public relations and marketing—to directly stimulate sales or to promote the brand.

On the home consumption side, we are solidly entrenched as market leaders in Quebec. Most of our growth potential therefore lies in the rest of Canada and in some niches in the U.S. In the past few years, we have expanded our supermarket presence in Ontario and Western Canada. The visibility and growing reputation of the Van Houtte brand on these markets, combined with our marketing efforts, should help us deepen our footprint in these networks and stimulate sales growth.

VKI's growth depends in part on that of our Coffee Services network. Developing outside sales is, however, top on its list.

Exercise strict cost management

Exercising strict management is a constant concern that has become all the more important in the past two fiscal years due to fluctuations in the cost price of green coffee and rising energy costs.

Our efficiency has improved considerably in recent years. For one, we streamlined Coffee Services operations in a number of regions by reorganizing work processes and consolidating multiple branches in some cities. In the Manufacturing and Marketing segment, we continually invest in our production infrastructure to make sure we are always on the cutting edge. This will not change. For example, in 2007 we invested in our Montreal plants and updated our production processes and logistics.

In 2007, we continued with our ERP rollout across the network. The deployment was completed in Canada, and we began the process in our wholly-owned branches in the U.S. Given the strategic importance of this management tool, the U.S. rollout will be stepped up and should be completed in 2008.

Optimize capital management

Capital is one of our most important resources. Securing a competitive return on this capital depends not only on dynamic, strict management of our operations but also of our capital.

We made strides in this area in 2007. For example, at the end of 2006, we used about $0.91 from each dollar of sales. By the end of 2007, this ratio was $0.80.

The sale of our interest in Keurig reflects our plan to optimize capital use and is in keeping with our overall strategy. Since we were a passive shareholder in Keurig, our strategic relationship with this company was and remains at arm's length. The fact that we sold it does not change this relationship.

Thanks to the ERP system, we now have access to much more detailed information than in the past. For instance, we can now measure the return on capital invested for each account. With this tool, we can also better adjust the equipment to our clients' needs and optimize the use of our installed base of coffeemakers.

Dividend policy

Every quarter, the Board of Directors evaluates whether it should pay out a quarterly dividend. During the year, the Company paid out four quarterly dividends of $0.08 per share for an annual rate of $0.32 per share.

In August 2006, following the sale of our investment in Keurig, the Board of Directors declared a special dividend of $0.50 per share, payable in two instalments of $0.25 each. The first payment was made on September 15, 2006 and the second will be made on June 15, 2007 to shareholders of record on June 7.

Under the terms of the agreement signed with Littlejohn, (see "Enhancing Shareholder Value," p. 17), the $0.25 dividend already declared will be paid on June 15. However, the Board of Directors will not declare a quarterly dividend.

Risks and uncertainties

Van Houtte's main product is coffee, a commodity subject to considerable price fluctuations. An increase in the cost price of coffee can adversely affect sales, profit margins or both. Van Houtte tempers the risk associated with fluctuations in the cost price of green coffee by covering its needs for three to six months using forward exchange contracts (see "Financial Instruments").

Van Houtte specializes in gourmet coffee, and past experience has shown that consumption in the gourmet coffee segment is fairly impervious to price hikes since consumers are already prepared to pay more for a superior product. However, there is no assurance that this behaviour will continue.

Coffee destined for retail channels represents nearly 25% of Van Houtte's total sales. Our access to this market depends on agreements signed with retailers, mostly supermarket chains. In most of their stores, we design, set up and stock the gourmet coffee department. A Van Houtte distributor then handles replenishment.

However, some of these agreements allow the retailers to vary the number of Van Houtte products they carry, in other words, to decide whether or not to offer our products at all. As well, some chains mandate Van Houtte to roast and package coffee under their private label. The margins on these coffees are much

lower than on coffees carrying the Van Houtte or any one of our other labels. There is no assurance that these agreements and the associated coffee volumes will be renewed. Moreover, some retailers may also change their marketing strategy and step up promotion of their brand to the detriment of ours.

Coffee Services account for more than 60% of sales and nearly 55% of EBITDA. Because these services are offered mainly to workplaces, particularly offices, demand fluctuates in direct proportion to the general economic and employment situation. A large portion of our Coffee Services costs are fixed in the near term, providing us with considerable operating leverage. When sales decrease, the corresponding decrease in EBITDA will be greater. However, when sales increase, the corresponding decrease in EBITDA will also be higher. Moreover, amortization also affects Coffee Services and further amplifies the leverage on net earnings.

We have spent the last few years developing coffee services in places other than work, for example, university campuses, hospitals and other public locations, especially convenience store chains and other retail environments. This development is positive in that it diversifies places where our coffees are consumed. It also creates a new class of large accounts whose agreements encompass hundreds of coffeemakers. For example, our largest Coffee Services account represented approximately 2% of this segment's sales in 2007.

Historically, the single-cup brewing technology developed by our subsidiary VKI has provided us with a solid strategic edge in the coffee services market. As comparable, sophisticated technologies become available on the market, our competitive advantage diminishes. We are therefore redefining our strategic positioning by playing up other competitive factors such as the quality of our coffees, the extent of our product and equipment line, our brands, our service quality and the uniqueness of our branch network.

Most of our loans are at variable interest rates determined based on Bankers' Acceptances rates or the prime rate. Since our loans are both in Canadian and U.S. dollars, the interest rates could fluctuate based on the monetary policies of the Bank of Canada and the U.S. Federal Reserve. Because a sudden rate jump would negatively impact profitability, the interest rates for part of our debt are fixed by interest rate swap agreements (see "Financial Instruments") that are evaluated at their fair value at the end of each quarter. Although these evaluations can create accounting gains and losses, they do not change the interest amount paid on the loans covered by these swap agreements.

Financial instruments

Interest rate swap agreements

The swap agreements mentioned above mature from July 2007 to October 2010. Under these contracts we exchange, at set intervals, the difference between contractually fixed interest rates and the floating rate stipulated in our credit agreements. We pay a fixed interest rate ranging from 3.99% to 4.86% on a face value of $57 million ($42 million and US$13 million) and obtain a floating rate based on 3-month Bankers' Acceptances rates. The fair value of these agreements is recorded in our results.

Forward exchange contracts

A significant portion of our business is conducted in U.S. dollars. We use various types of forward exchange contracts solely for the purpose of managing the exchange risk associated with doing business and never for speculation. As at May 25, 2007, we had forward exchange contracts with a face value of US$13.5 million at a fixed exchange rate of $1.1343. The negative fair value of these contracts is $0.7 million.

Forward coffee contracts

In order to manage the risk associated with fluctuations in the cost price of green coffee, we purchase forward coffee contracts to cover three to six months' supply. As at May 25, 2007, we had contracts with a positive fair value of $0.1 million.

Changes in accounting policies

In 2005, Van Houtte began recording the cost of executive compensation in the form of stock options based on their fair market value. Previously, this compensation was disclosed in a note to the financial statements but was not included in the computation of the Company's results, and therefore had no impact on earnings calculation.

We have changed the way we recognize our interest in certain joint ventures. Since April 3, 2005, the Company fully consolidates joint ventures that were proportionately consolidated up to this date. This change has no impact on the Company's net earnings or net assets.

At the end of 2006, we reclassified a portion of the goodwill, a non-depreciable asset, into two classes of depreciable assets: *Customer Relations* (new) and *Non-compete Clauses* (existing). Both appear on the balance sheet under *Other* assets. A portion of the *Non-compete Clauses* class was also reclassified as *Customer Relations*, which has a longer amortization period. The result of this change is a recurring net increase of $0.4 million in amortization per year. The full amount was recorded in the fourth quarter of 2006 along with a non-recurring amortization expense of $0.3 million in order to give retroactive effect to this change to 2004. In 2007, these changes gave rise to a $0.1 million increase per quarter.

New accounting principles in 2008

In 2005, The Canadian Institute of Chartered Accountants (CICA) published three new chapters in the CICA manual: Chapter 3855 entitled *Financial Instruments – Recognition and Measurement*, Chapter 3865 entitled *Hedges*, and Chapter 1530 entitled *Comprehensive Income*. These new chapters are in effect for the interim and annual periods commencing after October 1, 2006. They provide instructions on recognition and measurement of financial instruments as well as the standards for using hedge accounting.

Chapter 1530 requires companies to disclose comprehensive income. In addition to net earnings, this primarily includes unrealized gains and losses that do not appear in traditional income statements and are recorded directly in shareholders' equity. Other components of comprehensive income include unrealized gains and losses associated with foreign currency translation adjustments to financial statements, certain deferred profits and losses stemming from hedge activities, and unrealized gains and losses on certain securities investments.

The Company is currently evaluating the impact of these recommendations and will prospectively implement them in the first quarter of 2008.

Significant estimates

Some amounts in the financial statements or in this MD&A are estimates by management based on knowledge of current or anticipated events.

Goodwill

Goodwill is the difference between the acquisition cost of an enterprise over the fair value of its tangible and intangible net assets at the time of acquisition. Goodwill is revised downward if the fair value of an operating unit is less than its book value. This fair value is estimated annually.

Since they have an indefinite life, goodwill and intangible assets are not amortized.

Inventory

Every year, management reviews the inventory movement of brewers and other equipment, as well as maintenance parts to determine the obsolescence reserve required to cover potential losses associated with obsolete or low-turnover inventory.

Other

Management uses other estimates when preparing financial statements but these have no material impact on the Company's earnings or value and consequently are not relevant.

Related party transactions

There were no material related party transactions in 2007.

Disclosure controls and procedures

The Company's Chief Executive Officer and Chief Financial Officer are responsible for establishing and maintaining adequate disclosure controls and procedures. Disclosure controls and procedures are designed to provide reasonable assurance that material information required to be disclosed in reports filed with, or submitted to, securities regulatory authorities is recorded, processed, summarized and reported within the time periods specified under securities laws, and to ensure that information is accumulated and communicated to management, including the Chief Executive Officer and Chief Financial Officer, to allow timely decisions regarding required disclosure. While we regularly examine our disclosure controls and procedures, they cannot provide absolute assurance given that the control systems cannot prevent or detect all the inaccuracies associated with errors or fraud due to their inherent limitations.

As of March 31, 2007, an evaluation was carried out with the participation of management, including the Chief Executive Officer and Chief Financial Officer, of the effectiveness of the Company's disclosure controls and procedures. Based on that evaluation, the Chief Executive Officer and the Chief Financial Officer concluded that the design and operation of the Company's disclosure controls and procedures were effective as at March 31, 2007.

Internal controls over financial reporting

Management is responsible for establishing and maintaining adequate internal control over financial reporting to provide reasonable assurance regarding the reliability of financial reporting and the preparation of financial statements for external purposes in accordance with GAAP. The Chief Executive Officer and the Chief Financial Officer have evaluated whether there were changes to internal control over financial reporting during the year ended March 31, 2007 that have materially affected, or are reasonably likely to materially affect, its internal control over financial reporting. No such changes were identified through their evaluation.

During the quarter ended March 31 2007, the Company improved the design of disclosure controls and procedures and internal control over financial reporting toward certification of filings under Instrument 52-109 for fiscal year ended March 31, 2007. Improvements were made to the specific risks review and their documentation.

Forward-looking information

This analysis contains forward-looking statements reflecting Van Houtte's objectives, estimates and expectations. Such statements may be marked by the use of verbs such as "believe," "anticipate," "estimate" and "expect" as well as the use of the future or conditional tense. By their very nature, such statements involve risks and uncertainty. Consequently, results could differ materially from the Company's projections or expectations.

Management's Responsibility for Financial Statements

These financial statements have been prepared by management in conformity with Canadian generally accepted accounting principles and include amounts that are based on best estimates and judgments.

Management of the Company and of its subsidiaries, in furtherance of the integrity and objectivity of the data in the financial statements, has developed and maintains systems of internal accounting controls and supports a program of internal audit. Management believes that these systems of internal accounting controls provide reasonable assurance that financial records are reliable and form a proper basis for the preparation of the financial statements and that assets are properly accounted for and safeguarded, and that the preparation and presentation of other financial information are consistent with the financial statements.

The Board of Directors carries out its responsibility for the financial statements principally through its Audit Committee, consisting solely of independent directors. The Audit Committee reviews the Company's annual consolidated financial statements, and management's discussion and analysis and recommends them to the Board of Directors for approval. The Audit Committee meets with the Company's management and external auditors to discuss internal controls over the financial reporting process, auditing matters and financial reporting issues and formulates the appropriate recommendations to the Board of Directors. The auditors appointed by the shareholders have full access to the Audit Committee, with and without management being present.

These financial statements have been audited by the auditors appointed by the shareholders, KPMG LLP, chartered accountants, and their report is presented hereafter.

Jean-Yves Monette
President and Chief Executive Officer

Gérard Geoffrion
Executive Vice-President

Jean-Luc Deschamps
Chief Financial Officer

June 5, 2007

Auditors' Report to Shareholders

We have audited the consolidated balance sheets of Van Houtte Inc. as at March 31, 2007 and April 1, 2006 and the consolidated statements of earnings, shareholders' equity and cash flows for the years then ended. These financial statements are the responsibility of the Company's management. Our responsibility is to express an opinion on these financial statements based on our audits.

We conducted our audits in accordance with Canadian generally accepted auditing standards. Those standards require that we plan and perform an audit to obtain reasonable assurance whether the financial statements are free of material misstatement. An audit includes examining, on a test basis, evidence supporting the amounts and disclosures in the financial statements. An audit also includes assessing the accounting principles used and significant estimates made by management, as well as evaluating the overall financial statement presentation.

In our opinion, these consolidated financial statements present fairly, in all material respects, the financial position of the Company as at March 31, 2007 and April 1, 2006 and the results of its operations and its cash flows for the years then ended in accordance with Canadian generally accepted accounting principles.

KPMG LLP

Chartered Accountants
Montreal, Canada
June 5, 2007

Consolidated Statements of Earnings

Years ended March 31, 2007 and April 1, 2006
(In thousands of dollars, except for earnings per share data)

	2007	2006
Revenues (note 2)	$ 388,158	$ 376,173
Cost of goods sold and operating expenses	315,280	306,917
	72,878	69,256
Amortization	36,105	33,790
Write-down of the value of certain assets	1,337	-
Operating profit	35,436	35,466
Financial expenses (note 3)	4,271	2,382
Strategy review fees of value enhancement (note 22)	975	-
Materialized gain on disposal of investment (note 7)	(19,948)	-
Earnings before the income taxes	50,138	33,084
Income taxes (note 4a)	9,544	8,665
Prior years income taxes (note 4b)	13,712	-
Net earnings before the undernoted	26,882	24,419
Share in net earnings of companies subject to significant influence	-	31
Non-controlling interest	(1,921)	(1,944)
Net earnings	$ 24,961	$ 22,506
EARNINGS PER SHARE (note 5)		
Basic		
Net earnings	$ 1.17	$ 1.05
Diluted		
Net earnings	$ 1.16	$ 1.05
Weighted average number of shares outstanding (in thousands)	21,375	21,399
Diluted weighted average number of shares (in thousands)	21,428	21,454

See accompanying notes to consolidated financial statements.

Consolidated Statements of Shareholders' Equity

Years ended March 31, 2007 and April 1, 2006
(In thousands of dollars)

	Capital stock	Contributed Surplus	Retained Earnings	Currency Translation	Total
Balance, April 2, 2005	$ 128,250	$ 2,043	$ 114,603	$ (13,519)	$ 231,377
Net earnings	-	-	22,506	-	22,506
Dividends	-	-	(9,183)	-	(9,183)
Currency translation adjustment (note 14)	-	-	-	(3,652)	(3,652)
Redemption of subordinate voting shares (note 13b)	(2,040)	-	(3,160)	-	(5,200)
Issuance of shares (note 13b)	287	-	-	-	287
Stock-based compensation (note 13c)	-	418	-	-	418
Balance, April 1, 2006	126,497	2,461	124,766	(17,171)	236,553
Net earnings	-	-	24,961	-	24,961
Dividends	-	-	(17,550)	-	(17,550)
Currency translation adjustment (note 14)	-	-	-	(648)	(648)
Issuance of shares (note 13a)	3,545	(898)	-	-	2,647
Stock-based compensation (note 13c)	-	232	-	-	232
Balance, March 31, 2007	$ 130,042	$ 1,795	$ 132,177	$ (17,819)	$ 246,195

See accompanying notes to consolidated financial statements.

Consolidated Balance Sheets

March 31, 2007 and April 1, 2006
(In thousands of dollars)

	2007	2006
ASSETS		
Current assets :		
Cash	$ **4,884**	$ 5,796
Accounts receivable	**48,459**	43,036
Note receivable (note 7)	**8,320**	-
Inventories (note 6)	**29,539**	29,972
Prepaid expenses	**3,320**	3,553
Future income taxes (note 4)	**1,571**	1,804
	96,093	84,161
Investments (note 7)	**2,641**	20,121
Fixed assets (note 8)	**116,604**	118,474
Goodwill (note 9)	**136,676**	135,734
Other assets (note 10)	**14,878**	15,475
Future income taxes (note 4)	**3,228**	6,154
	$ 370,120	$ 380,119
LIABILITIES AND SHAREHOLDERS' EQUITY		
Current liabilities :		
Accounts payable and accrued liabilities	$ **39,003**	$ 34,434
Dividends payable	**5,366**	-
Income taxes payable	**14,097**	2,312
Deferred income	**747**	372
Current portion of long-term debt (note 11)	**1,407**	1,520
	60,620	38,638
Long-term debt (note 11)	**51,073**	93,589
Other liabilities (note 12)	**3,135**	1,799
Future income taxes (note 4)	**1,201**	1,498
Non-controlling interest	**7,896**	8,042
Shareholders' equity :		
Capital stock (note 13)	**130,042**	126,497
Contributed surplus (note 13)	**1,795**	2,461
Retained earnings	**132,177**	124,766
Currency translation adjustment (note 14)	**(17,819)**	(17,171)
	246,195	236,553
Commitments and guarantees (note 15)		
Contingencies (note 16)		
Subsequent events (notes 4b) and 22)		
	$ 370,120	$ 380,119

See accompanying notes to consolidated financial statements.

On behalf of the Board:

Jean-Yves Monette
Director

Roger Desrosiers, FCA
Director

Consolidated Statements of Cash Flows

Years ended March 31, 2007 and April 1, 2006
(In thousands of dollars)

	2007	2006
CASH FLOWS FROM OPERATING ACTIVITIES :		
Net earnings :	$ 24,961	$ 22,506
Adjustments for :		
Depreciation of fixed assets	33,644	31,061
Amortization of other assets	2,461	2,729
Amortization of financial expenses (note 3)	620	1,405
Future income taxes (note 4)	2,857	356
Pension expense and post employment benefits (note 12)	1,336	(2)
Change in fair value of interest rate swaps	119	(2,169)
Non-controlling interest	1,921	1,944
Increase in value of investment in preferred shares and dividends (note 7)	-	(1,559)
Stock-based compensation (note 13)	232	418
Gain on disposal of fixed assets	(358)	(314)
Gain on disposal of businesses	(897)	(921)
Materialized gain on disposal of investment (note 7)	(19,948)	-
Other elements	(15)	(21)
	46,933	55,433
Net change in non-cash balances related to working capital items (note 17)	10,492	(7,622)
	57,425	47, 811
CASH FLOWS FROM INVESTING ACTIVITIES :		
Business and asset acquisitions and disposals (note 18)	(435)	(9,545)
Additions to fixed assets	(32,957)	(30,589)
Proceeds from disposal of fixed assets	1,553	3,105
Proceeds from disposal of an investment (note 7)	29,096	-
Acquisition of investments	19	(177)
Increase in other assets	(1,274)	(1,187)
	(3,998)	(38,393)
CASH FLOWS FROM FINANCING ACTIVITIES :		
Issue of subordinate voting shares (note 13)	2,647	287
Redemption of subordinate voting shares for cancellation (note 13b)	-	(5,200)
Increase in long-term debt	41,081	65,197
Decrease in long-term debt	(83,776)	(57,778)
Dividends	(12,184)	(9,183)
Dividends paid to non-controlling shareholders of subsidiaries	(1,914)	(1,973)
	(54,146)	(8,650)
Effect of exchange rate changes on cash denominated in foreign currency	(193)	(310)
Increase (decrease) in cash	(912)	458
Cash, beginning of year	5,796	5,338
Cash, end of year	$ 4,884	$ 5,796

See accompanying notes to consolidated financial statements.

Notes to Consolidated Financial Statements

Years ended March 31, 2007 and April 1, 2006

(Tabular amounts are expressed in thousands of dollars)

Van Houtte Inc. is incorporated under the Canada Business Corporations Act. The Company is an important gourmet coffee roaster, marketer and distributor. It markets its gourmet coffees across Canada and the US through distribution channels that include coffee services, retail stores, cafés-bistros, on-line shopping and food service networks.

NOTE 1
Significant accounting policies

a) Consolidation and long-term investments

The consolidated financial statements include the accounts of Van Houtte Inc. and all its subsidiaries (the "Company"). The major subsidiaries are Van Houtte Coffee Services Inc., VKI Technologies Inc., Filterfresh Coffee Service, Inc., including its principal subsidiaries, Corporate Coffee Services, LLC and Potomac Coffee, LLC.

Investments in companies subject to significant influence are accounted for using the equity method. Investments in companies in which the Company believes it does not exercise a significant influence are classified as portfolio investments. Portfolio investment was recorded at cost and was written down in the case of a permanent impairment. However, cumulative dividends and accreted value of mandatory redeemable preferred shares are recorded provided the ultimate collection is reasonably assured.

Investments in joint ventures are consolidated. This basis of presentation results from the control that the Company exercises over the strategic operating, financing and investing policies.

b) Inventories

Raw materials are stated at the lower of cost, based on the first-in, first-out method, and replacement value. Finished goods and work-in-process are stated at the lower of average cost and net realizable value.

Raw materials purchased using commodity contracts are accounted for at the purchase price set out under the terms and conditions of these contracts.

c) Fixed assets

Fixed assets are stated at cost, net of any investment tax credits which are accounted for when qualified expenditures are incurred. Interest expenses and other direct costs relating to major capital projects are capitalized to the cost of fixed assets until the commercial production stage.

Depreciation is calculated using the straight-line method over the following periods:

Asset	Period
Buildings	20 to 30 years
Coffee service equipment for rental purposes	2 to 7 years
Vending equipment	12 years
Machinery and equipment	5 to 15 years
Furniture	10 years
Computer equipment	3 years
Software	5 years
Rolling stock	3 to 15 years
Leasehold improvements	Term of lease

d) Long-lived assets

The Company reviews long-lived assets whenever events or changes of circumstances indicate that the carrying amount of such assets may not be recoverable. An impairment loss is recognized when the carrying amount of a group of assets held for use exceeds the sum of the undiscounted cash flows expected from its use and eventual disposition. Measurement of an impairment loss is based on the amount by which the group of assets carrying amount exceeds its fair value. Fair value is determined using quoted market prices, when available, or using accepted valuation techniques such as the discounted future cash flows method.

e) Goodwill and other intangible assets

Goodwill is tested for impairment annually or more frequently if events or changes in circumstances indicate that the asset might be impaired. The impairment test is carried out in two steps. In the first step, the carrying amount of the reporting unit is compared with its fair value. When the fair value of a reporting unit exceeds its carrying amount, then goodwill of the reporting unit is considered not to be impaired and the second step of the impairment test is not required. The second step is carried out when the carrying amount of a reporting unit exceeds its fair value, in which case the implied fair value of the reporting unit's goodwill is compared with its carrying amount to measure the amount of the impairment loss. When the carrying amount of the reporting unit's goodwill exceeds the implied fair value of the goodwill, an impairment loss is recognized in an amount equal to the excess and is presented as a separate line item in the statement of earnings before extraordinary items and discontinued operations.

During the fourth quarter of 2006, the Company reviewed retroactively the allocation of the purchase price of acquired businesses since March 30, 2003. At April 1, 2006, the cumulative impact on the intangible asset Customer relations is $11.8 million, the decrease in goodwill is $9.9 million, $1.2 million for other assets and the future income tax liability is $0.7 million. This new purchase price allocation has had the effect of reducing earnings before income taxes of the fourth quarter of 2006 in an amount of $0.65 million following an additional amortization charge.

f)   Other assets

Development costs for coffee brewing equipment, net of applicable research and development tax credits, represent costs incurred to develop new coffee brewing equipment, brewers and other. Deferred costs are amortized on a straight-line basis over a period of three to five years.

Patents and licences are recorded at cost and are amortized using the straight-line method over 17 years.

The deferred financing costs related to long-term financing are amortized using the straight-line method over the term of the related long-term debt.

Other assets, which include start-up costs and non-compete agreements, are primarily amortized over a period of three to five years.

Customer relations are amortized on the straight-line basis over a period of 15 years.

Management reviews periodically the value and amortization period of other assets. An impairment, if such be the case, will be determined based on future undiscounted cash flows.

g) Income taxes

The Company follows the asset and liability method of accounting for income taxes. Under this method, future income tax assets and liabilities are recognized for the estimated future tax consequences attributable to differences between the financial statement carrying amounts of existing assets and liabilities and their respective tax bases. Future income tax assets and liabilities are measured using enacted or substantively enacted tax rates expected to apply when the assets are realized or the liabilities settled. Future income tax assets are recognized and, if realization is not considered "more likely than not", a valuation allowance is provided. The effect on future income tax assets and liabilities of a change in tax rates is recognized in earnings in the period during which that substantive enactment or enactment occurs.

h) Employee future benefits and pension plan

Employee future benefits

The Company accrues the estimated cost of the contractual termination benefits, when it is probable that employees will be entitled to benefits and the amount can be reasonably estimated.

Pension plan

Since April 3, 2005, the Company grants certain employees a supplementary defined benefit retirement plan and, since July 1, 2006, the Company grants a retirement program for management. The cost of the supplementary retirement plans is calculated according to actuarial methods that encompass management's best estimate regarding the future evolution of salary levels, the age of retirement of salaried employees and other actuarial factors. These plans are not funded and the payment of future benefits will be done from the funds of the Company. The pension expense is applied against earnings and includes the following items:

- The cost of pension benefits provided in exchange for employees' services rendered during the year.
- The amortization of cumulative unrecognized net actuarial gains and losses in excess of 10% of the benefit obligation over the expected average remaining service life of active employees covered by the plan.
- The amortization of prior service cost over the expected average remaining service life of active employees covered by the plan.
- Actuarial gains and losses resulting from modifications brought to actuarial assumptions used to determine the accrued benefit obligation.

The Company also offers to certain of its employees, defined contribution plans. Under these plans, employees can contribute a certain percentage of their salary and the Company can also make annual contributions to the plan.

i) Foreign currency translation

Net assets of self-sustaining foreign operations are translated using the current rate method. Adjustments arising from this translation are deferred and recorded as a separate item under shareholders' equity and are included in income only when a reduction in the net investment in these foreign operations is realized.

Other foreign currency transactions entered into by the Company are translated using the temporal method. Translation gains and losses are included in the statement of earnings.

j) Derivative financial instruments

The Company uses various derivative financial instruments to manage its exposure to fluctuations in interest rates, foreign currency exchange rates and commodity pricing.

The Company documents all relationships between hedging instruments and hedged items, as well as its risk management objective and strategy for undertaking various hedge transactions. This process includes linking all derivatives to specific assets and liabilities or to specific firm commitments or forecasted transactions.

The Company has entered into forward exchange contracts to manage the risk exchange on the purchase of raw materials it anticipates it will do in a foreign currency and on note receivable. According to hedge accounting, exchange gains and losses are recorded at the time the contract is carried out.

Realized and unrealized gains or losses associated with derivative instruments, which have been terminated or cease to be effective prior to maturity, are deferred under other current or non-current assets or liabilities on the balance sheet and recognized in earnings in the period in which the underlying hedged transaction is recognized. In the event a designated hedged item is sold, extinguished or matures prior to the termination of the related derivative instrument, any realized or unrealized gain or loss on such derivative instrument is recognized in earnings.

Inefficient derivative instruments, or, those which are not designated as hedged, are presented on a fair value basis in the consolidated financial statements. Changes in the fair value related to these instruments are recorded in earnings.

k) Revenue recognition

Revenue is recognized when goods are delivered or when services are provided. Rental fees are billed on a periodic or a monthly basis and recognized when services are provided. When clients are invoiced, the portion of unearned revenues is recorded under deferred revenues.

l) Stock-based compensation and other stock-based payments

The fair value of stock options to employees and directors is determined at the date of grant using the Black-Scholes option pricing model, and the compensation charge is expensed over the vesting period of the options with a corresponding increase to contributed surplus. When the stock options are exercised, capital stock is credited by the sum of the consideration paid with the related amount previously recorded to the contributed surplus for received services.

m) Consolidation of variable interest entities

During the year ended April 1, 2006, the Company adopted the Canadian Institute of Chartered Accountants (CICA) Accounting Guideline ("AcG") AcG-15 "Consolidation of Variable Interest Entities" (VIEs) that came into effect November 1, 2004. This guideline clarifies and addresses the application of consolidation guidance to those entities defined as VIEs which are entities that are subject to control on a basis other than voting interests. Such entities should be consolidated by the primary beneficiary, which is the entity that will absorb a majority of the VIE's expected losses or will receive a majority of its expected residual returns, or both.

The Company conducted a review of all its operations and determined that, in certain very particular circumstances, a notion of control, in the sense of the accounting guideline, could exist in one of the business sectors. In order to comply with the principles of the application of this accounting guideline, the Company has defined the criteria and inferior limits above which it considers it should consolidate the VIEs. Following the evaluation of the established criteria, the Company concluded that the application of the guideline would have no impact on the results of the Company.

n) Use of estimates

The preparation of financial statements requires management to make estimates and assumptions that affect the reported amounts of assets and liabilities, related amounts of revenues and expenses and disclosure of contingent assets and liabilities. Significant areas requiring the use of management estimates relate to the determination of the useful life of assets for amortization and evaluation of net recoverable amounts, the determination of the fair value of portfolio investments, the determination of the fair value of assets acquired and liabilities assumed in business combinations, implied fair value of goodwill, provisions for income taxes and determination of future income tax assets and liabilities that take into account the estimate of taxable benefits in the various jurisdictions and the determination of the fair value of financial instruments. Actual results could differ from those estimates.

NOTE 2
Revenues

	2007	2006
Manufacturing and coffee services	$ 340,020	$ 327,787
Equipment rental income	45,929	46,087
Franchising fees	2,209	2,299
	$ 388,158	$ 376,173

NOTE 3
Financial expenses

	2007	2006
Interest on long-term debt	$ 4,375	$ 4,843
Change in fair value of interest rate swaps	119	(2,169)
Amortization of financial expenses	620	1,405
Increase in the redemption value of portfolio investment in preferred shares and dividends	-	(1,559)
Other	(843)	(138)
	$ 4,271	$ 2,382

NOTE 4
a) Income taxes

Income tax expense, excluding prior year's income taxes, is detailed as follows:

	2007	2006
Current	$ 6,687	$ 8,309
Future	2,857	356
	$ 9,544	$ 8,665

The following table reconciles the statutory tax rate with the effective tax rate:

	2007	2006
Combined statutory tax rate	32.71 %	31.4 %
Earnings taxed (losses recovered) at a different rate than the statutory rate	-	(4.0)
Permanent differences	(6.30)	(0.7)
Tax benefit realized during the year related to capital losses	(6.85)	-
Adjustment to future income tax assets and liabilities for enacted changes in tax laws and rates	(0.7)	(0.4)
Other items	0.14	(0.1)
Effective tax rate	19.0 %	26.2 %

The tax effects of temporary differences that give rise to a significant portion of the future tax assets and future tax liabilities are as follows:

	2007	2006
Future income tax:		
Reserve deductible next year	$ **1,442**	$ 1,804
Pension benefit liability and post employment benetifs	**979**	694
Tax losses carried forward	**12,841**	17,401
Differences between book and tax bases of fixed assets	**4,726**	2,787
Valuation allowance	**(1,625)**	(1,855)
Total future income tax assets	**18,363**	20,831
Future income tax liabilities – non-current:		
Differences between book and tax bases of fixed assets	**2,365**	7,444
Differences between book and tax bases of other assets	**12,400**	6,927
Total future income tax liabilities	**14,765**	14,371
Net future income tax assets	$ **3,598**	$ 6,460

These future tax assets and liabilities are presented in the consolidated balance sheet as follows:

	2007	2006
Future income tax assets:		
Current	$ **1,571**	$ 1,804
Non-current	**3,228**	6,154
	4,799	7,958
Future income tax liabilities	**1,201**	1,498
	$ **3,598**	$ 6,460

The Company has not recognized a future tax liability for retained earnings of its subsidiaries in 2007 and in prior years because the Company does not expect those retained earnings to reverse and become taxable in the Company in a foreseeable future. A future tax liability will be recognized when the Company expects that it will recover these retained earnings in a way that will render them taxable.

As at March 31, 2007, the Company had net operating loss carryforwards, other than capital, for income tax purposes, available to reduce future federal, provincial and US federal taxable income of approximately $380,000, $382,000 and $32,612,000, respectively.

These losses will expire as follows:

	Federal	Provincial	US Federal
2014	$ 380	$ 380	$ -
2015	-	2	-
2021	-	-	1,843
2022	-	-	8,021
2023	-	-	7,872
2024	-	-	5,182
2025	-	-	4,614
2026	-	-	5,080
	$ 380	$ 382	$ 32,612

As at March 31, 2007, the Company also had capital losses to carry forward of $6,444,597 without expiry dates. The future tax asset related to these capital losses is partially recorded in the financial statements.

b) Prior years' income taxes

On June 13, 2006, the Quebec Government's National Assembly enacted Bill 15 to amend the Taxation Act and other legislative provisions. Bill 15 provides for retroactive changes to the Quebec taxation which would have the impact of increasing the Quebec taxable income of the Company for previous years.

During the first quarter ended 2007, the Company recorded a $15.8 million reserve for prior years' income taxes, including related charges. The Company initiated discussions with the government in order to resolve the issue.

On April 26, 2007, the Company received a confirmation from the Government of Quebec, permitting to reduce the tax expenses for prior years' income taxes from $15.8 million to $13.7 million.

NOTE 5
Earnings per share

Basic earnings per share are calculated by dividing the net earnings attributable to the common shareholders by the weighted average daily number of common shares outstanding during the year.

Diluted earnings per share are calculated by dividing the net earnings attributable to the common shareholders by the weighted average number of common shares outstanding restated to take into account the potential dilutive impact of the exercise of the stock options under the treasury stock method.

	2007	2006
	(in thousands)	*(in thousands)*
Weighted average number of outstanding common shares	**21,375**	21,399
Potential dilutive impact	**53**	55
Weighted average number of common and dilutive shares	**21,428**	21,454

The average share price for the year was $19.49 ($20,19 in 2006). At March 31, 2007, 357,700 options had an exercise price greater than this price (313,634 in 2006).

Price range	Number of options
	(in thousands)
$19.50 to $23	61
$23.01 to $25	122
$25.01 to $30	175
	358

NOTE 6
Inventories

	2007	2006
Raw materials	$ 9,206	$ 11,123
Goods in process	430	684
Finished goods	19,903	18,165
	$ 29,539	$ 29,972

NOTE 7
Investments

	2007	2006
Advances to companies subject to significant influence and to minority shareholders, with various interest rates and payment terms	$ 2,641	$ 3,142
Portfolio investment [1]	-	16,979
	$ 2,641	$ 20,121

[1] On May 3, 2006, the Company accepted to sell its interest in Keurig for US$34.1 million (Cdn$37.4 million) as part of a transaction that has transferred all the shares of Keurig to a third party. A gain of investment of Cdn$20 million was recorded in earnings and a corresponding income tax expense of Cdn$3.5 million was recorded as current income taxes.

Under the terms of the transaction, a cash portion amounting to US$26.7 million (Cdn $29.1 million) was received and the balance of the proceeds, amounting to US$7.4 million (Cdn $8.3 million), has been classified as a Note Receivable until payout in June 2007. This amount is held in escrow in order to guarantee the vendor's representations and there is no indication that the Company will not receive the full amount.

NOTE 8
Fixed assets

			2007
	Cost	Accumulated depreciation	Net book value
Land	$ 1,571	$ -	$ 1,571
Buildings	15,895	6,049	9,846
Retail equipment	12,273	7,593	4,680
Vending equipment	4,413	2,761	1,652
Coffee service equipment [1]	177,883	117,399	60,484
Machinery and equipment	41,036	21,718	19,318
Furniture, computer equipment and leasehold improvements	31,280	22,952	8,328
Software	4,630	2,374	2,256
Rolling stock	22,680	14,211	8,469
	$ 311,661	$ 195,057	$ 116,604

[1] The majority of coffee service equipment is for rental.

			2006
	Cost	Accumulated depreciation	Net book value
Land	$ 1,571	$ -	$ 1,571
Buildings	15,289	5,571	9,718
Retail equipment	9,392	5,992	3,400
Vending equipment	6,073	3,812	2,261
Coffee service equipment [1]	161,828	97,838	63,990
Machinery and equipment	37,476	19,832	17,644
Furniture, computer equipment and leasehold improvements	28,961	19,739	9,222
Software	3,796	1,547	2,249
Rolling stock	20,805	12,386	8,419
	$ 285,191	$ 166,717	$ 118,474

[1] The majority of coffee service equipment is for rental.

NOTE 9
Goodwill

For the year ended March 31, 2007, the changes in the carrying amounts of goodwill for each of the two business segments are as follows:

	Manufacturing and marketing	Coffee services	Total
Balance as at April 1, 2006	$ 29,178	$ 106,556	$ 135,734
Business acquisitions	145	1,171	1,316
Translation adjustments	-	(374)	(374)
Balance as at March 31, 2007	$ 29,323	$ 107,353	$ 136,676

NOTE 10
Other assets

	Cost	Accumulated depreciation	2007 Net book value
Customer relations	$ 12,846	$ 2,104	$ 10,742
Non-compete clauses	2,888	1,549	1,339
Development costs for coffee service equipment	6,278	5,134	1,144
Deferred financing and hedging costs	3,598	3,153	445
Deposits	436	-	436
Other deferred charges	1,667	1,243	424
Patents and licences	1,107	759	348
Start-up costs	1,143	1,143	-
	$ 29,963	$ 15,085	$ 14,878

	Cost	Accumulated depreciation	2006 Net book value
Customer relations	$ 11,773	$ 1,304	$ 10,469
Non-compete clauses	2,587	1,106	1,481
Development costs for coffee service equipment	5,514	4,451	1,063
Deferred financing and hedging costs	3,563	2,535	1,028
Deposits	444	-	444
Other deferred charges	1,508	965	543
Patents and licences	946	685	261
Start-up costs	1,143	957	186
	$ 27,478	$ 12,003	$ 15,475

NOTE 11
Long-term debt

	Effective interest rate March 31, 2007	2007	2006
Revolving bank credit facility	5.8%	$ 49,742	$ 92,159
Other	0 to 9.5%	2,738	2,950
		52,480	95,109
Less current portion		1,407	1,520
		$ 51,073	$ 93,589

The $150 million bank credit facility is a five-year revolving facility and allows borrowing in either Canadian or American currency, as the Company chooses so. This facility can, upon approval, be increased by $50 million. As at March 31, 2007 and April 1, 2006, amounts of $24 million and $28 million were borrowed in American currency, respectively (equivalent to Cdn$27,742,000 and Cdn$32,558,000). The borrowed amounts will be reimbursed in full in November 2010.

The credit agreement governing this bank credit facility contains certain covenants, among which is the obligation to maintain certain financial ratios. The borrowed amounts bear interest at floating rates based on Bankers' Acceptances, Libor or the bank prime rate.

In accordance with the terms of various borrowing agreements and excluding any refinancing options, the Company will make the following repayments over the next five years:

2008	$ 1,407
2009	657
2010	414
2011	165
2012	49,837

NOTE 12
Other liabilities

The Company grants, to certain employees, a supplementary final career defined benefit retirement plan and a retirement plan for the management employees. The plans were subject to an actuarial evaluation at the time they were set up and will be evaluated at least once again during the next three years.

The following tables reconcile the variation of obligations and of the plans' pension expense for the year ended March 31:

		2007		2006
Accumulated benefit obligations, beginning of year	$	1,932	$	1,591
Current benefit costs		328		125
Interest expense on accumulated benefit obligations		186		97
Benefits paid		(114)		(14)
Unamortized actuarial loss		341		133
Prior service costs		1,468		-
Other adjustments		(14)		-
Accumulated benefit obligations, end of year	$	4,127	$	1,932

Pension plan expense for the year is as follows:

		2007		2006
Cost of services rendered during the year	$	328	$	125
Interest expense on accumulated benefit obligations		186		97
Net actuarial loss		341		133
Prior service costs		1,468		-
Pension expense before adjustment to recognize its long-term nature		2,323		355
Difference between amortization and net actuarial loss		(340)		(133)
Difference between amortization and prior service costs		(1,029)		-
Amortization of transition obligation		476		477
Pension expense at end of year	$	1,430	$	699

		2007		2006
Accumulated benefit obligations	$	4,127	$	1,932
Unamortized actuarial loss		(486)		(160)
Unamortized prior service costs		(1,029)		-
Unamortized transitional obligation		(362)		(838)
Accrued pension benefit	$	2,250	$	934

Amounts shown on the balance sheets are as follows:

	2007	2006
Accrued pension benefit	$ 2,250	$ 934
Less: portion presented in accrued liabilities	(215)	(235)
Post employment benefits	1,100	1,100
Other liabilities	$ 3,135	$ 1,799

During the years ended March 31, 2007 and April 1, 2006, contributions in the amount of $350,000 and $358,000 were paid to the defined contribution plans, respectively. For the post employment benefits, the Company signed a guarantee letter of $248,638. The assumptions used to determine the pension expense are 5% as discount rate and 3% as rate of compensation increase.

NOTE 13
Capital stock

	2007	2006
Authorized:		
Unlimited number of multiple voting shares with voting rights of five votes per share, participating and without par value		
Unlimited number of subordinate voting shares with voting rights of one vote per share, participating and without par value		
Unlimited number of Classes A and B preferred shares, issuable only in series, non-voting and without par value		
Issued and paid:		
5,300,000 multiple voting shares	$ 353	$ 353
16,202,831 subordinate voting shares (16,062,331 shares in 2006)	129,689	126,144
	$ 130,042	$ 126,497

a) Issue and redemption of shares - 2007
During the year, 140,500 subordinate voting shares were issued upon the exercise of stock options, for a cash consideration of $2,646,735. Following the exercice of these options, $897,869 was transfered from the credited surplus to the capital stock.

b) Issue and redemption of shares - 2006
During the year, 260,000 subordinate voting shares were redeemed for a cash consideration of $5,200,000. The excess of the price paid over the average cost of these shares as well as the redemption expenses of $3,160,000 were recorded as a reduction of retained earnings.

During the year, 19,000 subordinate voting shares were issued upon the exercise of stock options, for a cash consideration of $287,000.

c) Stock option plan
Under a stock option plan, 1,650,000 subordinate voting shares are reserved for certain management employees of the Company. The exercise price of each option is determined based on the average price of the last five trading days immediately preceding the date on which the option is granted. Each option may be exercised during a period not exceeding ten years from the date it was granted. Options can generally be exercised during the year following their allotment at the rate of 20% per year.

The following table provides details regarding changes to outstanding options for the years ended March 31, 2007 and April 1, 2006.

	Options	2007 Weighted average exercise price	Options	2006 Weighted average exercise price
Balance at beginning of year	872,751	$ 20.67	844,687	$ 20.49
Granted	-	-	69,000	19.85
Cancelled	(23,470)	14.68	(21,936)	15.78
Exercised	(140,500)	18.84	(19,000)	15.11
Expired	(2,734)	26.75	-	-
Balance at end of year	706,047	$ 21.09	872,751	$ 20.67
Vested options at end of year	630,146	$ 21.46	732,492	$ 21.17

The following table summarizes the information regarding outstanding options as at March 31, 2007:

Range of prices	Options outstanding Number of outstanding options as at March 31, 2007	Weighted average years to maturity	Weighted average exercise price	Options exercisable Number exercisable as at March 31, 2007	Weighted average exercise price
$ 10 à 15	143,455	6.1	$ 14.12	137,500	$ 14.13
15 à 20	227,892	3.6	17.95	175,946	18.00
20 à 25	160,000	3.4	22.61	142,000	22.93
25 à 30	174,700	1.3	29.51	174,700	29.51
$ 10 à 30	706,047	3.5	$ 21.09	630,146	$ 21.46

During the year 2007, the Company granted no stock options to officers but cancelled 23,470 stock options and 2,734 stock options expired. Of those stock options, 17,270 were granted after March 31, 2002 at a weighted average exercise price of $15.26. The weighted average fair value of cancelled options was $4.77.

During the year 2006, the Company granted 69,000 stock options to officers at a weighted average exercise price of $19.85 and cancelled 21,936 stock options, of which 19,474 were granted after March 31, 2002 at a weighted average exercise price of $14.49. The weighted average fair value of stock options granted was $7.05 while that of cancelled options was $4.18. The fair value of each option granted was determined using the Black-Scholes option pricing model and the following weighted average assumptions:

	2006
Risk-free interest rate	4.54 %
Expected life	7.0 years
Expected volatility	32.03 %
Expected dividend yield	1.5 %

The compensation expense for the years ended March 31, 2007 and April 1, 2006 is $232,000 and $418,000 respectively. The total consideration was recorded under contributed surplus.

NOTE 14
Currency translation adjustment

	2007	2006
Balance at beginning	$ (17,171)	$ (13,519)
Effect of exchange rate variation on translation of net assets of US self-sustaining subsidiaries	(648)	(3,652)
Balance at end	$ (17,819)	$ (17,171)

Losses on foreign exchange transactions recorded in the consolidated statement of earnings amounted to $604,000 in 2007 and $191,000 in 2006.

NOTE 15
Commitments and guarantees

a) Commitments

The Company rents premises and equipment under operating leases which expire at various dates up to 2021 and for which gross rents total $26,831,000. Of this amount, a portion of $6,455,000 is assumed by the franchisees of the Company. Annual payments under these leases for the next five years are as follows:

	Gross	Franchisees	Net
2008	$ 6,896	$ 965	$ 5,931
2009	5,517	905	4,612
2010	4,023	705	3,318
2001	3,133	643	2,490
2012	2,741	630	2,111
2013 and thereafter	4,521	2,607	1,914

Leases expenses related to the operating leases amounted to $7.5 million and $7.4 million for the year ended March 31, 2007 and April 1, 2006.

b) Guarantees

Directors' and officers' indemnification agreements

The Company indemnifies its directors and officers, former directors and officers and individuals who act or who have acted at the Company's request as a director or officer of an entity in which the Company is a shareholder or creditor, to the extent permitted by law, against any and all charges, costs, expenses, amounts paid in settlement or investigative damages incurred by the directors and officers as a result of any lawsuit, or any judicial, administrative or investigating proceeding in which the directors and officers are sued as a result of their service. These indemnification claims are subject to any statutory or other legal limitation period. The nature of the indemnification agreements prevents the Company from making a reasonable estimate of the maximum potential amount it could be required to pay to counterparties.

The Company has purchased directors' and officers' liability insurance coverage in the amount of $30,000,000 which carries a $250,000 deductible. No amount has been accrued in the consolidated balance sheet with respect to these indemnifications. To the knowledge of the Company, there is no such claim against directors and officers.

Operating leases

The Company has guaranteed lease obligations for its franchisees expiring in 2012. If a franchisee defaults under its contractual obligation, the Company must, under certain conditions, compensate the lessor for the default. The maximum exposure in respect of these guarantees is $261,250 (2006 - $359,409). As at March 31, 2007, the Company has not recorded a liability associated with these guarantees since it is not probable that a franchisee will default under the agreement.

NOTE 16
Contingencies

The Company is involved in various lawsuits and claims. Management and legal advisers are of the opinion that the resolution of these claims will have no material impact on the Company's financial position or results of operations.

NOTE 17
Additional information on cash flows

	2007	2006
Operating activities:		
Changes in non-cash operating working capital items:		
Accounts receivable	$ (5,223)	$ (1,739)
Inventories	433	(1,927)
Prepaid expenses	233	(671)
Accounts payable and accrued liabilities	3,139	(4,943)
Deferred income	375	(320)
Income taxes payable	11,785	346
Working capital acquired (assumed)	(250)	1,258
Consolidation of joint ventures	-	374
	$ 10,492	$ (7,622)
Cash payments of interest and income taxes were as follows:		
Interest paid	$ 3,752	$ 4,754
Income taxes paid	$ 8,099	$ 7,691
Additions to fixed assets financed by accounts payable	$ 2,158	$ 1,643
Additions to fixed assets financed by capital lease obligations	$ 61	$ 215

NOTE 18
Business and asset acquisitions and disposals

Business acquisitions are accounted for using the purchase method. Results of the businesses acquired are included from the date of the acquisition in the consolidated financial statements of the Company.

a) 2007

During the year, the Company acquired 11 small coffee service businesses, four in the United States and seven in Canada. Furthermore, it concluded with some joint ventures the buyback of their minority interest. The Company sold five vending businesses in Canada. The total net consideration is $1,056,000.

The acquisitions and disposals are summarized as follows:

	Acquisitions	Disposals	Net 2007
Assets acquired and disposed of:			
Non-cash operating working capital	$ 30	$ 280	$ (250)
Fixed assets	625	978	(353)
Non-compete clause	314	-	314
Customer relations	984	-	984
Goodwill [1]	1,316	-	1,316
	3,269	1,258	2,011
Liabilities assumed:			
Long-term debt	175	-	175
Non-controlling interest	(113)	-	(113)
Gain on disposal	-	893	893
Net assets acquired at fair value	$ 3,207	$ 2,151	$ 1,056
Consideration:			
Cash	$ 2,357	$ 1,922	$ 435
Portion of purchase price unpaid	850	200	650
Shares without voting right	-	29	(29)
	$ 3,207	$ 2,151	$ 1,056
(1) Tax value of goodwill and customer relations	$ 2,300	$ -	$ 2,300

Notes to Consolidated Financial Statements

a)   2006

During the year, the Company acquired coffee service businesses, ten in the United States and seven in Canada, and sold one of its vending branches in the United States and two in Canada for a total net consideration of $10,004,000. The main acquisitions of the year are:

United States

On May 3, 2005, the Company purchased the remaining 75% interest in Filterfresh of Georgia, LLC.

On November 2, 2005, the Company purchased the Fresh Brew Coffee business.

Canada

On August 31, 2005, the Company purchased Dawson's Office Beverage Services Inc.

The acquisitions and disposals are summarized as follows:

	Acquisitions	Disposals	Net 2006
Assets acquired and disposed of:			
Non-cash operating working capital	$ 1,293	$ 35	$ 1,258
Fixed assets	3,081	765	2,316
Non-compete clause	675	-	675
Customer relations	3,703	-	3,703
Goodwill [(1)]	3,183	-	3,183
	11,935	800	11,135
Liabilities assumed:	-	-	-
Long-term debt	14	-	14
Non-controlling interest	196	-	196
Gain on disposal	-	921	921
Net assets acquired at fair value	$ 11,725	$ 1,721	$ 10,004
Consideration:			
Cash	$ 11,266	$ 1,721	$ 9,545
Portion of purchase price unpaid	5	-	5
Portion of purchase price paid during a previous year	454	-	454
	$ 11,725	$ 1,721	$ 10,004
(1) Tax value of goodwill and customer relations	$ 6,312	$ -	$ 6,312

NOTE 19
Financial instruments

a)   Fair value of financial instruments

The carrying value of cash, accounts receivable, accounts payable and accrued liabilities approximates their fair value because of the near-term maturity of these instruments. The carrying value of the revolving term loan and other debt approximates their fair value, as the interest rates vary based on market rate.

b)   Management of interest rate risk

The Company has entered into interest rate swaps to manage its interest rate exposure on a portion of the revolving bank credit facility. The Company is committed to exchange, at specific intervals, the difference between the fixed and floating interest rates calculated based on notional principal amounts. The Company pays a fixed interest rate ranging from 3.99% to 4.86% on a notional amount of $57,026,700 (Cdn$42,000,000 and US$13,000,000) and receives floating interest rates based on Bankers' Acceptance having a three-month maturity. The swaps will expire from July 2007 to October 2010. Hedge accounting is not applied for these financial instruments, and, therefore, the change in fair value of these swaps is recorded in earnings.

c)   Foreign exchange risk

The Company makes several purchases in US dollars and enters into various types of foreign exchange forward contracts in order to manage its foreign exchange risk. The Company does not hold nor issue such financial instruments for trading purposes. As at March 31, 2007, there were forward exchange contracts outstanding with an exchange rate of one US dollar for CDN 1.1398 for a notional amount of US$13,000,000 (2006 - US$28,350,000). These contracts expire from April to August 2007. The positive fair value of the forward exchange contracts is $163,020 as March 31, 2007 and there was a negative fair value of $570,036 as at April 1, 2006.

As at March 31, 2007, the Company owned a foreign exchange forward contract in order to manage its foreign exchange risk on the note receivable, at a fixed rate of one US dollar for CDN 1,1227 for a notional amount of US$7 000 000. This contract expires in June 2007. The negative fair value of the forward exchange contract is $232,400.

The Company foresees that third parties will meet their obligations seeing that these contracts are established with reputable Canadian banks. The fair value is estimated using the year-end market rate.

d)   Credit risk

The Company does not have a significant exposure to any individual customer nor counterparty. The Company reviews a new customer's credit history before extending credit and conducts regular reviews of its existing customers' credit performance. An allowance for doubtful accounts is established based upon factors such as the credit risk for specific customers, historical trends and other information.

e)   Other risks

The Company also has a significant exposure toward the fluctuation of the price of green coffee. The Company purchases coffee contracts on a public commodities market in order to manage its price risk. As at March 31, 2007, the Company had contracts for green coffee having a negative fair value of $291,113 and, as at April 1, 2006, the Company had contracts for green coffee having a positive fair value of $107,508.

The Company foresees that the third party, with whom it has closed these contracts, will meet its obligations. The fair value of those contracts is estimated using the public market rates.

NOTE 20
Segmented information

The segmented information comprises two significant segments:

a) The "Manufacturing and Marketing" segment encompasses coffee roasting and distribution for home consumption through retail channels such as supermarkets and other. It also includes café-bistros and the manufacturing of coffeemakers.

b) The "Coffee Services" segment focuses on the sale of coffee for consumption in the workplace and other public locations. Van Houtte's coffee services network also distributes complementary products such as condiments, snacks and various beverages. Moreover, this segment, which encompasses the Canadian and American activities, includes vending machine operations and food services.

These segments are managed separately and are assessed individually based on operating income before depreciation, amortization and financial expenses.

The accounting policies of each segment are identical to those policies used for the consolidated financial statements.

Segment income includes income from sales to third parties and inter-segment sales. These sales are accounted for at prevailing market prices.

	2007	2006
By business segment:		
Revenues:		
Manufacturing and marketing	$ 175,603	$ 172,680
Coffee services	278,766	267,469
	454,369	440,149
Intersegments	(66,211)	(63,976)
	$ 388,158	$ 376,173
Operating earnings before amortization and write-down of the value of certain assets		
Manufacturing and marketing	$ 35,754	$ 32,944
Coffee services	44,125	41,748
	79,879	74,692
General corporate expenses and other	(7,001)	(5,436)
	$ 72,878	$ 69,256
Capital assets and goodwill:		
Manufacturing and marketing	$ 67,735	$ 65,105
Coffee services	195,720	199,065
	$ 263,455	$ 264,170
Additions to capital assets and other assets:		
Manufacturing and marketing	$ 11,119	$ 9,101
Coffee services	23,585	22,946
	34,704	32,047
Intersegments	39	2,109
	$ 34,743	$ 34,156
Depreciation and amortization of fixed assets and other assets:		
Manufacturing and marketing	$ 8,141	$ 7,834
Coffee services	27,904	25,866
	36,045	33,700
General corporate expenses and other	60	90
	$ 36,105	$ 33,790

	2007	2006
By geographical segment:		
Revenues:		
Canada	$ 260,601	$ 252,205
United States	125,695	121,299
Other countries	1,862	2,669
	$ 388,158	$ 376,173
Capital assets and goodwill:		
Canada	$ 160,776	$ 162,769
United States	102,679	101,401
	$ 263,455	$ 264,170

NOTE 21
Comparative figures

Certain comparative figures have been reclassified to conform to the financial statement presentation adopted in the current year.

NOTE 22
Subsequent event

On May 7, 2007, the Company announced that it has entered into a definitive acquisition agreement to be acquired and take private by a company controlled by Littlejohn & Co LLC «Littlejohn», a Greenwich, United States based (Connecticut) private equity firm.

Under the terms of the agreement, Littlejohn will acquire all of the issued and outstanding shares of the Company for a consideration of $25.00 per share. The total enterprise value of the transaction is approximately $600 million, including the assumption of existing indebtedness.

As at March 31, 2007, the Company incurred expenses in the amount of $1.0 million related to the strategy review of value enhancement. Those expenses were charged to the statement of earnings. Furthermore, additional estimated costs of $3.5 million will be incurred during the next quarter.

Index